Lecture Notes in Computer Science 12493

Shiho Moriai · Huaxiong Wang (Eds.)

Advances in Cryptology – ASIACRYPT 2020

26th International Conference on the Theory and Application of Cryptology and Information Security Daejeon, South Korea, December 7–11, 2020 Proceedings, Part III

Springer

Editors
Shiho Moriai
Network Security Research Institute (NICT)
Tokyo, Japan

Huaxiong Wang
Nanyang Technological University
Singapore, Singapore

ISSN 0302-9743 ISSN 1611-3349 (electronic)
Lecture Notes in Computer Science
ISBN 978-3-030-64839-8 ISBN 978-3-030-64840-4 (eBook)
https://doi.org/10.1007/978-3-030-64840-4

LNCS Sublibrary: SL4 – Security and Cryptology

This Springer imprint is published by the registered company Springer Nature Switzerland AG
The registered company address is: Gewerbestrasse 11, 6330 Cham, Switzerland

Preface

The 26th Annual International Conference on Theory and Application of Cryptology and Information Security (ASIACRYPT 2020), was originally planned to be held in Daejeon, South Korea, during December 7–11, 2020. Due to the COVID-19 pandemic, it was shifted to an online-only virtual conference.

The conference focused on all technical aspects of cryptology, and was sponsored by the International Association for Cryptologic Research (IACR).

We received a total of 316 submissions from all over the world, the Program Committee (PC) selected 85 papers for publication in the proceedings of the conference. The two program chairs were supported by a PC consisting of 66 leading experts in aspects of cryptology. Each submission was reviewed by at least three PC members (or their sub-reviewers) and five PC members were assigned to submissions co-authored by PC members. The strong conflict of interest rules imposed by the IACR ensure that papers are not handled by PC members with a close working relationship with authors. The two program chairs were not allowed to submit a paper, and PC members were limited to two submissions each. There were approximately 390 external reviewers, whose input was critical to the selection of papers.

The review process was conducted using double-blind peer review. The conference operated a two-round review system with a rebuttal phase. After the reviews and first-round discussions, the PC selected 205 submissions to proceed to the second round, including 1 submission with early acceptance. The authors of 204 papers were then invited to provide a short rebuttal in response to the referee reports. The second round involved extensive discussions by the PC members.

The three volumes of the conference proceedings contain the revised versions of the 85 papers that were selected, together with the abstracts of 2 invited talks. The final revised versions of papers were not reviewed again and the authors are responsible for their contents.

The program of ASIACRYPT 2020 featured two excellent invited talks by Shweta Agrawal and Jung Hee Cheon. The conference also featured a rump session which contained short presentations on the latest research results of the field.

The PC selected three papers to receive the Best Paper Award, via a voting-based process that took into account conflicts of interest, which were solicited to submit the full versions to the *Journal of Cryptology*: "Finding Collisions in a Quantum World: Quantum Black-Box Separation of Collision-Resistance and One-Wayness" by Akinori Hosoyamada and Takashi Yamakawa; "New results on Gimli: full-permutation distinguishers and improved collisions" by Antonio Flórez Gutiérrez, Gaëtan Leurent, María Naya-Plasencia, Léo Perrin, André Schrottenloher, and Ferdinand Sibleyras; and "SQISign: Compact Post-Quantum signatures from Quaternions and Isogenies" by Luca De Feo, David Kohel, Antonin Leroux, Christophe Petit, and Benjamin Wesolowski.

Many people contributed to the success of ASIACRYPT 2020. We would like to thank the authors for submitting their research results to the conference. We are very grateful to the PC members and external reviewers for contributing their knowledge and expertise, and for the tremendous amount of work that was done with reading papers and contributing to the discussions. We are greatly indebted to Kwangjo Kim, the general chair, for his efforts and overall organization. We thank Michel Abdalla, McCurley, Kay McKelly, and members of the IACR's emergency pandemic team for their work in designing and running the virtual format. We thank Steve Galbraith, Joo Young Lee, and Yu Sasaki for expertly organizing and chairing the rump session. We are extremely grateful to Zhenzhen Bao for checking all the latex files and for assembling the files for submission to Springer. Finally, we thank Shai Halevi and the IACR for setting up and maintaining the Web Submission and Review software, used by IACR conferences for the paper submission and review process. We also thank Alfred Hofmann, Anna Kramer, and their colleagues at Springer for handling the publication of these conference proceedings.

December 2020

Shiho Moriai
Huaxiong Wang

Organization

General Chair

Kwangjo Kim	Korea Advanced Institute of Science and Technology (KAIST), South Korea

Program Chairs

Shiho Moriai	Network Security Research Institute (NICT), Japan
Huaxiong Wang	Nanyang Technological University, Singapore

Program Committee

Shweta Agrawal	IIT Madras, India
Gorjan Alagic	University of Maryland, USA
Shi Bai	Florida Atlantic University, USA
Zhenzhen Bao	Nanyang Technological University, Singapore
Paulo Barreto	University of Washington Tacoma, USA
Lejla Batina	Radboud University, The Netherlands
Amos Beimel	Ben-Gurion University, Israel
Sonia Belaïd	CryptoExperts, France
Olivier Blazy	University of Limoges, France
Jie Chen	East China Normal University, China
Yilei Chen	Visa Research, USA
Chen-Mou Cheng	Osaka University, Japan
Jun Furukawa	NEC Israel Research Center, Israel
David Galindo	University of Birmingham, Fetch.AI, UK
Jian Guo	Nanyang Technological University, Singapore
Swee-Huay Heng	Multimedia University, Malaysia
Xinyi Huang	Fujian Normal University, China
Andreas Hülsing	TU Eindhoven, The Netherlands
Takanori Isobe	University of Hyogo, Japan
David Jao	University of Waterloo, evolutionQ, Inc., Canada
Jérémy Jean	ANSSI, France
Zhengfeng Ji	University of Technology Sydney, Australia
Hyung Tae Lee	Jeonbuk National University, South Korea
Jooyoung Lee	KAIST, South Korea
Benoît Libert	CNRS, ENS, France
Dongdai Lin	Chinese Academy of Sciences, China
Helger Lipmaa	University of Tartu, Estonia, and Simula UiB, Norway
Feng-Hao Liu	Florida Atlantic University, USA

Giorgia Azzurra Marson	University of Bern, Switzerland, and NEC Laboratories Europe, Germany
Daniel Masny	Visa Research, USA
Takahiro Matsuda	AIST, Japan
Brice Minaud	Inria, ENS, France
Shiho Moriai	NICT, Japan
Kartik Nayak	Duke University, VMware Research, USA
Khoa Nguyen	Nanyang Technological University, Singapore
Svetla Nikova	KU Leuven, Belgium
Carles Padró	UPC, Spain
Jiaxin Pan	NTNU, Norway
Arpita Patra	Indian Institute of Science, India
Thomas Peters	UCL, Belgium
Duong Hieu Phan	University of Limoges, France
Raphael C.-W. Phan	Monash University, Malaysia
Josef Pieprzyk	CSIRO, Australia, and Institute of Computer Science, Polish Academy of Sciences, Poland
Ling Ren	VMware Research, University of Illinois at Urbana-Champaign, USA
Carla Ràfols	Universitat Pompeu Fabra, Spain
Rei Safavi-Naini	University of Calgary, Canada
Yu Sasaki	NTT laboratories, Japan
Jae Hong Seo	Hanyang University, South Korea
Ron Steinfeld	Monash University, Australia
Willy Susilo	University of Wollongong, Australia
Qiang Tang	New Jersey Institute of Technology, USA
Mehdi Tibouchi	NTT laboratories, Japan
Huaxiong Wang	Nanyang Technological University, Singapore
Xiaoyun Wang	Tsinghua University, China
Yongge Wang	The University of North Carolina at Charlotte, USA
Chaoping Xing	Shanghai Jiao Tong University, China, and NTU, Singapore
Yu Yu	Shanghai Jiao Tong University, China
Mark Zhandry	Princeton University, NTT Research, USA

External Reviewers

Behzad Abdolmaleki
Parhat Abla
Mamun Akand
Orestis Alpos
Hiroaki Anada
Benny Applebaum
Diego F. Aranha
Marcel Armour
Gilad Asharov
Man Ho Au
Benedikt Auerbach
Khin Mi Mi Aung
Sepideh Avizheh
Christian Badertscher
Saikrishna Badrinarayanan
Mir Ali Rezazadeh Baee
Joonsang Baek
Karim Baghery
Gustavo Banegas
Laasya Bangalore

Subhadeep Banik
James Bartusek
Carsten Baum
Rouzbeh Behnia
Aner Ben-Efraim
Fabrice Benhamouda
Francesco Berti
Luk Bettale
Tim Beyne
Shivam Bhasin
Nina Bindel
Nir Bitansky
Xavier Bonnetain
Katharina Boudgoust
Florian Bourse
Zvika Brakerski
Jaqueline Brendel
Olivier Bronchain
Benedikt Bunz
Seyit Camtepe
Ignacio Cascudo
Gaëtan Cassiers
Suvradip Chakraborty
Jorge Chávez Saab
Hao Chen
Hua Chen
Long Chen
Rongmao Chen
Yu Chen
Yuan Chen
Ding-Yuan Cheng
Ji-Jian Chin
Seongbong Choi
Wonseok Choi
Ashish Choudhury
Sherman S. M. Chow
Heewon Chung
Michele Ciampi
Benoît Cogliati
Craig Costello
Nicholas Courtois
Geoffroy Couteau
Alain Couvreur
Daniele Cozzo
Hongrui Cui
Edouard Cuvelier
Jan Czajkowski
João Paulo da Silva
Jan-Pieter D'anvers
Joan Daemen
Ricardo Dahab
Nilanjan Datta
Bernardo David
Gareth Davies
Yi Deng
Amit Deo
Patrick Derbez
Siemen Dhooghe
Hang Dinh
Christoph Dobraunig
Javad Doliskani
Jelle Don
Xiaoyang Dong
Dung Duong
Betül Durak
Avijit Dutta
Sabyasachi Dutta
Sébastien Duval
Ted Eaton
Keita Emura
Muhammed F. Esgin
Thomas Espitau
Xiong Fan
Antonio Faonio
Prastudy Fauzi
Hanwen Feng
Shengyuan Feng
Tamara Finogina
Apostolos Fournaris
Ashley Fraser
Philippe Gaborit
Steven Galbraith
Pierre Galissant
Chaya Ganesh
Romain Gay
Chunpeng Ge
Kai Gellert
Nicholas Genise
Alexandru Gheorghiu
Hossein Ghodosi
Satrajit Ghosh
Benedikt Gierlichs
Kristian Gjøsteen
Aarushi Goel
Huijing Gong
Junqing Gong
Zheng Gong
Alonso González
Rishab Goyal
Benjamin Grégoire
Jiaxin Guan
Cyprien de Saint Guilhem
Aldo Gunsing
Chun Guo
Fuchun Guo
Qian Guo
Felix Günther
Ariel Hamlin
Ben Hamlin
Jinguang Han
Kyoohyung Han
Keisuke Hara
Debiao He
Chloé Hébant
Javier Herranz
Shoichi Hirose
Deukjo Hong
Akinori Hosoyamada
Hector Hougaard
Qiong Huang
Shih-Han Hung
Kathrin Hövelmanns
Akiko Inoue
Tetsu Iwata
Ashwin Jha
Dingding Jia
Shaoquan Jiang
Chanyang Ju
Eliran Kachlon
Saqib A. Kakvi
Ghassan Karame
Sabyasachi Karati
Angshuman Karmakar
Shuichi Katsumata
Marcel Keller
Dongwoo Kim
Jihye Kim
Jinsu Kim

Jiseung Kim
Jongkil Kim
Minkyu Kim
Myungsun Kim
Seongkwang Kim
Taechan Kim
Elena Kirshanova
Fuyuki Kitagawa
Susumu Kiyoshima
Michael Kloss
François Koeune
Lisa Kohl
Markulf Kohlweiss
Chelsea Komlo
Yashvanth Kondi
Nishat Koti
Toomas Krips
Veronika Kuchta
Thijs Laarhoven
Jianchang Lai
Qiqi Lai
Huy Quoc Le
Byeonghak Lee
Changmin Lee
Moon Sung Lee
Liang Li
Shuaishuai Li
Shun Li
Xiangxue Li
Xinyu Li
Ya-Nan Li
Zhe Li
Bei Liang
Cheng-Jun Lin
Fuchun Lin
Wei-Kai Lin
Dongxi Liu
Fukang Liu
Guozhen Liu
Jia Liu
Joseph K. Liu
Meicheng Liu
Qipeng Liu
Shengli Liu
Yunwen Liu
Zhen Liu
Julian Loss
Yuan Lu
Zhenliang Lu
Lin Lyu
Fermi Ma
Hui Ma
Xuecheng Ma
Bernardo Magri
Monosij Maitra
Christian Majenz
Nathan Manohar
Ange Martinelli
Zdenek Martinasek
Ramiro Martínez
Pedro Maat C. Massolino
Loïc Masure
Bart Mennink
Lauren De Meyer
Peihan Miao
Kazuhiko Minematsu
Rafael Misoczki
Tarik Moataz
Tal Moran
Tomoyuki Morimae
Hiraku Morita
Travis Morrison
Pratyay Mukherjee
Sayantan Mukherjee
Pierrick Méaux
Helen Möllering
Michael Naehrig
Yusuke Naito
Maria Naya-Plasencia
Ngoc Khanh Nguyen
Jianting Ning
Ryo Nishimaki
Ariel Nof
Kazuma Ohara
Daniel Esteban Escudero Ospina
Giorgos Panagiotakos
Bo Pang
Lorenz Panny
Anna Pappa
Anat Paskin-Cherniavsky
Alain Passelègue
Shravani Patil
Sikhar Patranabis
Kateryna Pavlyk
Alice Pellet-Mary
Geovandro Pereira
Thomas Peyrin
Phuong Pham
Stjepan Picek
Zaira Pindado
Rafael del Pino
Rachel Player
Geong Sen Poh
David Pointcheval
Yuriy Polyakov
Ali Poostindouz
Frédéric de Portzamparc
Chen Qian
Tian Qiu
Sai Rahul Rachuri
Adrian Ranea
Divya Ravi
Jean-René Reinhard
Peter Rindal
Francisco Rodríguez-Henríquez
Mélissa Rossi
Partha Sarathy Roy
Ajith S.
Yusuke Sakai
Kosei Sakamoto
Amin Sakzad
Simona Samardjiska
Olivier Sanders
Partik Sarkar
Santanu Sarkar
John Schanck
André Schrottenloher
Jacob Schuldt
Mahdi Sedaghat
Ignacio Amores Sesar
Siamak Shahandashti
Setareh Sharifian
Yaobin Shen
Sina Shiehian
Kazumasa Shinagawa
Janno Siim

Javier Silva
Ricardo Dahab
Siang Meng Sim
Leonie Simpson
Daniel Slamanig
Daniel Smith-Tone
Fang Song
Yongcheng Song
Florian Speelman
Akshayaram Srinivasan
Jun Xu
Igors Stepanovs
Ling Sun
Shi-Feng Sun
Akira Takahashi
Katsuyuki Takashima
Benjamin Hong Meng Tan
Syh-Yuan Tan
Titouan Tanguy
Adrian Thillard
Miaomiao Tian
Ivan Tjuawinata
Yosuke Todo
Alin Tomescu
Junichi Tomida
Ni Trieu
Viet Cuong Trinh
Ida Tucker
Aleksei Udovenko
Bogdan Ursu
Damien Vergnaud
Fernando Virdia
Srinivas Vivek
Misha Volkhov
Quoc Huy Vu
Alexandre Wallet
Ming Wan
Chenyu Wang
Han Wang
Junwei Wang
Lei Wang
Luping Wang
Qingju Wang
Weijia Wang
Wenhao Wang
Yang Wang
Yuyu Wang
Zhedong Wang
Gaven Watson
Florian Weber
Man Wei
Weiqiang Wen
Thom Wiggers
Zac Williamson
Lennert Wouters
Qianhong Wu
Keita Xagawa
Zejun Xiang
Hanshen Xiao
Xiang Xie
Yanhong Xu
Haiyang Xue
Shota Yamada
Takashi Yamakawa
Sravya Yandamuri
Jianhua Yan
Zhenbin Yan
Bo-Yin Yang
Guomin Yang
Kang Yang
Rupeng Yang
Shao-Jun Yang
Wei-Chuen Yau
Kisoon Yoon
Yong Yu
Zuoxia Yu
Chen Yuan
Tsz Hon Yuen
Aaram Yun
Alexandros Zacharakis
Michal Zajac
Luca Zanolini
Arantxa Zapico
Ming Zeng
Bin Zhang
Bingsheng Zhang
Cong Zhang
Hailong Zhang
Jiang Zhang
Liang Feng Zhang
Xuc Zhang
Zhenfei Zhang
Zhifang Zhang
Changan Zhao
Yongjun Zhao
Zhongxiang Zheng
Yihong Zhu
Arne Tobias Ødegaard

Contents – Part III

Secret Sharing

Attribute-Based Encryption

Updatable Encryption

Zero Knowledge

Blockchains and Contact Tracing

Multi-party Computation

MOTIF: (Almost) Free Branching in GMW
Via Vector-Scalar Multiplication

David Heath(✉), Vladimir Kolesnikov, and Stanislav Peceny

Georgia Institute of Technology, Atlanta, GA, USA
{heath.davidanthony,kolesnikov,stan.peceny}@gatech.edu

Abstract. MPC functionalities are increasingly specified in high-level languages, where control-flow constructions such as conditional statements are extensively used. Today, concretely efficient MPC protocols are circuit-based and must evaluate *all* conditional branches at high cost to hide the taken branch.

The Goldreich-Micali-Wigderson, or GMW, protocol is a foundational circuit-based technique that realizes MPC for p players and is secure against up to $p-1$ semi-honest corruptions. While GMW requires communication rounds proportional to the computed circuit's depth, it is effective in many natural settings.

Our main contribution is MOTIF (Minimizing OTs for IFs), a novel GMW extension that evaluates conditional branches almost for free by amortizing Oblivious Transfers (OTs) across branches. That is, we simultaneously evaluate multiple *independent* AND gates, one gate from each mutually exclusive branch, by representing them as a *single* cheap vector-scalar multiplication (VS) gate.

For 2PC with b branches, we simultaneously evaluate up to b AND gates using only two 1-out-of-2 OTs of b-bit secrets. This is a factor $\approx b$ improvement over the state-of-the-art $2b$ 1-out-of-2 OTs of 1-bit secrets. Our factor b improvement generalizes to the multiparty setting as well: b AND gates consume only $p(p-1)$ 1-out-of-2 OTs of b-bit secrets.

We implemented our approach and report its performance. For 2PC and a circuit with 16 branches, each comparing two length-65000 bitstrings, MOTIF outperforms standard GMW in terms of communication by $\approx$9.4×. Total wall-clock time is improved by $4.1-9.2\times$ depending on network settings.

Our work is in the semi-honest model, tolerating all-but-one corruptions.

Keywords: MPC · GMW · Conditional branching

1 Introduction

Secure Multiparty Computation (MPC) enables mutually untrusting parties to compute a function of their private inputs while revealing only the function output. The Goldreich-Micali-Wigderson (GMW) protocol is a foundational technique that realizes MPC for p players and that tolerates up to $p-1$ semi-honest

S. Moriai and H. Wang (Eds.): ASIACRYPT 2020, LNCS 12493, pp. 3–30, 2020.
https://doi.org/10.1007/978-3-030-64840-4_1

corruptions. In GMW, the players jointly evaluate a circuit C by (1) randomly secret sharing their private input values, (2) privately evaluating C gate-by-gate, ensuring that the random secret shares encode the correct value for each wire, and (3) reconstructing secret shares on the output wires.

While `XOR` gates are evaluated without interaction, `AND` gates require communication in the form of oblivious transfer (OT). The bottleneck in GMW performance is communication incurred by OTs, both in terms of bandwidth consumption and latency.

In this work, **we improve the bandwidth consumption of the GMW protocol for circuits that include conditional branching.** In particular, we improve by up to the branching factor: for a circuit with b branches, we reduce bandwidth consumption by up to $b\times$.

The Cost of Round Complexity and GMW Use Cases. GMW requires a round of communication for each of the circuit's layers of `AND` gates[1]. Because in many scenarios the network latency is substantial, constant-round protocols, such as Garbled Circuit (GC) are often preferred.

Nevertheless, there are a number of scenarios where GMW is preferable to GC and other protocols:

- GMW efficiently supports multiparty computation and is resilient against a dishonest majority. While multiparty GC protocols exist, they are expensive: the GC is generated jointly among players such that no small subset of players can decrypt wire labels. Thus, the GC must be generated inside MPC, which is expensive.
- Many useful circuits are *low-depth* or have low-depth variants. GMW's multi-round nature is less impactful for low-depth circuits, and prior work has shown that the protocol can outperform GC in these cases [SZ13].
- It is possible to front-load most of GMW's bandwidth consumption to a *pre-computation* phase. When pre-computation is allowed, GMW can perform useful work even before the computed function is known. Indeed, given pre-computed random OTs, GMW consumes only 6 bits per `AND` gate in the 2PC setting (1-out-of-2 bit OT can be done by transferring a single one-bit secret and a single two-bit secret as introduced in [Bea95]); this holds for arbitrary C. In contrast, GC protocols cannot perform useful work until the circuit is known[2].

[1] Circuit depth can be reduced by rebalancing at the cost of increased overall circuit size [BCE91,BB94]. Further, in the 2PC setting, two-input/one-output gates can be aggregated into multi-input/multi-output gates and evaluated in one round at cost exponential in the number of inputs [KKW17,DKS+17].

[2] Universal circuits (UCs) can be programmed in an online phase to model any circuit up to a given size n. Hence, UCs technically allow GC protocols to precompute a garbling before the circuit topology is known, but at great cost. A UC of size n is implemented with $3n \log n$ gates [LYZ+20]. Further, large numbers of GC labels (of total size greater than the garbling of the underlying circuit) must be transferred in the online phase in order to program the UC.

In sum, GMW is suitable for a number of practical scenarios, and its improvement benefits many applications.

Goal: (Almost) Free Branching in GMW. GMW is a circuit-based protocol, and as such, all of C's branches must be evaluated by the players. Until the recent work of [HK20] (whose improvement is not for MPC, but for the simpler zero-knowledge setting), it was widely believed that the cost of branching is unavoidable in circuit-based protocols. In this work, we show how to essentially eliminate the cost of branching for GMW. Our technique is wholly different from that of [HK20]; their 'stacking' technique has no obvious analog in GMW due to the interactive nature of the protocol.

Semi-honest GMW requires two bit-OTs per AND gate per each pair of players. The cost of such OT includes the transfer of the secrets (cheap, 3 bits from [Bea95]) and consumes one row of the OT extension matrix (expensive, κ bits). Evaluation of all but one branch is ultimately discarded by the MPC, and our goal is to eliminate this waste.

We work in the semi-honest model, which is useful in many scenarios (e.g. protecting against players who may become corrupted in the future). Furthermore, advances in the semi-honest model often lead to similar advances in the malicious model. We leave exploring such improvements to future work.

1.1 Our Contributions

- **Efficient `VS` gate.** We extend the GMW protocol with gates that we call 'vector-scalar' gates (`VS`). `VS` gates allow p players to multiply a shared vector of b bits by a shared scalar bit for only $p \cdot (p-1)$ OTs. Standard GMW computes each multiplication separately and thus requires $b \cdot p \cdot (p-1)$ OTs. Thus, we reduce bandwidth consumption by $b\times$ when evaluating the `VS` gate.
- **(Almost) free conditional branching.** We show how to use `VS` to essentially eliminate the communication cost of inactive branches. Precisely, we amortize random OTs needed to securely compute `AND` gates across a conditional. The players must still broadcast several bits per `AND` gate, but this cost is small compared to the expensive κ-bit random OTs which we amortize. For a circuit with b branches, we improve communication by up to $b\times$ as compared to state-of-the-art GMW. Our computation costs are also slightly lower than standard GMW because we process fewer OTs.
- **Implementation and evaluation.** We implemented our approach in `C++` and report performance (see Sect. 9). For 2PC and a circuit with 16 branches, we improve communication by 9.4× and total wall-clock time by 5.1× on a LAN and 9.2× on a LAN with shared traffic (i.e. lower bandwidth).

1.2 Presentation Outline

We motivated our work in Sect. 1 and summarized the contributions in Sect. 1.1. We present related work in Sect. 2, review the basic GMW protocol in Sect. 3, and introduce notation in Sect. 4.

We present a technical summary of our approach in Sect. 5. We formally specify our protocols in Sect. 6 and provide proofs in Sect. 7. We discuss implementation details and evaluate performance in Sects. 8 and 9.

2 Related Work

We improve the state-of-the-art Goldreich-Micali-Wigderson (GMW) protocol [GMW87] by adding an efficient vector-scalar multiplication gate (`VS`) that is notably useful for executing conditional branches. We therefore review related work that improves (1) secure computation of conditional branches and (2) the classic GMW protocol.

Stacked Garbling. A recent line of work improves communication of GC with conditional branching in settings where one player knows the evaluated branch [Kol18, HK20]. [Kol18] is motivated by the use case where the GC generator knows the taken branch, e.g. while evaluating one of several DB queries. [HK20] is motivated by ZK proofs.

Prior to these works, it was generally believed that all circuit branches must be processed *and transmitted* according to the underlying protocol. [Kol18, HK20] break this assumption by using communication proportional to only the longest branch, given that one of the players knows which branch is taken.

Our research direction was inspired by these prior works: we show that communication reduction via conditional branching efficiently carries to GMW as well. In particular, the OTs used to compute `AND` gates can be amortized across branches. Unlike [Kol18, HK20], we do not require any player to know which branch is taken.

Universal Circuits. Our work improves conditional branching by adding a new gate primitive that amortizes OTs across branches. Another approach instead recompiles branches into a new form. Universal circuits (UCs) are programmable constructions that can evaluate arbitrary circuits up to a given size n. Thus, a single UC can be programmed to compute any single branch in a conditional, amortizing the gate costs of the individual branches.

Unfortunately, a UC representing circuits of size n incurs significant overhead in the number of gates. Decades after Valiant's original construction [Val76], UC enjoyed a renewed interest due to its use in MPC, and UC size has steadily improved [KS08, LMS16, GKS17, AGKS19, KS16, ZYZL18]. The state-of-the-art UC construction has size $3n \log n$ [LYZ+20]. Even with these improvements, representing conditional branches with UCs is often impractical. For example, if we consider branches of size $n = 2^{10}$ gates, the state-of-the-art UC construction has factor $3 \cdot \log(2^{10}) = 30\times$ overhead. In addition, programming the UC based on branch conditions known only to the MPC player is a difficult and expensive process. Thus, in use cases arising in evaluation of typical programs, UC-based branch evaluation is slower than naïve circuit evaluation.

[KKW17] observed that UCs are overly general for conditional branching: a UC can represent *any* circuit up to size n, while a conditional has a fixed and often small set of publicly known circuits. Correspondingly, [KKW17] generalized UCs to *Set* Universal Circuits ($\mathcal{S}$-UCs). An $\mathcal{S}$-UC can be programmed to implement any circuit in a fixed set $\mathcal{S}$, rather than the entire universe of circuits of size n. By constraining the problem to smaller sets, the authors improved UC overhead. [KKW17] used heuristics to exploit common sub-structures in the topologies of the circuits in $\mathcal{S}$ by *overlaying* the circuits with one another. For a specific set of 32 circuits, the authors achieved 6.1× size reduction compared to separately representing each circuit. For 32 circuits, our approach can improve by up to 32×. Additionally, we do not face the expensive problem of programming the conditional based on conditions known only to the MPC player. Finally, [KKW17] is a heuristic whose performance depends on the specific circuits. Our approach is much more general.

Oblivious Transfer (OT) Extension and Silent OT. Since OT requires expensive public-key primitives, efficient GMW relies on OT *extension* [Bea96,IKNP03]. Our implementation uses the highly performant 1-out-of-2 OT extension of [IKNP03] as implemented by the EMP-toolkit [WMK16]. More specifically, we precompute 1-out-of-2 *random* OTs in a precomputation phase and use the standard trick [Bea95] to cheaply construct 1-out-of-2 OT from random OT.

With [IKNP03], each 1-out-of-2 OT requires transmission of a κ-bit (e.g. 128-bit) OT matrix row, regardless of the length of the sent secrets. Reducing the number of consumed OT matrix rows is the source of our improvement: our `VS` gate takes advantage of the fact that a single 1-out-of-2 OT of b-bit strings is much cheaper than b 1-out-of-2 OTs of 1-bit strings, since in the former case only one κ-bit OT matrix row is consumed.

Silent OT is an exciting recent primitive that generates large numbers of random OTs from relatively short pseudorandom correlation generators [BCG+19]. It largely removes the communication overhead of random OT when a large batch is executed. Currently, [IKNP03] remains more efficient than Silent OT in many contexts because Silent OT incurs expensive computation and involves operations with high RAM consumption [BCG+19]. We stress that although we emphasize communication improvement via amortizing OTs, Silent OT does not replace our approach. Indeed, our approach yields improvement even if we use Silent OT, because we reduce the number of needed random OTs, thus allowing us to run a smaller Silent OT instance. Therefore, our approach significantly reduces the computation overhead of Silent OT, both in terms of RAM consumption and wall-clock time.

GMW with Multi-input/Multi-output Gates. Prior work [KK13,KKW17, DKS+17] noticed that the cost of OTs associated with GMW gate evaluation could be amortized across several gates. [KK13] improved OT for short secrets by extending [IKNP03] 1-out-of-2 OT to a 1-out-of-n OT at only double the cost. [KKW17,DKS+17] applied the [KK13] OT to larger gates with more than the standard two inputs/one output, thus amortizing the OT matrix cost across several gates. As a secondary benefit, merging several gates into larger gates reduces the circuit depth and latency overhead.

Unfortunately, the above multi-input gate constructions encounter two significant problems. First, the size of the truth table, and thus bandwidth consumption, grows exponentially in the number of inputs. Therefore, it is unrealistic to construct multi-gates with large numbers of inputs. Second, gates that encode arbitrary functions do not cleanly generalize from the two-party to the multi-party setting. To explain why, we contrast arbitrary gates with `AND` gates. `AND` gates generalize to the multi-party setting because logical `AND` distributes over `XOR` secret shares. Therefore, the multiple players can construct `XOR` shares of the `AND` gate truth table. In contrast, an arbitrary function *does not* distribute over shares, and thus players cannot construct shares of the table.

Our `VS` gate can be viewed as a particularly useful multi-input/multi-output gate that `AND`s (multiplies) any number of vector elements with a scalar. The advantage of our approach over prior multi-input/multi-output gates is that our approach is based on algebra, not on the brute-force encoding of truth-tables. This algebra scales well both to any number of inputs/outputs and to any number of players. Of course, the most important difference is the key application of our approach – efficient branching – which was not achievable with prior work.

Arithmetic MPC and Vector OLE. A number of works presented arithmetic generalizations of MPC in the GMW style, e.g. [IPS09, ADI+17]. Modern works in this area can efficiently multiply arbitrary field elements using a generalization of 1-out-of-2 string OT called 'vector oblivious linear function evaluation' (vOLE) [ADI+17, BCGI18, DGN+17]. In addition, these works point out that field scalar-vector multiplication can be efficiently achieved with two vOLEs, and emphasize the usefulness of this technique for efficient linear algebra operations (e.g., matrix multiplication). Because we work with Boolean circuits, we do not need generalized vOLEs, and instead more efficiently base our vectorization directly on the efficient OT extension technique [IKNP03]. Importantly, our branching application benefits from multiplication of relatively small vectors (of size equal to the branching factors), while break-even points of prior constructions imply their usefulness with much longer vectors.

Our work applies efficient scalar-vector multiplication to the unobvious and important use case of conditional branching.

Constant-Overhead MPC. Ishai et al. [IKOS08] proposed a constant-overhead GMW-based MPC. They observe that once sufficiently many random OTs are available to the players, the remainder of the protocol can be done with constant overhead per Boolean gate. They exhibit a construction of such a pool of OTs with constant cost per OT. For this, [IKOS08] relies on Beaver's non-black-box OT extension [Bea96], decomposable randomized encoding and an NC^0 PRG. While asymptotically [IKOS08]'s cost is optimal, in concrete terms, it is impractically high. Our work does not achieve constant factor overhead, but similarly improves OT utilization and is concretely efficient.

GMW Optimizations. [CHK+12] showed that GMW is particularly suitable in low-latency network settings and that it outperforms GCs in certain scenarios.

[CHK+12] further showed an application in a set of online marketplaces such as a mobile social network, where a provider helps its users connect according to mutual interests. Their implementation used multi-threaded programming to take advantage of inherent parallelism available in the execution of OT and the evaluation of AND gates of the same depth.

[SZ13] introduced several low-level computation improvements, such as using SIMD instructions and performing load-balancing, and circuit representation improvements, such as choosing low-depth circuits even at the cost of larger overall circuits. [SZ13] also elaborated on a number of examples where GMW is suitable, including a privacy-preserving face recognition with Eigenfaces [EFG+09,HKS+10,SSW10] or Hamming distance [OPJM10]. We draw our key evaluation benchmark, a log-depth bitstring comparison circuit, from [SZ13].

3 GMW Protocol Review

The GMW protocol allows p semi-honest players to securely compute a Boolean function of their private inputs. The key invariant is that on each wire, the p players together hold an XOR secret share of the truth value.

Consider p players $P_1, ..., P_p$ who together evaluate a Boolean circuit C. For a wire a, we denote P_i's share of a as a_i. The players step through C gate-by-gate:

- For each wire a corresponding to an input bit from player P_i, P_i uniformly samples a p-bit XOR secret share of a and sends a share to each player.
- To compute an XOR gate $c = a \oplus b$, the players locally add their shares:

$$(a_1 \oplus ... \oplus a_p) \oplus (b_1 \oplus ... \oplus b_p) = (a_1 \oplus b_1) \oplus ... \oplus (a_p \oplus b_p)$$

- To compute an AND gate, the players communicate. Consider an AND Gate $c = ab$ and the following equality:

$$c = ab = (a_1 \oplus ... \oplus a_p)(b_1 \oplus ... \oplus b_p) = \left(\bigoplus_{i,j \in 1..p} a_i b_j \right)$$

  That is, to compute an AND gate it suffices for each pair of players to multiply together their respective shares and then for the players to locally XOR the results. Consider two players P_i and P_j. The players compute shares of $a_i b_j$ and $a_j b_i$ via 1-out-of-2 OT: To compute $a_i b_j$, P_i first samples a uniform bit x_i. Then, the players perform 1-out-of-2 OT where P_j inputs b_j as her choice bit and P_i submits as input x_i and $x_i \oplus a_i$. Let x_j be P_j's OT output and note that $x_i \oplus x_j = a_i b_j$. P_i XORs together her OT outputs with $a_i b_i$ (which is computed locally) and outputs the sum.
- For each output wire a, the players reconstruct the cleartext output by broadcasting their share and then locally XORing all shares.

Thus, the GMW protocol securely computes an arbitrary function by consuming $p(p-1)$ OTs per AND gate. Our construction uses this same protocol, except that we replace AND gates by a generalized VS gate that ANDs an entire vector of bits with a scalar bit for $p(p-1)$ OTs. As our key use-case, we show that this improves conditional branching.

4 Notation

- We use p to denote the number of players.
- We use subscript notation to associate a variable with a player. E.g., a_i is the share of wire a held by player P_i.
- t denotes the 'active' branch in a conditional i.e. a branch that is taken during the oblivious execution. $\bar{t}$ implies an 'inactive' branch.
- In this work, we manipulate strings of bits as vectors:
  • Superscript notation denotes vector indexes. E.g. a^i refers to the i-th index of a vector a.
  • We denote a vector of bits by writing parenthesized comma-separated values. E.g., (a, b, c) is a vector of a, b, and c.
  • We use n to denote the length of a vector.
  • When two vectors are known to have the same length, we use $\oplus$ to denote the bitwise XOR sum:

$$(a^1, \ldots, a^n) \oplus (b^1, \ldots, b^n) = (a^1 \oplus b^1, \ldots, a^n \oplus b^n)$$

  • We indicate a vector scalar Boolean product by writing the scalar to the left of the vector:

$$a(b^1, \ldots, b^n) = (ab^1, \ldots, ab^n)$$

5 Technical Overview

Our approach amortizes OTs across conditional branches. Section 6 formalizes this approach in technical detail. In this section, we explain at a high level.

Recall, that GMW computes `AND` (Boolean multiplication) gates via 1-out-of-2 OT. Suppose that we wish to multiply an entire *vector* of Boolean bits $(b^1, \ldots, b^n)$ by the same scalar a. I.e., we wish to compute $(ab^1, \ldots, ab^n)$. `MOTIF` amortizes the expensive 1-out-of-2 OTs needed to multiply each shared vector element by a shared *scalar* (hence the notation `VS` for vector-scalar). Namely, to evaluate n `AND` gates of this form, instead of using $n \cdot p \cdot (p-1)$ OTs of length-1 secrets, we use only $p \cdot (p-1)$ OTs of length-n secrets. This reduces consumption of the OT extension matrix rows, the most expensive resource in the GMW evaluation.

We first show how we achieve this cheap vector scalar multiplication. Then, we show how this tool is used to reduce the cost of conditional branching.

In this section, for simplicity, we focus on the case of $b = 2$ branches and $p = 2$ players. Our approach naturally generalizes to arbitrary b and p, and we formally present our constructions in full generality in Sect. 6.

5.1 `VS` Gates

As we showed in Sect. 3, a single `AND` gate computed amongst p players requires $p(p-1)$ 1-out-of-2 OTs. Our `VS` gate construction consumes the same number of

OTs, but multiplies an entire vector of bits by a scalar bit. Suppose two players P_1, P_2 wish to compute the following vector operation:

$$a(b,c) = (ab, ac)$$

where $a = a_1 \oplus a_2, b = b_1 \oplus b_2$, and $c = c_1 \oplus c_2$ are GMW secret shared between P_1, P_2. Note the following equality:

$$\begin{aligned} a(b,c) &= (a_1 \oplus a_2)(b_1 \oplus b_2, c_1 \oplus c_2) && \text{XOR shares} \\ &= (a_1b_1 \oplus a_1b_2 \oplus a_2b_1 \oplus a_2b_2, a_1c_1 \oplus a_1c_2 \oplus a_2c_1 \oplus a_2c_2) && \text{distribute} \\ &= a_1(b_1, c_1) \oplus a_1(b_2, c_2) \oplus a_2(b_1, c_1) \oplus a_2(b_2, c_2) && \text{group} \end{aligned}$$

The first and fourth summands can be computed locally by the respective players. Thus, we need only show how to compute $a_1(b_2, c_2)$ (the remaining third summand is computed symmetrically). To compute this vector `AND`, the players perform a single 1-out-of-2 OT of length-2 secrets. Here, P_2 plays the OT sender and P_1 the receiver. P_2 draws two uniform bits x and y and allows P_1 to choose between the following two secrets:

$$(x, y) \qquad (x \oplus b_2, y \oplus c_2)$$

P_1 chooses based on a_1 and hence receives $(x \oplus a_1b_2, y \oplus a_1c_2)$. P_2 uses the vector (x, y) as her secret share of this summand. Thus, the players successfully hold shares of $a_1(b_2, c_2)$.

Put together, the full vector multiplication $a(b, c)$ uses only two 1-out-of-2 OTs of length-2 secrets. Our `VS` gate generalizes to arbitrary numbers of players and vector lengths: a vector scaling of b elements between p players requires $p(p-1)$ 1-out-of-2 OTs of length b secrets.

5.2 `MOTIF`: (Almost) Free Conditional Branching in GMW

We now show how `VS` gates allow improved conditional branching. We amortize OTs used by `AND` gates across conditional branches. Branches may be arbitrary, having different topologies and operating on independent wires.

For simplicity, consider a circuit that has only two branches and that is computed by only two players; our approach generalizes to b branches and n players. Since the two branches are conditionally composed, one branch is 'active' (i.e. taken) and one is 'inactive'.

Our key invariant is that on all wires of the inactive branch the players hold a share of 0, whereas on the active branch they hold valid shares. We begin by showing how `AND` gates interact with this invariant. In particular, the invariant allows `AND` gates across different conditional branches to be simultaneously computed by a single `VS` gate. Then we show how all gates maintain the invariant and how we enter/leave branches.

AND *Gates.* Our key optimization allows the players to consider simultaneously one AND gate from each branch. For example, suppose the players wish to compute both a^1b^1 and a^2b^2 where a^1, b^1 are wires in branch 1 and a^2, b^2 are wires in branch 2. Despite the fact that the players compute two gates, they need only two 1-out-of-2 OTs. Let t be the taken branch. Hence x^t, y^t are active wires and $x^{\bar{t}}, y^{\bar{t}}$ are both 0. Observe the following equalities:

$$(x^t \oplus x^{\bar{t}})y^t = (x^t \oplus 0)y^t = x^t y^t$$
$$(x^t \oplus x^{\bar{t}})y^{\bar{t}} = (x_t \oplus 0)0 = 0$$

Thus if we efficiently compute both $(x^t \oplus x^{\bar{t}})y^t$ and $(x^t \oplus x^{\bar{t}})y^{\bar{t}}$, then we propagate the invariant: the active branch's AND output wire receives the correct value while the inactive branch's wire receives 0. These products reduce to a vector-scalar product computed by our VS gate:

$$(x^t \oplus x^{\bar{t}})(y^t, y^{\bar{t}})$$

Thus, we compute two AND gates for the price of one. This technique generalizes to arbitrary numbers of branches: to compute b AND gates across b branches, our approach consumes two OTs of length b secrets.

Additional Details. Our optimization relies on ensuring all inactive wires hold 0. We now show how we establish this invariant upon entering a branch, how non-AND gates maintain the invariant, and how we leave conditionals.

- **Demultiplexing.** 'Entering' a conditional is controlled by a *condition bit*, a single bit whose value determines which of the two branches should be taken. To enter a conditional with two branches, we *demultiplex* the input values based on the condition bit. That is, we AND the branch inputs with the condition bit. More precisely, for the input to branch 1, i.e. the branch taken if the condition bit holds 1, we AND the input bits with the condition bit. Symmetrically, for branch 0, we AND each input bit with the NOT of the condition bit. Thus, we obtain a vector of valid inputs for the active branch and a vector of all 0s for the inactive branch. Because we multiply all inputs by the same two bits, we can use VS gates to efficiently implement the demultiplexer. In order to implement more than two branches, we nest conditionals.
- **XOR gates.** XOR gates trivially maintain our invariant: an XOR gate with two 0 inputs outputs 0.
- **NOT gates.** Native NOT gates would break our invariant: a NOT gate with input 0 outputs 1. Thus, we do not *natively* support NOT gates. Fortunately, we can construct NOT gates from XOR gates. To do so, we maintain a distinguished 'true' wire in each branch. We ensure, by demultiplexing, that the 'true' wire holds logical 1 on all active branches and logical 0 on all inactive branches. A NOT gate of a wire can thus be achieved by XORing the wire with 'true'.
- **Multiplexing.** To 'leave' a conditional, we resolve the output wires of the two branches: we propagate the output values on the active branch and discard

the output of the inactive branch. Fortunately, our invariant means that this operation is extremely cheap: to multiplex the output values of wires on the active and inactive branches, we simply XOR corresponding wires together.

Branch Layer Alignment. As GMW is an interactive scheme, at any time we can only evaluate gates whose input shares have already been computed (*ready* gates), and thus we cannot include 'future round' AND gates into the current VS computation. In each round of GMW computation, we can only amortize OTs over the ready gates.

That is, in p-party GMW, in each round our technique eliminates *all* OTs, except for the total of $p(p-1) \cdot \max(w_i)$ OTs, where w_i is the number of AND gates in the current layer of branch i. Clearly, the more aligned (i.e. having a similar number of AND gates in each circuit layer) the circuit branches are, the higher the performance improvement.

In our experiments, we demonstrate the maximum achievable benefit of our construction by evaluating perfectly aligned circuits. While typical circuits will not have perfectly aligned branches, we do not expect them to have a poor alignment either, particularly if the branching factor is high. We leave improving alignment, perhaps via compilation techniques, as future work.

6 MOTIF: Formalization and Protocol Construction

We now formalize MOTIF, our GMW extension that supports efficient branching. As in the standard GMW protocol, our approach represents functions as circuits composed from a collection of low-level gates. We presented the core technical ideas of our approach in Sect. 5; the following discussion assumes a familiarity with Sect. 5.

Underlying Idea. We implement efficient branching by simultaneous evaluation of multiple *independent* AND gates, one gate from each mutually exclusive branch, by representing them as a *single* cheap VS gate.

Presentation Roadmap. Our formalization involves intertwined low-level cryptographic, programming language, and circuit technical details.

In Sect. 6.1 we motivate our compilation sequence, which takes a program with `if` branches written in a high-level language and outputs a *straight-line circuit* that uses VS gates. We do not yet explain in detail how it is achieved, absent a necessary formalization of circuits and gates, which we provide in Sect. 6.2. Armed with the formalization, we explain in Sect. 6.3 how vectorized VS gates facilitate branching in a straight-line circuit: we provide a formal algorithm (Fig. 1) that generates a straight-line circuit with VS gates implementing branching over two circuits C_0, C_1.

Then, having converted a program/circuit with branching into a VS circuit defined in Sect. 6.2, we focus on efficient secure evaluation of the latter. In Sect. 6.4, we complete our formalization by defining cleartext semantics. In Sect. 6.5, we present a complete protocol, Π-MOTIF, with proofs in Sect. 7.

6.1 Compiling Conditionals to Straight-Line VS Circuits

Our approach is concerned primarily with the efficient handling of conditional branching. Therefore, we begin our formalization by discussing how conditional branches can be efficiently represented in terms of only `XOR` and `VS` gates.

Assume that the user's MPC functionality is encoded in some high-level language as a program with branching. The user hands this high-level functionality to a *compiler* which translates the high-level-language program into a low-level collection of gates. To interface with our approach, the compiler should output a circuit that contains `XOR` and `VS` gates.

It is thus the job of the compiler to translate conditionals into the `VS` circuit. Recall (from Sect. 5.2) that our key branching invariant requires that all inactive branches hold 0 values on all wires. Consider b branches, where each branch i computes the conjunction $x^i y^i$, and where x^i, y^i are independent values carried by i-th branch's wires. Due to the key invariant, and as discussed in detail in Sect. 5.2, the following vector-scalar product simultaneously computes these b `AND`s:

$$(x^1 \oplus \ldots \oplus x^b)(y^1, \ldots, y^b)$$

The compiler's job is to output `VS` gates that simultaneously compute `AND` gates in this manner. In Sect. 6.3 we show how a compiler can *merge* the gates of two branches in order to amortize `AND` gates as just described. First, we describe the syntax needed for this compiler algorithm and for our protocol.

6.2 Circuit Formal Syntax

Because we add a new gate primitive, we cannot use the community-held implicit syntax of Boolean circuits. Thus, we formalize the syntax and semantics of our modified circuits such that we can prove correctness and security.

Gate Syntax. Our approach handles two kinds of gates: `XOR` gates, which can be evaluated locally, and vector-scalar gates (`VS`), a new type of gate, which multiplies a vector of bits by a scalar for the cost of only $p(p-1)$ OTs. An `XOR` gate has two input wires a, b and an output wire c and computes $c \leftarrow a \oplus b$. We denote an `XOR` gate by writing $\texttt{XOR}(c, a, b)$. A vector-scalar gate `VS` takes as input a scalar a and a vector $(b^1, \ldots, b^n)$ and computes:

$$(c^1, \ldots, c^n) \leftarrow a(b^1, \ldots, b^n)$$

We denote a vector-scalar gate by writing $\texttt{VS}((c^1, \ldots, c^n), a, (b^1, \ldots, b^n))$. We also formalize the input/output wires of the circuit. We denote an input wire a whose value is given by player P by writing $\texttt{INPUT}(P, a)$. Finally, we indicate that wire a is an output wire by writing $\texttt{OUTPUT}(a)$. Formally, let variables $a, b, c, \ldots$ be arbitrary wires and let P be an arbitrary player. The space of gates is denoted:

$$\mathcal{G} ::= \texttt{XOR}(c, a, b) \mid \texttt{VS}((c^1, \ldots, c^n), a, (b^1, \ldots, b^n)) \mid \texttt{INPUT}(P, a) \mid \texttt{OUTPUT}(a)$$

`NOT` *Gates.* Typically, Boolean techniques support gates that perform logical `NOT`. As discussed in Sect. 5, we do not *natively* support `NOT` gates as they would break the correctness of `VS` implementation of conditional branches: our invariant requires *all* inactive wires to hold shares of 0, and `NOT` gates flip 0 to 1. Accordingly, our formal syntax does not include `NOT` gates. Instead, we build `NOT` gates from `XOR` gates and a per branch auxiliary distinguished wire **aux**, which is set by the MPC player to **aux** = 1 in the active branch, and to **aux** = 0 in all inactive branches. Then $\neg a = a \oplus \textbf{aux}$, which implements `NOT` in the active branch and preserves monotonicity in the inactive branches.

Circuit Syntax. A *circuit* is a list of gates. We do not need to "connect" the gates in the circuit, since gates already refer to specific wire ids. Formally, let $g_1, \ldots, g_k \in \mathcal{G}$ be arbitrary gates. The space of circuits with k gates is denoted:

$$\mathcal{C} ::= (g_1, \ldots, g_k)$$

We consider a circuit to be valid only if the gates are in a *topological order*: i.e., a wire must appear as a gate output before it is used as a subsequent gate input. In upcoming discussion, we assume circuits are valid.

Circuit Layers. In our implementation, our circuit syntax groups collections of gates into *layers*, such that all `VS` gates of the same depth can be computed in constant communication rounds. We omit this layering from our formalization to keep notation simple, but emphasize that the required change is straightforward.

6.3 Merging Conditional Branches

As discussed in Sect. 6.1, we view the problem of translating from programs with conditional branches to circuits in our syntax as a problem for a compiler. In this section, we specify an algorithm `merge` (Sect. 1) that demonstrates how a compiler can combine `VS` gates from each branch into a single `VS` gate (of course, the standard `AND` gate is a special case of the `VS` gate).

For simplicity, assume that the high-level source language contains only binary branching, perhaps through `if` statements. Even in this simplified model, the programmer can nest `if` statements to achieve arbitrary branching. We also assume that the compiler can translate low-level program statements into circuits (e.g., assignment statements are converted into circuits).

Consider two branches of an `if` statement, and suppose that the compiler already recursively compiled the body of both branches into two circuits C_0 and C_1. To finish translating the `if` statement while taking advantage of our approach, the compiler should *merge together* `VS` gates in C_0 and C_1. `merge` is one technique for performing this combining operation. `merge` takes C_0 and C_1 as arguments and outputs a single circuit that computes both input circuits, but that uses fewer `VS` gates than simply concatenating C_0 and C_1. At a high level, `merge` walks the two input circuits gate-by-gate. It eagerly moves `XOR` gates from the input circuits to the output circuit until the next gate in both circuits

```
def merge(C_0, C_1) :
  m ← |C_0| ; n ← |C_1|
  out ← λ
  ▷ Initialize counters that point into the two respective circuits.
  i ← 1 ; j ← 1
  ▷ Continue to loop until gates from both input circuits are exhausted.
  while(i ≤ m and j ≤ n) :
    ▷ Eagerly pull XOR gates from both input circuits.
    while(i ≤ m and C_0[i] is an XOR gate) :
      out.push(C_0[i])
      i ← i + 1
    while(j ≤ n and C_1[j] is an XOR gate) :
      out.push(C_1[j])
      j ← j + 1
    ▷ Now, the next gate in both circuits either
    ▷ does not exist (i.e. the branch has no gates left) or is a VS gate.
    if i ≤ m and j ≤ n :
      ▷ The general case: both branches have a VS gate that can be merged.
      VS((c_0^1, ..., c_0^k), a_0, (b_0^1, ..., c_0^k)) ← C_0[i]
      VS((c_1^1, ..., c_1^k), a_1, (b_1^1, ..., c_1^k)) ← C_1[j]
      ▷ The compiler allocates a fresh wire for the XOR output
      a ← freshWire()
      ▷ Recall, our invariant ensures that at runtime either a_0 or a_1 holds 0.
      out.push(XOR(a, a_0, a_1))
      out.push(VS((c_0^1, ..., c_0^k, c_1^1, ..., c_1^k), a, (b_0^1, ..., b_0^k, b_1^1, ..., b_1^k))
    else if i ≤ m :
      out.push(C_0[i])
      i ← i + 1
    else if j ≤ n :
      out.push(C_0[j])
      j ← j + 1
  return out
```

Fig. 1. merge, a compiler algorithm, demonstrates how two branch circuits can be merged into one while joining together VS gates. By using an algorithm like merge, a compiler can use our approach to amortize the cost of OTs across conditional branches.

is a `VS` gate. `merge` combines these two `VS` gates into one by concatenating the two vectors and by `XOR`ing the two scalars. `merge` assumes that circuits inside of conditionals do not contain `INPUT` or `OUTPUT` wires.

By recursively applying `merge` across many conditional branches, a compiler can achieve up to $b\times$ reduction in the number of `VS` gates.

Merging Layers. As discussed in Sect. 6.2, our formalization does not account for circuit layers (i.e. `VS` gates that occur at the same multiplicative depth) for simplicity. In order to avoid increasing latency, merging must take care to preserve layers: merging `VS` gates across layers can increase the overall multiplicative depth and add communication rounds. Thus, the compiler must be careful when merging gates.

One straightforward technique, which we implemented, is to only merge together `VS` gates of the same depth. That is, our implementation introduces an extra loop which combines all `VS` gates that are grouped in the same layer instead of handling `VS` gates one at a time. Even this straightforward strategy is likely to yield large improvements, particularly if the branching factor is high.

More optimal approaches exist, and the problem of maximally amortizing OTs across branches thus becomes a relatively interesting compilers problem. An intelligent compiler could allocate gates to different layers in order to maximally match up `VS` gates across branches without increasing depth. An even more intelligent compiler could account for network settings in order to decide when it is worth it to increase multiplicative depth in exchange for better layer alignment.

6.4 Circuit Cleartext Semantics

Prior discussion showed that a Boolean circuit with branches can be represented as a straight-line `VS` circuit. We present our MPC protocol for evaluating such circuits in formal detail in Sect. 6.5.

In order to demonstrate that our protocol is correct, we require a formal semantics. I.e., we require the functionality that the protocol achieves. In this section, we specify the formal semantics of circuits as the algorithm `eval` listed in Fig. 2. `eval` maintains a circuit wiring: a map from wire indexes to Boolean values. Each gate reads values from the wiring for input wires and/or writes values to the wiring for output wires.

6.5 Our Protocol

In this section, we formalize our protocol `Π-MOTIF`, which securely implements the semantics of `eval` (Fig. 2):

Construction 1. *(Protocol* `Π-MOTIF`*)* `Π-MOTIF` *is defined in Figs. 3 and 4.*

Theorems in Sect. 7 imply the following:

Theorem 1. *Construction 1 implements the functionality* `eval` *(Fig. 2) and is secure against up to $p-1$ semi-honest corruptions in the OT-hybrid model.*

```
def eval(C, inp_1, ..., inp_p) :
  ▷ Initialize an empty wiring map.
  wiring ← λ
  ▷ Initialize an empty output string.
  out ← λ
  ▷ Update the wiring for each gate in the circuit.
  for g ∈ C :
   switch g :
     case XOR(c, a, b) :
       wiring[c] ← wiring[a] ⊕ wiring[b]
     case VS((c^1, ..., c^n), a, (b^1, ..., b^n))
       for i ∈ [1..n] :
         ▷ AND each vector input by a.
         wiring[c^i] ← wiring[a] · wiring[b^i]
     case INPUT(i, a) :
       ▷ Read a bit of input from player i.
       wiring[a] ← inp_i.pop()
     case OUTPUT(a) :
       ▷ Update the output string with the wire value.
       out.push(wiring[a])
  return out
```

Fig. 2. The cleartext semantics for a circuit $C \in \mathcal{C}$ run between p players. Each player i's input is modeled as a string of bits $\texttt{inp}_i$. The method pop pops the first value from the string. Each gate manipulates a *wiring*, which is a map from wire indexes to values. The output of evaluation is a string of bits out.

Figure 3 lists our high level protocol Π-MOTIF from the perspective of an arbitrary player P_i. For the reader familiar with the detail of the classic GMW protocol, the only essential difference between the classic protocol and ours is that we handle VS gates by invoking an instance of our Π-VS protocol.

Π-MOTIF ensures that the p players hold random XOR secret shares of the truth values on the already computed wires. This invariant ensures both correctness and security: the protocol is correct because the output wires' secret shares can be reconstructed to the correct truth value. The protocol is secure because the XOR secret shares are uniformly random, and hence no player's share (or any strict subset's shares) gives any information about the truth value on a particular wire. We argue these facts in detail in our proofs (Sect. 7).

Like the functionality eval, Π-MOTIF proceeds by case analysis on gates:

Functionality:

- Players $P_1, \ldots, P_p$ agree on a circuit $C \in \mathcal{C}$.
- Each player P_i provides as input a bitstring $\mathtt{inp}_i$.
- Players output $\mathtt{eval}(C, \mathtt{inp}_1, \cdots, \mathtt{inp}_p)$.

Protocol:

```
Π-MOTIF_i(C, inp_i) :
  ▷ Each player sets up an empty wiring map and output string.
  wiring ← λ
  out ← λ
  ▷ The protocol proceeds by case analysis of each gate in C.
  for g ∈ C :
    switch g :
      case XOR(c, a, b) :
        ▷ XOR gates are computed locally by each player.
        wiring[c] ← wiring[a] ⊕ wiring[b]
      case VS((c^1, ..., c^n), a, (b^1, ..., b^n)) :
        ▷ We delegate VS gates to the protocol Π-VS.
        (ab^1, ···, ab^n) ← Π-VS_i(wiring[a], wiring[b^1], ..., wiring[b^n])
        ▷ Each player puts VS gate results into her wiring.
        for j ∈ [1..n]
          wiring[c^j] ← ab^j
      case INPUT(j, a) :
        if i == j :
          ▷ Player j draws fresh shares that XOR sum to her next input.
          ▷ sendShares outputs P_j's share, which she adds to her wiring.
          wiring[a] ← sendShares(inp_i.pop())
        else :
          ▷ Other players add random shares sent by j to their wiring.
          wiring[a] ← recvShare(j)
      case OUTPUT(j, a) :
        ▷ Each player broadcasts her output share and locally sums all shares.
        ▷ reconstruct performs the broadcasts and the local XOR.
        out.push(reconstruct(wiring[a]))
  return out
```

Fig. 3. Our protocol Π-MOTIF from the perspective of player i. Π-MOTIF performs the same tasks as the classic GMW protocol except for VS gates, where we delegate to the sub-protocol Π-VS.

- XOR. The players locally XOR their shares. Because XOR is commutative and associative, this local computation correctly implements the functionality.
- VS. We delegate VS gates to a separate protocol Π-VS (Fig. 4). Recall, VS simultaneously multiplies an entire n-element Boolean vector $(x^1, \ldots, x^n)$ by a Boolean scalar a, as follows: Let p be the number of players holding XOR shares of a and $x^1, ..., x^n$. Consider an arbitrary k-th vector element x^k. Π-VS is based on the following equivalence:

$$ax^k = (a_1 \oplus \ldots \oplus a_p)(x_1^k \oplus \ldots \oplus x_p^k) = \bigoplus_{i=1}^{p} \left(\bigoplus_{j=1}^{p} a_i x_j^k \right) \quad (1)$$

  Now, the sums $\bigoplus_{j=1}^{p} a_i x_j^k$ can be delivered to player P_i *simultaneously* for all $k \in [1, ..., n]$ via only $(p-1)$ n-bit string 1-out-of-2 OTs executed with the $p-1$ other players. Once this is done for all p players (using a total of $p(p-1)$ OTs of n-bit strings), the result is a secret sharing of the vector $(ax^1, ..., ax^n)$. OT senders introduce uniform masks to protect the secrecy of their shares x_j^k. The VS protocol is formalized in Fig. 4.
- INPUT. Each input wire has a designated player who provides the input value. In Π-MOTIF, this player distributes a share of a single bit from their input. Our formalization assumes two procedures: (1) `sendShares` constructs a uniform XOR secret share of a given value and sends the shares to all p players and (2) `recvShare` is the symmetric procedure that receives a single share from the sending player.
- OUTPUT. For output wires, the players simply reconstruct their XOR secret shares. Our formalization assumes a protocol `reconstruct` which handles these details. `reconstruct` instructs each player to broadcast their share to all other players. Then, each player locally XORs together all shares.

7 Proofs

Now that we have formalized Π-MOTIF, we prove that it is correct and secure.

7.1 Proof of Correctness

Π-MOTIF implements the functionality `eval` (Fig. 2):

Theorem 2 (Π-MOTIFCorrectness). *For all circuits* $C \in \mathcal{C}$ *and all input bit-strings* $\texttt{inp}_1, \ldots, \texttt{inp}_p$*:*

$$\texttt{eval}(C, \texttt{inp}_1, \ldots, \texttt{inp}_p) = \Pi\text{-}\texttt{MOTIF}(C, \texttt{inp}_1, \ldots, \texttt{inp}_p)$$

Proof. By induction on C. The invariant is that gate input wires hold XOR secret shares of corresponding cleartext values.

We proceed by case analysis of an individual gate g, showing that the invariant is propagated from input wires to output wires.

Functionality:

- Players $P_1, \ldots, P_p$ input XOR secret shares of $a, b^1, \ldots, b^n$.
- Players output XOR secret shares of $ab^1, \ldots, ab^n$.

Protocol:

```
Π-VS_i(a_i, b_i^1, ..., b_i^n) :
  ▷ Vector scaling is computed by having each player i interact with every player j.
  for j ∈ [1..p] :
    if i == j :
      ▷ P_i computes the AND of her two shares locally.
      c_j ← (a_i b_i^1, ..., a_i b_i^n)
    else if i < j :
      ▷ To AND shares with another player, the two players perform two OTs.
      ▷ The order of OT send/receive is chosen based on player IDs.
      ▷ When sending, P_i's share is a uniform mask.
      x ← draw {0,1}^n
      OTsend(x, x ⊕ (b_i^1, ..., b_i^n))
      y ← OTrecv(a_i)
      ▷ The sub-result computed with P_j is the XOR sum of both OT outputs.
      c_j ← x ⊕ y
    else if i > j :
      ▷ Symmetric to above: order of send and receive is swapped.
      y ← OTrecv(a_i)
      x ← draw {0,1}^n
      OTsend(x, x ⊕ (b_i^1, ..., b_i^n))
      c_j ← x ⊕ y
  ▷ The output vector is the XOR sum of all results computed with all players.
  return ⨁_j c_j
```

Fig. 4. Protocol Π-VS from the perspective of player i. Π-VS explains how the players perform a vector-scalar multiplication. draw uniformly draws a random bit-vector of the specified length. OTSend and OTRecv respectively send and receive a 1-out-of-2 OT of n-bit secrets. In practice, we precompute all random OTs at the start of the protocol.

- Suppose g is an input INPUT(i, a). Then P_i secret shares her input bit and distributes it amongst players, trivially establishing the invariant on wire a.
- Suppose g is an XOR gate XOR(c, a, b). By induction, the input wires a and b hold correct shares. In Π-MOTIF, the players locally sum their shares. Thus,

the output wire c holds a correct sharing of the XOR of the input shares:

$$(a_1 \oplus \ldots \oplus a_p) \oplus (b_1 \oplus \ldots \oplus b_p) = (a_1 \oplus b_1) \oplus \ldots \oplus (a_p \oplus b_p)$$

- Suppose g is a vector-scalar gate $\texttt{VS}((c^1, \ldots, c^n), a, (b^1, \ldots, b^n))$. By induction, $a, b^1, \ldots, b^n$ hold correct shares. Consider an arbitrary vector element b^k. The specification `eval` requires that the corresponding output wire c^k obtains a secret sharing of ab^k. Recall the crucial AND equality given by Equation (1):

$$ab^k = (a_1 \oplus \ldots \oplus a_p)(b_1^k \oplus \ldots \oplus b_p^k) = \bigoplus_{i=1}^{p} \left(\bigoplus_{j=1}^{p} a_i b_j^k \right)$$

  The protocol Π-VS (Fig. 4) uses local computation and OTs to simultaneously compute a secret sharing of the above XOR sum for each vector element. In particular, for each element b^k, each player P_i computes a share $\bigoplus_{j=1}^{p} a_i b_j^k$ (with added random masks). Thus, for each vector element b^k, the players hold correct XOR secret shares, which they store on the wire c^k.
- Suppose g is an output $\texttt{OUTPUT}(a)$. By induction, wire a holds correct secret shares. Thus, when the players reconstruct their shares they obtain the correct truth value for wire a.

Π-MOTIF is correct.

□

7.2 Proof of Security

We now prove Π-MOTIF secure in the OT-hybrid model. Π-MOTIF uses 1-out-of-2 OT as an oracle functionality.

Our proof is nearly identical to that of classic GMW. The difference between the two proofs is that our protocol uses VS gates whereas classic GMW uses AND gates. Both proofs show that interactions involving AND/VS gates can be simulated by uniform bits.

Theorem 3 (Π-MOTIFSecurity). *Π-MOTIF is secure against semi-honest corruption of up to $p - 1$ players in the OT-hybrid model.*

Proof. By construction of a simulator $\mathcal{S}$ that simulates the view of a player P_1, and an argument that $\mathcal{S}$ generalizes to arbitrary strict subsets of players.

At a high level, $\mathcal{S}$ computes simulated secret shares on all circuit wires and adds simulated messages to P_1's simulated view. The crucial property is that all wire values, except outputs and inputs belonging to P_1, are indistinguishable from uniform bits.

- Consider an input wire. First, suppose that this wire belongs to P_1. In this case, P_1 receives no messages. Hence, $\mathcal{S}$ need not modify P_1's view. Instead, $\mathcal{S}$ samples a uniform bit as an XOR secret share of P_1's input and adds it to the circuit wiring.

Next, suppose that the input wire belongs to some other player $P_{i \neq 1}$. Recall that $P_{i \neq 1}$ uniformly samples an XOR secret share of her input and sends one share to P_1. Thus, $\mathcal{S}$ simulates an input wire by drawing a uniform bit. $\mathcal{S}$ adds this bit to P_1's view and to the circuit wiring.

- XOR gates are computed locally. Hence, $\mathcal{S}$ need not modify P_1's view. Instead, $\mathcal{S}$ simply XORs the gate's simulated input shares and adds the output share to the wiring.
- Consider a VS gate. In the real world, P_1 interacts with OT twice per every other player (once as a sender and once as a receiver). On send interactions, P_1 receives no output, so the interaction is trivially simulated. Receiving OTs is more complex. Recall that for a VS gate (see Fig. 4), each player $P_{i \neq 1}$ sends via OT either a random string x or $x \oplus b$ where b is $P_{i \neq 1}$'s shares for all of the scaled wires. Note that in this second message, b is masked by x. Since P_1 obtains only one of these messages from the OT oracle, both are indistinguishable from uniform bits. Thus, $\mathcal{S}$ simulates each OT output by drawing uniform bits. Now, $\mathcal{S}$ updates the simulated wiring by XORing the simulated input shares with the simulated OT messages (see Fig. 4, Equation (1) for the required computation) and places the results on the VS gate output wires.
- Consider an output wire. In the real world, P_1 receives all other players' shares and XORs them with her own share. $\mathcal{S}$ must take care that P_1's view is consistent with this XORed output value. In particular, $\mathcal{S}$ draws uniform bits to simulate messages for all uncorrupted players except for one. For this last player, $\mathcal{S}$ simulates a message by XORing these drawn bits with P_1's simulated share (stored in the wiring) and the desired output.

Thus, $\mathcal{S}$ simulates P_1's view.

Now, we argue that $\mathcal{S}$ is generalizable to any strict subset of players. Because of the symmetry of the protocol, $\mathcal{S}$ is clearly applicable to any one player. Generalizing to more than one player relies on the fact that players' values are XOR secret shares. Thus, holding k player shares gives no information about the other players' views. $\mathcal{S}$ is easily modified to simulate more messages, i.e. to simulate the messages received by all simulated players.

Π-MOTIF is secure against semi-honest corruption of up to $p - 1$ players. □

8 Implementation

We implemented MOTIF in C++ using GCC's experimental support for C++20. Our implementation consists of a circuit compiler, which converts code with conditionals into circuits, and a circuit evaluator, which implements our protocol.

Our compiler accepts a C++ program written in a stylized vocabulary. This vocabulary allows programs with overloaded C++ Boolean operations that construct Boolean circuits (from the programmer's perspective, this stylized vocabulary is similar to that of EMP's circuit generation library). We add a special

IF/THEN/ELSE branching syntax that constructs circuits with conditionals of two branches. Higher branching factor is achieved by nesting.

The compiler outputs XOR and VS gates listed in order of depth. The compiler also optionally outputs standard GMW circuits (i.e., without our conditional optimization) for benchmarking purposes.

Our implementation of the MPC protocol Π-MOTIF is natural, but we point out some of its more interesting aspects. We use 1-out-of-2 [IKNP03] OT as implemented by EMP [WMK16]. Each pair of players precomputes enough OT matrix rows for the MPC evaluation. Players evaluate circuits layer-by-layer as specified by the compiler output. In the case of standard GMW, players evaluate each AND gate by consuming two OT matrix rows per each pair of players. In Π-MOTIF, players consume the same number of OT matrix rows, but evaluate our more expressive VS gates. The benefit of our approach is that up to $b\times$ fewer VS gates (vs AND gates) are needed to implement b branches, thus reducing the number of consumed OT rows. In both the reference protocol and our optimized protocol, we parallelize OTs for AND/VS gates in the same circuit layer. Thus, communication rounds are proportional to the circuit's multiplicative depth.

9 Performance Evaluation

We compare Π-MOTIF to the standard GMW protocol [GMW87]. All experiments were run on a commodity laptop running Ubuntu 19.04 with an Intel(R) Core(TM) i5-8350U CPU @ 1.70 GHz and 16 GB RAM. All players were run on the same machine, and network settings were configured with the tc command. We sampled data points over 200 runs, averaging the middle 100 results.

In our experiments, the computed circuit consists of b branches, each implementing the same log-depth string-comparison circuit, which checks the equality of two length-65000 bitstrings. The active branch is selected based on private variables chosen by the players. In more realistic circuits, each conditional branch would have a different topology. We use the same circuit across branches so that it is easy to understand branching improvement: all branches have the same size.

We emphasize that our compiler does not 'optimize away' conditionals: i.e., even though each branch is the same circuit, all branches are still evaluated by both protocols. We use a string-comparison circuit because it is indicative of the kinds of circuits where GMW excels: the string-comparison circuit has low-depth. This circuit was suggested as a useful application of GMW by [SZ13].

Choice of Benchmark Circuit and Layering. As discussed in Sect. 5.2, our approach cannot always fully amortize OTs across branches because we must preserve the circuit's multiplicative depth. Thus, in p-party GMW, in each round our technique eliminates all OTs, except for the total of $p(p-1) \cdot \max(w_i)$ OTs, where w_i is the number of AND gates in the current layer of branch i. The effectiveness of our approach thus varies depending on the relative *alignment* of branch layers. Branches that are highly aligned (i.e., have similar numbers of AND gates in each layer) enjoy significant improvement.

Because our experiment uses the same circuit in each branch, we achieve perfect alignment. Thus, our experiments show the maximum benefit that our technique can provide. We emphasize that our approach *always* reduces the number of required OTs, because each circuit layer of each branch must have at least 1 AND gate that can be combined into a VS gate. Additionally, as we discuss in Sect. 6.3, compiler technologies can be applied to improve the alignment of misaligned circuits, further improving the benefit of our approach.

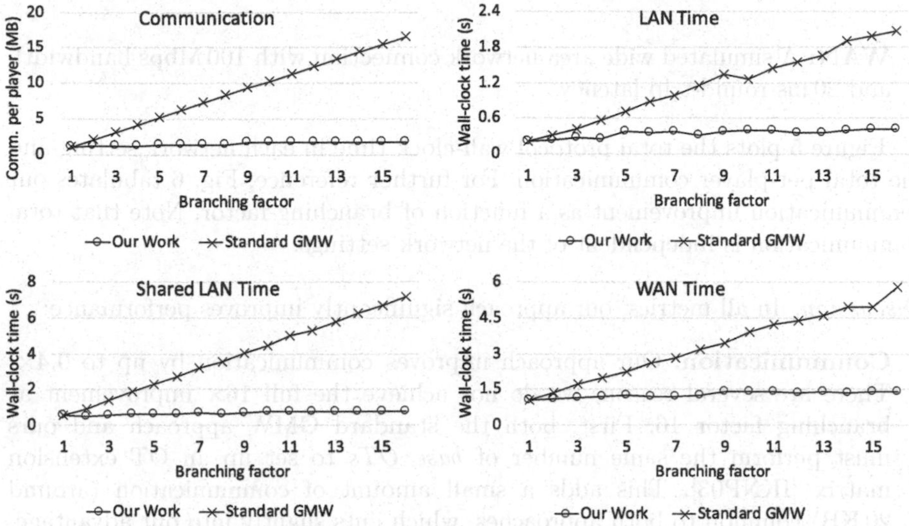

Fig. 5. 2PC comparison of Π-MOTIF against standard GMW. We plot the following metrics as functions of the *branching factor* (i.e. the number of branches in the overall conditional): the overall per-player communication (top-left), the wall-clock time to complete the protocol on a LAN (top-right), the wall-clock time to complete the protocol on a LAN where other processes share bandwidth (bottom-left), and the wall-clock time on a WAN (bottom-right).

9.1 2PC Improvement over Standard GMW

We first compare the performance of Π-MOTIF to that of standard GMW in the 2PC setting. Specifically, we run the branching string-comparison circuit between two players on 3 different simulated network settings:

1. **LAN:** A simulated gigabit ethernet connection with 1 Gbps bandwidth and 2 ms round-trip latency.
2. **Shared LAN:** A simulated shared local area network connection where the protocol shares network bandwidth with a number of other processes. The connection features 50 Mbps bandwidth and 2 ms round-trip latency.

# Branches	Π-MOTIF(MB)	Standard GMW (MB)	Improvement
1	1.04	1.04	1×
2	1.09	2.07	1.9×
4	1.18	4.11	3.5×
8	1.37	8.21	6×
16	1.74	16.39	9.4×

Fig. 6. Per-player communication improvement for our 2PC string comparison experiment as a function of the number of branches.

3. **WAN:** A simulated wide area network connection with 100 Mbps bandwidth and 20 ms round-trip latency.

Figure 5 plots the total protocol wall-clock time in each network setting and the total per-player communication. For further reference, Fig. 6 tabulates our communication improvement as a function of branching factor. Note that total communication is independent of the network settings.

Discussion. In all metrics, our approach significantly improves performance:

- **Communication.** Our approach improves communication by up to 9.4×. There are several reasons we do not achieve the full 16× improvement at branching factor 16. First, both the standard GMW approach and ours must perform the same number of *base OTs* to set up an OT extension matrix [IKNP03]. This adds a small amount of communication (around 20 KB) common to both approaches, which cuts slightly into our advantage. Second, the online communication for the body of each branch is the same in both approaches. That is, although we amortize the κ-bit strings sent for random OTs, we do not amortize the six bits per `AND` gate needed in the 'online' phase of the protocol. Finally, we pay communication cost for the demultiplexer at the start of each branch. Recall that we `AND` branch inputs with the branch condition to ensure that all inactive branches have 0 on each wire. Although the demultiplexer is achieved using only one `VS` gate (and hence two OTs) per branch, the 'online' cost of multiplying 65000 wires by the branch condition is significant. The relative cost of demultiplexers varies with the number of inputs to each branch: circuits with small inputs incur less demultiplexer overhead. The string comparison circuit has a particularly costly demultiplexer because the circuit has a large number of input bits relative to the number of gates in the circuit.
- **LAN wall-clock time.** On a fast LAN network, our approach's improvement is diminished compared to our communication improvement. Even so, we improve by approximately 5.1× over standard GMW at 16 branches. A 1Gbps network is very fast, and our modest hardware struggles to fill the communication pipe. With better hardware and low-level implementation improvements, our wall-clock improvement would approach 9.4×.

- **Shared LAN wall-clock time.** On the more constrained shared LAN network, our approach excels. We achieve an approximate 9.2× speedup compared to standard GMW at 16 branches. On this slower network, our hardware and implementation easily keep up with the network, and hence we very nearly match the 9.4× communication improvement.
- **WAN wall-clock time.** On this high-latency network our advantage is less pronounced. Still, we achieve a 4.1× speedup compared to standard GMW at 16 branches. This high-latency network highlights the weakness of GMW's multi-round nature. Because we do not reduce the number of rounds, our approach incurs the same total latency as standard GMW, and hence our improvement is diminished.

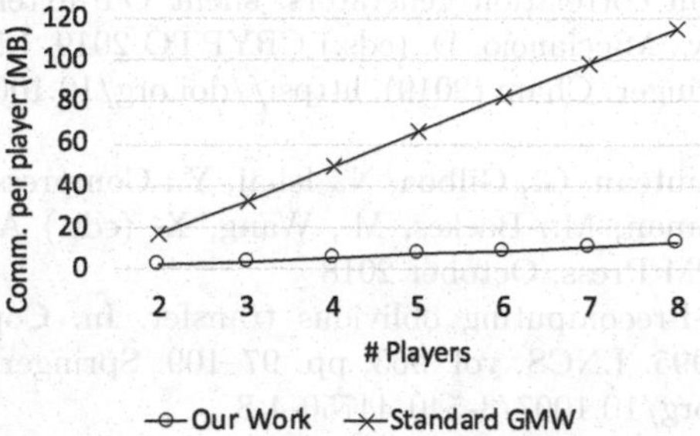

Fig. 7. MPC per-player communication usage of both Π-MOTIF and of standard GMW as a function of the number of players. Note that, like standard GMW, our approach uses per-player communication linear in the number of players.

9.2 Scaling to MPC

For our second experiment, we emphasize our approach's efficient scaling to the multiparty setting. This experiment uses the same branching string-comparison circuit as the first, but fixes the number of branches to 16. We run this 16-branch circuit among varying numbers of MPC players. We plot the results of this experiment in Fig. 7.

Discussion. The key takeaway of this second experiment is that MOTIF works well in the multiparty setting. In particular, our approach's branching optimization does not add extra costs compared to standard GMW: both techniques use total communication quadratic in the number of players.

References

[ADI+17] Applebaum, B., Damgård, I., Ishai, Y., Nielsen, M., Zichron, L.: Secure arithmetic computation with constant computational overhead. Cryptology ePrint Archive, Report 2017/617 (2017). http://eprint.iacr.org/2017/617

[AGKS19] Alhassan, M.Y., Günther, D., Kiss, Á., Schneider, T.: Efficient and scalable universal circuits. Cryptology ePrint Archive, Report 2019/348 (2019). https://eprint.iacr.org/2019/348

[BB94] Bonet, M.L., Buss, S.R.: Size-depth tradeoff for Boolean formulae. Inf. Process. Lett. **49**, 151–155 (1994)

[BCE91] Bshouty, N.H., Cleve, R., Eberly, W.: Size-depth tradeoffs for algebraic formulae. In: 32nd FOCS, pp. 334–341. IEEE Computer Society Press, October 1991

[BCG+19] Boyle, E., Couteau, G., Gilboa, N., Ishai, Y., Kohl, L., Scholl, P.: Efficient pseudorandom correlation generators: silent OT extension and more. In: Boldyreva, A., Micciancio, D. (eds.) CRYPTO 2019. LNCS, vol. 11694, pp. 489–518. Springer, Cham (2019). https://doi.org/10.1007/978-3-030-26954-8_16

[BCGI18] Boyle, E., Couteau, G., Gilboa, N., Ishai, Y.: Compressing vector OLE. In: Lie, D., Mannan, M., Backes, M., Wang, X. (eds.) ACM CCS 2018, pp. 896–912. ACM Press, October 2018

[Bea95] Beaver, D.: Precomputing oblivious transfer. In: Coppersmith, D. (ed.) CRYPTO 1995. LNCS, vol. 963, pp. 97–109. Springer, Heidelberg (1995). https://doi.org/10.1007/3-540-44750-4_8

[Bea96] Beaver, D.: Correlated pseudorandomness and the complexity of private computations. In: 28th ACM STOC, pp. 479–488. ACM Press, May 1996

[CHK+12] Choi, S.G., Hwang, K.-W., Katz, J., Malkin, T., Rubenstein, D.: Secure multi-party computation of Boolean circuits with applications to privacy in on-line marketplaces. In: Dunkelman, O. (ed.) CT-RSA 2012. LNCS, vol. 7178, pp. 416–432. Springer, Heidelberg (2012). https://doi.org/10.1007/978-3-642-27954-6_26

[DGN+17] Döttling, N., Ghosh, S., Nielsen, J.B., Nilges, T., Trifiletti, R.: TinyOLE: efficient actively secure two-party computation from oblivious linear function evaluation. In: Thuraisingham, B.M., Evans, D., Malkin, T., Xu, D. (eds.) ACM CCS 2017, pp. 2263–2276. ACM Press, October/November 2017

[DKS+17] Dessouky, G., Koushanfar, F., Sadeghi, A.-R., Schneider, T., Zeitouni, S., Zohner, M.: Pushing the communication barrier in secure computation using lookup tables. In: NDSS 2017. The Internet Society, February/March 2017

[EFG+09] Erkin, Z., Franz, M., Guajardo, J., Katzenbeisser, S., Lagendijk, I., Toft, T.: Privacy-preserving face recognition. In: Goldberg, I., Atallah, M.J. (eds.) PETS 2009. LNCS, vol. 5672, pp. 235–253. Springer, Heidelberg (2009). https://doi.org/10.1007/978-3-642-03168-7_14

[GKS17] Günther, D., Kiss, Á., Schneider, T.: More efficient universal circuit constructions. Cryptology ePrint Archive, Report 2017/798 (2017). http://eprint.iacr.org/2017/798

[GMW87] Goldreich, O., Micali, S., Wigderson, A.: How to play any mental game or A completeness theorem for protocols with honest majority. In: Aho, A. (ed.) 19th ACM STOC, pp. 218–229. ACM Press, May 1987

[HK20] Heath, D., Kolesnikov, V.: Stacked garbling for disjunctive zero-knowledge proofs. In: Canteaut, A., Ishai, Y. (eds.) EUROCRYPT 2020. LNCS, vol. 12107, pp. 569–598. Springer, Cham (2020). https://doi.org/10.1007/978-3-030-45727-3_19

[HKS+10] Henecka, W., Kögl, S., Sadeghi, A.-R., Schneider, T., Wehrenberg, I.: TASTY: Tool for automating secure two-party computations. Cryptology ePrint Archive, Report 2010/365 (2010). http://eprint.iacr.org/2010/365

[IKNP03] Ishai, Y., Kilian, J., Nissim, K., Petrank, E.: Extending oblivious transfers efficiently. In: Boneh, D. (ed.) CRYPTO 2003. LNCS, vol. 2729, pp. 145–161. Springer, Heidelberg (2003). https://doi.org/10.1007/978-3-540-45146-4_9

[IKOS08] Ishai, Y., Kushilevitz, E., Ostrovsky, R., Sahai, A.: Cryptography with constant computational overhead. In: Ladner, R.E., Dwork, C. (eds.) 40th ACM STOC, pp. 433–442. ACM Press, May 2008

[IPS09] Ishai, Y., Prabhakaran, M., Sahai, A.: Secure arithmetic computation with no honest majority. In: Reingold, O. (ed.) TCC 2009. LNCS, vol. 5444, pp. 294–314. Springer, Heidelberg (2009). https://doi.org/10.1007/978-3-642-00457-5_18

[KK13] Kolesnikov, V., Kumaresan, R.: Improved OT extension for transferring short secrets. In: Canetti, R., Garay, J.A. (eds.) CRYPTO 2013. LNCS, vol. 8043, pp. 54–70. Springer, Heidelberg (2013). https://doi.org/10.1007/978-3-642-40084-1_4

[KKW17] Kennedy, W.S., Kolesnikov, V., Wilfong, G.: Overlaying conditional circuit clauses for secure computation. In: Takagi, T., Peyrin, T. (eds.) ASIACRYPT 2017. LNCS, vol. 10625, pp. 499–528. Springer, Cham (2017). https://doi.org/10.1007/978-3-319-70697-9_18

[Kol18] Kolesnikov, V.: `Free IF`: how to omit inactive branches and implement $\mathcal{S}$-universal garbled circuit (almost) for free. In: Peyrin, T., Galbraith, S. (eds.) ASIACRYPT 2018. LNCS, vol. 11274, pp. 34–58. Springer, Cham (2018). https://doi.org/10.1007/978-3-030-03332-3_2

[KS08] Kolesnikov, V., Schneider, T.: A practical universal circuit construction and secure evaluation of private functions. In: Tsudik, G. (ed.) FC 2008. LNCS, vol. 5143, pp. 83–97. Springer, Heidelberg (2008). https://doi.org/10.1007/978-3-540-85230-8_7

[KS16] Kiss, Á., Schneider, T.: Valiant's universal circuit is practical. In: Fischlin, M., Coron, J.-S. (eds.) EUROCRYPT 2016. LNCS, vol. 9665, pp. 699–728. Springer, Heidelberg (2016). https://doi.org/10.1007/978-3-662-49890-3_27

[LMS16] Lipmaa, H., Mohassel, P., Sadeghian, S.: Valiant's universal circuit: Improvements, implementation, and applications. Cryptology ePrint Archive, Report 2016/017 (2016). http://eprint.iacr.org/2016/017

[LYZ+20] Liu, H., Yu, Y., Zhao, S., Zhang, J., Liu, W.: Pushing the limits of valiant's universal circuits: Simpler, tighter and more compact. IACR Cryptology ePrint Archive, 2020:161 (2020)

[OPJM10] Osadchy, M., Pinkas, B., Jarrous, A., Moskovich, B.: SCiFI - a system for secure face identification. In: 2010 IEEE Symposium on Security and Privacy, pp. 239–254. IEEE Computer Society Press, May 2010

[SSW10] Sadeghi, A.-R., Schneider, T., Wehrenberg, I.: Efficient privacy-preserving face recognition. In: Lee, D., Hong, S. (eds.) ICISC 2009. LNCS, vol. 5984, pp. 229–244. Springer, Heidelberg (2010). https://doi.org/10.1007/978-3-642-14423-3_16

[SZ13] Schneider, T., Zohner, M.: GMW vs. Yao? Efficient secure two-party computation with low depth circuits. In: Sadeghi, A.-R. (ed.) FC 2013. LNCS, vol. 7859, pp. 275–292. Springer, Heidelberg (2013). https://doi.org/10.1007/978-3-642-39884-1_23
[Val76] Valiant, L.G.: Universal circuits (preliminary report). In: STOC, pp. 196–203, New York, NY, USA. ACM Press (1976)
[WMK16] Wang, X., Malozemoff, A.J., Katz, J.: EMP-toolkit: Efficient MultiParty computation toolkit (2016). https://github.com/emp-toolkit
[ZYZL18] Zhao, S., Yu, Y., Zhang, J., Liu, H.: Valiant's universal circuits revisited: an overall improvement and a lower bound. Cryptology ePrint Archive, Report 2018/943 (2018). https://eprint.iacr.org/2018/943

Maliciously Secure Matrix Multiplication with Applications to Private Deep Learning

Hao Chen[1], Miran Kim[2], Ilya Razenshteyn[3], Dragos Rotaru[4,5], Yongsoo Song[3], and Sameer Wagh[6,7(✉)]

[1] Facebook, Menlo Park, USA
haoche@fb.com
[2] Ulsan National Institute of Science and Technology, Ulsan, South Korea
mirankim@unist.ac.kr
[3] Microsoft Research, Redmond, USA
{ilyaraz,yongsoo.song}@microsoft.com
[4] imec-COSIC, KU Leuven, Leuven, Belgium
[5] Cape Privacy, New York, USA
dragos@capeprivacy.com
[6] Princeton University, Princeton, NJ, USA
swagh@alumni.princeton.edu
[7] University of California, Berkeley, USA

Abstract. Computing on data in a manner that preserve the privacy is of growing importance. Multi-Party Computation (MPC) and Homomorphic Encryption (HE) are two cryptographic techniques for privacy-preserving computations. In this work, we have developed efficient UC-secure multiparty protocols for matrix multiplications and two-dimensional convolutions. We built upon the SPDZ framework and integrated the state-of-the-art HE algorithms for matrix multiplication. Our protocol achieved communication cost linear only in the input and output dimensions and not on the number of multiplication operations. We eliminate the "triple sacrifice" step of SPDZ to improve efficiency and simplify the zero-knowledge proofs. We implemented our protocols and benchmarked them against the SPDZ LowGear variant (Keller et al. Eurocrypt'18). For multiplying two square matrices of size 128, we reduced the communication cost from 1.54 GB to 12.46 MB, an improvement of over two orders of magnitude that only improves with larger matrix sizes. For evaluating all convolution layers of the ResNet-50 neural network, the communication reduces cost from 5 TB to 41 GB.

Keywords: Multi-party computation · Dishonest majority · Homomorphic encryption

Work done while Sameer, Dragos, and Hao were at Microsoft Research, Redmond.

S. Moriai and H. Wang (Eds.): ASIACRYPT 2020, LNCS 12493, pp. 31–59, 2020.
https://doi.org/10.1007/978-3-030-64840-4_2

1 Introduction

Secure Multiparty Computation (MPC) allows a set of parties to compute over their inputs while keeping them private. Over the span of few decades this field turned theoretical ideas into practical implementations that allow to compute even one billion Boolean gates per second [2] with an honest majority of parties. The growth of computing on encrypted data has sparked interest in combining MPC with Machine Learning (ML), which allows distrusting parties to perform ML tasks such as evaluating private decision trees and support vector machines [35] or evaluating and training neural networks, on their joint data [4,31,33,34,37].

One important building block in all these works is *secure matrix multiplication*, which is often achieved by computing many dot products $\boldsymbol{a} \cdot \boldsymbol{b}$. In the case of honest majority this problem has a straightforward solution: parties multiply locally each entry $a_i \cdot b_i$ and then re-randomize the sum $\sum_i a_i \cdot b_i$ to the other parties. Hence, the cost of a dot product is a single opening which is independent of the vector sizes. However, in the case of dishonest majority the dot product protocol must use some correlated randomness (e.g. *Beaver triples*) for each multiplication since the secret sharing scheme is no longer multiplicative. Such a triple requires expensive public key operations and a lot of research focused on computing triples more efficiently via somewhat homomorphic encryption (HE) or oblivious transfer [6,19,26,27].

The SPDZ framework [5,18,19,27] is a state-of-the-art protocol for dishonest-majority MPC under one of the strongest adversarial settings – it assumes all-but-one corruption and malicious security, meaning that all parties except one can be controlled by the adversary, and can arbitrarily deviate from the protocol description. Moreover, SPDZ is proven secure under the Universal Composability (UC) framework of Cannetti [11], which means in particular that it is still secure when composed arbitrarily with other MPC protocols. Under this framework, even if a fast matrix multiplication algorithm such as Strassen's algorithm is used, securely multiplying two $n \times n$ matrices in SPDZ uses at least $O(n^{2.8})$ authenticated Beaver triples. This is prohibitively expensive when targeting applications with a large number and sizes of matrix multiplications. For instance, the deep convolutional neural network (CNN) ResNet50 [24] requires more than 4 billion multiplications of plaintext values[1]. Currently, the best two-party triple generation algorithm over a 128-bit prime field produces 30,000 triples per second on modest hardware and requires a communication of 15 kbits per party [27]. Using such an approach, the preprocessing phase for evaluating convolution layers of ResNet50 will require each party to send 5 TB of data. Our work reduces the communication by a factor of about 121×, while keeping the same adversarial setting.

[1] This is considering the scenario that both the model (i.e., ResNet weights) and inference inputs are secret shared.

1.1 Our Contributions

We summarize our contributions below:

1. We integrate the idea of classical Beaver triples to multiple matrices into the dishonest majority SPDZ framework (this idea has been explored previously in the semi-honest setting in works such as [15,34,37]). This enables computing any bilinear operation efficiently in a *dishonest majority MPC setting.* We focus on two types of bilinear operations, matrix multiplications and two-dimensional convolutions. We call the correlated randomness 'matrix triple' and 'convolution triple', respectively. We then applied the state-of-the-art algorithm for HE matrix multiplication [25] to efficiently generate authenticated matrix triples with low communication complexity. Such algorithms allow us to have a communication cost linear in the size of the input and output, and independent of the complexity of the operation itself, in both offline and online phases. For example, in terms of matrix multiplication of n-by-n matrices, our method reduced the communication from $O(n^3)$ to $O(n^2)$ required by SPDZ, with similar computational overhead.
2. We introduced some further optimizations to the offline phase of SPDZ:
   - We avoid the "sacrifice" procedure in SPDZ via switching to slightly larger HE parameters which supports circuits of one more depth. By doing this, we saved a factor of (almost) two in overall communication and computation.
   - We optimized the zero-knowledge proof of plaintext knowledge in the offline phase of SPDZ, reducing the amortized communication overhead for proving each ciphertext from 2.5 to roughly 1.5.
3. We demonstrated the concrete efficiency of our protocols for (1) private matrix multiplications and (2) private neural network inference in the two-party case. In the former case, we benchmarked the private matrix multiplications over various matrix sizes while in the latter, we benchmarked evaluation of all convolution layers of ResNet-50, a massive, state-of-the-art neural network for image classification with 52 layers. The preprocessing phase improves by a factor of at least 121 compared to SPDZ. We integrated the convolution triples in MP-SPDZ [20] to evaluate the online phase ResNet-50 convolutions. Our approach reduces the online communication overhead from 86.9 GB to only 0.54 GB (for a plaintext modulus $p \approx 2^{128}$), which amounts to a factor of at least 150× improvement over the existing matrix multiplication in SPDZ using Strassen's algorithm.

1.2 Related Works

To the best of our knowledge, our work is the first to consider efficient linear algebra in the context of dishonest majority MPC. Previous research works primarily focused on evaluating relatively small ML models such as support vector machines or decision trees [16,32]. However, for deep convolutional neural networks (CNN) the linear operations occupy a significant part of the computation. We give a brief overview on some recent protocols for combining MPC with ML:

1. In ABY3 [33], Mohassel and Rindal mix secret sharing with garbled circuits for the three party case with honest majority. While their work introduces many clever techniques to perform share conversions, it is hard to estimate its performance on deep neural networks such as ResNet50 since their optimizations are circuit dependent and precision sensitive. It is also unclear how to extend their techniques to support an arbitrary number of parties with a dishonest majority.
2. SecureNN [37] operates under the same trust assumption as ABY3: three party protocols with honest majority. While they also introduced some clever techniques to compute the sign function in MPC over rings, these only work for their specific setting.
3. Barak et al. [4] used quantized datatypes instead of fixed point arithmetic to realize secure inference on Google's MobileNets. They have implemented secure quantized dot products to perform the convolutions in MobileNets for various adversary structures (semi-honest, honest majority, and dishonest majority). If the convolutions are done by evaluating dot products, they incur an $O(n^3)$ communication cost for convolving two $n \times n$ matrices in the dishonest majority case. Our work would cut down a factor of n from their communication cost.
4. Helen [38] proposed a protocol for distributed convex optimization by converting between SPDZ and the Paillier additively homomorphic encryption (AHE) scheme. They use zero-knowledge proofs on top of Paillier for secure matrix-vector multiplication in the dishonest majority setting. Instead, our work does not need costly conversions, utilizes more efficient lattice-based AHE scheme, and is fully compatible with the SPDZ framework.
5. Jiang et al. [25] is a more recent protocol and strictly outperforms [39] – the latter takes 19 s to multiply two 128×128 matrices whereas the former only takes 5 s and we outperform Jiang et al.

1.3 Roadmap

We present preliminary materials in Sect. 2. In Sect. 3, we introduce our changes to the SPDZ framework to better support bilinear operations, including an algorithm to generate authenticated matrix triples, an optimization which removes the sacrifice procedure, and optimizations on the ZKPoPK. We go on to present the experimental results for private matrix multiplication, private nearest neighbor search, and private evaluation of ResNet-50 in Sect. 4. Finally, we conclude in Sect. 5.

2 Preliminaries

2.1 Notation

We use $\boldsymbol{x}$ to denote vectors i.e., $\boldsymbol{x} = (x_1, \ldots, x_k)$ for some k specified in the context. We also use the notation $[k]$ to denote the set $\{1, 2, \ldots, k\}$. For a positive integer q, we identify $\mathbb{Z}_q = \mathbb{Z} \cap (-q/2, q/2]$. For a finite set S, $U(S)$ denotes a uniform distribution over S.

Adversarial Setting. Our protocols in this work follow the same adversarial setting as SPDZ, meaning that they are secure under all-but-one corruption and malicious security (we will refer to this setting as *dishonest majority* for short). Also, our protocol is proven secure under the UC framework [10], a property inherited from SPDZ.

2.2 Authenticated Shares in SPDZ

Let n be the number of parties involved in the multi-party computation. In the SPDZ framework, all computations are performed over the finite field $\mathbb{Z}_p$ with prime p. We use $[\![x]\!]_\alpha$ to denote "authenticated shares", i.e., the i-th party holds (x_i, m_i) such that $x \equiv x_0 + \ldots + x_{n-1} \pmod p$ and $\alpha \cdot x \equiv m_0 + \ldots + m_{n-1} \pmod p$. The parties also hold shares α_i of the global MAC key $\alpha \equiv \alpha_0 + \ldots + \alpha_{n-1} \pmod p$. In other words,

$$[\![x]\!]_\alpha := \{(x_i, m_i, \alpha_i)\}_{i=1}^n \text{ such that}$$
$$\sum_i m_i \equiv \left(\sum_i \alpha_i\right) \cdot \left(\sum_i x_i\right) \pmod p \tag{1}$$

2.3 Bilinear Triples

Beaver's multiplication triple technique is widely used in secure computation in both semi-honest and malicious settings. [6,19,34,37]. Let $\mathbb{F}$ be a finite field. Recall that a multiplication triple is a tuple $([a], [b], [c])$ where $a, b \in \mathbb{F}$ are random elements such that $c = a \cdot b$. Here $[x]$ represents an additive sharing of x where each party has a share x_i such that $\sum_{i=1}^n x_i = x$. These multiplication triples can be utilized to perform private multiplication: in order to multiply secret-shared values x and y. The parties reveal $x - a$ and $y - b$, and compute $[x \cdot y] = (x - a) \cdot (y - b) + [a] \cdot (y - b) + (x - a) \cdot [b] + [c]$. In the dishonest majority malicious adversarial setting, SPDZ enhances the above to authenticated triples $([\![a]\!], [\![b]\!], [\![c]\!])$.

Mohassel and Zhang [34] generalized the above notion to "matrix triples" and applied it to secure training of machine learning models in the semi-honest setting. We take this idea further and consider triples for any bilinear operation. Then, we integrate them with the SPDZ preprocessing framework to provide security in the dishonest majority malicious adversarial setting.

Bilinear Triples. Let l, m, k be positive integers and let $\circledast : \mathbb{F}^l \times \mathbb{F}^m \to \mathbb{F}^k$ be a bilinear function[2]. Then, we define a $\circledast$-*triple* as a tuple of secret sharings $[a], [b], [a \circledast b]$ where a, b are uniformly random. Given such a triple, it is simple to securely compute a secret sharing of $x \circledast y$ given secret sharings of x and y

[2] A function $\circledast$ is called *bilinear* if it satisfies the relations $(\alpha x_1 + x_2) \circledast y = \alpha(x_1 \circledast y) + x_2 \circledast y$ and $x \circledast (\alpha y_1 + y_2) = \alpha(x \circledast y_1) + x \circledast y_2$ for arbitrary $\alpha \in \mathbb{F}$, $x_1, x_2, x \in \mathbb{F}^l$ and $y_1, y_2, y \in \mathbb{F}^k$.

following Beaver's method verbatim. Note that when $\circledast$ is scalar multiplication, we get back Beaver's multiplication triple; when $\circledast$ is matrix multiplication, we get the matrix triple in [34]. Another example is convolution, described in more detail below.

Using $\circledast$-triples instead of Beaver triples for securely computing bilinear operations has an advantage of lower communication cost in the triple consumption phase. For example, multiplying two n-by-n matrices with Beaver triples would cost $O(n^3)$ field elements being communicated, or $O(n^{\log 7+o(1)})$ using Strassen's algorithm, whereas using matrix triple only amounts to $O(n^2)$ communication cost. Importantly, we will see that using $\circledast$-triples could also reduce the communication cost in the *triple generation phase*, via homomorphic encryption.

Convolutions. *Convolution* is a bilinear operation between tensors widely used by deep neural networks [28,30]. Here we will define and discuss *two-dimensional* convolutions, since they are used by a ResNet network [24] we use for benchmarking, but our approach can be easily generalized to all dimensions.

Let A_{ijk} be an input tensor, where $1 \le i \le h$ and $1 \le j \le w$ are spatial coordinates, and $1 \le k \le s$ is the channel. Suppose we would like to compute an $(2l+1) \times (2l+1)$-convolution for some $l \ge 0$, given by a tensor $B_{\Delta i,\Delta j,k,k'}$, where $-l \le \Delta i, \Delta j \le l$ are shifts of the spatial coordinates, and $1 \le k \le s$ and $1 \le k' \le s'$ are the channels. The resulting tensor $C_{ijk'} = \mathsf{conv}(A, B)$ has $h \times w$ spatial coordinates and s' channels and is defined via the formula:

$$C_{ijk'} = \sum_{\Delta i,\Delta j,k} A_{i+\Delta i,j+\Delta j,k} \cdot B_{\Delta i,\Delta j,k,k'},$$

where in the right-hand side, we set the entries of A to be zero if $i + \Delta i$ or $j + \Delta j$ are outside of the ranges $[1; h]$ and $[1; w]$, respectively. Since convolution is bilinear, we can consider *convolution triples*, that is secret shares of uniformly random tensors A, B and secret shares of $\mathsf{conv}(A, B)$.

We can reduce convolution to matrix multiplication as follows: we create an $wh \times (2l+1)^2 \cdot s$ matrix $\mathcal{A}$ with $\mathcal{A}_{(i,j)(\Delta i,\Delta j,k)} = A_{i+\Delta i,j+\Delta j,k}$, as well as an $(2l+1)^2 \cdot s \times s'$ matrix $\mathcal{B}$ defined as: $\mathcal{B}_{(\Delta i,\Delta j,k)k'} = B_{\Delta i,\Delta j,k,k'}$. Then one can extract C from the product $\mathcal{C} = \mathcal{AB}$ (which is of size $wh \times s'$) as follows: $C_{ijk'} = \mathcal{C}_{(i,j)k'}$. Note that 1×1 convolution ($l = 0$) is exactly matrix multiplication. When $l > 0$, one of the matrices $\mathcal{A}$ is obtained from $(2l+1)^2$ stacked permuted instances of the flattening of A. Overall, using this reduction, we can compute the convolution in $O((2l+1)^2 \cdot whss')$ operations[3]. Thus, evaluating the convolution using the authenticated Beaver triples in SPDZ requires $O((2l+1)^2 \cdot whss')$ communication. In contrast, using our convolution triples yields a communication cost of merely $O((wh + s') \cdot s \cdot (2l+1)^2)$. Sometimes, one is willing to *stride* the convolution. This simply corresponds to the regular sampling of the i, j coordinates of the answer. In terms of matrix multiplications, this corresponds to sampling a subset of rows of $\mathcal{A}$.

[3] In principle, one can speed it up using Fourier or Winograd transforms [29], but we leave the study of these algorithms in the secure setting for the future work.

2.4 The BFV Scheme

We use the Fan-Vercauteren variant of Brakerski's scale-invariant HE scheme [8, 21], which we shall refer to as the BFV scheme. For a power-of-two integer N, we denote by $R = \mathbb{Z}[X]/(X^N+1)$ and $R_q = \mathbb{Z}_q[X]/(X^N+1)$ the ring of integers of $(2N)$-th cyclotomic field and its residue ring modulo q. We define $\|a\|_\infty$ of an element $a \in R_q$ as the infinite norm of its coefficient vector in $\mathbb{Z}_q^N$. A secret key $\mathsf{sk} = s \in R$ is sampled uniformly from the set R_3 of ternary polynomials with coefficients in $\{0, \pm 1\}$. A public key of BFV is generated by

$$\mathsf{pk} = (-a \cdot s + e, a) \in R_q^2, \tag{2}$$

for $a \leftarrow U(R_q)$ and $e \leftarrow \chi$ from the error distribution χ over R. We set χ to be a discrete Gaussian with a small variance and let ρ be an upper bound of χ, i.e., $|e| \leq \rho$ holds with an overwhelming probability where $e \leftarrow \chi$. The BFV encryption and decryption procedures are given by the following formulas:

$$\begin{aligned} \mathsf{Enc} &: m \mapsto \mathfrak{c}_m = u \cdot \mathsf{pk} + (\Delta \cdot m + e_0, e_1) \pmod q, \\ \mathsf{Dec} &: \mathfrak{c}_m \mapsto m = \lfloor \Delta^{-1} \cdot (\mathfrak{c}_0 + \mathfrak{c}_1 \cdot s) \rceil \pmod p, \end{aligned} \tag{3}$$

where $\mathfrak{c}_m = (\mathfrak{c}_0, \mathfrak{c}_1)$, $m \in R_p$ is the message to be encrypted, $\Delta = \lfloor q/p \rfloor$, $u \leftarrow U(R_3)$, $e_0, e_1 \leftarrow \chi$, and $\lfloor \cdot \rceil$ denotes the nearest integer function. For the remainder of the paper, we use the shorthand $r_m = (u, e_0, e_1) \in R^3$ to denote the randomness used for encrypting a plaintext m. We write $\mathfrak{c}_m = \mathsf{Enc}(m, r_m)$ when the randomness is taken as input of encryption.

We define the *normalized norm* of randomness r_m by $\|r_m\| = \max\{\|u\|_\infty, \rho^{-1} \cdot \|e_0\|_\infty, \rho^{-1} \cdot \|e_1\|_\infty\}$. For $B > 0$, we call $\mathfrak{c}$ a *B-ciphertext* if there exists $m \in R_p$ and $r_m = (u, e_0, e_1) \in R^3$ such that $\|r_m\| \leq B$ and $\mathfrak{c} = \mathsf{Enc}_{\mathsf{pk}}(m, r_m)$. We also use U_B to denote a uniform distribution over the set of triples $r = (u, e_0, e_1) \in R^3$ such that $\|r\| \leq B$.

The native plaintext space of BFV is R_p, but we can exploit the Discrete Fourier Transform (DFT) over $\mathbb{Z}_p$ to pack multiple values in a single ciphertext and support parallel computation in a single instruction multiple data (SIMD) manner. We choose a plaintext modulus satisfying $p = 1 \pmod{2N}$ so that $X^N + 1 = \prod_{i \in \mathbb{Z}_{2N}^\times}(X - \zeta^i)$ for a primitive $2N$-th root of unity ζ of the finite field $\mathbb{Z}_p$. Hence, we can use the packing technique via the ring isomorphism $R_p \to \mathbb{Z}_p^N$, $m(X) \mapsto (m(\zeta^i))_{i \in \mathbb{Z}_{2N}^\times}$.

Recall that the multiplicative group $\mathbb{Z}_{2N}^\times$ is isomorphic to $\mathbb{Z}_2 \times \mathbb{Z}_{N/2}$. In our implementation, we encode two vectors of length $N/2$ into a single element of R_p using this algebraic structure. The BFV scheme support the simultaneous rotation of these two based on the homomorphic evaluation of automorphism $X \mapsto X^5$. More generally, we can perform an arbitrary linear transformation on these two vectors by combining homomorphic rotation and plaintext-ciphertext multiplication in BFV. The complexity of a linear transformation is mainly dominated by k rotations where $k \leq N/2$ is the number of nonzero diagonals $(A_{0,i}, A_{1,i+1} \ldots, A_{N/2-1,i-1})$ of its matrix representation $A \in \mathbb{Z}_p^{N/2 \times N/2}$. We refer the reader to [22] for details.

2.5 Matrix Multiplication Using HE

We recall the protocol from [25] which transforms square matrix multiplications into HE-friendly operations. For a $d \times d$ square matrix $A = (a_{i,j})_{0 \le i,j < d}$, we first define useful permutations σ, τ, ϕ, and ψ on the set $\mathbb{Z}_p^{d \times d}$. For simplicity, we assume that $N/2 = d^2$. All the indices will be considered as integers modulo d. Let $\sigma(A)_{i,j} = a_{i,i+j}$, $\tau(A)_{i,j} = a_{i+j,j}$, $\phi(A)_{i,j} = a_{i,j+1}$, and $\psi(A)_{i,j} = a_{i+1,j}$. Then for two square matrices A, B of order d, we can express the matrix product $A \times B$ as follows:

$$A \times B = \sum_{k=0}^{d-1} \left(\phi^k \circ \sigma(A)\right) \odot \left(\psi^k \circ \tau(B)\right), \tag{4}$$

where $\odot$ denotes the component-wise multiplication between matrices (see Sect. 3.1 of [25] for more detail).

We can identify a matrix of order $d \times d$ with a vector of length d^2 via the encoding map $\mathbb{Z}_p^{d^2} \to \mathbb{Z}_p^{d \times d}$, $\boldsymbol{a} = (a_0, \ldots, a_{d^2-1}) \mapsto A = (a_{d \cdot i+j})_{0 \le i,j < d}$. A ciphertext will be called an encryption of A if it is an encryption of the plaintext vector $\boldsymbol{a}$. Suppose that we are given two ciphertexts $\mathfrak{c}_A$ and $\mathfrak{c}_B$ that encrypt $\sigma(A)$ and $\tau(B)$, respectively. Then we define the homomorphic matrix product by

$$\mathfrak{c}_A \circledast \mathfrak{c}_B = \sum_{k=0}^{d-1} \left(\phi^k(\mathfrak{c}_A) \boxtimes \psi^k(\mathfrak{c}_B)\right), \tag{5}$$

where $\mathfrak{c} \boxtimes \mathfrak{c}'$ denotes the homomorphic multiplication between two ciphertexts $\mathfrak{c}$ and $\mathfrak{c}'$. The permutations ϕ^k and ψ^k are fixed linear transformations over $\mathbb{Z}_p^{d^2}$, which can be evaluated as described above. The evaluation of a permutation includes only two homomorphic rotations since the matrix representation of ϕ^k or ψ^k has two nonzero diagonals. It follows from Eq. (4) that $\mathfrak{c}_A \circledast \mathfrak{c}_B$ is an encryption of $A \times B$.

The authors of [25] implemented the matrix multiplication algorithm over the CKKS scheme [14], while we apply the same algorithm to the BFV scheme encrypting two vectors of dimension $(N/2)$ with entries in $\mathbb{Z}_p$. We will encrypt two square matrices A and B of size $d = \sqrt{N/2}$ in a single ciphertext. As noted in Sect. 2.4, the BFV scheme supports parallel arithmetic operations and permutations on two vectors. Hence, we can perform two homomorphic matrix multiplications simultaneously by fully utilizing the slots.

3 Protocol Specification

We describe our major contributions in this section. First, we propose our algorithm for generating authenticated matrix triples. Then, we introduce two other optimizations. The first one improves the triple generation phase, by carefully choosing the HE parameters to avoid the sacrifice stage. The second one improves the zero-knowledge proof of knowledge in SPDZ.

3.1 Generation of Bilinear Triples

In this section we present our main contribution, which can be thought of as an improvement to the SPDZ framework to support efficient bilinear operations, in particular matrix multiplications and convolutions. Recall that the offline phase of the SPDZ framework generates Beaver triples, which means that to multiply two square matrices of size d we need to consume $M(d)$ triples, where $M(d)$ is the complexity of the matrix multiplication algorithm of choice. In order to minimize the communication overhead, we designed new offline phases for generating matrix and convolution triples. We use HE algorithms to generate these triples in the offline phase. In the online phase, they are consumed in essentially the same way as Beaver triples. Such triples allow us to have communication linear in the size of the input and output, and independent of the number of multiplications, in both offline and online phases.

On a high level, our protocol for generating authenticated matrix triples works as follows. First, each party P_i select uniformly random matrices A_i, B_i and send an encryption of these matrix. Then, the parties engage in the n-party zero-knowledge proof, and obtain encryptions of $A = \sum A_i$ and $B = \sum B_i$ with bounded noise. Next, parties use the homomorphic matrix multiplication algorithm recalled in Sect. 2.5 to compute an encryption of $C = AB$. Finally, the parties use homomorphic multiplication to compute encryptions of $\alpha A, \alpha B, \alpha C$, and perform distributed decryption on the resulting ciphertexts. In this way, the parties end up with a valid authenticated triples $(\llbracket A \rrbracket_\alpha, \llbracket B \rrbracket_\alpha, \llbracket C \rrbracket_\alpha)$. We provide the formal description of our pre-processing protocol in Fig. 1, with the distributed decryption protocol in Fig. 2.

Theorem 1. *In the $(\mathcal{F}_{\mathsf{Prep}}, \mathcal{F}_{\mathsf{Commit}})$-hybrid model, the protocol Π_{Online} implements $\mathcal{F}_{\mathsf{Online}}$ with statistical security against any static, active adversary corrupting up to $n-1$ parties.*

Theorem 2. *If the underlying cryptosystem is somewhat homomorphic and IND-CPA secure, then Π_{Prep} (Fig. 1) implements $\mathcal{F}_{\mathsf{Prep}}$ with computational security against any static, active adversary corrupting up to $n-1$ parties, in the $(\mathcal{F}_{\mathsf{KeyGen}}, \mathcal{F}_{\mathsf{Rand}})$-hybrid model.*

Theorem 3. *The protocol Π_{DDec} securely implements $\mathcal{F}_{\mathsf{KeyGenDec}}$ in the $\mathcal{F}_{\mathsf{KeyGen}}$-hybrid model with statistical security against any static adversary corrupting upto $n-1$ parties if B' is an upper bound on the noise of the input ciphertext, and $B' \cdot 2n \cdot 2^{\mathsf{sec_{dd}}} < \Delta$.*

For proof of Theorems 1, 2, and 3 please refer to the extended version at https://eprint.iacr.org/2020/451.

3.2 Authenticating Triples Without Sacrifice

To introduce this optimization, we first recall the technique of authenticated multiplication triples as proposed by the SPDZ line of work [18,19]. In the framework, there is a global MAC key $\alpha \in \mathbb{F}_p$ and parties have access to a ciphertext

Π_{Prep}

Usage: We execute Π_{PoPK} by batching u ciphertexts together. At the same time, we use the SIMD properties of HE to optimally compute on N plaintext elements at the same time (cf. Sec 4.1). Calls to Π_{PoPK} are amortized in batches of u, a detail omitted for simplicity. Also, randomness used in the encryption is implicit and is the randomness used for a fresh ciphertext (cf. Sec 2)

Initialize: All parties first invoke $\mathcal{F}_{\mathsf{KeyGenDec}}$ to obtain the public key pk. Then, each party does the following:

1. Each party generates $\alpha^i \leftarrow \mathbb{Z}_p$. Let $\alpha := \sum_i \alpha^i \pmod p$.
2. Each party computes and broadcasts a fresh encryption $\mathfrak{c}^i_\alpha \leftarrow \mathsf{Enc}_{\mathsf{pk}}(\alpha^i)$ (Note that this ciphertext has α^i in all the N slots. Refer Sec. 2).
3. The parties invoke protocol Π_{PoPK} on ciphertexts $\mathfrak{c}_{\alpha_i}$ for $i \in [n]$.
4. All parties compute $\mathfrak{c}_\alpha \leftarrow \sum_i \mathfrak{c}^i_\alpha$.

Authenticated Singles: Parties run this protocol to generate $u \cdot N$ random authenticated shares in $\mathbb{Z}_p$ in one invocation. Let $i \in [n]$ and $k \in [u]$.

1. All parties sample random $r^i_k \leftarrow U(R_p)$. Each party computes and broadcasts $\mathfrak{c}^i_{r_k} = \mathsf{Enc}_{\mathsf{pk}}(r^i_k)$. Let $\mathfrak{c}_{r_k} \leftarrow \sum_i \mathfrak{c}^i_{r_k}$.
2. The parties invoke protocol Π_{PoPK} on the u ciphertexts $\mathfrak{c}^i_{r_k}$.
3. Parties run Π_{AddMacs} to generate $(\gamma(r_k)^1, \ldots, \gamma(r_k)^n) \leftarrow \mathsf{AddMacs}(\mathfrak{c}_{r_k})$.
4. Parties output $[\![r_k]\!]_\alpha = \left((r^1_k, \gamma(r_k)^1), \ldots, (r^n_k, \gamma(r_k)^n)\right)$.

Matrix Triples: For the ease of exposition, we encode one matrix in one ciphertext. Refer to Section 4.1 for more details on how to optimally use all the ciphertext slots. Let $\circledast$ refer to the HE ciphertext-ciphertext matrix multiplication relation defined in Section 2.5. Let $j \in [d_1], k \in [d_2]$, and $l \in [d_3]$. Steps 1-10 are done for all j, k, l in their respective ranges. Set $v = (\mathsf{sec_s} + 2)/\log_2(2N+1)$

1. Each party generates random $A^i_{jk} \leftarrow U(R_p)$ and $B^i_{kl} \leftarrow U(R_p)$.
2. Compute and broadcast $\mathfrak{c}^i_{A_{jk}} \leftarrow \mathsf{Enc}(\sigma(A^i_{jk}))$ and $\mathfrak{c}^i_{B_{kl}} \leftarrow \mathsf{Enc}(\tau(B^i_{kl}))$.
3. All parties invoke Π_{PoPK} for $\mathfrak{c}^i_{A_{jk}}$ and $\mathfrak{c}^i_{B_{kl}}$ for each $i \in [n]$.
4. All parties set $\mathfrak{c}_{A_{jk}} \leftarrow 2 \cdot \sum_i \mathfrak{c}^i_{A_{jk}}$ and $\mathfrak{c}_{B_{kl}} \leftarrow 2 \cdot \sum_i \mathfrak{c}^i_{B_{kl}}$.
5. All parties compute $\mathfrak{c}_{C_{jl}} \leftarrow \mathfrak{c}_{A_{jk}} \circledast \mathfrak{c}_{B_{kl}}$.
6. Parties run Π_{AddMacs} to generate $(\gamma(A_{jk})^1, \ldots \gamma(A_{jk})^n) \leftarrow \mathsf{AddMacs}(\mathfrak{c}_{A_{jk}})$ and $(\gamma(B_{kl})^1, \ldots \gamma(B_{kl})^n) \leftarrow \mathsf{AddMacs}(\mathfrak{c}_{B_{kl}})$.
7. Parties run Π_{DDec} to generate $(C^1_{jl}, \ldots C^n_{jl}) \leftarrow \mathsf{DDec}(\mathfrak{c}_{C_{jl}})$.
8. Parties run Π_{AddMacs} to generate $(\gamma(C_{jl})^1, \ldots \gamma(C_{jl})^n) \leftarrow \mathsf{AddMacs}(\mathfrak{c}_{C_{jl}})$.
9. Set $A^i_{jk} \leftarrow 2 \cdot A^i_{jk}$ and $B^i_{kl} \leftarrow 2 \cdot B^i_{kl}$.
10. Generate a large matrix by using A^i_{jk} as sub-matrix blocks – k blocks per row and j blocks per column. This forms a matrix of dimensions ($d_m \cdot$ **block size**) where $m \in \{1, 2\}$ Similarly, rearrange the $\gamma(A_{jk})^i$ and call this group of 2 matrices as $[\![A]\!]$. Similarly, set $[\![B]\!]$ and $[\![C]\!]$ (except without scaling by factor of 2 for C).

Convolution Triples: This uses matrix triples to generate convolution triples.

1. Parties call **Authenticated Singles** to generate 2D tensors $[\![X]\!], [\![Y]\!]$.
2. Parties call **Matrix Triples** (cf. Sec 2.3 for dimensions of the matrices) to get a matrix multiplication triple $[\![A]\!], [\![B]\!], [\![C]\!]$.
3. All parties open $\epsilon = [\![X' - A]\!]$ and $\delta = [\![Y' - B]\!]$, where X', Y' are matrices generated by converting convolutions into matrix multiplications.
4. Compute $[\![Z]\!] = [\![C]\!] + \epsilon \times [\![B]\!] + [\![A]\!] \times \delta + \epsilon \times \delta$. Output $[\![X]\!], [\![Y]\!], [\![Z]\!]$.

Fig. 1. Protocol for generating various preprocessing material

Π_{DDec}

Distributed Decryption: Parties run the following protocol:

1. Parties generate $r^i \leftarrow U(R_p)$. Let $\mathfrak{c}_m := (\mathfrak{c}_0, \mathfrak{c}_1)$.
2. Compute v^i as follows:
$$v^i = \begin{cases} \mathfrak{c}_0 + \mathfrak{c}_1 \cdot s^i & \text{if } i = 1 \\ \mathfrak{c}_1 \cdot s^i & \text{if } i \neq 1 \end{cases}$$
3. Broadcast $t^i \leftarrow \Delta \cdot r^i + v^i + e^i \pmod q$ where $e^i \leftarrow U(R_{B \cdot 2^{\mathsf{sec}_{\mathsf{dd}}}})$
4. Party $i = 1$ outputs $m^1 = \lfloor \Delta^{-1} \cdot (\sum_i t^i) \rceil - r^1 \pmod p$ while all other parties ($i \neq 1$) output $m^i = -r^i \pmod p$
5. Finally, $\mathsf{Decode}(m^i)$ to obtain of vector of plaintexts encoded in each m^i.

Fig. 2. Protocol for distributed decryption.

$\mathfrak{c}_\alpha$ encrypting α, here the ciphertext is generated via an HE scheme, whose public key is known to all parties and the secret key is secret-shared among the parties[4]. During the triple generation phase, parties obtain ciphertexts $\mathfrak{c}_x, \mathfrak{c}_y, \mathfrak{c}_z$ where supposedly the relation $z = xy$ holds. In order to authenticate the secret values x, y and z, the parties engage in an $\mathsf{AddMacs}$ subroutine (this is a common procedure to prevent malicious behavior for dishonest majority protocols, cf. [18,19]), in which parties compute and then jointly decrypt $\mathfrak{c}_\alpha \boxtimes \mathfrak{c}_t$ to obtain secret shares of $\alpha \cdot t$ for $t \in \{x, y, z\}$. However, a malicious adversary can inject an error term ϵ into z such that $z = xy + \epsilon$, and the $\mathsf{AddMacs}$ subroutine could authenticate such an incorrect triple, which corrupts the final computation result. In order to resolve this issue, a step called *sacrifice* was introduced, where one triple is consumed to check the correctness of the other. Sacrificing brings a two times overhead to the complexity of the triple generation phase.

We begin by noting that SPDZ only uses a depth-1 HE, i.e., the underlying HE scheme could support one multiplication. Recall that in the SPDZ triple generation, after computing a ciphertext $\mathfrak{c}_z = \mathfrak{c}_x \boxtimes \mathfrak{c}_y$, the $\mathsf{Reshare}$ procedure is called which outputs secret shares of z' and a new ciphertext $\mathfrak{c}_{z'}$ with smaller noise than $\mathfrak{c}_z$. Then, the $\mathsf{AddMacs}$ procedure is called, which produces authenticated share $[\![z']\!]_\alpha$. In particular, to generate shares of the MAC on z, prior work requires that the distributed decryption subroutine to be called on z to get a level-1 ciphertext (z') that enables adding the MAC on it. This way, an additive error introduced in z can be "authenticated" using the $\mathsf{AddMacs}$ procedure by the adversary. To prevent against such an attack, prior work required a sacrifice of one triple with other which was proved to ensure that the triples do not have an error. The $\mathsf{MacCheck}$ ensures that any such additive error introduced is caught with high probability.

[4] The initialize phase in Π_{Prep} will require Diag flag similar to [18,19] to ensure that the ciphertext encodes the same MAC key in the same slots.

In our work, we modify the HE parameters to support larger depth, in particular depth-2 computation. The homomorphic encryption product ($z = xy$) is done over public ciphertexts and hence z is guaranteed to equal xy. However, to add MACs to the product z, we do not need to run a distributed decryption protocol (we only need it for generating the shares of z but *not* for the MAC generation). In our work, we directly call the AddMacs routine on the public ciphertext for z, i.e., $\mathfrak{c}_{\alpha z} = \mathfrak{c}_z \boxtimes \mathfrak{c}_\alpha$, and perform distributed decryption on $\mathfrak{c}_{\alpha z}$ to obtain the MAC shares. This ensure that the additive error introduced by the adversary when running DDec on $\mathfrak{c}_z$ to get shares of z is *independent* of α from the additive error introduced in the DDec of $\mathfrak{c}_{\alpha z}$. This way, we eliminate the need for a sacrifice and simply rely on the MacCheck subroutine to catch malicious behavior.

Thus, we save the computation and communication by a factor of two, with a less-than-two additional overhead due to the need to increase underlying HE parameters to support larger depth computations. This optimization is particularly useful in our bilinear triple generation protocol, since in this case we already need to increase the HE parameters in order to run the homomorphic matrix multiplication algorithm, and the overhead of supporting just one more depth is small.

3.3 Improved ZKPoPK Based on BFV Scheme

In the SPDZ offline phase, parties need to use a homomorphic encryption scheme (the BGV scheme of Brakerski, Gentry, and Vaikuntanathan [9]) to encrypt random values, and broadcast these encryptions. Then, they run homomorphic evaluation and distributed decryption to generate the multiplication triples. Since parties could be malicious, each party needs to prove that it is providing a valid ciphertext. In the context of BGV, this means the coefficients of the message and randomness used in the encryption method must be bounded in size. This zero-knowledge proof of plaintext knowledge (ZKPoPK) follows a 3-move Schnorr protocol pattern. The goal is to prove knowledge of message x and encryption randomness r with bounded size, such that $\mathfrak{c}_{x,r} = \mathfrak{b}$. The prover chooses some random mask values y_x, y_r and sends $\mathfrak{c}_{y_x,y_r}$ to the verifier. After the verifier selects a challenge e the prover sends back the masked values $z_x = y_x + e \cdot x$ and $z_r = y_r + e \cdot r$. Finally, the verifier checks whether $\mathfrak{c}_{z_x,z_r} = \mathfrak{c}_{y_x,y_r} + e \cdot \mathfrak{b}$ and whether the noise and plaintext bounds are correct on producing $\mathfrak{c}_x$ by checking the norm of z_x and z_r. The state-of-the-art ZKPoPK in [5] enhances the above approach by designing an n-prover protocol which adds the ability to prove the validity of sum of n ciphertexts instead of proving each individual ones.

Our Modification. We note that the BFV homomorphic encryption scheme of Brakerski/Fan-Vercauteren [8,21] provides the same functionalities as the BGV scheme, while the two schemes have some subtle differences, which we will exploit for our improved zero-knowledge proof. In particular, BFV allows selecting the plaintext modulus p to divide the ciphertext modulus q, which is not allowed in BGV[5]. We will use this fact to simplify and reduce the complexity of the zero-knowledge proof of plaintext knowledge (ZKPoPK) component in SPDZ.

Recall that the BGV encryption of a message m with public key pk and randomness (u, e_0, e_1) is

$$\mathfrak{c} = u \cdot \mathsf{pk} + (m + pe_0, pe_1) \pmod{q}. \tag{6}$$

Although an honest party would encrypt a message $m \in R_p$ with $\|m\|_\infty \leq p/2$, a malicious party can use any $m \in R$, and the excess part $m - [m]_p$ goes into the noise of the ciphertext. Hence the prover needs to prove that $\|m\|_\infty$ is not too large. This is done by having the prover send encryptions of random messages y with $\log \|y\|_\infty \approx \mathsf{sec_{zk}} + \log p$ and later reveal a linear combination of y and m. On the other hand, in the BFV scheme, an encryption of m is the form of

$$\mathfrak{c} = u \cdot \mathsf{pk} + (\Delta \cdot m + e_0, e_1) \pmod{q}, \quad \text{where} \quad \Delta = \lfloor q/p \rceil. \tag{7}$$

Suppose p divides q, then $\Delta = q/p$ exactly, and using a message $m \in R$ in the encryption algorithm is equivalent to using $[m]_p$ due to the automatic reduction modulo q on the ciphertexts. Therefore, the prover in our ZKPoPK only needs to prove upper bounds on the encryption randomness, and it suffices to sample the "masking elements" y as random elements in R_p. This reduces the size of the proof, since we reduce the coefficients of the masked plaintexts sent by the prover (the terms z_i in [5, Figure 1]) from $\log p + \log \mathsf{sec_{zk}}$ bits down to $\log p$ bits.

ZKPoPK. The zero-knowledge proof of knowledge we describe next (Fig. 3) is a n-party ZKP used in the preprocessing phase. The n players all simultaneously act as the provers and the verifiers. $\mathsf{Sampling}$ is an algorithm that describes the behavior of honest parties to generate their ciphertexts and broadcast them to the other parties. This algorithm satisfies the relation given in Eq. 8. However, Π_{PoPK} provides weaker guarantees as given in Eq. 9 which will be sufficient for the preprocessing phase[6]. In particular, the protocol introduces a *soundness slack* in the bounds that can be proven on the witness. The protocol works in the standard 3-move Schnorr protocol pattern as described below:

1. Each party P_i independently runs the "commitment" algorithm on (x_i, w_i) to get $(\mathsf{comm}_i, \mathsf{state}_i) \leftarrow \mathsf{Commit}(x_i, w_i)$ and broadcasts comm_i to all the other parties.
2. The n parties jointly generate a challenge w (produced via a call to an ideal functionality $\mathcal{F}_{\mathsf{Rand}}$)
3. Each party P_i independently runs the "response" algorithm to get $\mathsf{resp}_i \leftarrow \mathsf{Response}(\mathsf{state}_i, w)$
4. Each party P_i independently runs the "verification" algorithm and accept if the output is true: $\mathsf{Verify}(\{\mathsf{comm}_i, \mathsf{resp}_i\}_{i \in [n]}, w) == \mathsf{True}$.

[5] $\gcd(p, q) = 1$ is required for security of BGV.

[6] This is the worst case guarantee when all provers are dishonest while at least one verifier is honest, which in the case when provers and verifiers are the same entities is the dishonest majority model.

$$
\begin{aligned}
\mathcal{R}_{\mathsf{PoPK}}^{u,\mathsf{Honest}} = \Big\{ & ((x^1,\ldots,x^n),(w^1,\ldots,w^n)), \\
& x^i = (\mathfrak{c}_1^i,\ldots,\mathfrak{c}_u^i), w^i = ((a_1^i, r_{a_1}^i),\ldots(a_u^i, r_{a_u}^i)) : \\
& \mathfrak{c}_{a_k} = \mathsf{Enc}_{\mathsf{pk}}(a_k, r_{a_k}) \text{ and} \\
& \|r_{a_k}\| \le n \text{ where} \\
& \mathfrak{c}_{a_k} = \sum_i \mathfrak{c}_{a_k}^i \text{ and } r_{a_k} = \sum_i r_{a_k}^i \Big\}
\end{aligned} \tag{8}
$$

$$
\begin{aligned}
\mathcal{R}_{\mathsf{PoPK}}^{u,2} = \Big\{ & ((x^1,\ldots,x^n),(w^1,\ldots,w^n)), \\
& x^i = (\mathfrak{c}_1^i,\ldots,\mathfrak{c}_u^i), w^i = ((a_1^i, r_{a_1}^i),\ldots(a_u^i, r_{a_u}^i)) : \\
& 2\cdot\mathfrak{c}_{a_k} = \mathsf{Enc}_{\mathsf{pk}}(2\cdot a_k, 2\cdot r_{a_k}) \text{ and} \\
& \|2r_{a_k}\| \le Nnu\cdot 2^{\mathsf{sec_{zk}}+1} \text{ where} \\
& \mathfrak{c}_{a_k} = \sum_i \mathfrak{c}_{a_k}^i \text{ and } r_{a_k} = \sum_i r_{a_k}^i \Big\}
\end{aligned} \tag{9}
$$

Before we describe the protocol, we reiterate some key notation. The *normalized norm* of randomness r_m by $\|r_m\| = \max\{\|u\|_\infty, \rho^{-1}\cdot\|e_0\|_\infty, \rho^{-1}\cdot\|e_1\|_\infty\}$. For $B > 0$, we call $\mathfrak{c}$ a *B-ciphertext* if there exists $m \in R_p$ and $r_m = (u, e_0, e_1) \in R^3$ such that $\|r_m\| \le B$ and $\mathfrak{c} = \mathsf{Enc}_{\mathsf{pk}}(m, r_m)$. We also use U_B to denote a uniform distribution over the set of triples $r = (u, e_0, e_1) \in R^3$ such that $\|r\| \le B$. We set $\rho = 20$ following [5] to ensure the randomness r from an honest party satisfies $\|r\| \le 1$ with overwhelming probability. Furthermore, we also use the following distributions (specifically the third) in the description of the protocol:

1. $\mathcal{ZO}(0.5, k)$: This distribution generates a vector of size k with elements $\{x_i\}_{i=1}^k$ chosen from $\{-1, 0, +1\}$ such that the $\Pr(x_i = -1) = 0.25, \Pr(x_i = +1) = 0.25$, and $\Pr(x_i = 0) = 0.5$ for all $i \in [k]$.
2. $\mathcal{DN}(\sigma^2, k)$: This distribution generates a vector of size k with elements drawn according to an approximation to the discrete Gaussian distribution with variance σ^2.
3. $\mathcal{RG}(0.5, \sigma^2, k)$: This distribution generates a triple of elements (u, e_0, e_1) where $u \leftarrow \mathcal{ZO}(0.5, k)$ and $e_0, e_1 \leftarrow \mathcal{DN}(\sigma^2, k)$.

Improvements Compared to Prior Work. In our protocol, the hiding on the message (z_l^i) is information-theoretic (as opposed to statistical hiding in TopGear) and hence does not need any check during the verification phase. This is due choosing $p \mid q$ in underlying BFV scheme. In addition, the ZKPoPK in [5] sends the polynomials z_l^i and $r_{z_l}^i$ as elements in R_q, which is more than necessary since q is typically large but these polynomials are supposed to have bounded norm. We can reduce this cost by sending z_l^i and $r_{z_l}^i$ in bounded size (since $z_l^i \in U(R_p)$ and all the coefficients of $r_{z_l}^i$ should be bounded by $u \cdot 2^{\mathsf{sec_{zk}}}$

Π_{PoPK}

Proof of Plaintext Knowledge (PoPK): This protocol is run between n parties – each acting as a prover and verifier simultaneously. The protocol flow is a standard three-move structure (commitment, challenge, and response) called Σ-protocol with a single challenge produced using an ideal functionality $\mathcal{F}_{\mathsf{Rand}}$. Let u, v be two proof parameters, $\mathsf{Flag} \in \{\mathsf{Diag}, \perp\}$. We use i to denote party index and k, l for variables iterating across ciphertexts ($k \in [u], l \in [v]$). Let n denote the number of parties and N denote the degree of the cyclotimic polynomial used for HE. Ensure that $v \geq (\mathsf{sec_s} + 2)/\log_2(2N+1)$.

Sampling (Sampling phase)

1. On input $i \in [n]$, if $\mathsf{Flag} = \perp$ sample $a_k^i \leftarrow U(R_p)$ for each $k \in [u]$. If $\mathsf{Flag} = \mathsf{Diag}$, sample a_k^i as a random diagonal element in $U(R_p)$ for each $k \in [u]$.
2. Generate $r_{a_k}^i \leftarrow \mathcal{RG}(0.5, \sigma^2, N)$.
3. Compute ciphertexts $\mathfrak{c}_{a_k}^i = \mathsf{Enc_{pk}}(a_k^i, r_{a_k}^i)$.
4. Define vectors $\mathfrak{c}_a = (\mathfrak{c}_{a_1}^i, \ldots, \mathfrak{c}_{a_u}^i)$, $\boldsymbol{a}^i = (a_1^i, \ldots a_u^i)$ and $\boldsymbol{r}_a^i = (r_{a_1}^i, \ldots r_{a_u}^i)$. Output $(x^i, w^i) = (\mathfrak{c}_a^i, (\boldsymbol{a}^i, \boldsymbol{r}_a^i))$.

Commit (Commitment phase)

1. Party P_i generates v ciphertexts $\mathfrak{c}_{y_l}^i = \mathsf{Enc_{pk}}(y_l^i, r_{y_l}^i)$ where $l \in [v], y_l^i \leftarrow U(R_p)$, and $r_{y_l}^i \leftarrow U_{u \cdot 2^{\mathsf{sec_{zk}}}}$.
2. Party P_i broadcasts a commitment $\mathsf{comm}_i \leftarrow \{\mathfrak{c}_{y_l}^i\}_{\forall l}$.

Challenge (Challenge phase)

1. Parties call $\mathcal{F}_{\mathsf{Rand}}$ to obtain a $v \times u$ challenge matrix w with random entries. If $\mathsf{Flag} = \perp$, entries of w come from $\{\pm X^j\}_{0 \leq j < N} \cup \{0\}$. If $\mathsf{Flag} = \mathsf{Diag}$, entries of w come from $\{0, 1\}$.

Response (Response phase)

1. Party P_i computes $z_l^i = y_l^i + (w \cdot \boldsymbol{a}^i)_l$ and $r_{z_l}^i = r_{y_l}^i + (w \cdot \boldsymbol{r}_a^i)_l$.
2. Party P_i sets $\mathsf{resp}_i \leftarrow \{z_l^i, r_{z_l}^i\}_{\forall l}$ and broadcasts resp_i.

Verify (Verification phase)
Each party then performs the following computations and verifications:

1. Compute $\mathfrak{c}_{z_l}^i = \mathsf{Enc_{pk}}(z_l^i, r_{z_l}^i)$.
2. Compute $\mathfrak{c}_a \leftarrow \sum_i \mathfrak{c}_a^i$, $\mathfrak{c}_{y_l} \leftarrow \sum_i \mathfrak{c}_{y_l}^i$, $\mathfrak{c}_{z_l} \leftarrow \sum_i \mathfrak{c}_{z_l}^i$, $z_l \leftarrow \sum_i z_l^i$, and $r_{z_l} \leftarrow \sum_i r_{z_l}^i$.
3. Verify $\mathfrak{c}_{z_l} = \mathfrak{c}_{y_l} + (w \cdot \mathfrak{c}_a)_l$ and $\|r_{z_l}\| \leq n \cdot u \cdot 2^{\mathsf{sec_{zk}}}$.
4. If $\mathsf{Flag} = \mathsf{Diag}$ then additionally verify that z_l is a diagonal plaintext element.
5. If all checks pass, parties accept otherwise they reject.

Fig. 3. Protocol for proof of plaintext knowledge.

or $\rho \cdot u \cdot 2^{\mathsf{sec_{zk}}}$). In this way, we can also omit the check on size of r_{z_l} in Step 3 of Verify phase.

Note that the "slack" in the ZKP provides looser bounds on the norms of values as well as multiplied the values themselves by a factor of 2. This is a consequence of the zero-knowledge proof. Figure 1 shows how to account for this by modifying the preprocessing protocol to takes these slacks into consideration. The above describes the zero-knowledge proof protocol. We define the security of the ZKPoPK similar to prior work [5] and present it below for completeness.

Theorem 4. *The n-party ZKPoPK-protocol defined by Π_{PoPK} satisfies the following three properties:*

1. ***Correctness:*** *If all parties P_i, with inputs sampled using the* Sampling *algorithm (in Π_{PoPK}, Fig. 3), follow the protocol honestly, then an honest verifier will accept with probability one.*
2. ***Soundness:*** *Let $\mathcal{A} = (\mathcal{A}_1, \mathcal{A}_2, \mathcal{A}_3)$ be a tuple of PPT algorithms and let $\epsilon \in [0, 1)$. Consider the following game:*
   - *(1a) $\mathcal{A}_1$ takes no input and outputs $I \subset [n]$, $\{x_i\}_{i \in I}$ and $\mathsf{state}_{\mathcal{A}_1}$.*
   - *(1b) Choose $(x_j, w_j) \leftarrow \mathsf{Sampling}(j)$ for each $P_j, j \notin I$.*
   - *(1c) Compute $(\mathsf{comm}_j, \mathsf{state}_j) \leftarrow \mathsf{Commit}(x_j, w_j)$ for $j \notin I$.*
   - *(2a) $\mathcal{A}_2$ on input $\mathsf{state}_{\mathcal{A}_1}, \{x_j, \mathsf{comm}_j\}_{j \notin I}$ output $\mathsf{state}_{\mathcal{A}_2}, \{\mathsf{comm}_i\}_{i \in I}$.*
   - *(3a) Choose a uniformly random w and compute $\mathsf{resp}_j \leftarrow \mathsf{Response}(\mathsf{state}_j, w)$ for $j \notin I$.*
   - *(4a) $\mathcal{A}_3$ on input $\mathsf{state}_{\mathcal{A}_2}, w, \{\mathsf{resp}_j\}_{j \notin I}$ outputs $\{\mathsf{resp}_i\}_{i \in I}$.*
   - *(4b) $\mathcal{A}$ wins the game if $\mathsf{Verify}(\{\mathsf{comm}_i, \mathsf{resp}_i\}_{i \in [n]}, w) = \mathsf{True}$.*

   Suppose $\mathcal{A}$ wins the game with probability $\delta > \epsilon$. Then there exists a PPT algorithm Extract *which for any fixed output of $\mathcal{A}_1$, honestly generated inputs given by $\{x_j, w_j, \mathsf{comm}_j, \mathsf{state}_j\}_{j \notin I}$, and black-box access to $\mathcal{A}_2, \mathcal{A}_3$ outputs $\{w_i\}_{i \in I}$ such that $\mathcal{R}^{u,2}_{\mathsf{PoPK}}$ (Eq. 9) holds in at most $f(\mathsf{sec_s})/(\delta - \epsilon)$ steps, where $f(\cdot)$ is a positive polynomial and $\epsilon = 2^{-\mathsf{sec_s}}$ ($\mathsf{sec_s}$ is the soundness security parameter).*
3. ***Honest-verifier zero knowledge:*** *There exists a PPT algorithm $\mathcal{S}_I$ indexed by a set $I \subset [n]$, which takes as input an element in the language given by relation $\mathcal{R}^{u,\mathsf{Honest}}_{\mathsf{PoPK}}$ (Eq. 8) and a challenge w, and outputs tuples $\{\mathsf{comm}_i, \mathsf{resp}_i\}_{i \in I}$ such that this output is statistically indistinguishable from a valid execution of the protocol (the statistical indistinguishability parameter is denoted by $\mathsf{sec_{zk}}$).*

Proof of Theorem 4 is presented in Appendix A.

4 Experimental Results

We present our experimental results for the applications of our protocols to private matrix multiplication and neural network inference. We start with describing some further optimizations. Then, we present noise growth estimates for the homomorphic matrix multiplication algorithms, followed by our concrete parameter instantiation, before proceeding to present our experimental results. The main results are presented over 3 application scenarios (1) private matrix multiplications (2) private nearest neighbor search and (3) private inference of ResNet-50.

4.1 Evaluation Set-Up and Parameter Estimation

Next, we describe the optimization used for the homomorphic matrix multiplication, the general noise estimation bounds, and lastly, describe a choice of parameters that satisfy all these constraints which we use in the following evaluations.

Further Optimizations. On top of the baseline implementation, we apply the following optimization techniques for the homomorphic matrix multiplication.

- A *lazy key-switching* technique can be applied to the last multiplication step of Eq. (5). To be precise, we compute tensor products between $\phi^k(\mathfrak{c}_A)$ and $\psi^k(\mathfrak{c}_B)$ and aggregate all the resulting ciphertexts. In the end, the key-switching operation is performed only once to relinearize the output ciphertext.
- The *hoisting* technique of [23] can be applied to our case to reduce the complexity of rotations in the generation of $\phi^k \circ \sigma(A)$ and $\psi^k \circ \tau(B)$. Since there are many rotations done on the same input ciphertext, one can compute the common part of computation that only depend on the input, and therefore it can be significantly faster than applying each rotation separately.
- As described in [25], homomorphic matrix multiplication can be extended to matrices of an arbitrary size. Given the packing structure of BFV (presented in Sect. 2), the two rows of BFV encoding operate identically and without interference, so it is easy to pack two matrices in a single ciphertext. Additionally, we can use the interlacing technique of [25] to encrypt multiple matrices in each plaintext row and carry out matrix operations in parallel, thereby amortizing it over many operations. On the other hand, when an input matrix is too large to be encrypted in a single ciphertext, we split it into *block-size* matrices and encrypt them separately in different ciphertexts. A large matrix operation can be expressed as a composition of several block-size matrix operations. Instead of computing block-wise multiplications separately, we precompute and store the permutations of block matrices not to repeat the same computation in individual products.

Noise Estimation of Homomorphic Matrix Multiplication. In order to optimally choose the parameters of the HE scheme, we perform a noise analysis of our algorithms. The noise bounds of ciphertexts are updated during the computation with respect to the following analysis.

- Encryption: Suppose that $\mathfrak{c} = \mathsf{Enc}_{\mathsf{pk}}(m, r_m)$ for a message m and randomness $r_m = (u, e_0, e_1)$ such that $\|r_m\| \leq B$. Then, we have

$$\mathfrak{c}[0] + \mathfrak{c}[1] \cdot s = \Delta \cdot m + (u \cdot e + e_0 + e_1 \cdot s) \pmod{q}$$

  and the encryption noise $e_{enc} = u \cdot e + e_0 + e_1 \cdot s$ is bounded by $\|e_{enc}\|_\infty \leq B\rho(1+2N)$. If a ciphertext is honestly generated, then we derive the bound $B_{\mathsf{clean}} = \rho(1+2N)$ since $\|r_m\| \leq 1$. However, our ZKPoPK only guarantees that $2\mathfrak{c}_m = Enc_{\mathsf{pk}}(2m, 2r_m)$ for some $\|2r_m\| \leq Nnu \cdot 2^{\mathsf{sec}_{\mathsf{zk}}+1}$ and so the noise of $2\mathfrak{c}_m$ is bounded by $B_{\mathsf{clean}}^{\mathsf{dishonest}} = Nnu \cdot 2^{\mathsf{sec}_{\mathsf{zk}}+1} \cdot \rho(1+2N)$.
- Plaintext-ciphertext product: The noise of resulting ciphertext is the product of an initial noise $e \in R$ and a plaintext $\mathfrak{p}$ such that $\|\mathfrak{p}\|_\infty \leq p$. Hence a new noise bound is $\|\mathfrak{p} \cdot e\|_\infty \leq N \cdot \|\mathfrak{p}\|_\infty \|e\|_\infty \leq Np \cdot \|e\|_\infty$.
- Rotation: In our protocols, all ciphertexts are generated with PoPKs which provide an upper bound $Nnu \cdot 2^{\mathsf{sec}_{\mathsf{zk}}}$ of the size of encryption randomness $r = (u, e_0, e_1)$. Hence the noise of a ciphertext $u \cdot (\mathsf{pk}[0] + \mathsf{pk}[1] \cdot s) + (e_0 + e_1 \cdot s)$ also has an exponential bound in $\mathsf{sec}_{\mathsf{zk}}$. Since we introduce a special modulus to use the modulus-raising technique in our key-switching algorithm, the noise from homomorphic rotation is $\tilde{O}(N)$ which is negligible compared to the noise parameter of ciphertexts. Hence the homomorphic rotation does not change the upper bound of noise.
- Multiplication: Given two ciphertexts $\mathfrak{c}_1, \mathfrak{c}_2$, we have $\mathfrak{c}_i[0] + \mathfrak{c}_i[1] \cdot s = qI_i + \Delta \cdot m_i + e_i$ over R for some $I_i \in R$, plaintext $m_i \in R_p$ and noise $e_i \in R$. Their product scaled by Δ is $\Delta \cdot m_1 m_2 + e'$ modulo q for some noise $e' \approx p(I_1 e_2 + I_2 e_1)$ (other terms are exponentially small compared to this dominating one). We note that $\|I_i\|_\infty \leq N$ and so $\|e'\|_\infty \leq 2N^2 p \cdot \max\{\|e_1\|_\infty, \|e_2\|_\infty\}$. In certain cases, multiplication is followed by a key-switching procedure, which introduces a negligible noise, similar to the case of rotation.
- Matrix product: The permutation $\psi^k(\cdot)$ is not simply a rotation but the composition of two *maskings* and rotations, where a masking refers a specific scalar multiplication which zeros out some values in plaintext slots. It increases the noise bound of input ciphertext by a factor of Np. To sum up, for input ciphertexts $\mathfrak{c}_A, \mathfrak{c}_B$ of noise e_A and e_B, respectively, the noise of each term $\sigma^k(\mathfrak{c}_A) \boxtimes \tau^k(\mathfrak{c}_B)$ is bounded by $2N^2 p \cdot 2Np \cdot \max\{\|e_A\|_\infty, \|e_B\|_\infty\}$ and their sum $\mathfrak{c}_A \circledast \mathfrak{c}_B$ has a noise with the upper bound $4dN^3 p^2 \cdot \max\{\|e_A\|_\infty, \|e_B\|_\infty\}$.

Concrete Parameter Choices. In our experiments, we set $\mathsf{sec}_{\mathsf{zk}} = 128$, $\mathsf{sec}_{\mathsf{dd}} = 80$, and $\log p = 128$. For the BFV scheme, we chose $N = 2^{15}$, $\log q = 720$ and the standard deviation $\sigma = 8/\sqrt{2\pi}$, same as in [5] and [27]. This parameter set enjoys computational security of more than 128 bits [12]. In the ZKPoPK protocol (Fig. 3), we use $u = 2v$ and similar to TopGear [5] set $v = 16$. For notational convenience, we let $|R_m|$ denote the set of polynomials of degree N with non-negative integer coefficients bounded above by m, and let $|R_m|$ denote the number of bits needed to represent an element of R_m. Hence $|R_m| = N \log m$.

4.2 Private Matrix Multiplication

Communication Cost. We calculate the communication cost of our private matrix multiplication protocol for 128×128 matrices, noting that the communication cost scales linearly with the number of entries in the matrix[7]. In the online phase, the parties open two matrices (say of size $d \times d$), so the communication is $2d^2 \log p$ bits per matrix multiplication. The dominating cost occurs in the offline phase, which we break down further into three parts: the ciphertexts, the ZKPoPK procedure, and the distributed decryption (i.e. DDec) procedure. Each ciphertext takes $2|R_q|$ bits; the ZKPoPK can be used to prove u ciphertexts while it sends $v = u/2$ additional ciphertexts together with v "openings". Here, as seen in Fig. 3, each opening consists of one element in R_p, one element in $R_{u \cdot 2^{\mathsf{sec}_{\mathsf{zk}}}}$ and two elements in $R_{\rho \cdot u \cdot 2^{\mathsf{sec}_{\mathsf{zk}}}}$; finally, the protocol requires 4 invocations to DDec, which requires each party to send $4|R_q|$ bits.

Note that one invocation of the protocol generates two matrix triples, due to the fact that we optimally use the $2^{15} = 128^2 \cdot 2$ slots in our HE scheme. Hence, the amortized communication cost *sent by each party* in the offline phase is

$$\begin{aligned} &\frac{1}{2}\left(6|R_q| + \frac{1}{u}v(2|R_q| + u \cdot \log_2 N + (1 + 2\log_2 \rho)|R_{u \cdot 2^{\mathsf{sec}_{\mathsf{zk}}}}| + |R_p|)\right) \\ &\approx \frac{1}{2}\left(6|R_q| + \frac{1}{u}v(2|R_q| + u \cdot \log_2 N + 9.64|R_{u \cdot 2^{\mathsf{sec}_{\mathsf{zk}}}}| + |R_p|)\right) \end{aligned} \tag{10}$$

With our parameter settings, this amounts to around 12.46MB of data sent by each party.

Comparison with LowGear [27]. We compare our communication cost with the preprocessing required by the SPDZ protocol to multiply 128×128 matrices: the LowGear protocol takes 15 kbits per triple, and we assume that we need $d^{2.8}$ triples. Setting $d = 128$, this amounts to a 1.54 GB communication cost of sent by each party. So we reduced the communication by roughly two orders of magnitude for 128-dimensional matrix multiplication.

Concrete Efficiency. We now present the performance of our secure matrix multiplication protocol over various matrix sizes. Our source code was developed in C++ with Microsoft SEAL version 3.3 [36]. All the experiments were done on a machine with an Intel Xeon Platinum 8168 2.7 GHz featuring 16 cores. The compiler was GNU version 7.4.0 (-O3), and we used GMP version 6.1.2 and NTL version 11.3.3.

Table 1 shows results for microbenchmarks on homomorphic matrix computation for a two party scenario and various components of the matrix triple generation process. We split the input matrices into 128×128 matrix blocks.

[7] Note that we did not include the cost of one-time set-up, which consists of generating all the required keys for the HE scheme and generating and proving the encryptions of shares of the MAC key.

We found that key generation takes about 83 s and it takes about 191 ms to encrypt two input square matrices of size 128 as a single ciphertext, yielding an amortized rate of 96 ms per matrix. The second column gives the amortized encryption timing per matrix. We note that a one time set-up cost is to prepare appropriate masking plaintext polynomials that will be used for performing permutation $\psi^k(\cdot)$, which takes around 14.5 s. In the third and fourth columns labeled "Permutation", we give timings per matrix for generating the encrypted permutations of blocks of A and B, respectively. The fifth column labeled "Block comp." gives the amortized time taken for additions and multiplications on block matrices.

Theoretical Complexity. Suppose the input matrix of size n is partitioned into k^2 blocks of size d (we have $d = 128$ in our experiments). Then the encryption cost is $O(k^2)$. On the other hand, the computational costs of generating permutations of block matrices and performing block computation are $O(k^2)$ and $O(k^3)$, respectively. These trends can be seen in Table 1.

In Table 2 we document the experimental latency associated with the communication cost of our protocol. In the LAN setting, two parties are deployed in the same geographic network (N. Virginia on Amazon EC2, bandwidth about 5Gbps, ping time 20 ms). In the WAN setting, they were deployed in different geographic settings (N. Virginia and N. California on Amazon EC2, bandwidth about 320 Mbps, ping time 70 ms). SPDZ uses a 25 Gbps link for LAN and 50 Mbps for WAN (WAN numbers are extrapolated from Overdrive [27]).

Table 1. Microbenchmarks: All timings measured in seconds; 16 threads were used for columns labeled "Permutation" and "Block comp", and a single thread was used for other operations; the ZkPoPK time is amortized over $u = 32$ ciphertexts.

Matrix size	Encrypt time	Permutation		Block comp.	ZkPoPK		AddMacs time	DDec time
		of A	of B		Prover	Verifier		
128 × 128	0.10	1.8	0.9	1.4	0.047	0.09	0.6	1
256 × 256	0.38	5.6	2.3	10.1	0.188	0.35	2.4	4
384 × 384	0.86	12.8	4.9	34.0	0.79	0.81	5.4	9
512 × 512	1.52	21.8	8.0	79.6	1.41	1.44	9.6	16
1024 × 1024	6.08	79.6	32.9	648	3	5.63	38.4	64

Finally, Tables 3 provides total time estimates on matrix multiplications in the LAN and WAN settings respectively. Total-16, SPDZ-16 refer to timings using 16 threads and Total-1, SPDZ-1 refer to single-threaded implementations. As can be seen from the table, our approach is between 16×–40× faster than prior art and improves with larger matrix sizes.

4.3 Private Nearest Neighbors

In the batched version of the private nearest neighbor search (NNS) problem, one party holds a dataset X of n vectors in d-dimensional Euclidean space, and the other party holds several d-dimensional query vectors $q_1, q_2, \cdots, q_b$. The task is to compute securely for each query k nearest data vectors with respect to the Euclidean distance. There is a large body of work on this topic (see [13] for an overview). However, we are not aware of any previous work that solves the problem in the dishonest majority malicious adversarial model. Most of the secure NNS algorithms first (securely) compute secret shares of distances between every query vector and every dataset vector and then perform top-k selection. Distance computation can easily be reduced to matrix multiplication for matrices of size $n \times d$ and $d \times b$ and thus in the dishonest majority security model, we can use our protocol to perform distance computation.

Table 2. Communication overhead accounting for the round complexity and amount of data sent between parties.

Matrix Sizes	Communication time	
	LAN	WAN
128×128	0.010 s	2.05 s
256×256	0.039 s	8.19 s
384×384	0.091 s	18.44 s
512×512	0.161 s	32.78 s
1024×1024	0.647 s	131.15 s

As an example, we will consider the largest NNS instance that was solved securely to date [13]: the subset of the Deep1B dataset [3] with $n = 10^7$, $d = 96$. If we would like to compute distances between $b = 128$ queries and the whole dataset, we would need to multiply 78125 pairs of square matrices of size 128. Since each matrix multiplication requires 12.46 MB of communication per party in the offline phase, the overall distance computation requires 7.6 GB per party per query. On 16 threads, our protocols roughly require 30 min per query. LowGear equipped with the Strassen algorithm, on the other hand, requires at least 500 million Beavers triples per query. Running on 16 threads, this amounts to at least 80 min, and takes more than 1 TB of communication. Note that these performances numbers are obtained from our microbenchmarks rather than from running actual experiments.

4.4 Private Inference of ResNet-50

We can use our protocol to perform convolutions of a neural network securely. Here we discuss it in the context of the ResNet-50 network [24]. Note that for this discussion we ignore ReLUs, batch normalization, and pooling layers and focus on convolutions only.

All the convolutions in the ResNet-50 network require 3298 multiplications of pairs of 128×128 matrices. We will now follow the benchmarks from Table 3

Table 3. Benchmarks for private matrix multiplication over various sizes. Note that the timings for SPDZ are obtained by measuring the throughput of triple generation.

	Matrix sizes	Total-16 time	Total-1 time	SPDZ-16	SPDZ-1
LAN	128 × 128	5.9 s	36.1 s	8.41 s	128 s
	256 × 256	25.5 s	214.5 s	58.9 s	900 s
	384 × 384	68.3 s	653.6 s	3 min	46.8 min
	512 × 512	2.3 min	24.5 min	6.87 min	105 min
	1024 × 1024	14.5 min	173 min	52.02 min	735 min
WAN	128 × 128	7.95 s	38.15 s	1.61 min	24.6 min
	256 × 256	33.5 s	222.6 s	11.32 min	2.88 h
	384 × 384	68.34 s	672.0 s	34.6 min	9 h
	512 × 512	2.35 min	25.0 min	1.32 h	20.2 h
	1024 × 1024	16.51 min	175.1 min	10 h	5.88 days

to estimate the preprocessing cost of computing these products securely. Since each multiplication requires 12.46 MB of communication per party, the total communication would be 41 GB per party. Estimating the running time for preprocessing phase on 16 threads, we obtain 7.4 h per query.

On the other hand doing Strassen multiplications with LowGear would require at least 2.7 billion Beavers triples, so when run with 16 triple generation threads, this amounts to at least 7.6 h of running time and 5 TB of communication.

Adding RELUs into the Costs. ResNet-50 architecture requires a total of 9,608,704 ReLUs. To compute a RELU in MPC, one needs to have access to a protocol for random shared bit generation $[\![b]\!]$. Using existing techniques, the cost of such a RELU protocol is two-fold: in terms of preprocessing, it requires 122 triples and 105 random bits[8] whereas the online cost of RELU is 8 rounds of communication and 1 extra openings. A more careful analysis of SCALE/MP-SPDZ implementation of RELU reveals that there are exactly 119 field elements sent per party in the online phase.

On top of the RELUs, each multiplication involving a Beaver triple requires two field elements opened per party hence some extra 256 bits. In Table 4 we summarize the estimated costs using LowGear and SPDZ-online versus our implementation of the online phase which uses convolution triples. Note that our current implementation does not support RELUs so we estimate that part. In Table 4 the "Conv" keyword denotes the evaluation of the convolution layers only. As can be seen from the table, our approach brings down the online cost of

[8] This is assuming $p \approx 2^{128}$ and a comparison with statistical security $\mathsf{sec_s} = 40$ - see SCALE-MAMBA documentation for more details [1].

the convolution layers by at least two orders of magnitude compared with classic SPDZ Beaver triples.

Table 4. Estimated communication costs for 2-party private inference in a dishonest majority malicious adversarial setting on ResNet-50 without the batch norm layers.

Protocol	Communication (GB)			
	Preprocessing		Online	
Conv [27]	5,092	124×	86.91	160×
Conv (ours)	41		0.54	
Conv + RELUs [27]	9,225	2.2×	105.2	5.6×
Conv + RELUs (ours)	4,133		18.83	

5 Conclusion

In this work, we reduced the overhead of computing linear operations in the SPDZ framework for dishonest-majority MPC. First, we demonstrate a novel way of generating pre-processing data for bilinear operations such as matrix multiplication and convolutions in the SPDZ framework, where the communication cost does not depend on the number of multiplications but only depends on the input and output size. We achieved this by leveraging state-of-the-art homomorphic encryption algorithms for linear operations into SPDZ. We generalized the notion of authenticated Beaver triples to arbitrary bilinear operations and adapted the state-of-the-art homomorphic matrix multiplication algorithm to generate authenticated "matrix triples" and "convolution triples." We also removed the sacrifice stage of SPDZ via increasing the parameters of the HE scheme to allow one more multiplication, and optimized the SPDZ zero-knowledge proof via the usage of BFV homomorphic encryption scheme, which further improved performance. Our protocol requires $O(n^2)$ total communication to multiply two $n \times n$ matrices, compared to $O(n^{2.8})$ from SPDZ. In terms of concrete efficiency, to securely multiply two 128×128 matrices, our protocol is at least *one order of magnitude* faster in terms of latency and as much as *two orders of magnitude* more communication efficient compared to prior art. Furthermore, this improvement only increases as the dimensions of the matrices increase. We believe our protocols improves the state-of-the-art in dishonest-majority secure computation, particularly in tasks that require a large number of linear operations such as private machine learning inference and training.

Acknowledgements. The authors thank the anonymous reviewers for their valuable comments and suggestions. The work of Miran Kim was supported by Institute of Information & communications Technology Planning & Evaluation (IITP) grant funded by the Korea government (MSIT) (No.2020-0-01336, Artificial Intelligence graduate school support (UNIST)). Dragos Rotaru has been supported in part by the Defense Advanced Research Projects Agency (DARPA) and Space and Naval Warfare Systems

Center, Pacific (SSC Pacific) under contract No. N66001-15-C-4070, by the Office of the Director of National Intelligence (ODNI), Intelligence Advanced Research Projects Activity (IARPA) via Contract No. 2019-1902070006, by the CyberSecurity Research Flanders with reference number VR20192203 and by ERC Advanced Grant ERC-2015-AdG-IMPaCT. Any opinions, findings and conclusions or recommendations expressed in this material are those of the author(s) and do not necessarily reflect the views of the ODNI, United States Air Force, IARPA, DARPA, the US Government, FWO or ERC. The U.S. Government is authorized to reproduce and distribute reprints for governmental purposes notwithstanding any copyright annotation therein.

A Security Proof of Our Zero Knowledge Protocol

We split the proof into the 3 components – completeness, soundness, and the zero-knowledge property.

Completeness. For completeness, a true statement must be verified correctly when both the prover and verifier are honest. In this case, completeness follows directly from the construction as the relation $\mathfrak{c}_{z_l} = \mathfrak{c}_{y_l} + (w \cdot \mathfrak{c}_a)_l$ is linear in its arguments and works component-wise as well as from the fact that the BFV encryption procedure is linear in the message and the randomness. The noise bound (in Verify 3 of Fig. 3) is obtained by:

$$\begin{aligned} \|r_{z_l}\| = \left\| \sum_i r^i_{z_l} \right\| &\le \sum_i \left(\left\| r^i_{y_l} \right\| + \left\| (w \cdot \boldsymbol{r}^i_a)_l \right\| \right) \\ &\le nu \cdot 2^{\mathsf{sec}_{\mathsf{zk}}} \end{aligned} \tag{11}$$

where the last equality holds with an overwhelming probability since $\left\|(w \cdot \boldsymbol{r}^i_a)_l\right\| \le u$ and $r^i_{y_l}$ is a sample from $U_{u \cdot 2^{\mathsf{sec}_{\mathsf{zk}}}}$.

Zero-Knowledge. To prove zero-knowledge, we need to show that for a true statement, the verifier learns nothing more than the fact that the statement is true. This is done by showing that the verifier (in this case all the parties), given access only to the statement to be proven ($\mathfrak{c}_{a_k} = \mathsf{Enc}_{\mathsf{pk}}(a_k, r_{a_k})$) but no access to prover, can produce a transcript that is statistically indistinguishable from the real transcript, in this case, $\{\mathfrak{c}^i_{a_k}\}, \{\mathfrak{c}^i_{y_l}\}, w, \{z^i_l\}, \{r^i_{z_l}\}$ where $k \in [u], l \in [v]$, and $i \in [n]$.

Assuming a set of corrupt parties $A \subset [n]$, we simulate an accepting transcript for the set of honest parties, i.e., P_i where $i \notin A$ by first choosing the challenge matrix w. Once w is fixed, generate $z^i_l \leftarrow R_p$ and $r^i_{z_l} \leftarrow U_{u \cdot 2^{\mathsf{sec}_{\mathsf{zk}}}}$ for $i \notin A$. Finally, compute $\mathfrak{c}^i_{y_l} \leftarrow \mathsf{Enc}_{\mathsf{pk}}(z^i_l, r^i_{z_l}) - (w \cdot \mathfrak{c}^i_a)_l$. Next, we argue that each of $\{r^i_{z_l}\}, \{z^i_l\}$, and $\{\mathfrak{c}^i_{y_l}\}$ has the same distribution in the real and simulated transcripts (w is straightforward and $\{\mathfrak{c}^i_{a_k}\}$ are in the proof statement). $r^i_{z_l}$ has the same distribution in both the transcripts as it is generated from the same distribution except for an additive factor which is from an exponentially smaller distribution. The distributions of z_l^i are uniformly random elements from R_p and hence are exactly the same. Finally, the distribution of $\mathfrak{c}_{y_l}^i$ is a uniformly random $u \cdot 2^{\mathsf{sec_{zk}}}$-ciphertext in both the real and simulated transcript as $(w \cdot \mathfrak{c}_a^i)_l$ is a u-ciphertext.

Soundness. To prove knowledge soundness, we follow the techniques of [5, 7]. Informally, we show that if there exists a prover $\mathcal{P}$ (as a function of the adversarial corruptions) that can succeed with probability $\epsilon > 2^{-\mathsf{sec_s}}$, then there exists a knowledge extractor running in $\mathsf{poly}(\mathsf{sec_s}) \cdot \epsilon^{-1}$ that can extract the witnesses $\{(a_k^i, r_{a_k}^i)\}_{k \in [u]}$. We effectively construct a polynomial time extractor $\mathcal{E}_k$ for each witness $(a_k^i, r_{a_k}^i)$ and $k \in [u]$. The extractor $\mathcal{E}_k$, which acts as the verifier, given access to such a prover P, performs the following steps:

(i) Send random challenges w to the prover $\mathcal{P}$ until it outputs an accepting transcript. Let us denote this accepting transcript by $(z_l^i, r_{z_l}^i)$. This runs in expected time $1/\epsilon$.
(ii) Select a new random challenge $\tilde{w}$ identical to w except the k-th column. This ensures that $w - \tilde{w}$ is a matrix with all zeros except in the k-th column, where the entries are elements of R of the form $a - b \neq 0$ where $a, b \in \{0\} \cup \{\pm X^j\}_{0 \leq j < N}$.
(iii) Send challenge matrices to the prover $\mathcal{P}$ until one of two things happen
   (a) A successful transcript is generated with $\tilde{w}$.
   (b) There are $t = \lceil \mathsf{sec_s} \cdot \epsilon^{-1} \rceil$ unsuccessful challenges.
(iv) The extractors aborts in case (iii)(b). In case (iii)(a), the extractor outputs the two successful transcripts along with the challenges.

If the extractor outputs two transcripts successfully, then we can use the resulting two conversations to compute the witness $(a_k^i, r_{a_k}^i)$ efficiently. We describe this argument next. However, it is important to note here that the soundness argument is not complete until we show that (1) the above extractor runs in $\mathsf{poly}(\mathsf{sec_s})/\epsilon$ time and (2) aborts with low probability. We break down the proof into the above three steps.

Runtime. The runtime is easiest to argue and follows directly from the description of the extractor.

Probability of Aborting. To bound the failure probability of the extractor, we follow the line of argument from [17]. Let w_k denote the k-th column of the challenge matrix w and w_{-k} the rest of the challenge matrix, i.e., w except the k-th column. We construct a binary matrix H such that each row corresponds to a choice of randomness σ used by the prover $\mathcal{P}$ and a choice of challenge w_{-k} and each column corresponds to a choice of w_k. The entry H_{σ, w_{-k}, w_k} is 1 if the verifier accepts the transcripts for this random choice σ and challenge w. When the extractor uses $\mathcal{P}$ as a blackbox and submits a random challenge w, it is equivalent to probing an entry in the matrix H. By rewinding the prover $\mathcal{P}$, we can probe another entry in the matrix H in the same row (same internal randomness, i.e., $\tilde{w}$) and these two transcripts can be used to extract the witness $(a_k^i, r_{a_k}^i)$ efficiently.

Now, we look at the number of ones in each row of H. We note that each row has $(2N+1)^v$ entries (the size of the challenge space w_k). A row is called heavy if it contains at least $(\epsilon/2) \times (2N+1)^v$ ones. A simple application of Markov inequality implies that at least half of the ones are located in the heavy rows since ϵ is the ratio of the number of ones to the size of entire matrix H. Setting $v \geq (\mathsf{sec_s}+2)/\log_2(2N+1)$, we get at least $(\epsilon/2)\cdot(2N+1)^v \geq 2$ ones in each of the heavy rows. Now, from the description, it is clear that the extractor aborts in the following two cases:

$$\begin{bmatrix} \mathfrak{c}_{d_1}^1 & \cdots & \mathfrak{c}_{d_1}^n \\ \vdots & \ddots & \vdots \\ \mathfrak{c}_{d_v}^1 & \cdots & \mathfrak{c}_{d_v}^n \end{bmatrix} = \begin{bmatrix} & e_{1k} & \\ \mathbf{0} & \vdots & \mathbf{0} \\ & e_{vk} & \end{bmatrix} \times \begin{bmatrix} \mathfrak{c}_{a_1}^1 & \cdots & \mathfrak{c}_{a_1}^n \\ \vdots & \ddots & \vdots \\ \mathfrak{c}_{a_u}^1 & \cdots & \mathfrak{c}_{a_u}^n \end{bmatrix}$$

Fig. 4. Visual aid to assist the exposition of the witness extraction. Here $\mathfrak{c}_{d_l}^i = \mathfrak{c}_{z_l}^i - \tilde{\mathfrak{c}}_{z_l}^i$ and $e = w - \tilde{w}$ is a matrix with zeros everywhere except the k-th column.

1. The first successful challenge is not in a heavy row.
2. The first successful challenge is in a heavy row but we do not hit another one in $t = \lceil 4\mathsf{sec_s}/\epsilon \rceil$ tries.

The first probability as we just saw is $\leq 1/2$. For second probability, each successful attempt happens with probability $\geq \epsilon/2 - (2N+1)^{-v} > \epsilon/4$. Hence, the probability of aborting from the second case is at most

$$(1-\epsilon/4)^t < \exp\left(-t \cdot \epsilon/4\right) < 2^{-\mathsf{sec_s}} \tag{12}$$

Adding these up, the probability that the extractor aborts is $< 1/2 + 2^{-\mathsf{sec_s}}$.

Witness Extraction. The final piece of completing the soundness proof is the witness extraction and associated bounds. Given two accepting transcripts $(w, \{z_l^i, r_{z_l}^i\})$ and $(\tilde{w}, \{\tilde{z}_l^i, \tilde{r}_{z_l}^i\})$, we set $\mathfrak{c}_{z_l}^i = \mathsf{Enc_{pk}}(z_l^i, r_{z_l}^i)$ and $\tilde{\mathfrak{c}}_{z_l}^i = \mathsf{Enc_{pk}}(\tilde{z}_l^i, \tilde{r}_{z_l}^i)$. Let us consider the matrix with entries $\mathfrak{c}_{d_l} = \mathfrak{c}_{z_l} - \tilde{\mathfrak{c}}_{z_l}$ and another matrix $w - \tilde{w}$ with 0's everywhere except the k-th column.

We can see that this set of linear constraints allows us to find the witness, one index at a time. In particular, at least one of the $e_{lk} \neq 0$ and consequently, $z_l^i, r_{z_l}^i, \tilde{z}_l^i$, and $\tilde{r}_{z_l}^i$ along with e_{lk} can be used to extract, respectively, the plaintext and randomness a_k^i and $r_{a_k}^i$ (which encrypts to C_k^i). The exact relations can be written as follows:

$$\begin{aligned} a_k^i &= e_{lk}^{-1} \cdot (z_l^i - \tilde{z}_l^i) \\ r_{a_k}^i &= e_{lk}^{-1} \cdot (r_{z_l}^i - \tilde{r}_{z_l}^i) \end{aligned} \tag{13}$$

Finally, to estimate the noise, we use the following result from [7]:

Lemma 1. *The quantity* $2/(X^i - X^j)$ *for* $0 \leq i \neq j < N$ *is a polynomial in* R *with coefficients in* $\{0, \pm 1\}$.

As a consequence of the above, $\left\|2/(X^i - X^j)\right\|_\infty \leq 1$. We use this to bound the norm of $2 \cdot a_k^i$ and $2 \cdot r_{a_k}^i$ from Eq. 13. In particular,

$$\left\|2 \cdot r_{a_k}^i\right\| \leq N \cdot \|2/e_{lk}\|_\infty \cdot \left\|r_{z_l}^i - \tilde{r}_{z_l}^i\right\| \leq 2N \cdot u \cdot 2^{\mathsf{sec_{zk}}}. \tag{14}$$

Therefore, $2 \cdot \mathfrak{c}_{a_k}^i = \mathsf{Enc}(2 \cdot a_k, 2 \cdot r_{a_k}^i)$ and $\|2 \cdot r_{a_k}\| \leq Nnu \cdot 2^{\mathsf{sec_{zk}}+1}$. This completes the proof. □

References

1. Aly, A., et al.: SCALE-MAMBA v1.2: Documentation (2018)
2. Araki, T., et al.: Optimized honest-majority MPC for malicious adversaries - breaking the 1 billion-gate per second barrier. In: 2017 IEEE Symposium on Security and Privacy, San Jose, CA, USA, 22–26 May 2017, pp. 843–862. IEEE Computer Society Press (2017)
3. Babenko, A., Lempitsky, V.: Efficient indexing of billion-scale datasets of deep descriptors. In: Proceedings of the IEEE Conference on Computer Vision and Pattern Recognition, pp. 2055–2063 (2016)
4. Barak, A., Escudero, D., Dalskov, A., Keller, M.: Secure evaluation of quantized neural networks. Cryptology ePrint Archive, Report 2019/131 (2019). https://eprint.iacr.org/2019/131
5. Baum, C., Cozzo, D., Smart, N.P.: Using topgear in overdrive: A more efficient zkpok for spdz. Cryptology ePrint Archive, Report 2019/035 (2019). https://eprint.iacr.org/2019/035
6. Bendlin, R., Damgård, I., Orlandi, C., Zakarias, S.: Semi-homomorphic encryption and multiparty computation. In: Paterson, K.G. (ed.) EUROCRYPT 2011. LNCS, vol. 6632, pp. 169–188. Springer, Heidelberg (2011). https://doi.org/10.1007/978-3-642-20465-4_11
7. Benhamouda, F., Camenisch, J., Krenn, S., Lyubashevsky, V., Neven, G.: Better zero-knowledge proofs for lattice encryption and their application to group signatures. In: Sarkar, P., Iwata, T. (eds.) ASIACRYPT 2014. LNCS, vol. 8873, pp. 551–572. Springer, Heidelberg (2014). https://doi.org/10.1007/978-3-662-45611-8_29
8. Brakerski, Z.: Fully homomorphic encryption without modulus switching from classical GapSVP. In: Safavi-Naini, R., Canetti, R. (eds.) CRYPTO 2012. LNCS, vol. 7417, pp. 868–886. Springer, Heidelberg (2012). https://doi.org/10.1007/978-3-642-32009-5_50
9. Brakerski, Z., Gentry, C., Vaikuntanathan, V.: (Leveled) fully homomorphic encryption without bootstrapping. ACM Trans. Comput. Theory (TOCT) **6**(3), 13 (2014)
10. Canetti, R.: Universally composable security: a new paradigm for cryptographic protocols. In: Proceedings of the 42Nd IEEE Symposium on Foundations of Computer Science, FOCS 2001, pp. 136–145 (2001)
11. Canetti, R.: Security and composition of multiparty cryptographic protocols. J. Cryptol. **13**(1), 143–202 (2000)

12. Chase, M., et al.: Security of homomorphic encryption. HomomorphicEncryption.org, Redmond WA, USA, Technical report (2017)
13. Chen, H., Chillotti, I., Dong, Y., Poburinnaya, O., Razenshteyn, I., Sanns, M.S.R.: Scaling up secure approximate k-nearest neighbors search. arXiv preprint arXiv:1904.02033 (2019)
14. Cheon, J.H., Kim, A., Kim, M., Song, Y.: Homomorphic encryption for arithmetic of approximate numbers. In: Takagi, T., Peyrin, T. (eds.) ASIACRYPT 2017. LNCS, vol. 10624, pp. 409–437. Springer, Cham (2017). https://doi.org/10.1007/978-3-319-70694-8_15
15. Cock, M.D., Dowsley, R., Nascimento, A.C., Newman, S.C.: Fast, privacy preserving linear regression over distributed datasets based on pre-distributed data. In: Proceedings of the 8th ACM Workshop on Artificial Intelligence and Security, pp. 3–14 (2015)
16. Damgård, I., Escudero, D., Frederiksen, T., Keller, M., Scholl, P., Volgushev, N.: New primitives for actively-secure MPC over rings with applications to private machine learning. In: 2019 IEEE Symposium on Security and Privacy (SP), pp. 1102–1120 (2019)
17. Damgård, I.: On σ-protocols. University of Aarhus, Department for Computer Science, Lecture Notes (2002)
18. Damgård, I., Keller, M., Larraia, E., Pastro, V., Scholl, P., Smart, N.P.: Practical covertly secure MPC for dishonest majority–or: breaking the SPDZ limits. In: Crampton, J., Jajodia, S., Mayes, K. (eds.) ESORICS 2013. LNCS, vol. 8134, pp. 1–18. Springer, Heidelberg (2013). https://doi.org/10.1007/978-3-642-40203-6_1
19. Damgård, I., Pastro, V., Smart, N., Zakarias, S.: Multiparty computation from somewhat homomorphic encryption. In: Safavi-Naini, R., Canetti, R. (eds.) CRYPTO 2012. LNCS, vol. 7417, pp. 643–662. Springer, Heidelberg (2012). https://doi.org/10.1007/978-3-642-32009-5_38
20. Data61. MP-SPDZ (2019). https://github.com/data61/MP-SPDZ
21. Fan, J., Vercauteren, F.: Somewhat practical fully homomorphic encryption. IACR Cryptol. ePrint Arch. **2012**, 144 (2012)
22. Halevi, S., Shoup, V.: Algorithms in HElib. In: Garay, J.A., Gennaro, R. (eds.) CRYPTO 2014. LNCS, vol. 8616, pp. 554–571. Springer, Heidelberg (2014). https://doi.org/10.1007/978-3-662-44371-2_31
23. Halevi, S., Shoup, V.: Faster homomorphic linear transformations in HElib. In: Shacham, H., Boldyreva, A. (eds.) CRYPTO 2018. LNCS, vol. 10991, pp. 93–120. Springer, Cham (2018). https://doi.org/10.1007/978-3-319-96884-1_4
24. He, K., Zhang, X., Ren, S., Sun, J.: Deep residual learning for image recognition. In: Proceedings of the IEEE Conference on Computer Vision and Pattern Recognition, pp. 770–778 (2016)
25. Jiang, X., Kim, M., Lauter, K., Song, Y.: Secure outsourced matrix computation and application to neural networks. In: ACM Conference on Computer and Communications Security (CCS), pp. 1209–1222 (2018)
26. Keller, M., Orsini, E., Scholl, P.: MASCOT: faster malicious arithmetic secure computation with oblivious transfer. In: Weippl, E.R., Katzenbeisser, S., Kruegel, C., Myers, A.C., Halevi, S. (eds.) ACM CCS 2016: 23rd Conference on Computer and Communications Security, Vienna, Austria, 24–28 October 2016, pp. 830–842. ACM Press (2016)
27. Keller, M., Pastro, V., Rotaru, D.: Overdrive: making SPDZ great again. In: Nielsen, J.B., Rijmen, V. (eds.) EUROCRYPT 2018. LNCS, vol. 10822, pp. 158–189. Springer, Cham (2018). https://doi.org/10.1007/978-3-319-78372-7_6

28. Krizhevsky, A., Sutskever, I., Hinton, G.E.: ImageNet classification with deep convolutional neural networks. In: Advances in Neural Information Processing Systems, pp. 1097–1105 (2012)
29. Lavin, A., Gray, S.: Fast algorithms for convolutional neural networks. In: Proceedings of the IEEE Conference on Computer Vision and Pattern Recognition, pp. 4013–4021 (2016)
30. Lawrence, S., Giles, C.L., Tsoi, A.C., Back, A.D.: Face recognition: a convolutional neural-network approach. IEEE Trans. Neural Netw. **8**(1), 98–113 (1997)
31. Liu, J., Juuti, M., Lu, Y., Asokan, N.: Oblivious neural network predictions via MiniONN transformations. In: Bhavani, M., Thuraisingham, D.E., Tal, M., Xu, D. (eds.) ACM CCS 2017: 24th Conference on Computer and Communications Security, Dallas, TX, USA, 31 October–2 November 2017, pp. 619–631. ACM Press (2017)
32. Makri, E., Rotaru, D., Smart, N.P., Vercauteren, F.: EPIC: efficient private image classification (or: learning from the masters). In: Matsui, M. (ed.) CT-RSA 2019. LNCS, vol. 11405, pp. 473–492. Springer, Cham (2019). https://doi.org/10.1007/978-3-030-12612-4_24
33. Mohassel, P., Rindal, P.: ABY^3: a mixed protocol framework for machine learning. In: Lie, D., Mannan, M., Backes, M., Wang, X.F. (eds.) ACM CCS 2018: 25th Conference on Computer and Communications Security, Toronto, ON, Canada, 15–19 October 2018, pp. 35–52. ACM Press (2018)
34. Mohassel, P., Zhang, Y.: SecureML: a system for scalable privacy-preserving machine learning. In: 2017 IEEE Symposium on Security and Privacy, San Jose, CA, USA, 22–26 May 2017, pp. 19–38. IEEE Computer Society Press (2017)
35. Riazi, M.S., Weinert, C., Tkachenko, O., Songhori, E.M., Schneider, T., Koushanfar, F.: Chameleon: a hybrid secure computation framework for machine learning applications. In: Kim, J., Ahn, G.J., Kim, S., Kim, Y., López, J., Kim, T. (eds.) ASIACCS 18: 13th ACM Symposium on Information, Computer and Communications Security, Incheon, Republic of Korea, 2–6 April 2018, pp. 707–721. ACM Press (2018)
36. Microsoft SEAL (release 3.3), Microsoft Research, Redmond, WA (2019).https://github.com/Microsoft/SEAL
37. Wagh, S., Gupta, D., Chandran, N.: SecureNN: 3-party secure computation for neural network training. In: Privacy Enhancing Technologies Symposium (PETS) (2019)
38. Zheng, W., Popa, R.A., Gonzalez, J.E., Stoica, I.: Helen: maliciously secure coopetitive learning for linear models. arXiv preprint arXiv:1907.07212 (2019)
39. Mishra, P.K., Rathee, D., Duong, D.H., Yasuda, M.: Fast secure matrix multiplications over ring-based homomorphic encryption. IACR Cryptol. ePrint Arch. **2018**, 663 (2018)

On the Exact Round Complexity of Best-of-Both-Worlds Multi-party Computation

Arpita Patra[1], Divya Ravi[1](✉), and Swati Singla[2]

[1] Indian Institute of Science, Bangalore, India
{arpita,divyar}@iisc.ac.in
[2] Google India, Bangalore, India
swatis@iisc.ac.in

Abstract. The two traditional streams of multiparty computation (MPC) protocols consist of– (a) protocols achieving guaranteed output delivery (god) or fairness (fn) in the honest-majority setting and (b) protocols achieving unanimous or selective abort (ua, sa) in the dishonest-majority setting. The favorable presence of honest majority amongst the participants is necessary to achieve the stronger notions of god or fn. While the constructions of each type are abound in the literature, one class of protocols does not seem to withstand the threat model of the other. For instance, the honest-majority protocols do not guarantee privacy of the inputs of the honest parties in the face of dishonest majority and likewise the dishonest-majority protocols cannot achieve god and fn, tolerating even a single corruption, let alone dishonest minority. The promise of the unconventional yet much sought-after species of MPC, termed as 'Best-of-Both-Worlds' (BoBW), is to offer the best possible security depending on the actual corruption scenario.

This work nearly settles the exact round complexity of two classes of BoBW protocols differing on the security achieved in the honest-majority setting, namely god and fn respectively, under the assumption of no setup (plain model), public setup (CRS) and private setup (CRS + PKI or simply PKI). The former class necessarily requires the number of parties to be strictly more than the sum of the bounds of corruptions in the honest-majority and dishonest-majority setting, for a feasible solution to exist. Demoting the goal to the second-best attainable security in the honest-majority setting, the latter class needs no such restriction.

Assuming a network with pair-wise private channels and a broadcast channel, we show that 5 and 3 rounds are necessary and sufficient for the class of BoBW MPC with fn under the assumption of 'no setup' and 'public and private setup' respectively. For the class of BoBW MPC with god, we show necessity and sufficiency of 3 rounds for the public setup case and 2 rounds for the private setup case. In the no setup setting, we show the sufficiency of 5 rounds, while the known lower bound is 4. All our upper bounds are based on polynomial-time assumptions and assume

Arpita Patra would like to acknowledge financial support from SERB MATRICS (Theoretical Sciences) Grant 2020 and Google India AI/ML Research Award 2020.

S. Moriai and H. Wang (Eds.): ASIACRYPT 2020, LNCS 12493, pp. 60–91, 2020.
https://doi.org/10.1007/978-3-030-64840-4_3

black-box simulation. With distinct feasibility conditions, the classes differ in terms of the round requirement. The bounds are in some cases different and on a positive note at most one more, compared to the maximum of the needs of the honest-majority and dishonest-majority setting. Our results remain unaffected when security with abort and fairness are upgraded to their identifiable counterparts.

1 Introduction

In secure multi-party computation (MPC) [1–3], n parties wish to jointly perform a computation on their private inputs in a way that no adversary $\mathcal{A}$ actively corrupting a coalition of t parties can learn more information than their outputs (*privacy*), nor can they affect the outputs of the computation other than by choosing their own inputs (*correctness*). MPC protocol comes in distinct flavours with varying degree of robustness– guaranteed output delivery (god), fairness (fn), unanimous abort (ua) and selective abort (sa). The strongest security, god, implies that all parties are guaranteed to obtain the output, regardless of the adversarial strategy. In the weaker notion of fn, the corrupted parties receive their output if and only if all honest parties do. In the further weaker guarantee of ua, fairness may be compromised, yet the adversary cannot break unanimity of honest parties. That is, either all or none of the honest parties receive the output. Lastly, sa security, the weakest in the lot, allows the adversary to selectively deprive some honest parties of the output.

While highly sought-after, the former two properties can only be realised, when majority of the involved population is honest [4]. In the absence of this favorable condition, only the latter two notions can be attained. With these distinct affordable goals, MPC with honest majority [5–11] and dishonest majority [1,12–17] mark one of the earlier demarcations in the world of MPC. With complementary challenges and techniques, each setting independently stands tall with spectacular body of work. Yet, the most worrisome shortcoming of these generic protocols is that: a protocol in *one* setting completely breaks down in the *other* setting i.e. the security promises are very rigid and specific to the setting. For example, a protocol for honest majority might no longer even be "private" or "correct" if half (or more) of the parties are corrupted. A protocol that guarantees security with ua for arbitrary corruptions cannot pull off the stronger security of god or fn even if only a "single" party is corrupt. In many real-life scenarios, it is highly unlikely for anyone to guess upfront how many parties the adversary is likely to corrupt. In such a scenario, the best a practitioner can do, is to employ the 'best' protocol from her favorite class and hope that the adversary will be within assumed corruption limit of the employed protocol. If the guess fails, the employed protocol, depending on whether it is an honest or dishonest majority protocol, will suffer from the above mentioned issues. The quest for attaining the best feasible security guarantee in the respective settings of honest and dishonest majority in a *single* protocol sets the beginning of a brand new class of MPC protocols, termed as 'Best of Both Worlds (BoBW)' [18–20]. In critical applications like voting [21,22], secure auctions [23], secure aggregation [24], federated learning and prediction [25,26], financial data analysis [27] and others, where privacy of the inputs of an honest party needs protection at any cost and yet a robust completion is called for (as much as theoretically feasible), BoBW protocols are arguably the best fit.

Denoting the threshold of corruption in honest and dishonest majority case by t and s respectively, an ideal BoBW MPC should promise the best possible security in each corruption scenario for any population of size n, as long as $t < n/2$ and $s < n$. Quite contrary to the expectation, the grand beginning of BoBW MPC with the works of [18–20] is mostly marred with pessimistic results showing the above goal is impossible for many scenarios. For reactive functionalities that receive inputs and provide outputs in multiple rounds maintaining a state information between subsequent invocations, it is impossible to achieve BoBW security [18]. While theoretical feasibility is not declined, non-reactive or standard functionalities are shown to be impossible to realise as long as $t+s \geq n$ in expected polynomial time (in the security parameter), making any positive result practically irrelevant [19,20]. A number of meaningful relaxations were proposed in the literature to get around the impossibility of BoBW security when $t+s \geq n$ [19,20]. The most relevant to our work is the relaxation proposed in [28] where the best possible security of god is compromised to the second-best notion of fn in the honest-majority setting. Other attempts to circumvent the impossibility result appear in [18] and [19,29] where the security in dishonest-majority setting is weakened to allowing the adversary to learn s evaluations of the function (each time with distinct inputs *exclusively* corresponding to the corrupt parties) in the former and achieving a weaker notion of $O(1/p)$-security with abort (actions of any polynomial-time adversary in the real world can be simulated by a polynomial-time adversary in the ideal world such that the distributions of the resulting outcomes cannot be distinguished with probability better than $O(1/p)$) in the latter. [18] shows yet another circumvention by weakening the adversary in dishonest-majority case from active to passive. On the contrary, constructions are known when $t + s < n$ is assumed [18], tolerating active corruptions and giving best possible security in both the honest and dishonest majority case.

In this work, we consider two types of BoBW MPC protocols and study their exact round complexity: (a) MPC achieving the best security of god and ua in the honest and dishonest majority setting respectively assuming $s+t < n$, referred as (god|ua)-BoBW; (b) MPC achieving second-best security notion of fn in the honest majority and the best possible security of ua in the dishonest majority for any n, referred as (fn|ua)-BoBW. The adversary is considered malicious, rushing and polynomially-bounded in either world. The latter notion (introduced in [28]) is an elegant and meaningful relaxation that brings back the true essence of BoBW protocols with no constraint on n, apart from the natural bounds of $t < n/2$ and $s < n$. Furthermore, fn is almost as good as god for many practical applications where the adversary is rational enough and does not wish to fail the honest parties at the expense of losing its own output. In spite of immense practical relevance of BoBW protocols, the question of their exact round complexity has not been tackled so far. Below, we review relevant literature on BoBW protocols and exact round complexity of MPC.

1.1 On the Round Complexity of BoBW MPC

The phenomenal body of work done on round complexity catering to various adversarial settings and network models emphasises its theoretical importance and practical relevance. For instance, the exact round complexity of MPC independently in honest and dishonest majority has been examined and the recent literature is awash with a bunch of upper bounds that eluded for quite a long time [16,17,30,31]. We review the round complexity of the honest-majority and dishonest-majority MPC in the cryptographic setting which define natural yet possibly loose bounds for the BoBW MPC. To begin with, 2 rounds are known to be necessary to realize any MPC protocol, regardless of the setting, no matter whether a setup is assumed or not as long as the setup (when assumed) is independent of the inputs of the involved parties [32]. In the dishonest-majority setting, when no setup is assumed (plain model) 4 rounds are necessary [33]. Tight upper bounds appear in [14–17,34], with the latter three presenting constructions under polynomial-time assumptions, yet with sa security. In the presence of a public setup (Common Reference String a.k.a. CRS setting), the lower bound comes down to 2 rounds [32]. A series of work present matching upper bounds under various assumptions [13,35,36], culminating with the works of [30,31] that attain the goal under the minimal assumption of 2-round oblivious transfer (OT). In the honest-majority setting and in plain model, 3 rounds are shown to be necessary for fn (and hence for god) protocols, in the presence of pairwise-private and broadcast channels for $t \geq 2$ active corruptions [37] and for any t as long as $n/3 < t < n/2$ [38]. The results of [37,38] hold in the presence of CRS but does not hold in the presence of correlated randomness setup such as PKI. Circumventing the lower bound of 3 for fn, [39] shows a 2-round 4PC protocol against a single active corruption achieving god even without a broadcast channel. The matching upper bounds appear in [11] for the general case under public-key assumption, and in [38] for the special case of 3PC under the minimal assumption of (injective) OWF. In the CRS model, 3 rounds remains to be the lower bound for fn in a setting where broadcast is the only medium of communication (broadcast-only setting) [40] and additionally with point-to-point channels [37,38,41]. Given PKI, the bound can be improved to 2 [40].

In the BoBW setting, constant-round protocols are presented in (or can be derived from) [18,20] for (god|ua)-BoBW and BoBW where only semi-honest corruptions are tolerated in the dishonest majority. The recent work of [42] settled the exact round complexity of the latter class, as a special case of a strong adversarial model that allows both active (with threshold t_a) and passive (with threshold t_p, which subsumes the active corruptions) corruption for a range of thresholds for (t_a, t_p) starting from $(\lceil n/2 \rceil - 1, \lfloor n/2 \rfloor)$ to $(0, n-1)$. Lastly, the round complexity of BoBW protocols of [29] that achieve $1/p$- security with abort in dishonest-majority (and god in honest majority), depends on the polynomial $p(\kappa)$ (where κ denotes the security parameter).

1.2 Our Results

This work nearly settles the exact round complexity for two classes of BoBW protocols, (god|ua)-BoBW and (fn|ua)-BoBW, under the assumption of no setup (plain model), public setup (CRS) and private setup (CRS + PKI or simply PKI). The adversary is assumed to be rushing, active and static. The parties are connected via pair-wise private channels and an additional broadcast channel. All our upper bounds are based on polynomial-time assumptions and assume black-box simulation. We summarise our results below.

(fn|ua)-BoBW. We settle the exact round complexity of this class of BoBW protocols by establishing the necessity and sufficiency of: (a) 5 rounds in the plain model and (b) 3 rounds in both the public (CRS) and private (CRS+PKI) setup setting. In the CRS model, the necessity of 3 rounds for honest-majority MPC achieving fn (and hence for (fn|ua)-BoBW) has been demonstrated in [37,38,40], the former in a setting where broadcast is the only mode of communication (broadcast-only) and the latter two additionally with pairwise-private channels. However, these results do not hold in the presence of PKI. Our lower bound argument, on the other hand, is resilient to the presence of both CRS and PKI, and further holds in the presence of broadcast and pairwise-private channels.

Table 1. Summary of results

	No setup (plain model)	Public setup (CRS)	Private setup (CRS + PKI)
Honest majority	Round: 3	Round: 3	Round: 2
$t < n/2$	Lower Bound: [37,38]	Lower Bound: [37,38]	Lower Bound: [32]
fn / god	Upper Bound: [11,43]	Upper Bound: [11,40,43]	Upper Bound: [40]
Dishonest majority	Round: 4	Round: 2	Round: 2
$s < n$	Lower Bound: [33]	Lower Bound: [32]	Lower Bound: [32]
sa / ua	Upper Bound: [16,17,34]	Upper Bound: [13,35]	Upper Bound: [13,35]
	(sa only)	[30,31,36]	[30,31,36]
(fn|ua)-BoBW	Round: 5	Round: 3	Round: 3
$t < n/2, s < n$	Lower Bound: **This paper**	Lower Bound: [37,38]	Upper Bound: **This paper**
fn & ua	Upper Bound: **This paper**	Lower Bound: **This paper**	Upper Bound: **This paper**
(god|ua)-BoBW	Round: –	Round: 3	Round: 2
$t < n/2, t + s < n$	Lower Bound: 4 [33]	Lower Bound: **This paper**	Lower Bound: [32]
god & ua	Upper Bound: 5 **This paper**	Upper Bound: **This paper**	Upper Bound: **This paper**

(god|ua)-BoBW. In this regime, we demonstrate that 4, 3 and 2 are the respective lower bounds in the no-setup, public setup and private setup setting.

The first lower bound follows from the fact that BoBW MPC in this class trivially subsumes the dishonest majority MPC when $t = 0$ and the lower bound for dishonest-majority MPC is 4 [33]. The last lower bound follows from the standard 2-round bound for MPC needed to counter "residual function attack" [32]. Regarding the lower bound of 3 for the public setup (CRS) setting, we point that it follows directly from the 2-round impossibility of MPC with fn for honest majority in the CRS model [37,38,40] for *most* values of (t, s, n) satisfying $s + t < n$. However, these existing results do not rule out the possibility of 2-round (god|ua)-BoBW MPC for $(t = 1, s > t, n \geq 4)$. (In fact the protocols of [39,44] circumvent the 3-round lower bound for fn when $t = 1, n \geq 4$). We address this gap by giving a *unified proof* that works even for $s > t$, for all values of t (including $t = 1$). This is non-trivial and it demonstrably breaks down in the presence of PKI. The bounds are totally different from the ones for previous class, owing to the different feasibility condition of $s + t < n$. While our upper bound falls merely one short of matching the first lower bound in case of no-setup, the upper bounds of the other two settings are tight. We leave the question of designing or alternately proving the impossibility of 4-round (god|ua)-BoBW MPC protocol as open. Our results summarised and put along with the bounds known in the honest and dishonest majority setting appear in Table 1.

Extensions. We can boost the security of all our protocols to offer identifiability (i.e. public identifiability of the parties who misbehaved) when abort happens– (fn|ua)-BoBW protocols with identifiable fairness and abort in honest and dishonest majority setting respectively and (god|ua)-BoBW protocols with identifiable abort in dishonest-majority setting. Our lower bound results hold as is when ua and fn are upgraded to their stronger variants with identifiability. Furthermore, all our upper bounds relying on CRS have instantiations based on a weaker setup, referred as common *random* string, owing to the availability of 2-round OT [45] and Non-Interactive Zero Knowledge (NIZK) [46] under the latter setup assumption. Lastly, we also propose few optimizations to minimize the use of broadcast channels in our compilers upon which our upper bounds are based. Specifically, these optimizations preserve the round complexity of our upper bounds at the cost of relaxing the security notion in dishonest majority setting to sa (as opposed to ua).

1.3 Techniques

(fn|ua)-BoBW. The lower bounds are obtained via a reduction to 3-round OT in plain model and 1-round OT in private setup setting, both of which are known to be impossible [32,33] (albeit under the black-box simulation paradigm which is of concern in this paper). The starting point is a protocol π between 3 parties which provides fn when 1 party is corrupt and ua when 2 parties are corrupt, in 4 rounds when no setup is assumed and 2 rounds when private/public setup is assumed. The heart of the proof lies in devising a function f such that the realization of f via π, barring its last round, leads to an OT.

The upper bounds are settled with a proposed generic compiler that turns an r-round dishonest-majority MPC protocol achieving ua to an $(r+1)$-round BoBW MPC protocol *information-theoretically*. The compiler churns out a 5-round and a 3-round BoBW protocol in the plain model and in the presence of a CRS respectively, when plugged with appropriate ua-secure dishonest-majority protocol in the respective setting. Since the constructions of the known 4-round dishonest-majority MPC relying on polynomial-time assumptions [16,17,34] provide only sa security, we transform them to achieve ua for our purpose which invokes non-triviality for [16]. With CRS, the known constructions of [30,31] achieve unanimity and readily generate 3-round BoBW protocols.

Our compiler motivated by [47] uses the underlying r-round protocol to compute authenticated secret sharing of the output y with a threshold $t(< n/2)$ enabling the output reconstruction to occur in the last round. Fairness is ensured given the unanimity of the underlying protocol and the fact that the adversary (controlling t corrupt parties) has no information about the output y from the t shares he owns. However, using pairwise MACs for authentication defies unanimity in case of arbitrary corruptions because a corrupt party can choose to provide a verified share to a selected set of honest parties enabling their output reconstruction while causing the rest to abort. To address this, a form of authentication used in the Information Checking Protocol (ICP) primitive of [48,49] and unanimously identifiable commitments (UIC) of [50] can be used. This technique maintains unanimity amongst the honest parties during output reconstruction.

(god|ua)-BoBW. The non-trivial lower bound for this class is for the CRS setting. The other bounds imply from the dishonest-majority case. In the CRS setting, we prove a lower bound of 3 rounds. We start with assuming a 2 round BoBW protocol π for a specifically articulated 4-party function f. Next, we consider a sequence of executions of π, with different adversarial strategies in the order of their increasingly malicious behaviour such that the views of a certain party stays the same between the executions. This sequence finally leads us to a strategy where the adversary is able to learn the input of an honest party breaching privacy, hence coming to a contradiction. The crux of the lower bound argument lies in the design of the adversarial strategies that shuffle between the honest and dishonest majority setting encapsulating the challenge in designing BoBW protocols. This is in contrast to existing lower bounds in traditional models that deal with a fixed setting and single security notion at a time.

In the presence of a CRS, we build a 3-round protocol in two steps: a) we provide a generic compiler that transforms a broadcast-only ua-secure 2-round semi-malicious protocol such as [30,31] to a 3-round broadcast-only BoBW protocol of this class against a semi-malicious adversary (that follows the protocol honestly but can choose bad random coins for each round which are available to the simulator) b) then, the round-preserving compiler of [51] (using NIZKs) is applied on the above protocol to attain malicious security. The first compiler, in spirit of [11], ensures god against t non-cooperating corrupt parties in the last round, via secret-sharing the last-round message of the underlying protocol during the penultimate round of the compiled protocol. This is achieved by means of a garbled circuit sent by each party outputting its last-round message of the underlying protocol and the shares of the encoded labels with a threshold of s so that $s+1$ parties (in case of honest majority) can come together in the final round to construct the last-round message of the corrupt parties. This garbled circuit of a party P_i also takes into account the case when some other parties abort in the initial rounds of the protocol by taking the list of aborting parties as input and hard-coding their default input and randomness such that P_i's last round message is computed considering default values for parties who aborted. The compiler is made round-preserving with additional provision of pairwise-private channels or alternately, PKI. The latter (with PKI) just like its 3-round avatar can be compiled to a malicious protocol via the compiler of [51].

In the plain model, we provide a 5-round construction which is substantially more involved than our other upper bounds. To cope up with the demands of (god|ua)-BoBW security in the plain model, we encountered several roadblocks that were addressed by adapting some existing techniques combined with new tricks. The construction proceeds in two steps: a) we boost the security of our broadcast-only 3-round semi-malicious BoBW protocol to a stronger notion of delayed-semi-malicious security (where the adversary is required to justify his messages by giving a valid witness only in the last but one round) and b) we plug this 3-round BoBW protocol in the compiler of [31] with some additional modifications to obtain a 5-round BoBW protocol secure against a malicious adversary. The compiler of [31] takes as input a $(k-1)$-round protocol secure *with abort* against a delayed-semi-malicious adversary and churns out a k-round protocol secure *with abort* against a malicious adversary for any $k \geq 5$. The major challenges in our construction surface in simulation, where we cannot terminate in the honest-majority case even if the adversary aborts on behalf of a corrupt party (unlike the compiler of [31] that achieves abort security only). Furthermore, we observed that the natural simulation strategy to retain the BoBW guarantee suffered from a subtle flaw, similar to the one pointed in the work of [52], which we resolve with the help of the idea suggested therein. To bound the simulation time by expected polynomial-time, we further needed to introduce two 'dummy' rounds (rounds which do not involve messages of the underlying protocol being compiled) in our compiler as opposed to one as in [31]. This does not inflate the round complexity as our underlying delayed-semi-malicious protocol only consumes 3 rounds (instead of 4 as in the case of [31]). As a step towards resolving the question left open in this work (namely proving the impossibility or alternately constructing a 4-round (god|ua)-BoBW protocol under polynomial-time assumption), we present a sketch of a 4-round (god|ua)-BoBW protocol based on sub-exponentially secure trapdoor permutations and ZAPs. This construction builds upon the work of [53]. The pictorial roadmap to obtain the upper bounds is given in the figure below.

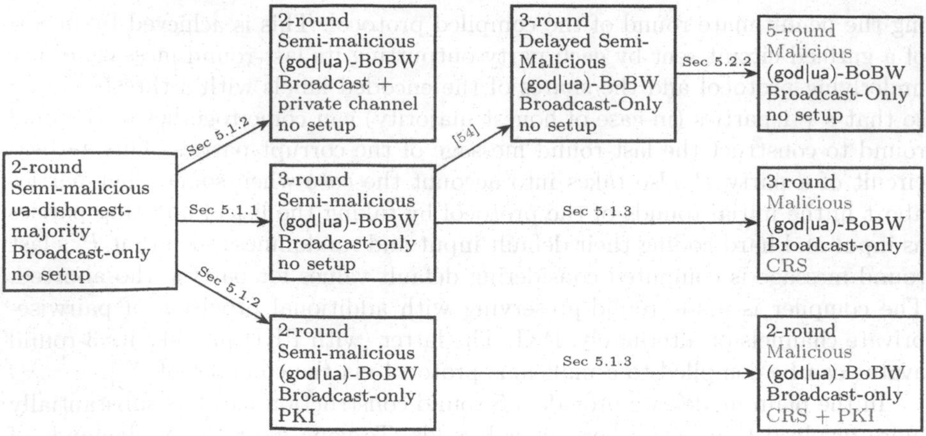

1.4 Related Works on BoBW MPC

An orthogonal notion of BoBW security is considered in [28,55,56] where information-theoretic and computational security is the desired goal in honest and dishonest majority setting respectively. Avoiding the relaxation to computational security in dishonest-majority setting, the work of [57] introduces the best possible information-theoretic guarantee achievable in the honest and dishonest majority settings simultaneously; i.e. the one that offers standard information-theoretic security in honest majority and offers residual security (the adversary cannot learn anything more than the residual function of the honest parties' inputs) in dishonest-majority setting. A more fine-grained graceful degradation of security is dealt with in the works of [28,42,58–60] considering a mixed adversary that can simultaneously corrupt in both active and semi-honest style. Lastly, [61] studies the communication efficiency in the BoBW setting.

1.5 Our Model

Before moving onto the technical section, we detail our model here. We consider a set of n parties $\mathcal{P} = \{P_1, \ldots P_n\}$ connected by pairwise-secure and authentic channels and having access to a broadcast channel. A few protocols in our work that are referred to as being *broadcast-only* do not assume private channels. Each party is modelled as a probabilistic polynomial time (PPT) Turing machine. We assume that there exists a PPT adversary $\mathcal{A}$, who can corrupt a subset of these parties. We denote the set of indices corresponding to parties controlled by $\mathcal{A}$ and the honest parties with $\mathcal{C}$ and $\mathcal{H}$ respectively. We denote the cryptographic security parameter by κ. A negligible function in κ is denoted by $\mathsf{negl}(\kappa)$. A function $\mathsf{negl}(\cdot)$ is negligible if for every polynomial $p(\cdot)$ there exists a value N such that for all $m > N$ it holds that $\mathsf{negl}(m) < \frac{1}{p(m)}$. Lastly, we denote the ideal functionalities for unanimous abort, fairness and guaranteed output delivery with $\mathcal{F}_{\mathsf{ua}}$, $\mathcal{F}_{\mathsf{fair}}$ and $\mathcal{F}_{\mathsf{god}}$ respectively (details appear in full version [54]).

Roadmap. Our lower and upper bounds for (fn|ua)-BoBW appear in Sect. 2–3. Our lower and upper bounds for (god|ua)-BoBW appear in Sect. 4–5. Our protocols are proven in real-world and ideal-world paradigm. The detailed security definitions, complete security proofs and formal definitions of the primitives used in our upper bounds are described in the full version [54].

2 Lower Bounds for (fn|ua)-BoBW

In this section, we show two lower bounds concerning (fn|ua)-BoBW protocols– one with no setup and the other with private setup. In the plain model, we show that it is impossible to design a 4-round (fn|ua)-BoBW protocol (with black-box simulation). In the CRS setting, the 3-round lower bound for (fn|ua)-BoBW protocols follows directly from the impossibility of 2-round protocol achieving fn [37,38,40]. However, they do not hold in the presence of PKI. While the argument of [40] crucially relies on the adversary being able to eavesdrop communication between two honest parties (which does not hold in the presence of PKI), the lower bounds of [37,38] also do not hold if PKI is assumed (as acknowledged/demonstrated in [37,41]). In the setting with CRS and PKI, we show impossibility of a 2-round protocol. The proof of both our lower bounds relies on the following theorem, which we formally state and prove below.

Theorem 1. *An n-party r-round* (fn|ua)*-BoBW protocol implies a 2-party $(r-1)$-round maliciously-secure oblivious transfer (OT).*

Proof. We prove the theorem for $n = 3$ parties with $t = 1$ and $s = 2$ which can be extended for higher values of n in a natural manner (elaborated in the full version). Let $\mathcal{P} = \{P_1, P_2, P_3\}$ denote the 3 parties and the adversary $\mathcal{A}$ may corrupt at most two parties. As per the hypothesis, we assume that there exists a r-round (fn|ua)-BoBW protocol protocol π_f that can compute the function f defined as $f((m_0, m_1), (c, R_2), R_3) = ((m_c + R_2 + R_3), m_c, m_c)$ which simultaneously achieves fn when $t = 1$ parties are corrupt and ua when $s = 2$ parties are corrupt. At a high-level, we transform the r-round 3-party protocol π_f among $\{P_1, P_2, P_3\}$ into a $(r-1)$-round 2-party OT protocol between a sender P_S with inputs (m_0, m_1) and a receiver P_R with input c.

Let $\mathsf{q} = 1 - \mathsf{negl}(\kappa)$ denote the overwhelming probability with which security of π_f holds, where the probability is defined over the choice of setup (in case a setup is assumed) and the random coins used by the parties. Before describing the transformation, we present the following lemma:

Lemma 1. *Protocol π_f must be such that the combined view of $\{P_2, P_3\}$ at the end of Round $(r-1)$ suffices to compute their output, with overwhelming probability.*

Proof. Consider an adversary $\mathcal{A}$ who corrupts only a minority of the parties ($t = 1$). $\mathcal{A}$ controls party P_1 with the following strategy: P_1 behaves honestly in the first $(r-1)$ rounds while he simply remains silent in Round r (last round). Since

P_1 receives all the desired communication throughout the protocol, it follows directly from correctness of π_f (which holds with overwhelming probability q) that $\mathcal{A}$ must be able to compute the output with probability q. Since π_f is assumed to be fair (with probability q) for the case of $t = 1$, it must hold that when P_1 learns the output, the honest parties P_2 and P_3 must also be able to compute the output with overwhelming probability $\mathsf{q} \times \mathsf{q} = \mathsf{q}^2$; without any communication from P_1 in Round r. This implies that the combined view of $\{P_2, P_3\}$ at the end of Round $(r - 1)$ must suffice to compute the output with overwhelming probability q^2. □

Our transformation from π_f to a $(r - 1)$-round OT protocol π_{OT} between a sender P_S with inputs (m_0, m_1) and a receiver P_R with input c goes as follows. P_S emulates the role of P_1 during π_f while P_R emulates the role of both parties $\{P_2, P_3\}$ during π_f using random inputs R_2, R_3 respectively. In more detail, let $\mathsf{m}^{\mathsf{r}}_{i \to j}$ denote the communication from P_i to P_j in round r of π_f. Then for $\mathsf{r} \in [r - 1]$, the interaction in round r of protocol π_{OT} is the following: P_S sends $\mathsf{m}^{\mathsf{r}}_{1 \to 2}$ and $\mathsf{m}^{\mathsf{r}}_{1 \to 3}$ to P_R while P_R sends $\mathsf{m}^{\mathsf{r}}_{2 \to 1}$ and $\mathsf{m}^{\mathsf{r}}_{3 \to 1}$ to P_S. P_R computes the output m_c using the combined view of $\{P_2, P_3\}$ at the end of Round $(r - 1)$. P_S outputs nothing. Recall that the output of the OT between (P_S, P_R) is $(\perp, m_c)$ respectively. We now argue that π_{OT} realizes the OT functionality.

Lemma 2. *Protocol π_{OT} realizes the* OT *functionality.*

Proof. We first prove that π_{OT} is correct. By Lemma 1, it follows that P_R emulating the role of both $\{P_2, P_3\}$ of π_f must be able to compute the correct output m_c with overwhelming probability by the end of Round $(r - 1)$. We now consider the security properties. First, we consider a corrupt P_R (emulating the roles of $\{P_2, P_3\}$ in π_f). Since by assumption, π_f is a protocol that should preserve privacy of P_1's input even in the presence of an adversary corrupting $\{P_2, P_3\}$ ($s = 2$ corruptions), the input m_{1-c} of P_S must remain private against a corrupt P_R. Next, we note that privacy of π_f against a corrupt P_1 ($t = 1$ corruption) guarantees that P_1 does not learn anything beyond the output $(m_c + R_2 + R_3)$ in the protocol π_f which leaks nothing about c. It thus follows that a corrupt P_S in π_{OT} emulating the role of P_1 in π_f will also not be able to learn anything about P_R's input c. More formally, we can construct a simulator for the OT protocol π_{OT} for the cases of corrupt P_R and corrupt P_S by invoking the simulator of π_f for the case of dishonest majority ($s = 2$) and honest majority ($t = 1$) respectively. In each case, it follows from the security of π_f (which holds with overwhelming probability) that the simulator of π_f would return a view indistinguishable from the real-world view with overwhelming probability; directly implying the security of the OT protocol π_{OT}. □

Thus, we can conclude that a $(r - 1)$-round 2-party OT protocol π_{OT} can be derived from r-round π_f. This concludes the proof of Theorem 1. □

Theorem 2. *There exists a function f for which there is no 4-round (resp. 2 round) protocol computing f in the plain model (resp. with CRS and PKI)* *that simultaneously realises– (1)* $\mathcal{F}_{\mathsf{fair}}$ *when* $t < n/2$ *parties are corrupted (2)* $\mathcal{F}_{\mathsf{ua}}$ *when* $s < n$ *parties are corrupted. In the former setting (plain model), we assume black-box simulation.*

Proof. We start with the proof in the plain model, followed by the proof with CRS and PKI. We assume for contradiction that there exists a 4-round (fn|ua)-BoBW protocol (with black-box simulation) in the plain model. Then, it follows from Theorem 1 that there must exist a 3-round 2-party maliciously-secure OT protocol with black-box simulation in the plain model. We point that this OT derived as per the transformation of Theorem 1 is a bidirectional OT, where each round consists of messages from both the OT sender and the receiver. Using the round-preserving transformation from bidirectional OT to alternating-message OT (where each round consists of a message from only one of the two parties) [34], we contradict the necessity of 4 rounds for alternating OT in the plain model with black-box simulation [33]. This completes the proof for plain model.

Next, we assume for contradiction that there exists a 2-round (fn|ua)-BoBW MPC protocol in the presence of CRS and PKI. Then, it follows from Theorem 1 that there exists 1-round OT protocol in this model. We have arrived at a contradiction since non-interactive OT is impossible to achieve in a model with input-independent setup that includes CRS and PKI (notably 1-round OT constructions which use an *input-dependent* PKI setup such as [62] exist). To be more specific, a 1-round OT protocol would be vulnerable to the following residual attack by a corrupt receiver P_R: P_R can participate in the OT protocol with input c and get the output m_c at the end of the 1-round OT protocol (where (m_0, m_1) denote the inputs of sender P_S). Now, since the Round 1 messages of P_S and P_R are independent of each other, P_R can additionally plug in his input as being $(1-c)$ to locally compute m_{1-c} as well which is a violation of sender's security as per the ideal OT functionality. □

3 Upper Bounds for (fn|ua)-BoBW

In this section, we construct two upper bounds for the (fn|ua)-BoBW class.

Our upper bounds take 5 and 3 rounds in the plain model and in the CRS setting respectively, tightly matching the lower bounds presented in Sect. 2. We begin with a general compiler that transforms any n-party r-round actively-secure MPC protocol achieving ua in dishonest majority into an $(r+1)$-round (fn|ua)-BoBW protocol.

3.1 The Compiler

At a high-level, our compiler uses the compiler of [47] and a form of authentication used in the Information Checking Protocol (ICP) primitive of [48,49] and unanimously identifiable commitments (UIC) of [50]. Drawing motivation from the compiler of [47] from ua to fn in the honest majority setting, our compiler uses the given r-round protocol achieving ua security to compute an "authenticated" secret sharing with a threshold of t of the output y and reconstruct the output y during the $(r+1)^{\text{th}}$ round. The correct reconstruction is guaranteed thanks to unanimity offered by the underlying protocol and the authentication mechanism that makes equivocation of a share hard. Alternatively termed as error-correcting secret sharing (ECSS) [47], the authenticated secret sharing was instantiated with pairwise information-theoretic or one-time MAC as a form of authentication. This, when taken as is in our case, achieves fairness in the honest majority setting as in the original transformation. The sharing threshold t ensures that the shares of the honest set, consisting of at least $t+1$ parties, dictate the reconstruction of the output, no matter whether the corrupted parties cooperate or not. The pairwise MAC, however, makes it challenging to maintain unanimity in the dishonest majority case of the transformed protocol, where a corrupt party may choose to verify its share to *selected* few enabling their output reconstruction. This seems to call for a MAC that cannot be manipulated partwise to keep the verifiers on different pages. A possible approach to achieve the property of public verifiability is by means of digital signatures i.e. each party obtains a signed output share which it broadcasts during reconstruction and can be verified by remaining parties using a common public verification key (that the parties obtain as part of the output of the r-round protocol achieving ua). Alternately, if the form of authentication used in the ICP of [48,49] and UIC of [50] is used, then digital signatures can be avoided and the compiler (transforming any n-party r-round actively-secure MPC protocol achieving ua in dishonest majority into an $(r+1)$-round (fn|ua)-BoBW protocol) achieves the desirable property of being information-theoretic (i.t).

Achieving i.t security is a worthwhile goal, as substantiated by its extensive study in various settings including those where achieving this desirable security notion demands additional tools. For instance, there are well-known results circumventing the impossibility of achieving i.t security in dishonest majority by relying on additional assistance such as tamper-proof hardware tokens [50,63] and Physically Uncloneable Functions (PUFs) [64,65]. Having an i.t compiler opens up the possibility of achieving i.t BoBW MPC by plugging in an i.t. secure dishonest majority protocol (say, that uses hardware tokens/PUFs or other assistance) in the compiler. The details of the i.t compiler appear in [54].

3.2 The Upper Bounds

Building our round-optimal (fn|ua)-BoBW protocols in the plain and CRS model involves constructing 2 and 4 round protocols that achieve ua security against dishonest majority in the respective models. Such protocols when plugged in our compiler of Sect. 3.1 would directly yield the round-optimal (fn|ua)-BoBW protocols.

In the CRS setting, the known 2-round protocols of [30,31] achieve ua and thereby lead to a 3-round (fn|ua)-BoBW protocol, matching the lower bound. Unfortunately, the existing 4-round MPC protocols in the plain model relying on polynomial-time assumptions [16,17,34], in spite of convenient use of broadcast, only satisfy the weaker notion of sa. We demonstrate how the protocol of [16] and [17,34] can be tweaked to achieve ua in the full version [54]. With respect to the above mentioned ua protocols, our (fn|ua)-BoBW MPC protocols rely on the assumption of 2-round OT in the common random/reference string model and 4-round OT in the plain model.

Theorem 3. *Assuming the existence of a 4 (resp., 2) round MPC protocol that realizes $\mathcal{F}_{\mathsf{ua}}$ for upto $n-1$ malicious corruptions in the plain (resp., CRS) model, there exists a 5 (resp., 3)-round MPC protocol in the plain (resp., CRS) model that simultaneously realises– (1) $\mathcal{F}_{\mathsf{fair}}$ when $t < n/2$ parties are corrupted (2) $\mathcal{F}_{\mathsf{ua}}$ when $s < n$ parties are corrupted.*

A minor observation regarding the use of broadcast in our compiler is that we can replace it with point-to-point communication at the expense of relaxing ua to sa security in the dishonest majority setting.

Security with Identifiability. Our compiler preserves the property of identifiability. Since the underlying dishonest-majority protocols [30,31] can be boosted to achieve identifiable abort (as shown by [66]), the upper bound in the CRS model achieves identifiable fairness and abort in the honest and dishonest majority setting respectively. With respect to the plain model, we show how security of [17] can be boosted to achieve identifiable abort with minor tweaks, in the full version. This variant, when compiled using our compiler of Sect. 3.1 would achieve identifiable fairness and abort in the honest and dishonest majority setting respectively.

4 Lower Bounds for (god|ua)-BoBW

In this section, we prove that it is impossible to design a 2-round (god|ua)-BoBW protocol with $t + s < n$ in the CRS model. Note that the necessity of 3 rounds for (god|ua)-BoBW protocol for most values of (n, s, t) follows from the 2-round impossibility of fair MPC for honest majority in the CRS model [37,38,40]. Accounting for the fact that these existing results do not rule out the possibility of 2-round (god|ua)-BoBW MPC for $(t = 1, s > t, n \geq 4)$, we present a *unified proof* that works even for $s > t$, for all values of t (including $t = 1$). Our proof approach deals with adversarial strategies that shuffle between the honest and dishonest majority setting, highlighting the challenge of designing protocols that simultaneously provide different guarantees for different settings. This is in contrast to the existing lower bounds of [37,38,40] which deal only with honest majority setting and single security notion of fn. Lastly, we demonstrate why our proof breaks down in the presence of PKI. Indeed, we construct a 2-round (god|ua)-BoBW protocol assuming CRS and PKI in this work.

Theorem 4. *Let n, t, s be such that $t + s < n$ and $t < n/2$. There exist functions f for which there is no two-round protocol in the CRS model computing f that simultaneously realizes– (1) $\mathcal{F}_{\mathsf{god}}$ when $t < n/2$ parties are corrupted (2) $\mathcal{F}_{\mathsf{ua}}$ when $s < n$ parties are corrupted.*

Proof. We prove the theorem for $n = 4$ parties with $t = 1$ and $s = 2$. The result then can be extended for higher values of n in a natural manner (elaborated in the full version). Let $\mathcal{P} = \{P_1, P_2, P_3, P_4\}$ denote the set of 4 parties and $\mathcal{A}$ may corrupt at most two among them. We prove the theorem by contradiction. We assume that there exists a 2-round (god|ua) BoBW protocol π in the CRS model that can compute the function $f(x_1, x_2, x_3, x_4)$ defined below for P_i's input x_i: $f(x_1, x_2, x_3, x_4) = 1$ if $x_1 = x_2 = 1; 0$ otherwise. By assumption, π achieves god when $t = 1$ parties are corrupt and ua security when $s = 2$ parties are corrupt (satisfying feasibility criteria $t + s < n$).

At a high level, we discuss three adversarial strategies $\mathcal{A}_1, \mathcal{A}_2$ and $\mathcal{A}_3$ of $\mathcal{A}$. While both $\mathcal{A}_1$ and $\mathcal{A}_3$ deal with $t = 1$ corruption with the adversary corrupting P_1, $\mathcal{A}_2$ involves $s = 2$ corruptions where the adversary corrupts $\{P_3, P_4\}$. We consider $\mathcal{A}_i$ strategy as being launched in execution Σ_i ($i \in [3]$) of π. The executions are assumed to be run for the same input tuple $(x_1, x_2, \perp, \perp)$ and the same random inputs (r_1, r_2, r_3, r_4) of the parties. (Same random inputs are considered for simplicity and without loss of generality. The same arguments hold for distribution ensembles as well.) Our executions and adversarial strategies are sequenced in the order of increasingly more non-cooperating malicious adversaries. Yet, keeping the views of a certain party between two consecutive executions same, we are able to conclude the party would output the correct value even in the face of stronger malicious behaviour. Finally, we reach to the final execution Σ_3 where we show that a party can deduce the output in the end of Round 1 itself. Lastly, we show a strategy for the party to explicitly breach the input privacy of one of the input-contributing parties.

We assume that the communication done in the second round of π is via broadcast alone. This holds without loss of generality since the parties can perform point-to-point communication by exchanging random pads in the first round and then use these random pads to unmask later broadcasts. We use the following notation: Let $\mathsf{p}^1_{i \to j}$ denote the pairwise communication from P_i to P_j in round 1 and b^r_i denote the broadcast by P_i in round r, where $r \in [2], \{i, j\} \in [4]$. These values may be function of CRS as per the working of the protocol. V^ℓ_i denotes the view of party P_i at the end of execution Σ_ℓ ($\ell \in [3]$) of π. Below we describe the strategies $\mathcal{A}_1, \mathcal{A}_2$ and $\mathcal{A}_3$.

- $\mathcal{A}_1$: $\mathcal{A}$ corrupts P_1 here. P_1 behaves honestly towards P_2 in Round 1, i.e. sends the messages $\mathsf{p}^1_{1 \to 2}, \mathsf{b}^1_1$ as per the protocol. However P_1 does not communicate privately to $\{P_3, P_4\}$ in Round 1. In Round 2, P_1 behaves honestly as per the protocol.
- $\mathcal{A}_2$: $\mathcal{A}$ corrupts $\{P_3, P_4\}$ here. $\{P_3, P_4\}$ behave honestly in Round 1 of the protocol. In Round 2, P_k ($k \in \{3, 4\}$) acts as per the protocol specification when no *private* message from P_1 is received in Round 1. Specifically, suppose P_k did not receive $\mathsf{p}^1_{1 \to k}$ in Round 1. Let $\overline{\mathsf{b}^2_k}$ denote the message that should be sent by P_k as per the protocol in Round 2 in such a scenario. Then as per $\mathcal{A}_2$, corrupt P_k sends $\overline{\mathsf{b}^2_k}$ in Round 2.

$\mathcal{A}_3$: Same as in $\mathcal{A}_1$ and in addition– during Round 2, P_1 simply remains silent i.e. waits to receive the messages from other parties, but does not communicate at all.

Next we present the views of the parties in Σ_1, Σ_2 and Σ_3 in Table 2. Here, $\overline{\mathsf{b}_k^2}$ ($k \in \{3,4\}$) denotes the message that should be sent by P_k according to the protocol in Round 2 in case P_k did not receive any private communication from P_1 in Round 1.

Table 2. Views of P_1, P_2, P_3, P_4 in Σ_1, Σ_2, Σ_3

	Σ_1				Σ_2				Σ_3			
	V_1^1	V_2^1	V_3^1	V_4^1	V_1^2	V_2^2	V_3^2	V_4^2	V_1^3	V_2^3	V_3^3	V_4^3
Input	(x_1, r_1)	(x_2, r_2)	r_3	r_4	(x_1, r_1)	(x_2, r_2)	r_3	r_4	(x_1, r_1)	(x_2, r_2)	r_3	r_4
R1	$\mathsf{p}_{2\to1}^1$, $\mathsf{p}_{3\to1}^1$ $\mathsf{p}_{4\to1}^1$, b_2^1, b_3^1, b_4^1	$\mathsf{p}_{1\to2}^1$, $\mathsf{p}_{3\to2}^1$, $\mathsf{p}_{4\to2}^1$, b_1^1, b_3^1, b_4^1	–, $\mathsf{p}_{2\to3}^1$, $\mathsf{p}_{4\to3}^1$, b_1^1, b_2^1, b_4^1	–, $\mathsf{p}_{2\to4}^1$, $\mathsf{p}_{3\to4}^1$, b_1^1, b_2^1, b_3^1	$\mathsf{p}_{2\to1}^1$, $\mathsf{p}_{3\to1}^1$ $\mathsf{p}_{4\to1}^1$, b_2^1, b_3^1, b_4^1	$\mathsf{p}_{1\to2}^1$, $\mathsf{p}_{3\to2}^1$, $\mathsf{p}_{4\to2}^1$, b_1^1, b_3^1, b_4^1	$\mathsf{p}_{1\to3}^1$, $\mathsf{p}_{2\to3}^1$, $\mathsf{p}_{4\to3}^1$, b_1^1, b_2^1, b_4^1	$\mathsf{p}_{1\to4}^1$, $\mathsf{p}_{2\to4}^1$, $\mathsf{p}_{3\to4}^1$, b_1^1, b_2^1, b_3^1	$\mathsf{p}_{2\to1}^1$, $\mathsf{p}_{3\to1}^1$ $\mathsf{p}_{4\to1}^1$, b_2^1, b_3^1, b_4^1	$\mathsf{p}_{1\to2}^1$, $\mathsf{p}_{3\to2}^1$, $\mathsf{p}_{4\to2}^1$, b_1^1, b_3^1, b_4^1	–, $\mathsf{p}_{2\to3}^1$, $\mathsf{p}_{4\to3}^1$, b_1^1, b_2^1, b_4^1	–, $\mathsf{p}_{2\to4}^1$, $\mathsf{p}_{3\to4}^1$, b_1^1, b_2^1, b_3^1
R2	b_2^2, $\overline{\mathsf{b}_3^2}$, $\overline{\mathsf{b}_4^2}$	b_1^2, $\overline{\mathsf{b}_3^2}$, $\overline{\mathsf{b}_4^2}$	b_1^2, b_2^2, $\overline{\mathsf{b}_4^2}$	b_1^2, b_2^2, $\overline{\mathsf{b}_3^2}$	b_2^2, $\overline{\mathsf{b}_3^2}$, $\overline{\mathsf{b}_4^2}$	b_1^2, $\overline{\mathsf{b}_3^2}$, $\overline{\mathsf{b}_4^2}$	b_1^2, b_2^2, $\overline{\mathsf{b}_4^2}$	b_1^2, b_2^2, $\overline{\mathsf{b}_3^2}$	b_2^2, $\overline{\mathsf{b}_3^2}$, $\overline{\mathsf{b}_4^2}$	–, $\overline{\mathsf{b}_3^2}$, $\overline{\mathsf{b}_4^2}$	–, b_2^2, $\overline{\mathsf{b}_4^2}$	–, b_2^2 $\overline{\mathsf{b}_3^2}$

We now prove a sequence of lemmas to complete our proof. Let y denote the output computed as per the inputs (x_1, x_2) provided by the honest P_1 and P_2. Let $\mathsf{q} = 1 - \mathsf{negl}(\kappa)$ denote the overwhelming probability with which security of π holds, where the probability is defined over choice of setup and the random coins used by the parties.

Lemma 3. *The view of P_2 is the same in Σ_1 and Σ_2 and it outputs y in both with overwhelming probability.*

Proof. We observe that as per both strategies $\mathcal{A}_1$ and $\mathcal{A}_2$, P_2 receives communication from P_1, P_3, P_4 as per honest execution in Round 1. In Round 2, according to $\mathcal{A}_1$, corrupt P_1 did not send private messages to P_3 and P_4 who therefore broadcast $\overline{\mathsf{b}_3^2}$ and $\overline{\mathsf{b}_4^2}$ respectively as per protocol specification. On the other hand, according to $\mathcal{A}_2$, corrupt P_3 and corrupt P_4 send the same messages respectively as per protocol specification for case when P_3, P_4 receive no private message from P_1 in Round 1. It is now easy to check (refer Table 2) that $\mathsf{V}_2^1 = \mathsf{V}_2^2$. Now, since Σ_1 involves $t = 1$ corruption, by assumption, π must be robust (with overwhelming probability q) and V_2^1 must lead to output computation, say of output y'. Due to view equality, P_2 in Σ_2 must also output y' with probability q. In Σ_2, P_1 and P_2 are honest and their inputs are x_1 and x_2 respectively. Due to correctness of π (which holds with overwhelming probability q) during Σ_2, it must then hold that $y' = y$ i.e. the output computed based on V_2^2 is according to honest P_1's input x_1 during Σ_2, with overwhelming probability $\mathsf{q} \times \mathsf{q} = \mathsf{q}^2$. □

Lemma 4. *The view of P_1 is the same in Σ_2 and Σ_3 and it outputs y in both, with overwhelming probability.*

Proof. An honest P_2 has the same view in both Σ_1 and Σ_2 and outputs y with overwhelming probability as per Lemma 3. As π achieves ua (with probability q) in the presence of $s = 2$ corruptions, when P_2 learns the output in Σ_2, P_1 must learn y in Σ_2 with overwhelming probability $\mathsf{q}^2 \times \mathsf{q} = \mathsf{q}^3$. We now show that P_1's view in Σ_2 and Σ_3 are the same and so it outputs y in Σ_3 with overwhelming probability q^3. First, it is easy to see that the Round 1 communication towards P_1 is as per honest execution in both Σ_2, Σ_3. Next, recall that as per $\mathcal{A}_2$, both corrupt $\{P_3, P_4\}$ send messages in Round 2 according to the scenario when they didn't receive any private communication from P_1 in Round 1. A similar message would be sent by honest $\{P_3, P_4\}$ in Σ_3 who did not receive private message from corrupt P_1 as per $\mathcal{A}_3$. Finally, since corrupt P_1 behaved honestly to P_2 in Round 1 of Σ_3 as per $\mathcal{A}_3$, the Round 2 communication from P_2 is similar to that in execution Σ_2. It is now easy to verify (refer Table 2) that $\mathsf{V}_1^2 = \mathsf{V}_1^3$ from which output y can be computed. □

Lemma 5. *P_2 in Σ_3 should learn the output y by the end of Round 1, with overwhelming probability.*

Proof. Firstly, it follows directly from Lemma 4 and the assumption that protocol π is robust against $t = 1$ corruption that all parties including P_2 must learn output y at the end of Σ_3 with overwhelming probability $\mathsf{q}^3 \times \mathsf{q} = \mathsf{q}^4$. Next, we note that as per strategy $\mathcal{A}_3$, P_1 only communicates to P_2 in Round 1. We argue that the second round communication from P_3, P_4 does not impact P_2's output computation as follows: we observe that the output y depends only on (x_1, x_2). Clearly, Round 1 messages of P_3, P_4 does not depend on x_1. Next, since there is no private communication to P_3, P_4 from P_1 as per strategy $\mathcal{A}_3$, the only communication that can possibly hold information on x_1 and can impact the round 2 messages of P_3, P_4 is b_1^1. However, since this is a broadcast message, P_2 also holds this by the end of Round 1 itself. Thus, P_2 must be able to compute the output y at the end of Round 1.

In more detail, P_2 can choose randomness r_3, r_4 on behalf of P_3, P_4 to locally emulate their following Round 1 messages $\{\mathsf{p}^1_{3\to2}, \mathsf{p}^1_{4\to2}, \mathsf{p}^1_{3\to4}, \mathsf{p}^1_{4\to3}, \mathsf{b}^1_3, \mathsf{b}^1_4\}$. Next, P_2 can now simulate P_3's Round 2 message $\overline{\mathsf{b}^2_3}$ which is a function of its view comprising of $\{\mathsf{p}^1_{2\to3}, \mathsf{p}^1_{4\to3}, \mathsf{b}^1_1, \mathsf{b}^1_2, \mathsf{b}^1_4\}$ (all of which are available to P_2, where b^1_1 was broadcast by P_1 in Round 1). Similarly, P_2 can locally compute P_4's Round 2 message $\overline{\mathsf{b}^2_4}$. We can thus conclude that P_2's view at the end of Σ_3 comprising of $\{\mathsf{p}^1_{1\to2}, \mathsf{p}^1_{3\to2}, \mathsf{p}^1_{4\to2}, \mathsf{b}^1_1, \mathsf{b}^1_3, \mathsf{b}^1_4, \overline{\mathsf{b}^2_3}, \overline{\mathsf{b}^2_4}\}$ can be locally simulated by him at the end of Round 1 itself from which the output y can be computed. □

Lemma 6. *A corrupt P_2 violates the privacy property of π.*

Proof. The adversary corrupting P_2 participates in the protocol honestly by fixing input $x_2 = 0$. Since P_2 can get the output at the end of Round 1 with overwhelming probability (Lemma 5), it must be true that P_2 can evaluate f locally by plugging in any value of x_2. Now a corrupt P_2 can plug in $x_2 = 1$ locally and learn x_1 (via the output $x_1 \wedge x_2$) with overwhelming probability. In the ideal world, corrupt P_2 must learn nothing beyond the output 0 as it has participated in the protocol with input 0. But in the execution of π (in which P_2 participated honestly with input $x_2 = 0$), P_2 has learnt x_1 with overwhelming probability. This is a breach of privacy as P_2 learns x_1 regardless of his input. □

Hence, we have arrived at a contradiction, completing proof of Theorem 4.□

We draw attention to the fact that Lemma 5 would not hold in the presence of any additional setup such as PKI. With additional setup, P_3, P_4 may possibly hold some private information (such as their secret key in case of PKI used to decode P_1's broadcast message in Round 1) that is not available to P_2. Due to this reason, we cannot claim that P_2 can emulate Round 2 messages of $\{P_3, P_4\}$ locally at the end of Round 1. However, this holds in case of CRS as the knowledge of CRS is available to all parties at the beginning of the protocol.

5 Upper Bounds for (god|ua)-BoBW

In this section, we present three (god|ua)-BoBW MPC protocols, assuming $t+s < n$ which is the feasibility condition for such protocols [20] consuming– *a*) 3-rounds with CRS *b*) 2-rounds with an additional PKI setup *c*) 5-rounds in plain model. The first two are round-optimal in light of the lower bound of Sect. 4 and [32] respectively. The third construction is nearly round-optimal (falls just one short of the 4-round lower bound of [33]). Among our upper bounds, the construction in the plain model is considerably more involved and uses several new tricks in conjugation with existing techniques.

5.1 (god|ua)-BoBW MPC with Public and Private Setup

To arrive at the final destination, the roadmap followed is: (i) A 2-round MPC achieving ua security is compiled to a 3-round (god|ua)-BoBW MPC protocol, both against a weaker semi-malicious adversary. With the additional provision of PKI, this compiler can be turned to a round-preserving one. (ii) The semi-malicious (god|ua)-BoBW MPC protocols are compiled to malicious ones in CRS setting via the known round-preserving compiler of [51] (using NIZKs). All the involved and resultant constructions are in *broadcast-only* setting. The protocol just with CRS tightly upper bounds the 3-round lower bound presented in Section 4, which accounts for both pair-wise and broadcast channels. The protocol with additional PKI setup works in 2 rounds, displaying the power of PKI and that our lower bound of 3-rounds in Theorem 4 breaks down in the presence of PKI. Yet, this construction is round optimal, in light of the known impossibility of 1-round MPC [32].

5.1.1 3-Round (god|ua)-BoBW MPC in Semi-malicious Setting

Here, we present a generic compiler that transforms any 2-round MPC protocol $\pi_{\mathsf{ua.sm}}$ achieving ua security into a 3-round broadcast-only (god|ua)-BoBW MPC protocol $\pi_{\mathsf{bw.god.sm}}$ assuming $t + s < n$. Our compiler borrows techniques from the compiler of [11] which is designed for the honest majority setting and makes suitable modifications to obtain BoBW guarantees. Recall that a semi-malicious adversary needs to follow the protocol specification, but has the liberty to decide the input and random coins in each round. Additionally, the parties controlled by the semi-malicious adversary may choose to abort at any step. The underlying and the resultant protocol use broadcast as the *only* medium of communication.

To transform $\pi_{\mathsf{ua.sm}}$ to guarantee BoBW security, the compiler banks on the idea of giving out the Round 2 message of $\pi_{\mathsf{ua.sm}}$ in a way that ensures god in case of honest majority. The dishonest majority protocols usually do not provide this feature even against a single corruption, let alone a minority. Mimicking the Round 1 of $\pi_{\mathsf{ua.sm}}$ as is, $\pi_{\mathsf{bw.god.sm}}$ achieves this property by essentially giving out a secret sharing of the Round 2 messages of $\pi_{\mathsf{ua.sm}}$ with a threshold of s. When at most t parties are corrupt, the set of $s+1$ honest parties pool their shares to reconstruct Round 2 messages of $\pi_{\mathsf{ua.sm}}$ and compute the output robustly as in $\pi_{\mathsf{ua.sm}}$. This idea is enabled by encoding (i.e. garbling) the next message functions of the second round of $\pi_{\mathsf{ua.sm}}$ and secret-sharing their encoding information using a threshold of s in Round 2 and reconstructing the appropriate input labels in the subsequent round. The next-message circuit of a party P_i hard-codes Round 1 broadcasts of $\pi_{\mathsf{ua.sm}}$, P_i's input and randomness and the default input and randomness of all the other parties. It takes n flags as input, the jth one indicating the alive/non-alive status of P_j. P_j turning non-alive (aborting) translates to the jth flag becoming 0 in which case the circuit makes sure P_j's default input is taken for consideration by internally recomputing P_j's first round broadcast and subsequently using that to compute the Round 2 message of P_i. Since the flag bits become public by the end of Round 2 (apparent as broadcast is the only mode of communication), the parties help each other by reconstructing the correct label, enabling all to compute the garbled next-message functions of all the parties and subsequently run the output computation of $\pi_{\mathsf{ua.sm}}$. The agreement of the flag bits further ensures output computation is done on a unique set of inputs. The transfer of the shares in broadcast-only setting is enabled via setting up a (public key, secret key) pair in the first round by every party. Broadcasting the encrypted shares emulates sending the share privately. This technique of garbled circuits computing the augmented next-message function (taking the list of alive (non-aborting) parties as input) followed by reconstruction of the appropriate input label was used in the work of [11] for the honest majority setting. The primary difference in our compiler is with respect to the threshold of the secret-sharing of the labels, to ensure BoBW guarantees. The formal description of protocol $\pi_{\mathsf{bw.god.sm}}$, its security and correctness proofs appear in the full version. We only state the theorems for correctness and security below.

Theorem 5. *Protocol $\pi_{\mathsf{bw.god.sm}}$ is correct, except with negligible probability.*

Theorem 6. *Let (n, s, t) be such that $s + t < n$. Let $\pi_{\mathsf{ua.sm}}$ realises $\mathcal{F}_{\mathsf{ua}}$ for upto $n-1$ semi-malicious corruptions. Then protocol $\pi_{\mathsf{bw.god.sm}}$ realises– (i) $\mathcal{F}_{\mathsf{god}}$ when at most $t < n/2$ parties are corrupt and (ii) $\mathcal{F}_{\mathsf{ua}}$ when at most $s < n$ parties are corrupt, semi-maliciously in both cases. It takes 3 rounds, assuming that $\pi_{\mathsf{ua.sm}}$ takes 2 rounds.*

5.1.2 2-Round (god|ua)-BoBW MPC in Semi-malicious Setting

The compiler of the previous section can be made round preserving by assuming pair-wise channels or alternately, PKI. The main difference lies in preponing the actions of Round 2 of $\pi_{\mathsf{bw.god.sm}}$ to Round 1, by exploiting the presence of private channels or PKI. We describe these extensions that can be used to obtain a 2-round semi-malicious (god|ua)-BoBW MPC assuming pair-wise channels (protocol $\phi_{\mathsf{bw.god.sm}}$) or alternately, PKI (protocol $\psi_{\mathsf{bw.god.sm}}$) in the full version.

5.1.3 The Upper Bounds with Public and Private Setup

The 2-round semi-malicious broadcast-only protocol of [30,31] can be plugged in as $\pi_{\mathsf{ua.sm}}$ in our compilers from previous sections to directly yield a 3-round broadcast-only protocol $\pi_{\mathsf{bw.god.sm}}$, 2-round protocol $\phi_{\mathsf{bw.god.sm}}$ that uses both broadcast and pairwise-private channels and 2-round broadcast-only protocol $\psi_{\mathsf{bw.god.sm}}$ assuming PKI, all in the semi-malicious setting. Next, the compiler of [51] that upgrades any broadcast-only semi-malicious protocol to maliciously-secure by employing NIZKs, can be applied on $\pi_{\mathsf{bw.god.sm}}$ and $\psi_{\mathsf{bw.god.sm}}$ to yield a 3-round (god|ua)-BoBW protocol in the CRS model and a 2-round (god|ua)-BoBW protocol given both CRS and PKI. Note that the compiler of [51] works only for broadcast-only protocols and cannot be used to boost security of $\phi_{\mathsf{bw.god.sm}}$ to malicious setting (details appear in full version). Assumption wise, our upper bound constructions rely on 2-round semi-malicious oblivious transfer and NIZK in the common random/reference string model upon using the protocols of [30,31] to realize $\pi_{\mathsf{ua.sm}}$. The formal description of the (god|ua)-BoBW upper bounds with public and private setup appear in the full version. We state the theorem below.

Theorem 7. *Let (n, s, t) be such that $s + t < n$. Assuming the existence of a 3-round (resp., 2-round with PKI) broadcast-only semi-malicious (god|ua)-BoBW MPC and NIZKs, there exists a 3 (resp., 2)-round MPC protocol in the presence of CRS (resp., CRS and PKI) that simultaneously achieves (i) $\mathcal{F}_{\mathsf{god}}$ when at most $t < n/2$ parties are corrupt and (ii) $\mathcal{F}_{\mathsf{ua}}$ when at most $s < n$ parties are corrupt, maliciously in both cases.*

Security with Identifiability. Since the compiler of [51] uses NIZKs to prove correctness of each round, it offers identifiability. Thus our maliciously-secure (god|ua)-BoBW protocols achieve the stronger notion of identifiable abort in case of dishonest majority, with no extra assumption. A minor observation is that we can replace the last round broadcast with point-to-point communication at the expense of relaxing ua to sa security in the dishonest majority setting.

5.2 Upper Bound for (god|ua)-BoBW MPC in Plain Model

In this section, we present a 5-round (god|ua)-BoBW protocol in the plain model. For our construction, we resort to the compiler of [31] that transforms any generic $(k-1)$-round delayed-semi-malicious MPC protocol to a k-round malicious MPC protocol for any $k \geq 5$. Our 5-round construction comes in two steps:

a) first, we show that our 3-round semi-malicious protocol $\pi_{\mathsf{bw.god.sm}}$ (described in Sect. 5.1.1) is delayed-semi-maliciously secure (refer full version for proof) and then b) we plug in this 3-round BoBW protocol in a modified compiler of [31] that carries over the BoBW guarantees, while the original compiler works for security with abort. Our final 5-round compiled protocol faces several technical difficulties in the proof, brought forth mainly by the need to continue the simulation in case the protocol must result in god, which needs deep and non-trivial redressals. The techniques we use to tackle the challenges in simulation are also useful in constructing a 4-round (god|ua)-BoBW protocol based on sub-exponentially secure trapdoor permutations and ZAPs. We give a sketch of this construction in the full version (built upon the protocol of [53]) as a step towards resolving the open question of proving the impossibility or alternately constructing a 4-round (god|ua)-BoBW protocol under polynomial-time assumptions.

5.2.1 The Compiler of [31]

Substituting $k = 5$, we recall the relevant details of the compiler of [31] that transforms a 4-round delayed-semi-malicious protocol ϕ_{dsm} to a 5-round maliciously-secure protocol π achieving security with abort. The tools used in this compiler appears in Fig. 1. Each party commits to her input and randomness using a 2-round statistically binding commitment scheme Com in the first two rounds. The four rounds of the delayed-semi-malicious protocol ϕ_{dsm} are run as it is in Round 1, 2, 4 and 5 respectively (Round 3 is skipped) with two additional sets of public-coin delayed-input witness indistinguishable proofs (WI). The first set of proofs (WI^1) which is completed by Round 4, is associated with the first 3 rounds of ϕ_{dsm}. In addition to proving honest behaviour in these rounds, this set of proofs enables the simulator of the malicious protocol to extract the inputs of the corrupt parties, in order to appropriately emulate the adversary for the delayed-semi-malicious simulator in the last but one round. The second set of proofs (WI^2) which is completed by Round 5, is associated with proving honest behaviour in *all* rounds of ϕ_{dsm}. To enable the simulator to pass the WI proofs without the knowledge of the inputs of the honest parties, it is endowed with a *cheat* route (facilitated by the *cheating* statement of the WI proof, while the *honest* statement involves proving honest behaviour wrt inputs committed via Com) which requires the knowledge of the trapdoor of the corrupt parties; which the simulator can obtain by rewinding the last 2 rounds of a trapdoor-generation protocol (Trap) run in the first 3 rounds of the final construction. To enable this cheat route of the simulator, the compiler has an additional component, namely 4-round non-malleable commitment NMCom run in Rounds 1–4. We refer to the full version for further details of the compiler.

Next, we give an overview of the simulator $\mathcal{S}$ (details appear in [31]) for the 5-round compiled protocol π that uses the simulator $\mathcal{S}_\phi$ of the underlying 4-round protocol ϕ_{dsm}. To emulate the ideal-world adversary corrupting parties in set $\mathcal{C}$, $\mathcal{S}$ invokes the malicious adversary $\mathcal{A}_\pi$ and simulates a real execution of π for $\mathcal{A}_\pi$ by acting on behalf of the honest parties in set $\mathcal{H}$. Recall that the delayed-semi-malicious security of ϕ_{dsm} guarantees that it is secure against an adversary $\mathcal{A}_\phi$

Tools used in the compiler [31]

- **A $(k-1)$-round delayed-semi-malicious protocol ϕ_{dsm} for computing a function f.**
- **A 2-message statistically binding commitment scheme Com from one-way functions.**
- **A 3-round protocol Trap to set up a trapdoor between a sender (S) and a receiver (R) as the following sequence of rounds:**
  R1: **S samples a signing and verification key pair $(\mathsf{sk}, \mathsf{vk})$ of a signature scheme and sends vk to R.**
  R2: **R sends a random message $m \leftarrow \{0,1\}^\lambda$ to S.**
  R3: **S computes a signature σ on m using sk and sends σ to R who accepts if (m, σ) is valid w.r.t. vk.**
  A valid trapdoor td w.r.t. a verification key vk constitutes of (m, σ, m', σ') such that $m' \neq m$ and σ and σ' are valid signatures of messages m and m' respectively corresponding to vk.
- **A 4-round non-malleable commitment scheme NMCom.**
- **A 4-round public-coin delayed-input witness indistinguishable proof WI.**

Fig. 1. Tools used in the compiler of [31]

who can choose to behave arbitrarily in the protocol as long as it writes a valid witness (which consists of an input randomness pair $(\{x_i, r_i\}_{i \in \mathcal{C}})$ on behalf of all corrupt parties) on the witness tape of the simulator $\mathcal{S}_\phi$ in the penultimate round such that the witness (x, r) can justify *all* the messages sent by him. In order to avail the services of $\mathcal{S}_\phi$, $\mathcal{S}$ needs to transform the malicious adversary $\mathcal{A}_\pi$ to a delayed-semi-malicious adversary $\mathcal{A}_\phi$ i.e. it needs a mechanism to write (x, r) on the witness tape of $\mathcal{S}_\phi$. This is enabled via extraction of witness i.e. $\{x_i, r_i\}_{i \in \mathcal{C}}$ from the WI^1 proofs sent by $\mathcal{A}_\pi$ as the prover via rewinding its last two rounds (Round $3, 4$ of π).

Apart from the above set of rewinds for extraction of corrupt parties' inputs, another set of rewinds is required for the following reason: Consider messages of honest parties simulated by $\mathcal{S}_\phi$ that are used by $\mathcal{S}$ to interact with $\mathcal{A}_\pi$ during the execution of π. Here, $\mathcal{S}$ cannot convince $\mathcal{A}_\pi$ in the two sets of WI proofs that these messages are honestly generated. Hence, he opts for the route of the *cheating* statement of the WI proofs which requires the knowledge of the trapdoor of the corrupt parties. The trapdoor of a party, say P_i consists of *two* valid message-signature pairs with respect to the verification key of P_i (described in Fig. 1). The simulator extracts the trapdoor of parties in $\mathcal{C}$ by rewinding the adversary $\mathcal{A}_\pi$ in Rounds 2 and 3 till he gets an additional valid message-signature pair. The trapdoor has been established this way to ensure that only the simulator (and not the adversary) is capable of passing the proofs via the *cheating* statement.

Finally, we point that the two sets of rewinds (Round 2–3 and Round 3–4 of π) can be executed by $\mathcal{S}$ while maintaining that the interaction with $\mathcal{S}_\phi$ is *straight-line* since Round 3 of the compiled protocol is 'dummy' i.e. does not involve messages of ϕ_{dsm}. This 'dummy' round is crucial to avoid rewinding of messages in ϕ_{dsm}. Since there are no messages of ϕ_{dsm} being sent in Round 3, $\mathcal{S}$ can simply replay the messages of ϕ_{dsm} (obtained via $\mathcal{S}_{\phi}$) to simulate Round 2 and Round 4 of π during the rewinds.

5.2.2 Our 5-round BoBW Construction

Our final goal of a (god|ua)-BoBW protocol $\pi_{\mathsf{bw.god.plain}}$ is obtained by applying the compiler of [31] to our delayed-semi-malicious-secure (god|ua)-BoBW protocol $\pi_{\mathsf{bw.god.sm}}$ (described in Sect. 5.1.1) with slight modifications. Broadly speaking, to preserve the BoBW guarantees from semi-malicious to malicious setting upon applying the compiler, the malicious behaviour of corrupt P_i in the compiled protocol is translated to an analogous scenario when semi-malicious P_i aborts (stops communicating) in the underlying protocol $\pi_{\mathsf{bw.god.sm}}$. Towards this, we make the following modification: Recall from the construction of $\pi_{\mathsf{bw.god.sm}}$ that each party P_i is unanimously assigned a boolean indicator i.e. flag_i by the remaining parties which is initialized to 1 and is later set to 0 if P_i aborts (stops) in the first two rounds. Accounting for malicious behavior, we now require the value of flag_i to be decided based on not just P_i's decision to abort in a particular round but also on whether he misbehaves in the publicly-verifiable Trap protocol or WI proofs. Specifically, if P_i misbehaves in Trap or the first set of proofs WI^1 with P_i as prover fails, flag_i is set to 0 (analogous to P_i aborting in Round 1 or 2 of $\pi_{\mathsf{bw.god.sm}}$). Further, if the second set of proofs WI^2 with P_i as prover fails, then the last round message of P_i is discarded (analogous to P_i aborting in last round of $\pi_{\mathsf{bw.god.sm}}$).

Next, we point that in our compiled protocol, the 3 rounds of the underlying semi-malicious protocol $\pi_{\mathsf{bw.god.sm}}$ are run in Rounds 1, 4 and 5 respectively. As opposed to compiler of [31] which needed a single 'dummy' round on top of the delayed-semi-malicious protocol, we face an additional simulation technicality (elaborated in the next section) that demands two 'dummy' rounds. This could be enabled while maintaining the round complexity of 5, owing to our 3 (and not 4) round delayed semi-malicious protocol. Furthermore, as described earlier, in order to simulate the WI proofs on behalf of an honest prover towards some corrupt verifier P_i, the simulator requires the knowledge of the trapdoor of P_i which would be possible only if P_i is alive (has not aborted) during the rounds in which trapdoor extraction occurs i.e. Round 2 and Round 3. While the simulator of [31] simply aborts incase any party aborts, the simulator of our BoBW protocol cannot afford to do so as god must be achieved even if upto $t < n/2$ parties abort. We handle this by adding a supplementary condition in our construction, namely, a prover needs to prove the WI proofs only to verifiers who have been alive until the round in consideration.

Table 3. $\pi_{\mathsf{bw.god.plain}}$

	$\pi_{\mathsf{bw.god.sm}}$	Com	Trap	NMCom	WI^1	WI^2
Round 1	R1	R1	R1	R1	R1	
Round 2		R2	R2	R2	R2	R1
Round 3			R3	R3	R3	R2
Round 4	R2			R4	R4	R3
Round 5	R3					R4

5-round Malicious (god|ua)-BoBW MPC Protocol $\pi_{\mathsf{bw.god.plain}}$ from 3-round delayed-semi-malicious BoBW protocol ϕ_{dsm}

Primitives: Tools mentioned in Fig 1 with ϕ_{dsm} instantiated with $\pi_{\mathsf{bw.god.sm}}$ (described in Section 5.1.1).

Round 1. Each party $P_i, i \in [n]$ does the following with $P_j, j \in [n] \setminus \{i\}$:
- Execute Round 1 of ϕ_{dsm}. Initialize $\mathsf{flag}_k = 1$ for all $k \in [n]$ as per ϕ_{dsm}.
- Run Round 1 of $\mathsf{Com}_{i \to j}$ to commit to his input and randomness (x_i, r_i) to P_j. Let the commitment be denoted by $c_{i \to j}$. Run Round 1 of $\mathsf{Com}_{j \to i}$ (where P_j acts as committer) as receiver.
- Run Round 1 of $\mathsf{Trap}_{i \to j}$ as sender, with $\mathsf{vk}_{i \to j}$ denoting the verification key.
- Run Round 1 of $\mathsf{NMCom}_{i \to j}$ as committer and Round 1 of $\mathsf{NMCom}_{j \to i}$ as receiver (with P_j as committer).
- Run Round 1 of $\mathsf{WI}^1_{i \to j}$ as prover and Round 1 of $\mathsf{WI}^1_{j \to i}$ as verifier (with P_j as prover).

Round 2. Each party $P_i, i \in [n]$ does the following with $P_j, j \in [n] \setminus \{i\}$:
- Run Round 2 of $\mathsf{Com}_{i \to j}$ and $\mathsf{Com}_{j \to i}$.
- Run Round 2 of $\mathsf{Trap}_{j \to i}$ (as receiver).
- Run Round 2 of $\mathsf{NMCom}_{i \to j}$ and $\mathsf{NMCom}_{j \to i}$.
- Run Round 2 of $\mathsf{WI}^1_{i \to j}$ and $\mathsf{WI}^1_{j \to i}$. Also, run Round 1 of $\mathsf{WI}^2_{i \to j}$ as prover and Round 1 of $\mathsf{WI}^2_{j \to i}$ as verifier (with P_j as prover).
- Set $\mathsf{flag}_j = 0$ if P_j aborts in Round 1 or Round 2.

Round 3. Each party $P_i, i \in [n]$ does the following with $P_j, j \in [n] \setminus \{i\}$:
- Run Round 3 of $\mathsf{Trap}_{i \to j}$ (as sender).
- Run Round 3 of $\mathsf{NMCom}_{i \to j}$ and $\mathsf{NMCom}_{j \to i}$.
- Run Round 3 of $\mathsf{WI}^1_{i \to j}$ and $\mathsf{WI}^1_{j \to i}$. Also, run Round 2 of $\mathsf{WI}^2_{i \to j}$ and $\mathsf{WI}^2_{j \to i}$.
- Set $\mathsf{flag}_j = 0$ if either P_j aborts in Round 3 or if there exists a $k \in [n], k \neq j$ such that the message-signature pair (m, σ) in $\mathsf{Trap}_{j \to k}$ is not valid w.r.t. $\mathsf{vk}_{j \to k}$. Broadcast enables everyone to agree on this.

Fig. 2. The Modified Compiler for (god|ua)-BoBW MPC (Part 1)

This completes the description of the modifications of our compiler over [31]. The round-by-round interplay of the different components is given in Table 3. We present our 5-round (god|ua)-BoBW MPC protocol $\pi_{\mathsf{bw.god.plain}}$ (incorporating the above modifications) in the plain model in Fig 2-3.

5.2.3 Proof-Sketch for 5-round (god|ua)-BoBW Protocol

The simulator for the compiler of [31] runs in different stages. Plugging it for our 5-round (god|ua)-BoBW construction with appropriate modifications, we present a high-level overview of the simulation. Let $\mathcal{S}_{\mathsf{bw.god.plain}}$ and $\mathcal{S}_{\mathsf{bw.god.sm}}$ denote the simulators corresponding to $\pi_{\mathsf{bw.god.plain}}$ and the underlying delayed semi-malicious protocol $\pi_{\mathsf{bw.god.sm}}$ respectively. Stage 1 involves running the first three rounds with the following changes compared to the real-execution of the protocol: a) Commit to 0 in Com instances (run in Round 1, 2) involving honest party as committer. b) Invoke the simulator for the semi-malicious protocol,

5-round Malicious (god|ua)-BoBW MPC Protocol $\pi_{\mathsf{bw.god.plain}}$ from 3-round delayed-semi-malicious BoBW protocol ϕ_{dsm}

Round 4. Each party $P_i, i \in [n]$ does the following with $P_j, j \in [n] \setminus \{i\}$:
- Execute Round 2 of ϕ_{dsm}.
- Run Round 4 of $\mathsf{NMCom}_{i \to j}$ in order to commit to a random string $s^0_{i \to j}$. Run Round 4 of $\mathsf{NMCom}_{j \to i}$ as receiver. Additionally, send another random string $s^1_{i \to j}$ on clear to P_j.
- Run Round 4 of $\mathsf{WI}^1_{j \to i}$ as verifier. If $\mathsf{flag}_j = 1$, run Round 4 of $\mathsf{WI}^1_{i \to j}$ to prove to P_j the correctness of the first 2 messages of ϕ_{dsm}. In detail, $\mathsf{WI}^1_{i \to j}$ proves correctness of one of the following statements: (1) *Honest Statement:* P_i has correctly generated the first 2 messages of ϕ_{dsm} using the input and randomness committed in $c_{i \to j}$. (2) *Cheating Statement:* XOR of the share $s^0_{i \to j}$ committed to in $\mathsf{NMCom}_{i \to j}$ and the share $s^1_{i \to j}$ is a valid trapdoor $\mathsf{td}_{j \to i}$ w.r.t. verification key $\mathsf{vk}_{j \to i}$.
- Run Round 3 of $\mathsf{WI}^2_{i \to j}$ and $\mathsf{WI}^2_{j \to i}$.
- Set $\mathsf{flag}_j = 0$ if either P_j aborts in Round 4 or if there exists a $k \in [n], k \neq j$ such that $\mathsf{WI}^1_{j \to k}$ leads to *reject*. Public verifiability of WI proofs enables this.

Round 5. Each party $P_i, i \in [n]$ does the following $P_j, j \in [n] \setminus \{i\}$:
- Execute Round 3 of ϕ_{dsm}.
- Run Round 4 of $\mathsf{WI}^2_{j \to i}$ as verifier. If $\mathsf{flag}_j = 1$, run Round 4 of $\mathsf{WI}^2_{i \to j}$ to prove to P_j the correctness of *all* messages of ϕ_{dsm} that he broadcasted. In detail, $\mathsf{WI}^2_{i \to j}$ proves correctness of one of the following statements: (1) *Honest Statement:* P_i has correctly generated *all* messages of ϕ_{dsm} using the input and randomness committed in $c_{i \to j}$ (2) *Cheating Statement:* XOR of the share $s^0_{i \to j}$ committed to in $\mathsf{NMCom}_{i \to j}$ and the share $s^1_{i \to j}$ is a valid trapdoor $\mathsf{td}_{j \to i}$ w.r.t. verification key $\mathsf{vk}_{j \to i}$.
- **Output Computation:** If any proof $\mathsf{WI}^2_{j \to k}$ is not accepting for any $k \in [n], k \neq j$, discard the message from P_j. Compute the output as per ϕ_{dsm}.

Fig. 3. The Modified Compiler for (god|ua)-BoBW MPC (Part 2)

$\mathcal{S}_{\mathsf{bw.god.sm}}$ to generate the first message of $\pi_{\mathsf{bw.god.sm}}$ in Round 1 on behalf of honest parties. The rest of the actions in Round 1–3 on behalf of honest parties are emulated by $\mathcal{S}_{\mathsf{bw.god.plain}}$ as per protocol specifications. Note that the simulator wrt compiler in [31] proceeds beyond the first stage only when the adversary did not cause an *abort* on behalf of any corrupt party in Stage 1. Else, it aborts. This works out because their protocol promises security with abort and hence, simply terminates if a party aborts. However our protocol, in case of honest majority, promises god with the output being computed on the actual input of the parties who have been alive till last but one round. To accommodate this, $\mathcal{S}_{\mathsf{bw.god.plain}}$ cannot simply afford to terminate in case a corrupt party aborts. It needs to continue the simulation with respect to corrupt parties who are alive, which demands rewinding. It can thus be inferred that $\mathcal{S}_{\mathsf{bw.god.plain}}$ must always proceed to rewinds unless all the corrupt parties are exposed by adversary in Stage 1.

The second and the fourth stage, in particular, are concerned with rewinding of the adversary to enable $\mathcal{S}_{\mathsf{bw.god.plain}}$ to extract some information. In Stage 2, the adversary is reset to the end of Round 1 and Rounds 2, 3 are rewound in order to enable $\mathcal{S}_{\mathsf{bw.god.plain}}$ to extract trapdoor of corrupt parties. In more detail, consider $\mathsf{Trap}_{j \to i}$ executed between corrupt sender P_j and honest P_i wrt verification key $\mathsf{vk}_{j \to i}$. Now, $\mathcal{S}_{\mathsf{bw.god.plain}}$ acting on behalf of P_i computes the trapdoor of P_j wrt $\mathsf{vk}_{j \to i}$ to be *two* message-signature pairs constituted by one obtained in Stage 1 and the other as a result of rewinding in Stage 2 (note that both signatures are wrt $\mathsf{vk}_{j \to i}$ sent in Round 1 of $\mathsf{Trap}_{j \to i}$; rewinds involve only Round 2, 3). To enable continuation of the simulation after Stage 2, which requires the knowledge of the trapdoors of corrupt parties who are alive, the logical *halt* condition for the rewinds is: *stop when you have enough!* This translates to- stop at the ℓth rewind if a valid trapdoor has been obtained for the set of corrupt parties alive across the ℓth rewind. Since the ℓth (last) rewind is expected to provide one valid (m, σ) pair (i.e. message, signature pair) out of two required for the trapdoor, all that is required is for the corrupt party to have been alive across at least one previous rewind. Let the set of parties alive across i^{th} rewind be denoted by $\mathbb{A}_{i+1}$ ($\mathbb{A}_1$ represents the set of parties that were alive in the execution preceeding the rewinds i.e. after Stage 1), then the condition formalizes to: halt at rewind ℓ if $\mathbb{A}_{\ell+1} \subseteq \mathbb{A}_1 \cup \cdots \cup \mathbb{A}_\ell$.

While this condition seems appropriate, it leads to the following subtle issue. The malicious adversary can exploit this stopping condition by coming up with a strategy to choose the set of aborting and the alive parties (say, according to some unknown distribution D pre-determined by the adversary) such that the final set of alive parties $\mathbb{A}$ in the transcript output by the simulator (when the rewinds halt) will be biased towards the set of parties that were alive in the earlier rewinds. (Ideally the distribution of the set of alive parties when simulator halts should be identical to D). This would lead to the view output by the simulator being distinguishable from the real view. A very similar subtle issue appears in zero-knowledge (ZK) protocol of [52] - While the details of this issue of [52] appear in the full version, we give a glimpse into how their scenario is analogous to ours below. Consider a basic 4-round ZK protocol with the following skeleton: the verifier commits to a challenge in Round 1 which is subsequently decommitted in Round 3. The prover responds to the challenge in Round 4. At a very high-level, the protocol of [52] follows a cut-and-choose paradigm involving N instances of the above basic protocol. Here, the verifier chooses a random subset $S \subset [N]$ of indices and decommits to the challenges made in those indices in Round 3. Subsequently, the prover completes the ZK protocol for instances with indices in S. The simulator for the zero-knowledge acting on behalf of the honest prover involves rewinds to obtain 'trapdoors' corresponding to the indices in S. However, note that the verifier can choose different S in different rewinds. Therefore, the simulator is in a position to produce an accepting transcript and stop at the ℓth rewind only when it has trapdoors corresponding to all indices in

S chosen by the adversary during the ℓth rewind. However, if the simulation is stopped at the execution where the above scenario happens for the 'first' time, their protocol suffers an identical drawback as ours. In particular, the malicious verifier can choose the set of indices S in a manner that the distribution of the views output by the simulator is not indistinguishable from the real view. Drawing analogy in a nutshell, the set of indices chosen by the malicious verifier is analogous to the set of alive corrupt parties in our context (details in full version). We thereby adopt the solution of [52] and modify our halting condition as: halt at rewind ℓ if $\mathbb{A}_{\ell+1} \subseteq \mathbb{A}_1 \cup \cdots \cup \mathbb{A}_\ell$ **and** $\mathbb{A}_{\ell+1} \nsubseteq \mathbb{A}_1 \cup \cdots \cup \mathbb{A}_{\ell-1}$. [52] gives an elaborate analysis showing why this simulation strategy results in the right distribution. With this change in simulation of Stage 2, the simulation of Stage 3 can proceed identical to [31] which involves simulating the WI^1 proofs via the *fake* statement using the knowledge of trapdoor.

Proceeding to simulation of Stage 4, we recall that the simulator of [31] involves another set of rewinds in Stage 4 which requires to rewind Round 3 and 4 to extract the witness i.e. the inputs and randomness of the corrupt parties from WI^1. Similar to Stage 2, two successful transcripts are sufficient for extraction. Thus, the simulator is in a position to halt at ℓ^{th} rewind if all the corrupt parties that are alive in Stage 4 have been alive across at least one previous rewind. Next, following the same argument as Stage 2, it seems like the *halting* condition for Stage 2 should work, as is, for Stage 4 too.

With this conclusion, we stumbled upon another hurdle elaborated in this specific scenario: Recall that the trapdoors extracted for corrupt parties in Stage 2 are used here to simulate the WI^1 proofs (as described in Stage 3). It is thereby required that $\mathcal{S}_{\mathsf{bw.god.plain}}$ already has the trapdoors for the corrupt parties that are alive in Stage 4. Let $\mathbb{T}$ be the set of trapdoors accumulated at the end of Stage 2. Consider a party, say P_i, which stopped participating in Round 3 of the last rewind ℓ of Stage 2 (P_i was alive till Round 2 of ℓth rewind). $\mathcal{S}_{\mathsf{bw.god.plain}}$ still proceeds to Stage 4 without being bothered about the trapdoor of P_i (as the halting condition is satisfied). However in Stage 4, when the adversary is reset to the end of Round 2 of ℓth rewind, P_i came back to life again in Round 3. The simulation of WI^1 proofs with P_i as a verifier will be stuck if $\mathbb{T}$ does not contain the trapdoor for P_i. Hence, it is required to accommodate the knowledge of set $\mathbb{T}$ during Stage 4. Accordingly $\mathcal{S}_{\mathsf{bw.god.plain}}$ does the following in Stage 4: During each rewind, if a party (say P_i) whose trapdoor is not known becomes alive during Round 3, store the signature sent by P_i in Round 3 (as part of Trap) and go back to Stage 2 rewinds (if P_i's trapdoor is still unknown). Looking ahead, storing the signature of P_i ensures that the missing trapdoor of P_i in $\mathbb{T}$ can cause $\mathcal{S}_{\mathsf{bw.god.plain}}$ to revert to Stage 2 rewinds at most once (if the same scenario happens again i.e. P_i becomes alive in Round 3 during Stage 4 rewinds, then another (message, signature) pair wrt verification key of P_i is obtained in this rewind by $\mathcal{S}_{\mathsf{bw.god.plain}}$; totaling upto 2 pairs which suffices to constitute valid trapdoor of P_i which can now be added to $\mathbb{T}$). Else, if $\mathbb{T}$ comprises of the trapdoor of all the corrupt parties that are alive during the rewind of Stage 4, then adhere to the same halting condition as Stage 2. This trick tackles the above described problematic scenario, while ensuring that the simulation terminates in polynomial time and maintains indistinguishability of views.

Before concluding the section, we highlight two important features regarding the simulation of $\pi_{\mathsf{bw.god.plain}}$: Despite the simulator $\mathcal{S}_{\mathsf{bw.god.plain}}$ reverting to Stage 2 rewinds in some cases (unlike the simulation of [31]), the simulation terminates in polynomial-time since this can occur at most once per corrupt party (as argued above). Lastly, since there is a possibility of reverting back to simulation of Round 2 after simulation of Round 4, we keep an additional 'dummy' Round 2 as well (on top of 'dummy' Round 3 as in [31]) in our construction. This allows us to maintain the invariant that $\mathcal{S}_{\mathsf{bw.god.sm}}$ is never rewound. To be more specific, as there are no messages of underlying semi-malicious protocol being sent in Round 2, 3; even if $\mathcal{S}_{\mathsf{bw.god.plain}}$ needs to return to Stage 2 from Stage 4 (after Round 4 has been simulated by obtaining the relevant message from $\mathcal{S}_{\mathsf{bw.god.sm}}$) and resume the simulation from Stage 2 onwards, the message of $\pi_{\mathsf{bw.god.sm}}$ sent in Round 4 can simply be replayed. We are able to accommodate two dummy rounds while maintaining the round complexity of 5 owing to the privilege that our delayed-semi-malicious protocol is just 3 rounds. This completes the simulation sketch. Assumption wise, our construction relies on 2-round semi-malicious oblivious transfer (a building block of our 3-round delayed-semi-malicious BoBW MPC $\pi_{\mathsf{bw.god.sm}}$). We state the formal theorem below.

Theorem 8. *Let (n, s, t) be such that $s + t < n$. Let $\pi_{\mathsf{bw.god.sm}}$ realises– (i) $\mathcal{F}_{\mathsf{god}}$ when at most $t < n/2$ parties are corrupt and (ii) $\mathcal{F}_{\mathsf{ua}}$ when at most $s < n$ parties are corrupt, delayed-semi-maliciously in both cases. Then $\pi_{\mathsf{bw.god.plain}}$ in the plain model realises– (i) $\mathcal{F}_{\mathsf{god}}$ when at most $t < n/2$ parties are corrupt and (ii) $\mathcal{F}_{\mathsf{ua}}$ when at most $s < n$ parties are corrupt, maliciously in both cases. It takes 5 rounds, assuming that $\pi_{\mathsf{bw.god.sm}}$ takes 3 rounds.*

Proof. The proof which includes the complete description of the simulator, a discussion about its indistinguishability to the real view and its running time appears in the full version [54]. □

Extension to Identifiability. We additionally point that the publicly-verifiable WI proofs render identifiability to our construction. Thus our maliciously-secure (god|ua)-BoBW protocol achieves the stronger notion of identifiable abort in case of dishonest majority, with no extra assumption. A minor observation is that we can replace the last round broadcast with point-to-point communication in our (god|ua)-BoBW protocol $\pi_{\mathsf{bw.god.plain}}$ at the expense of relaxing ua to sa security in the dishonest-majority setting.

References

1. Goldreich, O., Micali, S., Wigderson, A.: How to play any mental game or a completeness theorem for protocols with honest majority. In: ACM STOC (1987)
2. Chaum, D., Damgård, I.B., van de Graaf, J.: Multiparty computations ensuring privacy of each party's input and correctness of the result. In: Pomerance, C. (ed.) CRYPTO 1987. LNCS, vol. 293, pp. 87–119. Springer, Heidelberg (1988). https://doi.org/10.1007/3-540-48184-2_7

3. Yao, A.C.: Protocols for secure computations (extended abstract). In: FOCS (1982)
4. Cleve, R.: Limits on the security of coin flips when half the processors are faulty (extended abstract). In: ACM STOC (1986)
5. Ben-Or, M., Goldwasser, S., Wigderson, A.: Completeness theorems for non-cryptographic fault-tolerant distributed computation (extended abstract). In: ACM STOC (1988)
6. Chaum, D., Crépeau, C., Damgård, I.: Multiparty unconditionally secure protocols (extended abstract). In: ACM STOC (1988)
7. Rabin, T., Ben-Or, M.: Verifiable secret sharing and multiparty protocols with honest majority (extended abstract). In: ACM STOC (1989)
8. Beaver, D., Micali, S., Rogaway, P.: The round complexity of secure protocols (extended abstract). In: ACM STOC (1990)
9. Beaver, D.: Efficient multiparty protocols using circuit randomization. In: Feigenbaum, J. (ed.) CRYPTO 1991. LNCS, vol. 576, pp. 420–432. Springer, Heidelberg (1992). https://doi.org/10.1007/3-540-46766-1_34
10. Damgård, I., Nielsen, J.B.: Scalable and unconditionally secure multiparty computation. In: Menezes, A. (ed.) CRYPTO 2007. LNCS, vol. 4622, pp. 572–590. Springer, Heidelberg (2007). https://doi.org/10.1007/978-3-540-74143-5_32
11. Ananth, P., Choudhuri, A.R., Goel, A., Jain, A.: Round-optimal secure multiparty computation with honest majority. In: Shacham, H., Boldyreva, A. (eds.) CRYPTO 2018. LNCS, vol. 10992, pp. 395–424. Springer, Cham (2018). https://doi.org/10.1007/978-3-319-96881-0_14
12. Damgård, I., Orlandi, C.: Multiparty computation for dishonest majority: from passive to active security at low cost. In: Rabin, T. (ed.) CRYPTO 2010. LNCS, vol. 6223, pp. 558–576. Springer, Heidelberg (2010). https://doi.org/10.1007/978-3-642-14623-7_30
13. Garg, S., Gentry, C., Halevi, S., Raykova, M.: Two-round secure MPC from indistinguishability obfuscation. In: Lindell, Y. (ed.) TCC 2014. LNCS, vol. 8349, pp. 74–94. Springer, Heidelberg (2014). https://doi.org/10.1007/978-3-642-54242-8_4
14. Brakerski, Z., Halevi, S., Polychroniadou, A.: Four round secure computation without setup. In: Kalai, Y., Reyzin, L. (eds.) TCC 2017. LNCS, vol. 10677, pp. 645–677. Springer, Cham (2017). https://doi.org/10.1007/978-3-319-70500-2_22
15. Ananth, P., Choudhuri, A.R., Jain, A.: A new approach to round-optimal secure multiparty computation. In: Katz, J., Shacham, H. (eds.) CRYPTO 2017. LNCS, vol. 10401, pp. 468–499. Springer, Cham (2017). https://doi.org/10.1007/978-3-319-63688-7_16
16. Halevi, S., Hazay, C., Polychroniadou, A., Venkitasubramaniam, M.: Round-optimal secure multi-party computation. In: Shacham, H., Boldyreva, A. (eds.) CRYPTO 2018. LNCS, vol. 10992, pp. 488–520. Springer, Cham (2018). https://doi.org/10.1007/978-3-319-96881-0_17
17. Badrinarayanan, S., Goyal, V., Jain, A., Kalai, Y.T., Khurana, D., Sahai, A.: Promise zero knowledge and its applications to round optimal MPC. In: Shacham, H., Boldyreva, A. (eds.) CRYPTO 2018. LNCS, vol. 10992, pp. 459–487. Springer, Cham (2018). https://doi.org/10.1007/978-3-319-96881-0_16
18. Ishai, Y., Kushilevitz, E., Lindell, Y., Petrank, E.: On combining privacy with guaranteed output delivery in secure multiparty computation. In: Dwork, C. (ed.) CRYPTO 2006. LNCS, vol. 4117, pp. 483–500. Springer, Heidelberg (2006). https://doi.org/10.1007/11818175_29
19. Katz, J.: On achieving the "best of both worlds" in secure multiparty computation. In: ACM STOC (2007)

20. Ishai, Y., Katz, J., Kushilevitz, E., Lindell, Y., Petrank, E.: On achieving the "best of both worlds" in secure multiparty computation. SIAM J. Comput. **40**(1), 122–141 (2011)
21. Katz, J., Myers, S., Ostrovsky, R.: Cryptographic counters and applications to electronic voting. In: Pfitzmann, B. (ed.) EUROCRYPT 2001. LNCS, vol. 2045, pp. 78–92. Springer, Heidelberg (2001). https://doi.org/10.1007/3-540-44987-6_6
22. Nair, D.G., Binu, V.P., Kumar, G.S.: An improved e-voting scheme using secret sharing based secure multi-party computation. CoRR (2015)
23. Damgård, I., Geisler, M., Krøigaard, M.: Efficient and secure comparison for online auctions. In: Pieprzyk, J., Ghodosi, H., Dawson, E. (eds.) ACISP 2007. LNCS, vol. 4586, pp. 416–430. Springer, Heidelberg (2007). https://doi.org/10.1007/978-3-540-73458-1_30
24. Bonawitz, K., et al.: Practical secure aggregation for privacy-preserving machine learning. In: ACM CCS (2017)
25. Mohassel, P., Rindal, P.: ABY^3: a mixed protocol framework for machine learning. In: ACM CCS (2018)
26. Mohassel, P., Zhang, Y.: SecureML: a system for scalable privacy-preserving machine learning. In: IEEESP (2017)
27. Bogdanov, D., Talviste, R., Willemson, J.: Deploying secure multi-party computation for financial data analysis. In: Keromytis, A.D. (ed.) FC 2012. LNCS, vol. 7397, pp. 57–64. Springer, Heidelberg (2012). https://doi.org/10.1007/978-3-642-32946-3_5
28. Lucas, C., Raub, D., Maurer, U.M.: Hybrid-secure MPC: trading information-theoretic robustness for computational privacy. In: PODC (2010)
29. Beimel, A., Lindell, Y., Omri, E., Orlov, I.: $1/p$-secure multiparty computation without honest majority and the best of both worlds. In: Rogaway, P. (ed.) CRYPTO 2011. LNCS, vol. 6841, pp. 277–296. Springer, Heidelberg (2011). https://doi.org/10.1007/978-3-642-22792-9_16
30. Garg, S., Srinivasan, A.: Two-round multiparty secure computation from minimal assumptions. In: Nielsen, J.B., Rijmen, V. (eds.) EUROCRYPT 2018. LNCS, vol. 10821, pp. 468–499. Springer, Cham (2018). https://doi.org/10.1007/978-3-319-78375-8_16
31. Benhamouda, F., Lin, H.: k-round multiparty computation from k-round oblivious transfer via garbled interactive circuits. In: Nielsen, J.B., Rijmen, V. (eds.) EUROCRYPT 2018. LNCS, vol. 10821, pp. 500–532. Springer, Cham (2018). https://doi.org/10.1007/978-3-319-78375-8_17
32. Halevi, S., Lindell, Y., Pinkas, B.: Secure computation on the web: computing without simultaneous interaction. In: Rogaway, P. (ed.) CRYPTO 2011. LNCS, vol. 6841, pp. 132–150. Springer, Heidelberg (2011). https://doi.org/10.1007/978-3-642-22792-9_8
33. Garg, S., Mukherjee, P., Pandey, O., Polychroniadou, A.: The exact round complexity of secure computation. In: Fischlin, M., Coron, J.-S. (eds.) EUROCRYPT 2016. LNCS, vol. 9666, pp. 448–476. Springer, Heidelberg (2016). https://doi.org/10.1007/978-3-662-49896-5_16
34. Choudhuri, A.R., Ciampi, M., Goyal, V., Jain, A., Ostrovsky, R.: Round optimal secure multiparty computation from minimal assumptions. Cryptology ePrint Archive, Report 2019/216 (2019)
35. Mukherjee, P., Wichs, D.: Two round multiparty computation via multi-key FHE. In: Fischlin, M., Coron, J.-S. (eds.) EUROCRYPT 2016. LNCS, vol. 9666, pp. 735–763. Springer, Heidelberg (2016). https://doi.org/10.1007/978-3-662-49896-5_26

36. Garg, S., Srinivasan, A.: Garbled protocols and two-round MPC from bilinear maps. In: FOCS (2017)
37. Gennaro, R., Ishai, Y., Kushilevitz, E., Rabin, T.: On 2-round secure multiparty computation. In: Yung, M. (ed.) CRYPTO 2002. LNCS, vol. 2442, pp. 178–193. Springer, Heidelberg (2002). https://doi.org/10.1007/3-540-45708-9_12
38. Patra, A., Ravi, D.: On the exact round complexity of secure three-party computation. In: Shacham, H., Boldyreva, A. (eds.) CRYPTO 2018. LNCS, vol. 10992, pp. 425–458. Springer, Cham (2018). https://doi.org/10.1007/978-3-319-96881-0_15
39. Ishai, Y., Kumaresan, R., Kushilevitz, E., Paskin-Cherniavsky, A.: Secure computation with minimal interaction, revisited. In: Gennaro, R., Robshaw, M. (eds.) CRYPTO 2015. LNCS, vol. 9216, pp. 359–378. Springer, Heidelberg (2015). https://doi.org/10.1007/978-3-662-48000-7_18
40. Dov Gordon, S., Liu, F.-H., Shi, E.: Constant-round MPC with fairness and guarantee of output delivery. In: Gennaro, R., Robshaw, M. (eds.) CRYPTO 2015. LNCS, vol. 9216, pp. 63–82. Springer, Heidelberg (2015). https://doi.org/10.1007/978-3-662-48000-7_4
41. Patra, A., Ravi, D.: On the exact round complexity of secure three-party computation. Cryptology ePrint Archive, Report 2018/481 (2018)
42. Patra, A., Ravi, D.: Beyond honest majority: the round complexity of fair and robust multi-party computation. In: Galbraith, S.D., Moriai, S. (eds.) ASIACRYPT 2019. LNCS, vol. 11921, pp. 456–487. Springer, Cham (2019). https://doi.org/10.1007/978-3-030-34578-5_17
43. Badrinarayanan, S., Jain, A., Manohar, N., Sahai, A.: Threshold multi-key fhe and applications to round-optimal MPC. Cryptology ePrint Archive, Report 2018/580 (2018)
44. Ishai, Y., Kushilevitz, E., Paskin, A.: Secure multiparty computation with minimal interaction. In: Rabin, T. (ed.) CRYPTO 2010. LNCS, vol. 6223, pp. 577–594. Springer, Heidelberg (2010). https://doi.org/10.1007/978-3-642-14623-7_31
45. Peikert, C., Vaikuntanathan, V., Waters, B.: A framework for efficient and composable oblivious transfer. In: Wagner, D. (ed.) CRYPTO 2008. LNCS, vol. 5157, pp. 554–571. Springer, Heidelberg (2008). https://doi.org/10.1007/978-3-540-85174-5_31
46. De Santis, A., Di Crescenzo, G., Ostrovsky, R., Persiano, G., Sahai, A.: Robust non-interactive zero knowledge. In: Kilian, J. (ed.) CRYPTO 2001. LNCS, vol. 2139, pp. 566–598. Springer, Heidelberg (2001). https://doi.org/10.1007/3-540-44647-8_33
47. Ishai, Y., Kushilevitz, E., Prabhakaran, M., Sahai, A., Yu, C.-H.: Secure protocol transformations. In: Robshaw, M., Katz, J. (eds.) CRYPTO 2016. LNCS, vol. 9815, pp. 430–458. Springer, Heidelberg (2016). https://doi.org/10.1007/978-3-662-53008-5_15
48. Patra, A., Choudhary, A., Rangan, C.P.: Simple and efficient asynchronous byzantine agreement with optimal resilience. In: PODC (2009)
49. Patra, A., Rangan, C.P.: Communication and round efficient information checking protocol. CoRR (2010)
50. Ishai, Y., Ostrovsky, R., Seyalioglu, H.: Identifying cheaters without an honest majority. In: Cramer, R. (ed.) TCC 2012. LNCS, vol. 7194, pp. 21–38. Springer, Heidelberg (2012). https://doi.org/10.1007/978-3-642-28914-9_2
51. Asharov, G., Jain, A., López-Alt, A., Tromer, E., Vaikuntanathan, V., Wichs, D.: Multiparty computation with low communication, computation and interaction via threshold FHE. In: Pointcheval, D., Johansson, T. (eds.) EUROCRYPT 2012. LNCS, vol. 7237, pp. 483–501. Springer, Heidelberg (2012). https://doi.org/10.1007/978-3-642-29011-4_29

52. Hazay, C., Venkitasubramaniam, M.: Round-optimal fully black-box zero-knowledge arguments from one-way permutations. In: Beimel, A., Dziembowski, S. (eds.) TCC 2018. LNCS, vol. 11239, pp. 263–285. Springer, Cham (2018). https://doi.org/10.1007/978-3-030-03807-6_10
53. Ciampi, M., Ostrovsky, R.: Four-round secure multiparty computation from general assumptions. Cryptology ePrint Archive, Report 2019/214 (2019)
54. Patra, A., Ravi, D., Singla, S.: On the exact round complexity of best-of-both-worlds multi-party computation. Cryptology ePrint Archive, Report 2020/1050 (2020). https://eprint.iacr.org/2020/1050
55. Chaum, D.: The spymasters double-agent problem. In: Brassard, G. (ed.) CRYPTO 1989. LNCS, vol. 435, pp. 591–602. Springer, New York (1990). https://doi.org/10.1007/0-387-34805-0_52
56. Hirt, M., Maurer, U., Zikas, V.: MPC vs. SFE: unconditional and computational security. In: Pieprzyk, J. (ed.) ASIACRYPT 2008. LNCS, vol. 5350, pp. 1–18. Springer, Heidelberg (2008). https://doi.org/10.1007/978-3-540-89255-7_1
57. Halevi, S., Ishai, Y., Kushilevitz, E., Rabin, T.: Best possible information-theoretic MPC. In: Beimel, A., Dziembowski, S. (eds.) TCC 2018. LNCS, vol. 11240, pp. 255–281. Springer, Cham (2018). https://doi.org/10.1007/978-3-030-03810-6_10
58. Hirt, M., Lucas, C., Maurer, U., Raub, D.: Graceful degradation in multi-party computation (extended abstract). In: Fehr, S. (ed.) ICITS 2011. LNCS, vol. 6673, pp. 163–180. Springer, Heidelberg (2011). https://doi.org/10.1007/978-3-642-20728-0_15
59. Hirt, M., Lucas, C., Maurer, U., Raub, D.: Passive corruption in statistical multi-party computation. In: Smith, A. (ed.) ICITS 2012. LNCS, vol. 7412, pp. 129–146. Springer, Heidelberg (2012). https://doi.org/10.1007/978-3-642-32284-6_8
60. Hirt, M., Maurer, U., Lucas, C.: A dynamic tradeoff between active and passive corruptions in secure multi-party computation. In: Canetti, R., Garay, J.A. (eds.) CRYPTO 2013. LNCS, vol. 8043, pp. 203–219. Springer, Heidelberg (2013). https://doi.org/10.1007/978-3-642-40084-1_12
61. Genkin, D., Gordon, S.D., Ranellucci, S.: Best of both worlds in secure computation, with low communication overhead. In: Preneel, B., Vercauteren, F. (eds.) ACNS 2018. LNCS, vol. 10892, pp. 340–359. Springer, Cham (2018). https://doi.org/10.1007/978-3-319-93387-0_18
62. Bellare, M., Micali, S.: Non-interactive oblivious transfer and applications. In: Brassard, G. (ed.) CRYPTO 1989. LNCS, vol. 435, pp. 547–557. Springer, New York (1990). https://doi.org/10.1007/0-387-34805-0_48
63. Goyal, V., Ishai, Y., Sahai, A., Venkatesan, R., Wadia, A.: Founding cryptography on tamper-proof hardware tokens. In: Micciancio, D. (ed.) TCC 2010. LNCS, vol. 5978, pp. 308–326. Springer, Heidelberg (2010). https://doi.org/10.1007/978-3-642-11799-2_19
64. Ostrovsky, R., Scafuro, A., Visconti, I., Wadia, A.: Universally composable secure computation with (malicious) physically uncloneable functions. In: Johansson, T., Nguyen, P.Q. (eds.) EUROCRYPT 2013. LNCS, vol. 7881, pp. 702–718. Springer, Heidelberg (2013). https://doi.org/10.1007/978-3-642-38348-9_41
65. Brzuska, C., Fischlin, M., Schröder, H., Katzenbeisser, S.: Physically uncloneable functions in the universal composition framework. In: Rogaway, P. (ed.) CRYPTO 2011. LNCS, vol. 6841, pp. 51–70. Springer, Heidelberg (2011). https://doi.org/10.1007/978-3-642-22792-9_4
66. Cohen, R., Garay, J., Zikas, V.: Broadcast-optimal two-round MPC. In: Canteaut, A., Ishai, Y. (eds.) EUROCRYPT 2020. LNCS, vol. 12106, pp. 828–858. Springer, Cham (2020). https://doi.org/10.1007/978-3-030-45724-2_28

MPC with Synchronous Security and Asynchronous Responsiveness

Chen-Da Liu-Zhang[1(✉)], Julian Loss[2], Ueli Maurer[1], Tal Moran[3], and Daniel Tschudi[4]

[1] ETH Zurich, Zurich, Switzerland
{lichen,maurer}@inf.ethz.ch
[2] University of Maryland, College Park, USA
lossjulian@gmail.com
[3] IDC Herzliya, Herzliya, Israel
talm@idc.ac.il
[4] Concordium, Zurich, Switzerland
dt@concordium.com

Abstract. Two paradigms for secure MPC are synchronous and asynchronous protocols. While synchronous protocols tolerate more corruptions and allow every party to give its input, they are very slow because the speed depends on the conservatively assumed worst-case delay Δ of the network. In contrast, asynchronous protocols allow parties to obtain output as fast as the actual network allows, a property called *responsiveness*, but unavoidably have lower resilience and parties with slow network connections cannot give input.

It is natural to wonder whether it is possible to leverage synchronous MPC protocols to achieve responsiveness, hence obtaining the advantages of both paradigms: full security with responsiveness up to t corruptions, and *extended* security (full security or security with unanimous abort) with no responsiveness up to $T \geq t$ corruptions. We settle the question by providing matching feasibility and impossibility results:

- For the case of unanimous abort as extended security, there is an MPC protocol if and only if $T + 2t < n$.
- For the case of full security as extended security, there is an MPC protocol if and only if $T < \frac{n}{2}$ and $T + 2t < n$. In particular, setting $t = \frac{n}{4}$ allows to achieve a fully secure MPC for honest majority, which in addition benefits from having substantial responsiveness.

1 Introduction

In the context of multiparty computation (MPC), a set of mutually distrustful parties wish to jointly compute a function by running a distributed protocol. The protocol is deemed secure if every party obtains the correct output and if

---

T. Moran—Supported in part by ISF grant no. 1790/13 and by the Bar-Ilan Cyber-center.

D. Tschudi—Author was supported by advanced ERC grant MPCPRO.

S. Moriai and H. Wang (Eds.): ASIACRYPT 2020, LNCS 12493, pp. 92–119, 2020.
https://doi.org/10.1007/978-3-030-64840-4_4

it does not reveal any more information about the parties' inputs than what can be inferred from the output. Moreover, these guarantees should be met even if some of the parties can maliciously deviate from the protocol description. Broadly speaking, MPC protocols exist in two regimes of synchrony. First, there are *synchronous* protocols which assume that parties share a common clock and messages sent by honest parties can be delayed by at most some a priori known bounded time. Synchronous protocols typically proceed in rounds of length Δ, ensuring that any message sent at the beginning of a round by an honest party will arrive by the end of that round at its intended recipient. On the upside, such strong timing assumptions allow to obtain protocols with an optimal resilience of $\frac{1}{2}n$ corruptions for the case of *full security* [2,5,13,20,27,45], and of arbitrary number of corruptions for the case of *security with (unanimous) abort* and no fairness [23,29]. On the downside, especially in real-world networks where the *actual* maximal network delay δ is hard to predict, Δ has to be chosen rather pessimistically, and synchronous protocols fail to take advantage of a fast network.

The second type of protocols that we will study in this work are *asynchronous* protocols. Such protocols do not require synchronized clocks or an a priori known bounded network delay to work properly. As such, they function correctly under much more realistic network assumptions. Moreover, asynchronous protocols have the benefit of running at the *actual speed of the network*, i.e., they run in time that depends only on δ, but *not* on Δ; a notion that we shall refer to as *responsiveness* [41]. This speed and robustness comes at a price, however: it can easily be seen that no asynchronous protocol that implements an arbitrary function can tolerate $\frac{1}{3}n$ maliciously corrupted parties [6]. We ask the natural question of whether it is possible to leverage synchronous MPC protocols to also achieve responsiveness:

Is there a (synchronous) MPC protocol that allows to simultaneously achieve full security with responsiveness up to t corruptions, and some form of extended security (full security, unanimous abort) up to $T \geq t$ corruptions?

We settle the question with tight feasibility and impossibility results:

- For the case where unanimous abort is required as extended security, this is possible if and only if $T + 2t < n$.
- For the case where full security is required as extended security, this is possible if and only if $T < \frac{n}{2}$ and $T + 2t < n$.

1.1 Technical Overview of Our Results

The Model. We first introduce a new composable model of functionalities in the UC framework [11], which captures the guarantees that protocols from both asynchronous and synchronous worlds achieve in a very general fashion. Our model allows to capture multiple distinct guarantees such as privacy, correctness, or responsiveness, each of which is guaranteed to hold for (possibly) different thresholds of corruption. In contrast to previous works, we do not capture the guarantees as protocol properties, but rather as part of the ideal functionality. This allows to use the ideal functionality as an assumed functionality in further steps of the composition, without the need to keep track of the properties of the real-world protocols.

Real World Functionalities. Our protocols work with public-key infrastructure (PKI) and common-reference string (CRS) as setup. Parties have access to a synchronized global clock functionality $\mathcal{G}_{\text{CLK}}$ and a communication network of authenticated channels with *unknown* upper bound δ, corresponding to the maximal network delay. This value is unknown to the honest parties. Instead, protocols make use of a conservatively assumed worst-case delay $\Delta \gg \delta$. Within δ, the adversary can schedule the messages arbitrarily.

Ideal Functionality. In order to capture the guarantees that asynchronous and synchronous protocols achieve in a fine-grained manner, we describe an ideal functionality $\mathcal{F}_{\text{HYB}}$ which allows parties to jointly evaluate a function. At a high level, $\mathcal{F}_{\text{HYB}}$ is composed of two phases; an asynchronous and a synchronous phase, separated by some pre-defined time-out. Each party can obtain a unique identical output in either phase. As in asynchronous protocols, the outputs obtained during the asynchronous phase are obtained fast, i.e., at a time which depends on the actual maximal network delay δ, but not on the conservatively assumed worst-case network delay Δ. Let us describe the guarantees that $\mathcal{F}_{\text{HYB}}$ provides.

If there are up to t corruptions, $\mathcal{F}_{\text{HYB}}$ achieves full security with responsiveness. That is, honest parties obtain a correct and identical output, and honest parties' inputs remain private. Moreover, they obtain an output $y_{\mathtt{asynch}}$ by a time proportional to the actual network delay δ. Unavoidably, this means that $\mathcal{F}_{\text{HYB}}$ may ignore up to t inputs from honest parties.

If there are up to $T \geq t$ corruptions, $\mathcal{F}_{\text{HYB}}$ can give output at two different points in time $\tau_1 \leq \tau_2$. Either all parties obtain $y_{\mathtt{asynch}}$ before time τ_1 (there might be some parties which obtained $y_{\mathtt{asynch}}$ in the asynchronous phase), or all parties obtain the output $y_{\mathtt{sync}}$ by time τ_2, which is guaranteed to take into account all inputs from honest parties. For the output $y_{\mathtt{sync}}$, we consider two versions: $\mathcal{F}_{\text{HYB}}^{\mathtt{fs}}$ which guarantees full security up to T corruptions implying that $y_{\mathtt{sync}}$ is the correct output, and $\mathcal{F}_{\text{HYB}}^{\mathtt{ua}}$ which guarantees security with unanimous abort up to T corruptions, meaning that the adversary can set $y_{\mathtt{sync}}$ to $\bot$.

We depict in Fig. 1 a time-line showing the point in time at which the honest parties obtain the output, depending on the number of corruptions.

Black-Box Compiler. We give a generic black-box compiler that combines an asynchronous MPC protocol with a synchronous MPC protocol and gives a hybrid protocol that combines beneficial properties from both the synchronous and asynchronous regime, very roughly in the following way: Using threshold encryption and assuming 1) a *two-threshold* asynchronous protocol with full

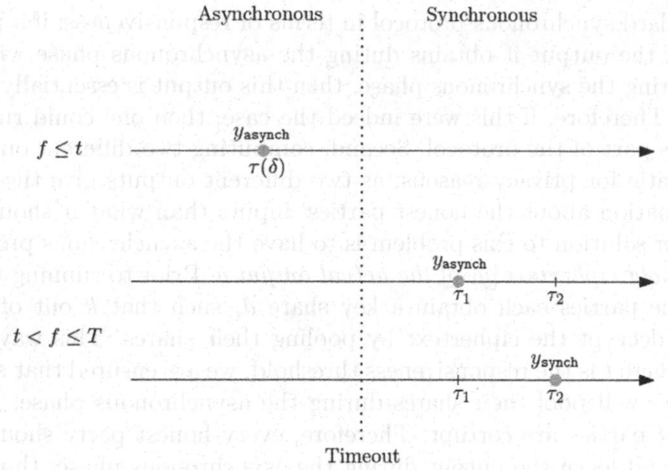

Fig. 1. The dotted vertical line separates the asynchronous and the synchronous phase. The orange dot shows the latest point in time when honest parties get output. The output y_{asynch} takes into account $n-t$ inputs, whereas y_{sync} takes into account all inputs. Up to t corruptions all parties obtain y_{asynch} fast. In the other case, either all parties obtain y_{asynch} by τ_1, or all parties obtain y_{sync} by τ_2, which is the correct output for $\mathcal{F}_{\text{HYB}}^{\text{fs}}$, and may be $\perp$ for $\mathcal{F}_{\text{HYB}}^{\text{ua}}$.

security up to t corruptions and security with no termination (correctness and privacy) up to $T \geq t$ corruptions, and 2) a synchronous protocol with *extended* security (full security or security with unanimous abort) up to T corruptions, the compiler provides full security with responsiveness up to t corruptions, and extended security up to T corruptions, for any $T + 2t < n$.

For the first sub-protocol 1), we show how to modify the asynchronous MPC protocol by Cohen [18] to obtain the trade-off mentioned above when used in our aforementioned compiler. We separate the termination threshold from all other security guarantees. That is, we achieve an asynchronous protocol that terminates (in a responsive and fully-secure manner) for any $t < \frac{1}{3}n$, and provides security without termination up to $T < n - 2t$ corruptions.

The second sub-protocol 2) can be achieved with known protocols; for $T < n$ in the case of security with unanimous abort (e.g. [23,29]) and for $T < n/2$ for full security (e.g. [2,5,13,20,27,45]).

Compiler Description. We now give an outline of our compiler. At a high level, the idea of our compiler is to first run an asynchronous protocol until some pre-defined timeout. Upon timing out, the parties switch to a synchronous computation. If sufficiently many parties are honest, the honest parties obtain their output at the actual speed of network. The main challenge is to ensure that if even a single party obtains output during the asynchronous phase, the output will not be changed during the synchronous phase. This would be problematic for two reasons: First, because the combined protocol would offer no improvement over a standard synchronous protocol in terms of responsiveness; if a party does not know if the output it obtains during the asynchronous phase will be later changed during the synchronous phase, then this output is essentially useless to that party. Therefore, if this were indeed the case, then one could run *just* the synchronous part of the protocol. Second, computing two different outputs may be problematic for privacy reasons, as two different outputs give the adversary more information about the honest parties' inputs than what it should be able to infer. Our solution to this problem is to have the asynchronous protocol output a *threshold ciphertext* $[y]$ *of the actual output* y. Prior to running the hybrid protocol, the parties each obtain a key share d_i such that k out of n parties can jointly decrypt the ciphertext by pooling their shares. This way, if we set $k = n - t$, where t is the responsiveness threshold, we are ensured that sufficiently many parties will pool their shares during the asynchronous phase, given that fewer than t parties are corrupt. Therefore, every honest party should be able to decrypt and learn the output during the asynchronous phase, thus ensuring responsiveness. On the other hand, our compiler ensures that if any honest party gives out its share during the asynchronous phase after seeing the ciphertext $[y]$ being output by the asynchronous protocol, then the only possible output during the synchronous phase can be y. Finally, our compiler has a mechanism to detect whether no honest party has made its share public yet. In this case, we can safely recompute the result during the synchronous phase of the hybrid protocol, as we can be certain that the adversary does not have sufficient shares to learn the output from the asynchronous phase.

Two-Threshold Asynchronous MPC Protocol. Finally, in Sect. 5, we show how to obtain an asynchronous MPC protocol to achieve trade-offs between termination and security (correctness and privacy). While many asynchronous MPC protocols (e.g. [14,15,18,32,43]) can be adapted to the two-threshold setting, we choose to adapt the protocol in [18] for simplicity.

The protocol in [18] achieves all guarantees simultaneously for the corruption threshold $\frac{1}{3}n$. At a high level, the idea of this protocol is to use a threshold fully homomorphic encryption scheme (TFHE) with threshold $k = \frac{1}{3}n$ and let parties distribute encryption shares of their inputs to each other. Then, parties agree on a common set of at least $\frac{2}{3}n$ parties, whose inputs will be taken into account during the function evaluation. In this step, n Byzantine Agreement protocols are run. Parties can then locally evaluate the function which is to be computed on their respective input shares by carrying out the corresponding (homomorphic) arithmetic operations on these shares. After this local computation has succeeded, parties pool their shares of the computation's result to decrypt the final output of the protocol. We modify the thresholds in this protocol in the following manner. Instead of setting $k = \frac{1}{3}n$, we set $k = \frac{3}{4}n$. Intuitively, assuming a perfect Byzantine Agreement (BA) functionality, this modification has the effect that the adversary needs to corrupt $\frac{3}{4}n$ parties to break privacy, but can prevent the protocol from terminating by withholding decryption shares whenever it corrupts more than $\frac{1}{4}n$ parties. However, one can see that if one realizes the BA functionality using a traditional protocol with validity and consistency thresholds $\frac{1}{3}n$, the overall statement will only have security $\frac{1}{3}n$.

We show how to improve the security threshold T of the protocol by using, as a sub-component, an asynchronous BA protocol which trades liveness for consistency without sacrificing validity. Our protocol inherits the thresholds of the improved BA protocol, achieving any $T < n - 2t$, where t is the termination threshold.

1.2 Synchronous Protocols over an Asynchronous Network

We argue that it is not trivial to enhance a synchronous MPC protocol to achieve responsiveness. Two ways to execute a synchronous protocol over a network with unknown delay δ are as follows:

Time-Out Based. Perhaps the easiest approach to execute a synchronous protocol over this network is to model each round using Δ clock ticks, where Δ is a known upper bound on the network delay. In this case, the output is obtained at a time which depends on Δ. Note that Δ has to be set high enough to accommodate any conditions, and such that any honest party has enough time to perform its local computation; if an honest party is slightly later than Δ in any round, it will be considered corrupted throughout the whole computation. In realistic settings where δ is hard to predict, we will have that $\Delta \gg \delta$. Hence, any synchronous protocol (even constant-round) is slow.

Notification Based. A well-known approach (see e.g. [39]) to "speed up" a synchronous protocol is to let the parties simulate a synchronized clock in an event-based fashion over an asynchronous network. More concretely, the idea is that each party broadcasts a notification once it finishes a particular round i and only advances to round $i + 1$ upon receiving a notification for round i from all parties. It is not hard to see that this approach does not achieve the responsiveness guarantees we aim for. To this end, observe that a **single** corrupted party P_j can make all parties wait Δ clock ticks in each round, simply by not sending a notification in this particular round. Note that parties cannot infer that P_i is corrupted, unless they wait for Δ clock ticks, because δ is unknown. Hence, unless there are *no corruptions*, an approach along these lines can not ensure responsiveness. In contrast, our protocol guarantees that parties obtain fast outputs as long as there are up to t corruptions.

1.3 Related Work

Despite being a very natural direction of research, compilers for achieving tradeoffs between asynchronous and synchronous protocol have only begun to be studied in relatively recent works.

Pass and Shi study a hybrid type of state-machine replication (SMR) protocol in [41] which confirms transactions at an asynchronous speed and works in the model of *mildly adaptive* malicious corruptions; such corruptions take a short time to take effect and as such model a slightly weaker adversary than one that is fully adaptive. Subsequently, Pass and Shi show a general paradigm for SMR protocols with optimistic confirmation of transactions called *Thunderella* [42]. In their work, they show how to achieve optimistic transaction confirmation (at asynchronous network speed) as long as the majority of some designated committee and a party called the 'accelerator' are honest and faithfully notarize transactions for confirmation. If the committee or the accelerator become corrupted, the protocol uses a synchronous SMR protocol to recover and eventually switch back to the asynchronous path of the protocol. Their protocol achieves safety and liveness against a fully adaptive adversary, but can easily be kept on the slow, synchronous path forever in this case. Subsequently, Loss and Moran [40] showed how to obtain compilers for the simpler case of BA that achieve tradeoffs between responsiveness and safety against a fully adaptive adversary.

The work by Guo et al. [30] introduced a model which weakens classical synchrony. There, the adversary can interrupt the communication between certain sets of parties, as long as in each round there is a (possibly different) connected component with an honest majority of the nodes. Although their focus is not on responsive protocols, the authors include an MPC responsive protocol, based on threshold FHE for the case of full-security as extended security. Our protocols differ from theirs in various aspects: 1) In contrast to their protocol, our approach is conceptually simpler and allows to plug-in any asynchronous and synchronous protocol in a black-box manner and automatically inherit the thresholds for each of the guarantees, and the assumptions from each of the protocols. For example, we can plug-in a synchronous protocol with full security and unanimous abort, and obtain the corresponding guarantees; one could further consider other types of guarantees, or design MPC protocols from different types of assumptions which would all be inherited automatically from our compiler; 2) We phrase all our results in the UC framework and capture in a very general fashion the guarantees that the protocol provides as part of the ideal functionality. This leads to some differences, e.g. our ideal functionality allows to capture responsiveness guarantees; also allows to take into account in the computation the inputs from all parties in some cases.

Further Related Work. Best-of-both worlds compilers for distributed protocols (in particular MPC protocols) come in many flavours and we are only able to list an incomplete summary of related work. Goldreich and Petrank [28] give a black-box compiler for Byzantine agreement which focuses on achieving protocols which have expected constant round termination, but in the worst case terminate after a fixed number of rounds. Kursawe [38] gives a protocol for Byzantine agreement that has an optimistic *synchronous path* which achieves Byzantine agreement if every party behaves honestly and the network is well-behaved. If the synchronous path fails, then parties fall back to an asynchronous path which is robust to network partitions. However, the overall protocol tolerates only $\frac{1}{3}n$ corrupted parties in order to still achieve safety and liveness. A recent line of works [7–9] studied protocols resilient to t_2 corruptions when run in a synchronous network and also to t_1 corruptions if the network is asynchronous, for $0 < t_1 < \frac{1}{3}n \leq t_2 < \frac{1}{2}n$. A line of works [3,4,16,44] consider the setting where parties have a few synchronous rounds before switching to fully asynchronous computation. Here, one can achieve protocols with better security guarantees than purely asynchronous ones. Finally, the line of works [24,25,31,34,35] consider different thresholds to achieve more fine-grained security guarantees.

Worth mentioning, are the works of [34,35], which consider MPC protocols with full security up for an honest majority t, and security with abort for a dishonest majority T. Our protocols achieve results in this direction as well, except that our threshold t includes responsiveness as well. Note that the impossibility of [35], where it is shown that $T + t \geq n$ is impossible does not apply to our work, since we consider a *weaker* trade-off $T + 2t < n$. Moreover, the fact that our threshold t for full security case includes responsiveness as well is essential to prove that the bound $T + 2t < n$ is tight.

2 Preliminaries

Threshold Encryption Scheme. We assume the existence of a secure public-key encryption scheme which enables threshold decryption.

Definition 1. *A threshold encryption scheme is a public-key encryption scheme which has the following two additional properties:*

- *The key generation algorithm is parameterized by (t, n) and outputs $(\mathtt{ek}, \mathtt{dk}) = \mathsf{Gen}_{(t,n)}(1^\kappa)$, where $\mathtt{ek}$ is the public key, and $\mathtt{dk} = (\mathtt{dk}_1, \ldots, \mathtt{dk}_n)$ is the list of private keys.*
- *Given a ciphertext c and a secret key share $\mathtt{dk}_i$, there is an algorithm that outputs $d_i = \mathtt{DecShare}_{\mathtt{dk}_i}(c)$, such that $(d_1, \ldots, d_n)$ forms a t-out-of-n sharing of the plaintext $m = \mathtt{Dec}_{\mathtt{dk}}(c)$. Moreover, with t decryption shares $\{d_i\}$, one can reconstruct the plaintext $m = \mathtt{Rec}(\{d_i\})$.*

Digital Signature Scheme. We assume the existence of a digital signature scheme unforgettable against adaptively chosen message attacks. Given a signing key $\mathtt{sk}$ and a verification key $\mathtt{vk}$, let $\mathsf{Sign}_{\mathtt{sk}}$ and $\mathsf{Ver}_{\mathtt{vk}}$ the signing and verification functions. We write $\sigma = \mathsf{Sign}_{\mathtt{sk}}(m)$ meaning using $\mathtt{sk}$, sign a plaintext m to obtain a signature σ. Moreover, we write $\mathsf{Ver}_{\mathtt{vk}}(m, \sigma) = 1$ to indicate that σ is a valid signature on m.

3 Model

Notation. We denote by κ the security parameter, $\mathcal{P} = \{P_1, \ldots, P_n\}$ the set of n parties and by $\mathcal{H}$ the set of honest parties.

3.1 Adversary

We consider a static adversary, who can corrupt up to f parties at the onset of the execution and make them deviate from the protocol arbitrarily. The adversary is also computationally bounded.

3.2 Communication Network and Clocks

We borrow ideas from a standard model for UC synchronous communication [36,37]. Parties have access to functionalities and global functionalities [12]. More concretely, parties have access to a synchronized global clock functionality $\mathcal{G}_{\text{CLK}}$, and a network functionality $\mathcal{F}^{\delta}_{\text{NET}}$ of pairwise authenticated channels with an unknown upper bound on the message delay δ.

At a high level, the model captures the two guarantees that parties have in the synchronous model of communication. First, every party must be activated each clock tick, and second, every party is able to perform all its local computation before the next tick. Both guarantees are captured via the clock functionality $\mathcal{G}_{\text{CLK}}$. It maintains the global time τ, initially set to 0, and a round-ready flag $d_i = 0$, for each party P_i. Each clock tick, $\mathcal{G}_{\text{CLK}}$ sets the flag to $d_i = 1$ whenever a party sends a confirmation (that it is ready) to the clock. Once the flag is set for every honest party, the clock counter is increased and the flags are reset to 0 again. This ensures that all honest parties are activated in each clock tick.

Functionality $\mathcal{G}_{\text{CLK}}$

The clock functionality stores a counter τ, initially set to 0. For each honest party P_i it stores flag d_i, initialized to 0.

ReadClock:

1: On input (ReadClock), return τ.

Ready:

1: On input (ClockReady) from honest party P_i set $d_i = 1$ and notify the adversary.

ClockUpdate: Every activation, the functionality runs the following code before doing anything else:

1: **if** for every honest party P_i it holds $d_i = 1$ **then**
2: Set $d_i = 0$ for every honest party P_i and $\tau = \tau + 1$.
3: **end if**

The UC standard communication network does not consider any delivery guarantees. Hence, we consider the functionality $\mathcal{F}^{\delta}_{\text{NET}}$ which models a complete network of pairwise authenticated channels with an *unknown* upper bound δ corresponding to the real delay in the network. The network is connected to the clock functionality $\mathcal{G}_{\text{CLK}}$. It works in a *fetch-based* mode: parties need to actively query for the messages in order to receive them. For each message m sent from P_i to P_j, $\mathcal{F}_{\text{NET}}$ creates a unique identifier $\mathtt{id}_m$ for the tuple $(T_{\mathtt{init}}, T_{\mathtt{end}}, P_i, P_j, m)$. This identifier is used to refer to a message circulating the network in a concise way. The field $T_{\mathtt{init}}$ indicates the time at which the message was sent, whereas $T_{\mathtt{end}}$ is the time at which the message is made available to the receiver. At first, the time $T_{\mathtt{end}}$ is initialized to $T_{\mathtt{init}} + 1$.

Whenever a new message is input to the buffer of $\mathcal{F}_{\text{NET}}$, the adversary is informed about both the content of the message and its identifier. It is then allowed to modify the delivery time $T_{\texttt{end}}$ by any finite amount. For that, it inputs an integer value T along with some corresponding identifier $\texttt{id}_m$ with the effect that the corresponding tuple $(T_{\texttt{init}}, T_{\texttt{end}}, P_i, P_j, m)$ is modified to $(T_{\texttt{init}}, T_{\texttt{end}} + T, P_i, P_j, m)$. Moreover, to capture that there is an upper bound on the delay of the messages, the network does not accept more than δ accumulated delay for any identifier $\texttt{id}_m$. That is, $\mathcal{F}_{\text{NET}}$ checks that $T_{\texttt{end}} \leq T_{\texttt{init}} + \delta$. Also, observe that the adversary has the power to schedule the delivery of messages: we allow it to input delays more than once, which are added to the current amount of delay. If the adversary wants to deliver a message during the next activation, it can input a negative delay. We remark, that the traditional model of an asynchronous network with eventual delivery can be modeled by setting $\delta = \infty$.

Functionality $\mathcal{F}_{\text{NET}}^{\delta}$

The functionality is connected to a clock functionality $\mathcal{G}_{\text{CLK}}$. It is parameterized by a positive constant δ (the real delay upper bound only known to the adversary). It also stores the current time τ and keeps a buffer of messages $\texttt{buffer}$ which initially is empty.
Each time the functionality is activated it first queries $\mathcal{G}_{\text{CLK}}$ for the current time and updates τ accordingly.

Message transmission:

1: At the onset of the execution, output δ to the adversary.
2: On input (SEND, i, j, m) from party P_i, $\mathcal{F}_{\text{NET}}$ creates a new identifier $\texttt{id}_m$ and records the tuple $(\tau, \tau+1, P_i, P_j, m, \texttt{id}_m)$ in $\texttt{buffer}$. Then, it sends the tuple $(\text{SENT}, P_i, P_j, m, \texttt{id}_m)$ to the adversary.
3: On input $(\text{FETCHMESSAGES}, i)$ from P_i, for each message tuple $(T_{\texttt{init}}, T_{\texttt{end}}, P_k, P_i, m, \texttt{id}_m)$ from $\texttt{buffer}$ where $T_{\texttt{end}} \leq \tau$, the functionality removes the tuple from $\texttt{buffer}$ and outputs (k, m) to P_i.
4: On input $(\text{DELAY}, D, \texttt{id})$ from the adversary, if there exists a tuple $(T_{\texttt{init}}, T_{\texttt{end}}, P_i, P_j, m, \texttt{id})$ in $\texttt{buffer}$ and $T_{\texttt{end}} + D \leq T_{\texttt{init}} + \delta$, then set $T_{\texttt{end}} = T_{\texttt{end}} + D$ and return (DELAY-OK) to the adversary. Otherwise, ignore the message.

3.3 Ideal World

We introduce ideal functionality $\mathcal{F}_{\text{HYB}}^{\texttt{fs}}$ (resp. $\mathcal{F}_{\text{HYB}}^{\texttt{ua}}$) which allows to capture the guarantees that asynchronous and synchronous protocols for secure function evaluation offer in a fine-grained manner. The functionality has access to the global functionality $\mathcal{G}_{\text{CLK}}$, and allows parties to evaluate a function f. The idea is that up to t corruptions, parties have full security and responsiveness. Moreover, in the case of $\mathcal{F}_{\text{HYB}}^{\texttt{fs}}$, if up to $t \leq T < n/2$ parties are corrupted, full security is guaranteed, i.e. all honest parties obtain the correct and identical output, and the inputs from honest parties remain secret. The functionality $\mathcal{F}^{\text{ua}}_{\text{HYB}}$ is the same, except that it guarantees security with unanimous abort up to $t \leq T < n$ corruptions instead of full security, i.e., honest parties obtain the correct output or unanimously obtain $\perp$.

The number of inputs that the function is guaranteed to take into account and the time at which it provides output depends the number of corruptions. The time-out divides the execution into two phases: an asynchronous and a synchronous phase.

- If there are up to t corruptions, parties are guaranteed to obtain an output at time $\tau_{\texttt{asynch}}$, which depends on δ. This fast output is identical to every party and is guaranteed to take into account at least $n - t$ inputs, i.e. can ignore the inputs from up to t honest parties.
- Otherwise, the parties are guaranteed to obtain the same output, but at a time which depends on Δ. More concretely, there are two latest points in time at which parties can obtain an output after the time-out occurs: $\tau_{\texttt{OD}} < \tau_{\texttt{OND}}$. Either all parties obtain the output by $\tau_{\texttt{OD}}$, which is guaranteed to take into account $n - t$ inputs, or all parties obtain output at a later time $\tau_{\texttt{OND}}$, which is guaranteed to take into account all inputs.

The adversary can in addition gain certain capabilities depending on the amount of corruption it performs. More technically, we introduce a tamper function Tamper, parametrized by a tuple of thresholds (t, T). This allows to naturally capture the different guarantees for the two corruption thresholds t and T. Basically, if the number of corruptions is greater than t, the adversary can prevent the parties to obtain fast outputs. And beyond T, no security guarantee is ensured, as the adversary learns the inputs from the honest parties and can choose the outputs as well.

Tamper Function. The ideal functionality is parameterized by a tamper function, which indicates the adversary's capabilities depending on the threshold. We consider two thresholds: T for full security, and t for responsiveness.

Definition 2. *We define the ideal functionality with parameters* (t, T) *if it has the following tamper function* $\mathsf{Tamper}^{\text{HYB}}_{t,T}$*:*

Function $\mathsf{Tamper}^{\text{HYB}}_{t,T}$

// Flags indicating violation of c correctness, p privacy, r responsiveness
$(c, p, r) = \mathsf{Tamper}^{\text{HYB}}_{t,T}$, *where:*
- $c = 1$, $p = 1$ *if and only if* $|\mathcal{P} \setminus \mathcal{H}| > T$.
- $r = 1$ *if and only if* $|\mathcal{P} \setminus \mathcal{H}| > t$

The ideal functionality has in addition a set of parameters. It contains a parameter $\tau_{\texttt{asynch}}$ which models the maximum output delay in the asynchronous phase, and parameters $\tau_{\texttt{OD}}$ and $\tau_{\texttt{OND}}$ which model the output delays for an output that takes into account $n-t$ inputs, or an output with all the inputs. One can think of $\tau_{\texttt{asynch}} = O(\delta)$, and $\tau_{\texttt{OD}} < \tau_{\texttt{OND}}$ are times which depend on Δ.

In addition, it keeps the following local variables:

- `FastOutput` indicates if the output contains $n-t$ inputs or all inputs.
- τ keeps the current time.
- $\tau_{\texttt{tout}}$ is the pre-defined time-out to switch between the two phases.
- `sync` indicates the phase being executed (asynchronous or synchronous).
- x_i, y_i the input and output for party P_i.
- w_i indicates if the adversary decided to not deliver output y_i in the asynchronous phase. The adversary can only use this capability if the number of corruptions is larger than t.
- $\mathcal{I}$ keeps the set of parties whose input are taken into account for the fast output.

Functionality $\mathcal{F}_{\text{HYB}}^{\text{fs}}$

The functionality is connected to a global clock $\mathcal{G}_{\text{CLK}}$.
The functionality is parametrized by δ, $\tau_{\texttt{asynch}}$, $\tau_{\texttt{OD}}$, $\tau_{\texttt{OND}}$, Tamper, $\tau_{\texttt{tout}}$ and the function to evaluate f.
The functionality stores variables `FastOutput`, τ, `sync`, x_i, y_i, w_i. These variables are initialized as `FastOutput` = `false`, $\tau = 0$, `sync` = `false`, $x_i = \bot$, and $y_i = w_i = \bot$.
It keeps $\mathcal{I} = \mathcal{H}$, where $\mathcal{H}$ is the set of honest parties, and a set $\mathcal{C} = \emptyset$.

Timeout/Clock :

Each time the functionality is activated, query $\mathcal{G}_{\text{CLK}}$ for the current time and update τ accordingly.
If $\tau \geq \tau_{\texttt{tout}}$, set `sync` = `true`. If `FastOutput` = `false`, compute $y_1 = \cdots = y_n = f(x_1, \ldots, x_n)$.

Asynchronous Phase If `sync` = `false` do the following:

At the onset of the execution, output δ and $\tau_{\texttt{asynch}}$ to the adversary.

- On input (INPUT, v_i, sid) from party P_i:
  - If some party has received output, ignore this message. Otherwise, set $x_i = v_i$.
  - If $x_i \neq \bot$ for each $P_i \in \mathcal{I}$, set each output to $y_j = f(x'_1, \ldots, x'_n)$, where $x'_i = x_i$ for each $P_i \in \mathcal{I} \cup (\mathcal{P} \setminus \mathcal{H})$ and $x'_i = \bot$ otherwise.
  - Output (INPUT, P_i, sid) to the adversary.
- On input (GETOUTPUT, sid) from P_i do the following:
  - If the output has not been set yet or is blocked, i.e., $y_i = \bot$ or w_i = `aBlocked`, ignore this message.
  - If $\tau \geq \tau_{\texttt{asynch}}$ output (OUTPUT, y_i, sid) to P_i and set `FastOutput` = `true`.
  - Otherwise, output (OUTPUT, P_i, sid) to the adversary.

Synchronous Phase If `sync` = `true` do the following:

- On input (GETOUTPUT, sid) from party P_i
  - If $\texttt{FastOutput} = \texttt{true}$ and $\tau \geq \tau_{\text{tout}} + \tau_{\text{OD}}$, it outputs (OUTPUT, y_i, sid) to P_i.
  - If $\texttt{FastOutput} = \texttt{false}$ and $\tau \geq \tau_{\text{tout}} + \tau_{\text{OND}}$, it outputs (OUTPUT, y_i, sid) to P_i.

Adversary

Upon each party corruption, update $(c, p, r) = \mathsf{Tamper}^{\text{HYB}}_{t,T}$.

// Core Set and Delivery of Outputs

1: Upon receiving a message (NO-INPUT, $\mathcal{P}'$, sid) from the adversary, if $\texttt{sync} = \texttt{false}$, $\mathcal{P}'$ is a subset of $\mathcal{P}$ of size $|\mathcal{P}'| \leq t_r$ and $y_1 = \cdots = y_n = \bot$, set $\mathcal{I} = \mathcal{H} \setminus \mathcal{P}'$.

2: On input (DELIVEROUTPUT, i, sid) from the adversary, if $y_i \neq \bot$ and $\texttt{sync} = \texttt{false}$, output (OUTPUT, y_i, sid) to P_i and set $\texttt{FastOutput} = \texttt{true}$.

// Adversary's capabilities

3: On input (TAMPEROUTPUT, P_i, y_i', sid) from the adversary, if $c = 1$, set $y_i = y_i'$.

4: If $p = 1$, output $(x_1, \ldots, x_n)$ to the adversary.

5: On input (BLOCKASYNCHOUTPUT, P_i, sid) from the adversary, if $r = 1$ and $\texttt{sync} = \texttt{false}$, set $w_i = \texttt{aBlocked}$.

In the version where $\mathcal{F}^{\text{ua}}_{\text{HYB}}$ provides security with unanimous abort and no fairness, the adversary can in addition choose to set the output to $\bot$ for all honest parties and learn the output $y_{\texttt{sync}}$, in the case $\texttt{FastOutput} = \texttt{false}$.

4 Compiler

In this section, we present a protocol which realizes the ideal functionality presented in the previous section. The protocol works with a setup $\mathcal{F}_{\text{SETUP}}$, where parties have access to a public-key infrastructure used to sign values, and keys for a threshold encryption scheme.

The protocol uses a number of sub-protocols:

- $\Pi_{\texttt{ZK}}$ is a bilateral zero-knowledge protocol which allows a party to prove knowledge of a witness corresponding to a statement.
- $\Pi_{\texttt{aMPC}}$ is an asynchronous MPC protocol that provides full security up to t corruptions, and security without termination (correctness and privacy) up to $T \geq t$ corruptions.
- $\Pi^{\texttt{fs}}_{\texttt{sMPC}}$ (resp. $\Pi^{\texttt{ua}}_{\texttt{sMPC}}$) is a synchronous MPC protocol with full security (resp. security with unanimous abort) up to T corruptions.
- $\Pi_{\texttt{sBC}}$ is a synchronous broadcast protocol secure up to T corruptions.

4.1 Key-Distribution Setup

The compiler works with a key distribution setup. The setup can be computed once for multiple instances of the protocol, without knowing the parties' inputs nor the function to evaluate.

As usual, we describe our compiler in a hybrid model where parties have access to an ideal functionality $\mathcal{F}_{\text{SETUP}}$. At a very high level, $\mathcal{F}_{\text{SETUP}}$ allows to distribute the keys for a threshold encryption scheme and a digital signature scheme. The threshold encryption scheme here does not need to be homomorphic. More concretely, it provides to each party P_i a global public key $\mathtt{ek}$ and a private key share $\mathtt{dk}_i$. Moreover, it gives a PKI infrastructure. That is, it gives to each party P_i a signing key $\mathtt{sk}_i$ and the verification keys of all parties $(\mathtt{vk}_1, \ldots, \mathtt{vk}_n)$.

We describe the two setups, PKI setup $\mathcal{F}_{\text{PKI}}$ and threshold encryption setup $\mathcal{F}_{\text{TE}}$ independently. The setup of the protocol consists of includes both functionalities $\mathcal{F}_{\text{SETUP}} = [\mathcal{F}_{\text{PKI}}, \mathcal{F}_{\text{TE}}]$.

Digital Signature Setup. The protocol assumes a signature setup. That is, each party P_i has a pair secret key and verification key $(\mathtt{sk}_i, \mathtt{vk}_i)$, where $\mathtt{vk}_i$ is known to all parties.

Threshold Encryption Setup. The protocol assumes also a threshold encryption setup, which allows each party to access a global public key $\mathtt{ek}$ and a private key share $\mathtt{dk}_i$.

4.2 Zero-Knowledge

The protocol Π_{ZK} is a bilateral zero-knowledge protocol which allows a party to prove knowledge of a witness corresponding to a statement. The protocol must be UC-secure, meaning that it has to UC-realize the $\mathcal{F}_{\text{ZK}}$ functionality, described in the full version for completeness. As shown in [21], such a protocol exists in the $\mathcal{F}_{\text{CRS}}$-hybrid model for any relation. For this protocol, we need *proofs of correct decryption*, where the relation is parametrized by a threshold encryption scheme. The statement consists of $\mathtt{ek}$, a ciphertext c, and a decryption share d. The witness is a decryption key share $\mathtt{dk}_i$ such that $d = \mathtt{Dec}_{\mathtt{dk}_i}(c)$.

4.3 Synchronous MPC

Classical synchronous MPC protocols [2,5,13,20,27,45], for $\Pi^{\mathtt{fs}}_{\mathtt{sMPC}}$ can be proven to UC-realize an ideal MPC functionality $\mathcal{F}^{\mathtt{fs}}_{\text{SYNC}}$ (described in the full version for completeness) up to $T < n/2$ corruptions, which allows a set of n parties to evaluate a specific function f. For the case of unanimous abort, where the adversary is allowed to set the output $\bot$, one can instantiate $\Pi^{\mathtt{ua}}_{\mathtt{sMPC}}$ for any $T < n$ [23,29].

4.4 Synchronous Byzantine Broadcast

A Byzantine broadcast primitive allows a party P_s, called the sender, to consistently distribute a message among a set of parties $\mathcal{P}$.

Definition 3. *Let Π be a protocol executed by parties $P_1, \ldots, P_n$, where a designated sender P_s initially holds an input v, and parties terminate upon generating output. Π is a T-secure broadcast protocol if the following conditions hold up to T corruptions:*

- *Validity: If the sender P_s is honest, every honest party outputs the sender's message v.*
- *Consistency: All honest parties output the same message.*

The classical result of Dolev-Strong [22] shows that synchronous broadcast protocol $\Pi_{\mathtt{sBC}}$ can be achieved for any $T < n$, assuming a public-key infrastructure. The protocol UC-realizes the synchronous broadcast functionality $\mathcal{F}_{\mathtt{sBC}}$ (which is a synchronous MPC functionality, where the output is the sender's input) for our setting with static corruptions [26,36].

4.5 Asynchronous MPC

In this section we formally define what it means for a protocol $\Pi_{\mathtt{aMPC}}$ to achieve full security up to t corruptions and security without termination (correctness and privacy) up to $T \geq t$ corruptions. In Sect. 5.2 we show how to achieve such a protocol.

In a nutshell, the idea is that the protocol realizes an ideal MPC functionality which is parametrized with the two thresholds (t, T). If the adversary corrupts up to t parties, all honest parties obtain all the security guarantees as a conventional asynchronous MPC functionality. If the adversary corrupts $t \leq f \leq T$ parties, it is allowed to block any party from obtaining output; however, those parties that obtain output, are ensured to obtain the correct output, and privacy is still guaranteed. Finally, if the adversary corrupts $f > T$ parties, no guarantees remain: the adversary learns the inputs from all honest parties and can choose the outputs to be anything.

To model formally an asynchronous MPC functionality, we borrow ideas from [19,36]. In traditional asynchronous protocols, the parties are guaranteed to *eventually* receive output, meaning that the adversary can delay the output of honest parties in an arbitrary but finite manner. The reason for this is that the assumed network guarantees eventual delivery. One can make the simple observation that if the network has an unknown upper bound δ, then the adversary can delay the outputs of honest parties up to time $\tau_{\mathtt{asynch}} = \tau(\delta)$, which is a function of δ. The guarantee obtained in an asynchronous MPC with eventual delivery (e.g. as in [19]) is a special case of our functionality, namely when $\tau_{\mathtt{asynch}} = \infty$. We describe it for the case where $\tau_{\mathtt{asynch}}$ is a fixed time, but one can model $\tau_{\mathtt{asynch}}$ to be probabilistic as well.

It is known that asynchronous protocols cannot achieve simultaneously fast termination (at a time which depends on δ) and input completeness. This is because δ is unknown and hence it is impossible to distinguish between an honest slow party and an actively corrupted party. If fast termination must be ensured even when up to t parties are corrupted, the parties can only wait for $n - t$ inputs. Since the adversary is able to schedule the delivery of messages from honest parties, it can also typically choose exactly a set of parties $\mathcal{P}' \subseteq \mathcal{P}$, $|\mathcal{P}'| \leq t$, whose input is not considered. Therefore, the ideal functionality also allows the simulator to choose this set. As in [19], and similar to the network functionality $\mathcal{F}^{\delta}_{\text{NET}}$, we use a "fetch-based" mode functionality and allow the simulator to specify a delay on the delivery to every party.

Functionality $\mathcal{F}_{\text{ASYNC}}$

$\mathcal{F}_{\text{ASYNC}}$ is connected to a global clock functionality $\mathcal{G}_{\text{CLK}}$. It is parameterized by a set $\mathcal{P}$ of n parties, a function f, a tamper function $\mathsf{Tamper}_{t,T}$, a delay δ, and a maximum delay $\tau_{\texttt{asynch}}$. It initializes the variables $x_i = y_i = \bot$, $\tau_{\texttt{in}} = \bot$ and $\tau_i = 0$ for each party $P_i \in \mathcal{P}$ and the variable $\mathcal{I} = \mathcal{H}$, where $\mathcal{H}$ is the set of honest parties.
Upon receiving input from any party or the adversary, it queries $\mathcal{F}_{\text{CLOCK}}$ for the current time and updates τ accordingly.

Party P_i:

1: On input (INPUT, v_i, sid) from party P_i:
 – If some party has received output, ignore this message. Otherwise, set $x_i = v_i$.
 – If $x_i \neq \bot$ for each $P_i \in \mathcal{I}$, set each output to $y_j = f(x'_1, \ldots, x'_n)$, where $x'_i = x_i$ for each $P_i \in \mathcal{I} \cup (\mathcal{P} \setminus \mathcal{H})$ and $x'_i = \bot$ otherwise. Set $\tau_{\texttt{in}} = \tau$.
 – Output (INPUT, P_i, sid) to the adversary.
2: On input (GETOUTPUT, sid) from P_i, if the output is not set or is blocked, i.e., $y_i \in \{\bot, \top\}$, ignore the message. Otherwise, if the current time is larger than the time set by the adversary, $\tau \geq \tau_i$, output (OUTPUT, y_i, sid) to P_i.

Adversary:

1: Upon receiving a message (NO-INPUT, $\mathcal{P}'$, sid) from the adversary, if $\mathcal{P}'$ is a subset of $\mathcal{P}$ of size $|\mathcal{P}'| \leq t$ and $y_1 = \cdots = y_n = \bot$, set $\mathcal{I} = \mathcal{H} \setminus \mathcal{P}'$.
2: On input (SETOUTPUTTIME, P_i, τ', sid) from the adversary, if $\tau_{\texttt{in}} \neq \bot$ and $\tau' < \tau_{\texttt{in}} + \tau_{\texttt{asynch}}$, set $\tau_i = \tau'$.

Upon each party corruption, update $(c, p, l) = \mathsf{Tamper}^{\text{ASYNCH}}_{t,T}$.

1: On input (TAMPEROUTPUT, P_i, y'_i, sid) from the adversary, if $c = 1$, set $y_i = y'_i$.
2: If $p = 1$, output $(x_1, \ldots, x_n)$ to the adversary.
3: On input (BLOCKOUTPUT, P_i, sid) from the adversary, if $l = 1$, set $y_i = \top$.

Similar to $\mathcal{F}_{\text{HYB}}$, we parametrize the functionality by a tamper function to capture the guarantees depending on the set of corrupted parties. The $\mathcal{F}_{\text{ASYNC}}$ functionality has the tamper function $\mathsf{Tamper}^{\text{ASYNCH}}_{t,T}$, where the adversary can tamper with the output value and learn the inputs if the number of corruptions is larger than T, and is allowed to block the delivery of the outputs if the number of corruptions is larger than t.

Definition 4. *We define an asynchronous MPC functionality with full security t and security without termination T, if it has the tamper function* $\mathsf{Tamper}^{\text{ASYNCH}}_{t,T}$:

Function $\mathsf{Tamper}_{t,T}^{\text{ASYNCH}}$

$(c, p, l) = \mathsf{Tamper}_{t,T}^{\text{ASYNCH}}$, *where:*
- $c = 1$, $p = 1$ *if and only if* $|\mathcal{P} \setminus \mathcal{H}| > T$.
- $l = 1$ *if and only if* $|\mathcal{P} \setminus \mathcal{H}| > t$.

4.6 Protocol Compiler

The protocol has two phases: an asynchronous phase and a synchronous phase, separated by a pre-defined timeout. The timeout is set large enough (using Δ and the number of asynchronous rounds) so that the asynchronous phase should have supposedly terminated if there were not too many corruptions.

During the asynchronous phase, parties may obtain an output $y_{\mathtt{asynch}}$. We need to ensure (1) that if an honest party obtains an output $y_{\mathtt{asynch}}$ during the asynchronous phase, then every other honest party obtains this output as well; and (2) that the adversary does not learn two outputs. We remark that even if the function to evaluate is the same, the output obtained from the synchronous MPC protocol $\Pi_{\mathtt{sMPC}}$ is not necessarily $y_{\mathtt{asynch}}$. This is because in an asynchronous protocol $\Pi_{\mathtt{aMPC}}$, up to t inputs from honest parties can be ignored. This is the reason why we require that $\Pi_{\mathtt{aMPC}}$ evaluates the function $f' = \mathtt{Enc}_{\mathtt{ek}}(f)$. During the synchronous phase, parties agree on whether they execute the synchronous protocol $\Pi_{\mathtt{sMPC}}$. The parties will invoke $\Pi_{\mathtt{sMPC}}$ only if it is guaranteed that the adversary did not obtain $y_{\mathtt{asynch}}$. Also, if the parties do not invoke $\Pi_{\mathtt{sMPC}}$, it is guaranteed that they can jointly decrypt the output $y_{\mathtt{asynch}}$.

Asynchronous Phase. In this phase, parties optimistically execute $\Pi_{\mathtt{aMPC}}$. When a party P_i obtains as output a ciphertext $c = [y]$ from $\Pi_{\mathtt{aMPC}}$, it sends a signature of c and collects a list L of $n-t$ signatures on the same c. Once such list L is collected, it runs a robust threshold decryption protocol. For that, P_i computes a decryption share $d_i = \mathtt{Dec}_{\mathtt{dk}_i}(c)$, and proves using $\Pi_{\mathtt{ZK}}$ to each P_j that d_i is a correct decryption share of c. Upon receiving d_i and a correct proof of decryption share for c from $n-t$ parties, compute and output $y_i = \mathtt{Rec}(\{d_j\})$.

Synchronous Phase. After the timeout, parties execute a synchronous broadcast protocol to send a pair list-ciphertext (c, L), where L contains at least $n-t$ signatures on c, if such a list was collected during the asynchronous phase. If a party receives via broadcast any valid L, then it sends its decryption share d_i and runs the same robust threshold decryption protocol as above. Otherwise, parties execute the synchronous MPC $\Pi_{\mathtt{sMPC}}$.

Observe that if an honest party collects a list L of $n - t$ signatures on a ciphertext $[y]$ during the asynchronous phase, it broadcasts the pair $([y], L)$ during the synchronous phase. Then, every honest party obtains at least a valid pair $([y], L)$ after the broadcast round finishes. By a standard quorum argument, if there are up to $T < n-2t$ corruptions, there cannot be two signature lists of size $n - t$ on different values. Given that honest parties only sign the correct output ciphertext $[y_{\mathtt{asynch}}]$ from $\Pi_{\mathtt{aMPC}}$, this is the only value that can gather a list of signatures. Hence, all parties are instructed to run the robust threshold decryption protocol, and if there are up to t corruptions, every honest party is guaranteed to receive enough decryption shares to obtain the output $y_{\mathtt{asynch}}$. On the other hand, if no honest party obtained such a pair during the asynchronous phase, it is guaranteed that the adversary did not learn $y_{\mathtt{asynch}}$, since no honest party sent its decryption share. However, it might be that the adversary collected a valid $([y_{\mathtt{asynch}}], L')$. The adversary can then decide whether to broadcast a valid pair. If it does, every party will hold this pair and everyone outputs $y_{\mathtt{asynch}}$ as before. And if it does not, no honest party holds a valid pair after the broadcast round, and every party can safely run the synchronous MPC protocol $\Pi_{\mathtt{sMPC}}$.

We remark that it is not enough that upon the timeout parties simply *send* $([y], L)$, because the parties need to have agreement on whether or not to invoke $\Pi_{\mathtt{sMPC}}$. It can happen that the adversary is the only one who collected $([y], L)$.

Protocol $\Pi^{\Delta}_{\mathrm{hyb}}(P_i)$

The party stores the current time τ, a flag $\mathtt{sync} = \mathtt{false}$ and a variable $\tau_{\mathtt{sync}} = \bot$. Let $\tau_{\mathtt{tout}} = T_{\mathtt{asynch}}(\Delta) + T_{\mathtt{zk}}(\Delta) + \Delta$ be a known upper bound on the time to execute the asynchronous phase, composed of protocols $\Pi_{\mathtt{aMPC}}$, $\Pi_{\mathtt{ZK}}$ and a network transmission message. Also, let $T_{zk}(\Delta)$ denote an upper bound on the time to execute $\Pi_{\mathtt{ZK}}$.

Clock / Timeout Each time the party is activated do the following:

1: Query $\mathcal{G}_{\mathrm{CLK}}$ for the current time and updates τ accordingly.
2: If $\tau \geq \tau_{\mathtt{tout}}$, set $\mathtt{sync} = \mathtt{true}$ and $\tau_{\mathtt{sync}} = \tau$.

Setup:

1: If activated for the first time input (GETKEYS, sid) to $\mathcal{F}_{\mathrm{SETUP}}$. We denote the public key $\mathtt{ek}$, a $(n-t, n)$-share $\mathtt{dk}_i$ of the corresponding secret key $\mathtt{dk}$, the signing key $\mathtt{sk}$ and the verification key $\mathtt{vk}$.

Asynchronous Phase: If $\mathtt{sync} = \mathtt{false}$ handle the following commands.

- On input (INPUT, x_i, sid) (and following activations) do
  1: Execute $\Pi_{\mathtt{aMPC}}$ with input x_i and wait until an output c is received.
  2: Send $(c, \mathsf{Sign}(c, \mathtt{sk}))$ to every other party using $\mathcal{F}_{\mathrm{NET}}$.
  3: Receive signatures and values via $\mathcal{F}_{\mathrm{NET}}$ until you received $n-t$ signatures $L = (\sigma_1, \ldots, \sigma_l)$ on a value c.
  4: Send (c, L) to every party using $\mathcal{F}_{\mathrm{NET}}$.
  5: Receive message lists (c, L'). For each such list send (c, L') to every party using $\mathcal{F}_{\mathrm{NET}}$.
  6: Once done with the above, compute $d_i = \mathtt{Dec}_{\mathtt{dk}_i}(c)$, and prove, using $\mathcal{F}_{\mathrm{ZK}}$, to each P_j, that d_i is a correct decryption share of c.
  7: Upon receiving $n-t$ correct decryption shares for c, compute and output $y = \mathtt{Rec}(\{d_j\})$.
- At every clock tick, if it is not possible to progress with the list above, send (CLOCKREADY) to $\mathcal{G}_{\mathrm{CLK}}$.

Synchronous Phase: If $\mathtt{sync} = \mathtt{true}$ and $\tau \geq \tau_{\mathsf{sync}}$, stop all previous steps and do the following commands.

- On input (ClockReady) do:
  1: Send (ClockReady) to $\mathcal{G}_{\text{CLK}}$.
  2: **if** $\tau \geq \tau_{\mathsf{sync}}$ **then**
  3: Use Π_{sBC} to broadcast (c, L), for each pair (c, L) received during the Asynchronous Phase.
  4: Wait until Π_{sBC} terminated. If a pair (c, L) was received as output, compute $d_i = \mathtt{Dec}_{\mathtt{dk}_i}(c)$, and prove, using $\mathcal{F}_{\text{ZK}}$, to each P_j, that d_i is a correct decryption share of c. Otherwise, if no pair (c, L) was received, run the synchronous MPC protocol $\Pi^{\mathtt{fs}}_{\mathtt{sMPC}}$ with input x_i.
  5: **end if**
- If there was an output (c', L') from Π_{sBC}, wait for $T_{zk}(\Delta)$ clock ticks. After that, if $n - t$ correct decryption shares d_j are received from $\mathcal{F}_{\text{NET}}$, compute and reconstruct the value $y = \mathtt{Rec}(\{d_j\})$ from c, and output y. Otherwise, if there was no output (c, L') from Π_{sBC}, output the output received from $\Pi^{\mathtt{fs}}_{\mathtt{sMPC}}$.

Let $T_{zk}(\delta)$, $T_{\mathtt{sync}}(\Delta)$, $T_{\mathtt{BC}}(\Delta)$, $T_{\mathtt{asynch}}(\delta)$ be the corresponding time to execute the protocols $\Pi_{\mathtt{ZK}}$, $\Pi_{\mathtt{sMPC}}$, $\Pi_{\mathtt{sBC}}$ and $\Pi_{\mathtt{aMPC}}$, respectively. We state the following theorem, and the proof is formally described in the full version. The communication complexity is inherited from the corresponding sub-protocols.

Theorem 1. *Assuming PKI and CRS, for any $\Delta \geq \delta$, $\Pi^{\Delta}_{\mathtt{hyb}}$ realizes $\mathcal{F}^{\mathtt{fs}}_{\text{HYB}}$ with full security with responsiveness t and full security $\min\{T, n-2t\}$. The maximum delay of the asynchronous phase is $\tau_{\mathtt{asynch}} = T_{\mathtt{asynch}}(\delta) + T_{\mathtt{zk}}(\delta) + \delta$, and of the synchronous phase is $\tau_{\mathtt{OD}} = T_{\mathtt{BC}}(\Delta) + T_{\mathtt{zk}}(\Delta)$ for a fast output with $n - t$ inputs, and otherwise is $\tau_{\mathtt{OND}} = T_{\mathtt{BC}}(\Delta) + T_{\mathtt{sync}}(\Delta)$ for an output with all the inputs.*

By replacing the invocation of $\Pi^{\mathtt{fs}}_{\mathtt{sMPC}}$ to $\Pi^{\mathtt{ua}}_{\mathtt{sMPC}}$, one realizes $\mathcal{F}^{\mathtt{ua}}_{\text{HYB}}$ for the same parameters. Let $\Pi^{\Delta}_{\mathtt{hyb\text{-}ua}}$ denote the same protocol as $\Pi^{\Delta}_{\mathtt{hyb}}$, except that the invocation of $\Pi^{\mathtt{fs}}_{\mathtt{sMPC}}$ is replaced by $\Pi^{\mathtt{ua}}_{\mathtt{sMPC}}$.

Theorem 2. *Assuming PKI and CRS, for any $\Delta \geq \delta$, $\Pi^{\Delta}_{\mathtt{hyb\text{-}ua}}$ realizes $\mathcal{F}^{\mathtt{ua}}_{\text{HYB}}$ with full security with responsiveness t and security with unanimous abort $\min\{T, n-2t\}$. The maximum delay of the asynchronous phase is $\tau_{\mathtt{asynch}} = T_{\mathtt{asynch}}(\delta) + T_{\mathtt{zk}}(\delta) + \delta$, and of the synchronous phase is $\tau_{\mathtt{OD}} = T_{\mathtt{BC}}(\Delta) + T_{\mathtt{zk}}(\Delta)$ for a fast output with $n-t$ inputs, and otherwise is $\tau_{\mathtt{OND}} = T_{\mathtt{BC}}(\Delta) + T_{\mathtt{sync}}(\Delta)$ for an output with all the inputs.*

5 Asynchronous Protocols

In this section, we show how to obtain $\Pi_{\mathtt{aMPC}}$ with full security with responsiveness up to t corruptions and security (correctness and privacy) up to T corruptions, for any $t < \frac{n}{3}$ and any $T < n - 2t$.

Technical Remark. In our model, parties have access to a synchronized clock. The asynchronous protocols do not read the clock, but in our model they need to specify at which point the parties send a (ClockReady) message to $\mathcal{G}_{\text{CLK}}$, so that the clock advances. Observe that we do not model time within a single asynchronous round (between fetching and sending messages), or computation time. Hence, in an asynchronous protocol, at every activation, each party P_i *fetches* the messages from the assumed functionalities, and then checks whether it has any message available that it can send. If so, it sends the corresponding message. Otherwise, it sends a (ClockReady) message to $\mathcal{G}_{\text{CLK}}$.

5.1 Asynchronous Byzantine Agreement

The goal of Byzantine agreement is to allow a set of parties to agree on a common value.

Definition 5. *Let Π be a protocol executed by parties $P_1, \ldots, P_n$, where each party P_i initially holds an input v_i and parties terminate upon generating output.*

- *Validity: Π is t-valid if the following holds whenever up to t parties are corrupted: if every honest party has the same input value v, then every honest party that outputs, outputs v.*
- *Consistency: Π is t-consistent if the following holds whenever up to t parties are corrupted: every honest party which outputs, outputs the same value.*
- *Liveness: Π is t-live if the following holds whenever up to t parties are corrupted: every honest party outputs a value.*

The first step is to obtain an asynchronous Byzantine Agreement protocol Π_{aBA} with higher consistency threshold. In the full version, we formally prove security of such a protocol Π_{aBA} in the UC framework for any validity t_v, consistency t_c and termination t_l, such that $t_l \le t_v < \frac{n}{3}$ and $t_c + 2t_l < n$.

The general idea is to trade termination by consistency, while keeping validity. The protocol is quite simple. First, each party P_i runs with input x_i a regular Byzantine agreement protocol secure up to a single threshold $t' = t_v < n/3$. Once an output x is obtained from the BA, it computes a signature $\sigma = \mathsf{Sign}(x, \mathsf{sk})$ and sends it to every other party. Once $n - t_l$ signatures on a value x' are collected, the party sends the list containing the signatures along with the value x' to every other party, and terminates with output x'. Since there cannot be two lists of $n - t_l$ signatures on different values if there are up to $t_c < n - 2t_l$ corruptions, this prevents parties to output different values if there are up to $t_c < n - 2t_l$ corruptions. On the other hand, termination is reduced to t_l. One can also verify that validity is inherited from the regular BA protocol: if every honest party starts with input x, no honest party signs any other value $x' \neq x$, and hence there cannot be a list of $n - t_l$ signatures on x', given that $t_l \le t_v$.

Lemma 1. *There is a Byzantine agreement protocol Π_{aBA} with validity, consistency and termination parameters (t_v, t_c, t_l), for any $t_l < \frac{n}{3}$, $t_l \le t_v < \frac{n}{3}$ and $t_c < n - 2t_l$, assuming a PKI infrastructure setup $\mathcal{F}_{\text{PKI}}$. The expected maximum delay for the output is $\tau_{aba} = O(\delta)$.*

5.2 Two-Threshold Asynchronous MPC

In order to realize $\mathcal{F}_{\text{ASYNC}}$ with full security up to t and security with no termination (correctness and privacy) up to T, where $t < \frac{n}{3}$ and $T + 2t < n$, we follow the ideas from [18, 32, 33], and replace the single-threshold asynchronous BA protocol for the one that we obtained in Sect. 5.1 with increased consistency $t_c < n - 2t_l$.

The protocol works with a threshold FHE setup, similar to [18], which we model with the functionality $\mathcal{F}_{\text{SETUP}}^{\text{FHE}}$, which is the same as $\mathcal{F}_{\text{SETUP}}$ from Sect. 4.1, except that the threshold encryption scheme is fully-homomorphic. For completeness, we review the definition in the full version.

The protocol uses in addition a number of sub-protocols:

- $\Pi_{\mathtt{aBA}}$ is a Byzantine agreement protocol with liveness threshold $t_l = t < n/3$, validity $t \le t_v < n/3$ and consistency $t_c = T < n - 2t$.
- $\Pi_{\mathtt{ZK}}$ is a bilateral zero-knowledge protocol, similar to the one in Sect. 4.

Very roughly, the protocol asks each party P_i to encrypt its input x_i and distribute it to all parties. Then, parties homomorphically evaluate the function over the encrypted inputs to obtain an encrypted output, and jointly decrypt the output. Of course, the protocol does not work like that. In order to achieve robustness, we need that every party proves in zero-knowledge the correctness of essentially every value provided during the protocol execution.

We are interested in zero-knowledge proofs for two relations, parametrized by a threshold encryption scheme with public encryption key $\mathtt{ek}$:

1. *Proof of Plaintext Knowledge:* The statement consists of $\mathtt{ek}$, and a ciphertext c. The witness consists of a plaintext m and randomness r such that $c = \mathtt{Enc}_{\mathtt{ek}}(m; r)$.
2. *Proof of Correct Decryption:* The statement consists of $\mathtt{ek}$, a ciphertext c, and a decryption share d. The witness consists of a decryption key share $\mathtt{dk}_i$, such that $d = \mathtt{Dec}_{\mathtt{dk}_i}(c)$.

The protocol proceeds in three phases: the input stage, the computation and threshold-decryption stage, and the termination stage.

Input Stage. The goal of the input stage is to define an encrypted input for each party. In order to ensure that the inputs are independent, the parties are required to perform a proof of plaintext knowledge of their ciphertext. It is known that input completeness and guaranteed termination cannot be simultaneously achieved in asynchronous networks, since one cannot distinguish between an honest slow party and an actively corrupted party. Given that we only guarantee termination up to t corruptions, we can take into account $n - t$ input providers.

The input stage is as follows: each party P_i encrypts its input to obtain a ciphertext c_i. It then constructs a certificate π_i that P_i knows the plaintext of c_i and that c_i is the only input of P_i, using bilateral zero-knowledge proofs and signatures. It then sends (c_i, π_i) to every other party, and constructs a *certificate of distribution* $\mathtt{dist}_i$, which works as a non-interactive proof that (c_i, π_i) was distributed to at least $n - t$ parties. This certificate is sent to every party.

After P_i collects $n-t$ certificates of distribution, it knows that at least $n-t$ parties have proved knowledge of the plaintext of their input ciphertext and distributed the ciphertext correctly to $n-t$ parties. If the number of corruptions is smaller than $n-t$, this implies that each of the $n-t$ parties have proved knowledge of the plaintext of their input ciphertext and also have distributed the ciphertext to at least 1 honest party. At this point, if each party is instructed to echo the certified inputs they saw, then every honest party will end up holding the $n-t$ certified inputs. To determine who they are, the parties compute a common set of input providers. For that, n asynchronous Byzantine Agreement protocols are run, each one to decide whether a party's input will be taken into account. To ensure that the size of the common set is at least $n-t$, each party P_i inputs 1 to the BAs of those parties for which it saw a certified input. It then waits until there are $n-t$ ones from the BAs before inputting any 0.

Protocol $\Pi_{\mathsf{aMPC}}^{\mathsf{input}}(P_i)$

The protocol keeps sets S_i and D_i, initially empty. Let x_i be the input for P_i.

Setup:

1: If activated for the first time input $(\textsc{GetKeys}, \mathrm{sid})$ to $\mathcal{F}_{\mathrm{SETUP}}^{\mathrm{FHE}}$. We denote the public key $\mathtt{ek}$, a $(n-t,n)$-share $\mathtt{dk}_i$ of the corresponding secret key $\mathtt{dk}$, the signing key $\mathtt{sk}$ and the verification key $\mathtt{vk}$.

Plaintext Knowledge and Distribution:

1: Compute $c_i = \mathtt{Enc}_{\mathtt{ek}}(x_i)$.
2: Prove to each P_j knowledge of the plaintext of c_i, using Π_{ZK}.
3: Upon receiving a correct proof of plaintext knowledge for a ciphertext c_j from P_j, send $\sigma_i^{\mathtt{popk}} = \mathsf{Sign}_{\mathtt{sk}_i}(c_j)$ to P_j.
4: Upon receiving $n-t$ signatures $\{\sigma_j^{\mathtt{popk}}\}$, compute $\pi_i = \{\sigma_j^{\mathtt{popk}}\}$ and send (c_i, π_i) to all parties.
5: Upon receiving a message (c_j, π_j) from P_j, send $\sigma_i^{\mathtt{dist}} = \mathsf{Sign}_{\mathtt{sk}_i}((c_j, \pi_j))$ to P_j. Add $(j, (c_j, \pi_j))$ to S_i.
6: Upon receiving $n-t$ signatures $\{\sigma_j^{\mathtt{dist}}\}$, compute $\mathtt{dist}_i = \{\sigma_j^{\mathtt{dist}}\}$ and send $((c_i, \pi_i), \mathtt{dist}_i)$ to all parties.
7: Upon receiving $((c_j, \pi_j), \mathtt{dist}_j)$ from P_j, add j to D_i.

Select Input Providers: Once $|D_i| > n-t$, stop the above rules and proceed as follows:

1: Send S_i to every party.
2: Once $n-t$ sets $\{S_j\}$ are collected, let $R = \bigcup_j S_j$ and enter n asynchronous Byzantine agreement protocols Π_{aBA} with inputs $v_1, \ldots, v_n \in \{0,1\}$, where $v_j = 1$ if $\exists (j, (c_j, \pi_j)) \in R$. Keep adding possibly new received sets to R.
3: Wait until there are at least $n-t$ outputs which are one. Then, input 0 for the BAs which do not have input yet.
4: Let $w_1, \ldots, w_n$ be the outputs of the BAs.
5: Let $\mathtt{CoreSet} := \{j | w_j = 1\}$.
6: For each $j \in \mathtt{CoreSet}$ with $(j, (c_j, \pi_j)) \in R$, send $(j, (c_j, \pi_j))$ to all parties. Wait until each tuple $(j, (c_j, \pi_j)), j \in \mathtt{CoreSet}$ is received.

Computation and Threshold-Decryption Stage. After input stage, parties have agreed on a common subset $\mathtt{CoreSet}$ of size at least $n-t$ parties, and each party holds the $n-t$ ciphertexts corresponding to the encryption of the input from each party in $\mathtt{CoreSet}$. In the computation stage, the parties homomorphically evaluate the function, resulting on the ciphertext c encrypting the output. In the threshold-decryption stage, each party P_i computes the decryption share $d_i = \mathtt{Dec}_{\mathtt{dk}_i}(c)$, and proves in zero-knowledge simultaneously towards all parties that the decryption share is correct. Once $n-t$ correct decryption shares on the same ciphertext are collected, P_i reconstructs the output y_i.

Protocol $\Pi^{\mathtt{comp}}_{\mathsf{aMPC}}(P_i)$

Start once $\Pi^{\mathtt{input}}_{\mathsf{aMPC}}(P_i)$ is completed. Let $\mathtt{CoreSet}$ be the resulting set of at least $n-t$ parties, and let the input ciphertexts be c_j, for each $j \in \mathtt{CoreSet}$.

Function Evaluation:

1: For each $j \notin \mathtt{CoreSet}$, assume a default valid ciphertext c_j for P_j.
2: Locally compute the homomorphic evaluation of the function $c = f_{\mathtt{ek}}(c_1, \ldots, c_n)$.

Threshold Decryption:

1: Compute a decryption share $d_i = \mathtt{Dec}_{\mathtt{dk}_i}(c)$.
2: Prove, using Π_{ZK}, to each P_j that d_i is a correct decryption share of c.
3: Upon receiving a correct proof of decryption share for a ciphertext c' and decryption share d_j from P_j, send $\sigma_i^{\mathtt{pocs}} = \mathsf{Sign}_{\mathtt{sk}_i}((d_j, c'))$ to P_j.
4: Upon receiving $n-t$ signatures $\{\sigma_j^{\mathtt{pocs}}\}$ on the same pair (d_i, c'), compute $\mathtt{ProofShare}_i = \{\sigma_j^{\mathtt{pocs}}\}$ and send $((d_i, c'), \mathtt{ProofShare}_i)$ to all parties.
5: Upon receiving $n-t$ valid pairs $((d_j, c'), \mathtt{ProofShare}_j)$ for the same c', compute the output $y_i = \mathtt{Rec}(\{d_j\})$.

Termination Stage. The termination stage ensures that all honest parties terminate with the same output. This stage is essentially a Bracha broadcast [10] of the output value. The idea is that each party P_i votes for one output y_i and continuously collects outputs votes. More concretely, P_i sends y_i to every other party. If P_i receives $n-2t$ votes on the same value y, it knows that y is the correct output (because at least an honest party obtained the value y as output if the security threshold $T < n-2t$ is satisfied). Hence, if no output was computed yet, it sets $y_i = y$ as its output and sends y_i to every other party. Observe that if the security threshold is not satisfied, the adversary can tamper the outputs, but so can the simulator. Once $n-t$ votes on the same value y are collected, terminate with output y. If a party receives $n-t$ votes on y, and termination should be guaranteed ($f \leq t$), there are $n-2t$ honest parties that voted for y, and hence every honest party which did not output will at some point collect $n-2t$ votes on y, and hence will also vote for y. Since each honest party which terminated voted for y and each honest party which did not terminated voted for y as well, this means that all honest parties which did not terminate will receive $n-t$ votes for y.

Protocol $\Pi^{\mathtt{term}}_{\mathtt{aMPC}}(P_i)$

During the overall protocol, execute this protocol concurrently.

Waiting for Output:

1: Wait until the output c is computed from $\Pi^{\mathtt{comp}}_{\mathtt{aMPC}}(P_i)$.

Adopt Output:

1: Wait until receiving $n-2t$ votes for the same value y.
2: Adopt y as output, and send y to every other party.

Termination:

1: Wait until receiving $n-t$ votes for the same value y.
2: Terminate.

Let us denote $\Pi_{\mathtt{aMPC}}$ the protocol that executes concurrently the protocols $\Pi^{\mathtt{input}}_{\mathtt{aMPC}}$, $\Pi^{\mathtt{comp}}_{\mathtt{aMPC}}$ and $\Pi^{\mathtt{term}}_{\mathtt{aMPC}}$. Each party, at every activation, tries to progress with any of the subprotocols. If they cannot, they output (ClockReady) to $\mathcal{G}_{\text{CLK}}$ so that the clock advances. In full version we prove the following theorem.

Theorem 3. *The protocol $\Pi_{\mathtt{aMPC}}$ uses $\mathcal{F}^{\text{FHE}}_{\text{SETUP}}$ as setup and realizes $\mathcal{F}_{\text{ASYNC}}$ on any function f on the inputs, with full security up to t corruptions and security without termination up to T, for any $t < n/3$ and $T+2t < n$. The total maximum delay for the honest parties to obtain output is $\tau_{\mathtt{asynch}} = \tau_{\mathtt{aba}}(\delta) + 2\tau_{\mathtt{zk}}(\delta) + 9\delta$.*

6 Impossibility Results

In this section we argue that the obtained trade-offs are optimal. We prove that any MPC protocol that achieves full security with responsiveness up to t corruptions, and extended security with unanimous abort up to T corruptions needs to satisfy $T + 2t < n$. Since full security is stronger than security with unanimous abort, these bounds also hold for the case where the extended security is full security.

Lemma 2. *Let t, T be such that $T + 2t \geq n$. There is no MPC protocol Π that achieves full security with responsiveness up to t corruptions, and extended security with unanimous abort up to $T \geq t$ corruptions.*

Proof. Let δ be the unknown delay upper bound. Moreover, let $\delta' \ll \delta$ be such that the time to execute Π when messages are scheduled within δ' is $\tau(\delta') < \delta$.

Assume without loss of generality that $3t = n$. We prove impossibility for the case where the function to be computed is the majority function. Consider three sets S_0, S_1 and S, where $|S_0| = |S_1| = t$ and $|S| = T$.

First, consider an execution where parties in S_0 and S are honest and have input 0, and parties in S_1 are corrupted and crash. Moreover, the adversary *instantly* delivers the messages between S_0 and S (within δ'). Since full security with responsiveness is guaranteed, parties in S_0 output 0 at time $\tau(\delta')$. Similarly, in an execution where parties in S_1 and S are honest and have input 1, the parties in S_1 output at time $\tau(\delta')$.

Now, consider an execution where S is corrupted, and the parties in S_0 and S_1 have inputs 0 and 1 respectively. The corrupted parties in S emulate an honest protocol execution with input $b \in \{0,1\}$ with the parties in S_b. Moreover, the adversary delays δ the messages between S_0 and S_1. A party in S_0 (resp. S_1) cannot distinguish between the two executions, because it outputs at time $\tau(\delta') < \delta$, and hence outputs 0 (resp. 1).

However, since T parties are corrupted, the protocol provides security with unanimous abort meaning that in the ideal world all honest parties output the same value (which may be $\perp$).

This contradicts the fact that Π achieves full security with responsiveness up to t corruptions and unanimous abort up to T corruptions. □

In addition, classical bounds in synchronous MPC with full security, show that full security for dishonest majority $T \geq n/2$ is impossible [17]. As a consequence, MPC with extended full security is impossible for dishonest majority.

7 Conclusions

We summarize all our results. Using the compiler from Sect. 4 and the following instantiations:

- A bilateral zero-knowledge protocol like in [21], which uses CRS.
- A synchronous MPC with full security (resp. unanimous abort) for $T < n/2$ (resp. $T < n$), using a protocol such as [5,27] (resp. [23,29]).
- A synchronous broadcast protocol for $T < n$ such as [22] from PKI.
- An asynchronous MPC with full security up to $t < n/3$ and security without termination up to $T < n - 2t$, as described in Sect. 5.2, based on PKI and threshold FHE (achievable from CRS [1]).

We obtain the following corollaries, where $T_{\mathtt{sync}}(\Delta)$ and $T_{\mathtt{BC}}(\Delta)$ are the running times for the synchronous MPC protocol and the synchronous broadcast:

Corollary 1. *There exists a protocol parametrized by $\Delta \geq \delta$, which realizes $\mathcal{F}_{\mathrm{HYB}}^{\mathtt{fs}}$ on any function f, with full security with responsiveness t and full security T for any $t < \frac{n}{3}$ and $T < \min\{n/2, n-2t\}$, in the $(\mathcal{G}_{\mathrm{CLK}}, \mathcal{F}_{\mathrm{NET}}^{\delta}, \mathcal{F}_{\mathrm{PKI}}, \mathcal{F}_{\mathrm{CRS}})$-hybrid world. The expected maximum delay of the asynchronous phase is $\tau_{\mathtt{asynch}} = O(\delta)$, and the maximum delay of the synchronous phase is $\tau_{\mathtt{OD}} = T_{\mathtt{BC}}(\Delta) + T_{\mathtt{zk}}(\Delta)$ if an output was delivered in the asynchronous phase, and otherwise is $\tau_{\mathtt{OND}} = T_{\mathtt{BC}}(\Delta) + T_{\mathtt{sync}}(\Delta)$.*

For $t_r = \frac{n}{4}$, we obtain $\mathcal{F}_{\mathrm{HYB}}^{\mathtt{fs}}$ with correctness with privacy for any $t_s < \frac{n}{2}$.

Corollary 2. *There exists a protocol parametrized by $\Delta \geq \delta$, which realizes $\mathcal{F}_{\mathrm{HYB}}^{\mathtt{ua}}$ on any function f, with full security with responsiveness t and full security T for any $t < \frac{n}{3}$ and $T < n - 2t$, in the $(\mathcal{G}_{\mathrm{CLK}}, \mathcal{F}_{\mathrm{NET}}^{\delta}, \mathcal{F}_{\mathrm{PKI}}, \mathcal{F}_{\mathrm{CRS}})$-hybrid world.*

The expected maximum delay of the asynchronous phase is $\tau_{\mathtt{asynch}} = O(\delta)$, *and the maximum delay of the synchronous phase is* $\tau_{\mathtt{OD}} = T_{\mathtt{BC}}(\Delta) + T_{\mathtt{zk}}(\Delta)$ *if an output was delivered in the asynchronous phase, and otherwise is* $\tau_{\mathtt{OND}} = T_{\mathtt{BC}}(\Delta) + T_{\mathtt{sync}}(\Delta)$.

References

1. Asharov, G., Jain, A., López-Alt, A., Tromer, E., Vaikuntanathan, V., Wichs, D.: Multiparty computation with low communication, computation and interaction via threshold FHE. In: Pointcheval, D., Johansson, T. (eds.) EUROCRYPT 2012. LNCS, vol. 7237, pp. 483–501. Springer, Heidelberg (2012). https://doi.org/10.1007/978-3-642-29011-4_29
2. Beaver, D., Micali, S., Rogaway, P.: The round complexity of secure protocols (extended abstract). In: 22nd ACM STOC, pp. 503–513. ACM Press, May 1990
3. Beerliova-Trubiniova, Z., Hirt, M., Buus Nielsen, J.: Almost-asynchronous MPC with faulty minority. Cryptology ePrint Archive, Report 2008/416 (2008). http://eprint.iacr.org/2008/416
4. Beerliová-Trubíniová, Z., Hirt, M., Buus Nielsen, J.: On the theoretical gap between synchronous and asynchronous MPC protocols. In: PODC, Zurich, Switzerland (2010)
5. Ben-Or, M., Goldwasser, S., Wigderson, A.: Completeness theorems for non-cryptographic fault-tolerant distributed computation (extended abstract). In: 20th ACM STOC, pp. 1–10. ACM Press, May 1988
6. Ben-Or, M., Kelmer, B., Rabin, T.: Asynchronous secure computations with optimal resilience (extended abstract). In: Anderson, J., Toueg, S. (eds.) 13th ACM PODC, pp. 183–192. ACM, August 1994
7. Blum, E., Katz, J., Loss, J.: Synchronous consensus with optimal asynchronous fallback guarantees. In: Theory of Cryptography Conference (2019)
8. Blum, E., Katz, J., Loss, J.: Network-agnostic state machine replication. Cryptology ePrint Archive, Report 2020/142 (2020). https://eprint.iacr.org/2020/142
9. Blum, E., Liu-Zhang, C.-D., Loss, J.: Always have a backup plan: fully secure synchronous MPC with asynchronous fallback. In: Micciancio, D., Ristenpart, T. (eds.) CRYPTO 2020. LNCS, vol. 12171, pp. 707–731. Springer, Cham (2020). https://doi.org/10.1007/978-3-030-56880-1_25
10. Bracha, G., Toueg, S.: Asynchronous consensus and broadcast protocols. J. ACM (JACM) **32**(4), 824–840 (1985)
11. Canetti, R.: Universally composable security: a new paradigm for cryptographic protocols. In: 42nd FOCS, pp. 136–145. IEEE Computer Society Press, October 2001
12. Canetti, R., Dodis, Y., Pass, R., Walfish, S.: Universally composable security with global setup. In: Vadhan, S.P. (ed.) TCC 2007. LNCS, vol. 4392, pp. 61–85. Springer, Heidelberg (2007). https://doi.org/10.1007/978-3-540-70936-7_4
13. Chaum, D., Crépeau, C., Damgård, I.: Multiparty unconditionally secure protocols (extended abstract). In: 20th ACM STOC, pp. 11–19. ACM Press, May 1988
14. Choudhury, A.: Optimally-resilient unconditionally-secure asynchronous multiparty computation revisited. Cryptology ePrint Archive, Report 2020/906 (2020). https://eprint.iacr.org/2020/906
15. Choudhury, A., Patra, A.: Optimally resilient asynchronous MPC with linear communication complexity. In: Proceedings of the 2015 International Conference on Distributed Computing and Networking, pp. 1–10 (2015)

16. Choudhury, A., Patra, A., Ravi, D.: Round and communication efficient unconditionally-secure MPC with t<n/3 in partially synchronous network. In: ICITS 2017 (2017)
17. Cleve, R.: Limits on the security of coin flips when half the processors are faulty (extended abstract). In: 18th ACM STOC, pp. 364–369. ACM Press, May 1986
18. Cohen, R.: Asynchronous secure multiparty computation in constant time. In: Cheng, C.-M., Chung, K.-M., Persiano, G., Yang, B.-Y. (eds.) PKC 2016. LNCS, vol. 9615, pp. 183–207. Springer, Heidelberg (2016). https://doi.org/10.1007/978-3-662-49387-8_8
19. Coretti, S., Garay, J., Hirt, M., Zikas, V.: Constant-round asynchronous multi-party computation based on one-way functions. In: Cheon, J.H., Takagi, T. (eds.) ASIACRYPT 2016. LNCS, vol. 10032, pp. 998–1021. Springer, Heidelberg (2016). https://doi.org/10.1007/978-3-662-53890-6_33
20. Cramer, R., Damgård, I., Nielsen, J.B.: Multiparty computation from threshold homomorphic encryption. In: Pfitzmann, B. (ed.) EUROCRYPT 2001. LNCS, vol. 2045, pp. 280–300. Springer, Heidelberg (2001). https://doi.org/10.1007/3-540-44987-6_18
21. De Santis, A., Di Crescenzo, G., Ostrovsky, R., Persiano, G., Sahai, A.: Robust non-interactive zero knowledge. In: Kilian, J. (ed.) CRYPTO 2001. LNCS, vol. 2139, pp. 566–598. Springer, Heidelberg (2001). https://doi.org/10.1007/3-540-44647-8_33
22. Dolev, D., Raymond Strong, H.: Authenticated algorithms for byzantine agreement. SIAM J. Comput. **12**(4), 656–666 (1983)
23. Fitzi, M., Gottesman, D., Hirt, M., Holenstein, T., Smith, A.: Detectable byzantine agreement secure against faulty majorities. In: Ricciardi, A. (ed.) 21st ACM PODC, pp. 118–126. ACM, July 2002
24. Fitzi, M., Hirt, M., Holenstein, T., Wullschleger, J.: Two-threshold broadcast and detectable multi-party computation. In: Biham, E. (ed.) EUROCRYPT 2003. LNCS, vol. 2656, pp. 51–67. Springer, Heidelberg (2003). https://doi.org/10.1007/3-540-39200-9_4
25. Fitzi, M., Holenstein, T., Wullschleger, J.: Multi-party computation with hybrid security. In: Cachin, C., Camenisch, J.L. (eds.) EUROCRYPT 2004. LNCS, vol. 3027, pp. 419–438. Springer, Heidelberg (2004). https://doi.org/10.1007/978-3-540-24676-3_25
26. Garay, J.A., Katz, J., Kumaresan, R., Zhou,H.-S.: Adaptively secure broadcast, revisited. In: Proceedings of the 30th Annual ACM SIGACT-SIGOPS Symposium on Principles of Distributed Computing, pp. 179–186 (2011)
27. Goldreich, O., Micali, S., Wigderson, A.: How to play any mental game or a completeness theorem for protocols with honest majority. In: Aho, A. (ed.) 19th ACM STOC, pp. 218–229. ACM Press, May 1987
28. Goldreich, O., Petrank, E.: The best of both worlds: guaranteeing termination in fast randomized byzantine agreement protocols. Tech. rep. Computer Science Department, Technion (1990)
29. Goldwasser, S., Lindell, Y.: Secure computation without a broadcast channel. In: 16th International Symposium on Distributed Computing (DISC). Citeseer (2002)
30. Guo, Y., Pass, R., Shi, E.: Synchronous, with a chance of partition tolerance. In: Boldyreva, A., Micciancio, D. (eds.) CRYPTO 2019. LNCS, vol. 11692, pp. 499–529. Springer, Cham (2019). https://doi.org/10.1007/978-3-030-26948-7_18
31. Hirt, M., Maurer, U., Lucas, C.: A dynamic tradeoff between active and passive corruptions in secure multi-party computation. In: Canetti, R., Garay, J.A. (eds.) CRYPTO 2013. LNCS, vol. 8043, pp. 203–219. Springer, Heidelberg (2013). https://doi.org/10.1007/978-3-642-40084-1_12

32. Hirt, M., Nielsen, J.B., Przydatek, B.: Cryptographic asynchronous multi-party computation with optimal resilience. In: Cramer, R. (ed.) EUROCRYPT 2005. LNCS, vol. 3494, pp. 322–340. Springer, Heidelberg (2005). https://doi.org/10.1007/11426639_19
33. Hirt, M., Nielsen, J.B., Przydatek, B.: Asynchronous multi-party computation with quadratic communication. In: Aceto, L., Damgård, I., Goldberg, L.A., Halldórsson, M.M., Ingólfsdóttir, A., Walukiewicz, I. (eds.) ICALP 2008. LNCS, vol. 5126, pp. 473–485. Springer, Heidelberg (2008). https://doi.org/10.1007/978-3-540-70583-3_39
34. Ishai, Y., Kushilevitz, E., Lindell, Y., Petrank, E.: On combining privacy with guaranteed output delivery in secure multiparty computation. In: Dwork, C. (ed.) CRYPTO 2006. LNCS, vol. 4117, pp. 483–500. Springer, Heidelberg (2006). https://doi.org/10.1007/11818175_29
35. Katz, J.: On achieving the "best of both worlds" in secure multiparty computation. In: Johnson, D.S., Feige, U. (eds.) 39th ACM STOC, pp. 11–20. ACM Press, June 2007
36. Katz, J., Maurer, U., Tackmann, B., Zikas, V.: Universally composable synchronous computation. In: Sahai, A. (ed.) TCC 2013. LNCS, vol. 7785, pp. 477–498. Springer, Heidelberg (2013). https://doi.org/10.1007/978-3-642-36594-2_27
37. Kiayias, A., Zhou, H.-S., Zikas, V.: Fair and robust multi-party computation using a global transaction ledger. In: Fischlin, M., Coron, J.-S. (eds.) EUROCRYPT 2016. LNCS, vol. 9666, pp. 705–734. Springer, Heidelberg (2016). https://doi.org/10.1007/978-3-662-49896-5_25
38. Kursawe, K.: Optimistic asynchronous byzantine agreement (2000)
39. Kushilevitz, E., Lindell, Y., Rabin, T.: Information-theoretically secure protocols and security under composition. In: Kleinberg, J.M. (ed.) 38th ACM STOC, pp. 109–118. ACM Press, May 2006
40. Loss, J., Moran, T.: Combining asynchronous and synchronous byzantine agreement: the best of both worlds. Cryptology ePrint Archive, Report 2018/235 (2018). https://eprint.iacr.org/2018/235
41. Pass, R., Shi, E.: Hybrid consensus: efficient consensus in the permissionless model. In: LIPIcs-Leibniz International Proceedings in Informatics, vol. 91. Schloss Dagstuhl-Leibniz-Zentrum fuer Informatik (2017)
42. Pass, R., Shi, E.: Thunderella: blockchains with optimistic instant confirmation. In: Nielsen, J.B., Rijmen, V. (eds.) EUROCRYPT 2018. LNCS, vol. 10821, pp. 3–33. Springer, Cham (2018). https://doi.org/10.1007/978-3-319-78375-8_1
43. Patra, A., Choudhary, A., Rangan, C.P.: Communication efficient statistical asynchronous multiparty computation with optimal resilience. In: Bao, F., Yung, M., Lin, D., Jing, J. (eds.) Inscrypt 2009. LNCS, vol. 6151, pp. 179–197. Springer, Heidelberg (2010). https://doi.org/10.1007/978-3-642-16342-5_14
44. Patra, A., Ravi, D.: On the power of hybrid networks in multi-party computation. IEEE Trans. Inf. Theo. **64**(6), 4207–4227 (2018)
45. Rabin, T., Ben-Or, M.: Verifiable secret sharing and multiparty protocols with honest majority (extended abstract). In: 21st ACM STOC, pp. 73–85. ACM Press, May 1989

Secure MPC: Laziness Leads to GOD

Saikrishna Badrinarayanan[1], Aayush Jain[2], Nathan Manohar[2(✉)], and Amit Sahai[2]

[1] Visa Research, Palo Alto, USA
sabadrin@visa.com

[2] UCLA and Center for Encrypted Functionalities, Los Angeles, USA
{aayushjain,nmanohar,sahai}@cs.ucla.edu

Abstract. Motivated by what we call "honest but lazy" parties in the context of secure multi party computation, we revisit the notion of multi-key FHE schemes (MFHE). In MFHE, any message encrypted using a public key pk_i can be "expanded" so that the resulting ciphertext is encrypted with respect to a set of public keys $(pk_1, .., pk_n)$. Such expanded ciphertexts can be homomorphically evaluated with respect to any circuit to generate a ciphertext ct. Then, this ciphertext ct can be partially decrypted using a secret key sk_i (corresponding to the public key pk_i) to produce a partial decryption p_i. Finally, these partial decryptions $\{p_i\}_{i \in [n]}$ can be combined to recover the output. However, this definition of MFHE works only for n-out-of-n access structures and, thus, each node in the system is a point of failure. In the context of "honest but lazy" parties, it is necessary to be able to decrypt even when only given a subset of partial decryptions (say t out of n). In order to solve this problem, we introduce a new notion of multi-key FHE designed to handle arbitrary access patterns that can reconstruct the output. We call it a threshold multi-key FHE scheme (TMFHE).

Our main contributions are the following:

- We formally define and construct TMFHE for any access structure given by a monotone boolean formula, assuming LWE.
- We construct the first simulation-extractable multi-string NIZK from polynomially hard LWE.
- We use TMFHE and our multi-string NIZK to obtain the first round-optimal (three round) MPC protocol in the plain model with *guaranteed output delivery* secure against malicious adversaries or, more generally, mixed adversaries (which supports "honest but lazy" parties), assuming LWE.
- Our MPC protocols simultaneously achieve security against the *maximum* number of corruptions under which guaranteed output delivery is achievable, depth-proportional communication complexity, and reusability.

1 Introduction

Starting with the breakthrough work of Gentry [21], fully homomorphic encryption (FHE) has been extensively studied over a long sequence of works (see

S. Moriai and H. Wang (Eds.): ASIACRYPT 2020, LNCS 12493, pp. 120–150, 2020.
https://doi.org/10.1007/978-3-030-64840-4_5

e.g. [6,8,9,21,22]). In an FHE scheme, given a public key pk and a ciphertext of a message m encrypted using this public key, a user can homomorphically evaluate this ciphertext with respect to any circuit C to generate a new ciphertext ct that is an encryption of $C(m)$ without learning anything about the message. Then, the decryptor, using the secret key sk can decrypt this message to recover the output $C(m)$. However, traditionally, FHE schemes are single-key in nature: that is, they can be used to perform arbitrary computation on data encrypted using the same public key.

In this work, we build a new multi-party generalization of FHE that we call Threshold Multi-Key FHE, which we build from the LWE assumption. We then use this new primitive to achieve efficient secure multi-party protocols (MPC) in a model that allows for some honest parties to be "lazy", as we discuss below. Subsequent to our work, our Threshold Multi-Key FHE was used in [26], which explicitly extends our MPC model with honest but lazy parties to also allow lazy parties to return in future rounds and builds upon our MPC protocol to achieve their results. We believe both our notion of Threshold Multi-Key FHE and our MPC model and protocol will continue to find other applications, as well (see e.g. [13], for another subsequent result that builds upon ours). We now elaborate on our contributions.

Multi-key FHE. Lopez-Alt et al. [32] introduced the notion of multi-key fully homomorphic encryption. Informally, in a multi-key FHE scheme, any message encrypted using a public key pk_i can be "expanded" so that the resulting ciphertext is encrypted with respect to a set of public keys $(pk_1, .., pk_n)$. Such expanded ciphertexts can be homomorphically evaluated with respect to any circuit to generate a ciphertext ct. Then, this ciphertext ct can be partially decrypted using a secret key sk_i (corresponding to the public key pk_i) to produce a partial decryption p_i. Finally, these partial decryptions $\{p_i\}_{i\in[n]}$ can be combined to recover the output. In addition to the semantic security of encryption, a multi-key FHE scheme also requires that given any expanded (and possibly evaluated) ciphertext ct encrypting a message m, any set of $(n-1)$ secret keys $\{sk_i\}_{i\neq i^*}$ for any i^*, and the message m, it is possible to statistically simulate the partial decryption p_{i^*}. Multi-key FHE has been extensively studied [7,14,33,34] and has proven particularly useful in the context of building round-efficient secure multiparty computation protocols for protocols achieving security with abort. Recall that in security with abort, a single party that aborts could potentially prevent all honest parties from receiving the output.

1.1 A New Primitive: Threshold Multi-key FHE

However, none of the existing multi-key FHE schemes enable the output to be reconstructed unless all the n partial decryptions are given out and hence they only "work" for n-out-of-n access structures. Unfortunately, this leads to situations where every secret key owner in the system represents a single point of failure, since if their partial decryption is not given out, it is not possible to recover the output. This is sufficient for protocols only achieving security with abort, as this security notion allows the functionality to fail if even a single party misbehaves. If we want to create schemes that are capable of handling failures, we would necessarily want one to be able to decrypt even when one only possesses a subset of partial decryptions (say t out of n).

At first glance, it seems that our goal is simply incompatible with the notion of multi-key FHE. For instance, suppose that a ciphertext encrypting m under a public key pk can be combined with two public keys pk' and pk'', and "expanded" into a ciphertext encrypting m under a 2-out-of-3 threshold under the triple of public keys $\{pk, pk', pk''\}$. Such a feature would imply the insecurity of the original encryption, since an adversary could sample the public keys $\{pk', pk''\}$ together with their secret keys $\{sk', sk''\}$, and then use the two secret keys $\{sk', sk''\}$ to obtain m using the expanded ciphertext.

In order to solve this problem, we introduce a new notion of *threshold* multi-key FHE[1] where ciphertexts cannot be "expanded." Instead, in our notion, given a collection of public keys $\{pk_1, \ldots, pk_n\}$, it is possible for an encryptor to encrypt a message m with respect to an access pattern such as t-out-of-n. Then this ciphertext would only be decryptable by combining partial decryptions obtained from holders of at least t corresponding secret keys. As we show in this work, it turns out that this functionality is sufficient for obtaining new applications to MPC (see below for details).

In this work, we first formally define threshold multi-key FHE in a general way, and then we show to construct this new primitive from the learning with errors (LWE) assumption. Formally, we show the following theorem:

Theorem 1 (Informal). *Assuming LWE, there exists a secure threshold multi-key FHE scheme for the class of access structures $\mathbb{A}$ induced by all monotone boolean formulas.*

In Sect. 2, we describe the challenges and techniques involved in our construction. Our next contribution is an application of threshold multi-key FHE in the context of round-optimal secure MPC protocols with guaranteed output delivery (GOD).

1.2 Application to Round-Optimal MPC

Secure multi-party computation (MPC) [23,36,37] has been a problem of fundamental interest in cryptography. In an MPC protocol, a set of mutually distrusting parties can evaluate a function on their joint inputs while maintaining privacy of their respective inputs. Over the last few decades, much of the work related to MPC has been devoted to achieving stronger security guarantees and improving efficiency with respect to various parameters such as round complexity and communication complexity. In this work, we further advance our understanding of this landscape with threshold multi-key FHE being the main technical tool.

[1] We remark that in fact, some existing standard multi-key FHE schemes [33] also sometimes used the term threshold multi-key FHE to refer to their primitive, which requires an n-out-of-n threshold. We will use threshold multi-key FHE to denote only our stronger notion supporting general thresholds.

MPC Supporting "Honest but Lazy" Parties. In traditional MPC, every party is required to remain online and participate completely in the protocol execution. This applies not only to "classical" MPC protocols where every party has to participate and send a message in every round of the protocol, but also to other interesting variants such as protocols in the client-server setting where all the servers are required to remain active until the end of the protocol execution. We refer the reader to Sect. 1.4 for a more detailed comparison with related works. In other words, traditional MPC protocols decide to treat a "lazy" party that just aborts midway into the protocol execution as a corrupt party that is colluding with the other corrupt parties, and this is addressed in different ways. In some cases, all parties abort the protocol execution while in other cases, the "lazy" party is just discarded and all the other parties compute the function on their joint inputs alone. We believe that such an outlook is undesirable as there are several reasons why even an honest party might have to abort and become "lazy" during the execution of a protocol without having to be deemed as colluding with the corrupt parties. A few potential reasons include:

- Connectivity - A party might lose connectivity and hence be unable to continue the protocol.
- Computational resources - A computationally weak party might be unable to perform intensive computation and hence be forced to exit the protocol.
- Interest - At some point, a party might just lose interest in that protocol execution due to other higher priority tasks that come up.

Motivated by the above realistic scenarios, we would like to construct MPC protocols that can handle "honest but lazy" parties without simply lumping them in with the other corrupted parties (since treating all aborting parties as "malicious" will unrealistically enhance the power of the adversary and limit our protocol's capabilities). Furthermore, we would like our protocol to be robust to aborting parties (that is, have guaranteed output delivery). Informally, this means that at the end of the protocol execution, regardless of the behavior of the adversary, the honest parties can still compute the output of the function on all their joint inputs (with either a default or the actual input for each of the corrupted parties). Ideally, we would like to achieve a stronger form of guaranteed output delivery, where, when possible, the output of the protocol is with respect to the actual input of all the "honest but lazy" parties, rather than some default input. This is akin to stating that provided an "honest but lazy" party actually sent a message dependent on its input, the protocol will compute the functionality with respect to this party's input, regardless of whether or not the party aborted during the rest of the protocol. We call this property *input fidelity.* In this work, we ask

Can we construct round-optimal protocols in the plain model that achieve the above desiderata?

If such protocols are achievable, then

Can these protocols handle the maximum number of possible corruptions?

What can we say about the assumptions, communication complexity, and reusability of such protocols?

Using our new primitive, threshold multi-key FHE, we are able to answer all the above satisfactorily. We construct the first round-optimal (three-round) MPC protocol in the plain model that achieves our desired properties. Moreover, our protocol is capable on handling the *maximum* number of corruptions that a protocol can possibly support while achieving the desired properties. Our protocol relies only on the learning with errors (LWE) assumption. Furthermore, our protocol has depth-proportional communication complexity and is reusable.

Formalizing Our Desired Properties. Formally, we study MPC with guaranteed output delivery in the presence of threshold mixed adversaries, introduced by Fitzi et al. [19,20]. In this setting, a threshold mixed adversary $\mathcal{A}$ is allowed to corrupt three sets of parties $(\mathcal{A}_{\mathbf{Mal}}, \mathcal{A}_{\mathbf{Sh}}, \mathcal{A}_{\mathbf{Fc}})$ such that the following holds: (i) $|\mathcal{A}_{\mathbf{Mal}}| \leq t_{\mathbf{Mal}}$, $|\mathcal{A}_{\mathbf{Sh}}| \leq t_{\mathbf{Sh}}$, and $|\mathcal{A}_{\mathbf{Fc}}| \leq t_{\mathbf{Fc}}$, for a tuple of thresholds $(t_{\mathbf{Mal}}, t_{\mathbf{Sh}}, t_{\mathbf{Fc}})$. (ii) The set of parties in $\mathcal{A}_{\mathbf{Mal}}$ are maliciously corrupted meaning that the adversary can choose to behave using any arbitrary polynomial time algorithm on behalf of each of them. (iii) The set of parties in $\mathcal{A}_{\mathbf{Sh}}$ are corrupted in a semi-honest manner and so the adversary is required to follow the protocol execution honestly on behalf of each of them. (iv) The set of parties in $\mathcal{A}_{\mathbf{Fc}}$ are corrupted in a fail-corrupt manner meaning that for each party in this set, the adversary can specify when that party is required to abort the protocol execution. Until then, these parties follow the protocol execution honestly. Note that the adversary never gets to see the inputs or internal state of any of the fail-corrupt parties and hence these parties capture our motivation of "honest but lazy" parties - where their laziness is enforced by the adversary in the security game.

In this work, our goal is to build a round-optimal MPC protocol with guaranteed output delivery in this model that also simultaneously satisfies the following desirable properties:

- **Security Against the Maximum Number of Corruptions:** Security should hold against a threshold mixed adversary that can corrupt the maximum number of parties under which guaranteed output delivery is achievable.
- **Input Fidelity:** In line with our motivation, we want our protocol to satisfy not only guaranteed output delivery, but also the stronger property that the output of the computation is a function of the joint inputs of all parties, including those that aborted after a "certain point". Intuitively, we would like our protocol to be divided into two phases - an input commitment phase and a computation phase. We refer to the end of the input commitment phase as this "point." That is, in the scenario where the adversary corrupts a set of parties in a fail-corrupt manner, for every fail-corrupt party P_i that aborts after the input commitment phase, its input y_i that is used to compute the final output $C(y_1, \ldots, y_n)$ is set to be its actual input x_i used in the protocol so far and not a default input $\perp$. Recall that this aligns with our original

motivation where we wish to not discard honest but lazy parties and deem them to be corrupt.

- **Depth-Proportional Communication Complexity:** For any function f, the communication complexity of the protocol should be $\mathsf{poly}(\lambda, d, N, \ell_{\mathsf{inp}})$ where N is the number of parties, λ is the security parameter, ℓ_{inp} is the input length for each party, d is the depth of the circuit computing f.
- **Reusability:** Given the transcript of the input commitment phase of the protocol, the computation phase of the protocol should be able to be reused across an unbounded polynomial number of executions to compute different functions on the same fixed joint inputs of all the parties.

Prior to our work, much of the focus in this model was on obtaining feasibility results, understanding under what corruption patterns is secure computation even possible, and improving the communication complexity. We refer to Sect. 1.4 for a more detailed discussion on the prior work in this model. In particular, Hirt et al. [27] showed that in the setting of a threshold mixed adversary, MPC with guaranteed output delivery is possible if and only if $2t_{\mathbf{Mal}} + t_{\mathbf{Sh}} + t_{\mathbf{Fc}} < N$, where N is the total number of parties. Since we are interested in guaranteed output delivery, we focus on constructing MPC protocols that are secure against $(t_{\mathbf{Mal}}, t_{\mathbf{Sh}}, t_{\mathbf{Fc}})$-threshold mixed adversaries, for any $(t_{\mathbf{Mal}}, t_{\mathbf{Sh}}, t_{\mathbf{Fc}})$ satisfying the above inequality. Furthermore, in light of the result of Gordon et al. [24] showing that three rounds are required for MPC with guaranteed output delivery in the traditional model (this can be viewed as a special case of the threshold mixed adversary model, where $t_{\mathbf{Sh}}$ and $t_{\mathbf{Fc}}$ are both 0), we observe that a three round protocol will be round-optimal in this setting.

Utilizing our new primitive, threshold multi-key FHE, given any tuple of thresholds $(t_{\mathbf{Mal}}, t_{\mathbf{Sh}}, t_{\mathbf{Fc}})$ satisfying the Hirt et al. [27] inequality, we construct the first round-optimal (three-round) MPC protocol with guaranteed output delivery that is secure against such a threshold mixed adversary. Since guaranteed output delivery is possible if and only if the Hirt et al. [27] inequality holds, our resulting protocol is *optimal* in terms of the best possible corruption we can tolerate. The first two rounds of our protocol form the input commitment phase, and round 3 is the computation phase. Our protocol has input fidelity, in the sense that the functionality is computed with respect to the inputs of all parties that did not abort in the first two rounds, *even* if that party aborts in round three. Additionally, given the transcript of the input commitment phase (the first two rounds of the protocol), the third round can be reused across an unbounded polynomial number of executions to compute different functions on the same fixed joint inputs of all parties. Our protocol also has depth-proportional communication complexity. Formally, we show the following result:

Theorem 2 (Informal). *Assuming learning with errors (LWE), for any function f on N inputs, for any tuple of thresholds $(t_{Mal}, t_{Sh}, t_{Fc})$ satisfying $2t_{Mal} + t_{Sh} + t_{Fc} < N$, there exists a three-round MPC protocol with guaranteed output delivery in the plain model that is secure against a $(t_{Mal}, t_{Sh}, t_{Fc})$-mixed adversary. The protocol has input fidelity, depth-proportional communication complexity, and is reusable.*

By instantiating Theorem 2 with the $(\lceil N/2-1 \rceil, 0, 0)$-mixed adversary we achieve an interesting result in the traditional MPC world in the plain model: in particular, notice that this setting corresponds to an honest majority of parties and as a result, we get a three round MPC protocol in the plain model with guaranteed output delivery. As mentioned previously, our protocol is round optimal for this setting as well due to the lower bound of Gordon et al. [24]. Formally, we achieve the following corollary, matching the round complexity of the recent independent work [1], but for the first time, also achieving input fidelity, reusability, and depth-proportional communication complexity, assuming only LWE.

Corollary 1 (Informal). *Assuming LWE, for any function f, there exists a three-round MPC protocol with guaranteed output delivery in the plain model in the presence of an honest majority.*

1.3 Multi-string NIZK from LWE

As a stepping stone to achieving Theorem 2, we first consider the weaker setting of a $(t_{\mathbf{Sm}}, t_{\mathbf{Sh}}, t_{\mathbf{Fc}})$-semi-malicious mixed adversary that corrupts the sets $(\mathcal{A}_{\mathbf{Sm}}, \mathcal{A}_{\mathbf{Sh}}, \mathcal{A}_{\mathbf{Fc}})$ of parties such that the first set of parties $\mathcal{A}_{\mathbf{Sm}}$, with $|\mathcal{A}_{\mathbf{Sm}}| \leq t_{\mathbf{Sm}}$, is only corrupted in a semi-malicious manner - that is, on behalf of each party in this set, the adversary can pick any arbitrary randomness of its choice but using this randomness, the party is required to execute the protocol honestly. We define this formally in the technical sections. Once we have constructed a protocol that is secure against a semi-malicious mixed adversary, we are able to bootstrap it to one that is secure against a (malicious) mixed adversary in the plain model using a multi-string non-interactive zero knowledge (NIZK) argument.

In a multi-string NIZK argument system, introduced in the work of Groth and Ostrovsky [25], a set of parties can each generate one CRS that can then be combined to compute one unified CRS which is used to compute NIZKs. The guarantee is that as long as a majority of the individual CRS strings are honestly generated, the argument system is correct and secure. Unfortunately, one of the tools in the construction of multi-string NIZKs in [25] was a Zap [16], which is not known from polynomially hard LWE. In order to obtain Theorem 2 assuming only polynomially hard LWE, we construct a (simulation-extractable) multi-string NIZK directly from LWE, which may be of independent interest. Formally, we show the following.

Theorem 3 (Informal). *Assuming polynomially hard LWE, there exists a simulation-extractable multi-string NIZK for NP.*

1.4 Independent and Subsequent Work

We discuss related work in detail in the full version of the paper.

Independent Work. Recently, in an independent work, Ananth et. al [1] also constructed a three-round honest majority MPC protocol with guaranteed output delivery in the plain model, assuming PKE and ZAPs. Their techniques are substantially different from ours, and we note that if we instantiate our protocol with the $(\lceil N/2-1\rceil, 0, 0)$ tuple of thresholds, we are able to match their result, assuming LWE, as shown in Corollary 1. Moreover, our protocol simultaneously achieves depth-proportional communication complexity and reusability, properties not achievable by their protocol. Furthermore, we note that our general protocol can handle threshold mixed adversaries, whereas their protocol is only secure against malicious adversaries in the honest majority setting.

Subsequent Works. The work of [15] (which cites us as prior work) can use a threshold PKI model, which is a very strong form of certified PKI model, to achieve some of our results (guaranteed output delivery, depth proportional communication) in 2 rounds. In this work, we do not make any trust assumptions. However, we observe that our protocol already gives a 2-round protocol with a much weaker form of PKI where the public keys can be any arbitrary string. Thus, our work also implies results in a "plain" PKI setting. Last-round reusability, which we achieve, was also not studied in [15]. However, we note that the focus of [15] was to understand adaptive security in the context of communication efficient protocols, which we do not study.

A recent series of works [10,11,28,31,35] have developed a framework for instantiating the Fiat-Shamir transform [18] using a hash function that satisfies a property called correlation-intractability [12]. This culminated in the work of Peikert and Shiehian [35], who were able to obtain the first NIZK from LWE by constructing a correlation-intractable hash function family for (bounded) circuits from LWE. Following this, there have been two works [2,30], subsequent to ours, that construct two message statistically witness indistinguishable ZAP arguments from quasipolynomial LWE. From this, using the work of [25] one can construct a multi-string NIZK from quasipolynomial LWE. We obtain a multi-string NIZK argument system assuming only the polynomial hardness of LWE.

2 Technical Overview

We first describe the challenges involved in defining and constructing our new primitive of threshold multi-key FHE in the next subsection. This is followed by the techniques involved in constructing our round-optimal MPC protocol with guaranteed output delivery. Finally, we discuss the techniques used to construct a multi-string NIZK from LWE.

2.1 Threshold Multi-key FHE (TMFHE)

Definitional Challenges. Recall that we would like to construct a version of multi-key FHE that only requires some (say t out of n) of the partial decryption shares in order to reconstruct the output as opposed to all n partial decryptions, as is required in all existing multi-key FHE schemes.

At first glance, it is not even clear how to define such a notion. The most direct approach leads to a definition that is impossible to achieve. Consider for example the $n/2$-out-of-n access structure. In this case, if we follow the standard procedure used by known multi-key FHE schemes, any evaluator can expand a ciphertext encrypting a message m with respect to public key pk_n to a ciphertext ct with respect to the set of public keys $(pk_1, ..., pk_n)$. Then, the evaluator can use secret keys $sk_1, .., sk_{n/2}$ to learn the value of m, as the set $\{1 ..., n/2\}$ satisfies the access structure. However, in doing so, an adversary can learn m without knowing sk_n, breaking the semantic security of the encryption scheme with respect to (pk_n, sk_n) and leading to a notion that provides no security.

Although we seem to have arrived at a notion that is not meaningful at all, we note that the issue with the above approach is that a ciphertext encrypted with respect to a public key pk can be expanded to one encrypted with respect to many public keys. However, if we prevent ciphertexts from being expanded, there is hope of achieving a meaningful notion. Expanding on this idea, we arrive at the following (informal) definition. Any party can generate its own key pair (pk, sk). Any encryptor can compute $ct \leftarrow \mathsf{Encrypt}(pk_1, .., pk_n, \mathbb{A}, m)$. Given two (or more) ciphertexts encrypted with respect to the same set of public keys and the same access structure $\mathbb{A}$, it is possible to homomorphically evaluate a circuit on these ciphertexts and partially decrypt the resulting ciphertext using any secret key sk_i to recover a partial decryption p_i. Given $\{p_i\}_{i \in B}$ for some B satisfying $\mathbb{A}$, one can reconstruct the output. Roughly, we require two security guarantees from the scheme.

1. Given $\{sk_i\}_{i \in S}$ for some $S \notin \mathbb{A}$,
$$\mathsf{Encrypt}(pk_1, \ldots, pk_n, \mathbb{A}, m_0) \approx_c \mathsf{Encrypt}(pk_1, .., pk_n, \mathbb{A}, m_1)$$
for any two equal length messages m_0, m_1.
2. Given a ciphertext ct for an underlying message m and $\{sk_i\}_{i \in S}$ for any maximally unqualified set[2] $S \notin \mathbb{A}$ (for example $(n/2 - 1)$ of the parties for the example above), it is possible to statistically simulate a partial decryption p_i for any $i \in [n]$.

For technical reasons, we require a more nuanced security definition, and we refer the reader to Sect. 4 for the details.

Construction Overview. In order to construct TMFHE, one could try many approaches to build on top of existing multi-key FHE schemes. For example, one could try the following. Given any set of public keys $(pk_1, .., pk_n)$, generate ciphertexts $ct_S \leftarrow \mathsf{Encrypt}(\{pk_i\}_{i \in S}, m)$ for all minimally valid sets $S \in \mathbb{A}$. However, such an approach is not feasible for access structures such as $n/2$–out-of-n

[2] By maximally unqualified set S, we mean that for any $i \in [n] \backslash S$, $(S \cup \{i\}) \in \mathbb{A}$. Similarly, a set S is minimally qualified if for any $i \in [S]$, $(S \backslash \{i\}) \notin \mathbb{A}$.

as then the encryptor has to compute encryptions for roughly $\binom{n}{n/2}$ subsets, which is super-polynomial.

To overcome this limitation, we use the tool of threshold FHE introduced in the work of Boneh et al. [4]. In a threshold FHE scheme, the setup algorithm samples a single public key fpk and n secret key shares $(\mathsf{fsk}_1, .., \mathsf{fsk}_n)$ for a secret key fsk that are shared according to the access structure $\mathbb{A}$. Using the public key fpk, an encryptor can encrypt a message m to receive a ciphertext ct (which may be evaluated). This ciphertext can then be partially decrypted independently using key shares sk_i to compute a partial decryption p_i. Then using these $\{p_i\}_{i \in S}$ for any set $S \in \mathbb{A}$, one can recover m. Security properties are two fold:

- Given $\{sk_i\}_{i \in S}$ for some $S \notin \mathbb{A}$, $\mathsf{Encrypt}(pk, \mathbb{A}, m_0) \approx_c \mathsf{Encrypt}(pk, \mathbb{A}, m_1)$ for any two equal length messages m_0, m_1.
- Second, given a ciphertext ct with underlying message m and $\{sk_i\}_{i \in S}$ for any maximally unqualified $S \notin \mathbb{A}$, it is possible to statistically simulate partial decryptions p_i for any $i \in [n]$.

We make the following useful observations about threshold FHE which will aid us in our construction.

1. The setup algorithm of the scheme of [4] first samples $(pk, sk) \leftarrow \mathsf{FHE.Setup}(1^\lambda)$ and then secret shares sk according to the access structure using a "special purpose" secret sharing scheme to compute shares $(sk_1, .., sk_n)$ so that the reconstruction involves just addition of some subset of shares. Looking ahead to the security proof, this feature allows us to easily simulate partial decryptions.
2. The encryption procedure just involves encrypting the message m using an underlying FHE scheme.
3. The underlying FHE scheme can be instantiated using most of the known homomorphic encryption schemes satisfying a few general properties.

Thus, we observe that, in particular, the multi-key FHE schemes of both [7,33], can be used to instantiate the underlying FHE scheme in threshold FHE. This can then be used to evaluate on multiple ciphertexts encrypted with respect to different public keys - since, using multi-key FHE, one can expand on various ciphertexts and evaluate jointly on them. However, at this point, it is still not clear how to compute (or simulate) partial decryptions, especially since the threshold FHE construction of [4] only handled underlying FHE schemes where the ciphertext was encrypted with respect to a single public key. However, we observe the following property of the multi-key FHE schemes of both [7,33]. Suppose we have two ciphertexts, ct_1 and ct_2 that are encrypted under public keys fpk_1 and fpk_2, respectively. In the multi-key FHE scheme, we can expand these ciphertexts to $\hat{ct}_1$ and $\hat{ct}_2$, each encrypted under the set of public keys $\{\mathsf{fpk}_1, \mathsf{fpk}_2\}$. If the secret keys corresponding to fpk_1 and fpk_2 are fsk_1 and fsk_2, respectively, then the secret key for decryption of $\hat{ct}_1$ and $\hat{ct}_2$ (and any ciphertext computed by evaluating on these ciphertexts) is $[\mathsf{fsk}_1, \mathsf{fsk}_2]$. In a standard threshold FHE scheme, the secret key would be secret shared across n parties.

For simplicity, assume that we secret share according to the n out of n access structure. Let party i's shares of fsk_1 and fsk_2 be denoted by $\mathsf{fsk}_{1,i}$ and $\mathsf{fsk}_{2,i}$, respectively. Since the decryption procedure of the multi-key FHE scheme is linear and the secret sharing of fsk_1 and fsk_2 is also linear and, crucially, with respect to the *same* access structure, one could have party i partially decrypt by running the decryption procedure of the multi-key FHE scheme using the secret key $[\mathsf{fsk}_{1,i}, \mathsf{fsk}_{2,i}]$. Given these partial decryptions, one could combine them to recover the message by adding them as specified by the reconstruction procedure of the secret sharing scheme.

The above gives intuition as to how one might construct threshold multi-key FHE, but several points are still unclear. In particular, we noted that in order to achieve a meaningful notion, we want an encryptor to encrypt with respect to a public key set and an access structure. The idea is that the public key set that an encryptor encrypts with respect to is *not* a public key set of the underlying MFHE scheme, but rather simply a set of public keys for a public-key encryption scheme. These public keys serve as a means to send the corresponding multi-key FHE secret key shares to the other parties. At a high level, encryption works by generating a multi-key FHE public key fpk and secret key shares $\mathsf{fsk}_1, \ldots, \mathsf{fsk}_n$ corresponding to the access structure $\mathbb{A}$. The encryptor then encrypts fsk_i under pk_i and includes this in the ciphertext. This allows a set of parties satisfying the access structure to use their secret keys sk_i of the public-key scheme to recover the necessary fsk_i's to decrypt the ciphertext. Furthermore, as we noted above, standard multi-key FHE expansion and evaluation will result in a ciphertext that can be decrypted by concatenating the secret key shares for each of the ciphertexts.

The above discussion is highly simplified and is meant to provide the reader with some intuition behind our construction. We ignored various subtle points and refer the reader to the main technical sections for the details. As a consequence of our techniques, we are able to directly simulate partial decryptions against an adversary that corrupts *any* set $S \notin \mathbb{A}$, not only a maximally unqualified one. The constructions of [7,33] could only simulate against a maximally unqualified set ($N-1$ out of the N parties in their case) and relied on a transformation to achieve simulation security against any unqualified corrupted set.

2.2 MPC with Guaranteed Output Delivery

Recall that a $(t_{\mathbf{Mal}}, t_{\mathbf{Sh}}, t_{\mathbf{Fc}})$-threshold mixed adversary is one which corrupts three sets of parties $(\mathcal{A}_{\mathbf{Mal}}, \mathcal{A}_{\mathbf{Sh}}, \mathcal{A}_{\mathbf{Fc}})$ with $|\mathcal{A}_{\mathbf{Mal}}| \leq t_{\mathbf{Mal}}$, $|\mathcal{A}_{\mathbf{Sh}}| \leq t_{\mathbf{Sh}}$, and $|\mathcal{A}_{\mathbf{Fc}}| \leq t_{\mathbf{Fc}}$ that behave as follows: the set of parties in $\mathcal{A}_{\mathbf{Mal}}$ are completely malicious and can behave arbitrarily as per the adversary's choice, the set of parties in $\mathcal{A}_{\mathbf{Sh}}$ are corrupted in a semi-honest manner meaning that they are required to follow the protocol behavior correctly and the set of parties in $\mathcal{A}_{\mathbf{Fc}}$ are corrupted in a fail-corrupt manner meaning that for each party in this set, the adversary can choose to abort the protocol execution at any point. Crucially, the adversary does not get to see the internal state of any fail-corrupt party. Intuitively, we can imagine these fail-corrupt parties as honest "lazy" parties whose aborting/laziness is controlled by the adversary. In this work, we focus on the setting of static corruptions where the adversary is required to specify all three sets apriori. Of course, note that for each fail-corrupt party, the adversary still has the luxury to determine adaptively when each party is expected to abort.

Our three-round MPC protocol secure against a threshold mixed adversary follows the same recipe as in the works of Mukherjee and Wichs [33] and Brakerski et al. [7] who construct MPC protocols from multi-key FHE. We adapt it to instead use the underlying system as a threshold multi-key FHE scheme. Further, we will parametrize our protocol using an access structure $\mathbb{A}$ which will be used to run the setup of the threshold multi-key FHE scheme. Recall that since we are interested in the setting where guaranteed output delivery is possible, we require that $(t_{\mathbf{Mal}}, t_{\mathbf{Sh}}, t_{\mathbf{Fc}})$ respect the Hirt et al. [27] inequality. That is, $2t_{\mathbf{Mal}} + t_{\mathbf{Sh}} + t_{\mathbf{Fc}} < N$. In our protocol, given a threshold tuple $(t_{\mathbf{Mal}}, t_{\mathbf{Sh}}, t_{\mathbf{Fc}})$, $\mathbb{A}$ will be set as the $(N - t_{\mathbf{Mal}} - t_{\mathbf{Fc}})$-out-of-$N$ access structure. This ensures that $t_{\mathbf{Mal}} + t_{\mathbf{Sh}}$, the maximum number of parties for which the adversary can view the internal state is less than the required threshold to satisfy the access structure.

Security Against Semi-Malicious Mixed Adversaries. Let's first consider the simpler setting where the first set of corrupted parties $\mathcal{A}_{\mathbf{Mal}}$ can only be semi-malicious. That is, on behalf of each of them, the adversary can pick randomness of its choice but the parties are required to follow the protocol behavior honestly using this randomness. The adversary may also choose to have these parties abort at any time. A more formal definition is given in the full version. The overall structure of our MPC protocol with respect to any access structure is the following:

- In round 1, each party generates its parameters and public key for the threshold multi-key FHE scheme.
- In round 2, each party individually encrypts its input with respect to the combined set of public keys and access structure and broadcasts the ciphertext.
- All parties can now homomorphically compute a threshold multi-key FHE encryption of the output, with respect to the functionality under consideration. Then, each party broadcasts a partial decryption of the output using its secret key. The partial decryptions can be combined to recover the output in plaintext.

It can be readily observed from the definition of threshold multi-key FHE that this protocol satisfies correctness and security even in the presence of a threshold mixed adversary (with semi-malicious corruptions), where some lazy honest parties could drop off from the protocol execution at any point as determined by the fail-corrupt corruption. Furthermore, the fact that the protocol has guaranteed output delivery can be observed by noting that at most $t_{\mathbf{Mal}} + t_{\mathbf{Fc}}$ parties will abort. So, at least $N - t_{\mathbf{Mal}} - t_{\mathbf{Fc}}$ parties will remain, which is sufficient to recover the output. Note that since we have restricted the adversary to behave semi-maliciously instead of maliciously on the set $\mathcal{A}_{\mathsf{Mal}}$, every message sent will be "valid."

One key difference from the previous works [7,33] is the following: in the standard model MPC protocols of [7,33], due to the design of the multi-key FHE primitive, the protocol is secure only against a semi-malicious adversary that corrupts all but one party. They then need to transform it to a protocol that is secure against an adversary that can corrupt any arbitrary number of parties up to all but one of them. In our MPC protocol, the security guarantee given by the threshold multi-key FHE scheme allows us to prove a more general statement that our protocol is in fact secure even if the adversary chooses to corrupt fewer parties than it is capable of (it chooses to corrupt less than the threshold number of parties).

Handling Malicious Adversaries. The final step in achieving our MPC protocol is to allow the set $\mathcal{A}_{\mathsf{Mal}}$ to be maliciously corrupted. One way to do this would be to use a NIZK and have each party send a proof in each round that they computed their message properly; if the NIZK proof does not verify, the party would be treated as malicious and ignored. Unfortunately, using a NIZK would require us to introduce a CRS, and we want our protocol to be in the plain model.

Round One: Malicious. To do so, the first crucial observation we make is that the underlying semi-malicious protocol (without a NIZK) in the plain model is already in fact secure against an adversary that can behave maliciously only in the first round. The reason is that the first round message, which consists of the adversary's parameters for the threshold multi-key FHE scheme, is simply a random matrix and a public key. To argue semi-malicious security, we only needed the following two properties:

- The honest parties' matrices are generated uniformly at random.[3]
- The simulator, before the beginning of round three, only needs to know the randomness used by the adversary in the second round to generate its ciphertext. In particular, the simulator does not need to know a corresponding secret key for the public key sent by the adversary in round 1.

As a result, we did not require the input or randomness used by the adversary to generate its round one messages, and hence our protocol is secure against an adversary that can behave maliciously in round one.

Multi-string NIZK. Armed with the above property, we note that our protocol no longer needs to prove correctness of round one messages using a NIZK. Therefore, we will use the first round messages of all parties to try to collectively generate a valid CRS that can then be used to generate the NIZKs and achieve a construction in the plain model. The notion of multi-string NIZKs, introduced in the work of Groth and Ostrovsky [25] exactly fits this requirement. As discussed

[3] This was a wonderful observation made in the work of Brakerski et al. [7].

previously, in a multi-string NIZK argument system, a set of parties can each generate one CRS that can then be combined to compute one unified CRS which is used to compute NIZKs. The guarantee is that as long as a majority of the individual CRS strings are honestly generated, the argument system is correct and secure[4].

In our protocol, we can use this primitive as follows: in round 1, each party generates an individual CRS for the multi-string NIZK system. At the end of round 1, all parties can combine the above set of CRS strings to compute one unified CRS that can then be used to compute NIZKs. In rounds 2 and 3, each party also sends a NIZK along with their message, and the other parties make sure the NIZK verifies. If the NIZK does not verify, the party that submitted an invalid message is ignored for the rest of the protocol and treated as if it had aborted instead.

There is one additional hurdle to ensuring that a multi-string NIZK suffices for our setting. The multi-string NIZK is only secure if a *majority* of the CRSs are honestly generated. However, we want our protocol to be secure against any $(t_{\mathbf{Mal}}, t_{\mathbf{Sh}}, t_{\mathbf{Fc}})$- mixed adversary, where $2t_{\mathbf{Mal}} + t_{\mathbf{Sh}} + t_{\mathbf{Fc}} < N$. In particular, we need the multi-string NIZK to be secure in settings without an honest majority! Fortunately, the multi-string NIZK is still secure in our setting, provided that the CRSs are *uniformly random* strings. To see why this is the case, we first observe that $t_{\mathbf{Fc}}$, the number of fail-corrupt parties does not present any difficulties. This is because these parties fall under the "honest but lazy" parties in our motivation, and so while the adversary can force them to abort, the adversary can never learn any internal state information of these parties or cause them to behave dishonestly. Therefore, any CRS output by these parties will be an honest CRS, and so choosing to not have these parties abort prior to round 1 only increases the number of honest CRSs that are output. The second observation is that any semi-honest corruptions also do not cause any difficulties. This is because the honest procedure for generating a CRS is to simply sample a random string. Therefore, even if an adversary semi-honestly corrupts a party, it can neither prevent it from outputting an honestly generated random string nor learn any state information that could compromise the random string. Therefore, all the CRSs output by the semi-honest corrupt and fail-corrupt parties are honest, and since $2t_{\mathbf{Mal}} + t_{\mathbf{Sh}} + t_{\mathbf{Fc}} < N$, it follows that a majority of the CRSs are honestly generated. Therefore, security of the multi-string NIZK system holds and we obtain a plain model construction. In this work, we construct a multi-string NIZK from LWE that satisfies this additional property required of the CRS and we elaborate more on this construction now.

2.3 Multi-string NIZK from LWE

The above demonstrated that a simulation-extractable multi-string NIZK would allow us to obtain our round-optimal MPC protocol. However, a multi-string

[4] As is the case with compiling semi-malicious protocols into malicious secure ones, we need the NIZK to be simulation-extractable.

NIZK is not known to exist from LWE. Previously it was known from statistically sound ZAPS as shown in the work of [25]. However, ZAPs are not known to exist from polynomially hard LWE. One might think that we could use the recent result of Peikert and Shiehian [35], which constructs either a statistically-sound NIZK in the common reference string model or a computationally-sound NIZK in the common random string model. One might think that we could use the transformation of Dwork and Naor [16] to obtain a ZAP from LWE and then apply the transformation of [25]. However, this does not work, since their transformation crucially requires a *statistically-sound* NIZK in the common *random* string model, which is not known from polynomially hard LWE (the recent works of [2,30] construct such ZAPs from quasipolynomial LWE). Therefore, we require a different approach. We construct the first multi-string NIZK from LWE and use it as a tool in obtaining our round-optimal MPC result.

Our construction proceeds in two main steps. We first build a multi-string non-interactive witness indistinguishable (NIWI) argument from LWE and then show how to bootstrap it to obtain a simulation-extractable multi-string NIZK.

A recent series of works [10,11,28,31,35] have developed a framework for instantiating the Fiat-Shamir transform [18] using a hash function that satisfies a property called correlation-intractability [12]. This culminated in the work of Peikert and Shiehian [35], who were able to obtain the first NIZK from LWE by constructing a correlation-intractable hash function family for (bounded) circuits from LWE. The notion of a correlation-intractable hash function family is defined formally in the full version. Informally, a hash function family $\mathcal{H}$ is correlation-intractable for a relation $\mathcal{R}$ if given a sampled key K, it is hard to find an x such that $(x, \mathcal{H}_K(x)) \in \mathcal{R}$. Following the formula introduced in the above works, we will apply the Fiat-Shamir transform to the Σ protocol for Graph Hamiltonicity by Blum [3] in order to obtain our multi-string NIZK.

Multi-string NIWI from LWE. The first step is to construct a multi-string NIWI from LWE. A multi-string NIWI is defined analogously to a multi-string NIZK. That is, in a multi-string NIWI, a set of parties can each generate one CRS that can then be combined to compute one unified CRS which is used to compute NIWIs. The guarantee is that as long as a majority of the individual CRS strings are honestly generated, the argument system is correct and secure.

To construct the multi-string NIWI, we first construct a non-interactive commitment scheme in the multi-string model with the property that the scheme remains hiding and binding provided that a majority of the CRSs are honestly generated. At a high level, this is done by having each CRS be a public key pk_i of a public key encryption (PKE) scheme. To commit to a message m, one simply secret shares m using a $\lfloor n/2 \rfloor + 1$-out-of-n secret sharing scheme to obtain shares $(m_1, \ldots, m_n)$, then encrypts m_i under pk_i, and outputs these n ciphertexts as the commitment. Since a majority of the public keys were generated honestly, a majority of the shares are hidden by the encryption, so the commitment scheme satisfies hiding. By the correctness of the PKE scheme, the resulting commitment scheme must also be binding. Furthermore, we observe that this commitment scheme also has an associated trapdoor that facilitates extraction of the message committed. In particular, any majority of the secret keys sk_i can be used as a trapdoor as they can recover a majority of message shares from the commitment and, therefore, the message.

The multi-string NIWI is built by having each party generate its CRS in the setup phase as a public key pk_i of a PKE scheme and a hash key K_i from the correlation hash function family $\mathcal{H}$. To prove a statement $x \in L$ using a witness w, we run λ parallel repetitions of the Σ protocol using the above commitment scheme as the underlying commitment scheme and making it non-interactive via the Fiat-Shamir transformation, with the hash function instantiated using $\mathcal{H}_{K_i}$. A proof is the transcript of all the parallel executions of the Σ protocol. Soundness follows from the correlation-intractability of the hash function family $\mathcal{H}$, the binding property of the commitment scheme and the soundness of the underlying Σ protocol. Witness indistinguishability follows from the witness indistinguishability of the underlying Σ protocol and the fact that the commitment scheme is hiding even if a minority of shares are learned. We refer the reader to the full version for more details.

Obtaining a Multi-string NIZK. In order to obtain a multi-string NIZK from our multi-string NIWI, we use the standard trick found in [17,25] each party also generates a random string r_i as part of their CRS and the statement that is proven using the multi-string NIWI now is that $x \in L$ OR a majority of the r_i's are actually the output of a pseudorandom generator G. Soundness and zero knowledge then follow via standard arguments, and we refer the reader to the full version for more details. We then observe that we can also prove simulation-extractability of our multi-string NIZK if we additionally use the commitment scheme from before once again and require the prover to commit to its witness using this scheme. The statement being proved using the multi-string NIWI would now be that either $x \in L$ using a witness w that was committed OR a majority of the r_i's are actually the output of a pseudorandom generator G. Further, in order to prove that the scheme is simulation extractable, here, we will instantiate all the underlying PKE schemes inside the extra commitment scheme (for the witness) with CCA-secure PKE schemes. As a result, our extractor for the simulation-extractable NIZK can use the secret keys of all the honest parties for this extra commitment scheme as a trapdoor to learn the witness associated with the adversary's proof. We refer the reader to the full version for more details about the proof.

Finally, recall that in order to use the multi-string NIZK in our MPC protocol, we require that the CRS generated by each party is a uniformly random string. However, in our construction, in addition to the random string r, the CRS consists of two public keys (one for committing to the witness and one for the commitment used in the Σ protocol) and a hash key K for a correlation-intractable hash function family $\mathcal{H}$. We will use an encryption scheme whose public keys are statistically-close to uniform and we also observe that the hash key is statistically-close to uniform. This ensures that the CRS is also statistically-close to uniform. We then prove that this is in fact sufficient for the MPC application and we don't require the CRS to be a uniformly random string. We refer to the full version for more details.

Roadmap. We define some preliminaries in Sect. 3. Then, we formally define threshold multi-key FHE in Sect. 4 and give our construction in Sect. 5. In Sect. 6, we describe our round optimal MPC protocol with guaranteed output delivery against threshold mixed adversaries. Finally, in Sect. 7, we construct multi-string NIZKs.

3 Preliminaries

We denote the security parameter by λ. For an integer $n \in \mathbb{N}$, we use $[n]$ to denote the set $\{1, 2, \ldots, n\}$. We use $\mathcal{D}_0 \cong_c \mathcal{D}_1$ to denote that two distributions $\mathcal{D}_0, \mathcal{D}_1$ are computationally indistinguishable. We use $\mathsf{negl}(\lambda)$ to denote a function that is negligible in λ. We use $x \leftarrow \mathcal{A}$ to denote that x is the output of a randomized algorithm $\mathcal{A}$, where the randomness of $\mathcal{A}$ is sampled from the uniform distribution. We use PPT as an abbreviation for probabilistic polynomial-time. Whenever we write $\{x_j\}_{j \in S}$ for a set of parties S, we assume that the party j that x_j corresponds to is included in S. When we say an error distribution is E-bounded, we mean that the errors are in $[-E, E]$.

Cryptographic Primitives. We formally define secret sharing, correlation intractable hash functions, simulation-extractable multi-string NIZKs, and Sigma protocols in the full version. We also define MPC against a threshold mixed adversary with guaranteed output delivery following the works of [19,20] in the full version of the paper.

Guaranteed Output Delivery (GOD). Consider an MPC protocol π amongst N parties. Informally, π is said to possess guaranteed output delivery (GOD) if for every PPT malicious adversary, for all possible sets of inputs $\{x_1, \ldots, x_N\}$, for any function f, the following holds: At the end of the execution of π, every honest party outputs $f(y_1, \ldots, y_n)$ where $y_i = x_i$ for every honest party P_i and $y_j = x_j/\perp$ for every corrupt party P_j.

3.1 Multi-key FHE

We recall the definition of multi-key FHE in the plain model with distributed setup as found in [7].

Definition 1 (MFHE). *A multi-key fully homomorphic encryption scheme is a tuple of PPT algorithms*

$$\mathsf{MFHE} = (\mathsf{DistSetup}, \mathsf{KeyGen}, \mathsf{Enc}, \mathsf{Eval}, \mathsf{PartDec}, \mathsf{FinDec})$$

satisfying the following specifications:

$\mathsf{params}_i \leftarrow \mathsf{DistSetup}(1^\lambda, 1^d, 1^N, i)$: *It takes as input a security parameter* λ, *a circuit depth* d, *the maximal number of parties* N, *and a party index* i. *It outputs the public parameters* params_i *associated with the ith party, where* $\mathsf{params}_i \in \{0,1\}^{\mathsf{poly}(\lambda,d,N)}$ *for some polynomial* poly. *We assume implicitly that all the following algorithms take the public parameters of all parties as input, where we define* $\mathsf{params} = \mathsf{params}_1 || \ldots || \mathsf{params}_N$.

$(pk, sk) \leftarrow \mathsf{KeyGen}(\mathsf{params})$: *It takes as input the public parameters* params *and outputs a key pair* (pk, sk).

$ct \leftarrow \mathsf{Encrypt}(pk, m)$: *It takes as input a public key* pk *and a plaintext* $m \in \{0,1\}^\lambda$ *and outputs a ciphertext* ct. *Throughout, we will assume that all ciphertexts include the public key(s) that they are encrypted under.*

$\widehat{ct} \leftarrow \mathsf{Eval}(C, ct_1, \ldots, ct_\ell)$: *It takes as input a boolean circuit* $C\colon (\{0,1\}^\lambda)^\ell \to \{0,1\} \in \mathcal{C}_\lambda$ *of depth* $\leq d$ *and ciphertexts* $ct_1, \ldots, ct_\ell$ *for* $\ell \leq N$. *It outputs an evaluated ciphertext* $\widehat{ct}$.

$p_i \leftarrow \mathsf{PartDec}(i, sk, \hat{ct})$: *It takes as input an index* i, *a secret key* sk *and an evaluated ciphertext* $\hat{ct}$ *and outputs a partial decryption* p_i.

$\widehat{\mu} \leftarrow \mathsf{FinDec}(p_1, \ldots, p_\ell)$: *It takes as input partial decryptions* $p_1, \ldots, p_\ell$ *and deterministically outputs a plaintext* $\widehat{\mu} \in \{0, 1, \perp\}$.

We require that for any parameters $\{\mathsf{params}_i \leftarrow \mathsf{Setup}(1^\lambda, 1^d, 1^N, i)\}_{i \in [N]}$, *any key pairs* $\{(pk_i, sk_i) \leftarrow \mathsf{KeyGen}(\mathsf{params})\}_{i \in [N]}$, *any plaintexts* $m_1, \ldots, m_\ell \in \{0,1\}^\lambda$ *for* $\ell \leq N$, *any sequence* $I_1, \ldots, I_\ell \in [N]$ *of indices, and any boolean circuit* $C\colon \{0,1\}^\ell \to \{0,1\} \in \mathcal{C}_\lambda$ *of depth* $\leq d$, *the following is satisfied:*

Correctness. *Let* $ct_i = \mathsf{Encrypt}(pk_{I_i}, m_i)$ *for* $1 \leq i \leq \ell$, $\hat{ct} = \mathsf{Eval}(C, ct_1, \ldots, ct_\ell)$, *and* $p_i = \mathsf{PartDec}(i, sk_{I_i}, \hat{ct})$ *for all* $i \in [\ell]$. *With all but negligible probability in* λ *over the coins of* Setup, KeyGen, Encrypt, *and* PartDec,

$$\mathsf{FinDec}(p_1, \ldots, p_\ell) = C(m_1, \ldots, m_\ell).$$

Compactness of Ciphertexts. *There exists a polynomial,* poly, *such that* $|ct| \leq \mathsf{poly}(\lambda, d, N)$ *for any ciphertext* ct *generated from the algorithms of* MFHE.

Semantic Security of Encryption. *Any PPT adversary* $\mathcal{A}$ *has only negligible advantage as a function of* λ *over the coins of all the algorithms in the following game:*

1. *On input the security parameter* 1^λ, *a circuit depth* 1^d, *and the number of parties* 1^N, *the adversary* $\mathcal{A}$ *outputs a non-corrupted party* i.
2. *Run* $\mathsf{DistSetup}(1^\lambda, 1^d, 1^N, i) \to \mathsf{params}_i$. *The adversary is given* params_i.
3. *The adversary outputs* $\{\mathsf{params}_j\}_{j \in [N] \setminus \{i\}}$.
4. params *is set to* $\mathsf{params}_1 || \ldots || \mathsf{params}_N$. *Run* $\mathsf{KeyGen}(\mathsf{params}) \to (pk_i, sk_i)$. *The adversary is given* pk_i.
5. *The adversary outputs two messages* $m_0, m_1 \in \{0,1\}^\lambda$.
6. *The adversary is given* $ct \leftarrow \mathsf{Encrypt}(pk_i, m_b)$ *for a random* $b \in \{0,1\}$.
7. *The adversary outputs* b' *and wins if* $b = b'$.

Simulation Security. *There exists a stateful PPT algorithm* Sim *such that for any PPT adversary* $\mathcal{A}$, *we have that the experiments* $\mathsf{Expt}_{\mathcal{A},Real}(1^\lambda, 1^d, 1^N)$ *and* $\mathsf{Expt}_{\mathcal{A},\mathsf{Sim}}(1^\lambda, 1^d, 1^N)$ *as defined below are statistically close as a function of* λ *over the coins of all the algorithms. The experiments are defined as follows:*

$\mathsf{Expt}_{\mathcal{A},Real}(1^\lambda, 1^d, 1^N)$:

1. *On input the security parameter* 1^λ, *a circuit depth* 1^d, *and the number of parties* 1^N, *the adversary* $\mathcal{A}$ *a non-corrupted party* i.
2. *Run* $\mathsf{DistSetup}(1^\lambda, 1^d, 1^N, i) \rightarrow \mathsf{params}_i$. *The adversary is given* params_i.
3. *The adversary outputs* $\{\mathsf{params}_j\}_{j\in[N]\setminus\{i\}}$.
4. params *is set to* $\mathsf{params}_1 || \dots || \mathsf{params}_N$. *Sample* $N-1$ *key pairs* $\mathsf{KeyGen}(\mathsf{params}) \rightarrow (pk_j, sk_j)$ *for* $j \in [N]\setminus\{i\}$. *The adversary is given* $\{(pk_j, sk_j)\}_{j\in[N]\setminus\{i\}}$.
5. *The adversary outputs randomness* r_i^{KeyGen} *used to generate* (pk_i, sk_i), $m_1, \dots, m_\ell \in \{0,1\}^\lambda$, $I_1, \dots, I_\ell \in [N]$, *and a set of circuits* $\{C_k : (\{0,1\}^\lambda)^\ell \rightarrow \{0,1\}\}_{k\in[t]}$ *with each* $C_k \in \mathcal{C}$ *for some* $\ell \leq N$ *and some* $t = \mathsf{poly}(\lambda, d, N)$.
6. *Set* $(pk_i, sk_i) \leftarrow \mathsf{KeyGen}(\mathsf{params}; r_i^{\mathsf{KeyGen}})$. *The adversary is given* $ct_j \leftarrow \mathsf{Enc}(pk_{I_j}, m_j)$ *for* $1 \leq j \leq \ell$ *and the evaluated ciphertexts* $\hat{ct}_k \leftarrow \mathsf{Eval}(C_k, ct_1, \dots, ct_\ell)$ *for all* $k \in [t]$.
7. *The adversary is given* $p_{i,k} \leftarrow \mathsf{PartDec}(i, sk_i, \hat{ct}_k)$ *for all* $k \in [t]$.
8. $\mathcal{A}$ *outputs* out. *The output of the experiment is* out.

$\mathsf{Expt}_{\mathcal{A},\mathsf{Sim}}(1^\lambda, 1^d, 1^N)$:

1. *On input the security parameter* 1^λ, *a circuit depth* 1^d, *and the number of parties* 1^N, *the adversary* $\mathcal{A}$ *a non-corrupted party* i.
2. *Run* $\mathsf{DistSetup}(1^\lambda, 1^d, 1^N, i) \rightarrow \mathsf{params}_i$. *The adversary is given* params_i.
3. *The adversary outputs* $\{\mathsf{params}_j\}_{j\in[N]\setminus\{i\}}$.
4. params *is set to* $\mathsf{params}_1 || \dots || \mathsf{params}_N$. *Sample* $N-1$ *key pairs* $\mathsf{KeyGen}(\mathsf{params}) \rightarrow (pk_j, sk_j)$ *for* $j \in [N]\setminus\{i\}$. *The adversary is given* $\{(pk_j, sk_j)\}_{j\in[N]\setminus\{i\}}$.
5. *The adversary outputs randomness* r_i^{KeyGen} *used to generate* (pk_i, sk_i), $m_1, \dots, m_\ell \in \{0,1\}^\lambda$, $I_1, \dots, I_\ell \in [N]$, *and a set of circuits* $\{C_k : (\{0,1\}^\lambda)^\ell \rightarrow \{0,1\}\}_{k\in[t]}$ *with each* $C_k \in \mathcal{C}$ *for some* $\ell \leq N$ *and some* $t = \mathsf{poly}(\lambda, d, N)$.
6. *Set* $(pk_i, sk_i) \leftarrow \mathsf{KeyGen}(\mathsf{params}; r_i^{\mathsf{KeyGen}})$. *The adversary is given* $ct_j \leftarrow \mathsf{Enc}(pk_{I_j}, m_j)$ *for* $1 \leq j \leq \ell$ *and the evaluated ciphertexts* $\hat{ct}_k \leftarrow \mathsf{Eval}(C_k, ct_1, \dots, ct_\ell)$ *for all* $k \in [t]$.
7. *Define* $\mu_k = C_k(m_1, \dots, m_\ell)$. *For all* $k \in [t]$, *the adversary is given* $p_{i,k} \leftarrow \mathsf{Sim}(\mu_k, \hat{ct}, i, \{sk_j\}_{j\in[N]\setminus\{i\}})$.
8. $\mathcal{A}$ *outputs* out. *The output of the experiment is* out.

4 Threshold Multi-key FHE: Definition

In this section, we present the definition of threshold multi-key fully homomorphic encryption (TMFHE) in the plain model with distributed setup[5]. TMFHE will be the main building block in our MPC protocol.

Definition 2 (TMFHE). *Let $P = \{P_1, \ldots, P_N\}$ be a set of parties and let $\mathbb{S}$ be a class of efficient access structures on P. A threshold multi-key fully homomorphic encryption scheme supporting up to N parties is a tuple of PPT algorithms*

$$\mathsf{TMFHE} = (\mathsf{DistSetup}, \mathsf{KeyGen}, \mathsf{Enc}, \mathsf{Eval}, \mathsf{PartDec}, \mathsf{FinDec})$$

satisfying the following specifications:

$\mathsf{params}_i \leftarrow \mathsf{DistSetup}(1^\lambda, 1^d, 1^N, i)$: *It takes as input a security parameter λ, a circuit depth d, the maximal number of parties N, and a party index i. It outputs the public parameters* params_i *associated with the ith party. We define* $\mathsf{params} = \mathsf{params}_1 || \cdots || \mathsf{params}_N$.

$(pk, sk) \leftarrow \mathsf{KeyGen}(1^\lambda)$: *It takes as input the security parameter λ and outputs a key pair (pk, sk).*

$ct \leftarrow \mathsf{Encrypt}(\mathsf{params}, pk_1, \ldots, pk_N, \mathbb{A}, m)$: *It takes as input the public parameters* params, *public keys $pk_1, \ldots, pk_N$, an access structure $\mathbb{A}$ over P and a plaintext $m \in \{0,1\}^\lambda$ and outputs a ciphertext ct. Throughout, we will assume that all ciphertexts include the public parameters, the public keys, and the access structure that they are encrypted under.*

$\widehat{ct} \leftarrow \mathsf{Eval}(C, ct_1, \ldots, ct_\ell)$: *It takes as input a boolean circuit $C\colon (\{0,1\}^\lambda)^\ell \to \{0,1\} \in \mathcal{C}_\lambda$ of depth $\leq d$ and ciphertexts $ct_1, \ldots, ct_\ell$ for $\ell = \mathsf{poly}(N)$. It outputs an evaluated ciphertext $\widehat{ct}$.*

$p_i \leftarrow \mathsf{PartDec}(i, sk, \hat{ct})$: *It takes as input an index i, a secret key sk and an evaluated ciphertext $\hat{ct}$ and outputs a partial decryption p_i.*

$\widehat{\mu} \leftarrow \mathsf{FinDec}(B)$: *It takes as input a set $B = \{p_i\}_{i \in S}$ for some $S \subseteq \{P_1, \ldots, P_N\}$ where we recall that we identify a party P_i with its index i. It deterministically outputs a plaintext $\widehat{\mu} \in \{0, 1, \perp\}$.*

We require that for any parameters $\{\mathsf{params}_i \leftarrow \mathsf{DistSetup}(1^\lambda, 1^d, 1^N, i)\}_{i\in[N]}$, *any key pairs* $\{(pk_i, sk_i) \leftarrow \mathsf{KeyGen}(1^\lambda)\}_{i\in[N]}$, *any supported access structure $\mathbb{A}$ over P, any plaintexts $m_1, \ldots, m_\ell \in \{0,1\}^\lambda$ for $\ell = \mathsf{poly}(N)$, and any boolean circuit $C\colon (\{0,1\}^\lambda)^\ell \to \{0,1\} \in \mathcal{C}_\lambda$ of depth $\leq d$, the following is satisfied:*

Correctness. *Let* $ct_i = \mathsf{Encrypt}(\mathsf{params}, pk_1, \ldots, pk_N, \mathbb{A}, m_i)$ *for* $1 \leq i \leq \ell$, $\hat{ct} = \mathsf{Eval}(C, ct_1, \ldots, ct_\ell)$, *and* $B = \{\mathsf{PartDec}(i, sk_i, \hat{ct})\}_{i\in S}$. *With all but negligible probability in λ over the coins of* DistSetup, KeyGen, Encrypt, *and* PartDec,

$$\mathsf{FinDec}(B) = \begin{cases} C(m_1, \ldots, m_\ell), & S \in \mathbb{A} \\ \perp & S \notin \mathbb{A}. \end{cases}$$

[5] Note that we can instead define TMFHE with a single trusted setup, which will allow us to construct MPC protocols in the CRS model as in [33]. However, our main focus is on the plain model, and therefore, we use decentralized setup as in [7].

Compactness of Ciphertexts. *There exists a polynomial,* poly*, such that* $|ct| \leq \mathsf{poly}(\lambda, d, N)$ *for any ciphertext ct generated from the algorithms of* TMFHE.

Simulation Security. *There exist PPT algorithms* $\mathsf{Sim}_1, \mathsf{Sim}_2$ *such that for any PPT adversary* $\mathcal{A}$*, we have that the experiments* $\mathsf{Expt}_{\mathcal{A},Real}(1^\lambda, 1^d, 1^N)$ *and* $\mathsf{Expt}_{\mathcal{A},\mathsf{Sim}}(1^\lambda, 1^d, 1^N)$ *are computationally indistinguishable.*

$\mathsf{Expt}_{\mathcal{A},Real}(1^\lambda, 1^d, 1^N)$:

1. *On input the security parameter* 1^λ*, a circuit depth* 1^d*, and the maximal number of parties* 1^N*, the adversary* $\mathcal{A}$ *outputs an access structure* $\mathbb{A} \in \mathbb{S}$ *over* N *parties and a maximal set* $S \subseteq [N]$ *such that* $S \notin \mathbb{A}$.
2. *For* $i \in [N]$*, run* $\mathsf{DistSetup}(1^\lambda, 1^d, 1^N, i) \rightarrow \mathsf{params}_i$*. The adversary is given* $\{\mathsf{params}_i\}_{i \in [N]}$*. Sample key pairs* $\mathsf{KeyGen}(1^\lambda) \rightarrow (pk_i, sk_i)$ *for* $i \in [N]$*. The adversary is given* $\{pk_i\}_{i \in [N]}$ *and* $\{sk_i\}_{i \in S}$.
3. *The adversary then outputs messages* $m_1, \ldots, m_\ell \in \{0,1\}^\lambda$ *for* $\ell = \mathsf{poly}(N)$.
4. params *is set to the concatenation of the* params_i*'s for* $i \in [N]$*. Let* $\mathcal{PK} = \{pk_i\}_{i \in [N]}$*. The adversary is given* $ct_i \leftarrow \mathsf{Enc}(\mathsf{params}, \mathcal{PK}, \mathbb{A}, m_i)$ *for* $i \in [\ell]$.
5. *The adversary issues polynomially many queries of the form* $(C_k : (\{0,1\}^\lambda)^\ell \rightarrow \{0,1\})$*, where* $C_k \in \mathcal{C}$*. Let the evaluated ciphertext be* $\hat{ct}_k \leftarrow \mathsf{Eval}(C_k, ct_1, \ldots, ct_\ell)$*. After each query, the adversary receives* $p_{i,k} \leftarrow \mathsf{PartDec}(i, sk_i, \hat{ct}_k)$ *for all* $i \in [N] \backslash S$.
6. $\mathcal{A}$ *outputs* out*. The output of the experiment is* out.

$\mathsf{Expt}_{\mathcal{A},Sim}(1^\lambda, 1^d, 1^N)$:

1. *On input the security parameter* 1^λ*, a circuit depth* 1^d*, and the maximal number of parties* 1^N*, the adversary* $\mathcal{A}$ *outputs an access structure* $\mathbb{A} \in \mathbb{S}$ *over* N *parties and a maximal set* $S \subseteq [N]$ *such that* $S \notin \mathbb{A}$.
2. *For* $i \in [N]$*, run* $\mathsf{DistSetup}(1^\lambda, 1^d, 1^N, i) \rightarrow \mathsf{params}_i$*. The adversary is given* $\{\mathsf{params}_i\}_{i \in [N]}$*. Sample key pairs* $\mathsf{KeyGen}(1^\lambda) \rightarrow (pk_i, sk_i)$ *for* $i \in [N]$*. The adversary is given* $\{pk_i\}_{i \in [N]}$ *and* $\{sk_i\}_{i \in S}$.
3. *The adversary then outputs messages* $m_1, \ldots, m_\ell \in \{0,1\}^\lambda$ *for* $\ell = \mathsf{poly}(N)$.
4. params *is set to the concatenation of the* params_i*'s for* $i \in [N]$*. Let* $\mathcal{PK} = \{pk_i\}_{i \in [N]}$*. The adversary is given* $\{ct_i\}_{i \in [\ell]} \leftarrow \mathsf{Sim}_1(\mathsf{params}, \mathcal{PK}, \mathbb{A})$.
5. *The adversary issues polynomially many queries of the form* $(C_k : (\{0,1\}^\lambda)^\ell \rightarrow \{0,1\})$*, where* $C_k \in \mathcal{C}$*. Let the evaluated ciphertext be* $\hat{ct}_k \leftarrow \mathsf{Eval}(C_k, ct_1, \ldots, ct_\ell)$*. After each query, the adversary receives* $\{p_{i,k}\}_{i \notin S} \leftarrow \mathsf{Sim}_2(\mu_k, \hat{ct}_k, S, \{sk_i\}_{i \in S})$*, where* $\mu_k = C_k(\{m_i\}_{i \in [\ell]})$.
6. $\mathcal{A}$ *outputs* out*. The output of the experiment is* out.

The security notion is inspired by the security definitions of multi-key FHE [7, 33] suitably adapted to the context of general access structures. Observe that the above definition captures both the semantic security of ciphertexts and the simulation security of partial decryptions.

Looking ahead to our MPC protocol, we will actually need some stronger guarantees from the TMFHE scheme, which adds complexity to the security definition. In our MPC protocol, the adversary is allowed to choose which honest parties abort in each round and is rushing, so he is allowed to control the randomness of corrupted parties as a function of the honest parties. We capture this by allowing the simulator of the TMFHE scheme to be stateful. Additionally, since the adversary in MPC is rushing, it is allowed to see the honest parameters/ciphertexts before it picks its parameters/ciphertexts.

The (more general) formal definition we use is deferred to the full version.

5 Threshold Multi-key FHE: Construction

In this section, we construct threshold multi-key FHE as defined in Sect. 4. Formally, we show the following.

Theorem 4 (TMFHE). *Assuming LWE, there exists a secure threshold multi-key FHE scheme for the class of access structures* $\{0,1\}$-LSSSD. *In particular, there exists a secure TMFHE scheme for any access structure induced by a monotone boolean formula and any* t *out of* N *access structure.*

We use several ingredients. First, we initialize a multi-key FHE scheme using the construction in [7]. Then, we utilize the techniques in the construction of threshold FHE in [29][6], which shows how to transform a generic FHE scheme satisfying several properties into a threshold FHE scheme. We observe that the multi-key FHE construction of [7] is "compatible" with the thresholdizing transformation described in [29]. Finally, we use a public key encryption scheme to tie everything together.

In more detail, examining the construction of [29], we note that it is compatible with a generic FHE scheme where:

1. The secret key sk is a vector in $\mathbb{Z}_q^m$ for some prime q.
2. The decryption function Dec can be broken into two algorithms $\mathsf{Dec}_0, \mathsf{Dec}_1$ where $\mathsf{Dec}_0(sk, ct)$ computes a linear function in sk and ct to output $\mu\lceil q/2\rceil + e$ for some bounded error $e \in [-E, E]$ with $E << q$, where ct is an encryption of μ. Dec_1 then takes this resulting value and rounds to recover μ.

We note that the construction of multi-key FHE in [7] satisfies these required properties. Furthermore, it satisfies the following additional properties that will be useful to note in the construction.

1. An evaluated ciphertext $\hat{ct}$ that encrypts a bit μ with respect to public keys $pk_1, \ldots, pk_\ell$ is a matrix that satisfies

$$\boldsymbol{s} \cdot \hat{ct} \approx \mu \boldsymbol{s} \cdot G$$

for a gadget matrix G and $\boldsymbol{s} = (sk_1 || \ldots || sk_\ell)$, where sk_i is the secret key corresponding to public key pk_i. Each sk_i is of the form $(s_i||1)$.

[6] We note that the work of Boneh et al. [4] is a merge of [29] and [5].

2. There exists a low-norm vector $\boldsymbol{v}$ such that $G\boldsymbol{v} = (0, 0, \ldots, \lceil q/2 \rceil)^T$. Decryption proceeds by evaluating $\boldsymbol{s} \cdot \hat{ct} \cdot \boldsymbol{v}$ and then outputs 1 if the resulting value is closer to $\lceil q/2 \rceil$ than 0 and 0 otherwise.

Furthermore, [29] shows the following result.

Theorem 5. **([29]).** *For any access structure* $\mathbb{A}$ *on* N *parties induced by a monotone boolean formula, there exists a* $\{0,1\}$*-LSSSD scheme of a vector* $s \in \mathbb{Z}_q^m$ *where each party* P *receives at most* w *shares of the form* $s_i \in \mathbb{Z}_q^m$ *for* $w = \mathsf{poly}(N)$.

5.1 Construction

Let $\mathsf{MFHE} = (\mathsf{DistSetup}, \mathsf{KeyGen}, \mathsf{Enc}, \mathsf{Eval}, \mathsf{PartDec}, \mathsf{FinDec})$ be a multi-key FHE scheme instantiated with the construction in [7]. Let $\mathsf{PKE} = (\mathsf{Setup}, \mathsf{Enc}, \mathsf{Dec})$ be a public-key encryption scheme. Let χ^{sm} denote the uniform distribution on the interval $[-E_{sm}, E_{sm}]$ for a value E_{sm} to be determined.

Our threshold multi-key FHE construction TMFHE is given as follows:

$\mathsf{DistSetup}(1^\lambda, 1^d, 1^N, i)$: Run $\mathsf{MFHE.DistSetup}(1^\lambda, 1^d, 1^N, i) \to \mathsf{params}_i$ and output params_i.

$\mathsf{KeyGen}(1^\lambda)$: Run $\mathsf{PKE.Setup}(1^\lambda) \to (pk, sk)$ and output (pk, sk).

$\mathsf{Encrypt}(\mathsf{params}, pk_1, \ldots, pk_N, \mathbb{A}, m)$: Run $\mathsf{MFHE.KeyGen}(\mathsf{params}) \to (\mathsf{fpk}, \mathsf{fsk})$. Compute $\{\mathsf{fsk}_{i,j}\}_{i \in [N], j \in [w]}$ for some $w = \mathsf{poly}(N)$ by applying the $\{0,1\}$-LSSSD scheme associated with $\mathbb{A}$ to fsk to . Set $ct' \leftarrow \mathsf{MFHE.Enc}(\mathsf{fpk}, m)$ and for $i \in [N]$, set $ct_i = \mathsf{PKE.Enc}(pk_i, \{\mathsf{fsk}_{i,j}\}_{j \in [w]})$. Output

$$ct = (ct', ct_1, \ldots, ct_N).$$

$\mathsf{Eval}(C, ct_1, \ldots, ct_\ell)$: Parse ct_i as $(ct'_i, ct_{i,1}, \ldots, ct_{i,N})$. Let fpk_i be the MFHE public key associated with ct'_i. Run $\mathsf{MFHE.Eval}(C, ct'_1, \ldots, ct'_\ell) \to \hat{ct}'$. Output

$$\hat{ct} = (\hat{ct}', \{ct_{i,j}\}_{(i,j) \in [\ell] \times [N]}).$$

$\mathsf{PartDec}(i, sk, \hat{ct})$: Parse $\hat{ct}$ as $(\hat{ct}', \{ct_{k,j}\}_{(k,j) \in [\ell] \times [N]})$. For every $k \in [\ell]$, run $\mathsf{PKE.Dec}(sk, ct_{k,i}) \to \{\mathsf{fsk}_{k,i,j}\}_{j \in [w]}$. For $t \in [w]$, compute

$$(\mathsf{fsk}_{1,i,t} || \mathsf{fsk}_{2,i,t} || \ldots || \mathsf{fsk}_{\ell,i,t}) \cdot \hat{ct}' \cdot \boldsymbol{v} + e_t^{sm} \to p'_t,$$

where $e_t^{sm} \leftarrow \chi^{sm}$ and $\boldsymbol{v}$ is the low-norm vector used for decryption in [7] described above. Output $p_i = (i, \{p'_t\}_{t \in [w]})$.

$\mathsf{FinDec}(B)$: Parse B as $\{(i, \{p'_t\}_{t \in [w]})\}_{i \in S}$ for some set S of indices. If $S \notin \mathbb{A}$, output $\perp$. If $S \in \mathbb{A}$, apply the $\{0,1\}$-LSSSD reconstruction to get $\approx \hat{\mu} \lceil q/2 \rceil$. Then, round to recover $\hat{\mu}$.

We defer the proofs of correctness, compactness, and security to the full version.

Instantiation. In order for correctness to hold, we required that $E + NwE_{sm} < q/4$. For security, we required that $NwE/E_{sm} = \mathsf{negl}(\lambda)$. Recall that $w = \mathsf{poly}(N)$. Let $W = \mathsf{poly}(N)$ be an upper bound for the set of access structures supported by the scheme. Then, setting $E/E_{sm} < \lambda^{-\log_2 \lambda}$ and $E_{sm} < q/8NW$ gives us an instantiation that satisfies both correctness and security. The MFHE scheme of [7] can be instantiated with such properties assuming a variant of the learning with errors assumption, which is as hard as approximating the shortest vector problem to within a subexponential factor.

6 Round-Optimal MPC with Guaranteed Output Delivery Secure Against Threshold Mixed Adversaries

In this section, we use threshold multi-key FHE to construct a round-optimal (three-round) MPC protocol in the plain model with guaranteed output delivery that is secure against a threshold mixed adversary (defined in the full version), assuming LWE. Our protocol supports all functionalities computable by polynomial-sized circuits and is parameterized by a tuple of thresholds $(t_{\mathbf{Mal}}, t_{\mathbf{Sh}}, t_{\mathbf{Fc}})$ that represent the number of malicious, semi-honest, and fail-corrupt corruptions that the adversary is allowed to make, respectively. Our protocol has guaranteed output delivery and is secure provided that $2t_{\mathbf{Mal}} + t_{\mathbf{Sh}} + t_{\mathbf{Fc}} < N$, the Hirt et al. [27] inequality that characterizes the threshold values under with guaranteed output delivery is possible to achieve.

Thus, our resulting protocol is both *optimal* in terms of the best possible corruption we can tolerate and also *round-optimal* (since at least three rounds are required for a protocol to have guaranteed output delivery, as shown by Gordon et al. [24]). Moreover, our protocol has depth-proportional communication complexity, is reusable, and has input fidelity for "honest but lazy" parties. Formally, we show the following.

Theorem 6. *Assuming LWE, for any function f, for any tuple of thresholds $(t_{Mal}, t_{Sh}, t_{Fc})$ satisfying $2t_{Mal} + t_{Sh} + t_{Fc} < N$, there exists a three-round MPC protocol with guaranteed output delivery in the plain model that is secure against a $(t_{Mal}, t_{Sh}, t_{Fc})$-mixed adversary. Furthermore, the protocol is reusable, has communication complexity* $\mathsf{poly}(\lambda, d, N)$, *where d is the depth of the circuit computing f and the functionality is computed with respect to the inputs of all parties that send valid messages in the first two rounds.*

Note that our result in the mixed adversary setting is in fact broader and more general than the traditional MPC setting. By instantiating Theorem 6 with the $(\lceil N/2 - 1 \rceil, 0, 0)$-mixed adversary (this corresponds to the honest-majority setting against a malicious adversary), we immediately obtain the following corollary.

Corollary 2. *Assuming LWE, for any function f, there exists a three-round MPC protocol with guaranteed output delivery in the plain model that is secure against a malicious adversary in the honest majority setting. Furthermore, the protocol is reusable and has communication complexity* $\mathsf{poly}(\lambda, d, N)$, *where d is the depth of the circuit computing f.*

Like Theorem 6, this result is round-optimal and supports the maximum possible number of corruptions.

6.1 Security Against a Semi-malicious Mixed Adversary

As a stepping stone to showing Theorem 6, we first construct a protocol that satisfies all the properties of Theorem 6, except that it is only secure against a semi-malicious mixed adversary (defined in the full version), which is simply a mixed adversary that corrupts some parties *semi-maliciously*, rather than maliciously. We describe below our three-round MPC protocol that is secure against a $(t_{\mathbf{Sm}}, t_{\mathbf{Sh}}, t_{\mathbf{Fc}})$-semi-malicious mixed adversary $\mathcal{A} = (\mathcal{A}_{\mathbf{Sm}}, \mathcal{A}_{\mathbf{Sh}}, \mathcal{A}_{\mathbf{Fc}})$ for $2t_{\mathbf{Sm}} + t_{\mathbf{Sh}} + t_{\mathbf{Fc}} < N$.

Notation: Consider N parties $P_1, \ldots, P_N$ with inputs $x_1, \ldots, x_N$, respectively, who wish to evaluate a boolean circuit C with depth $\leq d$. Without loss of generality, assume $|x_i| = \lambda\ \forall i \in [N]$. Let $(\mathsf{DistSetup}, \mathsf{KeyGen}, \mathsf{Enc}, \mathsf{Eval}, \mathsf{PartDec}, \mathsf{FinDec})$ be the previously constructed threshold multi-key FHE scheme. Fix $(t_{\mathbf{Sm}}, t_{\mathbf{Sh}}, t_{\mathbf{Fc}})$ satisfying $2t_{\mathbf{Sm}} + t_{\mathbf{Sh}} + t_{\mathbf{Fc}} < N$. Let $\mathbb{A}$ be the $(N - t_{\mathbf{Sm}} - t_{\mathbf{Fc}})$-out-of-$N$ threshold access structure.

Protocol: We now describe our construction.

- **Input Commitment Phase:**
  - **Round 1:** Each party P_i does the following:
    1. Run $\mathsf{TMFHE.DistSetup}(1^\lambda, 1^d, 1^N, i)$ to obtain params_i.
    2. Run $\mathsf{TMFHE.KeyGen}(1^\lambda)$ to compute (pk_i, sk_i).
    3. Output $(\mathsf{params}_i, pk_i)$.
  - **Round 2:** Each party P_i does the following:
    1. Parse the message (if one was sent) from P_j as $(\mathsf{params}_j, pk_j)$. Let $S_1 \subseteq [N]$ be the set of parties that sent a message in round 1.
    2. Truncate each params_j for $j \in S_1$ to the appropriate size given $|S_1|$[7]. Set params as the concatenation of the truncated params_j's for $j \in S_1$. Set $\mathcal{PK} = \{pk_j\}_{j \in S_1}$. Let $\mathbb{A}'$ be the access structure induced by restricting $\mathbb{A}$ to the parties in S_1 (that is, the $(N - t_{\mathbf{Sm}} - t_{\mathbf{Fc}})$-out-of-$|S_1|$ access structure).
    3. Run $\mathsf{TMFHE.Encrypt}(\mathsf{params}, \mathcal{PK}, \mathbb{A}', x_i)$ to compute ct_i.
    4. Output ct_i.
- **Computation Phase:**
  - **Round 3:** Each party P_i does the following:
    1. Parse the previous message (if one was sent) from P_j as ct_j. Let $S_2 \subseteq [N]$ be the set of parties that sent a message in round 2. Let $\mathcal{CT} = \{ct_j\}_{j \in S_2}$. Let C' be the circuit induced by hardcoding the inputs to C corresponding to parties not in S_2 to be 0^λ.

[7] Note that the params_i of each party in the MFHE construction in [7] and, therefore, also in our TMFHE construction, are simply random matrices A_i of a size dependent on N. Therefore, truncating the matrix to the appropriate size for a scheme with $|S_1|$ parties is equivalent to having run the distributed setup algorithm for $|S_1|$ parties.

2. Run $\mathsf{TMFHE.Eval}(C', \mathcal{CT})$ to obtain $\hat{ct}$.
3. Run $\mathsf{TMFHE.PartDec}(i, sk_i, \hat{ct})$ to obtain p_i.
4. Output p_i.

– **Output Computation:** Each party P_i does the following:
1. Parse the previous message (if one was sent) from P_j as p_j. Let $S_3 \subseteq [N]$ be the set of parties that sent a message in round 3.
2. Take any set $S \subseteq S_3$ with $S \in \mathbb{A}$ and run $\mathsf{TMFHE.FinDec}(B)$ where $B = \{p_j\}_{j \in S}$ to recover $\hat{\mu}$. If no such set exists, output $\perp$.

We defer the proofs of correctness, security, and the properties of the above protocol to the full version.

6.2 Handling a Malicious Mixed Adversary

In the above protocol, the adversary can only corrupt some subset $\mathcal{A}_{\mathbf{Sm}}$ of the parties semi-maliciously, some subset $\mathcal{A}_{\mathbf{Sh}}$ in a semi-honest manner and another subset $\mathcal{A}_{\mathbf{Fc}}$ in a fail-corrupt manner. In order to show Theorem 6, we need to allow the adversary to corrupt the first subset $\mathcal{A}_{\mathbf{Sm}}$ maliciously.

Our first observation is that the protocol is secure even against mixed adversaries that are allowed make parties in $\mathcal{A}_{\mathbf{Sm}}$ behave *maliciously* in round 1, but only semi-maliciously in rounds 2 and 3. After noting this, we further observe that if we had a simulation-extractable multi-string NIZK [25] in the plain model where the honest party's behavior when generating a CRS is to simply sample a uniformly random string[8], then we could upgrade to security against malicious mixed adversaries. We simply have each party send a reference string CRS in round 1 and then require each party to also provide a NIZK argument in rounds 2 and 3 using these CRSs to ensure that they submitted a valid message in that round. As mentioned previously, the multi-string NIZK is only secure if a *majority* of the CRSs are honestly generated. However, we want our protocol to be secure against any $(t_{\mathbf{Mal}}, t_{\mathbf{Sh}}, t_{\mathbf{Fc}})$- mixed adversary, where $2t_{\mathbf{Mal}}+t_{\mathbf{Sh}}+t_{\mathbf{Fc}} < N$. In particular, we are no longer in the honest majority setting. As discussed earlier, this is not an issue because only the CRSs corresponding to a maliciously-corrupted party could be dishonestly generated and since the honest-generation behavior is to simply output a uniformly random string, a party that is semi-honestly corrupted will also output a perfectly good CRS. Furthermore, since the number of maliciously-corrupted parties is a minority of the total number of parties that send a CRS, a majority of the CRSs will be honestly generated and security of the multi-string NIZK holds.

Security Against a Round 1 Malicious Mixed Adversary. We begin by showing security of the protocol in Sect. 6.1 against a semi-malicious mixed adversary that can behave maliciously in round 1. Since params_i in the MFHE

[8] For ease of exposition, we assume here that the honest CRS is a uniformly random string. However, there is a subtle technical issue, which we handle in Sect. 7 where we construct the multi-string NIZK.

construction in [7] is simply a matrix A_i of random entries, it follows that every A_i output of a malicious adversary could also have been output by a semi-malicious adversary that chose the appropriate randomness (we can simply truncate the message or pad it with 0's if the malicious adversary sends a message of inappropriate length). However, a malicious adversary may send a pk_i that does not correspond to any possible public key output by the $\mathsf{TMFHE.KeyGen}$ algorithm. So, in the proof, the simulator does not receive the randomness r_i^{KeyGen} used by the adversary to compute the round 1 message for a corrupted party and therefore does not receive sk_i for corrupted parties. However, as we saw in Sect. 5, the simulator does not need to know sk_i or r_i^{KeyGen}. Rather, it suffices to know $(x_i, r_i^{\mathsf{Encrypt}})$, the input and randomness used to compute a corrupted party's round 2 message in order to simulate. Thus, an analogous simulator and proof can be used to show security against this adversary.

Upgrading to Malicious Security via Multi-string NIZKs. We now show how to use a simulation-extractable multi-string NIZK with uniformly random CRSs to upgrade the protocol in Sect. 6.1 to one that achieves Theorem 6. The final step is to show that such a multi-string NIZK can be built from LWE. This was not previously known, and we show this in Sect. 7.

Construction. Let $\mathsf{TMFHE} = (\mathsf{DistSetup}, \mathsf{KeyGen}, \mathsf{Enc}, \mathsf{Eval}, \mathsf{PartDec}, \mathsf{FinDec})$ be the previously constructed threshold multi-key FHE scheme from Sect. 5 with the underlying PKE scheme instantiated with one where any string is a valid public key (a dense cryptosystem). Fix $(t_{\mathbf{Mal}}, t_{\mathbf{Sh}}, t_{\mathbf{Fc}})$ satisfying $2t_{\mathbf{Mal}} + t_{\mathbf{Sh}} + t_{\mathbf{Fc}} < N$. Let $\mathbb{A}$ be the $N - t_{\mathbf{Mal}} - t_{\mathbf{Fc}}$-out-of-$N$ threshold access structure. Let $\mathsf{NIZK} = (\mathsf{Gen}, \mathsf{Prove}, \mathsf{Verify})$ be a simulation-extractable multi-string NIZK. To compare against our previous protocol in Sect. 6.1, we highlight the changes in red.

- **Round 1:** Each party P_i does the following:
  1. Run $\mathsf{TMFHE.DistSetup}(1^\lambda, 1^d, 1^N, i)$ to obtain params_i.
  2. Run $\mathsf{TMFHE.KeyGen}(1^\lambda)$ to compute (pk_i, sk_i).
  3. Run $\mathsf{NIZK.Gen}(1^{\lambda'})$ to compute crs_i, where $\lambda' = \mathsf{poly}(\lambda, d, N)$ is the size of statements that will be proven.
  4. Output $(\mathsf{params}_i, pk_i, \mathsf{crs}_i)$.
- **Round 2:** Each party P_i does the following:
  1. Parse the message (if one was sent) from P_j as $(\mathsf{params}_j, pk_j, \mathsf{crs}_j)$ by appropriately truncating or padding with 0's if it was of incorrect length. Let $S_1 \subseteq [N]$ be the set of parties that sent a message in round 1.
  2. Truncate each params_j for $j \in S_1$ to the appropriate size given $|S_1|$. Set params as the concatenation of the truncated params_j's for $j \in S_1$. Set $\mathcal{PK} = \{pk_j\}_{j \in S_1}$. Let $\mathcal{CRS} = \{\mathsf{crs}_j\}_{j \in S_1}$. Let $\mathbb{A}'$ be the access structure induced by restricting $\mathbb{A}$ to the parties in S_1 (that is, the $(N - t_{\mathbf{Sm}} - t_{\mathbf{Fc}})$-out-of-$|S_1|$ access structure).
  3. Sample randomness r_i and run $\mathsf{TMFHE.Encrypt}(\mathsf{params}, \mathcal{PK}, \mathbb{A}', x_i; r_i)$ to compute ct_i.

4. Run $\mathsf{NIZK.Prove}(\mathcal{CRS}, y_i, (x_i, r_i))$ to compute π_i, where y_i is the statement that there exists some input x and randomness r such that $\mathsf{TMFHE.Encrypt}(\mathsf{params}, \mathcal{PK}, \mathbb{A}', x; r) = ct_i$.
5. Output (ct_i, π_i).

- **Round 3:** Each party P_i does the following:
  1. Parse the previous message (if one was sent) from P_j as (ct_j, π_j) and check that $\mathsf{NIZK.Verify}(\mathcal{CRS}, y_j, \pi_j) = 1$. Let $S_2 \subseteq S_1$ be the set of parties that sent a message in round 2 that passed the verification. Let $\mathcal{CT} = \{ct_j\}_{j \in S_2}$. Let C' be the circuit induced by hardcoding the inputs to C corresponding to parties not in S_2 to be 0^λ.
  2. Run $\mathsf{TMFHE.Eval}(C', \mathcal{CT})$ to compute $\hat{ct}$.
  3. Sample randomness r'_i and run $\mathsf{TMFHE.PartDec}(i, sk_i, \hat{ct}; r'_i)$ to compute p_i.
  4. Run $\mathsf{NIZK.Prove}(\mathcal{CRS}, z_i, (sk_i, r'_i))$ to compute π'_i, where z_i is the statement that there exists randomness r, r' such that $\mathsf{TMFHE.KeyGen}(1^\lambda; r) = (pk_i, sk)$ and $\mathsf{TMFHE.PartDec}(i, sk, \hat{ct}; r') = p_i$.
  5. Output (p_i, π'_i).
- **Output Computation:** Each party P_i does the following:
  1. Parse the previous message (if one was sent) from P_j as (p_j, π'_j) and check that $\mathsf{NIZK.Verify}(\mathcal{CRS}, z_j, \pi'_j) = 1$. Let $S_3 \subseteq S_2$ be the set of parties that sent a message in round 3 that passed verification.
  2. Take any set $S \subseteq S_3$ with $S \in \mathbb{A}'$ and run $\mathsf{TMFHE.FinDec}(B)$ where $B = \{p_j\}_{j \in S}$ to recover $\hat{\mu}$. If no such set exists, output $\perp$.

We defer the formal proofs to the full version.

7 Multi-string NIZKs

In this section, we build a simulation-extractable multi-string NIZK argument system for NP based on the learning with errors (LWE) assumption. We first show how to build a multi-string non-interactive witness indistinguishable argument system (NIWI) from LWE. We then give a transformation from multi-string NIWI to multi-string simulation-extractable NIZK that follows along the lines of the work of Groth and Ostrovsky [25]. Formally, we show the following results:

Theorem 7. *Assuming LWE, there exists a multi-string non-interactive witness indistinguishable argument system for NP.*

Theorem 8. *Assuming LWE, there exists a multi-string simulation-extractable NIZK argument system for NP.*

We defer this section to the full version.

Acknowledgements. Saikrishna Badrinarayanan, Aayush Jain, Nathan Manohar, and Amit Sahai were supported in part from DARPA SAFEWARE and SIEVE awards, NTT Research, NSF Frontier Award 1413955, and NSF grant 1619348, BSF grant 2012378, a Xerox Faculty Research Award, a Google Faculty Research Award, an equipment grant from Intel, and an Okawa Foundation Research Grant. This material is based upon work supported by the Defense Advanced Research Projects Agency through Award HR00112020024 and the ARL under Contract W911NF-15-C- 0205. The views expressed are those of the authors and do not reflect the official policy or position of the Department of Defense, the National Science Foundation, NTT Research, or the U.S. Government. Saikrishna Badrinarayanan was also partially supported by an IBM PhD fellowship. Aayush Jain was also partially supported by a Google PhD fellowship.

References

1. Ananth, P., Choudhuri, A.R., Goel, A., Jain, A.: Round-optimal secure multiparty computation with honest majority. In: Shacham, H., Boldyreva, A. (eds.) CRYPTO 2018. LNCS, vol. 10992, pp. 395–424. Springer, Cham (2018). https://doi.org/10.1007/978-3-319-96881-0_14
2. Badrinarayanan, S., Fernando, R., Jain, A., Khurana, D., Sahai, A.: Statistical ZAP arguments. In: Canteaut, A., Ishai, Y. (eds.) EUROCRYPT 2020. LNCS, vol. 12107, pp. 642–667. Springer, Cham (2020). https://doi.org/10.1007/978-3-030-45727-3_22
3. Blum, M.: How to prove a theorem so no one else can claim it. In: Proceedings of the International Congress of Mathematicians. vol. 1, p. 2. Citeseer (1986)
4. Boneh, D., et al.: Threshold cryptosystems from threshold fully homomorphic encryption. In: Shacham, H., Boldyreva, A. (eds.) CRYPTO 2018. LNCS, vol. 10991, pp. 565–596. Springer, Cham (2018). https://doi.org/10.1007/978-3-319-96884-1_19
5. Boneh, D., Gennaro, R., Goldfeder, S., Kim, S.: A lattice-based universal thresholdizer for cryptographic systems. IACR Cryptol. ePrint Arch. **2017**, 251 (2017). http://eprint.iacr.org/2017/251
6. Brakerski, Z., Gentry, C., Vaikuntanathan, V.: (leveled) fully homomorphic encryption without bootstrapping. In: ITCS, pp. 309–325 (2012)
7. Brakerski, Z., Halevi, S., Polychroniadou, A.: Four round secure computation without setup. In: Theory of Cryptography (2017)
8. Brakerski, Z., Vaikuntanathan, V.: Efficient fully homomorphic encryption from (standard) LWE. In: FOCS, pp. 97–106 (2011)
9. Brakerski, Z., Vaikuntanathan, V.: Fully homomorphic encryption from Ring-LWE and security for key dependent messages. In: Rogaway, P. (ed.) CRYPTO 2011. LNCS, vol. 6841, pp. 505–524. Springer, Heidelberg (2011). https://doi.org/10.1007/978-3-642-22792-9_29
10. Canetti, R., et al.: Fiat-Shamir: from practice to theory (2019)
11. Canetti, R., Chen, Y., Reyzin, L., Rothblum, R.D.: Fiat-Shamir and correlation intractability from strong KDM-secure encryption. In: Nielsen, J.B., Rijmen, V. (eds.) EUROCRYPT 2018. LNCS, vol. 10820, pp. 91–122. Springer, Cham (2018). https://doi.org/10.1007/978-3-319-78381-9_4
12. Canetti, R., Goldreich, O., Halevi, S.: The random oracle methodology, revisited. J. ACM **51**(4), 557–594 (2004)
13. Chan, T.H., Chung, K., Lin, W., Shi, E.: MPC for MPC: secure computation on a massively parallel computing architecture. In: ITCS (2020)

14. Clear, M., McGoldrick, C.: Multi-identity and multi-key leveled FHE from learning with errors. In: Gennaro, R., Robshaw, M. (eds.) CRYPTO 2015. LNCS, vol. 9216, pp. 630–656. Springer, Heidelberg (2015). https://doi.org/10.1007/978-3-662-48000-7_31
15. Cohen, R., Shelat, A., Wichs, D.: Adaptively secure MPC with sublinear communication complexity. In: Boldyreva, A., Micciancio, D. (eds.) CRYPTO 2019. LNCS, vol. 11693, pp. 30–60. Springer, Cham (2019). https://doi.org/10.1007/978-3-030-26951-7_2
16. Dwork, C., Naor, M.: Zaps and their applications. SIAM J. Comput. **36**(6), 1513–1543 (2007). https://doi.org/10.1137/S0097539703426817
17. Feige, U., Lapidot, D., Shamir, A.: Multiple noninteractive zero knowledge proofs under general assumptions. SIAM J. Comput. **29**(1), 1–28 (1999)
18. Fiat, A., Shamir, A.: How to prove yourself: practical solutions to identification and signature problems. In: Odlyzko, A.M. (ed.) CRYPTO 1986. LNCS, vol. 263, pp. 186–194. Springer, Heidelberg (1987). https://doi.org/10.1007/3-540-47721-7_12
19. Fitzi, M., Hirt, M., Maurer, U.: Trading correctness for privacy in unconditional multi-party computation. In: Krawczyk, H. (ed.) CRYPTO 1998. LNCS, vol. 1462, pp. 121–136. Springer, Heidelberg (1998). https://doi.org/10.1007/BFb0055724
20. Fitzi, M., Hirt, M., Maurer, U.: General adversaries in unconditional multi-party computation. In: Lam, K.-Y., Okamoto, E., Xing, C. (eds.) ASIACRYPT 1999. LNCS, vol. 1716, pp. 232–246. Springer, Heidelberg (1999). https://doi.org/10.1007/978-3-540-48000-6_19
21. Gentry, C.: Fully homomorphic encryption using ideal lattices. In: STOC, pp. 169–178 (2009)
22. Gentry, C., Sahai, A., Waters, B.: Homomorphic encryption from learning with errors: conceptually-simpler, asymptotically-faster, attribute-based. In: Canetti, R., Garay, J.A. (eds.) CRYPTO 2013. LNCS, vol. 8042, pp. 75–92. Springer, Heidelberg (2013). https://doi.org/10.1007/978-3-642-40041-4_5
23. Goldreich, O., Micali, S., Wigderson, A.: How to play any mental game. In: STOC, pp. 218–229. ACM (1987)
24. Dov Gordon, S., Liu, F.-H., Shi, E.: Constant-round MPC with fairness and guarantee of output delivery. In: Gennaro, R., Robshaw, M. (eds.) CRYPTO 2015. LNCS, vol. 9216, pp. 63–82. Springer, Heidelberg (2015). https://doi.org/10.1007/978-3-662-48000-7_4
25. Groth, J., Ostrovsky, R.: Cryptography in the multi-string model. In: Menezes, A. (ed.) CRYPTO 2007. LNCS, vol. 4622, pp. 323–341. Springer, Heidelberg (2007). https://doi.org/10.1007/978-3-540-74143-5_18
26. Guo, Y., Pass, R., Shi, E.: Synchronous, with a chance of partition tolerance. In: Boldyreva, A., Micciancio, D. (eds.) CRYPTO 2019. LNCS, vol. 11692, pp. 499–529. Springer, Cham (2019). https://doi.org/10.1007/978-3-030-26948-7_18
27. Hirt, M., Maurer, U., Zikas, V.: MPC vs. SFE: unconditional and computational security. In: Pieprzyk, J. (ed.) ASIACRYPT 2008. LNCS, vol. 5350, pp. 1–18. Springer, Heidelberg (2008). https://doi.org/10.1007/978-3-540-89255-7_1
28. Holmgren, J., Lombardi, A.: Cryptographic hashing from strong one-way functions (or: one-way product functions and their applications). In: FOCS (2018)
29. Jain, A., Rasmussen, P.M.R., Sahai, A.: Threshold fully homomorphic encryption. ePrint (2017). https://eprint.iacr.org/2017/257
30. Jain, A., Jin, Z.: Statistical zap arguments from quasi-polynomial LWE. IACR Crypt. ePrint Arch. **2019**, 839 (2019)

31. Kalai, Y.T., Rothblum, G.N., Rothblum, R.D.: From obfuscation to the security of Fiat-Shamir for proofs. In: Katz, J., Shacham, H. (eds.) CRYPTO 2017. LNCS, vol. 10402, pp. 224–251. Springer, Cham (2017). https://doi.org/10.1007/978-3-319-63715-0_8
32. López-Alt, A., Tromer, E., Vaikuntanathan, V.: On-the-fly multiparty computation on the cloud via multikey fully homomorphic encryption. In: STOC, pp. 1219–1234 (2012)
33. Mukherjee, P., Wichs, D.: Two round multiparty computation via multi-key FHE. In: Fischlin, M., Coron, J.-S. (eds.) EUROCRYPT 2016. LNCS, vol. 9666, pp. 735–763. Springer, Heidelberg (2016). https://doi.org/10.1007/978-3-662-49896-5_26
34. Peikert, C., Shiehian, S.: Multi-key FHE from LWE, revisited. In: TCC Part II (2016)
35. Peikert, C., Shiehian, S.: Noninteractive zero knowledge for NP from (plain) learning with errors. In: Boldyreva, A., Micciancio, D. (eds.) CRYPTO 2019. LNCS, vol. 11692, pp. 89–114. Springer, Cham (2019). https://doi.org/10.1007/978-3-030-26948-7_4
36. Yao, A.C.: Protocols for secure computations. In: SFCS (1982)
37. Yao, A.C.C.: How to generate and exchange secrets (extended abstract). In: FOCS, pp. 162–167 (1986)

Asymptotically Good Multiplicative LSSS over Galois Rings and Applications to MPC over $\mathbb{Z}/p^k\mathbb{Z}$

Mark Abspoel[1(✉)], Ronald Cramer[1,2], Ivan Damgård[3], Daniel Escudero[3], Matthieu Rambaud[4], Chaoping Xing[5], and Chen Yuan[1]

[1] Centrum Wiskunde and Informatica (CWI), Amsterdam, The Netherlands
abspoel@cwi.nl
[2] Mathematisch Instituut, Leiden University, Leiden, The Netherlands
[3] Aarhus University, Aarhus, Denmark
[4] Telecom Paris, Institut Polytechnique de Paris, Paris, France
[5] School of Electronic Information and Electric Engineering, Shanghai Jiaotong University, Shanghai, China

Abstract. We study information-theoretic multiparty computation (MPC) protocols over rings $\mathbb{Z}/p^k\mathbb{Z}$ that have good asymptotic communication complexity for a large number of players. An important ingredient for such protocols is arithmetic secret sharing, i.e., linear secret-sharing schemes with multiplicative properties. The standard way to obtain these over fields is with a family of linear codes C, such that C, $C^\perp$ and C^2 are asymptotically good (strongly multiplicative). For our purposes here it suffices if the square code C^2 is not the whole space, i.e., has codimension at least 1 (multiplicative).

Our approach is to lift such a family of codes defined over a finite field $\mathbb{F}$ to a Galois ring, which is a local ring that has $\mathbb{F}$ as its residue field and that contains $\mathbb{Z}/p^k\mathbb{Z}$ as a subring, and thus enables arithmetic that is compatible with both structures. Although arbitrary lifts preserve the distance and dual distance of a code, as we demonstrate with a counterexample, the multiplicative property is not preserved. We work around this issue by showing a dedicated lift that preserves *self-orthogonality* (as well as distance and dual distance), for $p \geq 3$. Self-orthogonal codes are multiplicative, therefore we can use existing results of asymptotically good self-dual codes over fields to obtain arithmetic secret sharing over Galois rings. For $p = 2$ we obtain multiplicativity by using existing techniques of secret-sharing using both C and $C^\perp$, incurring a constant overhead. As a result, we obtain asymptotically good arithmetic secret-sharing schemes over Galois rings.

With these schemes in hand, we extend existing field-based MPC protocols to obtain MPC over $\mathbb{Z}/p^k\mathbb{Z}$, in the setting of a submaximal adversary corrupting less than a fraction $1/2 - \varepsilon$ of the players, where $\varepsilon > 0$ is arbitrarily small. We consider 3 different corruption models. For passive and active security with abort, our protocols communicate $O(n)$ bits per multiplication. For full security with guaranteed output delivery we use a preprocessing model and get $O(n)$ bits per multiplication in the online

S. Moriai and H. Wang (Eds.): ASIACRYPT 2020, LNCS 12493, pp. 151–180, 2020.
https://doi.org/10.1007/978-3-030-64840-4_6

phase and $O(n \log n)$ bits per multiplication in the offline phase. Thus, we obtain true linear bit complexities, without the common assumption that the ring size depends on the number of players.

1 Introduction

A secret-sharing scheme is a mathematical object that disperses a secret element into n shares. Combined, the shares determine the secret, but individual shares, and limited subsets of them, contain no information about the secret. In linear secret-sharing schemes (LSSS), given several secret-shared elements, linear operations on the secrets correspond to linear operations on the shares. LSSS are the cornerstone of information-theoretic multiparty computation (MPC) protocols, but they also have applications in other domains of cryptography.

LSSS and MPC are typically defined over finite fields (e.g., the secret and the shares are elements of the same finite field), which have a rich algebraic structure. A natural question is whether we can extend some of these techniques to other structures, such as rings $\mathbb{Z}/p^k\mathbb{Z}$ where $k > 0$ is an integer and p is a prime. This question is not only motivated in theory: some results [3,18] show that MPC over $\mathbb{Z}/2^k\mathbb{Z}$ with $k = 32$ or $k = 64$ can offer many practical benefits compared to fields, partly due to the compatibility of binary arithmetic in modern hardware. Feasibility of LSSS and MPC over these rings, as well as theoretical benefits, were already demonstrated back in 2003 based on *black-box secret sharing* [14].

Recently, MPC *directly* over these rings has been shown, in both the cryptographic dishonest majority setting [12] as well as the information-theoretic setting [2], by extending and generalizing existing techniques over fields. Both of these approaches use a single LSSS defined over $\mathbb{Z}/p^k\mathbb{Z}$: additive secret sharing and a variant of Shamir's secret sharing, respectively. It is natural to wonder whether techniques for other LSSS can be extended to these rings, to obtain desirable properties such as good asymptotic complexity.

In this work, we study the lifting of linear codes defined over finite fields to *Galois rings*, which are a natural generalization of *both* finite fields and our rings of interest $\mathbb{Z}/p^k\mathbb{Z}$. In a way, Galois rings are analogues of finite fields: informally, a Galois ring is to $\mathbb{Z}/p^k\mathbb{Z}$, what a finite field is to the prime field $\mathbb{F}_p$. Therefore, to extend existing techniques over finite fields to work over $\mathbb{Z}/p^k\mathbb{Z}$, it is necessary to consider Galois rings. As shown in Sect. 3, lifting preserves the essential properties of linear codes (distance, dual distance) that make them suitable as LSSS.

However, extending the theory of LSSS to Galois rings is not straightforward, due to the reduced structure and the presence of non-invertible elements. Thus, a priori it is not clear if properties of LSSS over fields carry over when considering these constructions over Galois rings. The above leads to the following question: *Can we obtain "good" LSSS over a Galois ring?* More precisely, we focus on realizing families of LSSS indexed by n, the number of shares, with privacy and reconstruction thresholds arbitrarily close to $n/2$, and with the information rate tending to a positive constant. The most widely known construction of LSSS over fields, Shamir secret sharing, does not satisfy the rate condition as it is based on polynomial interpolation and therefore the shares have to be at least $\log(n)$ in length. This issue was addressed over fields in the work of [10], using non-trivial results on random codes.

The above question is relevant for MPC that is asymptotically optimal, i.e., secure multiplication that has a total communication complexity linear in the number of players [16]. For information-theoretic MPC we typically care about *arithmetic secret-sharing schemes*, or synonymously, LSSS with multiplicativity: given two secret-shared elements, their product is a linear function of the pairwise products of shares. However, as we shall demonstrate with a counterexample in Sect. 3, multiplicativity does not directly lift.

True linear complexity is hard to achieve, and in fact conjectured to be impossible in the maximal adversary case $n = 2t+1$ for the single-circuit setting.[1] Many state-of-the-art protocols such as [5,21] state a linear complexity, but the complexity is given in the number of field elements communicated. If the field is fixed and the number of players tends to infinity, this obscures a $\log(n)$ factor in the bit-complexity of the protocol. Over fields, this asymptotic factor does not affect the complexity for practical ranges of parameters, since the field size is usually much larger than the number of players. However, for our rings $\mathbb{Z}/p^k\mathbb{Z}$ this issue is more pressing, since the comparable requirement is that $p > n$ rather than $p^k > n$ [2], thus leading to a $\log(n)$ factor immediately if for example $p = 2$. Removing this $\log(n)$ overhead is thus worthwhile and in fact highly desired, since it would achieve a *constant* complexity per party: even if more parties join the computation, the communication per party does not increase.

1.1 Our Contributions

We show that some of the results for LSSS over a finite field $\mathbb{F}$ also hold over a Galois ring R that contains $\mathbb{F}$ as a residue field, by *arbitrarily* lifting the associated code over $\mathbb{F}$ to R, and showing that certain relevant properties are preserved.

First, in Sect. 3, we show that we can obtain explicit good families of linear codes over Galois rings. In what follows, R is a large enough Galois ring.

Theorem 1 (informal). *There exists an explicit family of R-linear codes over R with $|R| = O_\varepsilon(1)$ such that its relative distance is at least $\frac{1}{2} - \varepsilon$ and relative dual distance is at least $\frac{1}{2} - \varepsilon$. In particular, there exists an explicit family of self-dual codes over R with relative distance at least $\frac{1}{2} - \varepsilon$.*

It is well-known that any linear code over a field with good parameters yields a good linear secret-sharing scheme [25], and it is straightforward to show this also holds over Galois rings. However, to get the arithmetic secret-sharing schemes that we need, we also need good parameters for the square of the code.

---

[1] LSSS with these parameters are equivalent to MDS codes, hence if the MDS conjecture if true, then the field size has to grow with the number of players. When evaluating a circuit multiple times in parallel, this can be mitigated [9].

We demonstrate with a counterexample that these parameters are not preserved by arbitrary lifts.

We work around this issue by showing a *dedicated* lift for $p > 2$ that preserves self-orthogonality in Sect. 3.1. For $p = 2$ we secret-share elements using both C and $C^{\perp}$, at the expense of increasing the share size by a factor of two. Both of these approaches rely on techniques from [13] to obtain arithmetic secret sharing via a code and its dual, and we demonstrate in Sect. 4 that these extend to Galois rings. We capture the asymptotic result in the following theorem.

Theorem 2 (informal). *There exists a family of R-arithmetic secret-sharing schemes* $\Sigma_1, \Sigma_2, \ldots$ *over* R *with* $|R| = O_{\varepsilon}(1)$ *such that the number of players* $n(\Sigma_i) \to \infty$, *and the schemes have* $t(\Sigma_i) \geq (1/2 - \varepsilon)n(\Sigma_i)$*-privacy and* $r(\Sigma_i) \geq (1/2 - \varepsilon)n(\Sigma_i)$*-reconstruction.*

To illustrate the power of our results on arithmetic secret sharing, we apply them to the problem of communication-efficient honest-majority MPC over $\mathbb{Z}/p^k\mathbb{Z}$. This problem has only recently been studied in [2], but the authors were more concerned with feasibility rather than achieving optimal communication complexity. In particular, their protocol is based on the (no longer state-of-the-art) protocol of [4], which has $O(n^2 \log(n))$ complexity in the number of parties. Here, the $\log(n)$ factor comes from polynomial interpolation, as discussed above. Plugging in our LSSS we immediately remove this $\log(n)$ factor and obtain true quadratic complexity for the adversary regime of $t < (1/2 - \varepsilon)n$, analogously to the work of [10] over fields.

We further improve the complexity, for three different regimes:

1. (Section 5) For passive security, we present a protocol that obtains an amortized communication complexity of $O(n)$ bits per multiplication gate.
2. (Section 6) For active security with abort, we present a protocol with an amortized communication complexity of $O(n)$ bits per multiplication gate.
3. (Section 7) For full active security with guaranteed output delivery, we obtain an amortized communication complexity of $O(n \log(n))$ bits for the offline phase and $O(n)$ bits for online phase. This solves the open problem from [2].

The last protocol is the most involved, since we adapt the protocol of [6] to work over Galois rings. Here we achieve linear complexity only in the online phase, as we still rely on polynomial interpolation to efficiently verify multiplication triples in the preprocessing phase. This matches the state-of-the-art over fields until the very recent result of [22]. However, since their protocol also uses the constructions of [6], our techniques can be combined with theirs to achieve linear complexity for the preprocessing phase.[2]

1.2 Overview of Our Techniques

We mainly use elementary (arbitrary) liftings from codes C over a finite field $\mathbb{F}$ to a Galois ring that contains $\mathbb{F}$ as its residue field, and $\mathbb{Z}/p^k\mathbb{Z}$ as a subring. This way

[2] Ignoring terms that are sublinear in the circuit size.

we leverage results from codes over fields directly. For example, since there exist explicit families of codes with asymptotically good distance and dual distance over a finite field $\mathbb{F}$, we also obtain explicit families of codes with asymptotically good distance and dual distance over R.

Once we obtain arithmetic secret sharing over R we can use it to get MPC over $\mathbb{Z}/p^k\mathbb{Z}$. Our general template to obtain an MPC protocol is to first develop protocols over R itself, and since $\mathbb{Z}/p^k\mathbb{Z}$ is a subring of R, we can supply inputs in $\mathbb{Z}/p^k\mathbb{Z}$ and then evaluate a circuit over R to securely obtain the correct output in $\mathbb{Z}/p^k\mathbb{Z}$[3,4].

Our passively secure protocol over R follows the template of [17], which consists of preprocessing so-called "double-sharings" and then using them to compute secure multiplications in the online phase. Since our construction of arithmetic secret sharing does not come directly from a code, we abstract the underlying technique to work on arbitrary arithmetic secret-sharing schemes. We do not have access to Vandermonde matrices over R directly, but we fix this by moving to an extension of Galois rings without amortized overhead using the "tensoring trick" from [9] together with the interpolation theorems from [2].

To get our actively secure protocol with abort, we make the simple but powerful observation that our protocol above is already actively secure up to additive attacks, i.e., the only attack that an adversary may carry out is to add a chosen value to the outputs of multiplications that is independent of the inputs. We obtain our actively secure protocol with abort by compiling our passively secure protocol with the recent work of [3], preserving linear complexity.[5]

Finally, for our actively secure protocol with guaranteed output delivery we use our arithmetic secret-sharing scheme as a building block and extend the protocol of [6], which is defined over a field in the $t < n/2$ regime. We show the check of authentication tags generalizes to our setting, and show how to compute the authentication tags (based on "twisted sharings") using our secret-sharing scheme. We also adapt the batch verification of triples.

1.3 Related Work

Honest majority MPC over rings has been already studied in [14] via black-box secret sharing, but their computational overhead is rather large. This problem was not revisited until very recently, with the work of [2], which presented efficient constructions using Galois rings, showing their potential benefits in the

[3] One may think initially that R is more general than $\mathbb{Z}/p^k\mathbb{Z}$ and thefore computation over $\mathbb{Z}/p^k\mathbb{Z}$ is implied trivially by computation over R by taking the degree of the extension to be 1. However, note that the degree of the extension is constrained to be $\Omega(\log_p(\varepsilon^{-1}))$, which is constant for a fixed $\varepsilon > 0$, but it is not necessarily equal to 1.

[4] For passive security the condition on the inputs is trivial to satisfy, but for active security some extra check needs to be added, which was already addressed in [2] for the case of Galois rings.

[5] Although their compiler is described for $\mathbb{Z}/p^k\mathbb{Z}$, it also applies to arbitrary Galois rings.

theory of MPC. They provide a protocol for multiplication with $O(n \log n)$ bits of total communication per gate, for the $t < n/3$ setting. This $\log(n)$ factor comes from using Shamir's scheme, and removing it requires codes with good distance of the square, or asymptotically good families of reverse multiplication-friendly embeddings, which as we illustrate in Example 2 are out of reach of our elementary lifting methods. Both were very recently claimed by [15], and illustrated with protocols for the $t < n/3$ setting. The tools developed in the present work enable up to honest majority, so are therefore complementary. Also, the recent work of [3] considers honest majority MPC over $\mathbb{Z}/2^k\mathbb{Z}$, but they achieve only security with abort and they do so with a communication complexity of $O(n \log(n))$ for both online and offline phases.

On the other hand, there are several other works in the context of honest-majority MPC over *fields*. We have already mentioned the work of Ben-Sasson et al. [6], that proposes a protocol in the honest-majority setting with guaranteed output delivery and near-linear communication complexity, and constitutes the basis of our protocol in Sect. 7. More recently, the protocol of [22] improves upon the protocol in [6] by introducing a novel method for verifying the correctness of multiplication triples. In the setting of security with abort the line of research is richer, with many protocols proposed in the last few years that aim at providing concrete practical efficiency. For example, an efficient general compiler from active security up to additive attacks to active security is presented in [11], which improves upon the methods built in [24]. The work of [26] also improves upon [24] by extending it using similar ideas as the batch triple check presented in [6]. Also, very recently, an efficient method to achieve actively secure three party computation was presented [8], building on top of the distributed zero knowledge proof techniques introduced in [7]. Although the authors of this work do consider an extension of their protocol to the ring $\mathbb{Z}/2^k\mathbb{Z}$, but it is unlikely to be efficient in practice as they make use of a Galois ring of a degree that is roughly equal to the security parameter.

2 Preliminaries

2.1 Linear Codes over Finite Fields

Let $\mathbb{F}_q$ be the finite field with q elements, and let $\mathbb{F}_q^n$ be the $\mathbb{F}_q$-vector space consisting of n copies of $\mathbb{F}_q$. A code $C \subseteq \mathbb{F}_q^n$ is a set of row vectors in $\mathbb{F}_q^n$. The rate of C is defined as $\frac{\log_q |C|}{n}$. For a vector $\mathbf{x} = (x_1, \dots, x_n)$ its Hamming weight is the number of nonzero coordinates: $w_H(\mathbf{x}) = |\{i \in [n] \mid x_i \neq 0\}|$, where we write $[n] := \{1, \dots, n\}$. If $\mathbf{y} = (y_1, \dots, y_n) \in \mathbb{F}_q^n$ is another vector, the Hamming distance between $\mathbf{x}$ and $\mathbf{y}$ is the number of coordinates in which they differ $d(\mathbf{x}, \mathbf{y}) = |\{i \in [n] \mid x_i \neq y_i\}| = w_H(\mathbf{x} - \mathbf{y})$. The minimum distance of a code C is defined as $d(C) = \min_{\mathbf{x} \neq \mathbf{y} \in C} d(\mathbf{x}, \mathbf{y})$.

In the following, let $C \subseteq \mathbb{F}_q^n$ be a linear subspace; we then say C is a linear code. The dimension of C is the dimension of C as a vector space. If C has $k = \dim(C)$ and $d = d(C)$, we say C is a $[n, k, d]$-linear code over $\mathbb{F}_q$. A matrix

G is a generator matrix for C if its rows form a basis for C. The dual code of C is defined as $C^{\perp} = \{\mathbf{x} \in \mathbb{F}_q^n \mid \forall \mathbf{y} \in C : \mathbf{x}\mathbf{y}^T = 0\}$. One can see that $C^{\perp}$ is a linear code with dimension $n - \dim_{\mathbb{F}_q}(C)$. The dual distance of C is defined as the minimum distance of $C^{\perp}$, and is denoted as $d^{\perp}(C)$.

In this paper, we are mostly concerned with the minimum distance d and dual distance $d^{\perp}$ of a linear code C. For applications to secret sharing, we want both of these to be large, since they imply $(n-d+1)$-reconstruction and $(d^{\perp}-1)$-privacy for secret-sharing scheme associated to the code. There is a large body of works dedicated to determining the achievable distance and dual distance of a code. In this work, we are particularly interested in the asymptotic behavior of d and $d^{\perp}$. To characterize this asymptotic behavior, we look at the relative distance $\delta = \frac{d}{n}$ and relative dual distance $\delta^{\perp} = \frac{d^{\perp}}{n}$.

Definition 1. *A family $C_1, C_2, \ldots$ of linear codes over a fixed finite field, where each C_i has parameters $[n_i, k_i, d_i]$ and dual distance $d_i^{\perp}$, is said to have relative distance δ and relative dual distance $\delta^{\perp}$ if the following holds:*

$$1. \lim_{i\to\infty} n_i = \infty$$

$$2. \liminf_{i\to\infty} \frac{d_i}{n_i} \geq \delta, \quad \liminf_{i\to\infty} \frac{d_i^{\perp}}{n_i} \geq \delta^{\perp}.$$

We stress that we study this asymptotic behaviour only for a family of codes defined over the same finite field.

In general, there are two ways to construct a family of codes with large relative distance and relative dual distance. One way is through a random argument that gives a family of codes reaching the Gilbert-Varshamov bound. For a finite field $\mathbb{F}_q$ with $q < 49$, this Gilbert-Varshamov Bound is the best lower bound known. When $q \geq 49$ is a square, there exists an explicit construction of algebraic geometric codes outperforming the random codes, i.e., there exists a family of algebraic geometric codes attaining the celebrated Vlăduţ-Drinfeld bound [19]. We skip the details of these codes and refer the interested reader to [28]. The family of algebraic geometric codes attaining the celebrated Vlăduţ-Drinfeld bound meets the following condition.

Proposition 1. *Let q be any prime power. Then there exists an explicit family of codes over a fixed finite field $\mathbb{F}_{q^2}$ with relative distance δ and relative dual distance $\delta^{\perp}$ as long as δ and $\delta^{\perp}$ satisfy*

$$\delta + \delta^{\perp} \leq 1 - \frac{2}{q-1}. \tag{1}$$

A similar result holds for self-dual codes [27], i.e., there exists an explicit family of self-dual codes reaching the Vlăduţ-Drinfeld bound.

Proposition 2. *Let $\varepsilon > 0$ be any small constant. Then, for any $q \geq 2/\varepsilon$ there exists an explicit family of codes over a fixed finite field $\mathbb{F}_{q^2}$ such that its relative* *distance* $\delta \geq \frac{1}{2} - \varepsilon$ *and its relative dual distance* $\delta^{\perp} \geq \frac{1}{2} - \varepsilon$. *Moreover, there exists an explicit family of self-dual codes over a fixed finite field* $\mathbb{F}_{q^2}$ *with relative distance* $\delta \geq \frac{1}{2} - \varepsilon$.

2.2 Galois Rings

Galois rings are a natural analogue to finite fields: roughly, Galois rings are to $\mathbb{Z}/p^k\mathbb{Z}$ what finite fields are to prime-order fields $\mathbb{F}_p$. As such, these rings have rich structure and they share many properties with finite fields. In fact, Galois rings are a strict generalization of finite fields, since setting $k = 1$ one obtains exactly the finite fields.

Definition 2. *Let* p *be a prime number and let* k *be a positive integer. Let* $g(Y) \in (\mathbb{Z}/p^k\mathbb{Z})[Y]$ *be a monic polynomial such that its reduction modulo* p *is an irreducible polynomial in* $\mathbb{F}_p[Y]$. *The ring*

$$R := (\mathbb{Z}/p^k\mathbb{Z})[Y]/\left(g(Y)\right)$$

is called a Galois ring.

Proposition 3. *R has the following properties:*

1. *It is a local ring, i.e. it has a unique maximal ideal* $(p) \subsetneq R$. *We have that* $R/(p) \cong \mathbb{F} := \mathbb{F}_{p^h}$, *where* h *denotes the degree of* g.
2. *The Lenstra constant of* R *is* p^h, *which gives the maximum number of interpolation points in Shamir's (because the pairwise differences must be invertible)*
3. *For any prime* p, *positive integer* k, *and positive integer* h *there exists a Galois ring as defined above, and any two of them with identical parameters* p, k, h *are isomorphic. We may therefore write* $R = \mathsf{GR}(p^k, h)$.
4. *If* e *is any positive integer, then* R *is a subring of* $\hat{R} = \mathsf{GR}(p^k, h \cdot e)$. *There is a polynomial* $\hat{g} \in R[X]$ *that is irreducible modulo* p, *such that* $\hat{R} = R[X]/(\hat{g}(X))$. *There is a natural* R*-module isomorphism* $R^e \to \hat{R}$.

Remark 1. Also, we have a natural ring embedding $\mathbb{Z}/p^k\mathbb{Z} \hookrightarrow R$, given by mapping $x \mapsto x \bmod g(Y)$. Moreover, there is another way to uniquely represent the elements of R. Since $R/(p) \cong \mathbb{F}$, let ξ be a non-zero element of order $p^h - 1$ in R and define the subset

$$\mathcal{I} = \{0, 1, \xi, \dots, \xi^{p^h-2}\} \subset R\,. \tag{2}$$

Then, any element $a \in R$ can be uniquely written as

$$a = a_0 + a_1 p + a_2 p^2 + \cdots + a_{k-1} p^{k-1} \text{ where } a_0, \dots, a_{k-1} \in \mathcal{I}\,.$$

This decomposition also allows us to define "division by powers of p". Indeed, notice that given an element $a = a_0 + a_1 p + a_2 p^2 + \cdots + a_{k-1} p^{k-1} \in R$ and a positive integer u, we have that p^u divides a if and only if $a_i = 0$ for all $i < u$. If this is the case, we then define $a/p^u := a_u + a_{u+1} p + \cdots + a_{k-1} p^{k-u-1} \in$

$\mathsf{GR}(p^{k-u}, h)$; notice that $a/p^u \equiv a_u \pmod{p}$. If u is maximal and a is non-zero in R, then $a/p^u \in R^*$.

Finally, Item 1 of Proposition 3 gives rise to the canonical map $\pi : R \to \mathbb{F}$ ("reduction modulo p"), which we shall frequently use. It is easy to see that $\pi|_{\mathcal{I}}$ is bijection, and in particular we have a one-to-one correspondence between $\mathcal{I}$ and $\mathbb{F}_{p^h}$. Given $x \in R$ we shall also write $\overline{x} = \pi(x)$.

3 Codes over Galois Rings

In this section, we show how to obtain codes over Galois rings. Although there is a large body of works dedicated to linear codes, most of it only deals with codes over finite fields. For the purpose of asymptotically good secret-sharing schemes, we need a family of codes over Galois rings whose rate and relative distance tends to a positive constant.

We obtain such codes by *arbitrarily* lifting linear codes defined over some finite field $\mathbb{F}$, such as the ones from Proposition 1, to a Galois ring whose residue field is $\mathbb{F}$. We show that the lifted codes have at least the same distance and dual distance as the original codes, hence using Proposition 1 we obtain a good family of codes over Galois rings of arbitrary characteristic p^k.

For the particular case of self-orthogonal codes defined over a field of characteristic $\neq 2$, we give an *explicit* lift that preserves self-orthogonality in Sect. 3.1. Self-orthogonal codes satisfy a multiplicative property that is needed for arithmetic secret sharing. In Sect. 4 we show how to extend existing techniques to obtain multiplication for $p = 2$, but this comes at the cost of doubling the share size.

Let $R = \mathsf{GR}(p^k, h)$ be a Galois ring with residue field $\mathbb{F} = \mathbb{F}_{p^h}$. We define a linear code C of length n over R to be a free R-submodule of R^n. We define its dimension as $\dim(C) = \mathrm{rank}_R(C)$. Recall the canonical homomorphism $\pi : R \to \mathbb{F}$. For convenience we will also write π for the induced map on vectors or matrices defined over R, and write $\overline{\mathbf{x}} := \pi(\mathbf{x})$ for $\mathbf{x} \in R^n$ and $\overline{M} = \pi(M)$ for a matrix M over R.

Proposition 4. *Let C be a linear code over R. Then the following statements hold:*

1. *$\mathrm{rank}_R\, C = \dim_{\mathbb{F}} \overline{C}$, where $\overline{C} = \pi(C) \subseteq \mathbb{F}^n$ is the reduction of C modulo p.*
2. *If $\mathbf{c} \neq \mathbf{0} \in C$ we may write $\mathbf{c} = p^m \mathbf{y}$, for $0 \leq m < k$ and $\pi(\mathbf{y}) \neq \mathbf{0} \in \overline{C}$.*

Proof. Let us prove the first claim. Since $C \subseteq R^n$ is a linear code, it has an R-basis $\mathbf{e}_1, \ldots, \mathbf{e}_t \in R^n$. Then, it is clear that $\overline{C}$ is an $\mathbb{F}$-linear code spanned by $\pi(\mathbf{e}_1), \ldots, \pi(\mathbf{e}_t)$. If we can show that $\pi(\mathbf{e}_1), \ldots, \pi(\mathbf{e}_t)$ are linearly independent over $\mathbb{F}$, then we are done. Assume this is false, so there exist $\lambda_1, \ldots, \lambda_k \in \mathbb{F}$ not all equal to 0 such that $\sum_{i=1}^{t} \lambda_i \pi(\mathbf{e}_i) = 0$. Let $\lambda'_i = \pi^{-1}(\lambda_i) \in \mathcal{I} \subseteq R$, then it holds that $\sum_{i=1}^{t} \lambda'_i \mathbf{e}_i \in pR$, since

$$\pi\left(\sum_{i=1}^{t} \lambda'_i \mathbf{e}_i\right) = \sum_{i=1}^{t} \lambda_i \pi(\mathbf{e}_i) = 0.$$

It follows that $\sum_{i=1}^{t} p^{k-1}\lambda_i'\mathbf{e}_i = 0$ and $p^{k-1}\lambda_1', \ldots, p^{k-1}\lambda_t'$ are not all zero. This contradicts the claim that $\mathbf{e}_1, \ldots, \mathbf{e}_t$ form a basis of C.

We turn to the second claim. Let G be a $t \times n$ matrix over R whose rows form a basis $\mathbf{e}_1, \ldots, \mathbf{e}_t$ of C. We may represent $C = \{\mathbf{x}G : \mathbf{x} \in R^t\}$. We call G the generator matrix of C, which gives a linear isomorphism between R^t and C. Let $\mathbf{c} = \mathbf{x}G$ be any nonzero codeword in C. Since G is an isomorphism, $\mathbf{x}$ is also a nonzero vector. By Remark 1, we write $\mathbf{x} = p^m\mathbf{x}_1$ with $0 \le m < k$ and $\mathbf{x}_1 \neq \mathbf{0} \in \mathcal{I}^t$. This follows that $\mathbf{c} = p^m\mathbf{x}_1G$. Let $\mathbf{y} = \mathbf{x}_1G$ and the desired result follows as $\pi(\mathbf{y}) = \pi(\mathbf{x}_1)\pi(G) \in \overline{C}$ is a nonzero codeword. □

Lemma 1. *Let $C \subseteq R^n$ be a linear code. We have $d(C) \ge d(\overline{C})$.*

Proof. Let G be the generator matrix of C. Since C is a linear code, it suffices to bound the weight of its codewords. For any $\mathbf{c} \neq \mathbf{0} \in C$, by Proposition 4 we can write $\mathbf{c} = p^m\mathbf{y}$ for some $\overline{\mathbf{y}} \neq \mathbf{0} \in \overline{C}$ and $m < k$. Note that $\overline{\mathbf{y}}$ is a nonzero codeword of $\overline{C}$. Thus, $w_H(\mathbf{c}) \ge w_H(\mathbf{y}) \ge d(\overline{C})$. The proof is completed. □

Example 1. It is hopeless to control the minimum distance without the freeness assumption. Consider the code $\overline{C} := \langle(1, 1, \ldots, 1)\rangle$ of two elements code over $(\mathbb{F}_2)^n$, with distance n. We can lift the code to $\mathbb{Z}/2^2\mathbb{Z}$ as $C := \langle(1, 1, \ldots, 1), (2, 0, \ldots, 0)\rangle$ which is non-free, because of the bad element $(2, 0, \ldots, 0)$. Then $d(C) = 1 \ll d(\overline{C}) = n$.

Like for codes over a field, we can similarly define the dual code over R. The dual code of C is defined as $C^{\perp} = \{\mathbf{c} \in R^n \mid \mathbf{c}\mathbf{y}^T = \mathbf{0} \text{ for all } \mathbf{y} \in C\}$.

Lemma 2. *Assume that $C \subseteq R^n$ is a t-dimensional R-linear code. Then, $C^{\perp} \subseteq R^n$ is a $(n-t)$-dimensional R-linear code. Moreover, the minimum distance of $C^{\perp}$ is lower bounded by the minimum distance of the dual code of $\overline{C}$.*

Proof. Let G be the generator matrix of C. Every element in $C^{\perp}$ is a solution to the linear equation $G\mathbf{x}^T = \mathbf{0}$ over R, and vice versa. This implies that $C^{\perp}$ is the kernel $\ker(G)$ of the R-linear map $G\mathbf{x}^T$. The image $\operatorname{im}(G)$ of $G\mathbf{x}^T$ is C, a free module of R^n with rank t. The homomorphism theorem of modules states that $R^n/\ker(G) \cong \operatorname{im}(G)$. Thus, the kernel is also free and has rank $n-t$. By our definition, $\ker(G)$ is a linear code of dimension $n-t$ over R.

It remains to lower bound the minimum distance of $C^{\perp}$. Given any codeword $\mathbf{c} \neq \mathbf{0} \in C^{\perp}$, we have $G\mathbf{c}^T = \mathbf{0}$. Moreover, by Remark 1, we can write $\mathbf{c} = p^m\mathbf{y}$ for $0 \le m < k$ and $\mathbf{y} \neq \mathbf{0} \in \mathcal{I}^t$. Reducing modulo p gives $\overline{G}\overline{\mathbf{y}}^T = 0$ over $\mathbb{F}_{p^h}$. This implies that $\overline{\mathbf{y}}$ is a nonzero codeword in the dual code of $\overline{C}$. Then, the desired result follows. □

We now define the square of a linear code C over R. Given $\mathbf{x} = (x_1, \ldots, x_n)$, $\mathbf{y} = (y_1, \ldots, y_n) \in R^n$ denote their componentwise (Schur) product as $\mathbf{x} * \mathbf{y} = (x_1y_1, \ldots, x_ny_n) \in R^n$. The square code C^{*2} is defined as $\text{span}_R\{\mathbf{x} * \mathbf{y} \in R^n \mid \mathbf{x}, \mathbf{y} \in C\}$. We emphasize that this square code C^{*2} is an R-module but not necessarily a free R-module. We say C is t-strongly multiplicative if the minimum distance $d(C)$, its dual distance $d^{\perp}(C)$ and the distance of the square $d(C^{*2})$ are at least t.

One may wonder whether strong multiplication is preserved when lifting. Unfortunately, our next example shows that we can have poor distance of the square code C^{*2} even if $\overline{C}^{*2}$ is a square code with large distance.

Example 2. Let C_1 and C_2 be linear code over $\mathbb{F}_{p^h}$ such that C_1^{*2} and C_2^{*2} have distance d_1 and d_2 respectively. Let $S = GR(p^3, h)$ and C be a code over S defined as $C = \{(\pi^{-1}(\mathbf{c}_1), p\,\pi^{-1}(\mathbf{c}_2)) \mid \mathbf{c}_1 \in C_1, \mathbf{c}_2 \in C_2\}$. It is clear that $\overline{C} = \{(\mathbf{c}_1, 0) \mid \mathbf{c}_1 \in C_1\}$ whose square code has minimum distance d_1. On the other hand, since C_2^{*2} has distance d_2, let $\mathbf{y}_2 \in C_2^{*2}$ be a codeword with weight d_2. Then, we have that $(\mathbf{0}, p^2\pi(\mathbf{y}_2)) \in C^{*2}$, and therefore the minimum distance of C^{*2} is at most d_2. The desired result follows if we pick d_2 to be a small number and d_1 to a big number.

Unlike the distance and dual distance of the lifted code, strong multiplication does not automatically carry over. We now give a brief argument for uniformity, which shall be important when using our codes for secret sharing later on.

Lemma 3. *Let $C \subseteq R^n$ be a submodule, and let $U \subseteq [n]$ be an index set with $|U| \leq d(C^{\perp}) - 1$. Then the projection C_U of C onto the coordinates of U equals the whole space $R^{|U|}$.*

Proof. We argue by contradiction. Note that C_U is also an R-module, so we may write $C_U = \sum_{i=1}^{t} R\mathbf{x}_i$ with $t \leq |U|$. Here, C_U may be non-free. Let M be an $t \times |U|$ matrix whose rows are $\mathbf{x}_1, \ldots, \mathbf{x}_t$. Recall $\overline{M} = \pi(M)$ is the reduction of M modulo p.

We first show that if $|C_U| < R^{|U|}$, then the rank of $\overline{M}$ is less than $|U|$. It is obvious if $t < |U|$. When $t = |U|$, since $|C_U| < R^{|U|}$, $\mathbf{x}_1, \ldots, \mathbf{x}_t$ are linearly dependent over R. Therefore, there exist $\lambda_1, \ldots, \lambda_t \in R$, not all equal to 0, such that $\sum_{i=1}^{t} \lambda_i \mathbf{x}_i = 0$. Let m be maximal such that p^m divides all of $\lambda_1, \ldots, \lambda_t$. Then, we have $\sum_{i=1}^{t} \frac{\lambda_i}{p^m}\mathbf{x}_i = 0$. This implies that $\sum_{i=1}^{t} \pi(\frac{\lambda_i}{p^m})\pi(\mathbf{x}_i) = 0$ over $\mathbb{F}$ where $\pi(\frac{\lambda_1}{p^m}), \ldots, \pi(\frac{\lambda_t}{p^m}) \in \mathbb{F}$ are not all zero. Therefore, $\pi(\mathbf{x}_1), \ldots, \pi(\mathbf{x}_t)$ are linearly dependent and the rank of $\overline{M}$ is less than $|U|$.

Let $\mathbf{c}^T$ be the nonzero solution to $\overline{M}\mathbf{c}^T = \mathbf{0}$ over $\mathbb{F}$. Then, we have $Mp^{k-1}\pi^{-1}(\mathbf{c})^T = \mathbf{0}$ over R. Extend $p^{k-1}\pi^{-1}(\mathbf{c})^T$ to a vector $\mathbf{c}'$ in R^n by setting i-th component with $i \notin U$ to be zero. Clearly, $\mathbf{c}'$ is a codeword of the dual code $C^{\perp}$. However, $w_H(\mathbf{c}') = w_H(\mathbf{c}) \leq |U|$ and a contradiction occurs. □

3.1 Constructing a Self-orthogonal Code over R

By a judicious choice of lift, we show that for $p \geq 3$ we can preserve self-orthogonality of a code over $\mathbb{F}$ when lifting to R.

Theorem 3. *Assume that there is a $[n, t, d]$ self-orthogonal code C over the finite field $\mathbb{F}_{p^h}$ with dual distance $d^{\perp}$ and $p \geq 3$. Then, there is a $[n, t, d]$ self-orthogonal code C_k with dual distance $d^{\perp}$ over the Galois ring $\mathsf{GR}(p^k, h)$ for* *any positive integer k. Moreover, given an explicit generator matrix of C the generator matrix of C_k is explicit.*

Proof. We lift the self-orthogonal code C increasing k step by step. For each step, we specify the lifted code by its generator matrix. Define $R_k := \mathsf{GR}(p^k, h)$. By Definition 2, R_k contains $\mathbb{Z}/p^k\mathbb{Z}$ as a subring, and its residue field is $\mathbb{F}_{p^h}$.

Our first step is to lift self-orthogonal code from $\mathbb{F}_{p^h}$ to $R_2 = \mathsf{GR}(p^2, h)$. Let C be an $[n, t, d]$ self-orthogonal code over $\mathbb{F}_{p^h}$ and $\overline{G} = (\overline{I}\,\overline{A})$[6] be the generator matrix of C. Due to the bijection between $\mathcal{I}$ and $\mathbb{F}_{p^h}$, we could find a matrix $G = (I\,A)$ with $G \in \pi^{-1}(\overline{G})$ whose entries are in $\mathcal{I}$. Self-orthogonality of C implies that

$$GG^T = AA^T + I = \overline{A} \times \overline{A}^T + \overline{I} = 0 \pmod{p}.$$

That means that all the entries in GG^T are elements in the ideal pR. By Remark 1, we can find a matrix S_1 over $\mathcal{I}$ such that $I + AA^T = pS_1 \pmod{p}^2$. It is clear that we can choose S_1 to be symmetric. Note that 2 is a unit in R_k as $p \neq 2$ and we can define $A_1 = A + 2^{-1}pS_1A$. Let $G_1 = (I\,A_1)$ and let C_1 be the code whose generator matrix is G_1. Obviously, G_1 is defined over R_2. Next, we show that C_1 is indeed a self-orthogonal code over R_2. To see this, we have

$$\begin{aligned} G_1G_1^T &= I + AA^T + \frac{p}{2}(S_1AA^T + AA^TS_1) \\ &= pS_1 + \frac{p}{2}S_1(pS_1 - I) + \frac{p}{2}(pS_1 - I)S_1 \\ &= pS_1 - pS_1 = 0 \pmod{p^2}. \end{aligned}$$

The first equality follows from the fact that S_1 is a symmetric matrix. It remains to bound the minimum distance of C_1. Observe that the reduced code of C_1 is C. By Lemma 1, the distance of C_1 is lower bounded by that of C. We can apply the same argument to its dual distance by observing that the generator matrix of $C_1^\perp$ is $(-A_1^T\,I)$, whose reduction modulo p, the matrix $(-A^T\,I)$, is the generator matrix of $C^\perp$, and therefore C_1 is free. Now, C_2 is a self-orthogonal code over R_2 satisfying all the claims in our theorem. In a same manner, we can the lift code C_2 to a code C_3 over R_3. By induction, we obtain a code C_k over R_k for any $k \geq 1$ satisfying all the claims in our theorem. □

Note that a self-dual code is also a self-orthogonal code. Theorem 3 together with Proposition 2 gives the following.

Corollary 1. *Let $\varepsilon > 0$ be any small constant, k any positive integer and $p^h \geq \frac{4}{\varepsilon^2}$ be any square with p an odd prime. Then there exists an explicit family of self-dual codes over Galois ring $\mathsf{GR}(p^k, h)$ with relative distance $\delta \geq \frac{1}{2} - \varepsilon$.*

[6] We use bar notation to represent the fact that these matrices are defined over $\mathbb{F}_{p^h}$.

3.2 Code and Dual Code over R

In our last subsection, we constructed a self-orthogonal code C over the Galois ring $\mathsf{GR}(p^k, h)$ with $p \geq 3$, by lifting a self-orthogonal code over the finite field $\mathbb{F}_{p^h}$. We may use these to construct an arithmetic secret-sharing scheme, as we will see in Section 4. However, our technique only works for $p \geq 3$, and of course especially for MPC purposes the case $p = 2$ is also very interesting. The existence of asymptotically good self-orthogonal codes over these rings is not yet known. To get around this obstacle, we replace the self-orthogonal code with code and its dual code in our secret-sharing scheme. This will incur the cost of doubling the share size, and hence doubling the communication complexity of the MPC protocols build on top of it.

The following is dedicated to lifting a code together with its dual code from the finite field $\mathbb{F}_{p^h}$ to the Galois ring $\mathsf{GR}(p^k, h)$. Our lifting technique maintains the minimum distance of our code and its dual code.

Theorem 4. *Assume that there is a $[n, t, d]$ linear code C over the finite field $\mathbb{F}_{p^h}$ with dual distance $d^\perp$. Then, there is a $[n, t, d]$ linear code C_k with dual distance $d^\perp$ over the Galois ring $\mathsf{GR}(p^k, h)$, for any integer k. Moreover, the generator matrices of C_k and its dual code are explicit as long as the generator matrix of C is explicit.*

Proof. Let G and H be the generator matrix and parity check matrix, respectively, of C. Note that H is also the generator matrix of $C^\perp$, the dual code of C over $\mathbb{F}_{p^h}$. We have $GH^T = 0 \pmod p$ and thus $GH^T = pM \pmod{p^2}$, for some matrix M defined over $\mathbb{F}_{p^h}$. Since G is a generator matrix of C, its rank is t. There exists $(n-t) \times n$ matrix A_1 such that $GA_1^T = -M \pmod p$. It follows that $G(H + pA_1)^T = GH^T + pGA_1^T = 0 \pmod{p^2}$.

Let C_2 be the linear code over $\mathsf{GR}(p^2, h)$ with generator matrix G. We claim that the dual code $C_2^\perp$ of C_2 has generator matrix $H + pA_1$. By Lemma 2, the dual code $C_2^\perp$ has dimension $n-t$. To see this, we first note that $H+pA_1$ has rank $\mathrm{rank}_{\mathbb{F}_{p^h}}(H) = n - t$ due to Proposition 4. Moreover, any codeword generated by $H + pA_1$ is a solution to $G\mathbf{x} = 0$ over R_2 since $G(H + pA_1)^T = 0 \pmod{p^2}$.

These two facts lead to the conclusion that $H + pA_1$ is indeed the generator matrix of $C_2^\perp$ over $\mathsf{GR}(p^2, h)$. The distance and dual distance comes from Lemma 1 and Lemma 2. In the same manner, one can show that C_k is a linear code over $\mathsf{GR}(p^k, h)$ with generator matrix G for any $k \geq 1$. In the meantime, by Lemma 1 the minimum distance and dual distance of C_k are lower bounded by d and $d^\perp$ respectively. The dual code of C_k is specified by its generator matrix $H + pA_1 + \cdots + p^{k-1}A_{k-1}$. □

Theorem 4 combined with Proposition 2 gives the following result.

Theorem 5. *Let $\varepsilon > 0$ be any small constant and $p^h \geq \frac{4}{\varepsilon^2}$ be any square. There exists an explicit family of codes over the Galois ring $\mathsf{GR}(p^k, h)$ with relative distance $\delta \geq \frac{1}{2} - \varepsilon$ and relative dual distance $\delta^\perp \geq \frac{1}{2} - \varepsilon$ for any integer k.*

4 Arithmetic Secret-Sharing over Galois Rings

In this section we construct an arithmetic secret-sharing scheme over a Galois ring R starting from an R-linear code C together with its dual $C^\perp$, by extending techniques from [13]. In this section, let $R = \mathsf{GR}(p^k, h)$, and suppose $C \subseteq R^{n+1}$ is a linear code with distance d and dual distance $d^\perp$. We first provide a brief overview of the techniques, before fixing the slightly heavier notation in Sect. 4.1 that we use to write the protocols in the remaining sections of this paper.

As for nomenclature, note that the difference between arithmetic and linear secret sharing is that the former is an LSSS with multiplication. We say an LSSS has multiplication if there exists a multiplication operator $*$ on shares, such that given secrets x and y with respective share vectors $(x_1, \dots, x_n)$ and $(y_1, \dots, y_n)$ then the product $x \cdot y$ is linearly determined by the $*$-products of shares $x_1 * y_1, \dots, x_n * y_n$. Here we are explicit about the operator $*$ because in the arithmetic secret-sharing scheme that we construct, the shares are not elements of R, but rather each share is given by 2 elements in R. These pairs of R-elements form an R-algebra with the operator $*$, which we define below.

Informally, a secret-sharing scheme has t-privacy if for any share vector, any t coordinates are independent of the secret, and it has r-reconstruction if any r coordinates of a share vector jointly determine the secret. For a full formalization of an arithmetic secret-sharing scheme over R, we refer to the full version of our paper [1].

Via Massey's construction [25] we may obtain an LSSS from a code over a field with good parameters, and this generalizes to Galois rings, as follows. To share $s \in R$, we sample a codeword $\mathbf{c} = (s, c_1, \dots, c_n) \in C$ uniformly at random and let c_i be the i-th share. Due to properties of the dual distance $d^\perp$, we can show that for any subset $T \subseteq [n]$ with $|T| \leq d^\perp - 2$ and $s \in R$, $\{(c_i)_{i \in T} : (s, c_1, \dots, c_n) \in C\} = R^{|T|}$. This implies $(d^\perp - 2)$-privacy. From the minimum distance of C it follows that the LSSS has $(n - d + 1)$-reconstruction.

To use a secret-sharing scheme for MPC, we need the multiplicative property. The LSSS constructed above has multiplication if and only if its square code C^{*2} has minimum distance $d(C^{*2}) \geq 1$. Unfortunately, the codes from Theorem 5 do not satisfy this property. However, by simultaneously secret-sharing values in C and in the dual code $C^\perp$, we can obtain multiplication with the following construction from [13].

To secret-share $s \in R$, we sample a codeword $\mathbf{x} = (s, x_1, \dots, x_n) \in C$ and a codeword $\mathbf{y} = (s, y_1, \dots, y_n) \in C^\perp$ uniformly at random. The i-th share is now a pair (x_i, y_i). The privacy of this scheme is $\min\{d - 2, d^\perp - 2\}$ and it is $\min\{n - d + 1, n - d^\perp + 1\}$-reconstruction. Now suppose we have another secret-shared element $u \in R$ shared as $\mathbf{x}' = (u, x'_1, \dots, x'_n) \in C$ and $\mathbf{y}' = (u, y'_1, \dots, y'_n) \in C^\perp$. For the product su, we see that $\sum_{i=1}^n x_i y'_i = -su$ (and also $\sum_{i=1}^n y_i x'_i = -su$).

4.1 Formalization

We now formalize the scheme and define the notation which we shall use in the remaining sections. Recall C is of length $n+1$. Let $\widetilde{C} \subseteq R^n$ denote the projection of C onto its last n coordinates, and similarly for $\widetilde{C^\perp} \subseteq R^n$. Let $\psi : \widetilde{C} \to R$ be the R-module homomorphism given by $\psi(x_1, \ldots, x_n) = x$ where $x \in R$ is the unique element such that $(x, x_1, \ldots, x_n) \in C$. Note that this map is well-defined if $d \geq 2$. Similarly define $\psi' : \widetilde{C^\perp} \to R$ as $(x_1', \ldots, x_n') \mapsto x'$. We equip $R \oplus R$ with the product $(a, b) \star (c, d) = (ad, bc)$; this defines an R-algebra which we denote A.

Consider the R-submodule of A^n given by

$$D = \{((x_1, x_1'), \ldots, (x_n, x_n')) \mid \mathbf{x} \in \widetilde{C}, \mathbf{x}' \in \widetilde{C^\perp}, \psi(\mathbf{x}) = \psi'(\mathbf{x}')\} \subseteq A^n,$$

and define the map $\psi : D \to R$ by $((x_1, x_1'), \ldots, (x_n, x_n')) \mapsto \psi(\mathbf{x})(= \psi'(\mathbf{x}'))$. We may think of D as the space of consistent sharings, and ψ as the map that reconstructs the secret. For $s \in R$ we write $[s]$ to denote an element of D that maps to s under ψ.

When we use the secret-sharing scheme in the protocol, we also occasionally need to operate on publicly known values. Let $\theta \in \psi^{-1}(1) \subset D$ be a fixed publicly known sharing of $1 \in R$. A public value $x \in R$ can be associated with the canonical sharing $x\theta \in D$.

Now consider the R-module homomorphism $\phi : R^n \to R$ given by $\phi(\mathbf{x}) = -\sum_{i=1}^n x_i$. Define the R-submodule of A^n given by

$$M = \{((x_1, x_1'), \ldots, (x_n, x_n')) : \phi(\mathbf{x}) = \phi(\mathbf{x}')\} \subseteq A^n,$$

which intuitively corresponds to redundant additive shares. The reason why we have the redundancy will be made clear in a moment, but at a high level it exists due to the fact that additive shares of the product of two $[\cdot]$-shared secrets can be obtained in two different ways. As we did with D, we define the R-module homomorphism $\phi : M \to R$ given by $((x_1, x_1'), \ldots, (x_n, x_n')) \mapsto \phi(\mathbf{x})(= \phi(\mathbf{x}'))$, and for $s \in R$ we write $\langle s \rangle$ to denote an element of M that maps to s under ϕ.

For $\boldsymbol{x}, \boldsymbol{y} \in A^n$ we define $\boldsymbol{x} * \boldsymbol{y}$ as the point-wise product of these vectors (under the product in A, which is $\star$). We define

$$D^{*2} = \mathsf{span}_R\{\boldsymbol{x} * \boldsymbol{y} \mid \boldsymbol{x}, \boldsymbol{y} \in D\} \subseteq A^n,$$

which corresponds at a high level to the operations we performed in the previous paragraphs to obtain additive shares of the product of two secrets.

Proposition 5. *Let $\boldsymbol{x}, \boldsymbol{y} \in D$. Then $\boldsymbol{x} * \boldsymbol{y} \in M$ and moreover $\phi(\boldsymbol{x} * \boldsymbol{y}) = \psi(\boldsymbol{x}) \cdot \psi(\boldsymbol{y})$.*

Proof. Write (x_i, x_i') and (y_i, y_i') for the i-th entry of $\boldsymbol{x}$ and $\boldsymbol{y}$, respectively, for $i = 1, \ldots, n$. The i-th entry of $\boldsymbol{x} * \boldsymbol{y}$ is $(x_i y_i', x_i' y_i)$, via the $\star$-product. There exists $(x_0, x_1, \ldots, x_n) \in C$ and $(y_0', y_1', \ldots, y_n') \in C^\perp$, hence $\sum_{i=1}^n x_i y_i' = -x_0 y_0' = -\psi(\mathbf{x})\psi(\mathbf{y}')$. Similarly, there exists $(x_0', x_1', \ldots, x_n') \in C$ and $(y_0, y_1, \ldots, y_n) \in C^\perp$, hence $\sum_{i=1}^n x_i' y_i = -x_0' y_0 = -\psi(\mathbf{x}')\psi(\mathbf{y})$. The claim follows. □

In terms of shares, we may write the proposition above as $[x] * [y] = \langle x \cdot y \rangle$. We obtain the following properties.

Theorem 6. *The scheme above* $(n - d + 2)$*-reconstruction and* $(d(\overline{C}^{\perp}) - 2)$*-privacy.*

Proof. ψ is a well-defined R-module homomorphism. Also ψ is surjective, since by Lemma 3 the projection of C onto the zero-th coordinate (corresponding to the secret) is surjective. The map $\phi : D^{*2} \to Z$ is surjective and satisfies $\overline{\psi}(\boldsymbol{x} * \boldsymbol{y}) = \psi(\boldsymbol{x})\psi(\boldsymbol{y})$.

If $U \subseteq \{0, \dots, n\}$ is an index set of cardinality $d(\overline{C}^{\perp}) - 2$ then projecting C onto $\{0\} \cup U$ is uniform by Lemma 3, and privacy follows. If $\boldsymbol{x} \in D$ has $\boldsymbol{x}_U = \boldsymbol{0}$ for $|U| = n - d + 2$ then since the only codeword in C with weight $\leq n - (n - d + 2) + 1 = d - 1$ is $\boldsymbol{0}$, we have $\psi(\boldsymbol{x}) = 0$, and reconstruction follows.
□

As a corollary, by instantiating these codes with the ones we obtained in Corollary 1, we get our main result.

Theorem 7. *Let* $\varepsilon > 0$*, and let* h *be an integer such that* $p^h \geq \frac{4}{\varepsilon^2}$*. Then there exists a family of* R*-ASSS* $\Sigma_1, \Sigma_2, \dots$ *with* $R = \mathsf{GR}(p^k, h)$*, such that the number of players* $n(\Sigma_i) \to \infty$*, and the schemes have* $t(\Sigma_i) \geq (1/2 - \varepsilon)n(\Sigma_i)$ *privacy and* $r(\Sigma_i) \geq (1/2 - \varepsilon)n(\Sigma_i)$ *reconstruction.*

5 Passive Security

In this and the upcoming sections, we fix $\varepsilon > 0$ and consider the Galois ring R of degree $h = \Omega(\log_p(\varepsilon^{-1}))$ over $\mathbb{Z}/p^k\mathbb{Z}$. We consider the family of LSSS over R from Theorem 7. We reuse the notation from Sect. 4.1: fixing $n \in \mathbb{N}$, we denote by $[x]$ the shares of a secret element $x \in R$, and each of these shares belong to the share space $A = R^2$. We denote by $\langle x \rangle$ shares under the "square" secret-sharing scheme, and recall that given $[x]$ and $[y]$, the parties can perform local computation on their shares to obtain $\langle x \cdot y \rangle$, and we denote this by $\langle x \cdot y \rangle = [x] * [y]$. Whenever we say that parties *reconstruct* a secret $[x]$ (or $\langle x \rangle$), we mean that the parties send their shares to P_1, who uses the reconstruction function to compute x and then sends x to all other parties.

To get a passively secure protocol with perfect security we use the standard approach in MPC of preprocessing some data that can be used to handle multiplication gates efficiently. We follow the template from [17], except that instead of using Reed-Solomon codes, which would lead to a complexity of $O(n \log(n))$, we use our linear secret-sharing scheme $[\cdot]$, allowing us to obtain complexity linear in the number of players.

The techniques from [17] consist, in general, of four main phases:

1. The parties generate "random double-sharings" in a preprocessing phase.
2. The parties use the preprocessed material to distribute inputs.

3. The parties compute the circuit in a gate-by-gate basis. Addition gates are computed locally. Multiplication gates make use of the double-sharings.
4. The output wires are reconstructed towards the parties.

Most of these techniques extend seamlessly to the R setting. The biggest issue lies in the generation of the random double-sharings, which uses a Vandermonde matrix in order to achieve linear complexity, and although these matrices do exist over $R = \mathsf{GR}(p^k, h)$ if $h = \Omega(\log(n))$ [2], our goal here is to avoid this overhead. In Sect. 5.1, we show how to get around this issue by moving to a Galois ring extension.

The protocol we describe in the next few subsections proves the following theorem.

Theorem 8. *For every $n, p, k \in \mathbb{N}$, with p a prime, for every $\varepsilon > 0$ and for every arithmetic circuit C over $R = \mathsf{GR}(p^k, h)$ with $h = \Omega(\log_p(\varepsilon^{-1}))$, there exists an n-party MPC protocol that securely computes C against an unbounded semi-honest adversary corrupting up to $t < \left(\frac{1}{2} - \varepsilon\right) \cdot n$ players with a communication complexity of $O(k \cdot \log p \cdot h \cdot |C| \cdot n)$.*

For constant p, k, ε, and by embedding $\mathbb{Z}/p^k\mathbb{Z}$ in R, we obtain the following as a simple corollary.

Theorem 9. *For every $n \in \mathbb{N}$ and for every arithmetic circuit C over $\mathbb{Z}/p^k\mathbb{Z}$ there exists an n-party MPC protocol that securely computes C against an unbounded semi-honest adversary corrupting up to $t < \left(\frac{1}{2} - \varepsilon\right) \cdot n$ players with an amortized communication complexity per multiplication gate of $O(n)$.*

5.1 Offline Phase

As preprocessed material the parties need many shares of the form $([r], \langle r \rangle)$, where $r \in R$ is uniformly random. The basic template used in the literature to achieve this comes from [17], and it uses the fact that Vandermonde matrices are good randomness extractors. However, we cannot use these matrices in our setting since they require the prime p to be at least n, which is not the case for us. Naively, one can use a Galois ring extension in which these matrices exist, as in [2], but this would lose linear complexity. There are two solutions to this problem.

One solution is instead of a hyperinvertible matrix to use the generator matrix of a $[n, u, d]$ linear code over R, with $d \geq t + 1$. This yields u random elements at the cost of n^2 elements of R communicated, which if the rate and distance are linear in n leads to linear complexity. By Theorem 5 we know such codes exist.

The second solution is to move to a Galois ring extension S with high enough Lenstra constant, such that there is a non-singular $n \times n$ Vandermonde matrix. Instead of simply embedding $R \hookrightarrow S$, we use a tensor product $R^s \cong R \otimes_R S \cong S$, where s is the degree of the extension [2,9]. We can take the tensor product of the secret-sharing scheme; the result is a secret-sharing scheme that can be interpreted as s parallel sharings of R. In this way $n - t$ random elements of

S can be obtained at the cost of n^2 elements of S communicated. Since each random sharing of S can be interpreted as s random sharings of R, this leads to linear communication per random sharing.

5.2 Online Phase

Now we describe how the parties can securely compute any circuit assuming they have preprocessed enough random sharings $([r], \langle r \rangle)$.

Online Phase

Input Phase. P_i secret-shares its input $x_i \in R$ as follows.
1. The parties take a preprocessed $([r], \langle r \rangle)$ and reconstruct $[r]$ towards P_i.
2. P_i broadcasts the difference $x_i - r$ to all parties.
3. The parties compute $[x_i] = (x_i - r) + [r]$.

Addition Gates. The parties compute locally $[x + y] = [x] + [y]$.

Multiplication Gates. To multiply $[x]$ and $[y]$, the parties use a preprocessed value $([r], \langle r \rangle)$ as follows.
1. The parties compute $\langle x \cdot y \rangle \leftarrow [x] \cdot [y]$.
2. The parties compute $\langle x \cdot y - r \rangle = \langle x \cdot y \rangle - \langle r \rangle$ and reconstruct this value.
3. The parties compute $[x \cdot y] = [r] + (x \cdot y - r)$.

Output Wires. For every shared output wire $[w]$, the parties reconstruct w.

The complexity of the protocol above is dominated by the reconstructions in the multiplication gates. Each such reconstruction involves sending $O(n)$ elements in A. Since these elements have bit-length $O(k \cdot \log(p) \cdot h)$, the overall complexity of these reconstructions is $O(k \cdot \log(p) \cdot h \cdot |C| \cdot n)$.

6 Active Security with Abort

Even though we present an actively secure protocol with guaranteed output delivery in Sect. 7, it is still worth mentioning that a much simpler protocol can be envisioned if one is aiming for security with abort.

Our starting observation is that the online multiplication protocol presented previously is secure up to additive attacks, as defined in [20], or, put more precisely, the only attack that an active adversary can carry out is to cause the result of the multiplication to be wrong by an additive amount that is known by him and that is completely independent of the inputs. To see why this is the case, we observe that if the preprocessed pair $([r], \langle r \rangle)$ is correctly shared, then the only thing that the adversary can do in the online phase is broadcasting[7] an

[7] To handle the active case we must have a proper broadcast channel, that is, we need to assume a the existence of a broadcast functionality. This is required in the setting of honest majority setting with statistical security, that is, a statistically secure protocol that instantiates a broadcast functionality cannot exist [23].

incorrect difference $r - xy + \delta$ (assuming that P_1 is corrupted), but the effect of this is that the final shares the parties get are $[xy + \delta]$, which constitutes an additive attack. Furthermore, the preprocessed pairs can be guaranteed to be consistent by a simple extension to the preprocessing protocol in Sect. 5.1 that adds a consistency check at the end (for instance as in done in [2] or in [12]).

Very recently it was shown in [3] how to compile *any* protocol over rings that is secure up to additive attacks to an actively secure protocol. Given that our multiplication protocol satisfies this condition (and it can be verified that it satisfies the other conditions required by the compiler), we obtain an actively secure protocol by feeding our protocol from the previous section through the compiler from [3]. The resulting protocol has linear communication in the number of parties.

7 Active Security with Guaranteed Output Delivery

The main theorem we prove in this section is the following.

Theorem 10. *For every $n, p, k \in \mathbb{N}$, with p a prime, for every $\varepsilon > 0$ and for every arithmetic circuit C over $R = \mathsf{GR}(p^k, h)$ with $h = \Omega(\log_p(\varepsilon^{-1}))$, there exists an n-party MPC protocol that securely computes C with guaranteed output delivery against an unbounded active adversary corrupting up to $t < \left(\frac{1}{2} - \varepsilon\right) \cdot n$ players, with negligible failure probability in $\kappa \in \mathbb{N}$, offline communication complexity of $O(k \cdot \log p \cdot (h \cdot |C| \cdot n \cdot \log(n) + n^7 \cdot \kappa))$, and online communication complexity of $O(k \cdot \log p \cdot h \cdot |C| \cdot n)$.*

Typically, we regard p, k and ε (and therefore h) as constants, so that the only variables are n, C and κ. In this case, we see that the amortized complexity per multiplication is $O(n)$ for the online phase, and $O(n \log(n))$ for the offline phase. Furthermore, computation over $\mathbb{Z}/p^k\mathbb{Z}$ can be obtained by embedding the computation into a Galois ring R of constant degree h, and adding a check of input correctness as in [2]. The following theorem is thus obtained as a corollary.

Theorem 11. *For every constants $p, k \in \mathbb{N}$, with p a prime, every constant $\varepsilon > 0$, and for every arithmetic circuit C over $\mathbb{Z}/p^k\mathbb{Z}$ there exists an n-party MPC protocol that securely computes C with guaranteed output delivery against an unbounded active adversary corrupting up to $t < \left(\frac{1}{2} - \varepsilon\right) \cdot n$ players, with negligible failure probability in κ, amortized offline communication complexity of $O(n \log(n))$ per multiplication gate and amortized online communication complexity of $O(n)$ per multiplication gate.*

The rest of this section is devoted to proving Theorem 10. We do so by adapting the protocol from [6] over fields, which we refer to as the BFO protocol, to work over a Galois ring R, while also making use of our LSSS from Sect. 4. Due to space constraints, we only detail the most essential modifications to the BFO protocol, and assume some of the terminology from [6] as given. An overview of the BFO protocol and more details can be found in the full version of this paper [1].

In order to extend the BFO protocol to our setting while preserving its efficiency, we mostly need to adapt the preprocessing phase. Arguments regarding dispute control carry over immediately, since they are essentially combinatorial in nature. In the next sections we discuss how to adapt the preprocessing: the verification of multiplication triples is in Sect. 7.4, and the computation of the tags is sketched in Sect. 7.3. Additionally, the fact that these tags provide the required authentication features when instantiated over Galois rings is not trivial, and we discuss this thoroughly in Sect. 7.3.

We stress that our goal here is not to present a full-fledged self-contained MPC protocol, but rather to describe our novel techniques and extensions to the BFO protocol. Hence, we assume familiarity with the work of [6] and we omit most of its heavy machinery, especially everything that extends seamlessly to Galois rings. We also remark that, even though we assume the existence of a broadcast channel implicitly (as the dispute control layer requires it), our complexity analysis does not include the cost of these broadcasts, which is equal to the corresponding cost in [6] and is independent of the circuit size.

Finally, we notice that the techniques from [22], which improve the complexity of the protocol from [6] by removing an additive term of $n^2 d$, where d is the depth of the circuit, rely mostly on the batch triple check from [6], which we extend in Sect. 7.4 to the Galois ring setting. Hence, the optimizations from [22] can be also applied to Galois rings, resulting in a much more efficient protocol that does not have a quadratic communication complexity in terms of the numbers of parties and the depth of the circuit.

7.1 Different Types of Shares

From now on, we fix $R = \mathsf{GR}(p^k, h)$ and $S = \mathsf{GR}(p^k, \kappa)$. Notice that we may view S as an extension of R of degree κ/h. The BFO protocol follows the template from Sect. 5, except that it has an additional mechanism to ensure that whenever the adversary cheats this can be detected and the computation can continue. This is achieved by using different types of secret-sharings (especially 2-level sharings, defined below), which create enough "redundancy" for the parties to be able to interactively[8] correct any error the adversary may introduce.

The multiple types of sharings considered for our extension of the BFO protocol are found below—for the intuition on these definitions we refer the reader to [6]. Note that these sharings were originally defined purely in the context of Shamir's secret-sharing scheme. We plug in the family of LSSS over R from Theorem 7 and get a more general setting: not only because our LSSS is defined over a Galois ring, but also because it does not have information rate 1, i.e., the shares do not have the same size as the secret.

Single sharing. These are the sharings $[x]$ as defined using our LSSS. The secret space is R, and the share space is A. They are the analogue to the degree-t Shamir sharings from [6].

[8] In contrast to the $t < n/3$ case in which an appropriate choice of the code allows for non-interactive error correction.

Square sharing. These are the shares $\langle x \rangle$ under the "square" secret-sharing scheme. The secret space is R, and the share space is A. As in Sect. 5, they are the analogue to the degree-$2t$ Shamir sharings from [6].

Twisted single sharing. These are defined with respect to a coordinate $i \in \{1,\ldots,n\}$. Let $x \in A$. We denote by $\lceil x \rfloor^i$ an element $\boldsymbol{x} = (x_1,\ldots,x_n) \in D$ such that $\psi(\boldsymbol{x}) = 0$ and $x_i = x$. One may view this as a sharing of 0 such that i-th share equals x.

Twisted square sharing. These are defined with respect to a coordinate $i \in \{1,\ldots,n\}$. Let $x \in A$. We denote by $\langle x \rangle^i$ an element $\boldsymbol{x} = (x_1,\ldots,x_n) \in M$ such that $\phi(\boldsymbol{x}) = 0$ and $x_i = x$. One may view this as square sharing of 0 such that the i-th share equals x.

Two-level single sharing. The secret space is R and the share space is A^n. For $x \in R$, we define $[\![x]\!]$ as an $n \times n$ matrix $(x_{i,j})_{i=1,\ldots,n}^{j=1,\ldots,n} \in A^{n\times n}$, such that:

1. The j-th share is the j-th column.
2. Each i-th row $\boldsymbol{x}_i = (x_{i,1},\ldots,x_{i,n})$ is a vector in D, i.e., it constitutes a single sharing $[x_i]$ of some element $x_i \in R$.
3. We have $x_1 + \cdots + x_n = x$.

Two-level square sharing. Denoted $\langle\!\langle x \rangle\!\rangle$. It is identical to a two-level single sharing, except the rows are vectors in M, and hence constitute square sharings $\langle x_i \rangle$.

7.2 Secret Sharing over a Galois Ring Extension

In [6], some subprotocols need a field size that is exponential in the security parameter in order to ensure negligible cheating probability. To this end, most of the protocol is defined over a smaller field, but occasionally they move to a large field extension, in a way such that the overall complexity is not negatively affected. Over fields and using Shamir secret sharing, it is straightforward to use shares defined over the base field and the extension field together, since the arithmetic is compatible. For our protocols, we use a Galois ring extension and we show that the arithmetic is compatible as well.

Let L be a Galois ring extension of R of degree r, i.e., $L = GR(p^k, h \cdot r)$. Intuitively, the secret-sharing scheme $[\cdot]$ (and similarly for $\langle\cdot\rangle$) over R can be extended to L as follows. First, fix an R-basis $\omega_1,\ldots,\omega_r$ of L. To secret-share an element $\alpha \in L$, write $\alpha = \sum_{i=1}^{r} a_i \cdot \omega_i$, and set $[\alpha]_L := ([a_1],\ldots,[a_r])$. More details can be found in the full version of this paper [1].

7.3 Authentication Tags

In the BFO protocol, whenever some cheating is detected, parties resort to dispute control in order to partially identify the cheater. One of the critical points in which the adversary can cheat in the protocol is when sending shares in order to reconstruct shared values, since in principle any corrupt party can lie about its own share. In order to be able to detect who sent a wrong share, the parties need an additional mechanism that somehow "binds" a party to its own share. This is precisely the purpose of the two-level shares defined in Sect. 7.1: the share of each party P_i is also shared among the other parties, so the parties can check whether P_i is lying about its share by reconstructing it from the two-level shares.

Unfortunately, nothing prevents the parties to also lie in the reconstruction of the two-level shares themselves. In order to deal with this situation, authentication tags are put in place, which allow a party to announce a share and prove that it is *correct*, or more precisely, prove that it is the same share that was created at the beginning of the protocol, which was guaranteed to be correct.

At a high level, the tags over fields in the BFO protocol work as follows.[9] Consider a value $s \in \mathbb{F}_q$ that is shared as $[s] = (s_1, \dots, s_n) \in \mathbb{F}_q^n$ using Shamir LSSS. Player P_i holds share $s_i \in \mathbb{F}_q^n$, and to prevent him from lying about his share, P_i is given a *tag* $\tau = \mu \cdot s_i + \nu$, where the key $\mu, \nu \in \mathbb{F}_q^n$ is random and only known by some verifier P_j. At the time of opening, P_i has to present a share $s'_i = s_i + \delta$ plus a tag $\tau' = \tau + \Delta$, where $\delta, \Delta \in \mathbb{F}_q$ may be nonzero for the case of a corrupt P_i, and the verifier P_j checks whether $\tau' \stackrel{?}{=} \mu \cdot s'_i + \nu$. This check passes if and only if $\Delta = \mu \cdot \delta$. If P_i attempts to cheat (i.e., $\delta \neq 0$) and if the verifier P_j is honest, then P_i does not know the random μ, and therefore check must fail with high probability (assuming the field is large). This can be seen by using that $\delta \neq 0$ is invertible, so $\Delta \cdot \delta^{-1} = \mu$, which due to the randomness of μ cannot be satisfied.

Adapting this to our setting is not straightforward because of two reasons. First, Galois rings are not fields for $k > 1$ and therefore the argument above does not apply directly, since $\delta \neq 0$ need not be invertible. Fortunately, using the ideas from [2] we still can show that the equation $\Delta = \mu \cdot \delta$ holds with negligible probability. However, the second issue is more delicate and it has to do with the fact that in our setting each share in $[s]$ is not a single Galois ring element but it is actually an element of $A = R^2$.

We handle this second issue by extending the authentication scheme from above not only from $\mathbb{F}_q$ to R, but to A. At a high level, the tag corresponding to a share $s_i \in A$ is computed as $\tau = \mu \star s_i + \nu \in A$, for the key $\mu, \nu \in A$. Cheating in this new MAC scheme corresponds to solving equations of the form $\Delta = \mu \star \delta$, for some $\Delta, \delta \in A$, which intuitively cannot be satisfied since it corresponds to two similar equations over R. We develop the details in what follows.

Definition and Properties of the Tags. We use the same template as the MAC scheme from [6], which authenticates batches instead of individual values. Let $\{(s_{j,1}, \dots, s_{j,\kappa/h})\}_{j=1}^{\ell} \in (R^h)^\ell$. Recall from Proposition 3 that $R^{\kappa/h} \cong S$, so we may think of each $(s_{j,1}, \dots, s_{j,\kappa/h})$ as one single element $\sigma_j \in S$. Following Sect. 7.2, we consider shares $[\sigma_j]_S$ which can be obtained by sharing each of its coordinates as $[s_{j,i}]$. By writing $[s_{j,i}] = (s_{j,i,1}, \dots, s_{j,i,n}) \in D^n$ and considering the vector $(s_{j,1,w}, \dots, s_{j,\kappa/h,w}) \in A^{\kappa/h}$ for $j \in \{1, \dots, \ell\}$ and $w \in \{1, \dots, n\}$, which we identify with an element $\sigma_{j,w} \in A_S$ where $A_S = \mathsf{span}_S(A)$, we can see that $[\sigma_j]_S = (\sigma_{j,1}, \dots, \sigma_{j,n}) \in (A_S)^n$.

[9] As we will see, the scheme is a bit more complex since the values are tagged in blocks rather than individually, but we will not consider this for now.

Notice that the S-algebra A_S can be seen simply as S^2, with the product operation defined as $(\alpha, \alpha') \star (\beta, \beta') = (\alpha \cdot \beta', \alpha' \cdot \beta)$. With this in hand we can define what it means for the shares of σ to be authenticated.

Definition 3. *(Informal.)*[10] *We say that the* $\ell \cdot \frac{\kappa}{h}$ *shares* $\{[s_{j,i}]\}_{j=1,i=1}^{\ell,\kappa/h}$ *are authenticated if for every pair of players* P_u, P_v *the following holds:*

- P_v *has a random key* $\boldsymbol{\mu} \in (A_S)^\ell$ *and* $\nu \in A_S$.
- P_u *has a tag* $\tau \in A_S$
- $\tau = \boldsymbol{\mu} \odot \boldsymbol{\sigma} + \nu$, *where* $\boldsymbol{\sigma} = (\sigma_{1,u}, \ldots, \sigma_{\ell,u}) \in (A_S)^\ell$ *and* $\odot$ *denotes the dot product operator.*

Proposition 6 argues that the tags defined above serve their purpose, i.e. a corrupt P_u cannot lie about any of his shares $s_{j,i,u}$ and still present a valid tag without an honest P_v detecting this. The proof follows a similar argument as the one sketched before over fields for the BFO protocol. However, we first need to show that the S-algebra A_S, even though it is not a field, and not even a Galois ring, does have good properties in terms of roots of linear equations. This is shown in the following lemma, which can be seen as an analogue of Lemma 6 to the S-algebra A_S, but considers multivariate polynomials of degree 1.

Lemma 4. *Let* $L = \mathsf{GR}(p^k, r)$ *and let* $B = L^2$ *be the* L*-algebra with multiplication given by* $(\alpha, \alpha') \star (\beta, \beta') = (\alpha\beta', \alpha'\beta)$. *Let* $\boldsymbol{\alpha} \in B^\ell$ *and* $\gamma \in B$. *If* $\boldsymbol{\alpha} \neq 0$, *then* $\Pr_{\boldsymbol{\beta} \leftarrow B^\ell}[\boldsymbol{\alpha} \odot \boldsymbol{\beta} = \gamma] \leq \frac{\ell}{p^r}$.

Proof. Suppose that $(\alpha_1, \ldots, \alpha_\ell) \odot (\beta_1, \ldots, \beta_\ell) = \gamma$, and suppose that $\boldsymbol{\alpha} \neq 0$. Without loss of generality, assume that $\alpha_1 \neq 0$, so $\alpha_1 \star \beta_1 = \rho$, with $\rho = \gamma - \sum_{j=2}^{\ell} \alpha_j \star \beta_j$. Let π_1, π_2 be the canonical L-algebra homomorphisms $B \to L$ of projection onto the first and second coordinate, respectively. Since $\alpha_1 \neq 0$, for at least one of $i = 1$ or $i = 2$ we have $\pi_i(\alpha_1) \neq 0$. Then $\pi_i(\rho) = \pi_i(\alpha_1 \star \beta_1) = \pi_i(\alpha_1)\pi_i(\beta_1)$ is a nonzero polynomial of degree 1 over L (in the variable $\pi_i(\beta_1)$), which occurs with probability at most $1/p^r$ according to Lemma 6. □

Proposition 6. *(Informal) Suppose that the shares* $\{[s_{j,i}]\}_{j=1,i=1}^{\ell,\kappa/h}$ *are authenticated, and let* P_u, P_v *be two players, where* P_v *is honest. If* P_u *announces potentially incorrect shares* $s'_{j,i,u} = s_{j,i,u} + \delta_{j,i,u}$ *and a potentially incorrect tag* $\tau' = \tau + \Delta$, *then the check* $\tau' \stackrel{?}{=} \boldsymbol{\mu} \odot \boldsymbol{\sigma}' + \nu$ *will succeed with probability at most* $\frac{1}{p^\kappa}$.

Proof. The errors $\delta_{j,i,u}$ translate into an error vector $\boldsymbol{\delta} \in (A_L)^\ell$ such that the check is performed on $\boldsymbol{\sigma}' = \boldsymbol{\sigma} + \boldsymbol{\delta}$. Furthermore, $\boldsymbol{\delta} = 0$ if and only if $\delta_{j,i,u} = 0$ for all $i \in \{1, \ldots, \kappa/h\}$ and $j \in \{1, \ldots, \ell\}$, so checking that the shares announced by P_u are correct amounts to checking that $\boldsymbol{\delta} = 0$.

It is easy to see that the check passes if and only if $\Delta = \boldsymbol{\mu} \odot \boldsymbol{\delta} + \nu$. Invoking Lemma 4 completes the proof. □

[10] The statement is incomplete since we are deliberately omitting many details like the dispute control layer, which determines which parties should get which type of tags, or how the keys are reused. We refer to [6] for these details.

We conclude that once the tags are in place, these can be used to prevent corrupt parties to lie about their shares whenever some fault localization is required at the dispute control layer. We refer the reader to [6] for the details about how these tags are exactly used.

Computation of the Tags. In the previous paragraphs we showed that the tags, once computed and distributed, provide the required authentication properties. However, we did not deal with the way that these tags are computed. An important contribution of [6] was showing an efficient method for the computation of these tags, which saves in communication and that is crucial for the overall efficiency.

At a very high level, their method works as follows: First, observe that the task of computing the tags can be seen as a two-party protocol between party P_u and party P_v, where P_u inputs the share vector $\boldsymbol{\sigma}$, P_v inputs the keys $\boldsymbol{\mu} \in (A_S)^\ell$, $\nu \in A_S$, and P_u gets the output τ. The idea is to use a "Mini-MPC" protocol for this computation, but to ensure efficiency of the whole protocol distributing the inputs must be done with little communication. This is where the concept of twisted shares defined in Sect. 7.1 comes into play: one of the inputs, $\boldsymbol{\sigma}$, is actually a share, and therefore it is already "shared". We discuss this idea in a bit more detail in what follows, but first we begin with the crucial property of twisted shares that motivates their consideration in a first place.

Lemma 5. *Let* $R = \mathsf{GR}(p^k, h)$*, let* $x, y \in R$ *and suppose they are shared as* $[x] = (x_1, \dots, x_n) \in A^n$*,* $\lceil y \rfloor^i = (y_1, \dots, y_n) \in A^n$*. Then* $[x] * \lceil y \rfloor^i = \langle\!\langle x_i \star y \rangle\!\rangle$*. Furthermore, an analogous property holds for the LSSS obtained by extending to a Galois ring extension L.*

Proof. By definition, $\lceil y \rfloor^i$ can be seen as $[0]$. Then, using Proposition 5, we see that $[x] * \lceil y \rfloor^i = [x] * [0] = \langle 0 \rangle$. Furthermore, the i-th entry of this vector is $x_i \star y_i = x_i \star y$, which concludes the proof of the lemma. □

With this lemma in hand we can sketch the Mini-MPC protocol that the parties P_u, P_v use to compute the tags. First, let us assume for simplicity that $\ell = 1$ and that $R = S$, so the MAC is simply $\tau = \mu \star \sigma + \nu \in A$. Let $[s]$ be such that its u-th share is σ (recall that the tags are used to authenticate shares, so σ is a share of some secret). The protocol, at a high level, proceeds as follows:

1. P_v samples $\mu, \nu \in A$.
2. P_v distributes twisted shares of μ and double twisted shares of ν, i.e., $\lceil \mu \rfloor^u, \langle \nu \rangle^u$.
3. The parties compute $[s] * \lceil \mu \rfloor^u + \langle \nu \rangle^u$, which by Lemma 5 equals $\langle\!\langle \sigma \star \mu + \nu \rangle\!\rangle$.
4. The parties send these shares to P_u for reconstruction.
5. The correctness of the tags is verified via standard cut-and-choose techniques.

We refer the reader to protocol $\mathsf{TagComp}$ in [6] for the full details of the protocol to compute the tags. We remark that the core aspects of this protocol that depend on working over a field have been already addressed above, and the rest of the protocol translates directly to our setting.

Complexity Analysis. With the due modifications the resulting TagComp protocol over R has a communication complexity of $O(k \cdot \log_2(p) \cdot (m \cdot n \cdot h + n^5 \cdot \kappa))$ for computing the tags in one single segment. Since $m = O(|C|)/n^2$, multiplying by the n^2 segments yields $O(k \cdot \log_2(p) \cdot (|C| \cdot n \cdot h + n^7 \cdot \kappa))$.

7.4 Batched Triple Sacrifice

The task here is to compute the $M = O(|C|)$ multiplication triples necessary for the execution of online phase. Computing them can be done in a similar way as in Sect. 5, but their correctness will not be guaranteed. As before, due to the dispute control layer, $m = M/n^2$ triples are checked in each segment. One of the key novelties of the BFO protocol is a technique for checking these triples with a complexity that is roughly $O(n \log(n) + \kappa)$ per triple.[11] This is achieved by dividing the m triples to be checked into batches of size $N = n^2$ each, developing a procedure that checks these N triples with complexity $O(N \cdot n \cdot \log(n) + n^2 \cdot \kappa)$, which, by multiplying by the number of batches m/N, yields $O(m \cdot (n \cdot \log(n) + \kappa))$.

Before we adapt their protocol to our setting, we begin by revisiting their techniques over fields here. Consider a field $\mathbb{F}_q$ with at least $2N$ elements, where $N = n^2$, and let $x_1, \ldots, x_{2N-1}$ be different points in $\mathbb{F}_q$. Suppose the parties have shares over this field $\{[\![a_i]\!], [\![b_i]\!], [\![c_i]\!]\}_{i=1}^N$ where c_i is supposed to be $a_i \cdot b_i$. The parties check their consistency as follows:

1. Define $f(X), g(X) \in \mathbb{F}_q[X]$ to be the polynomials of degree at most $N - 1$ such that $f(x_k) = a_k$ and $g(x_k) = b_k$ for $k = 1, \ldots, N$.
2. The parties compute shares of $a_k := f(x_k)$ and $b_k := g(x_k)$ for $k = N + 1, \ldots, 2N - 1$ by taking an appropriate linear combination (over $\mathbb{F}_q$) of the shares $\{[\![a_k]\!]\}_{k=1}^N$ and $\{[\![b_k]\!]\}_{k=1}^N$, respectively.
3. Define $h(X)$ as the polynomial of degree at most $2N - 2$ given by $h(X) = f(X) \cdot g(X)$, notice that it should be the case that $c_k = h(x_k)$ for $k = 1, \ldots, N$.
4. Use a passively secure multiplication protocol to compute (potentially incorrectly) $[\![c_k]\!] := [\![a_k]\!] \cdot [\![b_k]\!]$ for $k = N + 1, \ldots, 2N - 1$. Now the parties have shares of $2N - 1$ points on the polynomial $h(X)$.
5. Sample a random $\sigma \in \mathbb{F}_{q^\kappa}$ and compute shares over $\mathbb{F}_{q^\kappa}$ of $f(\sigma), g(\sigma), h(\sigma) \in \mathbb{F}_{q^\kappa}$ by taking a linear combination over $\mathbb{F}_{q^\kappa}$ of $\{[\![a_k]\!]\}_{k=1}^N$, $\{[\![b_k]\!]\}_{k=1}^N$ and $\{[\![c_k]\!]\}_{k=1}^{2N-1}$, respectively.
6. Perform some check over these shares to verify that $f(\sigma) \cdot g(\sigma) = h(\sigma)$.

When extending the above protocol over rings there are several complications that appear. One immediate concern is the argument that shows that checking the polynomial equality $f(X) \cdot g(X) = h(X)$ can be done by evaluating a random point. To show this still holds, we invoke the following lemma from [2, Lemma 2].

Lemma 6. *Let $f \in R[X]$ polynomial of arbitrary degree $\ell > 0$. Then $\Pr_{x \leftarrow R}[f(x) = 0] \leq \frac{\ell}{p^\kappa}$, where x is drawn uniformly from R.*

[11] A simple optimization in [6] transforms this into $O(n \log(n))$ for the case in which $\kappa = \mathsf{poly}(n)$. This optimization also applies to our setting.

One issue that appears is that we do not necessarily have enough points $x_1, \ldots, x_{2N-1} \in R$ for interpolation over our ring R. We fix this by using a Galois ring extension L of degree $O(\log(N)) = O(\log(n))$ for the interpolation, which introduces an overhead of $\log(n)$ in the multiplications $[\![c_k]\!] = [\![a_k]\!] \cdot [\![b_k]\!]$ for $k = N+1, \ldots, 2N-1$. We remark that this is the *only* place of the whole protocol where the $\log(n)$ overhead appears.

The final effect of this is that the complexity of the preprocessing phase becomes $O(|C| \cdot (n \cdot \log(n) + \kappa))$, which is not fully linear, but it is already better than the best protocol known for this setting [2], which has a complexity of $O(|C| \cdot n^2 \cdot \log(n))$.[12] Furthermore, our online phase is fully linear, i.e., $O(|C| \cdot n)$. This has an interpretation in practice: in the offline phase the communication per party increases logarithmically as the number of parties gets larger, but in the online phase, this communication remains constant. This supports the rationale of the offline/online paradigm: expensive computations can be pushed to a function-independent preprocessing phase, and in the online phase where the inputs and the function are actually instantitated, the computation is cheaper.

We describe our protocol for batched triple generation in Fig. 1. It is very similar to the corresponding protocol in [6] except that in our case we use properties of Galois rings to argue about the security of the construction. The security of our construction is argued below in proposition 7. It shows that if there is at least one triple that is incorrect then it will be detected in the final check with high probability.

Proposition 7. *Let* $\{([\![a_i]\!]_R, [\![b_i]\!]_R, [\![c_i]\!]_R)\}_{i=1}^N$ *be the triples inputted to Protocol* BatchedTriples, *and suppose that* $c_i = a_i \cdot b_i + d_i$ *for* $i = 1, \ldots, N$. *If the honest parties output* OK *at the end of the protocol, then* $d_i = 0$ *for all* i *with probability at least* $1 - \frac{1}{p^\kappa}$.

Thanks to the properties of Galois rings that we have exploited throughout the paper, the proof follows along the same lines as the corresponding proof in [6], and we will not replicate it here.

Complexity Analysis. Similar to the analysis in the field case done at the beginning of this section, the complexity of checking the m triples in one segment using BatchedTriples is $O(k \cdot \log_2(p) \cdot m \cdot (n \cdot \log(N) \cdot h + \kappa))$. By multiplying by the number of segments n^2, and recalling that $N = n^2$ and $m = O(|C|)/n^2$, we obtain $O(k \cdot \log_2(p) \cdot |C| \cdot (n \cdot \log(n) \cdot h + \kappa))$. Furthermore, the optimization in [6] of using $N = n^{2+c}$ where $\kappa(n) = O(n^c)$ applies also in our case and results in a complexity of $O(k \cdot \log_2(p) \cdot |C| \cdot n \cdot \log(n) \cdot h)$.

---

[12] We notice, however, that the extension of Shamir secret sharing to R from [2] is likely to be compatible with the BFO protocol using some of the ideas introduced in our work. The resulting protocol would have the same offline complexity as our construction, but the online complexity would be $O(|C| n \log(n))$, unlike ours which is $O(|C| n)$. On the other hand, the threshold would be maximal.

BatchedTriples

Input: N potentially incorrect triples $\{(\llbracket a_i \rrbracket_R, \llbracket b_i \rrbracket_R, \llbracket c_i \rrbracket_R)\}_{i=1}^N$.

– Let L be a Galois-ring extension of $\mathbb{Z}/p^k\mathbb{Z}$ of degree $\log_p(2N)$, and let $\chi_1, \ldots, \chi_{2N-1} \in L$ be an exceptional sequence. We may think of S as a Galois-ring extension of L of degree $\kappa / \log_p(2N)$.

The parties execute the following in order to check the correctness of these triples:

1. Define $f(X), g(X) \in L[X]$ as the polynomials of degree at most $N-1$ such that $f(\chi_k) = a_k$ and $g(\chi_k) = b_k$ for $k = 1, \ldots, N$.
2. The parties compute shares of $a_k := f(\chi_k) \in L$ and $b_k := g(\chi_k) \in L$ for $k = N+1, \ldots, 2N-1$ by taking an appropriate linear combination $\llbracket a_k \rrbracket_L = \sum_{j=1}^N \lambda_j \cdot \llbracket a_j \rrbracket_R$ and $\llbracket b_k \rrbracket_L = \sum_{j=1}^N \lambda_j \cdot \llbracket b_j \rrbracket_R$, where $\lambda_j \in L$.
3. Define $h(X)$ as the polynomial of degree at most $2N-2$ given by $h(X) = f(X) \cdot g(X)$. Notice that it should be the case that $c_k = h(\chi_k)$ for $k = 1, \ldots, N$.
4. For $i = N+1, \ldots, 2N-1$ use the passively secure multiplication protocol to compute (possibly incorrect) shares $\llbracket a_i \cdot b_i \rrbracket_L = \llbracket a_i \rrbracket_L \cdot \llbracket b_i \rrbracket_L$.
5. Sample a random $\sigma \in S$ and compute shares of $f(\sigma), g(\sigma) \in S$ as $\llbracket f(\sigma) \rrbracket_S = \sum_{j=1}^N \mu_j \cdot \llbracket a_j \rrbracket_R$ and $\llbracket g(\sigma) \rrbracket_S = \sum_{j=1}^N \mu_j \cdot \llbracket b_j \rrbracket_R$ where $\mu_j \in S$.
6. Compute shares $\llbracket h(\sigma) \rrbracket_S = \sum_{i=1}^{2N-1} \omega_i \cdot \llbracket a_i \cdot b_i \rrbracket_L$, where $\omega_i \in S$.
7. The parties execute a *sacrifice* step in order to check the correctness of $(\llbracket f(\sigma) \rrbracket_S, \llbracket g(\sigma) \rrbracket_S, \llbracket h(\sigma) \rrbracket_S)$:[a]
   (a) Sample a potentially incorrect triple $(\llbracket \alpha \rrbracket_S, \llbracket \beta \rrbracket_S, \llbracket \gamma = \alpha \cdot \beta \rrbracket_S)$.
   (b) Sample a random value $\lambda \in S$.
   (c) Open sequentially $\alpha' = \llbracket \alpha \rrbracket_S + \lambda \cdot \llbracket f(\sigma) \rrbracket_S$ and $\nu = \llbracket \gamma \rrbracket_S + \gamma \cdot \llbracket h(\sigma) \rrbracket_S - \alpha' \cdot \llbracket g(\sigma) \rrbracket_S$.
   (d) If $v \neq 0$ then proceed to the fault localization phase as in [6]. Otherwise output OK.

[a] This corresponds to protocol SingleVerify in [6].

Fig. 1. Protocol for checking the correctness of several triples

Remark 2. The $\log(n)$ overhead we have in the preprocessing appears in a very specific stage, and we can even remove it assuming a functionality that produces additive shares of matrix outer products efficiently.

Optimizing the Batch Triple Verification. We can use the tools we have developed to further optimize our triple check procedure by adapting the more recent protocol of [22]. Their batch check protocol builds on top of the one we use from [6], and also makes use of polynomial interpolation, which as we have shown extends to Galois rings. This would lead to a more efficient protocol.

7.5 Putting the Pieces Together

Using the building blocks described in previous sections, we obtain a protocol over $R = \mathsf{GR}(p^k, h)$ whose offline phase has a total communication complexity of $O(k \cdot \log p \cdot (h \cdot |C| \cdot n \cdot \log(n) + n^7 \cdot \kappa))$. The online phase, which follows the exact same template as in [6, Section 3.4], has a total communication complexity of $O(k \cdot \log p \cdot h \cdot |C| \cdot n)$. This proves Theorem 10.

8 Conclusions and Future Work

Our work shows that results from coding theory over fields can be leveraged to obtain corresponding results over the more general Galois rings, which include as a particular case the practically relevant ring $\mathbb{Z}/2^k\mathbb{Z}$. Although not all properties automatically lift (e.g., multiplicativity), we presented techniques to overcome these issues and still get meaningful coding-theoretic tools over Galois rings, that can be applied to MPC.

We showed that information-theoretic honest-majority MPC over rings which scales well with the number of parties is possible. Our protocols have linear communication complexity, except for the offline phase of our protocol with guaranteed output delivery from Sect. 7, which has a $\log(n)$ overhead. The complexity can be further reduced by combining our results with the work of [21].

Finally, like in [6], the communication complexity of our construction remains linear if the circuit is not too narrow. This restriction was removed in [21] for the case of $t < n/3$, and then in [22] for the case of $t < n/2$. As we mentioned in Sect. 7, the techniques from that paper can also be adapted to Galois rings.

Acknowledgements. The authors thank Gabriele Spini for helpful discussions in the early stages of this research project. This work has been supported by the European Union Horizon 2020 research and innovation programme under grant agreements No. 74079 (ALGSTRONGCRYPTO) and No. 669255 (MPCPRO), and by an SJTU-Huawei project.

References

1. Abspoel, M., et al.: Asymptotically good multiplicative LSSS over Galois rings and applications to MPC over $\mathbb{Z}/p^k\mathbb{Z}$. Cryptology ePrint Archive (2020)
2. Abspoel, M., Cramer, R., Damgård, I., Escudero, D., Yuan, C.: Efficient information-theoretic secure multiparty computation over $\mathbb{Z}/p^k\mathbb{Z}$ via Galois rings. In: Hofheinz, D., Rosen, A. (eds.) TCC 2019. LNCS, vol. 11891, pp. 471–501. Springer, Cham (2019). https://doi.org/10.1007/978-3-030-36030-6_19
3. Abspoel, M., Dalskov, A., Escudero, D., Nof, A.: An efficient passive-to-active compiler for honest-majority MPC over rings. Cryptology ePrint Archive, Report 2019/1298 (2019). https://eprint.iacr.org/2019/1298
4. Beerliová-Trubíniová, Z., Hirt, M.: Efficient multi-party computation with dispute control. In: Halevi, S., Rabin, T. (eds.) TCC 2006. LNCS, vol. 3876, pp. 305–328. Springer, Heidelberg (2006). https://doi.org/10.1007/11681878_16

5. Beerliová-Trubíniová, Z., Hirt, M.: Perfectly-secure MPC with linear communication complexity. In: Canetti, R. (ed.) TCC 2008. LNCS, vol. 4948, pp. 213–230. Springer, Heidelberg (2008). https://doi.org/10.1007/978-3-540-78524-8_13
6. Ben-Sasson, E., Fehr, S., Ostrovsky, R.: Near-linear unconditionally-secure multiparty computation with a dishonest minority. In: Safavi-Naini, R., Canetti, R. (eds.) CRYPTO 2012. LNCS, vol. 7417, pp. 663–680. Springer, Heidelberg (2012). https://doi.org/10.1007/978-3-642-32009-5_39
7. Boneh, D., Boyle, E., Corrigan-Gibbs, H., Gilboa, N., Ishai, Y.: Zero-Knowledge proofs on secret-shared data via fully linear PCPs. In: Boldyreva, A., Micciancio, D. (eds.) CRYPTO 2019. LNCS, vol. 11694, pp. 67–97. Springer, Cham (2019). https://doi.org/10.1007/978-3-030-26954-8_3
8. Boyle, E., Gilboa, N., Ishai, Y., Nof, A.: Practical fully secure three-party computation via sublinear distributed zero-knowledge proofs. In: Cavallaro, L., Kinder, J., Wang, X., Katz, J. (eds.) ACM CCS 2019, pp. 869–886. ACM Press (2019)
9. Cascudo, I., Cramer, R., Xing, C., Yuan, C.: Amortized complexity of information-theoretically secure MPC revisited. In: Shacham, H., Boldyreva, A. (eds.) CRYPTO 2018. LNCS, vol. 10993, pp. 395–426. Springer, Cham (2018). https://doi.org/10.1007/978-3-319-96878-0_14
10. Chen, H., Cramer, R., Goldwasser, S., de Haan, R., Vaikuntanathan, V.: Secure computation from random error correcting codes. In: Naor, M. (ed.) EUROCRYPT 2007. LNCS, vol. 4515, pp. 291–310. Springer, Heidelberg (2007). https://doi.org/10.1007/978-3-540-72540-4_17
11. Chida, K., et al.: Fast large-scale honest-majority MPC for malicious adversaries. In: Shacham, H., Boldyreva, A. (eds.) CRYPTO 2018. LNCS, vol. 10993, pp. 34–64. Springer, Cham (2018). https://doi.org/10.1007/978-3-319-96878-0_2
12. Cramer, R., Damgård, I., Escudero, D., Scholl, P., Xing, C.: SPD $\mathbb{Z}_{2^k}$: efficient MPC mod 2^k for dishonest majority. In: Shacham, H., Boldyreva, A. (eds.) CRYPTO 2018. LNCS, vol. 10992, pp. 769–798. Springer, Cham (2018). https://doi.org/10.1007/978-3-319-96881-0_26
13. Cramer, R., Damgård, I., Maurer, U.: General secure multi-party computation from any linear secret-sharing scheme. In: Preneel, B. (ed.) EUROCRYPT 2000. LNCS, vol. 1807, pp. 316–334. Springer, Heidelberg (2000). https://doi.org/10.1007/3-540-45539-6_22
14. Cramer, R., Fehr, S., Ishai, Y., Kushilevitz, E.: Efficient multi-party computation over rings. In: Biham, E. (ed.) EUROCRYPT 2003. LNCS, vol. 2656, pp. 596–613. Springer, Heidelberg (2003). https://doi.org/10.1007/3-540-39200-9_37
15. Cramer, R., Rambaud, M., Xing, C.: Asymptotically-good arithmetic secret sharing over $\mathbb{Z}/p^k\mathbb{Z}$ with strong multiplication and its applications to efficient MPC. IACR Cryptol. ePrint Arch. **2019**, 832 (2019)
16. Damgård, I., Larsen, K.G., Nielsen, J.B.: Communication lower bounds for statistically secure MPC, with or without preprocessing. In: Boldyreva, A., Micciancio, D. (eds.) CRYPTO 2019. LNCS, vol. 11693, pp. 61–84. Springer, Cham (2019). https://doi.org/10.1007/978-3-030-26951-7_3
17. Damgård, I., Nielsen, J.B.: Scalable and unconditionally secure multiparty computation. In: Menezes, A. (ed.) CRYPTO 2007. LNCS, vol. 4622, pp. 572–590. Springer, Heidelberg (2007). https://doi.org/10.1007/978-3-540-74143-5_32
18. Damgård, I., Escudero, D., Frederiksen, T., Keller, M., Scholl, P., Volgushev, N.: New primitives for actively-secure MPC over rings with applications to private machine learning. In: 2019 IEEE Symposium on Security and Privacy (SP), Los Alamitos, CA, USA, May 2019, pp. 1325–1343. IEEE Computer Society (2019)

19. Garcia, A., Stichtenoth, H.: A tower of Artin-Schreier extensions of function fields attaining the Drinfeld-Vladut bound. Inventiones mathematicae **121**(1), 211–222 (1995)
20. Genkin, D., Ishai, Y., Prabhakaran, M., Sahai, A., Tromer, E.: Circuits resilient to additive attacks with applications to secure computation. In: Shmoys, D.B. (ed.) 46th ACM STOC, pp. 495–504. ACM Press (2014)
21. Goyal, V., Liu, Y., Song, Y.: Communication-efficient unconditional MPC with guaranteed output delivery. In: Boldyreva, A., Micciancio, D. (eds.) CRYPTO 2019. LNCS, vol. 11693, pp. 85–114. Springer, Cham (2019). https://doi.org/10.1007/978-3-030-26951-7_4
22. Goyal, V., Song, Y., Zhu, C.: Guaranteed output delivery comes free in honest majority MPC. In: Micciancio, D., Ristenpart, T. (eds.) CRYPTO 2020. LNCS, vol. 12171, pp. 618–646. Springer, Cham (2020). https://doi.org/10.1007/978-3-030-56880-1_22
23. Lamport, L., Shostak, R., Pease, M.: The byzantine generals problem. In: Concurrency: The Works of Leslie Lamport, pp. 203–226 (2019)
24. Lindell, Y., Nof, A.: A framework for constructing fast MPC over arithmetic circuits with malicious adversaries and an honest-majority. In: Thuraisingham, B.M., Evans, D., Malkin, T., Xu, D. (eds.) ACM CCS 2017, pp. 259–276. ACM Press (2017)
25. Massey, J.L.: Some applications of coding theory in cryptography. In: Farrell, P.F. (ed.) Codes and Ciphers, Cryptography and Coding IV, pp. 33–47. Formara Lt., Esses (1995)
26. Nordholt, P.S., Veeningen, M.: Minimising communication in honest-majority MPC by batchwise multiplication verification. In: Preneel, B., Vercauteren, F. (eds.) ACNS 2018. LNCS, vol. 10892, pp. 321–339. Springer, Cham (2018). https://doi.org/10.1007/978-3-319-93387-0_17
27. Stichtenoth, H.: Transitive and self-dual codes attaining the Tsfasman-Vlăduţ-Zink bound. IEEE Trans. Inf. Theor. **52**(5), 2218–2224 (2006)
28. Stichtenoth, H.: Algebraic Function Fields and Codes, 2nd edn. Springer, Heidelberg (2008). https://doi.org/10.1007/978-3-540-76878-4

Towards Efficiency-Preserving Round Compression in MPC

Do Fewer Rounds Mean More Computation?

Prabhanjan Ananth[1(✉)], Arka Rai Choudhuri[2], Aarushi Goel[2], and Abhishek Jain[2]

[1] University of California, Santa Barbara, USA
prabhanjan@cs.ucsb.edu
[2] Johns Hopkins University, Baltimore, USA
{achoud,aarushig,abhishek}@cs.jhu.edu

Abstract. Reducing the rounds of interaction in secure multiparty computation (MPC) protocols has been the topic of study of many works. One popular approach to reduce rounds is to construct *round compression compilers*. A round compression compiler is one that takes a highly interactive protocol and transforms it into a protocol with far fewer rounds. The design of round compression compilers has traditionally focused on preserving the security properties of the underlying protocol and in particular, not much attention has been given towards preserving their computational and communication efficiency. Indeed, the recent round compression compilers that yield round-optimal MPC protocols incur large computational and communication overhead.

In this work, we initiate the study of *efficiency-preserving* round compression compilers, i.e. compilers that translate the efficiency benefits of the underlying highly interactive protocols to the fewer round setting. Focusing on the honest majority setting (with near-optimal corruption threshold $\frac{1}{2} - \varepsilon$, for any $\varepsilon > 0$), we devise a new compiler that yields two round (i.e., round optimal) semi-honest MPC with similar communication efficiency as the underlying (arbitrary round) protocol. By applying our compiler on the most efficient known MPC protocols, we obtain a two-round semi-honest protocol based on one-way functions, with total communication (and per-party computation) cost $\widetilde{O}(s + n^4)$ – a significant improvement over prior two-round protocols with cost $\widetilde{O}(n^\tau s + n^{\tau+1} d)$, where $\tau \geq 2$, s is the size of the circuit computing the function and d the corresponding depth. Our result can also be extended to handle malicious adversaries, either using stronger assumptions in the public key infrastructure (PKI) model, or in the plain model using an extra round.

An artifact of our approach is that the resultant protocol is "unbalanced" in the amount of computation performed by different parties. We give evidence that this is *necessary* in our setting. Our impossibility result makes novel use of the "MPC-in-the-head" paradigm which has typically been used to demonstrate feasibility results.

S. Moriai and H. Wang (Eds.): ASIACRYPT 2020, LNCS 12493, pp. 181–212, 2020.
https://doi.org/10.1007/978-3-030-64840-4_7

1 Introduction

Understanding the minimal rounds of interaction required to carry out a cryptographic task has been the subject of extensive study over the past few decades. While ad-hoc techniques are often used to obtain low round complexity solutions, a more systematic approach adopted in the literature is to build a *round compression compiler*. As the name suggests, a round compression compiler transforms a highly interactive protocol into one with far fewer rounds. The celebrated compiler of Fiat and Shamir [22] is one such example that transforms a public-coin interactive proof system into a non-interactive one (in the random oracle model).

Recently, a sequence of works have designed round compression compilers to resolve major open problems in cryptography. For instance, the recent result on non-interactive zero knowledge proofs for NP from learning with errors was designed by instantiating the Fiat-Shamir methodology [11,38]. In the context of secure multiparty computation (MPC) [6,12,29,40] – the focus of this work – a recent sequence of exciting works devised novel round compression compilers to construct round-optimal MPC protocols based on minimal assumptions [1–4,7,24,25].

Rounds vs Computation in MPC. In this work, we continue the study of round compression in MPC. Starting from [5], round compression in MPC has been extensively studied over the years in a variety of models. Traditionally, most works have focused on devising compilers that preserve the security properties of the underlying protocol. However, not much emphasis has been placed on preserving the *computational and communication efficiency.*

Indeed, the recent round compression compilers that yield round-optimal MPC [1–4,7,24,25] incur a large overhead in computation and communication. Some of these compilers work in the setting where a majority of parties are allowed to be dishonest, while others require a majority of the parties to be honest. In this work, we focus on the latter setting, referred to as *honest majority.* In this setting, consider an arbitrary round MPC protocol with total computational work $W = W(n, s)$, where n denotes the number of parties executing the protocol and s denotes the size of the circuit implementing the function being computed. Then, applying the compilers of [1–4,24] on such a protocol yields a two round protocol with total communication and per-party computation $\widetilde{O}(n^\tau \cdot W)$, where $\tau \geq 2$, ignoring multiplicative factors in security parameter. Plugging in the most efficient known multi-round MPC protocols [15,16,26] with total cost $\widetilde{O}(s+nd)$ (where d is the circuit depth), we obtain a two round protocol with significantly worse total communication (and per-party computation) $\widetilde{O}(n^\tau s + n^{\tau+1}d)$.

The above state of affairs raises the question: does round compression necessarily require high computational and communication cost? If not, can we design *efficiency-preserving* round compression compilers for MPC that preserve both the security as well as the computational and communication efficiency of the underlying protocol?

1.1 Our Results

We study efficiency-preserving round compression compilers for MPC. As a first step in this direction, we narrow our focus on the honest majority setting.

Our main result stated below holds with respect to *semi-honest* adversaries. Later, we also discuss extensions to the case of *malicious* adversaries.

Theorem 1 (Informal). *Let n be the number of parties and let λ be the security parameter, such that n is polynomially related to λ. Assuming one-way functions, there is a round compression compiler that transforms a semi-honest secure MPC protocol Π for any n-party functionality $\mathcal{F}$ into a two-round semi-honest secure protocol Π' for $\mathcal{F}$ with the following properties:*

- *If Π tolerates corruption threshold ε, then Π' tolerates ε', for arbitrary constants $\varepsilon' < \varepsilon < \frac{1}{2}$.*
- *If the total computation cost of Π is $W = W(n, s)$, where s is the circuit size representation of $\mathcal{F}$, then the amortized per-party computation cost and total communication cost of Π' is*

$$\widetilde{O}\left(\left(W(\log^2(n), s) + n^4\right)\right),$$

where the $\widetilde{O}$ notation suppresses polynomial factors in λ and polylog factors in n.

To handle smaller values of n, we can use a *hybrid mode* of compilation: if n is small, simply use existing compilers; for larger values of n, one should use our compiler.

Comparison with Prior Work. Our compiler performs significantly better than previous compilers [1,3,4] that yield two-round protocols with total communication and per-party computation cost of $\tilde{O}(n^{\tau} W(n, s))$, where $\tau \geq 2$. All of these existing two round compilers [1,3,4] rely on the following high level idea[1]- they view the entire computation done in the underlying protocol as a circuit and then require all the parties to communicate at least one-bit for each gate in this circuit, with every other party over pair-wise private channels in the first round. This adds a multiplicative overhead of at least n^2 in the complexity of the resulting protocol. Infact, the exact overhead in these compilers might even be more than n^2, because these are not the only messages that the parties compute and send in those compilers. However, for comparison, it suffices for us to use a conservative approximation, i.e., $\tau \geq 2$.

On the other hand, by applying our compiler on the most asymptotically efficient MPC protocols [15,16,26] with total computation cost $W(n, s) = \widetilde{O}(s + nd)$, we obtain a two-round protocol with total communication and per-party computation cost $\tilde{O}(s + n^4)$. In contrast, applying previous compilers on the same protocols yields two-round protocols with total communication and per-party computation cost $\tilde{O}(n^{\tau} \cdot s + n^{\tau+1} d)$, where $\tau > 2$.

---

[1] While this idea is made explicit in [3,4], it is easy to observe that [1] also implicitly uses the same idea.

Extensions. With suitable modifications to the above compiler, we can obtain additional results that achieve different tradeoffs, both in the case of semi-honest and malicious adversaries.

- *Semi-honest:* The above compiler can be easily modified such that the *total* (as opposed to amortized per-party) computation cost is $\widetilde{O}(W(\log^2(n), s) + n^4)$, at the cost of increasing a round of interaction.[2]
- *Malicious:* The above compiler can also be easily modified to work against *malicious* adversaries, yielding either two round protocols in the PKI model assuming verifiable random functions [37], or three round protocols in the plain model without additional assumptions. Both these protocols achieve the standard notion of security with abort, assuming that the underlying protocol also achieves the same security.

Impossibility of Balanced Protocols. Our compiler utilizes a committee-based approach which has been used in many prior works in the larger round setting. A caveat of this approach is that it results in *unbalanced* protocols where a small subset of parties (namely, the committee members) perform much of the "heavy" computation, while other parties only do "light" computation. Furthermore, this approach also yields a sub-optimal corruption threshold (i.e., $n > 2t + 1$, where t is the number of corrupted parties). In view of this, we investigate whether this is inherent.

We give evidence that our approach is "tight" by showing that there exists some functionality for which there does not exist a *balanced* constant round (even insecure) MPC protocol with total computational cost $\widetilde{O}(s)$. In contrast, our compiler yields an unbalanced constant-round secure MPC protocol with roughly the same total cost (ignoring additive terms).

1.2 Our Techniques

In this section we describe the main ideas underlying our results. In Sect. 1.2.1 we give an overview of our techniques for designing efficiency-preserving round-compression compilers. Later, in Sect. 1.2.2, we describe ideas for proving impossibility of balanced constant-round MPC protocols with total computation cost $\widetilde{O}(s)$. Throughout this section we assume $\tau \geq 2$, and is hereby omitted for clarity of exposition.

1.2.1 Efficiency-Preservation via Committees

We now proceed to describe the techniques used in our compiler. At a high-level, we devise a two step approach:

- **Step 1: Special Two Round MPC.** First, given a potentially highly interactive MPC protocol with total computational work $W = W(n, s)$, where s

[2] If there are only a constant number of parties that are recipients of the output, then the resultant protocol from Theorem 1 already achieves this result.

is the size of the circuit and n is the number of parties, we apply a round-compression compiler to obtain a *special* two round protocol with some specific structural properties. The total computational complexity of this *special MPC* is proportional to $\tilde{O}(n^{\tau} \cdot W)$.[3] Even though it does not achieve our desired efficiency, its structural properties are crucially used in the second step.
- **Step 2: Efficiency Boost.** We then leverage the structural properties of the special two round MPC to transform it into a new protocol with the same round complexity, but improved asymptotic computational and communication complexity.

We postpone the discussion on the structural properties required from the two round protocol. Instead, we first focus on Step 2; the efficiency boosting transformation would then guide us towards identifying these structural properties.

Starting Ideas for Efficiency Boost. We first focus on the semi-honest setting, and defer the malicious case to later. Given a special two-round MPC, our starting idea for improving its efficiency is to use the classical *committee-based approach*, where the bulk of the computation is "delegated" to a small committee of parties, while the remaining parties do very little work.

More specifically, the main idea in a committee-based approach is to first elect a "small" committee, while ensuring that a majority of the parties in the committee are honest and letting these elected parties run the actual protocol. Since the parties not elected to the committee are no longer doing any work, we need a mechanism to allow these parties to transfer their inputs to the committee members. To ensure privacy of their inputs, the parties who are not elected in the committee, secret-share their inputs amongst the committee members. The elected committee then runs an MPC computing a modified functionality $\mathcal{F}'$, that collects all the secret shares of all the non-elected parties, reconstructs their inputs, and computed the original function $\mathcal{F}$. Unlike the original function $\mathcal{F}$, $\mathcal{F}'$ requires inputs from only the elected committee members, which as described above, also implicitly contains the remaining parties' inputs. Since the cost of the computation is dominated by the number of parties involved in the "heavy" computation, it suffices to use a committee of size poly-logarithmic in the total number of parties to yield non-trivial savings in the total cost.

In order to prevent an adversary from corrupting a majority of the members in the committee, it is important to choose the committee at random. This means that the identities of the committee members are unknown to all parties at the start of the protocol; instead, we must implement a committee election mechanism during the protocol execution. Let Π be the two-round protocol obtained by applying the round-compression compiler in the first step. Now,

[3] While special MPC with total computation proportional to $\tilde{O}(n^{\tau} \cdot W)$ can be constructed (as we discuss later), the second step of our approach is actually less sensitive to the exact asymptotic complexity of special MPC. In particular, the exact dependence on n is not very important as long the total computation in special MPC has only linear dependence on W.

applying the committee-based approach over Π, we get the following five round protocol Π':

1. **Round 1.** Each party tosses an appropriately biased coin to decide whether or not it will be in the committee and reveals the result to all other parties.
2. **Round 2.** The parties that are not part of the committee secret share their inputs amongst the committee members.
3. **Round 3.** The committee members compute and send their first round messages in π.
4. **Round 4.** The committee members compute and send their second round messages in π.
5. **Round 5.** The committee members reconstruct the output and then send the output to all other parties.

Since the bulk of the computation is performed by the committee members, the amortized per-party computation in Π' depends only on $\mathsf{polylog}(n)$ as opposed to $\mathsf{poly}(n)$. The main problem however, is that Π' requires five rounds, while we seek a two round protocol.

Committee-Based Approach in Two-Rounds. Towards obtaining a two round protocol, we start with the observation that if protocol Π allows for public reconstruction of output based on the transcript of the last round, then Rounds 4 and 5 of Π' can be parallelized. Indeed, this property is satisfied by the protocol output by our compiler in Step 1[4] and is also true for other recent round-compression compilers [2,7,25]. While this yields a saving of one round, it is not clear how to proceed further. Indeed, to obtain a two-round protocol, the task of electing a committee and sharing of inputs by the remaining parties must be parallelized with the computation done by the committee members using Π. In other words, Rounds 1, 2 and 3 must seemingly be executed in the first round of Π', and Round 4 in the second round. This, however, raises some fundamental challenges:

1. **Challenge 1: Sharing of Inputs.** If the committee election happens in parallel with input sharing, the non-committee members (henceforth referred to as the *clients*) would not know the identities of the committee members (henceforth referred to as the *servers*) at the time of distributing their inputs. How can the clients secret share their inputs with the servers, without knowing their identities? It seems like there is no way to get around this, which means that the servers must start their computation without knowing their "entire input". But parallelizing committee election and input sharing is crucial both for the correctness and security. Indeed, in any two round MPC protocol, the private inputs of all parties must be "fixed" in the first round to prevent input resetting attacks [32].

[4] Protocols obtained by applying the compiler from [1] always satisfy this property, while the compilers in [3,4], yield protocols that satisfy the "public reconstruction of outputs" property only when applied to a (multi-round) protocols that also satisfy this property.

2. **Challenge 2: Blind Computation.** All known two-round honest majority MPC protocols based on minimal assumptions [1–4, 24] necessarily rely on the use of private channels in the first round. Since the committee election and computation must happen simultaneously, it is not clear how the servers would exchange private channel messages in the first round without knowing each other's identities. It seems like we require the servers to start their computation "in the blind".

To address these two challenges, we require some structural properties from Π. We now describe them.

Special Two Round MPC. We require the following two structural properties from the special two round MPC in Step 1:

1. **Decomposability:** The first round messages of each party in a special two round MPC protocol can be decomposed into: **(i)** "light" messages that depend on the input but whose computational complexity is independent of W, and **(ii)** "heavy" messages that are independent of the input but whose computational complexity may depend on W. The light and heavy messages may share common randomness.
2. **Independence:** The private channel messages in a special two round MPC protocol should be independent of the inputs of the parties.

At a first glance, these properties may seem quite unconventional and strong. Indeed, our main technical contribution is in identifying these rather unconventional and specific structural properties of two-round protocols and then leveraging these properties for efficiency gains in the setting of two rounds. In particular, as we describe below, the decomposability property, with additional delegation of computation techniques, is used to address Challenge 1 and the independence property is used to address Challenge 2. Moreover, as we discuss later, these properties can, in fact, be achieved generically.

Solving Challenge 1. Towards explaining our main ideas, let us first consider a simpler scenario where Π only consists of broadcast channel messages (we deal with private channel messages later while addressing challenge 2). As noted earlier, the main issue in parallelizing input distribution and committee election is that the servers cannot know their entire input in the first round, yet the first round messages of the protocol must fix the inputs of all the parties. Moreover, the second round messages of all parties can also depend on the entire first round transcript (which in turn must depend on the inputs).

To address these problems, a natural starting idea is to require the clients to *aid* the servers in the computation of the first and second round messages of Π while still achieving the desired efficiency. Let us first focus on the second round messages of Π; specifically, that of a particular server (say) S_i. Our first idea is to run a separate *helper protocol* involving all parties (servers and clients) to help compute the second round messages of S_i. This helper protocol can take the input shares from all clients and the randomness from all servers to first internally compute the first round messages of all servers and then compute and output the second round message of S_i. A naive implementation of this approach, however, runs into an obvious problem: since the per-party complexity for computing second round messages of the servers in Π is $\tilde{O}(n^\tau \cdot W)$, the size of the functionality implemented by the helper protocol, and thereby the per-party computation performed by the clients, also has the same total complexity of $\tilde{O}(n^\tau \cdot W)$.

Towards addressing this problem, we first use a delegation of computation approach implemented via garbled circuits and a modified two-round helper protocol as follows:

- We require the server S_i to garble and send its second round next-message function of Π in the second round of Π'. This circuit takes as input the entire first round transcript of Π and computes, and outputs, S_i's second round messages in Π.
- The input wire labels for this garbled circuit are computed via a modified two-round helper protocol for a specific functionality. This functionality takes as input, secret-shares from the clients and randomness used to compute the first round messages from the servers. It also takes as input all of the garbled circuit input wire labels from S_i. It internally computes the first round message of all servers and then selects and outputs the corresponding input wire labels.

Thus far we have ignored the first round messages and an observant reader may notice that this solution still does not suffice; indeed, since the size of the first round messages in Π is also proportional to $\tilde{O}(n^\tau \cdot W)$, the clients still need to spend the same computational effort.

Our main conceptual idea to overcome this problem is to leverage the decomposability property of special MPC. Recall that the decomposability property requires that in the first round, each party sends computationally light messages depend on its input and computationally heavy messages that are independent of its input. We leverage this property as follows: we require the servers to compute (on their own) and send the heavy messages in the first round, which can then be hardwired in the *circuit* that S_i garbles in the second round. The *helper protocol* involving all parties is now only required to compute the input wire labels corresponding to the light messages, as opposed to the entire first round messages, which is efficient. Moreover, this also ensures that the inputs of all parties are indeed fixed in the first round, which is necessary for security.

Finally, we remark that if the light messages in Π can be computed using a degree-1 computation over the parties' inputs, then we can use lightweight protocols such as [36] (satisfying security with abort) for quadratic functionalities to further reduce the work done by clients. We later show that our compiler from Step 1 achieves this property as well.

Solving Challenge 2. While so far we have only considered the simplified setting of broadcast-only protocols, in reality, our protocol Π from the first step (necessarily) consists of both the broadcast and P2P messages. As described earlier, this creates the challenge that the servers cannot send P2P messages to each other in the first round without knowing their identities. Since the computation must start in the first round itself, we need a mechanism for "computing in the blind".

We implement such a mechanism by allowing the servers to encrypt their private channel messages and broadcasting them in the first round and then enabling others to somehow compute on these encrypted messages. To help compute on the encrypted messages, we again utilize a delegation of computation approach:

- Each server garbles a circuit that takes the decryption key as input and decrypts the corresponding first round encrypted message that was intended for it and computes its second round message.
- Wire labels corresponding to the decryption key are computed via a helper protocol involving all properties, similar to the solution to the previous challenge. Since the helper protocol is only responsible for computing labels corresponding to the decryption keys, the total work done by the parties (especially clients) in this helper protocol does not depend upon the complexity of the next-message functions of the parties in Π.

An observant reader, however, may notice that this approach fails completely, if the P2P messages in Π were dependent on the input. Indeed, since the servers do not have access to their entire input in the first round, it is unclear how they would compute and encrypt these messages in such a case.

Our next conceptual idea to overcome this problem is to leverage the independence property of special MPC. Recall that this property requires all of the private channel messages in Π to be independent of the inputs. Given this property, the above solution already works.

Realizing Special Two Round MPC. Recall that a special two-round MPC must satisfy the following requirements:

1. **Structural Properties:** It must satisfy the decomposability and independence properties defined earlier.
2. **Complexity:** The total communication complexity of the special MPC must be $\tilde{O}(n^{\tau} \cdot W)$. (As discussed earlier, the key requirement here is the linear dependence on W, whereas the exact multiplicative dependence on n is less important since this special MPC is only executed by $\mathsf{polylog}(n)$-sized) committee of parties.)

We address each of these requirements separately. There is a surprisingly simple approach for achieving the structural properties *generically*. Specifically, we show that any two-round protocol π with the delayed-function property[5] can be made to achieve these structural properties without affecting its asymptotic efficiency. The idea is to have each party P_i sample a random mask r_i for its input x_i,

[5] At a high level, a two-round MPC protocol satisfies the delayed-function property if the first round messages of the honest parties are computed independent of the functionality, but may depend on the size of the circuit implementing the functionality.

and broadcast $x_i \oplus r_i$ in the first round. Additionally, the parties run π on a modified functionality $f'_{x_1 \oplus r_i,\ldots,x_n \oplus r_n}$ that has $x_1 \oplus r_i, \ldots, x_n \oplus r_n$ hardwired in its description, such that

$$f'_{x_1 \oplus r_i,\ldots,x_n \oplus r_n}(r_1, \ldots, r_n) = f(x_1, \ldots, x_n),$$

where f is the original functionality. It is easy to see that because of this simple modification, the first round messages of party P_i in the modified protocol Π can now be decomposed into a "light" message $x_i \oplus r_i$ that depends on its input and "heavy" messages which correspond to its first round messages in π. Moreover, because of the delayed-function property of π, these "heavy" first round messages in Π are independent of their actual inputs. This already achieves decomposability. With regards to independence property, we first note that the above transformation already ensures that the first round private channel messages in Π are independent of the parties' inputs. However, their second round private channel messages may still depend on their inputs. Towards this, we observe that any two-round protocol that makes use of private channel messages in the second round can be modified into one that only uses broadcast channel messages in the second round. This can be done by letting the parties exchange one-time pads with each other in the first round, and then broadcasting their second round messages encrypted under these one-time pads. With this modification, we can also achieve independence.

Since the above approach works generically with any protocol that satisfies the delayed-function property, it can also be applied to a delayed-function variant of [1,3,4]. We note that while [1] already satisfies the delayed function property, the two-round compilers of [3,4] do not. A simple modification to this construction can yield two-round protocols with delayed-function property without compromising its efficiency. We refer the reader to the full version for details on this modification.

Moreover, when applied to an interactive protocol with total computation W, the compilers of [1,3,4] already yield two-round protocols with total communication at least $\tilde{O}(n^\tau \cdot W)$. Hence, in summary, either of the recent two-round protocols [1,3,4] in the honest majority setting, with the above modifications, can be used to obtain a two-round special MPC with all of the required properties.

Summary (so far). Putting the above solutions together, we now obtain a two-round semi-honest protocol that achieves total communication complexity $\tilde{O}(W(\mathsf{polylog}(n), s) + n^4)$[6] and total computation complexity $\tilde{O}(nW(\mathsf{polylog}(n), s) + n^5)$ if we elect a committee of size $\mathsf{polylog}(n)$. The computation complexity is higher than the communication complexity. This is because in order to reconstruct the output, all the parties must locally compute on all the second round messages of all parties, which adds a multiplicative overhead of n

[6] For this technical overview, some details of the protocol are omitted. The resultant protocol incurs an additive term of n^4, which is elaborate upon in the technical section.

to the computation complexity. We note that we are limited to this computation complexity in two rounds, since we do not know of any two round compilers with better and more efficient output reconstruction algorithms. However, if we add another round such that only one of the parties the output at the second round and broadcasts it to others in the third round, we can get optimal computational efficiency.[7]

Handling Malicious Adversaries. The above approach only works against semi-honest adversaries. For the malicious setting, we need to start with a malicious special two round MPC protocol. We are now faced with the following additional issues in the malicious setting:

1. **Input Consistency.** Recall that in the semi-honest protocol proposed above, the servers are required to use the same randomness as input in multiple sub-protocols: (1) for computing its "heavy" first round messages in Π and (2) in the helper protocol for computing its "light" first round messages. Since the light messages depend on the inputs of clients, if a malicious server does not use the input randomness consistently in the two sub-protocols, it could potentially change the input share of an honest client.
2. **Malicious Secure Committee Election.** Our naive way of doing a committee election where the parties can randomly elect themselves to be in the committee, clearly does not work in the malicious setting. A corrupt party can always elect it self to be in the committee.

Towards describing our solution to the first problem, let us first address why simply compiling a maliciously secure protocol Π with the compiler described above is not sufficient. Recall that in general, a maliciously secure protocol cannot prevent adversarial parties from choosing their inputs arbitrarily. However, in the above compiler, since the underlying (maliciously secure) protocol Π is only run amongst the committee members and their inputs also contain input shares of the honest clients, we cannot afford to let them choose their entire input arbitrarily.

To prevent this, we make use of one-time message authentication codes (MACs). The honest clients compute a MAC over each of their input shares. For the MAC's to be verified, they must be checked, and hence require the key. However, providing a (potentially corrupt) server with the MAC key defeats the purpose, since there is no longer any security. Therefore, for each input share, we shall create MACs with each of the server keys, i.e., one corresponding to each server. These keys are sent to the respective servers, while the input share and all the corresponding MAC tags are sent only to the designated server. The functionality computed by the protocol Π is modified to first check if for each input share that it gets as input, all its corresponding MACs are valid. As long as there is an honest party, for which the adversary does not have access to the key, it cannot create a mauled tag that will verify with that key. We use the

[7] Alternatively, if the number of parties computing the output are already a constant, then even the two round protocol achieves optimal computation.

helper protocols exactly as described earlier with the only exception that now instead of just their input shares, the clients also communicate these MACs and MAC keys to the servers via the helper protocol.

To implement a maliciously secure committee election protocol, we use the following standard techniques:

- **Using VRFs:** We use the strategy from Algorand [27] based on verifiable random functions (VRFs) [37]. This is implemented in the reusable[8] correlated randomness model where the adversarial corruption may happen after the setup. We note that since VRFs are known from non-interactive witness indistinguishability proofs (NIWIs) [8,30], we get a resulting maliciously secure two-round protocol in the correlated randomness model based on NIWI, whose communication complexity is $\tilde{O}(W(\mathsf{polylog}(n), s) + n^{\tau+4})$ and total computation complexity is $\tilde{O}(nW(\mathsf{polylog}(n), s) + n^{\tau+5})$.[9]
- **Feige's Lightest Bin Protocol** [21]**:** This gives a statistically secure committee election protocol. However each party learns whether or not it is in the committee only at the end of this protocol, so it adds another round at the start of the two-round protocol. As a result we get a three-round maliciously secure protocol in the plain model, whose communication complexity is $\tilde{O}(W(\mathsf{polylog}(n), s) + n^{\tau+4})$ and total computation complexity is $\tilde{O}(nW(\mathsf{polylog}(n), s) + n^{\tau+5})$.

Comparison with Existing Maliciously Secure Compilers: By applying our compiler on the most asymptotically efficient MPC protocols [15,16,26] with total computation cost $W(n, s) = \widetilde{O}(s+nd)$, we obtain a two-round protocol with total communication and per-party computation cost $\tilde{O}(s + n^{\tau+4})$. In contrast, applying previous maliciously secure compilers on the same protocols yields two-round protocols with total communication and per-party computation cost $\tilde{O}(n^{\tau} \cdot s + n^{\tau+1}d + n^{\tau+2})$, where $\tau > 2$.

1.2.2 Impossibility of Balanced Protocols

While our approach gives an efficiency preserving compiler in 3 rounds, a drawback of our compiler is that it yields unbalanced protocols with sub-optimal corruption threshold of $t < n/2$. This is a consequence of our committee-based approach. Next, we provide some evidence towards the fact that a committee-based approach is necessary. In particular, we show that it is impossible to obtain a constant round MPC protocol with equal division of labor, where the total work done by parties is $\tilde{O}(|C|)$, where $|C|$ is the size of the circuit implementing the functionality. We show this impossibility using the player emulation methodology [13,33,35]. To the best of our knowledge, this is the first time that this paradigm is used for proving a negative result.

[8] A simpler solution using non-reusable correlated randomness can be obtained using regular digital signatures which are known from one-way functions.

[9] As for the semi-honest setting, the additive term will be elaborated upon in the technical sections.

Let us assume that there exists an $r-$round MPC protocol Π, where the total work done by each party is approximately $\tilde{O}(|C|)/n$, where r is some constant. In other words, the size (and depth) of the circuit implementing the next-message function of each party is $\tilde{O}(|C|)/n$. In every round, we can recursively use protocol Π to implement the next-message function of each party. The total number of rounds in the resulting protocol is r^2, while the total work done by each party in each round is still $\tilde{O}(|C|)/n$, it can now be computed using n-parallel circuits each of depth $\tilde{O}(|C|)/n^2$.

If we repeat this approach of recursively replacing the next-message function of each party in each round with an execution of Π for k iterations, we get a protocol with r^k rounds where in each round, the next message function of each party can be computed using a circuit of depth $\tilde{O}(|C|)/n^k$. Let k, c be constants such that $\tilde{O}(|C|)/n^k = c$. In each round the total computation done by the parties can be viewed as an execution of n-parallel circuits, each of depth at most c. Overall, the total work done by the parties in the final protocol, can be viewed as an execution of $n-$parallel circuits, each of depth at most $c \cdot r^k = O(1)$.

This approach can be used to reduce any arbitrary-depth circuit C into a constant-depth circuit, which is a contradiction since we know that functions like parity are not computable in constant depth.

1.3 Related Work

The study of multiparty computation was initiated in the seminal works of [6, 12, 29, 40]. Beaver et al. [5] initiated the study of constant round protocols in the honest majority setting. Subsequently, there has been extensive work in the study of constant round protocols, resulting in round optimal protocols both in the honest majority and dishonest majority settings [1–4, 7, 23–25].

Further, the design of efficient protocols have been studied in both the computational and information theoretic settings [9, 14–18, 20, 34, 39, 41]. Some of these results [15, 16] achieve optimal computational and communication complexity of $\tilde{O}(s)$. Similar to us, their results also have an additive factors which are polynomial in both the security parameter and number of parties.

Committee based techniques have been used primarily in the context of scalable computation, where the goal is to build secure computation protocols that scale well with a large number of parties. Of these, the works of [9, 10, 19, 39, 41] seek to reduce computational and communication complexity work in the large round setting. See [39] and the references therein for for a detailed survey of the use of committee based techniques in the context of scalable computation. To the best of our knowledge no prior works apply committee based approaches in the two round setting. This is perhaps unsurprising given the recency of the two round protocols based on standard assumptions.

1.4 Full Version

Due to space constraints, preliminaries, details of the proofs, and complexity calculations have been omitted from this manuscript, and can be found in the full version of the paper.

2 Two-Round Efficiency Preserving Compiler in the Client-Server Model

In order to describe our compiler in a manner that easily extends to the malicious setting, we will present our solution in two steps, spread across Sects. 2 and 3. In this section, we construct a maliciously secure efficiency preserving, round compression compiler in the Client-Server model.

Recall that in the client-server model, every party is designated to be either a client or a server, and is additionally aware of the roles of all the other parties. The clients share their inputs among all the servers (servers may additionally have inputs), who in turn do the computation and broadcast the result. Later in Sect. 3, we will show how this protocol in the client-server model can be extended to obtain an efficiency preserving compiler in the *plain model*, namely, where the parties do not have any pre-designated roles assigned to them.

The rest of this section is organized as follows. First, we present a two-round *special* MPC with some specific structural properties in Sect. 2.1. Then in Sect. 2.2, we make use of the properties of this protocol to present a two-round, maliciously secure, efficiency preserving compiler in the client server model.

2.1 Special Two-Round MPC

As discussed in the technical overview, given an interactive protocol with total computation work W, as a starting step, we need to transform it into a two-round *special* MPC protocol that satisfies the following properties:

1. **Decomposability**: The first round messages of each party in Π can be decomposed into "light" messages that depend on the input but not W, and "heavy" messages that depend on W but not on the input; however they may share common randomness.
2. **Independence:** The private channel messages in Π are independent of the inputs.
3. **Complexity:** The total computation complexity of the resulting protocol should only be linearly dependent on W.

We state the following lemma proven in the full version of our paper.

Lemma 1. *Let λ be the security parameter. There is a round compression compiler that transforms a maliciously (and semi-honest, resp.) secure MPC protocol π for any n-party functionality $\mathcal{F}$ into a two-round maliciously (and semi-honest, resp) secure protocol Π for $\mathcal{F}$ with the following properties:*

1. *If π tolerates corruption threshold ϵ, then Π tolerates ϵ', for arbitrary constants $\epsilon' < \epsilon < 1/2$.*
2. *If the computational cost of π is $W = W(n, s)$, where s is the circuit size representation of $\mathcal{F}$, then the amortized per-party computational cost of Π is $O(n^{\tau} W)$ and the per-party communication cost of Π is $O(n^{\tau-1} W)$.*
3. *Each party in Π sends messages over both private channels and a broadcast channel in the first round. While in the second round, each party only sends messages over a broadcast channel.*
4. *Each party P_i in Π broadcasts its masked input $(x_i \oplus \gamma_i)$ in the first round, where x_i is its input and γ_i is a random value. The rest of its first round broadcast messages are independent of its input but may depend on r_i.*
5. *The private channel message of each party P_i in Π is independent of its input x_i but may depend on r_i.*

Remark 1. We note that we consider the computation of functions represented by circuits consisting of AND, OR and NOT gates.

2.2 From Special MPC to Efficiency Preserving Compiler in the Client-Server Model

Now that we have a two-round protocol Π with the desired structural properties from Lemma 1, we use it to present a two-round maliciously secure, efficiency preserving compiler in the client-server model. Since our protocol works in the client server model, for ease of presentation we use indices with different fonts for referring to specific servers and clients: $\mathbb{i} \in \mathbb{n}$ for servers (double-struck) and $\mathbf{i} \in \mathbf{n}$ for clients (bold).

Protocol Overview. At a high level, given $\mathbb{n}$ servers and $\mathbf{n}$ clients, where $\mathbb{n} + \mathbf{n} = n$, the semi-honest protocol works as follows. Each client generates $\mathbb{n}$ additive secret shares of its input - one for each server. The servers then engage in a single execution of the two round protocol Π to compute the function. As mentioned in the introduction, this doesn't work directly and requires servers delegating their second round computation to a garbled circuit. The corresponding keys for the circuit are computed by a two round helper protocol Π_{help} that *all* parties participate in.

For security against malicious adversaries, we must prevent a malicious server from modifying the input shares of an honest client and make use of one-time message authentication codes (MACs) to enforce consistency checks. So, in addition to secret sharing their inputs, the clients compute $\mathbb{n}$ MAC's on each of their shares using a different MAC key. The functionality computed by the protocol Π first checks if inputs and their corresponding MACs are valid. Only if this check succeeds, does it start computing on them. We use the helper protocol Π_{help} exactly as described earlier with the only addition that now instead of just their input shares, the clients also communicate these MACs and MAC keys to the servers via the helper protocol.

Formally, we prove the following theorem. In this theorem we also enlist additional properties achieved by our resulting protocol. These properties are crucially used by our compiler in Sect. 3 to obtain an efficiency preserving compiler in the plain model. We refer the reader to Sect. 3 for a detailed discussion on the relevance of these properties.

Theorem 2. *Let n be the number of parties and λ be the security parameter. Assuming one-way functions, there is a round compression compiler that transforms a maliciously (and semi-honest, resp.) secure MPC protocol Π for any n-input functionality $\mathcal{F}$ into a two-round maliciously (and semi-honestly, resp.) secure protocol Φ for $\mathcal{F}$ in the client-server model with the following properties:*

1. *Let $\mathbb{n}$ be the number of servers and $\mathbf{n} = n - \mathbb{n}$ be the number of clients. If the computational cost of π is $W = W(n, s)$, where s is the circuit size representation of $\mathcal{F}$, then the amortized per-party computational cost and total communication of maliciously (and semi-honest, resp.) secure protocol Φ is $\widetilde{O}(W(\mathbb{n}, s) + n^{\tau+4})$, (and $\widetilde{O}(W(\mathbb{n}, s) + n^4)$, resp.), where the $\widetilde{O}$ notation suppresses suppresses polynomial factors in λ and $\mathbb{n}$.*
2. *If π tolerates corruption threshold ϵ, then Φ tolerates ϵ', for arbitrary constants $\epsilon' < \epsilon < 1/2$ corruptions in the server set and ϵ corruptions in the client set.*
3. *Each party can send messages over both private channels and a broadcast channel in the first round in Φ. While in the second round, each party only sends messages over a broadcast channel.*
4. *The private channel messages sent by clients in Φ are independent of the role (client/server) of the receiving party in the protocol.*
5. *The total length of messages sent by all clients is $O(\mathbb{n}^2 n \mathbf{n}^3 \lambda^3)$ in the semi-honest case and $\widetilde{O}(n^{\tau-1}\mathbb{n}^3\mathbf{n}^3\lambda^3 + \mathbb{n}\mathbf{n}^3 n^{\tau+1}\lambda)$ in the malicious case.*
6. *The private channel messages sent by servers in Φ can be divided into messages that are independent of the role (client/server) of the receiving party and ones that are specifically intended for other server parties.*
7. *The total length of messages sent by all servers in Φ is $O(\mathbb{n}^4 n \mathbf{n}\lambda^3 + \mathbb{n}^{\tau+1} W\lambda)$ in the semi-honest case and $\widetilde{O}(n^{\tau-1}\mathbb{n}^5\mathbf{n}\lambda^3 + \mathbb{n}^3\mathbf{n}n^{\tau+1}\lambda) + \mathbb{n}^{\tau+1}W\lambda$ in the malicious case.*

We now give a constructive proof of Theorem 2 using the protocol described below.

2.2.1 Construction

We start by establishing some notations that will be used throughout this section.

Notations. We use various underlying protocols for different functionalities in our construction. We use Π_X to denote the underlying protocol used for computing functionality $\mathcal{F}_X$. The rth next message function of protocol Π_X is denoted by Π_X^r. We use multiple instantiations of these underlying protocols. In the rth round of the yth instantiation of Π_X, we use $\mathtt{M}_X^{r,y}[\mathbb{i}, \mathbf{j}]$ to the message that server i sends to client j and $\mathtt{M}_X^{r,y}[\mathbb{i}]$ denotes the message that it broadcasts. $\mathtt{I}_X^y[\mathbb{i}]$ denotes the input of server i in the yth instantiation of Π_X. Often times, we replace some indices in the above notations with symbols such as $\bullet, \diamond$ or $*$ to denote a set. For instance $\mathtt{M}_X^{r,y}[\mathbb{i}, \bullet] = \{\mathtt{M}_X^{r,y}[\mathbb{i}, \mathbf{j}]\}_{\mathbf{j}\in\mathbf{n}}$. Similarly, $\diamond$ is used to denote all servers and

$*$ is used for referring to all clients and all parties respective. The collection of labels (of a garbled circuit) are denoted as $\overline{\mathsf{lab}} := \{\mathsf{lab}_{i,0}, \mathsf{lab}_{i,0}\}_{i \in [L]}$. Projection of a string of $c \in \{0, 1, \perp\}^L$ is defined as $\mathsf{Projection}(c, \overline{\mathsf{lab}}) = \{\mathsf{lab}_{i,c[i]}\}_{i \in [L]}$, where $\mathsf{lab}_{i,\perp}$ is defined to be $\perp$. The output of $\mathsf{Projection}$ is treated as a string. For convenience, we also specify that $\perp$ under the XOR operation remains unchanged. Specifically, $\forall b \in \{0, 1\}$, $b \oplus \perp = \perp$. Wherever necessary, we augment the protocol description with comments denoted as /\/comment.

Next, we list the building blocks used in our construction.

Building Blocks. The main primitives required in this construction for computing an n-input functionality $\mathcal{F}$ are the following:

1. An unconditionally secure message authentication scheme ($\mathsf{MAC}, \mathsf{Verify}$).
2. A two-round protocol Π_{aug} [4] for $\mathbb{n}$ parties output by the compiler in Lemma 1, for the function $\mathcal{F}_{\mathsf{aug}}$ defined in Fig. 1.

Function: $\mathcal{F}_{\mathsf{aug}}$

Parties: $\mathbb{n}$ parties $P_1, \cdots, P_{\mathbb{n}}$.

Inputs: Each party has input $X_{\mathbb{i}} := x_{\mathbb{i}} || \left\{ x[\mathsf{j}, \mathbb{i}] || \{\mathsf{tag}^{\ell}_{\mathsf{j} \to \mathbb{i}}\}_{\ell \in [n]} || \{\mathsf{k}^{\mathbb{i}}_{\mathsf{j} \to \ell}\}_{\ell \in [\mathbb{n}]} \right\}_{\mathsf{j} \in [\mathsf{n}]}$

Output:

- $\forall \mathbb{i}, \ell \in [\mathbb{n}], \mathsf{j} \in [\mathsf{n}]$, check if $\mathsf{Verify}\left(x[\mathsf{j}, \mathbb{i}], \mathsf{tag}^{\ell}_{\mathsf{j} \to \mathbb{i}}, \mathsf{k}^{\ell}_{\mathsf{j} \to \mathbb{i}} \right) = 1$
  If all checks verify, set $x_{\mathsf{j}} := \bigoplus_{\mathbb{i}=1}^{\mathbb{n}} x[\mathsf{j}, \mathbb{i}]$, output $:= \mathcal{F}\left(\{x_{\mathbb{i}}\}_{\mathbb{i} \in [\mathbb{n}]}, \{x_{\mathsf{j}}\}_{\mathsf{j} \in [\mathsf{n}]}\right)$
- Else, if any of the checks failed, set output to be $\perp$.

Return output.

Fig. 1. The augmented function $\mathcal{F}_{\mathsf{aug}}$

$\mathcal{F}_{\mathsf{aug}}$ takes inputs from n parties, and parses each input as: (1)its own input; (2) input shares (from parties not involved in the computation of $\mathcal{F}'$); (3) MAC tags for each share; (4) MAC keys to verify tags.[10]
Upon aggregation the functionality checks if *all* the MAC tags verify. If the verification succeeds, input shares are used to reconstruct inputs of the parties not involved in the computation. Output the result on evaluating $\mathcal{F}$ on the inputs (both parties' own and reconstructed).
3. A Garbled Circuit scheme $\mathsf{GC} = \{\mathsf{Gen}, \mathsf{Garb}, \mathsf{Eval}\}$ based on one-way functions.
4. A two-round maliciously secure honest majority protocol [4] Π_{help} computing function $\mathcal{F}_{\mathsf{help}}$, which helps the client select labels, of a garbled circuit, corresponding to its input share (Fig. 2).

[10] The MAC keys correspond to tags held by other parites.

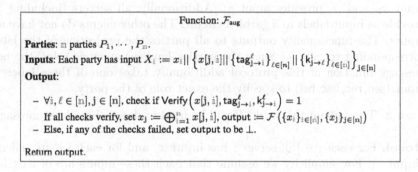

Function: $\mathcal{F}_{\mathsf{help}}$

Parties: Clients $\mathcal{C} = \{C_1, \cdots, C_n\}$ and servers $\mathcal{S} = \{S_1, \cdots, S_n\}$
Inputs:

- Client C_i (called *sender*) has input x_i.
- Server S_j (called *receiver*) has input γ_j and $\{y^j_{w,0}, y^j_{w,1}\}_{w\in[|x_i|]}$
- Each server $S_k \in \mathcal{S} \setminus \{S_j\}$ (called *label receiver*) has input $\{y^k_{w,0}, y^k_{w,1}\}_{w\in[|x_i|]}$.
- Each client $C_k \in \mathcal{C} \setminus \{C_i\}$, (called *helper*) has no input.

Output: $\forall S_k \in \mathcal{S}$, set $\mathsf{out}^k_{\mathsf{help}} = \mathsf{Projection}(x_i[w] \oplus \gamma_j[w], \{y^k_{w,0}, y^k_{w,1}\}_{w\in[|x_i|]})$.
Output $\mathsf{out}_{\mathsf{help}} := \{\mathsf{out}^k_{\mathsf{help}}\}_{k\in[n]}$ to all parties.

Fig. 2. The function $\mathcal{F}_{\mathsf{help}}$

$\mathcal{F}_{\mathsf{help}}$ separates out its participants into two sets, clients and servers. In addition, it designates two special parties: client C_i, and server S_j. C_i provides input x_i, and S_j provides input γ_j. Additionally, all servers (including S_j) provide as input labels to a garbled circuit. The other clients do not have any inputs. The functionality outputs to all parties the projection of the labels corresponding to $x_i \oplus \gamma_j$. Since the parties have asymmetric roles, the next message function of this protocol additionally takes one of these labels as input ($\mathsf{sen}, \mathsf{rec}, \mathsf{lrec}, \mathsf{hel}$) to specify the exact role of the party.

Remark 2. Throughout this work, B will be used to denote broadcast messages.

Protocol. For each $i \in [n]$, server i has input x_i and for each $\mathbf{i} \in [\mathbf{n}]$, client $\mathbf{i}$ has input $x_{\mathbf{i}}$. For simplicity we assume that each these inputs are of length 1. Our protocol easily extends to the setting with longer inputs. We assume that every party samples a sufficiently long random string at the start of the protocol, which is used appropriately throughout the protocol. Therefore we remove the randomness from protocol description and assume that it is implicit in all the algorithms used in the protocol.

Round 1. Each client $C_{\mathbf{i}}$ for $\mathbf{i} \in [\mathbf{n}]$ computes the following:

1. Computes n additive shares of $x_{\mathbf{i}}$: $\bigoplus_{j=1}^{n} x[\mathbf{i}, j] = x_{\mathbf{i}}$
2. Authentication tags for each share: $\forall j, \ell \in [n]$, sample $\mathsf{k}^{\ell}_{\mathbf{i}\to j} \leftarrow_\$ \{0,1\}^\lambda$ and compute $\mathsf{tag}^{\ell}_{\mathbf{i}\to j} := \mathsf{MAC}(\mathsf{k}^{\ell}_{\mathbf{i}\to j}, x[\mathbf{i}, j])$.
3. Aggregate inputs: $\forall j \in [n]$, $\mathsf{I}_{\mathsf{help}}[\mathbf{i}, j] := x[\mathbf{i}, j] \circ \{\mathsf{tag}^{\ell}_{\mathbf{i}\to j}\}_{\ell\in[n]} \circ \left\{\mathsf{k}^{j}_{\mathbf{i}\to\ell}\right\}_{\ell\in[n]}$
4. First round of Π_{help}:
   1. $\forall j \in [n]$: $(\mathbf{i}, j)$-th instance as *sender*, $\mathsf{M}^{1,(\mathbf{i},j)}_{\mathsf{help}}[\mathbf{i}, *] \leftarrow \Pi^1_{\mathsf{help}}(\mathbf{i}, \mathsf{sen}, \mathsf{I}_{\mathsf{help}}[\mathbf{i}, j])$
   2. $\forall \mathbf{j} \in [\mathbf{n}] \setminus \{\mathbf{i}\}, k \in [n]$: $(\mathbf{j}, k)$-th instance as *helper*, $\mathsf{M}^{1,(\mathbf{j},k)}_{\mathsf{help}}[\mathbf{i}, *] \leftarrow \Pi^1_{\mathsf{help}}(\mathbf{i}, \mathsf{hel}, \perp)$
5. $\forall j \in [n]$, send $\mathsf{M}^{1,(\bullet,\diamond)}_{\mathsf{help}}[\mathbf{i}, j]$ to server S_j.
6. $\forall \mathbf{j} \in [\mathbf{n}]$, send $\mathsf{M}^{1,(\bullet,\diamond)}_{\mathsf{help}}[\mathbf{i}, \mathbf{j}]$ to client $C_{\mathbf{j}}$.

Each server $S_{\mathbb{i}}$ for $\mathbb{i} \in [\mathbb{n}]$ computes the following:

1. Sets $\mathtt{I}_{\mathsf{aug}}[\mathbb{i}] := x_{\mathbb{i}} \circ \mathtt{I}_{\mathsf{help}}[\bullet, \mathbb{i}]$, where $\mathtt{I}_{\mathsf{help}}[\bullet, \mathbb{i}] = \bot$ of appropriate length. //This indicates the missing inputs that are contributed by the clients.
2. Computes first round messages of Π with random mask $\gamma_{\mathbb{i}} \leftarrow_{\$} \{0,1\}^{|\mathtt{I}_{\mathsf{aug}}[\mathbb{i}]|}$: $((\mathtt{I}_{\mathsf{aug}}[\mathbb{i}] \oplus \gamma_{\mathbb{i}}), \mathtt{M}^1_{\mathsf{aug}}[\mathbb{i}, \diamond], \mathtt{M}^1_{\mathsf{aug}}[\mathbb{i}]) \leftarrow \Pi^1_{\mathsf{aug}}(\mathbb{i}, \mathtt{I}_{\mathsf{aug}}[\mathbb{i}], \gamma_{\mathbb{i}})$
3. Samples wire labels for a garbled circuit: $\overline{\mathsf{lab}}_{\mathbb{i}}[\bullet, \diamond] \leftarrow \mathsf{Gen}(1^\lambda)$.
4. First round of Π_{help}:
   (a) $\forall \mathbf{j} \in [\mathbf{n}]$: $(\mathbf{j}, \mathbb{i})$-th instance as *receiver*, set $\mathtt{I}^{(\mathbf{j},\mathbb{i})}_{\mathsf{help}}[\mathbb{i}] = \gamma_{\mathbb{i}|\mathbf{j}} \circ \overline{\mathsf{lab}}_{\mathbb{i}}[\mathbf{j}, \mathbb{i}]$ and computes $\mathtt{M}^{1,(\mathbf{j},\mathbb{i})}_{\mathsf{help}}[\mathbb{i}, *] \leftarrow \Pi^1_{\mathsf{help}}\left(\mathbb{i}, \mathsf{rec}, \mathtt{I}^{(\mathbf{j},\mathbb{i})}_{\mathsf{help}}[\mathbb{i}]\right)$
   //$\gamma_{\mathbb{i}|\mathbf{j}}$ denotes the part of $\gamma_{\mathbb{i}}$ that is used to mask input $\mathtt{I}_{\mathsf{aug}}[\mathbb{i}, \mathbf{j}]$.
   (b) $\forall \mathbb{k} \in [\mathbb{n}] \backslash \{\mathbb{i}\}, \mathbf{j} \in [\mathbf{n}]$: $(\mathbf{j}, \mathbb{k})^{th}$ instance as *label receiver*, set $\mathtt{I}^{(\mathbf{j},\mathbb{k})}_{\mathsf{help}}[\mathbb{i}] = \overline{\mathsf{lab}}_{\mathbb{i}}[\mathbf{j}, \mathbb{k}]$ and computes $\mathtt{M}^{1,(\mathbf{j},\mathbb{k})}_{\mathsf{help}}[\mathbb{i}, *] \leftarrow \Pi^1_{\mathsf{help}}\left(\mathbb{i}, \mathsf{lrec}, \mathtt{I}^{(\mathbf{j},\mathbb{k})}_{\mathsf{help}}[\mathbb{i}]\right)$
5. $\forall \mathbb{j} \in [\mathbb{n}]$, send $\mathtt{M}^{1,(\bullet,\diamond)}_{\mathsf{help}}[\mathbb{i}, \mathbb{j}], \mathtt{M}^1_{\mathsf{aug}}[\mathbb{i}, \mathbb{j}]$ to server $S_{\mathbb{j}}$
6. $\forall \mathbf{j} \in [\mathbf{n}]$, send $\mathtt{M}^{1,(\bullet,\diamond)}_{\mathsf{help}}[\mathbb{i}, \mathbf{j}]$ to client $C_{\mathbf{j}}$.
7. Broadcast $\mathtt{M}^1[\mathbb{i}] := (\mathtt{M}^1_{\mathsf{aug}}[\mathbb{i}], (\mathtt{I}_{\mathsf{aug}}[\mathbb{i}] \oplus \gamma_{\mathbb{i}}))$

Round 2.

- Each client $C_{\mathbf{i}}$ for $\mathbf{i} \in [\mathbf{n}]$ computes and broadcasts second round messages of Π_{help}: $\forall \mathbb{k} \in [\mathbb{n}], \mathbf{j} \in [\mathbf{n}]$, $(\mathbf{j}, \mathbb{k})$-th instance: $\mathtt{M}^{2,(\mathbf{j},\mathbb{k})}_{\mathsf{help}}[\mathbf{i}] \leftarrow \Pi^2_{\mathsf{help}}\left(\mathbf{i}, \mathtt{M}^{1,(\mathbf{j},\mathbb{k})}_{\mathsf{help}}[*, \mathbf{i}]\right)$
- Each server $S_{\mathbb{i}}$ for $\mathbb{i} \in [\mathbb{n}]$:
  1. Second round of Π_{help}: $\forall \mathbb{k} \in [\mathbb{n}], \mathbf{j} \in [\mathbf{n}]$ $(\mathbf{j}, \mathbb{k})$-th instance: computes $\mathtt{M}^{2,(\mathbf{j},\mathbb{k})}_{\mathsf{help}}[\mathbb{i}] \leftarrow \Pi^2_{\mathsf{help}}\left(\mathbb{i}, \mathtt{M}^{1,(\mathbf{j},\mathbb{k})}_{\mathsf{help}}[*, \mathbb{i}]\right)$
  2. Garbled circuit: sets $\mathsf{ckt}_{\mathbb{i}} := \mathsf{P}\left[\mathbb{i}, \mathtt{M}^1_{\mathsf{aug}}[\diamond], \mathtt{M}^1_{\mathsf{aug}}[\diamond, \mathbb{i}], \{(\mathtt{I}_{\mathsf{aug}}[\mathbb{j}] \oplus \gamma_{\mathbb{j}})\}_{\mathbb{j} \in [\mathbb{n}]}\right]$ and computes $\tilde{\mathsf{P}}_{\mathbb{i}} \leftarrow \mathsf{Garb}\left(\mathsf{P}_{\mathbb{i}}, \overline{\mathsf{lab}}_{\mathbb{i}}[\bullet, \diamond]\right)$, where program P is as defined in figure 3.
  3. Broadcast $\left(\mathtt{M}^{2,(\bullet,\diamond)}_{\mathsf{help}}[\mathbb{i}], \tilde{\mathsf{P}}_{\mathbb{i}}\right)$

Output Computation. Each every client and server computes the following:

1. Output of Π_{help}: $\forall \mathbf{j} \in [\mathbf{n}], \mathbb{k} \in [\mathbb{n}]$ $\widetilde{\mathsf{lab}}_{\mathbb{i}}[\mathbf{j}, \mathbb{k}] := \Pi^3_{\mathsf{help}}(\mathtt{M}_{\mathsf{help},(\mathbf{j},\mathbb{k})}[*])$
2. Evaluate garbled circuits: $\forall \mathbb{i} \in [\mathbb{n}]$, $\mathtt{M}^2_{\mathsf{aug}}[\mathbb{i}] := \mathsf{Eval}(\tilde{\mathsf{P}}_{\mathbb{i}}, \widetilde{\mathsf{lab}}_{\mathbb{i}}[\diamond, \bullet])$
3. Output of Π, $y := \Pi^3_{\mathsf{aug}}(\mathtt{M}^2_{\mathsf{aug}}[\diamond])$
4. Output y.

Program: P

Input: $\{\mathtt{I}_{\mathsf{help}}[\mathbf{k}, \mathbb{j}] \oplus \gamma_{\mathbb{j}|\mathbf{k}}\}_{\mathbf{k} \in [\mathbf{n}], \mathbb{j} \in [\mathbb{n}]}$
Hardcoded: $\mathbb{i}, \mathtt{M}^1_{\mathsf{aug}}[\diamond], \mathtt{M}^1_{\mathsf{aug}}[\diamond, \mathbb{i}], \{(\mathtt{I}_{\mathsf{aug}}[\mathbb{j}] \oplus \gamma_{\mathbb{j}})\}_{\mathbb{j} \in [\mathbb{n}]}$
Function:

- For each $\mathbb{j} \in [\mathbb{n}]$, update $\mathtt{I}_{\mathsf{aug}}[\mathbb{j}] \oplus \gamma_{\mathbb{j}}$ with values $\{\mathtt{I}_{\mathsf{help}}[\mathbf{k}, \mathbb{j}] \oplus \gamma_{\mathbb{j}|\mathbf{k}}\}_{\mathbf{k} \in [\mathbf{n}]}$.
- Compute and output the second round messages using these updated values of the first round.

$$\mathtt{M}^2_{\mathsf{aug}}[\mathbb{i}] \leftarrow \Pi^2_{\mathsf{aug}}\left(\mathbb{i}, \mathtt{M}^1_{\mathsf{aug}}[\diamond], \mathtt{M}^1_{\mathsf{aug}}[\diamond, \mathbb{i}], \{(\mathtt{I}_{\mathsf{aug}}[\mathbb{j}] \oplus \gamma_{\mathbb{j}})\}_{\mathbb{j} \in [\mathbb{n}]}\right)$$

Fig. 3. Program P

The security proof of the protocol can be found in the full version.

Semi Honest Protocol. We note that for the semi-honest variant of the above protocol, the MAC checks are no longer needed. Therefore, $\mathcal{F}_{\mathsf{help}}$ can be simplified. The rest of the protocol remains the same, except that we can instantiate the underlying protocols used in this protocol with their semi-honest variants.

Complexity. Note that there are $\mathbf{n} \cdot \mathbb{n}$ instances of Π_{help}. Given that Π_{help} implements a quadratic functionality, the resulting circuit computed by each instance has size $O(\lambda^2 \cdot \mathbb{n}^2)$. Also, each instance is run by all n parties. Importantly, the circuit size is independent of s, size of circuit representing the underlying protocol. There is also a single instance of Π_{aug} computing a circuit of size s with $\mathbb{n}$ parties. From the described properties of the underlying protocols, this gives us a protocol with the desired complexity. The details of the exact calculations are presented in the full version.

3 Efficiency Preserving Compiler in the Plain Model

In this section we go from the compiler in the client-server model in Sect. 2 to present our main result, namely an efficient two-round compiler in the plain model. Formally we prove the following theorem.

Theorem 3. *Let n be the number of parties and λ be the security parameter, such that n is polynomially related to λ and let k be set to $\log^2(n)$.*

1. *Assuming one-way functions, there is a round compression compiler that transforms a semi-honest MPC protocol π for any n-party functionality $\mathcal{F}$ into a two-round semi-honest protocol Π' for $\mathcal{F}$ with the following properties:*
   (a) *If π tolerates corruption threshold ε, then Π' tolerates ε', for arbitrary constants $\varepsilon' < \varepsilon < \frac{1}{2}$.*
   (b) *If the computational cost of π is $W = W(n, s)$, where s is the circuit size representation of $\mathcal{F}$, then the amortized per-party computational cost and total communication cost of Π' is $O\left((W(k, s + kn) + n^4\lambda^2) \cdot \lambda \cdot k^3\right)$. We will denote this by $\widetilde{O}(W(k, s + kn)k^{\tau-2} + n^4)$, where the $\widetilde{O}$ notation suppresses polynomial factors in k and λ. For most known protocols, the additive term in the circuit size (kn) will be suppressed by the additive term of n^4 simplifying the expression to $\widetilde{O}(W(k, s) + n^4)$.*
2. *Assuming one-way functions, there is a round compression compiler that transforms a maliciously secure MPC protocol π for any n-party functionality $\mathcal{F}$ into a three-round maliciously secure protocol Π' for $\mathcal{F}$ that satisfies properties 1(a) and amortized per-party computational cost $\widetilde{O}(W(k, s) + n^{\tau+4})$.*
3. *Assuming NIWIs, there is a round compression compiler that transforms a maliciously secure MPC protocol π for any n-party functionality $\mathcal{F}$ into a two-round maliciously secure protocol Π' in the reusable correlated randomness setup model for $\mathcal{F}$ that satisfies properties 1(a) and amortized per-party computational cost $\widetilde{O}(W(k, s) + n^{\tau+4})$.*

Overview. We now present an overview of the compiler that builds on the protocol output by the compiler from Sect. 2 (Theorem 2) in the client-server model to get a compiler in the plain model. Along the way, we shall discuss the relevant properties used from Theorem 2. We shall do this in two steps.

1. **Phase One:** Compile the protocol in Sect. 2 to a protocol in the $\mathcal{F}_{\mathsf{election}}$-hybrid model. In this model, at the start of the protocol, each party receives a bit from $\mathcal{F}_{\mathsf{election}}$ indicating whether it is in the committee. The functionality $\mathcal{F}_{\mathsf{election}}$ is described in Fig. 4.
2. **Phase Two:** Instantiate $\mathcal{F}_{\mathsf{election}}$ based on the desired security properties of the final protocol.

Function: $\mathcal{F}_{\mathsf{election}}$

Parameter: k
Parties: $\mathcal{P} := \{P_1, \ldots, P_n\}$
Inputs: Parties do not have inputs.
Select, in expectation, a random k-sized subset of the parties to be elected to the committee.

Output: For each P_i: if P_i was selected, send 1. Else, send 0.

Fig. 4. The randomized functionality that selects a k-sized committee in expectation

The main challenge in going from the client model to the plain model is that parties are no longer aware of the roles of the other parties, i.e. which parties are clients and which are servers. To get around this issue, we will leverage the fact that $\mathcal{F}_{\mathsf{election}}$ guarantees that every party knows whether it is a server, but doesn't know its index in the server set.

Since the party doesn't know its role (index) in the server (resp. client) set, it computes messages assuming all m (resp. **n**) roles. At the end of the first round, when all parties are aware of the elected committee based on the messages sent, the irrelevant messages are discarded. But a problem with this approach is that the protocol involves private messages, which require knowledge of the recipient's role. Based on the properties listed in Theorem 2 from Sect. 2, we can divide the private messages into two categories which are handled differently:

Private Message Independent of the Role of the Receiving Party. This is the case for all private messages sent by the clients, and some of the private messages sent by the servers. This is an easy setting to handle since these messages can be sent privately without the need to know the recipient's role.

Private Message Intended for the Parties in the Server Set. This is of concern only to parties that are elected into the committee. Since a party is not aware of other elected parties, these messages cannot be sent privately. Instead, the party masks these messages, and broadcasts the masked messages.

But we want the designated party to receive the mask, and unmask the message to proceed with the computation. We seem to be back where we started, but we use a solution similar to Sect. 2, where the second round computation of the server parties are delegated to a garbled circuit. Now, the party generating the mask initiates a helper protocol that will enable the appropriate party's garbled circuit to receive the mask, thereby allowing to proceed with the computation. To ensure there is no complexity blow-up by involving all parties, we make sure that the size of the computation involving all parties is independent of the underlying circuit. This is easily done by utilizing a pseudo-random generator (PRG) to generate the masks.

The relevance of the other properties listed in Theorem 2 is in the efficiency of the resultant protocol.

3.1 Phase One: $\mathcal{F}_{\mathsf{election}}$-hybrid Model

In this section, we shall perform the first step of our compilation. Namely, we shall compile the protocol in Sect. 2 from the client-server model to a protocol in the $\mathcal{F}_{\mathsf{election}}$-hybrid model. To differentiate from the client-server models, we shall refer to parties "elected" to be in the server set to be a part of a committee.

Building Blocks. The main primitives required in this construction are the following:

1. The two-round protocol $\Pi_{f_{\mathsf{c\text{-}s}}}$ from Sect. 2 in the client-server model.
   For this section, we shall use the following notation to refer to the first round messages of $\Pi_{f_{\mathsf{c\text{-}s}}}$. There are special first round messages[11] that are privately sent among the servers, these will be denoted by an additional $\mathbb{S}$: $\mathtt{M}^1_{f_{\mathsf{c\text{-}s}}}[\mathbb{i}, \mathbb{j}, \mathbb{S}]$ indicates the special message sent from server indexed by $\mathbb{i}$ to the server indexed by $\mathbb{j}$. Other messages are denoted as previous sections with $\mathtt{M}^1_{f_{\mathsf{c\text{-}s}}}[i, j]$ indicating a message from party i to j (with appropriate font to differentiate between clients and severs). Broadcast messages correspondingly defined. Additionally, as before, we group messages corresponding clients ($\bullet$), servers ($\diamond$) or all parties ($*$).
2. A Garbled Circuit scheme $\mathsf{GC} = \{\mathsf{Gen}, \mathsf{Garb}, \mathsf{Eval}\}$.
3. A two-round maliciously secure honest majority protocol Π_{mOT} computing function $\mathcal{F}_{\mathsf{mOT}}$ described in Fig. 5.
   $\mathcal{F}_{\mathsf{mOT}}$ is similar to a multi-party variant of oblivious transfer. There are two designated parties, sender (sen) and receiver (rec) with inputs b and (x_0, x_1) respectively, while all other parties are referred to as helper (hel) parties. $\mathcal{F}_{\mathsf{mOT}}$ outputs x_b to all the parties.
   Our protocol will use multiple instance of the Π_{mOT} protocol, which is indexed by indices corresponding to (sender, receiver).
4. A pseudo-random generator $\mathsf{PRG} : \{0,1\}^\lambda \to \{0,1\}^{\mathsf{poly}(\lambda)}$.

[11] This will correspond to the messages whose size depend on the size of the circuit being computed.

Function: $\mathcal{F}_{\mathsf{mOT}}$

Parties: $\mathcal{P} := \{P_1, \ldots, P_n\}$
Inputs:

- Party P_i (also called the receiver) has input $\{x_{i,0}, x_{i,1}\}_{i\in[q]}$
- Party P_j (also called the sender) has input $b \in \{0,1\}^q$.
- For each $P_k \in \mathcal{P} \setminus \{P_i, P_j\}$ (also called the helper parties) have no inputs.

Output: Every party receives $\{x_{i,b[i]}\}_{i\in[q]}$.

Fig. 5. The function $\mathcal{F}_{\mathsf{mOT}}$ where P_i acts as the sender and P_j acts as receiver

As explained earlier, prior to sending the first round messages, a party is only aware if it is in the committee, but not its role (index) in the committee (or outside). In our protocol, depending on whether party P_i is in the committee (resp. outside), P_i computes the first round message for *every* possible role in the committee (resp. outside). The index of the sender in the protocol message is thus denoted by $(i, \mathbb{j})$ (resp. $(i, \mathbf{j})$) to indicate P_i's message for role $\mathbb{j}$ in the committee (resp. role $\mathbf{j}$ outside).

Although no party is aware of the roles of the other parties at the start of the first round of the protocol, there is an implicit mapping from the set of all parties to the corresponding role in the committee (or outside). $\mathbb{Q}$ (resp. $\mathbf{Q}$) denotes this mapping. At the end of the first round, all parties will be able to locally compute both the mappings and discard the relevant messages. We shall also abuse notation slightly and use $\mathbb{Q}$ and $\mathbf{Q}$ to denote the corresponding sets.

Protocol. Let $\mathcal{P} = \{P_1, \cdots, P_n\}$ be the set of parties in the protocol and let the corresponding inputs be $x_1, \cdots, x_n$. We now give a formal description of the protocol in the $\mathcal{F}_{\mathsf{election}}$-hybrid model. We assume parties sample appropriate random strings in the protocol description.

Initialization-Election. At the start of the protocol, each party P_i receives a bit from $\mathcal{F}_{\mathsf{election}}$. If the received bit is 1, then P_i is a committee member, else it is a non-committee member.

Round 1. Each non-committee member P_i for $i \in \mathbf{Q}$ computes the following:

1. For $\mathbf{i} \in [\mathbf{n}]$ compute the first round of the following assuming role $\mathbf{i}$:
   - Client message in $\Pi_{f_{\mathsf{c\text{-}s}}}$: $\mathtt{M}^1_{f_{\mathsf{c\text{-}s}}}[(i,\mathbf{i}),*] \leftarrow \Pi^1_{f_{\mathsf{c\text{-}s}}}(\mathbf{i}, x_i)$
   - $\forall \mathbb{j}, \mathbb{k} \in [\mathbb{n}]$, $(\mathbb{j}, \mathbb{k})$-th instance of Π_{mOT} as helper: $\mathtt{M}^{1,(\mathbb{j},\mathbb{k})}_{\mathsf{mOT}}[(i,\mathbf{i}),*] \leftarrow \Pi^1_{\mathsf{mOT}}(\mathsf{hel}, \perp)$
2. For every j, send $\left(i,\ \mathtt{M}^1_{f_{\mathsf{c\text{-}s}}}[(i,\bullet),j],\ \mathtt{M}^{1,(\diamond,\diamond)}_{\mathsf{mOT}}[(i,\bullet),j]\right)$ to P_j privately.
3. Broadcast $\mathtt{M}^1_{f_{\mathsf{c\text{-}s}}}[(i,\bullet),B]$.

Each committee members P_i for $i \in \mathbb{Q}$ computes the following:

1. For $\mathbb{i} \in [\mathbb{n}]$ compute the first round of the following assuming role $\mathbb{i}$:

(a) First round server messages in $\Pi_{f\text{c-s}}$: $\mathtt{M}^1_{f\text{c-s}}[(i,\mathbb{i}),*], \mathtt{M}^1_{f\text{c-s}}[(i,\mathbb{i}),\diamond,\mathbb{S}] \leftarrow \Pi^1_{f\text{c-s}}(\mathbb{i}, x_i)$
(b) Sample PRG seeds $s[(i,\mathbb{i}),\diamond]$
(c) Wire labels for a garbled circuit: $\overline{\mathsf{lab}}_{(i,\mathbb{i})}[\diamond,(i,\mathbb{i})] \leftarrow \mathsf{Gen}(1^\lambda)$
(d) $\forall \mathbb{j} \in [\mathbb{n}]$: $\mathsf{ct}[(i,\mathbb{i}),\mathbb{j}] := \mathtt{M}^1_{f\text{c-s}}[(i,\mathbb{i}),\mathbb{j},\mathbb{S}] \oplus \mathsf{PRG}(s[(i,\mathbb{i}),\mathbb{j}])$
(e) First round of Π_{mOT}, for every $\mathbb{j} \in [\mathbb{n}]$,
   i. $(\mathbb{i},\mathbb{j})$-th instance as sender: $\mathtt{M}^{1,(\mathbb{i},\mathbb{j})}_{\mathsf{mOT}}[(i,\mathbb{i}),*] \leftarrow \Pi^1_{\mathsf{mOT}}(\mathsf{sen}, s[(i,\mathbb{i}),\mathbb{j}])$.
   ii. $(\mathbb{j},\mathbb{i})$-th instance as receiver: $\mathtt{M}^{1,(\mathbb{j},\mathbb{i})}_{\mathsf{mOT}}[(i,\mathbb{i}),*] \leftarrow \Pi^1_{\mathsf{mOT}}(\mathsf{rec}, \overline{\mathsf{lab}}_{(i,\mathbb{i})}[\mathbb{j},(i,\mathbb{i})])$.
   iii. for every $\mathbb{k} \in [\mathbb{n}]$, $(\mathbb{j},\mathbb{k})$-th instance as helper: $\mathtt{M}^{1,(\mathbb{j},\mathbb{k})}_{\mathsf{mOT}}[(i,\mathbb{i}),*] \leftarrow \Pi^1_{\mathsf{mOT}}(\mathsf{hel},\perp)$.

2. For every $j \in [n]$, send $\left(i,\ \mathtt{M}^1_{f\text{c-s}}[(i,\diamond),j],\ \mathtt{M}^{1,(\diamond,\diamond)}_{\mathsf{mOT}}[(i,\diamond),j]\right)$ to P_j.
3. Broadcast $\mathsf{msg}^1_i := \left(i,\ \mathtt{M}^1_{f\text{c-s}}[(i,\diamond),B],\ \mathsf{ct}[(i,\diamond),\diamond]\right)$

At the end of Round 1. Each party locally computes the mappings $\mathbb{Q}$ and $\mathbf{Q}$, discards the extra messages and updates sender index from $(i,\mathbb{Q}(i))$ to $\mathbb{i}(=\mathbb{Q}(i))$ for P_i in the committee and $(i,\mathbf{Q}(i))$ to $\mathbf{i}(=\mathbf{Q}(i))$ for P_i not in the committee.

Round 2. Each committee member P_i for $i \in \mathbb{Q}$ sets $\mathbb{i} := \mathbb{Q}(i)$ and computes:

1. A garbled circuit as $\overline{\mathsf{P}}_{\mathbb{i}} \leftarrow \mathsf{Garb}(\mathsf{P}_{\mathbb{i}}, \overline{\mathsf{lab}}_{\mathbb{i}}[\diamond,\mathbb{i}])$ where $\mathsf{P}_{\mathbb{i}}$ is computed as $\mathsf{P}_{\mathbb{i}} := \mathsf{P}_{\mathsf{plain}}[x_{\mathbb{i}}, \mathsf{ct}[\diamond,\mathbb{i}], \mathtt{M}^1_{f\text{c-s}}[*,B], \mathtt{M}^1_{f\text{c-s}}[*,\mathbb{i}]]$ where $\mathsf{P}_{\mathsf{plain}}$ defined in Figure 6.
2. $\forall \mathbb{j},\mathbb{k} \in [\mathbb{n}]$, $(\mathbb{j},\mathbb{k})$-th instance of Π_{mOT}: $\mathtt{M}^{2,(\mathbb{j},\mathbb{k})}_{\mathsf{mOT}}[\mathbb{i},B] \leftarrow \Pi^2_{\mathsf{mOT}}(\mathtt{M}^{1,(\mathbb{j},\mathbb{k})}_{\mathsf{mOT}}[*,\mathbb{i}])$.
3. Broadcast $\overline{\mathsf{P}}_{\mathbb{i}}, \mathtt{M}^{2,(\diamond,\diamond)}_{\mathsf{mOT}}[\mathbb{i},B]$

Each non-committee member P_i for $i \in \mathbf{Q}$ sets $\mathbf{i} := \mathbf{Q}(i)$ and computes:

1. Client messages in $\Pi_{f\text{c-s}}$: $\mathtt{M}^2_{f\text{c-s}}[\mathbf{i},B] \leftarrow \Pi^2_{f\text{c-s}}(\mathtt{M}^1_{f\text{c-s}}[*,B], \mathtt{M}^1_{f\text{c-s}}[*,\mathbf{i}])$
2. $\forall \mathbb{j},\mathbb{k} \in [\mathbb{n}]$, $(\mathbb{j},\mathbb{k})$-th instance of Π_{mOT}: $\mathtt{M}^{2,(\mathbb{j},\mathbb{k})}_{\mathsf{mOT}}[\mathbf{i},B] \leftarrow \Pi^2_{\mathsf{mOT}}(\mathtt{M}^{1,(\mathbb{j},\mathbb{k})}_{\mathsf{mOT}}[*,\mathbf{i}])$.
3. Broadcast $\mathtt{M}^2_{f\text{c-s}}[\mathbf{i},B], \mathtt{M}^{2,(\diamond,\diamond)}_{\mathsf{mOT}}[\mathbf{i},B]$.

Output Computation. Each party does the following:

1. $\forall \mathbb{j},\mathbb{k} \in [\mathbb{n}]$ output of Π_{mOT}: $\widetilde{\mathsf{lab}}_{\mathbb{k}}[\mathbb{j},\mathbb{k}] \leftarrow \Pi^{\mathsf{out}}_{\mathsf{mOT}}(\mathtt{M}^{2,(\mathbb{j},\mathbb{k})}_{\mathsf{mOT}}[*,B])$.
2. $\forall \mathbb{i} \in [\mathbb{n}]$, evaluate the garbled circuits: $\mathtt{M}^2_{f\text{c-s}}[\mathbb{i},B] \leftarrow \mathsf{Eval}(\overline{\mathsf{P}}_{\mathbb{i}}, \widetilde{\mathsf{lab}}_{\mathbb{k}}[\diamond,\mathbb{k}])$
3. Output $y \leftarrow \Pi^{\mathsf{out}}_{f\text{c-s}}(\mathtt{M}^2_{f\text{c-s}}[*,B])$

Program: $\mathsf{P}_{\mathsf{plain}}$

Input: $s[\diamond,\mathbb{i}]$
Hardcoded: $x_{\mathbb{i}}, \mathsf{ct}[\diamond,\mathbb{i}], \mathtt{M}^1_{f\text{c-s}}[*,B], \mathtt{M}^1_{f\text{c-s}}[*,\mathbb{i}]$
Function:

- For each $\mathbb{j} \in [\mathbb{n}]$, $\mathtt{M}^1_{f\text{c-s}}[\mathbb{j},\mathbb{i},\mathbb{S}] := \mathsf{ct}[\mathbb{j},\mathbb{i}] \oplus \mathsf{PRG}(s[\mathbb{j},\mathbb{i}])$
- Compute server messages in $\Pi_{f\text{c-s}}$: $\mathtt{M}^2_{f\text{c-s}}[\mathbb{i},B] \leftarrow \Pi^2_{f\text{c-s}}(\mathtt{M}^1_{f\text{c-s}}[*,B], \mathtt{M}^1_{f\text{c-s}}[*,\mathbb{i}], \mathtt{M}^1_{f\text{c-s}}[*,\mathbb{i},\mathbb{S}])$
- Output $\mathtt{M}^2_{f\text{c-s}}[\mathbb{i},B]$

Fig. 6. Program $\mathsf{P}_{\mathsf{plain}}$ unmasks the first round messages sent via broadcast, and computes the second round messages of $\Pi_{f\text{c-s}}$.

The security proof of the protocol can be found in the full version of the paper.

Complexity. Note that there are $\mathbbm{m}^2$ instances of Π_{mOT}, where the sender has inputs of length $O(\lambda)$, while the receiver has inputs of length $O(\lambda^2)$. Given that Π_{mOT} implements a quadratic functionality, the resulting circuit computed by each instance has size $O(\lambda^2)$. Also, each instance is run by all n parties. Importantly, the circuit size is independent of s, size of circuit representing the underlying protocol. There is an additional overhead of parties not knowing their own role in the committee. Finally, there is a single instance of $\Pi_{f_{\mathsf{c\text{-}s}}}$ computed by all parties. The cost then follows from the properties of the underlying protocols and the details are presented in the full version.

3.2 Phase Two

We can now complete the description of our compiler by instantiating the randomized functionality $\mathcal{F}_{\mathsf{election}}$ used in the protocol described in the $\mathcal{F}_{\mathsf{election}}$-hybrid model. We consider three different settings, which will lead to corresponding results. The settings are (a) semi-honest; (b) malicious in the reusable correlated randomness model; (c) malicious in the plain model.

Semi-honest. For the semi-honest setting, the protocol idea is simple: every party tosses appropriately biased coins to determine if it is in the committee. The only thing left to do is to determine the right parameters so that we have a committee with poly-logarithmic size and honest majority. This is a non-interactive process, and the resultant protocol is given below. The committee size will be $(1-\delta)\cdot k$, where δ is any non-zero constant.

Round 1. Each party does the following:
- Toss a coin that outputs 1 with probability $p = \frac{k}{n}$. If output 1, it assumes it is a part of the committee and computes the messages
- If it is in the committee, pick an element $a_i \leftarrow_{\$} \mathbb{Z}_q$, from an exponentially sized field $\mathbb{Z}_q$. This is to pick the relative position within the committee and trim the committee if needed.
- All parties compute the client messages, and the parties that assumed they were in the committee additionally compute server messages. This is because the committee might be larger than the final size, and a party make not make it to the final committee.
- Only parties that assumed they were in the committee broadcast their a_i value.

Round 2. On receiving the first round messages, each party knows both (a) which parties are in the committee; and (b) the relative roles of each party in the committee. This follows from picking the committee to be the ordered set of first $(1-\delta)\cdot k$ parties based on their broadcast a_i. It then executed the rest of the protocol appropriately.

Since each party independently samples coins to determine if it is in the committee, the expected party size is k. If we set $k = \Omega(\log^2(n))$, from the

Chernoff bound, other than with negligible probability, the size of the committee is $> (1-\delta)\log^2(n)$, and thus will not end up with a smaller committee. By a similar argument, it is easy to see that other than with negligible probability, honest majority is maintained in the committee. This gives us a resultant *two round semi-honest protocol in the plain model.*

Lemma 2. *Assuming the that the fraction of adversarial parties are bounded by $\left(\frac{1}{2}-\epsilon\right)$ for some $\epsilon > 0$, our constructed protocol is a two round semi-honest protocol.*

Remark 3. While our protocol is proven in the malicious setting, we instantiate the underlying protocols with their corresponding semi-honest versions. The semi-honest versions also satisfy Lemma 1.

The security of the protocol follows from the composition theorem for semi-honest protocols [28].

Malicious in the Reusable Correlated Randomness Model. We consider the setting of the reusable correlated randomness model, where the trusted set up can select the public and private keys for a verifiable random function (VRF)[37]. We then follow the same strategy of selecting a committee as done in Algorand [27]. While they select committees by weight, we set the weights for each party to be identical (say 1).

Specifically, the trusted parties select public/private key pairs $(\mathsf{pk}_i, \mathsf{sk}_i)$ for each party i, and a random seed. Additionally, a threshold τ is picked based on the required size of the committee.

Round 1. Each party receives the public key for all parties, and a public/private key pair $(\mathsf{pk}_i, \mathsf{sk}_i)$ unique to it. It then evaluates the VRF to determine if it is in the committee. It then computes the first round messages of the Phase one protocol, and also broadcasts the messages indicating it is in the committee.

Round 2. Compute the second round messages of the Phase one protocol.

We allow the adversary to adaptively pick the parties it corrupts having seen only the public keys for all parties and the private keys for the parties it has corrupted thus far.

As stated in [27], we have the following two properties. Given a random seed, VRF outputs a pseudorandom value. Hence the parties are randomly picked into the committee. An adversary that does not know the secret key sk_i for party i cannot guess if i was chosen at all (more precisely, the adversary cannot guess any better than just by randomly guessing).

This lets us allow the adversary to adaptively corrupt parties based on the public keys, seed and the secret keys of the parties it has corrupted thus far. This would give us a *two round protocol, maliciously secure against an adaptive adversary in the presence of trusted set up.*

Lemma 3. *Assuming the that the fraction of adversarial parties are bounded by $\left(\frac{1}{2}-\epsilon\right)$ for some $\epsilon > 0$, our constructed protocol is a two round protocol in the trusted set up model secure against malicious adversaries.*

We note that the best known constructions for VRFs are based on non-interactive witness indistinguishable proofs (NIWIs) [8,30], which are in turn known from the assumption of bilinear maps [31].

Malicious in the Plain Model. In the malicious setting, we cannot let the parties locally sample coins. Instead, we run Feige's lightest bin protocol [21] to determine the committee. The protocol gives a method of selecting a committee of approximately k parties for a given parameter k. It is a single round protocol, where the parties broadcast their choice of a random bin in the set $\left[\frac{n}{k}\right]$. This adds an additional round to the start of the protocol.

Round 1. Every party broadcasts a random bin in the set $\left[\frac{n}{\log^2(n)}\right]$.

Round 2. Each party knows whether they are in the committee based on the received broadcast, by picking the $(1-\delta)\cdot k$ lightest bins. In fact at the end of this round, we get a stronger property that every party is aware of the role of every party in the protocol, i.e. whether a given party is in the committee.

Now each party can compute first round messages of the protocol from Phase one.

Round 3. Each party computes second round messages of the protocol from Phase one.

The following lemma from [21] is relevant to us.

Lemma 4 ([21]). *For $k = \log^2 n$, if the number of corrupted parties is βn, for any constant $\delta > 0$, other than with negligible probability in n, the size of the committee $\mathcal{C}$ will be elected such that:*

Bound on Size: $(1-\beta-\delta)\log^2 n \leq |\mathcal{C}| \leq \log^2 n$;

Honest Parties in Committee: *# honest parties in the committee is* $\geq ((1-\beta-\delta)\log^2 n)$.

In our setting, $\beta < \left(\frac{1}{2}-\epsilon\right)$, which guarantees an honest majority in the committee. This gives us a resultant *three round maliciously secure protocol in the plain model.*

Lemma 5. *Assuming the that the fraction of adversarial parties are bounded by $\left(\frac{1}{2}-\epsilon\right)$ for some $\epsilon > 0$, our constructed protocol is a three round protocol secure against malicious adversaries.*

The security of the protocol follows from the sequential composition theorem [28].

Remark 4. We note that both $\mathcal{F}_{\mathsf{help}}$ and $\mathcal{F}_{\mathsf{mOT}}$ resemble the multiparty homomorphic OT (M-OT) functionality described in [1]. These functionalities can be seen as special cases of the M-OT functionality, but we've described them separately for ease of notation.

4 Impossibility Result

In this section we prove our impossibility result showing that our committee based approaches are inherent to the results we achieve.

Theorem 4. *There exists an n-party function $\mathcal{F}$, such that there does not exist an n-party, r-round balanced scalable (possibly insecure) MPC protocol, where each party does asymptotically equal amount of work, computing a circuit C of size s, where r is some constant, and the protocol can be represented by a circuit of size $\tilde{O}(s)$ defined over the basis* {AND, OR, NOT}.

Proof. We make a novel use of the "MPC in the head" paradigm [35] to prove this theorem.

Let us assume for contradiction that for every n-party functionality $\mathcal{F}$, there exists an r-round scalable MPC protocol Π computing $\mathcal{F}$, where r is a constant and each party can be represented as a circuit over the basis {AND, OR, NOT} of size $\tilde{O}(s)/n$. Let $\Pi.\mathsf{NMF}i, j$ be the next-message function of party i (for each $i \in [n]$) in round j (for each $j \in [r]$). Since r is a constant, the size of the circuit implementing the next-message function of each party $i \in [n]$ in each round $j \in [r]$ is

$$|\Pi.\mathsf{NMF}_{i,j}| = \frac{\tilde{O}(s)}{rn} = \frac{\tilde{O}(s)}{n}$$

Hence, depth of each next message function $|\Pi.\mathsf{NMF}_{i,j}|_d = \tilde{O}(s)/n$.

Base Step. We now modify Π to Π_1 as follows: for each $i \in [n]$, $j \in [r]$, we execute MPC protocol Π (let us denote this execution by $\Pi_{1,i,j}$) to implement $\Pi.\mathsf{NMF}_{i,j}$. The size of the circuit implementing the next-message function of each party $i' \in [n]$ in each round $j' \in [r]$ of this sub-protocol $\Pi_{1,i,j}$ is

$$|\Pi_{1,i,j}.\mathsf{NMF}_{i',j'}| = \frac{\tilde{O}(|\Pi.\mathsf{NMF}_{i,j}|)}{n} = \frac{\tilde{O}(s)}{n^2}$$

Hence, depth of each next message function in each sub-protocol $|\Pi_{1,i,j}.\mathsf{NMF}_{i',j'}|_d = \tilde{O}(s)/n^2$.

The total number of rounds in the resulting protocol Π_1 is r^2 and in each round $j' \in [r^2]$, the next message function of each party $i' \in [n]$ is

$$\Pi_1.\mathsf{NMF}_{i',j'} = \Pi_{1,1,j}.\mathsf{NMF}_{i',j'}||\ldots||\Pi_{1,n,j}.\mathsf{NMF}_{i',j'}$$

where $j = j' \mod r$. Note that since this is a parallel composition of n circuits, each of depth $\tilde{O}(s)/n^2$, the depth of each next message function in the modified protocol $\Pi_1 = \tilde{O}(s)/n^2$.

Let p be a constant such that $\tilde{O}(s)/n^p$ is some constant c. Now for each $k \in \{2, \ldots, p-1\}$, we perform the following recursion step.

Recursion Step. We modify the r^k-round protocol Π_{k-1} to obtain Π_k as follows: for each $i \in [n]$, $j \in [r^k]$, we execute MPC protocol Π (let us denote this execution by $\Pi_{k,i,j}$) to implement $\Pi_{k-1}.\mathsf{NMF}_{i,j}$. Similar to before, the depth of the circuit implementing the next-message function of each party $i' \in [n]$ in each round $j' \in [r]$ of this sub-protocol $\Pi_{k,i,j}$ is

$$|\Pi_{k,i,j}.\mathsf{NMF}_{i',j'}|_d = \frac{\tilde{O}(|\Pi_{k-1}.\mathsf{NMF}_{i,j}|_d)}{n} = \frac{\tilde{O}(s)}{n^{k+1}}$$

The total number of rounds in the resulting protocol Π_1 is r^2 and in each round $j' \in [r^{k+1}]$, the next message function of each party $i' \in [n]$ is

$$\Pi_k.\mathsf{NMF}_{i',j'} = \Pi_{k,1,j}.\mathsf{NMF}_{i',j'}||\ldots||\Pi_{k,n,j}.\mathsf{NMF}_{i',j'}$$

where $j = j' \mod r$. Again since this is a parallel composition of n circuits, each of depth $\tilde{O}(s)/n^{k+1}$, the depth of each next message function in the resulting modified protocol $\Pi_1 = \tilde{O}(s)/n^{k+1}$.

Protocol Π_{p-1}. The depth of the next message function of each party in each round, in the final r^p-round protocol Π_{p-1} is

$$\frac{\tilde{O}(s)}{n^p} = c$$

Thus the final modified protocol Π_{p-1} can be viewed as a circuit of depth ($c\times$ No. of rounds) $= c \cdot r^p = O(1)$. Moreover, the size of this circuit is poly(s).

This means that every n-party functionality $\mathcal{F}$ representable by a polynomial-sized circuit, also admits a constant-depth polynomial-sized circuit over the basis $\{\text{AND}, \text{OR}, \text{NOT}\}$ and thus is in AC^0. However note that there are functions like parity and majority that are not in AC^0. Therefore, this is a clear contradiction.

Acknowledgments. Arka Rai Choudhuri, Aarushi Goel and Abhishek Jain are supported in part by DARPA/ARL Safeware Grant W911NF-15-C-0213, NSF CNS-1814919, NSF CAREER 1942789, Samsung Global Research Outreach award and Johns Hopkins University Catalyst award. Arka Rai Choudhuri is also supported by NSF Grants CNS-1908181, CNS-1414023, and the Office of Naval Research Grant N00014-19-1-2294. Aarushi Goel is also supported in part by NSF Grants CNS-1653110 and CNS-1801479 and the Office of Naval Research under contract N00014-19-1-2292.

References

1. Ananth, P., Choudhuri, A.R., Goel, A., Jain, A.: Round-optimal secure multiparty computation with honest majority. In: Shacham, H., Boldyreva, A. (eds.) CRYPTO 2018. LNCS, vol. 10992, pp. 395–424. Springer, Cham (2018). https://doi.org/10.1007/978-3-319-96881-0_14
2. Ananth, P., Choudhuri, A.R., Goel, A., Jain, A.: Two round information-theoretic MPC with malicious security. In: Ishai, Y., Rijmen, V. (eds.) EUROCRYPT 2019. LNCS, vol. 11477, pp. 532–561. Springer, Cham (2019). https://doi.org/10.1007/978-3-030-17656-3_19
3. Applebaum, B., Brakerski, Z., Tsabary, R.: Perfect secure computation in two rounds. In: Beimel, A., Dziembowski, S. (eds.) TCC 2018. LNCS, vol. 11239, pp. 152–174. Springer, Cham (2018). https://doi.org/10.1007/978-3-030-03807-6_6

4. Applebaum, B., Brakerski, Z., Tsabary, R.: Degree 2 is complete for the round-complexity of malicious MPC. In: Ishai, Y., Rijmen, V. (eds.) EUROCRYPT 2019. LNCS, vol. 11477, pp. 504–531. Springer, Cham (2019). https://doi.org/10.1007/978-3-030-17656-3_18
5. Beaver, D., Micali, S., Rogaway, P.: The round complexity of secure protocols (extended abstract). In: 22nd ACM STOC, pp. 503–513. ACM Press, May 1990. https://doi.org/10.1145/100216.100287
6. Ben-Or, M., Goldwasser, S., Wigderson, A.: Completeness theorems for non-cryptographic fault-tolerant distributed computation (extended abstract). In: 20th ACM STOC, pp. 1–10. ACM Press, May 1988. https://doi.org/10.1145/62212.62213
7. Benhamouda, F., Lin, H.: k-round multiparty computation from k-round oblivious transfer via Garbled interactive circuits. In: Nielsen, J.B., Rijmen, V. (eds.) EUROCRYPT 2018. LNCS, vol. 10821, pp. 500–532. Springer, Cham (2018). https://doi.org/10.1007/978-3-319-78375-8_17
8. Bitansky, N.: Verifiable random functions from non-interactive witness-indistinguishable proofs. In: Kalai, Y., Reyzin, L. (eds.) TCC 2017. Lecture Notes in Computer Science, vol. 10678, pp. 567–594. Springer, Cham (2017). https://doi.org/10.1007/978-3-319-70503-3_19
9. Boyle, E., Chung, K.-M., Pass, R.: Large-scale secure computation: multi-party computation for (Parallel) RAM programs. In: Gennaro, R., Robshaw, M. (eds.) CRYPTO 2015. Lecture Notes in Computer Science, vol. 9216, pp. 742–762. Springer, Heidelberg (2015). https://doi.org/10.1007/978-3-662-48000-7_36
10. Boyle, E., Goldwasser, S., Tessaro, S.: Communication locality in secure multi-party computation. In: Sahai, A. (ed.) TCC 2013. LNCS, vol. 7785, pp. 356–376. Springer, Heidelberg (2013). https://doi.org/10.1007/978-3-642-36594-2_21
11. Canetti, R., et al.: Fiat-Shamir: from practice to theory. In: STOC (2019)
12. Chaum, D., Crépeau, C., Damgård, I.: Multiparty unconditionally secure protocols (extended abstract). In: 20th ACM STOC, pp. 11–19. ACM Press, May 1988. https://doi.org/10.1145/62212.62214
13. Cohen, G., Damgård, I.B., Ishai, Y., Kölker, J., Miltersen, P.B., Raz, R., Rothblum, R.D.: Efficient multiparty protocols via log-depth threshold formulae. In: Canetti, R., Garay, J.A. (eds.) CRYPTO 2013. LNCS, vol. 8043, pp. 185–202. Springer, Heidelberg (2013). https://doi.org/10.1007/978-3-642-40084-1_11
14. Damgård, I., Ishai, Y.: Scalable secure multiparty computation. In: Dwork, C. (ed.) CRYPTO 2006. LNCS, vol. 4117, pp. 501–520. Springer, Heidelberg, August 2006. https://doi.org/10.1007/11818175_30
15. Damgård, I., Ishai, Y., Krøigaard, M.: Perfectly secure multiparty computation and the computational overhead of cryptography. In: Gilbert, H. (ed.) EUROCRYPT 2010. LNCS, vol. 6110, pp. 445–465. Springer, Heidelberg (2010). https://doi.org/10.1007/978-3-642-13190-5_23
16. Damgård, I., Ishai, Y., Krøigaard, M., Nielsen, J.B., Smith, A.: Scalable multiparty computation with nearly optimal work and resilience. In: Wagner, D. (ed.) CRYPTO 2008. LNCS, vol. 5157, pp. 241–261. Springer, Heidelberg (2008). https://doi.org/10.1007/978-3-540-85174-5_14
17. Damgård, I., Nielsen, J.B.: Scalable and unconditionally secure multiparty computation. In: Menezes, A. (ed.) CRYPTO 2007. LNCS, vol. 4622, pp. 572–590. Springer, Heidelberg (2007). https://doi.org/10.1007/978-3-540-74143-5_32
18. Dani, V., King, V., Movahedi, M., Saia, J.: Brief announcement: breaking the O(nm) bit barrier, secure multiparty computation with a static adversary. In: ACM

Symposium on Principles of Distributed Computing, PODC 2012, 16–18 July 2012, Funchal, Madeira, Portugal, pp. 227–228 (2012)
19. Dani, V., King, V., Movahedi, M., Saia, J.: Quorums quicken queries: efficient asynchronous secure multiparty computation. In: Chatterjee, M., Cao, J., Kothapalli, K., Rajsbaum, S. (eds.) ICDCN 2014. LNCS, vol. 8314, pp. 242–256. Springer, Heidelberg (2014). https://doi.org/10.1007/978-3-642-45249-9_16
20. Dani, V., King, V., Movahedi, M., Saia, J., Zamani, M.: Secure multi-party computation in large networks. Distrib. Comput. **30**(3), 193–229 (2017)
21. Feige, U.: Noncryptographic selection protocols. In: 40th FOCS, pp. 142–153. IEEE Computer Society Press, October 1999. https://doi.org/10.1109/SFFCS.1999.814586
22. Fiat, A., Shamir, A.: How to prove yourself: practical solutions to identification and signature problems. In: Odlyzko, A.M. (ed.) CRYPTO 1986. LNCS, vol. 263, pp. 186–194. Springer, Heidelberg, August 1987. https://doi.org/10.1007/3-540-47721-7_12
23. Garg, S., Gentry, C., Halevi, S., Raykova, M.: Two-round secure MPC from indistinguishability obfuscation. In: Lindell, Y. (ed.) TCC 2014. LNCS, vol. 8349, pp. 74–94. Springer, Heidelberg (2014). https://doi.org/10.1007/978-3-642-54242-8_4
24. Garg, S., Ishai, Y., Srinivasan, A.: Two-round MPC: information-theoretic and black-box. In: Beimel, A., Dziembowski, S. (eds.) TCC 2018. LNCS, vol. 11239, pp. 123–151. Springer, Cham (2018). https://doi.org/10.1007/978-3-030-03807-6_5
25. Garg, S., Srinivasan, A.: Two-round multiparty secure computation from minimal assumptions. In: Nielsen, J.B., Rijmen, V. (eds.) EUROCRYPT 2018. LNCS, vol. 10821, pp. 468–499. Springer, Cham (2018). https://doi.org/10.1007/978-3-319-78375-8_16
26. Genkin, D., Ishai, Y., Polychroniadou, A.: Efficient multi-party computation: from passive to active security via secure SIMD circuits. In: Gennaro, R., Robshaw, M. (eds.) CRYPTO 2015. LNCS, vol. 9216, pp. 721–741. Springer, Heidelberg (2015). https://doi.org/10.1007/978-3-662-48000-7_35
27. Gilad, Y., Hemo, R., Micali, S., Vlachos, G., Zeldovich, N.: Algorand: scaling byzantine agreements for cryptocurrencies. In: Proceedings of the 26th Symposium on Operating Systems Principles, 28–31 October 2017, Shanghai, China, pp. 51–68 (2017)
28. Goldreich, O.: The Foundations of Cryptography, vol. 2, Basic Applications. Cambridge University Press, Cambridge (2004)
29. Goldreich, O., Micali, S., Wigderson, A.: How to play any mental game or a completeness theorem for protocols with honest majority. In: Aho, A. (ed.) 19th ACM STOC, pp. 218–229. ACM Press, May 1987. https://doi.org/10.1145/28395.28420
30. Goyal, R., Hohenberger, S., Koppula, V., Waters, B.: A generic approach to constructing and proving verifiable random functions. In: Kalai, Y., Reyzin, L. (eds.) TCC 2017. LNCS, vol. 10678, pp. 537–566. Springer, Cham (2017). https://doi.org/10.1007/978-3-319-70503-3_18
31. Groth, J., Ostrovsky, R., Sahai, A.: New techniques for noninteractive zero-knowledge. J. ACM **59**(3), 11:1–11:35 (2012)
32. Halevi, S., Lindell, Y., Pinkas, B.: Secure computation on the web: computing without simultaneous interaction. In: Rogaway, P. (ed.) CRYPTO 2011. LNCS, vol. 6841, pp. 132–150. Springer, Heidelberg (2011). https://doi.org/10.1007/978-3-642-22792-9_8
33. Hirt, M., Maurer, U.: Player simulation and general adversary structures in perfect multiparty computation. J. Cryptol. **13**(1), 31–60 (2000)

34. Hirt, M., Nielsen, J.B.: Robust multiparty computation with linear communication complexity. In: Dwork, C. (ed.) CRYPTO 2006. LNCS, vol. 4117, pp. 463–482. Springer, Heidelberg (2006). https://doi.org/10.1007/11818175_28
35. Ishai, Y., Kushilevitz, E., Ostrovsky, R., Sahai, A.: Zero-knowledge proofs from secure multiparty computation. SIAM J. Comput. **39**(3), 1121–1152 (2009)
36. Ishai, Y., Kushilevitz, E., Paskin, A.: Secure multiparty computation with minimal interaction. In: Rabin, T. (ed.) CRYPTO 2010. LNCS, vol. 6223, pp. 577–594. Springer, Heidelberg (2010). https://doi.org/10.1007/978-3-642-14623-7_31
37. Micali, S., Rabin, M.O., Vadhan, S.P.: Verifiable random functions. In: 40th FOCS, pp. 120–130. IEEE Computer Society Press, October 1999. https://doi.org/10.1109/SFFCS.1999.814584
38. Peikert, C., Shiehian, S.: Noninteractive zero knowledge for NP from (plain) learning with errors. Tech. rep., Cryptology ePrint Archive Report 2019/158 (2019). https://eprint.iacr.org/2019/158
39. Saia, J., Zamani, M.: Recent results in scalable multi-party computation. In: SOFSEM 2015: Proceedings of the Theory and Practice of Computer Science - 41st International Conference on Current Trends in Theory and Practice of Computer Science, 24–29 January 2015, Pec pod Sněžkou, Czech Republic, pp. 24–44 (2015)
40. Yao, A.C.C.: How to generate and exchange secrets. In: 27th Annual Symposium on Foundations of Computer Science, pp. 162–167. IEEE (1986)
41. Zamani, M., Movahedi, M., Saia, J.: Millions of millionaires: multiparty computation in large networks. IACR Cryptol. ePrint Arch. **2014**, 149 (2014). https://eprint.iacr.org/2014/149

Circuit Amortization Friendly Encodingsand Their Application to Statistically Secure Multiparty Computation

Anders Dalskov[1(✉)], Eysa Lee[2], and Eduardo Soria-Vazquez[1]

[1] Aarhus University, Aarhus, Denmark
{anderspkd,eduardo}@cs.au.dk
[2] Northeastern University, Boston, USA
eysa@ccs.neu.edu

Abstract. At CRYPTO 2018, Cascudo et al. introduced *Reverse Multiplication Friendly Embeddings* (RMFEs). These are a mechanism to compute δ parallel evaluations of the same arithmetic circuit over a field $\mathbb{F}_q$ at the cost of a single evaluation of that circuit in $\mathbb{F}_{q^d}$, where $\delta < d$. Due to this inequality, RMFEs are a useful tool when protocols require to work over $\mathbb{F}_{q^d}$ but one is only interested in computing over $\mathbb{F}_q$. In this work we introduce Circuit Amortization Friendly Encodings (CAFEs), which generalize RMFEs while having concrete efficiency in mind. For a Galois Ring $R = GR(2^k, d)$, CAFEs allow to compute certain circuits over $\mathbb{Z}_{2^k}$ at the cost of a single secure multiplication in R. We present three CAFE instantiations, which we apply to the protocol for MPC over $\mathbb{Z}_{2^k}$ via Galois Rings by Abspoel et al. (TCC 2019). Our protocols allow for efficient switching between the different CAFEs, as well as between computation over $GR(2^k, d)$ and $\mathbb{F}_{2^d}$ in a way that preserves the CAFE in both rings. This adaptability leads to efficiency gains for e.g. Machine Learning applications, which can be represented as highly parallel circuits over $\mathbb{Z}_{2^k}$ followed by bit-wise operations. From an implementation of our techniques, we estimate that an SVM can be evaluated on 250 images in parallel up to $\times 7$ more efficiently using our techniques, compared to thc protocol from Abspoel et al. (TCC 2019).

1 Introduction

Secure Multi-Party Computation (MPC) protocols allow any n parties to compute any function on their secret data, while revealing nothing beyond the function's output. This is guaranteed even in the presence of an adversary $\mathcal{A}$ who corrupts and coordinates up to t of the participants. The capabilities of $\mathcal{A}$ determine the main limitations of MPC, as well as the most relevant techniques to construct such protocols.

One of the main distinctions is whether corrupted parties follow the protocol (but try to extract additional information from its execution) or if they arbitrarily deviate from it. The former is known as *passive* corruption, whereas the latter

S. Moriai and H. Wang (Eds.): ASIACRYPT 2020, LNCS 12493, pp. 213–243, 2020.
https://doi.org/10.1007/978-3-030-64840-4_8

is *active*. Additionally, $\mathcal{A}$ could have limited computational resources, or rather be unbounded. Finally, one of the most important aspects is whether corrupted parties constitute a minority ($t < n/2$) or not and, if so, whether $t < n/3$.

All *practical* protocols capable of resisting a computationally unbounded, active adversary are based in *linear secret sharing schemes* (LSSS), such as Shamir's LSSS [18]. Most of them follow a "gate-by-gate" paradigm[1], where a boolean (or arithmetic) circuit is computed on secret-shared inputs one gate at a time. As the secret sharing scheme is linear, addition gates can then be computed without interaction among the parties. Non-linear operations, such as multiplying two secrets together, are more complicated. In fact, for all known protocols in this setting which are able to compute *any* function efficiently, multiplication gates require running some interactive sub-protocol. If some preprocessed correlated randomness is assumed, this usually consists in "opening" (i.e. reconstructing to all parties) a linear combination of such randomness with either the inputs (e.g. when using Beaver triples [4]) or the outputs (e.g. when using double-shares [5]) of the multiplication gate. The protocol maintains the invariant that inputs and outputs of any processed gate are secret-shared in the same way, so that they can be combined and used as inputs to other gates.

Frequently, one is interested in computing functions which are naturally represented as either a boolean circuit or an arithmetic circuit over $\mathbb{Z}_{2^k}$. Nevertheless, be it in order to achieve some security parameter [15] or because the number of parties is bounded by the LSSS and the ring where computation takes place [1,18], it is often required to "lift" the computation to a large enough extension ring. As a concrete example, when the goal is to evaluate a boolean circuit (resp. a circuit over $\mathbb{Z}_{2^k}$) using Shamir-style MPC, the computation has to take place over $\mathbb{F}_{2^d}$ (resp. $GR(2^k, d)$, the degree-d Galois extension of $\mathbb{Z}_{2^k}$), where $d = \log(n + 1)$. This incurs on a multiplicative overhead of d in communication and d^2 in computation, where the latter can be asymptotically reduced to quasi-linear in d using FFT-style techniques.

Having the above in mind, the authors in [8] and [10] introduced *Reverse Multiplication Friendly Embeddings* (RMFEs), which exploit the inherent overhead induced by the extension degree d as a mechanism to compute in parallel $\delta < d$ copies of the boolean (resp. $\mathbb{Z}_{2^k}$) circuit that was the original target. Namely, through RMFEs, a single multiplication in $\mathbb{F}_{2^d}$ (resp. $GR(2^k, d)$) translates into a component-wise multiplication in $\mathbb{F}_2^\delta$ (resp. $\mathbb{Z}_{2^k}^\delta$). Interested in asymptotic results, most of the RMFE constructions provided by the authors involved algebraic geometry tools[2], whose concrete computational efficiency is unclear and for which the exact ratio δ/d might only become interesting for very large values of d.

In this work we propose Circuit Amortization Friendly Encodings (CAFEs) as a generalization of the RMFE paradigm, where we compute certain *subcircuits*

---

[1] A notable exception here are protocols based on lookup tables, such as those described in [9] or [14].

[2] As an exception, their most practical construction, given in [8] for boolean circuits, builds on polynomial interpolation.

Table 1. Encoding schemes. All rows assume a single "opening" in $R = GR(2^k, d)$.

Name	#Inputs (in R)	Expressiveness (as a $\mathbb{Z}_{2^k}$-subcircuit)
Naïve [1]	2	Circuits with 1 multiplication and 1 output
InnerProd	2	Inner products of length $\approx d/2$
SIMD	2	$\approx d^{0.6}$ parallel circuits w/ 1 mult. and 1 output each
Naïve [1]	m	Depth 1 circuit with m multiplications and 1 output
FLEX	m	Depth 1 circuit with m multiplications and d outputs

over $\mathbb{Z}_{2^k}$ at the cost of a *single* multiplication in $R = GR(2^k, d)$. Furthermore, as the extension degree d is usually very small, we focus our attention on concrete rather than asymptotic efficiency and provide an implementation which experimentally validates our claims. We apply our techniques to the protocol for MPC over $\mathbb{Z}_{2^k}$ via Galois Rings by Abspoel et al. [1], but we expect our framework to be useful for other protocols as well. Note that by setting $k = 1$ we obtain CAFEs for boolean circuits at the cost of a multiplication in $\mathbb{F}_{2^d}$.

The use of CAFEs allows us to match the efficiency improvements they provide with a "subcircuit-by-subcircuit" rather than "gate-by-gate" view of computation. Such view (and more general ones) is shared among many people programming MPC, who view LSSS-based protocols as a series of linear combinations and "openings" (secret reconstruction) rather than addition and multiplication gates. In Table 1 we show our three CAFE proposals, which allow computing commonly found subcircuits, and compare them with using the protocol by Abspoel et al. [1]. The RMFEs from [10] can be seen as a different proposal for the Single Instruction Multiple Data (SIMD) CAFE.

From a more theoretical perspective, Circuit Amortization Friendly Encodings (and RMFEs in particular) constitute a partial answer to the question *"what can we securely compute at the cost of one multiplication?"*, rather than the more usual *"what is the cost of securely computing one multiplication?"*. This means, among other things, that our CAFEs can be naturally combined with packed secret sharing techniques such as [13].

Bit-Wise Operations. Our previous discussion focused on the matter of computing circuits over $\mathbb{Z}_{2^k}$. Many practical applications, however, make use of *bit-wise* operations in order to compute e.g. comparisons between integers. These operations can be emulated in $\mathbb{Z}_{2^k}$ even when $k > 1$, but doing so loses the advantage of XOR being "for free": Whereas XOR is linear in $\mathbb{Z}_2$, it is not in $\mathbb{Z}_{2^k}$. In fact, for $a, b \in \{0, 1\}$, we have that $a \texttt{ XOR } b = a + b - 2ab \mod 2^k$, so XOR reduces to a multiplication in $\mathbb{Z}_{2^k}$, which requires communication.

A solution to this problem is the use of *doubly-authenticated bits* (daBits) [17], which are secret, random bits shared in two different algebraic structures. In our case, these structures are $GR(2^k, d)$ and $\mathbb{F}_{2^d}$, where we further make use our CAFEs in order to compute sub-circuits over $\mathbb{Z}_{2^k}$ and $\mathbb{F}_2$, respectively.

1.1 Technical Overview and Contributions

The fact of being constantly switching between different algebraic structures ($\mathbb{Z}_{2^k}, GR(2^k, d), \mathbb{F}_2$ and $\mathbb{F}_{2^d}$) in an actively secure way introduces several technical challenges in our protocols, as we do not want the costs introduced by these transformations to outweigh the benefit from using CAFEs. In order to deal with these, we devise efficient protocols for creating *correlated encoded randomness*.

Both for efficiency and simplicity of presentation, we restrict ourselves to the non-robust MPC scenario, where the adversary is able to abort the protocol after seeing its outputs. This way we avoid describing (now standard) player elimination techniques [1,5], the absence of which allows us to introduce *batch checking* mechanisms for double-shares and daBits. Concretely, the use of our batch checking allows us to *duplicate* the throughput of correlated randomness production via hyper-invertible matrices [1,3,5,8]. Furthermore, even when using hyper-invertible matrices over $R = GR(2^k, d)$, the batch check is compatible with the production of double-shares which are bound by $\mathbb{Z}_{2^k}$-linear relations, such as those required for our CAFEs.

To the best of our knowledge, this is the first time batch checking is applied to MPC protocols using hyper-invertible matrices, even in non-robust protocols such as [3]. We remark that our non-robust preprocessing protocols using this technique can still be used in the robust scenario in an *optimistic* way: Namely, if an abort is induced by the batch check failure, parties can switch to the slower, robust protocols. As no actual inputs to the MPC protocol have been provided yet, our optimistic variant remains both secure and robust.

We would like to highlight that our concrete CAFE constructions are mostly a clever combination of combinatorics, circuit randomization and multilinear algebra. The individual components are generally simple, which we see as a positive rather than a negative aspect of our work. Simple protocols usually lead to more efficient implementations, which is something we back with our experiments. Finally, we make a conscious effort to present our techniques in the most elementary way, so that they are as broadly accessible as possible within the community. In particular, we avoid using formal abstractions such as *d-fold generalized linear secret sharing* from [8], which are useful and we implicitly use, but we feel they could clog our presentation.

2 Preliminaries

We use n to denote the number of parties, among which $t < n/3$ are corrupted. Denote by $\mathcal{P} = \{\mathsf{P}_1, \dots, \mathsf{P}_n\}$ the set of parties. We use boldface letters $\mathbf{x}$ to denote vectors, for which we index their elements starting at 0, i.e., if $\boldsymbol{x} \in R^{\delta}$, $\mathbf{x} = (x_0, \dots, x_{\delta-1})$. If X is a set, $x \leftarrow X$ denotes a uniform random sampling from X, the result of which is assigned to the variable x. Finally, $[n]$ is used to denote the set $\{0, \dots, n-1\}$ and $[a, b]$ with $a < b$ to denote the set $\{a, \dots, b\}$. Let λ be the statistical security parameter.

2.1 Commutative Algebra

We briefly recall some previous results from commutative ring theory, as well as the background for Galois Rings we will need. In this subsection, R denotes a commutative ring with identity.

Definition 1. *Let $\alpha_0, \ldots, \alpha_{m-1} \in R$. We call $A = \{\alpha_0, \ldots, \alpha_{m-1}\}$ an* exceptional set *if and only if $\alpha_i - \alpha_j \in R^*$ for all $i, j \in [m]$ with $i \neq j$. We define the* Lenstra constant *of R to be the size of the biggest exceptional subset of R.*

The following is a generalization of the Schwartz-Zippel lemma which we will need throughout the paper.

Lemma 1 ([6]). *Let R be a commutative ring and $f : R^n \to R$ be an n-variate non-zero polynomial. Let $A \subseteq R$ be an exceptional set. Then*

$$\Pr_{\mathbf{x} \leftarrow A^n}[f(\mathbf{x}) = 0] \leq \frac{\deg f}{|A|}.$$

2.2 Galois Rings

Galois Rings are the unique degree-d Galois extension of rings of the form $\mathbb{Z}_{p^k}$, where p is a prime. Whereas for $k = 1$ such an extension yields the Galois Field $\mathbb{F}_{p^d}$, for $k > 1$ Galois Rings contain zero-divisors, in particular the multiples of p. We will use the following, equivalent definition of Galois Rings, as it is better suited for our purposes.

Definition 2. *A* Galois Ring *is a ring of the form $R = \mathbb{Z}_{p^k}[X]/(h(X))$ where p is a prime, $k \geq 1$ and $h(X) \in \mathbb{Z}_{p^k}[X]$ is a monic polynomial of degree $d \geq 1$ such that its reduction modulo p yields an irreducible polynomial in $\mathbb{F}_p[X]$.*

Once p, k and d has been fixed in Definition 2, any valid choice of $h(X) \in \mathbb{Z}_{p^k}[X]$ will result in the same R, up to isomorphism. Hence, we shall denote such a ring as $R = GR(p^k, d)$.

The ring $R = GR(p^k, d)$ is of characteristic p^k and all its ideals (p^i) form the chain

$$R \supset (p) \supset (p^2) \supset \cdots \supset (p^{k-1}) \supset (p^k) = 0.$$

Thus, for $i \in [1, k]$ we can define the natural homomorphisms $\pi_i : R \to R/(p^i)$ which are computed by "reducing modulo p^i". Notice that $R/(p^i) \cong GR(p^i, d)$, so by computing the quotient of R with its unique maximal ideal (p) we will obtain the finite field $\mathbb{F}_{p^d}$. Furthermore, all non-units of R are nilpotent and they constitute (p). We will need the following lemma:

Lemma 2. *The Lenstra constant of $GR(p^k, d)$ is p^d.*

In order to reason about Galois Ring elements and their arithmetic, we will sometimes describe them as it naturally follows from Definition 2. We will refer to such explicit description as the *additive representation of a*. More concretely, any element of $a \in GR(p^k, d)$ can be described as

$$a = a_0 + a_1 \cdot \xi + \ldots + a_{d-1} \cdot \xi^{d-1}, \quad (1)$$

where $a_i \in \mathbb{Z}_{p^k}$ and ξ is a root of $h(X)$, i.e. $GR(p^k, d) \cong \mathbb{Z}_{p^k}[\xi]$.

Our work focuses in Galois Rings of the form $R = GR(2^k, d)$, hence of characteristic 2^k, maximal ideal (2), Lenstra constant 2^d and such that $R/(2) \cong \mathbb{F}_{2^d}$. Notice that in such case $a \in R$ is a unit (i.e. $a \notin (2)$) if and only if, given its additive representation, there is at least one $i \in [d]$ such that $a_i \equiv 1 \mod 2$.

2.3 Shamir's Secret Sharing over Galois Rings

Shamir's secret sharing scheme [18] extends to any commutative ring with identity, as long as it contains an exceptional set of size at least $n+1$ [1]. Given the fact that the Lenstra constant of a Galois Ring $R = GR(2^k, d)$ is 2^d, we can construct Shamir's secret sharing for R if $d \geq \log(n+1)$. We provide the precise construction in $\Pi_{\mathsf{Share}}(s, t)$ (Protocol 1).

Protocol 1. $\Pi_{\mathsf{Share}}(s, t)$ — Degree-t Shamir's LSSS over Galois Rings.

Let $R = GR(2^k, d)$ be a Galois Ring such that $\log(n+1) \leq d$ and let $A = \{\alpha_0, \alpha_1, \ldots, \alpha_n\} \subset R$ be an exceptional set. Let P_i be the Dealer of the secret, with input $s \in R$.

1. P_i samples a random degree-t polynomial $p(X) \in R[X]$ such that $p(\alpha_0) = s$.
2. P_i defines its own share as $p(\alpha_i)$ and sends $p(\alpha_j)$ to P_j for all $j \neq i$.

Denote the output as $\langle s \rangle_t^R = (p(\alpha_1), \ldots, p(\alpha_n))$, a "degree-$t$ sharing" of s.

Since $\{\alpha_i\}_{i=0}^n$ is an exceptional set, Lagrange interpolation can be used with $t+1$ points to interpolate $p(X)$ and thus recover the secret. We denote the sharing of a value a as $\langle a \rangle$. Whenever there could be confusion about whether a is shared in one of two rings R or $\tilde{R}$, we will use $\langle a \rangle^R$ and $\langle a \rangle^{\tilde{R}}$ to avoid misunderstandings.

To run MPC using Shamir's scheme we also need the following protocols, which are standard and we provide in the full version.

- Private reconstruction $\Pi_{\mathsf{rPriv}}(\mathsf{P}_i, s)$: This reconstructs a Shamir secret shared value to a single party. This only requires every party apart from P_i communicate a single element for a total of $n-1$ elements.
- Public reconstruction $\Pi_{\mathsf{rPub}}(s_0, \ldots, s_{n-t-1})$: This reconstructs $n-t$ Shamir secret shared values simultaneously to all parties. To do so, parties privately reconstruct a single share to each party, followed by each party sending the reconstructed value to all other parties. This protocol requires communicating a total of $2 \cdot n \cdot (n-1)$ elements.

2.4 Hyper-Invertible Matrices over Galois Rings

Hyper-Invertible Matrices (HIMs) were introduced in [5] as a tool to generate secret correlated randomness in information-theoretic MPC. Their original description was limited to matrix whose entries are Finite Field elements, but HIMs naturally generalize to rings having big enough exceptional sets, as shown in [1].

Definition 3. *Let M be a r-by-c matrix. We say that M is* Hyper-Invertible *if, for all $A \subseteq [r]$, $B \subseteq [c]$ with $|A| = |B| > 0$, the sub-matrix M_A^B is invertible, where M_A denotes the matrix consisting of the rows $i \in A$ of M, M^B denotes the matrix consisting of the columns $j \in B$ of M, and $M_A^B = (M_A)^B$.*

For constructions of hyper-invertible matrices over Finite Fields and rings, we refer the reader to [5] and [1].

The technical reason why hyper-invertible matrices are a powerful instrument in MPC is the following lemma from [5].

Lemma 3. *Let $M \in R^{m\times m}$ be a hyper-invertible matrix, and let $\boldsymbol{y} = M\boldsymbol{x}$. Then, for all $A, B \subseteq [m]$ with $|A|+|B| = m$, there exists a R-linear isomorphism $\phi : R^m \to R^m$ such that $\phi(\boldsymbol{x}_A, \boldsymbol{y}_B) = (\boldsymbol{x}_{\bar{A}}, \boldsymbol{y}_{\bar{B}})$, where $\bar{A} = [m] \setminus A$ and $\bar{B} = [m] \setminus B$.*

Informally, it states that any combination of m inputs/outputs of the R-linear isomorphism induced by a square hyper-invertible matrix are uniquely determined by the remaining m inputs/outputs. This is key in enabling the "player elimination" mechanism, which relies in revealing each of $2t$ outputs to a different party. Player elimination enables, in turn, robust MPC.

Lemma 4. *Let $P_1, \ldots, P_n$ be parties out of which at most t are corrupted. Let $M \in R^{(n-t)\times n}$ be a hyper-invertible matrix. Let $\boldsymbol{y} = M \cdot \boldsymbol{x}$, where $\boldsymbol{y} = (y_1, \ldots, y_{n-t})$, $\boldsymbol{x} = (x_1, \ldots, x_n)$ and each $x_i \in R$ is a secret, uniformly random input chosen by party P_i. No Adversary can distinguish any $y_j \in R$ from uniformly random.*

Proof. Let $H \subset [1, n]$ be a set of indices corresponding to any $n - t$ honest parties. We have that $\boldsymbol{y} = M \cdot \boldsymbol{x} = M^H \cdot \boldsymbol{x}_H + M^{\bar{H}} \cdot \boldsymbol{x}_{\bar{H}}$. Denote $\boldsymbol{z}_H = M^H \cdot \boldsymbol{x}_H$. As M is hyper-invertible, M^H and all its entries are invertible. Then, as $\boldsymbol{x}_H$ consists only of secret, random values; we have that $\boldsymbol{z}_H \in R^{n-t}$ is uniformly random. Thus, so is $\boldsymbol{y} = (y_1, \ldots, y_{n-t})$. □

3 Switching Between Galois Rings and Galois Fields

Computation over $\mathbb{Z}_{2^k}$, while attractive for many applications, is not the best choice for operating on the level of bits. In fact, for many applications where $\mathbb{Z}_{2^k}$ shines, such as machine learning, specialized conversion protocols are often employed to deal with certain computations that cannot easily be expressed as arithmetic in $\mathbb{Z}_{2^k}$. For example, comparing two numbers a and b is equivalent to computing the result of the comparison $0 < a - b$, which amounts to extracting the most significant bit of $a - b$ (in two's complement, this bit is 1 if the result is negative, i.e., $b > a$ and 0 otherwise). Common for many protocols for MSB extraction, is a need for a secret-shared representation of the *bit-decomposition* of a number. If we know $v_0, \ldots, v_{k-1}$ such that $v = \sum_{i=0}^{k-1} 2^i v_i$ then MSB extraction is easy. Obtaining secret-shares of $v_0, \ldots, v_{k-1}$ given a secret-sharing of v can be done in the following way. Suppose we have k pairs of values $(\langle b_i \rangle^{\mathbb{F}_{2^d}}, \langle b_i \rangle^R)$; that is, the same bit b_i secret-shared in R as well as in $\mathbb{F}_{2^d}$. First we open the value $z = \langle v \rangle^R + \langle \sum_i 2^i b_i \rangle^R$ after which z is decomposed into bits. Notice that everyone now has a masked version of $v + b$ in its bit representation (where $b = \sum_{i=0}^{k-1} 2^i b_i$), as well as secret-shares of the bits of b. Finally, shares of the bits of v can be obtained by computing a binary adder.

Efficiently generating tuples of the kind $(\langle b_i \rangle^{\mathbb{F}_{2^d}}, \langle b_i \rangle^R)$ has been the topic of recent work such as [17], and more recently [12]. Both these works present a generic approach (i.e., generating bits for any two algebraic structures). We will instead focus on the specific case where the bits are shared over $R = GR(2^k, d)$ and the residue field of R, that is $\mathbb{F}_{2^d}$.

Let $\tilde{R} = GR(2^{\tilde{k}}, d)$ and $R = GR(2^k, d)$ be two Galois Rings such that $\tilde{k} > k$. Let $\pi_k : \tilde{R} \to R$ be the "reduction modulo 2^k" map.

Lemma 5. *Let $\tilde{A} = \{\alpha_0, \ldots, \alpha_{m-1}\} \subset \tilde{R}$ be an exceptional set. Then $A = \pi_k(\tilde{A}) = \{\pi_k(\alpha_0), \ldots, \pi_k(\alpha_{m-1})\}$ is an exceptional set in R.*

Proof. For any $\alpha_i, \alpha_j \in \tilde{A}$ such that $\alpha_i \neq \alpha_j$, let $\beta_{i,j} \in \tilde{R}$ be the inverse of $\alpha_i - \alpha_j \in \tilde{R}$. We have the following equalities, all derived form the fact that π_k is an homomorphism:

$$\begin{aligned}\pi_k(\beta_{i,j}) \cdot (\pi_k(\alpha_i) - \pi_k(\alpha_j)) &= \pi_k(\beta_{i,j}) \cdot \pi_k(\alpha_i - \alpha_j) = \pi_k(\beta_{i,j} \cdot (\alpha_i - \alpha_j)) \\ &= \pi_k(1_{\tilde{R}}) = 1_R.\end{aligned}$$

Hence, $A = \{\pi_k(\alpha_0), \ldots, \pi_k(\alpha_{m-1})\} \subset R$ is an exceptional set. □

Proposition 1. *The "reduction modulo 2^k" map $\pi_k : \tilde{R} \to R$ commutes with Shamir secret sharing. More precisely, given $a \in \tilde{R}$ shared as $\langle a \rangle^{\tilde{R}}$ using an exceptional set $\tilde{A} \subset \tilde{R}$, then*

$$\pi_k(\langle a \rangle^{\tilde{R}}) = \langle \pi_k(a) \rangle^R,$$

where the shares of $\langle \pi_k(a) \rangle^R$ use the exceptional set $A = \pi_k(\tilde{A}) \subset R$ and they are computed by applying π_k to the shares of $\langle a \rangle^{\tilde{R}}$.

Proof. Let $\tilde{p}(X) \in \tilde{R}[X]$ be the polynomial such that $\langle a \rangle^{\tilde{R}} = (\tilde{p}(\alpha_1), \ldots, \tilde{p}(\alpha_n))$ and denote $p(X) = \pi_k(\tilde{p}(X)) \in R[X]$. As $\tilde{p}(X)$ is of degree at most $m - 1$, so is $p(X)$. Additionally, observe that $\pi_k(\tilde{p}(\alpha_i)) = \pi_k(\tilde{p}(\pi_k(\alpha_i))) = p(\pi_k(\alpha_i))$. As shown in [1, Theorem 3], which follows from the Chinese Remainder Theorem over rings, there is an isomorphism between $p(X) \in R[X]$ and any m evaluations of $p(X)$ at points of the same exceptional set $A \subset R$. We conclude that

$$\begin{aligned}\langle \pi_k(a) \rangle^R &= (p(\pi_k(\alpha_1)), \ldots, p(\pi_k(\alpha_n))) \\ &= (\pi_k(\tilde{p}(\alpha_1)), \ldots, \pi_k(\tilde{p}(\alpha_n))) = \pi_k(\langle a \rangle^{\tilde{R}}).\end{aligned}$$ □

Notice that, as a corollary of the previous proposition, we have that for any $\tilde{k} \geq 1$, $\pi_1(\langle a \rangle^{\tilde{R}}) = \langle \pi_1(a) \rangle^{\mathbb{F}}$, where $\mathbb{F} = \mathbb{F}_{2^d}$ is the residue field of $\tilde{R}$.

3.1 Double Authenticated Bits

In Sect. 4 we present concrete protocols for generating shares of random bits. Here we outline the general technique that we will be using.

With the properties of R outlined in the previous section, a pair of secret-shared bits—one in R and the other in $\mathbb{F}_{2^d}$—is easy to obtain: We first generate a secret shared bit $\langle b \rangle^R$ in R and then use the observation in Proposition 1 to obtain $\langle b \rangle^{\mathbb{F}_{2^d}}$ by simply having each party locally truncate their share of $\langle b \rangle^R$ modulo 2.

It remains to discuss how to produce a random $\langle b \rangle^R, b \in \{0,1\}$. For this, we will adapt the RandBit protocol from [11], which produces such values when $R = \mathbb{Z}_{2^k}$. We will make use of their following lemma when proving our protocols.

Lemma 6 ([11]). *Let $\ell > 2$. If $a \in \mathbb{Z}$ is such that $a^2 \equiv 1 \mod 2^\ell$, then a is congruent modulo 2^ℓ to one among $\{1, -1, 2^{\ell-1} - 1, 2^{\ell-1} + 1\}$.*

4 Circuit Amortization Friendly Encodings

Given some private $a_1, \ldots, a_m \in \mathbb{Z}_{2^k}$, consider that we want to securely compute some circuit C taking them as inputs. In what we will call the *naïve* encoding (which is the approach in [1] and [2]), sharings of the inputs $\langle a_1 \rangle_t, \ldots, \langle a_m \rangle_t$ would have to be produced by first embedding each $a_i \in \mathbb{Z}_{2^k}$ into $R = GR(2^k, d)$, individually. Any multiplication gate in C would then be computed in the usual way, that is, given $\langle a \rangle_t, \langle b \rangle_t$ and a double sharing $(\langle r \rangle_t, \langle r \rangle_{2t})$:

Protocol 2. $\Pi_{\text{online-ds}}$ — Standard Online use of double-shares.

1. Parties locally compute $\langle c \rangle_{2t} = \langle a \rangle_t \cdot \langle b \rangle_t$.
2. Publicly reconstruct $\langle z \rangle = \langle c \rangle_{2t} - \langle r \rangle_{2t}$.
3. Compute $\langle c \rangle_t = z + \langle r \rangle_t$.

However, this approach makes no use of the extension degree of R, and as we previously outlined in Table 1, it would incur on more communication (and computation) than the encodings we are about to present.

By making explicit the act of encoding the $\mathbb{Z}_{2^k}$ elements on which we want to compute into elements in R, we can generalize the above protocol in the following way. For a circuit C with $2 \cdot \delta_1$ inputs, δ_2 outputs, and where $\delta_2 \leq \delta_1$, define two $\mathbb{Z}_{2^k}$-linear homomorphisms $\mathsf{E}_{in} : (\mathbb{Z}_{2^k})^{\delta_1} \rightarrow R$ and $\mathsf{E}_{out} : (\mathbb{Z}_{2^k})^{\delta_2} \rightarrow R$ satisfying

$$\mathsf{E}_{in}(\mathbf{a}) \cdot \mathsf{E}_{in}(\mathbf{b}) + \mathsf{E}_{out}(\mathbf{c}) = \mathsf{E}_{out}(C(\mathbf{a}, \mathbf{b}) + \mathbf{c}). \quad (2)$$

Using E_{in} and E_{out}, Protocol 2 can be generalized as shown in Protocol 3:

Protocol 3. $\Pi_{\text{online-enc-ds}}$ — Online use of encoded double-shares.

1. Parties locally compute $\langle \mathsf{E}_{in}(\boldsymbol{a}) \cdot \mathsf{E}_{in}(\boldsymbol{b}) \rangle_{2t} = \langle \mathsf{E}_{in}(\boldsymbol{a}) \rangle_t \cdot \langle \mathsf{E}_{in}(\boldsymbol{b}) \rangle_t$.
2. Publicly reconstruct $\langle \mathsf{E}_{out}(C(\boldsymbol{a}, \boldsymbol{b}) - \boldsymbol{r}) \rangle_{2t} = \langle \mathsf{E}_{in}(\boldsymbol{a}) \cdot \mathsf{E}_{in}(\boldsymbol{b}) \rangle_{2t} - \langle \mathsf{E}_{out}(\boldsymbol{r}) \rangle_{2t}$.
3. From $\mathsf{E}_{out}(C(\boldsymbol{a}, \boldsymbol{b}) - \boldsymbol{r})$, compute $\mathsf{E}_{in}(C(\boldsymbol{a}, \boldsymbol{b}) - \boldsymbol{r})$.
4. Finally, define $\langle \mathsf{E}_{in}(C(\boldsymbol{a}, \boldsymbol{b})) \rangle_t = \mathsf{E}_{in}(C(\boldsymbol{a}, \boldsymbol{b}) - \boldsymbol{r}) + \langle \mathsf{E}_{in}(\boldsymbol{r}) \rangle_t$.

Notice that by setting $C(a, b) = a \cdot b$ and encodings $\mathsf{E}_{in}(a) = \mathsf{E}_{out}(a) = a$ we get the naïve encoding and Protocol 2.

In the following, we present alternative definitions of E_{in} and E_{out} which work for the more expressive circuits from Table 1: In Sect. 4.2 we give what we call FLEX encoding, InnerProd encoding in Sect. 4.3, and finally SIMD encoding in Sect. 4.4. The main challenge will be to produce pairs $(\langle \mathsf{E}_{out}(\mathbf{r}) \rangle_{2t}, \langle \mathsf{E}_{in}(\mathbf{r})_t \rangle)$ in an efficient manner. We also show how to produce random bits $\langle b \rangle \in \{0, 1\} \subset \mathbb{Z}_{2^k}$ compatible with each CAFE: For example, for the SIMD encoding we produce sharings of the form $\langle \mathsf{E}_{out}(\boldsymbol{b}) \rangle_t^R$, where $\boldsymbol{b} = (b_0, \ldots, b_{\delta-1})$ and each $b_i \leftarrow \{0, 1\}$ independently. Each presentation is concluded with an analysis of the technique's efficiency and expressiveness. An overview of our CAFEs and how they relate to each other is given in Fig. 1. By setting $k = 1$, we obtain the finite field equivalent of our protocols, but without exploiting the fact of being in a structure of characteristic two. Finally, note that, through the use of daBits, we can switch between values with a given encoding in $GR(2^k, d)$ and their bit decomposition, using the same encoding, in $\mathbb{F}_{2^d}$

We briefly note that parties must check if private secret-shared inputs in the online phase are correctly encoded and not arbitrary elements from R. In the naïve case, this corresponds to verifying that parties input $\mathbb{Z}_{2^k}$ elements [1]. In our CAFEs, this can be done with the aid of preprocessing by making use of the fact that E_{in}-encoded (resp. E_{out}-encoded) values will constitute a $\mathbb{Z}_{2^k}$-module. In the offline phase, parties generate shares of random encodings. Then, in the online phase, to verify that some share is of the form $\langle \mathsf{E}_{in}(\mathbf{a}) \rangle_t$, parties can use a random share $\langle \mathsf{E}_{in}(\mathbf{r}) \rangle_t$ to open and check that the sum $\mathsf{E}_{in}(\mathbf{a} + \mathbf{r}) = \mathsf{E}_{in}(\mathbf{a}) + \mathsf{E}_{in}(\mathbf{r})$ is in the $\mathbb{Z}_{2^k}$-module defined by E_{in}.

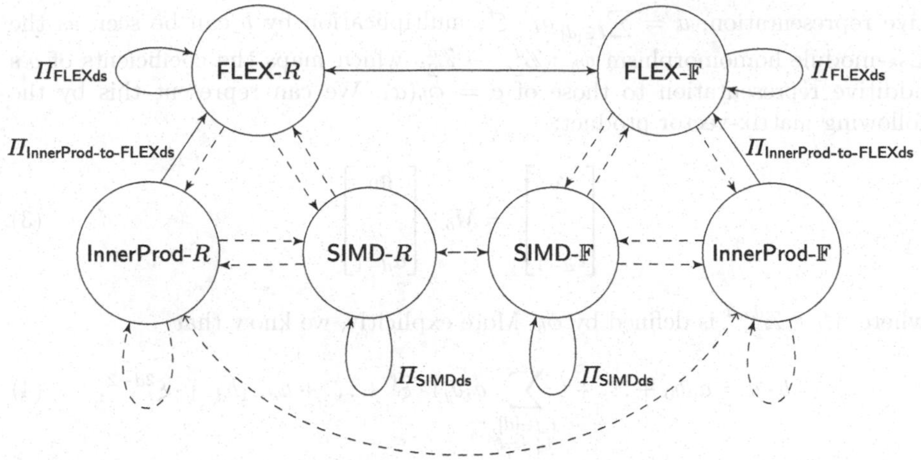

Fig. 1. Overview of how our Circuit Amortization Friendly Encodings relate to one another. The direction of an edge indicates the transformation from one type of encoding to another. Dashed lines indicate protocols which we do not explicitly provide in this work, but which are easy to build from the ones we give.

4.1 Hyper-Invertible Matrices and $\mathbb{Z}_{2^k}$-Modules

Let $\Phi_M : R^n \to R^{n-t}$ be the R-module homomorphism defined by multiplication with a hyper-invertible matrix $M \in R^{(n-t)\times n}$, i.e. $\Phi_M(\boldsymbol{x}) = \boldsymbol{y}$, where $\boldsymbol{y} = M\boldsymbol{x}$. Φ_M is trivial to define, as all the elements of $M, \boldsymbol{x}$, and $\boldsymbol{y}$ belong to the ring R. As the input and output encodings of CAFEs can be seen as some $\mathbb{Z}_{2^k}$-module N, we also need to define a $\mathbb{Z}_{2^k}$-module homomorphism from multiplication by $M \in R^{(n-t)\times n}$ which preserves the properties of hyper-invertible matrices. We will denote such homomorphism by $\Psi_M : (N^d)^n \to (N^d)^{n-t}$.

As N^d is a $\mathbb{Z}_{2^k}$-module, we know how to multiply its elements with scalars from $\mathbb{Z}_{2^k}$. But how can we multiply the elements of N^d with scalars from R, the degree-d extension of $\mathbb{Z}_{2^k}$? For the reader familiar with tensor products the answer is simple: N^d is isomorphic to $R \otimes_{\mathbb{Z}_{2^k}} N$ as a $\mathbb{Z}_{2^k}$-module, but $R \otimes_{\mathbb{Z}_{2^k}} N$ can also be seen as an R-module compatible with the $\mathbb{Z}_{2^k}$-module structure N^d. Aiming for a broader audience, our following exposition will refrain from using tensor products, giving instead explicit formulas to compute $\boldsymbol{y} = \Psi_M(\boldsymbol{x})$. We refer those interested in a more systematic path towards the tensor product argument to the sections on *interleaved generalized secret sharing schemes* in [8], where all the mentions to vector spaces and finite fields can be replaced by modules and Galois Rings without any harm. The tensoring technique was also implicitly used by the authors of [1] when producing double-shares of $\mathbb{Z}_{p^k}$ elements using matrices in $(GR(p^k, d))^{n\times n}$.

$\mathbb{Z}_{2^k}$-linear action of $b \in R$ on N^d: Towards our goal of defining the $\mathbb{Z}_{2^k}$-module homomorphism $\Psi_M : (N^d)^n \to (N^d)^{n-t}$, let us start by looking at how the product between any $a, b \in R$ is computed. If we express a in its additive representation, $a = \sum_{\ell \in [d]} a_\ell \cdot \xi^\ell$, multiplication by b can be seen as the $\mathbb{Z}_{2^k}$-module homomorphism $\phi_b : \mathbb{Z}_{2^k}^d \to \mathbb{Z}_{2^k}^d$ which maps the coefficients of a's additive representation to those of $c = \phi_b(a)$. We can represent this by the following matrix-vector product:

$$\begin{bmatrix} c_0 \\ \vdots \\ c_{d-1} \end{bmatrix} = M_b \cdot \begin{bmatrix} a_0 \\ \vdots \\ a_{d-1} \end{bmatrix} \tag{3}$$

where $M_b \in \mathbb{Z}_{2^k}^{d \times d}$ is defined by ϕ_b. More explicitly, we know that

$$c = b \cdot a = a_0 b_0 + \ldots + (\sum_{\substack{i,j \in [d], \\ i+j=\ell}} a_i b_j) \cdot \xi^\ell + \ldots + a_{d-1} b_{d-1} \cdot \xi^{2d-2}, \tag{4}$$

from which we reduce to the coefficients $(c_0, \ldots, c_{d-1}) \in \mathbb{Z}_{2^k}^d$ of c's additive representation, according to the polynomial $h(X)$ such that $R = \mathbb{Z}_{2^k}[X]/(h(X))$. Hence, M_b can be written as the following sum, where the first matrix is lower diagonal and H_b represents the reduction by the quotient polynomial in Eq. (4):

$$M_b = \begin{bmatrix} b_0 & & & \\ b_1 & b_0 & & \\ \vdots & \vdots & \ddots & \\ b_{d-1} & b_{d-2} & \ldots & b_0 \end{bmatrix} + H_b$$

As R is isomorphic $\mathbb{Z}_{2^k}^d$, what we have shown in Eq. (3) is the $\mathbb{Z}_{2^k}$-linear action of "multiplying by b" on an element $a \in N^d$ when $N = \mathbb{Z}_{2^k}$. Informally, we can simply substitute the $a_i \in \mathbb{Z}_{2^k}$ coefficients in Eq. (3) with $a_i \in N$, where N is a $\mathbb{Z}_{2^k}$-module. As each c_i would then be a $\mathbb{Z}_{2^k}$-linear combination of the a_i's, we have that $c_i \in N$.

The $\mathbb{Z}_{2^k}$-module homomorphism $\Psi_M : (N^d)^n \to (N^d)^{n-t}$: Now, let $M \in R^{(n-t) \times n}$ be a (hyper-invertible) matrix and $\boldsymbol{x} = (x_1, \ldots, x_n) \in R^n$, $\boldsymbol{y} = (y_1, \ldots, y_{n-t}) \in R^{n-t}$ be vectors such that $\boldsymbol{y} = M\boldsymbol{x}$. We then have that

$$y_i = m_{i,1} \cdot x_1 + \ldots + m_{i,n} \cdot x_n = \phi_{m_{i,1}}(x_1) + \ldots + \phi_{m_{i,n}}(x_n)$$

where $(m_{i,1}, \ldots, m_{i,n}) \in R^n$ is the i-th row of M and $\phi_{m_{i,j}}$ is the "multiplication by $m_{i,j}$" map. Hence, if we represent $x_j, y_i \in R$ in their additive representations and each of the $\mathbb{Z}_{2^k}$-module homomorphisms $\phi_{m_{i,j}}$ as in Eq. (3), we obtain:

$$(y_{i,0}, \ldots, y_{i,d-1}) = M_{m_{i,1}}(x_{1,0}, \ldots, x_{1,d-1}) + \ldots + M_{m_{i,n}}(x_{n,0}, \ldots, x_{n,d-1})$$

This leads to a "block-wise" view of the product of hyper-invertible matrices with elements from $R^n \cong (\mathbb{Z}_{2^k}^d)^n$, which we depict in Eq. (5).

$$\begin{bmatrix} y_{1,0} \\ \vdots \\ y_{1,d-1} \\ \hline \vdots \\ \hline y_{n-t,0} \\ \vdots \\ y_{n-t,d-1} \end{bmatrix} = \left[\begin{array}{c|c|c} M_{m_{1,1}} & \cdots & M_{m_{1,n}} \\ \hline \vdots & \ddots & \vdots \\ \hline M_{m_{n-t,1}} & \cdots & M_{m_{n-t,n}} \end{array}\right] \begin{bmatrix} x_{1,0} \\ \vdots \\ x_{1,d-1} \\ \hline \vdots \\ \hline x_{n,0} \\ \vdots \\ x_{n,d-1} \end{bmatrix} \tag{5}$$

The same way we did in Eq. (3), we can replace $\boldsymbol{x} \in (\mathbb{Z}_{2^k}^d)^n, \boldsymbol{y} \in (\mathbb{Z}_{2^k}^d)^{n-t}$ with $\boldsymbol{x} \in (N^d)^n, \boldsymbol{y} \in (N^d)^{n-t}$. In other words, we can simply substitute each $x_{i,\ell}, y_{j,\ell} \in \mathbb{Z}_{2^k}$ in Eq. (5) with $x_{i,\ell}, y_{j,\ell} \in N$. This way, we have defined the $\mathbb{Z}_{2^k}$-module homomorphism $\Psi_M : (N^d)^n \to (N^d)^{n-t}$. When writing $\boldsymbol{y} = \Psi_M(\boldsymbol{x})$ while specifying each $x_{i,\ell}, y_{j,\ell} \in N$, we will use semicolons to preserve the lines breaking up $\boldsymbol{x} \in (N^d)^n$ and $\boldsymbol{y} \in (N^d)^{n-t}$ into blocks of size d as in Eq. (5).

Finally, the following lemma tells us that Ψ_M preserves the guarantees provided by Lemma 4.

Lemma 7. *Let $R = GR(2^k, d)$ and let N be a $\mathbb{Z}_{2^k}$-module. Consider the same hypothesis as in Lemma 4 but with $\boldsymbol{x} \in (R \otimes_{\mathbb{Z}_{2^k}} N)^n$ and $\boldsymbol{y} \in (R \otimes_{\mathbb{Z}_{2^k}} N)^{n-t}$, so that now $x_i, y_j \in N^d$. For $j \in [1, n-t]$, parse $y_j = (y_{j,0}, \ldots, y_{j,d-1}) \in N^d$. No Adversary can distinguish any $y_{j,\ell} \in N$ from uniformly random.*

Proof. Let $H \subset [1, n]$ be a set of indices corresponding to any $n-t$ honest parties. Express $\boldsymbol{y} = M \cdot \boldsymbol{x} = M^H \cdot \boldsymbol{x}_H + M^{\bar{H}} \cdot \boldsymbol{x}_{\bar{H}}$ and denote $\boldsymbol{z}_H = M^H \cdot \boldsymbol{x}_H$. As M is hyper-invertible, M^H and all its entries are invertible. If we adopt the "block-wise" view from Eq. (5), H is selecting among the pre-established size-d blocks and $m_{i,j}$ being invertible translates into $M_{m_{i,j}}$ being invertible. Due to this and the fact that $\boldsymbol{x}_H \in (N^d)^{n-t}$ consist only of secret, random values, we have that $\boldsymbol{z}_H \in (N^d)^{n-t}$ is uniformly random. Thus, so is $\boldsymbol{y} \in (N^d)^{n-t}$, which in turn implies that the values $y_{j,\ell} \in N$ are i.i.d. uniformly random. □

4.2 FLEX Encodings

Given m secret-shared values encoded as in the naïve [1] setting, our FLEX encoding shows how to compute a circuit C with d outputs and multiplication depth one. Such a circuit could of course be computed in the naïve setting, using d openings in R; however we show how to compute it using only a single opening.

The encoding works as follows: During preprocessing, parties produce "double-shares" of the form $(\langle r_0 \rangle_t, \langle r_1 \rangle_t, \ldots, \langle r_{d-1} \rangle_t, \langle r \rangle_{2t})$ where $r = \sum_{i=0}^{d-1} r_i \cdot \xi^i$. Given inputs $\{\langle a_i \rangle_t\}_{i \in [m]}$, parties compute $C(\langle a_0 \rangle_t, \ldots, \langle a_{m-1} \rangle_t)$. Let $\langle z_j \rangle_{2t}$

for $j \in [d]$ denote the resultant shares. To reduce the degree of these d shares, parties do the following:

1. Locally compute $\langle z \rangle_{2t} = \sum_{i=0}^{d-1} \langle z_i \rangle_{2t} \cdot \xi^i$.
2. Open $\langle w \rangle_{2t} = \langle z \rangle_{2t} - \langle r \rangle_{2t}$.
3. Parse w in its additive form as $w \equiv \sum_{i=0}^{d-1} w_i \cdot \xi^i$.
4. Each party defines $\langle z_j \rangle_t$ as $\langle z_j \rangle_t := w_j + \langle r_j \rangle_t$ for $j \in [d]$.

Double Share Generation. It remains to be shown how to generate a double-sharing for this encoding. Π_{FLEXds} in Protocol 4 shows how to do so using Hyper-Invertible matrices. We remark that our protocol takes a different approach than previous work, in that we utilize the Hyper-Invertible matrices *only* for generating the double-sharings. By separating generation of the double-sharings from their checking, we produce double-shares much more efficiently than [1], as we can now batch check *all* the generated double-shares at once.

Protocol 4. Π_{FLEXds} — Double-sharings for FLEX encoding.

Let $M \in R^{(n-t)\times n}$ be a Hyper-Invertible matrix and let $\Psi_M : (N^d)^n \to (N^d)^{n-t}$ be as defined in Section 4.1 and depicted in Equation (5).

Generate. Parties produce a batch of $d \cdot (n-t)$ random double-shares as follows:

1. For $i \in [n]$, $\ell \in [d]$, each P_i samples at random $s_\ell^i \in \mathbb{Z}_{2^k}$ and computes $s^i = \sum_{\ell=0}^{d-1} s_\ell^i \cdot \xi^\ell$. Call $\Pi_{\mathsf{Share}}(s_\ell^i, t)$ and $\Pi_{\mathsf{Share}}(s^i, 2t)$ to distribute $\langle s_\ell^i \rangle_t$ and $\langle s^i \rangle_{2t}$ shares to all parties in $\mathcal{P}$.
2. Parties compute $(\langle r^1 \rangle_{2t}, \ldots, \langle r^{(n-t)} \rangle_{2t}) = M \cdot (\langle s^1 \rangle_{2t}, \ldots, \langle s^n \rangle_{2t})$.
3. Parties compute:

$$(\langle r_0^1 \rangle, \ldots, \langle r_{d-1}^1 \rangle; \ldots; \langle r_0^{n-t} \rangle, \ldots, \langle r_{d-1}^{n-t} \rangle) \\ = \Psi_M \left(\langle s_0^1 \rangle, \ldots, \langle s_{d-1}^1 \rangle; \ldots; \langle s_0^n \rangle, \ldots, \langle s_{d-1}^n \rangle \right)$$

Batch Check. Let m be the number of batches generated in the previous step. Assume that $m(n-t) > \lambda$. Throughout, $j \in [m]$ identifies each batch.

I. $\mathbb{Z}_{2^k}$**-outputs:** We check that each $\langle r_{j,\ell}^i \rangle_t$ is a sharing of a $\mathbb{Z}_{2^k}$ element.

1. For each $\langle r_{j,\ell}^i \rangle_t$ and $\tau \in [\lambda]$, call $\chi_{j,\ell}^{i,\tau} \leftarrow \mathcal{F}_{\mathsf{rand}}(\{0,1\})$ to obtain a random bit.
2. For each $\tau \in [\lambda]$, compute:

$$\langle x_\tau \rangle_t = \sum_{j=0}^{m-1} \sum_{i=1}^{n-t} \sum_{\ell=0}^{d-1} \chi_{j,\ell}^{i,\tau} \cdot \langle r_{j,\ell}^i \rangle_t.$$

3. Call $\Pi_{\mathsf{rPub}}(x_0, \ldots, x_{\lambda-1})$. If $x_\tau \notin \mathbb{Z}_{2^k}$ for $\tau \in [\lambda]$, abort.

4. For $\tau \in [\lambda]$ pick a tuple $(i_\tau, j_\tau, \ell_\tau) \in ([m]\times[1, n-t]\times[d])$ such that $\chi^{i_\tau,\tau}_{j_\tau,\ell_\tau} = 1$ and discard the shares $\langle r^{i_\tau}_{j_\tau,0}\rangle_t, \ldots, \langle r^{i_\tau}_{j_\tau,d-1}\rangle_t, \langle r^{i_\tau}_{j_\tau}\rangle_{2t}$. These shares are considered as having acted like masks in the computation of $\langle x_\tau\rangle_t$ as a linear combination.

II. Equality: Next we check that each double-share satisfies $\langle r^i_j\rangle_{2t} = \sum_{\ell=0}^{d-1}\langle r^i_{j,\ell}\rangle_t \cdot \xi^\ell$. Let $\bar{\lambda}$ such that $\bar{\lambda}d > \lambda$.

1. For $\tau \in [\bar{\lambda}], j \in [m]$ and $i \in [1, n-t]$. Call $\chi^{i,\tau}_j \leftarrow \mathcal{F}_{\mathsf{rand}}(A)$, where A is an exceptional set of R of length 2^d.
2. For $\tau \in [\bar{\lambda}]$, compute:

$$\langle y_\tau\rangle_{2t} = \sum_{j=0}^{m-1}\sum_{i=1}^{n-t}\chi^{i,\tau}_j \cdot \left(\langle r^i_j\rangle_{2t} - \sum_{\ell=0}^{d-1}\langle r^i_{j,\ell}\rangle_t \cdot \xi^\ell\right).$$

Call $\Pi_{\mathsf{rPub}}(y_0, \ldots, y_{\bar{\lambda}-1})$. If $y_\tau \neq 0$ for any $\tau \in [\bar{\lambda}]$, abort.

Output. Let $D = \{(i_\tau, j_\tau) \mid \tau \in [\lambda]\}$ be a set of indices corresponding to the discarded values in Step I.4 of Batch Check. For $(i,j) \in ([m]\times[1, n-t])\setminus D$ output the double-shares $\langle r^i_{j,0}\rangle_t, \ldots, \langle r^i_{j,d-1}\rangle_t, \langle r^i_j\rangle_{2t}$ as valid.

Theorem 1. *Π_{FLEXds} in Protocol 4 securely produces a minimum of $m\cdot(n-t)-\lambda$ valid double-sharings for the* FLEX *encoding.*

Proof. Let $\mathbb{A} \subset [1, n]$ denote the indices of the parties corrupted by $\mathcal{A}$ and assume a non-aborting execution Π_{FLEXds}. We do not care about the abort scenario, as in such case all double-shares are discarded and, furthermore, no private MPC inputs have been yet provided.

Correctness. In an honest protocol execution, it follows from the discussion in Sect. 4.1 that Π_{FLEXds} produces double-shares of the right form. When $\mathcal{A}$ deviates from the protocol, we need to look at what is implied by the non-aborting execution of **Batch Check.**

I. $\mathbb{Z}_{2^k}$-outputs: See each shared value $\langle r^i_{j,\ell}\rangle_t$ in its unique additive representation, i.e. $r^i_{j,\ell} = \sum_{\iota=0}^{d-1} r^i_{j,\ell,\iota}\cdot\xi^\iota$ where $r^i_{j,\ell,\iota} \in \mathbb{Z}_{2^k}$. What we want to prove is that $\langle r^i_{j,\ell}\rangle_t = \langle r^i_{j,\ell,0}\rangle_t$ or, in other words, that $r^i_{j,\ell,\iota} = 0$ for $\iota \in [1, d-1]$. For $\tau \in [\lambda]$, define also $x_\tau = \sum_{\iota=0}^{d-1} x_{\tau,\iota}\cdot\xi^\iota$. Then we have that:

$$x_{\tau,\iota} = \sum_{j=1}^{m}\sum_{i=1}^{n-t}\sum_{\ell=0}^{d-1}\chi^{i,\tau}_{j,\ell}\cdot r^i_{j,\ell,\iota}, \quad \iota \in \{1, \ldots, d-1\}.$$

Let $M = m\cdot(n-t)\cdot d$. We can look at $x_{\tau,\iota}$ as the evaluation in $\chi^{i,\tau}_{j,\ell}$ of an M-variate polynomial f of degree one with coefficients $r^i_{j,\ell,\iota} \in \mathbb{Z}_{2^k}$. Assume f is not the zero polynomial (i.e. that there exists any $r^i_{j,\ell,\iota} \neq 0$). Then, by applying the Schwartz-Zippel Lemma (c.f. Lemma 1), as each variable is evaluated only in elements of the exceptional set $A = \{0,1\} \subset \mathbb{Z}_{2^k}$, we have that $\Pr_{\chi^\tau \leftarrow \{0,1\}^M}[x_{\tau,\iota} = 0] = \Pr_{\chi^\tau \leftarrow \{0,1\}^M}[f(\chi^\tau) = 0] \leq 1/2$. Let $\chi = (\chi^1, \ldots, \chi^\lambda)$. We conclude that for $\iota \in \{1, \ldots, d-1\}$:

$$\Pr_{\chi \leftarrow \{0,1\}^{M \cdot \lambda}}[x_{0,\iota} = \ldots = x_{\lambda,\iota} = 0] \leq 2^{-\lambda}.$$

Applying a union bound, the previous equation implies that the Adversary can produce a $r^i_{j,\ell} \notin \mathbb{Z}_{2^k}$ (i.e. a $r^i_{j,\ell,\iota} \neq 0$ for $\iota \neq 0$) with a success probability of at most $(d-1) \cdot 2^{-\lambda}$.

II. Equality: Let $\tilde{m} = m \cdot (n-t) \cdot d$. We apply the Schwartz-Zippel Lemma (c.f. Lemma 1), where each variable is evaluated only in elements of the exceptional set $A \subset GR(2^k, d)$ of size $|A| = 2^d$. For $\tau \in [\tilde{\lambda}]$, we have that $\Pr_{\chi^\tau \leftarrow A^{\tilde{m}}}[y_\tau = 0] = \Pr_{\chi^\tau \leftarrow A^{\tilde{m}}}[f(\chi^\tau) = 0] \leq 2^{-d}$. Let $\chi = (\chi^1, \ldots, \chi^{\tilde{\lambda}})$, we conclude:

$$\Pr_{\chi \leftarrow A^{\tilde{m} \cdot \tilde{\lambda}}}[y_0 = \ldots = y_{\tilde{\lambda}} = 0] \leq 2^{-\tilde{\lambda} \cdot d},$$

As $\tilde{\lambda} \cdot d > \lambda$, we are done.

Privacy. Let's first look at the **Generate** step. The Adversary knows at most t of the degree-$2t$ inputs to which the hyper-invertible matrix M is applied, namely $\{\langle s^i \rangle_{2t}\}_{i \in \mathbb{A}}$. By Lemma 4, we know that the values $\{\langle r^i \rangle_{2t}\}_{i \in [1,n]}$ are secret and uniformly random. For the degree-t sharings, $\mathcal{A}$ know t blocks of inputs, namely $\{\langle s^i_0 \rangle_t, \ldots, \langle s^i_{d-1} \rangle_t\}_{i \in \mathbb{A}}$. By Lemma 7, we know that the values $\{\langle r^i_\ell \rangle_t\}_{i \in [1,n], \ell \in [d]}$ are secret and i.i.d. uniformly random from $\mathcal{A}$'s perspective.

Finally, the outputs of **Batch Check** do not leak any information on the output $\langle r \rangle$ values. This follows from the fact that $y_\tau = 0$ and that each revealed x_τ is one-time padded by the discarded $\langle r \rangle$ values indexed by the set $D = \{(i_\tau, j_\tau) \mid \tau \in [\lambda]\}$. □

Generation of Random Bits for FLEX Encoding. In Protocol 5 Π_{FLEXbits}, we give an adaptation of the RandBit protocol of [11] to producing shares over R. Moreover, applying FLEX encoding enables us to produce batches of d random bits, compared to producing a single random bit if we were to only replace the arithmetic sharing with Shamir secret sharing over R.

Protocol 5. Π_{FLEXbits}—Random bits for the FLEX encoding.

Let $\tilde{R} = GR(2^{k+2}, d)$, $R = GR(2^k, d)$. Parties produce m batches of d random bits as follows:

1. For $j \in [m]$, $\ell \in [d]$ parties produce shares $\langle u_{j,\ell} \rangle^{\tilde{R}}_t$ of secret, random $u_{j,\ell} \in \mathbb{Z}_{2^{k+2}}$. This can be done as in the Π_{FLEXds} (Protocol 4) by skipping steps related to the degree $2t$ sharings, including skipping Step II. of Batch Check.

---

2. Compute $\langle a_{j,\ell}\rangle_t^{\tilde{R}} = 2 \cdot \langle u_{j,\ell}\rangle_t^{\tilde{R}} + 1$ and $\langle (a_{j,\ell})^2\rangle_{2t}^{\tilde{R}} = \langle a_{j,\ell}\rangle_t^{\tilde{R}} \cdot \langle a_{j,\ell}\rangle_t^{\tilde{R}}$.
3. Compute $\langle e_j\rangle_{2t}^{\tilde{R}} = \langle (a_{j,0})^2\rangle_{2t}^{\tilde{R}} + \langle (a_{j,1})^2\rangle_{2t}^{\tilde{R}} \cdot \xi + \cdots + \langle (a_{j,d-1})^2\rangle_{2t}^{\tilde{R}} \cdot \xi^{d-1}$.
4. Call Π_{rPub} to reconstruct e_j for all $j \in [m]$ and parse each revealed value e_j in its additive form as $e_j = e_{j,0} + e_{j,1} \cdot \xi + \cdots + e_{j,d-1} \cdot \xi^{d-1}$
5. For $j \in [m]$, $\ell \in [d]$, let $c_{j,\ell}$ be the smallest square root modulo 2^{k+2} of $e_{j,\ell}$ and let $c_{j,\ell}^{-1}$ be its inverse.
6. Each party computes $\langle d_{j,\ell}\rangle_t^{\tilde{R}} = c_{j,\ell}^{-1} \cdot \langle a_{j,\ell}\rangle_t^{\tilde{R}} + 1$.
7. Parties then divides their shares of $d_{j,\ell}$ by 2. This division is well-defined, and we denote the result of this operation $\langle \tilde{b}_{j,\ell}\rangle_t^{\tilde{R}}$.
8. Parties output $\langle b_{j,\ell}\rangle_t^R = \pi_k(\langle \tilde{b}_{j,\ell}\rangle_t^{\tilde{R}})$.

Proposition 2. *Π_{FLEXbits} in Protocol 5 securely produces $m \cdot d$ shares of random bits for the* FLEX *encoding.*

Proof. Our proof, as our protocol, is very similar to that of [11, Proposition IV.1]. We limit our discussion to correctness, as privacy follows from the properties of the secret sharing scheme. Observe that the coefficients $e_{j,\ell} \in \mathbb{Z}_{2^{k+2}}$ of e_j's additive representation are all odd integers, since $a_{j,\ell} = 2 \cdot u_{j,\ell} + 1$. Hence, $c_{j,\ell}$ is also odd, which implies the existence of $c_{j,\ell}^{-1}$. Now, as both $c_{j,\ell}^{-1}$ and $a_{j,\ell}$ are square roots of $e_{j,\ell}$, we have that:

$$(c_{j,\ell}^{-1} \cdot a_{j,\ell})^2 \equiv c_{j,\ell}^{-2} \cdot a_{j,\ell}^2 \equiv e_{j,\ell}^{-1} \cdot e_{j,\ell} \equiv 1 \mod 2^{k+2}$$

Thus, by Lemma 6, $c_{j,\ell}^{-1} \cdot a_{j,\ell} \equiv \pm 1 \mod 2^{k+1}$. Moreover, 1 and -1 are as likely in this last congruence, since $a_{j,\ell}$ is guaranteed to be a uniformly random odd value (because $u_{j,\ell}$ is uniformly random) and $c_{j,\ell}^{-1}$ is chosen in a unique, pre-established way. Hence, $d_{j,\ell} = c_{j,\ell}^{-1} \cdot a_{j,\ell} + 1$ is congruent to a uniformly random value among $\{0, 2\}$ modulo 2^{k+1}.

Finally, we need to argue about the "division by two" of $d_{j,\ell}$, which results in a $\tilde{b}_{j,\ell}$ that is congruent (with the same probability) to either 0 or 1 modulo 2^k. We perform such "division" by looking at the shares of $\langle d_{j,\ell}\rangle^{\tilde{R}}$ as elements of $\mathbb{Z}$, so this operation is well-defined as long as each share of $d_{j,\ell}$ is an even number. Notice that this is the case, since:

$$\langle d_{j,\ell}\rangle_t^{\tilde{R}} = c_{j,\ell}^{-1} \cdot (2 \cdot \langle u_{j,\ell}\rangle_t^{\tilde{R}} + 1) + 1 = 2 \cdot c_{j,\ell}^{-1} \cdot \langle u_{j,\ell}\rangle_t^{\tilde{R}} + (1 + c_{j,\ell}^{-1})$$

As $c_{j,\ell}^{-1}$ is invertible in $\mathbb{Z}_{2^{k+2}}$, it is odd. Hence, an even public constant $(1 + c_{j,\ell}^{-1})$ is added to $2 \cdot c_{j,\ell}^{-1} \cdot \langle u_{j,\ell}\rangle_t^{\tilde{R}}$. As the shares of the latter value are clearly even (since they are the result of multiplying by an even public constant), we can conclude that all the shares of $\langle d_{j,\ell}\rangle_t^{\tilde{R}}$ are even. Finally, observe that if we re-interpret the new divided shares of $d_{j,\ell}$ as elements of $\mathbb{Z}_{2^{k+1}}$, it could be that their reconstruction is not an element among $\{0, 1\}$, but rather among $\{0, 1, 2^k, 2^k+1\}$. Hence, we need to compute $\langle \pi_k(\tilde{b}_{j,\ell})\rangle_t^R$, which we can just do by computing $\pi_k(\langle \tilde{b}_{j,\ell}\rangle^{\tilde{R}})$ as shown in Proposition 1. □

Analysis. We now analyze the FLEX encoding. This works over naïve shares (i.e. by embedding $\mathbb{Z}_{2^k}$ into $GR(2^k, d)$, as in [1]) and outputs naïve shares. Online, it can be used to compute any depth 1 circuit with any number of inputs and d outputs at the cost of opening a single element in R.

Double shares for the FLEX encoding can be precomputed in batches of $d\cdot(n-t)$ with $n \cdot d$ calls to $\Pi_{\mathsf{Share}}(\cdot, t)$ and n calls to $\Pi_{\mathsf{Share}}(\cdot, 2t)$. Checking these double shares requires $(\lambda + \lambda)/(n-t)$ invocations of Π_{rPub}. Notice the communication cost of the **Batch Check** step of Π_{FLEXds} is independent of the number of shares being checked as long as $m \cdot (n-t) > \lambda$, where m is the number of batches of shares generated. The amortized communication cost is therefore approximately $\frac{3(d+1)}{2}$ calls to Π_{Share} per double-share.

Π_{FLEXds} can be adapted to generate shares of random $\mathbb{Z}_{2^k}$ elements by skipping steps related to degree-$2t$ shares. Doing so yields batches of $d\cdot(n-t)$ random shares with d calls to Π_{Share}, and only requires $\lambda/(n-t)$ calls to Π_{rPub} for the **Batch Check**. Producing shares of ℓ random bits in Π_{FLEXbits} then only requires generating shares of ℓ random $\mathbb{Z}_{2^{k+2}}$ elements and $\ell/(d\cdot(n-t))$ calls to Π_{rPub}.

4.3 InnerProd Encodings

Given sharings of the inputs, inner products can be computed with a single opening in our previous FLEX encoding, which incurs very little communication. Nevertheless, there are two major problems with such an approach: First, one still needs to individually share each of the elements in the input vectors. Second, the amount of multiplications to be computed is the same as in the naïve case.

In order to overcome such limitations, we introduce our InnerProd encoding technique. Let δ be the encoding capacity of the encoding and consider the following two Galois Ring elements $a, b \in R$ given in their additive representation:

$$\begin{aligned} a &= a_0 + a_1 \cdot \xi + \cdots + a_{\delta-1} \cdot \xi^{\delta-1}, \\ b &= b_{\delta-1} \cdot \xi^{\delta} + b_{\delta-2} \cdot \xi^{\delta+1} + \cdots + b_0 \cdot \xi^{2\delta-1}. \end{aligned} \tag{6}$$

Our goal is that, by computing $c = a \cdot b$, one can retrieve the value $\sum_{i=0}^{\delta-1} a_i \cdot b_i$ as the coefficient associated to $\xi^{2\delta-1}$ in c. In order to achieve this, we need to impose two restrictions on δ. Let $h(X)$ be the degree-d polynomial used to represent the Galois Ring, i.e. $R = \mathbb{Z}_{2^k}[X]/(h(X))$. Define $\tilde{d}$ to be the degree of the second-highest monomial in $h(X)$. The following bounds on δ need to be imposed:

1. $\delta < (d+1)/2$. This is to ensure that b can be defined in Eq. (6).
2. $\delta < d - \tilde{d} + 1$. This is in order to avoid "wrap-around" terms to be added to the coefficient associated to $\xi^{2\delta-1}$ in c.

More precisely, we define encodings $\mathsf{E}^{inn}_{in,L}, \mathsf{E}^{inn}_{in,R}, \mathsf{E}^{inn}_{out}$ of $\mathbf{a}, \mathbf{b} \in (\mathbb{Z}_{2^k})^\delta, c \in \mathbb{Z}_{2^k}$ as follows:

$$\mathsf{E}^{inn}_{in,L}(\boldsymbol{a}) = a_0 + a_1 \cdot \xi + \cdots + a_{\delta-1} \cdot \xi^{\delta-1},$$
$$\mathsf{E}^{inn}_{in,R}(\boldsymbol{b}) = b_{\delta-1} \cdot \xi^{\delta} + b_{\delta-2} \cdot \xi^{\delta+1} + \cdots + b_0 \cdot \xi^{2\delta-1},$$
$$\mathsf{E}^{inn}_{out}(c) = c \cdot \xi^{2\delta-1} + \sum_{\ell \in [d], \ell \neq 2\delta-1} r_\ell \cdot \xi^\ell, \quad r_\ell \leftarrow \mathbb{Z}_{2^k}.$$

Double Shares from InnerProd to FLEX ($\Pi_{\mathsf{InnerProd\text{-}to\text{-}FLEXds}}$). The results of the InnerProd encoding can be easily converted into inputs of the FLEX encoding by producing double shares. For a randomly sampled $r \leftarrow GR(2^k, d)$, $r = \sum_{i=0}^{d-1} r_i \cdot \xi^i$, these are of the form $\langle r \rangle_{2t}, \langle r_{2\delta-1} \rangle_t$ or, what is the same, $\langle \mathsf{E}^{inn}_{out}(r_{2\delta-1}) \rangle_{2t}, \langle r_{2\delta-1} \rangle_t$. Thus, these double shares can be produced exactly as in Π_{FLEXds} (Protocol 4) by ignoring $d-1$ of the degree-t shares.

Generation of Random Bits for InnerProd Encoding. Random bits can be generated in exactly the same way as in the previous encoding (see Π_{FLEXbits} Protocol 5). Nevertheless, those bits are not quite enough for values in the InnerProd encoding. In particular, they cannot be used as-is for masking a value encoded according to E^{inn}_{out}. Let $c = \mathsf{E}^{inn}_{in,L}(\boldsymbol{a}) \cdot \mathsf{E}^{inn}_{in,R}(\boldsymbol{b})$. If we write $c = \sum_{i=0}^{d-1} c_i \cdot \xi^i$, we have that $c_{2\delta-1}$ has the result of the inner product between $\boldsymbol{a}$ and $\boldsymbol{b}$, but the other components of c leak further information on the input vectors. Hence, when reconstructing c, we will need a single random mask r satisfying that $r = \sum_{\ell \in [d], \ell \neq 2\delta-1} r_\ell \cdot \xi^\ell$, i.e. ensuring that $r_{2\delta-1} = 0$. Such values can be produced using the same ideas as in Π_{FLEXds} or, more efficiently as we only need to produce one such mask for each bit decomposition in the protocol, by adapting the RandEl protocol of [1].

Analysis. As input, InnerProd encoding takes two sharings encoded as described above. The output is an element of $R \cong \mathbb{Z}^d_{2^k}$ with the inner product as its $(2\delta-1)$'th coefficient. The online cost is a single opening in R, and the offline cost is the same as for FLEX encoding (since double-shares are produced with the same protocol). It is worth remarking here that one can compute inner products with naïve shares as well, at the same online communication cost. I.e., given naïve sharings $\langle a_0 \rangle, \ldots, \langle a_{k-1} \rangle$ and $\langle b_0 \rangle, \ldots, \langle b_{k-1} \rangle$ for some k, the inner product can be computed as $\langle c \rangle = \sum_{i=0}^{k-1} \langle a_i \rangle \langle b_i \rangle$, because addition does not increase the degree of a share. However, InnerProd encoding allows us to decrease local computation (in the online phase) by around a factor of $d/2$, which is significant as operations in R are non-trivial.

4.4 SIMD Encodings

Our final encoding allows us to compute multiple circuits in parallel. Hence, we dub it SIMD, i.e., *Single Instruction Multiple Data.* Reverse Multiplication Friendly Embeddings (RMFEs), as introduced in [8,10], can also be seen as a SIMD encoding. On a technical level, the combinatorial problem behind our SIMD construction has been previously applied in the context of packing for homomorphic encryption [16] and leakage-resilient MPC [7].

Let δ denote the encoding capacity, and let $I = \{i_0, \ldots, i_{\delta-1}\}$ and $J = \{j_0, \ldots, j_{\delta-1}\}$ be index sets. The sets I, J will describe in which positions of an element in R we will "store" encoded $\mathbb{Z}_{2^k}$ elements. More precisely, we define two $\mathbb{Z}_{2^k}$-linear encodings $\mathsf{E}^{\mathsf{SIMD}}_{in}$, $\mathsf{E}^{\mathsf{SIMD}}_{out}$ of $\mathbf{a} \in (\mathbb{Z}_{2^k})^\delta$ as follows:

$$\mathsf{E}^{\mathsf{SIMD}}_{in}(\mathbf{a}) = a_0 \cdot \xi^{i_0} + a_1 \cdot \xi^{i_1} + \cdots + a_{\delta-1} \cdot \xi^{i_{\delta-1}},$$

$$\mathsf{E}^{\mathsf{SIMD}}_{out}(\mathbf{a}) = \sum_{k=0}^{\delta-1} a_k \cdot \xi^{j_k} + \sum_{\ell \in [d] \setminus J} r_\ell \cdot \xi^\ell, \quad r_\ell \leftarrow \mathbb{Z}_{2^k}$$

Regardless of how we choose I and J, we have that adding $\mathsf{E}^{\mathsf{SIMD}}_{in}$-encodings (resp. $\mathsf{E}^{\mathsf{SIMD}}_{out}$-encodings) results in an $\mathsf{E}^{\mathsf{SIMD}}_{in}$-encoding (rep. $\mathsf{E}^{\mathsf{SIMD}}_{out}$-encodings). Nevertheless, we further ask our encodings to satisfy the relation given by Eq. (2). In particular, we want following equality to hold:

$$\mathsf{E}^{\mathsf{SIMD}}_{in}(\mathbf{a}) \cdot \mathsf{E}^{\mathsf{SIMD}}_{in}(\mathbf{b}) + \mathsf{E}^{\mathsf{SIMD}}_{out}(\mathbf{c}) = \mathsf{E}^{\mathsf{SIMD}}_{out}(\mathbf{a} * \mathbf{b} + \mathbf{c}) \tag{7}$$

where $*$ denotes the component-wise product. In order to achieve this, we need to introduce the following restrictions to the way the index sets are chosen.

1. $j_\ell = 2 \cdot i_\ell$. This implies that the product $a_\ell b_\ell$ ends up in the degree j_ℓ monomial.
2. For all $i_\ell \in I$ we require that $i_\ell < d/2$, so that no wrap-around happens during reduction in R.
3. For all $i_\ell, i_\iota \in I$ that are pairwise different, then $i_\ell + i_\iota \notin J$. This implies that cross products between a_ℓ and b_ι (and a_ι and b_δ) do not end up on a monomial of J.

Under these restrictions, we obtain the following when multiplying $\mathsf{E}^{\mathsf{SIMD}}_{in}(\boldsymbol{a})$ and $\mathsf{E}^{\mathsf{SIMD}}_{in}(\boldsymbol{b})$:

$$\begin{aligned}\mathsf{E}^{\mathsf{SIMD}}_{in}(\boldsymbol{a}) \cdot \mathsf{E}^{\mathsf{SIMD}}_{in}(\boldsymbol{b}) &= (a_0 \cdot \xi^{i_0} + \cdots + a_{\delta-1} \cdot \xi^{i_{\delta-1}}) \cdot (b_0 \cdot \xi^{i_0} + \cdots + b_{\delta-1} \cdot \xi^{i_{\delta-1}}) \\ &= \sum_{\ell \in [\delta]} \left(a_\ell b_\ell \cdot \xi^{j_\ell} + \sum_{\iota \in ([\delta] \setminus \{\ell\})} (a_\ell b_\iota + a_\iota b_\ell) \cdot \xi^{i_\ell + i_\iota} \right).\end{aligned}$$

Notice that this is different from $\mathsf{E}^{\mathsf{SIMD}}_{out}(\mathbf{a} * \mathbf{b})$, as the monomials of degree $j \notin J$ have coefficients which have not been sampled independently and uniformly at random from $\mathbb{Z}_{2^k}$. Yet, we have that Eq. (7) holds.

Turning our attention to δ, asymptotically we have $\delta \sim d^{0.6}$, as pointed out by [16]. However, for small values of d this allows for relatively large values of δ. Taking into account that in Shamir secret sharing over Galois Rings (or small finite fields) we would have that $d = O(\log n)$, we get reasonable values for δ despite the poor asymptotic. Table 2 provides some examples of the index sets defining $\mathsf{E}^{\mathsf{SIMD}}_{in}$ and $\mathsf{E}^{\mathsf{SIMD}}_{out}$ for different values of d.

Table 2. Examples of I and J for different values of d.

d	δ	I	J
3–6	2	$\{0, 1\}$	$\{0, 2\}$
7–8	3	$\{0, 1, 3\}$	$\{0, 2, 6\}$
9–16	4	$\{0, 1, 3, 4\}$	$\{0, 2, 6, 8\}$
17	5	$\{0, 1, 3, 7, 8\}$	$\{0, 2, 6, 14, 16\}$

Double Share Generation. Protocol 6 shows how to generate double-shares for SIMD encoding. As in our previous protocols, this is a two-step process, where we first generate shares in batches and then we check for correctness all of them at once.

Protocol 6. Π_{SIMDds} — Double-sharings for SIMD encoding.

Let $M \in R^{(n-t)\times n}$ be a Hyper-Invertible matrix and δ the packing capability of R. Let $\Psi_M : (N^d)^n \to (N^d)^{n-t}$ be as defined in Section 4.1 (Equation (5)).

Generate. Parties produce a batch of $d \cdot (n-t)$ random double-shares as follows:

1. For $\ell \in [d]$, each party P_i samples $\mathbf{s}^i_\ell \leftarrow (\mathbb{Z}_{2^k})^\delta$ and calls both $\Pi_{\mathsf{Share}}(\mathsf{E}_{in}(\mathbf{s}^i_\ell), t)$ and $\Pi_{\mathsf{Share}}(\mathsf{E}_{out}(\mathbf{s}^i_\ell), 2t)$.
2. Parties apply Ψ_M to their degree-t and degree-$2t$ shares in the same way:

$$(\langle \mathsf{E}_{in}(\mathbf{r}^1_0)\rangle, \ldots, \langle \mathsf{E}_{in}(\mathbf{r}^1_{d-1})\rangle; \ldots; \langle \mathsf{E}_{in}(\mathbf{r}^{n-t}_0)\rangle, \ldots, \langle \mathsf{E}_{in}(\mathbf{r}^{n-t}_{d-1})\rangle)$$
$$= \Psi_M\left(\langle \mathsf{E}_{in}(\mathbf{s}^1_0)\rangle, \ldots, \langle \mathsf{E}_{in}(\mathbf{s}^1_{d-1})\rangle; \ldots; \langle \mathsf{E}_{in}(\mathbf{s}^n_0)\rangle, \ldots, \langle \mathsf{E}_{in}(\mathbf{s}^n_{d-1})\rangle\right)$$

$$(\langle \mathsf{E}_{out}(\mathbf{r}^1_0)\rangle, \ldots, \langle \mathsf{E}_{out}(\mathbf{r}^1_{d-1})\rangle; \ldots; \langle \mathsf{E}_{out}(\mathbf{r}^{n-t}_0)\rangle, \ldots, \langle \mathsf{E}_{out}(\mathbf{r}^{n-t}_{d-1})\rangle)$$
$$= \Psi_M\left(\langle \mathsf{E}_{out}(\mathbf{s}^1_0)\rangle, \ldots, \langle \mathsf{E}_{out}(\mathbf{s}^1_{d-1})\rangle; \ldots; \langle \mathsf{E}_{out}(\mathbf{s}^n_0)\rangle, \ldots, \langle \mathsf{E}_{out}(\mathbf{s}^n_{d-1})\rangle\right)$$

Batch Check. Let m be the number of batches produced in the previous step. We need to check that the degree t and degree $2t$ shares are using their respective encodings (I and J). We also verify that both shares encode the same vector $\boldsymbol{r}$. Throughout, $j \in [m]$ identifies each batch.

1. For each $\langle \mathsf{E}_{in}(\mathbf{r}^i_{j,\ell})\rangle$, $\langle \mathsf{E}_{out}(\mathbf{r}^i_{j,\ell})\rangle$ and $\tau \in [\lambda]$, parties generate a random bit $\chi^{i,\tau}_{j,\ell} \leftarrow \mathcal{F}_{\mathsf{rand}}(\{0, 1\})$.

2. For $\tau \in [\lambda]$, parties compute:

$$\langle x_\tau \rangle_t = \sum_{j=0}^{m-1} \sum_{i=1}^{n-t} \sum_{\ell=0}^{d-1} \chi_{j,\ell}^{i,\tau} \cdot \langle \mathsf{E}_{in}(\mathbf{r}_{j,\ell}^i) \rangle_t$$

$$\langle y_\tau \rangle_{2t} = \sum_{j=0}^{m-1} \sum_{i=1}^{n-t} \sum_{\ell=0}^{d-1} \chi_{j,\ell}^{i,\tau} \cdot \langle \mathsf{E}_{out}(\mathbf{r}_{j,\ell}^i) \rangle_{2t}$$

and call Π_{rPub} to reconstruct both x_τ, y_τ.
3. If for any $\tau \in [\lambda]$ parties observe either that
   - x_τ is not a I-encoding (i.e. $x_\tau \notin Im(\mathsf{E}_{in})$), or
   - $\mathsf{E}_{in}^{-1}(x_\tau) \neq \mathsf{E}_{out}^{-1}(y_\tau)$

   then they abort.
4. For $\tau \in [\lambda]$, let $(i_\tau, j_\tau, \ell_\tau) \in \{[m] \times [1, n-t] \times [d]\}$ be a triplet of indices such that $\chi_{j_\tau,\ell_\tau}^{i_\tau,\tau} = 1$. Define $D = \{(i_\tau, j_\tau, \ell_\tau) \mid \tau \in [\lambda]\}$.

Output. For $(i, j, \ell) \in \{[m] \times [1, n-t] \times [d]\} \setminus D$, where D is defined on Step 4 of Batch Check, output the double sharings $(\langle \mathsf{E}_{in}(\mathbf{r}_{j,\ell}^i) \rangle_t, \langle \mathsf{E}_{out}(\mathbf{r}_{j,\ell}^i) \rangle_{2t})$.

Theorem 2. *Π_{SIMDds} in Protocol 6 securely produces $m \cdot (n-t) \cdot d - \lambda$ valid double-sharings for the* SIMD *encoding.*

Proof. Let $\mathbb{A} \subset [1, n]$ denote the indices of the parties corrupted by $\mathcal{A}$ and assume a non-aborting execution Π_{SIMDds}. We do not care about the abort scenario, as in such case all double-shares are discarded and, furthermore, no private MPC inputs have been yet provided.

Correctness. In an honest protocol execution, it follows from the discussion in Sect. 4.1 that Π_{SIMDds} produces double-shares of the right form. When $\mathcal{A}$ deviates from the protocol, we need to look at what is implied by the non-aborting execution of **Batch Check**.

Denote by $\langle r_{j,\ell}^i \rangle$ (resp. $\langle \tilde{r}_{j,\ell}^i \rangle$) the output from **Generate** that in a fully honest execution would be $\langle \mathsf{E}_{in}(\boldsymbol{r}_{j,\ell}) \rangle_t$ (resp. $\langle \mathsf{E}_{out}(\boldsymbol{r}_{j,\ell}) \rangle_{2t}$). **Batch Check** has two goals. The first one is ensuring that $\langle r_{j,\ell}^i \rangle$ (resp. $\langle \tilde{r}_{j,\ell}^i \rangle$) is actually an E_{in}-encoding (resp. E_{out}-encoding). In particular, if we see each $r_{j,\ell}^i \in R$ in its unique additive representation $r_{j,\ell}^i = \sum_{\iota=0}^{d-1} r_{j,\ell,\iota}^i \cdot \xi^\iota$ (where $r_{j,\ell,\iota}^i \in \mathbb{Z}_{2^k}$), we want to prove that $\forall \iota \notin I$, $r_{j,\ell,\iota}^i = 0$. Applying the same reasoning as in the proof of the $\mathbb{Z}_{2^k}$**-outputs** step of Π_{FLEXds} (see Theorem 1), we conclude from the Schwartz-Zippel Lemma that this happens with probability at most $(d - |I|) \cdot 2^{-\lambda}$.

Express $\tilde{r}_{j,\ell}^i, x_\tau, y_\tau$ in their unique additive representations, i.e. $\tilde{r}_{j,\ell}^i = \sum_{\iota=0}^{d-1} \tilde{r}_{j,\ell,\iota}^i \cdot \xi^\iota$ and similarly for the others. The second goal of **Batch Check** is proving that $\forall \iota \in I$, $r_{j,\ell,\iota}^i = \tilde{r}_{j,\ell,2\iota}^i$. Let $M = m \cdot (n-t) \cdot d$. We can look at $f_{\tau,\iota} = x_{\tau,\iota}^i - y_{\tau,2\iota}^i$ as an M-variate linear polynomial, where the coefficients are

$r^i_{j,\ell,\iota} - \tilde{r}^i_{j,\ell,2\iota}$ and the variables are evaluated at $\chi^{i,\tau}_{j,\ell} \in \{0,1\}$. Once again, by the Schwartz-Zippel Lemma, we have that if $f_{\tau,\iota}$ is not identically equal to zero, then $\Pr_{\chi^\tau \leftarrow A^M}[f_{\tau,\iota}(\chi^\tau) = 0] \leq 1/2$. Hence, $\forall \iota \in I$, if we let $\chi = (\chi^1, \ldots, \chi^\lambda)$, then $\Pr_{\chi \leftarrow \{0,1\}^{M \cdot \lambda}}[f_{0,\iota} = \ldots = f_{\lambda,\iota} = 0] \leq 2^{-\lambda}$. Applying a union bound we can conclude that, if the test passes, it is at most with probability $|I| \cdot 2^{-\lambda}$ that we do not have the same $\boldsymbol{r}^i_{j,\ell}$ on the E_{in} and the E_{out} encodings.

Privacy. Let's first look at the **Generate** step. For the degree-t and the degree-$2t$ shares, respectively, the Adversary knows at most t blocks of inputs, namely $\{\langle \mathsf{E}_{in}(\boldsymbol{s}^i_0)\rangle_t, \ldots, \langle \mathsf{E}_{in}(\boldsymbol{s}^i_{d-1})\rangle_t\}_{i \in \mathbb{A}}$ and $\{\langle \mathsf{E}_{out}(\boldsymbol{s}^i_0)\rangle_{2t}, \ldots, \langle \mathsf{E}_{out}(\boldsymbol{s}^i_{d-1})\rangle_{2t}\}_{i \in \mathbb{A}}$. By Lemma 7, we know that the values $\{\langle \mathsf{E}_{in}(\boldsymbol{r}^i_\ell)\rangle_t, \langle \mathsf{E}_{out}(\boldsymbol{r}^i_\ell)\rangle_{2t}\}_{i \in [1,n], \ell \in [d]}$ are secret and i.i.d. uniformly random from $\mathcal{A}$'s perspective.

Finally, the outputs of **Batch Check** do not leak any information on the output values. This follows from the fact that each revealed (x_τ, y_τ) is one-time padded by the discarded values indexed by the set $D = \{(i_\tau, j_\tau) \mid \tau \in [\lambda]\}$. $\square$

Random Bit Generation for SIMD. This section we give a way for producing shares of random bits for SIMD, but first we introduce an intermediate protocol for producing shares of $\mathsf{E}^{\mathsf{SIMD}}_{out}(\mathbf{a})$, where $\mathbf{a} \in (\mathbb{Z}_{2^k})^\delta$ is some fixed, known vector. This is given in Protocol 7 as Π_{SIMDOut}.

At a high level, Π_{SIMDOut} works by having parties generate zero shares and offsetting these zero shares by $\boldsymbol{a}$. Producing shares of zero is done in the same manner as producing random $\mathsf{E}^{\mathsf{SIMD}}_{out}$ shares in Π_{SIMDds} by having parties instead use $\mathbf{s} = \mathbf{0}$. Batch checking also works in the same way as in Π_{SIMDds}, with parties checking $y_\tau = \mathsf{E}^{\mathsf{SIMD}}_{out}(\mathbf{0})$. Proof of Proposition 3 follows the proof of Theorem 2.

Protocol 7. Π_{SIMDOut} — Producing $\langle \mathsf{E}_{out}(\boldsymbol{a})\rangle$ for a fixed $\boldsymbol{a}$.

Let $M \in R^{(n-t) \times n}$ a Hyper-Invertible matrix and let $\Psi_M : (N^d)^n \to (N^d)^{n-t}$ be as defined in Section 4.1 and depicted in Equation (5). Let δ the packing capability of R. Denote by $\mathbf{0}$ the all-zero vector of length δ and parse the input $\boldsymbol{a} \in \mathbb{Z}^\delta_{2^k}$ as $\boldsymbol{a} = (a_0, \ldots, a_{\delta-1})$. Recall that E_{out} is defined by $J = \{j_0, \ldots, j_{\delta-1}\}$.

Generate. Parties produce a batch of $d \cdot (n-t)$ random E_{out}-sharings of zero as follows:

1. For $\ell \in [d]$, each P_i samples $z^i_\ell = \mathsf{E}_{out}(\mathbf{0})$ and calls $\Pi_{\mathsf{Share}}(z^i_\ell, t)$.
2. Parties apply Ψ_M to their shares in the following way:

$$(\langle Z^1_0\rangle, \ldots, \langle Z^1_{d-1}\rangle, \ldots, \langle Z^{n-t}_0\rangle, \ldots, \langle Z^{n-t}_{d-1}\rangle) = \Psi_M\left(\langle z^1_0\rangle, \ldots, \langle z^1_{d-1}\rangle, \ldots, \langle z^n_0\rangle, \ldots, \langle z^n_{d-1}\rangle\right)$$

Batch Check. Let m be the number of batches produced in the previous step. For $j \in [m], \ell \in [d]$ and $i \in [1, n-t]$, we need to verify that $\langle Z^i_{j,\ell}\rangle = \mathsf{E}_{out}(\mathbf{0})$.

1. For each $\langle Z^i_{j,\ell}\rangle$ and $\tau \in [\lambda]$, parties sample $\chi^{i,\tau}_{j,\ell} \leftarrow \mathcal{F}_{\mathsf{rand}}(\{0,1\})$.
2. For $\tau \in [\lambda]$, parties compute:
$$\langle x_\tau\rangle = \sum_{j=0}^{m-1}\sum_{i=1}^{n-t}\sum_{\ell=0}^{d-1} \chi^{i,\tau}_{j,\ell} \cdot \langle Z^i_{j,\ell}\rangle$$
and call Π_{rPub} to reconstruct x_τ.
3. If for any $\tau \in [\lambda]$ parties observe that $\mathsf{E}^{-1}_{out}(x_\tau) \neq \mathbf{0}$, they abort.
4. For $\tau \in [\lambda]$, let $(i_\tau, j_\tau, \ell_\tau) \in \{[m] \times [1, n-t] \times [d]\}$ be a triplet of indices such that $\chi^{i_\tau,\tau}_{j_\tau,\ell_\tau} = 1$. Define $D = \{(i_\tau, j_\tau, \ell_\tau) \mid \tau \in [\lambda]\}$.

Output. Let $A = \sum_{k=0}^{\delta-1} a_k \cdot X^{j_k}$. For $(i, j, \ell) \in \{[m] \times [1, n-t] \times [d]\} \setminus D$, where D is defined on Step 4 of Batch Check, output the $m \cdot (n-t) \cdot d - \lambda$ different sharings of $\boldsymbol{a}$ as $\langle \mathsf{E}_{out}(\boldsymbol{a})\rangle = \langle Z^i_{j,\ell}\rangle + A$.

Proposition 3. *Π_{SIMDOut} in Protocol 7 securely produces a minimum of $m \cdot (n-t) \cdot d - \delta$ shares of a public value for the* SIMD *encoding.*

Π_{SIMDbits} in Protocol 8 gives a way of generating shares of the form $\langle \mathsf{E}^{\mathsf{SIMD}}_{out}(\mathbf{b})\rangle$, where $\mathbf{b} \leftarrow \{0,1\}^\delta$. Similar to Π_{FLEXbits}, this follows the outline of the RandBit protocol of [11]. The main differences are in Steps 3 and 6 where add $\mathsf{E}^{\mathsf{SIMD}}_{out}$ shares of some publicly know values, which we produce using Π_{SIMDOut}. The reason for this is that elements in $\mathsf{E}^{\mathsf{SIMD}}_{out}$ have uniformly random coefficients in the positions $j \notin J$. As the multiplication of two $\mathsf{E}^{\mathsf{SIMD}}_{in}$ values introduces the result of some cross-products of the $\mathbb{Z}_{2^k}$ encoded values in such positions, we need to add these secret sharings of $\mathsf{E}^{\mathsf{SIMD}}_{out}(\mathbf{0})$ and $\mathsf{E}^{\mathsf{SIMD}}_{out}(\mathbf{1})$ as a masking mechanism. By Eq. (7), we obtain the displayed results.

Protocol 8. Π_{SIMDbits} — Random bits for SIMD encoding.

Let $\tilde{R} = GR(2^{k+2}, d)$, $R = GR(2^k, d)$, and δ the packing capability of R. Denote $\mathbf{0}$ and $\mathbf{1}$ be the all-zero and all-one vectors of length δ, respectively. For $j \in [m]$, parties produce $\langle \mathsf{E}_{out}(\boldsymbol{b}_j)\rangle_t$, where $\boldsymbol{b}_j \leftarrow \{0,1\}^\delta$ as follows:

1. For $j \in [m]$ parties produce shares $\langle \mathsf{E}_{in}(\mathbf{u}_j)\rangle^{\tilde{R}}_t$ of secret, random $\mathbf{u}_j = (u_{j,0}, \ldots, u_{j,\delta-1}) \in (\mathbb{Z}_{2^{k+2}})^\delta$. This can be done as in Π_{SIMDds} (Protocol 6) by skipping the generation of E_{out} values there and hence the computation of y_τ.
2. Compute $\langle \mathsf{E}_{in}(\mathbf{a}_j)\rangle^{\tilde{R}}_t = 2 \cdot \langle \mathsf{E}_{in}(\mathbf{u}_j)\rangle^{\tilde{R}}_t + \mathsf{E}_{in}(\mathbf{1})$.
3. Compute $\langle \mathsf{E}_{out}(\mathbf{a}^2_j)\rangle^{\tilde{R}}_{2t} = \langle \mathsf{E}_{in}(\mathbf{a}_j)\rangle^{\tilde{R}}_t \cdot \langle \mathsf{E}_{in}(\mathbf{a}_j)\rangle^{\tilde{R}}_t + \langle \mathsf{E}_{out}(\mathbf{0})\rangle^{\tilde{R}}_t$ where $\langle \mathsf{E}_{out}(\mathbf{0})\rangle^{\tilde{R}}_t$ is produced using Protocol 7.
4. Call Π_{rPub} to reconstruct $\langle \mathsf{E}_{out}(\mathbf{a}^2_j)\rangle^{\tilde{R}}_{2t}$ for all $j \in [m]$ and parse the revealed $\mathbf{a}^2_j$ as a vector $(a^2_{j,0}, \ldots, a^2_{j,\delta-1}) \in (\mathbb{Z}_{2^{k+2}})^\delta$.

5. For $\ell \in [\delta]$, let $c_{j,\ell}$ be the smallest root modulo 2^{k+2} of $a_{j,\ell}^2$ and let $c_{j,\ell}^{-1}$ be its inverse. Write $\mathbf{c}_j^{-1} = (c_{j,0}^{-1}, \ldots, c_{j,\delta-1}^{-1})$.
6. Compute $\langle \mathsf{E}_{out}(\mathbf{d}_j) \rangle_t^{\tilde{R}} = \mathsf{E}_{in}(\mathbf{c}_j^{-1}) \cdot \langle \mathsf{E}_{in}(\mathbf{a}_j) \rangle_t^{\tilde{R}} + \langle \mathsf{E}_{out}(\mathbf{1}) \rangle_t^{\tilde{R}}$, where $\langle \mathsf{E}_{out}(\mathbf{1}) \rangle_t^{\tilde{R}}$ is produced using Protocol 7.
7. Finally, each party divides their share of $\langle \mathsf{E}_{out}(\mathbf{d}_j) \rangle_t^{\tilde{R}}$ by 2. We denote the result of this operation $\langle \mathsf{E}_{out}(\boldsymbol{b}_j) \rangle_t^{R}$, which is our final output.

Proposition 4. *Π_{SIMDbits} in Protocol 8 securely produces shares of $m \cdot \delta$ random bits for the* SIMD *encoding, where δ is the SIMD packing capacity of $R = GR(2^k, d)$.*

Analysis. We now discuss the SIMD encoding. This encoding can compute in parallel $\delta \approx d/4 + 1$ circuits that each have one multiplication and one output.

Batches of $d \cdot (n-t)$ double shares for SIMD encoding can be generated in the offline phase with $2 \cdot d \cdot n$ calls to Π_{Share}. Similar to the FLEX **Batch Check**, the communication cost of the **Batch Check** of SIMD double shares is independent of the number of batches produced. Checking m batches of double shares can be done with $2 \cdot \lambda/(n-t)$ calls to Π_{rPub}.

Producing $d \cdot (n-t)$ shares of encodings (both fixed values or random) takes d calls to Π_{Share}. The cost of the batch check in either of these cases takes $\lambda/(n-t)$ calls to Π_{rPub}. Producing m random bits takes $m/(n-t)$ calls to Π_{Share}, $(\lambda + m)/(n-t)$ calls to Π_{rPub}, and $2 \cdot m$ calls to Π_{SIMDout}.

5 Efficiency Analysis

We implemented Π_{FLEXds} and Π_{SIMDds} and compared them with a double-share generation protocol extracted from [1, Figure 2] as a baseline.[3] We provide various microbenchmarks for different stages of these protocols, as well as our InnerProd encoding scheme. For each of these protocols, we are mainly interested in their throughput, but we also compare our approach with that of [1] for a specific circuit in Sect. 5.5.

5.1 Experiment Setup

We set $k = 64$ and $d = 4$. With $k = 64$, all operations in $\mathbb{Z}_{2^k}$ can take place on `uint64_t` types, and setting $d = 4$ lets us support up to 15 parties. Our Galois Ring is therefore $GR(2^{64}, 4) = \mathbb{Z}_{2^{64}}[X]/(h(X))$ where $h(X) = X^4 + X + 1$. Our

[3] Although the protocol in [1] is used to generate sharings of random elements, it is trivial to modify it to generate double-shares to use for multiplication: The same random element is shared twice with degree t and $2t$, and when the check is performed we additionally check that the opened shares are equal.

implementation was written in C++ and the code can be found at https://github.com/eysalee/cafe. Openmp was used in various places to speed up local computation.

Experiments were run on `c5.9xlarge` machines on a local network. Each machine is equipped with 36 cores, 76 gb of memory, and are connected with a 10 Gpbs network. The average rtt between machines is 0.29 ms.

Everlasting/Computational Security. Our experiments constitute a prototype and hence are not a statistically secure implementation of our protocols. If we ignore the (obvious) fact that we do not use pure randomness in Π_{Share}, we actually implement an *everlasting* version of our protocols [19]. In more detail, our protocols are secure against adversaries that are computationally unlimited *after* the protocol execution. This stems from the fact that we implement $\mathcal{F}_{\mathsf{rand}}$ in a computationally secure fashion, so that we can toss coins non-interactively once a PRG seed is sampled. Thus, our overall protocol is everlasting-secure, since we only require $\mathcal{F}_{\mathsf{rand}}$ to be computationally unpredictable *during* the protocol execution, but once the randomness has already been sampled, an unbounded adversary breaking the PRG cannot harm the protocol.

5.2 Experiments

We experimentally investigate the efficiency of the preprocessing protocols presented in Protocol 4 (Π_{FLEXds}) and Protocol 6 (Π_{SIMDds}) by comparing them against a double share procedure presented extracted from [1]. For each protocol, we measured the running time of the generation step as well as the batch check. For the protocol in [1], the generation step encompasses generating randomness, sending shares and evaluating the hyper-invertible matrices. The check step involves reconstructing $2t$ double-shares per batch and verifying that (1) the reconstructed tuple are $\mathbb{Z}_{2^k}$ elements and (2) that the two shares are the shame (thus being a valid double share). We note that our implementation of [1] uses Π_{rPub} rather than Π_{rPriv}, making it somewhat sub-optimal. Nevertheless, we remark that the communication complexity of Π_{rPub} is roughly just twice that of Π_{rPriv}, and that the extra round in Π_{rPub} will not affect much our reported numbers due to the low network latency. Hence, even with this quantitative inaccuracies, the qualitative results of our experiments remain the same.

We ran each protocol several times and took the average of the running time. Each protocol was run with n set to 4, 7, 10 and 13 parties (thus giving us thresholds 1, 2, 3 and 4). For each n we generated 1260, 12 600, 63 000, 126 000 and 630 000 double-shares.[4] For our InnerProd encoding, we report on *local computation* times. Since generating double shares for this encoding is captured by the experiments pertaining to Π_{FLEXds}, looking at the speedup in terms of local computation is more insightful.

[4] A quirk in our implementation requires the number of double shares that are generated to be divisible by the different batch sizes.

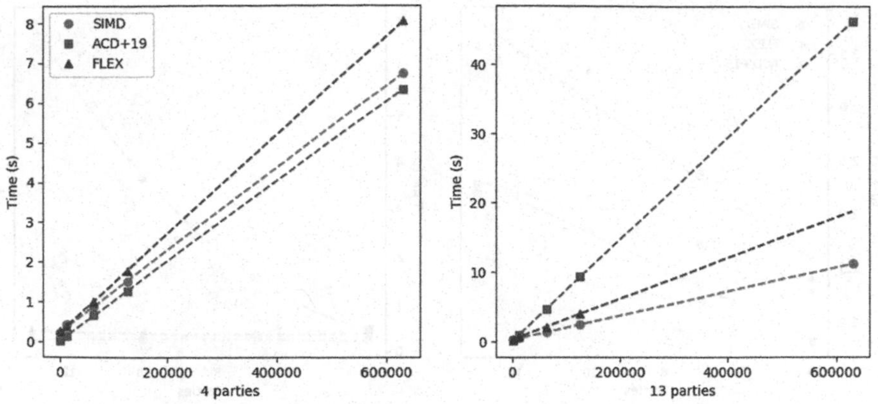

Fig. 2. Running time generating a varying number of shares for fixed number of parties.

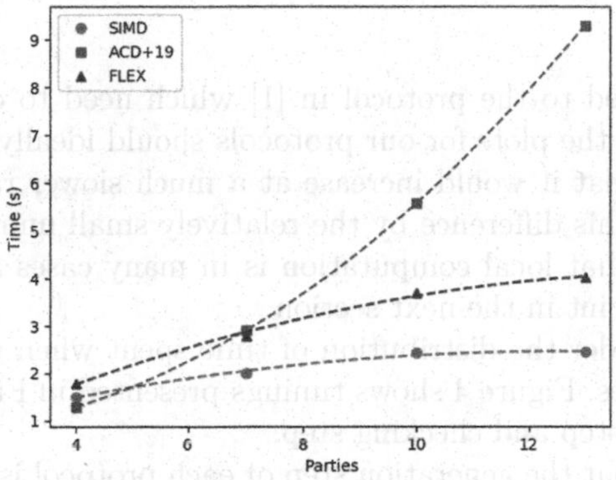

Fig. 3. Varying the number of parties who generate 126k double-shares.

Finally, we use our results to analytically obtain the running time of evaluating an SVM on 100 inputs in parallel. This is done both to get an intuition about the cost of our protocols in connection with a real application, as well as to showcase the functionality of our SIMD encoding.

5.3 Results

Figure 2 shows running time for increasing number of double share generation for a fixed number of parties (4 and 13).[5] Interestingly, we see that the naïve double-share protocol of [1] is faster for a smaller number of parties. However, when the number of parties increase, our protocols are a lot more efficient.

We can further see this fact in Fig. 3. Indeed, the running time of both our protocols increase only slightly when the number of parties increase. This demonstrates the benefit of the check we utilize, which does not depend on the number

[5] Our experiments lack a data point for FLEX in the case of 630k shares.

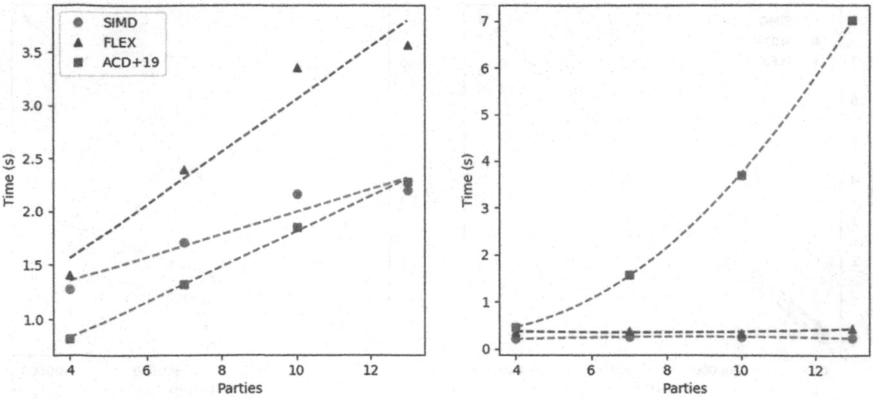

Fig. 4. Running time for the generation (left) and check (right) step of double share protocols, for variable number of parties generating 126k double-shares.

of parties, as opposed to the protocol in [1] which need to open $2t$ shares per batch. We note that the plots for our protocols should ideally follow a parabolic curve as well, but that it would increase at a much slower rate than the curve for [1]. We explain this difference by the relatively small number of data points as well as the fact that local computation is in many cases a dominant factor. We return to this point in the next section.

Finally, we consider the distribution of time spent when generating, respectively checking shares. Figure 4 shows timings presented in Fig. 3, but separated into the generation step and checking step.

We clearly see that the generation step of each protocol is not that different. On the other hand, the right graph in Fig. 4 clearly shows the benefit of the check step in our protocol. This graph also shows that we are not making an unfair comparison by having sub optimal protocol for [1]. Indeed, even if this protocol communicated half the number of bits, the general trend we see would still be present, and the extra round does not impact the result as the round-trip-time in our setup is less than 0.3 ms.

5.4 Micro Benchmarks

We also run a number of micro-benchmarks. First, we look at the speedup by using our InnerProd encoding. Not surprisingly, we see a speedup approaching ×2. The table below shows local computation times of computing inner products of varying lengths (with the length denoted as multiplies of 100 000).

Length	0.1	1	10	100	500
Naïve [1] (ns)	298.7	320.7	404.9	421.0	461.1
InnerProd (ns)	207.2	104.0	289.5	350.5	347.1

We further perform timings of the local computation that is performed in the generation step of Π_{FLEXds} and Π_{SIMDds}, as this is where the majority of computation is spent. The table below provides some insight in this regard.

# double-shares	1 260	12 600	63 000	126 000	630 000
SIMD (s)	0.03	0.12	0.47	0.91	4.44
FLEX (s)	0.05	0.13	0.51	0.99	4.87
Naïve [1] (s)	0.01	0.07	0.31	0.61	3.00

We see a small difference in times between our protocols and the one in [1]; besides slight variations in programming style (which may affect compiler optimizations), the main difference comes from the added processing (e.g., encoding) of the random values that is needed in our protocols; something which does not exist in the protocol of [1].

5.5 Extrapolation to Practical Applications

Finally, we examine the running time of evaluating an SVM using our SIMD encoding, and compare this with the protocol of [1]. To be concrete, we consider a linear SVM on a dataset of 3072 features and 10 classes.[6] Thus, the function we wish to evaluate is $f(\mathbf{x}) = \text{argmax}_i(\mathbf{w}_i\mathbf{x}+b_i)$ where $\mathbf{w}_i$ and b_i are the parameters of the model, and i denotes a class. This computation can be expressed as follows: Compute $\mathbf{z} = \mathbf{W}\mathbf{x} + \mathbf{b}$, where $\mathbf{W}$ is a matrix with the vectors $\mathbf{w}_i$ arranged in the rows. $\mathbf{z}$ will be a $10 \times k$ vector, where k denotes the number of images, and the remaining step is to find the index of the entry with the highest value, for which we can use a bit-sliced circuit which requires 1216 AND gates since we have 10 classes and 64 bit wide values. We present here two cost formulas that can be used to derive the number of double-shares required to evaluate an SVM on k images. How we arrive at these formulas is described in the full version:

Naïve case: $C_0(k) = k(1216 + 2 \cdot 64 \cdot 10)$.

SIMD case: $C_{\mathsf{SIMD}}(k) = k/2(1216 + 2.5 \cdot 64 \cdot 10)$.

Acknowledgements. We thank the Asiacrypt 2020 reviewers for their useful feedback. Eduardo Soria-Vazquez was supported by the Carlsberg Foundation under the Semper Ardens Research Project CF18-112 (BCM). Anders Dalskov was supported by the Danish Independent Research Council under Grant-ID DFF-6108-00169 (FoCC). Eysa Lee was supported by the National Science Foundation grant 1646671 and Office of the Director of National Intelligence (ODNI), Intelligence Advanced Research Project Activity (IARPA) under contract number 2019-19-020700009 (ACHILLES).

References

1. Abspoel, M., Cramer, R., Damgård, I., Escudero, D., Yuan, C.: Efficient information-theoretic secure multiparty computation over $\mathbb{Z}/p^k\mathbb{Z}$ via Galois rings. In: Hofheinz, D., Rosen, A. (eds.) TCC 2019. LNCS, vol. 11891, pp. 471–501. Springer, Cham (2019). https://doi.org/10.1007/978-3-030-36030-6_19

[6] This matches an SVM trained on the CIFAR10 image prediction problem.

2. Abspoel, M., Dalskov, A., Escudero, D., Nof. A.: An efficient passive-to-active compiler for honest-majority MPC over rings. Cryptology ePrint Archive, Report 2019/1298 (2019). https://eprint.iacr.org/2019/1298
3. Barak, A., Hirt, M., Koskas, L., Lindell, Y.: An end-to-end system for large scale P2P MPC-as-a-service and low-bandwidth MPC for weak participants. In: Lie, D., Mannan, M., Backes, M., Wang, X. (eds.) ACM CCS 2018, pp. 695–712. ACM Press, October 2018
4. Beaver, D.: Efficient multiparty protocols using circuit randomization. In: Feigenbaum, J. (ed.) CRYPTO 1991. LNCS, vol. 576, pp. 420–432. Springer, Heidelberg (1992). https://doi.org/10.1007/3-540-46766-1_34
5. Beerliová-Trubíniová, Z., Hirt, M.: Perfectly-secure MPC with linear communication complexity. In: Canetti, R. (ed.) TCC 2008. LNCS, vol. 4948, pp. 213–230. Springer, Heidelberg (2008). https://doi.org/10.1007/978-3-540-78524-8_13
6. Bishnoi, A., Clark, P.L., Potukuchi, A., Schmitt, J.R.: On zeros of a polynomial in a finite grid. Comb. Prob. Comput. **27**(3), 310–333 (2018)
7. Block, A.R., Maji, H.K., Nguyen, H.H.: Secure computation based on leaky correlations: high resilience setting. In: Katz, J., Shacham, H. (eds.) CRYPTO 2017. LNCS, vol. 10402, pp. 3–32. Springer, Cham (2017). https://doi.org/10.1007/978-3-319-63715-0_1
8. Cascudo, I., Cramer, R., Xing, C., Yuan, C.: Amortized complexity of information-theoretically secure MPC revisited. In: Shacham, H., Boldyreva, A. (eds.) CRYPTO 2018. LNCS, vol. 10993, pp. 395–426. Springer, Cham (2018). https://doi.org/10.1007/978-3-319-96878-0_14
9. Couteau, G.: A note on the communication complexity of multiparty computation in the correlated randomness model. In: Ishai, Y., Rijmen, V. (eds.) EUROCRYPT 2019. LNCS, vol. 11477, pp. 473–503. Springer, Cham (2019). https://doi.org/10.1007/978-3-030-17656-3_17
10. Cramer, R., Rambaud, M., Xing, C.: Asymptotically-good arithmetic secret sharing over $\mathbb{Z}/p^{\ell}\mathbb{Z}$ with strong multiplication and its applications to efficient MPC. Cryptology ePrint Archive, Report 2019/832 (2019). https://eprint.iacr.org/2019/832
11. Damgård, I., Escudero, D., Frederiksen, T.K., Keller, M., Scholl, P., Volgushev, N.: New primitives for actively-secure MPC over rings with applications to private machine learning. In: 2019 IEEE Symposium on Security and Privacy, pp. 1102–1120. IEEE Computer Society Press, May 2019
12. Escudero, D., Ghosh, S., Keller, M., Rachuri, R., Scholl, P.: Improved primitives for MPC over mixed arithmetic-binary circuits. In: Micciancio, D., Ristenpart, T. (eds.) CRYPTO 2020. LNCS, vol. 12171, pp. 823–852. Springer, Cham (2020). https://doi.org/10.1007/978-3-030-56880-1_29
13. Franklin, M.K., Yung, M.: Communication complexity of secure computation (extended abstract). In: 24th ACM STOC, pp. 699–710. ACM Press, May 1992
14. Keller, M., Orsini, E., Rotaru, D., Scholl, P., Soria-Vazquez, E., Vivek, S.: Faster secure multi-party computation of AES and DES using lookup tables. In: Gollmann, D., Miyaji, A., Kikuchi, H. (eds.) ACNS 2017. LNCS, vol. 10355, pp. 229–249. Springer, Cham (2017). https://doi.org/10.1007/978-3-319-61204-1_12
15. Keller, M., Orsini, E., Scholl, P.: MASCOT: faster malicious arithmetic secure computation with oblivious transfer. In: Weippl, E.R., Katzenbeisser, S., Kruegel, C., Myers, A.C., Halevi, S. (eds.) ACM CCS 2016, pp. 830–842. ACM Press, October 2016

16. Orsini, E., Smart, N.P., Vercauteren, F.: Overdrive2k: efficient secure MPC over $\mathbb{Z}_{2^k}$ from somewhat homomorphic encryption. In: Jarecki, S. (ed.) CT-RSA 2020. LNCS, vol. 12006, pp. 254–283. Springer, Heidelberg (2020)
17. Rotaru, D., Wood, T.: MArBled circuits: mixing arithmetic and Boolean circuits with active security. In: Hao, F., Ruj, S., Sen Gupta, S. (eds.) INDOCRYPT 2019. LNCS, vol. 11898, pp. 227–249. Springer, Cham (2019). https://doi.org/10.1007/978-3-030-35423-7_12
18. Shamir, A.: How to share a secret. Commun. Assoc. Comput. Mach. **22**(11), 612–613 (1979)
19. Unruh, D.: Everlasting multi-party computation. In: Canetti, R., Garay, J.A. (eds.) CRYPTO 2013. LNCS, vol. 8043, pp. 380–397. Springer, Heidelberg (2013). https://doi.org/10.1007/978-3-642-40084-1_22

Efficient Fully Secure Computation via Distributed Zero-Knowledge Proofs

Elette Boyle[1], Niv Gilboa[2], Yuval Ishai[3], and Ariel Nof[3(✉)]

[1] IDC Herzliya, Herzliya, Israel
eboyle@alum.mit.edu
[2] Ben-Gurion Univeristy, Beersheba, Israel
gilboa@bgu.ac.il
[3] Technion, Haifa, Israel
{yuvali,ariel.nof}@cs.technion.ac.il

Abstract. Secure computation protocols enable mutually distrusting parties to compute a function of their private inputs while revealing nothing but the output. Protocols with *full security* (also known as *guaranteed output delivery*) in particular protect against denial-of-service attacks, guaranteeing that honest parties receive a correct output. This feature can be realized in the presence of an honest majority, and significant research effort has gone toward attaining full security with good asymptotic and concrete efficiency.

We present an efficient protocol for *any constant* number of parties n, with full security against $t < n/2$ corrupted parties, that makes a black-box use of a pseudorandom generator. Our protocol evaluates an arithmetic circuit C over a finite ring R (either a finite field or $R = \mathbb{Z}_{2^k}$) with communication complexity of $\frac{3t}{2t+1}S + o(S)$ R-elements per party, where S is the number of multiplication gates in C (namely, < 1.5 elements per party per gate). This matches the best known protocols for the semi-honest model up to the sublinear additive term. For a small number of parties n, this improves over a recent protocol of Goyal *et al.* (Crypto 2020) by a constant factor for circuits over large fields, and by at least an $\Omega(\log n)$ factor for Boolean circuits or circuits over rings.

Our protocol provides new methods for applying the distributed zero-knowledge proofs of Boneh *et al.* (Crypto 2019), which only require logarithmic communication, for compiling semi-honest protocols into fully secure ones in the more challenging case of $t > 1$ corrupted parties. Our protocol relies on *replicated secret sharing* to minimize communication and simplify the mechanism for achieving full security. This results in computational cost that scales exponentially with n.

E. Boyle—Supported by ISF grant 1861/16, AFOSR Award FA9550-17-1-0069, and ERC Project HSS (852952).
N. Gilboa—Supported by ISF grant 2951/20, ERC grant 876110, and a grant by the BGU Cyber Center.
Y. Ishai and A. Nof—Supported by ERC Project NTSC (742754), ISF grant 2774/20, NSF-BSF grant 2015782, and BSF grant 2018393.

S. Moriai and H. Wang (Eds.): ASIACRYPT 2020, LNCS 12493, pp. 244–276, 2020.
https://doi.org/10.1007/978-3-030-64840-4_9

Our main protocol builds on a new honest-majority protocol for verifying the correctness of multiplication triples by making a *general* use of distributed zero-knowledge proofs. While the protocol only achieves the weaker notion of *security with abort*, it applies to any linear secret-sharing scheme and provides a conceptually simpler, more general, and more efficient alternative to previous protocols from the literature. In particular, it can be combined with the Fiat-Shamir heuristic to simultaneously achieve logarithmic communication complexity and constant round complexity.

1 Introduction

Protocols for secure computation [2,7,19,38] enable a set of parties with private inputs to compute a joint function of their inputs while revealing nothing but the output. Secure computation protocols provide a general-purpose tool for computing on sensitive data while eliminating single points of failure.

Beyond privacy and correctness, a highly desirable feature of such protocols is *guaranteed output delivery*, also known as *full security*, where honest parties are guaranteed to receive the final output of computation. This is in contrast to weaker notions of security, such as *security with abort* or *fairness*, which leave protocols vulnerable to denial-of-service attacks.

Full security can be achieved with an honest majority, namely when there are $n \geq 3$ parties of which at most $t < n/2$ are corrupted. This holds unconditionally given secure point-to-point channels and a broadcast primitive [35] (where the latter can be realized from a public-key infrastructure using digital signatures [12]), or alternatively using only secure channels assuming $t < n/3$ [2,7]. However, despite intensive research efforts, there is still a significant efficiency gap between the best known protocols achieving full security and those achieving weaker notions. We focus on the *communication* complexity of such protocols, which in the domain of concretely efficient protocols typically dominates overall cost. In this work, "concretely efficient" is interpreted as making only black-box use of a pseudo-random generator (PRG).[1]

A useful metric for measuring efficiency of fully secure protocols is the ratio between the communication cost of the protocol and that of the best known protocol with a "minimal" level of security, namely security against *semi-honest* parties, who act as prescribed by the protocol but try to learn additional information from messages they receive. Minimizing the overhead of full security has been the subject of a large body of work; see [5,6,21,23,26] and references therein. Here we focus on the more challenging case of a minimal honest majority ($t < n/2$). The ultimate goal is to obtain full security with the *same communication complexity* as the best known protocols that achieve semi-honest security, up to sublinear additive terms.

[1] As opposed to expensive cryptographic tools such as fully homomorphic encryption [17,36], where communication is asymptotically small but overall concrete costs are high. In the context of protecting against malicious parties, a PRG is not known to imply sublinear-communication arguments for NP in the standard setting.

The most relevant state of the art toward this goal is captured by two recent works: Boyle et al. [5] in the special case of 3 parties (i.e., $n = 3, t = 1$), and Goyal et al. [23] that approaches the goal for general n.

For the special case of 3 parties, the fully secure protocol of Boyle et al. [5] matches the amortized cost of the best known semi-honest protocol in this setting (due to Araki et al. [1]). More specifically, the protocol from [5] evaluates an arithmetic circuit C over a finite ring R with an amortized communication cost of a *single* R-element per party per multiplication gate.[2] The protocol applies to rings R that are either finite fields or rings of the form $R = \mathbb{Z}_{2^k}$, and in particular applies to Boolean circuits with an amortized cost of just 1 bit per party per AND gate.

Very recently, Goyal et al. [23] presented a fully secure protocol for arbitrary n that applies to the case where R is a large finite field, and provides information theoretic security. In the case that parties do not deviate from the protocol, the amortized per-party communication cost is 5.5 field elements, matching that of the best known information-theoretic semi-honest protocol. However, several gaps remain to the ultimate goal. If cheating occurs, the amortized communication cost of the protocol increases to 7.5 field elements per party, above the 5.5 semi-honest baseline. Further, by allowing black-box use of PRGs in the place of information theoretic security, the semi-honest baseline can be improved. Finally, the protocol of [23] only applies to the case that R is a finite field, as opposed to more general rings, and the quoted communication complexity is achieved only when the field is large. For instance, for Boolean circuits the protocol induces an additional $\log n$ factor. Overall, removing these limitations introduces several challenges which require new techniques.

In this work, we make progress toward closing the remaining gaps, focusing our attention on the practically motivated case of a *constant* number of parties[3] n. Even in this setting, designing fully secure protocols is a challenging task. Indeed, concretely efficient protocols in an even more restricted settings of $n = 3, 4$ or 5 parties, of which only $t = 1$ may be corrupted, have been the target of several previous works (e.g., [5,6,20,25,31,33]). However, these protocols are heavily tailored to the case $t = 1$, and there are multiple difficulties one encounters when trying to efficiently extend them to larger t.

For a constant threshold t and $n = 2t + 1$, the relevant semi-honest baseline is a protocol from [4] that optimizes a protocol of Damgård and Nielsen [11] using pseudorandom secret sharing [10,18]. The amortized communication cost is $\frac{3t}{2t+1}$ (< 1.5) R-elements per party per multiplication gate. This sets our target communication goal for full security.

[2] Namely, communication of $S + o(S)$ ring elements per party, where S is the number of multiplication gates in C.

[3] More generally, our main protocol incurs computation and storage costs that scale exponentially with n. However, these costs involve only symmetric cryptography and can be shifted almost entirely to an offline phase, before the inputs are known.

Relaxing full security to *security with abort*, this goal was recently met by Boyle et al. [4]. For the case of non-constant t, the amortized overhead of security with abort was also eliminated recently, first for $n = 3t + 1$ parties by Furukawa and Lindell [15] and then for $n = 2t + 1$ parties by Goyal and Song [22]. (A similar result, with a bigger sublinear additive term, can be obtained from the technique of [4].) However, in all these protocols, the parties immediately abort whenever cheating is detected. As always, the challenge of full security is in safely recovering to completion in the case corrupt parties send improper messages, withhold information, or exit the computation prematurely.

1.1 Our Contributions

Our main contribution is a secure computation protocol for *any constant* number of parties $n = 2t + 1$ that achieves full security against up to t malicious parties with the *same amortized communication* as for the best known semi-honest protocol mentioned above. Our protocol applies to both Boolean and arithmetic circuits, and even over the rings $\mathbb{Z}_{2^k}$. It uses a broadcast channel $\mathcal{F}_{\text{bc}}$ (necessary to achieve full security in this setting, where broadcast is not possible without setup [34]), and makes only black-box use of a PRG. The total size of strings communicated over $\mathcal{F}_{\text{bc}}$ is sublinear in the circuit size.

A basic building block in our construction is an arbitrary n-party protocol Π_{mult} for *private multiplication* based on replicated secret-sharing [27]. In such a protocol, inputs to a multiplication gate are shared by replicated secret sharing, and if all parties act honestly then in the end of the protocol the product of the inputs is also shared by the same scheme. Furthermore, even if t malicious parties act dishonestly in the protocol, they do not obtain information on the inputs of the honest parties. The usefulness of replicated secret sharing for simplifying general secure computation protocols was first pointed out by Maurer [30]. The most communication-efficient instance of a protocol of this type was given by Boyle et al. [4], combining the approach of Damgård and Nielsen [11] with the pseudorandom secret sharing technique of Cramer et al. [10] (see also [18]).

Our first result shows how to use this building block *in a generic way* to achieve full security with only sublinear additive communication overhead when no cheating occurs. When cheating does occur, there is an additional additive term that grows linearly with a circuit "width" parameter W. Intuitively, the circuit width captures the amount of space required by the computation.

At a very high level, the protocol starts by using Π_{mult} to privately compute shares of the outputs of all multiplication gates, without reconstructing them. It then ensures that these outputs are correct by applying *distributed zero-knowledge proofs*, i.e., proofs of a statement on an input that is distributed between several verifiers. Such proofs for simple languages, including the "degree-2 languages" we require, can have sublinear (in fact, logarithmic) length in the size of the statement [4], which we use to achieve low communication overhead. A major challenge that we solve is efficient recovery from failures. We achieve this by a careful combination of a player elimination approach (cf. [24]) with an authentication mechanism (cf. [35]). Our particular way of combining these techniques takes advantage of the redundancy provided by replicated secret sharing and the amortization enabled by pseudorandom secret sharing.

Using the concrete instantiation of Π_{mult} from [4,11], we can eliminate the extra $O(W)$ additive overhead and obtain the following main result.

Theorem 1.1 (Efficient fully secure MPC for constant n). *Let R be a finite field or a ring of the form $\mathbb{Z}_{2^k}$, let $t \geq 1$ be a constant security threshold and $n = 2t + 1$. Then, assuming a black-box access to a PRG, there is a fully t-secure n-party protocol that evaluates an arithmetic circuit over R, with S multiplication gates, by communicating $\frac{3t}{2t+1}S + o(S)$ ring elements per party.*

Compared to the recent protocol from [23], this improves the worst-case amortized communication by at least a factor of 5 over big fields, and by at least a $5 \log_2 n$ factor for Boolean circuits and circuits over $\mathbb{Z}_{2^k}$. Moreover, unlike the protocol from [23], here we can match the amortized cost of the best known semi-honest protocol even when cheating occurs. However, unlike the protocol from [23], our protocol is restricted to a constant number of parties and provides computational (rather than information-theoretic) security.

The Simpler Case of Security-with-Abort. As an intermediate step in constructing fully secure protocols, we develop a protocol that is only secure-with-abort, i.e., the adversary can force the honest parties to abort without receiving an output. Unlike our main protocol, here we apply a general compilation technique that is not restricted to replicated secret sharing or a small number of parties. Instead, we give a simple protocol for verifying the correctness of secret-shared multiplication triples by making a *general* use of (sublinear-communication) distributed zero-knowledge proofs. The main difference between the triple verification task and distributed zero knowledge is that in the latter there is a prover who knows all of the (distributed) secrets, whereas in the former there is no such prover. Nevertheless, we show that triple verification can be efficiently reduced to distributed zero knowledge. The high-level idea is to view the shares held by all parties *except* P_i as a secret-sharing of the share held by P_i. This allows each party to prove to the other parties that a computation it locally performed on its shares was done correctly using distributed zero knowledge.

We stress that unlike similar verification protocols from [3,4,22], our approach is very general and can rely on any instantiation of the underlying distributed proofs primitives. In particular, using the distributed zero-knowledge protocols from [4,5], the verification cost is logarithmic in the size of the circuit. This is similar to a verification procedure from [22] and better than the square-root complexity of an earlier triple verification protocol from [4]. Compared to the protocol from [22], our approach is more general, and can rely on any distributed zero-knowledge protocol for degree-2 languages, which in fact reduces to a "zero-knowledge fully-linear IOP" for such languages [4]. Another advantage of our triple verification protocol over that of [22] is that it can be combined with the Fiat-Shamir heuristic to simultaneously achieve logarithmic communication complexity and *constant* (as opposed to logarithmic) round complexity. See Sect. 4.3 for a detailed discussion of concrete efficiency.

As in the generic version of our main theorem, we can apply the above technique to compile any semi-honest MPC protocol that builds on a private multiplication sub-protocol into a similar protocol that achieves security-with-abort. However, in the current case the private multiplication sub-protocol Π_{mult} can use any linear secret-sharing scheme, in particular Shamir's scheme [37]. As a result, our compiler can yield protocols that are efficient for any (super-constant) number of parties n. This is captured by the following theorem.

Theorem 1.2 (Security-with-abort compiler for any n, informal). *Let R be either a finite field or a ring of the form $\mathbb{Z}_{2^k}$, let $t \geq 1$ be a security threshold, and $n = 2t + 1$. Then, assuming a black-box access to any n-party t-private protocol Π_{mult} for multiplying linearly shared secrets over R, there is an n-party protocol Π for arithmetic circuits over R with the following security and efficiency properties. The protocol Π is t-secure-with-abort, with the same type of security (information-theoretic or computational) as Π_{mult}. It evaluates an arithmetic circuit with S multiplication gates using communication complexity of $|\Pi_{\text{mult}}| \cdot S + o_n(S)$ elements of R, where $|\Pi_{\text{mult}}|$ is the communication complexity of Π_{mult}, and o_n hides polynomial terms in n.*

Theorem 1.2 can be viewed as a more general alternative to the recent protocol from [22], which is tailored to a special kind of semi-honest protocol. Our approach is more general both in its treatment of the underlying multiplication sub-protocol and in the use of general distributed zero-knowledge proofs.

2 Preliminaries

Notation. Let $P_1, \ldots, P_n$ be the set of parties and let t be such that $n = 2t + 1$. In this work, we assume that there exists an honest majority and so the number of corrupted parties is at most t. We use $[n]$ to denote the set $\{1, \ldots, n\}$. We denote by $\mathbb{F}$ a finite field and by $\mathbb{Z}_{2^k}$ the ring of integers modulo 2^k. We use the notation R to denote a ring that can either be a finite field or the ring $\mathbb{Z}_{2^k}$. We use $[\![x]\!]$ to denote a secret sharing of x with threshold t (as defined below) and $\langle x \rangle$ to denote an additive sharing of x.

2.1 Computation Model

In this work, we model the computation that represent the functionality the parties wish to compute, as a straight-line program, with addition and multiplication instructions [9]. The advantage of this representation is that it captures the notion of *width*, which is defined to be the maximal numbers of registers required to store memory during the computation.

Definition 2.1 (Straight-line programs). *A* straight-line program *over a ring R consists of an arbitrary sequence of the four following instructions, each with a unique identifier id:*

- *Load an input into memory:* $(id, \hat{R}_j \leftarrow x_i)$.
- *Add values in memory:* $(id, \hat{R}_k \leftarrow \hat{R}_i + \hat{R}_j)$.
- *Multiply two values in memory:* $(id, \hat{R}_k \leftarrow \hat{R}_i \cdot \hat{R}_j)$.
- *Output value from memory, as element of R:* $(id, O_i \leftarrow \hat{R}_j)$.

where $x_1, \ldots, x_n$ are the inputs, $O_1, \ldots, O_n$ are the outputs and $\hat{R}_1, \ldots, \hat{R}_W$ are registers holding memory. We define the size *of a program P as the number of multiplication instructions and denote it by S. We define the* width *of P as the number of registers W.*

Every arithmetic circuit with S multiplication gates can be converted into a straight-line program of size S by sorting its gates in an arbitrary topological order. We will assume for simplicity that each party has a single input and receives a single output. Our constructions can be easily adapted to the setting of multiple inputs and outputs per party.

2.2 Threshold Linear Secret Sharing Schemes

Definition 2.2 *A t-out-of-n secret sharing scheme is a protocol for a* dealer *holding a secret value v and n parties $P_1, \ldots, P_n$. The scheme consists of two interactive algorithms:* $\mathsf{share}(v)$, *which outputs shares $[\![v]\!] = (v_1, \ldots, v_n)$ and* $\mathsf{reconstruct}([\![v]\!]_T, i)$, *which given the shares $v_j, j \in T \subseteq \{1, \ldots, n\}$ outputs v or $\perp$. The dealer runs* $\mathsf{share}(v)$ *and provides P_i with a share of the secret v_i. A subset of users T run* $\mathsf{reconstruct}([\![v]\!]_T, i)$ *to reveal the secret to party P_i by sending their shares to P_i. The scheme must ensure that no subset of t shares provide any information on v, but that $v =$* $\mathsf{reconstruct}([\![v]\!]_T, i)$ *for any T, $|T| \geq t+1$. We say that a sharing is* consistent *if* $\mathsf{reconstruct}([\![v]\!]_T, i) = \mathsf{reconstruct}([\![v]\!]_{T'}, i)$ *for any two sets of honest parties $T, T' \subseteq \{1, \ldots, n\}$, and $|T|, |T'| \geq t+1$.*

Verifiable Secret Sharing (VSS). We say that $\mathsf{share}(v)$ is verifiable if at the end of $\mathsf{share}(v)$, either the parties hold a consistent sharing of the secret or the honest parties abort. This is achieved by adding a consistency check after each party receives its shares from the dealer. We will describe consistency checks for the secret sharing schemes used in our work below.

Authenticated Secret Sharing. We say that a secret sharing scheme is *authenticated* if, assuming that the sharing phase was correctly executed, malicious parties cannot prevent the correct reconstruction of the secret by tampering with their shares. (Authenticated secret sharing is sometimes also referred to as *robust* secret sharing.) We remark that it is not straightforward to achieve this when $t \geq n/3$, as standard error-correcting techniques do not suffice. In fact, perfect reconstruction is provably impossible to achieve in this setting, and one must settle for statistically small error probability. There is a recent line of work on optimizing the efficiency of authenticated secret sharing; see [13] and references therein. However, the asymptotically good constructions are quite complex and are not attractive when the number of parties are small. In this work, we only need to make minimal use of this primitive which is independent of the size of the circuit. Thus, any implementation will suffice. An example for such a simple implementation is the well-known construction of Rabin and Ben-Or [35] based on pairwise authentication of shares.

Local Linear Operations and Multiplication. In this work, we require that linear operations over a ring for a given secret sharing scheme can be carried out locally. In particular, given $[\![x]\!]$, $[\![y]\!]$ and some public constant c, the parties can compute: (1) $[\![x+y]\!]$ (2) $[\![c \cdot x]\!]$ and (3) $[\![c+x]\!]$. We use the notation $[\![x]\!] + [\![y]\!]$, $c \cdot [\![x]\!]$ and $c + [\![x]\!]$ to denote the three local procedures respectively that achieve this. Thus, we have $[\![x+y]\!] = [\![x]\!] + [\![y]\!]$, $[\![c \cdot x]\!] = c \cdot [\![x]\!]$ and $[\![c+x]\!] = c + [\![x]\!]$.

While a linear secret sharing scheme does not allow multiplication of shares without interaction, we assume that given $[\![x]\!]$ and $[\![y]\!]$, the parties can locally compute $\langle x \cdot y \rangle$ (thus the interaction is required for reducing the threshold). We denote the operation of computing the product's additive sharing by $[\![x]\!] \cdot [\![y]\!]$.

Local Conversion From $[\![x]\!]$ *to* $[\![x^i]\!]$. Given a consistent sharing $[\![x]\!]$, we require that the parties are able to locally generate a consistent sharing $[\![x^i]\!]$, where x^i is the share of x held by party P_i.

Instantiation 1: Replicated Secret Sharing [27]. To share a secret $x \in R$, for each subset T of t parties the dealer hands a random share x_T to the parties in $\overline{T} = \{P_1, \dots, P_n\} \setminus T$, under the constraint that $x = \sum_{T \subset \{P_1, \dots, P_n\}:\, |T|=t} x_T$. The share held by each party P_i is the tuple consisting of all x_T such that $P_i \in T$. Thus, the number of shares is $\binom{n}{t}$ and each party holds $\binom{n-1}{t}$ shares.

It is easy to see that replicated secret sharing scheme is linear over R and allows local multiplication to obtain an additive sharing of the product when $t < n/2$. Local conversion from $[\![x]\!]$ to $[\![x^i]\!]$ can be done by sharing each component x_T that P_i holds separately. For each T for which $P_i \in T$, every party $P_j \in T$ will hold x_T, while parties not it T will set their share to be 0.

Pairwise Consistency. Observe that since $n = 2t + 1$ in our setting, each share is held by a subset of $t + 1$ parties. Thus, a sharing is inconsistent if a cheating dealer hands different values to honest parties in the same subset. In order to verify that a sharing is consistent, it suffices that every pair of parties verify that they hold the same share for each subset T, which includes both parties. This can be done with low communication by having these parties compare a hash of their joint shares. Observe that if pairwise inconsistency is detected then this pair can ask the dealer to publish the conflicted share, as in this case, this share is already known to the adversary.

Instantiation 2: Shamir's Secret Sharing [37]. In this well-known scheme, the dealer defines a random polynomial $p(x)$ of degree t over a finite field $\mathbb{F}$ such that the constant term is the secret. Each party is associated with a distinct non-zero field element $\alpha \in \mathbb{F}$ and receives $p(\alpha)$ as its share of the secret. Linear operations on secrets can be computed locally on the shares, since polynomial interpolation is a linear operation. In addition, given shares of x and y, the parties can locally multiply their shares to obtain a sharing of degree $2t$ of $x \cdot y$.

Finally, observe that since each share is a point on a polynomial, then a consistent sharing $[\![x]\!]$ is also a consistent sharing of P_i's share x^i, written as $[\![x^i]\!]$ (the only difference is that now the secret is not stored at the point 0 but at the point α_i).

Polynomial Consistency. A Shamir secret sharing is consistent if all shares $(p(\alpha_1) = \beta_1, \ldots, p(\alpha_n) = \beta_n)$ lie on the same degree-t polynomial. A simple way to check the consistency of m sharings: $(\beta_{1,1}, \ldots, \beta_{1,n}), \ldots, (\beta_{m,1}, \ldots, \beta_{m,n})$ together in a batch is to generate n random coefficients $c_1, \ldots, c_n \in \mathbb{F}$ and a random degree-t polynomial $q(x)$, compute $(\sum_{i=1}^{m} c_i\beta_{i,1} + q(\alpha_1), \ldots, \sum_{i=1}^{m} c_i\beta_{i,n} + q(\alpha_n))$, open the shares, and check that they lie on a degree t polynomial.

We stress that Shamir's scheme can be used only in our base secure-with-abort construction. The fully secure construction relies on properties that hold only for replicated secret sharing.

2.3 Π_{mult} – Private Multiplication Protocol

In our main protocol, the parties first compute each multiplication instruction using a protocol Π_{mult} that satisfies only the following a weak notion of security and then run a verification protocol to detect and recover from cheating.

Definition 2.3. *Let Π_{mult} be an n-party protocol that takes as inputs $[\![x]\!]$ and $[\![y]\!]$ and outputs $[\![z]\!]$. We say that Π_{mult} is a* private *multiplication protocol in the presence of a malicious adversary controlling up to t parties if it satisfies two properties.*

Correctness. *If $[\![x]\!]$ and $[\![y]\!]$ are consistent sharings and all the parties follow the protocol's instructions, then $[\![z]\!]$ is a consistent sharing of $z = x \cdot y$.*

Privacy. *Denote the set of honest parties by J and denote the vector of all input shares held by the honest parties by $\boldsymbol{u}_J$. Then, for every adversary $\mathcal{A}$ controlling up to t parties, and for every two vectors of shares $\boldsymbol{u}_J, \boldsymbol{u}'_J$ the view that $\mathcal{A}$ has in the protocol when the honest parties hold $\boldsymbol{u}_J$ is computationally indistinguishable from its view when the honest parties hold $\boldsymbol{u}'_J$.*

We say that Π_{mult} is a replicated *and private multiplication protocol if in addition to the correctness and privacy properties it holds that if $[\![x]\!]$ and $[\![y]\!]$ are consistent sharings of x and y in a replicated secret sharing scheme for threshold t, and all the parties follow the protocol's instructions, then $[\![z]\!]$ is a consistent sharing of $z = x \cdot y$ in the same replicated secret sharing scheme for threshold t.*

The latter property in the above definition will be used in our fully secure construction.

Instantiation: The DN [11] Multiplication Protocol. In the DN protocol, the parties prepare in advance two random sharings $[\![r]\!], \langle r \rangle$ which are used in the following way. First, the parties locally compute $\langle x \cdot y - r \rangle = [\![x]\!] \cdot [\![y]\!] - \langle r \rangle$ and send the result to P_1. Then, P_1 reconstructs $x \cdot y - r$ and sends it back to the parties. The parties then locally compute $[\![x \cdot y]\!] = x \cdot y - r + [\![r]\!]$. A simple optimization to the second step is having P_1 share $x \cdot y - r$ to the parties instead of sending it in the clear. Then, we can let the shares of t parties be 0 and let the shares of the remaining parties be computed given the value of $xy - r$ and the t zero shares (for replicated secret sharing this translates into having the share given to one subset of $t+1$ parties being $x \cdot y - r$ and the remaining shares being 0). Thus, we can have P_1 send $xy - r$ to t parties, and then P_1 and these t parties can locally compute their shares of $xy - r$ and add them to their shares of r, while the remaining parties set their output to be their shares of r. Thus, the overall communication in the online step is $n - 1 + t$ elements, and so $\frac{2t+1-1+t}{2t+1} \leq 1.5$ elements per party. The masking of all sent messages in this protocol with random value guarantees that the protocol satisfies the privacy requirement. For the offline step, it is possible to produce $[\![r]\!], \langle r \rangle$ without any interaction [10] or using interaction but with reduced computational overhead for large number of parties [11] (using hyper-invertible matrices). We refer the reader to [8,29] for exact analysis.

In the full version of this paper, we describe other instantiations for Π_{mult} that can be usefull in some settings.

2.4 Other Basic Ideal Functionalities

Let $\mathcal{F}_{\mathrm{rand}}(t)$ be an ideal functionality that hands the parties a sharing of a random secret value with threshold t, while allowing the adversary to choose the corrupted parties' shares. This functionality can be realized for both Shamir and the replicated secret sharing scheme [10,11]. We remark that for replicated secret sharing, the functionality can be realized without any interaction (except for a setup step) [10], which makes the protocol fully secure. This is of high importance for our fully secure construction.

Let $\mathcal{F}_{\mathrm{coin}}$ be an ideal functionality that hands the parties fresh random coins. In the security with abort model, it can be realized by calling $\mathcal{F}_{\mathrm{rand}}$ and opening the result. To achieve full security, heavier machinery is required. Nevertheless, we can reduce the number of calls to this functionality to the size of the security parameter (as it is possible to call it only to generate a seed r from which all the required randomness is derived.

Finally, Let $\mathcal{F}_{\mathsf{bc}}$ be a secure broadcast functionality which allows the parties to broadcast a message to all the other parties. We remark that use of a broadcast channel is necessary to achieve full security within this setting, where broadcast is not possible without setup [34]. Full security of $\mathcal{F}_{\mathsf{bc}}$ is achievable given PKI setup [35]. The number of times this functionality is called will be sublinear in the size of the circuit and so any reasonable implementation will suffice.

3 Prove Correctness of Degree-2 Relations over Shared Data

In this section, we present the main building block for our constructions: a protocol that allows the parties to prove that a degree-2 computation over their shares was carried-out correctly. Specifically, in our protocol, we have a party P_i who wishes to prove that the following equation holds:

$$c - \sum_{k=1}^{L}(a_k \cdot b_k) = 0 \tag{1}$$

where c, $\{a_k\}_{k=1}^{L}$ and $\{b_k\}_{k=1}^{L}$ are known to P_i and are secret shared among the parties via a consistent t-out-of-n linear secret sharing scheme (see Definition 2.2). We note that the above task can be seen as an application of the distributed zero-knowledge proof system defined in [4]. In the setting of distributed zero-knowledge proofs there is a prover who wishes to prove a statement in zero-knowledge, where the statement is held in a distributed manner across multiple verifiers. An example for a statement that is distributed across verifiers, is our setting in which the statement is secret shared among the verifiers. As in any zero-knowledge proof system, the definition of distributed zero-knowledge interactive proofs requires that three properties will be satisfied: *completeness* (if the statement is correct and the parties follow the protocol, then the verifiers will output accept with probability 1), *soundness* (if the statement is incorrect, then the honest verifiers will output accept only with a small probability) and *zero-knowledge* (no information about the inputs is leaked during the execution). However, in distributed zero-knowledge proof protocols, the above requirements should be met even if the prover colludes with a subset of verifiers. As shown in [4], for low-degree relations it is possible to construct zero-knowledge proof protocols with sub-linear communication complexity. In Sect. 3.1, we rely on one of their ideas to design a highly-efficient protocol to prove that Eq. (1) holds. In Sect. 3.2 we take a step further and provide a protocol where an honest prover can also identify a cheating verifier in case the proof is rejected.

3.1 The Functionality $\mathcal{F}^{\text{abort}}_{\text{proveDeg2Rel}}$ - Prove Correctness with Abort

We begin with a protocol that is secure with abort, i.e., it allows a malicious verifier to cause honest parties to reject even when the statement is correct. In this section, we assume that the prover knows also $[\![c]\!]$ (i.e., the shares of all parties of c)[4]. In contrast, for the a_ks and b_ks, P_i does not need to know the other parties' shares, and in fact, in this case, P_i's share is the secret itself. We compute the ideal functionality $\mathcal{F}^{\text{abort}}_{\text{proveDeg2Rel}}$. The functionality checks that Eq. (1) holds using the honest parties' shares. This is sufficient since in the honest majority setting, the honest parties' shares fully determine both the secret and the corrupted parties' shares. Observe that in case the equation holds, $\mathcal{F}^{\text{abort}}_{\text{proveDeg2Rel}}$ lets the adversary determine the output (i.e., accept or reject) for each party, whereas if the equation does not hold, the output is always reject. Note also that in case the prover is corrupt, $\mathcal{F}^{\text{abort}}_{\text{proveDeg2Rel}}$ hands the adversary $\mathcal{S}$ also the inputs, and all shares of c (since these are known anyway to the real world adversary).

FUNCTIONALITY 3.1. ($\mathcal{F}^{\text{abort}}_{\text{proveDeg2Rel}}$**- Prove Correctness of a Shared Secret**)
Let $\mathcal{S}$ be the ideal world adversary controlling a subset $< n/2$ of corrupted parties.
The functionality $\mathcal{F}^{\text{abort}}_{\text{proveDeg2Rel}}$ works with $\mathcal{S}$ and honest parties holding consistent t-out-of-n secret sharings $[\![c]\!], \{[\![a_k]\!]\}_{k=1}^{L}, \{[\![b_k]\!]\}_{k=1}^{L}$.
$\mathcal{F}^{\text{abort}}_{\text{proveDeg2Rel}}$ is invoked by an index i sent from the honest parties and works as follows:

1. $\mathcal{F}^{\text{abort}}_{\text{proveDeg2Rel}}$ receives from the honest parties their shares of c, $\{a_k\}_{k=1}^{L}$ and $\{b_k\}_{k=1}^{L}$.
2. $\mathcal{F}^{\text{abort}}_{\text{proveDeg2Rel}}$ computes c, $\{a_k\}_{k=1}^{L}$ and $\{b_k\}_{k=1}^{L}$. Then, it computes the corrupted parties' shares of these values and sends them to $\mathcal{S}$. If P_i is corrupted, then it sends also $[\![c]\!], \{a_k\}_{k=1}^{L}$ and $\{b_k\}_{k=1}^{L}$ to $\mathcal{S}$.
3. $\mathcal{F}^{\text{abort}}_{\text{proveDeg2Rel}}$ checks that Eq. (1) holds.
   If it holds, then it sends accept to $\mathcal{S}$ to receive back $\text{out}_j \in \{\text{accept}, \text{reject}\}$ for each honest party P_j, which is handed to party P_j.
   Otherwise, it sends reject to $\mathcal{S}$ and the honest parties.

Computing $\mathcal{F}^{\text{abort}}_{\text{proveDeg2Rel}}$ Using Distributed Zero-Knowledge Proofs. While the definition of $\mathcal{F}^{\text{abort}}_{\text{proveDeg2Rel}}$ yields a setting which is similar to the setting of distributed zero-knowledge proofs defined in [4], there is still one difference. The zero-knowledge property in the definition of [4] considers only privacy in the presence of a subset of verifiers. Here however we assume that the prover does not know the verifiers' shares of the a_ks and b_ks. Thus, the proof protocol must also prevent the prover from learning any information on these shares. Thus,

[4] It is possible to avoid this assumption, but it nevertheless holds for our verification protocol that uses this proof as a building block.

any distributed zero-knowledge proof used to realize $\mathcal{F}^{\text{abort}}_{\text{proveDeg2Rel}}$ must provide this stronger requirement.

A Concrete Protocol to Compute $\mathcal{F}^{\text{abort}}_{\text{proveDeg2Rel}}$. We next show how to compute this functionality using the fully linear interactive oracle proof from [4] with low communication. The idea works as follows. First, the parties define a g-gate $g(\nu_1, \ldots, \nu_L) = \sum_{\ell=1}^{L/2} \nu_{2\ell-1} \cdot \nu_{2\ell}$. We now can write Eq. (1) as

$$c - g\left(a_1, b_1, \ldots, a_{L/2}, b_{L/2}\right) - g\left(a_{L/2+1}, b_{L/2+1}, \ldots, a_L, b_L\right) = 0.$$

Next, the prover P_i, who knows all inputs, computes the output of the two g gates and verifiably secret shares them to the parties. Let $g_1 = g\left(a_1, b_1, \ldots, a_{L/2}, b_{L/2}\right)$ and $g_2 = g\left(a_{L/2+1}, b_{L/2+1}, \ldots, a_L, b_L\right)$. Thus, the parties hold now a t-out-of-n secret sharing of c, g_1 and g_2. Hence, the parties can locally compute $[\![b]\!] = [\![c]\!] - [\![g_1]\!] - [\![g_2]\!]$ and check that $b = 0$ by revealing their shares of b. Since an honest majority exists, the adversary cannot do any harm in the opening beyond causing the parties to abort. However, this is not enough; a corrupted P_i may cheat when sharing g_1 and g_2. To prevent this, the parties carry-out an additional test. Let $f_1, \ldots f_L$ be polynomials defined in the following way: for each $e \in [L]$, $f_e(1)$ is the eth input to the first g-gate, and $f_e(2)$ is the eth input to the second g-gate. It follows that f_e is a linear function (i.e., polynomial of degree-1). Next, define the polynomial $q(x) = g(f_1(x), \ldots, f_L(x))$. From the definition of q, it follows that: (1) $q(1)$ is the output of the first g-gate and $q(2)$ is the output of the second; (2) q is of degree-2 (since g is a circuit of of multiplicative depth-1 and the f polynomials are of degree-1). Now, to check that P_i shared the correct $q(1)$ and $q(2)$, it suffices to check that $q(r) = g(f_1(r), \ldots, f_L(r))$ for some random r in the ring/field. To carry-out the check, the parties can locally compute a t-out-of-n secret sharings of $q(r)$ and $f_1(r), \ldots, f_L(r)$ via Lagrange interpolation over their shares (note that this is a local linear operation), open these sharings and check the equality in the clear. This requires that P_i will share also $q(3)$, so that the parties have enough points on q (and so r cannot be in $\{1, 2, 3\}$)). Note however that opening L shares results with communication cost that is linear in L. To achieve communication that is logarithmic in L, instead of opening, we let P_i prove that

$$q(r) - g(f_1(r), \ldots, f_L(r)) = 0 \tag{2}$$

by repeating *the exact same process as above*. This is possible since Eq. (2) has the same form as Eq. (1) and since all parties hold a consistent sharing of all the inputs to Eq. (2). Note that this time we only have L inputs (instead of $2L$). Thus, the parties can repeat the process $\log L$ times, until there are only small constant number of inputs and then check equality to 0 by opening. One subtle security issue that arise here is that $f_e(r)$ is a linear combination of inputs. Thus, to securely open it, the parties randomize the f polynomials by adding (only in the last step) a random point to each polynomial. This is achieved by using $\mathcal{F}_{\text{rand}}$ to generate an additional shared point for each of f polynomials. Note that the degree of q is now 4 (since the degree of f was increased to 2) and so P_i needs to share 5 points on q instead of 3. As an additional optimization, we also deffer the check of equality to 0 of the b values to the end, and then perform a single check by taking a random linear combination of all b values generated in each step of the recursion. As we will argue below, the cost per step in the recursion is constant, and so since we have $\log L$ steps, the overall communication cost is logarithmic in L. The protocol is formalized in Protocol 3.2.

Cheating Probability for Finite Fields. We now compute the probability that the parties output accept, even though Eq. (1) does not hold, when the protocol is executed over finite fields. Note that for this to hold, the prover P_i has two choices: (i) not to cheat in the protocol, hoping that the linear combination of the b values will yield 0. This will happen with probability $\frac{1}{\mathbb{F}}$; (ii) cheat when sharing the points on the polynomial q. This means that $q \neq g(f_1, \ldots, f_L)$ and so the polynomial $h(x) = q(x) - g(f_1(x), \ldots, f_L(x))$ is not the zero polynomial. Thus, by the Schwartz–Zippel lemma, the probability that $h(r) = 0$ for a randomly chosen $r \in \mathbb{F} \setminus \{1, 2, 3\}$ is bounded by $\frac{2}{|\mathbb{F}|-3}$ (since the degree of the polynomial h is 2) in the first $\log L - 1$ rounds and $\frac{4}{|\mathbb{F}|-5}$ in the last round (since then the degree of h is 4). Observe that for the prover to successfully cheat, this event should happen in *one* of the iterations of the protocol. Thus, the overall cheating probability is bounded by $\frac{2(\log L-1)}{|\mathbb{F}|-3} + \frac{4}{|\mathbb{F}|-5} < \frac{2\log L+4}{|\mathbb{F}|-5}$. Finally, note that $\frac{1}{\mathbb{F}} < \frac{2\log L}{|\mathbb{F}|-3}$ and so a malicious prover will increase its success cheating probability by cheating as in (ii). If the field is not large enough to achieve the desired level of security, the parties can repeat the protocol several times.

We prove that Protocol 3.2 securely computes $\mathcal{F}^{\text{abort}}_{\text{proveDeg2Rel}}$ in the full version of the paper.

Extending the Protocol to the Ring $\mathbb{Z}_{2^k}$. The main challenge in extending the verification protocol to rings, and in particular the ring $\mathbb{Z}_{2^k}$, is that we require interpolation and not all elements in a ring have an inverse. To overcome this, the solution suggested in [4,5] is to work over the extension ring $\mathbb{Z}_{2^k}[x]/f(x)$, i.e., the ring of all polynomials with coefficients in $\mathbb{Z}_{2^k}$ working modulo a polynomial f that is of the right degree and is irreducible over $\mathbb{Z}_2$. As shown in [4,5], this enables to define enough points on the polynomial that allow interpolation.

We note that the cheating probability when working with the extension ring and hence the statistical error of the protocol is different, since the number of roots of a polynomial defined over a ring, is larger than its degree. For a program with m multiplication instructions, the error will be roughly $\frac{2\log m+4}{2^d}$, where d is the extension degree. We refer the reader to [4,5] for more details. Nevertheless, the main observation here is that the communication when using this solution blows up only by a *constant*, and so asymptotically the complexity remains the same.

Cost Analysis. In the first $\log L - 1$ iterations, the prover shares 3 ring elements in each iteration. In the last round, the prover shares 5 elements, followed by opening 4 shared elements. Using a PRG, it is possible to share a secret by sending $t \approx n/2$ ring elements, and opening a secret requires transmission of n^2 elements. To realize $\mathcal{F}_{\text{coin}}$ (with abort) it suffices to open a random sharing. Hence, in this case, the overall communication cost per party is

$$(1.5 + n - 1)\log(L-1) + 2.5 + 4(n-1) \approx n \cdot \log(L) + 4n \text{ field elements.}$$

PROTOCOL 3.2. (Securely Computing $\mathcal{F}_{\text{proveDeg2Rel}}^{\text{abort}}$)

- **Inputs:** Prover P_i holds $2L+1$ inputs $c, \{a_k\}_{k=1}^{L}, \{b_k\}_{k=1}^{L}$. The parties hold a consistent t-out-of-n secret sharing of each of these inputs. P_i knows all shares of c.
- **The protocol:**
  1. The parties set $\bar{L} = L$.
  2. For $l = 1$ to $\log \bar{L} - 1$:
     (a) The parties define linear polynomials $f_1, f_2 \ldots, f_L$ such that for each $e \in [L]$ the polynomial f_e is defined by the two points:
     $$f_e(1) = \begin{cases} a_{\lceil \frac{e}{2} \rceil} & \text{if } e \bmod 2 = 1 \\ b_{\frac{e}{2}} & \text{if } e \bmod 2 = 0 \end{cases} \quad f_e(2) = \begin{cases} a_{\frac{L}{2}+\lceil \frac{e}{2} \rceil} & \text{if } e \bmod 2 = 1 \\ b_{\frac{L}{2}+\frac{e}{2}} & \text{if } e \bmod 2 = 0 \end{cases}$$
     (b) Let $q(x) = g(f_1(x), \ldots, f_L(x))$ be a polynomial of degree 2, where
     $$g(f_1(x), \ldots, f_L(x)) = \sum_{\ell=1}^{L/2} f_{2\ell-1}(x) \cdot f_{2\ell}(x).$$
     Then, P_i locally computes $q(1), q(2), q(3)$ and verifiably secret shares (VSS) them to the other parties (If the check consistency fails for some party, then it outputs reject).
     (c) The parties locally compute $[\![b_l]\!] = [\![c]\!] - [\![q(1)]\!] - [\![q(2)]\!]$ and store the result.
     (d) The parties call $\mathcal{F}_{\text{coin}}$ to receive a random $r \in R \setminus \{1, 2, 3\}$.
     (e) The parties locally compute $[\![q(r)]\!]$ and $[\![f_1(r)]\!], \ldots, [\![f_L(r)]\!]$ via Lagrange interpolation.
     (f) The parties set $c \leftarrow q(r)$, and $\forall k \in [L/2] : a_k \leftarrow f_{2k-1}(r), b_k \leftarrow f_{2k}(r)$ and $L \leftarrow L/2$.
  3. The parties exit the loop with $L = 2$ and inputs c, a_1, a_2, b_1, b_2 that are known to P_i and are secret shared among the parties. Then:
     (a) The parties call $\mathcal{F}_{\text{rand}}$ to receive $[\![w_1]\!]$ and $[\![w_2]\!]$, where $w_1, w_2 \in R$ are P_i's shares. Then, they define two polynomials f_1, f_2 of degree-2 such that: $f_1(0) = w_1, f_1(1) = a_1, f_1(2) = a_2$ and $f_2(0) = w_2, f_2(1) = b_1, f_2(2) = b_2$.
     (b) Party P_i defines a polynomial $q(x) = g(f_1(x), f_2(x))$ where $g(f_1(x), f_2(x)) = f_1(x) \cdot f_2(x)$. Thus, q is of degree-4. Then, P_i computes $q(0), q(1), \ldots, q(4)$.
     (c) Party P_i verifiably secret shares (VSS) the points $q(0), q(1), \ldots,$ $q(4)$ to the other parties (If the check consistency fails for some party, then it outputs reject).
     (d) The parties locally compute $[\![b_{\log L}]\!] = [\![c]\!] - [\![q(1)]\!] - [\![q(2)]\!]$.
     (e) The parties call $\mathcal{F}_{\text{coin}}$ to receive random $r, \gamma_1, \ldots \gamma_{\log L} \in R$.
     (f) The parties locally compute $[\![b]\!] = \sum_{l=1}^{\log L} \gamma_l \cdot [\![b_l]\!]$.
     (g) The parties locally compute $[\![f_1(r)]\!], [\![f_2(r)]\!]$ and $[\![q(r)]\!]$ via Lagrange interpolation.
     (h) The parties run reconstruct$([\![b]\!], j)$, reconstruct$([\![q(r)]\!], j)$, reconstruct$([\![f_1(r)]\!], j)$ and reconstruct$([\![f_2(r)]\!], j)$ for each $j \in [n]$. If any party received $\perp$ in any of these executions or if $b \neq 0$ or $q(r) \neq f_1(r) \cdot f_2(r)$, then it outputs reject. Otherwise, the parties output accept.

The asymptotic communication complexity is thus $O(n \log L + n)$. When the verified shared triples are defined over a *ring*, then the cost is multiplied with the degree of extension d. We ignore here the cost of consistency checks (in the VSS protocol) that can typically be batched together with a small constant cost.

For the computational cost, we remark that while our protocol requires many interpolations, all polynomials used in the protocol are of small degree (up to 4). Thus, the number of operations (i.e., multiplications and additions) required for each interpolation is a small constant. The number of polynomials that we have in the protocol is $L+1$ in the first iteration, $L/2+1$ in the second, $L/4+1$ in the third and so on. Over $\log L$ iterations, we thus have $O(L)$ polynomials and so the overall computational cost is also $O(L)$ operations.

A Constant-Round Protocol Using the Fiat-Shamir Transform. The number of rounds in Protocol 3.2 is logarithmic in the size of the input. In the full version of the paper, we show how to use the Fiat-Shamir transform [14] to reduce interaction and achieve constant number of rounds. This transform applies to public-coin protocols and proceeds by letting the prover generating the challenge in each round on its own, by applying a random oracle $H : \{0,1\}^* \to \{0,1\}^\kappa$ to the concatenation of the messages exchanged so far. In our protocol, the prover secret shares 3 elements in each round. This means that the random oracle should be applied on the shares sent to all the parties. This seems problematic, since the shares are private information which cannot be revealed, and so the verifiers have no way to compute the public randomness. Nevertheless, we show how to solve it by changing slightly the protocol.

Batching n Proofs Together. In our protocols, we will call Protocol 3.2 n times in parallel, each time for one of the parties participating in the multi-party computation. Naively, this means that the communication cost per party will be $O(n^2 \log L + n^2)$. We now show how to batch together these n proofs, reducing the cost to $O(n \log L + n)$.

To reduce the term $O(n^2 \log L)$ to $O(n \log L)$, one simply need to call $\mathcal{F}_{\text{coin}}$ once for each round of the n proofs. The parties can jointly generate a seed from which all the randomness is derived.

To reduce the term $O(n^2)$ to $O(n)$, recall first that in our proof the parties perform two tests: (i) they check that $b = 0$ and (ii) they check that $q(r) = f_1(r) \cdot f_2(r)$. These checks are carried-out by opening the secret shared $b, f_1(r), f_2(r)$ and $q(r)$ and checking that (i) and (ii) hold in the clear.

It is immediate to see that the first check can be compressed to one single check by taking a random linear combination of the b values in n proofs and opening the result. For the second check, we observe that verifying (ii) across n proofs is equivalent to check the correctness of n multiplication triples. This can be done in $O(n)$ complexity and $O(1)$ rounds via the verification technique of [32]. We present the details in the full version, where we show that the overall communication per party for running n proofs in parallel is

$$n \log L + 8n \text{ field elements}$$

and the asymptotic complexity is $O(n \log L + n)$ as required.

3.2 The Ideal Functionality $\mathcal{F}^{\text{cheatIdntfy}}_{\text{proveDeg2Rel}}$- Prove Correctness with Cheating Identification

In this section, we augment our protocol to prove degree-2 relations over shared data to achieve an additional property: if the protocol ends with the parties rejecting the proof, then in addition to reject, the parties will also output a pair of parties, with the guarantee that one of these parties belongs to the set of corrupted parties. Our protocol computes the ideal functionality $\mathcal{F}^{\text{cheatIdntfy}}_{\text{proveDeg2Rel}}$ defined in Functionality 3.3. The functionality works the same as the $\mathcal{F}^{\text{abort}}_{\text{proveDeg2Rel}}$ functionality defined in the previous section, with one addition: in case the output is reject, it outputs a pair of parties' indices. These contain the index of the prover and of an additional party chosen by the ideal world adversary $\mathcal{S}$. If P_i is corrupted, then $\mathcal{S}$ is allowed to pick any party it wishes. Otherwise, it must pick an index of a corrupted party. This ensures that one of the chosen parties is corrupted: in the first case, it is the prover, whereas in the second case $\mathcal{S}$ hands a corrupted party's index. Note also that in this functionality, unlike $\mathcal{F}^{\text{abort}}_{\text{proveDeg2Rel}}$, all honest parties output the same output.

FUNCTIONALITY 3.3. ($\mathcal{F}^{\text{cheatIdntfy}}_{\text{proveDeg2Rel}}$**- Prove Correctness - Identify Cheating)**

Let $\mathcal{S}$ be the ideal world adversary controlling a subset $< n/2$ of corrupted parties. The functionality $\mathcal{F}^{\text{cheatIdntfy}}_{\text{proveDeg2Rel}}$ is invoked by an index i sent from the honest parties and works exactly as $\mathcal{F}^{\text{abort}}_{\text{proveDeg2Rel}}$ with the following modification:

If Eq. (1) holds, then $\mathcal{F}^{\text{cheatIdntfy}}_{\text{proveDeg2Rel}}$ sends accept to $\mathcal{S}$, to receive back out $\in$ {accept, reject}. Then, $\mathcal{F}^{\text{cheatIdntfy}}_{\text{proveDeg2Rel}}$ sends out to the honest parties. If Eq. (1) does not hold, then $\mathcal{F}^{\text{cheatIdntfy}}_{\text{proveDeg2Rel}}$ sends reject to the honest parties.
If the output handed to the honest parties is reject:

- If P_i is corrupted, then $\mathcal{S}$ sends an index $j \in [n]$ to $\mathcal{F}^{\text{cheatIdntfy}}_{\text{proveDeg2Rel}}$. If P_i is honest, then $\mathcal{S}$ send an index j where P_j is corrupted.
- $\mathcal{F}^{\text{cheatIdntfy}}_{\text{proveDeg2Rel}}$ sends the pair (i, j) to the honest parties.

To compute functionality we use Protocol 3.2 from the previous section, with one additional step: in case that the parties reject the proof, the prover is asked to identify a party who cheated in the execution. Then, the pair of parties outputted by the protocol includes the prover and the party that was pointed at by the prover. Clearly, if the prover is corrupted, then regardless of the party it chooses, the output pair will contain a corrupted party. However, it is not clear how an honest prover will identify a party who cheated in the protocol (note that in this case, we know that the degree-2 relation holds, and so if the protocol ends with a reject, then it means that someone sent incorrect messages during the execution of the proof-of-correctness protocol). To allow an honest prover to correctly identify cheaters, we require the following additional property from our protocol: *the shares held by the parties should be known to the prover.* To leverage this property, we first observe the following fact:

Fact 3.4. *Each message sent by each verifier P_j in Protocol 3.2 is a deterministic function of (1) messages received from the prover P_i; (2) its inputs to the protocol; and (3) randomness received from $\mathcal{F}_{\text{coin}}$ and $\mathcal{F}_{\text{rand}}$.*

This implies that if the inputs of all parties and the randomness chosen during the execution are known to P_i, then it can compute by himself the messages that should be sent by the other parties, and so P_i can identify cheating parties that send incorrect messages. We stress that this fact does not mean that P_i knows *in advance* what messages should be sent in the execution, since these depend on randomness received in the execution only *after* P_i sends his messages. Thus, knowing the shares held by all parties does not break the soundness of the protocol, which rely on the randomness of the evaluated point r - randomness which P_i cannot predict.

Our protocol is described and proved in the full version of the paper. It is identical to Protocol 3.2 with the following modifications in the last steps: (i) the random sharings of $f_1(0)$ and $f_2(0)$ are now verifiably secret shared by P_i (this is allowed since P_i knows now all the inputs and essential to achieve the property of P_i knowing the messages that should be sent by all other parties); (ii) the messages to reconstruct the secrets are now broadcast (to ensure anonymous output) and (iii) if the parties reject the proof, the prover P_i identify a cheating party and broadcasts its index to the other parties.

Batching n Proofs Together and Communication Cost. In Sect. 3.1 we showed a way to batch n proofs together when only security with abort is considered. This enabled us to reduce communication complexity of n proofs ran in parallel from $O(n^2 \log L + n^2)$ to $O(n \log L + n)$ elements sent per party. While the optimization to reduce the term $O(n^2 \log L)$ to $O(n \log L)$ can be used here as well (call $\mathcal{F}_{\text{coin}}$ once for each round for all protocols), we note that it is impossible to batch all the checks at the end of the protocol together, since then the prover will lose the ability to identify cheaters.

Thus, the communication cost of running n proofs together per party is

$$n \log L + 4n \cdot |\mathcal{F}_{\text{bc}}| \text{ field elements.}$$

4 Secure Computation of Any Straight-Line Program with Abort

In this section we present a base construction, which is only secure with abort. Given a straight-line program P, the protocol computes $P(x)$ in two stages. It first executes a protocol which computes $P(x)$ using a private multiplication protocol, as defined in Sect. 2.3. It then runs a verification protocol which requires communication that is sublinear in the program's size S. If the verification protocol accepts then the value of $P(x)$ is correct, while if the verification protocol rejects then the honest parties abort the protocol.

The protocol can be based on any linear threshold secret-sharing as defined in Sect. 2.2 and works for both finite fields and the ring $\mathbb{Z}_{2^k}$. When instantiating the protocol with Shamir's secret sharing scheme, the obtained protocol matches the complexity achieved by the protocol of [22] for finite fields and arbitrary number of parties. When using replicated secret sharing as the underlying secret sharing scehme, the obtained protocol improves upon the result of [4] for constant number of parties over the ring $\mathbb{Z}_{2^k}$; while the additive sub-linear term in [4] is square root of the size of the program, in our protocol it is *logarithmic* in the program's size.

4.1 Verifying Correctness of Multiplications with Abort

In this section, we show how the parties can verify correctness of many multiplication triples with sub-linear communication complexity in the number of triples. A multiplication triple in a ring R is a secret shared tuple $[\![x]\!], [\![y]\!], [\![z]\!]$ such that $z = x \cdot y$. In other words, a triple shares both the inputs and the output of a multiplication instruction.

At the beginning of the protocol, the parties hold sharings of many multiplication triples denoted by $([\![x_1]\!], [\![y_1]\!], [\![z_1]\!]), \ldots, ([\![x_m]\!], [\![y_m]\!], [\![z_m]\!])$ and want to verify that $z_i = x_i \cdot y_i$ for each $i \in [m]$. The ideal functionality we compute is defined in Functionality 4.1. Observe that it allows the ideal world adversary $\mathcal{S}$ to force rejection even if all triples are correct. In contrast, if there exists a triple which is incorrect, then the output will always be reject. Note also that $\mathcal{F}_{\mathsf{vrfy}}^{\mathsf{abort}}$ hands $\mathcal{S}$ the corrupted parties' shares of all triples and the additive difference $d_k = z_k - x_k \cdot y_k$ when $d_k \neq 0$ (i.e., the triple is incorrect). This is justified by the fact that, as we will see, these are known anyway to the adversary in the main protocol that works in the $\mathcal{F}_{\mathsf{vrfy}}^{\mathsf{abort}}$-hybrid model. Moreover, in many private multiplication protocols, the adversary is even allowed to choose the additive difference (see [8,16,29]).

FUNCTIONALITY 4.1. ($\mathcal{F}_{\mathsf{vrfy}}^{\mathsf{abort}}$- Verify Correctness of Multiplications)
Let $\mathcal{S}$ be the ideal world adversary controlling a subset of $< n/2$ corrupted parties. The functionality $\mathcal{F}_{\mathsf{vrfy}}^{\mathsf{abort}}$ is invoked by the honest parties sending their shares of m multiplication triples $\{(x_k, y_k, z_k)_{k=1}^m\}$ to $\mathcal{F}_{\mathsf{vrfy}}^{\mathsf{abort}}$.
Then, $\mathcal{F}_{\mathsf{vrfy}}^{\mathsf{abort}}$ computes all secrets and the corrupted parties' shares which are sent to $\mathcal{S}$.
Then, it checks that $z_k = x_k \cdot y_k$ for all $k \in [m]$. If this holds, it sends accept to $\mathcal{S}$. In this case, it waits for $\mathcal{S}$ to send $\mathsf{out}_j \in \{\mathsf{accept}, \mathsf{reject}\}$ which is then handed to the honest party P_j. Otherwise, $\mathcal{F}_{\mathsf{vrfy}}^{\mathsf{abort}}$ sends reject to $\mathcal{S}$ and the honest parties. In addition, it sends $d_k = z_k - x_k \cdot y_k$ for each $k \in [m]$ for which $d_k \neq 0$ to $\mathcal{S}$.

To compute this functionality efficiently, the parties take a random linear combination $\beta = \sum_{k=1}^{m} \theta_k \cdot (z_k - x_k \cdot y_k)$ (where θ_k is random and jointly chosen by the parties) and wish to check that $\beta = 0$. Observe that since β is a 2-degree function of $\{(x_k, y_k, z_k)_{k=1}^{m}\}$, and these are secret shared via a linear threshold scheme among the parties, it follows that the parties can locally compute an additive sharing of β. At this point, we would want the parties to open the sharing of β and check equality to 0. However, an additive sharing has no robustness in it and so the parties have no way to verify that the received shares are correct. To overcome this, we first ask the parties to secret share their additive shares of $\psi = \sum_{k=1}^{m} \theta_k \cdot (x_k \cdot y_k)$ in a verifiable way. Denote by ψ^i the additive share of ψ held by party P_i. Once the parties hold $[\![\psi^i]\!]$ for each $i \in [n]$, the parties can compute $[\![\beta]\!] = \sum_{k=1}^{m} \theta_k \cdot [\![z_k]\!] - \sum_{i=1}^{n} [\![\psi^i]\!]$ and reconstruct the value of β. By the properties of the reconstruct procedure, the corrupted parties cannot do any harm beyond causing an abort. However, this is not enough since a corrupted party can share any value it wishes. Thus, the parties need to verify that each party shared the correct value. Towards achieving this, recall that one of the properties of the secret sharing scheme, is that it allows local conversion from $[\![x_k]\!], [\![y_k]\!]$ to $[\![x_k^i]\!], [\![y_k^i]\!]$ where x_k^i, y_k^i are the shares of x_k, y_k held by party P_i respectively. Thus, the parties wish to verify that

$$\forall i \in [n] : \sum_{k=1}^{m} \theta_k \cdot ([\![x_k^i]\!] \cdot [\![y_k^i]\!]) - [\![\psi^i]\!] = 0. \tag{3}$$

Letting $[\![c^i]\!] = [\![\psi^i]\!]$, $[\![a_k^i]\!] = \theta_k \cdot [\![x_k^i]\!]$ and $[\![b_k^i]\!] = [\![y_k^i]\!]$ we have that the parties ensure that $\forall i \in [n] : [\![c^i]\!] - \sum_{k=1}^{m} [\![a_k^i]\!] \cdot [\![b_k^i]\!] = 0$. This is exactly the type of statement that can be verified using $\mathcal{F}_{\mathsf{proveDeg2Rel}}^{\mathsf{abort}}$ defined in Sect. 3. Hence, the parties call $\mathcal{F}_{\mathsf{proveDeg2Rel}}^{\mathsf{abort}}$ and proceed only if it outputs accept. The formal description of the protocol and a security proof appear in the full version of the paper.

Extending the Protocol to the Ring $\mathbb{Z}_{2^k}$. If the parties work over the ring $\mathbb{Z}_{2^k}$, then the statistical error of the protocol is only 1/2. To achieve an error which is sufficiently small, the parties can choose $\theta_1, \ldots, \theta_m$ from a larger ring $\mathbb{Z}_{2^{k+s}}$. Then, the probability that $\beta = 0$ when $\exists k \in [m] : \ d_k = z_k - x_k \cdot y_k \neq 0$ will be at most 2^{-s}.

Communication Complexity. Note that in the protocol each party only shares one element and reconstructs one element. The cost of computing $\mathcal{F}_{\mathsf{vrfy}}^{\mathsf{abort}}$ thus equals to the cost of calling n copies of $\mathcal{F}_{\mathsf{proveDeg2Rel}}^{\mathsf{abort}}$ plus a small constant cost. By the analysis in Sect. 3.1, we conclude that the cost is $O(n \log m + n)$.

4.2 The Main Protocol

Our main protocol works in the $\mathcal{F}_{\mathsf{vrfy}}^{\mathsf{abort}}$-hybrid model. In the protocol, the parties first verifiably secret shares their inputs to the other parties. Then, they compute

Table 1. Field elements sent per party in the verification of m multiplication triples, per one triple, when Shamir's secret sharing is used, for different sizes of m and number of parties n. The numbers are computed via the formula $(10n + n \cdot \log m) \cdot \frac{1}{m}$ and the statistical error is $\frac{2 \log m+4}{|\mathbb{F}|-5}$.

# of multiplication triples (m)	Field elements per party per triple $n = 25$	$n = 50$	$n = 500$	$n = 1000$
2^{15}	0.02	0.03	0.38	0.76
2^{20}	0.0007	0.001	0.01	0.02
2^{25}	0.00002	0.00005	0.0005	0.001
2^{30}	0.0000009	0.000002	0.00002	0.0003

the program using Π_{mult}. Before revealing the outputs, they call $\mathcal{F}_{\mathsf{vrfy}}^{\mathsf{abort}}$ to verify the correctness of all multiplication triples. If the output received from $\mathcal{F}_{\mathsf{vrfy}}^{\mathsf{abort}}$ is reject, then they abort. Otherwise, they proceed to reconstruct the output. The formal description appears in the full version of the paper.

Communication Complexity. Let m be the number of multiplication gates in the program and let $|\Pi_{\mathsf{mult}}|$ be the communication cost per party when running Π_{mult}. Thus, the communication cost is $|\Pi_{\mathsf{mult}}| \cdot m + O(\log m \cdot n)$. Amortized over the size of the program and assuming that $m >> n$, we have that the cost per gate is $|\Pi_{\mathsf{mult}}|$.

Practical Instantiations. Our protocol can be instantiated using both replicated and Shamir's secret sharing schemes (see Sect. 2.2). The former is usually used for small number of parties and when working over rings, whereas the latter is usually preferred when the number of parties grows, due to the fact that the size of each share grows at most logarithmically with n. For Π_{mult}, it is possible to use protocols such as [1,28] (for 3 parties) or the DN protocol [11] for any number of parties. As shown in Sect. 2.3 (see also [4], the communication cost of the semi-honest DN protocol with replicated secret-sharing and pseudorandom secret sharing is less than 1.5 ring elements per party per multiplication. This dominates the amortized cost of our main protocol.

4.3 Concrete Efficiency

To illustrate the efficiency of our protocol, we measured the exact communication cost of our verification protocol, for various program sizes and number of parties. In Table 1, we present the number of *field elements* sent per party amortized over the size of the program, when instantiating our protocol with Shamir's secret sharing scheme. The reported numbers in the table can be seen as the cost of strengthening security from semi-honest to malicious, per multiplication instruction. As can be seen, the communication overhead of our verification protocol is so low, that even when the number of parties is increased to 1000,

Table 2. Ring elements sent per party in the verification of m multiplication triples, per one triple, for different sizes of m and number of parties n, when the semi-honest computation is over the ring $\mathbb{Z}_{2^k}$ and using replicated secret sharing scheme. The numbers are computed via the formula $\left(\binom{n-1}{t} \cdot 2 + 2.5n + n\log(m)\right) \cdot \frac{1}{m} \cdot d$, where the extension degree d satisfies the condition $d > 40 + \log(2\log m + 4)$ to achieve statistical error of 2^{-40}.

# of multiplication triples (m)	Ring elements sent per party per triple				
	$n = 3$	$n = 5$	$n = 7$	$n = 9$	$n = 11$
2^{15}	0.002	0.13	0.22	0.41	0.97
2^{20}	0.00008	0.005	0.008	0.01	0.03
2^{25}	0.000003	0.0002	0.0003	0.0005	0.001
2^{30}	0.0000001	0.000007	0.00001	0.00001	0.00005

the cost is still less just 0.76 field element per instruction. We note that when the field is small, the verification protocol can be "lifted" to an extension field $\mathbb{F}$ of the same characteristic, without changing the base semi-honest protocol. As a result, the statistical error can be reduced to (roughly) an inverse of the size of the extension field.

In Table 2 we present the communication cost when our protocol is used to compute a program defined over the ring $\mathbb{Z}_{2^k}$ for some $k \geq 1$ (when $k = 1$ this is equivalent to computing a binary circuit), with replicated secret sharing as the underlying secret sharing scheme. Recall that in this case, the verification protocol is carried-out over an extension ring (see the end of Sect. 3.1). To compute the number of ring elements sent in the verification protocol, we thus multiply the communication cost obtained over fields with the degree extension d (since the size of each element is increased by a factor of d). The extension degree depends on the desired statistical error, which is approximately $\frac{2\log m+4}{2^d}$. This means in particular that for security of s bits, the extension degree should satisfy the condition $d > s + \log(2\log m + 4)$. In Table 2, we report the number of sent ring elements per instruction for each party, with statistical error of at most 2^{-40}, and so it suffices to set $d = 46$. In addition, each opening of a secret requires each party to send $\binom{n-1}{t}$ elements. However, note that this is not the case for sharing a secret, since here we can have all subsets except one derive their share from a pre-distributed seed (known also to the dealer), and have the dealer send just one share (to adjust the secret) to one subset of $t+1$ shares. This means that sharing a secret yields cost of 0.5 ring elements per party, exactly as for Shamir's secret sharing. Due to the fast increase of the share's size in this scheme, we report the cost up to 11 parties. Note that even for $n = 11$, programs of size $\geq 2^{15}$) can be computed in the presence of malicious adversaries, while paying an extra cost of *less than 1 ring elements per instruction* beyond the cost of semi-honest security.

For the computational cost, we saw that in $\mathcal{F}^{\text{abort}}_{\text{proveDeg2Rel}}$ the number of local operations is $O(m)$ with small constants. Observe that in $\mathcal{F}^{\text{abort}}_{\text{vrfy}}$ the parties only

Table 3. Comparison to previous works of communication and round complexity, when verifying m multiplication triples by n parties.

	Communication per party (field elements)	# of rounds
Nordholt et al. [32]	$O(m+n)$	$O(1)$
Boneh et al. [4]	$O(n\sqrt{m}+n)$	$O(1)$
Goyal et al. [22]	$O(n\log m+n)$	$O(\log m)$
This work (with Fiat-Shamir)	$\mathbf{O(n\log m+n)}$	$\mathbf{O(1)}$

need to compute a linear combination of m inputs and so the cost is roughly m operations. Since we have n calls to $\mathcal{F}^{\text{abort}}_{\text{proveDeg2Rel}}$, the overall cost is $n \cdot O(m)$.

Comparison to Previous Works. In Table 3 we compare our security-with-abort verification protocol with previous works. As can be seen, our work as well as [4,22] achieve sublinear communication, whereas [32] achieves only linear communication in the amount of verified triples m. Our improvement compared to [4] is that our sublinear additive term is logarithmic in m rather than just square root of m. Compared to [22], we are able to use the Fiat-Shamir transform to achieve constant number of rounds (see Sect. 3.1), whereas in their protocol, the parties carry out a joint multiparty computation is each step of the protocol, and so it is unclear how to reduce interaction via the Fiat-Shamir transform.

5 Achieving Full Security for Constant Number of Parties

In this section, we show how to augment our base construction to full security, including fairness and guaranteed output delivery, without changing the amortized communication cost.

Our protocol works by having the parties divide the program into segments and compute each segment separately. For each segment, the parties work in the same way as before, that is, computing it first using a private multiplication protocol and then running a verification protocol. However, we change the verification protocol so that it will give the parties more information besides outputting merely accept or reject. Specifically, in the case of reject, the verification protocol will also output a pair of parties in conflict, such that at least one of them is guaranteed to be corrupted. Once such a pair is known, the parties will remove both parties from the protocol and recompute the segment without them. Since one of the eliminated parties is corrupt, it follows that an honest majority is maintained even though the number of parties was reduced by two. Removing two parties and restarting the segment computation without them raises several challenges. In particular, the parties need to carefully move from a t-out-of-n sharing to a $(t-1)$-out-of-$(n-2)$ secret sharing. Our solution to this includes having authentication tags over the shares, which prevent corrupted parties from cheating in the process. We present a novel technique for computing these tags efficiently, requiring a single tag for all the shares held by a subset of $t+1$ parties and using sublinear communication in the number of shares. We stress that authentication is required only for the *secrets that are stored in memory when moving from one layer to the next layer.* This fact together with the sublinear communication of our verification protocol implies that the overall amortized communication cost per multiplication instruction remains $|\Pi_{\text{mult}}|$.

The construction in this section is designed for replicated secret sharing scheme only and thus we assume that the number of parties n is *constant.* Our construction depends on two properties that hold for replicated secret sharing: (1) Pair-wise consistency: when opening a secret, the opening will fail if there exist two parties which do not agree on a certain share. If we know in advance that the sharing was consistent, such a disagreement can occur only with a corrupted party. This is used in our protocol to find a pair of disputed parties, where at least one of them is guaranteed to be corrupt. (2) For each input held by a party P_i, we can define a consistent secret sharing of this input, which is known to P_i. This holds since any secret held by P_i is known to t other parties and so it is possible to define a sharing where the share of one subset of $t+1$ parties is the input itself, whereas the shares of the other subsets is 0. This property is required in our verification protocol when each party proves it behaved honestly when sharing a secret.

This section is organized as follows. In Sect. 5.1 we present the updated verification protocol which allows identification of a pair of conflicting parties to eliminate. In Sect. 5.2 we present two additional sub-protocols which are required for our construction. Finally, in Sect. 5.3 we present the main protocol for computing any arithmetic program.

5.1 Joint Verification of Multiplications with Cheating Identification

In this section, we present the verification protocol, with the property that when cheating took place in the execution of the private multiplication protocol, the parties will be able to identify a pair of conflicting parties (and not just reject the computation). Our protocol realizes the functionality $\mathcal{F}_{\mathsf{vrfy}}^{\mathsf{full}}$ formally described in Functionality 5.1, which is defined similarly to $\mathcal{F}_{\mathsf{vrfy}}^{\mathsf{abort}}$ but with two differences: first, the parties always receive the same output. Second, if the trusted party computing $\mathcal{F}_{\mathsf{vrfy}}^{\mathsf{full}}$ outputs reject (which means that there exists an incorrect multiplication triple), then the ideal world adversary can pick one of two options: provide a pair of parties to eliminate, where at least one of them is a corrupted party, or let $\mathcal{F}_{\mathsf{vrfy}}^{\mathsf{full}}$ detect such pair. In the latter, $\mathcal{F}_{\mathsf{vrfy}}^{\mathsf{full}}$ receives the inputs, randomness and views of the honest parties when computing some incorrect multiplication triple. Then, based on this information, $\mathcal{F}_{\mathsf{vrfy}}^{\mathsf{full}}$ finds a pair of conflicting parties and outputs it to the parties.

Our protocol to compute $\mathcal{F}_{\mathsf{vrfy}}^{\mathsf{full}}$ is an extension of our protocol from Sect. 4.1. In order to add the cheating identification property to our verification protocol, we need to provide a mechanism to identify a pair of conflicting parties in each step for which the parties may output reject in the original protocol. There are 4

FUNCTIONALITY 5.1. ($\mathcal{F}_{\mathsf{vrfy}}^{\mathsf{full}}$**- Verify Mult. with Cheating Identification**)
Let $\mathcal{S}$ be the ideal world adversary controlling a subset $< n/2$ of corrupted parties. The functionality $\mathcal{F}_{\mathsf{vrfy}}^{\mathsf{full}}$ is invoked by the honest parties sending their shares of m multiplication triples $\{(x_k, y_k, z_k)_{k=1}^{m}\}$ to $\mathcal{F}_{\mathsf{vrfy}}^{\mathsf{full}}$.
Then, $\mathcal{F}_{\mathsf{vrfy}}^{\mathsf{full}}$ computes all secrets and the corrupted parties' shares. These shares are sent to $\mathcal{S}$.
Then, it checks that $z_k = x_k \cdot y_k$ for all $k \in [m]$. If this holds, it sends accept to $\mathcal{S}$. Otherwise, it sends reject to $\mathcal{S}$ and $d_k = z_k - x_k \cdot y_k$ for each $k \in [m]$ such that $d_k \neq 0$. Then:

- If $\mathcal{F}_{\mathsf{vrfy}}^{\mathsf{full}}$ sent accept, then it waits for $\mathcal{S}$ to send out $\in$ {accept, reject} which is then handed to the honest parties. If out = reject, then $\mathcal{S}$ is required to send a pair of indices (i, j) to $\mathcal{F}_{\mathsf{vrfy}}^{\mathsf{full}}$ with at least one of them being a corrupted party. Then, $\mathcal{F}_{\mathsf{vrfy}}^{\mathsf{full}}$ hands (i, j) to the honest parties.
- If $\mathcal{F}_{\mathsf{vrfy}}^{\mathsf{full}}$ sent reject, then $\mathcal{S}$ chooses one of the next two options:
  - Send a pair of indices (i, j) to $\mathcal{F}_{\mathsf{vrfy}}^{\mathsf{full}}$ with at least one of them being a corrupted party. Then, $\mathcal{F}_{\mathsf{vrfy}}^{\mathsf{full}}$ hands (i, j) to the honest parties.
  - Ask $\mathcal{F}_{\mathsf{vrfy}}^{\mathsf{full}}$ to find a pair of conflicting parties in the $\bar{k}$th multiplication. Then, $\mathcal{F}_{\mathsf{vrfy}}^{\mathsf{full}}$ commands the honest parties to send their inputs, randomness and views in the execution to compute $\bar{k}$th triple. Then, based on this information, $\mathcal{F}_{\mathsf{vrfy}}^{\mathsf{full}}$ computes the messages that should have been sent by each corrupted party, and find a pair of parties P_i, P_j , where P_j received an incorrect message. Then, $\mathcal{F}_{\mathsf{vrfy}}^{\mathsf{full}}$ sends (i, j) to the honest parties and $\mathcal{S}$.

such steps: (i) when the VSS protocol to share the additive shares fails due to inconsistency; (ii) when $\mathcal{F}_{\mathrm{proveDeg2Rel}}^{\mathrm{abort}}$ returns reject; (iii) when the opening of β fails due to inconsistency; and (iv) when the parties output reject since $\beta \neq 0$.

Note that in (i), we can simply ask the dealer to broadcast any share for which pair-wise inconsistency exist. Since this can happen only with shares that are known to the adversary, no secret information is never revealed. To identify a pair of conflicting parties in case (iii), we use the pairwise-consistency check of replicated secret sharing to identify a disputed pair. Namely, that inconsistency can occur only when an honest party and a corrupted party disagree on the value of a share held by both of them. Note that in addition we need that the messages in the consistency check will broadcast (via $\mathcal{F}_{\mathsf{bc}}$), otherwise the parties may not agree on the disputed pair they output. For (ii), we simply use $\mathcal{F}_{\mathrm{proveDeg2Rel}}^{\mathrm{cheatIdntfy}}$. Recall that our protocol to realize $\mathcal{F}_{\mathrm{proveDeg2Rel}}^{\mathrm{cheatIdntfy}}$ requires that the proving party will know the shares held by the other parties. This indeed holds for replicated secret sharing, since the parties convert $[\![x_k]\!], [\![y_k]\!], [\![z_k]\!]$ to $[\![x_k^i]\!], [\![y_k^i]\!], [\![z_k^i]\!]$ by setting the shares of all subsets T for which $P_i \notin T$ to be 0 (see Sect. 2.2). Finally, for case (iv), if the parties reject since $\beta \neq 0$, we observe that this means that no one cheated in the verification protocol itself (with high probability). Thus, the parties can conclude that cheating took place in one of the calls to the private multiplication protocol to compute the program. The parties thus continue to localize the fault by running a binary search on the set of multiplication triples, aiming to find the *first* triple k where the corrupted party have cheated and $z_k \neq x_k \cdot y_k$. In each step of the search, the parties repeat the verification protocol on a smaller set of triples. The search will continue at the worst case (i.e., if no execution have ended with obtaining a pair of conflicting parties), until the parties are left with one incorrect triple. Finally, the parties can check the execution of the multiplication protocol for computing this triple, and use it to find a pair of disputing parties. For this final check, we define an ideal functionality $\mathcal{F}_{\mathsf{miniMPC}}$ that receives the input, randomness and view of each honest party in the multiplication protocol and output the first pair of parties for which incoming and sent messages do not match. Observe that this functionality is called just once for the entire computation and so its cost is amortized away, regardless of the way it is realized. We provide a formal description of the protocol and proof of security in the full version of the paper.

Cheating Probability. Assume that there is one incorrect triple. Then, if the adversary does not cheat in the verification protocol, then this triple will be tested in at most $\log m$ executions of the protocol. In each execution, the probability that it will pass the test is bounded by $\frac{1}{|\mathbb{F}|}$. This holds since the parties will output accept in this case only if the random linear combination cause the opened value to be 0. Note that if the output of the parties is accept when examining a set of triples, then they stop the search in this set. Thus, an incorrect triple has $\log m$ attempts to be accepted. The overall cheating probability is therefore bounded by $\log m \cdot \frac{1}{|\mathbb{F}|}$.

We remark that the protocol can be extended to work over a ring in the same way as for $\mathcal{F}^{\mathsf{abort}}_{\mathsf{vrfy}}$. See the remark at the end of Sect. 4.1.

Communication Cost. Our protocol is recursive. In jth step of the recursion, the parties secret share one element, reconstruct one element (using $\mathcal{F}_{\mathsf{bc}}$) and call $\mathcal{F}^{\mathrm{cheatIdntfy}}_{\mathrm{proveDeg2Rel}}$ for each party over a set of triples of size $m/2^j$. Sharing a secret requires each party to send $\binom{n}{t}$ elements (we ignore here the consistency check which can be typically done with constant cost), reconstruction requires sending $\binom{n-1}{t}$ elements by each party and the cost of n invocations of $\mathcal{F}^{\mathrm{cheatIdntfy}}_{\mathrm{proveDeg2Rel}}$, as shown in Sect. 3.2, is $n\log(m/2^j) + 4n \cdot \binom{n-1}{t} \cdot |\mathcal{F}_{\mathsf{bc}}|$ per party. Overall, the obtained cost per party is roughly

$$\binom{n}{t} \cdot \log m + \binom{n-1}{t} \cdot \log m \cdot 4n \cdot |\mathcal{F}_{\mathsf{bc}}| + n \cdot \log m \cdot \log \sqrt{m} \ \ \text{ring elements.} \tag{4}$$

For constant number of parties, the asymptotic cost is roughly $O\left(\log m \cdot \log \sqrt{m}\right)$, which is sublinear in m. We remind the reader that when the triples were computed over the ring $\mathbb{Z}_{2^k}$, then the verification protocol is carried-out over an extension ring; see the end of Sect. 4.2 for more details.

5.2 Two Additional Building Blocks

Computing Authentication Tags. We next show how to compute an authentication tag over shares held by a subset T of $t+1$ parties. Let $x_1^T, \ldots, x_L^T$ be the shares held by the parties in T. The authentication tag τ^T is computed as follows: $\tau^T = \sum_{k=1}^{L} u_k^T \cdot x_k^T + v^T$, where $\boldsymbol{u}^T = (u_1^T, \ldots, u_L^T)$ and v^T are random secret keys that are shared among the parties using *authenticated* secret sharing (see definition in Sect. 2). Observe that for the long vector u^T it is possible to secret share a random seed from which the key is expanded, thus using the expensive mechanism of authenticated secret sharing only small constant number of times.

To compute the tag we observe that the parties can first locally compute an additive sharing of $\sum_{k=1}^{m} u_k^T \cdot x_k^T$. This is done by taking $[\![u_k^T]\!] \cdot [\![x_k^T]\!]$, where $[\![x_k^T]\!]$ is simply defined such that the share held by subset T is x_k^T and the shares held by the other subsets is 0. Then, we let each party secret share each additive share and prove that it shared the correct secret. The observation here is that we can utilize the functionality $\mathcal{F}_{\text{proveDeg2Rel}}^{\text{cheatIdntfy}}$ for this proof, as the additive share each party computes and shares to the other parties, is a 2-degree function of inputs that are verifiably shared among the other parties. If all proofs passed the check, then the parties can locally add the shared secrets, add $[\![v^T]\!]$ to the result and reconstruct the obtained tag. If the reconstructions fails due to pair-wise inconsistency, then the parties obtain a conflicting pair of parties.

Formally, The parties work as follows:

$\Pi_{auth}(x_1^T, \ldots, x_L^T, [\![\boldsymbol{u}^T]\!], [\![v^T]\!])$:

1. The parties locally compute $\langle z^T \rangle = \left\langle \sum_{k=1}^{L} u_k^T \cdot x_k^T \right\rangle = \sum_{k=1}^{L} [\![u_k^T]\!] \cdot [\![x_k^T]\!]$
2. Let $z^{T,i}$ the additive share of z^T held by P_i. Note that by definition $z^{T,i} = 0$ for each $P_i \notin T$. Then, each party $P_i \in T$ verifiably secret shares (VSS) $z^{T,i}$ to the other parties.
3. For each $i \in [n]$ such that $P_i \in T$, the parties convert $[\![u_k^T]\!]$ to $[\![u_k^{T,i}]\!]$ for each $k \in [L]$ and send $[\![z^{T,i}]\!]$ and $\left([\![u_k^T]\!], [\![x_k^T]\!]\right)_{k=1}^{L}$ to $\mathcal{F}_{\text{proveDeg2Rel}}^{\text{cheatIdntfy}}$.
4. If the parties received reject, (i,j) from $\mathcal{F}_{\text{proveDeg2Rel}}^{\text{cheatIdntfy}}$ in any of the calls in the previous step, then the parties output the first pair of conflicting parties (P_i, P_j). Otherwise, they proceed to the next step.
5. The parties locally compute $[\![\tau^T]\!] = \sum_{i \mid P_i \in T} [\![z^{T,i}]\!] + [\![v^T]\!]$.
6. The parties reveal τ^T by sending their shares via $\mathcal{F}_{\mathsf{bc}}$ to each other. If the shares are inconsistent, then the parties output the first pair of parties for which pair-wise consistency exists. Otherwise, they output τ^T.

Communication Complexity. We note that in practice the parties can call $\mathcal{F}_{\text{proveDeg2Rel}}^{\text{cheatIdntfy}}$ once per party for all shares (over the same layer of instructions). Thus, the cost is dominated by each party secret sharing its additive sharing of z^T, and opening the shared tag at the end. Overall, this means that for each subset T of $t+1$ parties, the cost per party is $\binom{n}{t} + |\mathcal{F}_{\text{proveDeg2Rel}}^{\text{cheatIdntfy}}| + \binom{n-1}{t} \cdot |\mathcal{F}_{\mathsf{bc}}|$.

Player Elimination and Recovery. We next show how the parties can remove a pair of conflicting parties and restart the computation without them.

Denote the parties to eliminate by P_i and P_j. The goal is to recompute the segment, but with less parties. Since we are guaranteed that at least one of the parties is corrupted, then we move from a t-out-of-n secret sharing to a $(t-1)$-out-of-$(n-2)$ secret sharing (i.e., the number of parties is reduced by 2 and the threshold is reduced by 1). In order to achieve this, we distinguish between three types of shares:

- *Shares that are known to either P_i or P_j*: In this case, no action is needed by the parties, as each such share is now known to t active parties, which is exactly what needed by the updated threshold.
- *Shares that are known to both P_i and P_j*: Shares in this category are held by a subset T of $t+1$ parties, with $P_i, P_j \in T$. Since we require that from now on each share will be held by a subset of t parties, it suffices to reveal this share to a subset T' of t parties, which will add the share to its current share. To minimize communication, we can take $T' = T \setminus \{P_i, P_j\} \cup \{P_k\}$ for some $P_k \notin T$. This implies that we need all parties in T to send the share to P_k.This is where the authentication tags are being used. Each party that holds the share sends it to P_k. However, corrupted parties may send incorrect values. Thus, the keys used to authenticate the share are also being revealed (recall that they are secret shared using an authentication secret sharing scheme and so cheating is not possible when opening these values). Once the keys are revealed, party P_k checks for each share it received, that the tag is correct given the authentication keys (i.e., that $\tau^T = \sum_{k=1}^{L} u_k^T \cdot x_k^T + v^T$). Since in each subset there exists at least one honest party, then at least one of the possible shares is correct, and so the check will pass for this share.
- *Shares that are not known to both P_i and P_j*: Note that each such share is known to a set of $t+1$ active parties. Since the threshold is now reduced to t, we just let one subset of t parties (there are exactly $\binom{t+1}{t} = t+1$ such subsets) locally add this share to the share already held by it. Note that the parties can locally update the authentication tag for the updated share of this subset, by simply adding the tag of the added share to the existing tag.

Observe that only for shares in the second category interaction is required. There are $\binom{n-2}{t-1}$ such shares, which are transmitted from $t+1$ parties to a single party. Recall that this cost is paid only for shares that are stored between segments of the program. Nevertheless, later we will see that for specific instantiations, it is possible to eliminate this cost completely.

5.3 The Main Protocol

In this section, we describe our main protocol to compute any straight-line program. Our protocol computes the program segment by segment. Throughout the protocol we maintain the following invariant: at the beginning of each segment's computation, the parties hold a consistent sharing of the values on the input layer of the segment, an authentication tag for the shares held by each subset of $t+1$ parties on the input layer and an authenticated secret sharing of the keys used to compute the tag. A computation of a segment includes using private multiplication and computing authentication tags for the shares on the output layer of the segment. Then, the parties use the verification protocol to verify that the output is correct. If the verification succeeds, then the parties can proceed to the next segment. Otherwise, the parties hold a pair of parties to eliminate. In this case, they apply the player elimination and recovery subprotocol and recompute the segment with less two parties and updated secret sharing of the input layer. To achieve fairness when outputs are revealed we use again the authentication mechanism. Here however, we cannot authenticate all shares held by a subset T together, since the shares may be intended to different parties. Thus, for the output layer of the entire program, the parties compute new authentication tags for each subset of shares intended to party P_i and held by a subset of parties T. The formal description can be found in the full version of this paper.

Size of the Segments. Each time we repeat the computation of a segment, it means that one corrupted party was eliminated. Thus, each segment can be computed at most t times. If we split the program to $O(n^2)$ equally sized segments (i.e., with the same amount of multiplication instructions), then amortized over the entire program, it can be shown that the average number of repetitions per instruction is approximately 1.

Communication Complexity for Constant Number of Parties. For each segment with $m/O(n^2)$ multiplication instructions, we call Π_{mult} for each multiplication, call Π_{auth} for each subset of $t+1$ parties at the output layer and call $\mathcal{F}_{\mathsf{vrfy}}^{\mathsf{full}}$ once. The asymptotic cost of $\mathcal{F}_{\mathsf{vrfy}}^{\mathsf{full}}$ per party for a segment of size m/n^2 is $O(\log(m/n^2)\cdot\log\sqrt{m/n^2})$. Thus, the cost of computing the segment is $\frac{m}{n^2}\cdot|\Pi_{\mathsf{mult}}|+O(\log(m/n^2)\cdot\log\sqrt{m/n^2})$. Summing over all $O(n^2)$ segments, the cost per party is thus $m\cdot|\Pi_{\mathsf{mult}}|+O(n^2\log(m/n^2)\cdot\log\sqrt{m/n^2})$. Letting the program's size S be its number of multiplication instructions, and assuming that n is constant, the cost of our protocol per multiplication per party is $|\Pi_{\mathsf{mult}}|+o(S)$.

If cheating took place, then the parties need to recover shares held by the eliminated parties for each secret stored in memory between the segments. The number of such secrets is bounded by the width of the program W. Thus, in case of cheating the cost per party is $|\Pi_{\mathsf{mult}}|\cdot S+O(W)+o(S)$. Note that $W\leq S$ and in many cases, W will be much smaller than S, and so $O(W)$ can be ignored.

Removing the $O(W)$ Term when Π_{mult} is Instantiated with [11]**.** If we instantiate Π_{mult} with the DN protocol [11], then as explained in Sect. 2.3, the cost of Π_{mult} is *1.5 elements per party.* We next show how it is possible to recover from cheating without increasing the communication cost, improving upon our general construction from Sect. 5.2. Recall that in the DN protocol, the output shares (of each multiplication) are computed by taking $[\![r]\!]+(xy-r)$, where

$[\![r]\!]$ is a sharing of a random r that was generated in the offline step (possibly without any interaction), and $xy - r$ is computed by party P_1 (the parties send him masked additive shares of $x \cdot y$). Note that $xy - r$ is in fact sent from P_1 only to one subset of $t + 1$ parties (including P_1 itself), denoted by T. Now, assume that cheating was detected and two parties, say P_i and P_j are eliminated. To recover the computation, it suffices that the parties will generate a new $[\![r]\!]$ with the updated $t - 1$ threshold, and that one subset of t active parties will add $xy - r$ to its share of r. If the eliminated parties are not both in T, then this can be done without interaction. However, if both of them are in T, then $xy - r$ is known now only to $t - 1$ active parties. Thus, we require that some party $P_k \notin T$ will learn $xy - r$. To this end, we ask party $P_\ell \in T$ $(\ell \neq i, j)$ to send $xy - r$ to P_k. To detect whether P_ℓ sent the correct value, we use the authentication mechanism as before. Specifically, the parties compute authentication tags for all $xy - r$ received during the computation (for secrets that are outputs of segments only). Thus, if the authentication succeeds, then P_k has the correct $xy - r$ and the parties can recompute the segment. Otherwise, P_k accuse P_ℓ of sending him an incorrect value. Note that in this case, we know again that either P_k or P_ℓ are corrupted. Moreover, this is a new pair of conflicted parties that does not overlap with the original pair. In this case, we restart the recovery process to remove 4 parties and update the sharings to a $(t-2)$-out-of-$(n-4)$ secret sharing. As before, we ask a party from T to send $xy - r$ to a party outside of T, with both parties not being one of the eliminated parties, and so on. Note that the process can end with two outcomes: (1) At some point, no one complains. In this case, the parties successfully removed $t' < t$ pair of parties, where in each pair, one of the parties is guaranteed to be corrupted. The parties thus can continue the computation. (2) The parties keep adding pair of conflicted parties to the list, until we are left with one honest party. This holds since we started with $t - 1$ active parties in T, and t outside of T. Thus, at some point there will remain one party outside of T. This party must be honest since we overall eliminated t pairs of semi-corrupted parties, with the property that one of them must be corrupted. Since there are t corrupted parties, the remaining party is honest. In this case, following the 3-party construction of [5], this honest party can be used as a trusted party and complete the computation. Note that in the above process, each pair that is eliminated requires the transmission of one element. However, in future multiplications, the overall communication is reduced by at least one element, since a party that is eliminated, will not be part of the interaction anymore. Thus, amortized over the circuit, the recovery process is communication-free. The overall cost of our entire protocol is thus $1.5 \cdot S + o(S)$, with no dependency on the width of the circuit.

References

1. Araki, T., Furukawa, J., Lindell, Y., Nof, A., Ohara, K.: High-throughput semi-honest secure three-party computation with an honest majority. In: ACM CCS (2016)
2. Ben-Or, M., Goldwasser, S., Wigderson, A.: Completeness theorems for non-cryptographic fault-tolerant distributed computation (extended abstract). In: ACM Symposium on Theory of Computing (1988)
3. Ben-Sasson, E., Fehr, S., Ostrovsky, R.: Near-linear unconditionally-secure multiparty computation with a dishonest minority. In: Safavi-Naini, R., Canetti, R. (eds.) CRYPTO 2012. LNCS, vol. 7417, pp. 663–680. Springer, Heidelberg (2012). https://doi.org/10.1007/978-3-642-32009-5_39
4. Boneh, D., Boyle, E., Corrigan-Gibbs, H., Gilboa, N., Ishai, Y.: Zero-knowledge proofs on secret-shared data via fully linear PCPs. In: Boldyreva, A., Micciancio, D. (eds.) CRYPTO 2019. LNCS, vol. 11694, pp. 67–97. Springer, Cham (2019). https://doi.org/10.1007/978-3-030-26954-8_3
5. Boyle, E., Gilboa, N., Ishai, Y., Nof, A.: Practical fully secure three-party computation via sublinear distributed zero-knowledge proofs. In: ACM CCS (2019)
6. Byali, M., Hazay, C., Patra, A., Singla, S.: Fast actively secure five-party computation with security beyond abort. In: ACM CCS (2019)
7. Chaum, D., Crépeau, C., Damgård, I.: Multiparty unconditionally secure protocols (extended abstract). In: ACM Symposium on Theory of Computing (1988)
8. Chida, K., et al.: Fast large-scale honest-majority MPC for malicious adversaries. In: Shacham, H., Boldyreva, A. (eds.) CRYPTO 2018. LNCS, vol. 10993, pp. 34–64. Springer, Cham (2018). https://doi.org/10.1007/978-3-319-96878-0_2
9. Cleve, R.: Towards optimal simulations of formulas by bounded-width programs. In: ACM Symposium on Theory of Computing (1990)
10. Cramer, R., Damgård, I., Ishai, Y.: Share conversion, pseudorandom secret-sharing and applications to secure computation. In: Kilian, J. (ed.) TCC 2005. LNCS, vol. 3378, pp. 342–362. Springer, Heidelberg (2005). https://doi.org/10.1007/978-3-540-30576-7_19
11. Damgård, I., Nielsen, J.B.: Scalable and unconditionally secure multiparty computation. In: Menezes, A. (ed.) CRYPTO 2007. LNCS, vol. 4622, pp. 572–590. Springer, Heidelberg (2007). https://doi.org/10.1007/978-3-540-74143-5_32
12. Dolev, D., Strong, H.R.: Authenticated algorithms for Byzantine agreement. SIAM J. Comput. **12**(4), 656–666 (1983)
13. Fehr, S., Yuan, C.: Towards optimal robust secret sharing with security against a rushing adversary. In: Ishai, Y., Rijmen, V. (eds.) EUROCRYPT 2019. LNCS, vol. 11478, pp. 472–499. Springer, Cham (2019). https://doi.org/10.1007/978-3-030-17659-4_16
14. Fiat, A., Shamir, A.: How to prove yourself: practical solutions to identification and signature problems. In: Odlyzko, A.M. (ed.) CRYPTO 1986. LNCS, vol. 263, pp. 186–194. Springer, Heidelberg (1987). https://doi.org/10.1007/3-540-47721-7_12
15. Furukawa, J., Lindell, Y.: Two-thirds honest-majority MPC for malicious adversaries at almost the cost of semi-honest. In: ACM CCS (2019)
16. Genkin, D., Ishai, Y., Prabhakaran, M., Sahai, A., Tromer, E.: Circuits resilient to additive attacks with applications to secure computation. In: STOC (2014)
17. Gentry, C.: Fully homomorphic encryption using ideal lattices. In: ACM symposium on Theory of computing (2009)

18. Gilboa, N., Ishai, Y.: Compressing cryptographic resources. In: Wiener, M. (ed.) CRYPTO 1999. LNCS, vol. 1666, pp. 591–608. Springer, Heidelberg (1999). https://doi.org/10.1007/3-540-48405-1_37
19. Goldreich, O., Micali, S., Wigderson, A.: How to play any mental game or a completeness theorem for protocols with honest majority. In: ACM Symposium on Theory of Computing (1987)
20. Gordon, S.D., Ranellucci, S., Wang, X.: Secure computation with low communication from cross-checking. In: Peyrin, T., Galbraith, S. (eds.) ASIACRYPT 2018. LNCS, vol. 11274, pp. 59–85. Springer, Cham (2018). https://doi.org/10.1007/978-3-030-03332-3_3
21. Goyal, V., Liu, Y., Song, Y.: Communication-efficient unconditional mpc with guaranteed output delivery. In: Boldyreva, A., Micciancio, D. (eds.) CRYPTO 2019. LNCS, vol. 11693, pp. 85–114. Springer, Cham (2019). https://doi.org/10.1007/978-3-030-26951-7_4
22. Goyal, V., Song, Y.: Malicious security comes free in honest-majority MPC. IACR Cryptol. ePrint Arch. (2020)
23. Goyal, V., Song, Y., Zhu, C.: Guaranteed output delivery comes free in honest majority MPC. In: Micciancio, D., Ristenpart, T. (eds.) CRYPTO 2020. LNCS, vol. 12171, pp. 618–646. Springer, Cham (2020). https://doi.org/10.1007/978-3-030-56880-1_22
24. Hirt, M., Maurer, U., Przydatek, B.: Efficient secure multi-party computation. In: Okamoto, T. (ed.) ASIACRYPT 2000. LNCS, vol. 1976, pp. 143–161. Springer, Heidelberg (2000). https://doi.org/10.1007/3-540-44448-3_12
25. Ishai, Y., Kumaresan, R., Kushilevitz, E., Paskin-Cherniavsky, A.: Secure computation with minimal interaction, revisited. In: Gennaro, R., Robshaw, M. (eds.) CRYPTO 2015. LNCS, vol. 9216, pp. 359–378. Springer, Heidelberg (2015). https://doi.org/10.1007/978-3-662-48000-7_18
26. Ishai, Y., Kushilevitz, E., Prabhakaran, M., Sahai, A., Yu, C.-H.: Secure protocol transformations. In: Robshaw, M., Katz, J. (eds.) CRYPTO 2016. LNCS, vol. 9815, pp. 430–458. Springer, Heidelberg (2016). https://doi.org/10.1007/978-3-662-53008-5_15
27. Ito, M., Saito, A., Nishizeki, T.: Secret sharing scheme realizing general access structure. Electron. Commun. Jpn. **72**(9), 56–64 (1989)
28. Katz, J., Kolesnikov, V., Wang, X.: Improved non-interactive zero knowledge with applications to post-quantum signatures. In: ACM CCS (2018)
29. Lindell, Y., Nof, A.: A framework for constructing fast MPC over arithmetic circuits with malicious adversaries and an honest-majority. In: ACM CCS (2017)
30. Maurer, U.M.: Secure multi-party computation made simple. Discret. Appl. Math. **154**(2), 370–381 (2006)
31. Mohassel, P., Rosulek, M., Zhang, Y.: Fast and secure three-party computation: the garbled circuit approach. In: ACM CCS (2015)
32. Nordholt, P.S., Veeningen, M.: Minimising communication in honest-majority MPC by batchwise multiplication verification. In: Preneel, B., Vercauteren, F. (eds.) ACNS 2018. LNCS, vol. 10892, pp. 321–339. Springer, Cham (2018). https://doi.org/10.1007/978-3-319-93387-0_17
33. Patra, A., Ravi, D.: On the exact round complexity of secure three-party computation. In: Shacham, H., Boldyreva, A. (eds.) CRYPTO 2018. LNCS, vol. 10992, pp. 425–458. Springer, Cham (2018). https://doi.org/10.1007/978-3-319-96881-0_15
34. Pease, M.C., Shostak, R.E., Lamport, L.: Reaching agreement in the presence of faults. J. ACM **27**(2), 228–234 (1980)

35. Rabin, T., Ben-Or, M.: Verifiable secret sharing and multiparty protocols with honest majority. In: ACM Symposium on Theory of Computing (1989)
36. Rivest, R.L., Adleman, L., Dertouzos, M.L., et al.: On data banks and privacy homomorphisms. In: Demillo, R.D., et al. (eds.) Foundations of Secure Computation. Academic Press, New York (1978)
37. Shamir, A.: How to share a secret. Commun. ACM **22**(11), 612–613 (1979)
38. Yao, A.C.: How to generate and exchange secrets (extended abstract). In: Symposium on Foundations of Computer Science (1986)

Efficient and Round-Optimal Oblivious Transfer and Commitment with Adaptive Security

Ran Canetti[1(✉)], Pratik Sarkar[1], and Xiao Wang[2]

[1] Boston University, Boston, USA
{canetti,pratik93}@bu.edu
[2] Northwestern University, Evanston, USA
wangxiao@cs.northwestern.edu

Abstract. We construct the most efficient two-round adaptively secure bit-OT in the Common Random String (CRS) model. The scheme is UC secure under the Decisional Diffie-Hellman (DDH) assumption. It incurs $\mathcal{O}(1)$ exponentiations and sends $\mathcal{O}(1)$ group elements, whereas the state of the art requires $\mathcal{O}(\kappa^2)$ exponentiations and communicates poly(κ) bits, where κ is the computational security parameter. Along the way, we obtain several other efficient UC-secure OT protocols under DDH:

- The *most efficient yet* two-round adaptive string-OT protocol assuming global programmable random oracle. Furthermore, the protocol can be made non-interactive in the simultaneous message setting, assuming random inputs for the sender.
- The *first* two-round string-OT with amortized constant exponentiations and communication overhead which is secure in the global observable random oracle model.
- The *first* two-round receiver equivocal string-OT in the CRS model that incurs constant computation and communication overhead.

We also obtain the first non-interactive adaptive string UC-commitment in the CRS model which incurs a sublinear communication overhead in the security parameter. Specifically, we commit to polylog(κ) bits while communicating $\mathcal{O}(\kappa)$ bits. Moreover, it is additively homomorphic.

We can also extend our results to the single CRS model where multiple sessions share the same CRS. As a corollary, we obtain a two-round adaptively secure MPC protocol in this model.

1 Introduction

Oblivious Transfer (OT), introduced in [23,41], is one of the main pillars of secure distributed computation. Indeed, OT is a crucial building block for many MPC protocols, e.g. [4,5,27,28,33,42]. As a result, significant amount of research has been dedicated to constructing OT protocols that are efficient enough and secure enough to be of practical use.

This work was supported by the IARPA ACHILLES project, the NSF MACS project and NSF grant CNS-1422965. The first author is a member of the Check Point Institute for Information Security.

S. Moriai and H. Wang (Eds.): ASIACRYPT 2020, LNCS 12493, pp. 277–308, 2020.
https://doi.org/10.1007/978-3-030-64840-4_10

Table 1. Comparing our actively-secure UC-OT protocols with state-of-the-art DDH-based 2-round actively-secure UC-OT protocols.

Setting	Protocols	Setup	Security	Sender-input size (bits)	Exponentiations	Communication (bits)
1	[36]	GPRO	Adaptive	κ	6	$4\log\lvert\mathbb{G}\rvert + 2\kappa$
	[6]		Adaptive	κ	11	6κ
	$\pi_{\mathsf{aOT\text{-}GPRO}}$ (Fig. 4)[1]		Adaptive	κ	5	$2\log\lvert\mathbb{G}\rvert+2\kappa$
2	[10]	GORO	Static	κ	$\mathcal{O}(\kappa)$	$\mathcal{O}(\kappa^2)$
	$\pi_{\mathsf{sOT\text{-}GORO}}$ (Fig. 6)[2]			κ	5	$2\log\lvert\mathbb{G}\rvert+2\kappa$
3	[40][3]	CReS	Static	$\log\lvert\mathbb{G}\rvert$	11	$6\log\lvert\mathbb{G}\rvert$
	$\pi_{\mathsf{sOT\text{-}CRS}}$(Fig. 8)	CRS		$\log\lvert\mathbb{G}\rvert$	8	$5\log\lvert\mathbb{G}\rvert$
4	[25]	CRS	Receiver equivocal	$\log\lvert\mathbb{G}\rvert$	poly(κ)	poly(κ)
	[5][3]	CReS		$\log\lvert\mathbb{G}\rvert$	$\mathcal{O}(\kappa)$	$\mathcal{O}(\kappa^2)$
	$\pi_{\mathsf{reOT\text{-}CRS}}$(Fig. 7)	CRS		$\log\lvert\mathbb{G}\rvert$	9	$5\log\lvert\mathbb{G}\rvert$
5	[5][3]	CReS	Adaptive	1	$\Omega(\kappa^2) + 2\cdot\mathsf{NCE}_E = \mathcal{O}(\kappa^2)$	poly(κ)
	$\pi_{\mathsf{aOT\text{-}CRS}}$ (Fig. 10)[4]	CRS		1	$11 + 2\,\mathsf{NCE}_E = \mathcal{O}(1)$	$6\log\lvert\mathbb{G}\rvert + 2\,\mathsf{NCE}_C = \mathcal{O}(\kappa)$

Note: The computational security parameter is κ and $\mathbb{G}$ denotes a group where DDH holds with $\log|\mathbb{G}| = \mathcal{O}(\kappa)$. NCE_E and NCE_C denotes the exponentation and communication cost of an augmented NCE on a bit respectively. It can be instantiated using the DDH-based scheme of [16] where $\mathsf{NCE}_C = \mathcal{O}(\kappa)$ and $\mathsf{NCE}_E = \mathcal{O}(1)$. [1] $\pi_{\mathsf{aOT\text{-}GPRO}}$ requires a one-time communication of 2 group elements and κ bits and computation of 4 exponentiations. [2] $\pi_{\mathsf{sOT\text{-}GORO}}$ requires a one-time communication of 2 group elements and κ bits and computation of 2 NIZKPoKs and 5 exponentiations. [3] Can be instantiated from QR and LWE too. [4] $\pi_{\mathsf{aOT\text{-}CRS}}$ has a one-time communication cost of $\log|\mathbb{G}|$ and one exponentiation.

Designing good OT protocols is a multi-dimensional challenge: One obvious dimension is the complexity, in terms of computational and communication overhead, as well as the number of rounds. Another dimension is the level of security guaranteed. Here the standard measure is Universally Composable (UC) security [8], in order to enable seamless modular composition into larger MPC protocols. Yet another dimension is the setup used. Commonplace models include the common random string model (CRS), the common reference string (CReS) model and the random oracle (RO) model. (Recall that UC-secure OT does not exist in the plain model [9], thus it is essential to use *some* sort of setup.) Yet another dimension is the computational hardness assumptions used.

A final dimension, which is the focus of this work, is whether security is guaranteed for adaptive corruption of one or both of the participants, or alternatively only for the static case where one of the parties is corrupted, and the corruption takes place before the computation starts. Indeed, most of the recent works towards efficient OT concentrates on the static case, e.g. [10,22,36,40].

We concentrate on the case of two-round, adaptively UC-secure OT. We only consider the case of malicious adversaries. It is easy to see that two rounds is the minimum possible, even for static OT. Furthermore, two-round OT enables two-round MPC [3–5,27] which is again round-optimal. More importantly, the efficiency of the two-round MPC protocol crucially depends on the efficiency of the underlying two-round UC-OT protocol. Still, there is a dearth of efficient two-round adaptively UC-secure OT protocols which can tolerate malicious corruptions.

1.1 Our Contributions

We present a number of two-round UC-secure OT protocols. Our protocols are all based on the plain DDH assumption and work with any group where DDH is hard. While the protocols are quite different and in particular work in very different settings, they all use the same underlying methodology, which we sketch in Sect. 1.2. But first we summarize our results and compare it with the relevant state-of-the-art protocols. We organize the presentation and comparison based on the setup assumptions - the global random oracle (GRO) model, and the common reference and random string models. A stronger notion of RO is the GRO model where the same instance of RO is shared globally among different sessions. We have results in the global observable random oracle (GORO) model and the global programmable random oracle (GPRO) model. Our results are further subdivided into cases based on static and adaptive corruptions. A detailed comparison can be found in Table 1. We assume that the number of bits required to represent a group element (for which DDH holds) is $\mathcal{O}(\kappa)$. For example, the DDH assumption holds in the elliptic curve groups and a group element can be represented with $\mathcal{O}(\kappa)$ bits.

Global Random Oracle Model. Our protocols are proven to be secure in the well established GRO [7,10] model. Our results in the GRO model are as follows:

- **Efficient Adaptive OT in Programmable GRO Model.** The work of "Simplest OT" [18] presented a 3-round OT in the programmable RO (PRO) model, which was later shown as not UC-statically secure [6,34]. Inspired by their protocol, we design a 2-round adaptively secure OT $\pi_{\mathsf{aOT\text{-}GPRO}}$ in the GPRO model. Our protocol requires roughly 5 exponentiations and communicates 2 group elements and 2κ bits when the sender's input messages are κ bits long and the computational security parameter is κ.

  State-of-the-Art. The work of [6] presents an adaptively secure OT assuming DDH. They require 11 exponentiations and 5κ bits of communication. The work of [36] obtains a two-round OT based on DDH using 6 exponentiations. They obtained static security assuming PRO. We observe that it can be proven to be adaptively secure under the same assumptions. They also provide an optimized variant requiring 4 exponentiations under the non-standard assumption of Interactive DDH, which is not known to be reducible to standard DDH. The work of [29] presented a 8 round adaptive OT protocol from semi-honest UC adaptive-OT and observable GRO (i.e. GORO) model in the tamper-proof hardware model. We do not compare with them due to difference in the underlying setup assumptions. A detailed comparison with other protocols is shown as Setting 1 in Table 1.
- **One-Round Random OT in the GPRO + Short Single CRS Model.** Our GPRO-based protocol can be further improved to obtain a one-round

random OT (where the sender's messages are randomly chosen) $\pi_{\text{aROT-GPRO}}$ in the simultaneous message (where the parties can send messages in parallel) setting assuming a single short CRS of two group elements. By single CRS, we refer to the setting of [11] where the same CRS is shared among all sessions and the simulator knows the trapdoor of the CRS. In our protocols, each random OT requires communicating 2 group elements and computing roughly 5 exponentiations. This is particularly useful to compute the base OT in OT extension [32,39] non-interactively during the offline phase.

State-of-the-Art. In comparison, the work of [36] can obtain a one-round random OT in the simultaneous message setting from non-interactive Key Agreement protocols. Assuming DDH, they can instantiate their protocol using 6 exponentiations.[1] The work of [14] presented an OT with selective failure from CDH assumption and proven its security for $\mathcal{O}(\kappa)$ OTs together. The work by Doerner et al. [21] presented an OT with selective failure based on observable RO (ORO) and used it to obtain OT extension while computing roughly 3 exponentiations per base-OT and 1 NIZKpok. However, their OT requires 5 rounds of interaction and communication of 4 group elements and 3κ bit strings, yielding a 6 round OT extension. On the other hand, our protocol would give a 3 round OT extension with communication of 2 group elements per base-OT and it should outperform theirs in the WAN setting where interaction dominates the computation time.

- **Static OT in the Observable GRO Model.** We replace the GPRO by a non-programmable GORO, with an extra one-time cost of 2 NIZKPoKs for Discrete Log and 5 exponentiations, which can be reused across multiple executions. One-time cost is a cost that is incurred only once per session/subsession even if multiple OT protocols are run in that session/subsession between the pair of parties. The remaining per-OT cost of this protocol is 5 exponentiations, except that now the protocol is only statically secure.

  State-of-the-Art. In comparison, the only two-round OT protocol from GORO is known from [10]. The authors generate a statically-secure one-sided simulatable OT under DDH assumption. It is used to obtain a UC-secure 2PC protocol using garbled circuits [3]. The 2PC can be instantiated as an UC-secure OT protocol. Each such OT would cost $\mathcal{O}(\kappa)$ exponentiations, which cannot be amortized for large number of OTs. A detailed comparison can be found in Setting 2 of Table 1.

Common Random String Model. Next we present our results in the CRS model. We would like to note that the state-of-the-art protocols are in a stronger

[1] They have an optimized variant (in Appendix D.2 of their paper) from Interactive DDH requiring 4 exponentiations based on a non-standard assumption, not known to be reducible to standard DDH assumption.

model, i.e. the common reference string model and yet we work in the common random string model and still outperform them. Our results and detailed comparison follows:

- **Static OT in the CRS Model.** We replace the GRO with a non programmable CRS. This gives us an efficient two-round static OT $\pi_{\mathsf{sOT\text{-}CRS}}$ which requires 8 exponentiations and communication of 5 group elements.

  State-of-the-Art. In contrast, The state-of-the-art is obtained by [40] in the common reference string model from DDH, Quadratic Residuosity (QR) and Learning with Errors (LWE). Their DDH based instantiation required 11 exponentiations and communicated 6 group elements, while other instantiations required more. Following this, [17] presented constructions in the single common reference string model (of [11]), which is a weaker setup assumption. They have a 2 round construction from Decision Linear Assumption which requires 20 exponentiations and they have a 4 round construction from DDH and Decisional Composite Residuosity Assumption. The recent work of [22] presents a theoretical construction based on CDH and Learning with Parity. Detailed comparison can be found in Setting 3 of Table 1.

- **Receiver Equivocal OT in the CRS Model.** Next, we add security against adaptive corruption of receiver at the cost of one extra exponentiation. This yields a receiver equivocal OT $\pi_{\mathsf{reOT\text{-}CRS}}$ which requires 9 exponentiations and communication of 5 group elements. Such an OT can find useful applications in efficient adaptively-secure zero knowledge [24] schemes.

  State-of-the-Art. Previous receiver equivocal OT protocol of [25] required somewhere equivocal encryption leading to a practically infeasible solution. On the other hand, [5] required $\mathcal{O}(\kappa)$ instances of static string-OTs and non-blackbox usage of non-interactive equivocal commitment to construct a receiver equivocal OT. A detailed comparison can be found in Setting 4 of Table 1.

- **Adaptive OT in the CRS Model.** Finally, we add sender equivocation in our receiver equivocal OT to obtain a semi-adaptive OT (which is secure against static corruption of one party and adaptive corruption of another party) $\pi_{\mathsf{saOT\text{-}CRS}}$ in two rounds. Then, we apply the transformation of [5] to obtain our adaptively-secure bit OT $\pi_{\mathsf{aOT\text{-}CRS}}$ in two rounds. Their transformation upgrades a semi-adaptively secure OT to an adaptively secure OT in the augmented NCE model. Our final protocol $\pi_{\mathsf{aOT\text{-}CRS}}$ computes 11 exponentiations and communicates 7 group elements. In addition, it encrypts 2 bits using augmented NCE. Upon instantiating the NCE scheme using the DDH-based protocol of [16], we obtain the first two round adaptively secure bit-OT which has constant communication and computation overhead.

Table 2. Comparing our protocol with state-of-the-art adaptively secure (without erasures) UC commitment schemes where the commitment size is $\mathcal{O}(\kappa)$ bits

Protocols	Message bit length	No. of rounds		Setup	Assumptions
		COMMIT	DECOMMIT		
[9]	1	1	1	CReS	DDH + UOWHF
[11]	1	1	1	CReS	TDP
[1]	1	1	1	CReS	SXDH
[2]	1	1	1	CReS	DDH
[20]	κ	3	1	CReS	DCR
[19]	κ	3	1	CReS	DCR + SRSA
Our DDH-based protocol (Fig. 12)	polylog(κ)	1	1	CRS	DDH

Notations:
UOWHF - Universal One-Way Hash Functions
TDP - Trapdoor Permutations, SXDH - Symmetric External Diffie–Hellman,
DCR - Decisional Composite Residuosity, SRSA - Strong RSA

State-of-the-Art. In this setting, few works [12,26,26] achieve adaptive security based on general two-round MPC protocol using indistinguishability obfuscation. The only round optimal adaptively-secure protocol under standard computational assumption is due to [5] from DDH, LWE, and QR. They obtain a semi-adaptive bit-OT by garbling a non-interactive equivocal commitment scheme using equivocal garbling techniques of [13]. The construction also requires $\mathcal{O}(\kappa^2)$ invocations to a static string OT with oblivious sampleability property. Then, they provide a generic transformation to obtain an adaptively secure bit OT from a semi-adaptively secure bit-OT in the augmented NCE model. On efficiency measures, the work of [5] constructs the equivocal garbled circuit by communicating poly(κ) bits and their semi-adaptive bit OT requires $\mathcal{O}(\kappa^2)$ exponentiations, thus yielding a feasibility result. In contrast, our protocol is concretely efficient. We have compared with their protocol in Setting 5 of Table 1.

- **Non-interactive Adaptive Commitment.** As an independent result, we demonstrate that the first message of any two-round receiver equivocal OT behaves as an adaptively-secure commitment. By applying this result to our receiver equivocal OT $\pi_{\mathsf{reOT\text{-}CRS}}$, we obtain the *first* non-interactive adaptive string commitment scheme with sublinear communication in κ. More specifically, we commit polylog(κ) bits using 4 exponentiations and communicating 2 group elements. Interestingly, our scheme is additively homomorphic.

  State-of-the-Art. On the other hand, the previous non-interactive adaptively-secure commitment schemes [1,2,9,11] in the common reference string model were bit commitments requiring $\mathcal{O}(1)$ exponentiations and $\mathcal{O}(\kappa)$ bits communication to commit a bit. There are string commitments [19,20] but they require 3 rounds of interaction for commitment. The work of [30] presented a theoretical construction from the minimal assumption of public key encryption with oblivious ciphertext generation. It has an interactive commitment phase and communicates $\mathcal{O}(\kappa^2)$ bits to commit to a single bit. Table 2 provides a qualitative comparison of our protocol with other schemes.

Single Common Random String Model. Currently, our results in this subsection are in the local CRS model. We can extend it to the single common random string, i.e. sCRS model of [11], where all parties share the same sCRS for their subsessions. A subsession is computed between a pair of parties with unique roles (party A is the sender of an OT subsession and Party B is the receiver). The local CRS is generated from sCRS by the parties during the protocol. There can be multiple instances of the same protocol within a subsession with the same local CRS between same parties with their roles preserved, i.e. A will be the sender and B will be the receiver. The simulator knows the hidden trapdoors for sCRS. This benefit comes at a cost of keeping the sCRS length to $4\kappa + 2$ group elements. The length is independent of the number of parties or the number of instances of the protocol being run. However, we assume that the subsession ids are chosen statically by the environment $\mathcal{Z}$ before seeing sCRS. Using our adaptive OT and commitment protocol in the sCRS model, we obtain a two-round adaptively secure MPC protocol in the sCRS model. Similar result was observed in the work of [5].

1.2 Key Insights

Our OT protocols are in the dual-mode [35,40] paradigm. In this paradigm, the protocol can be either in *extractable* mode or *equivocal* mode based on the mode of the setup assumption. In the extractable mode, the input of a corrupt receiver can be extracted by a simulator(playing the role of sender) using a trapdoor; whereas in the equivocal mode the simulator(playing the role of honest receiver) can use the trapdoor to compute randomness that would equivocate the receiver's message to both bit values $b \in \{0,1\}$. This would enable the simulator to extract a corrupt sender's input messages corresponding to both bit values. Previous protocols ensured that the real world protocol was always in the extractable mode by programming the setup distribution [35,40]. However, this required programming the setup based on which party is statically corrupt and this was incompatible with adaptive security.

The novelty of our paper lies in programming the mode of the protocol, during the protocol execution, without explicitly programming the setup. We achieve this by relying on the Computational Diffie-Hellman(CDH) and DDH assumption. The protocols either start off with a common random string - (g, h, T_1) or generate one by invoking the GRO on a random string. The receiver is required to generate T_2 and execute the OT protocol using (g, h, T_1, T_2) as the setup tuple. The protocol ensures that if the tuple is non-DDH then the protocol is in extractable mode, else it is in equivocal mode. The CDH assumption guarantees that the tuple is a non-DDH tuple and hence the real world protocol is in extractable mode. Meanwhile, the simulator can compute $T_2 = h^{\mathsf{td}}$ s.t. the tuple is in equivocal mode by using the trapdoor $\mathsf{td} = \log_g T_1$. The simulated tuple is indistinguishable from real tuple due to DDH assumption. This trick follows by carefully tweaking the DDH based instantiation of the PWV framework such that it satisfies an additional property, i.e. the CRS for the protocol will be in extractable mode (a.k.a messy mode according to PVW) and it can be set to equivocal mode (a.k.a decryption mode according to PVW) by the simulator, given a trapdoor. This enables simulation in the adaptive setting as the simulator can conveniently program the CRS based on which party gets corrupted. Extending our techniques to hold under additional assumptions is an intriguing open question, especially LWE and QR since PVW can be instantiated from them. See Sect. 3 for a more detailed overview.

Paper Organization. In the next section, we introduce some notations and important concepts used in this paper. In Sect. 3, we present the key intuitions behind our protocols. This is followed by our results in the global random oracle model in Sect. 4. Then, we replace the random oracle assumption with a CRS setup to obtain a receiver equivocal OT in Sec. 5. Our optimized static-OT is present in the same section. In Sect. 6 we add sender equivocation in our receiver equivocal OT to obtain adaptively-secure OT in the CRS model. We present our independent result on adaptively-secure commitment scheme in Sect. 7. Finally, we conclude by replacing our local CRS with a single CRS in Sect. 8. In the same section we provide our two round adaptive MPC protocol in the single CRS model.

2 Preliminaries

Notations. We denote by $a \leftarrow D$ a uniform sampling of an element a from a distribution D. The set of elements $\{1, \ldots, n\}$ is represented by $[n]$. We denote polylog(a) and poly(b) as polynomials in $\log a$ and b respectively. We denote a probabilistic polynomial time algorithm as PPT. We denote the computational security parameter by κ. Let $\mathbb{Z}_q$ denote the field of order q, where $q = \frac{p-1}{2}$ and p are primes. Let $\mathbb{G}$ be the multiplicative group corresponding to $\mathbb{Z}_p^*$ with generator g, where DDH assumption holds. We denote the set of natural numbers as N. When a party S gets corrupted we denote it by S^*. Our protocols have the following naming convention $\pi_{\langle \mathsf{sec} \rangle \langle \mathsf{prot} \rangle \text{-} \langle \mathsf{setup} \rangle}$ where $\langle \mathsf{sec} \rangle$ refers to the security model and it can be either s (static), re (receiver equivocal) or a (adaptive). $\langle \mathsf{prot} \rangle$ refers to the protocol which is either OT or ROT or COM based on OT or random OT or commitment protocol respectively. Similarly, $\langle \mathsf{setup} \rangle$ refers to the setup assumption where it can be either PRO (PRO model) or ORO (ORO model) or CRS (CRS). Our security proofs are in the Universal Composability (UC) framework of [8]. We refer to the original paper for details.

Global Random Oracle Model. We present the global random oracle functionality from [7] in Fig. 1. It allows a simulator to observe illegitimate queries that are made by the adversary from outside the session by invoking the

$\mathcal{F}_{\mathsf{GRO}}$

$\mathcal{F}_{\mathsf{GRO}}$ is parameterized by a domain D and range R and it proceeds as follows, running on security parameter κ:

- $\mathcal{F}_{\mathsf{GRO}}$ maintains a list L (which is initially empty) of pairs of values $(\hat{\mathsf{sid}}, \hat{m}, \hat{h})$, s.t. $\hat{m} \in D$, $\hat{h} \in R$ and $\hat{\mathsf{sid}}$ is a session id.
- Upon receiving a value (QUERY, m, sid') (where $m \in D$) from a party $\mathcal{P}$, from session with session id sid, perform the following: If there is a pair $(\mathsf{sid}', m, \hat{h})$, for some $\hat{h} \in R$, in the list L, set $h := \hat{h}$. If there is no such pair, sample $h \leftarrow_R R$ and store the pair (sid', m, h) in L. If $\mathsf{sid} \neq \mathsf{sid}'$, then add (sid', m, h) to the illegitimate query set Q_{sid}. Once h is set, reply to the activating machine with (HASHCONFIRM, h).
- Upon receiving a value (OBSERVE, sid) from the adversary: If Q_{sid} does not exist then set $Q_{\mathsf{sid}} = \bot$. Output Q_{sid} to the adversary.
- Upon receiving a value (PROGRAM, m, h', sid) from the adversary, if there exists an entry (sid, m, h) and $h \neq h'$ then ignore this input. Else, set $\mathsf{L} = \mathsf{L} \cup (\mathsf{sid}, m, h)$ and PROG $=$ PROG $\cup\, m$ and return (PROGRAMCONFIRM) to adversary.
- Upon receiving a value (ISPROGRAMMED, m, sid') from a party $(\mathcal{P}, \mathsf{sid})$, if $\mathsf{sid} \neq \mathsf{sid}'$ then ignore the input. Else, set $b = 1$ if $m \in$ PROG. Otherwise set $b = 0$. Return (ISPROGRAMMEDRESULT, b) to the calling entity.

Fig. 1. The ideal functionality $\mathcal{F}_{\mathsf{GRO}}$ for global random oracle

OBSERVE command. It also enables the simulator to program (using the PROGRAM command) the random oracle on unqueried input points. Meanwhile, an adversary can also program (using the PROGRAM command) the random oracle on a point but an honest party can check whether that point has been programmed or not by invoking the ISPROGRAMMED command. In the ideal world, a simulator can successfully program the RO since it can always return the result of ISPROGRAMMED command as 0 when the adversary invokes it to verify whether a point has been programmed or not. More details can be found in Sect. 8 of [7]. In our OT protocols we require multiple instances of the GRO due different distributions on the domain and range of the GRO. We denote them as $\mathcal{F}_{\mathsf{GRO1}}$, $\mathcal{F}_{\mathsf{GRO2}}$ and so on. We assume $\mathcal{F}_{\mathsf{GRO}i}$ is indexed by a parameter $i \in \mathsf{N}$, in addition to sid. We avoid writing i as part of the parameters to avoid notation overloading.

Common Random String Model. In this assumption, the parties of a session sid have access to a string randomly sampled from a distribution. A CRS is local to the session sid and should not be used for protocols outside the session. In the security proof, the simulator would have access to the trapdoors of the CRS which would enable him to simulate the ideal world adversary. In the MPC literature, the acronym CRS can also refer to common reference string which is a stronger assumption than common random string. In this paper, we always use CRS for common random string unless explicitly mentioned. We also use the

$\mathcal{F}_{\mathsf{OT}}$

$\mathcal{F}_{\mathsf{OT}}$ interacts with a sender S and a receiver R as follows:

- On input $(\text{CHOOSE}, \mathsf{rec}, \mathsf{sid}, b)$ from R where $b \in \{0, 1\}$; if no message of the form $(\mathsf{rec}, \mathsf{sid}, b)$ has been recorded in the memory, store $(\mathsf{rec}, \mathsf{sid}, b)$ and send $(\mathsf{rec}, \mathsf{sid})$ to S.
- On input $(\text{TRANSFER}, \mathsf{sen}, \mathsf{sid}, (a_0, a_1))$ from S with $a_0, a_1 \in \{0, 1\}^n$, if no message of the form $(\mathsf{sen}, \mathsf{sid}, (a_0, a_1))$ is recorded and a message of the form $(\mathsf{rec}, \mathsf{sid}, b)$ is stored, send $(\mathsf{sent}, \mathsf{sid}, a_b)$ to R and $(\mathsf{sent}, \mathsf{sid})$ to S. Ignore future messages with the same sid.

Fig. 2. The ideal functionality $\mathcal{F}_{\mathsf{OT}}$ for oblivious transfer

$\mathcal{F}_{\mathsf{COM}}$

$\mathcal{F}_{\mathsf{COM}}$ interacts with committer C and verifier V as follows:

- On receiving input $((\text{COMMIT}, \mathsf{V}), \mathsf{C}, \mathsf{sid}, m)$ from C, if $(\mathsf{sid}, \mathsf{C}, \mathsf{V}, m')$ has been recorded, ignore the input. Else record the tuple $(\mathsf{sid}, \mathsf{C}, \mathsf{V}, m)$ and send $(\text{RECEIPT}, \mathsf{sid}, \mathsf{C}, \mathsf{V})$ to V.
- On receiving input $(\text{DECOMMIT}, \mathsf{C}, \mathsf{sid})$ from C, if there is a record of the form $(\mathsf{sid}, \mathsf{C}, \mathsf{V}, m')$ return $(\text{DECOMMIT}, \mathsf{sid}, \mathsf{C}, \mathsf{V}, m')$ to V. Otherwise, ignore the input.

Fig. 3. The ideal functionality $\mathcal{F}_{\mathsf{COM}}$ for commitment scheme

single CRS model [11] where a single CRS - sCRS is shared among all sessions and the simulator knows the trapdoor of the sCRS.

Oblivious Transfer. In a 1-out-of-2 OT, we have a sender (S) holding two inputs $a_0, a_1 \in \{0, 1\}^n$ and a receiver (R) holding a choice bit b. The correctness of OT means that R will obtain a_b as the outcome of the protocol. At the same time, S should learn nothing about b, and R should learn nothing about the other input of S, namely $a_{\bar{b}}$. The ideal OT functionality $\mathcal{F}_{\mathsf{OT}}$ is shown in Fig. 2. We also consider the multi-session variant $\mathcal{F}_{\mathsf{mOT}}$ (Fig. 13) where multiple parties can run pairwise OT protocols, while sharing the same setup resources. This captures our OT protocols in the single CRS model.

Adversarial Model. We initially consider security against static corruptions by a malicious adversary. Later, we need different levels of adaptive security and we enlist them as follows:

- *Static Corruption:* The adversary corrupts the parties at the beginning of the protocol.
- *Receiver Equivocal Corruption:* The adversary corrupts sender statically and he corrupts the receiver adaptively.
- *Sender Equivocal Corruption:* The adversary corrupts receiver statically and he corrupts the sender adaptively.

- *Semi-adaptive Corruption:* The adversary corrupts one party statically and the other party adaptively.
- *Adaptive Corruption:* The adversary corrupts both parties adaptively. This scenario covers the previous corruption cases.

Commitment. A commitment scheme allows a committing party C to compute a commitment c to a message m, using randomness r, towards a party V in the COMMIT phase. Later in the DECOMMIT phase, C can open c to m by sending the decommitment to V. The commitment should hide m from a corrupt V*. Binding ensures that a corrupt C* cannot open c to a different message $m' \neq m$. In addition, UC-secure commitments require a simulator (for honest V) to extract the message committed by C*. Also, it enables a simulator (for honest C) to commit to 0 and later open it to any valid message by using the trapdoor. The ideal commitment functionality $\mathcal{F}_{\mathsf{COM}}$ is shown in Fig. 3. We also consider the multi-session [11] variant $\mathcal{F}_{\mathsf{mCOM}}$ (Fig. 14) where multiple parties can run pairwise commitment schemes protocols, while sharing the same setup resources. This captures our commitment scheme in the single CRS model.

Non-committing Encryption. A non-committing encryption consists of three algorithms NCE = (Gen; Enc; Dec). It is a public key encryption scheme which allows a simulator to encrypt a plaintext in the presence of an adaptive adversary. Given a trapdoor, the simulator (on behalf of the honest party) can produce some dummy ciphertext c without the knowledge of any plaintext m. Later when the honest party gets corrupted and the simulator produces matching randomness (or decryption key) s.t. c decrypts to m. More formally, it is defined as follows.

Definition 1. (Non-committing Encryption). *A non-committing (bit) encryption scheme (NCE) consists of a tuple (NCE.Gen, NCE.Enc, NCE.Dec, NCE.S) where (NCE.Gen, NCE.Enc, NCE.Dec) is an IND-CPA public key encryption scheme and NCE.S is the simulation satisfying the following property: for $b \in \{0,1\}$ the following distributions are computationally indistinguishable:*

$$\{(pk, c, r_G, r_E) : (pk, sk) \leftarrow \mathsf{NCE.Gen}(1^\kappa; r_G), c = \mathsf{NCE.Enc}(pk, b; r_E)\}_{\kappa,b} \approx$$

$$\{(pk, c, r_G^b, r_E^b) : (pk, c, r_G^0, r_E^0, r_G^1, r_E^1) \leftarrow \mathsf{NCE}.\mathcal{S}(1^\kappa)\}_{\kappa,b}.$$

Definition 2. (Augmented Non-committing Encryption). *An augmented NCE scheme consists of a tuple of algorithms (NCE.Gen, NCE.Enc, NCE.Dec, NCE.S, NCE.Gen$_{Obl}$, NCE.Gen$_{Inv}$) where (NCE.Gen, NCE.Enc, NCE.Dec, NCE.S) is an NCE and:*

- *Oblivious Sampling: NCE.Gen$_{Obl}(1^\kappa)$ obliviously generates a public key pk (without knowing the associated secret key sk.*
- *Inverse Key Sampling: NCE.Gen$_{Inv}(pk)$ explains the randomness for the key pk satisfying the following property.*
  Obliviousness: The following distributions are indistinguishable:

$$\{(pk, r) : pk \leftarrow \mathsf{NCE.Gen}_{Obl}(1^\kappa; r)\}_\kappa \approx$$
$$\{(pk, r') : (pk, sk) \leftarrow \mathsf{NCE.Gen}(1^\kappa); r' \leftarrow \mathsf{NCE.Gen}_{Inv}(pk)\}_\kappa.$$

Definition 3. (Computational Diffie-Hellman Assumption). *We say that the CDH assumption holds in a group* $\mathbb{G}$ *if for any PPT adversary* $\mathcal{A}$,

$$\Pr[\mathcal{A}(g, h, T) = Z] = \mathsf{neg}(\kappa).$$

holds, where $h, T \leftarrow \mathbb{G}$, *and* $T = g^t$, $Z = h^t$.

Definition 4. (Decisional Diffie-Hellman Assumption). *We say that the DDH assumption holds in a group* $\mathbb{G}$ *if for any PPT adversary* $\mathcal{A}$,

$$|\Pr[\mathcal{A}(g, h, T, Y) = 1] - \Pr[\mathcal{A}(g, h, T, Z) = 1]| = \mathsf{neg}(\kappa).$$

holds, where $h, T, Y \leftarrow \mathbb{G}$ *and* $T = g^t$, $Z = h^t$.

3 Technical Overview

In this section, we will provide a high-level overview of our main constructions. Full technical details can be found in later sections.

3.1 Adaptively Secure OT in the Global Programmable RO Model

The "Simplest OT protocol" [18] is a three-round OT protocol in the programmable RO model. S sends the first message as $T = g^r$, using some secret randomness $r \leftarrow \mathbb{Z}_q$. R uses the sender's message to compute the second message as $B = g^\alpha T^b$ based on his input bit b using some secret receiver randomness $\alpha \leftarrow \mathbb{Z}_q$. Upon receiving B, the sender reuses the secret randomness r to compute the OT third message as follows:

$$\begin{aligned} c_0 &= \mathcal{F}_{\mathsf{GRO}}\left(B^r\right) \oplus m_0 \\ c_1 &= \mathcal{F}_{\mathsf{GRO}}\left(\left(\frac{B}{T}\right)^r\right) \oplus m_1 \end{aligned} \tag{1}$$

The receiver decrypts $m_b = c_b \oplus \mathcal{F}_{\mathsf{GRO}}(\mathsf{sid}, T^\alpha)$. A corrupt R^* cannot obtain both messages as it requires computing T^r (as it involves querying B^r and $(\frac{B}{T})^r$) to the RO. Such a computation is hard by CDH assumption as $T = g^r$ is randomly sampled by S and kept secret from R. On the other hand, a corrupted S^* cannot guess b as b is perfectly hidden in B (since α and $\alpha - r$ are valid receiver randomness for bits 0 and 1). This also disrupts a corrupt receiver's input extraction by the simulator as b is not binded to B. The only way to extract the input of R^* is when he invokes $\mathcal{F}_{\mathsf{GRO}}$ on B^α to decrypt m_b. However, such a weak extraction process is insufficient for UC-secure protocols (GC-based protocols) where this OT protocol might be used and it has been pointed out by the work of [6,34]. To tackle this issue, the protocol should bind the receiver's input bit b to the receiver's message. Here our goals are: 1) fix this protocol to be fully UC-secure; 2) reduce the round complexity of the protocol to two rounds.

Our Solution. We reduce the round complexity by generating T as an OT parameter using a GRO. The receiver generates T by invoking the GRO on a randomly sampled seed. He constructs $B = g^{\alpha}T^{b}$ based on bit b. The sender samples a random r from $\mathbb{Z}_q$ and encrypt his message as in Eq. 1. The sender also sends $z = g^r$ so that the receiver can decrypt $m_b = c_b \oplus \mathcal{F}_{\mathsf{GRO}}(\mathsf{sid}, z^{\alpha})$. Security follows from the the security of Simplest OT. And sender's messages are hidden due to CDH assumption. However, the receiver's bit cannot be extracted from the receiver's message as it is perfectly hidden.

Now we will add a mechanism such that the receiver's bit can be extracted from the receiver's message. Intuitively, the protocol is modified in such a way that the receiver runs two instances (using two different OT parameters) of the modified Simplest OT using the same randomness α. The sender encrypts his message by combining these two instances. Finally, the receiver uses α to decrypt m_b. Security ensures that a corrupt receiver cannot decrypt m_0 or m_1 if the two instances are not computed using α. And a simulator can extract the corrupt receiver's input bit from the two instances if they are correctly constructed. This ensures input extraction of a corrupt receiver, thus giving us a round optimal UC-secure OT with high concrete efficiency.

More formally, the receiver R generates (h, T_1, T_2) as receiver OT parameters using the GRO. He constructs two instances as $B = g^{\alpha}T_1^{b}$ and $H = h^{\alpha}T_2^{b}$ using the same randomness α. He sends seed and (B, H) to the sender S. Next, S samples r, s from $\mathbb{Z}_q$ and computes the sender OT parameter $z = g^r h^s$. The sender combines the two OT instance by computing the ciphertexts:

$$c_0 = \mathcal{F}_{\mathsf{GRO}}(\mathsf{sid}, B^r H^s) \oplus m_0, \text{ and } c_1 = \mathcal{F}_{\mathsf{GRO}}\left(\mathsf{sid}, \left(\frac{B}{T_1}\right)^r \cdot \left(\frac{H}{T_2}\right)^s\right) \oplus m_1.$$

The receiver computes $m_b = c_b \oplus \mathcal{F}_{\mathsf{GRO}}(\mathsf{sid}, z^{\alpha})$. This new scheme supports extraction of a corrupt receiver's input bit if the simulator knows x s.t. $h = g^x$. The simulator extracts $b = 0$ if $H = B^x$, else if $\frac{H}{T_2} = (\frac{B}{T_1})^x$ then he sets $b = 1$. Otherwise, the receiver message is malformed and b is set as $\perp$. Extraction always succeeds unless (g, h, T_1, T_2) forms a DDH tuple. In such a case $(g, h, T_1, T_2) = (g, g^x, g^t, g^{xt})$ and both extraction cases will satisfy. However, such an event occurs with negligible probability since (h, T_1, T_2) is generated using a random oracle. Sender's messages are hidden from a corrupt receiver due to CDH assumption. Simulation against a corrupt sender proceeds by programming the GRO s.t (g, h, T_1, T_2) is a DDH tuple. The simulator (playing the role of honest R) sets $B = g^{\alpha}$ and $H = h^{\alpha}$ as receiver message. Upon obtaining the second OT message from the corrupt sender, the simulator extracts m_0 and m_1 by using randomness α and $\alpha - t$ respectively. The corrupt sender cannot distinguish between the real and ideal world OT parameters due to DDH assumption. Also, B and H perfectly hides b in the ideal world.

Our protocol is more efficient than the state-of-the-art two-round UC-secure OT [36,40]. Furthermore, if we are interested in random OTs, then S needs to communicate only the OT parameter z for all the OTs. This would yield a non-interactive random OT at the cost of 5 exponentiations and 2 group elements (i.e.

R communicates (B, H) for each random OT). The same protocol is adaptively secure in the programmable random oracle model, and can be modified to use an global observable RO but only provide static security. See Sect. 4 for full details.

3.2 Receiver Equivocal Oblivious Transfer in the CRS Model

Our next goal is to obtain efficient UC-secure OT with only a common random string setup. We replace the GRO by partially setting the receiver OT parameters as the CRS, consisting of three random group elements (g, h, T_1). The receiver is required to generate T_2 as part of the protocol and use it to compute B and H following the previous protocol (Sect. 3.1). T_2 will be reused for multiple OT instances in the same session. It is guaranteed that a corrupt receiver will compute T_2 s.t. the tuple is non-DDH due to the CDH assumption. In such a case, the simulator for a corrupt receiver can extract b from B and H given x, where $h = g^x$. On the other hand, the simulator (playing role of honest receiver) for a corrupt sender can compute T_2 s.t. (g, h, T_1, T_2) is a DDH tuple, given the trapdoor t s.t. $T_1 = g^t$. It would allow him to extract corrupt sender's input messages from (c_0, c_1) and equivocate $(B, H) = (g^\alpha, h^\alpha)$ to open to bit b by opening the receiver's randomness as $\alpha - bt$. This provides security against adaptive corruption of receiver. The sender's algorithm is similar to the one in Sect. 3.1 where the ciphertexts are formed as follows:

$$c_0 = B^r H^s \cdot m_0, \text{ and } c_1 = \left(\frac{B}{T_1}\right)^r \cdot \left(\frac{H}{T_2}\right)^s \cdot m_1$$

However, the sender's randomness (r, s) has to be unique for each OT instance, else the sender's OT messages - (c_0, c_1), will leak about the sender's input messages - (m_0, m_1). Thus, we obtain a two-round OT protocol which is secure against static corruption of the sender and adaptive corruption of the receiver in the common random string model. Our protocol requires 9 exponentiations and communication of 6 group elements, where one group element (i.e. T_2) can be reused; reducing the communication overhead to 5 group elements. We can further optimize our computation cost to 8 exponentiations if we sacrifice receiver equivocal property and instead settle for static security. In contrast, the only other two-round protocol [40] in this model requires 11 exponentiations and communication of 6 group elements in the common reference string model. Note that the protocol here is receiver-equivocal, which will be made fully adaptive in the following subsection.

3.3 Adaptively Secure Oblivious Transfer in the CRS Model

Finally, we would like to add sender equivocation to the above protocol. It requires a simulator to simulate the OT second message without the knowledge of sender's input. Upon post-execution corruption of sender, the simulator should provide the randomness s.t. the OT second message corresponds to sender's original input (m_0, m_1). In our current protocol, the second OT message is computed based on B and H using the randomness r and s. The simulator (playing the role of an honest sender) sets $c_{\bar{b}}$ randomly and opening it to $m_{\bar{b}}$ requires the knowledge of receiver's randomness - α. Also, such an equivocation would be possible only if the tuple - CRS and T_2, is a non-DDH tuple as z and $p_{\bar{b}} = \frac{c_{\bar{b}}}{m_{\bar{b}}}$ are two separate equations in r and s. When the tuple is a DDH one (which is required for receiver equivocation when the receiver is corrupted post-execution) then we can write $p_{\bar{b}} = z^{\alpha+(-1)^b t}$. It is not possible to provide r and s s.t. a random $c_{\bar{b}}$ opens to $p_{\bar{b}} \cdot m_{\bar{b}}$, where $p_{\bar{b}}$ gets fixed by α and z, and $m_{\bar{b}}$ is chosen by the adaptive adversary in post-execution corruption. Thus, it seems receiver and sender equivocation will not be possible simultaneously if we follow this approach.

We address this challenge by modifying the sender protocol. We construct a semi-adaptive OT protocol by slightly tweaking our receiver equivocal OT protocol. Then we apply the transformation of [5] which uplifts a semi-adaptive OT into to an adaptively secure OT using augmented NCE. A semi-adaptive OT is one which is secure against static corruption of one party and adaptive corruption of another party. Our semi-adaptive OT construction is described as follows. The sender encrypts only bit messages $m_i \in \{0,1\}$ in ciphertext (z_i, c_i), for $i \in \{0,1\}$, using independent randomness (r_i, s_i). If $m_i = 1$ then sender encrypts it using the sender protocol as follows:

$$z_i = g^{r_i} h^{s_i}$$

$$c_i = \left(\frac{B}{T_i^i}\right)^{r_i} \left(\frac{H}{T_2^i}\right)^{s_i} \cdot m_i = \left(\frac{B}{T_i^i}\right)^{r_i} \left(\frac{H}{T_2^i}\right)^{s_i} \cdot 1 = \left(\frac{B}{T_i^i}\right)^{r_i} \left(\frac{H}{T_2^i}\right)^{s_i}$$

If $m_i = 0$, then sender samples z_i and c_i as random group elements. Upon receiving (z_0, c_0, z_1, c_1), the receiver computes $y = c_b \cdot z_b^{-\alpha}$. If $y = 1$, then receiver outputs $m_b = 1$, else he outputs $m_b = 0$. In this new construction, $m_{\bar{b}}$ remains hidden in $c_{\bar{b}}$ from the corrupt receiver due to DDH assumption. Moreover, it solves our previous problem of equivocating sender's OT message - $c_{\bar{b}}$. Here, the simulator (playing the role of honest sender) can always compute $(z_{\bar{b}}, c_{\bar{b}})$ s.t. they encrypt $m_{\bar{b}} = 1$ using randomness $(r_{\bar{b}}, s_{\bar{b}})$. Later, when sender gets corrupted post-execution, the simulator can claim $(z_{\bar{b}}, c_{\bar{b}})$ was randomly sampled if $m_{\bar{b}} = 0$, else provide the randomness as $(r_{\bar{b}}, s_{\bar{b}})$ if $m_{\bar{b}} = 1$. Adversary cannot decrypt $m_{\bar{b}}$ from $c_{\bar{b}}$ since $T_1^{r_{\bar{b}}}$ makes $c_{\bar{b}}$ pseudorandom due to DDH assumption.

Thus, our new protocol is secure against semi-adaptive corruptions of parties. Next, we use the transformation of [5] to make it adaptively secure using augmented NCE. The receiver generates an NCE key pair $(\mathsf{pk}_b, \mathsf{sk})$ corresponding to his input bit b. He samples another NCE public key $\mathsf{pk}_{\bar{b}}$ obliviously for bit $\bar{b}$. He sends these two public keys to the sender. The sender additively secret shares his inputs:

$$m_0 = x_0 \oplus y_0, m_1 = x_1 \oplus y_1.$$

He runs the semi-adaptive OT protocol with inputs (x_0, x_1) and encrypts y_0 and y_1 using pk_0 and pk_1 respectively.

$$e_0 = \mathsf{NCE.Enc}(\mathsf{pk}_0, y_0), e_1 = \mathsf{NCE.Enc}(\mathsf{pk}_1, y_1).$$

The sender sends the semi-adaptive OT messages and (e_0, e_1) to the receiver. The honest receiver obtains x_b from the OT and y_b. A corrupt receiver can obtain $y_{\bar{b}}$ in addition, if he sampled $(\mathsf{pk}_{\bar{b}}, \mathsf{sk}_{\bar{b}})$ using the NCE.Gen algorithm. Our final protocol is secure against adaptive corruption of both parties. Consider the setting where both parties are honest initially and the simulator has to construct their view. The adaptive simulator runs the semi-adaptive simulator for the underlying semi-adaptive OT with static corruption of sender and adaptive corruption of receiver. The honest sender algorithm is run with inputs (x_0, x_1), sampled as random bits. Suppose the sender gets corrupted first in post-execution then e_0 and e_1 can be equivocated s.t. $y_0 = x_0 \oplus m_0$ and $y_1 = x_1 \oplus m_1$. Indistinguishability proceeds due to the NCE property. Next, when the receiver gets corrupted the simulator obtains b. He uses the adaptive simulator for receiver in the semi-adaptive OT. The simulator also uses the inverse samplability property of the NCE to claim that pk_b was generated honestly and $\mathsf{pk}_{\bar{b}}$ obliviously. If the receiver gets corrupted first, then the receiver's simulation doesn't change. For the sender side, the simulator sets $y_b = x_b \oplus m_b$. Later, when sender gets corrupted and simulator obtains $m_{\bar{b}}$ the simulator equivocates $e_{\bar{b}}$ s.t. $y_{\bar{b}} = x_{\bar{b}} \oplus n_{\bar{b}}$. Indistinguishability proceeds since the adversary does not posses the secret key $\mathsf{sk}_{\bar{b}}$ as $\mathsf{pk}_{\bar{b}}$ was supposed to be obliviously sampled. As a result, the simulator successfully equivocates $e_{\bar{b}}$. More details of our protocol can be found in Sect. 6.

3.4 Non-interactive Commitment with Adaptive Security

As an independent result, we prove that the first (i.e. receiver's) message of any two-round 1-out-of-$\mathcal{M}$ *receiver equivocal* OT can be considered as an UC-secure non-interactive commitment to receiver's input. It can also withstand adaptive corruption of the parties involved in the commitment scheme. The committer C commits to his message $b \in \mathcal{M}$ (where $\mathcal{M}$ is the message space for the commitment) as c by invoking the receiver algorithm on choice b with randomness α. Decommitment follows by providing the randomness α for the receiver's OT message.

We can show that the commitment scheme satisfies the properties of an UC commitment- binding, hiding, extractable and equivocal, by relying on the security of the underlying receiver equivocal OT protocol. Binding of the commitment follows from sender security as a corrupt receiver cannot produce different randomness α' s.t. c can be used to decrypt $m_{\bar{b}}$ (where m_i is S's ith message for $i \in \mathcal{M}$) where $\bar{b} \in \mathcal{M}$ and $\bar{b} \neq b$. Hiding of b is ensured from the OT security guarantees for an honest receiver against a corrupt sender. A corrupter committer's input b is extracted by running the extraction algorithm of the OT simulator for a corrupt receiver. Finally, the commitment can be opened correctly by running the simulator (who is playing the role of honest OT receiver) and its equivocation algorithm (when receiver gets corrupted adaptively in post-execution). The commitment scheme is also secure against adaptive corruption as the simulator (for the honest committer in the commitment scheme) can always produce randomness α', which is consistent with message b, by running the adaptive simulator for the OT.

$\pi_{\mathsf{aOT\text{-}GPRO}}$

- **Public Inputs:** Group $\mathbb{G}$, field $\mathbb{Z}_q$ and generator g of group $\mathbb{G}$.
- **Private Inputs:** S has two κ-bit inputs $(m_0, m_1) \in \{0,1\}^\kappa$ and R has a choice bit b.
- **Functionalities:** Global Random Oracles $\mathcal{F}_{\mathsf{GRO1}} : \{0,1\}^\kappa \to \mathbb{G}^3$ and $\mathcal{F}_{\mathsf{GRO2}} : \mathbb{G} \to \{0,1\}^\kappa$.

Choose:

- R samples $\mathsf{seed} \leftarrow \{0,1\}^\kappa$ and computes $(h, T_1, T_2) \leftarrow \mathcal{F}_{\mathsf{GRO1}}(\mathsf{sid}, \mathsf{seed})$.
- R samples $\alpha \leftarrow \mathbb{Z}_q$ and sets $B = g^\alpha T_1^b$ and $H = h^\alpha T_2^b$.
- Receiver Parameters: R sends seed as OT parameters.
- R sends (B, H) to S.

Transfer:

- S invokes $\mathcal{F}_{\mathsf{GRO1}}$ on $(\textsc{IsProgrammed}, \mathsf{seed}, \mathsf{sid})$ and aborts if it returns 1.
- S computes $(h, T_1, T_2) \leftarrow \mathcal{F}_{\mathsf{GRO1}}(\mathsf{sid}, \mathsf{seed})$.
- S samples $r, s \leftarrow \mathbb{Z}_q$ and computes $z = g^r h^s$.
- S computes $c_0 = \mathcal{F}_{\mathsf{GRO2}}(\mathsf{sid}, B^r H^s) \oplus m_0$ and $c_1 = \mathcal{F}_{\mathsf{GRO2}}\left(\mathsf{sid}, (\frac{B}{T_1})^r (\frac{H}{T_2})^s\right) \oplus m_1$.
- Sender Parameters: S sends z to R as OT parameters.
- S sends (c_0, c_1) to R.

Local Computation by R:

- R computes $m_b = c_b \oplus \mathcal{F}_{\mathsf{GRO2}}(\mathsf{sid}, z^\alpha)$.

Fig. 4. Adaptively secure oblivious transfer in the global programmable random oracle model

When we compile our $\pi_{\mathsf{reOT\text{-}CRS}}$ protocol with this result, we obtain a non-interactive commitment $c = (B, H) = (g^\alpha T_1^m, h^\alpha T_2^m)$ for polylog(κ) bit messages using four exponentiations and communication of two group elements. We can only commit to polylog(κ)-bit messages or messages from poly(κ)-sized message space $\mathcal{M}$ since our PPT simulator runs in $\mathcal{O}(|\mathcal{M}|)$ time to extract a corrupt receiver's input by matching the following condition for each $i \in \mathcal{M}$:

$$\text{if } \frac{H}{T_2^i} \stackrel{?}{=} \left(\frac{B}{T_1^i}\right)^x \text{ output } i.$$

Our detailed transformation from a receiver equivocal OT to an adaptive commitment can be found in Sect. 7.

4 Oblivious Transfer in the Global Random Oracle Model

In Sect. 4.1, we first show an efficient 2-round OT in the Global programmable RO model secure against adaptive adversaries. Then, we present a set of optimizations that can bring the efficiency at par with the Simplest OT by Chou and Orlandi [18] while requiring only one simultaneous round. In Sect. 4.2, we will show how to adapt our protocol to work in the global observable RO model but with only static security.

$\pi_{\mathsf{aROT\text{-}GPRO}}$

- **Public Inputs:** Group $\mathbb{G}$, field $\mathbb{Z}_q$, generator g of group $\mathbb{G}$ and global CRS $= (g, h)$.
- **Functionalities:** Random Oracles $\mathcal{F}_{\mathsf{GRO1}} : \{0,1\}^\kappa \rightarrow \mathbb{G}^3$ and $\mathcal{F}_{\mathsf{GRO2}} : \mathbb{G} \rightarrow \{0,1\}^\kappa$.

Receiver's Simultaneous Message:
- R samples seed $\leftarrow \{0,1\}^\kappa$ and computes $(T_1, T_2) \leftarrow \mathcal{F}_{\mathsf{GRO1}}(\mathsf{sid}, \mathsf{seed})$.
- R samples $b \leftarrow \{0,1\}$ and $\alpha \leftarrow \mathbb{Z}_q$
- R sets $B = g^\alpha T_1^b$ and $H = h^\alpha T_2^b$.
- Receiver Parameters: R sends seed as OT parameters.
- R sends (B, H) to S.

Sender's Simultaneous Message:
- S samples $r, s \leftarrow \mathbb{Z}_q$ and computes $z = g^r h^s$.
- Sender Parameters: S sends z to R as OT parameters.

Local Computation by R:
- R computes $p_b = \mathcal{F}_{\mathsf{GRO2}}(\mathsf{sid}, z^\alpha)$ and outputs (b, p_b).

Local Computation by S:
- S outputs $p_0 = \mathcal{F}_{\mathsf{GRO2}}(\mathsf{sid}, B^r H^s)$ and $p_1 = \mathcal{F}_{\mathsf{GRO2}}\left(\mathsf{sid}, \left(\frac{B}{T_1}\right)^r \left(\frac{H}{T_2}\right)^s\right)$.

Fig. 5. Fully optimized random oblivious transfer with one simultaneous round

4.1 Adaptively Secure OT in the Global Programmable RO Model

As we have discussed in details the main intuition behind our protocol in Sect. 3.1, we will proceed to the full description. Our protocol $\pi_{\mathsf{aOT\text{-}GPRO}}$ in the PRO model is presented in Fig. 4. Security of our protocol has been summarized in Theorem 1 and the full proof can be found in [15].

Theorem 1. *Assuming the Decisional Diffie-Hellman holds in group $\mathbb{G}$, then $\pi_{\mathsf{aOT\text{-}GPRO}}$ UC-securely implements $\mathcal{F}_{OT}$ functionality in presence of adaptive adversaries in the global programmable random oracle model.*

Practical Optimizations. The above OT protocol requires computing 9 exponentiations and communication of 3 group elements and 3 strings of length κ for one OT. However, the sender can reuse r, s for multiple instances of the OT protocol. Let B_i and H_i be the receiver's message for the i-th OT instance. The sender will compute his OT message by reusing T_1^r, T_2^s and z. He can compute $c_{i,0} = \mathcal{F}_{\mathsf{GRO2}}(\mathsf{sid}, i, B^r H^s) \oplus m_{i,0}$ and $c_{i,1} = \mathcal{F}_{\mathsf{GRO2}}\left(\mathsf{sid}, i, \left(\frac{B}{T_1}\right)^r \left(\frac{H}{T_2}\right)^s\right) \oplus m_{i,1}$.

This reduces the overhead to 5 exponentiations and communication of 2 group elements and 2κ bit strings in the amortized setting. Our second observation is that many practical use of OT depends on OT extension [31] which in turn needs a base OT protocol on random messages, namely random OT. In the random OT

$\pi_{\mathsf{sOT\text{-}GORO}}$

– **Functionalities :** Random oracles $\mathcal{F}_{\mathsf{GRO1}} : \{0,1\}^\kappa \to \mathbb{G}^2$, $\mathcal{F}_{\mathsf{GRO2}} : \mathbb{G} \to \{0,1\}^\kappa$.
– **Public Inputs :** Group $\mathbb{G}$, field $\mathbb{Z}_q$ and generator g of group $\mathbb{G}$.
– **Private Inputs :** S has κ-bit inputs (m_0, m_1) and R has input choice bit b.

Choose:

– R samples $x \leftarrow \mathbb{Z}_q$ and computes $h = g^x$. He also computes an NIZKPoK $\pi_R = (\exists x : h = g^x)$. He samples seed $\leftarrow \{0,1\}^\kappa$ and sets $(T_1, T_2) = \mathcal{F}_{\mathsf{GRO1}}(\mathsf{sid}, \mathsf{sid}, \mathsf{seed})$.
– R samples $\alpha \leftarrow \mathbb{Z}_q$ and computes $B = g^\alpha T_1^b$ and $H = h^\alpha T_2^b$.
– Receiver Parameters: R sends $(h, \pi_R, \mathsf{seed})$ as OT parameters to S.
– R sends (B, H) to S.

Transfer:

– S verifies π_R using h and computes $(T_1, T_2) \leftarrow \mathcal{F}_{\mathsf{GRO1}}(\mathsf{sid}, \mathsf{seed})$.
– S samples $r, s \leftarrow \mathbb{Z}_q$ and computes $z = g^r h^s$. He also computes an NIZKPoK $\pi_S = (\exists r, s : w = g^r h^s)$.
– S computes $c_0 = \mathcal{F}_{\mathsf{GRO2}}(\mathsf{sid}, B^r H^s) \oplus m_0$ and $c_1 = \mathcal{F}_{\mathsf{GRO2}}(\mathsf{sid}, (\frac{B}{T_1})^r (\frac{H}{T_2})^s) \oplus m_1$.
– Sender Parameters: S sends (z, π_S) as OT parameters to R.
– S sends (c_0, c_1) to R.

Local Computation by R :

– R verifies π_S using z.
– R computes $m_b = c_b \oplus \mathcal{F}_{\mathsf{GRO2}}(\mathsf{sid}, z^\alpha)$.

Fig. 6. Statically secure oblivious transfer in the observable random oracle model

variant of our OT protocol, the sender's messages will be random pads (p_0, p_1) where $p_0 = \mathcal{F}_{\mathsf{GRO2}}(\mathsf{sid}, B^r H^s)$ and $p_1 = \mathcal{F}_{\mathsf{GRO2}}\left(\mathsf{sid}, \left(\frac{B}{T_1}\right)^r \left(\frac{H}{T_2}\right)^s\right)$.

The receiver obtains $p_b = \mathcal{F}_{\mathsf{GRO2}}(\mathsf{sid}, z^\alpha)$ as output. In such a case, the receiver needs to send (B, H) for each OT and the sender only needs to send $z = g^r h^s$, which can be reused for multiple OT instances. One can observe that the sender's and receiver's messages are independent of each other and depends only on (g, h). Thus, we can consider a setup consisting of a global CRS $= (g, h)$ and a global programmable RO. The receiver computes (B, H) and sends it to the sender. Simultaneously, the sender can compute z and send it over to the receiver; thus resulting in a non-interactive random OT which requires 5 exponentiations and communication of 2 group elements per OT. This protocol is also secure against mauling attacks by a rushing adversary, who can either corrupt the sender or the receiver. A corrupt receiver can break security only if (g, h, T_1, T_2) is a DDH tuple where (g, h, T_1) is the CRS; which occurs with negligible probability due to CDH assumption. Security against a corrupt sender is ensured by programming the GRO s.t. the tuple is a DDH tuple. In such a case R's message, i.e. (B, H), perfectly hides R's input. Indistinguishability of the tuple follows from DDH.

Our protocol $\pi_{\mathsf{aROT\text{-}GPRO}}$ is presented in Fig. 5. To compute n OTs, we only need $4 + 5n$ exponentiations and communication of $2n + 1$ group elements and one κ-bit string. In contrast, the state-of-the-art OT extension protocol (from PRO based OT) of [36] requires $6n$ exponentiations and requires sending $4n$ group elements. The protocol of [21] requires lesser computation but they need 5 rounds of interaction for their OT. Thus, our protocol will outperform them in WAN setting where interaction is expensive.

4.2 Statically Secure OT in the Global Observable RO Model

The work of [37] has shown a separation between programmable RO and non-programmable RO. Therefore, we show how to change our protocol to work with an observable GRO. Our protocol is statically secure and has the same computation and communication overhead as the GPRO-based protocol, except now the parties need to compute one NIZKPoK each. We present the GORO-based OT protocol $\pi_{\mathsf{sOT\text{-}GORO}}$ in Fig. 6.

The only difference from the PRO-based scheme lies in the generation of the CRS and the OT parameters. The (T_1, T_2) is generated by invoking $\mathcal{F}_{\mathsf{GRO1}}$ on seed. The other group element h is generated by R and he also produces an NIZKPoK of x s.t. $h = g^x$. We perform this because the simulator for a corrupt receiver needs the knowledge of x to extract the receiver's input, which would not be possible if all three elements were generated using the ORO. However, this limits the possibility of extracting a corrupt sender's input by programming the RO to return a DDH tuple. So, the sender is required to produce an NIZKPoK of r and s. This allows the simulator for a corrupt sender to extract r and s; thus extracting the input messages of the corrupt sender. The rest of the proof follows from the static security proof of our PRO-based scheme Security is summarized in Theorem 2 and the full proof can be found in [15].

Theorem 2. *Assuming the Decisional Diffie-Hellman holds in group $\mathbb{G}$, then $\pi_{\mathsf{sOT\text{-}GORO}}$ UC-securely implements $\mathcal{F}_{\mathsf{OT}}$ functionality in presence of static adversaries in the observable random oracle model.*

We would like to point out that NIZK is known to be impossible in the ORO model [38]. However, we only need a relaxed NIZK and allow programming the RO in the security reduction while the simulator is restricted only to the observability feature. Such a relaxation is also utilized to circumvent the impossibility of NIZKs in ORO domain in prior related work [21].

Our protocol needs 5 exponentiations and communication of 2 group elements and two κ-bit strings. In addition, we require a one-time computation of 2 NIZKPoKs and 5 exponentiations and one-time communication of 2 group elements and κ bits. The only other 2 round GORO-based OT protocol is a feasibility result by [10].

5 Receiver Adaptively Secure OT in the CRS Model

In this section, we replace our use of GRO in $\pi_{\mathsf{aOT\text{-}GPRO}}$ by a common random string (CRS). Such a relaxation in the setup assumption results in degradation

$\pi_{\mathsf{reOT\text{-}CRS}}$

- **Public Inputs:** Group $\mathbb{G}$ with a generator g, field $\mathbb{Z}_q$, and CRS $= (g, h, T_1)$.
- **Private Inputs:** S has inputs (m_0, m_1) where $m_0, m_1 \in \mathbb{G}$; R has input choice bit b.

Choose:

- R samples $T_2 \leftarrow \mathbb{G}$.
- R samples $\alpha \leftarrow \mathbb{Z}_q$ and sets $B = g^\alpha T_1^b$ and $H = h^\alpha T_2^b$.
- R sends T_2 and (B, H) to S.

Transfer:

- S samples $r, s \leftarrow \mathbb{Z}_q$ and computes $z = g^r h^s$.
- S computes $c_0 = B^r H^s \cdot m_0$ and $c_1 = (\frac{B}{T_1})^r (\frac{H}{T_2})^s \cdot m_1$.
- S sends z and (c_0, c_1) to R.

Local Computation by R:

- R computes $m_b = c_b . z^{-\alpha}$.

Fig. 7. Oblivious transfer secure against adaptive receiver corruption

of the security and efficiency of the protocol. We lose security against adaptive corruption of sender, resulting in a receiver-equivocal OT which is secure against adaptive corruption of receiver. The computation overhead also increases to 9 exponentiations and 5 group elements as the sender's randomness cannot be reused for multiple instances of the OT protocol as it will leak the individual sender messages from the OT messages. The intuition of our protocol has been discussed in Sect. 3.2 and Fig. 7 gives a detailed description of our protocol. The CRS consists of 3 group elements CRS $= (g, h, T_1)$ and it requires to satisfy two properties for the security to hold.

Properties of CRS. The CRS for the subprotocols should satisfy the following two properties:

- *Property 1:* Given (g, h, T_1) it should be computationally infeasible to obtain a T_2 s.t. (g, h, T_1, T_2) is a DDH tuple. This is ensured in our protocol since an adversary computing such a T_2 (i.e. the tuple is DDH) can be used to break the CDH assumption in a blackbox manner by invoking it in a OT session. The CDH adversary will set the CRS s.t. (h, T_1) is the CDH challenge and it will return T_2 as the CDH response.
- *Property 2:* Given a simulated tuple (g, h, T_1, T_2), where $T_2 = h^t$ and $T_1 = g^t$, it should be indistinguishable from a random tuple. An adversary who can distinguish the tuples can be used to break the DDH assumption. The DDH adversary forwards the DDH challenge tuple as the tuple to this adversary and forwards the answer of this adversary as the DDH answer. In addition, or simulation purposes we provide the simulator with the trapdoors- (x, t) for the CRS $= (g, h, T_1)$ s.t. $h = g^x$ and $T_1 = g^t$.

$\pi_{\mathsf{sOT\text{-}CRS}}$

- **Public Inputs:** Group $\mathbb{G}$, field $\mathbb{Z}_q$ and generator g of group $\mathbb{G}$, CRS $= (g, h, T)$.
- **Private Inputs:** S has κ-bit inputs (m_0, m_1) and R has input choice bit b.

Choose:

- R samples $\alpha \leftarrow \mathbb{Z}_q$ and sets $B = g^{\alpha} T^b$ and $H = h^{\alpha}$.
- R sends (B, H) to S.

Transfer:

- S samples $r, s \leftarrow \mathbb{Z}_q$ and computes $z = g^r h^s$.
- S computes $c_0 = B^r H^s \cdot m_0$ and $c_1 = (\frac{B}{T})^r H^s \cdot m_1$.
- S sends z and (c_0, c_1) to R.

Local Computation by R:

- R computes $m_b = c_b . z^{-\alpha}$.

Fig. 8. Static oblivious transfer in the CRS model

We require the first property for arguing security against a statically corrupt receiver. Given the CRS the corrupt receiver should not be able to set it in the equivocal mode. It will be in the extractable mode to ensure extraction of receiver's input. On the other hand, if the receiver is honest, then the simulated receiver can set the CRS in the equivocal by using Property 2. This allows extracting both messages of the sender and simulate the honest receiver's view during post-execution corruption. Security of our protocol is summarized in Theorem 3 and the full proof can be found in [15].

Theorem 3. *Assuming the Decisional Diffie-Hellman holds in group $\mathbb{G}$, then $\pi_{\mathsf{reOT\text{-}CRS}}$ UC-securely implements $\mathcal{F}_{\mathsf{OT}}$ functionality in presence of a statically corrupted sender and an adaptively corrupted receiver in the common random string model.*

5.1 Efficient Static OT

We can further optimize our protocol $\pi_{\mathsf{reOT\text{-}CRS}}$ for static corruption by removing T_2 from the protocol and henceforth renaming T_1 to T. In $\pi_{\mathsf{reOT\text{-}CRS}}$, the element T_2 was required solely for the purpose of equivocating receiver's view. Our modified protocol $\pi_{\mathsf{sOT\text{-}CRS}}$ is presented in Fig. 8. This gives us a two-round static OT in the common random string model which computes 8 exponentiations and communicates 5 group elements. This outperforms the state-of-the-art [40] protocol which requires 11 exponentiations and communication of 6 group elements to obtain a two-round static OT in the common reference string model.

$\pi_{\mathsf{saOT\text{-}CRS}}$

- **Public Inputs :** Group $\mathbb{G}$, field $\mathbb{Z}_q$ and generator g of group $\mathbb{G}$, CRS = (g, h, T_1).
- **Private Inputs :** S has bit inputs (m_0, m_1) and R has input choice bit b.

Choose:

- R samples $T_2 \leftarrow \mathbb{G}$.
- R samples $\alpha \leftarrow \mathbb{Z}_q$ and sets $B = g^{\alpha}T_1^b$ and $H = h^{\alpha}T_2^b$.
- R sends T_2 and (B, H) to S.

Transfer:

- If $m_0 = 1$, S samples $r_0, s_0 \leftarrow \mathbb{Z}_q$ and computes $z_0 = g^{r_0}h^{s_0}$ and $c_0 = B^{r_0}H^{s_0}$. Else, he samples $c_0, z_0 \leftarrow \mathbb{G}$
- If $m_1 = 1$, S samples $r_1, s_1 \leftarrow \mathbb{Z}_q$ and computes $z_1 = g^{r_1}h^{s_1}$ and $c_1 = (\frac{B}{T_1})^{r_1}(\frac{H}{T_2})^{s_1}$. Else, he samples $c_1, z_1 \leftarrow \mathbb{G}$.
- S sends (z_0, c_0) and (z_1, c_1) to R.

Local Computation by R :

- R computes $y_b = \mathsf{NCE.Dec}(\mathsf{sk}, e_b)$.
- R sets $x_b = 1$ if $c_b = z_b^{\alpha}$ else he sets $x_b = 0$.
- R outputs $m_b = y_b \oplus x_b$.

Fig. 9. Semi-adaptively secure oblivious transfer

$\pi_{\mathsf{aOT\text{-}CRS}}$

- **Primitives :** Semi-adaptive OT $\pi_{\mathsf{saOT\text{-}CRS}} = (\mathsf{R}_1, \mathsf{S}, \mathsf{R}_2)$, Augmented Non Committing Encryption $\mathsf{NCE} = (\mathsf{NCE.Gen}, \mathsf{NCE.Enc}, \mathsf{NCE.Dec}, \mathsf{NCE.Gen_{Obl}}, \mathsf{NCE.Gen_{Inv}})$.
- **Public Inputs :** CRS of $\pi_{\mathsf{saOT\text{-}CRS}}$.
- **Private Inputs :** S has bit inputs (m_0, m_1) and R has input choice bit b.

Choose:

- R invokes $(\mathsf{OT_R}, \mathsf{st_R}) \leftarrow \pi_{\mathsf{saOT\text{-}CRS}}.\mathsf{R}_1(\mathrm{CRS}, b)$.
- R generates $\{\mathsf{pk}_b, \mathsf{sk}\} \leftarrow \mathsf{NCE.Gen}(1^{\kappa})$ and $\mathsf{pk}_{\bar{b}} \leftarrow \mathsf{NCE.Gen}(1^{\kappa})$.
- R sends $(\mathsf{OT_R}, \mathsf{pk}_0, \mathsf{pk}_1)$ to S.

Transfer:

- S randomly samples $y_0, y_1 \leftarrow \{0, 1\}$ and computes $x_0 = y_0 \oplus m_0$ and $x_1 = y_1 \oplus m_1$.
- S invokes $(\mathsf{OT_S}, \mathsf{st_S}) \leftarrow \pi_{\mathsf{saOT\text{-}CRS}}.\mathsf{S}(\mathrm{CRS}, (x_0, x_1), \mathsf{OT_R})$ and sends $\mathsf{OT_S}$ to R.
- S sends $e_0 = \mathsf{NCE.Enc}(\mathsf{pk}, y_0)$ and $e_1 = \mathsf{NCE.Enc}(\mathsf{pk}, y_1)$ to R.

Local Computation by R :

- R decrypts $y_b = \mathsf{NCE.Dec}(\mathsf{sk}, e_b)$ and computes $x_b = \pi_{\mathsf{saOT\text{-}CRS}}.\mathsf{R}_2(\mathrm{CRS}, \mathsf{st_R}, b, \mathsf{OT_S})$.
- R outputs $m_b = y_b \oplus x_b$.

Fig. 10. Adaptively secure oblivious transfer from semi-adaptively secure OT protocol using augmented NCE by [5]

$\pi_{\text{aCOM-CRS}}$

- **Private Inputs:** C has private input $b \in \mathcal{M}$.
- **Public Inputs:** Both parties have a common random string CRS_{OT} in $\pi_{\text{reOT-CRS}}$.

Commit Phase: C samples some randomness α, computes $c = \text{OT}_1(b; \alpha)$, and sends c as commitment to V.
Decommit Phase: C sends (b, α) as the decommitment.
Verification Phase: Upon receiving c and (b, α), V checks if $c \stackrel{?}{=} \text{OT}_1(b; \alpha)$.

Fig. 11. Adaptively secure non-interactive commitment from $\pi_{\text{reOT-CRS}} = (\text{OT}_1, \text{OT}_2)$

6 Adaptively Secure Oblivious Transfer in the CRS Model

Our protocol $\pi_{\text{reOT-CRS}}$ presented in the previous section is only secure against adaptive corruption of receiver. In this section, we make it secure against full adaptive corruption. In the overview section we constructed a semi-adaptive protocol first and then applied the [5] transformation using an augmented NCE to obtain our final protocol. See Sect. 3.3 for a high-level introduction. We first present our semi-adaptive OT protocol in Fig. 9 and then we present our complete protocol in Fig. 10.

6.1 Semi-adaptively Secure OT

We first present our semi-adaptive OT $\pi_{\text{saOT-CRS}}$ protocol in Fig. 9. Security of our protocol is summarized in Theorem 4 and the full proof can be found in [15].

Theorem 4. *Assuming the Decisional Diffie-Hellman holds in group $\mathbb{G}$, then $\pi_{\text{saOT-CRS}}$ UC-securely implements $\mathcal{F}_{\text{OT}}$ functionality in presence of semi-adaptively corrupted malicious parties in the common random string model.*

6.2 Obtaining Full Adaptive Security

Next, we apply the transformation of [5] to obtain our adaptively secure OT protocol $\pi_{\text{aOT-CRS}}$ from our semi-adaptively secure OT protocol $\pi_{\text{saOT-CRS}}$ in the augmented NCE model. For completeness we have presented the [5] transformation in Fig. 10 and it is summarized in Theorem 5.

Theorem 5. *[5] Assuming $\pi_{\text{saOT-CRS}}$ is a two-round semi-adaptively secure OT protocol and NCE is an augmented non-committing encryption scheme then protocol $\pi_{\text{aOT-CRS}}$ UC-securely implements $\mathcal{F}_{\text{OT}}$ functionality in presence of adaptively corrupted malicious parties in the common random string model.*

$\pi_{\mathsf{COM\text{-}DDH}}$

- **Private Inputs:** C has private input $b \in \mathcal{M}$.
- **Public Inputs:** Both parties have a CRS $= (g, h, T_1)$ where $g, h, T_1 \in \mathbb{G}$.

Commit Phase: C samples $T_2 \leftarrow \mathbb{G}$. He sends T_2 as the commitment scheme parameter. C samples $\alpha \leftarrow \mathbb{Z}_q$ and computes $B = g^\alpha T_1^b$ and $H = h^\alpha T_2^b$. He sends $c = (B, H)$ as commitment to V.
Decommit Phase: C sends (b, α) as the decommitment.
Verification Phase: Upon receiving $\{T_2, (c, \alpha, b)\}$, V interprets $c = (B, H)$ and verifies $B \stackrel{?}{=} g^\alpha T_1^b$ and $H \stackrel{?}{=} h^\alpha T_2^b$. R aborts if verification fails; otherwise R accepts the decommitment.

Fig. 12. Adaptively secure non-interactive commitment in the CRS model

Assuming DDH, $\pi_{\mathsf{saOT\text{-}CRS}}$ (Fig. 9) is a semi-adaptively secure OT from 4. Upon instantiating the NCE by the DDH-based augmented NCE scheme of [16] we obtain an adaptively secure bit-OT scheme from DDH. Thus, we can solely construct our adaptively secure OT from DDH.

Theorem 6. *Assuming DDH assumption holds, our protocol $\pi_{\mathsf{aOT\text{-}CRS}}$ (Fig. 10) UC-securely implements $\mathcal{F}_{OT}$ functionality in presence of adaptively corrupted malicious parties in the common random string model.*

Efficiency. Our final protocol requires 11 exponentiations and communication of 7 group elements. One of the group element, i.e. T_2 can be reused. In addition, it requires communicating 2 augmented NCE public keys and computing augmented NCE encryptions of 2 bits. We can instantiate our NCE scheme using the DDH-based protocol of [16] which computes $\mathcal{O}(1)$ exponentiations and communicates $\mathcal{O}(\kappa)$ bits for encrypting each bit. This yields the first two round adaptively secure bit-OT which has constant communication and computation overhead.

In contrast, the only other two round adaptive OT protocol of [5] uses communication-intensive tools likc cquivocal garblcd circuits communicating poly(κ) bits. They also incur a computation overhead of $\mathcal{O}(\kappa^2)$ exponentiations.

7 Adaptively Secure Non-Interactive Commitment in the CRS Model

In this section, we present a transformation from any two-round receiver equivocal OT to a non-interactive adaptive commitment scheme. The high-level description can be found in Sect. 3.4. Let $\pi_{\mathsf{reOT\text{-}CRS}} = (\mathsf{OT}_1, \mathsf{OT}_2)$ denote a two-round receiver equivocal OT, where both OT_1 and OT_2 are PPT algorithms: OT_1 outputs the receiver's OT message c and internal state st. Then our commitment to message $b \in \mathcal{M}$ with randomness α will be c where $\{c, \mathsf{st}\} = \mathsf{OT}_1(b; \alpha)$. The decommitment for c will be (b, α). The verifier V runs OT_1 algorithm on (b, α) to check the validity of the decommitment. Our protocol is presented in Fig. 11 and the security is summarized in Theorem 7. The proof of the theorem can be found in [15].

Theorem 7. *Assuming that $\pi_{\mathsf{reOT\text{-}CRS}} = (OT_1, OT_2)$ is a secure receiver equivocal OT, in the CRS model, then our protocol $\pi_{\mathsf{aCOM\text{-}CRS}}$ (Fig. 11) UC-securely implements $\mathcal{F}_{\mathsf{COM}}$ functionality against adaptive adversaries in the CRS model.*

7.1 Concrete Instantiation and Efficiency

We apply our DDH-based receiver equivocal OT in Fig. 7 to the above compiler and get a concretely efficient adaptive commitment as shown in Fig. 12. It requires four exponentiations and communicating two group elements for committing to a polylog(κ) bit message in the common random string model. Decommitment incurs similar computation overhead and communicating the message and a field element. This gives us the *first* adaptive string commitment with a constant number of exponentiations and $\mathcal{O}(\kappa)$ communication. The current state of the art non-interactive protocols with adaptive security [1,2,9,11] are all bit commitments. Moreover, our protocol also supports additive homomorphism which can be verified as $\textsc{Commit}(m_1; \alpha_1) + \textsc{Commit}(m_2; \alpha_2) = \textsc{Commit}(m_1 + m_2; \alpha_1 + \alpha_2)$.

8 Results in the Single CRS Model

In this section, we replace the per-session local CRS with a single "master" random string sCRS that can be reused by multiple pairs of parties for multiple sessions. Specifically, the parties will use the master random string sCRS to generate a per-session CRS – (g, h, T_1) and will then use the protocol from the previous section with that CRS. We present our multi-session OT and multi-session commitment functionalities $\mathcal{F}_{\mathsf{mOT}}$ and $\mathcal{F}_{\mathsf{COM}}$ in Figs. 13 and 14 respectively. For simplicity, we will describe $\mathcal{F}_{\mathsf{mOT}}$ and the same holds true for $\mathcal{F}_{\mathsf{mCOM}}$. The parties participate in one session, with id sid, which implements $\mathcal{F}_{\mathsf{mOT}}$. One of the parties intializes the session by invoking Initialization with the list L of all the subsession ids. Then each subsession consists of multiple instances of $\mathcal{F}_{\mathsf{OT}}$ between a specific pair of parties with unique roles. This is ensured by considering a counter j alongwith subsession id ssid in the functionality.

While implementing the functionalities, each subsession is associated with a unique ℓ-bit identifier, which we call the sub-session id ssid. The ssid may contain the identities of the two parties, as well as additional information that makes the session unique. Each participant will locally compute the session-specific reference string from the master reference string and the ssid. We assume that the ssid strings are generated by the environment $\mathcal{Z}$ before seeing the sCRS by invoking the Initialization phase with a list L of subsession ids through a

$\mathcal{F}_{\mathsf{mOT}}$

$\mathcal{F}_{\mathsf{mOT}}$ interacts with a sender S, having party id (ssid, sen) and a receiver R, having party id (ssid, rec, in a session with id sid as follows:

- On input (INITIALIZATION, sid, L) from a party, where L is the list of subsession ids; store $s = \mathsf{sid}$ and L, and send (INITIALIZED, sid) to the party. Ignore future initialization messages with same sid.
- On input (CHOOSE, (sid, ssid, j, rec), b) from R, where $b \in \{0,1\}, j > 0$; abort if $\mathsf{sid} \neq s$ or $\mathsf{ssid} \notin \mathsf{L}$, if no message of the form (ssid, j, rec, b) has been recorded in the memory, store (ssid, j, rec, b) and send (ssid, j, rec) to S.
- On input (TRANSFER, (sid, ssid, j, sen), (a_0, a_1)) from S with $a_0, a_1 \in \{0,1\}^n, j > 0$, abort if $\mathsf{sid} \neq s$ or $\mathsf{ssid} \notin \mathsf{L}$, if no message of the form (ssid, j, sen, (a_0, a_1)) is recorded and a message of the form (ssid, j, rec, b) is stored, send (sent, ssid, j, sen, a_b) to R and (sent, ssid, j, rec) to S. Ignore future messages with the ids - (ssid, j, sen) and (ssid, j, rec).

Fig. 13. The ideal functionality $\mathcal{F}_{\mathsf{mOT}}$ for multi-session oblivious transfer

$\mathcal{F}_{\mathsf{mCOM}}$

$\mathcal{F}_{\mathsf{COM}}$ interacts with committer C, having party id (ssid, C), and verifier V, having party id (ssid, V) in a session with id sid as follows:

- On input (INITIALIZATION, sid, L) from a party, where L is the list of subsession ids; store $s = \mathsf{sid}$ and L, and send (INITIALIZED, sid) to the party. Ignore future initialization messages with same sid.
- On receiving input ((COMMIT, V), (sid, ssid, j, C), m) from C for $j > 0$, abort if $\mathsf{sid} \neq s$ or $\mathsf{ssid} \notin \mathsf{L}$, if (ssid, j, C, V, m') has been recorded, ignore the input. Else record the tuple (ssid, j.C, V, m) and send (RECEIPT, ssid, j, C, V) to V.
- On receiving input (DECOMMIT, (sid, ssid, j, C)) for $j > 0$ from C, abort if $\mathsf{sid} \neq s$ or $\mathsf{ssid} \notin \mathsf{L}$, if there is a record of the form (ssid, j, C, V, m) return (DECOMMIT, ssid, j, C, V, m) to V. Otherwise, ignore the input.

Fig. 14. The ideal functionality $\mathcal{F}_{\mathsf{COM}}$ for multi-session commitment scheme

party. The master random string sCRS will contain (g, h) and 2ℓ random group elements- $(u_{i,0}, u_{i,1})$ for $i \in [\ell]$:

$$\mathrm{sCRS} = \begin{bmatrix} (g, h), \{u_{i,0}, u_{i,1}\}_{i \in [\ell]} \end{bmatrix}$$

The random string $\mathrm{CRS}_{\mathsf{ssid}}$ for some ssid will consist of (g, h, T_1), where ssid_i denotes the ith bit of ssid and T_1 is constructed as follows:

$$T_1 = \Pi_{i \in [\ell]} u_{i,\mathsf{ssid}_i}.$$

Once the $\mathrm{CRS}_{\mathsf{ssid}}$ for the session is computed, the parties run protocol $\pi_{\mathsf{aOT\text{-}CRS}}$ from Sect. 6 (for OT), or protocol $\pi_{\mathsf{COM\text{-}DDH}}$ from Sect. 7 (for Commitment), using $\mathsf{CRS}_{\mathsf{ssid}}$ as the reference string for the session. For security reasons, we need $\ell = 2\kappa$ as the security degrades by a factor $\frac{|\mathsf{L}|^2}{2^\ell}$. In [15] we demonstrate that $\mathsf{CRS}_{\mathsf{ssid}}$ satisfies the two properties (Sect. 5) that are required for arguing security of each OT/commitment in the subsessions.

On Statically Chosen List L *of* ssid*s.* We require that the subsession ids be chosen by the environment $\mathcal{Z}$ before seeing sCRS. This has been ensured since $\mathcal{Z}$ has to invoke the INITIALIZATION phase (in Figs. 13 and 14) with a list L of subsession ids through a party. This allows us to construct an adversary for CDH (or DDH) from an adversary who breaks the security of property 1 (or 2) of $\mathsf{CRS}_{\mathsf{ssid}}$. The reduction works by modifying the sCRS and planting an instance of CDH/DDH in one of the subsessions based on the coresponding ssid. Instead, if we allowed $\mathcal{Z}$ to adaptively choose the subsession ids after accessing sCRS, then the reduction fails. It would require guessing the subsession id since the adversary chooses the subsession id adaptively. There are 2^ℓ possible subsession ids, where $|\mathsf{ssid}| = \ell = \mathcal{O}(\kappa)$. Thus, the reduction succeeds only with negligible probability. We leave it as an interesting open question to obtain such protocols where we allow the environment to adaptively choose the subsession ids after seeing sCRS.

8.1 Adaptively Secure OT in the sCRS Model

We obtain a two round adaptively secure OT protocol in sCRS model where in each subsession ssid the parties run $\pi_{\mathsf{aOT\text{-}CRS}}$ using $\mathsf{CRS}_{\mathsf{ssid}}$. Our OT protocol and its security proof can be found in [15].

Theorem 8. *Assuming that $\pi_{\mathsf{aOT\text{-}CRS}}$ implements $\mathcal{F}_{\mathsf{OT}}$ in the local CRS model, then there exists an OT protocol that UC-securely implements $\mathcal{F}_{\mathsf{mOT}}$ functionality (Fig. 13) against adaptive adversaries in the sCRS model.*

8.2 Adaptively Secure Non-interactive Commitment in the sCRS Model

We obtain a non-interactive adaptively secure commitment scheme in sCRS model. In each subsession ssid the parties run $\pi_{\mathsf{COM\text{-}DDH}}$ with $\mathsf{CRS}_{\mathsf{ssid}}$. The commitment scheme and its security proof can be found in [15].

Theorem 9. *Assuming $\pi_{\mathsf{COM\text{-}DDH}}$ implements $\mathcal{F}_{\mathsf{COM}}$ in local CRS model, then there exists a non-interactive commitment protocol that UC-securely implements $\mathcal{F}_{\mathsf{mCOM}}$ functionality (Fig. 14) against adaptive adversaries in sCRS model.*

8.3 Adaptively Secure MPC in the sCRS Model

We discuss our two round adaptively-secure MPC protocol π in the sCRS model.

Theorem 10. *Let π' be a two round adaptively secure MPC protocol in the $(\mathcal{F}_{OT}, \mathcal{F}_{COM})$ model. Then π is a two round adaptively secure MPC protocol in the sCRS model.*

Proof. By applying Theorem 8 and Theorem 9 we obtain an OT and commitment protocol that implements $\mathcal{F}_{\mathsf{mOT}}$ and $\mathcal{F}_{\mathsf{mCOM}}$ functionality in sCRS model. Multiple sessions of $\mathcal{F}_{\mathsf{OT}}$ is simulated given access to a session of $\mathcal{F}_{\mathsf{mOT}}$. Each session of $\mathcal{F}_{\mathsf{OT}}$ with session id s is simulated as a subsession with id s in $\mathcal{F}_{\mathsf{mOT}}$. Similarly, each session of $\mathcal{F}_{\mathsf{COM}}$ with session id s' is simulated as a subsession with id s' in $\mathcal{F}_{\mathsf{mCOM}}$.

Two round adaptively secure MPC protocol π' in the $(\mathcal{F}_{\mathsf{OT}}, \mathcal{F}_{\mathsf{COM}})$ model can be obtained from [5]. They compiled a N-party malicious constant-round adaptively secure MPC protocol π'' into a 2 round N-party malicious constant-round adaptively secure MPC protocol π', in the presence of $\mathcal{F}_{\mathsf{OT}}$. The work of [13] obtained π'' in the $\mathcal{F}_{\mathsf{COM}}$ and $\mathcal{F}_{\mathsf{ZK}}$ by applying the adaptive malicious transformation of [11] on the semi-honest constant round MPC protocol obtained from equivocal garbled circuits. Finally, $\mathcal{F}_{\mathsf{ZK}}$ is implemented by [9] in the presence of adaptive corruptions in the $\mathcal{F}_{\mathsf{COM}}$-model.

Acknowledgements. We would like to thank the anonymous reviewers (and the subreviewers) of the Asiacrypt'20 program committee for their valuable feedback.

References

1. Abdalla, M., Benhamouda, F., Blazy, O., Chevalier, C., Pointcheval, D.: SPHF-friendly non-interactive commitments. In: Sako, K., Sarkar, P. (eds.) ASIACRYPT 2013. LNCS, vol. 8269, pp. 214–234. Springer, Heidelberg (2013). https://doi.org/10.1007/978-3-642-42033-7_12
2. Abdalla, M., Benhamouda, F., Pointcheval, D.: Removing erasures with explainable Hash proof systems. In: Fehr, S. (ed.) PKC 2017. LNCS, vol. 10174, pp. 151–174. Springer, Heidelberg (2017). https://doi.org/10.1007/978-3-662-54365-8_7
3. Afshar, A., Mohassel, P., Pinkas, B., Riva, B.: Non-interactive secure computation based on cut-and-choose. In: Nguyen, P.Q., Oswald, E. (eds.) EUROCRYPT 2014. LNCS, vol. 8441, pp. 387–404. Springer, Heidelberg (2014). https://doi.org/10.1007/978-3-642-55220-5_22
4. Benhamouda, F., Lin, H.: k-round multiparty computation from k-round oblivious transfer via garbled interactive circuits. In: Nielsen, J.B., Rijmen, V. (eds.) EUROCRYPT 2018. LNCS, vol. 10821, pp. 500–532. Springer, Cham (2018). https://doi.org/10.1007/978-3-319-78375-8_17
5. Benhamouda, F., Lin, H., Polychroniadou, A., Venkitasubramaniam, M.: Two-round adaptively secure multiparty computation from standard assumptions. In: Beimel, A., Dziembowski, S. (eds.) TCC 2018. LNCS, vol. 11239, pp. 175–205. Springer, Cham (2018). https://doi.org/10.1007/978-3-030-03807-6_7
6. Byali, M., Patra, A., Ravi, D., Sarkar, P.: Fast and universally-composable oblivious transfer and commitment scheme with adaptive security. Cryptology ePrint Archive, Report 2017/1165 (2017). https://eprint.iacr.org/2017/1165

7. Camenisch, J., Drijvers, M., Gagliardoni, T., Lehmann, A., Neven, G.: The wonderful world of global random oracles. In: Nielsen, J.B., Rijmen, V. (eds.) EUROCRYPT 2018. LNCS, vol. 10820, pp. 280–312. Springer, Cham (2018). https://doi.org/10.1007/978-3-319-78381-9_11
8. Canetti, R.: Universally composable security: a new paradigm for cryptographic protocols. In: 42nd FOCS, pp. 136–145. IEEE Computer Society Press, October 2001
9. Canetti, R., Fischlin, M.: Universally composable commitments. In: Kilian, J. (ed.) CRYPTO 2001. LNCS, vol. 2139, pp. 19–40. Springer, Heidelberg (2001). https://doi.org/10.1007/3-540-44647-8_2
10. Canetti, R., Jain, A., Scafuro, A.: Practical UC security with a global random oracle. In: Ahn, G.J., Yung, M., Li, N. (eds.) ACM CCS 2014, pp. 597–608. ACM Press, November 2014
11. Canetti, R., Lindell, Y., Ostrovsky, R., Sahai, A.: Universally composable two-party and multi-party secure computation. In: 34th ACM STOC, pp. 494–503. ACM Press, May 2002
12. Canetti, R., Poburinnaya, O., Venkitasubramaniam, M.: Better two-round adaptive multi-party computation. In: Fehr, S. (ed.) PKC 2017. LNCS, vol. 10175, pp. 396–427. Springer, Heidelberg (2017). https://doi.org/10.1007/978-3-662-54388-7_14
13. Canetti, R., Poburinnaya, O., Venkitasubramaniam, M.: Equivocating Yao: constant-round adaptively secure multiparty computation in the plain model. In: Hatami, H., McKenzie, P., King, V. (eds.) 49th ACM STOC, pp. 497–509. ACM Press, June 2017
14. Canetti, R., Sarkar, P., Wang, X.: Blazing fast OT for three-round UC OT extension. In: Kiayias, A., Kohlweiss, M., Wallden, P., Zikas, V. (eds.) PKC 2020. LNCS, vol. 12111, pp. 299–327. Springer, Cham (2020). https://doi.org/10.1007/978-3-030-45388-6_11
15. Canetti, R., Sarkar, P., Wang, X.: Efficient and round-optimal oblivious transfer and commitment with adaptive security. IACR Cryptol. ePrint Arch. **2020**, 545 (2020). https://eprint.iacr.org/2020/545
16. Choi, S.G., Dachman-Soled, D., Malkin, T., Wee, H.: Improved non-committing encryption with applications to adaptively secure protocols. In: Matsui, M. (ed.) ASIACRYPT 2009. LNCS, vol. 5912, pp. 287–302. Springer, Heidelberg (2009). https://doi.org/10.1007/978-3-642-10366-7_17
17. Choi, S.G., Katz, J., Wee, H., Zhou, H.-S.: Efficient, adaptively secure, and composable oblivious transfer with a single, global CRS. In: Kurosawa, K., Hanaoka, G. (eds.) PKC 2013. LNCS, vol. 7778, pp. 73–88. Springer, Heidelberg (2013). https://doi.org/10.1007/978-3-642-36362-7_6
18. Chou, T., Orlandi, C.: The simplest protocol for oblivious transfer. In: Lauter, K., Rodríguez-Henríquez, F. (eds.) LATINCRYPT 2015. LNCS, vol. 9230, pp. 40–58. Springer, Cham (2015). https://doi.org/10.1007/978-3-319-22174-8_3
19. Damgård, I., Groth, J.: Non-interactive and reusable non-malleable commitment schemes. In: 35th ACM STOC, pp. 426–437. ACM Press, June 2003
20. Damgård, I., Nielsen, J.B.: Perfect hiding and perfect binding universally composable commitment schemes with constant expansion factor. In: Yung, M. (ed.) CRYPTO 2002. LNCS, vol. 2442, pp. 581–596. Springer, Heidelberg (2002). https://doi.org/10.1007/3-540-45708-9_37
21. Doerner, J., Kondi, Y., Lee, E., Shelat, A.: Secure two-party threshold ECDSA from ECDSA assumptions. In: 2018 IEEE Symposium on Security and Privacy, pp. 980–997. IEEE Computer Society Press, May 2018

22. Döttling, N., Garg, S., Hajiabadi, M., Masny, D., Wichs, D.: Two-round oblivious transfer from CDH or LPN. In: Canteaut, A., Ishai, Y. (eds.) EUROCRYPT 2020. LNCS, vol. 12106, pp. 768–797. Springer, Cham (2020). https://doi.org/10.1007/978-3-030-45724-2_26
23. Even, S., Goldreich, O., Lempel, A.: A randomized protocol for signing contracts. In: Chaum, D., Rivest, R.L., Sherman, A.T. (eds.) CRYPTO 1982, pp. 205–210. Plenum Press, New York, USA (1982)
24. Ganesh, C., Kondi, Y., Patra, A., Sarkar, P.: Efficient adaptively secure zero-knowledge from Garbled circuits. In: Abdalla, M., Dahab, R. (eds.) PKC 2018. LNCS, vol. 10770, pp. 499–529. Springer, Cham (2018). https://doi.org/10.1007/978-3-319-76581-5_17
25. Garg, S., Miao, P., Srinivasan, A.: Two-round multiparty secure computation minimizing public key operations. In: Shacham, H., Boldyreva, A. (eds.) CRYPTO 2018. LNCS, vol. 10993, pp. 273–301. Springer, Cham (2018). https://doi.org/10.1007/978-3-319-96878-0_10
26. Garg, S., Polychroniadou, A.: Two-round adaptively secure MPC from indistinguishability obfuscation. In: Dodis, Y., Nielsen, J.B. (eds.) TCC 2015, Part II. LNCS, vol. 9015, pp. 614–637. Springer, Heidelberg (Mar (2015)
27. Garg, S., Srinivasan, A.: Two-round multiparty secure computation from minimal assumptions. In: Nielsen, J.B., Rijmen, V. (eds.) EUROCRYPT 2018. LNCS, vol. 10821, pp. 468–499. Springer, Cham (2018). https://doi.org/10.1007/978-3-319-78375-8_16
28. Goldreich, O., Micali, S., Wigderson, A.: How to play any mental game or a completeness theorem for protocols with honest majority. In: Aho, A. (ed.) 19th ACM STOC, pp. 218–229. ACM Press, May 1987
29. Hazay, C., Polychroniadou, A., Venkitasubramaniam, M.: Constant round adaptively secure protocols in the Tamper-Proof Hardware model. In: Fehr, S. (ed.) PKC 2017. LNCS, vol. 10175, pp. 428–460. Springer, Heidelberg (2017). https://doi.org/10.1007/978-3-662-54388-7_15
30. Hazay, C., Venkitasubramaniam, M.: On black-box complexity of universally composable security in the CRS model. In: Iwata, T., Cheon, J.H. (eds.) ASIACRYPT 2015. LNCS, vol. 9453, pp. 183–209. Springer, Heidelberg (2015). https://doi.org/10.1007/978-3-662-48800-3_8
31. Ishai, Y., Kilian, J., Nissim, K., Petrank, E.: Extending oblivious transfers efficiently. In: Boneh, D. (ed.) CRYPTO 2003. LNCS, vol. 2729, pp. 145–161. Springer, Heidelberg (2003). https://doi.org/10.1007/978-3-540-45146-4_9
32. Keller, M., Orsini, E., Scholl, P.: Actively secure OT extension with optimal overhead. In: Gennaro, R., Robshaw, M. (eds.) CRYPTO 2015. LNCS, vol. 9215, pp. 724–741. Springer, Heidelberg (2015). https://doi.org/10.1007/978-3-662-47989-6_35
33. Kilian, J.: Zero-knowledge with log-space verifiers. In: 29th FOCS, pp. 25–35. IEEE Computer Society Press, October 1988
34. Li, B., Micciancio, D.: Equational security proofs of oblivious transfer protocols. In: Abdalla, M., Dahab, R. (eds.) PKC 2018, Part I. LNCS, vol. 10769, pp. 527–553. Springer, Heidelberg (Mar (2018)

35. Lindell, Y.: An efficient transform from Sigma protocols to NIZK with a CRS and non-programmable random oracle. In: Dodis, Y., Nielsen, J.B. (eds.) TCC 2015. LNCS, vol. 9014, pp. 93–109. Springer, Heidelberg (2015). https://doi.org/10.1007/978-3-662-46494-6_5
36. Masny, D., Rindal, P.: Endemic oblivious transfer. In: Cavallaro, L., Kinder, J., Wang, X., Katz, J. (eds.) ACM CCS 2019, pp. 309–326. ACM Press, November 2019
37. Nielsen, J.B.: Separating random oracle proofs from complexity theoretic proofs: the non-committing encryption case. In: Yung, M. (ed.) CRYPTO 2002. LNCS, vol. 2442, pp. 111–126. Springer, Heidelberg (2002). https://doi.org/10.1007/3-540-45708-9_8
38. Pass, R.: On deniability in the common reference string and random oracle model. In: Boneh, D. (ed.) CRYPTO 2003. LNCS, vol. 2729, pp. 316–337. Springer, Heidelberg (2003). https://doi.org/10.1007/978-3-540-45146-4_19
39. Patra, A., Sarkar, P., Suresh, A.: Fast actively secure OT extension for short secrets. In: NDSS 2017. The Internet Society, February/March 2017
40. Peikert, C., Vaikuntanathan, V., Waters, B.: A framework for efficient and composable oblivious transfer. In: Wagner, D. (ed.) CRYPTO 2008. LNCS, vol. 5157, pp. 554–571. Springer, Heidelberg (2008). https://doi.org/10.1007/978-3-540-85174-5_31
41. Rabin, M.O.: How to exchange secrets with oblivious transfer. Cryptol. ePrint Arch. Rep. **2005**, 187 (2005). http://eprint.iacr.org/2005/187
42. Yao, A.C.C.: Protocols for secure computations (extended abstract). In: 23rd FOCS, pp. 160–164. IEEE Computer Society Press, November 1982

Secret Sharing

ALBATROSS: Publicly AttestabLe BATched Randomness Based On Secret Sharing

Ignacio Cascudo[1(✉)] and Bernardo David[2]

[1] IMDEA Software Institute, Madrid, Spain
ignacio.cascudo@imdea.org
[2] IT University of Copenhagen, Copenhagen, Denmark
bernardo@bmdavid.com

Abstract. In this paper we present ALBATROSS, a family of multiparty randomness generation protocols with guaranteed output delivery and public verification that allows to trade off corruption tolerance for a much improved amortized computational complexity. Our basic stand alone protocol is based on publicly verifiable secret sharing (PVSS) and is secure under in the random oracle model under the decisional Diffie-Hellman (DDH) hardness assumption. We also address the important issue of constructing Universally Composable randomness beacons, showing two UC versions of Albatross: one based on simple UC NIZKs and another one based on novel efficient "designated verifier" homomorphic commitments. Interestingly this latter version can be instantiated from a global random oracle under the weaker Computational Diffie-Hellman (CDH) assumption. An execution of ALBATROSS with n parties, out of which up to $t = (1/2 - \epsilon) \cdot n$ are corrupt for a constant $\epsilon > 0$, generates $\Theta(n^2)$ uniformly random values, requiring in the worst case an amortized cost per party of $\Theta(\log n)$ exponentiations per random value. We significantly improve on the SCRAPE protocol (Cascudo and David, ACNS 17), which required $\Theta(n^2)$ exponentiations per party to generate one uniformly random value. This is mainly achieved via two techniques: first, the use of packed Shamir secret sharing for the PVSS; second, the use of linear t-resilient functions (computed via a Fast Fourier Transform-based algorithm) to improve the randomness extraction.

1 Introduction

Randomness is essential for constructing provably secure cryptographic primitives and protocols. While in many cases it is sufficient to assume that each party executing a cryptographic construction has access to a local trusted source of unbiased uniform randomness, many applications (*e.g.* electronic voting [1] and

---

B. David—Work partially done while visiting IMDEA Software Institute. This work was supported by a grant from Concordium Foundation, DFF grant number 9040-00399B (TrA^{2}C) and Protocol Labs grant S^{2}LEDGE.

S. Moriai and H. Wang (Eds.): ASIACRYPT 2020, LNCS 12493, pp. 311–341, 2020.
https://doi.org/10.1007/978-3-030-64840-4_11

anonymous messaging [35,36]) require a randomness beacon [30] that can periodically provide fresh random values to all parties. Constructing such a randomness beacon without relying on a trusted third party requires a multiparty protocol that can be executed in such a way that all parties are convinced that an unbiased random value is obtained after the execution terminates, even if a fraction of these parties are corrupted. Moreover, in certain scenarios (*e.g.* in electronic voting [1]) it might be necessary to employ a publicly verifiable randomness beacon, which allows for third parties who did not participate in the beacon's execution to verify that indeed a given random value was successfully obtained after a certain execution. To raise the challenge of constructing such randomness beacons even more, there are classes of protocols that require a publicly verifiable randomness beacon with guaranteed output delivery, meaning that the protocol is guaranteed to terminate and output an unbiased random value no matter what actively corrupted parties do. A prominent class of protocols requiring publicly verifiable randomness beacons with guaranteed output delivery is that of Proof-of-Stake based blockchain consensus protocols [18,23], which are the main energy-efficient alternative to wasteful Proof-of-Work based blockchain consensus protocols [21,25].

Related Works: A number of randomness beacons aiming at being amenable to blockchain consensus applications have been proposed based on techniques such as Verifiable Delay Functions (VDF) [6], randomness extraction from data in the blockchain [2], Publicly Verifiable Secret Sharing [12,23,33] or Verifiable Random Functions [15,18]. However, most of these schemes do not guarantee either the generation of perfectly uniformly random values [2,15,18] or that a value will be generated regardless of adversarial behavior [33]. Those methods that do have those two guarantees suffer from high computational and communication complexity [23] or even higher computational complexity in order to improve communication complexity [6]. Another issue with VDF based approaches is that their security relies on very precise estimates of the average concrete complexity of certain computational tasks (*i.e.* how much time it takes an adversary to compute a VDF), which are hard to obtain for real world systems. While SCRAPE [12] does improve on [23], it can still be further improved, as is the goal of this work. Moreover, none of the protocols that guarantee generation of truly unbiased uniformly random values have any composability guarantees. This is a very important issue, since these protocols are not used in isolation but as building blocks of more complex systems and thus need composability.

Our Contributions: We present ALBATROSS, a family of multiparty randomness generation protocol with guaranteed output delivery and public verification, where parties generate $\Theta(n^2)$ independent and uniformly random elements in a group and where the computational complexity for each party in the worst case is of $\Theta(\log n)$ group exponentiations (the most computationally expensive operation in the protocol) per random element generated, as long as the number of corrupted parties is $t = n/2 - \Theta(n)$. Our contributions are summarized below:

- The first randomness beacon with $\Theta(\log n)$ group exponentiations per party.

- The first Universally Composable randomness beacon producing unbiased uniformly random values.
- The first randomness beacon based on the Computational Diffie-Hellman (CDH) assumption via novel "designated verifier" homomorphic commitments, which might be of independent interest.

Our basic stand alone protocol builds on SCRAPE [12], a protocol based on publicly verifiable secret sharing (PVSS). We depart from the variant of SCRAPE based on the Decisional Diffie-Hellman (DDH) assumption, which required $\Theta(n^2)$ group exponentiations per party to generate just one uniformly random element in the group, but tolerated any dishonest minority. Therefore, what we obtain is a trade-off of corruption tolerance in exchange for a much more efficient randomness generation, under the same assumptions (DDH hardness, RO model). We gain efficiency for ALBATROSS in the suboptimal corruption scenario by introducing two main techniques on top of SCRAPE, that in fact can be applied independently from each other: the first one is the use of "packed" (or "ramp") Shamir secret sharing in the PVSS, and the second is the use of privacy amplification through t-resilient functions that allows to extract more uniform randomness from a vector of group elements from which the adversary may control some of the coordinates. Applying these techniques requires us to overcome significant obstacles (see below) but using them together allows ALBATROSS to achieve the complexity of $\Theta(\log n)$ exponentiations per party and random group element. Moreover, this complexity is worst case: the $\log n$ factor only appears if a large number of parties refuse to open the secrets they have committed to, thereby forcing the PVSS reconstruction on many secrets, and a less efficient output phase. Otherwise (if e.g. all parties act honestly) the amortized complexity is of $O(1)$ exponentiation per party and element generated.

Our Techniques: In order to create a uniformly random element in a group in a multiparty setting, a natural idea is to have every party select a random element of that group and then have the output be the group operation applied to all those elements. However, the last party in acting can see the choices of the other parties and change her mind about her input, so a natural solution is to have every party commit to their random choice first. Yet, the adversary can still wait until everyone else has opened their commitments and decide on whether they want to open or not based on the observed result, which clearly biases the output. In order to solve this, we can have parties commit to the secrets by using a publicly verifiable secret sharing scheme to secret-share them among the other parties as proposed in [12,23]. The idea is that public verifiability guarantees that the secret will be able to be opened even if the dealer refuses to reveal the secrets. The final randomness is constructed from all these opened secrets.

In the case of SCRAPE the PVSS consists in creating Shamir shares σ_i for a secret s in a finite field $\mathbb{Z}_q$, and publishing the encryption of σ_i under the public key pk_i of party i. More concretely, the encryption is $pk_i^{\sigma_i}$, and $pk_i = h^{sk_i}$ for h a generator of a DDH-hard group $\mathbb{G}_q$ of cardinality q; what party i can decrypt is not really the Shamir share σ_i, but rather h^{σ_i}. However these values are enough to reconstruct h^s which acts as a uniformly random choice in the group by the party who chose s. The final randomness is $\prod h^{s^a}$. Public verifiability of the secret sharing is achieved in SCRAPE by having the dealer commit to the shares independently via some other generator g of the group (i.e. they publish g^{σ_i}), proving that these commitments contain the same Shamir shares via discrete logarithm equality proofs, or DLEQs, and then having verifiers use a procedure to check that the shares are indeed evaluations of a low-degree polynomial. In this paper we will use a different proof, but we remark that the latter technique, which we call $Local_{LDEI}$ test, will be of use in another part of our protocol (namely it is used to verify that h^s is correctly reconstructed).

In ALBATROSS we assume that the adversary corrupts at most t parties where $n - 2t = \ell = \Theta(n)$. The output of the protocol will be ℓ^2 elements of $\mathbb{G}_q$.

Larger Randomness via Packed Shamir Secret Sharing. In this suboptimal corruption scenario, we can use *packed* Shamir secret sharing, which allows to secret-share a vector of ℓ elements from a field (rather than a single element). The key point is that every share is still one element of the field and therefore the sharing has the same computational cost ($\Theta(n)$ exponentiations) as using regular Shamir secret sharing. However, there is still a problem that we need to address: the complexity of the reconstruction of the secret vector from the shares increases by the same factor as the secret size (from $\Theta(n)$ to $\Theta(n^2)$ exponentiations). To mitigate this we use the following strategy: each secret vector will be reconstructed only by a random subset of c parties (independently of each other). Verifying that a reconstruction is correct only requires $\Theta(n)$ exponentiations, by using the aforementioned $Local_{LDEI}$. The point is that if we assign $c = \log n$, then with large probability there will be only at most a small constant number of secret tuples that were not correctly reconstructed by any of the $c(n)$ parties and therefore it does not add too much complexity for the parties to compute those. The final complexity of this phase is then $O(n^2 \log n)$ exponentiations for each party, in the worst case.

Larger Randomness via Resilient Functions. To simplify, let us first assume that packed secret sharing has not been used. In that case, right before the output phase from SCRAPE, parties will know a value h^{s_a} for each of the parties P_a in the set $\mathcal{C}$ of parties that successfully PVSS'ed their secrets (to simplify, let us say $\mathcal{C} = \{P_1, P_2, \dots, P_{|\mathcal{C}|}\}$), where h is a generator of a group of order q. In the original version of SCRAPE, parties then compute the final randomness as $\prod_{a=1}^{|\mathcal{C}|} h^{s_a}$, which is the same as $h^{\sum_{a=1}^{|\mathcal{C}|} s_a}$.

Instead, in ALBATROSS, we use a randomness extraction technique based on a linear t-resilient function, given by a matrix M, in such a way that the parties instead output a vector of random elements $(h^{r_1}, ..., h^{r_m})$ where $(r_1, ..., r_m) = M(s_1, \dots, s_{|\mathcal{C}|})$. The resilient function has the property that the output vector is uniformly distributed as long as $|\mathcal{C}| - t$ inputs are uniformly distributed, even if the other t are completely controlled by the adversary. If in addition packed secret sharing has been used, one can simply use the same strategy for each of the ℓ coordinates of the secret vectors created by the parties. In this way we can create ℓ^2 independently distributed uniformly random elements of the group.

An obstacle to this randomness extraction strategy is that, in the presence of corrupted parties some of the inputs s_i may not be known if the dealers of these values have refused to open them, since PVSS reconstruction only allows to retrieve the values h^{s_i}. Then the computation of the resilient function needs to be done in the exponent which in principle appears to require either $O(n^3)$ exponentiations, or a distributed computation like in the PVSS reconstruction.

Fortunately, in this case the following idea allows to perform this computation much more efficiently: we choose M to be certain type of Vandermonde matrix so that applying M is evaluating a polynomial (with coefficients given by the s_i) on several n-th roots of unity. Then we adapt the Cooley-Tukey fast Fourier transform algorithm to work in the exponent of the group and compute the output with $n^2 \log n$ exponentiations, which in practice is almost as fast as the best-case scenario where the s_i are known. This gives the claim amortized complexity of $O(\log n)$ exponentiations per party and random element computed.

Additional Techniques to Decrease Complexity. We further reduce the complexity of the PVSS used in ALBATROSS, with an idea which can also be used in SCRAPE [12]. It concerns public verification that a published sharing is correct, i.e. that it is of the form $pk_i^{p(i)}$ for some polynomial of bounded degree, say at most k. Instead of the additional commitment to the shares used in [12], we use standard Σ-protocol ideas that allow to prove this type of statement, which turns out to improve the constants in the computational complexity. We call this type of proof a low degree exponent interpolation (LDEI) proof.

Universal Composability. We extend our basic stand alone protocol to obtain two versions that are secure in the Universal Composability (UC) framework [10], which is arguably one of the strongest security guarantees one can ask from a protocol. In particular, proving a protocol UC secure ensures that it can be used as a building block for more complex systems while retaining its security guarantees, which is essential for randomness beacons. We obtain the first UC-secure version of ALBATROSS by employing UC non-interactive zero knowledge proofs (NIZKs) for discrete logarithm relations, which can be realized at a reasonable overhead. The second version explores a new primitive that we introduce and construct called "designated verifier" homomorphic commitments, which allows a sender to open a commitment towards one specific receiver in such a way that this receiver can later prove to a third party that the opening revealed a certain message. Instead of using DDH based encryption schemes as before, we now have the parties commit to their shares using our new commitment scheme and rely on its homomorphic properties to perform the LDEI proofs that ensure share validity. Interestingly, this approach yields a protocol secure under the weaker CDH assumption in the random oracle model.

2 Preliminaries

$[n]$ denotes the set $\{1, 2, \ldots, n\}$ and $[m, n]$ denotes the set $\{m, m+1, \ldots, n\}$. We denote vectors with black font lowercase letters, i.e. $\mathbf{v}$. Given a vector $\mathbf{v} =$

$(v_1, \ldots, v_n)$ and a subset $I \subseteq [n]$, we denote by $\mathbf{v}_I$ the vector of length $|I|$ with coordinates $v_i, i \in I$ in the same order they are in $\mathbf{v}$. Throughout the paper, q will be a prime number and $\mathbb{Z}_q = \mathbb{Z}/q\mathbb{Z}$ is a finite field of q elements. For a field $\mathbb{F}$, $\mathbb{F}^{m \times n}$ is the set of $m \times n$ matrices with coefficients in $\mathbb{F}$. Moreover, we denote by $\mathbb{F}[X]_{\leq m}$ the vector space of polynomials in $\mathbb{F}[X]$ with degree at most m. For a set $\mathcal{X}$, let $x \overset{\$}{\leftarrow} \mathcal{X}$ denote x chosen uniformly at random from $\mathcal{X}$; and for a distribution $\mathcal{Y}$, let $y \overset{\$}{\leftarrow} \mathcal{Y}$ denote y sampled according to the distribution $\mathcal{Y}$.

Polynomial Interpolation and Lagrange Basis. We recall a few well known facts regarding polynomial interpolation in fields.

Definition 1 (Lagrange basis). *Let $\mathbb{F}$ be a field, and $S = \{a_1, \ldots, a_r\} \subseteq \mathbb{F}$. A basis of $\mathbb{F}[X]_{\leq r-1}$, called the Lagrange basis for S, is given by $\{L_{a_i,S}(X) : i \in [r]\}$ defined by*

$$L_{a_i,S}(X) = \prod_{a_j \in S \setminus \{a_i\}} \frac{X - a_j}{a_i - a_j}.$$

Lemma 1. *Let $\mathbb{F}$ be a field, and $S = \{a_1, \ldots, a_r\} \subseteq \mathbb{F}$. Then the map $\mathbb{F}[X]_{\leq r-1} \to \mathbb{F}^r$ given by $f(X) \mapsto (f(a_1), \ldots, f(a_r))$ is a bijection, and the preimage of $(b_1, \ldots, b_r) \in \mathbb{F}^r$ is given by $f(X) = \sum_{i=1}^r b_i \cdot L_{a_i,S}(X)$.*

Packed Shamir Secret Sharing. From now on we work on the finite field $\mathbb{Z}_q$. Shamir secret sharing scheme [32] allows to share a secret $s \in \mathbb{Z}_q$ among a set of n parties (where $n < q$) so that for some specified $1 \leq t < n$, the secret can be reconstructed from any set of $t+1$ shares via Lagrange interpolation ($t+1$-reconstruction), while any t or less shares convey no information about it (t-privacy). In Shamir scheme each share is also in $\mathbb{Z}_q$ and therefore of the same size of the secret.

Packed Shamir secret sharing scheme [5,20] is a generalization that allows for sharing a vector in $\mathbb{Z}_q^\ell$ while each share is still one element of $\mathbb{Z}_q$. Standard Shamir is the case $\ell = 1$. Packing comes at the inevitable cost of sacrificing the threshold nature of Shamir's scheme, which is replaced by an (optimal) quasithreshold (often called "ramp") behavior, namely there is t-privacy and $t + \ell$ reconstruction. The description of the sharing and reconstruction (from $t + \ell$ shares) algorithms can be found in Fig. 1.

Remark 1. The points $0, -1, \ldots, -(\ell - 1)$ (for the secret) and $1, \ldots, n$ (for the shares) can be replaced by any set of $n + \ell$ pairwise distinct points. In this case the reconstruction coefficients should be changed accordingly. Choosing other evaluation points may be beneficial due to efficient algorithms for both computing the shares and the Lagrange coefficients [34]. In this work we will not focus on optimizing this aspect and use the aforementioned points for notational simplicity.

Linear Codes. The Hamming weight of a vector $\mathbf{c} \in \mathbb{Z}_q^n$ is the number of nonzero coordinates of $\mathbf{c}$. An $[n, k, d]_q$-linear error correcting code C is a vector

Packed Shamir secret sharing

Packed Shamir secret sharing over $\mathbb{Z}_q$ for ℓ secrets with n parties, t-privacy and $t+\ell$-reconstruction. We require $n+\ell \leq q$, $1 \leq t$, $t+\ell \leq n$.

Sharing algorithm.

On input $(s_0, s_1, \ldots, s_{\ell-1}) \in \mathbb{Z}_q^\ell$:

- The dealer chooses a polynomial uniformly at random in the affine space

$$\{f \in \mathbb{Z}_q[X]_{\leq t+\ell-1}, f(0) = s_0, f(-1) = s_1, \ldots, f(-(\ell-1)) = s_{\ell-1}\}.$$

- For $i = 1, \ldots, n$, the dealer sends $f(i)$ to the i-th party.

Reconstruction algorithm.

On input the shares $\sigma_i = f(i), i \in \mathcal{Q}$ for a set of parties $\mathcal{Q} \subseteq [n]$, with $|\mathcal{Q}| = t + \ell$.

- For $m = 0, \ldots, \ell-1$, parties compute

$$s_m = \sum_{i \in \mathcal{Q}} \sigma_i L_{i,\mathcal{Q}}(-m) = \sum_{i \in \mathcal{Q}} \sigma_i \prod_{j \in \mathcal{Q}, j \neq i} \frac{-m-j}{i-j}$$

- Output $(s_0, s_1, \ldots, s_{\ell-1})$

Fig. 1. Packed Shamir secret sharing (sharing algorithm)

subspace of $\mathbb{Z}_q^n$ of dimension k and minimum distance d, i.e., the smallest Hamming weight of a nonzero codeword in C is exactly d. A generator matrix is a matrix $M \in \mathbb{Z}_q^{k \times n}$ such that $C = \{\mathbf{m} \cdot M : \mathbf{m} \in \mathbb{Z}_q^k\}$.

Given n pairwise distinct points $x_1, \ldots, x_n$ in $\mathbb{Z}_q^n$, a Reed Solomon of length n and dimension k is defined as $= \{(f(x_1), \ldots, f(x_n)) : f \in \mathbb{Z}_q[X], \deg f < k\}$. It is well known that this is an $[n, k, n-k+1]_q$-linear code, and therefore achieves the largest possible minimum distance for a code of that length and dimension. These codes are called MDS (maximum distance separable).

The dual code of a code C, denoted $C^\perp$, is the vector space consisting of all vectors $\mathbf{c}^\perp \in \mathbb{Z}_q^n$ such that $\langle \mathbf{c}, \mathbf{c}^\perp \rangle = 0$ for all $\mathbf{c} \in C$ where $\langle \cdot, \cdot \rangle$ denotes the standard inner product. For the Reed-Solomon code above, its dual is the following so-called generalized Reed-Solomon code

$$C^\perp = \{(u_1 \cdot f_*(x_1), \ldots, u_n \cdot f_*(x_n)) : g \in \mathbb{Z}_q[X], \deg f_* < n-k\}$$

where $u_1, \ldots, u_n$ are fixed elements of $\mathbb{Z}_q^n$, namely $u_i = \prod_{j=1, j \neq i}^n (x_i - x_j)^{-1}$.

Linear Perfect Resilient Functions. Our optimizations make use of randomness extractors which are linear over $\mathbb{Z}_q$ and hence given by a matrix $M \in \mathbb{Z}_q^{u \times r}$ satisfying the following property: the knowledge of any t coordinates of the input gives no information about the output (as long as the other $r-t$ coordinates are chosen uniformly at random). This notion is known as linear perfect t-resilient function [16].

Definition 2. *A $\mathbb{Z}_q$-linear (perfect) t-resilient function (t-RF for short) is a linear function $\mathbb{Z}_q^r \to \mathbb{Z}_q^u$ given by $\mathbf{x} \mapsto M \cdot \mathbf{x}$ such that for any $I \subseteq [r]$ of size t,* *and any* $\mathbf{a}_I = (a_j)_{j\in I} \in \mathbb{Z}_q^t$, *the distribution of* $M \cdot \mathbf{x}$ *conditioned to* $\mathbf{x}_I = \mathbf{a}_I$ *and to* $\mathbf{x}_{[r]\setminus I}$ *being uniformly random in* $\mathbb{Z}_q^{r-t}$, *is uniform in* $\mathbb{Z}_q^u$.

Note that such a function can only exist if $u \leq r - t$. We have the following characterization in terms of linear codes.

Theorem 1 [16]. *An* $u \times r$ *matrix* M *induces a linear t-RF if and only if* M *is a generator matrix for an* $[r, u, t+1]_q$*-linear code.*

Remark 2. Remember that with our notation for linear codes, the generator matrix acts on the right for encoding a message, i.e. $\mathbf{m} \mapsto \mathbf{m} \cdot M$. In other words the encoding function for the linear code and the corresponding resilient function given by the generator matrix as in Theorem 1 are "transpose from each other".

A t-RF for the optimal case $u = r - t$ is given by any generator matrix of an $[r, r-t, t+1]_q$ MDS code, for example a matrix M with $M_{ij} = a_j^{i-1}$ for $i \in [r-t]$, $j \in [r]$, where all a_j's are distinct, which generates a Reed-Solomon code. It will be advantageous for us to fix an element $\omega \in \mathbb{Z}_q^*$ of order at least $r-t$ and set $a_j = \omega^{j-1}$, that is we will use the matrix $M = M(\omega, r-t, r)$ where

$$M_{ij} = \omega^{(i-1)(j-1)}, i \in [r-t], j \in [r]$$

Then $M \cdot \mathbf{x} = (f(1), f(\omega), \cdots, f(\omega^{r-t-1}))$ where $f(X) := x_0 + x_1 X + x_2 X^2 + \cdots + x_{r-1} X^{r-1}$, and we can use the Fast Fourier transform to compute $M \cdot \mathbf{x}$ very efficiently, as we explain later.

3 Basic Algorithms and Protocols

In this section we introduce some algorithms and subprotocols which we will need in several parts of our protocols, and which are relatively straight-forward modifications of known techniques.

3.1 Proof of Discrete Logarithm Equality

We will need a zero-knowledge proof that given $g_1, ..., g_m$ and $x_1, ..., x_m$ the discrete logarithms of every x_i with base g_i are equal. That is $x_i = g_i^\alpha$ for all $i \in [m]$ for some common $\alpha \in \mathbb{Z}_q$. Looking ahead, these proofs will be used by parties in the PVSS to ensure they have decrypted shares correctly. A sigma-protocol performing DLEQ proofs for $m = 2$ was given in [14]. We can easily adapt that protocol to general m as follows:

1. The prover samples $w \leftarrow \mathbb{Z}_q$ and, for all $i \in [m]$, computes $a_i = g_i^w$ and sends a_i to the verifier.
2. The verifier sends a challenge $e \leftarrow \mathbb{Z}_q$ to the prover.
3. The prover sends a response $z = w - \alpha e$ to the verifier.
4. The verifier accepts if $a_i = g_i^z x_i^e$ for all $i \in [m]$.

We transform this proof into a non-interactive zero-knowledge proof of knowledge of α in the random oracle model via the Fiat-Shamir heuristic [19,29]:

- The prover computes $e = H(g_1, \ldots, g_m, x_1, \ldots, x_m, a_1, \ldots, a_m)$, for $H(\cdot)$ a random oracle (that will be instantiated by a cryptographic hash function) and z as above. The proof is $(a_1, \ldots, a_m, e, z)$.
- The verifier checks that $e = H(g_1, \ldots, g_m, x_1, \ldots, x_m, a_1, \ldots, a_m)$ and that $a_i = g_i^z x_i^e$ for all i.

This proof requires m exponentiations for the prover and $2m$ for the verifier.

3.2 Proofs and Checks of Low-Degree Exponent Interpolation

We consider the following statement: given generators $g_1, g_2, \ldots, g_m$ of a cyclic group $\mathbb{G}_q$ of prime order q, pairwise distinct elements $\alpha_1, \alpha_2, \ldots, \alpha_m$ in $\mathbb{Z}_q$ and an integer $1 \leq k < m$, known by prover and verifier, the claim is that a tuple $(x_1, x_2, \ldots, x_m) \in \mathbb{G}_q^m$ is of the form $(g_1^{p(\alpha_1)}, g_2^{p(\alpha_2)}, \ldots, g_m^{p(\alpha_m)})$ for a polynomial $p(X)$ in $\mathbb{Z}_q[X]_{\leq k}$. We will encounter this statement in two different versions:

- In the first situation, we need a zero-knowledge proof of knowledge of $p(X)$ by the prover. This type of proof will be used for a dealer in the publicly verifiable secret sharing scheme to prove correctness of sharing. We call this proof $LDEI((g_i)_{i \in [m]}, (\alpha_i)_{i \in [m]}, k, (x_i)_{i \in [m]})$.
- In the second situation, we have no prover, but on the other hand we have $g_1 = g_2 = \cdots = g_m$. In that case we will use a locally computable check from [12]: indeed, verifiers can check by themselves that the statement is correct with high probability. This type of check will be used to verify correctness of reconstruction of a (packed) secret efficiently. We call such check $Local_{LDEI}((\alpha_i)_{i \in [m]}, k, (x_i)_{i \in [m]})$.[1]

In [12], the first type of proof was constructed by using a DLEQ proof of knowledge of common exponent to reduce that statement to one of the second type and then using the local check we just mentioned. However, this is unnecessarily expensive both in terms of communication and computation. Indeed, a simpler Σ-protocol for that problem is given in Fig. 2.

Proposition 1. *Protocol LDEI in Fig. 2 is an honest-verifier zero-knowledge proof of knowledge for the given statement.*

Proof. The proof of this proposition follows standard arguments in Σ-protocol theory and is given in the full version of this paper [13].

Applying Fiat-Shamir heuristic we transform this into a non-interactive proof:

[1] This type of statement is independent of the generator g_1 of the group we choose: it is true for a given generator if and only if it is true for all of them.

Protocol *LDEI* (ZK PoK of Low-Degree Exponent Interpolation)

Public parameters: prime q, cyclic group $\mathbb{G}_q$ of prime order q, $g_1, ..., g_m$ generators of $\mathbb{G}_q$, $\alpha_1, \alpha_2, \ldots, \alpha_m$ pairwise distinct elements in $\mathbb{Z}_q$, integer $1 \leq k < m$.
Statement: $(x_1, x_2, \ldots, x_m) \in \left\{ \left(g_1^{p(\alpha_1)}, g_2^{p(\alpha_2)}, \ldots, g_m^{p(\alpha_m)} \right) : p \in \mathbb{Z}_q[X], \deg p \leq k \right\}$ and the prover knows p.

Protocol:
- Sender chooses $r(X) \in \mathbb{Z}_q[X]_{\leq k}$ uniformly at random and sends $a_i = g_i^{r(\alpha_i)}$ for all $i \in [m]$ to the verifier.
- Verifier chooses $e \in \mathbb{Z}_q$ uniformly at random.
- Sender sends $z(X) = e \cdot p(X) + r(X)$ to the verifier
- Verifier checks that $z(X) \in \mathbb{Z}_q[X]_{\leq k}$ and $x_i^e \cdot a_i = g_i^{z(\alpha_i)}$ for all $i \in [m]$.

Fig. 2. Protocol *LDEI* zero-knowledge proof of knowledge of low-degree exponent interpolation.

- The sender chooses $r \in \mathbb{Z}_q[X]_{\leq k}$ uniformly at random and computes $a_i = g_i^{r(\alpha_i)}$ for all $i = 1, \ldots, m$, $e = H(x_1, x_2, \ldots, x_m, a_1, a_2, \ldots, a_m)$ and $z = e \cdot p + r$. The proof is then $(a_1, a_2, \ldots, a_m, e, z)$.
- The verifier checks that $z \in \mathbb{Z}_q[X]_{\leq k}$, that $x_i^e \cdot a_i = g_i^{z(\alpha_i)}$ holds for all $i = 1, \ldots, m$ and that $e = H(x_1, x_2, \ldots, x_m, a_1, a_2, \ldots, a_m)$.

Now we consider the second type of situation mentioned above. The local check is given in Fig. 3.

Algorithm $Local_{LDEI}$ to Verify Low-Degree Exponent Interpolation

Public parameters: prime q, cyclic group $\mathbb{G}_q$ of prime order q, integer m.
Input: pairwise distinct elements $(\alpha_1, \alpha_2, \ldots, \alpha_m)$ in $\mathbb{Z}_q$, integer $1 \leq k < m$, tuple $(x_1, x_2, \ldots, x_m) \in \mathbb{G}_q$, a group generator g.
Statement: $(x_1, x_2, \ldots, x_m) \in \left\{ \left(g^{p(\alpha_1)}, g^{p(\alpha_2)}, \ldots, g^{p(\alpha_m)} \right) : p \in \mathbb{Z}_q[X], \deg p \leq k \right\}$.
Algorithm:
- Verifier defines $u_i = 1/\prod_{\ell \neq i}(\alpha_i - \alpha_\ell)$ for all $i = 1, \ldots, m$.
- Verifier chooses a polynomial p_* uniformly at random in $\mathbb{Z}_q[X]_{\leq m-k-2} \setminus \{0\}$ and computes $v_i = u_i \cdot p_*(\alpha_i)$ for all i.
- Verifier checks that $\prod_{i=1}^m x_i^{v_i} = 1$ and accepts if and only if that is the case.

Fig. 3. Algorithm $Local_{LDEI}$ to verify low-degree exponent interpolation

Proposition 2. *The local test $Local_{LDEI}$ in Fig. 3 always accepts if the statement is true and rejects with probability at least $1 - 1/q$ if the statement is false.*

Correctness is based on the fact that the vector $(u_1p_*(\alpha_1),\ldots,u_np_*(\alpha_m))$ is in the dual code $C^\perp$ of the Reed Solomon code C given by the vectors $(p(\alpha_1),\ldots,p(\alpha_m))$ with $\deg p \leq k$, hence if the exponents of the x_i's (in base g) indeed form a codeword in C, the verifier is computing the inner product of two orthogonal vectors in the exponent. Soundness follows from the fact that, if the vector is not a codeword in C, then a uniformly random element in $C^\perp$ will only be orthogonal to that vector of exponents with probability less than $1/q$. See [12, Lemma 1] for more information about this claim.

3.3 Applying Resilient Functions "in the Exponent"

In our protocol we will need to apply resilient functions in the following way. Let $h_1,\ldots,h_r$ be public elements of $\mathbb{G}_q$, chosen by different parties, so that $h_i = h^{x_i}$ (for some certain public generator h of the group) and x_i is only known to the party that has chosen it. Our goal is to extract $(\widehat{h}_1,\ldots,\widehat{h}_u) \in \mathbb{G}_q^u$ which is uniformly random in the view of an adversary who has control over up to t of the initial elements x_i. In order to do that, we take a t-resilient function from $\mathbb{Z}_q^r$ to $\mathbb{Z}_q^u$ given by a matrix M and apply it to the exponents, i.e., we define $\widehat{h}_i = h^{y_i}$ where $\mathbf{x} \mapsto \mathbf{y} = M \cdot \mathbf{x}$; this satisfies the desired properties. Because the resilient function is linear, the values $\widehat{h}_i$ can be computed from the h_i by group operations, without needing the exponents x_i. We define the following notation.

Definition 3. *As above, let $\mathbb{G}_q$ be a group of order q in multiplicative notation. Given a matrix $M = (M_{ij})$ in $\mathbb{Z}_q^{u\times r}$ and a vector $\mathbf{h} = (h_1, h_2,\ldots,h_r) \in \mathbb{G}_q^r$, we define $\widehat{\mathbf{h}} = M \diamond \mathbf{h} \in \mathbb{G}_q^u$, as $\widehat{\mathbf{h}} = (\widehat{h}_1,\widehat{h}_2,\ldots,\widehat{h}_r)$, where $\widehat{h}_i = \prod_{k=1}^u h_k^{M_{ik}}$.*

Remark 3. Given a generator h of $\mathbb{G}_q$, if we write $\mathbf{h} = (h^{x_1}, h^{x_2},\ldots,h^{x_r})$, $\mathbf{x} = (x_1, x_2,\ldots,x_r)$, then $M \diamond \mathbf{h} = (h^{y_1}, h^{y_2},\ldots,h^{y_r})$ where $(y_1, y_2,\ldots,y_r) = M \cdot \mathbf{x}$.

Now let $M = M(\omega, r-t, r)$ as in Sect. 2. In order to minimize the number of exponentiations that we need to compute $M \diamond \mathbf{h}$ recall first that $M \cdot \mathbf{x} = (f(1), f(\omega),\ldots,f(\omega^{r-t-1}))$, where f is the polynomial with coefficients $f_i = x_{i+1}$, for $i \in [0, r-1]$. Assuming there exists $n > r-t-1$ a power of 2 that divides $q-1$, we can choose ω to be a n-th root of unity for n and use the well known Cooley-Tukey recursive algorithm [17] for computing the Fast Fourier Transform. The algorithm in fact evaluates a polynomial of degree up to $n-1$ on all powers of ω up to ω^{n-1} with $O(n \log n)$ multiplications. We can just set $f_j = 0$ for $j \geq r$, and ignore the evaluations in ω^i, for $i \geq r-t$. In our situation the x_i's are not known; we use the fact that in the Cooley-Tukey algorithm all operations on the x_i are linear, so we can operate on the values $h_i = h^{x_i}$ instead. The resulting algorithm is then given in Fig. 4 (since we denoted $f_i = x_{i+1}$, then $h_i = h^{f_{i-1}}$).

At every recursion level of the algorithm, it needs to compute in total n exponentiations, and therefore the total number of exponentiations in $\mathbb{G}_q$ is $n \log_2 n$. In fact, half of these are inversions, which are typically faster.

"Cooley-Tukey FFT in the exponent" algorithm $FFTE$

Parameters: A large prime q, and a group $\mathbb{G}_q$ of cardinality q.
Input: An integer $n = 2^k$ dividing $q-1$, a tuple $\mathbf{h} = (h_1, h_2, \ldots, h_n) \in \mathbb{G}_q^n$, and an n-th root of unity $\omega \in \mathbb{Z}_q$.
Output: The tuple $\widehat{\mathbf{h}} = (\widehat{h}_1, \widehat{h}_2, \ldots, \widehat{h}_n) = M' \diamond \mathbf{h} \in \mathbb{G}_q^n$, where $M' \in \mathbb{Z}_q^{n\times n}$ is given by $M'_{ij} = \omega^{(i-1)(j-1)}$ for $i, j \in [n]$.

If $n = 1$, return h_1.
Else:

- For $j = 1, \ldots, n/2$, compute $v_j = h_j \cdot h_{j+n/2}$, $v_j^* = (h_j \cdot (h_{j+n/2})^{-1})^{\omega^{j-1}}$. Set $\mathbf{v} = (v_1, v_2, \ldots, v_{n/2})$, $\mathbf{v}^* = (v_1^*, v_2^*, \ldots, v_{n/2}^*)$.
- Apply the algorithm recursively to $(n/2, \mathbf{v}, \omega^2)$ and on $(n/2, \mathbf{v}^*, \omega^2)$ obtaining outputs $\widehat{\mathbf{v}} = (\widehat{v}_1, \widehat{v}_2, \ldots, \widehat{v}_{n/2})$ and $\widehat{\mathbf{v}^*} = (\widehat{v^*}_1, \widehat{v^*}_2, \ldots, \widehat{v^*}_{n/2})$ respectively.
- Return $(\widehat{v}_1, \widehat{v^*}_1, \widehat{v}_2, \widehat{v^*}_2, \ldots, \widehat{v}_{n/2}, \widehat{v^*}_{n/2})$.

Fig. 4. Algorithm $FFTE$ (Cooley-Tukey FFT in the exponent)

4 ALBATROSS Protocols

We will now present our main protocols for multiparty randomness generation. We assume n participants, at most $t < (n-1)/2$ of which can be corrupted by some active static adversary. We define then $\ell = n - 2t > 0$. Note that $n - t = t + \ell$, so we use these two quantities interchangeably. For asymptotics, we consider that both t and ℓ are $\Theta(n)$, in particular $t = \tau \cdot n$ for some $0 < \tau < 1/2$. The n participants have access to a public ledger, where they can publish information that can be seen by the other parties and external verifiers.

Our protocols take place in a group $\mathbb{G}_q$ of prime cardinality q, where we assume that the Decisional Diffie-Hellman problem is hard. Furthermore, in order to use the FFTE algorithm we require that $\mathbb{G}_q$ has large 2-adicity, i.e., that $q-1$ is divisible by a large power of two 2^u. Concretely we need $2^u > n - t$. DDH-hard elliptic curve groups with large 2-adicity are known, for example both the Tweedledee and Tweedledum curves from [8] satisfy this property for $u = 33$, which is more than enough for any practical application.

4.1 A PVSS Based on Packed Shamir Secret Sharing

As a first step, we show a generalization of a PVSS from [12], where we use packed Shamir secret sharing in order to share several secrets at essentially the same cost for the sharing and public verification phases. In addition, correctness of the shares is instead verified using the $LDEI$ proof. This is different than in [12] where the dealer needed to commit to the shares using a different generator of the group, and correctness of the sharing was proved using a combination of DLEQ proofs and the $Local_{LDEI}$ check, which is less efficient. In Fig. 5, we

Protocol π_{PPVSS}

Let h be a generator of a group $\mathbb{G}_q$ of order q. Let $H(\cdot)$ be a random oracle. Protocol π_{PPVSS} is run between n parties $P_1, \ldots, P_n$, a dealer D and an external verifier V (in fact any number of external verifiers) who have access to a public ledger where they can post information for later verification.

1. **Setup:** Party P_i generates a secret key $sk_i \leftarrow \mathbb{Z}_q$, a public key $pk_i = h^{sk_i}$ and registers the public key pk_i by posting it to the public ledger, for $1 \le i \le n$.
2. **Distribution:** The dealer D samples a polynomial $p(X) \leftarrow \mathbb{Z}_q[X]_{\le t+\ell-1}$ and sets $s_0 = p(0), s_1 = p(-1), \ldots, s_{\ell-1} = p(-(\ell-1))$. The secrets are defined to be $S_0 = h^{s_0}, S_1 = h^{s_1}, \ldots, S_{\ell-1} = h^{s_{\ell-1}}$. D computes Shamir shares $\sigma_i = p(i)$ for $1 \le i \le n$. D encrypts the shares as $\hat{\sigma}_i = pk_i^{\sigma_i}$ and publishes $(\hat{\sigma}_1, \ldots, \hat{\sigma}_n)$ in the public ledger along with the proof $LDEI$ that $\hat{\sigma}_i = pk_i^{p(i)}$ for some p of degree at most $t + \ell - 1$.
3. **Verification:** The verifier checks the proof $LDEI$.

Fig. 5. Protocol π_{PPVSS}

present the share distribution and verification of the correctness of the shares of the new PVSS. We discuss the reconstruction of the secret later.

Under the DDH assumption, π_{PPVSS} satisfies the property of IND1-secrecy as defined in [12] (adapted from [22,31]), which requires that given t shares and a vector $\mathbf{x}' = (s'_0, s'_1, \ldots, s'_{\ell-1})$, the adversary cannot tell whether $\mathbf{x}'$ is the actual vector of secrets.

Definition 4. ***Indistinguishability of secrets (IND1-secrecy).*** *We say that the PVSS is IND1-secret if for any polynomial time adversary $\mathcal{A}_{Priv}$ corrupting at most $t-1$ parties, $\mathcal{A}_{Priv}$ has negligible advantage in the following game played against a challenger.*

1. *The challenger runs the Setup phase of the PVSS as the dealer and sends all public information to $\mathcal{A}_{Priv}$. Moreover, it creates secret and public keys for all honest parties, and sends the corresponding public keys to $\mathcal{A}_{Priv}$.*
2. *$\mathcal{A}_{Priv}$ creates secret keys for the corrupted parties and sends the corresponding public keys to the challenger.*
3. *The challenger chooses values $\mathbf{x}_0$ and $\mathbf{x}_1$ at random in the space of secrets. Furthermore it chooses $b \leftarrow \{0,1\}$ uniformly at random. It runs the Distribution phase of the protocol with x_0 as secret. It sends $\mathcal{A}_{Priv}$ all public information generated in that phase, together with $\mathbf{x}_b$.*
4. *$\mathcal{A}_{Priv}$ outputs a guess $b' \in \{0,1\}$.*

The advantage of $\mathcal{A}_{Priv}$ is defined as $|\Pr[b = b'] - 1/2|$.

Proposition 3. *Protocol π_{PPVSS} is IND1-secret under the DDH assumption.*

We prove this proposition in the full version of the paper [13], but we note that the proof follows from similar techniques as in the security analysis of the PVSS in SCRAPE [12] and shows IND1-secrecy based on the ℓ-DDH hardness assumption, which claims that given $(g, g^{\alpha}, g^{\beta_0}, g^{\beta_1}, \cdots, g^{\beta_{\ell-1}}, g^{\gamma_0}, g^{\gamma_1}, \cdots, g^{\gamma_{\ell-1}})$ where the γ_i either have all been sampled at random from $\mathbb{Z}_q$ or are equal to $\alpha \cdot \beta_i$, it is hard to distinguish both situations. However, when ℓ is polynomial in the security parameter (as is the case here) ℓ-DDH is equivalent to DDH, see [26].

We now discuss how to reconstruct secrets in π_{PPVSS}. Rather than giving one protocol, in Fig. 6 we present a number of subprotocols that can be combined in order to reconstruct a secret. The reason is to have some flexibility about which parties will execute the reconstruction algorithm and which ones will verify the reconstruction in the final randomness generation protocol.

In the share decryption protocol party P_i, using secret key sk_i, decrypts the share $\hat{\sigma}_i$ and publishes the obtained value h^{σ_i}. Moreover P_i posts a DLEQ proof to guarantee correctness of the share decryption; if several secret tuples need to be reconstructed, this will be done by a batch DLEQ proof.

Once $n - t$ values h^{σ_i} have been correctly decrypted (by a set of parties $\mathcal{Q}$), any party can compute the ℓ secret values $S_j = h^{s_j}$ using the reconstruction algorithm $Rec_{\mathcal{Q}}$, which boils down to applying Lagrange interpolation in the exponent. Note that since Lagrange interpolation is a linear operation, the exponents σ_i do not need to be known, one can operate on the values h^{σ_i} instead.

However, the computational complexity of this algorithm is high ($O(n^2)$ exponentiations) so we introduce the reconstruction verification algorithm $RecVer_{\mathcal{Q}}$ which allows any party to check whether a claimed reconstruction is correct at a reduced complexity ($O(n)$ exponentiations). $RecVer_{\mathcal{Q}}$ uses the local test $Local_{LDEI}$ that was presented in Fig. 3.

We remark that the most expensive computation is reconstruction of a secret which requires $O(n^2)$ exponentiations.

4.2 Scheduling of Non-private Computations

In ALBATROSS, parties may need to carry out a number of computations of the form $M \diamond \mathbf{h}$, where $M \in \mathbb{Z}_q^{r \times m}$, $\mathbf{h} \in \mathbb{G}_q^m$ for some $r, m = O(n)$. This occurs if parties decide not to reveal their PVSSed secrets, and it happens at two moments of the computation: when reconstructing the secrets from the PVSS and when applying the resilient function at the output phase of the protocol.

These computations do not involve private information but especially in the PVSS they are expensive, requiring $O(n^2)$ exponentiations. Applying a resilient function via our $FFTE$ algorithm is considerably cheaper (it requires $O(n \log n)$ exponentiations), but depending on the application it still may make sense to apply the distributed computation techniques we are going to introduce.

On the other hand, given a purported output for such a computation, verifying their correctness can be done locally in a cheaper way ($O(n)$ exponentiations) using respectively the tests $Local_{LDEI}$ for verifying PVSS reconstruction and a similar test which we call $Local_{LExp}$ for verifying the correct application of $FFTE$ (since we will not strictly need $Local_{LExp}$, we will not describe it here but it can be found in the full version of our paper).

Reconstruction protocol and algorithms in π_{PPVSS}

Protocols used in the reconstruction of secrets in PVSS π_{PPVSS} from Figure 5. Same conditions and notations as there.

- **Share decryption (for P_i):** On input $\hat{\sigma}_i, pk_i$, decrypt share $\tilde{\sigma}_i = \hat{\sigma}_i^{\frac{1}{sk_i}} = h^{\sigma_i}$ and publish it in the ledger together with $PROOF_i = DLEQ((h, \tilde{\sigma}_i), (pk_i, \hat{\sigma}_i))$ (showing that the decrypted share $\tilde{\sigma}_i$ corresponds to $\hat{\sigma}_i$).
- **Amortized share decryption (for P_i):** If the PVSS has been used several times where P_i has received in each case a share $\hat{\sigma}_i^a$, P_i can decrypt shares as above but publish one single proof $PROOF_i = DLEQ((h, (\tilde{\sigma}_i^a)_a), (pk_i, (\hat{\sigma}_i^a)_a))$.
- **Share decryption verification:** Apply the verification algorithm of the DLEQ proof $PROOF_i$ and complain if this is not correct.
- **Secret reconstruction algorithm $Rec_{\mathcal{Q}}$:** On input $\{\tilde{\sigma}_i\}_{i\in\mathcal{Q}}$ for a set $\mathcal{Q}$ of exactly $n-t$ indices, for $j \in [\ell-1]$:
  - Set $\lambda_i^{(j)} = \prod_{m:m\in\mathcal{Q}, m\neq i} \frac{-j-m}{i-m}$ for all $i \in \mathcal{Q}$ and compute
  $$S_j = \prod_{i\in\mathcal{Q}} (\tilde{\sigma}_i)^{\lambda_i^{(j)}} = \prod_{i\in\mathcal{Q}} h^{p(i)\lambda_i^{(j)}} = h^{p(-j)} = h^{s_j},$$
  - Publish the values S_j.
- **Reconstruction verification algorithm $RecVer_{\mathcal{Q}}$:** On input $(S_0, S_1, \ldots, S_{\ell-1}, \{\tilde{\sigma}_i\}_{i\in\mathcal{Q}})$, and calling $\mathcal{Q} = \{i_1, \ldots, i_{n-t}\}$ execute
  $$Local_{LDEI}((\alpha_j)_{j\in[-(\ell-1),n-t]}, t+\ell-1, (\Sigma_j)_{j\in[-(\ell-1),n-t]}),$$
  where $\alpha_j = j$ and $\Sigma_j = S_{-j}$ for $j \in [-(\ell-1), 0]$ and $\alpha_j = i_j$, $\Sigma_j = \tilde{\sigma}_{i_j}$ for $j \in [1, n-t]$.

Fig. 6. Reconstruction protocols and algorithms in π_{PPVSS}

In the worst case where $\Theta(n)$ parties abort after having correctly PVSSed their secrets, $\Theta(n)$ computations of each type need to be carried out. We balance the computational complexity of the parties as follows: for each of the tasks $\texttt{task}_i$ to be computed, a random set of computing parties A_i is chosen of cardinality around some fixed value $c(n)$, who independently compute the task and publish their claimed outputs; the remaining parties verify which one of the outputs is correct, and if none of them is, they compute the tasks themselves.

Remark 4. The choice of A_i has no consequences for the correctness and security of our protocols. The adversary may at most slow down the computation if it can arrange too many sets A_i to contain no honest parties, but this requires a considerable amount of biasing of the randomness source. We will derive this randomness using a random oracle applied to the transcript of the protocol up to that moment, and assume for simplicity that each party has probability roughly $c(n)/n$ to belong to each A_i.

Let $T = \{\texttt{task}_1, \ldots, \texttt{task}_{f(n)}\}$ be a set of computation tasks, each of which consists of applying the same algorithm $AlgComp$ to an input $\texttt{in}_i$. Likewise, let $AlgVer$ be a verifying algorithm that given an input $\texttt{in}$ and a purported output $\texttt{out}$ always accepts if the output is correct and rejects it with very large probability if it is incorrect. We apply the protocol in Fig. 7.

Computational Complexity. We assume that $|\mathcal{P}| = \Theta(n)$, and that $AlgComp$ requires $\texttt{ccost}(n)$ group exponentiations while $AlgVer$ needs $\texttt{vcost}(n)$. On expectation, each party will participate as computing party for $O(f(n) \cdot c(n)/n)$ tasks and as verifier for the rest, in each case needing to verify at most $c(n)$ computations. Note that we schedule the verifications so that parties check first the most common claimed output, as this will likely be the correct one. For a given $\texttt{task}_i$, if A_i contains at least one honest party, then one of the verifications will be correct. A_i contains only corrupt parties with probability $\tau^{c(n)}$ where $\tau = t/n$ and therefore we can assume that the number of i's for which this happens will be at most $O(\tau^{c(n)} f(n))$, so parties will need to additionally apply $AlgComp$ on this number of tasks. Therefore the number of exponentiations per party is $\texttt{ccost}(n) \cdot O((c(n)/n + \tau^{c(n)}) \cdot f(n)) + \texttt{vcost}(n) \cdot O\left(c(n) \cdot (1 - c(n)/n) \cdot f(n)\right)$.

Distributed computation protocol $DistComp(\mathcal{T}, \mathcal{P}, c(n))$

For each $i = 1, \dots, f(n)$:
- A random subset $A_i \subseteq \mathcal{P}$ of $c(n)$ parties is selected.
- Each party $P_j \in A_i$ independently executes $AlgComp(\texttt{in}_i)$ and publishes $\texttt{out}_{P_j}$. Let $\mathcal{L}_i$ be the list of published claimed outputs for $\texttt{task}_i$ ordered from most frequent (the one that is claimed to be the output by more parties in A_i) to least frequent.
- Each party $P_k \in \mathcal{P} \setminus A_i$ does the following
  - P_k applies $AlgVer(\texttt{in}_i, \texttt{out})$ for $\texttt{out} \in \mathcal{L}_i$ in the order they appear in $\mathcal{L}_i$ until she finds a correct one, and accepts this as output of $\texttt{task}_i$.
  - If none of the $\texttt{out} \in \mathcal{L}_i$ passes the test, P_k computes $AlgComp(\texttt{in}_i)$ and sets the result as output for $\texttt{task}_i$.

Fig. 7. Distributed computation protocol $DistComp(\mathcal{T}, \mathcal{P}, c(n))$

PVSS Reconstruction. In the case of reconstruction of the PVSS'ed values, we have $AlgComp = Rec$ (Fig. 6), which has complexity $\texttt{ccost}(n) = O(n^2)$ and $AlgVer$ is $RecVer$ where $\texttt{vcost}(n) = O(n)$. The number of computations $f(n)$ equals the number of corrupted parties that correctly share a secret but later decide not to reveal it. In the worst case $f(n) = \Theta(n)$. In that case, setting $c(n) = \log n$ gives a computational complexity of $O(n^2 \log n)$ exponentiations. In fact the selection $c(n) = \log n$ is preferable unless $f(n)$ is small ($f(n) = O(\log n)$) where $c(n) = n$ (everybody reconstructs the $f(n)$ computations independently) is a better choice. For the sake of simplicity we will use $c(n) = \log n$ in the description of the protocols.

Output Reconstruction via $FFTE$. For this case we always have $f(n) = \ell = \Theta(n)$. We use $FFTE$ as $AlgComp$, so $\mathtt{ccost}(n) = O(n \log n)$, while $AlgVer$ is $Local_{LExp}$ where $\mathtt{vcost}(n) = O(n)$. Setting $c(n) = |\mathcal{P}|$, $c(n) = \log n$ or $c(n) = \Theta(1)$ all give $O(n^2 \log n)$ exponentiations in the worst case.

Setting $c(n) = \Theta(1)$ (a small constant number of parties computes each task, the rest verify) has a better best case asymptotic complexity: if every party acts honestly each party needs $O(n^2)$ exponentiations.

On the other hand, $c(n) = |\mathcal{P}|$ corresponds to every party carrying out the output computation by herself, so we do not really need $DistComp$ (and hence neither do we need $Local_{LExp}$). This requires less use of the ledger and a smaller round complexity, as the output of the majority is guaranteed to be correct. Moreover the practical complexity of $FFTE$ is very good, so in practice this option is computationally fast. We henceforth prefer this option, and leave $c(n) = \Theta(1)$ as an alternative.

4.3 The ALBATROSS Multiparty Randomness Generation Algorithm

Next we present our randomness generation protocol ALBATROSS. We first introduce the following notation for having a matrix act on a matrix of group elements, by being applied to the matrix formed by their exponents.

Definition 5. *As above, let $\mathbb{G}_q$ be a group of order q, and h be a generator. Given a matrix $A = (A_{ij})$ in $\mathbb{Z}_q^{m_1 \times m_2}$ and a matrix $B = (B_{ij}) \in \mathbb{G}_q^{m_2 \times m_3}$, we define $C = A \diamond B \in \mathbb{G}_q^{m_1 \times m_3}$ with entries $C_{ij} = \prod_{k=1}^{m_2} B_{kj}^{A_{ik}}$.*

Remark 5. An alternative way to write this is $C = h^{A \cdot D}$, where D in $\mathbb{Z}_q^{m_2 \times m_3}$ is the matrix containing the discrete logs (in base h) of B, i.e. $D_{ij} = DLog_h(B_{ij})$. But we remark that we do not need to know D to compute C.

The protocol can be found in Fig. 8 and Fig. 9. In Fig. 8 we detail the first two phases Commit and Reveal: in the Commit phase the parties share random tuples $(h^{s_0^a}, \ldots, h^{s_{\ell-1}^a})$ and prove correctness of the sharing. In the Reveal phase parties first verify correctness of other sharings. Once $n-t$ correct sharings have been posted,[2] the set $\mathcal{C}$ of parties that successfully posted correct sharings now open the sharing polynomials. The remaining parties verify this is consistent with the encrypted shares. If all parties in $\mathcal{C}$ open secrets correctly, then all parties learn the exponents s_i^a and compute the final output by applying the resilient function in a very efficient manner, as explained in Fig. 9, step 4'.

If some parties do not correctly open their secret tuples, the remaining parties will use the PVSS reconstruction routine to retrieve the values $h^{s_j^a}$, and then compute the final output from the reconstructed values, now computing the resilient functions in the exponent. This is explained in Fig. 9.

[2] This is since $n - t$ is the maximum we can guarantee if t parties are corrupted. However we can also adapt our protocol to work with more than $n - t$ parties in $\mathcal{C}$ if these come before a given time limit.

Note that once a party gets into the set $\mathcal{C}$, her PVSS is correct (with overwhelming probability) and her tuple of secrets will be used in the final output, no matter the behaviour of that party from that point on. This is important: it prevents that the adversary biases the final randomness by initially playing honestly so that corrupted parties get into $\mathcal{C}$, and at that point deciding whether or not to open the secrets of each corrupted party conditioned on what other parties open. The fact that the honest parties can reconstruct the secrets from any party in $\mathcal{C}$ makes this behaviour useless to bias the output. On the other hand, the properties of the resilient function prevent the corrupted parties from biasing the output before knowing the honest parties' inputs.

Theorem 2. *With overwhelming probability, the protocol Π_{ALB} has guaranteed output delivery and outputs a tuple of elements uniformly distributed in $\mathbb{G}_q^{\ell^2}$, as long as the active, static, computationally bounded adversary corrupts at most t parties (where $2t + \ell = n$).*

Proof. This theorem is based on the remarks above and formally proven in the full version of this paper [13].

Computational Complexity: Group Exponentiations. In Table 1 we collect the complexity of ALBATROSS in terms of number of group exponentiations per party, comparing it with the SCRAPE protocol, where for ALBATROSS we assume $\ell = \Theta(n)$. For the figures in the table, we consider both the worst case where $\Theta(n)$ parties in $\mathcal{C}$ do not open their secrets in the Reveal phase, and the best case where all the parties open their secrets. As we can see the amortized cost for generating a random group element goes down from $O(n^2)$ exponentiations to $O(\log n)$ in the first case and $O(1)$ in the second.

More in detail, in the Commit phase, both sharing a tuple of ℓ elements in the group costs $O(n)$ exponentiations and proving their correctness take $O(n)$ exponentiations. The Reveal phase takes $O(n^2)$ exponentiations since every party checks the $LDEI$ proofs of $O(n)$ parties, each costing $O(n)$ exponentiations, and similarly they later execute, for every party that reveals their sharing polynomial, $O(n)$ exponentiations to check that this is consistent with the encrypted shares.

In the worst case $O(n)$ parties from $\mathcal{C}$ do not open their secrets. The Recovery phase requires each then $O(n^2 \log n)$ exponentiations per party, as explained in Sect. 4.2. The Output phase also requires $O(n^2 \log n)$ exponentiations since $FFTE$ is used $O(n)$ times (or if the alternative distributed technique is used, the complexity is also $O(n^2 \log n)$ by the discussion in Sect. 4.2.

In the best case, all parties from $\mathcal{C}$ reveal their sharing polynomials correctly, the Recovery phase is not necessary and the Output phase requires $O(n^2)$ exponentiations per party as parties can compute the result directly by reconstructing the exponents first (where in addition one can use the standard FFT in $\mathbb{Z}_q$).

Computational Complexity: Other Operations. The total number of additional computation of group operations (aside from the ones involved in computing group exponentiations) is $O(n^2 \log n)$. With regard to operations in the field $\mathbb{Z}_q$, parties need to carry out a total of $O(n)$ computations of polynomials

Protocol Π_{ALB} (Commit and Reveal phases)

Protocol Π_{ALB} is run between a set $\mathcal{P}$ of n parties $P_1, \ldots, P_n$ who have access to a public ledger where they can post information for later verification. It is assumed that the Setup phase of π_{PPVSS} is already done and the public keys pk_i of each party P_i are already registered in the ledger. In addition, the parties have agreed on a Vandermonde $(n-2t) \times (n-t)$-matrix $M = M(\omega, n-2t, n-t)$ with $\omega \in \mathbb{Z}_q^*$ as specified in section 2.

1. **Commit:** For $1 \leq j \leq n$:
   - Party P_j executes the Distribution phase of the PVSS as Dealer for $\ell = n - 2t$ secrets, publishing the encrypted shares $\hat{\sigma}_1^j, \ldots, \hat{\sigma}_n^j$ and sharing correctness verification information $LDEI^j$ on the public ledger, also learning the secrets $h^{s_0^j}, \ldots, h^{s_{\ell-1}^j}$ and the exponents $s_0^j, \ldots, s_{\ell-1}^j$.
2. **Reveal:**
   - For every set of encrypted shares $\hat{\sigma}_1^j, \ldots, \hat{\sigma}_n^j$ and the verification information $LDEI^j$ published in the public ledger, all parties run the Verification phase of the PVSS sub protocol.
   - Once $n - t$ parties have posted a valid sharing on the ledger (we call $\mathcal{C}$ the set of these parties) each party $P_j \in \mathcal{C}$ reveals her sharing polynomial p_j.
   - Every party now verifies that indeed p_j is the sharing polynomial that P_j used in step 1 by reproducing the Distribution phase of P_j, i.e., computing the secrets s_i^j and shares σ_i^j of P_j, and verifying that $\hat{\sigma}_i^j$ is indeed equal to $pk_i^{\sigma_i^j}$. Note that at the same time they have computed the vector of secrets of P_j, i.e., $(s_0^j, \ldots, s_{\ell-1}^j)$.
   - At this point, if every party in $\mathcal{C}$ has opened their secrets correctly, go to step 4′ in Figure 9. Otherwise proceed to step 3 in Figure 9

Fig. 8. Protocol Π_{ALB} (commit and reveal phases)

of degree $O(n)$ in sets of $O(n)$ points, which are always subsets of the evaluation points for the secrets and share. In order to speed this computation up we can use $2n - th$ roots of unity as evaluation points (instead of $[-\ell - 1, n]$) and make use of the FFT yielding a total of $O(n^2 \log n)$ basic operations in $\mathbb{Z}_q$. We also need to compute Lagrange coefficients and the values u_i in $Local_{LDEI}$ but this is done only once per party. In addition, the recent article [34] has presented efficient algorithms for all these computations.

Smaller Outputs. ALBATROSS outputs $O(n^2)$ random elements in the group $\mathbb{G}_q$. However, if parties do not need such large output, the protocol can be adapted to have a smaller output and a decreased complexity (even though the amortized complexity will be worse than the full ALBATROSS). In fact there are a couple of alternatives to achieve this: The first is to use standard (i.e., "non-packed" Shamir's secret sharing, so a single group element is shared per party, as in SCRAPE; yet the resilient function based technique is still used to achieve an output of $O(n)$ (assuming $t = (1/2 - \epsilon)n$). This yields a total computational complexity per party of $O(n^2)$ exponentiations ($O(n)$ per output). A similar

Protocol Π_{ALB} continued (Recovery and Output phase)

3 **Recovery:** Let $\mathcal{C}_A$ be the set of parties $P_a \in \mathcal{C}$ that do not publish the openings of their secrets in the Reveal phase, or that publish an erroneous opening.
- Every party $P_j \in \mathcal{P}$ executes the Amortized Share Decryption protocol for all PVSSs where a party $P_a \in \mathcal{C}_A$ was the dealer as described in Figure 6. That is, P_j posts all decrypted shares $\tilde{\sigma}_j^a$ and a unique $PROOF_j = DLEQ((h, (\tilde{\sigma}_j^a)_{P_a \in \mathcal{C}_A})(pk, (\hat{\sigma}_j^a)_{P_a \in \mathcal{C}_A}))$ to the public ledger.
- Each party $P_i \in \mathcal{P}$ verifies each proof $PROOF_j$ published by some P_j.
- Once a set $\mathcal{Q}$ of $n - t$ parties publish valid decrypted shares, the secrets are reconstructed as follows:
  For every $P_a \in \mathcal{C}_A$, we define $\mathtt{task}_{Rec,a}$ to be the computation of $(h^{s_0^a}, \ldots, h^{s_{\ell-1}^a})$ from the decrypted shares with $AlgComp = Rec_{\mathcal{Q}}$ as described in PVSS reconstruction. Let $\mathcal{T}_{Rec} = \{\mathtt{task}_{Rec,a}\}_{P_a \in \mathcal{C}_A}$.
  Parties call $DistComp(\mathcal{T}_{Rec}, \mathcal{P}, \log n)$, where $DistComp$ is as described in Figure 7 (where $AlgVer = RecVer_{\mathcal{Q}}$, as in Figure 6) using as randomness the output of a random oracle applied to the transcript so far.

4 **Output:** Let T be the $(n-t) \times \ell$ matrix with rows indexed by the parties in $\mathcal{C}$ and where the row corresponding to $P_a \in \mathcal{C}$ is $(h^{s_0^a}, \ldots, h^{s_{\ell-1}^a})$.
- Each computes the $\ell \times \ell$-matrix $R = M \diamond T$ by applying $FFTE$ to each column $T^{(j)}$ of T, resulting in column $R^{(j)}$ of R (since $R^{(j)} = M \diamond T^{(j)}$ and M is Vandermonde) for $j \in [0, \ell - 1]$. [a].
- Parties output the ℓ^2 elements of R as final randomness.

4' **Alternative output:** if every party in $\mathcal{C}$ has opened her secrets correctly in step **Reveal**, then:
- Parties compute $R = M \diamond T$ in the following way:
  Let S be the $(n-t) \times \ell$ matrix with rows indexed by the parties in $\mathcal{C}$ and where the row corresponding to $P_a \in \mathcal{C}$ is $(s_0^a, \ldots, s_{\ell-1}^a)$. Then each party computes $U = M \cdot S \in \mathbb{Z}_q^{\ell \times \ell}$ (using the standard FFT in $\mathbb{Z}_q$ to compute each column) and $R = h^U$. [b]
- Parties output the ℓ^2 elements of R as final randomness.

[a] Alternatively $DistComp$ can be used to distribute the computation, using committees of size $O(1)$ to compute each column and a local test to verify these computations, see discussion in Section 4.2 and full version of the paper

[b] Meaning the (i, j)-th element in R is h^y where y is the (i, j)-th element in U

Fig. 9. Protocol Π_{ALB} continued

alternative is to instead use ALBATROSS as presented until the Recovery phase, and then only a subset $I \subset [0, \ell - 1]$ of the coordinates of the secret vectors is used to construct a smaller output, and the rest is ignored. Then parties only need to recover those coordinates and apply the output phase to them. The advantage is that at a later point the remaining unused coordinates can be used on demand, if more randomness is needed (however it is important to note this unused randomness can not be considered secret anymore at this point, as it is computable from the information available to every party). If initially only $O(n)$

Table 1. Computational complexity in terms of numbers of exponentiations for each phase of the protocols, and exponentiations per created element (per party).

Scheme	Output size	Complexity (# group exponentiations)					Amortized complexity
		Commit	Reveal	Recovery	Output	Total	
SCRAPE	1	$O(n)$	$O(n^2)$	$O(n^2)$	$O(1)$	$O(n^2)$	$O(n^2)$
ALBATROSS, worst case	$O(n^2)$	$O(n)$	$O(n^2)$	$O(n^2 \log n)$	$O(n^2 \log n)$	$O(n^2 \log n)$	$O(\log n)$
ALBATROSS, best case	$O(n^2)$	$O(n)$	$O(n^2)$	-	$O(n^2)$	$O(n^2)$	$O(1)$

random elements are needed, we set $|I| = O(1)$ and need $O(n^2)$ exponentiations per party ($O(n)$ per output). We give more details in the full version.

Implementation. A toy implementation of some of the algorithms used in ALBATROSS can be found in [27].

5 Making ALBATROSS Universally Composable

In the previous sections, we constructed a packed PVSS scheme π_{PPVSS} and used it to construct a guaranteed output delivery (G.O.D.) randomness beacon Π_{ALB}. However, as in previous G.O.D. unbiasable randomness beacons [12,23], we only argue stand alone security for this protocol. In the remainder of this work, we show that Π_{ALB} can be lifted to achieve Universally Composability by two different approaches: 1. using UC-secure zero knowledge proofs of knowledge for the LDEI and DLEQ relations defined above, and 2. using UC-secure additively homomorphic commitments. We describe the UC framework, ideal functionalities and additional modelling details in the full version [13].

Modeling Randomness Beacons in UC. We are interested in realizing a publicly verifiable G.O.D. coin tossing ideal functionality that functions as a randomness beacon (*i.e.* it allows any third party verifier to check whether a given output was previously generated by the functionality). We define such a functionality $\mathcal{F}_{\mathsf{CT}}^{m,\mathcal{D}}$ in Fig. 10. Notice that it provides random outputs once all honest parties activate it with (Toss, *sid*) independently from dishonest parties' behavior. We realize this simple functionality for single shot coin tossing because it allows us to focus on the main aspects of our techniques. In order to obtain a stream of random values as in a traditional beacon, all parties can periodically call this functionality with a fresh *sid*.

5.1 Using UC-Secure Zero Knowledge Proofs

Our first approach is to modify the commit and reveal phases of Protocol Π_{ALB} and use NIZK ideal functionalities as setup (along with an authenticated public bulletin board ideal functionality $\mathcal{F}_{APBB}$ as defined in the full version [13]) in order to obtain an UC-secure version of protocol. The crucial difference is that instead of having all parties reveal the randomness of the PVSS sharing

Functionality $\mathcal{F}_{\mathsf{CT}}^{k,\mathcal{D}}$

$\mathcal{F}_{\mathsf{CT}}^{k,\mathcal{D}}$ is parameterized by $k \in \mathbb{N}$ and a distribution $\mathcal{D}$, interacting with a set of parties $\mathcal{P} = \{\mathcal{P}_1, \ldots, \mathcal{P}_n\}$, a set of verifiers $\mathcal{V}$ and an adversary $\mathcal{S}$ through the following interfaces:

Toss: Upon receiving (TOSS, *sid*) from all honest parties in $\mathcal{P}$, uniformly sample k random elements $x_1, \ldots, x_k \xleftarrow{\$} \mathcal{D}$ and send (TOSSED, $sid, x_1, \ldots, x_k$) to all parties in $\mathcal{P}$.
Verify: Upon receiving (VERIFY, $sid, x_1, \ldots, x_k$) from $\mathcal{V}_j \in \mathcal{V}$, if (TOSSED, $sid, x_1, \ldots, x_k$) has been sent to all parties in $\mathcal{P}$ set $f = 1$, otherwise, set $f = 0$. Send (VERIFIED, $sid, x_1, \ldots, x_k, f$) to $\mathcal{V}_j$.

Fig. 10. Functionality $\mathcal{F}_{\mathsf{CT}}^{k,\mathcal{D}}$ for G.O.D. publicly verifiable coin tossing.

algorithm (*i.e.* the polynomial $p(X)$) in the reveal phase in order to verify that certain random inputs were previously shared in the commit phase, we have the parties commit to their random inputs using an equivocal commitment and then generate a NIZK proof that the random inputs in the commitments correspond to the ones shared by the PVSS scheme in the commit phase. In the reveal phase, the parties simply open their commitments. In case a commitment is not opened, the honest parties use the PVSS reconstruction to recover the random input. Intuitively, using an equivocal commitment scheme and ideal NIZKs allows the simulator to first extract all the random inputs shared by the adversary and later equivocate the simulated parties' commitment openings in order to trick the adversary into accepting arbitrary random inputs from simulated honest parties that result in the same randomness as obtained from $\mathcal{F}_{\mathsf{CT}}$. Protocol Π_{CT-ZK} is presented in Figs. 11 and 12.

Pedersen Commitments. We will use a Pedersen commitment [28], which is an *equivocal commitment*, *i.e.* it allows a simulator who knows a trapdoor to open a commitment to any arbitrary message. In this scheme, all parties are assumed to know generators g, h of a group $\mathbb{G}_q$ of prime order q chosen uniformly at random such that the discrete logarithm of h on base g is unknown. In order to commit to a message $m \in \mathbb{Z}_q$, a sender samples a randomness $r \xleftarrow{\$} \mathbb{Z}_q$ and computes a commitment $c = g^m h^r$, which can be later opened by revealing (m, r). In order to verify that an opening (m', r') for a commitment c is valid, a receiver simply checks that $c = g^{m'} h^{r'}$. However, a simulator who knows a trapdoor td such that $h = g^{\mathsf{td}}$ can open $c = g^m h^r$ to any arbitrary message m' by computing $r' = \frac{m + \mathsf{td} \cdot r - m'}{\mathsf{td}}$ and revealing (m', r'). For a message $m \in \mathbb{Z}_q$ and randomness $r \in \mathbb{Z}_q$, we denote a commitment c as $\mathsf{Com}(m, r)$, the opening of c as $\mathsf{Open}(m, r)$ and the opening of c to an arbitrary message $m' \in \mathbb{Z}_q$ given trapdoor td as $\mathsf{TDOpen}(m, r, m', \mathsf{td})$.

Protocol Π_{CT-ZK} (Initialization, Commit and Reveal)

It is assumed that $\mathcal{F}_{\mathsf{CRS}}$ provides Pedersen commitment parameters $g_p, h_p \in \mathbb{G}_q$ and a Vandermonde $(n-2t) \times (n-t)$-matrix $M = M(\omega, n-2t, n-t)$ with $\omega \in \mathbb{Z}_q^*$ as specified in section 2. We denote the commitment and open procedures of a Pedersen commitment as $\mathsf{Com}(m, r)$ and $\mathsf{Open}(m, r)$, respectively. Protocol Π_{CT-ZK} is run between a set $\mathcal{P} = \{P_1, \ldots, P_n\}$ (out of which at most t are corrupted) and a set of verifiers $\mathcal{V}$ interacting with each other and with functionalities $\mathcal{F}_{\mathsf{CRS}}, \mathcal{F}_{APBB}, \mathcal{F}_{\mathsf{NIZK}}^{LDEI}, \mathcal{F}_{\mathsf{NIZK}}^{DLEQ}, \mathcal{F}_{\mathsf{NIZK}}^{COMC}$ as follows:

1. **Initialization:** Upon being activated for the first time, all parties in $\mathcal{P}$ and $\mathcal{V}$ send (CRS, sid) to $\mathcal{F}_{\mathsf{CRS}}$, obtaining $(\mathrm{CRS}, sid, g_p, h_p, M)$. Each party $\mathcal{P}_i \in \mathcal{P}$ samples $sk_i \leftarrow \mathbb{Z}_q$, computes $pk_i = h^{sk_i}$ and sends $(\textsc{Post}, sid, \mathrm{MID}, pk_i)$ to $\mathcal{F}_{APBB}$ using a fresh MID. Finally, all parties obtain all pk_i from $\mathcal{F}_{APBB}$.
2. **Commit:** For $1 \le j \le n$:
   (a) Party P_j executes the Distribution phase of of π_{PPVSS} (Figure 5) as Dealer for $\ell = n-2t$ random inputs using $\mathcal{F}_{\mathsf{NIZK}}^{LDEI}$ to compute the NIZKs, obtaining encrypted shares $\hat{\sigma}_1^j, \ldots, \hat{\sigma}_n^j$, a NIZK proof π_{LDEI}^j, secrets $h^{s_0^j}, \ldots, h^{s_{\ell-1}^j}$ and exponents $s_0^j, \ldots, s_{\ell-1}^j$.
   (b) P_j computes $\mathsf{Com}(s_0^j, r_0^j), \ldots, \mathsf{Com}(s_{\ell-1}^j, r_{\ell-1}^j)$ (with fresh randomness $r_0^j, \ldots, r_{\ell-1}^j \leftarrow \mathbb{Z}_q$) and obtains from $\mathcal{F}_{\mathsf{NIZK}}^{COMC}$ a NIZK proof π_{COMC}^j that these commitments contain the same secrets $s_0^j, \ldots, s_{\ell-1}^j$ as $\hat{\sigma}_1^j, \ldots, \hat{\sigma}_n^j$.
   (c) P_j sends $(\textsc{Post}, sid, \mathrm{MID}, (\hat{\sigma}_1^j, \ldots, \hat{\sigma}_n^j, \pi_{LDEI}^j, \mathsf{Com}(s_0^j, r_0^j), \ldots, \mathsf{Com}(s_{\ell-1}^j, r_{\ell-1}^j), \pi_{COMC}^j))$ to $\mathcal{F}_{APBB}$ using a fresh MID.
3. **Reveal:**
   (a) All parties in $\mathcal{P}$ send $(\textsc{Read}, sid)$ to $\mathcal{F}_{APBB}$, receive $(\textsc{Read}, sid, \mathcal{M})$ and, for every new $(\mathcal{P}_i, sid, \mathrm{MID}, (\hat{\sigma}_1^j, \ldots, \hat{\sigma}_n^j, \pi_{LDEI}^j, \mathsf{Com}(s_0^j, r_0^j), \ldots, \mathsf{Com}(s_{\ell-1}^j, r_{\ell-1}^j), \pi_{COMC}^j))$ in $\mathcal{M}$, verify proof π_{COMC}^j using $\mathcal{F}_{\mathsf{NIZK}}^{COMC}$ and run the Verification phase of π_{PPVSS} (Figure 5) using $\mathcal{F}_{\mathsf{NIZK}}^{LDEI}$.
   (b) Once $n-t$ parties have posted valid $\hat{\sigma}_1^j, \ldots, \hat{\sigma}_n^j$, π_{LDEI}^j and $\mathsf{Com}(s_0^j, r_0^j), \ldots, \mathsf{Com}(s_{\ell-1}^j, r_{\ell-1}^j), \pi_{COMC}^j$ on $\mathcal{F}_{APBB}$ (we call $\mathcal{C}$ the set of these parties) each party $P_j \in \mathcal{C}$ sends $(\textsc{Post}, sid, \mathrm{MID}, (\mathsf{Open}(s_0^j, r_{0,j}), \ldots, \mathsf{Open}(s_{\ell-1}^j, r_{\ell-1,j})))$ to $\mathcal{F}_{APBB}$ using a fresh MID, for $j \in \mathcal{C}$.
   (c) All parties in $\mathcal{P}_i$ send $(\textsc{Read}, sid)$ to $\mathcal{F}_{APBB}$, receive $(\textsc{Read}, sid, \mathcal{M})$ and check that $(\mathcal{P}_i, sid, \mathrm{MID}, (\mathsf{Open}(s_0^j, r_{0,j}), \ldots, \mathsf{Open}(s_{\ell-1}^j, r_{\ell-1,j})))$ is in $\mathcal{M}$ for all $j \in \mathcal{C}$. Once this check succeeds, all parties in $\mathcal{P}$ verify that these correspond to the secrets that were shared, by computing all $h^{s_i^j}$ and checking the consistency of these values with the published shares with the check $Local_{LDEI}$, in the same way that they would do in Figure 6.
   (d) If any of the checks in the previous step fails, proceed to the recovery phase of Figure 12. Otherwise, if every party in $\mathcal{C}$ has opened their secrets correctly, parties compute $R = M \diamond T$ as follows. Let S be the $(n-t) \times \ell$ matrix with rows indexed by the parties in $\mathcal{C}$ and where the row corresponding to $P_a \in \mathcal{C}$ is $(s_0^a, \ldots, s_{\ell-1}^a)$. All parties in $\mathcal{P}$ compute $U = M \cdot S \in \mathbb{Z}_q^{\ell \times \ell}$ and $R = h^U$, outputting the ℓ^2 elements of R as final randomness.

Fig. 11. Protocol Π_{CT-ZK}, optimistic case (initialization, commit and reveal).

Protocol Π_{CT-ZK} continued, pessimistic case (Recovery phase)

4 **Recovery:** Let $\mathcal{C}_A$ be the set of parties $P_a \in \mathcal{C}$ that do not publish a valid opening of their commitments in the reveal phase. Every party $\mathcal{P}_j \in \mathcal{P}$ proceed as follows:
  (a) Execute the Share Decryption protocol for each PVSS where a party $P_a \in \mathcal{C}_A$ was the dealer as described in Figure 6 using $\mathcal{F}_{\mathsf{NIZK}}^{DLEQ}$ to compute π^j_{DLEQ}. $\mathcal{P}_j$ sends (Post, *sid*, MID, $(\{\tilde{\sigma}^a_j\}_{P_a \in \mathcal{C}_A}, \pi^j_{DLEQ})$) to $\mathcal{F}_{APBB}$ using a fresh MID.
  (b) Send (Read, *sid*) to $\mathcal{F}_{APBB}$, receive (Read, *sid*, $\mathcal{M}$) and, for every new $(\mathcal{P}_i, sid, \text{MID}, (\{\tilde{\sigma}^a_j\}_{P_a \in \mathcal{C}_A}, \pi^j_{DLEQ}))$ in $\mathcal{M}$, verify proof π^j_{DLEQ} using $\mathcal{F}_{\mathsf{NIZK}}^{DLEQ}$.
  (c) Once a set $\mathcal{Q}$ of $n-t$ parties have posted valid decrypted shares on $\mathcal{F}_{APBB}$, the secrets are reconstructed as follows. For every $P_a \in \mathcal{C}_A$, we define $\mathtt{task}_{Rec,a}$ to be the computation of $(h^{s^a_0}, \dots, h^{s^a_{\ell-1}})$ from the decrypted shares with $Rec_{\mathcal{Q}}$ as described in PVSS reconstruction. Let $\mathcal{T}_{Rec} = \{\mathtt{task}_{Rec,a}\}_{P_a \in \mathcal{C}_A}$. Then call $DistComp(\mathcal{T}_{Rec}, \mathcal{P}, \log n)$, where $DistComp$ is as described in Figure 7 with $AlgComp = Rec_{\mathcal{Q}}$ and $AlgVer = RecVer_{\mathcal{Q}}$ (Figure 6), taking all inputs from $\mathcal{F}_{APBB}$ and posting all outputs to $\mathcal{F}_{APBB}$.
  (d) Send (Read, *sid*) to $\mathcal{F}_{APBB}$, obtaining $\mathcal{M}$. Let T be the $(n-t) \times \ell$ matrix with rows indexed by the parties in $\mathcal{C}$ and where the row corresponding to $P_a \in \mathcal{C}$ is $(h^{s^a_0}, \dots, h^{s^a_{\ell-1}})$, which are obtained from $\mathcal{M}$.
  (e) Each computes the $\ell \times \ell$-matrix $R = M \diamond T$ by applying $FFTE$ to each column $T^{(j)}$ of T, resulting in column $R^{(j)}$ of R (since $R^{(j)} = M \diamond T^{(j)}$ and M is Vandermonde) for $j \in [0, \ell-1]$.
  (f) Output the ℓ^2 elements of R as final randomness.

5 **Verify:** On input (Verify, *sid*, $x_1, \dots, x_k$), a verifier $\mathcal{V}_i \in \mathcal{V}$ checks that the protocol transcript registered in $\mathcal{F}_{APBB}$ is valid using the verification interfaces of $\mathcal{F}_{\mathsf{NIZK}}^{LDEI}, \mathcal{F}_{\mathsf{NIZK}}^{DLEQ}, \mathcal{F}_{\mathsf{NIZK}}^{COMC}$. If the transcript is valid and results in output $x_1, \dots, x_k$, $AlgVer_i$ sets $b = 1$, else, it sets $b = 0$. $\mathcal{V}_i$ outputs (Verified, *sid*, $x_1, \dots, x_k, b$).

Fig. 12. Protocol Π_{CT-ZK} continued, pessimistic case (recovery phase)

NIZKs. We use three instances of functionality $\mathcal{F}_{\mathsf{NIZK}}^{R}$. The first one is $\mathcal{F}_{\mathsf{NIZK}}^{LDEI}$, which is parameterized with relation $LDEI$ (Sect. 3). The second one is $\mathcal{F}_{\mathsf{NIZK}}^{DLEQ}$, which is parameterized with relation $DLEQ$ for multiple statements $DLEQ((h, (\tilde{\sigma}^i_j)_{i \in I})(pk, (\hat{\sigma}^i_j)_{i \in I}))$ (Sect. 3). The third and final one is $\mathcal{F}_{\mathsf{NIZK}}^{COMC}$, which is parameterized with a relation $COMC$ showing that commitments $\mathsf{Com}(s^j_0, r^j_0), \dots, \mathsf{Com}(s^j_{\ell-1}, r^j_{\ell-1})$ contain the same secrets $s^j_0, \dots, s^j_{\ell-1}$ as in the encrypted shares $\hat{\sigma}^j_1, \dots, \hat{\sigma}^j_n$ generated by π_{PPVSS} (Fig. 5).

CRS and Bulletin Board. In order to simplify our protocol description and security analysis, we assume that parties have access to a CRS containing the public parameters for the Pedersen equivocal commitment scheme and Vandermonde matrix for the PVSS scheme π_{PPVSS}. Moreover, a CRS would be necessary to realize the instances of $\mathcal{F}_{\mathsf{NIZK}}^{R}$ we use. Nevertheless, we remark that the parties could generate all of these values in a publicly verifiable way through a multiparty computation protocol [7] and register them in the authenticated public bulletin board functionality in the beginning of the protocol.

Communication Model. Formally, for the sake of simplicity, we describe our protocol using an ideal authenticated public bulletin board $\mathcal{F}_{APBB}$ that guarantees all messages appear immediately in the order they are received and become immutable. However, we remark that our protocols can be proven secure in a semi-synchronous communication model with a public ledger where messages are arbitrarily delayed and re-ordered by the adversary but eventually registered (*i.e.* the adversary cannot drop messages or induce an infinite delay). Notice that the protocol proceeds to each of its steps once $n-t$ parties (*i.e.* at least all honest parties) post their messages to $\mathcal{F}_{APBB}$, so it is guaranteed to terminate if honest party messages are delivered eventually regardless of the order in which these messages appear or of the delay for such messages to become immutable. Using the terminology of [3,21], if we were to use a blockchain based public ledger instead of $\mathcal{F}_{APBB}$, each point we state that the parties wait for $n-t$ valid messages to be posted to $\mathcal{F}_{APBB}$ could be adapted to having the parties wait for enough rounds such that it is guaranteed by the chain growth property that a large number enough blocks are added to the ledger in such a way that the chain quality property guarantees that at least one of these blocks is honest (*i.e.* containing honest party messages) and that enough blocks are guaranteed to be added after this honest block so that the common prefix property guarantees that all honest parties have this block in their local view of the ledger. A similar analysis has been done in [18,23] in their constructions of randomness beacons.

Complexity. We execute essentially the same steps of Protocol Π_{ALB} with the added overhead of having each party compute Pedersen Commitments to their secrets and generate a NIZK showing these secrets are the same as the ones shared through the PVSS scheme. Using the combined approaches of [9,24] to obtain these NIZKs, the approximate extra overhead of using UC NIZKs in relation to the stand alone NIZKs of Π_{ALB} will be that of computing 2 evaluations of the Paillier cryptosystem's homomorphism and 4 modular exponentiations over $\mathbb{G}_q$ per each secret value in the witness for each NIZK. In the Commit and Reveal phases, this yields an approximate fixed extra cost of $4n^2$ evaluations of the Paillier cryptosystem's homomorphism and $8n^2$ modular exponentiations over $\mathbb{G}_q$ for generating and verifying NIZKs with $\mathcal{F}_{\mathsf{NIZK}}^{LDEI}$ and $\mathcal{F}_{\mathsf{NIZK}}^{COMC}$. In the recovery phase, if a parties fail to open their commitments, there is an extra costs of $2a(n-t)$ evaluations of the Paillier cryptosystem's homomorphism and $4a(n-t)$ modular exponentiations over $\mathbb{G}_q$ for generating and verifying NIZKs with $\mathcal{F}_{\mathsf{NIZK}}^{DLEQ}$. In terms of communication, the approximate extra overhead is of one Paillier ciphertext and two integer commitments per each secret value in the witness for each NIZK, yielding an approximate total overhead of $(n^2+a(n-t))\cdot|\mathsf{Paillier}|+(2n^2+a(n-t))\cdot|\mathbb{G}_q|$ bits where $|\mathsf{Paillier}|$ is the length of a Paillier ciphertext and $|\mathbb{G}_q|$ is the length of a $\mathbb{G}_q$ element.

Theorem 3. *Protocol Π_{CT-ZK} UC-realizes $\mathcal{F}_{\mathsf{CT}}^{k,\mathcal{D}}$ for $k = \ell^2 = (n-2t)^2$ and $\mathcal{D} = \{h^s | h \in \mathbb{G}_q, s \xleftarrow{\$} \mathbb{Z}_q\}$ in the $\mathcal{F}_{\mathsf{CRS}}, \mathcal{F}_{APBB}, \mathcal{F}_{\mathsf{NIZK}}^{LDEI}, \mathcal{F}_{\mathsf{NIZK}}^{DLEQ}, \mathcal{F}_{\mathsf{NIZK}}^{COMC}$-hybrid model with static security against an active adversary $\mathcal{A}$ corrupting corrupts at most t parties (where $2t + \ell = n$) parties under the DDH assumption.*

Proof. We prove this theorem in the full version [13].

5.2 Using Designated Verifier Homomorphic Commitments

In the stand alone version of ALBATROSS and the first UC-secure version we construct, the main idea is to encrypt shares of random secrets obtained from packed Shamir secret sharing and prove in zero knowledge that those shares were consistently generated. Later on, zero knowledge proofs are used again to prove that decrypted were correctly obtained from the ciphertexts that have already been verified for consistency, ensuring secrets can be properly reconstructed. We now explore an alternative where we instead commit to their shares using a UC additively homomorphic commitment scheme and perform a version the $Local_{LDEI}$ check on the committed shares and open the resulting commitment in order to prove that their shares were correctly generated. In order to do that, we need a new notion of a UC additively homomorphic commitment that allows for the sender to open a commitments to an specific share towards a specific party (so that only that party learns its share) but allows for those parties to later prove that they have received a valid opening or not, allowing the other parties to reconstruct the secrets from the opened shares. In the remainder of this section, we introduce our new definition of such a commitment scheme and show how it can be used along with $\mathcal{F}_{APBB}$ to realize $\mathcal{F}_{\mathsf{CT}}^{k,\mathcal{D}}$.

Designated Verifier Commitments. We define a new flavor of multi-receiver commitments that we call Designated Verifier Commitments, meaning that they allow a sender to open a certain commitment only towards a certain receiver in such a way that this receiver can later prove that the commitment was correctly opened (also revealing its message) or that the opening was not valid. Moreover, we give this commitments the ability to evaluate linear functions on committed values and reveal only the result of these evaluations but not the individual values used as input, a property that is called additive homomorphism. We depart from the multi-receiver additively homomorphic commitment functionality from [11] and augment it with designated verifier opening and verification interfaces. Functionality $\mathcal{F}_{\mathrm{DVHCOM}}$ is presented in Fig. 13. The basic idea to realize this functionality is that we make two important changes to the protocol of [11]: 1. all protocol messages are posted to the authenticated bulletin board $\mathcal{F}_{APBB}$; 2. designated openings are done by encrypting the opening information from the protocol of [11] with the designated verifier's public key for a cryptosystem with plaintext verification [4], which allows the designated verifier to later publicly prove that a certain (in)valid commitment opening was in the ciphertext. Interestingly, $\mathcal{F}_{\mathrm{DVHCOM}}$ can be realized in the global random oracle model under the Computational Diffie Hellman (CDH) assumption. We show how to realize $\mathcal{F}_{\mathrm{DVHCOM}}$ in the full version [13].

Functionality $\mathcal{F}_{\text{DVHCOM}}$

$\mathcal{F}_{\text{DVHCOM}}$ keeps two initially empty lists $\mathsf{open}_{\mathsf{des}}$ and $\mathsf{open}_{\mathsf{pub}}$. $\mathcal{F}_{\text{DVHCOM}}$ interacts with a sender P_S, a set of receivers $P = \{P_1, \ldots, P_t\}$, a set of verifiers $\mathcal{V}$ and an adversary $\mathcal{S}$ and proceeds as follows:

- **Commit Phase**: The length of the committed messages λ is fixed and known to all parties.
  - Upon receiving a message $(\text{COMMIT}, sid, ssid, P_S, P, \boldsymbol{m})$ from P_S, where $\boldsymbol{m} \in \{0,1\}^\lambda$, record the tuple $(ssid, P_S, P, \boldsymbol{m})$ and send the message $(\text{RECEIPT}, sid, ssid, P_S, P)$ to every receiver $P_i \in P$ and $\mathcal{S}$. Ignore any future commit messages with the same $ssid$ from P_S to P.
  - If a message (ABORT, sid) is received from $\mathcal{S}$, the functionality halts.
- **Addition**: Upon receiving a message $(\mathsf{add}, sid, ssid_1, ssid_2, ssid_3, P_S, P)$ from P_S: If tuples $(ssid_1, P_S, P, \boldsymbol{m}_1)$, $(ssid_2, P_S, P, \boldsymbol{m}_2)$ were previously recorded and $ssid_3$ is unused, record $(ssid_3, P_S, P, \boldsymbol{m}_1 + \boldsymbol{m}_2)$ and send the message $(\mathsf{add}, sid, ssid_1, ssid_2, ssid_3, P_S, P, \mathsf{success})$ to P_S, every $P_i \in P$ and $\mathcal{S}$.
- **Schedule Public Open**: Upon receiving a message $(\mathsf{P-Open}, sid, ssid)$ from P_S, if a tuple $(ssid, P_S, P, \boldsymbol{m})$ was previously recorded, append $ssid$ to $\mathsf{open}_{\mathsf{pub}}$.
- **Schedule Designated Open**: Upon receiving a message $(\mathsf{D-Open}, sid, P_d, ssid)$ from P_S for $P_d \in P$, if a tuple $(ssid, P_S, P, \boldsymbol{m})$ was previously recorded, append $(P_d, ssid)$ to $\mathsf{open}_{\mathsf{des}}$.
- **Execute Open**: Upon receiving a message $(\mathsf{Do-Open}, sid)$ from P_S:
  - For every $ssid \in \mathsf{open}_{\mathsf{pub}}$, send $(\text{P-REVEAL}, sid, P_S, P, ssid, \boldsymbol{m})$ to every receiver $P_i \in P$ where $\boldsymbol{m}$ is in the recorded tuple $(ssid, P_S, P, \boldsymbol{m})$.
  - For every pair $(P_d, ssid) \in \mathsf{open}_{\mathsf{des}}$ send $(\text{D-REVEAL}, sid, P_S, P_d, ssid)$ to every receiver in P and send $(\text{D-REVEAL}, sid, P_S, P_d, ssid, \boldsymbol{m})$ to P_d where $\boldsymbol{m}$ is in the recorded tuple $(ssid, P_S, P, \boldsymbol{m})$.

  Stop responding to $\mathsf{P-Open}$, $\mathsf{D-Open}$ and $\mathsf{Do-Open}$ queries.
- **Reveal Designated Open** Upon receiving message $(\text{REVEAL-D-OPEN}, sid, P_d, ssid)$ from P_d, if $(P_d, ssid) \in \mathsf{open}_{\mathsf{des}}$ and Execute Open has happened, send $(\text{P-REVEAL}, sid, P_S, P, ssid, \boldsymbol{m})$ to every receiver $P_i \in P$ where $\boldsymbol{m}$ is in the recorded tuple $(ssid, P_S, P, \boldsymbol{m})$.
- **Verify** Upon receiving $(\text{VERIFY}, sid, ssid, P_S, \boldsymbol{m})$ from $\mathcal{V}_j \in \mathcal{V}$, if $(\text{P-REVEAL}, sid, P_S, P, ssid, \boldsymbol{m})$ was sent to every receiver $P_i \in P$, set $f = 1$, else, set $f = 0$. Send $(\text{VERIFIED}, sid, ssid, P_S, \boldsymbol{m}, f)$ to $\mathcal{V}_j$.

Fig. 13. Functionality $\mathcal{F}_{\text{DVHCOM}}$

Realizing $\mathcal{F}_{\text{CT}}^{k,\mathcal{D}}$ with Π_{CT-COM}. The main idea in constructing Protocol Π_{CT-COM} is to have each party compute shares of their random secrets using packed Shamir secret sharing and then generate designated verifier commitments $\mathcal{F}_{\text{DVHCOM}}$ to each share. Next, each party proves that their committed shares are valid by executing the $Local_{LDEI}$ test on the committed shares (instead of group exponents), which involves evaluating a linear function on the committed shares and publicly opening the commitment containing the result of this evaluation. At the same time, each party performs designated openings of each committed share towards one of the other parties, who verify that they have

Protocol Π_{CT-COM}

Let $\ell = n - 2t$. We assume the parties have a Vandermonde $(\ell) \times (n-t)$-matrix $M = M(\omega, \ell, n-t)$ with $\omega \in \mathbb{Z}_q^*$ as specified in section 2. Protocol Π_{CT-COM} is run between a set $\mathcal{P} = \{P_1, \ldots, P_n\}$ (out of which at most t are corrupted) and a set of verifiers $\mathcal{V}$ interacting with each other and with functionalities $\mathcal{F}_{APBB}, \mathcal{F}_{\text{DVHCOM}}$ as follows:

1. **Commit:** On input (Toss, sid), every party $\mathcal{P}_i \in \mathcal{P}$ proceeds as follows:
   (a) $\mathcal{P}_i$ acts as dealer in Shamir packed secret sharing, sampling a polynomial $p(X) \leftarrow \mathbb{Z}_q[X]_{\leq t+\ell-1}$ such that $s_0 = p(0), s_1 = p(-1), \ldots, s_{\ell-1} = p(-(\ell-1))$ and computing shares $\sigma_i = p(i)$ for $1 \leq i \leq n$.
   (b) For $1 \leq j \leq n$, $\mathcal{P}_i$ picks an unused $ssid_j^i$ and sends (COMMIT, $sid, ssid_j, \mathcal{P}_i, \mathcal{P}, \sigma_j$) to $\mathcal{F}_{\text{DVHCOM}}$.
   (c) $\mathcal{P}_i$ uses the Addition interface of $\mathcal{F}_{\text{DVHCOM}}$ to evaluate the $Local_{LDEI}$ test on the committed shares identified by $ssid_1^i, \ldots, ssid_n^i$ obtaining a new commitment identified by $ssid_{LDEI}^i$. The random polynomial used by $Local_{LDEI}$ is sampled via de Fiat-Shamir heuristic using the output of a global random oracle queried on the protocol transcript so far.
   (d) $\mathcal{P}_i$ sends ($\mathsf{P-Open}$, $sid, ssid_{LDEI}^i$) to $\mathcal{F}_{\text{DVHCOM}}$ (scheduling a public opening the commitment with the $Local_{LDEI}$ result) and, for $1 \leq j \leq n$, sends ($\mathsf{D-Open}$, $sid, \mathcal{P}_j, ssid_j^i$) to $\mathcal{F}_{\text{DVHCOM}}$ (scheduling the delegated opening of share σ_j towards $\mathcal{P}_j$). Finally, $\mathcal{P}_i$ sends ($\mathsf{Do-Open}$, sid) to $\mathcal{F}_{\text{DVHCOM}}$ execute all openings and sends (Post, sid, MID, $\boldsymbol{m}_{LDEI}^i$) to $\mathcal{F}_{APBB}$ using a fresh MID (registering the result of the LDEI test on the bulletin board).
   (e) For $1 \leq j \leq n$, $\mathcal{P}_i$ checks that it has received (P-REVEAL, $sid, \mathcal{P}_j, \mathcal{P}, ssid_{LDEI}^j, 0$) (meaning that the shares from $\mathcal{P}_j$ passed the $Local_{LDEI}$ test), (D-REVEAL, $sid, \mathcal{P}_j, \mathcal{P}_i, ssid_i^j, \sigma_i^j$) and (D-REVEAL, $sid, \mathcal{P}_j, \mathcal{P}_i, ssid_{j'}^j$) for every $j' = 1, \ldots, n, j' = j$ (meaning that $\mathcal{P}_j$ opened each committed share towards the right designated verifier) from $\mathcal{F}_{\text{DVHCOM}}$. We call the set of parties for which this check succeeds $\mathcal{C}$, which is guaranteed to contain at least $n-t$ parties (all honest parties).
2. **Reveal and Output:** Every party $\mathcal{P}_i \in \mathcal{P}$ proceeds as follows:
   (a) For every party $\mathcal{P}_j \in \mathcal{C}$, $\mathcal{P}_i$ sends (Reveal-D-Open, $sid, \mathcal{P}_i, ssid_i^j$) to $\mathcal{F}_{\text{DVHCOM}}$ and (Post, sid, MID, σ_i^j) to $\mathcal{F}_{APBB}$ using a fresh MID.
   (b) After the $n-t$ honest parties open their committed shares, perform the recovery procedure of Π_{ALB} directly on the set of shares σ_o^j such that $\mathcal{P}_j \in \mathcal{C}$ and $\mathcal{P}_o$ revealed its shares in the previous step (which is guaranteed to contain at least $n-t$ shares revealed by the honest parties). Output the ℓ^2 elements of R as final randomness.
3. **Verify:** On input (Verify, $sid, x_1, \ldots, x_k$), a verifier $\mathcal{V}_i \in \mathcal{V}$ checks that the protocol transcript registered in $\mathcal{F}_{APBB}$ is valid using the verification interface of $\mathcal{F}_{\text{DVHCOM}}$. If the transcript is valid and results in output $x_1, \ldots, x_k$, $AlgVer_i$ sets $b = 1$, else, it sets $b = 0$. $\mathcal{V}_i$ outputs (Verified, $sid, x_1, \ldots, x_k, b$).

Fig. 14. Protocol Π_{CT-COM}.

obtained a valid designated opening and post a message to $\mathcal{F}_{APBB}$ confirming that this check succeeded. After a high enough number of parties successfully confirms this check for each of the sets of committed shares, each party publicly opens all of their committed shares, allowing the other parties to reconstruct the secrets. If one of the parties does not open all of their shares, the honest parties can still reconstruct the secrets by revealing the designated openings they received for their shares. We present Protocol Π_{CT-COM} in Fig. 14 and state its security in Theorem 4. Since $\mathcal{F}_{\mathsf{DVHCOM}}$ can be realized in the global random oracle model under the Computational Diffie Hellman (CDH) assumption as shown in the full version [13], we obtain an instantiation of $\mathcal{F}_{\mathsf{CT}}^{k,\mathcal{D}}$ with security based on CDH.

Theorem 4. *Protocol Π_{CT-COM} UC-realizes $\mathcal{F}_{\mathsf{CT}}^{k,\mathcal{D}}$ for $k = \ell^2 = (n-2t)^2$ and $\mathcal{D} = \{h^s | h \in \mathbb{G}_q, s \xleftarrow{\$} \mathbb{Z}_q\}$ in the $\mathcal{F}_{\mathsf{DVHCOM}}, \mathcal{F}_{APBB}$-hybrid model with static security against an active adversary $\mathcal{A}$ corrupting at most t parties (where $2t + \ell = n$).*

Proof. This theorem is proven in the full version [13].

Acknowledgements. The authors would like to thank the anonymous reviewers for their suggestions, Diego Aranha, Ronald Cramer and Dario Fiore for useful discussions and Eva Palandjian for the implementation in [27] and remarks about the initial draft.

References

1. Adida, B.: Helios: web-based open-audit voting. In: Proceedings of the 17th USENIX Security Symposium, pp. 335–348 (2008)
2. Azouvi, S., McCorry, P., Meiklejohn, S.: Winning the caucus race: continuous leader election via public randomness. CoRR, abs/1801.07965 (2018)
3. Badertscher, C., Maurer, U., Tschudi, D., Zikas, V.: Bitcoin as a transaction ledger: a composable treatment. In: Katz, J., Shacham, H. (eds.) CRYPTO 2017. LNCS, vol. 10401, pp. 324–356. Springer, Cham (2017). https://doi.org/10.1007/978-3-319-63688-7_11
4. Baum, C., David, B., Dowsley, R.: A framework for universally composable publicly verifiable cryptographic protocols. Cryptology ePrint Archive, Report 2020/207 (2020). https://eprint.iacr.org/2020/207
5. Blakley, G.R., Meadows, C.: Security of ramp schemes. In: Blakley, G.R., Chaum, D. (eds.) CRYPTO 1984. LNCS, vol. 196, pp. 242–268. Springer, Heidelberg (1985). https://doi.org/10.1007/3-540-39568-7_20
6. Boneh, D., Bonneau, J., Bünz, B., Fisch, B.: Verifiable delay functions. In: Shacham, H., Boldyreva, A. (eds.) CRYPTO 2018. LNCS, vol. 10991, pp. 757–788. Springer, Cham (2018). https://doi.org/10.1007/978-3-319-96884-1_25
7. Bowe, S., Gabizon, A., Green, M.D.: A multi-party protocol for constructing the public parameters of the Pinocchio zk-SNARK. In: Zohar, A., et al. (eds.) FC 2018. LNCS, vol. 10958, pp. 64–77. Springer, Heidelberg (2019). https://doi.org/10.1007/978-3-662-58820-8_5
8. Bowe, S., Grigg, J., Hopwood, D.: Halo: recursive proof composition without a trusted setup. IACR Cryptology ePrint Archive, 2019:1021 (2019)

9. Camenisch, J., Krenn, S., Shoup, V.: A framework for practical universally composable zero-knowledge protocols. In: Lee, D.H., Wang, X. (eds.) ASIACRYPT 2011. LNCS, vol. 7073, pp. 449–467. Springer, Heidelberg (2011). https://doi.org/10.1007/978-3-642-25385-0_24
10. Canetti, R.: Universally composable security: a new paradigm for cryptographic protocols. In: 42nd FOCS, pp. 136–145. IEEE Computer Society Press, October 2001
11. Cascudo, I., Damgård, I., David, B., Döttling, N., Dowsley, R., Giacomelli, I.: Efficient UC commitment extension with homomorphism for free (and applications). In: Galbraith, S.D., Moriai, S. (eds.) ASIACRYPT 2019, Part II. LNCS, vol. 11922, pp. 606–635. Springer, Cham (2019). https://doi.org/10.1007/978-3-030-34621-8_22
12. Cascudo, I., David, B.: SCRAPE: scalable randomness attested by public entities. In: Gollmann, D., Miyaji, A., Kikuchi, H. (eds.) ACNS 2017. LNCS, vol. 10355, pp. 537–556. Springer, Cham (2017). https://doi.org/10.1007/978-3-319-61204-1_27
13. Cascudo, I., David, B.: ALBATROSS: publicly attestable batched randomness based on secret sharing (full version). Cryptology ePrint Archive, Report 2020/644 (2020). https://eprint.iacr.org/2020/644
14. Chaum, D., Pedersen, T.P.: Wallet databases with observers. In: Brickell, E.F. (ed.) CRYPTO 1992. LNCS, vol. 740, pp. 89–105. Springer, Heidelberg (1993). https://doi.org/10.1007/3-540-48071-4_7
15. Chen, J., Micali, S.: Algorand: a secure and efficient distributed ledger. Theor. Comput. Sci. **777**, 155–183 (2019)
16. Chor, B., Goldreich, O., Håstad, J., Friedman, J., Rudich, S., Smolensky, R.: The bit extraction problem of t-resilient functions. In: 26th Annual Symposium on Foundations of Computer Science, Portland, Oregon, USA, 21–23 October 1985, pp. 396–407 (1985)
17. Cooley, J.W., Tukey, J.W.: An algorithm for the machine calculation of complex Fourier series. Math. Comp. **19**, 297–301 (1965)
18. David, B., Gaži, P., Kiayias, A., Russell, A.: Ouroboros Praos: an adaptively-secure, semi-synchronous proof-of-stake blockchain. In: Nielsen, J.B., Rijmen, V. (eds.) EUROCRYPT 2018. LNCS, vol. 10821, pp. 66–98. Springer, Cham (2018). https://doi.org/10.1007/978-3-319-78375-8_3
19. Fiat, A., Shamir, A.: How to prove yourself: practical solutions to identification and signature problems. In: Odlyzko, A.M. (ed.) CRYPTO 1986. LNCS, vol. 263, pp. 186–194. Springer, Heidelberg (1987). https://doi.org/10.1007/3-540-47721-7_12
20. Franklin, M.K., Yung, M.: Communication complexity of secure computation (extended abstract). In: Proceedings of the 24th Annual ACM Symposium on Theory of Computing, Victoria, British Columbia, Canada, 4–6 May 1992, pp. 699–710 (1992)
21. Garay, J., Kiayias, A., Leonardos, N.: The bitcoin backbone protocol: analysis and applications. In: Oswald, E., Fischlin, M. (eds.) EUROCRYPT 2015, Part II. LNCS, vol. 9057, pp. 281–310. Springer, Heidelberg (2015). https://doi.org/10.1007/978-3-662-46803-6_10
22. Heidarvand, S., Villar, J.L.: Public verifiability from pairings in secret sharing schemes. In: Avanzi, R.M., Keliher, L., Sica, F. (eds.) SAC 2008. LNCS, vol. 5381, pp. 294–308. Springer, Heidelberg (2009). https://doi.org/10.1007/978-3-642-04159-4_19

23. Kiayias, A., Russell, A., David, B., Oliynykov, R.: Ouroboros: a provably secure proof-of-stake blockchain protocol. In: Katz, J., Shacham, H. (eds.) CRYPTO 2017. LNCS, vol. 10401, pp. 357–388. Springer, Cham (2017). https://doi.org/10.1007/978-3-319-63688-7_12
24. Lindell, Y.: An efficient transform from sigma protocols to NIZK with a CRS and non-programmable random oracle. In: Dodis, Y., Nielsen, J.B. (eds.) TCC 2015, Part I. LNCS, vol. 9014, pp. 93–109. Springer, Heidelberg (2015). https://doi.org/10.1007/978-3-662-46494-6_5
25. Nakamoto, S.: Bitcoin: a peer-to-peer electronic cash system. Manuscript (2008). https://bitcoin.org/bitcoin.pdf
26. Naor, M., Reingold, O.: Number-theoretic constructions of efficient pseudo-random functions. J. ACM **51**(2), 231–262 (2004)
27. Palandjian, E.: Implementation of ALBATROSS. https://github.com/evapln/albatross
28. Pedersen, T.P.: Non-interactive and information-theoretic secure verifiable secret sharing. In: Feigenbaum, J. (ed.) CRYPTO 1991. LNCS, vol. 576, pp. 129–140. Springer, Heidelberg (1992). https://doi.org/10.1007/3-540-46766-1_9
29. Pointcheval, D., Stern, J.: Security proofs for signature schemes. In: Maurer, U. (ed.) EUROCRYPT 1996. LNCS, vol. 1070, pp. 387–398. Springer, Heidelberg (1996). https://doi.org/10.1007/3-540-68339-9_33
30. Rabin, M.O.: Transaction protection by beacons. J. Comput. Syst. Sci. **27**(2), 256–267 (1983)
31. Ruiz, A., Villar, J.L.: Publicly verfiable secret sharing from Paillier's cryptosystem. In: WEWoRC 2005, pp. 98–108 (2005)
32. Shamir, A.: How to share a secret. Commun. ACM **22**(11), 612–613 (1979)
33. Syta, E., et al.: Scalable bias-resistant distributed randomness. In: 2017 IEEE Symposium on Security and Privacy, SP 2017, pp. 444–460 (2017)
34. Tomescu, A., et al.: Towards scalable threshold cryptosystems. In: IEEE Symposium on Security and Privacy, pp. 1367–1383 (2020)
35. van den Hooff, J., Lazar, D., Zaharia, M., Zeldovich, N.: Vuvuzela: scalable private messaging resistant to traffic analysis. In: Proceedings of the 25th Symposium on Operating Systems Principles, SOSP 2015, pp. 137–152 (2015)
36. Wolinsky, D.I., Corrigan-Gibbs, H., Ford, B., Johnson, A.: Dissent in numbers: making strong anonymity scale. In: Proceedings of the 10th USENIX Conference on Operating Systems Design and Implementation, OSDI 2012, pp. 179–192 (2012)

Secret-Shared Shuffle

Melissa Chase[1(✉)], Esha Ghosh[1(✉)], and Oxana Poburinnaya[2(✉)]

[1] Microsoft Research, Redmond, USA
melissac@microsoft.com, Esha.Ghosh@microsoft.com
[2] University of Rochester/Ligero Inc., Rochester, USA
oxanapob@bu.edu

Abstract. Generating additive secret shares of a *shuffled* dataset - such that neither party knows the order in which it is permuted - is a fundamental building block in many protocols, such as secure collaborative filtering, oblivious sorting, and secure function evaluation on set intersection. Traditional approaches to this problem either involve expensive public-key based crypto or using symmetric crypto on permutation networks. While public-key-based solutions are bandwidth efficient, they are computation-heavy. On the other hand, constructions based on permutation networks are communication-bound, especially when the dataset contains large elements, for e.g., feature vectors in an ML context.

We design a new 2-party protocol for this task of computing secret shares of shuffled data, which we refer to as secret-shared shuffle. Our protocol is secure against a static semi-honest adversary. At the heart of our approach is a new primitive we define (which we call "Share Translation") that generates two sets of pseudorandom values "correlated via the permutation". This allows us to reduce the problem of shuffling the dataset to the problem of shuffling pseudorandom values, which enables optimizations both in computation and communication. We then design a Share Translation protocol based on oblivious transfer and puncturable PRFs.

Our final protocol for secret-shared shuffle uses lightweight operations like XOR and PRGs, and in particular doesn't use public-key operations besides the base OTs. As a result, our protocol is concretely more efficient than the existing solutions. In particular, we are two-three orders of magnitude faster than public-key-based approach and one order of magnitude faster compared to the best known symmetric-key approach when the elements are moderately large.

Keywords: Secure shuffle · Secure function evaluation · Puncturable PRF

O. Poburinnaya—Work was partially done while doing internship at Microsoft Research.

Electronic supplementary material The online version of this chapter (https://doi.org/10.1007/978-3-030-64840-4_12) contains supplementary material, which is available to authorized users.

S. Moriai and H. Wang (Eds.): ASIACRYPT 2020, LNCS 12493, pp. 342–372, 2020.
https://doi.org/10.1007/978-3-030-64840-4_12

1 Introduction

Machine Learning algorithms are data-hungry: more data leads to more accurate models. On the other hand, privacy of data is becoming exceedingly important, for social, business and policy compliance reasons (e.g. GDPR). There has been decades of groundbreaking work in the academic literature in developing cryptographic technology for collaborative computation, but it still has some significant bottlenecks in terms of wide-scale adoption. Although theoretical results demonstrate the possibility of generic secure computation, they are not efficient enough to be adopted, both in terms of computation and communication size. For instance, Google cited network cost as a major hindrance in adopting cryptographic secure computation solution [12].

Secret-Shared Shuffle. In this work, we focus on computation and communication efficiency of a building block used in many important secure computation protocols, which we call "secret-shared shuffle". Secret-shared shuffle is a protocol which allows two parties to jointly shuffle data and obtain additive secret shares of the result - without any party learning the permutation corresponding to the shuffle. (In the remainder of this paper, by secret sharing we will always mean *additive* secret sharing.)

Motivation. To see the importance of secret-shared shuffle, consider the task of securely evaluating some function on the intersection of two sets belonging to two parties - in particular, the intersection itself should also remain secret. As a concrete example, consider a merchant who wants to analyze efficiency of its online ads by running some ML algorithm on the data which contains the information about users who both (a) saw the ad and (b) made a purchase. Such data is split between the ad supplier (who knows which person clicked which add) and the merchant (who knows which person made a purchase). Thus, ML should be run on set intersection of the two databases - and both ML and set intersection have to be computed using secure multi-party computation protocols (MPC).

To do this securely, ideally we would use a private set intersection protocol which outputs an intersection in some "encrypted" form - e.g. by encrypting or secret sharing elements in the intersection - and then evaluate the ML function securely under MPC. However, currently known efficient protocols for private set intersection do not output an encrypted intersection: instead they output an encrypted indicator vector - i.e. a vector of bits indicating if each element is in the intersection or not [5]. This difference is very important, since in the former case one could run the ML function (under MPC) directly on the encrypted intersection, whereas in the latter case such MPC has to be run on the whole database, and the elements not in the intersection have to be filtered out under the MPC. Needless to say, this incurs unnecessary overhead, especially in cases where the intersection is relatively small compared to the input sets.

In other words, ideally we would want to get rid of non-intersection elements before running the rest of the MPC. A natural way to do this without compromising security is to shuffle the encrypted elements together with the encrypted indicator vector. Then parties can reveal the indicator vector and discard elements which are not in the intersection. Note that it is crucial that neither party learns how exactly the elements were permuted; otherwise this party could learn whether some of its elements are in the intersection or not. Also note that the requirement on the secrecy of the permutation implies that the result of the shuffle has to be in some encrypted or secret-shared form (in order to prevent linking original and shuffled elements), hence naturally leading to the notion of secret-shared shuffle.

Known Techniques and Their Limitations. For convenience, let us look at "a half" of a secret-shared shuffle, which we call Permute+Share: in this protocol P_0 holds a permutation π and P_1 holds the database $\boldsymbol{x}$, and they would like to learn secret shares of permuted database[1]. While this problem can be solved by any generic MPC, to the best of our knowledge, there are two specialized solutions for this problem, which differ in how exactly the permuting happens. One approach is to give P_0's shares of $\boldsymbol{x}$ to P_1 in some encrypted form, let P_1 permute them according to π under the encryption, rerandomize them, and return them to P_0. This is a folklore solution that uses rerandomizable additively homomorphic public-key encryption, and because of that it is compute-intensive. We elaborately describe this solution in the full version. The other approach is to start with secret-shared $\boldsymbol{x}$ and jointly compute atomic swaps, until all elements arrive to their target location. To prevent linking, each atomic swap should also rerandomize the shares. This approach is taken by [15,22], who let parties jointly apply a permutation network to the shares, where each atomic swap is implemented using oblivious transfer (OT) in [22] and garbled circuit in [15]. The downside of this approach is its communication complexity which is proportional to $\ell \cdot N \log N$, where N is the number of elements in the database and ℓ is the bitlength of each element. This overhead seems to be inherent in approaches based on joint computation of atomic swaps, since each element has to be fully fed into at least $\log N$ swaps.

We also note that there exist efficient protocols for secure shuffle in the 3 party setting (e.g. see [4] and references within). We note that our 2 party setting is very different from 3 party setting, which allows for honest majority and thus for simpler and more efficient constructions.

Our Contribution. We propose a novel approach to design a protocol for secret-shared shuffle, secure in the semi-honest model. Our protocol is parameterized by a value T, which can be chosen to optimize performance for a given tradeoff between network bandwith and computation cost. Our protocol runs in 3 rounds (6 messages) with communication only proportional to $\lambda N \log N + N\ell \log N / \log T$, where λ is security parameter, N is the number of elements in the database and ℓ is the size of each element. In our experiments on databases of size 2^{20}-2^{32} the optimal value for T is between 16 and 256, so we can

[1] Note that one can get secret-shared shuffle by combining two instance of Permute+Share.

think of $\log T$ as a number between 4 an 8. Note that the size ℓ of the element could be very large (e.g. each element could be a feature vector in ML algorithm), in which case the term $N\ell \log N/\log T$ dominates, and thus it could be a significant improvement compared to communication in permutation-network-based approach, which is proportional to $\ell N \log N$. While the computation cost of our protocol, dominated by $(NT \log N/\log T)(\ell/\lambda)$, is asymptotically worse than that of a PKE-based or permutation network-based approach, our protocol uses lightweight crypto primitives (XORs and PRGs) and does not require any public-key operations besides a set of base OTs, thus resulting in a concretely efficient protocol. We compute the concrete cost of our protocol and estimate its performance over different networks (bandwidth 1 Gbps, 100 Mbps and 72 Mbps). For large values of ℓ, we see a two to three orders of magnitude improvement over the best known public key based approach and an order of magnitude improvement over the best known symmetric key approach. The details of our experiment are in Sect. 7.

At the heart of our construction is a new primitive which we call Share Translation functionality. This functionality outputs two sets of pseudorandom values - one per party - with a special permutation-related dependency between them, and we show that this is enough to implement secret-shared shuffle. Conceptually, this functionality allows us to push the problem of permuting the *data* down to the problem of permuting *preudorandom values*[2]. This can be seen as the analogue of beaver triples or tiny tables for permutations rather than arithmetic or boolean computations.

Our Share Translation has quadratic running time (in N), and thus implementing secret-shared shuffle directly using Share Translation protocol becomes too prohibitive, even with lightweight operations like XOR and PRG. This brings us to the second crucial part of our construction: we devise a way to represent any permutation as a combination of several permutations π_i, where each π_i itself consists of several *disjoint* permutations, each acting on few elements. We find such decomposition using the special structure of Benes permutation network. This decomposition allows us to apply our Share Translation protocol to *small* individual disjoint permutations rather than *big* final permutation, allowing our protocol for secret-shared shuffle to achieve the claimed running time. We leverage the particular structure of our Share Translation protocol to make sure that this transformation doesn't increase the number of rounds.

1.1 Applications

Collaborative Filtering. One immediate application of our shuffle protocol is to allow two parties who hold shares of a set of elements to filter out elements that satisfy a certain criterion. This could include removing poorly formed or outlier elements. Or it could be used after a PSI protocol [5,23,24] or in database

[2] This in particular allows us to avoid the $\ell N \log N$ communication price of the permutation network-based approach (which stems from the fact that one has to feed the whole ℓ-bit element into each atomic swap of a permutation network, to retain security).

join [21] to remove elements that were not matched. If we are willing to reveal the number of elements meeting this criterion, we can use a shuffle to securely remove these elements so that subsequent operations can be evaluated only on the resulting smaller set, which is particularly valuable if the subsequent computation is expensive (e.g. a machine learning task [20]). To do this, we first shuffle the set, then apply a 2PC to each element to evaluate the criterion, revealing the result bit in the clear, and finally remove those items whose result is 1.

Sorting Under 2PC. Our secret shared shuffle protocol can also be used to build efficient protocols for other fundamental operations. For example, in order to sort a list of secret shared elements and output the resulting secret shares, we can use the shuffle-and-reveal approach proposed by [14] together with our secret-shared shuffle. The idea in [14] is that if the data is shuffled first, then sorting algorithms can reveal the result of each comparison operation in the clear without compromizing security. Thus their approach is to first shuffle the data, and then run a sorting algorithm where each comparison is done under 2PC, with the result revealed in the clear. This yields more efficient protocols than the standard oblivious sorting protocol based on sorting networks; those protocols either have huge constants [1] or require $O(N \log^2 N)$ running time (using Bitonic Sorting network), where N is the number of elements in the database. Note that in many cases we want to sort not just a set of elements, but also some associated data for each element.

Sort, in addition to being a fundamental operation, can be used to find the top k results in a list, to evaluate the median or quantiles, to find outliers, and so on.

Secure Computation for RAM Programs. There has been a line of work starting with [8,9,11,17–19,26,28] that looks at secure computation for RAM programs (as opposed to circuits). The primary building block in these constructions is oblivious RAM (ORAM), which allows to hide memory accesses made by the computation. A naive way to initialize ORAM is to perform an ORAM write operation for each input item, but the concrete costs on this are very high. [17,28] show that this can be made much more efficient using a shuffle: the parties simply permute their entries using a random secret shared permutation and then store them as the ORAM memory. [28] achieve significant improvements by using garbled circuits to implement a permutation network; as we will see in Sect. 7 our solution far outperforms this approach, so we should get significant performance improvements for this application. Note that in ORAM it is often beneficial to have somewhat large block size, and our protocol for secret-shared shuffle is especially advantageous in the setting where elements are large.

1.2 Technical Overview

Notation. By bold letters $\boldsymbol{x}, \boldsymbol{a}, \boldsymbol{b}, \boldsymbol{r}, \boldsymbol{\Delta}$ we denote vectors of N elements, and by $\boldsymbol{x}[j]$ we denote the j-th element of $\boldsymbol{x}$. By $\pi(\boldsymbol{x})$, where π is a permutation, we denote the permuted vector $(\boldsymbol{x}[\pi(1)], \ldots, \boldsymbol{x}[\pi(N)])$.

Secret-Shared Shuffle. Recall that the goal of the secret-shared shuffle is to let parties learn secret shares of a shuffled dataset. More concretely, consider parties P_0, P_1, where P_1 owns database $\boldsymbol{x}$. Our goal is to build a protocol which allows P_0 to learn $\boldsymbol{r}$ and P_1 to learn $\boldsymbol{r} \oplus \pi(\boldsymbol{x})$, but nothing more; here $\boldsymbol{r}$ is a random vector of the same size as the database, and π is a random permutation of appropriate size. Our protocol also works for the case when $\boldsymbol{x}$ was secret shared between P_0 and P_1 to begin with (instead of being an input of one party).

Secret-shared shuffle can be easily built given its variant, which we call Permute+Share, where one of the parties *chooses* the permutation. That is, in this protocol P_0 holds π and P_1 holds $\boldsymbol{x}$, and as before, they would like to learn $\boldsymbol{r}$ and $\boldsymbol{r} \oplus \pi(\boldsymbol{x})$, respectively. Indeed, secret-shared shuffle can be obtained by executing Permute+Share twice, where first P_0 and then P_1 chooses the permutation (note that in the second execution the database is itself already secret-shared). Thus, in the rest of the introduction we describe how to build Permute+Share.

Our construction proceeds in several steps: first we explain how to build Permute+Share using another protocol called Share Translation. Then we build the latter from oblivious punctured vector primitive, which can be in turn implemented using a GGM-based PRF and oblivious transfer with low communication. Note that we are going to describe our protocols using $\oplus$ (XOR) operation for simplicity, however, in the main body we instead use a more general syntax with addition and subtraction, to allow our protocols to work in different groups.

Building Simplified Permute+Share *from* Share Translation. We first describe a simplified and inefficient version of Permute+Share; the running time of this protocol is proportional to the square of the size of the database. Later in the introduction we explain how we exploit the structure of Benes permutation network [2] to achieve our final protocol.

As a starting point, consider the following idea: P_1 chooses random masks $\boldsymbol{a} = (\boldsymbol{a}[1], \ldots, \boldsymbol{a}[N])$ and sends its masked data $\boldsymbol{x} \oplus \boldsymbol{a}$ to P_0. Now P_0 and P_1 together hold a secret-shared $\boldsymbol{x}$, albeit not permuted. Note that P_0 knows the permutation π and could easily locally rearrange its shares in order of $\pi(\boldsymbol{x} \oplus \boldsymbol{a})$. However, P_1 doesn't know π and thus cannot rearrange $\boldsymbol{a}$ into $\pi(\boldsymbol{a})$. Further, any protocol which allows P_1 to learn $\pi(\boldsymbol{a})$ would immediately reveal π to P_1, since P_1 also knows $\boldsymbol{a}$.

Therefore, instead of choosing a single set of masks, P_1 should choose two different and independent sets of masks, $\boldsymbol{a}$ and $\boldsymbol{b}$, where $\boldsymbol{a}$, as before, is used to hide $\boldsymbol{x}$ from P_0, and $\boldsymbol{b}$ will become the final P_1's share of $\pi(\boldsymbol{x})$. However, now P_0 has a problem: since P_1's share is $\boldsymbol{b}$, P_0's share should be $\pi(\boldsymbol{x}) \oplus \boldsymbol{b}$; however, P_0 only receives $\boldsymbol{x} \oplus \boldsymbol{a}$ from P_1, and has no way of "translating" it into $\pi(\boldsymbol{x}) \oplus \boldsymbol{b}$. Thus we additionally let parties execute a Share Translation protocol to allow P_0 obtain a "translation function" $\boldsymbol{\Delta} = \pi(\boldsymbol{a}) \oplus \boldsymbol{b}$, as we explain next in more detail:

Share Translation protocol takes as input permutation π from P_0 and outputs vectors $\boldsymbol{\Delta}$ to P_0 and $\boldsymbol{a}, \boldsymbol{b}$ to P_1, such that $\boldsymbol{\Delta} = \pi(\boldsymbol{a}) \oplus \boldsymbol{b}$, and, roughly speaking,

$\boldsymbol{a}, \boldsymbol{b}$ look random[3]. A simple version of Permute+Share can be obtained from Share Translation as follows:

1. P_0 and P_1 execute a Share Translation protocol, where P_0 holds input π, receives output $\boldsymbol{\Delta}$, and P_1 receives output $\boldsymbol{a}, \boldsymbol{b}$.
2. P_1 sends $\boldsymbol{x} \oplus \boldsymbol{a}$ to P_0 and sets its final share to $\boldsymbol{b}$.
3. P_0 sets its share to $\pi(\boldsymbol{x} \oplus \boldsymbol{a}) \oplus \boldsymbol{\Delta}$. Note that this is equal to $\pi(\boldsymbol{x}) \oplus \pi(\boldsymbol{a}) \oplus \pi(\boldsymbol{a}) \oplus \boldsymbol{b} = \pi(\boldsymbol{x}) \oplus \boldsymbol{b}$, and therefore the parties indeed obtain secret-shared $\pi(\boldsymbol{x})$.

In other words, the share translation vector $\boldsymbol{\Delta}$ allows P_0 to translate "shares of x under $\boldsymbol{a}$" into "shares of permuted x under $\boldsymbol{b}$".

Note that the Share Translation protocol can be viewed as a variant of Permute+Share protocol, with a difference that the "data" which is being permuted and shared is pseudorandom and out of parties' control (i.e. it is chosen by the protocol): indeed, in Share Translation protocol P_1 receives the "pseudorandom data" $\boldsymbol{a}$, and in addition P_0 and P_1 receive $\boldsymbol{\Delta} = \pi(\boldsymbol{a}) \oplus \boldsymbol{b}$ and $\boldsymbol{b}$, respectively, which can be thought of as shares of $\pi(\boldsymbol{a})$. In other words, we reduced the problem of permuting the fixed data $\boldsymbol{x}$ to the problem of permuting some pseudorandom, out-of-control data $\boldsymbol{a}$. In the following paragraphs we explain how we can exploit pseudorandomness of $\boldsymbol{a}$ and $\boldsymbol{b}$ to build Share Translation protocol with reduced communication complexity.

Building Share Translation *from Oblivious Punctured Vector.* We start with defining an Oblivious Punctured Vector protocol (OPV), which is essentially an $(n-1)$-out-of-n random oblivious transfer[4]: this protocol, on input $j \in [N]$ from P_0, allows parties to jointly generate vector $\boldsymbol{v}$ with random-looking elements such that:

- P_0 learns all vector elements except for its j-th element $\boldsymbol{v}[j]$;
- P_1 learns the whole vector $\boldsymbol{v}$ (but doesn't learn index j)[5].

We use OPV to build Share Translation as follows: the parties are going to run N executions of OPV protocol to generate N vectors $\boldsymbol{v}_1, \ldots, \boldsymbol{v}_N$, where P_0's input in execution i is $\pi(i)$. Consider an $N \times N$ matrix $\{\boldsymbol{v}_i[j]\}_{i,j \in N^2}$. By the properties of OPV protocol, P_1 learns the whole matrix, and P_0 learns the matrix except for elements corresponding to the permutation, i.e. it learns nothing about $\boldsymbol{v}_1[\pi(1)], \ldots, \boldsymbol{v}_N[\pi(N)]$ (see Fig. 1).

Then P_1 sets elements of $\boldsymbol{a}, \boldsymbol{b}$ to be column- and row-wise sums of the matrix elements, i.e. for all $i \in N$ it sets $\boldsymbol{a}[i] \leftarrow \bigoplus_j \boldsymbol{v}_j[i]$, and for all $j \in N$ it sets $\boldsymbol{b}[j] \leftarrow$

[3] More precisely, P_1 shouldn't learn anything about π, and P_0 shouldn't learn $\boldsymbol{a}, \boldsymbol{b}$, except for what is revealed by π and $\boldsymbol{\Delta}$ (note that it still learns, e.g., $\boldsymbol{a}_{\pi(1)} \oplus \boldsymbol{b}_1$).

[4] We note that similar definitions were developed independently in [3,25].

[5] Note that this is very similar to 1-out of-N OT- except that j specifies which element P_0 *doesn't* learn - and in fact is almost the same as $N-1$-out of-N OT. The difference is that in our primitive vector $\boldsymbol{v}$ is pseudorandom and given by the protocol to the parties (rather than chosen by the sender as in standard OT). We use this fact to save on communication.

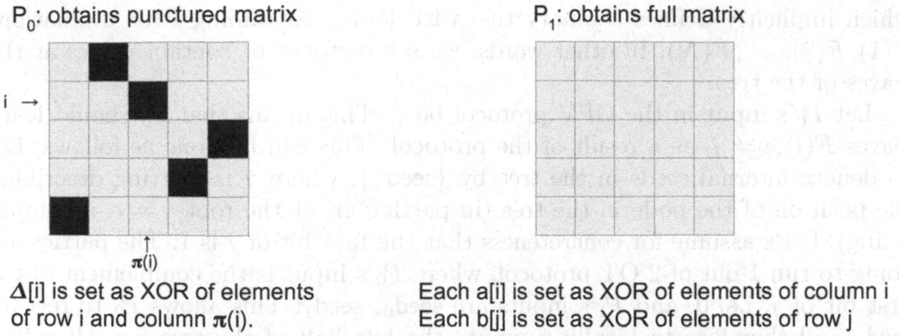
P0: obtains punctured matrix
i →
π(i)
Δ[i] is set as XOR of elements of row i and column π(i).
P1: obtains full matrix
Each a[i] is set as XOR of elements of column i
Each b[j] is set as XOR of elements of row j

Fig. 1. (left) P_0 receives a "punctured" matrix, which is missing elements at positions $(i, \pi(i))$. Note that the missing elements are not needed to compute $\boldsymbol{\Delta}$. (right) P_1 receives the full matrix and uses it to compute masks $\boldsymbol{a}, \boldsymbol{b}$.

$\bigoplus_i \boldsymbol{v}_j[i]$. P_0 computes $\boldsymbol{\Delta}[i]$ by taking the sum of column $\pi(i)$ (except the element $\boldsymbol{v}_i[\pi(i)]$ which it doesn't know) and adding the sum of row i (again, except the element $\boldsymbol{v}_i[\pi(i)]$ which it doesn't know), i.e. it sets $\boldsymbol{\Delta}[i] \leftarrow \left(\bigoplus_{j \neq i} \boldsymbol{v}_j[\pi(i)]\right) \oplus \left(\bigoplus_{j \neq \pi(i)} \boldsymbol{v}_i[j]\right)$.

Correctness of this protocol can be immediately verified: indeed, each $\boldsymbol{\Delta}[i] = \boldsymbol{a}[\pi(i)] \oplus \boldsymbol{b}[i]$, since the missing value $\boldsymbol{v}_i[\pi(i)]$ participates in the sum $\boldsymbol{a}[\pi(i)] \oplus \boldsymbol{b}[i]$ twice and therefore doesn't influence the result. For security, note that P_0 doesn't learn anything about $\boldsymbol{a}, \boldsymbol{b}$ (except for $\boldsymbol{\Delta}$), since it is missing exactly one element from each row and column of the matrix; the missing element acts as a one-time pad and hides each $\boldsymbol{a}[i], \boldsymbol{b}[j]$ from P_0. P_1 doesn't learn anything about the permutation π due to index hiding property of the OPV protocol.

Note that this protocol has running time proportional to N^2 - we will show how to reduce this below.

Building Oblivious Punctured Vector from OT and PRFs. Oblivious Punctured Vector can be implemented using any $(n-1)$-out-of-n OT, but in order to make it communication-efficient, we devise a new technique which was inspired by the protocol for distributed point function by Doerner and Shelat [6]. The same technique appears in concurrent and independent works[6] of Schoppmann et al. and Boyle et al. [3, 25] in the context of silent OT extension and vector-OLE.

In the beginning of the protocol P_1 computes $\boldsymbol{v}$ by choosing key for GGM PRF at random, denoted seed_ϵ, and setting each $\boldsymbol{v}[i] \leftarrow PRF(\mathsf{seed}_\epsilon; i)$, $i \in [N]$. Recall that in GGM construction the key is treated as a prg seed,

6 Our work was submitted to Eurocrypt 2020 on September 26, 2019, and [3, 25] appeared in the public domain (ePrint) roughly at at the same time.

which implicitly defines a binary tree with leaves containing PRF evaluations $F(1), F(2), \ldots, F(N)$. In other words, we set vector $\boldsymbol{v}$ to contain values at the leaves of the tree.

Let P_0's input in the OPV protocol be j. This means that P_0 should learn leaves $F(i), i \neq j$, as a result of the protocol. This can be done as follows. Let us denote internal seeds in the tree by $\{\mathsf{seed}_\gamma\}$, where γ is a string describing the position of the node in the tree (in particular, at the root $\gamma = \epsilon$, an empty string). Let's assume for concreteness that the first bit of j is 1. The parties are going to run 1-out of-2 OT protocol, where P_0's input is the complement of the first bit of j, i.e. 0, and P_1's inputs are seed_0, seed_1. This allows P_0 to recover seed_0 and therefore to locally compute the left half of the tree, i.e. all values $F(1), \ldots, F(N/2)$, and corresponding intermediate seeds.

Next, assume the second bit of j is 0. Note that the parties could run 1-out of-4 OT to let P_0 learn seed_{11} and therefore locally compute the right quarter of the tree $F(3N/4), \ldots, F(N)$, then run 1-out of-8 OT and so on. However, this approach would require eventually sending 1-out of N OT, which defeats the initial purpose of having $\log N$ 1-out of-2 OTs only.

Instead, we let P_0 learn seed_{11} in a different way: we let P_1 send only *two* values, via 1-out-of-2-OT: the first value is the sum of seeds which are left children, i.e. $\mathsf{seed}_{00} \oplus \mathsf{seed}_{10}$, and the second value is the sum of seeds which are right children, i.e. $\mathsf{seed}_{01} \oplus \mathsf{seed}_{11}$. Since P_0 already knows the whole left subtree and in particular seed_{00} and seed_{01}, it can receive $\mathsf{seed}_{01} \oplus \mathsf{seed}_{11}$ from the OT protocol and add seed_{01} to it to obtain seed_{11}. (We note that this idea of sending the sums of left and right children is coming from the work of Doerner and Shelat [6]).

More generally, the parties execute $\log N$ 1-out-of-2 OTs - one for each level of the tree - where at each level k the first input to OT is the sum of all odd seeds at that level, and the second input to OT is the sum of all even seeds at that level. It can be seen that each sum contains exactly one term which P_0 doesn't know yet, and therefore it can receive the appropriate sum (depending on the k-th bit of j) and subtract other seeds from it to learn the next seed of the subtree. Note that these OT's can be executed in parallel.

Note that the running time of the parties is proportional to the vector size, but their communication size only depends on its logarithm.

Applying Share Translation *to the Decomposed Permutation.* Recall that, while communication complexity in our protocol is low, computation complexity is proportional to the size of the database squared, and thus is only efficient for a small database. To deal with this issue, we change the way how Permute+Share is built from Share Translation : instead of applying Share Translation to the whole permutation π directly, we first split the permutation π into smaller permutations in a special way, then apply Share Translation to each separate permutation to get multiple shares, and then recombine these shares to obtain shares with respect to π.

More concretely, the idea is to split the permutation π into a composition of multiple permutations $\pi_1 \circ \ldots \circ \pi_d$, such that each π_i is itself a composition

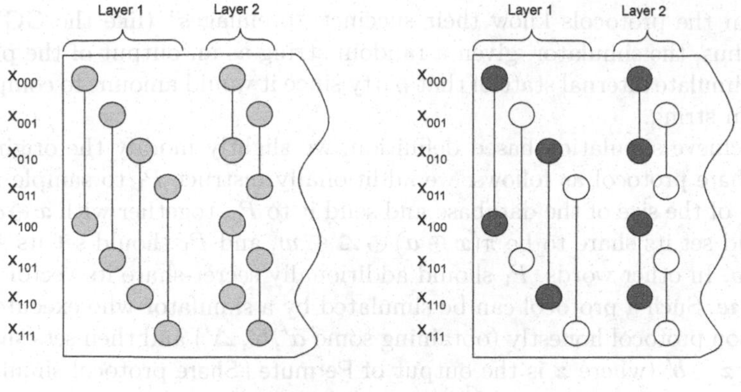

Fig. 2. *(left)* The first two layers of the Benes permutation network for 8 elements. A link indicates that the corresponding elements are potentially swapped, depending on the underlying permutation. *(right)* A grouping of these layers into two disjoint permutations acting on 4 elements each: one acting on white elements and the other acting on black elements.

of several disjoint permutations, each acting on T elements, for some parameter T. We refer to this as (T, d)–subpermutation representation of π. Such a representation can be found using a special structure of Benes permutation network. For instance, as shown on Fig. 2, the first two layers of a network on 8 elements can be split into two permutations, acting on $T = 4$ elements each, where the first permutation acts on odd elements and the second permutation acts on even elements. We present the full description of our decomposition in Sect. 6.2.

With such a decomposition in place, parties can run parallel executions of Share Translation , each acting on domain of size T. Note that, since the running time of a single Share Translation is proportional to the domain size squared, it is better to choose relatively small T. In our experiments, the typical optimal values of T were 16, 128, 256, depending on other parameters.

Note that setting $T = N$ corresponds to our simplified Permute+Share protocol described before, and setting $T = 2$ results in essentially computing the permutation network, where each swap is implemented in a somewhat-complicated way (using Share Translation protocol). Thus, this scheme can be thought of as a golden middle between the two approaches.

It remains to note that parties can run all executions of Share Translation in parallel (as opposed to taking multiple rounds, following the layered structure of the permutation network). To achieve this, in all execution except for the first ones, P_1 instead of sending initial masked data $\boldsymbol{x} \oplus \boldsymbol{a}$ should send correction vector $\boldsymbol{a}^{new} \oplus \boldsymbol{b}^{old}$, which can be added to the shares of P_0 in order to obtain $\boldsymbol{x} \oplus \boldsymbol{a}^{new}$. We refer the reader to Sect. 6.2 for more details.

Achieving Simulation-Based Definition. We note that the protocols we described so far only achieve indistinguishability-based definition, but not simulation-based definition. The problem is that the output values are only *pseudo*-random, and parties in the protocols know their succinct "preimages" (like the GGM PRF root). Thus, the simulator, given a random string as an output of the protocol, cannot simulate internal state of that party since it would amount to compressing a random string.

To achieve simulation-based definition, we slightly modify the original Permute+Share protocol as follows: we additionally instruct P_1 to sample random string $\boldsymbol{w}$ of the size of the database and send it to P_0, together with $\boldsymbol{x} \oplus \boldsymbol{a}$. Then P_0 should set its share to be $\pi(\boldsymbol{x} \oplus \boldsymbol{a}) \oplus \boldsymbol{\Delta} \oplus \boldsymbol{w}$, and P_1 should set its share to be $\boldsymbol{b} \oplus \boldsymbol{w}$. In other words, P_1 should additionally secret-share its vector $\boldsymbol{b}$ using random $\boldsymbol{w}$. Such a protocol can be simulated by a simulator who executes Share Translation protocol honestly (obtaining some $\boldsymbol{a}', \boldsymbol{b}', \boldsymbol{\Delta}'$) and then sets simulated $\boldsymbol{w}$ to be $\boldsymbol{z} \oplus \boldsymbol{b}'$ (where $\boldsymbol{z}$ is the output of Permute+Share protocol simulated by an external simulator).

2 Notations

We denote the security parameter as λ. The bit length of each element in the input set is ℓ, $\ell = \mathsf{poly}(\lambda)$. We denote an upper bound on the size of the database as N. Ideal functionality is denoted as $\mathcal{F}$. We will denote vectors with bold fonts and individual elements with indices. For example, $\boldsymbol{v}$ is a vector of N elements where each individual element is denoted as v_i. $\leftarrow^{\$}$ denotes selected uniformly at random from a domain. By S_N we denote the group of all permutations on N elements.

We also make use of the following notation:

Exec: Let Π be a two-party protocol. By $(\mathsf{output}_0, \mathsf{output}_1) \leftarrow \mathsf{exec}^{\Pi}(\lambda; x_0, x_1; r_0, r_1)$ we denote the concatenated outputs of all parties after the execution of the protocol Π with security parameter λ on inputs x_0, x_1 using randomness r_0, r_1.

View: Let Π be a two-party protocol. By $\mathsf{view}_b^{\Pi}(\lambda; x_0, x_1; r_0, r_1)$ we denote the view of party b when parties P_0 and P_1 run the protocol Π with security parameter λ on inputs x_0, x_1 using randomness r_0, r_1. The view of each party includes its inputs, random coins, all messages it receives, and its outputs. When the context is clear, we also write view_b for short.

Honest-but-Curious Security for a 2PC: Honest-but-curious security for a 2PC protocol Π evaluating function $\mathcal{F}$ is defined in terms of the following two experiments:

$IDEAL^{\mathcal{F}}_{\mathsf{sim},b}(\lambda, x_0, x_1)$ evaluates $\mathcal{F}(x_0, x_1)$ to obtain output (y_0, y_1) runs the stateful simulator $\mathsf{sim}(1^\lambda, b, x_b, y_b)$ which produces a simulated view view_b for party P_b. The output of the experiment is $(\mathsf{view}_b, y_{1-b})$.

$REAL^{\Pi}_b(\lambda, x_0, x_1)$ runs the protocol with security parameter λ between honest parties P_0 with input x_0 and P_1 with input x_1 who obtain outputs y_0, y_1 respectively. It outputs $(\mathsf{view}_b, y_{1-b})$.

Definition 1. *Protocol Π realizes $\mathcal{F}$ in the honest-but-curious setting if there exists a PPT simulator* sim *such that for all inputs x_0, x_1, and corrupt parties $b \in \{0,1\}$ the two experiments are indistinguishable.*

Pseudo Random Generator. Let $\{\mathsf{G}\}_\lambda$ be a family of polynomial size circuits where each $\mathsf{G}_\lambda : \{0,1\}^{m(\lambda)} \to \{0,1\}^{l(\lambda)}$, $l(\lambda) \geq m(\lambda)$. $\{\mathsf{G}\}_\lambda$ is a PRG if the following distributions are computationally indistinguishable:

$$\{\mathcal{D}_1\}_\lambda = \{\mathsf{G}(\mathsf{s}) : \mathsf{s} \leftarrow \{0,1\}^{m(\lambda)}\}, \{\mathcal{D}_2\}_\lambda = \{x : x \leftarrow \{0,1\}^{l(\lambda)}\}$$

We will omit the dependence of m and l on λ for simplicity. When $l = 2m$, we call this a length doubling PRG.

Oblivious Transfer (OT). OT is a secure 2-party protocol that realizes the functionality $\mathcal{F}_{\mathsf{OT}} : ((\mathsf{str}_0, \mathsf{str}_1), b) = (\perp, \mathsf{str}_b)$ where $\mathsf{str}_0, \mathsf{str}_1 \in \{0,1\}^k, b \in \{0,1\}$.

3 Oblivious Punctured Vector (OPV)

3.1 Definition and Security Properties

An Oblivious Punctured Vector (OPV) for domain $\mathbb{D}$ is an interactive protocol between two parties, P_0 and P_1, where parties' inputs are $((1^\lambda, \mathsf{n}), (1^\lambda, \mathsf{n}, i))$ and their outputs are $(\boldsymbol{v}_0, \boldsymbol{v}_1)$, respectively. Here λ is the security parameter that determines the running time of the protocol, $\boldsymbol{v}_b, b \in \{0,1\}$ are vectors of length n, $i \in [\mathsf{n}]$ and $\boldsymbol{v}_b \in [\mathbb{D}]^{\mathsf{n}}$.

This protocol lets the two parties jointly generate vector $\boldsymbol{v}$ with random-looking elements such that: 1) P_0 learns the whole vector $\boldsymbol{v}$ but doesn't learn index i. 2) P_1 learns all vector elements except for its i-th element $\boldsymbol{v}[i]$. So we define the protocol to be *correct* if $\boldsymbol{v}_1[j] = \boldsymbol{v}_0[j]\ \forall j \neq i$.

To capture the first property, we want to say that an adversarial P_0, who is given two distinct indices $i, i' \in [\mathsf{n}]$, $i \neq i'$ and participates in two executions of the protocol, one where party P_1 holds i, and the other, where P_1 holds i', cannot tell the two executions apart. We call this property *Position hiding.* To capture the second property, we want to say that an adversarial P_1, who, in addition to its view in the protocol execution, receives the vector $\boldsymbol{v}_0$, cannot differentiate between the two cases: when $\boldsymbol{v}_0$ is generated according to exec and when $\boldsymbol{v}_0$ is generated according to exec, then $\boldsymbol{v}_0[i]$ is replaced a random string from the domain. We call this security property *Value hiding.* We define the properties formally below.

Correctness. For any sufficiently large security parameter $\lambda \in \mathbb{N}$, for any $\mathsf{n} \in \mathbb{N}, i \in [\mathsf{n}]$, if $(\boldsymbol{v}_0, \boldsymbol{v}_1) \leftarrow \mathsf{exec}^{\mathsf{OPV}}((\lambda \mathsf{n}), (\lambda, \mathsf{n}, i))$ and $\boldsymbol{v}_b \in [\mathbb{D}]^{\mathsf{n}}, b \in \{0,1\}$, then $\boldsymbol{v}_1[j] = \boldsymbol{v}_0[j]\ \forall j \neq i$.

Position Hiding. For any sufficiently large security parameter $\lambda \in \mathbb{N}$, $\mathsf{n} \in \mathbb{N}, i, i' \in [\mathsf{n}]$, the following distributions are computationally indistinguishable:

$$\mathcal{D}_1 = \{(\boldsymbol{v}_0, \boldsymbol{v}_1) \leftarrow \mathsf{exec}^{\mathsf{OPV}}((1^\lambda, \mathsf{n}), (1^\lambda, \mathsf{n}, i)) : (1^\lambda, \mathsf{n}, i, i', \mathsf{view}_0)\}$$
$$\mathcal{D}_2 = \{(\boldsymbol{v}_0, \boldsymbol{v}_1) \leftarrow \mathsf{exec}^{\mathsf{OPV}}((1^\lambda, \mathsf{n}), (1^\lambda, \mathsf{n}, i')) : (1^\lambda, \mathsf{n}, i, i', \mathsf{view}_0)\}$$

Value Hiding. For any sufficiently large security parameter $\lambda \in \mathbb{N}$, for any $\mathsf{n} \in \mathbb{N}, i \in [\mathsf{n}]$, the following distributions are computationally indistinguishable:

$$\mathcal{D}_1 = \{(\boldsymbol{v}_0, \boldsymbol{v}_1) \leftarrow \mathsf{exec}^{\mathsf{OPV}}((1^\lambda, \mathsf{n}), (1^\lambda, \mathsf{n}, i)) : (1^\lambda, \mathsf{n}, i, \boldsymbol{v}_0, \mathsf{view}_1)\}$$
$$\mathcal{D}_2 = \{((\boldsymbol{v}_0, \boldsymbol{v}_1) \leftarrow \mathsf{exec}^{\mathsf{OPV}}((1^\lambda, \mathsf{n}), (1^\lambda, \mathsf{n}, i)), \boldsymbol{v}_0[i] := r \text{ where } r \leftarrow^{\$} \mathbb{D} : (1^\lambda, \mathsf{n}, i, \boldsymbol{v}_0, \mathsf{view}_1)\}\}$$

Construction: We defer the formal construction and security proof of Theorem 1 to the full version. For an informal description of the construction, please refer to Sect. 1.2.

Please note that we only count the cryptographic operations while analyzing the computation complexity of our protocols.

Theorem 1. *The OPV construction satisfies position and value hiding as defined in Definition Sect. 3.1. The protocol runs* n *(1-out-of-2)* OT *on messages of length* λ *bits in parallel. The communication cost is that of the* OT*s and the computation cost is the cost of these* OT*s +* n *length-doubling PRG computations for each party*[7]*, where* λ *is a security parameter and* n *is the number of elements in the vector.*

3.2 OPV Construction for Longer Strings

Let $\mathsf{OPV}_{\mathbb{D}}$ denote the interactive protocol between two parties, P_0 and P_1, where parties' inputs are $((1^\lambda, \mathsf{n}), (1^\lambda, \mathsf{n}, i))$ and their outputs are $(\boldsymbol{v}_0, \boldsymbol{v}_1)$, where $\boldsymbol{v}_b \in [\mathbb{D}]^{\mathsf{n}}$ and $\mathbb{D}$ is strings of length λ. We construct $\mathsf{OPV}_{\mathbb{D}'}$ where $\mathbb{D}'$ is strings of length $\ell \geq \lambda$ using $\mathsf{OPV}_{\mathbb{D}}$ and a PRG $\mathsf{G} : \{0,1\}^\lambda \to \{0,1\}^\ell$ as follows.

- Run $(\boldsymbol{v}_0, \boldsymbol{v}_1) \leftarrow \mathsf{exec}^{\mathsf{OPV}_{\mathbb{D}}}((1^\lambda, \mathsf{n}), (1^\lambda, \mathsf{n}, i)$
- Party P_b, $b \in \{0,1\}$ does the following: for each $\boldsymbol{v}_b[j], j \in [1, \mathsf{n}]$, expand it to a ℓ-bit string using $\mathsf{G}(\boldsymbol{v}_b[j])$, i.e., $\boldsymbol{v}'_b[j] \leftarrow \mathsf{G}(\boldsymbol{v}_b[j])$. P_b's output is $\boldsymbol{v}'_b$.

Theorem 2. *If* $\mathsf{OPV}_{\mathbb{D}}$ *satisfies correctness, position and value hiding as defined in Definition Sect. 3.1, and* G *is a secure PRG, then our construction for* $\mathsf{OPV}_{\mathbb{D}'}$ *satisfies correctness, position and value hiding as well. The round complexity and communication cost is the same as the cost of* $\mathsf{OPV}_{\mathbb{D}}$*. The computation cost includes the computation cost of* $\mathsf{OPV}_{\mathbb{D}}$ *+* n *λ-bit-to-ℓ-bit PRGs.*

Proof. Correctness: By the correctness of $\mathsf{OPV}_{\mathbb{D}}$, $\boldsymbol{v}_0[j] = \boldsymbol{v}_1[j]$, $\forall j \neq i$. Therefore, by our construction, $\boldsymbol{v}'_0[j] = \boldsymbol{v}'_1[j]$, $\forall j \neq i$.

Position Hiding: For the sake of contradiction, suppose not. Then, there exists a distinguisher D that breaks the position hiding property of $\mathsf{OPV}_{\mathbb{D}'}$. We use D to build a distinguisher $\mathcal{A}$ that breaks the position hiding property of $\mathsf{OPV}_{\mathbb{D}}$ as follows. $\mathcal{A}$ receives $(1^\lambda, \mathsf{n}, i, i', \mathsf{view}_0^{\mathsf{OPV}_{\mathbb{D}}})$ as input, where $\mathsf{view}_0^{\mathsf{OPV}_{\mathbb{D}}}$ contains $\boldsymbol{v}_0$. For

[7] We give the concrete cost of OT and OPV in Sect. 7.

every $v_0[j], j \in [1, \mathsf{n}]$, $\mathcal{A}$ computes $v'_0[j] = \mathsf{G}(v_0[j])$. Then it constructs $\mathsf{view}_0^{\mathsf{OPV}_{\mathbb{D}'}}$, which is $\mathsf{view}_0^{\mathsf{OPV}_{\mathbb{D}}}$, augmented with $v'_0[j]$. $\mathcal{A}$ forwards $(1^\lambda, \mathsf{n}, i, i', \mathsf{view}_0^{\mathsf{OPV}_{\mathbb{D}'}})$ to D. Thus, $\mathcal{A}$ directly inherits the success probability D.

Value Hiding: Recall that we are trying to prove the following two distributions are computationally indistinguishable.

$$\mathcal{D}_1 = \{(v'_0, v'_1) \leftarrow \mathsf{exec}^{\mathsf{OPV}_{\mathbb{D}'}}((1^\lambda, \mathsf{n}), (1^\lambda, \mathsf{n}, i)) : (1^\lambda, \mathsf{n}, i, v'_0, \mathsf{view}_1^{\mathsf{OPV}_{\mathbb{D}'}})\}$$
$$\mathcal{D}_2 = \{((v'_0, v'_1) \leftarrow \mathsf{exec}^{\mathsf{OPV}_{\mathbb{D}'}}((1^\lambda, \mathsf{n}), (1^\lambda, \mathsf{n}, i)), v'_0[i] := r \text{ where } r \leftarrow^{\$} \mathbb{D}' : (1^\lambda, \mathsf{n}, i, v'_0, \mathsf{view}_1^{\mathsf{OPV}_{\mathbb{D}'}})\}$$

The proof will proceed through a series of hybrid steps. We define a series of distributions as follows.

H_0: $\mathcal{D}_1 = \{(v'_0, v'_1) \leftarrow \mathsf{exec}^{\mathsf{OPV}_{\mathbb{D}'}}((1^\lambda, \mathsf{n}), (1^\lambda, \mathsf{n}, i)) : (1^\lambda, \mathsf{n}, i, v'_0, \mathsf{view}_1^{\mathsf{OPV}_{\mathbb{D}'}})\}$

H_1: Identical to the previous distribution except the following: generate $(v_0, v_1) \leftarrow \mathsf{exec}^{\mathsf{OPV}_{\mathbb{D}}}((1^\lambda, \mathsf{n}), (1^\lambda, \mathsf{n}, i))$, then set $v_0[i] := r$ where $r \leftarrow^{\$} \mathbb{D}$ and set $v'_0[i] \leftarrow \mathsf{G}(v'_0[i])$. By the value-hiding property of $\mathsf{OPV}_{\mathbb{D}}$, H_0, H_1 are identical.

H_2: Identical to the previous distribution except the following: instead of computing $v'_0[i] \leftarrow \mathsf{G}(v'_0[i])$, set $v'_0[i] := r'$ where $r' \leftarrow^{\$} \mathbb{D}'$. By the security property of PRG, H_1, H_2 are identical. Note that distribution H_2 is identical to $\mathcal{D}_2$. So this concludes the proof of value hiding. □

4 Share Translation Protocol

4.1 Definition

Share Translation (ST) protocol with parameters (N, ℓ) is an interactive protocol between two parties, P_0 and P_1, where parties' inputs are $(\pi, \perp)$ and their outputs are $(\boldsymbol{\Delta}, (\boldsymbol{a}, \boldsymbol{b}))$, respectively. Here π is a permutation on N elements, and $\Delta, \boldsymbol{a}, \boldsymbol{b}$ are all vectors of N elements in group $\mathbb{G}$, where each element can be represented with ℓ bits. The protocol should satisfy the following correctness and security guarantees:

Correctness: For each sufficiently large security parameter λ, for each $\pi \in S_N$, and for each r_0, r_1 of appropriate length, let $(\boldsymbol{\Delta}, (\boldsymbol{a}, \boldsymbol{b})) \leftarrow \mathsf{exec}^{\mathsf{ST}}(\lambda; \pi, \perp; r_0, r_1)$. Then it should hold that $\boldsymbol{\Delta} = \boldsymbol{b} - \pi(\boldsymbol{a})$.

This definition can be modified in a straightforward way for statistical or computational correctness.

Permutation Hiding: For all sufficiently large λ it should hold that for all $\pi, \pi' \in S_N$,

$$\mathsf{view}_1^{\mathsf{ST}}(\lambda; \pi, \perp; r_0, r_1) \approx \mathsf{view}_1^{\mathsf{ST}}(\lambda; \pi', \perp; r_0, r_1),$$

where indistinguishability holds over uniformly chosen r_0, r_1.

Share Hiding: For all sufficiently large λ it should hold that for any $\pi \in S_N$,

$$(\boldsymbol{a}, \boldsymbol{b}, \mathsf{view}_0^{\mathsf{ST}}(\lambda; \pi, \perp; r_0, r_1)) \approx (\boldsymbol{a}', \boldsymbol{b}', \mathsf{view}_0^{\mathsf{ST}}(\lambda; \pi, \perp; r_0, r_1)),$$

where $(\boldsymbol{\Delta}, \boldsymbol{a}, \boldsymbol{b}) = \mathsf{exec}_{\mathsf{ST}}(\lambda; \pi, \perp; r_0, r_1)$, $\boldsymbol{a}' \leftarrow^{\$} \mathbb{G}^N$, $\boldsymbol{b}' = \boldsymbol{\Delta} + \pi(\boldsymbol{a}')$, and indistinguishability holds over uniformly chosen r_0, r_1.

4.2 Construction

We build Share Translation protocol out of an Oblivious Punctured Vector (OPV) protocol for domain $\mathbb{D} = \mathbb{G}$. Let π be P_0's input in Share Translation protocol. The protocol proceeds as follows:

1. P_0 and P_1 run N executions of the OPV protocol in parallel, where P_0 uses $\pi(i)$ as its input in execution i, for $i \in [N]$. Denote $\boldsymbol{v}_i', \boldsymbol{v}_i$ to be the outputs of the OPV protocol in execution i, for parties P_0 and P_1, respectively, and denote $\boldsymbol{v}_i'[j], \boldsymbol{v}_i[j]$ to be j-th elements of these vectors.
2. For each $i \in [N]$ P_0 sets $\boldsymbol{\Delta}[i] \leftarrow \sum_{j \neq \pi(i)} \boldsymbol{v}_i'[j] - \sum_{j \neq i} \boldsymbol{v}_j'[\pi(i)]$. It sets its output to be $\boldsymbol{\Delta} = (\boldsymbol{\Delta}[1], \ldots, \boldsymbol{\Delta}[N])$.
3. For each $i \in [N]$ P_1 sets $\boldsymbol{b}_i \leftarrow \sum_j \boldsymbol{v}_i[j]$, $\boldsymbol{a}_i \leftarrow \sum_j \boldsymbol{v}_j[i]$. It sets $(\boldsymbol{a}, \boldsymbol{b})$ as its output, where $\boldsymbol{a} = (\boldsymbol{a}[1], \ldots, \boldsymbol{a}[N])$, $\boldsymbol{b} = (\boldsymbol{b}[1], \ldots, \boldsymbol{b}[N])$.

Theorem 3. *The construction described above satisfies correctness, permutation hiding and share hiding, assuming underlying OPV protocol satisfies correctness, value hiding and position hiding. The round complexity, communication and computation cost of this protocol are equal to those of N instances of OPV run in parallel.*

Correctness. For any $i \in [N]$ we have

$$\boldsymbol{\Delta}_i = \sum_{j \neq \pi(i)} \boldsymbol{v}_i'[j] - \sum_{j \neq i} \boldsymbol{v}_j'[\pi(i)] \overset{(1)}{=} \sum_{j \neq \pi(i)} \boldsymbol{v}_i[j] - \sum_{j \neq i} \boldsymbol{v}_j[\pi(i)] \overset{(2)}{=}$$

$$\overset{(2)}{=} \sum_{j \in [N]} \boldsymbol{v}_i[j] - \sum_{j \in [N]} \boldsymbol{v}_j[\pi(i)] = \boldsymbol{b}_i - \boldsymbol{a}_{\pi(i)}.$$

Here (1) follows from correctness of the OPV protocol, and (2) holds since we add and subtract the same value $\boldsymbol{v}_i[\pi(i)]$. Note that a computationally (resp., statistically, perfectly) correct OPV protocol results in a computationally (resp., statistically, perfectly) correct ST protocol.

Permutation Hiding. Recall that we need to show that for all $\pi, \pi' \in S_N$,

$$\mathsf{view}_1^{\mathsf{ST}}(\lambda; \pi, \perp; r_0, r_1) \approx \mathsf{view}_1^{\mathsf{ST}}(\lambda; \pi', \perp; r_0, r_1).$$

We show this indistinguishability in a sequence of hybrids $H_0, H_1, \ldots, H_N$, where:

- $H_0 = \mathsf{view}_1^{\mathsf{ST}}(\lambda; \pi, \perp; r_0, r_1)$, for uniformly chosen r_0, r_1,
- $H_N = \mathsf{view}_1^{\mathsf{ST}}(\lambda; \pi', \perp; r_0, r_1)$, for uniformly chosen r_0, r_1,
- For $1 \leq i < N$, $H_i = \mathsf{view}_1^{(i)}(\lambda; (\pi, \pi'), \perp; r_0, r_1)$, where $\mathsf{view}_1^{(i)}(\lambda; (\pi, \pi'), \perp; r_0, r_1)$ is a view of P_1 in the modified Share Translation protocol where party P_0 uses $\pi'(j)$ as its input in OPV executions $1 \leq j \leq i$ and $\pi(j)$ as its input in OPV executions $i < j \leq N$. r_0, r_1 are uniformly chosen.

We argue that for each $1 \leq i \leq N$ $H_i \approx H_{i-1}$ due to position-hiding property of the OPV protocol, and therefore $H_0 \approx H_N$.

Indeed, note that the only difference between H_i and H_{i-1} is that in i-th execution of OPV party P_0 uses input $\pi'(i)$ instead of $\pi(i)$. Therefore if some PPT adversary distinguishes between H_i and H_{i-1}, then we break position hiding of OPV as follows. Given the challenge in the OPV position hiding game $(\pi(i), \pi'(i), \mathsf{view}_1^{\mathsf{OPV}}(\lambda; x, \perp; r_0^{\mathsf{OPV}}, r_1^{\mathsf{OPV}}))$, where $r_0^{\mathsf{OPV}}, r_1^{\mathsf{OPV}}$ are uniformly chosen randomness of P_0 and P_1 in the OPV protocol, and $\mathsf{view}_1^{\mathsf{OPV}}$ is a view of P_1 in OPV protocol (which uses randomness $r_0^{\mathsf{OPV}}, r_1^{\mathsf{OPV}}$ and P_0's input x which is either $\pi(i)$ or $\pi'(i)$), we execute the rest $N-1$ OPV protocols honestly using uniform randomness for each party and setting P_0's input to $\pi'(j)$ (for executions $j < i$) and $\pi(j)$ (for executions $j > i$). Let $\boldsymbol{v}_j, j = 1, \ldots, N$, be the output of P_1 in j-th execution of OPV.

We give the adversary P_1's view in all N OPV executions (including $\mathsf{view}_1^{\mathsf{OPV}}(\lambda; x, \perp; r_0^{\mathsf{OPV}}, r_1^{\mathsf{OPV}})$ of i-th execution which we received as a challenge). Depending on whether challenge input x was $\pi(i)$ or $\pi'(i)$, the distribution the adversary sees is either H_{i-1} or H_i. Therefore, if the adversary distinguishes between the two distributions, we can break position hiding of OPV protocol with the same success probability.

Share Hiding. Recall that we need to show that for any $\pi \in S_N$,

$$(\boldsymbol{a}, \boldsymbol{b}, \mathsf{view}_0^{\mathsf{ST}}(\lambda; \pi, \perp; r_0, r_1)) \approx (\boldsymbol{a}', \boldsymbol{b}', \mathsf{view}_0^{\mathsf{ST}}(\lambda; \pi, \perp; r_0, r_1)),$$

where $\boldsymbol{a}, \boldsymbol{b}$ are true shares produced by the protocol, and $\boldsymbol{a}', \boldsymbol{b}'$ are uniformly random, subject to $\boldsymbol{\Delta} = \boldsymbol{b} - \pi(\boldsymbol{a})$.

We show this indistinguishability in a sequence of hybrids $H_0, H_1, \ldots, H_N$, where:

- $H_0 = (\boldsymbol{a}, \boldsymbol{b}, \mathsf{view}_0^{\mathsf{ST}}(\lambda; \pi, \perp; r_0, r_1))$, for uniformly chosen r_0, r_1,
- $H_N = (\boldsymbol{a}', \boldsymbol{b}', \mathsf{view}_0^{\mathsf{ST}}(\lambda; \pi, \perp; r_0, r_1))$, for uniformly chosen $r_0, r_1, \boldsymbol{a}'$, and $\boldsymbol{b}' = \boldsymbol{\Delta} + \pi(\boldsymbol{a})$, where $(\boldsymbol{\Delta}, \boldsymbol{a}, \boldsymbol{b}) = \mathsf{exec}_{\mathsf{ST}}(\lambda; \pi, \perp; r_0, r_1)$,

- $H_i = (\boldsymbol{a}^{(i)}, \boldsymbol{b}^{(i)}, \mathsf{view}_0^{\mathsf{ST}}(\lambda; \pi, \perp; r_0, r_1))$, where $(\boldsymbol{\Delta}, \boldsymbol{a}, \boldsymbol{b}) = \mathsf{exec}_{\mathsf{ST}}(\lambda; \pi, \perp; r_0, r_1)$ is the output of the Share Translation protocol for random r_1, r_2, $\boldsymbol{a}^{(i)} = (\boldsymbol{a}_1^{(i)}, \ldots, \boldsymbol{a}_N^{(i)})$ is such that $\boldsymbol{a}_j^{(i)}$ is uniformly chosen for $1 \leq j \leq i$, $\boldsymbol{a}_j^{(i)} = \boldsymbol{a}_j$ for $i < j \leq N$, and $\boldsymbol{b}^{(i)} = \Delta + \pi(\boldsymbol{a}^{(i)})$.

We argue that for each $1 \leq i \leq N$ $H_i \approx H_{i-1}$, by reducing it to value hiding of OPV protocol. Indeed, note that the only difference between H_i and H_{i-1} is that $\boldsymbol{a}_i^{(i)}$ is generated uniformly at random, rather then set to the true output of the protocol. Therefore if some PPT adversary distinguishes between H_i and H_{i-1}, then we break security of OPV as follows. Assume we are given the challenge $(\boldsymbol{v}_i, \mathsf{view}_0^{\mathsf{OPV}}(\lambda; \pi(i), \perp; r_0^{\mathsf{OPV}}, r_1^{\mathsf{OPV}}))$, where $r_0^{\mathsf{OPV}}, r_1^{\mathsf{OPV}}$ are uniformly chosen randomness of P_0 and P_1 in the OPV protocol, and $\mathsf{view}_0^{\mathsf{OPV}}$ is a view of P_0 in OPV protocol (which uses randomness $r_0^{\mathsf{OPV}}, r_1^{\mathsf{OPV}}$ and P_0's input $\pi(i)$), and challenge $\boldsymbol{v}_i$ is either the true output of P_1, or the output of P_1 except that $\boldsymbol{v}_i[\pi(i)]$ is set to a uniform value. We execute the rest $N-1$ OPV protocols honestly using uniform randomness for each party and setting P_0's input to $\pi(j)$, for $j \neq i$. Let's denote the outputs of each OPV execution $j \neq i$ as $(\boldsymbol{v}_j, \boldsymbol{v}'_j)$.

Then we compute $\boldsymbol{a}^{(i)}$, $\boldsymbol{b}^{(i)}$ as follows:

- $\boldsymbol{b}^{(i)}[k] \leftarrow \sum_j \boldsymbol{v}_k[j]$, for each $k \in [N]$,
- $\boldsymbol{a}^{(i)}[k] \leftarrow \sum_j \boldsymbol{v}_j[k]$, for each $k \in [N]$,

Then we give the adversary $\boldsymbol{a}^{(i)}, \boldsymbol{b}^{(i)}$, and the views of party P_0 in all N OPV executions (including the challenge view $\mathsf{view}_0^{\mathsf{OPV}}(\lambda; \pi(i), \perp; r_0^{\mathsf{OPV}}, r_1^{\mathsf{OPV}})$ of i-th execution). Depending on whether challenge $\boldsymbol{v}_i[\pi(i)]$ was uniform or not, the distribution the adversary sees is either H_{i-1} or H_i.

Thus, we showed that H_0 and H_N are indistinguishable, as required.

5 $(T, d)-$Subpermutation Representation Based on Benes Permutation Network

In this section we describe how to obtain $(T, d)-$subpermutation representation, which is used in our final construction of Share Translation and secret-shared shuffle in Sect. 6. That is, we show how to represent any permutation $\pi \in S_N$, where $N = 2^n$ for some integer n, as a composition of permutations $\pi_1 \circ \ldots \circ \pi_d$, such that each π_i is itself a composition of several disjoint permutations, each acting on T elements, for some parameter T. In our construction $d = 2\lceil \frac{\log N}{\log T} \rceil - 1$.

Our decomposition is based on the special structure of the Benes permutation network. This network has $2 \log N - 1$ layers, each containing $N/2$ 2-element permutations (that is, each is either an identity permutation or a swap). Specifically, if inputs are numbered with index $1, \ldots, N$, where each index is expressed in binary as $\sigma_1, \ldots, \sigma_n$, then the $j-$th layer and the $2 \log N - j$-th layer contain 2-element permutations, each acting on elements number $\sigma_1 \ldots \sigma_{j-1} 0 \sigma_{j+1}, \ldots \sigma_n$ and $\sigma_1 \ldots \sigma_{j-1} 1 \sigma_{j+1}, \ldots \sigma_n$, for all $\sigma_1, \ldots \sigma_{j-1}, \sigma_{j+1}, \ldots, \sigma_n \in \{0, 1\}^{n-1}$.

Now we describe our decomposition of π into $\pi_1 \circ \ldots \circ \pi_d$. For any parameter $T = 2^t$, $t \in \mathbb{N}$, set $d = 2\lceil \frac{n}{t} \rceil - 1$, and consider Benes network for π. We set π_1 to consist of first t layers $1, \ldots, t$ of this network, π_2 to consist of next t layers $t+1, \ldots, 2t$, and so on, except for the middle permutation $\pi_{\lfloor \frac{d}{2} \rfloor + 1}$ which consists of $2t - 1$ layers in the middle[8]. That is, we set each π_i, for $i = 1, \ldots, \lfloor \frac{d}{2} \rfloor$, to consist of t consecutive layers number $i \cdot t - (t-1), \ldots, i \cdot t - 1, i \cdot t$, and π_i for $i = \lfloor \frac{d}{2} \rfloor + 2, \ldots, d$ are defined symmetrically. From the description of Benes layers above, it follows that these t consecutive layers do not permute all N elements together, but instead only permute elements within each group of the form $\sigma_1, \ldots, \sigma_{i(t-1)} x \sigma_{i \cdot t+1}, \ldots, \sigma_n$, where x includes all t-bit strings, and the remaining $n - t$ bits $\sigma_1, \ldots, \sigma_{i(t-1)}, \sigma_{i \cdot t+1}, \ldots, \sigma_n$ are fixed. Therefore it follows that each π_i, $i \neq \lfloor \frac{d}{2} \rfloor + 1$, consists of $2^{n-t} = N/T$ disjoint permutations, each acting on $2^t = T$ elements. Similarly, the middle permutation $\pi_{\lfloor \frac{d}{2} \rfloor + 1}$, consisting of $2t - 1$ layers in the middle of the network, only permutes elements within each group of the form $\sigma_1, \ldots, \sigma_{n-t} x$, and thus can also be represented as a combination of N/T disjoint permutations each acting on T elements.

Finally, note that the total number of permutations is $\lceil \frac{(2n-1)-(2t-1)}{t} \rceil + 1 = 2\lceil \frac{n}{t} \rceil - 1$. Therefore, $\pi = \pi_1 \circ \ldots \circ \pi_d$ is indeed a (T, d)-subpermutation representation of π, for $d = 2\lceil \frac{n}{t} \rceil - 1$.

6 Permute and Share and Secret-Shared Shuffle

Recall that we use $\pi(\boldsymbol{x})$ for a permutation π and vector $\boldsymbol{x}$ to mean the permutation which produces $x_{\pi(1)}, \ldots, x_{\pi(N)}$.

We will use the Share Translation scheme we presented in the previous scheme to construct first a secure computation for permuting and secret sharing elements where one party chooses the permutation and the other the elements, and then a construction for a full secret-shared shuffle.

6.1 Definitions

We consider the following functionality, which we call Permute+Share, in which one party provides as input a permutation π, and the other party provides as input a set of elements $\boldsymbol{x}$ in group $\mathbb{G}$, and the output is secret shares of the permuted elements:

$$\mathcal{F}_{\mathsf{Permute+Share}[N,\ell]}(\pi, \boldsymbol{x}) = (\boldsymbol{r}, \pi(\boldsymbol{x}) - \boldsymbol{r}), \text{ where } \boldsymbol{r} \leftarrow^{\$} \mathbb{G}^N.$$

We can also consider the equivalent functionality when the permutation or the initial database is secret shared as input. (Here we consider a secret sharing of permutation π which consists of two permutations π_0, π_1 such that $\pi = \pi_0 \circ \pi_1$.)

[8] For a more general case, when $\log T$ doesn't divide $\log N$, there are $2n - 1 - t(d-1)$ layers in the middle.

Finally, we define the secret shared shuffle functionality:

$$\mathcal{F}_{\mathsf{SecretSharedShuffle}[N,\ell]}(\boldsymbol{x}_0, \boldsymbol{x}_1) = (\boldsymbol{r}, \pi(\boldsymbol{x}_0 + \boldsymbol{x}_1) - \boldsymbol{r}),$$

where $\boldsymbol{r} \leftarrow^{\$} \mathbb{G}^N$ and π is a random permutation over N elements.

6.2 Permute + Share from Share Translation

Let $\mathsf{ShareTrans}_T$ be a protocol satisfying the definition in Sect. 4 for permutations on T elements in group $\mathbb{G}$, where each element can be represented in ℓ bits. Let T, d be some parameters such that any permutation in S_N has $(T, d)-$subpermutation representation (e.g. $d = 2\lceil \frac{\log N}{\log T} \rceil - 1$ for any $T = 2^t$, as described in Sect. 5). We construct our permute and share protocol $\mathsf{Permute} + \mathsf{Share}$ using $(T, d)-$subpermutation representation as follows.

1. P_0 computes the (T, d)-subpermutation representation $\pi_1, \ldots, \pi_d$ of its input π.
2. For each layer i, the parties run N/T instances of $\mathsf{ShareTrans}_T$, with P_0 providing as input the N/T permutations making up π_i. (Note that all of these instances and layers can be run in parallel.) For each i, P_1 obtains $\boldsymbol{a}^{(i,1)}, \ldots, \boldsymbol{a}^{(i,N/T)}$ and $\boldsymbol{b}^{(i,1)}, \ldots, \boldsymbol{b}^{(i,N/T)}$. Call the combined vectors $\boldsymbol{a}^{(i)}$ and $\boldsymbol{b}^{(i)}$. Similarly, P_0 obtains $\boldsymbol{\Delta}^{(i,1)}, \ldots, \boldsymbol{\Delta}^{(i,N/T)}$, which we will call $\Delta^{(i)}$.
3. For each $i \in 1, \ldots, d-1$, P_1 computes $\boldsymbol{\delta}^{(i)} = \boldsymbol{a}^{(i+1)} - \boldsymbol{b}^{(i)}$ and sends it to P_0. P_1 also sends $\boldsymbol{m} = \boldsymbol{x} + \boldsymbol{a}^{(1)}$, and samples and sends random $\boldsymbol{w}$. P_1 outputs $\boldsymbol{b} = \boldsymbol{w} - \boldsymbol{b}^{(d)}$
4. P_0 computes $\boldsymbol{\Delta} = \boldsymbol{\Delta}^{(d)} + \pi_d(\boldsymbol{\delta}^{(d-1)} + \boldsymbol{\Delta}^{(d-1)} + \pi_{d-1}(\boldsymbol{\delta}^{(d-2)} + \boldsymbol{\Delta}^{(d-2)} + \ldots. + \pi_2(\boldsymbol{\delta}^{(1)} + \boldsymbol{\Delta}^{(1)})$ and outputs $\pi(\boldsymbol{m}) + \boldsymbol{\Delta} - \boldsymbol{w}$.

Theorem 4. *Let N and ℓ be the number of elements in the database and the size of each element, respectively, and let T, d be arbitrary parameters such that any permutation in S_N has $(T, d)-$subpermutation representation. Then the construction described above is a* Permute+Share *protocol secure against static semi-honest corruptions with the following efficiency:*

- *The communication cost is $(d+1)N\ell$ bits together with the cost of dN/T* Share Translation *protocols on T elements each, run in parallel,*
- *The computation cost is equal to the cost of dN/T* Share Translation *protocols on T elements each, run in parallel.*[9]

Correctness. By correctness of $\mathsf{ShareTrans}_T$, for all i $\boldsymbol{\Delta}^{(i)} = \boldsymbol{b}^{(i)} - \pi_i(\boldsymbol{a}^{(i)})$. This means that for all i, $\boldsymbol{\delta}^{(i)} + \boldsymbol{\Delta}^{(i)} = \boldsymbol{a}^{(i+1)} - \boldsymbol{b}^{(i)} + \boldsymbol{b}^{(i)} - \pi_i(\boldsymbol{a}^{(i)}) = \boldsymbol{a}^{(i+1)} - \pi_i(\boldsymbol{a}^{(i)})$.

[9] We give a concrete cost analysis on Sect. 7.

Thus, the final $\boldsymbol{\Delta}$ produced by P_0 is

$$
\begin{aligned}
&\boldsymbol{\Delta}^{(d)} + \pi_d(\boldsymbol{\delta}^{(d-1)} + \boldsymbol{\Delta}^{(d-1)} + \pi_{d-1}(\boldsymbol{\delta}^{(d-2)} + \boldsymbol{\Delta}^{(d-2)} + \ldots + \pi_2(\boldsymbol{\delta}^{(1)} + \boldsymbol{\Delta}^{(1)}) \\
=&\boldsymbol{\Delta}^{(d)} + \pi_d(\boldsymbol{a}^{(d)} - \pi_{d-1}(\boldsymbol{a}^{(d-1)}) + \pi_{d-1}(\boldsymbol{a}^{(d-1)} - \pi_{d-2}(\boldsymbol{a}^{(d-2)}) + \ldots + \pi_2(\boldsymbol{a}^{(2)} - \pi_1\boldsymbol{a}^{(1)}))) \\
=&\boldsymbol{\Delta}^{(d)} + \pi_d(\boldsymbol{a}^{(d)} - \pi_{d-1}(\ldots \pi_2(\pi_1\boldsymbol{a}^{(1)}))) \\
=&\boldsymbol{b}^{(d)} - \pi_d(\boldsymbol{a}^{(d)}) + \pi_d(\boldsymbol{a}^{(d)} - \pi_{d-1}(\ldots \pi_2(\pi_1\boldsymbol{a}^{(1)}))) \\
=&\boldsymbol{b}^{(d)} - \pi_d(\pi_{d-1}(\ldots \pi_2(\pi_1(\boldsymbol{a}^{(1)})))) \\
=&\boldsymbol{b}^{(d)} - \pi(\boldsymbol{a}^{(1)})
\end{aligned}
$$

The output for P_0, P_1 is:

$$
\begin{aligned}
&\pi(\boldsymbol{m}) + \boldsymbol{\Delta} - \boldsymbol{w}, &&\boldsymbol{w} - \boldsymbol{b}^{(d)} \\
=&\pi(\boldsymbol{x} + \boldsymbol{a}^{(1)}) + \boldsymbol{\Delta} - \boldsymbol{w}, &&\boldsymbol{w} - (\boldsymbol{\Delta} + \pi(\boldsymbol{a}^{(1)})) \\
=&\pi(\boldsymbol{x}) + \pi(\boldsymbol{a}^{1}) + \boldsymbol{\Delta} - \boldsymbol{w}, &&-\boldsymbol{\Delta} - \pi(\boldsymbol{a}^{(1)}) + \boldsymbol{w}
\end{aligned}
$$

If we let $\boldsymbol{r} = \pi(\boldsymbol{x}) + \pi(\boldsymbol{a}^{(1)}) + \boldsymbol{\Delta} - \boldsymbol{w}$, we see that this has the correct distribution.

Security. Our simulator behaves as follows: If $b = 0$ (i.e. P_0 is corrupt): $\mathsf{sim}(1^\lambda, 0, \pi, \boldsymbol{y}_0)$ will first generate the subpermutations for π as described above, and then internally run all of the $\mathsf{ShareTrans}_T$ protocols to obtain simulated view for P_0 and $\boldsymbol{a}^{(1)}, \ldots, \boldsymbol{a}^{(d)}, \boldsymbol{b}^{(1)}, \ldots, \boldsymbol{b}^{(d)}$. Let $\boldsymbol{\Delta}^{(1)}, \ldots, \boldsymbol{\Delta}^{(d)}$ be the corresponding values computed by P_0 in these protocols. Choose random $\boldsymbol{\delta}^{(1)}, \ldots, \boldsymbol{\delta}^{(d-1)}$. It then computes $\boldsymbol{\Delta}$ as in step 4 of the protocol and sets $\boldsymbol{w} = -\boldsymbol{y}_0 + \pi(\boldsymbol{m}) + \boldsymbol{\Delta}$. It outputs the views from the $\mathsf{ShareTrans}_T$ protocols and the messages $\boldsymbol{m}, \boldsymbol{w}, \boldsymbol{\delta}^{(1)}, \ldots, \boldsymbol{\delta}^{(d)}$.

If $b = 1$ (i.e. P_1 is corrupt): $\mathsf{sim}(1^\lambda, 1, \boldsymbol{x}, \boldsymbol{y}_1)$ will pick random π', compute the subpermutations, internally run the $\mathsf{ShareTrans}_T$ protocols with these permutations to obtain the views for P_1, and compute $\boldsymbol{b}^{(d)}$ from these runs as in the real protocol. It will set the random tape $\boldsymbol{w} = \boldsymbol{y}_1 + \boldsymbol{b}^{(d)}$. It outputs the view from the $\mathsf{ShareTrans}_T$ protocols and the random tape $\boldsymbol{w}$.

We show that this simulator produces an ideal experiment that is indistinguishable from the real experiment. We start with the case where $b = 0$ and show this through a series of games:

Real Game: Runs the real experiment. The output is P_0's view (its input, the view_0s from the Share Translation protocols and the messages $\boldsymbol{m}$, $\boldsymbol{w}$, and $\boldsymbol{\delta}^{(1)}, \ldots, \boldsymbol{\delta}^{(d-1)}$ it receives), and the honest P_1's input $\boldsymbol{x}$ and output $\boldsymbol{w} - \boldsymbol{b}$.

Game 1: As in the previous game except in step 2, compute $\boldsymbol{\Delta}^{(i)}$ as $\boldsymbol{b}^{(i)} - \pi_i(\boldsymbol{a}^{(i)}$ instead of through the $\mathsf{ShareTrans}_T$ protocols. This is identical by correctness of Share Translation .

Game 2: As in the previous game except after step 2 for each i we sample random $\boldsymbol{a}'^{(i)}$ and compute $\boldsymbol{b}'^{(i)} = \pi_i(\boldsymbol{a}'^{(i)}) + \boldsymbol{\Delta}^{(i)}$, and then use these values in place of $\boldsymbol{a}^{(i)}, \boldsymbol{b}^{(i)}$ in steps 3 and 4.

We can show that this is indistinguishable via a series of hybrids, where in hybrid H_i, we use $\boldsymbol{a}'^{(j)}, \boldsymbol{b}'^{(j)}$ for the output of the first i $\mathsf{ShareTrans}_T$ protocols and $\boldsymbol{a}^{(j)}, \boldsymbol{b}^{(j)}$ for the rest. Then H_i, H_{i+1} are indistinguishable by the share hiding property of $\mathsf{ShareTrans}_T$.

Game 3: As above, but choose random $\boldsymbol{m}, \boldsymbol{\delta}^{(1)}, \ldots, \boldsymbol{\delta}^{(d-1)}$. Set $\boldsymbol{a}'^{(1)} = \boldsymbol{m} - \boldsymbol{x}$. For $i = 1 \ldots d$, compute $\boldsymbol{b}'^{(i)} = \pi_i(\boldsymbol{a}'^{(i)}) + \boldsymbol{\Delta}^{(i)}$ as above, and then set $\boldsymbol{a}'^{(i+1)} = \boldsymbol{\delta}^{(i)} - \boldsymbol{b}^{(i)}$. Note that this is distributed identically to Game 2.

Game Simulated: The only difference between the simulated game and Game 3 is that in Game 3, $\boldsymbol{w}$ is chosen at random, and P_1's output is computed as $\boldsymbol{w} - \boldsymbol{b}'^{(d)}$, while in Game Simulated, P_1's output is random $\boldsymbol{r}$ and $\boldsymbol{w}$ is set to $-\boldsymbol{y}_0 + \pi(\boldsymbol{m}) + \boldsymbol{\Delta} = -(\pi(\boldsymbol{x}) - \boldsymbol{r}) + \pi(\boldsymbol{m}) + \boldsymbol{\Delta} = \pi(\boldsymbol{a}'^{(1)}) + \boldsymbol{r} + \boldsymbol{\Delta} = \boldsymbol{b}'^{(d)} + \boldsymbol{r}$ by construction of $\boldsymbol{\Delta}$. Thus, the two games are identical.

We argue the case when $b = 1$ as follows:

Real Game: Runs the real experiment. The output is P_1's view (it's input $\boldsymbol{x}$, view_1 from the Share Translation protocol and the random string $\boldsymbol{w}$ it chooses) and the honest P_0's input π and output $\pi(\boldsymbol{m}) + \boldsymbol{\Delta} - \boldsymbol{w}$ where $\boldsymbol{\Delta}$ is as computed in step 4 of the protocol.

Game 1: As in the previous game, but P_0's output is $\pi(x) + \boldsymbol{b}^{(d)} - \boldsymbol{w}$. Note that $\pi(x) + \boldsymbol{b}^{(d)} - \boldsymbol{w} = \pi(\boldsymbol{x} + \boldsymbol{a}^{(1)}) + \boldsymbol{b}^{(d)} - \pi(\boldsymbol{a}^{(1)}) - \boldsymbol{w} = \pi(\boldsymbol{m}) + \boldsymbol{\Delta} - \boldsymbol{w}$ where $\boldsymbol{a}^{(1)}, \boldsymbol{b}^{(d)}$ are the values P_1 obtains from the first and last layer $\mathsf{ShareTrans}_t$ protocols.

Game 2: As in the previous game except run the $\mathsf{ShareTrans}_T$ protocols with $\pi'_1, \ldots, \pi'_d$ derived from a random permutation π'.
We can show that this is indistinguishable via a series of hybrids, where in hybrid H_i, we use the subpermutations derived from π' for the first i protocols, and the subpermutations derived from π for the rest. Then H_i, H_{i+1} are indistinguishable by the permutation hiding property of $\mathsf{ShareTrans}_T$.

Game Simulated: As in the previous game except choose random $\boldsymbol{r}$ and set $\boldsymbol{w} = \pi(\boldsymbol{x}) - \boldsymbol{r} + \boldsymbol{b}^{(d)}$. *This is identically distributed to Game 1 and identical to the ideal experiment.*

6.3 Secret Shared Shuffle from Permute+Share

The Secret Shared Shuffle protocol proceeds as follows:

0. P_0 and P_1 each choose a random permutation $\pi_0, \pi_1 \leftarrow S_N$.
1. P_0 and P_1 run the Permute+Share protocol to apply π_0 to $\boldsymbol{x}_1$, resulting in shares $\boldsymbol{x}_0^{(1)}$ for P_0 and $\boldsymbol{x}_1^{(1)}$ for P_1.
2. P_0 computes $\boldsymbol{x}_0^{(2)} = \pi_0(\boldsymbol{x}_0) + \boldsymbol{x}_0^{(1)}$.
3. P_1 and P_0 run the Permute + Share protocol to apply π_1 to $\boldsymbol{x}_0^{(2)}$, resulting in shares $\boldsymbol{x}_1^{(3)}$ for P_1 and $\boldsymbol{x}_0^{(3)}$ for P_0.
4. P_1 computes $\boldsymbol{x}_1^{(4)} = \pi_1(\boldsymbol{x}_1^{(1)}) + \boldsymbol{x}_1^{(3)}$.
5. P_0 outputs $\boldsymbol{x}_0^{(3)}$ and P_1 outputs $\boldsymbol{x}_1^{(4)}$.

Theorem 5. *The construction above is a* Secret Shared Shuffle *protocol secure against static semi-honest corruptions. It's communication and computation cost is that of invokes 2 sequential* Permute+Share*'s. (See footnote 9).*

Correctness. The output for P_0, P_1 is:

$$\begin{aligned} & \boldsymbol{x}_0^{(3)}, && \boldsymbol{x}_1^{(4)} \\ =& \boldsymbol{x}_0^{(3)}, && \pi_1(\boldsymbol{x}_1^{(1)}) + \boldsymbol{x}_1^{(3)} \\ =& \pi_1(\boldsymbol{x}_0^{(2)}) - \boldsymbol{r}^{(3)}, && \pi_1(\boldsymbol{x}_1^{(1)}) + \boldsymbol{r}^{(3)} \\ =& \pi_1(\pi_0(\boldsymbol{x}_0) + \boldsymbol{x}_0^{(1)}) - \boldsymbol{r}^{(3)}, && \pi_1(\boldsymbol{x}_1^{(1)}) + \boldsymbol{r}^{(3)} \\ =& \pi_1(\pi_0(\boldsymbol{x}_0) + \boldsymbol{r}^{(1)}) - \boldsymbol{r}^{(3)}, && \pi_1(\pi_0(\boldsymbol{x}_1) - \boldsymbol{r}^{(1)}) + \boldsymbol{r}^{(3)} \\ =& \pi_1(\pi_0(\boldsymbol{x}_0)) + \pi_1(\boldsymbol{r}^{(1)}) - \boldsymbol{r}^{(3)}, && \pi_1(\pi_0(\boldsymbol{x}_1)) - (\pi_1(\boldsymbol{r}^{(1)}) - \boldsymbol{r}^{(3)}) \end{aligned}$$

Where $\boldsymbol{r}^{(1)}$ and $\boldsymbol{r}^{(3)}$ are the values generated by the first and second invocations of Permute+Share. If we let $\boldsymbol{r} = \pi_1(\pi_0(\boldsymbol{x}_0)) + \pi_1(\boldsymbol{r}^{(1)}) - \boldsymbol{r}^{(3)}$ and $\pi = \pi_1 \circ \pi_0$ we see that this has the correct distribution.

Security. Our simulator behaves as follows:

If $b = 0$ (i.e. P_0 is corrupt): $\mathsf{sim}(1^\lambda, 0, \boldsymbol{x}_0, \boldsymbol{y}_0)$ will choose random $\pi_0, \boldsymbol{x}_0^{(1)}$, set $\boldsymbol{x}_0^{(2)} = \pi_0(\boldsymbol{x}_0) + \boldsymbol{x}_0^{(1)}$, simulate the view from the first Permute+Share with $\mathsf{sim}^{\mathsf{Permute+Share}}(1^\lambda, 0, \pi_0, \boldsymbol{x}_0^{(1)})$, and simulate the view from the second Permute+Share with $\mathsf{sim}^{\mathsf{Permute+Share}}(1^\lambda, 1, \boldsymbol{x}_0^{(2)}, \boldsymbol{y}_0)$.

If $b = 1$ (i.e. P_1 is corrupt): $\mathsf{sim}(1^\lambda, 1, \boldsymbol{x}_1, \boldsymbol{y}_1)$ will choose random $\pi_1, \boldsymbol{x}_1^{(1)}$, set $\boldsymbol{x}_1^{(3)} = \boldsymbol{y}_1 - \pi_1(\boldsymbol{x}_1^{(1)})$, simulate the view from the first Permute+Share with $\mathsf{sim}^{\mathsf{Permute+Share}}(1^\lambda, 1, \boldsymbol{x}_1, \boldsymbol{x}_1^{(1)})$, and simulate the view from the second Permute+Share with $\mathsf{sim}^{\mathsf{Permute+Share}}(1^\lambda, 0, \pi_1, \boldsymbol{x}_1^{(3)})$.

We show that this simulator produces an ideal experiment that is indistinguishable from the real experiment. We start with the case where $b = 0$ and show this through a series of games:

Real Game: Runs the real experiment.
The output is P_0's view (its input $\boldsymbol{x}_0$, $\mathsf{view}_0^{(1)}$, $\mathsf{view}_0^{(2)}$ from the two Permute+Share protocols including the outputs $\boldsymbol{x}_0^{(1)}, \boldsymbol{x}_0^{(3)}$, and the honest P_1's input $\boldsymbol{x}_1$ and output $\boldsymbol{x}_1^{(4)} = \pi_1(\boldsymbol{x}_1^{(1)}) + \boldsymbol{x}_1^{(3)}$.

Game 1: In step 1, first compute $\mathcal{F}_{\mathsf{Permute+Share}}(\pi_0, \boldsymbol{x}_1)$, i.e. choose random $\boldsymbol{r}^{(1)}$, and set $\boldsymbol{x}_0^{(1)} = \boldsymbol{r}^{(1)}$ and $\boldsymbol{x}_1^{(1)} = \pi_0(\boldsymbol{x}_1) - \boldsymbol{r}^{(1)}$. Then run the Permute+Share simulator to generate the view $\mathsf{view}_0^{(1)'}$ for the first Permute+Share.
The output is P_0's view (its input $\boldsymbol{x}_0$, $\mathsf{view}_0^{(1)'}$, $\mathsf{view}_0^{(2)}$ from the two Permute+Share protocols including its outputs from those protocols $\boldsymbol{x}_0^{(1)} = \boldsymbol{r}^{(1)}$ and $\boldsymbol{x}_0^{(3)}$), and the honest P_1's input $\boldsymbol{x}_1$ and output $\boldsymbol{x}_1^{(4)} = \pi_1(\boldsymbol{x}_1^{(1)}) + \boldsymbol{x}_1^{(3)} = \pi_1(\pi_0(\boldsymbol{x}_1) - \boldsymbol{r}^{(1)}) + \boldsymbol{x}_1^{(3)}$.
This is indistinguishable by security of the Permute+Share*protocol.*

Game 2: In step 3, first compute $\mathcal{F}_{\mathsf{Permute+Share}}(\pi_1, \boldsymbol{x}_0^{(2)})$, i.e. choose random $\boldsymbol{r}^{(3)}$ and set $\boldsymbol{x}_1^{(3)} = \boldsymbol{r}^{(3)}$ and $\boldsymbol{x}_0^{(3)} = \pi_1(\boldsymbol{x}_0^{(2)}) - \boldsymbol{r}^{(3)}$. Then run the Permute+Share simulator to generate the view $\mathsf{view}_0^{(2)'}$ for the second Permute+Share.
The output is P_0's view (its input $\boldsymbol{x}_0$, $\mathsf{view}_0^{(1)'}, \mathsf{view}_0^{(2)'}$ from the two Permute+Share protocols including its outputs from those protocols $\boldsymbol{x}_0^{(1)} = \boldsymbol{r}^{(1)}$ and $\boldsymbol{x}_0^{(3)} = \pi_1(\boldsymbol{x}_0^{(2)}) - \boldsymbol{r}^{(3)}$), and the honest P_1's input $\boldsymbol{x}_1$ and output $\boldsymbol{x}_1^{(4)} = \pi_1(\pi_0(\boldsymbol{x}_1) - \boldsymbol{r}^{(1)}) + \boldsymbol{x}_1^{(3)} = \pi_1(\pi_0(\boldsymbol{x}_1) - \boldsymbol{r}^{(1)}) + \boldsymbol{r}^{(3)}$.
This is again indistinguishable by security of the Permute+Share *protocol.*

Game 3: Choose random $\pi, \boldsymbol{r}, \boldsymbol{x}_0^{(1)}$. Set $\pi_1 = \pi \circ \pi_0^{-1}$, $\boldsymbol{r}^{(1)} = \boldsymbol{x}_0^{(1)}$ and $\boldsymbol{r}^{(3)} = \pi_1(\pi_0(\boldsymbol{x}_0)) + \pi_1(\boldsymbol{r}^{(1)}) - \boldsymbol{r}$. Other than that, proceed as in Game 2.
The output is P_0's view (its input $\boldsymbol{x}_0$, $\mathsf{view}_0^{(1)'}, \mathsf{view}_0^{(2)'}$ from the two Permute+Share protocols including its outputs from those protocols $\boldsymbol{x}_0^{(1)} = \boldsymbol{r}^{(1)}$ and $\boldsymbol{x}_0^{(3)}$), and the honest P_1's input $\boldsymbol{x}_1$ and output $\boldsymbol{x}^{(4)}$).
This is identically distributed to Game 2. P_1's *output in this game is*

$$\begin{aligned}
\boldsymbol{x}_1^{(4)} &= \pi_1(\boldsymbol{x}_1^{(1)}) + \boldsymbol{x}_1^{(3)} \\
&= \pi_1(\boldsymbol{x}_1^{(1)}) + \pi_1(\boldsymbol{x}_0^{(2)}) - \boldsymbol{x}_0^{(3)} \\
&= \pi_1(\boldsymbol{x}_1^{(1)}) + \pi_1(\pi_0(\boldsymbol{x}_0) + \boldsymbol{x}_0^{(1)}) - \boldsymbol{x}_0^{(3)} \\
&= \pi_1(\pi_0(\boldsymbol{x}_1) - \boldsymbol{x}_0^{(1)}) + \pi_1(\pi_0(\boldsymbol{x}_0) + \boldsymbol{x}_0^{(1)}) - \boldsymbol{x}_0^{(3)} \\
&= \pi_1(\pi_0(\boldsymbol{x}_1 + \boldsymbol{x}_0)) - \boldsymbol{x}_0^{(3)} \\
&= \pi(\boldsymbol{x}_1 + \boldsymbol{x}_0) - \boldsymbol{x}_0^{(3)}
\end{aligned}$$

Thus, this is identical to the ideal experiment.

Next, we turn to the case where $b = 1$.

Real Game: Runs the real experiment

Game 1: In step 1, first compute $\mathcal{F}_{\mathsf{Permute+Share}}(\pi_0, \boldsymbol{x}_1)$, i.e. choose random $\boldsymbol{x}_0^{(1)}$, and then compute $\boldsymbol{x}_1^{(1)} = \pi_0(\boldsymbol{x}_1) - \boldsymbol{x}_0^{(1)}$. Then run the Permute+Share simulator to generate the view for the first Permute+Share. *This is indistinguishable by security of the* Permute+Share *protocol.*

Game 2: In step 3, first compute $\mathcal{F}_{\mathsf{Permute+Share}}(\pi_1, \boldsymbol{x}_0^{(2)})$, i.e. choose random $\boldsymbol{x}_1^{(3)}$, and then compute $\boldsymbol{x}_0^{(3)} = \pi_1(\boldsymbol{x}_0^{(2)}) - \boldsymbol{x}_1^{(3)}$. Then run the Permute+Share simulator to generate the view for the second Permute+Share. *This is again indistinguishable by security of the* Permute+Share *protocol.*

Game 3: Choose random $\boldsymbol{x}_0^{(3)}$. Set $\boldsymbol{x}_1^{(3)} = \pi_1(\boldsymbol{x}_0^{(2)}) - \boldsymbol{x}_0^{(3)}$. Other than that, proceed as in Game 2. *This is identically distributed to Game 2.*

Game 4: Choose random π, set $\pi_0 = \pi_1^{-1} \circ \pi$ and set $\boldsymbol{x}_1^{(3)} = \pi(\boldsymbol{x}_0 + \boldsymbol{x}_1) - \pi_1(\boldsymbol{x}_1^{(1)}) - \boldsymbol{x}_0^{(3)}$. *Note that this means* $\boldsymbol{x}_1^{(4)} = \pi(\boldsymbol{x}_0 + \boldsymbol{x}_1) - \boldsymbol{x}_0^{(3)}$ *so this is distributed identically to the ideal experiment. Note also that this is distributed identically to Game 3, because:*

$$\begin{aligned}\pi_1(\boldsymbol{x}_0^{(2)}) - \boldsymbol{x}_0^{(3)} \\ &= \pi_1(\pi_0(\boldsymbol{x}_0) + \boldsymbol{x}_0^{(1)}) - \boldsymbol{x}_0^{(3)} \\ &= \pi_1(\pi_0(\boldsymbol{x}_0) + \pi_0(\boldsymbol{x}_1) - \boldsymbol{x}_1^{(1)}) - \boldsymbol{x}_0^{(3)} \\ &= \pi_1(\pi_0(\boldsymbol{x}_0 + \boldsymbol{x}_1)) - \pi_1(\boldsymbol{x}_1^{(1)}) - \boldsymbol{x}_0^{(3)} \\ &= \pi(\boldsymbol{x}_0 + \boldsymbol{x}_1) - \pi_1(\boldsymbol{x}_1^{(1)}) - \boldsymbol{x}_0^{(3)}\end{aligned}$$

7 Experimental Evaluation

In this section, we compare the solution for our Permute + Share with public key based solution and with the best previous permutation network based solution [22]. We consider Permute + Share where party P_0 starts with a permutation π and party P_1 starts with a input vector $\boldsymbol{x}$ of N strings in $\{0,1\}^\ell$.

We take a microbenchmarking approach to estimating the cost of the two protocols, where we first empirically estimate the cost of the individual operations (AES computations or RSA group operations), and then use that number to estimate the cost of the full protocol, by plugging the time of individual operations into the formula for execution time of the protocol. For example, for our protocol and the protocol of [22], both of which are dominated by AES operations, we estimate the cost as follows:

1. We compute the computation cost in terms of number of AES calls.
2. We empirically estimate the cost for a computing fixed key AES (per 128-bit block).
3. We compute the communication cost in bits.
4. Then we compute the time to communicate the calculated number of bits using various networks (bandwidth 72 Mbps, 100 Mbps and 1 Gbps).
5. The total time reported is number of AES calls × the cost of a single AES + the size of communication/sbandwidth.

In the following we will describe our cost estimates in more detail and then present a detailed comparison. First we discuss some specifics on how we implement AES and how we analyze the cost of OT, then we present formulas for the number of basic operations required for each solution, then we describe how we estimate the cost of these operations, and finally we present the detailed efficiency comparison.

7.1 More Detail on Cost of OT and AES

Fixed key Block Ciphers. The symmetric key based protocols (ours and the one described in [22]) rely on two fundamental building blocks, namely, Oblivious Transfer extension (OTe) [16] and GGM PRG [10]. Typically, published OTe protocols are based on a hash function that is modeled as a random oracle.

However, in most of the recent implementations, the hash function is instantiated, somewhat haphazardly, using fixed key block ciphers (AES). In a recent work [13], the authors provided a principled way of implementing [16] using fixed key AES and formally proved that it is secure. The authors also propose that the length doubling PRG used in GGM [10] can be implemented using fixed key AES for better efficiency, though they do not prove it. Here, we first prove that it is safe to use this optimized PRG construction [13], and then use it in our experiments. In our experiments, we will also use the fixed-key AES-based length extension technique for stretching short messages into longer ones (both for OTe and for OPV message length extension) described in Section 6.1 in [13].

The optimized PRG construction is based on correlation-robust hash (CRH) function [13,16]. Roughly, H is said to be correlation-robust if the keyed function $f_R(x) = H(x \oplus R)$ is pseudorandom, as long as R is sufficiently random. Given a CRH H, the length doubling PRG is constructed as follows: $\mathsf{G}(x) = H(1 \oplus x) \circ H(2 \oplus x)$. We give more details in the full version.

In our experiments, we will use the following concrete instantiation of CRH [13]: $H(x) = \pi(x) \oplus x$ where $\pi(.)$ is a fixed key block cipher, e.g. AES.

OT Extension Costs. The computation in OT extension consists of $O(m\ell)$ bit-wise operations (ANDs an XORs), running λ public key OTs, and $O(m + m\ell/\lambda)$ AES operations as discussed above. This means that for sufficiently large m, like those we consider, the cost is dominated by the AES operations, as can be verified empirically using any standard OT library. For example, we benchmark Naor-Pinkas base OT (dubbed NPOT) using [27] and the average time to run 128 base OTs is 13 ms. As a result, we can focus our analysis of computational costs on the AES operations.

In our experiments, we simulate the cost of OT-extension as follows. The cost is reported in number of fixed-key AES calls for sender and receiver and communication is reported in number of bits. For random OT's on strings of length $\ell > \lambda = 128$ bits, we use IKNP OT-extension protocol with fixed-key AES optimization [13]. The cost of m Random OTs on messages of length ℓ bits is shown in Table 1, where the terms $2m\ell/\lambda$ for sender and $m\ell/\lambda$ for receiver are for extending the random messages from λ to ℓ bits. We denote this functionality as ROT_ℓ^m. For $\ell = \lambda$, no message length extension is required (both for ROT and SOT). Fixed message OT's or standard OTs (SOT) are obtained from ROT by using the ROT messages as one-time pads for the actual messages. So SOT_ℓ^m adds an additional $2m\ell$ bits of communication over ROT_ℓ^m, i.e., the communication cost of SOT_ℓ^m is $m(\lambda + 2\ell)$ bits. There is no additional computation overhead (except some additional XORs, which we ignore).

Table 1. The computation and communication cost for variants of OT extension.

OT	Sender	Receiver	Communication (bits)
$\mathsf{ROT}_{\lambda}^{m}$	$3m$	$3m$	$m\lambda$
ROT_{ℓ}^{m}	$3m + 2m\ell/\lambda$	$3m + m\ell/\lambda$	$m\lambda$
SOT_{ℓ}^{m}	$3m + 2m\ell/\lambda$	$3m + m\ell/\lambda$	$m(\lambda + 2\ell)$
$\mathsf{SOT}_{\lambda}^{m}$	$3m$	$3m$	$3m\lambda$

7.2 Analyzing the Cost of Each Solution

As discussed above, in the following estimates we only count computation time of AES, not base OTs or XORs, since the latter are fairly small.

Let N be the number of elements in the database, ℓ be the length of each element, λ be the security parameter, and T be the size of subpermutations. Let $d = 2\lceil \log N / \log T \rceil - 1$.

Our Protocol: The compute cost of our $\mathsf{Permute} + \mathsf{Share}$ protocol is the compute cost of dN/T $\mathsf{ShareTrans}_T$'s, where $d = 2\lceil \log N / \log T \rceil - 1$. The communication includes the cost of dN/T $\mathsf{ShareTrans}_T$'s $+ (d+1)N\ell$ bits.

Each $\mathsf{ShareTrans}_T$ protocol requires $\mathsf{SOT}_{\lambda}^{T \log T}$ and $T^2(2 + \ell/\lambda)$ local fixed key AES calls (for both parties) which includes PRG calls in the GGM tree and message length extension and for the underlying OPV protocol. There is no additional communication over the cost of $\mathsf{SOT}_{\lambda}^{T \log T}$.

Computation Cost. The number of AES calls (for each of sender and receiver) is the following:

$$3dN \log T + dNT(2 + \ell/\lambda)$$

Communication Cost. Communication in number of bits is the following:

$$3dN\lambda \log T + (d+1)N\ell$$

Protocol from [22]: This $\mathsf{Permute} + \mathsf{Share}$ requires $\mathsf{SOT}_{2\ell}^{N \log N - N/2}$ and has an additional $2N\ell$ bits communication overhead.

So, the total computation and computation costs are the following:

Computation Cost: Number of AES calls for receiver (receiver is slightly more efficient than sender) in the protocol of [22] is the following:

$$3(N \log N - N/2) + 2(\ell/\lambda)(N \log N - N/2)$$

Communication Cost: Communication in number of bits in the protocol of [22] is the following:

$$(N \log N - N/2)(\lambda + 4\ell) + 2\,N\ell$$

Paillier Based Solution. In the full version we describe a solution based on additively homomorphic encryption in which P_1 encrypts his data and sends it to P_0, who permutes the ciphertexts, randomizes them, and adds a random share to each before returning them to P_0; P_0 outputs the decryptions and P_1 outputs the random shares he added.

In this protocol, since every element of $\boldsymbol{x}$ has to be encrypted and the encryption message space in defined to be $\mathbb{Z}_n$, each element has to be broken into blocks of size n. This means that P_0 computes $N * \lceil \ell/n \rceil$ encryptions and P_1 computes $N * \lceil \ell/n \rceil$ ciphertext randomizations and ciphertext-plaintext multiplications. The communication for this protocol is $N * \lceil \ell/n \rceil * 2n$ bits. To get a very rough estimate of the cost of Paillier encryption and randomization+multiplication, we measure the cost of an RSA signing operation with modulus n. Note that this is a significant underestimate since Paillier operations actually happen in $\mathbb{Z}_n^2$, and since the RSA signer knows the factorization of n, while P_1 does not.

7.3 Microbenchmarking

To estimate the per block cost of AES, we use the *permute_block* function in prp of [27] to benchmark the cost of a fixed key AES-ECB 128 per 128-bit block (we use security parameter $\lambda = 128$ for our experiments). To get this cost, we run fixed key AES for different numbers of blocks (4096, 8192, 12288) to get the amortized cost of a single AES. We repeat each experiment 100 times and then report the average amortized cost per 128-bit block (no significant variance was noticeable).

For estimating the cost of a single encryption and a single ciphertext randomization for the Paillier based protocol, we use the RSA signing cost for modulus of size 4096. We get this cost using the OpenSSL benchmark [7] by running the command *openssl speed.*

The costs we get are the following: *AES-ECB 128:* 3.5 ns, *RSA 4096 signing* 0.17 s. All the benchmarks are run on a Macbook Pro 2017 with a 3.1 GHz Intel core i-7 processor and 16 GB of 2133 MHz LPDDR3 RAM.

7.4 Performance Comparison

We estimate the performance of the different constructions described above. For this estimation, we experiment with three different database sizes, $N = 2^{20}, 2^{24}$ and 2^{32} elements and three different network bandwidths, 72 Mbps, 100 Mbps and 1 Gbps. We vary the length of each element in the database from 640 bits to 64000 bits. This range of values is roughly inspired from Machine Learning training applications which has 100s to 1000s of features (with each feature represented by a 64 bit integer).

In the following graphs on Figs. 3, 4 and 5 we report the estimated running time of our protocol and the protocol from [22]. We do not report the running time of the PKE based protocol in the graphs since they are 2–3 orders of magnitude slower compared to our protocol. Instead we summarize their performance in Table 2.

Table 2. Comparative performance of our protocol vs PKE based protocol

N	T	Bandwidth	PKE time/Our time
2^{20}	16	1 Gbps	3000–7000x
2^{20}	128	72 bps	400–600x
2^{32}	16	1 Gbps	1900–4000x
2^{32}	256	72 Mbps	260-400x

Table 3. Comparative performance of our protocol vs [22] based protocol for $N = T = 128$

Bandwidth	[22] time/Our time
1 Gbps	3–5x
100 Gbps	4–11x
72 Mbps	5–12x

In addition, we summarize how we compare with the protocol from [22] for relatively small N but long elements (640–64000 bits) in Table 3. We get a performance gain of 3–12x depending on the speed of the network.

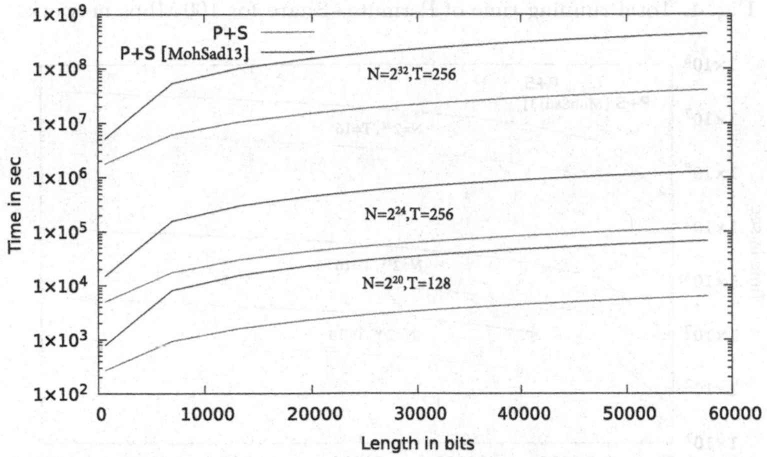

Fig. 3. Total running time of Permute+Share for 72 Mbps network

7.5 Choosing Optimal Subpermutation Size T

We choose the best value of T empirically: by fixing desired N, ℓ, enumerating over all possible T from 2 to N, and using the following formula to find the running time for each value of T (as before, d is set to be $2\lceil \log N / \log T \rceil - 1$), which is: $(3dN \log T + dNT(2 + \ell/\lambda)) \cdot \mathsf{TimePerAES} + (3dN\lambda \log T + (d+1)N\ell) \cdot \mathsf{TimePerBitSent}$. We give more details in the full version.

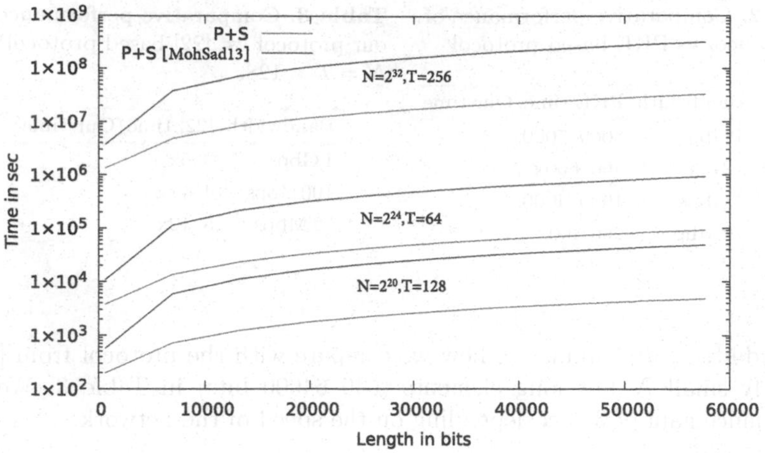

Fig. 4. Total running time of Permute+Share for 100 Mbps network

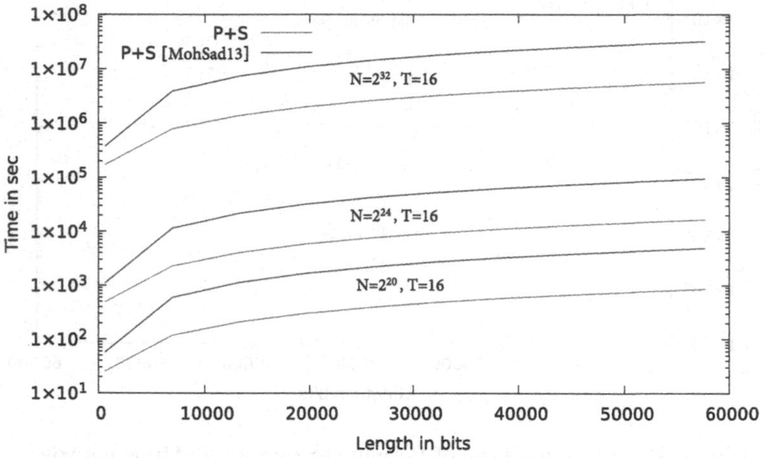

Fig. 5. Total running time of Permute+Share for 1 Gbps network

Acknowledgements. We are very grateful to the anonymous reviewers of Asiacrypt 2020, who have found inconsistencies in our experimental data, which was caused by a bug in our script. This version contains an updated estimates.

References

1. Ajtai, M., Komlós, J., Szemerédi, E.: An o(n log n) sorting network. In: Proceedings of the 15th Annual ACM Symposium on Theory of Computing, 25–27 April, 1983, Boston, Massachusetts, USA, pp. 1–9 (1983)
2. Benes, V.E.: Optimal rearrangeable multistage connecting networks. Bell Syst. Techn. J. **43**(4), 1641–1656 (1964)

3. Boyle, E., et al.: Efficient two-round ot extension and silent non-interactive secure computation. In: Proceedings of the 2019 ACM SIGSAC Conference on Computer and Communications Security, CCS 2019, pp. 291–308. Association for Computing Machinery, New York (2019). https://doi.org/10.1145/3319535.3354255
4. Chida, K., Hamada, K., Ikarashi, D., Kikuchi, R., Kiribuchi, N., Pinkas, B.: An efficient secure three-party sorting protocol with an honest majority. IACR Cryptol. ePrint Arch. 2019, 695 (2019). https://eprint.iacr.org/2019/695
5. Ciampi, M., Orlandi, C.: Combining private set-intersection with secure two-party computation. In: Proceedings of the Security and Cryptography for Networks - 11th International Conference, SCN 2018, Amalfi, Italy, 5–7 September, 2018, pp. 464–482 (2018)
6. Doerner, J., Shelat, A.: Scaling ORAM for secure computation. In: Proceedings of the 2017 ACM SIGSAC Conference on Computer and Communications Security, CCS 2017, Dallas, TX, USA, October 30–03 November, 2017, pp. 523–535 (2017)
7. Foundation, O.S.: OpenSSL. https://www.openssl.org/
8. Garg, S., Gupta, D., Miao, P., Pandey, O.: Secure multiparty RAM computation in constant rounds. In: Hirt, M., Smith, A. (eds.) TCC 2016. LNCS, vol. 9985, pp. 491–520. Springer, Heidelberg (2016). https://doi.org/10.1007/978-3-662-53641-4_19
9. Gentry, C., Halevi, S., Lu, S., Ostrovsky, R., Raykova, M., Wichs, D.: Garbled RAM revisited. In: Nguyen, P.Q., Oswald, E. (eds.) EUROCRYPT 2014. LNCS, vol. 8441, pp. 405–422. Springer, Heidelberg (2014). https://doi.org/10.1007/978-3-642-55220-5_23
10. Goldreich, O., Goldwasser, S., Micali, S.: How to construct random functions. J. ACM **33**(4), 792–807 (1986). https://doi.org/10.1145/6490.6503, http://doi.acm.org/10.1145/6490.6503
11. Gordon, S.D., et al.: Secure two-party computation in sublinear (amortized) time. In: the ACM Conference on Computer and Communications Security, CCS 2012, Raleigh, NC, USA, 16–18 October, 2012, pp. 513–524 (2012)
12. Group, B.C.: Bristol Cryptography Blog. http://bristolcrypto.blogspot.com/2017/01/rwc-2017-secure-mpc-at-google.html
13. Guo, C., Katz, J., Wang, X., Yu, Y.: Efficient and secure multiparty computation from fixed-key block ciphers. Cryptology ePrint Archive, Report 2019/074 (2019). https://eprint.iacr.org/2019/074
14. Hamada, K., Ikarashi, D., Chida, K., Takahashi, K.: Oblivious radix sort: an efficient sorting algorithm for practical secure multi-party computation. IACR Cryptology ePrint Archive 2014, 121 (2014). http://eprint.iacr.org/2014/121
15. Huang, Y., Evans, D., Katz, J.: Private set intersection: are garbled circuits better than custom protocols? In: NDSS (2012)
16. Ishai, Y., Kilian, J., Nissim, K., Petrank, E.: Extending oblivious transfers efficiently. In: Boneh, D. (ed.) CRYPTO 2003. LNCS, vol. 2729, pp. 145–161. Springer, Heidelberg (2003). https://doi.org/10.1007/978-3-540-45146-4_9
17. Keller, M., Scholl, P.: Efficient, oblivious data structures for MPC. In: Sarkar, P., Iwata, T. (eds.) ASIACRYPT 2014. LNCS, vol. 8874, pp. 506–525. Springer, Heidelberg (2014). https://doi.org/10.1007/978-3-662-45608-8_27
18. Liu, C., Huang, Y., Shi, E., Katz, J., Hicks, M.W.: Automating efficient ram-model secure computation. In: 2014 IEEE Symposium on Security and Privacy, SP 2014, Berkeley, CA, USA, 18–21 May 2014, pp. 623–638 (2014)
19. Liu, C., Wang, X.S., Nayak, K., Huang, Y., Shi, E.: ObliVM: a programming framework for secure computation. In: 2015 IEEE Symposium on Security and Privacy, SP 2015, San Jose, CA, USA, May 17–21, 2015, pp. 359–376 (2015)

20. Mohassel, P., Zhang, Y.: Secureml: a system for scalable privacy-preserving machine learning. In: 2017 IEEE Symposium on Security and Privacy (SP), pp. 19–38, May 2017. https://doi.org/10.1109/SP.2017.12
21. Mohassel, P., Rindal, P., Rosulek, M.: Fast database joins for secret shared data. Cryptology ePrint Archive, Report 2019/518 (2019). https://eprint.iacr.org/2019/518
22. Mohassel, P., Sadeghian, S.: How to hide circuits in MPC an efficient framework for private function evaluation. In: Johansson, T., Nguyen, P.Q. (eds.) EUROCRYPT 2013. LNCS, vol. 7881, pp. 557–574. Springer, Heidelberg (2013). https://doi.org/10.1007/978-3-642-38348-9_33
23. Pinkas, B., Schneider, T., Tkachenko, O., Yanai, A.: Efficient circuit-based psi with linear communication. Cryptology ePrint Archive, Report 2019/241 (2019). https://eprint.iacr.org/2019/241
24. Pinkas, B., Schneider, T., Weinert, C., Wieder, U.: Efficient Circuit-Based PSI via Cuckoo Hashing. In: Nielsen, J.B., Rijmen, V. (eds.) EUROCRYPT 2018. LNCS, vol. 10822, pp. 125–157. Springer, Cham (2018). https://doi.org/10.1007/978-3-319-78372-7_5
25. Schoppmann, P., Gascón, A., Reichert, L., Raykova, M.: Distributed vector-ole: improved constructions and implementation. In: Proceedings of the 2019 ACM SIGSAC Conference on Computer and Communications Security, CCS 2019, pp. 1055–1072. Association for Computing Machinery, New York (2019). https://doi.org/10.1145/3319535.3363228
26. Wang, X., Gordon, S.D., McIntosh, A., Katz, J.: Secure computation of MIPS machine code. In: Askoxylakis, I., Ioannidis, S., Katsikas, S., Meadows, C. (eds.) ESORICS 2016. LNCS, vol. 9879, pp. 99–117. Springer, Cham (2016). https://doi.org/10.1007/978-3-319-45741-3_6
27. Wang, X., Malozemoff, A.J., Katz, J.: EMP-toolkit: efficient MultiParty computation toolkit (2016). https://github.com/emp-toolkit
28. Zahur, S., et al.: Revisiting square-root ORAM: efficient random access, pp. 218–234 (2016)

Attribute-Based Encryption

Adaptively Secure Inner Product Encryption from LWE

Shuichi Katsumata[1], Ryo Nishimaki[2], Shota Yamada[1], and Takashi Yamakawa[2](✉)

[1] AIST, Tokyo, Japan
{shuichi.katsumata,yamada-shota}@aist.go.jp
[2] NTT Secure Platform Laboratories, Tokyo, Japan
{ryo.nishimaki.zk,takashi.yamakawa.ga}@hco.ntt.co.jp

Abstract. Attribute-based encryption (ABE) is an advanced form of encryption scheme allowing for access policies to be embedded within the secret keys and ciphertexts. By now, we have ABEs supporting numerous types of policies based on hardness assumptions over bilinear maps and lattices. However, one of the distinguishing differences between ABEs based on these two breeds of assumptions is that the former can achieve *adaptive* security for quite expressible policies (e.g., inner-products, boolean formula) while the latter can not. Recently, two adaptively secure lattice-based ABEs have appeared and changed the state of affairs: a non-zero inner-product (NIPE) encryption by Katsumata and Yamada (PKC'19) and an ABE for t-CNF policies by Tsabary (CRYPTO'19). However, the policies supported by these ABEs are still quite limited and do not embrace the more interesting policies that have been studied in the literature. Notably, constructing an adaptively secure *inner-product encryption* (IPE) based on lattices still remains open.

In this work, we propose the first adaptively secure IPE based on the learning with errors (LWE) assumption with sub-exponential modulus size (without resorting to complexity leveraging). Concretely, our IPE supports inner-products over the integers $\mathbb{Z}$ with polynomial sized entries and satisfies adaptively weakly-attribute-hiding security. We also show how to convert such an IPE to an IPE supporting inner-products over $\mathbb{Z}_p$ for a polynomial-sized p and a fuzzy identity-based encryption (FIBE) for small and large universes. Our result builds on the ideas presented in Tsabary (CRYPTO'19), which uses constrained pseudorandom functions (CPRF) in a semi-generic way to achieve adaptively secure ABEs, and the recent lattice-based adaptively secure CPRF for inner-products by Davidson et al. (CRYPTO'20). Our main observation is realizing how to weaken the *conforming* CPRF property introduced in Tsabary (CRYPTO'19) by taking advantage of the specific linearity property enjoyed by the lattice evaluation algorithms by Boneh et al. (EUROCRYPT'14).

1 Introduction

An attribute-based encryption (ABE) [44] is an advanced form of public-key encryption (PKE) that allows the sender to specify in a more general way about

S. Moriai and H. Wang (Eds.): ASIACRYPT 2020, LNCS 12493, pp. 375–404, 2020.
https://doi.org/10.1007/978-3-030-64840-4_13

who should be able to decrypt. In an ABE for predicate $\mathsf{P} : \mathcal{X} \times \mathcal{Y} \to \{0,1\}$, decryption of a ciphertext associated with an attribute $\mathbf{y}$ is only possible by a secret key associated with an attribute $\mathbf{x}$ such that $\mathsf{P}(\mathbf{x}, \mathbf{y}) = 1$. For instance, identity-based encryption (IBE) [9,22] is a special form of ABE where an equality predicate is considered.

Over the past decade and a half, we have seen exciting progress in the design and security analysis of ABEs. Each subsequent work provides improvements in various aspects including security, expressiveness of predicates, or underlying assumptions. While the earlier constructions were mainly based on bilinear maps, e.g., [8,11,32,34,44,45], by now we have plenty of constructions based on lattices as well, e.g., [1,3,10,19,25,28]. Some of the types of ABEs that have attracted more attention than others in the literature include (but not limited to), fuzzy IBE [2,44], inner-product encryption (IPE) [3,34,36], ABE for boolean formulae [32,36], and ABE for $\mathsf{P/poly}$ circuits [10,28]. Regarding the expressiveness of predicates, lattice-based ABEs seem to achieve stronger results than bilinear map-based ABEs since the former allows for predicates expressible by $\mathsf{P/poly}$ circuits, whereas the latter is restricted to boolean formulae.

Adaptive Security. While lattice-based ABEs have richer expressiveness, bilinear map-based ABEs can realize stronger security. Specifically, they can address *adaptive* security (in the standard model) for quite expressive predicates. Here, adaptive security states that, even if an adversary can obtain polynomially many secret keys for any attribute $\mathbf{x}$ and adaptively query for a challenge ciphertext associated with an attribute $\mathbf{y}^*$ such that $\mathsf{P}(\mathbf{x}, \mathbf{y}^*) = 0$, it still cannot learn the message encrypted within the challenge ciphertext. This clearly captures the real-life scenario where an adversary can adaptively choose which attributes to attack. In some cases, we may consider the much weaker *selective* security, where an adversary must declare which attribute $\mathbf{y}^*$ it will query as the challenge at the beginning of the security game. In general, we can convert a selectively secure scheme to an adaptively secure scheme by employing complexity leveraging, where the reduction algorithm simply guesses the challenge attribute at the outset of the game. However, this is often undesirable as such proofs incur an exponential security loss and necessitate in relying on exponentially hard assumptions. Using bilinear maps, we know how to directly construct adaptively secure fuzzy IBE [20,49], IPE [20,36,38,49], and even ABE for boolean formulae [5,6,20,36,39,49] from standard (polynomial) assumptions.

On the other hand, our knowledge of adaptively secure lattice-based ABEs is still quite limited. Notably, most of the lattice-based ABEs are only selectively secure. For almost a decade, the only adaptively secure scheme we knew how to construct from lattices was limited to the most simplistic form of ABE, an IBE [1,19]. Considering that we had a lattice-based selectively secure ABE for the powerful predicate class of $\mathsf{P/poly}$ circuits, this situation on adaptive security was unsatisfactory. Recently, the state of affairs changed: Katsumata and Yamada [33] proposed an adaptively secure non-zero IPE (NIPE), and Tsabary [46] proposed an adaptively secure ABE for t-CNF predicates. The latter predicate consists of formulas in conjunctive normal form where each clause depends on at most t bits of the input, for any constant t. The former work is based on a generic construction from adaptively secure functional encryption for inner-products [4], whereas the latter work ingeniously extends the adaptively secure bilinear map-based IBE of Gentry [24] to the lattice setting by utilizing a special type of *constrained* pseudorandom function (CPRF) [12,13,35]. Unfortunately, NIPE nor ABE for t-CNF is not expressive enough to capture the more interesting types of ABE such as fuzzy IBE or IPE, let al.one ABE for boolean formulae or P/poly. Therefore, the gap between the bilinear map setting and the lattice setting regarding adaptive security still remains quite large and dissatisfying. Indeed, constructing an adaptively secure IPE based on lattices is widely regarded as one of the long-standing open problems in lattice-based ABE.

1.1 Our Contribution

In this work, we propose the first lattice-based *adaptively* secure IPE over the integers $\mathbb{Z}$. In addition, we show several extensions of our main result to realize other types of ABEs such as fuzzy IBE. The results are summarized below and in Table 1. All of the following schemes are secure under the learning with errors (LWE) assumption with sub-exponential modulus size.

- We construct an adaptively secure IPE over the integers ($\mathbb{Z}$) with polynomial sized entries. The predicate is defined as $\mathsf{P} : \mathcal{Z} \times \mathcal{Z} \to \{0,1\}$, where $\mathcal{Z}$ is a subset of $\mathbb{Z}^\ell$ with bounded polynomial sized entries and $\mathsf{P}(\mathbf{x}, \mathbf{y}) = 1$ if and only if $\langle \mathbf{x}, \mathbf{y} \rangle = 0$ over $\mathbb{Z}$.
- We construct an adaptively secure IPE over the ring $\mathbb{Z}_p$ for $p = \mathsf{poly}(\kappa)$. The predicate $\mathsf{P}_{\mathsf{mod}} : \mathbb{Z}_p^\ell \times \mathbb{Z}_p^\ell \to \{0,1\}$ is defined similarly to above, where now $\mathsf{P}_{\mathsf{mod}}(\mathbf{x}, \mathbf{y}) = 1$ if and only if $\langle \mathbf{x}, \mathbf{y} \rangle = 0 \mod p$.
- We construct an adaptively secure fuzzy IBE for small and large universe with threshold T. Specifically, the predicate is defined as $\mathsf{P}_{\mathsf{fuz}} : \mathcal{D}^n \times \mathcal{D}^n \to \{0,1\}$, where $\mathcal{D}$ is a set of either polynomial size (i.e., small universe) or exponential size (i.e., large universe) and $\mathsf{P}_{\mathsf{fuz}}(\mathbf{x}, \mathbf{y}) = 1$ if and only if $\mathsf{HD}(\mathbf{x}, \mathbf{y}) \leq n - T$. Here, HD denotes the hamming distance. That is, if $\mathbf{x}$ and $\mathbf{y}$ are identical in more than T-positions, then $\mathsf{P}_{\mathsf{fuz}}(\mathbf{x}, \mathbf{y}) = 1$.

Though we mainly focus on proving payload-hiding for these constructions, we can generically upgrade payload-hiding ABE to be weakly-attribute-hiding by using lockable obfuscation, which is known to exist under the LWE assumption with sub-exponential modulus size [31,50]. Therefore, we obtain adaptively weakly-attribute-hiding ABE for the above classes of predicates under the LWE assumption with sub-exponential modulus size. We note that this does not require an additional assumption since our payload-hiding constructions already rely on the same assumption.

The first construction is obtained by extending the recent result by Tsabary [46], while the second and third constructions are obtained by a generic transformation of the first construction.

Table 1. Existing adaptively secure lattice-based ABE.

Reference	Type of predicate	LWE Asmp.
ABB'10 [1], CHKP'10 [19]	IBE and HIBE w/ $O(1)$-hierarchy	poly
	$\mathbb{Z}$ w/ poly-size entries	poly
KY'19 [33]	NIPE over $\mathbb{Z}$ w/ exp-size entries	poly
	$\mathbb{Z}_p$ w/ poly and exp-size $p^{\dagger}$	subexp
Tsabary'19 [46]	(CP-)ABE for t-CNF where $t = O(1)$	subexp
Ours	IPE over $\mathbb{Z}$ w/ poly-size entries	subexp
Ours	IPE over $\mathbb{Z}_p$ w/ poly-size p	subexp
Ours	Fuzzy IBE w/ small and large universe	subexp

$\dagger$: The key generation algorithm is stateful for NIPE over $\mathbb{Z}_p$.

1.2 Technical Overview

We provide a detailed overview of our first (main) result regarding an adaptively secure IPE over the integers ($\mathbb{Z}$) and provide some discussions on how to extend it to ABE with other types of useful predicates. For our first result, we first extend the framework of Tsabary [46] and exploit a specific linearity property of the lattice evaluation algorithms of Boneh et al. [10]. We then make a subtle (yet crucial) modification to the CPRF for inner-products over the integer by Davidson et al. [23] so as to be compatible with our extended framework for achieving adaptively secure ABEs.

Note. In the following, to make the presentation clearer, we treat ABE as either a *ciphertext-policy* (CP) ABE or a *key-policy* (KP) ABE interchangeably. In CP-ABE, an attribute associated to a ciphertext represents a policy $f \in \mathcal{Y}$, which is described as a circuit, and we define the predicate $\mathsf{P}(\mathbf{x}, f) := f(\mathbf{x})$. That is, the predicate is satisfied if $f(\mathbf{x}) = 1$. KP-ABE is defined analogously. Note that IPE can be viewed as both a CP and KP-ABE since the roles of the attributes associated with the secret key and the ciphertext are symmetric.

Reviewing Previous Results. Due to the somewhat lattice-heavy nature of our result, we review the relevant known results. For those who are up-to-date with the result of Tsabary [46] may safely skip to "Our Results". We first provide some background on lattice evaluation algorithms [10]. We then review the framework developed by Tsabary [46] for achieving adaptively secure ABEs (for t-CNF).

***Selectively* Secure (KP-)ABE Based on Homomorphic Evaluation.** We recall the selectively secure ABE by Boneh et al. [10], which is the basic recipe for constructing lattice-based ABEs. Let $\mathbf{A} \in \mathbb{Z}_q^{n \times \ell m}$ be a public matrix and $\mathbf{G} \in \mathbb{Z}_q^{n \times m}$ be the so-called (public) gadget matrix whose trapdoor is known [37]. Then, there exists two deterministic efficiently computable lattice evaluation algorithms $\mathsf{PubEval}$ and CtEval such that for any $f : \{0,1\}^\ell \to \{0,1\}$ and $\mathbf{x} \in \{0,1\}^\ell$, the following property holds.[1]

- $\mathsf{PubEval}(f, \mathbf{A}) \to \mathbf{A}_f$,

[1] We note that f can also be represented as an arithmetic circuit.

– $\mathsf{CtEval}(f, \mathbf{x}, \mathbf{A}, \mathbf{s}^\top(\mathbf{A} - \mathbf{x}^\top \otimes \mathbf{G}) + \mathsf{noise}) \to \mathbf{s}^\top(\mathbf{A}_f - f(\mathbf{x}) \otimes \mathbf{G}) + \mathsf{noise}$,

where noise denotes some term whose size is much smaller than q which we can ignore. In words, CtEval is an algorithm that allows to convert a ciphertext (or an encoding) of $\mathbf{x}$ w.r.t. matrix $\mathbf{A}$ into a ciphertext of $f(\mathbf{x})$ w.r.t. matrix $\mathbf{A}_f$, where $\mathbf{A}_f$ is the same matrix output by PubEval. In the following, we assume that the output of CtEval statistically hides the value $\mathbf{x}$, which is possible by adding sufficiently large noise.

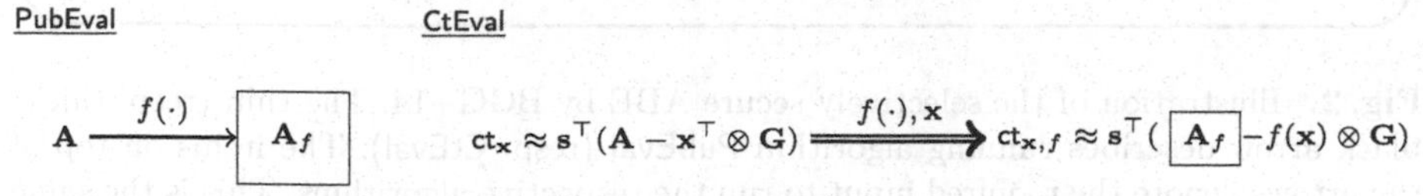

Fig. 1. PubEval and CtEval. In all figures, symbol $\approx$ means that we hide (or ignore) the noise part in ciphertexts.

We provide an overview of how to construct a (KP-)ABE. The public parameters consist of a matrix $\mathbf{A}$ and a vector $\mathbf{u}$. Let $\hat{f}$ be a negation of the function f, that is, $\hat{f}(\mathbf{x}) := 1 - f(\mathbf{x})$. To generate a secret key for function f, the KeyGen algorithm first runs $\mathbf{A}_{\hat{f}} \leftarrow \mathsf{PubEval}(\hat{f}, \mathbf{A})$ as in Equation (1) below. Then the secret key sk_f is sampled as a short vector $\mathbf{e}_f$ such that $\mathbf{A}_{\hat{f}}\mathbf{e}_f = \mathbf{u}$.[2] To generate a ciphertext for attribute $\mathbf{x}$ with message $\mathsf{M} \in \{0,1\}$, the Enc algorithm generates a LWE sample of the form $\mathsf{ct}_0 := \mathbf{s}^\top\mathbf{u} + \mathsf{noise} + \mathsf{M} \cdot \lfloor q/2 \rfloor$ and $\mathsf{ct}_\mathbf{x}$ as depicted on the l.h.s. of Equation (2). To decrypt with a secret key sk_f, the Dec algorithm first runs $\mathsf{CtEval}(\hat{f}, \mathbf{x}, \mathbf{A}, \mathsf{ct}_\mathbf{x})$ to generate $\mathsf{ct}_{\mathbf{x},\hat{f}}$ as depicted on the r.h.s. of Equation (2). Here, notice that the ciphertext is converted into a ciphertext that encodes the matrix $\mathbf{A}_{\hat{f}}$ used during KeyGen (both boxed in Equations (1) and (2)). Then, if the predicate is satisfied, i.e., $f(\mathbf{x}) = 1 \Leftrightarrow \hat{f}(\mathbf{x}) = 0$, then $\mathsf{ct}_{\mathbf{x},f} = \mathbf{s}^\top\mathbf{A}_{\hat{f}} + \mathsf{noise}$. Therefore, using $\mathbf{e}_f$, the message can be recovered by computing $\mathsf{ct}_0 - \langle \mathsf{ct}_{\mathbf{x},f}, \mathbf{e}_f \rangle$ and rounding appropriately.

Now, *selective* security follows by embedding the LWE problem in the challenge ciphertext. Specifically, the reduction algorithm is given an LWE instance $([\mathbf{u}|\mathbf{B}], [\mathbf{v}_0|\mathbf{v}])$, where $[\mathbf{v}_0|\mathbf{v}]$ is either random or of the form $[\mathbf{v}_0|\mathbf{v}] = \mathbf{s}^\top[\mathbf{u}|\mathbf{B}] + \mathsf{noise}$. It then implicitly sets $\mathbf{A} := \mathbf{B}\mathbf{R} + \mathbf{x}^{*\top} \otimes \mathbf{G}$ where $\mathbf{x}^*$ is the challenge attribute the adversary commits to at the outset of the security game and $\mathbf{R}$ is a random matrix with small entries and sets the challenge ciphertext as $(\mathsf{ct}_0 := \mathbf{v}_0 + \mathsf{M} \cdot \lfloor q/2 \rfloor, \mathsf{ct}_{\mathbf{x}^*} := \mathbf{v})$. It can be checked that if $[\mathbf{v}_0|\mathbf{v}]$ is a valid LWE instance, then the challenge is distributed as in the actual security game. Otherwise, the challenge ciphertext is uniformly random. Finally, we remark that simulating secret keys for policy f such that $f(\mathbf{x}^*) = 0$ is possible since there exists

[2] To be accurate, we require an extra matrix $\mathbf{A}_0$ for which we know a trapdoor in order to sample such a short vector. However, we simplify the exposition for the sake of clarity.

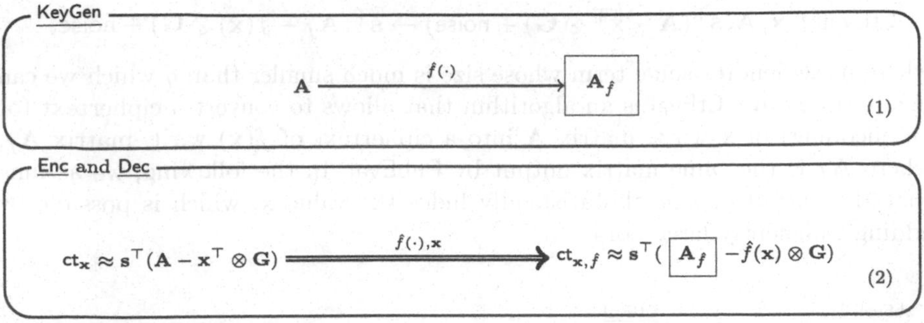

Fig. 2. Illustration of the selectively secure ABE by BGG+14. The thin (resp. thick) black arrow describes running algorithm PubEval (resp. CtEval). The items on top of the arrows denote the required input to run the respective algorithms. This is the same for all subsequent figures. In Equation (2), the l.h.s. and r.h.s. are generated by Enc and Dec, respectively.

a special lattice evaluation algorithm (only used during the security proof) that allows the reduction algorithm to convert $\mathbf{A}_{\hat{f}}$ into $\mathbf{BR}_{\hat{f}} + \hat{f}(\mathbf{x}^*) \otimes \mathbf{G} = \mathbf{BR}_{\hat{f}} + \mathbf{G}$, where $\mathbf{R}_{\hat{f}}$ is a matrix with short norm. We omit the details on what or how to use $\mathbf{R}_{\hat{f}}$ as it is not important for this overview and refer the readers to [10].

We end by emphasizing that the above reduction technique only works in the selective setting because the adversary commits to $\mathbf{x}^*$ at the outset of the game; if it did not, then the reduction algorithm will not be able to set $\mathbf{A}$ as $\mathbf{B} + \mathbf{x}^{*\top} \otimes \mathbf{G}$ in the public parameter.

Adaptively Secure IBE à la Gentry [24] **and Tsabary** [46].[3] Before getting into adaptively secure ABEs, we first consider the simpler adaptively secure IBEs. We overview the so-called "tagging" technique [24,46]. In the real scheme, a secret key and a ciphertext for an identity id are associated with random "tags" r_{id}. The scheme is set up so that decryption only works if the tag value r_{id} of the secret key $\mathsf{sk}_{\mathsf{id}}$ is different from the tag value $\tilde{r}_{\mathsf{id}}$ of the ciphertext for an identity id. In case the tags are sampled from an exponentially large space, such a scheme only has a negligible probability of a decryption failure. At a high level, the scheme will be tweaked so that the reduction algorithm assigns exactly one random tag r_{id} per identity id; a secret key and a challenge ciphertext for the same identity id are tagged by the same r_{id}. In addition, the reduction algorithm will only be able to simulate a secret key and a challenge ciphertext w.r.t. this unique tag r_{id}. Here, this tweak will remain unnoticed by the adversary since a valid adversary never asks for a secret key and a challenge ciphertext for the same identity id.

We briefly review how Tsabary [46] cleverly carried out this idea in the lattice-setting. The public parameter now includes a description of a pseudo-

[3] One can also see this construction as an analogy of Waters' dual system framework [48].

random function PRF, and the master secret key includes a seed k for the PRF. To generate a secret key for identity id, the KeyGen algorithm computes the random tag $r_{\mathsf{id}} \leftarrow \mathsf{PRF.Eval}(\mathsf{k}, \mathsf{id})$. It then sequentially runs $\mathbf{A}^{\mathsf{eval}}_{\mathsf{id}} \leftarrow \mathsf{PubEval}(\mathsf{PRF.Eval}(\cdot, \mathsf{id}), \mathbf{A})$ and $\mathbf{A}^{\mathsf{eq}}_{\mathsf{id}, r_{\mathsf{id}}} \leftarrow \mathsf{PubEval}(\mathsf{Eq}_{r_{\mathsf{id}}}(\cdot), \mathbf{A}^{\mathsf{eval}}_{\mathsf{id}})$ as in Equation (3) below, where $\mathsf{Eq}_{r_{\mathsf{id}}}(\widetilde{r}_{\mathsf{id}}) = 1$ if and only if $r_{\mathsf{id}} = \widetilde{r}_{\mathsf{id}}$. As before, it then samples a short vector $\mathbf{e}_{\mathsf{id}}$ such that $\mathbf{A}^{\mathsf{eq}}_{\mathsf{id}, r_{\mathsf{id}}} \mathbf{e}_{\mathsf{id}} = \mathbf{u}$. The final secret key is $\mathsf{sk}_{\mathsf{id}} := (r_{\mathsf{id}}, \mathbf{e}_{\mathsf{id}})$. To generate a ciphertext for identity id with message M, the Enc algorithm first samples a random PRF key $\widetilde{\mathsf{k}}$ and generates $\mathsf{ct}_0 := \mathbf{s}^\top \mathbf{u} + \mathsf{noise} + \mathsf{M} \cdot \lfloor q/2 \rfloor$ as before. It then generates $\mathsf{ct}_{\widetilde{\mathsf{k}}}$ as depicted in the l.h.s of Equation (4) and further executes $\mathsf{ct}^{\mathsf{eval}}_{\mathsf{id}} \leftarrow \mathsf{CtEval}(\mathsf{PRF.Eval}(\cdot, \mathsf{id}), \widetilde{\mathsf{k}}, \mathbf{A}, \mathsf{ct}_{\widetilde{\mathsf{k}}})$ as depicted in the r.h.s of Equation (4). The final ciphertext is $\mathsf{ct} := (\widetilde{r}_{\mathsf{id}}, \mathsf{ct}_0, \mathsf{ct}^{\mathsf{eval}}_{\mathsf{id}})$, where $\widetilde{r}_{\mathsf{id}} \leftarrow \mathsf{PRF.Eval}(\widetilde{\mathsf{k}}, \mathsf{id})$. Effectively, the Enc algorithm has constructed a ciphertext that is bound to an identity id and a random tag $\widetilde{r}_{\mathsf{id}}$; observe that $\mathbf{A}^{\mathsf{eval}}_{\mathsf{id}}$ is the same matrix that appears during KeyGen (in a single-framed box). Here, we note that the noise term in $\mathsf{ct}_{\mathsf{id}}$ does not leak any information on the PRF key $\widetilde{\mathsf{k}}$ by our assumption. Now, to decrypt, the Dec algorithm, with knowledge of both the random tag r_{id} and $\widetilde{r}_{\mathsf{id}}$, runs $\mathsf{ct}^{\mathsf{eq}}_{\mathsf{id}, r_{\mathsf{id}}} \leftarrow \mathsf{CtEval}(\mathsf{Eq}_{r_{\mathsf{id}}}(\cdot), \widetilde{r}_{\mathsf{id}}, \mathbf{A}^{\mathsf{eval}}_{\mathsf{id}}, \mathsf{ct}^{\mathsf{eval}}_{\mathsf{id}})$ as depicted in the r.h.s. of Equation (5). At this point, the ciphertext is converted into a ciphertext that encodes the matrix $\mathbf{A}^{\mathsf{eq}}_{\mathsf{id}, r_{\mathsf{id}}}$ used during KeyGen (in a double-framed box), and we have $\mathsf{Eq}_{r_{\mathsf{id}}}(\widetilde{r}_{\mathsf{id}}) = 0$ since $r_{\mathsf{id}} \neq \widetilde{r}_{\mathsf{id}}$ with all but a negligible probability. Hence, since $\mathsf{ct}^{\mathsf{eq}}_{\mathsf{id}, r_{\mathsf{id}}} = \mathbf{s}^\top \mathbf{A}^{\mathsf{eq}}_{\mathsf{id}, r_{\mathsf{id}}} + \mathsf{noise}$, the Dec algorithm can decrypt the ciphertext using the short vector $\mathbf{e}_{\mathsf{id}}$ included in the secret key following the same argument as before.

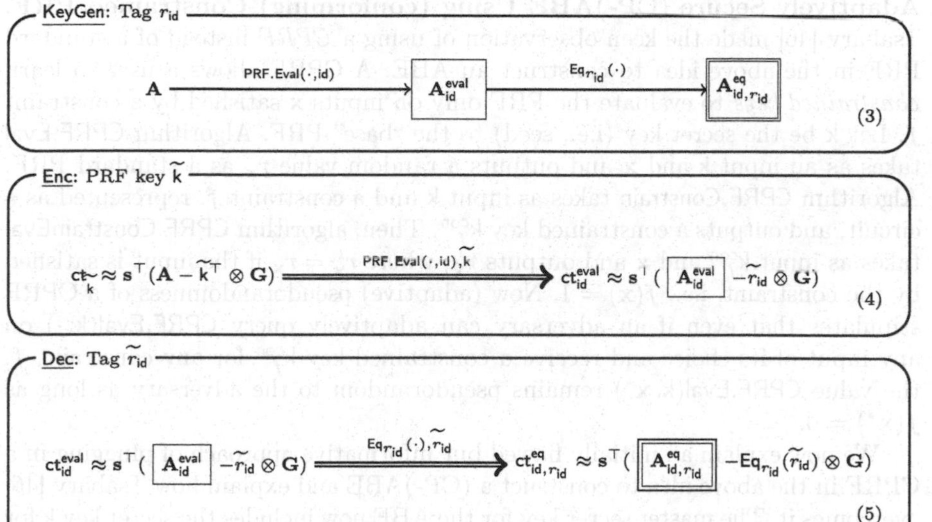

Fig. 3. Illustration of the adaptively secure IBE by Tsabary.

The key observation is that a ciphertext for an identity id is generated from $\mathsf{ct}_{\widetilde{\mathsf{k}}}$ that *only depends on the* PRF *key*. Notably, *adaptive* security can be achieved (informally) because the reduction algorithm no longer needs to guess the challenge identity id and by the *adaptive* pseudorandomness of the PRF. We provide a proof sketc.h to get a better intuition for the more complex subsequent ABE construction: We first modify the security game so that the challenger no longer needs to explicitly embed $\widetilde{\mathsf{k}}$ in the ciphertext. Namely, the challenger simply computes $\mathbf{A}_{\mathsf{id}}$ using $\mathsf{PubEval}$, which it can run without knowledge of $\widetilde{\mathsf{k}}$, and directly generates $\mathsf{ct}^{\mathsf{eval}}_{\mathsf{id}}$ using $\tilde{r}_{\mathsf{id}}$. This is statistically the same as in the real scheme since the noise term statistically hides $\widetilde{\mathsf{k}}$ due to the assumption. Now, we can invoke the adaptive pseudorandomness of the PRF. The reduction algorithm generates the random tag associated with the challenge ciphertext by implicitly using the seed k included in the master secret key (by querying its own PRF challenger) instead of sampling a fresh $\widetilde{\mathsf{k}}$. Note that the random tag associated with the secret key and challenge ciphertext for the same id are identical now. We then switch back to the real scheme where the Enc algorithm first constructs ct_{k}, where the only difference is that k is encoded rather than a random PRF seed $\widetilde{\mathsf{k}}$. At this point, we can rely on the same argument as the selective security of [10] since k is known at the outset of the game and the reduction algorithm (which is the LWE adversary) can set $\mathbf{A} := \mathbf{B} + \mathsf{k}^\top \otimes \mathbf{G}$. The challenge ciphertext for any id^* can be computed by simply running CtEval on $\mathsf{ct}_{\mathsf{k}} = \mathbf{v}$, where $\mathbf{v} = \mathbf{s}^\top \mathbf{B} + \mathsf{noise}$ for a valid LWE instance. In addition, a secret key for any id can be simulated as well since we have $\mathbf{A}^{\mathsf{eq}}_{\mathsf{id},r_{\mathsf{id}}} = \mathbf{B}\mathbf{R}^{\mathsf{eq}}_{\mathsf{id},r_{\mathsf{id}}} + \mathsf{Eq}_{r_{\mathsf{id}}}(r_{\mathsf{id}}) \otimes \mathbf{G} = \mathbf{B}\mathbf{R}^{\mathsf{eq}}_{\mathsf{id},r_{\mathsf{id}}} + \mathbf{G}$ for a matrix $\mathbf{R}^{\mathsf{eq}}_{\mathsf{id},r_{\mathsf{id}}}$ with low norm.

Adaptively Secure (CP-)ABE Using (conforming) Constrained PRF. Tsabary [46] made the keen observation of using a *CPRF* instead of a standard PRF in the above idea to construct an ABE. A CPRF allows a user to learn *constrained keys* to evaluate the PRF only on inputs $\mathbf{x}$ satisfied by a constraint f. Let k be the secret key (i.e., seed) to the "base" PRF. Algorithm $\mathsf{CPRF.Eval}$ takes as an input k and $\mathbf{x}$ and outputs a random value $r_{\mathbf{x}}$ as a standard PRF. Algorithm $\mathsf{CPRF.Constrain}$ takes as input k and a constraint f, represented as a circuit, and outputs a constrained key $\mathsf{k}^{\mathsf{con}}_f$. Then, algorithm $\mathsf{CPRF.ConstrainEval}$ takes as input $\mathsf{k}^{\mathsf{con}}_f$ and $\mathbf{x}$ and outputs $r'_{\mathbf{x}}$, where $r'_{\mathbf{x}} = r_{\mathbf{x}}$ if the input is satisfied by the constraint, i.e., $f(\mathbf{x}) = 1$. Now (adaptive) pseudorandomness of a CPRF stipulates that even if an adversary can adaptively query $\mathsf{CPRF.Eval}(\mathsf{k}, \cdot)$ on any input of its choice and receive a constrained key $\mathsf{k}^{\mathsf{con}}_f$ for any constraint f, the value $\mathsf{CPRF.Eval}(\mathsf{k}, \mathbf{x}^*)$ remains pseudorandom to the adversary as long as $f(\mathbf{x}^*) = 0$.

We now explain an initially flawed but informative approach of plugging in a CPRF in the above idea to construct a (CP-)ABE and explain how Tsabary [46] overcomes it. The master secret key for the ABE now includes the secret key k for the CPRF. To generate a secret key for an attribute $\mathbf{x}$, the KeyGen algorithm first computes a random tag $r_{\mathbf{x}} \leftarrow \mathsf{CPRF.Eval}(\mathsf{k}, \mathbf{x})$. It then sequentially runs $\mathbf{A}^{\mathsf{eval}}_{\mathbf{x}} \leftarrow \mathsf{PubEval}(\mathsf{CPRF.Eval}(\cdot, \mathbf{x}), \mathbf{A})$ and $\mathbf{A}^{\mathsf{eq}}_{\mathbf{x},r_{\mathbf{x}}} \leftarrow \mathsf{PubEval}(\mathsf{Eq}_{r_{\mathbf{x}}}(\cdot), \mathbf{A}^{\mathsf{eval}}_{\mathbf{x}})$ as in Equation (6) below. Finally, a short vector $\mathbf{e}_{\mathbf{x}}$ such that $\mathbf{A}^{\mathsf{eq}}_{\mathbf{x},r_{\mathbf{x}}} \mathbf{e}_{\mathbf{x}} = \mathbf{u}$ is sampled. The final secret key is $\mathsf{sk}_{\mathbf{x}} := (r_{\mathbf{x}}, \mathbf{e}_{\mathbf{x}})$. To encrypt with respect to a policy f, the Enc algorithm prepares a constrained key for f, which will later be used to derive random tags for any $\mathbf{x}$ during decryption. Specifically, it first samples a fresh secret key $\widetilde{\mathsf{k}}$ for the CPRF and generates $\mathsf{ct}_0 := \mathbf{s}^\top \mathbf{u} + \mathsf{noise} + \mathsf{M} \cdot \lfloor q/2 \rceil$ as before. It then generates $\mathsf{ct}_{\widetilde{\mathsf{k}}}$ and further executes $\mathsf{ct}_f^{\mathsf{con}} \leftarrow \mathsf{CtEval}(\mathsf{CPRF.Constrain}(\cdot, f), \widetilde{\mathsf{k}}, \mathbf{A}, \mathsf{ct}_{\widetilde{\mathsf{k}}})$ as depicted in Equation (7). The final ciphertext is $\mathsf{ct} := (\widetilde{\mathsf{k}}_f^{\mathsf{con}}, \mathsf{ct}_0, \mathsf{ct}_f^{\mathsf{con}})$, where $\widetilde{\mathsf{k}}_f^{\mathsf{con}} \leftarrow \mathsf{CPRF.Constrain}(\widetilde{\mathsf{k}}, f)$ is a constrained key and note that $\mathsf{ct}_f^{\mathsf{con}}$ statistically hides the information on $\widetilde{\mathsf{k}}$. Observe that the ciphertext encodes the policy f.

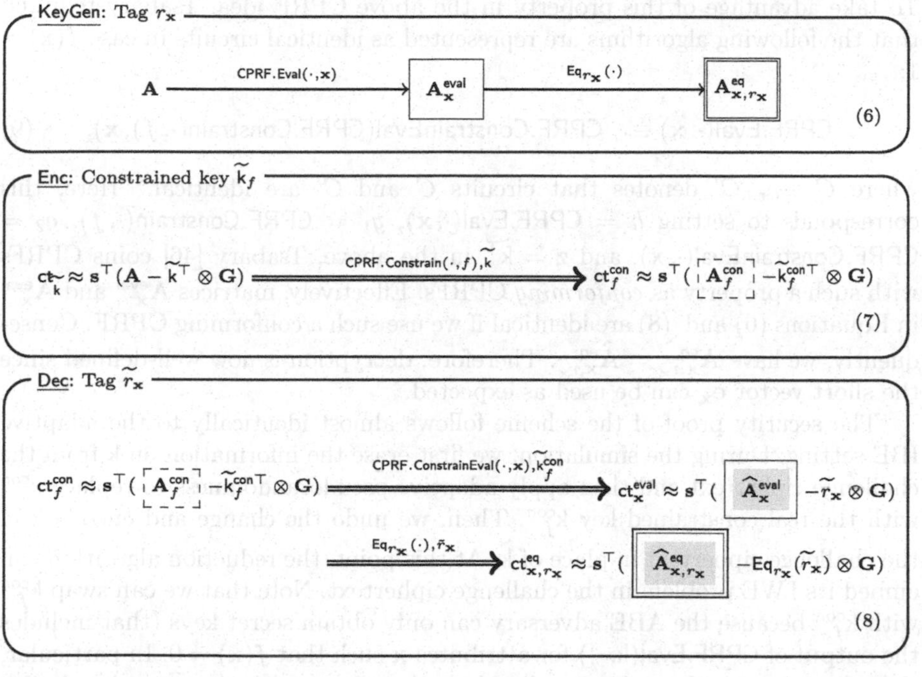

Fig. 4. Illustration of the high-level structure of the adaptively secure CP-ABE by Tsabary.

However, at this point, the problem becomes apparent: Decryption no longer works. What the decryptor in possession of secret key $\mathsf{sk}_{\mathbf{x}}$ can do is to convert the ciphertext $\mathsf{ct}_f^{\mathsf{con}}$ into $\mathsf{ct}_{\mathbf{x}}^{\mathsf{eval}} \leftarrow \mathsf{CtEval}(\mathsf{CPRF.ConstrainEval}(\cdot, \mathbf{x}), \widetilde{\mathsf{k}}_f^{\mathsf{con}}, \mathbf{A}_f^{\mathsf{con}}, \mathsf{ct}_f^{\mathsf{con}})$ as depicted in Equation (8). In addition, it can further convert it into $\mathsf{ct}_{\mathbf{x},r_{\mathbf{x}}}^{\mathsf{eq}} \leftarrow \mathsf{CtEval}(\mathsf{Eq}_{r_{\mathbf{x}}}(\cdot), \tilde{r}_{\mathbf{x}}, \widehat{\mathbf{A}}_{\mathbf{x}}^{\mathsf{eval}}, \mathsf{ct}_{\mathbf{x}}^{\mathsf{eval}})$, where $\tilde{r}_{\mathbf{x}} = \mathsf{CPRF.ConstrainEval}(\widetilde{\mathsf{k}}_f^{\mathsf{con}}, \mathbf{x})$. However, the secret key $\mathbf{e}_{\mathbf{x}}$ satisfying $\mathbf{A}_{\mathbf{x},r_{\mathbf{x}}}^{\mathsf{eq}} \mathbf{e}_{\mathbf{x}} = \mathbf{u}$ is useless for decryption because the (intermediate) matrices $\mathbf{A}_{\mathbf{x}}^{\mathsf{eval}}$ and $\widehat{\mathbf{A}}_{\mathbf{x}}^{\mathsf{eval}}$ in the single-framed box and the shadowed single-framed box, respectively, are different. Therefore, the tagging via CPRFs idea even fails to provide a correct ABE.

The main idea of Tsabary [46] to overcome this issue was taking advantage of the particular composition property of the lattice evaluation algorithms [10]. Specifically, for any matrix $\mathbf{A}$ and circuits h, g_1, and g_2, where h and $g_2 \circ g_1$ are described identically as circuits, the following evaluated matrices $\mathbf{A}_h$ and $\mathbf{A}_{g_2 \circ g_1}$ are the same, that is, $\mathbf{A}_h = \mathbf{A}_{g_2 \circ g_1}$:

1. $\mathbf{A}_h \leftarrow \mathsf{PubEval}(h, \mathbf{A})$,
2. $\mathbf{A}_{g_2 \circ g_1} \leftarrow \mathsf{PubEval}(g_2, \mathsf{PubEval}(g_1, \mathbf{A}))$.

Then, due to the correctness of PubEval and CtEval, when $\mathsf{ct} = \mathbf{s}^\top(\mathbf{A} - \mathbf{z} \otimes \mathbf{G}) + \mathsf{noise}$, ciphertexts ct_h and $\mathsf{ct}_{g_2 \circ g_1}$ are both of the form $\mathbf{s}^\top(\mathbf{A}_h - h(\mathbf{z}) \otimes \mathbf{G}) + \mathsf{noise}$. To take advantage of this property in the above CPRF idea, Tsabary required that the following algorithms are represented as identical circuits in case $f(\mathbf{x}) = 1$:

$$\mathsf{CPRF.Eval}(\cdot, \mathbf{x}) \equiv_{\mathsf{cir}} \mathsf{CPRF.ConstrainEval}(\mathsf{CPRF.Constrain}(\cdot, f), \mathbf{x}), \tag{9}$$

where $C \equiv_{\mathsf{cir}} C'$ denotes that circuits C and C' are identical.[4] Here, this corresponds to setting $h = \mathsf{CPRF.Eval}(\cdot, \mathbf{x})$, $g_1 = \mathsf{CPRF.Constrain}(\cdot, f)$, $g_2 = \mathsf{CPRF.ConstrainEval}(\cdot, \mathbf{x})$, and $\mathbf{z} = \widetilde{\mathsf{k}}^\top$ in the above. Tsabary [46] coins CPRFs with such a property as *conforming* CPRFs. Effectively, matrices $\mathbf{A}^{\mathsf{eval}}_{\mathbf{x}}$ and $\widehat{\mathbf{A}}^{\mathsf{eval}}_{\mathbf{x}}$ in Equations (6) and (8) are identical if we use such a conforming CPRF. Consequently, we have $\mathbf{A}^{\mathsf{eq}}_{\mathbf{x}, r_{\mathbf{x}}} = \widehat{\mathbf{A}}^{\mathsf{eq}}_{\mathbf{x}, r_{\mathbf{x}}}$. Therefore, decryption is now well-defined since the short vector $\mathbf{e}_{\mathbf{x}}$ can be used as expected.

The security proof of the scheme follows almost identically to the adaptive IBE setting: During the simulation, we first erase the information on $\widetilde{\mathsf{k}}$ from the challenge ciphertext and then apply adaptive pseudorandomness to replace $\widetilde{\mathsf{k}}^{\mathsf{con}}_f$ with the real constrained key $\mathsf{k}^{\mathsf{con}}_f$. Then, we undo the change and encode k in the challenge ciphertext in place of $\widetilde{\mathsf{k}}$. At this point, the reduction algorithm can embed its LWE problem in the challenge ciphertext. Note that we can swap $\widetilde{\mathsf{k}}^{\mathsf{con}}_f$ with $\mathsf{k}^{\mathsf{con}}_f$ because the ABE adversary can only obtain secret keys (that includes the output of $\mathsf{CPRF.Eval}(\mathsf{k}, \cdot)$) for attributes $\mathbf{x}$ such that $f(\mathbf{x}) = 0$. In particular, the adversary cannot use k_f to check whether the random tag associated with the secret key is generated by k or not.

The final remaining issue is whether such an adaptively secure conforming CPRF exists or not. Fortunately, the CPRF for bit-fixing predicates by Davidson et al. [23] (with a minor tweak) enjoyed such properties. Tsabary [46] further extended this CPRF to predicates expressed by t-CNF. Therefore, combining everything together, Tsabary obtained an adaptively secure (CP-)ABE for t-CNF policies.

Our Results. We are now prepared to explain our result. We first show why and how to weaken the conforming CPRF property required in the (semi-)generic

[4] More precisely, Tsabary [46] required that the circuit representation of $\mathsf{CPRF.Eval}(\cdot, \mathbf{x})$ and the effective *sub-circuit* of $\mathsf{CPRF.ConstrainEval}(\mathsf{CPRF.Constrain}(\cdot, f), \mathbf{x})$ are required to be the same.

construction of Tsabary [46]. We then present how to obtain such a CPRF for inner-products over $\mathbb{Z}$ from LWE building on top of the recent CPRF proposal of Davidson et al. [23]. By carefully combining them, we obtain the first lattice-based IPE over $\mathbb{Z}$. Finally, we briefly mention how to extend our IPE over $\mathbb{Z}$ to other types of useful ABE.

Weakening the Condition on Conforming CPRF. Combining the discussion thus far, an adaptively secure conforming CPRF for a more expressive constraint class $\mathcal{F}$ will immediately yield a (CP-)ABE for the policy class $\mathcal{F}$ based on Tsabary's proof methodology. Put differently, the goal now is to construct an adaptively secure CPRF such that for all $f \in \mathcal{F}$ and $\mathbf{x}$ where $f(\mathbf{x}) = 1$, Equation (9) holds. However, this turns out to be an extremely strong requirement which we only know how to construct using the CPRF for t-CNF [23,46]. This CPRF for t-CNF is based on a combinatoric approach using PRFs and differs significantly from all other (selectively secure) CPRFs for more expressive constraints that rely on algebraic tools such as bilinear-maps or lattices, e.g., [7,15,16,18,21,41]. That being said, there is one recent lattice-based CPRF for inner-products over $\mathbb{Z}$ by Davidson et al. [23] that comes somewhat close to what is required. Let us review their CPRF and explain how it fails short to fit in Tsabary's proof methodology.

A CPRF for inner-products over $\mathbb{Z}$ is a CPRF where the inputs and constraints are provided by vectors $\mathbf{x}, \mathbf{y} \in [-B, B]^\ell$ for some integer B. A constrained key $\mathsf{k}^{\mathsf{con}}_{\mathbf{y}}$ for vector $\mathbf{y}$ should allow to compute the same random value as the secret key k (i.e., the "base" seed) for all inputs $\mathbf{x}$ such that $\langle \mathbf{x}, \mathbf{y} \rangle = 0$ over $\mathbb{Z}$. In Davidson et al. [23] the secret key k is simply a random matrix-vector pair $(\mathbf{S}, \mathbf{d})$ sampled uniformly random over $[-\bar{\beta}, \bar{\beta}]^{n \times \ell} \times [-\beta, \beta]^n$ for some integers $\bar{\beta}$ and β, where $\bar{\beta}$ is sub-exponentially large.[5] In addition, a matrix $\mathbf{B} \xleftarrow{\$} \mathbb{Z}_{q'}^{n \times m}$ is provided as a public parameter. To evaluate on $\mathbf{x}$ using the secret key k, the $\mathsf{CPRF.Eval}$ algorithm first converts $\mathbf{B}$ to a specific matrix $\mathbf{B}_{\mathbf{x}}$ associated to $\mathbf{x}$ (whose detail is irrelevant for this overview). Then, it computes a vector $\mathsf{k}^{\mathsf{int}}_{\mathbf{x}} := \mathbf{S}\mathbf{x} \in \mathbb{Z}^n$ called an *intermediate key*, and finally outputs the random value $r_{\mathbf{x}} = \lfloor \mathsf{k}^{\mathsf{int}\top}_{\mathbf{x}} \mathbf{B}_{\mathbf{x}} \rceil_p \in \mathbb{Z}_p^m$. Here, $\lfloor a \rceil_p$ denotes rounding of an element $a \in \mathbb{Z}_{q'}$ to $\mathbb{Z}_p$ by multiplying it by (p/q') and rounding the result.[6] The constrained key $\mathsf{k}^{\mathsf{con}}_{\mathbf{y}}$ is simply defined as $\mathsf{k}^{\mathsf{con}}_{\mathbf{y}} := \mathbf{S} + \mathbf{d} \otimes \mathbf{y}^\top \in \mathbb{Z}^{n \times \ell}$. To evaluate on $\mathbf{x}$ using the constrained key $\mathsf{k}^{\mathsf{con}}_{\mathbf{y}}$, the $\mathsf{CPRF.ConstrainEval}$ algorithm first prepares $\mathbf{B}_{\mathbf{x}}$ as done by $\mathsf{CPRF.Eval}$ and then computes the *constrained* intermediate key $\mathsf{k}^{\mathsf{con\text{-}int}}_{\mathbf{y},\mathbf{x}} := (\mathbf{S} + \mathbf{d} \otimes \mathbf{y}^\top)\mathbf{x} \in \mathbb{Z}^{n \times \ell}$, and finally outputs the random value $r'_{\mathbf{x}} = \lfloor \mathsf{k}^{\mathsf{con\text{-}int}\top}_{\mathbf{y},\mathbf{x}} \mathbf{B}_{\mathbf{x}} \rceil_p \in \mathbb{Z}_p^m$. Observe that if $\langle \mathbf{x}, \mathbf{y} \rangle = 0$ over $\mathbb{Z}$, then $\mathsf{k}^{\mathsf{int}}_{\mathbf{x}} = \mathsf{k}^{\mathsf{con\text{-}int}}_{\mathbf{y},\mathbf{x}}$. Therefore, $\mathsf{CPRF.Eval}(\mathsf{k}, \mathbf{x}) = \mathsf{CPRF.ConstrainEval}(\mathsf{k}_{\mathbf{y}}, \mathbf{x})$ in case $\langle \mathbf{x}, \mathbf{y} \rangle = 0$ as desired. Davidson et al. [23] proved that such a CPRF is adaptively secure based on the LWE assumption with sub-exponential modulus size.

---

[5] In their original scheme, $\mathbf{d}$ is not included in the secret key but generated when constraining the secret key. However, this modification is w.l.o.g and will be vital for our purpose.

[6] Looking ahead, we note the moduli (q', p) used by the CPRF is different from the modulus q used by the ABE.

On first glance this CPRF may seem to satisfy the conforming property (Equation (9)) since the secret key $\mathsf{k} = \mathbf{S}$ and the constrained key $\mathsf{k}^{\mathsf{con}}_{\mathbf{y}} = \mathbf{S} + \mathbf{d} \otimes \mathbf{y}^{\top}$ are both matrices over $\mathbb{Z}^{n\times\ell}$, and the intermediate keys $\mathsf{k}^{\mathsf{int}}_{\mathbf{x}}$ and $\mathsf{k}^{\mathsf{con\text{-}int}}_{\mathbf{y},\mathbf{x}}$ are equivalent in case $\langle \mathbf{x}, \mathbf{y}\rangle = 0$ and are used identically (as a circuit) to compute $r_{\mathbf{x}}$. However, under closer inspection, it is clear that Equation (9) does not hold. Specifically, $\mathsf{CPRF.Constrain}(\mathsf{k}, \mathbf{y})$ computes $\mathsf{k}^{\mathsf{con}}_{\mathbf{y}} = (\mathbf{S} + \mathbf{d} \otimes \mathbf{y}^{\top})$; a computation that depends on the constraint vector $\mathbf{y}$, while $\mathsf{CPRF.Eval}(\mathsf{k}, \mathbf{x})$ does not internally perform such computation. Therefore, $\mathsf{CPRF.Eval}(\cdot, \mathbf{x})$ cannot be identical as a circuit as $\mathsf{CPRF.ConstrainEval}(\mathsf{CPRF.Constrain}(\cdot, \mathbf{y}), \mathbf{x})$. In the context of ABE, this means that the KeyGen algorithm and Enc/Dec algorithms will not be able to agree on the same matrix, and hence, correctness no longer holds. Although both algorithms CPRF.Eval and CPRF.ConstrainEval share a striking resemblance, it seems one step short of satisfying the conforming property of Tsabary.

Our main idea to overcome this issue is weakening the conforming property required by Tsabary [46] by noticing another particular *linearity* property of the lattice evaluation algorithms of [10]. Specifically, for any matrix $\mathbf{A}$ and *linear functions* h, g_1, and g_2 such that h and $g_2 \circ g_1$ are *functionally equivalent*, the matices $\mathbf{A}_h$ and $\mathbf{A}_{g_2 \circ g_1}$ evaluated using PubEval as in Items 1 and 2 are in fact equivalent (i.e., $\mathbf{A}_h = \mathbf{A}_{g_2 \circ g_1}$). By correctness of PubEval and CtEval, we then also have $\mathsf{ct}_h = \mathsf{ct}_{g_2 \circ g_1}$. Here, the main observation is that we no longer require the strong property of $h \equiv_{\mathsf{cir}} g_2 \circ g_1$, but only require a slightly milder property of h and $g_2 \circ g_1$ being functionally equivalent, that is, have the same input/output.

Let us see how this property can be used. Notice that the above CPRF of Davidson et al. [23] has the following structure. Algorithm $\mathsf{CPRF.Eval}(\mathsf{k}, \mathbf{x})$ can be broken up in linear and non-linear algorithms: $\mathsf{CPRF.EvalLin}(\mathsf{k}, \mathbf{x}) \to \mathsf{k}^{\mathsf{int}}_{\mathbf{x}}$ and $\mathsf{CPRF.EvalNonLin}(\mathsf{k}^{\mathsf{int}}_{\mathbf{x}}, \mathbf{x}) \to r_{\mathbf{x}}$.[7] Namely, we have

$$\mathsf{CPRF.Eval}(\mathsf{k}, \mathbf{x}) = \mathsf{CPRF.EvalNonLin}(\mathsf{CPRF.EvalLin}(\mathsf{k}, \mathbf{x}), \mathbf{x}).$$

Similarly, $\mathsf{CPRF.ConstrainEval}(\mathsf{k}_{\mathbf{y}}, \mathbf{x})$ can be broken up in linear and non-linear algorithms: $\mathsf{CPRF.ConstrainEvalLin}(\mathsf{k}^{\mathsf{con}}_{\mathbf{y}}, \mathbf{x}) \to \mathsf{k}^{\mathsf{con\text{-}int}}_{\mathbf{y},\mathbf{x}}$ and $\mathsf{CPRF.ConstrainEvalNonLin}$ $(\mathsf{k}^{\mathsf{con\text{-}int}}_{\mathbf{y},\mathbf{x}}, \mathbf{x}) \to r_{\mathbf{x}}$. In addition, from above, we know that we have the following property:

1. if $\langle \mathbf{x}, \mathbf{y}\rangle = 0$ over $\mathbb{Z}$, then $\mathsf{CPRF.EvalLin}(\cdot, \mathbf{x})$ and $\mathsf{CPRF.ConstrainEvalLin}(\mathsf{CPRF.Constrain}(\cdot, \mathbf{y}), \mathbf{x})$ are both *linear* functions that are *functionally equivalent* (in particular, $\mathsf{k}^{\mathsf{int}}_{\mathbf{x}} = \mathsf{k}^{\mathsf{con\text{-}int}}_{\mathbf{y},\mathbf{x}}$), and
2. the non-linear algorithms satisfy $\mathsf{CPRF.EvalNonLin}(\cdot, \mathbf{x}) \equiv_{\mathsf{cir}} \mathsf{CPRF.ConstrainEvalNonLin}(\cdot, \mathbf{x})$. Namely, they are *identical circuits.*

Importing these properties to the ABE setting, we get a transition of matrices and ciphertext for KeyGen, Enc, and Dec as in Figure 5.

Notice the matrices in red ($\mathbf{A}^{\mathsf{int}}_{\mathbf{x}}$ and $\mathbf{A}^{\mathsf{con\text{-}int}}_{\mathbf{y},\mathbf{x}}$) are identical due to the property in Item 1 and the linearity property of PubEval and CtEval. Moreover, due to

[7] Concretely, the non-linear part does a rounding operation modulo a certain integer p followed by an evaluation of a hash function.

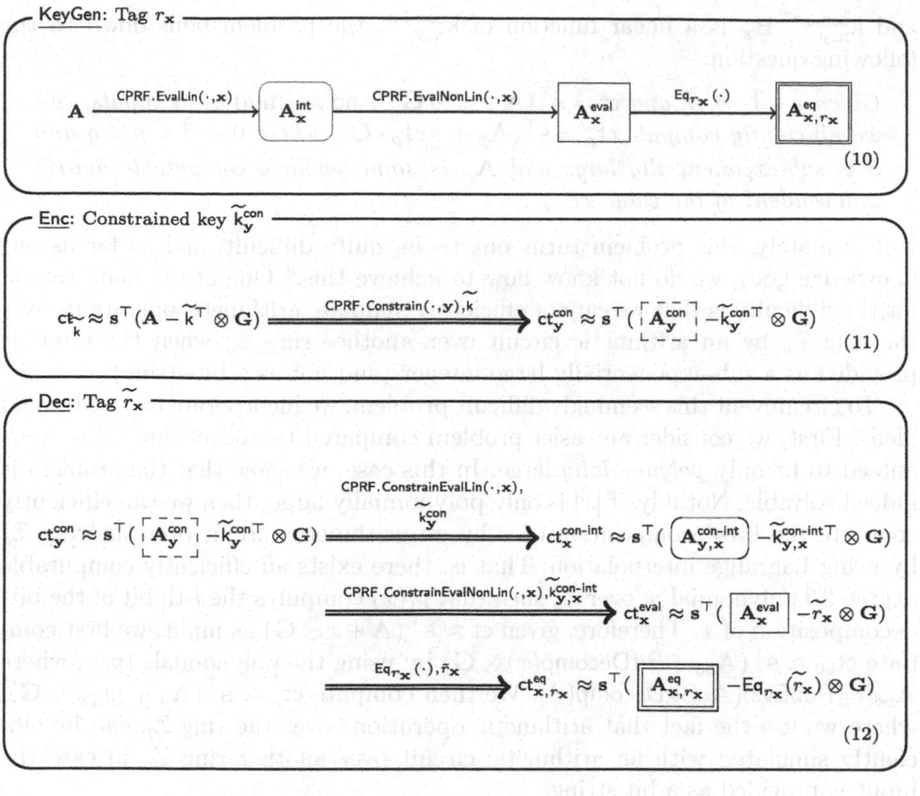

Fig. 5. Illustration of our adaptively secure IPE.

the property in Item 2, the subsequent evaluated ciphertexts $\mathsf{ct}^{\mathsf{eval}}_{\mathbf{x}}$ and $\mathsf{ct}^{\mathsf{eq}}_{\mathbf{x},r_{\mathbf{x}}}$ correctly encode the matrices $\mathbf{A}^{\mathsf{eval}}_{\mathbf{x}}$ and $\mathbf{A}^{\mathsf{eq}}_{\mathbf{x},r_{\mathbf{x}}}$, respectively, which correspond to those computed during KeyGen. Combining all of these observations, it seems we have successfully weakened the conforming property required by Tsabary [46] and showed that the CPRF of Davidson et al. [23] suffices to instantiate the generic (CP-)ABE construction. However, we show that a problem still remains.

Bit Decomposing and Tweaking Davidson et al.'s CPRF [23]. To understand the problem, let us take a closer look at how the CtEval algorithm is used in Equations (11) and (12). First, observe that the output of the linear function $\mathsf{CPRF.EvalLin}(\mathsf{k}, \mathbf{x})$, or equivalently, the output of $\mathsf{CPRF.ConstrainEvalLin}(\mathsf{CPRF.Constrain}(\mathsf{k}, \mathbf{y}), \mathbf{x})$ is over $\mathbb{Z}$ rather than over $\{0, 1\}$. More specifically, the output $\mathsf{k}^{\mathsf{int}}_{\mathbf{x}} (= \mathsf{k}^{\mathsf{con\text{-}int}}_{\mathbf{y},\mathbf{x}})$ is of the form $\mathbf{S}\mathbf{x} \in [-\widetilde{\beta}, \widetilde{\beta}]^n$, where $\widetilde{\beta}$ is some *sub-exponentially* large integer. Therefore, the ciphertext $\mathsf{ct}^{\mathsf{con\text{-}int}}_{\mathbf{x}} \approx \mathbf{s}^\top (\mathbf{A}^{\mathsf{con\text{-}int}}_{\mathbf{y},\mathbf{x}} - \widetilde{\mathsf{k}}^{\mathsf{con\text{-}int}\top}_{\mathbf{y},\mathbf{x}} \otimes \mathbf{G})$ computed within the Dec algorithm encodes $\widetilde{\mathsf{k}}^{\mathsf{con\text{-}int}}_{\mathbf{y},\mathbf{x}}$ as *integers* over $[-\widetilde{\beta}, \widetilde{\beta}]^n$. Now, the Dec algorithm must further convert this ciphertext to $\mathsf{ct}^{\mathsf{eval}}_{\mathbf{x}} \approx \mathbf{s}^\top (\mathbf{A}^{\mathsf{eval}}_{\mathbf{x}} - \widetilde{r}_{\mathbf{x}} \otimes \mathbf{G})$, where $\widetilde{r}_{\mathbf{x}} = \mathsf{CPRF.ConstrainEvalNonLin}(\mathsf{k}^{\mathsf{con\text{-}int}}_{\mathbf{y},\mathbf{x}}, \mathbf{x}) = \lfloor \mathsf{k}^{\mathsf{con\text{-}int}\top}_{\mathbf{x},\mathbf{y}} \mathbf{B}_{\mathbf{x}} \rceil_p \in \mathbb{Z}^m_p$. The problem is: is this efficiently computable? Since $\mathbf{B}_{\mathbf{x}}$ can be precomputed and $\mathsf{k}_{\mathbf{x},\mathbf{y}}^{\mathsf{con\text{-}int}\top}\mathbf{B}_{\mathbf{x}}$ is a linear function of $\mathsf{k}_{\mathbf{x},\mathbf{y}}^{\mathsf{con\text{-}int}}$, the problem boils down to the following question:

> *Given* $x \in [-\tilde{\beta}, \tilde{\beta}]$ *and* $\mathsf{ct} = \mathbf{s}^\top(\mathbf{A} + x \otimes \mathbf{G}) + \mathsf{noise} \pmod{q}$ *as inputs, can we efficiently compute* $\mathsf{ct}_p \approx \mathbf{s}^\top(\mathbf{A}_p + \lfloor x \rfloor_p \cdot \mathbf{G})$, *where* $0 < \tilde{\beta} < p < q$ *and* $\tilde{\beta}$ is *sub-exponentially large and* $\mathbf{A}_p$ *is some publicly computable matrix independent of the value* x*?*

Unfortunately, this problem turns out to be quite difficult, and as far as our knowledge goes, we do not know how to achieve this.[8] One of the main reason for the difficulty is that we cannot efficiently simulate arithmetic operations over the ring $\mathbb{Z}_p$ by an arithmetic circuit over another ring $\mathbb{Z}_q$ when the input is provided as a sub-exponentially large integer (and not as a bit-string).

To circumvent this seemingly difficult problem, we incorporate two additional ideas. First, we consider an easier problem compared to above where $\tilde{\beta}$ is guaranteed to be only *polynomially* large. In this case, we show that the problem is indeed solvable. Notably, if $|x|$ is only polynomially large, then we can efficiently compute the bit-decomposition of x by an arithmetic circuit over the ring $\mathbb{Z}_q$ by using Lagrange interpolation. That is, there exists an efficiently computable degree-$2\tilde{\beta}$ polynomial p_i over $\mathbb{Z}_q$ such that $p_i(x)$ computes the i-th bit of the bit-decomposition of x. Therefore, given $\mathsf{ct} \approx \mathbf{s}^\top(\mathbf{A} + x \otimes \mathbf{G})$ as input, we first compute $\mathsf{ct}_{\mathsf{bd}} \approx \mathbf{s}^\top(\mathbf{A}_{\mathsf{bd}} + \mathsf{BitDecomp}(x) \otimes \mathbf{G})$ by using the polynomials $(p_i)_i$, where $\mathbf{A}_{\mathsf{bd}} = \mathsf{PubEval}(\mathbf{A}, \mathsf{BitDecomp}(\cdot))$. We then compute $\mathsf{ct}_p \approx \mathbf{s}^\top(\mathbf{A}_p + \lfloor x \rfloor_p \otimes \mathbf{G})$, where we use the fact that arithmetic operations over the ring $\mathbb{Z}_p$ can be efficiently simulated with an arithmetic circuit over another ring $\mathbb{Z}_q$ in case the input is provided as a bit-string.

The remaining problem is whether $\tilde{\beta}$ in the CPRF of Davidson et al. [23] can be set to be polynomially large rather than sub-exponentially large. Very roughly, Davidson et al. required $\tilde{\beta}$ to be sub-exponentially large to argue that with all but a negligible probability, the absolute value of *all the entries* in $\mathbf{S} \in \mathbb{Z}^{n \times \ell}$ is smaller than some specified value. However, we notice that we can complete the same security proof by only requiring that the absolute value of *most of the entries* in $\mathbf{S}$ is smaller than a specified value. This small change allows us to use a finer probabilistic argument on the entries of $\mathbf{S}$, which in return, allows us to set $\tilde{\beta}$ only polynomially large.

By combining all the pieces, we obtain the first lattice-based adaptively secure IPE over $\mathbb{Z}$ with polynomial-sized entries. We note that our construction requires LWE with a sub-exponential modulus since the underlying CPRF of [23] requires it, and also, since we need to homomorphically compute the non-linear circuit $\mathsf{CPRF.EvalNonLin}$.

Extending IPE Over $\mathbb{Z}$ to Other ABEs. Finally, we also show how to extend our adaptively secure IPE over $\mathbb{Z}$ with polynomial-sized entries to other useful ABE using generic conversions. That is, the ideas are not limited to our specific lattice-based construction. Specifically, we obtain the following three lattice-based adaptively secure ABEs for the first time: IPE over the ring $\mathbb{Z}_p$ for $p =$

[8] We note that a solution to this question will directly give us the desired result.

$\mathsf{poly}(\kappa)$, fuzzy IBE for small and large universes with threshold T. The first two generic conversions are almost folklore. To obtain fuzzy IBE for large universe, we use error correcting codes with a polynomial-sized alphabet (such as Reed-Solomon codes [42]) to encode an exponentially large element to a string of polynomially large elements with polynomial length. We then use the fuzzy IBE for small universe with an appropriate threshold to simulate the large universe.

1.3 Related Works

Brakerski and Vaikuntanathan [17] constructed a lattice-based ABE for all circuits with a weaker adaptive security called the *semi-adaptive security*, where an adversary can declare the challenge attribute after seeing the public parameter but before making any key query. Subsequently, Goyal, Koppula and Waters [30] showed that we can convert any selectively secure ABE into a semi-adaptively secure one.

Recently, Wang et al. [47] gave a framework to construct lattice-based adaptively secure ABE by extending the dual system framework [48] into the lattice setting. However, their instantiation based on the LWE assumption only yields *bounded collusion-resistant* ABE where an adversary can obtain only bounded number of decryption keys that is fixed at the setup phase. We note that such an ABE trivially follows from the bounded collusion-resistant functional encryption scheme based on any PKE by Gorbunov, Vaikuntanathan, and Wee [27].

2 Preliminaries

We use standard cryptographic notations and refer the readers to the full version for reference.

2.1 Lattices

In this work, we only use standard tools from lattices such as bounding norms of discrete Gaussian distributions, gadget matrices, and sampling with trapdoors. Therefore, we omit the details to the full version. Below, we introduce the main hardness assumption we use in this work for completeness.

Definition 2.1 ([43], Learning with Errors). *For integers n, m, a prime $q > 2$, an error distribution χ over $\mathbb{Z}$, and a PPT algorithm $\mathcal{A}$, the advantage for the* learning with errors problem $\mathsf{LWE}_{n,m,q,\chi}$ *of $\mathcal{A}$ is defined as follows:*

$$\mathsf{Adv}_{\mathcal{A}}^{\mathsf{LWE}_{n,m,q,\chi}} = \left| \Pr\left[\mathcal{A}(\mathbf{A}, \mathbf{s}^\top \mathbf{A} + \mathbf{z}^\top) = 1\right] - \Pr\left[\mathcal{A}(\mathbf{A}, \mathbf{b}^\top) = 1\right] \right|$$

where $\mathbf{A} \leftarrow \mathbb{Z}_q^{n\times m}$, $\mathbf{s} \leftarrow \mathbb{Z}_q^n$, $\mathbf{b} \leftarrow \mathbb{Z}_q^m$, $\mathbf{z} \leftarrow \chi^m$. We say that the LWE *assumption holds if $\mathsf{Adv}_{\mathcal{A}}^{\mathsf{LWE}_{n,m,q,\chi}}$ is negligible for all PPT algorithm $\mathcal{A}$.*

The (decisional) $\mathsf{LWE}_{n,m,q,D_{\mathbb{Z},\alpha q}}$ for $\alpha q > 2\sqrt{n}$ has been shown by Regev [43] via a quantum reduction to be as hard as approximating the worst-case SIVP and GapSVP problems to within $\tilde{O}(n/\alpha)$ factors in the ℓ_2-norm in the worst case. In the subsequent works (partial) dequantumization of the reduction were achieved [14,40]. The worst-case problems are believed to be hard even for subexponential approximation factors, and in particular, the LWE problem with subexponential modulus size is believed to be hard. We note that this is different from assuming the subexponential LWE assumption where we allow for adversaries even with subexponentially small advantage.

2.2 Attribute-Based Encryption

Let $\mathsf{P} : \mathcal{X} \times \mathcal{Y} \to \{0, 1\}$ where $\mathcal{X}$ and $\mathcal{Y}$ are sets. An attribute-based encryption (ABE) for P (with the message space $\{0, 1\}$) consists of PPT algorithms ($\mathsf{Setup}, \mathsf{KeyGen}, \mathsf{Enc}, \mathsf{Dec}$): $\mathsf{Setup}(1^\kappa)$ outputs a pair public parameter and master secret key ($\mathsf{pp}, \mathsf{msk}$); $\mathsf{KeyGen}(\mathsf{pp}, \mathsf{msk}, x)$ outputs a secret key sk_x for attribute x; $\mathsf{Enc}(\mathsf{pp}, y, M)$ outputs a ciphertext ct_y for attribute y and message $\mathsf{M} \in \{0, 1\}$; and $\mathsf{Dec}(\mathsf{pp}, \mathsf{sk}_x, \mathsf{ct}_y)$ outputs M if $\mathsf{P}(x, y) = 1$.

An ABE is said to be (adaptively) payload-hiding, if it is infeasible for an adversary to tell apart a random ciphertext and a valid ciphertext for attribute y^* and message M^* of its choice, even if it is given polynomially many secret keys sk_x for $\mathsf{P}(x, y) = 0$. Here, adaptive security dictates that an adversary can adaptively choose the challenge attribute y^* even after seeing polynomially many secret keys sk_x. The formal definition is omitted to the full version.

Inner-product Encryption. In this study, we consider ABEs for the following predicate. Let P be the inner-product predicate with domain $\mathcal{X} = \mathcal{Y} = \mathcal{Z}^n$ where $\mathcal{Z}$ is a subset of $\mathbb{Z}$. That is, for $\mathbf{x}, \mathbf{y} \in \mathcal{Z}^n$, $\mathsf{P}(\mathbf{x}, \mathbf{y}) = 1$ if $\langle \mathbf{x}, \mathbf{y} \rangle = 0$ and $\mathsf{P}(\mathbf{x}, \mathbf{y}) = 0$ otherwise. We call this inner-production encryption (IPE) *over the integers* ($\mathbb{Z}$).

We also consider a variant where the inner-product is taken over $\mathbb{Z}_p$ for p a prime. Concretely, let $\mathsf{P}_{\mathsf{mod}}$ be the inner-product predicate with domain $\mathcal{X} = \mathcal{Y} = \mathbb{Z}_p^n$ such that for $\mathbf{x}, \mathbf{y} \in \mathbb{Z}_p^n$, $\mathsf{P}_{\mathsf{mod}}(\mathbf{x}, \mathbf{y}) = 1$ if $\langle \mathbf{x}, \mathbf{y} \rangle = 0 \mod p$ and $\mathsf{P}(\mathbf{x}, \mathbf{y}) = 0$ otherwise. We call this IPE *over* $\mathbb{Z}_p$.

Fuzzy Identity-based Encryption. We also consider the following predicate. Let $\mathsf{P}_{\mathsf{fuz}}$ be the fuzzy predicate with domain $\mathcal{X}^n = \mathcal{Y}^n = \mathcal{D}^n$ and *threshold* $T (> 0)$ such that for $\mathbf{x}, \mathbf{y} \in \mathcal{D}^n$, $\mathsf{P}_{\mathsf{fuz}}(\mathbf{x}, \mathbf{y}) = 1$ if $\mathsf{HD}(\mathbf{x}, \mathbf{y}) \leq n - T$ and $\mathsf{P}_{\mathsf{fuz}}(\mathbf{x}, \mathbf{y}) = 0$ otherwise. Here, $\mathsf{HD} : \mathcal{D}^n \times \mathcal{D}^n \to [0, n]$ denotes the hamming distance. That is, if $\mathbf{x}$ and $\mathbf{y}$ are identical in more than T-positions, then $\mathsf{P}_{\mathsf{fuz}}(\mathbf{x}, \mathbf{y}) = 1$. We call this fuzzy identity-based encryption (IBE) for *small universe* when $|\mathcal{D}| = \mathsf{poly}(\kappa)$, and fuzzy IBE for *large universe* when $|\mathcal{D}| = \exp(\kappa)$.

2.3 Constrained Pseudorandom Functions

A constrained pseudorandom function for $(\mathcal{D}, \mathcal{R}, \mathcal{K}, \mathcal{C})$ is defined by the five PPT algorithms $\Pi_{\mathsf{CPRF}} = (\mathsf{CPRF.Setup}, \mathsf{CPRF.Gen}, \mathsf{CPRF.Eval}, \mathsf{CPRF.Constrain},$

CPRF.ConstrainEval) where: $\mathsf{CPRF.Setup}(1^\kappa)$ outputs a set of public parameter pp; CPRF.Gen(pp) outputs a master key K; $\mathsf{CPRF.Eval}(\mathsf{pp}, \mathsf{K}, x)$ outputs a random value r; $\mathsf{CPRF.Constrain}(\mathsf{K}, C)$ outputs a constrained key $\mathsf{K}_C^{\mathsf{con}}$ associated with constraint C; and $\mathsf{CPRF.ConstrainEval}(\mathsf{pp}, \mathsf{K}_C^{\mathsf{con}}, x)$ outputs the same value as $\mathsf{CPRF.Eval}(\mathsf{pp}, \mathsf{K}, x)$ when $C(x) = 1$.

A CPRF is said to be (adaptive) *pseudorandomness on constrained points*, when informally, it infeasible for an adversary to evaluate on a point when only given constrained keys that are constrained on that particular point. Here, adaptive security dictates that an adversary can adaptively query the constrained keys even after seeing polynomially many evaluations. The formal definition is omitted to the full version.

3 Lattice Evaluations

In this section, we show various lattice evaluation algorithms that will be used in the description of our IPE scheme in Sec. 5. We start by recalling the following lemma, which is an abstraction of the evaluation algorithms developed in a long sequence of works [10,26,29,37].

Lemma 3.1 ([46, Theorem 2.5]). *There exist efficient deterministic algorithms* EvalF *and* EvalFX *such that for all $n, q, \ell \in \mathbb{N}$ and $m \geq n\lceil \log q \rceil$, for any depth d boolean circuit $f : \{0,1\}^\ell \to \{0,1\}^k$, input $x \in \{0,1\}^\ell$, and matrix $\mathbf{A} \in \mathbb{Z}_q^{n \times m(\ell+1)}$, the outputs $\mathbf{H} := \mathsf{EvalF}(f, \mathbf{A})$ and $\widehat{\mathbf{H}} := \mathsf{EvalFX}(f, x, \mathbf{A})$ are both in $\mathbb{Z}^{m(\ell+1) \times m(k+1)}$ and it holds that $\|\mathbf{H}\|_\infty, \|\widehat{\mathbf{H}}\|_\infty \leq (2m)^d$, and*

$$[\mathbf{A} - (1, x) \otimes \mathbf{G}]\widehat{\mathbf{H}} = \mathbf{A}\mathbf{H} - (1, f(x)) \otimes \mathbf{G} \mod q.$$

Moreover, for any pair of circuits $f : \{0,1\}^\ell \to \{0,1\}^k$, $g : \{0,1\}^k \to \{0,1\}^t$ and for any matrix $\mathbf{A} \in \mathbb{Z}_q^{n \times m(\ell+1)}$, the outputs $\mathbf{H}_f := \mathsf{EvalF}(f, \mathbf{A})$, $\mathbf{H}_g := \mathsf{EvalF}(g, \mathbf{A}\mathbf{H}_f)$ and $\mathbf{H}_{g \circ f} := \mathsf{EvalF}(g \circ f, \mathbf{A})$ satisfy $\mathbf{H}_f \mathbf{H}_g = \mathbf{H}_{g \circ f}$.

Here, we note that unlike in the original theorem [46, Theorem 2.5], we would require the constant 1 term to handle functions with a constant term. More details are provided in the full version.

In the following, we generalize the above lemma so that we can treat the case where x and $f(x)$ are integer vectors rather than bit strings. We first consider the case where function f is a linear function over $\mathbb{Z}^\ell$ in Sec. 3.1. The algorithm we give is essentially the same as that given in the previous work [10], but we will make a key observation that the evaluation results of two functions are the same as long as they are functionally equivalent *even if they are expressed as different (arithmetic) circuits*. In Sec. 3.2, we consider the case where f is a specific type of non-linear function taking a vector $\mathbf{x} \in \mathbb{Z}^\ell$ as input; f initially computes a binary representation of the input $\mathbf{x}$, and then computes an arbitrary function represented by a boolean circuit over that binarized input. We note that an evaluation algorithm for arithmetic circuits over $\mathbb{Z}$ in previous work [10] is not enough for our purpose. This is because the binary representation of an integer may not be efficiently computable by an arithmetic circuit over $\mathbb{Z}$ in case the integer is super-polynomially large.

3.1 Linear Evaluation

Here, we deal with linear functions over $\mathbb{Z}$ that are expressed by arithmetic circuits.

Definition 3.1. *For a (homogeneous) linear function $f : \mathbb{Z}^\ell \to \mathbb{Z}^k$, we denote the unique matrix that represents f by $\mathbf{M}_f$. That is, $\mathbf{M}_f = (m_{i,j})_{i\in[\ell],j\in[k]} \in \mathbb{Z}^{\ell\times k}$ is the matrix such that we have $f(\mathbf{x})^\top = \mathbf{x}^\top \cdot \mathbf{M}_f$. We denote $\|f\|_\infty$ to mean $\|\mathbf{M}_f\|_\infty$ and call $\|f\|_\infty$ the norm of f.*

The following lemma gives an evaluation algorithm for linear functions. The proof can be checked easily and is omitted to the full version.

Lemma 3.2. *There exist efficient deterministic algorithms* $\mathsf{EvalLin}$ *such that for all $n, m, q, \ell \in \mathbb{N}$, for any linear function $f : \mathbb{Z}^\ell \to \mathbb{Z}^k$, input $\mathbf{x} \in \mathbb{Z}^\ell$, and matrix $\mathbf{A} \in \mathbb{Z}_q^{n\times m(\ell+1)}$, the output $\overline{\mathbf{M}}_f := \mathsf{EvalLin}(f)$ is in $\mathbb{Z}^{m(\ell+1)\times m(k+1)}$ and it holds that $\|\overline{\mathbf{M}}_f\|_\infty = \max\{1, \|f\|_\infty\}$, and*

$$[\mathbf{A} - (1, \mathbf{x}^\top) \otimes \mathbf{G}]\overline{\mathbf{M}}_f = \mathbf{A}\overline{\mathbf{M}}_f - (1, f(\mathbf{x})^\top) \otimes \mathbf{G} \mod q.$$

Moreover, for any tuple of linear functions $f : \mathbb{Z}^\ell \to \mathbb{Z}^k$, $g : \mathbb{Z}^k \to \mathbb{Z}^t$, and $h : \mathbb{Z}^\ell \to \mathbb{Z}^t$ such that $g \circ f(\mathbf{x}) = h(\mathbf{x})$ for all $\mathbf{x} \in \mathbb{Z}^\ell$, the outputs $\overline{\mathbf{M}}_f := \mathsf{EvalLin}(f)$, $\overline{\mathbf{M}}_g := \mathsf{EvalLin}(g)$ and $\overline{\mathbf{M}}_h := \mathsf{EvalLin}(h)$ satisfy $\overline{\mathbf{M}}_f\overline{\mathbf{M}}_g = \overline{\mathbf{M}}_h$.

Looking ahead, the latter part of the above lemma is a key property for our generalization of the Tsabary's framework [46] when constructing adaptively secure ABE. Note that in the general non-linear case, an analogue of this property only holds when $g \circ f$ and h are expressed exactly as the same circuit (See Lemma 3.1).

3.2 Non-linear Evaluation

Next, we consider the non-linear case where f takes as input a vector $\mathbf{x} \in \mathbb{Z}^\ell$. Specifically, f first computes the binary decomposition of $\mathbf{x}$, and then performs an arbitrary computation represented by a boolean circuit. Since the latter part of the computation can be handled by Lemma 3.1, all we have to do is to give a homomorphic evaluation algorithm that handles the former part of the computation. The following lemma enables us to do this as long as $\|\mathbf{x}\|_\infty$ is bounded by some polynomial in κ. At a high level, when $\|\mathbf{x}\|_\infty$ is only a polynomial, we would be able to efficiently compute the bit-decomposition of $\mathbf{x}$ using Lagrange interpolation. We omit the proof to the full version. In the statement below, we focus on the case of $\ell = 1$.

Lemma 3.3. *There exist efficient deterministic algorithms* EvalBD *and* $\mathsf{EvalBDX}$ *such that for all $n, m, M \in \mathbb{N}$, prime q satisfying $q > 2M + 1$ and $m \geq n\lceil\log q\rceil$, $x \in [-M, M]$, and for any matrix $\mathbf{A} \in \mathbb{Z}_q^{n\times 2m}$, the outputs*

$\mathbf{H} := \mathsf{EvalBD}(1^M, \mathbf{A})$ *and* $\widehat{\mathbf{H}} := \mathsf{EvalBDX}(1^M, x, \mathbf{A})$ *are both in* $\mathbb{Z}^{2m \times m\lceil \log q \rceil}$ *and it holds that* $\|\mathbf{H}\|_\infty, \|\widehat{\mathbf{H}}\|_\infty \leq (2mM)^{2M+1}$, *and*

$$[\mathbf{A} - (1, x) \otimes \mathbf{G}]\widehat{\mathbf{H}} = \mathbf{A}\mathbf{H} - \mathsf{BitDecomp}(x) \otimes \mathbf{G} \mod q \tag{13}$$

where $\mathsf{BitDecomp}(x) \in \{0,1\}^{\lceil \log q \rceil}$ *denotes the bit decomposition of* x.

Finally, we combine Lemmata 3.1 and 3.3, to obtain our desired lemma. Let q and M be integers such that $q > 2M+1$. In the following lemma, we deal with function $f : [-M, M]^\ell \rightarrow \{0,1\}^k$ that can be represented by a Boolean circuit $\tilde{f} : \{0,1\}^{\ell\lceil \log q \rceil} \rightarrow \{0,1\}^k$ in the sense that we have

$$f(\mathbf{x}) = \tilde{f}(\mathsf{BitDecomp}(x_1), \ldots, \mathsf{BitDecomp}(x_\ell))$$

for any $\mathbf{x} \in [-M, M]^\ell$. The proof is quite standard and is omitted to the full version.

Lemma 3.4. *There exist efficient deterministic algorithms* $\mathsf{EvalF}^{\mathsf{bd}}$ *and* $\mathsf{EvalFX}^{\mathsf{bd}}$ *such that for all* $n, m, \ell, M \in \mathbb{N}$, *prime* q *satisfying* $q > 2M + 1$ *and* $m \geq n\lceil \log q \rceil$, *for any function* $f : [-M, M]^\ell \rightarrow \{0,1\}^k$ *that can be expressed as an efficient depth* d *boolean circuit* $\tilde{f} : \{0,1\}^{\ell\lceil \log q \rceil} \rightarrow \{0,1\}^k$, *for every* $\mathbf{x} \in [-M, M]^\ell$, *and for any matrix* $\mathbf{A} \in \mathbb{Z}_q^{n \times m(\ell+1)}$, *the outputs* $\mathbf{H} := \mathsf{EvalF}^{\mathsf{bd}}(1^M, f, \mathbf{A})$ *and* $\widehat{\mathbf{H}} := \mathsf{EvalFX}^{\mathsf{bd}}(1^M, f, \mathbf{x}, \mathbf{A})$ *are both in* $\mathbb{Z}^{m(\ell+1) \times m(k+1)}$ *and it holds that* $\|\mathbf{H}\|_\infty, \|\widehat{\mathbf{H}}\|_\infty \leq \ell\lceil \log q \rceil (2mM)^{d+2M+2}$ *and*

$$[\mathbf{A} - (1, \mathbf{x}^\top) \otimes \mathbf{G}]\widehat{\mathbf{H}} = \mathbf{A}\mathbf{H} - (1, f(\mathbf{x})) \otimes \mathbf{G} \mod q. \tag{14}$$

4 IPE-Conforming CPRF

In this section, we introduce the notion of *IPE-conforming* CPRF and instantiate it from the LWE assumption. An IPE-conforming CPRF is the main building block for our adaptively secure IPE schemes. Although Tsabary presents how to achieve adaptively secure ABE by using *conforming* CPRFs, the requirements on conforming CPRFs are quite strong and it seems very difficult to achieve such conforming CPRFs for inner-products. To achieve adaptively secure IPE, we relax the requirements.

4.1 Definition

Here, we define an IPE-conforming CPRF.

Definition 4.1. *A CPRF scheme* $\Pi_{\mathsf{CPRF}} = (\mathsf{CPRF.Setup}, \mathsf{CPRF.Eval}, \mathsf{CPRF.Constrain}, \mathsf{CPRF.ConstrainEval})$ *that supports inner products over* $\mathcal{D} := [-B, B]^\ell \subset \mathbb{Z}^\ell$ *is said to be IPE-conforming if it satisfies the following properties:*

- *Partial linear evaluation (Definition 4.2)*
- *Key simulation (Definition 4.3)*
- *Uniformity (Definition 4.4)*

The partial linear evaluation property is a relaxed variant of the gradual evaluation property for conforming CPRFs defined by Tsabary [46]. Recall that the gradual evaluation property of Tsabary [46] requires that (a sub-circuit of) the composition of $\mathsf{CPRF.Constrain}$ and $\mathsf{CPRF.ConstrainEval}$ is identical to $\mathsf{CPRF.Eval}$ *as a circuit.* On the other hand, we only require that they are identical as (arithmetic) circuits *excluding the linear computation.* The precise definition follows.

Definition 4.2 (Partial linear evaluation). *The algorithm* $\mathsf{CPRF.Eval}$ *(resp.* $\mathsf{CPRF.ConstrainEval}$*) can be divided into a linear part* $\mathsf{CPRF.EvalLin}$ *(resp.* $\mathsf{CPRF.ConstrainEvalLin}$*) and a non-linear part* $\mathsf{CPRF.EvalNonLin}$ *(resp.* $\mathsf{CPRF.ConstrainEvalNonLin}$*) with the following syntax:*

- $\mathsf{CPRF.EvalLin}(\mathsf{K}, \mathbf{x}) \to \mathsf{K}_{\mathbf{x}}^{\mathsf{int}} \in \mathbb{Z}^{\xi}$,
- $\mathsf{CPRF.EvalNonLin}(\mathsf{pp}, \mathsf{K}_{\mathbf{x}}^{\mathsf{int}}, \mathbf{x}) \to \mathsf{PRF}(\mathsf{K}, \mathbf{x})$,
- $\mathsf{CPRF.ConstrainEvalLin}(\mathsf{K}_{\mathbf{y}}^{\mathsf{con}}, \mathbf{x}) \to \mathsf{K}_{\mathbf{y},\mathbf{x}}^{\mathsf{con\text{-}int}} \in \mathbb{Z}^{\xi}$,
- $\mathsf{CPRF.ConstrainEvalNonLin}(\mathsf{pp}, \mathsf{K}_{\mathbf{y},\mathbf{x}}^{\mathsf{con\text{-}int}}, \mathbf{x}) \to \mathsf{PRF}(\mathsf{K}, \mathbf{x})$,

where the superscript int *stands for "intermediate key" and* $\mathsf{K}_{\mathbf{y}}^{\mathsf{con}}$ *denotes the constrained key for the inner-product constraint for vector* $\mathbf{y}$*. Specifically, we have*

$$\mathsf{CPRF.EvalNonLin}(\mathsf{pp}, \mathsf{CPRF.EvalLin}(\mathsf{K}, \mathbf{x}), \mathbf{x}) = \mathsf{CPRF.Eval}(\mathsf{K}, \mathbf{x})$$

and

$$\mathsf{CPRF.ConstrainEvalNonLin}(\mathsf{pp}, \mathsf{CPRF.ConstrainEvalLin}(\mathsf{K}, \mathbf{x}), \mathbf{x}) = \mathsf{CPRF.ConstrainEval}(\mathsf{K}, \mathbf{x}).$$

We require the following:

1. $\mathsf{CPRF.EvalNonLin}$ *and* $\mathsf{CPRF.ConstrainEvalNonLin}$ *are exactly the same algorithms. That is, they are expressed identically as circuits.*
2. *For any* $\mathbf{x}, \mathbf{y}$ *such that* $\langle \mathbf{x}, \mathbf{y} \rangle = 0$ *and* $\mathsf{K} \xleftarrow{\$} \mathsf{CPRF.Setup}(\mathsf{pp})$ *where* $\mathsf{pp} \xleftarrow{\$} \mathsf{CPRF.Setup}(1^{\kappa})$*, we have*
$$\mathsf{CPRF.EvalLin}(\mathsf{K}, \mathbf{x}) = \mathsf{CPRF.ConstrainEvalLin}(\mathsf{CPRF.Constrain}(\mathsf{K}, \mathbf{y}), \mathbf{x}).$$
Or equivalently, we have $\mathsf{K}_{\mathbf{x}}^{\mathsf{int}} = \mathsf{K}_{\mathbf{y},\mathbf{x}}^{\mathsf{con\text{-}int}}$.
3. K, $\mathsf{K}_{\mathbf{y}}^{\mathsf{con}}$, $\mathsf{K}_{\mathbf{x}}^{\mathsf{int}}$, *and* $\mathsf{K}_{\mathbf{y},\mathbf{x}}^{\mathsf{con\text{-}int}}$ *are integer vectors. Also, for any* $\mathbf{x}, \mathbf{y} \in \mathcal{D}$*, algorithms* $\mathsf{CPRF.Constrain}(\cdot, \mathbf{y})$, $\mathsf{CPRF.EvalLin}(\cdot, \mathbf{x})$ *and* $\mathsf{CPRF.ConstrainEvalLin}(\cdot, \mathbf{x})$ *are linear functions over* $\mathbb{Z}$*. Moreover, their norms are at most* $\mathsf{poly}(\kappa, \ell, B)$*. (See Definition 3.1 for the definition of a norm of a linear function.)*

4. We have $\|\mathsf{K}^{\mathsf{int}}_{\mathbf{x}}\|_\infty = \mathsf{poly}(\kappa, \ell, B)$ *where* $\mathsf{pp} \xleftarrow{\$} \mathsf{CPRF.Setup}(1^\kappa)$, $\mathsf{K} \xleftarrow{\$} \mathsf{CPRF.Setup}(\mathsf{pp})$, *and* $\mathsf{K}^{\mathsf{int}}_{\mathbf{x}} := \mathsf{CPRF.EvalLin}(\mathsf{K}, \mathbf{x})$.

We stress that, in the second item above, we *do not* require that $\mathsf{CPRF.EvalLin}(\mathsf{K}, \mathbf{x})$ and $\mathsf{CPRF.ConstrainEvalLin}(\mathsf{CPRF.Constrain}(\mathsf{K}, \mathbf{y}), \mathbf{x})$ to be identical as (arithmetic) circuits; they are only required to have the same input/output. This is a crucial difference from the notion of conforming CPRF by Tsabary [46].

The key simulation property is essentially the same as defined by Tsabary [46].

Definition 4.3 (Key simulation). *The key simulation security is defined by the following game between an adversary* $\mathcal{A}$ *and a challenger:*

Setup: *At the beginning of the game, the challenger generates the public parameter* $\mathsf{pp} \xleftarrow{\$} \mathsf{CPRF.Setup}(1^\kappa)$ *and master key* $\mathsf{K} \xleftarrow{\$} \mathsf{CPRF.Gen}(\mathsf{pp})$, *and sends* pp *to* $\mathcal{A}$.

Queries: $\mathcal{A}$ *can adaptively make unbounded number of evaluation queries. Upon a query* $\mathbf{x} \in \mathcal{D}$, *the challenger returns* $r \xleftarrow{\$} \mathsf{CPRF.Eval}(\mathsf{pp}, \mathsf{K}, \mathbf{x})$.

Challenge Phase: *At some point,* $\mathcal{A}$ *makes a challenge query* $\mathbf{y}^* \in \mathcal{D}$. *Then the challenger uniformly picks* $\mathsf{coin} \xleftarrow{\$} \{0, 1\}$. *If* $\mathsf{coin} = 0$, *then the challenger samples* $\widetilde{\mathsf{K}} \xleftarrow{\$} \mathsf{CPRF.Gen}(\mathsf{pp})$ *and returns* $\widetilde{\mathsf{K}}^{\mathsf{con}}_{\mathbf{y}^*} \xleftarrow{\$} \mathsf{CPRF.Constrain}(\widetilde{\mathsf{K}}, \mathbf{y}^*)$ *and otherwise returns* $\mathsf{K}^{\mathsf{con}}_{\mathbf{y}^*} \xleftarrow{\$} \mathsf{CPRF.Constrain}(\mathsf{K}, \mathbf{y}^*)$.

Queries: *After the challenge phase,* $\mathcal{A}$ *may continue to adaptively make unbounded number of evaluation queries. Upon a query* $\mathbf{x} \in \mathcal{D}$, *the challenger returns* $r \xleftarrow{\$} \mathsf{CPRF.Eval}(\mathsf{pp}, \mathsf{K}, \mathbf{x})$.

Guess: *Eventually,* $\mathcal{A}$ *outputs* $\widehat{\mathsf{coin}}$ *as a guess for* coin.

We say the adversary $\mathcal{A}$ *wins the game if* $\widehat{\mathsf{coin}} = \mathsf{coin}$ *and for any evaluation query* $\mathbf{x}$, *we have* $\langle \mathbf{x}, \mathbf{y}^* \rangle \neq 0$. *We require that for all PPT adversary* $\mathcal{A}$, $|\Pr[\mathcal{A}\ wins] - 1/2| = \mathsf{negl}(\kappa)$ *holds.*

We note that the key simulation property easily follows from the adaptive single-key security of a standard CPRF.

Lemma 4.1 (Implicit in [46]**).** *If* Π_{CPRF} *is adaptively single-key secure, then it also satisfies the key simulation property.*

The uniformity requires that for any fixed input, the PRF value is uniform over the random choice of a key.

Definition 4.4 (Uniformity). *For all* $x \in \mathcal{D}$ *and* $r \in \mathcal{R}$, *we have*

$$\Pr[\mathsf{CPRF.Eval}(\mathsf{K}, \mathbf{x}) = r : \mathsf{pp} \xleftarrow{\$} \mathsf{CPRF.Setup}(1^\kappa), \mathsf{K} \xleftarrow{\$} \mathsf{CPRF.Setup}(\mathsf{pp})] = 1/|\mathcal{R}|.$$

We note that this is a very mild property, and we can generically add this property by applying a one-time pad. Namely, suppose that we include a uniform string $R \in \mathcal{R}$ in K, and slightly modify the evaluation algorithm so that it outputs the XOR of the original output and R. Then it is clear that the resulting scheme satisfies the uniformity property. Moreover, it is easy to see that this conversion preserves the partial linear evaluation property and key simulation property. Combining this observation with Lemma 4.1, we obtain the following lemma.

Lemma 4.2. *If there exists a CPRF for inner-products that satisfies the partial linear evaluation property and the adaptive single-key security, then there exists an IPE-conforming CPRF that satisfies the partial linear evaluation, key simulation, and uniformity properties.*

Following [46], we use the following notations in Sec. 5:

- $U^{\mathsf{lin}}_{\mathbf{k}\to\mathbf{x}}$: A linear function computing $\mathsf{CPRF.EvalLin}(\cdot, \mathbf{x})$.
- $U^{\mathsf{lin}}_{\mathbf{k}\to\mathbf{y}}$: A linear function computing $\mathsf{CPRF.Constrain}(\cdot, \mathbf{y})$.
- $U^{\mathsf{lin}}_{\mathbf{y}\to\mathbf{x}}$: A linear function computing $\mathsf{CPRF.ConstrainEvalLin}(\cdot, \mathbf{x})$.
- $U^{\mathsf{non\text{-}lin}}_{\mathbf{x}}$: A (not necesarily linear) function that computes $\mathsf{CPRF.EvalNonLin}(\mathsf{pp}, \cdot, \mathbf{x})$ $(= \mathsf{CPRF.ConstrainEvalNonLin}(\mathsf{pp}, \cdot, \mathbf{x}))$.

Note that $U^{\mathsf{lin}}_{\mathbf{k}\to\mathbf{x}}$ and $U^{\mathsf{lin}}_{\mathbf{y}\to\mathbf{x}} \circ U^{\mathsf{lin}}_{\mathbf{k}\to\mathbf{y}}$ are functionally equivalent for any $\mathbf{x}, \mathbf{y} \in \mathcal{D}$ such that $\langle \mathbf{x}, \mathbf{y} \rangle = 0$ by Item 2 of Definition 4.2.

4.2 Construction

We show that a variant of the LWE-based CPRF recently proposed by Davidson et al. [23] satisfies the required property. The scheme and security proof are largely the same as theirs. The detais can be found in the full version. Then we obtain the following theorem.

Theorem 4.1. *There exists an IPE-conforming CPRF assuming the LWE assumption with sub-exponential modulus size.*

5 Adaptively Secure IPE

In this section, we give a construction of an adaptively secure IPE scheme. The scheme will deal with inner products over vectors $\mathcal{D} := [-B, B]^\ell \subset \mathbb{Z}^\ell$ for any arbitrarily chosen $B(\kappa) = \mathsf{poly}(\kappa)$ and $\ell(\kappa) = \mathsf{poly}(\kappa)$. The main ingredient of the construction is a CPRF scheme $\Pi_{\mathsf{CPRF}} = (\mathsf{CPRF.Setup}, \mathsf{CPRF.Gen}, \mathsf{CPRF.Eval}, \mathsf{CPRF.Constrain}, \mathsf{CPRF.ConstrainEval})$ for inner products over vectors in $\mathcal{D} := [-B, B]^\ell \subset \mathbb{Z}^\ell$ with IPE conforming property (See Definition 4.1). We assume that the size of the range $\mathcal{R}$ of the CPRF is super-polynomial in κ. We can instantiate such CPRF by the scheme in Theorem 4.1. To describe our scheme, we introduce the following parameters.

- For simplicity of notation, we assume that K, $\mathsf{K}^{\mathsf{int}}_{\mathbf{x}}$, and $\mathsf{K}^{\mathsf{con}}_{\mathbf{y}}$ are integer vectors with the same dimension $s(\kappa)$. This can be realized by choosing $s(\kappa)$ to be the maximum length of these vectors and padding the vectors with smaller dimensions by zeros. It is easy to see that the partial linear evaluation property and the security of the CPRF are preserved with this modification. Furthermore, by the efficiency of the CPRF, we can set $s(\kappa) = \mathsf{poly}(B(\kappa), \ell(\kappa)) = \mathsf{poly}(\kappa)$.

- We let $M(\kappa)$ be an upper bound on $\|\mathsf{K}_{\mathbf{x}}^{\mathsf{int}}\|_\infty$ and the norms of $U_{\mathbf{k}\to\mathbf{x}}^{\mathsf{lin}}$, $U_{\mathbf{k}\to\mathbf{y}}^{\mathsf{lin}}$, and $U_{\mathbf{x}}^{\mathsf{non\text{-}lin}}$, where we refer to Definition 3.1 for the definition of norm for linear functions. By Items 3 and 4 of Definition 4.2, these quantities are bounded by $\mathsf{poly}(\kappa, \ell(\kappa), B(\kappa)) \leq \mathsf{poly}(\kappa)$. We therefore can set $M(\kappa) = \mathsf{poly}(\kappa)$.
- We let $\eta(\kappa)$ to be the length of the output of the CPRF represented as a binary string. Namely, we have $\mathcal{R} \subseteq \{0,1\}^\eta$, where $\mathcal{R}$ is the range of the CPRF. We also assume $1/|\mathcal{R}| = \mathsf{negl}(\kappa)$ without loss of generality. If the CPRF does not satisfy the property, we can satisfy this by running $\omega(\kappa)$ number of the CPRF in parallel. We can easily see that this preserves the partial linear evaluation (Definition 4.2), key simulation security (Definition 4.3), and uniformity (Definition 4.4) properties.
- We let $d(\kappa)$ be an upper bound on the depth of the circuits $U_{\mathbf{x}}^{\mathsf{non\text{-}lin}}$ and Eq_r, where $\mathsf{Eq}_r : \{0,1\}^\eta \to \{0,1\}$ is the circuit that on input $\widetilde{r} \in \{0,1\}^\eta$ returns 1 if and only if $r = \widetilde{r}$ for $r \in \{0,1\}^\eta$. We have that $d(\kappa) = \mathsf{poly}(\kappa, \ell(\kappa), B(\kappa)) \leq \mathsf{poly}(\kappa)$ by the efficiency of the CPRF.

Then our IPE scheme $\Pi_{\mathsf{IPE}} = (\mathsf{IPE.Setup}, \mathsf{IPE.Enc}, \mathsf{IPE.KeyGen}, \mathsf{IPE.Dec})$ is described as follows. The lattice dimension $n(\kappa)$ and $m(\kappa)$, LWE modulus $q(\kappa)$, LWE noise distribution χ, Gaussian parameters $\tau_0(\kappa)$ and $\tau(\kappa)$, and width of noise $\Gamma(\kappa)$ in the scheme will be specified right after the description of the scheme.

$\mathsf{IPE.Setup}(1^\kappa)$: On input the security parameter 1^κ, it generates $\mathsf{pp}_{\mathsf{CPRF}} \overset{\$}{\leftarrow} \mathsf{CPRF.Setup}(1^\kappa)$, $\mathbf{k} \overset{\$}{\leftarrow} \mathsf{CPRF.Gen}(\mathsf{pp}_{\mathsf{CPRF}})$,[9] samples $(\mathbf{B}, \mathbf{B}_{\tau_0}^{-1}) \overset{\$}{\leftarrow} \mathsf{TrapGen}(1^n, 1^m, q)$, $\mathbf{A} \overset{\$}{\leftarrow} \mathbb{Z}_q^{n\times m(s+1)}$, and $\mathbf{v} \overset{\$}{\leftarrow} \mathbb{Z}_q^n$, and outputs $\mathsf{pp} := (\mathbf{B}, \mathbf{A}, \mathbf{v}, \mathsf{pp}_{\mathsf{CPRF}})$ and $\mathsf{msk} := (\mathbf{B}_{\tau_0}^{-1}, \mathbf{k})$.

$\mathsf{IPE.Enc}(\mathsf{pp}, \mathbf{y}, \mathsf{M})$: On input the public parameter pp, a vector $\mathbf{y} \in [-B, B]^\ell$, and a message $\mathsf{M} \in \{0,1\}$, it generates $\widetilde{\mathbf{k}} \overset{\$}{\leftarrow} \mathsf{CPRF.Gen}(\mathsf{pp}_{\mathsf{CPRF}})$ and samples $\mathbf{s} \overset{\$}{\leftarrow} \mathbb{Z}_q^n$, $\mathbf{e}_0 \overset{\$}{\leftarrow} \chi^m$, $\mathbf{e}_1 \overset{\$}{\leftarrow} [-\Gamma, \Gamma]^{m(s+1)}$, and $e_2 \overset{\$}{\leftarrow} \chi$. It then computes $\widetilde{\mathbf{k}}_{\mathbf{y}}^{\mathsf{con}} \leftarrow \mathsf{CPRF.Constrain}(\widetilde{\mathbf{k}}, C_{\mathbf{y}})$, sets

$$\mathbf{c}_0 = \mathbf{s}^\top\mathbf{B} + \mathbf{e}_0^\top, \quad \mathbf{c}_1 = \mathbf{s}^\top[\mathbf{A}_{\mathbf{y}}^{\mathsf{con}} - (1(\widetilde{\mathbf{k}}_{\mathbf{y}}^{\mathsf{con}})^\top)\otimes\mathbf{G}] + \mathbf{e}_1^\top, \quad c_2 = \mathbf{s}^\top\mathbf{v} + e_2 + \mathsf{M}\lfloor q/2\rfloor$$

where $\mathbf{A}_{\mathbf{y}}^{\mathsf{con}} = \mathbf{A}\overline{\mathbf{M}}_{\mathbf{k}\to\mathbf{y}}$ for $\overline{\mathbf{M}}_{\mathbf{k}\to\mathbf{y}} \leftarrow \mathsf{EvalLin}(U_{\mathbf{k}\to\mathbf{y}}^{\mathsf{lin}})$, and outputs $\mathsf{ct} := (\widetilde{\mathbf{k}}_{\mathbf{y}}^{\mathsf{con}}, \mathbf{c}_0, \mathbf{c}_1, c_2)$.

$\mathsf{IPE.KeyGen}(\mathsf{pp}, \mathsf{msk}, \mathbf{x})$: On input the master secret key $\mathsf{msk} = (\mathbf{B}_{\tau_0}^{-1}, \mathbf{k})$ and a vector $\mathbf{x} \in [-B, B]^\ell$, it computes $r := \mathsf{CPRF.Eval}(\mathbf{k}, \mathbf{x})$,

$$\overline{\mathbf{M}}_{\mathbf{k}\to\mathbf{x}} \leftarrow \mathsf{EvalLin}(U_{\mathbf{k}\to\mathbf{x}}^{\mathsf{lin}}), \qquad \mathbf{A}_{\mathbf{x}}^{\mathsf{int}} := \mathbf{A}\overline{\mathbf{M}}_{\mathbf{k}\to\mathbf{x}},$$
$$\mathbf{H}_{\mathbf{x}} \leftarrow \mathsf{EvalF}^{\mathsf{bd}}(1^M, U_{\mathbf{x}}^{\mathsf{non\text{-}lin}}, \mathbf{A}_{\mathbf{x}}^{\mathsf{int}}), \qquad \mathbf{A}_{\mathbf{x}}^{\mathsf{eval}} := \mathbf{A}_{\mathbf{x}}^{\mathsf{int}}\mathbf{H}_{\mathbf{x}}$$
$$\mathbf{H}_r \leftarrow \mathsf{EvalF}(\mathsf{Eq}_r, \mathbf{A}_{\mathbf{x}}^{\mathsf{eval}}), \qquad \mathbf{A}_{\mathbf{x},r}^{\mathsf{eq}} := \mathbf{A}_{\mathbf{x}}^{\mathsf{eval}}\mathbf{H}_r,$$

[9] We use $\mathbf{k}$ instead of K to denote the master secret key of CPRF for making it clear that it is a vector.

It then parses

$$\mathbf{A}^{\mathsf{eq}}_{\mathbf{x},r} \to [\mathbf{A}^{\mathsf{eq}}_{\mathbf{x},r,0} || \mathbf{A}^{\mathsf{eq}}_{\mathbf{x},r,1}] \in \mathbb{Z}_q^{n\times m} \times \mathbb{Z}_q^{n\times m},$$

samples $\mathbf{u} \xleftarrow{\$} [\mathbf{B}||\mathbf{A}^{\mathsf{eq}}_{\mathbf{x},r,1}]^{-1}_{\tau}(\mathbf{v})$ by using the trapdoor $\mathbf{B}^{-1}_{\tau_0}$, and outputs $\mathsf{sk}_{\mathbf{x}} := (r, \mathbf{u})$.

$\mathsf{IPE.Dec}(\mathsf{pp}, \mathsf{sk}_{\mathbf{x}}, \mathsf{ct}, \mathbf{y}, \mathbf{x})$: On input a secret key $\mathsf{sk}_{\mathbf{x}} = (r, \mathbf{u})$, a ciphertext $\mathsf{ct} = (\widetilde{\mathbf{k}}^{\mathsf{con}}_{\mathbf{y}}, \mathbf{c}_0, \mathbf{c}_1, c_2)$, and vectors $\mathbf{y} \in [-B, B]^{\ell}$ and $\mathbf{x} \in [-B, B]^{\ell}$, it computes $\widetilde{\mathbf{k}}^{\mathsf{int}}_{\mathbf{x}} := U^{\mathsf{lin}}_{\mathbf{y}\to\mathbf{x}}(\widetilde{\mathbf{k}}^{\mathsf{con}}_{\mathbf{y}})$ and $\widetilde{r} := U^{\mathsf{non\text{-}lin}}_{\mathbf{x}}(\widetilde{\mathbf{k}}^{\mathsf{int}}_{\mathbf{x}})$ and aborts if $r = \widetilde{r}$. Otherwise, it computes

$$\overline{\mathbf{M}}_{\mathbf{y}\to\mathbf{x}} \leftarrow \mathsf{EvalLin}(U^{\mathsf{lin}}_{\mathbf{y}\to\mathbf{x}}), \quad \widehat{\mathbf{H}}_{\mathbf{x}} \leftarrow \mathsf{EvalFX}^{\mathsf{bd}}(1^M, U^{\mathsf{non\text{-}lin}}_{\mathbf{x}}, \widetilde{\mathbf{k}}^{\mathsf{int}}_{\mathbf{x}}, \mathbf{A}^{\mathsf{int}}_{\mathbf{x}}),$$
$$\widehat{\mathbf{H}}_r \leftarrow \mathsf{EvalFX}(\mathsf{Eq}_r, \widetilde{r}, \mathbf{A}^{\mathsf{eval}}_{\mathbf{x}})$$

where $\mathbf{A}^{\mathsf{int}}_{\mathbf{x}}$, and $\mathbf{A}^{\mathsf{eval}}_{\mathbf{x}}$ are computed as in $\mathsf{IPE.KeyGen}$. Then it computes $u := c_2 - [\mathbf{c}_0||\mathbf{c}_1\overline{\mathbf{M}}_{\mathbf{y}\to\mathbf{x}}\widehat{\mathbf{H}}_{\mathbf{x}}\widehat{\mathbf{H}}_r[\mathbf{0}_m||\mathbf{I}_m]^{\top}]\mathbf{u}$, and output 1 if $|u| \geq q/4$ and 0 otherwise.

A concrete parameter candidate and the correctness of the scheme are provided in the full version. We note that the parameters are set in a way that the LWE assumption with sub-exponential modulus size is believed to be hard. The security of our scheme is provided by the following theorem.

Theorem 5.1. *Under the hardness of the* $\mathsf{LWE}_{n,m,q,D_{\mathbb{Z},\chi}}$ *problem,* Π_{IPE} *is adaptively payload-hiding if* Π_{CPRF} *is IPE-conforming.*

Proof. (sketc.h) We consider the following sequance of games between a valid adversary $\mathcal{A}$ and a challenger. In the following, we only give brief explanations on why each game is indistinguishable from the previous game. A full proof can be found in the full version. Below, let E_i denote the probability that $\widehat{\mathsf{coin}} = \mathsf{coin}$ holds in Game_i.

Game_0: This is the original adaptive security game. Specifically the game proceeds as follows:

- The challenger generates $\mathsf{pp}_{\mathsf{CPRF}} \xleftarrow{\$} \mathsf{CPRF.Setup}(1^{\kappa})$, $\mathbf{k} \xleftarrow{\$} \mathsf{CPRF.Gen}(\mathsf{pp}_{\mathsf{CPRF}})$, samples $(\mathbf{B}, \mathbf{B}^{-1}_{\tau_0}) \xleftarrow{\$} \mathsf{TrapGen}(1^n, 1^m, q)$, $\mathbf{A} \xleftarrow{\$} \mathbb{Z}_q^{n\times m(s+1)}$, and $\mathbf{v} \xleftarrow{\$} \mathbb{Z}_q^n$, sets $\mathsf{pp} := (\mathbf{B}, \mathbf{A}, \mathbf{v}, \mathsf{pp}_{\mathsf{CPRF}})$, and gives pp to $\mathcal{A}$.
- Given pp, $\mathcal{A}$ makes unbounded number of key generation queries and one challenge query in arbitrary order.

Key Generation: When $\mathcal{A}$ makes a key generation query $\mathbf{x} \in [-B, B]^{\ell}$, the challenger computes $r := \mathsf{CPRF.Eval}(\mathbf{k}, \mathbf{x})$,

$$\overline{\mathbf{M}}_{\mathbf{k}\to\mathbf{x}} \leftarrow \mathsf{EvalLin}(U^{\mathsf{lin}}_{\mathbf{k}\to\mathbf{x}}), \qquad \mathbf{A}^{\mathsf{int}}_{\mathbf{x}} := \mathbf{A}\overline{\mathbf{M}}_{\mathbf{k}\to\mathbf{x}},$$
$$\mathbf{H}_{\mathbf{x}} \leftarrow \mathsf{EvalF}^{\mathsf{bd}}(1^M, U^{\mathsf{non\text{-}lin}}_{\mathbf{x}}, \mathbf{A}^{\mathsf{int}}_{\mathbf{x}}), \qquad \mathbf{A}^{\mathsf{eval}}_{\mathbf{x}} := \mathbf{A}^{\mathsf{int}}_{\mathbf{x}}\mathbf{H}_{\mathbf{x}}$$
$$\mathbf{H}_r \leftarrow \mathsf{EvalF}(\mathsf{Eq}_r, \mathbf{A}^{\mathsf{eval}}_{\mathbf{x}}), \qquad \mathbf{A}^{\mathsf{eq}}_{\mathbf{x},r} := \mathbf{A}^{\mathsf{eval}}_{\mathbf{x}}\mathbf{H}_r,$$
$$\mathbf{A}^{\mathsf{eq}}_{\mathbf{x},r,1} := \mathbf{A}^{\mathsf{eq}}_{\mathbf{x},r}[\mathbf{0}_m||\mathbf{I}_m]^{\top},$$

samples $\mathbf{u} \xleftarrow{\$} [\mathbf{B}||\mathbf{A}^{\mathsf{eq}}_{\mathbf{x},r,1}]^{-1}_{\tau}(\mathbf{v})$ by using the trapdoor $\mathbf{B}^{-1}_{\tau_0}$, and returns $\mathsf{sk}_{\mathbf{x}} := (r, \mathbf{u})$ to $\mathcal{A}$.

Challenge: When $\mathcal{A}$ makes a challenge query $\mathbf{y}^*$, the challenger randomly picks $\mathsf{coin} \xleftarrow{\$} \{0,1\}$, generates $\widetilde{\mathbf{k}} \xleftarrow{\$} \mathsf{CPRF.Gen}(\mathsf{pp}_{\mathsf{CPRF}})$ and $\widetilde{\mathbf{k}}^{\mathsf{con}}_{\mathbf{y}^*} \leftarrow \mathsf{CPRF.Constrain}(\widetilde{\mathbf{k}}, C_{\mathbf{y}^*})$, samples $\mathbf{s} \xleftarrow{\$} \mathbb{Z}_q^n$, $\mathbf{e}_0 \xleftarrow{\$} \chi^m$, $\mathbf{e}_1 \xleftarrow{\$} [-\Gamma, \Gamma]^{m(s+1)}$, $e_2 \xleftarrow{\$} \chi$, and sets

$$\mathbf{c}_0 = \mathbf{s}^\top \mathbf{B} + \mathbf{e}_0^\top, \quad \mathbf{c}_1 = \mathbf{s}^\top [\mathbf{A}^{\mathsf{con}}_{\mathbf{y}^*} - (1(\widetilde{\mathbf{k}}^{\mathsf{con}}_{\mathbf{y}^*})^\top) \otimes \mathbf{G}] + \mathbf{e}_1^\top,$$
$$c_2 = \mathbf{s}^\top \mathbf{v} + e_2 + \mathsf{coin}\lfloor q/2 \rfloor$$

where $\mathbf{A}^{\mathsf{con}}_{\mathbf{y}^*} = \mathbf{A}\overline{\mathbf{M}}_{\mathbf{k}\to\mathbf{y}^*}$ for $\overline{\mathbf{M}}_{\mathbf{k}\to\mathbf{y}^*} \leftarrow \mathsf{EvalLin}(U^{\mathsf{lin}}_{\mathbf{k}\to\mathbf{y}^*})$, and returns $\mathsf{ct}^* := (\widetilde{\mathbf{k}}^{\mathsf{con}}_{\mathbf{y}^*}, \mathbf{c}_0, \mathbf{c}_1, c_2)$ to $\mathcal{A}$.

– Finally, $\mathcal{A}$ outputs its guess $\widehat{\mathsf{coin}}$.

By the definition of E_0, the advantage of $\mathcal{A}$ is $|\Pr[\mathsf{E}_0] - 1/2|$.

Game_1**:** This game is identical to the previous game except that $\widetilde{\mathbf{k}}^{\mathsf{con}}_{\mathbf{y}^*}$ used in the challenge ciphertext is replaced with $\mathbf{k}^{\mathsf{con}}_{\mathbf{y}^*} \xleftarrow{\$} \mathsf{CPRF.Constrain}(\mathbf{k}, \mathbf{y}^*)$.

By a straightforward reduction to key-simulatability of the CPRF, we have $|\Pr[\mathsf{E}_1] - \Pr[\mathsf{E}_0]| = \mathsf{negl}(\kappa)$.

Game_2**:** This game is identical to the previous game except that $\mathbf{A}$ is generated as $\mathbf{A} := \mathbf{B}\mathbf{R} + (1, \mathbf{k}^\top) \otimes \mathbf{G}$ where $\mathbf{R} \xleftarrow{\$} \{-1, 0, 1\}^{m \times m(s+1)}$.

By the leftover hash lemma, we have $|\Pr[\mathsf{E}_2] - \Pr[\mathsf{E}_1]| = \mathsf{negl}(\kappa)$.

Game_3**:** This game is identical to the previous game except that $\mathbf{c}_1$ is generated as $\mathbf{c}_1 := \mathbf{c}_0 \mathbf{R}\overline{\mathbf{M}}_{\mathbf{k}\to\mathbf{y}^*} + \mathbf{e}_1^\top$.
By Lemma 3.2, we can show that we have

$$\mathbf{c}_0 \mathbf{R}\overline{\mathbf{M}}_{\mathbf{k}\to\mathbf{y}^*} + \mathbf{e}_1^\top = \mathbf{s}^\top [\mathbf{A}^{\mathsf{con}}_{\mathbf{y}^*} - (1(\mathbf{k}^{\mathsf{con}}_{\mathbf{y}^*})^\top) \otimes \mathbf{G}] + \mathbf{e}_0^\top \mathbf{R}\overline{\mathbf{M}}_{\mathbf{k}\to\mathbf{y}^*} + \mathbf{e}_1^\top.$$

Moreover, by our choice of parameters, we can show that the distribution of $\mathbf{e}_0^\top \mathbf{R}\overline{\mathbf{M}}_{\mathbf{k}\to\mathbf{y}^*} + \mathbf{e}_1^\top$ is statistically close to that of $\mathbf{e}_1^\top$. Therefore, we have $|\Pr[\mathsf{E}_3] - \Pr[\mathsf{E}_2]| = \mathsf{negl}(\kappa)$.

Game_4**:** This game is identical to the previous game except that in each key generation, $\mathbf{u}$ is generated as $\mathbf{u} \xleftarrow{\$} [\mathbf{B}||\mathbf{B}\mathbf{R}\overline{\mathbf{M}}_{\mathbf{k}\to\mathbf{x}}\widehat{\mathbf{H}}_{\mathbf{x}}\widehat{\mathbf{H}}_r[\mathbf{0}_m||\mathbf{I}_m]^\top + \mathbf{G}]^{-1}_{\tau}(\mathbf{v})$ where $\widehat{\mathbf{H}}_{\mathbf{x}} \leftarrow \mathsf{EvalFX}^{\mathsf{bd}}(1^M, U^{\mathsf{non\text{-}lin}}_{\mathbf{x}}, \mathbf{k}^{\mathsf{int}}_{\mathbf{x}}, \mathbf{A}^{\mathsf{int}}_{\mathbf{x}})$ and $\widehat{\mathbf{H}}_r \xleftarrow{\$} \mathsf{EvalFX}(\mathsf{Eq}_r, r, \mathbf{A}^{\mathsf{eq}}_{\mathbf{x}})$. We note that this can be done using $\mathbf{R}\overline{\mathbf{M}}_{\mathbf{k}\to\mathbf{x}}\widehat{\mathbf{H}}_{\mathbf{x}}\widehat{\mathbf{H}}_r[\mathbf{0}_m||\mathbf{I}_m]^\top$ instead of using $\mathbf{B}^{-1}_{\tau_0}$ if the norm of $\mathbf{R}\overline{\mathbf{M}}_{\mathbf{k}\to\mathbf{x}}\widehat{\mathbf{H}}_{\mathbf{x}}\widehat{\mathbf{H}}_r[\mathbf{0}_m||\mathbf{I}_m]^\top$ is small enough by a standard lattice trapdoor technique [1,37].

By Lemma 3.2 and Lemma 3.4, we can show that we have

$$\mathbf{B}\mathbf{R}\overline{\mathbf{M}}_{\mathbf{k}\to\mathbf{x}}\widehat{\mathbf{H}}_{\mathbf{x}}\widehat{\mathbf{H}}_r \begin{bmatrix} \mathbf{0}_m \\ \mathbf{I}_m \end{bmatrix} + \mathbf{G} = \mathbf{A}^{\mathsf{eq}}_{\mathbf{x},r,1}.$$

Moreover, by our choice of parameters, we can show that the norm of $\mathbf{R}\overline{\mathbf{M}}_{\mathbf{k}\to\mathbf{x}}\widehat{\mathbf{H}}_{\mathbf{x}}\widehat{\mathbf{H}}_r[\mathbf{0}_m||\mathbf{I}_m]^\top$ is small enough for sampling $\mathbf{u}$ in the above way. Therefore, $|\Pr[\mathsf{E}_4] - \Pr[\mathsf{E}_3]| = \mathsf{negl}(\kappa)$.

Game_5: This game is identical to the previous game except that $\mathbf{B}$ is generated as $\mathbf{B} \xleftarrow{\$} \mathbb{Z}_q^{n\times m}$ instead of being generated with the trapdoor $\mathbf{B}_{\tau_0}^{-1}$. We note that this can be done since $\mathbf{B}_{\tau_0}^{-1}$ is no longer used due to the modification made in Game_4.

Since a matrix sampled with a trapdoor is almost uniformly distributed [25], we have $|\Pr[\mathsf{E}_5] - \Pr[\mathsf{E}_4]| = \mathsf{negl}(\kappa)$.

Game_6: This game is identical to the previous game except that $\mathbf{c}_0$ and c_2 are generated as $\mathbf{c}_0 \xleftarrow{\$} \mathbb{Z}_q^m$ and $c_2 \xleftarrow{\$} \mathbb{Z}_q$.
We can show that we have $|\Pr[\mathsf{E}_6] - \Pr[\mathsf{E}_5]| = \mathsf{negl}(\kappa)$ by a straightforward reduction to the LWE assumption. Moreover, we have $\Pr[\mathsf{E}_6] = 1/2$ since no information of coin is given to $\mathcal{A}$ in this game.

Combining the above, we obtain $|\Pr[\mathsf{E}_0] - 1/2| = \mathsf{negl}(\kappa)$, which concludes the proof of Theorem 5.1.

6 Extensions to Other Adaptively Secure Predicate Encryptions

In this section, we show how to extend our IPE over the integers $\mathbb{Z}$ from the previous section to other types of ABEs. Specifically, we provide the following type of adaptive ABEs: IPE over $\mathbb{Z}_p$ for $p = \mathsf{poly}(\kappa)$ and fuzzy IBE for small and large universe. We achieve these extensions by encoding the attributes for one predicate to attributes in another predicate. Thus, our transformations are simple and the security reductions are straightforward. Since the former two generic constructions are almost folklore, we provide the formal description in the full version.

In the following, we first show how to encode a fuzzy predicate for large universe D (i.e., D is exponentially large) into a fuzzy predicate for small universe D' (i.e., D is polynomially large). First, we define some parameters and functions. Let $D = \{0,1\}^d$ be the alphabet domain of a FIBE for large universe where $d = \mathsf{poly}(\kappa)$. That is, $\mathbf{a} = (\mathbf{a}_1, \dots, \mathbf{a}_L) \in D^L$ is a (row) vector of identities in FIBE for large universe. Let T be the threshold that satisfies $1 \le T \le L$. For a set S, a positive integer k, and a vector $\mathbf{x}, \mathbf{y} \in S^k$, let $\mathsf{HD}_{S^k}(\mathbf{x}, \mathbf{y})$ be the number of $i \in [k]$ such that $\mathbf{x}[i] \neq \mathbf{y}[i]$.

We use an error correcting code (ECC) $\mathsf{ECC} : D \to G^n$ such that $|G| = \mathsf{poly}(\kappa)$ and $n > d$. For simplicity, we use Reed-Solomon code [42]. More concretely, we consider $a \in D$ as a polynomial $p_a(X) := \sum_{i=1}^{d} a[i]X^{i-1}$ over $G := \mathbb{F}_q$ where q is a prime such that $n < q = \mathsf{poly}(\kappa)$ and a codeword is $f(a) = (p_a(1), ..., p_a(n))$. Then, $\mathsf{HD}_{G^n}(f(a), f(b)) \ge n-d+1$ holds for $a \neq b \in D$. We naturally extend the domain of f to D^L. That is, $\mathsf{ECC} : D^L \to (G^n)^L$

By the property of ECC, it holds that

$$0 \le \mathsf{HD}_{D^L}(\mathbf{a}, \mathbf{b}) \le L - T \Longrightarrow 0 \le \mathsf{HD}_{G^{nL}}(f(\mathbf{a}), f(\mathbf{b})) \le (L-T)n$$
$$L - T + 1 \le \mathsf{HD}_{D^L}(\mathbf{a}, \mathbf{b}) \le L \Longrightarrow (L-T+1)(n-d+1) \le \mathsf{HD}_{G^{nL}}(f(\mathbf{a}), f(\mathbf{b})) \le Ln$$

for two identities $\mathbf{a} = (a_1, ..., a_L), \mathbf{b} = (b_1, ..., b_L) \in D^L$. Therefore, for a fixed T, we will set (n, d) as

$$(L - T)n < (L - T + 1)(n - d + 1). \tag{15}$$

This allows us to argue that a "gap" exists in the hamming distance defined over polynomially large domains if there is a "gap" in the hamming distance defined over exponentially large domains.

Notably, we can reduce a fuzzy predicate $\mathsf{P}_{\mathsf{exp}}$ for exponentially large alphabet strings to a fuzzy predicate $\mathsf{P}_{\mathsf{poly}}$ for polynomially large alphabet strings. That is, we first encode $\mathbf{a} \in D^L$ into $f(\mathbf{a}) \in G^{nL}$ by using an ECC. Then, if the threshold of $\mathsf{P}_{\mathsf{exp}}$ is T, we set the threshold of $\mathsf{P}_{\mathsf{poly}}$ to be Tn. Lastly, we set $n > (d-1)(L-T+1)$ to satisfy Equation (15). Notice n is some polynomial in κ since $d = \mathsf{poly}(\kappa)$, $L = \mathsf{poly}(\kappa)$, and $0 \leq T \leq L$.

Translating the above encoding technique to the ABE context is straightforward and is omitted to the full version.

Acknowledgement. We thank anonymous reviewers for their helpful comments. The first and the third authors were supported by JST CREST Grant Number JPMJCR19F6 and JSPS KAKENHI Grant Number JP19H01109.

References

1. Agrawal, S., Boneh, D., Boyen, X.: Efficient lattice (H)IBE in the standard model. In: Gilbert, H. (ed.) EUROCRYPT 2010. LNCS, vol. 6110, pp. 553–572. Springer, Heidelberg (2010). https://doi.org/10.1007/978-3-642-13190-5_28
2. Agrawal, S., Boyen, X., Vaikuntanathan, V., Voulgaris, P., Wee, H.: Functional encryption for threshold functions (or fuzzy ibe) from lattices. In: Fischlin, M., Buchmann, J., Manulis, M. (eds.) PKC 2012. LNCS, vol. 7293, pp. 280–297. Springer, Heidelberg (2012)
3. Agrawal, S., Freeman, D.M., Vaikuntanathan, V.: Functional encryption for inner product predicates from learning with errors. In: Lee, D.H., Wang, X. (eds.) ASIACRYPT 2011. LNCS, vol. 7073, pp. 21–40. Springer, Heidelberg (2011). https://doi.org/10.1007/978-3-642-25385-0_2
4. Agrawal, S., Libert, B., Stehlé, D.: Fully secure functional encryption for inner products, from standard assumptions. In: Robshaw, M., Katz, J. (eds.) CRYPTO 2016. Part III, volume 9816 of LNCS, pp. 333–362. Springer, Heidelberg (2016)
5. Attrapadung, N.: Dual system encryption via doubly selective security: framework, fully secure functional encryption for regular languages, and more. In: Nguyen, P.Q., Oswald, E. (eds.) EUROCRYPT 2014. LNCS, vol. 8441, pp. 557–577. Springer, Heidelberg (2014)
6. Attrapadung, N.: Dual system encryption framework in prime-order groups via computational pair encodings. In: Cheon, J.H., Takagi, T. (eds.) ASIACRYPT 2016. LNCS, vol. 10032, pp. 591–623. Springer, Heidelberg (2016). https://doi.org/10.1007/978-3-662-53890-6_20
7. Attrapadung, N., Matsuda, T., Nishimaki, R., Yamada, S., Yamakawa, T.: Constrained PRFs for NC^1 in traditional groups. In: Shacham, H., Boldyreva, A. (eds.) CRYPTO 2018. Part II, volume 10992 of LNCS, pp. 543–574. Springer, Heidelberg (2018)

8. Boneh, D., Boyen, X.: Efficient selective identity-based encryption without random oracles. J. Cryptol. **24**(4), 659–693 (2011)
9. Boneh, D., Franklin, M.K.: Identity-based encryption from the weil pairing. SIAM J. Comput. **32**(3), 586–615 (2003)
10. Boneh, D., et al.: Fully key-homomorphic encryption, arithmetic circuit ABE and compact garbled circuits. In: Nguyen, P.Q., Oswald, E. (eds.) EUROCRYPT 2014. LNCS, vol. 8441, pp. 533–556. Springer, Heidelberg (2014)
11. Boneh, D., Waters, B.: Conjunctive, subset, and range queries on encrypted data. In: Vadhan, S.P. (ed.) TCC 2007. LNCS, vol. 4392, pp. 535–554. Springer, Heidelberg (2007)
12. Boneh, D., Waters, B.: Constrained pseudorandom functions and their applications. In: Sako, K., Sarkar, P. (eds.) ASIACRYPT 2013. Part II, volume 8270 of LNCS, pp. 280–300. Springer, Heidelberg (2013)
13. Boyle, E., Goldwasser, S., Ivan, I.: Functional signatures and pseudorandom functions. In: Krawczyk, H. (ed.) PKC 2014. LNCS, vol. 8383, pp. 501–519. Springer, Heidelberg (2014)
14. Brakerski, Z., Langlois, A., Peikert, C., Regev, O., Stehlé, D.: Classical hardness of learning with errors. In: Boneh, D., Roughgarden, T., Feigenbaum, J. (eds.) 45th ACM STOC, pp. 575–584. ACM Press, June 2013
15. Brakerski, Z., Tsabary, R., Vaikuntanathan, V., Wee, H.: Private constrained PRFs (and more) from LWE. In: Kalai, Y., Reyzin, L. (eds.) TCC 2017. Part I, volume 10677 of LNCS, pp. 264–302. Springer, Heidelberg (2017)
16. Brakerski, Z., Vaikuntanathan, V.: Constrained key-homomorphic PRFs from standard lattice assumptions. In: Dodis, Y., Nielsen, J.B. (eds.) TCC 2015. LNCS, vol. 9015, pp. 1–30. Springer, Heidelberg (2015). https://doi.org/10.1007/978-3-662-46497-7_1
17. Brakerski, Z., Vaikuntanathan, V.: Circuit-ABE from LWE: unbounded attributes and semi-adaptive security. In: Robshaw, M., Katz, J. (eds.) CRYPTO 2016. Part III, volume 9816 of LNCS, pp. 363–384. Springer, Heidelberg (2016)
18. Canetti, R., Chen, Y.: Constraint-hiding constrained PRFs for NC^1 from LWE. In: Coron, J., Nielsen, J.B. (eds.) EUROCRYPT 2017. LNCS, vol. 10210, pp. 446–476. Springer, Cham (2017). https://doi.org/10.1007/978-3-319-56620-7_16
19. Cash, D., Hofheinz, D., Kiltz, E., Peikert, C.: Bonsai trees, or how to delegate a lattice basis. J. Cryptol. **25**(4), 601–639 (2012)
20. Chen, J., Gay, R., Wee, H.: Improved dual system ABE in prime-order groups via predicate encodings. In: Oswald, E., Fischlin, M. (eds.) EUROCRYPT 2015. Part II, volume 9057 of LNCS, pp. 595–624. Springer, Heidelberg (2015)
21. Chen, Y., Vaikuntanathan, V., Wee, H.: GGH15 beyond permutation branching programs: proofs, attacks, and candidates. In: Shacham, H., Boldyreva, A. (eds.) CRYPTO 2018. Part II, volume 10992 of LNCS, pp. 577–607. Springer, Heidelberg (2018)
22. Cocks, C.: An identity based encryption scheme based on quadratic residues. In: Honary, B. (ed.) Cryptography and Coding 2001. LNCS, vol. 2260, pp. 360–363. Springer, Heidelberg (2001). https://doi.org/10.1007/3-540-45325-3_32
23. Davidson, A., Katsumata, S., Nishimaki, R., Yamada, S., Yamakawa, T.: Adaptively secure constrained pseudorandom functions in the standard model. CRYPTO **2020**, 111 (2020)
24. Gentry, C.: Practical identity-based encryption without random oracles. In: Vaudenay, S. (ed.) EUROCRYPT 2006. LNCS, vol. 4004, pp. 445–464. Springer, Heidelberg (2006). https://doi.org/10.1007/11761679_27

25. Gentry, C., Peikert, C., Vaikuntanathan, V.: Trapdoors for hard lattices and new cryptographic constructions. In: Ladner, R.E., Dwork, C. (eds.) 40th ACM STOC, pp. 197–206. ACM Press, May 2008
26. Gentry, C., Sahai, A., Waters, B.: Homomorphic encryption from learning with errors: conceptually-simpler, asymptotically-faster, attribute-based. In: Canetti, R., Garay, J.A. (eds.) CRYPTO 2013. Part I, volume 8042 of LNCS, pp. 75–92. Springer, Heidelberg (2013)
27. Gorbunov, S., Vaikuntanathan, V., Wee, H.: Functional encryption with bounded collusions via multi-party computation. In: Safavi-Naini, R., Canetti, R. (eds.) CRYPTO 2012. LNCS, vol. 7417, pp. 162–179. Springer, Heidelberg (2012)
28. Gorbunov, S., Vaikuntanathan, V., Wee, H.: Attribute-based encryption for circuits. J. ACM **62**(6), 45:1–45:33 (2015)
29. Gorbunov, S., Vaikuntanathan, V., Wichs, D.: Leveled fully homomorphic signatures from standard lattices. In: Servedio, R.A., Rubinfeld, R. (eds.) 47th ACM STOC, pp. 469–477. ACM Press, June 2015
30. Goyal, R., Koppula, V., Waters, B.: Semi-adaptive security and bundling functionalities made generic and easy. In: Hirt, M., Smith, A. (eds.) TCC 2016. LNCS, vol. 9986, pp. 361–388. Springer, Heidelberg (2016). https://doi.org/10.1007/978-3-662-53644-5_14
31. Goyal, R., Koppula, V., Waters, B.: Lockable obfuscation. In: Umans, C. (ed.) 58th FOCS, pp. 612–621. IEEE Computer Society Press, October 2017
32. Goyal, V., Pandey, O., Sahai, A., Waters, B.: Attribute-based encryption for fine-grained access control of encrypted data. In: Juels, A., Wright, R.N., De Capitani di Vimercati, S. (eds.)ACM CCS 2006, pp. 89–98. ACM Press, October / November 2006. Available as Cryptology ePrint Archive Report 2006/309
33. Katsumata, S., Yamada, S.: Non-zero inner product encryption schemes from various assumptions: LWE, DDH and DCR. In: Lin, D., Sako, K. (eds.) PKC 2019. Part II, volume 11443 of LNCS, pp. 158–188. Springer, Heidelberg (2019)
34. Katz, J., Sahai, A., Waters, B.: Predicate encryption supporting disjunctions, polynomial equations, and inner products. J. Cryptol. **26**(2), 191–224 (2013)
35. Kiayias, A., Papadopoulos, S., Triandopoulos, N., Zacharias, T.: Delegatable pseudorandom functions and applications. In: Sadeghi, A-R., Gligor, V.D., Yung, M. (eds.) ACM CCS 2013, pp. 669–684. ACM Press, November 2013
36. Lewko, A., Okamoto, T., Sahai, A., Takashima, K., Waters, B.: Fully secure functional encryption: attribute-based encryption and (Hierarchical) inner product encryption. In: Gilbert, H. (ed.) EUROCRYPT 2010. LNCS, vol. 6110, pp. 62–91. Springer, Heidelberg (2010). https://doi.org/10.1007/978-3-642-13190-5_4
37. Micciancio, D., Peikert, C.: Trapdoors for lattices: simpler, tighter, faster, smaller. In: Pointcheval, D., Johansson, T. (eds.) EUROCRYPT 2012. LNCS, vol. 7237, pp. 700–718. Springer, Heidelberg (2012)
38. Okamoto, T., Takashima, K.: Adaptively attribute-hiding (hierarchical) inner product encryption. In: Pointcheval, D., Johansson, T. (eds.) EUROCRYPT 2012. LNCS, vol. 7237, pp. 591–608. Springer, Heidelberg (2012)
39. Okamoto, T., Takashima, K.: Fully secure functional encryption with a large class of relations from the decisional linear assumption. J. Cryptol. **32**(4), 1491–1573 (2019)
40. Peikert, C.: Public-key cryptosystems from the worst-case shortest vector problem: extended abstract. In: Mitzenmacher, M. (ed.) 41st ACM STOC, pp. 333–342. ACM Press, May / June 2009

41. Peikert, C., Shiehian, S.: Privately constraining and programming PRFs, the LWE way. In: Abdalla, M., Dahab, R. (eds.) PKC 2018. Part II, volume 10770 of LNCS, pp. 675–701. Springer, Heidelberg (2018)
42. Reed, I.S., Solomon, G.: Polynomial codes over certain finite fields. SIAM J. Comput. **8**(2), 300–304 (1960)
43. Regev, O.: On lattices, learning with errors, random linear codes, and cryptography. J. ACM **56**(6), 34:1–34:40 (2009)
44. Sahai, A., Waters, B.R.: Fuzzy identity-based encryption. In: Cramer, R. (ed.) EUROCRYPT 2005. LNCS, vol. 3494, pp. 457–473. Springer, Heidelberg (2005)
45. Shi, E., Bethencourt, J., Chan, H.T.-H., Song, X.D., Perrig, A.: Multi-dimensional range query over encrypted data. In: 2007 IEEE Symposium on Security and Privacy, pp. 350–364. IEEE Computer Society Press, May 2007
46. Tsabary, R.: Fully secure attribute-based encryption for t-CNF from LWE. In: Boldyreva, A., Micciancio, D. (eds.) CRYPTO 2019. Part I, volume 11692 of LNCS, pp. 62–85. Springer, Heidelberg (2019)
47. Wang, G., Wan, M., Liu, Z., Dawu, G.: Dual system in lattice: fully secure abe from lwe assumption. IACR Cryptol. ePrint Arch. **2020**, 64 (2020)
48. Waters, B.: Dual system encryption: realizing fully secure IBE and HIBE under simple assumptions. In: Halevi, S. (ed.) CRYPTO 2009. LNCS, vol. 5677, pp. 619–636. Springer, Heidelberg (2009)
49. Wee, H.: Dual system encryption via predicate encodings. In: Lindell, Y. (ed.) TCC 2014. LNCS, vol. 8349, pp. 616–637. Springer, Heidelberg (2014)
50. Wichs, D., Zirdelis, G.: Obfuscating compute-and-compare programs under LWE. In: Umans, C. (ed.) 58th FOCS, pp. 600–611. IEEE Computer Society Press, October 2017

Unbounded Dynamic Predicate Compositions in ABE from Standard Assumptions

Nuttapong Attrapadung[1(✉)] and Junichi Tomida[2(✉)]

[1] National Institute of Advanced Industrial Science and Technology (AIST), Tokyo, Japan
n.attrapadung@aist.go.jp
[2] NTT Corporation, Tokyo, Japan
junichi.tomida.vw@hco.ntt.co.jp

Abstract. At Eurocrypt'19, Attrapadung presented several transformations that dynamically compose a set of attribute-based encryption (ABE) schemes for simpler predicates into a new ABE scheme for more expressive predicates. Due to the powerful unbounded and modular nature of his compositions, many new ABE schemes can be obtained in a systematic manner. However, his approach heavily relies on q-type assumptions, which are not standard. Devising such powerful compositions from standard assumptions was left as an important open problem. In this paper, we present a new framework for constructing ABE schemes that allow unbounded and dynamic predicate compositions among them, and show that the adaptive security of these composed ABE will be preserved by relying only on the standard matrix Diffie-Hellman (MDDH) assumption. This thus resolves the open problem posed by Attrapadung. As for applications, we obtain various ABEs that are the first such instantiations of their kinds from standard assumptions. These include the following adaptively secure *large-universe* ABEs for Boolean formulae under MDDH:

- The first completely unbounded monotone key-policy (KP)/ ciphertext-policy (CP) ABE. Such ABE was recently proposed, but only for the KP and *small-universe* flavor (Kowalczyk and Wee, Eurocrypt'19).
- The first completely unbounded non-monotone KP/CP-ABE. Especially, our ABEs support a new type of non-monotonicity that subsumes previous two types of non-monotonicity, namely, by Ostrovsky *et al.* (CCS'07) and by Okamoto and Takashima (CRYPTO'10).
- The first (non-monotone) KP and CP-ABE with constant-size ciphertexts and secret keys, respectively.
- The first KP and CP-ABE with constant-size secret keys and ciphertexts, respectively.

At the core of our framework lies a new *partially symmetric* design of the core 1-key 1-ciphertext oracle component called Key Encoding Indistinguishability, which exploits the symmetry so as to obtain compositions.

S. Moriai and H. Wang (Eds.): ASIACRYPT 2020, LNCS 12493, pp. 405–436, 2020.
https://doi.org/10.1007/978-3-030-64840-4_14

Keywords: Attribute-based encryption · Predicate compositions · k-Lin · Completely unbounded ABE · Non-monotone ABE · Succinct ABE · Boolean formula

1 Introduction

Attribute-based encryption (ABE) is a generalized form of public-key encryption that allows fine-grained access control over encrypted data [24,33]. In a broader sense of ABE, each scheme specifies a predicate $\mathsf{P} : \mathcal{X} \times \mathcal{Y} \to \{0,1\}$, where $\mathcal{X}$ and $\mathcal{Y}$ are ciphertext and secret-key attribute universes, respectively. All users can encrypt a message with an arbitrary attribute $x \in \mathcal{X}$. An owner of a master secret key can generate a secret key for an arbitrary attribute $y \in \mathcal{Y}$. A ciphertext for attribute x is decryptable with a secret key for attribute y if and only if x and y satisfy the predicate P, i.e., $\mathsf{P}(x,y) = 1$. This is in contrast to the traditional public-key encryption, in which only one legitimate user can decrypt a ciphertext.

One of central research topics in ABE is to explore what kind of predicates for which ABE can be realized. This is important in practice since if one attempts to realize an access control system based on ABE, the underlying predicate must be able to express all decryption conditions that appear in the system. A line of works has shown that we can realize ABE for various predicates: ABE for span programs, (non-)deterministic finite automata, polynomial-sized circuits, and so on [4,14,23–25,31,33,37]. These works directly construct ABE schemes for targeting predicates. In contrast, there is also another approach to construct ABE schemes for more expressive new predicates by transformations and combinations of known predicates [6,7,9,13]. The state of the art on this approach is the work by Attrapadung [9], who proposed a framework for dynamic predicate compositions and introduced new ABE schemes such as ABE for key-policy (KP)/ciphertext-policy (CP) augmentation over predicate sets, nested-policy ABE, and mixed-policy ABE. The salient feature of these ABE schemes is that they allow *unbounded* and *dynamic* predicate compositions, that is, they do not impose any restriction on the size and structure of composition policy. This is in contrast to previous works [6,7,13], which allow only *static* (*i.e.,* a-priori fixed) compositions. He also showed that his framework captures predicates that are known but whose adaptively secure ABE instance was still open such as the predicate for completely unbounded non-monotone ABE.

The framework of [9] modularly constructs new predicates with corresponding pair encoding schemes (PES), which are encoding systems that yield concise expressions of ABE schemes [7]. It is shown in [9] that a nested application of three transformations of predicates, namely, direct sum, dual transformation, and KP augmentation over a single predicate (we call it just KP augmentation in what follows), is sufficiently powerful to obtain expressive predicates, such as the predicates for KP/CP augmentation over predicate sets, nested-policy ABE, and completely unbounded non-monotone ABE. He also demonstrates the transformations of PESs that correspond to the three transformations of the predicates. Hence, starting from known predicates and corresponding PESs, one can obtain

Table 1. Comparison among frameworks that compose multiple predicates over ABE.

Framework	Composition type	Comp. class	Input primitive	Assumption
ABS17 [6]	Static	Boolean formulae	Predicate encodings (info.-theoretic)	MDDH
Att19 [9]	Unbounded, Dynamic	SP, BP, DFA	Pair encodings with symbolic security	q-ratio
This work	Unbounded, Dynamic	Boolean formulae	Pair encodings with info.-theoretic security or with Key-Encoding Indistinguishability	MDDH

Note: SP, BP, DFA stand for span programs, branching programs, deterministic, finite automata, respectively.

a new transformed predicate along with its PES. Additionally, all PESs obtained in his framework can be used to instantiate a secure ABE scheme.

A crucial fact that his framework relies on is that the transformations of PESs preserve the symbolic property, introduced by Agrawal and Chase [3]. That is, he proved that all transformed PESs in his framework satisfy the symbolic property if the starting PESs satisfy the symbolic property. Agrawal and Chase showed that an ABE scheme induced by a PES with the symbolic property is adaptively secure under the q-ratio assumption [3]. Thus, we can use known predicates that have a PES with the symbolic property to construct a new expressive predicate and the corresponding PES, which results in a secure ABE scheme.

One drawback of his framework is the necessity of the q-ratio assumption, which is one of so-called q-type assumptions. The q-ratio assumption is parametrized with two parameters d_1 and d_2 and becomes stronger as they grow. We require that the q-ratio assumption holds with respect to sufficiently large d_1 and d_2 to assure the security of most ABE schemes because these parameters depend on adversary's behavior. However, the q-ratio assumption is a new complex assumption and thus not well-understood. Hence, it is desirable if we can transform PESs and instantiate an ABE scheme from a transformed PES under well-understood standard assumptions like the matrix Diffie-Hellman assumption (which includes k-Lin as a special case), instead of q-type assumptions. The realization of such a framework yields many important new ABEs from standard assumptions but has been left as an open problem by Attrapadung [9].

1.1 Our Contributions

New Framework. We give an affirmative answer to the problem and present a new framework for transforming predicates and constructing ABE schemes on prime-order bilinear groups, which relies on only the standard matrix Diffie-Hellman (MDDH) assumption. Following [9], our framework also composes a new predicate by combining three essential transformations, namely, the direct sum, dual transformation, and KP augmentation. Nested applications of these transformations yield various expressive predicates and ABE schemes. Our framework introduces a new property on PESs that satisfies the two requirements under the

Table 2. Comparison among *unbounded* ABE schemes.

References	Large universe	Adaptive security	Multi-use	Static assumption	Without RO	Non-monotonicity	Prime-order	KP/CP
LW11 [27]	✓		✓	✓	✓			KP
OT12 [30]	✓	✓		✓	✓	✓(OT)	✓	KP, CP
RW13 [32]	✓		✓		✓		✓	KP, CP
YAHK14 [39]	✓		✓		✓	✓(OSW)	✓	KP, CP
Att14 [7]	✓	✓	✓		✓			KP
AY15 [13]	✓	✓	✓		✓			CP
Att16 [8]	✓	✓	✓		✓		✓	KP, CP
AC17a [3]	✓	✓	✓		✓		✓	KP, CP
AC17b [2]	✓	✓		✓			✓	KP, CP
CGKW18 [16]		✓		✓	✓		✓	KP, CP
KW19 [26]		✓	✓	✓	✓		✓	KP
Att19 [9]	✓	✓	✓		✓	✓(OSW)	✓	KP, CP
TKN19 [35]	✓	✓	✓	✓		✓(OT)	✓	KP, CP
Ours 1	✓	✓	✓	✓	✓		✓	KP, CP
Ours 2	✓	✓	✓	✓	✓	✓(OSWOT)	✓	KP, CP

Note: KP, CP is for key-policy, ciphertext-policy. RO is for random oracles. We consider three types of non-monotone ABE: OT-type (Okamoto-Takashima [30]), OSW-type (Ostrovsky-Sahai-Waters [31]), and a new unified type (OSWOT) (see Sect. 6).

MDDH assumption: the preservation of the property in the transformations and the induction of the adaptive security of the resulting ABE scheme.

Note that there are two differences between our framework and that by Attrapadung [9] (we provide a comparison among composition frameworks in Table 1). First, our KP augmentation is done with Boolean formulae, whereas that by Attrapadung is augmentation with span programs, branching programs, and deterministic finite automata (realizing them from standard assumptions is an interesting open problem). Second, starting predicates need to have a PES with a certain information-theoretic property, whereas those in his framework only require a PES with the symbolic property. Note that the latter may be attainable by larger classes of predicates (but the symbolic property would require q-type assumptions). Nevertheless, our framework is still sufficiently powerful to realize many ABE schemes of which instantiations under the standard assumptions have remained open before our work.

New Instantiations. Via our new framework, we obtain the following ABE instantiations for important specific predicates. We emphasize that all the instantiations are *large-universe* constructions, which have a super-poly size attribute domain. Their comparisons to previous schemes are given in Tables 2, 3, 4 and 5.

1. The first adaptively secure completely unbounded KP/CP-ABE for monotone Boolean formulae under MDDH.[1] Previously, such an adaptively secure

[1] To be more precise, we describe some terms. *Unbounded ABE* [27] refers to schemes that have no bounds on the sizes of attribute sets (inputs to a Boolean formula) and policies (Boolean formulae). *Multi-use* refers to the property that any attribute can be used arbitrarily many times in one policy. *Completely unbounded ABE* refers to unbounded *large-universe* ABE with multi-use (see *e.g.,* [9]).

Table 3. Closer comparison among *adaptively secure unbounded* ABE with *multi-use* in the standard model.

References	KP/CP	Large univ.	Static assump.	Non-monoton.	|pk|	|ct|	|sk|
Att14 [7], Att16 [8], AC17a [3]	KP	✓			$O(1)$	$O(t)$	$O(n)$
KW19 [26]	KP		✓		$O(1)$	$O(t)$	$O(n)$
Att19 [9]	KP	✓		✓(OSW)	$O(1)$	$O(t)$	$O(n)$
Ours 1	KP	✓	✓		$O(1)$	$O(t)$	$O(n)$
Ours 2	KP	✓	✓	✓(OSWOT)	$O(1)$	$O(t)$	$O(n)$
AY15 [13], Att16 [8], AC17a [3]	CP	✓			$O(1)$	$O(n)$	$O(t)$
Att19 [9]	CP	✓		✓(OSW)	$O(1)$	$O(n)$	$O(t)$
Ours 1	CP	✓	✓		$O(1)$	$O(n)$	$O(t)$
Ours 2	CP	✓	✓	✓(OSWOT)	$O(1)$	$O(n)$	$O(t)$

Table 4. Comparison among ABE with *constant-size ciphertexts* ($|\mathsf{ct}| = O(1)$).

References	KP/CP	Large univ.	Adapt. security	Static assumptn.	Non-monoton.	Prime-order	|pk|	|sk|
ALP11 [11]	KP	✓			✓(OSW)	✓	$O(T)$	$O(Tn)$
Att14 [7]	KP	✓	✓			✓	$O(T)$	$O(Tn)$
CW14 [17]	KP			✓			$O(T)$	$O(Tn)$
Tak14 [34]	KP	✓		✓	✓(OSW)	✓	$O(T)$	$O(Tn)$
Att16 [8]	KP	✓	✓			✓	$O(T)$	$O(Tn)$
AC17a [3]	KP	✓	✓			✓	$O(T)$	$O(Tn)$
Att19 [9]	KP	✓	✓		✓(OSW)	✓	$O(T^2)$	$O(T^3 n)$
Ours 3	KP	✓	✓	✓	✓(OSW)	✓	$O(T)$	$O(Tn)$
AHY15 [10]	CP	✓	✓		✓(OSW)	✓	$O((TN)^2\lambda)$	$O((TN)^4\lambda^2)$
AC16 [1]	CP			✓		✓	$O(N(T+M))$	$O(N^2T+NM)$
Att19 [9]	CP	✓	✓		✓(OSW)	✓	$O(N^2+NM)$	$O(t(N^3+N^2M))$
Ours 5	CP	✓	✓	✓		✓	$\tilde{O}((M+T\lambda)^2)$	$\tilde{O}((M+T\lambda)^4)$

Table 5. Comparison among ABE with *constant-size keys* ($|\mathsf{sk}| = O(1)$).

References	KP/CP	Large univ.	Adapt. security	Static assumptn.	Non-monoton.	Prime-order	|pk|	|ct|
AY15 [13]	CP	✓	✓				$O(T)$	$O(Tn)$
Att16 [8]	CP	✓	✓			✓	$O(T)$	$O(Tn)$
AC17a [3]	CP	✓	✓			✓	$O(T)$	$O(Tn)$
Att19 [9]	CP	✓	✓		✓(OSW)	✓	$O(T^2)$	$O(T^3 n)$
Ours 4	CP	✓	✓	✓	✓(OSW)	✓	$O(T)$	$O(Tn)$
AHY15 [10]	KP	✓	✓		✓(OSW)	✓	$O((TN)^2\lambda)$	$O((TN)^4\lambda^2)$
Att19 [9]	KP	✓	✓		✓(OSW)	✓	$O(N^2+NM)$	$O(t(N^3+N^2M))$
Ours 6	KP	✓	✓	✓		✓	$\tilde{O}((M+T\lambda)^2)$	$\tilde{O}((M+T\lambda)^4)$

Notes for Table 3, 4 and 5: we denote $t = |\text{attribute set}|$, n is the input length of a Boolean formula, while T, N are the maximum bound for t, n, respectively (if required). M is the maximum bound for the size of Boolean formulae (if required). λ is the security parameter, *i.e.*, $\lambda = \lceil \log p \rceil$.

KP/CP-ABE relies on either q-type assumptions [3,8,9] or the one-use restriction (each attribute is usable at most once in a policy) [16,30]. Note that the recent unbounded KP-ABE with multi-use by Kowalczyk and Wee [26, Sect. A] is a *small-universe* construction, i.e., the attribute domain size is (a priori unbounded) polynomial.

2. The first adaptively secure completely unbounded KP/CP-ABE for *non-monotone* Boolean formulae under MDDH. Furthermore, our ABE schemes support a new type of non-monotonicity that conflates the two types of existing non-monotonicity by Ostrovsky, Sahai, and Waters (OSW) [31] and by Okamoto and Takashima (OT) [29]. In other words, both OSW-non-monotone ABE and OT-non-monotone ABE can be captured as a special case of our non-monotone ABE. Previously, an adaptively secure unbounded ABE for non-monotone formulae is either the OSW-type and based on q-type assumption [9] or the OT-type with the one-use restriction [30].
3. The first adaptively secure KP/CP-ABE with constant-size ciphertexts/secret keys under MDDH for (OSW-non-)monotone Boolean formulae, respectively.
4. The first (adaptively secure) KP/CP-ABE with constant-size secret keys/ciphertexts under MDDH for monotone Boolean formulae, respectively.

Note that almost all previous ABE with constant-size ciphertexts or keys rely on q-type assumptions [1,3,7–10,13], even when considering only selective security. There are only two exceptions: KP-ABE with constant-size ciphertexts of [17,34], but these only achieves semi-adaptive security.

Discussions. We clarify that our framework allows us to construct ABEs that are hard to obtain even if given the recent groundbreaking work by Kowalczyk and Wee (KW), who solved the multi-use problem in the adaptive setting and also presented an unbounded KP-ABE scheme with multi-use [26]. Most notably, we can construct completely unbounded OSW-non-monotone KP/CP-ABEs via our framework in a systematic manner (our newly defined non-monotone ABE subsumes OSW-non-monotone ABE). Prior to our work, there are no unbounded OSW-non-monotone ABE schemes based on static assumptions *even with the one-use restriction* (Table 2). This means that the KW technique, which is useful for the multi-use problem, does not directly help to realize unbounded OSW-non-monotone ABE.

We next highlight that our ABE for the newly defined non-monotonicity is practically meaningful, besides providing a theoretical interest. Intuitively, it allows a ciphertext to be assigned with multiple attribute sets each with a "tag". This, in turns, allows flexible blacklisting access controls in dynamic systems where new attributes can be added on into the system *after deployment*. We will describe it in Sect. 6 (with more details and formal definitions in the full version). We remark that, in small universe ABE, we can use monotone ABE as non-monotone ABE by preparing both positive and negative attributes [31]. However, this is not the case in large-universe ABE since we cannot attach an exponentially large number of negative attributes to ciphertexts or secret keys. Hence, for large-universe ABE, non-monotone variant is essentially more difficult to obtain.

From these, we believe that it is challenging and important to devise a modular framework that allows us to construct such ABEs from standard assumptions.

1.2 Technical Overview of Our Framework

We first recall the three main basic predicate transformations/compositions similarly to [9], namely, the *Dual*, the *KP augmentation*, and the *Direct sum*. For a predicate $\mathsf{P} : \mathcal{X} \times \mathcal{Y} \to \{0,1\}$, we define the first two, $\mathsf{Dual}[\mathsf{P}]$, $\mathsf{KP1}[\mathsf{P}]$, as[2]

$$\mathsf{Dual}[\mathsf{P}]\,(y, x) = \mathsf{P}(x, y)$$

$$\mathsf{KP1}[\mathsf{P}]\Big(x,\ Y = \big((y_1, \ldots, y_n), f\big)\Big) = f\big(\mathsf{P}(x, y_1), \ldots, \mathsf{P}(x, y_n)\big).$$

We remark two things: a composition policy $f : \{0,1\}^n \to \{0,1\}$ is a part of the key attribute Y; the "1" in $\mathsf{KP1}$ refers to the *single* predicate P and a *single* ciphertext attribute x. Next, for a set of predicates $\mathcal{P} = \{\mathsf{P}_1, \ldots, \mathsf{P}_k\}$, we define its direct sum $\mathsf{DS}[\mathcal{P}]$ as follows. Here i, j specifies predicate P_i, P_j, respectively.

$$\mathsf{DS}[\mathcal{P}]\,\big((i, x),\ (j, y)\big) = 1 \quad \text{iff} \quad i = j \wedge \mathsf{P}_i(x, y) = 1.$$

It is shown in [9] that the three transforms imply the "full" KP augmentation over *predicate sets*, denoted $\mathsf{KP}[\mathcal{P}]$ (notice the absent of "1"), defined as follows. For a set $X = \{(i_1, x_1), \ldots, (i_t, x_t)\}$ and vector $Y = ((j_1, y_1), \ldots, (j_n, y_n), f)$, let

$$\mathsf{KP}[\mathcal{P}]\,(X, Y) = f(b_1, \ldots, b_n) \quad \text{where } b_v = 1 \text{ iff } \exists_{i_u = j_v} : \mathsf{P}_{j_v}(x_u, y_v) = 1$$

It is this full composition that we quantify the static vs dynamic, bounded vs unbounded features: it is *static* if f is fixed (and hence so does n), otherwise it is *dynamic* over the class of f; it is *unbounded* when n is unbounded.

We briefly explain its direct applications. Setting $\mathcal{P}' = \{\mathsf{E}\}$, where E is the equality predicate (IBE), we obtain the completely unbounded KP-ABE for monotone policies, that is, ABE for $\mathsf{KP}[\mathcal{P}']$ implies Ours 1 in Table 2. Similarly, setting $\mathcal{P}'' = \{\mathsf{E}, \bar{\mathsf{E}}\}$, where $\bar{\mathsf{E}}$ is the negation of E, basically yields that for non-monotone policies (see other precise ways to define its variants in the full version).

As motivated in [9], the seemingly unrelated Dual indeed plays a crucial role in bootstrapping $\mathsf{KP1}$ to KP (*i.e.*, even when considering bootstrapping over *sole* key-policy flavors, and not considering *across* dual flavors, namely ciphertext-policy). Intuitively, this is since the full KP "intrinsically" contains a *ciphertext-policy* predicate as given by $\mathsf{Dual}[\mathsf{KP1}[\mathsf{P}]]\,\big(X' = ((x_1, \ldots, x_t), f_{\mathsf{OR}}),\ y\big)$, where X' with the OR policy here is another way to express the set X in KP. "Nesting" $\mathsf{KP1}$ and $\mathsf{Dual} \circ \mathsf{KP1}$ together then yields KP (*cf.* [9]). Note also that the direct sum is used to "glue" predicates in $\mathcal{P}$ to single predicate; it is not needed for the case of a singleton $\mathcal{P}$ (such as $\mathcal{P}'$ above). Now that KP is reduced to the much simpler $\mathsf{KP1}$, Dual (and DS), we will deal with these basic transforms.

Background on PES. We now briefly recall PES [7], as refined in [3]. Informally, a PES for $\mathsf{P} : \mathcal{X} \times \mathcal{Y} \to \{0,1\}$ is represented by a variable α, five vectors of variables $(\mathbf{w}, \mathbf{s}, \hat{\mathbf{s}}, \mathbf{r}, \hat{\mathbf{r}})$, and two sets of polynomials (called ciphertext and key

[2] For simplicity, we omit writing their domains here. See formal treatments in Sect. 4.

encodings, resp.) on these variables $(\mathbf{c}_x(\mathbf{s},\hat{\mathbf{s}},\mathbf{w}),\mathbf{k}_y(\alpha,\mathbf{r},\hat{\mathbf{r}},\mathbf{w}))$ that depend on $x \in \mathcal{X}$ and $y \in \mathcal{Y}$, respectively. We require that $\mathbf{s}$ contains a variable s_0. Let $N = p_1p_2$ for primes p_1, p_2, and $e : G \times H \to G_T$ be bilinear groups of order N. Let g_i, h_i be generators of the subgroups G_i, H_i of order p_i for $i \in \{1,2\}$, respectively, and $g = g_1g_2, h = h_1h_2$. Then, an ABE scheme in composite-order groups based on PES can be described as follows: $\mathsf{pk} = (g_1^{\mathbf{w}}, e(g_1,h)^{\alpha})$ and

$$\mathsf{ct}_x = (g_1^{\mathbf{s}}, g_1^{\mathbf{c}_x(\mathbf{s},\hat{\mathbf{s}},\mathbf{w})}, e(g_1,h)^{s_0\alpha}m), \qquad \mathsf{sk}_y = (h_1^{\mathbf{r}}, h_1^{\mathbf{k}_y(\alpha,\mathbf{r},\hat{\mathbf{r}},\mathbf{w})}h_2^{\mathbf{k}_y(\alpha,\mathbf{0},\hat{\mathbf{r}},\mathbf{0})}),$$

where $(\alpha,\mathbf{w},\mathbf{s},\hat{\mathbf{s}},\mathbf{r},\hat{\mathbf{r}}) \leftarrow \mathbb{Z}_N^t$ (t is the total number of the variables). We require that each polynomial of $\mathbf{c}_x$ is a linear combination of monomials s_iw_j and $\hat{s}_k$ (where $s_i \in \mathbf{s}$, $\hat{s}_k \in \hat{\mathbf{s}}$, $w_j \in \mathbf{w}$). This yields the linearity of $\mathbf{c}_x$ over $\mathbf{s},\hat{\mathbf{s}}$, when fixing $\mathbf{w}$. Analogous properties go for key encodings. As an example, a PES for IBE [7] has the form $\mathbf{c}_x = s_0(w_1x + w_2)$, $\mathbf{k}_y = \alpha + r_1(w_1y + w_2)$, where $\mathbf{w} = (w_1, w_2)$, $\mathbf{s} = s_0$, $\mathbf{r} = r_1$ (and no $\hat{\mathbf{s}},\hat{\mathbf{r}}$). In what follows in this section, we write $\mathbf{c}_x(\mathbf{s},\hat{\mathbf{s}},\mathbf{w})$ and $\mathbf{k}_y(\alpha,\mathbf{r},\hat{\mathbf{r}},\mathbf{w})$ to implicitly include $\mathbf{s}$ and $\mathbf{r}$, respectively.

Our Goal: Three Main Implications. Since the symbolic property works only with the q-ratio assumption, we need a completely different new notion on PES that is preserved via the transformations, and that, at the same time, implies the adaptive security of the induced ABE scheme under standard assumptions. To this end, in this work, we introduce a new central notion called Key-Encoding Indistinguishability for PES, denoted KE-ind. Our goal is to design KE-ind in such a way that the following theorems (stated informally below) hold. The first states the preservation of KE-ind under the transformation. The second states that KE-ind implies adaptively secure ABE under MDDH.

Informal Theorem 1. *For a composition* $\mathsf{C} \in \{\mathsf{Dual},\mathsf{DS},\mathsf{KP1}\}$, *if there exists a PES for* P *that satisfies* KE-ind, *then there exists a PES for* $\mathsf{C}[\mathsf{P}]$ *that satisfies* KE-ind *under MDDH. (Note that for* DS, *its input is a predicate set* $\mathcal{P}$.*)*

Informal Theorem 2. *If there exists a PES for* P *that satisfies* KE-ind, *then there exists an adaptively secure ABE scheme for* P *under MDDH.*

The third theorem finally tells us how to achieve KE-ind via the existing information-theoretic notion of PES called perfect master-key hiding (PMH) of PES as defined in [7]. PMH requires that the following two distributions are identical with respect to $(\alpha,\mathbf{w},\mathbf{s},\hat{\mathbf{s}},\mathbf{r},\hat{\mathbf{r}}) \leftarrow \mathbb{Z}_N^t$:

$$\{\mathbf{c}_x(\mathbf{s},\hat{\mathbf{s}},\mathbf{w}),\mathbf{k}_y(\alpha,\mathbf{r},\hat{\mathbf{r}},\mathbf{w})\} \text{ and } \{\mathbf{c}_x(\mathbf{s},\hat{\mathbf{s}},\mathbf{w}),\mathbf{k}_y(0,\mathbf{r},\hat{\mathbf{r}},\mathbf{w})\}. \tag{1}$$

Informal Theorem 3. *If a PES satisfies the PMH property, then the same PES also satisfies* KE-ind *under MDDH.*

From these theorems, we have the following corollary.

Informal Corollary 1. *If there exists a PES for* P *satisfying the PMH, then there exists an adaptively secure ABE for the composed predicate* $\mathsf{C}_1 \circ \cdots \circ \mathsf{C}_n[\mathsf{P}]$ *under MDDH, where* $\mathsf{C}_i \in \{\mathsf{Dual},\mathsf{DS},\mathsf{KP1}\}$. *(For* DS *inputs are sets.)*

We can start from such information-theoretic PESs for basic predicates in [6,7], such as IBE, and obtain adaptively secure ABE for composed predicates.

To obtain these theorems, it remains to properly design KE-ind.

Designing Key-Encoding Indistinguishability. For simplicity, we explain our framework in composite-order bilinear groups in this overview since we can basically convert ABE constructions in composite-order groups into those in prime-order groups via the framework by Chen *et al.* [15,16,20]. Note that the MDDH assumption in prime-order groups corresponds to the subgroup (SG) assumptions in composite-order groups (see e.g., [16]).

Our starting point is to define KE-ind to be exactly the *computationally master-key hiding* (CMH) property [7], which is a relaxed notion of PMH (and we would obtain Theorem 3 above). We say that a PES Γ specified by $(\alpha, \mathbf{w}, \mathbf{s}, \hat{\mathbf{s}}, \mathbf{r}, \hat{\mathbf{r}}, \mathbf{c}_x, \mathbf{k}_y)$ for P satisfies CMH if the following advantage of $\mathcal{A}$ is negligible:

$$\mathsf{Adv}^{\mathsf{CMH}}_{\mathcal{A},\Gamma}(\lambda) = \left| \Pr\left[\beta = \beta' \middle| \begin{array}{l} \beta \leftarrow \{0,1\} \\ \beta' \leftarrow \mathcal{A}^{\mathsf{cO}(\cdot), \mathsf{kO}_\beta(\cdot)}(g_1, g_2, h_1, h_2) \end{array} \right] - \frac{1}{2} \right|,$$

where the ciphertext encoding oracle cO takes $x \in \mathcal{X}$ and outputs $g_2^{\mathbf{c}_x(\mathbf{s},\hat{\mathbf{s}},\mathbf{w})}$, while the key encoding oracle kO_β takes $y \in \mathcal{Y}$ and outputs $h_2^{\mathbf{k}_y(\beta\alpha,\mathbf{r},\hat{\mathbf{r}},\mathbf{w})}$, where $\alpha, \mathbf{w}, \mathbf{s}, \hat{\mathbf{s}}, \mathbf{r}, \hat{\mathbf{r}}$ are random. Here $\mathcal{A}$ can query each oracle once with $R(x,y)= 0$. Attrapadung showed that if we have a PES for P with CMH, then we can obtain an adaptively secure ABE scheme for P assuming the SG assumption [7] (this implies Theorem 2). Thus, if we could show that CMH is preserved via the transformations black(this would imply Theorem 1), we would achieve the goal.

Unfortunately, we quickly found out that this approach fails; in particular, we do not know how to preserve CMH via the KP1 transformation. Assume that we use the same KP1 transformation as in [9], which transforms a PES Γ for P to a PES Γ' for KP1[P] to be exactly the same as Γ except that

$$\mathbf{k}'_Y(\alpha, \mathbf{r}', \hat{\mathbf{r}}', \mathbf{w}) = \{\mathbf{k}_{y_i}(\sigma_i, \mathbf{r}_i, \hat{\mathbf{r}}_i, \mathbf{w})\}_{i\in[n]}$$

and $\mathbf{r}' = \{\mathbf{r}_i\}_{i\in[n]}$, $\hat{\mathbf{r}}' = \{\hat{\mathbf{r}}_i\}_{i\in[n]}$, where $\{\sigma_i\}_{i\in[n]}$ are secret shares of α with respect to f. (Here, primed variables are for Γ'.) Our goal here is to construct a reduction that breaks CMH of Γ internally using an adversary that breaks CMH of Γ'. One hopeful strategy is to limit f to Boolean formulae and consider a series of hybrids as the KW framework [26]. However, this idea does not work as the reduction cannot simulate $\{h_2^{\mathbf{k}_{y_i}(\sigma_i,\mathbf{r}_i,\hat{\mathbf{r}}_i,\mathbf{w})}\}_{i\neq j}$ when randomizing $h_2^{\mathbf{k}_{y_j}(\sigma_j,\mathbf{r}_j,\hat{\mathbf{r}}_j,\mathbf{w})}$ due to the absence of $h_2^{\mathbf{w}}$. Including $h_2^{\mathbf{w}}$ in the input of the CMH adversary does not solve the problem since this makes PMH not imply CMH, and Theorem 3 does not hold in such a definition (observe that in Eq. (1), $\mathbf{w}$ is not given out). Our next observation here is that we will need a property on indistinguishability of H_2 elements where the output of kO_β is simulatable *without* $h_2^{\mathbf{w}}$.

First Step: Subgroups vs Entire Groups. Our first idea is to make the outputs of cO and kO_β use *entire* groups G, H instead of only *subgroups* G_2, H_2, which can be seen as an extension of the technique by Tomida *et al.* [35]. A new candidate property (say, $\mathsf{Cand1}$) for Γ is then defined as follows:

$$\mathsf{Adv}^{\mathsf{Cand1}}_{\mathcal{A},\Gamma}(\lambda) = \left| \Pr\left[\beta = \beta' \,\middle|\, \begin{array}{l} \beta \leftarrow \{0,1\},\ \ \mathbf{w} \leftarrow \mathbb{Z}_N^{\omega} \\ \beta' \leftarrow \mathcal{A}^{\mathsf{cO}(\cdot),\mathsf{kO}_\beta(\cdot)}(g_1, h_1, h_2, g_1^{\mathbf{w}}, h_1^{\mathbf{w}}) \end{array} \right] - \frac{1}{2} \right|,$$

where $g^{\mathbf{c}_x(\mathbf{s},\hat{\mathbf{s}},\mathbf{w})} \leftarrow \mathsf{cO}(x)$ and $h_1^{\mathbf{k}_y(0,\mathbf{r},\hat{\mathbf{r}},\mathbf{w})} h_2^{\mathbf{k}_y(\beta\alpha,\mathbf{0},\hat{\mathbf{r}},\mathbf{0})} \leftarrow \mathsf{kO}_\beta(y)$ where $\alpha, \mathbf{s}, \hat{\mathbf{s}}, \mathbf{r}, \hat{\mathbf{r}}$ are random. Crucially, now, g_2 is not given out to $\mathcal{A}$.

$\mathsf{Cand1}$ implies an adaptive security of the ABE scheme from Γ (and we obtain Theorem 2). Intuitively, the indistinguishability of the H_2 elements in the output of kO_β implies the indistinguishability between normal and semi-functional keys, which then implies the adaptive security of the ABE scheme via the dual system technique [36]. Next, $\mathsf{Cand1}$ can be shown to be implied by PMH and the SG assumption (and we obtain Theorem 3) as follows (also recall linearity of $\mathbf{k}_y$):

$$h_1^{\mathbf{k}_y(0,\mathbf{r},\hat{\mathbf{r}},\mathbf{w})} h_2^{\mathbf{k}_y(0,\mathbf{0},\hat{\mathbf{r}},\mathbf{0})} \underset{\text{SG}}{\approx_c} - \cdot h_2^{\mathbf{k}_y(0,\underline{\mathbf{r}},\hat{\mathbf{r}},\underline{\mathbf{w}})} \underset{\text{PMH}}{\approx_s} - \cdot h_2^{\mathbf{k}_y(\underline{\alpha},\mathbf{r},\hat{\mathbf{r}},\mathbf{w})} \underset{\text{SG}}{\approx_c} - \cdot h_2^{\mathbf{k}_y(\alpha,\underline{\mathbf{0}},\hat{\mathbf{r}},\underline{\mathbf{0}})}.$$

Note that "$-$" is the same element in H_1, and $\approx_c, \approx_s$ are computational and statistical indistinguishability, respectively. The purpose for making g_2 absent in $\mathcal{A}$'s input is to use the SG assumption that claims $h_1^{\mathbf{r}} \approx_c h^{\mathbf{r}}$. In this way, we can prove that $\mathsf{Cand1}$ is preserved in $\mathsf{KP1}$ for Boolean formulae by extending the KW framework. Intuitively, the reduction goes through as it can simulate $K_i = h_1^{\mathbf{k}_{y_i}(0,\mathbf{r}_i,\hat{\mathbf{r}}_i,\mathbf{w})} h_2^{\mathbf{k}_{y_i}(\sigma_i,\mathbf{0},\hat{\mathbf{r}}_i,\mathbf{0})}$ without $h_2^{\mathbf{w}}$ (observe that there is no $\mathbf{w}$ in the exponent to h_2 in K_i).

However, it turns out that $\mathsf{Cand1}$ is not preserved in Dual. Assume that we use the same Dual transformation as in [3], which transforms a PES Γ for P to a PES $\overline{\Gamma}$ for $\mathsf{Dual}[\mathsf{P}]$ as follows: first let the variables for $\overline{\Gamma}$ be $\mathbf{w}' = (w_0, \mathbf{w})$, $\mathbf{s}' = (s_{\mathsf{new}}, \mathbf{r})$, $\hat{\mathbf{s}}' = \hat{\mathbf{r}}$, $\mathbf{r}' = \mathbf{s}$, $\hat{\mathbf{r}}' = \hat{\mathbf{s}}$ and define the two encodings for $\overline{\Gamma}$ as

$$\mathbf{c}'_y(\mathbf{s}', \hat{\mathbf{s}}', \mathbf{w}') = \mathbf{k}_y(s_{\mathsf{new}} w_0, \mathbf{r}, \hat{\mathbf{r}}, \mathbf{w}), \quad \mathbf{k}'_x(\alpha, \mathbf{r}', \hat{\mathbf{r}}', \mathbf{w}') = (\mathbf{c}_x(\mathbf{s}, \hat{\mathbf{s}}, \mathbf{w}), \alpha - s_0 w_0),$$

where w_0, s_{new} are new variables, and s_{new} takes a role of s_0 in $\overline{\Gamma}$. To prove the preservation of $\mathsf{Cand1}$ in Dual, we need to construct a reduction $\mathcal{R}$ that breaks $\mathsf{Cand1}$ of Γ internally using an adversary $\mathcal{A}$ against ($\mathsf{Cand1}$ of) $\overline{\Gamma}$. A crucial fact here is that the roles of G and H are "switched", that is, $\mathcal{R}$ uses its input G and H as H and G for the input of $\mathcal{A}$, respectively. This is since $\mathcal{R}$ needs the reply of $\mathsf{cO}^{\mathcal{R}}$ to answer $\mathcal{A}$'s query to $\mathsf{kO}^{\mathcal{A}}$ (and analogously for $\mathsf{kO}^{\mathcal{R}}$ to $\mathsf{cO}^{\mathcal{A}}$). Now the problem arises as $\mathcal{R}$ does not possess g_2, but this very term will be needed to supply to $\mathcal{A}$'s input as h_2 (recall the "switching" of G and H). Also recall that h_2 was necessary to prove Theorem 2 (to simulate semi-functional keys).

Second Step: Parametrized vs Same-at-once. To solve the above problem, instead of preserving the *same* property from Γ to $\overline{\Gamma}$, we will establish an implication over *slightly different* properties on Γ and $\overline{\Gamma}$. Namely, we use more subgroups by letting $N = p_1 \cdots p_z$ and parametrize the candidate property as (z,ℓ)-$\mathsf{Cand2}$, where $z, \ell \in \mathbb{N}$ s.t. $z \geq \ell$. Defining bilinear groups $e : G \times H \rightarrow G_{\mathsf{T}}$

of order N and its subgroups naturally, we then define $\mathsf{Adv}_{\mathcal{A},\Gamma}^{(\mathsf{z},\ell)\text{-}\mathsf{Cand2}}(\lambda)$ as

$$\left|\Pr\left[\beta=\beta' \,\middle|\, \begin{array}{l}\beta \leftarrow \{0,1\},\ \ \mathbf{w} \leftarrow \mathbb{Z}_N^{\omega} \\ \beta' \leftarrow \mathcal{A}^{\mathsf{cO}(\cdot),\mathsf{kO}_\beta(\cdot)}(g_1, h_1, g_{\ell+1}, \ldots, g_z, h_\ell, \ldots, h_z, g_1^{\mathbf{w}}, h_1^{\mathbf{w}})\end{array}\right] - \frac{1}{2}\right| \tag{2}$$

where $g^{\mathbf{c}_x(\mathbf{s},\hat{\mathbf{s}},\mathbf{w})} \leftarrow \mathsf{cO}(x)$ and $h_1^{\mathbf{k}_y(0,\mathbf{r},\hat{\mathbf{r}},\mathbf{w})} h_\ell^{\mathbf{k}_y(\beta\alpha,\mathbf{0},\hat{\mathbf{r}},\mathbf{0})} \leftarrow \mathsf{kO}_\beta(y)$. In this way, we have that g_ℓ is absent (generalizing the absence of g_2, so as to establish Theorem 3 as in the first step), but now, at the same time, we can also potentially establish the implication over Dual that $(z, \ell-1)$-Cand2 of Γ implies (z,ℓ)-Cand2 of $\overline{\Gamma}$ for $\ell \geq 2$ in the sense that the reduction $\mathcal{R}$ possesses $g_\ell, \ldots, g_z$ (as per the former notion) which can be used to exactly simulate $h_\ell, \ldots, h_z$ (giving to the adversary $\mathcal{A}$ against the latter notion), where we recall the switching of G and H.

Final Step: Wrapping up (Partial) Symmetries in Two Oracles. In the above, we generalize the functionality of the subgroups G_2, H_2 directly to G_ℓ, H_ℓ and hence obtain the above design of the oracle kO. However, this design fails when we try to use the reply of $\mathsf{cO}^{\mathcal{R}}$ to answer $\mathcal{A}$'s query to $\mathsf{kO}^{\mathcal{A}}$ (as presumably required in the reduction). This is since the former is an element of the entire group, while the latter is in the subgroup with generators h_1, h_ℓ; however, $\mathcal{A}$ possesses $g_{\ell+1}$ and thus can simply distinguish the two. A similar failure occurs analogously when relating $\mathsf{kO}^{\mathcal{R}}$ to $\mathsf{cO}^{\mathcal{A}}$. To solve this, we need to re-design also the two oracles carefully (satisfying not only this particular preservation of Dual that we are discussing but also all the required 3 theorems). To this end, our solution is to define them in partially (and not fully) *symmetrical* manner:

$$\begin{aligned} g_1^{\mathbf{c}_x(\mathbf{s},\mathbf{0},\mathbf{w})}\, g_{[2,\ell]}^{\mathbf{c}_x((s_0,\mathbf{0}),\mathbf{0},\mathbf{w})}\, g^{\mathbf{c}_x(\mathbf{0},\hat{\mathbf{s}},\mathbf{0})} &\leftarrow \mathsf{cO}(x), \\ h_1^{\mathbf{k}_y(0,\mathbf{r},\mathbf{0},\mathbf{w})}\, h_\ell^{\mathbf{k}_y(\beta\alpha,\mathbf{0},\mathbf{0},\mathbf{0})}\, h^{\mathbf{k}_y(0,\mathbf{0},\hat{\mathbf{r}},\mathbf{0})} &\leftarrow \mathsf{kO}_\beta(y), \end{aligned}$$

and also additionally give out $T = (g_{[1,\ell]}, \ldots, g_{[1,z]}, h_{[1,\ell+1]}, \ldots, h_{[1,z]})$ (as inputs to $\mathcal{A}$ in Eq. (2)), where we denote $g_{[a,b]} = g_a \cdots g_b$ for $a \leq b$. Intuitively, the forms of $\mathsf{cO}^{\mathcal{R}}$ and $\mathsf{kO}^{\mathcal{A}}$ are now *somewhat symmetric*, except the difference lying in the subgroups with indexes $2, \ldots, \ell-1$, and we observe that the adversary does not possess an element from these subgroups so as to distinguish the two; therefore, we can use the former to simulate the latter, under the SG assumption. The additional input T is essential for the other oracle simulation (from $\mathsf{kO}^{\mathcal{R}}$ to $\mathsf{cO}^{\mathcal{A}}$). Crucially, giving out individual generators such as $g_2, \ldots, g_\ell$ would destroy the "absence" requirement (essential for Theorem 3); while, on the other hand, giving out the elements like $g_{[1,i]}$ do work.

This completes our design rational of (z,ℓ)-KE-ind (in the composite-order-groups flavor). Note that ℓ is incremented by 1 after applying one Dual conversion. Starting from $(z,1)$-KE-ind, we have that $z-1$ is the maximum number of Dual applications. Thus, by choosing z depending on the number of dual applications to obtain a target predicate P, we can instantiate a secure ABE scheme for P. Also note that (z,ℓ)-KE-ind will require $\mathbf{s}$ to consist of only s_0 so that it is implied by PMH. We call it single-variable PMH. Note that PESs with single-variable PMH are still more general encodings than predicate encodings [6,38].

All in all, our conceptually new insight is the *partially symmetric* design of the core 1-key 1-ciphertext component (our KE-ind) so as to incorporate Dual (crucial in bootstrapping KP1 to KP). This differs to other similar core components in the literature, notably, the "1-ABE" in [26]. We discuss more in the next subsection.

1.3 Technical Comparisons to Previous Unbounded ABE and More

Our framework allows us to modularly construct unbounded ABE schemes. Thus, one may wonder how our framework compares to previous unbounded ABE schemes from static assumptions [16,26,27,30]. Basically, these ABE schemes rely on so-called "nested dual system technique", in which entropy in secret keys is increased via entropy propagation between a secret key and ciphertext. All these works uses the IBE predicate as a source of entropy.

Intuitively, when instantiating our framework to completely unbounded monotone ABE, such an entropy propagation can be viewed as being decomposed into modular parts, namely, the PMH (of a PES for IBE), the KP1 transform, and the Dual transform (recall that we apply KP1 and Dual∘KP1 to IBE in a nested manner to achieve such an ABE instance [9]). This predicate transformations implicitly trace a similar hybrid sequence to that by Lewko and Waters (LW) [27], borrowing the power of the KW framework (the piecewise guessing framework) to do it in the adaptive setting. An important fact here is that our framework uses the KW framework in a "nested" manner. Intuitively, this is the reason why our ABE schemes can be constructed as large-universe constructions similarly to the LW unbounded scheme. On the other hand, the KW unbounded scheme [26] is obtained by directly applying the KW framework (not in a nested manner) to the unbounded *small-universe* ABE scheme in [16]. This, in turn, *inherently* poses a linear cost of the universe size U in the security loss (and hence U cannot be super-polynomially large) for the KW scheme (see Table 6).

Another advantage of our framework over the KW scheme is that we do not use the subgroup DDH assumption [16], which requires a k-dimensional semi-functional space for the k-Lin assumption. In contrast, 1-dimensional semi-functional spaces suffice for our framework. This yields asymptotically smaller ciphertexts and keys than the KW scheme (asymptotic in k, see Table 6).

Table 6. Comparison with unbounded KP-ABE from $\mathcal{D}_k$-MDDH by KW19 [26].

References	Security loss	$\lvert\mathsf{pk}\rvert$	$\lvert\mathsf{ct}\rvert$	$\lvert\mathsf{sk}\rvert$
KW19 [26]	$O(Uq_{\mathsf{sk}})2^{O(B)}$	$(5k^2+k)\lvert G_1\rvert$ $+k\lvert G_T\rvert$	$((3k+1)t+2k+1)\lvert G_1\rvert$ $+\lvert G_T\rvert$	$((5k+2)n+(2k+1)m)\lvert G_2\rvert$
Ours 1	$O(q_{\mathsf{sk}})2^{O(B)}$	$(4k^2+8k)\lvert G_1\rvert$ $+k\lvert G_T\rvert$	$((2k+4)t+k+2)\lvert G_1\rvert$ $+\lvert G_T\rvert$	$(3k+6)n\lvert G_2\rvert$

Note: U is the attribute domain size, q_{sk} is the maximum number of secret key queries, B is the maximum depth of formulae, $t = \lvert\text{attribute set}\rvert$, m and n are the number of gates and the input length of a formula, respectively.

Full Version of This paper. Due to limited spaces, we defer details such as omitted proofs, details on instantiations, and discussions regarding more recent related works (such as [4,5,21,22,28]) to the full version of this paper [12].

2 Preliminaries

Notation. For a natural number $m, n \in \mathbb{N}$, $[m]$ denotes a set $\{1, \ldots, m\}$, $[m]^+$ denotes a set $\{0, \ldots, m\}$, and $[m, n]$ denotes a set $\{m, \ldots, n\}$. For a set S, $s \leftarrow S$ denotes that s is uniformly chosen from S. We treat vectors as column vectors unless specified otherwise. For a generator g_i of a cyclic group G_i of order p and $a \in \mathbb{Z}_p$, $[a]_i$ denotes g_i^a. Furthermore, for a matrix $\mathbf{A} = (a_{j,\ell})_{j,\ell}$ over $\mathbb{Z}_p$, $[\mathbf{A}]_i$ denotes a matrix over G_i whose (j, ℓ)-th entry is $g_i^{a_{j,\ell}}$. For vectors $\mathbf{x} = (x_1, \ldots, x_n)$ and $\mathbf{y} = (y_1, \ldots, y_n) \in \mathbb{Z}_p^n$, let $e([\mathbf{x}]_1, [\mathbf{y}]_2) = e(g_1, g_2)^{\langle \mathbf{x}, \mathbf{y} \rangle}$ be a function that computes the inner product on the exponent by $\prod_{i \in [n]} e([x_i]_1, [y_i]_2)$. A function $f : \mathbb{N} \rightarrow \mathbb{R}$ is called negligible if $f(\lambda) = \lambda^{-\omega(1)}$ and denotes $f(\lambda) \leq \mathsf{negl}(\lambda)$. For families of distributions $X = \{X_\lambda\}_{\lambda \in \mathbb{N}}$ and $Y = \{Y_\lambda\}_{\lambda \in \mathbb{N}}$, we denote $X \approx_c Y$ (resp. $X \approx_s Y$) as computational indistinguishability (resp. statistical indistinguishability). For an interactive game G, $\langle \mathcal{A}, \mathsf{G} \rangle$ denotes the output of $\mathcal{A}$ in G.

Matrix Notation. Throughout the paper, we use the following matrix notation. For a regular matrix $\overline{\mathbf{M}} \in \mathsf{GL}_{k+\zeta}(\mathbb{Z}_p)$, we define $\mathbf{M}$, $\mathbf{m}_i$, $\mathbf{M}^*$, and $\mathbf{m}_i^*$ as follows. $\mathbf{M}$ and $\mathbf{m}_i$ denote a matrix and a vector consist of the first k columns and the $(k+i)$-th column of $\overline{\mathbf{M}}$, respectively. Similarly, $\mathbf{M}^*$ and $\mathbf{m}_i^*$ denote a matrix and vector consist of the first k columns and the $(k+i)$-th column of $(\overline{\mathbf{M}}^\top)^{-1}$, respectively. We have the relations, $\mathbf{M}^\top \mathbf{m}_i^* = \mathbf{0}$ and $\mathbf{m}_i^\top \mathbf{m}_i^* = 1$ for $i \in [\zeta]$. We also uses the following notations:

$$\mathsf{span}(\mathbf{M}, \mathbf{m}_1, \ldots, \mathbf{m}_n) = \{\mathbf{v} \mid \exists \mathbf{u} \in \mathbb{Z}_p^{k+n}, \mathbf{v} = (\mathbf{M} || \mathbf{m}_1 || \ldots || \mathbf{m}_n)\mathbf{u}\},$$
$$\mathsf{Ker}(\mathbf{M}, \mathbf{m}_1, \ldots, \mathbf{m}_n) = \{\mathbf{v} \mid (\mathbf{M} || \mathbf{m}_1 || \ldots || \mathbf{m}_n)^\top \mathbf{v} = \mathbf{0}\}.$$

2.1 Basic Definitions and Tools

Boolean Formula and NC^1. A monotone Boolean formula can be represented by a Boolean circuit of which all gates have fan-in 2 and fan-out 1. More precisely, we specify a monotone Boolean formula by a tuple $f = (n, w, m, G)$ where $n, w, m \in \mathbb{N}$ represents the number of input wires, the number of all wires (including the input wires), and the number of gates, respectively, while $G : [m] \rightarrow \{\text{AND}, \text{OR}\} \times [w]^3$ is a function that specifies the gate type, the two incoming wires, and the outgoing wire of each gate. To specify G, we first let all the wires and gates to be numbered. The wire numbers range from 1 to w; while those of gates range from 1 to m. For each gate $i \in [m]$, the information $G(i) = (T, a, b, c)$ tells us that T is the type of the gate i, while a and b specify its incoming wires, and c specifies its outgoing wire. By convention, we always number the wires so that $a < b < c$. The computation of Boolean formula f on an input in $\{0,1\}^n$ is defined naturally; we often abuse the notation and treat f as a function $f\colon \{0,1\}^n \to \{0,1\}$.

A non-monotone Boolean formula additionally contains NOT gates, which have fan-in 1 and fan-out 1. It is well-known that, via De Morgan's law, we can express any non-monotone Boolean formula by one in which all the NOT gates are placed on the input wires (and the number of gates of the latter formula is two times of that of the former). Hence, we can specify a non-monotone Boolean formula as a tuple $f = (n, w, m, G, \Sigma)$, where $\Sigma : [n] \to \{\text{Positive}, \text{Negative}\}$ naturally specifies if the input wire $i \in [n]$ is a negative one or not.

Standard complexity theory tells us that circuit complexity class NC^1 and Boolean formulae are equivalent. It is known also that NC^1 is equivalent to the class captured by log-depth Boolean formulae (see *e.g.*, [26]). Thus, the circuit complexity class captured by Boolean formulae is equivalent to the class captured by log-depth Boolean formulae.

Definition 1 (Linear Secret Sharing Scheme). A linear secret sharing scheme (LSSS) for a function class $\mathcal{F}$ consists of two algorithms Share and Rec.

$\mathsf{Share}(f, \mathbf{h})$: It takes a function $f \in \mathcal{F}$ where $f : \{0,1\}^n \to \{0,1\}$ and a vector $\mathbf{h} \in \mathbb{Z}_p^{\gamma}$. Then, outputs shares $\mathbf{h}_1, \ldots, \mathbf{h}_n \in \mathbb{Z}_p^{\gamma}$.

$\mathsf{Rec}(f, x, \{\mathbf{h}_i\}_{x_i=1})$: It takes $f : \{0,1\}^n \to \{0,1\}$, a bit string $x = (x_1, \ldots, x_n) \in \{0,1\}^n$ and shares $\{\mathbf{h}_i\}_{x_i=1}$. Then, outputs a vector $\mathbf{h}'$ or $\perp$.

In particular, Rec computes a linear function on shares to reconstruct a secret; $\mathbf{h} = \sum_{x_i=1} a_i \mathbf{h}_i$ where each a_i is determined by f. A LSSS has two properties.

Correctness: For any $f \in F$, $x \in \{0,1\}^n$ such that $f(x) = 1$,

$$\Pr[\mathsf{Rec}(f, x, \{\mathbf{h}_i\}_{x_i=1}) = \mathbf{h} \mid \mathbf{h}_1, \ldots, \mathbf{h}_n \leftarrow \mathsf{Share}(f, \mathbf{h})] = 1.$$

Security: For any $f \in F$, $x \in \{0,1\}^n$ such that $f(x) = 0$, and $\mathbf{h}_1, \ldots, \mathbf{h}_n \leftarrow \mathsf{Share}(f, \mathbf{h})$, shares $\{\mathbf{h}_i\}_{x_i=1}$ have no information about $\mathbf{h}$.

Definition 2 (Bilinear Groups). A description of bilinear groups $\mathbb{G} = (p, G_1, G_2, G_\mathsf{T}, g_1, g_2, e)$ consist of a prime p, cyclic groups G_1, G_2, G_T of order p, generators g_1 and g_2 of G_1 and G_2 respectively, and a bilinear map $e : G_1 \times G_2 \to G_\mathsf{T}$, which has two properties.

- (Bilinearity): $\forall h_1 \in G_1, h_2 \in G_2, a, b \in \mathbb{Z}_p, e(h_1^a, h_2^b) = e(h_1, h_2)^{ab}$.
- (Non-degeneracy): For generators g_1, g_2; $g_\mathsf{T} = e(g_1, g_2)$ is a generator of G_T.

A bilinear group generator $\mathcal{G}_{\mathsf{BG}}(1^\lambda)$ takes a security parameter 1^λ and outputs a description of bilinear groups $\mathbb{G}$ with a $\Omega(\lambda)$-bit prime p.

Definition 3 ($\mathcal{D}_{j,k}$-MDDH Assumption [19]). For $j > k$, let $\mathcal{D}_{j,k}$ be a matrix distribution over matrices in $\mathbb{Z}_p^{j \times k}$, which outputs a full-rank matrix with overwhelming probability. Denote $\mathcal{D}_{k+1,k} = \mathcal{D}_k$. We can assume that, wlog, the first k rows of a matrix chosen from $\mathcal{D}_{j,k}$ form an invertible matrix. We consider the following distribution: $\mathbb{G} \leftarrow \mathcal{G}_{\mathsf{BG}}(1^\lambda)$, $\mathbf{A} \leftarrow \mathcal{D}_{j,k}$, $\mathbf{v} \leftarrow \mathbb{Z}_p^k$, $\mathbf{t}_0 = \mathbf{A}\mathbf{v}$, $\mathbf{t}_1 \leftarrow$

$\mathbb{Z}_p^j$, $P_{i,\beta} = (\mathbb{G}, [\mathbf{A}]_i, [\mathbf{t}_\beta]_i)$. We say that the $\mathcal{D}_{j,k}$-MDDH assumption holds with respect to $\mathcal{G}_{\mathsf{BG}}$ if, for any PPT adversary $\mathcal{A}$,

$$\mathsf{Adv}_{\mathcal{A}}^{\mathcal{D}_{j,k}\text{-MDDH}}(\lambda) = \max_{i \in \{1,2\}} |\Pr[1 \leftarrow \mathcal{A}(P_{i,0})] - \Pr[1 \leftarrow \mathcal{A}(P_{i,1})]| \leq \mathsf{negl}(\lambda).$$

Uniform Distribution. Let $\mathcal{U}_{j,k}$ be a uniform distribution over $\mathbb{Z}_p^{j \times k}$. Then, the following hold with tight reductions: $\mathcal{D}_k$-MDDH $\Rightarrow \mathcal{U}_k$-MDDH $\Rightarrow \mathcal{U}_{j,k}$-MDDH.

Random Self-reducibility. We can obtain arbitrarily many instances of the $\mathcal{D}_k$-MDDH problem without additional security loss. For any $n \in \mathbb{N}$, we define the following distribution: $\mathbb{G} \leftarrow \mathcal{G}_{\mathsf{BG}}(1^\lambda)$, $\mathbf{A} \leftarrow \mathcal{D}_k$, $\mathbf{V} \leftarrow \mathbb{Z}_p^{k \times n}$, $\mathbf{T}_0 = \mathbf{AV}$, $\mathbf{T}_1 \leftarrow \mathbb{Z}_p^{(k+1) \times n}$, $P_{i,\beta} = (\mathbb{G}, [\mathbf{A}]_i, [\mathbf{T}_\beta]_i)$. The n-fold $\mathcal{D}_k$-MDDH assumption is similarly defined to the $\mathcal{D}_k$-MDDH assumption. Then, n-fold $\mathcal{D}_k$-MDDH is tightly reduced to $\mathcal{D}_k$-MDDH. That is, $\mathcal{D}_k$-MDDH $\Rightarrow n$-$\mathcal{D}_k$-MDDH.

2.2 Attribute-Based Encryption

Predicate Family. Let $\mathsf{P} = \{\mathsf{P}_\kappa : \mathcal{X}_\kappa \times \mathcal{Y}_\kappa \to \{0, 1\} \mid \kappa \in \mathcal{K}\}$ be a predicate family where $\mathcal{X}_\kappa$ and $\mathcal{Y}_\kappa$ denote "ciphertext attribute" and "key attribute" spaces. The index κ denotes a list of some parameters such as bounds on some quantities (hence $\mathcal{K}$ depends on that predicate). We often omit κ if the context is clear.

Definition 4 (Attribute-Based Encryption). An attribute-based encryption (ABE) scheme for a predicate family P consists of four algorithms:

$\mathsf{Setup}(1^\lambda, \kappa)$]: It takes a security parameter 1^λ, and an index κ as inputs, and outputs a public key pk and a master secret key msk.

$\mathsf{Enc}(\mathsf{pk}, x, M)$]: It takes pk, an attribute $x \in \mathcal{X}$ and a message $M \in \mathcal{M}$ as inputs, and outputs a ciphertext ct_x. (Note that we let $\mathcal{M}$ be specified in pk.)

$\mathsf{KeyGen}(\mathsf{pk}, \mathsf{msk}, y)$]: It takes $\mathsf{pk}, \mathsf{msk}$, and an attribute $y \in \mathcal{Y}$ as inputs, and outputs a secret key sk_y.

$\mathsf{Dec}(\mathsf{pk}, \mathsf{ct}_x, \mathsf{sk}_y)$]: It takes $\mathsf{pk}, \mathsf{ct}_x$ and sk_y as inputs, and outputs a message M' or a symbol $\perp$.

Correctness/Security. The standard correctness is specified by the property if $\mathsf{P}(x, y) = 1$ then ct_x can be decrypted by sk_y. The standard security notion is called adaptive security. We refer these to the full version.

3 Pair Encoding Schemes

A pair encoding scheme (PES), introduced by Attrapadung [7], is an encoding system used in a general framework to construct ABE. Structures of a ciphertext and secret keys of an ABE scheme can be concisely captured by polynomials, and its decryption procedure can be represented by matrices. A PES is defined as a set of algorithms that output these polynomials or matrices. Intuitively, the polynomials specify the structures of exponent of group elements in a ciphertext and secret key, and the matrices specify coefficients used in the decryption.

3.1 Pair Encoding Scheme Definition

Definition 5 (Pair Encoding Schemes). Let $\mathsf{P}_\kappa : \mathcal{X}_\kappa \times \mathcal{Y}_\kappa \rightarrow \{0,1\}$ be a predicate family, indexed by $\kappa = (N, \mathsf{par})$, where par specifies some parameters. A PES for P_κ is given by four deterministic polynomial-time algorithms:

- $\mathsf{Param}(\mathsf{par}) \rightarrow \omega$. When given par as input, Param outputs $\omega \in \mathbb{N}$ that specifies the number of *common* variables, which we denote by $\mathbf{w} = (w_1, \ldots, w_\omega)$.
- $\mathsf{EncCt}(x, N) \rightarrow (n_1, n_2, \mathbf{c}(\mathbf{s}, \hat{\mathbf{s}}, \mathbf{w}))$. On input $N \in \mathbb{N}$, $x \in \mathcal{X}_{(N,\mathsf{par})}$, EncCt outputs a vector of polynomial $\mathbf{c} = (c_1, \ldots, c_{n_3})$ in *non-lone* variables $\mathbf{s} = (s_0, s_1, \ldots, s_{n_1})$ and *lone* variables $\hat{\mathbf{s}} = (\hat{s}_1, \ldots, \hat{s}_{n_2})$ as follows, where $\theta_{i,z}, \theta_{i,t,j} \in \mathbb{Z}_N$:

$$\mathbf{c}(\mathbf{s}, \hat{\mathbf{s}}, \mathbf{w}) = \{ \sum_{z \in [n_2]} \theta_{i,z}\hat{s}_z + \sum_{t \in [n_1]^+, j \in [\omega]} \theta_{i,t,j} w_j s_t \}_{i \in [n_3]}.$$

- $\mathsf{EncKey}(y, N) \rightarrow (m_1, m_2, \mathbf{k}(\mathbf{r}, \hat{\mathbf{r}}, \mathbf{w}))$. On input $N \in \mathbb{N}$ and $y \in \mathcal{Y}_{(N,\mathsf{par})}$, EncKey outputs a vector of polynomial $\mathbf{k} = (k_1, \ldots, k_{m_3})$ in *non-lone* variables $\mathbf{r} = (r_1, \ldots, r_{m_1})$ and *lone* variables $\hat{\mathbf{r}} = (\alpha, \hat{r}_1, \ldots, \hat{r}_{m_2})$ as follows, where $\phi_i, \phi_{i,u}, \phi_{i,v,j} \in \mathbb{Z}_N$:

$$\mathbf{k}(\mathbf{r}, \hat{\mathbf{r}}, \mathbf{w}) = \{\phi_i \alpha + \sum_{u \in [m_2]} \phi_{i,u}\hat{r}_u + \sum_{v \in [m_1], j \in [\omega]} \phi_{i,v,j} w_j r_v\}_{i \in [m_3]}.$$

- $\mathsf{Pair}(x, y, N) \rightarrow (\mathbf{E}, \overline{\mathbf{E}})$. On input N, and both x, and y, Pair outputs two matrices $\mathbf{E}, \overline{\mathbf{E}}$ of sizes $(n_1 + 1) \times m_3$ and $n_3 \times m_1$, respectively.

Correctness. A PES is said to be correct if for every $\kappa = (N, \mathsf{par})$, $x \in \mathcal{X}_\kappa$ and $y \in \mathcal{Y}_\kappa$ such that $\mathsf{P}_\kappa(x, y) = 1$, then $\mathbf{s}\mathbf{E}\mathbf{k}^\top + \mathbf{c}\overline{\mathbf{E}}\mathbf{r}^\top = \alpha s_0$ holds symbolically. The left-hand side is indeed a linear combination of $s_t k_p$ and $c_q r_v$, for $t \in [n_1]^+, p \in [m_3], q \in [n_3], v \in [m_1]$. Hence, an equivalent way to describe Pair and correctness together at once is to show such a linear combination that evaluates to αs_0.

Terminology. We denote $(\hat{r}_1, \ldots, \hat{r}_{m_2})$ by $\hat{\mathbf{r}}_{-\alpha}$. Following [3], a variable is called *lone* as it is not multiplied with any w_j (otherwise called *non-lone*). Furthermore, since α, s_0 are treated distinguishably in defining correctness, we also often call them the *special* lone and non-lone variable, respectively. Throughout the paper, we fix N in index κ as prime p, which is an order of bilinear groups used to construct an ABE scheme. For notational conciseness, we consider that κ only specifies par, and p is hard-coded in EncCt, EncKey, and Pair.

Evaluating PES with Vectors/Matrices. We can evaluate ciphertext encoding $\mathbf{c}(\mathbf{s}, \hat{\mathbf{s}}, \mathbf{w})$ with the following substitution from scalar variables to vectors/matrices as follows. Let $d \in \mathbb{N}$. Each s_t is substituted by a vector $\mathbf{s}_t \in \mathbb{Z}_N^d$. Each $\hat{s}_z$ is substituted by a vector $\hat{\mathbf{s}}_z \in \mathbb{Z}_N^d$. Each w_j is substituted by a matrix

$\mathbf{W}_j \in \mathbb{Z}_N^{d\times d}$. Let $\mathbf{S} = (\mathbf{s}_0, \ldots, \mathbf{s}_{n_1}) \in \mathbb{Z}_N^{d\times(n_1+1)}$, $\hat{\mathbf{S}} = (\hat{\mathbf{s}}_1, \ldots, \hat{\mathbf{s}}_{n_2}) \in \mathbb{Z}_N^{d\times n_2}$, and $\mathbb{W} = (\mathbf{W}_1, \ldots, \mathbf{W}_\omega)$, we then define

$$\mathbf{c}(\mathbf{S}, \hat{\mathbf{S}}, \mathbb{W}) = \{\sum_{z\in[n_2]} \theta_{i,z}\hat{\mathbf{s}}_z + \sum_{t\in[n_1]^+, j\in[\omega]} \theta_{i,t,j}\mathbf{W}_j^\top \mathbf{s}_t\}_{i\in[n_3]},$$

$$\mathbf{k}(\mathbf{R}, \hat{\mathbf{R}}, \mathbb{W}) = \{\phi_i\mathbf{h} + \sum_{u\in[m_2]} \phi_{i,u}\hat{\mathbf{r}}_u + \sum_{v\in[m_1], j\in[\omega]} \phi_{i,v,j}\mathbf{W}_j\mathbf{r}_v\}_{i\in[m_3]}.$$

3.2 Security Properties of PESs

Definition 6 (Perfect Master-Key Hiding (PMH) [7]). Let $\Gamma = (\mathsf{Param}, \mathsf{EncCt}, \mathsf{EncKey}, \mathsf{Pair})$ be a PES for a predicate faimily $\mathsf{P}_\kappa : \mathcal{X}_\kappa \times \mathcal{Y}_\kappa \to \{0, 1\}$. We say that Γ satisfies perfect master-key hiding (PMH) if the following holds. Let $\omega \leftarrow \mathsf{Param}(\mathrm{par})$, $(n_1, n_2, \mathbf{c}(\mathbf{s}, \hat{\mathbf{s}}, \mathbf{w})) \leftarrow \mathsf{EncCt}(x)$, and $(m_1, m_2, \mathbf{k}(\mathbf{r}, \hat{\mathbf{r}}, \mathbf{w})) \leftarrow \mathsf{EncKey}(y)$. Then, for all κ and $(x, y) \in \mathcal{X}_\kappa \times \mathcal{Y}_\kappa$ such that $\mathsf{P}_\kappa(x, y) = 0$, the two distributions are identical, where the probability is taken over $\mathbf{s} \leftarrow \mathbb{Z}_p^{n_1+1}$, $\hat{\mathbf{s}} \leftarrow \mathbb{Z}_p^{n_2}$, $\mathbf{r} \leftarrow \mathbb{Z}_p^{m_1}$, $\alpha \leftarrow \mathbb{Z}_p$, $\hat{\mathbf{r}}_{-\alpha} \leftarrow \mathbb{Z}_p^{m_2}$, and $\mathbf{w} \leftarrow \mathbb{Z}_p^{\omega}$.

$$\{\mathbf{s}, \mathbf{r}, \mathbf{c}(\mathbf{s}, \hat{\mathbf{s}}, \mathbf{w}), \mathbf{k}(\mathbf{r}, (0, \hat{\mathbf{r}}_{-\alpha}), \mathbf{w})\} \quad \text{and} \quad \{\mathbf{s}, \mathbf{r}, \mathbf{c}(\mathbf{s}, \hat{\mathbf{s}}, \mathbf{w}), \mathbf{k}(\mathbf{r}, (\alpha, \hat{\mathbf{r}}_{-\alpha}), \mathbf{w})\}.$$

Definition 7 (Single-Variable PMH). We say that Γ satisfies single-variable PMH if Γ is PMH and $n_1 = 0$ for all $x \in \mathcal{X}_\kappa$, where $(n_1, n_2, \mathbf{c}(\mathbf{s}, \hat{\mathbf{s}}, \mathbf{w})) \leftarrow \mathsf{EncCt}(x)$. In other words, EncCt uses only s_0 for non-lone variable.

Note that Ambrona *et al.* showed that all predicate encodings [38] can be seen as a PES with single-variable PMH [6].

We next introduce the (ζ, ℓ)-key-encoding indistinguishability ((ζ, ℓ)-$\mathsf{KE\text{-}ind}$), which is a central security property in our framework, where we consider several transformations of PESs. The crucial feature on (ζ, ℓ)-$\mathsf{KE\text{-}ind}$ is two-fold: it is preserved after transformations, and it leads to the adaptive security of the resulting ABE scheme.

Definition 8 ((ζ, ℓ)-KE-ind). Let $\Gamma = (\mathsf{Param}, \mathsf{EncCt}, \mathsf{EncKey}, \mathsf{Pair})$ be a PES for a predicate family $\mathsf{P}_\kappa : \mathcal{X}_\kappa \times \mathcal{Y}_\kappa \to \{0, 1\}$. Let $\zeta, \ell \in \mathbb{N}$ such that $\ell \leq \zeta$. We say that Γ satisfies (ζ, ℓ)-$\mathsf{KE\text{-}ind}$ if the following holds. Consider a game $\mathsf{G}_\beta^{(\zeta,\ell)\text{-}\mathsf{KE\text{-}ind}}$ defined in Fig. 1, in which an adversary $\mathcal{A}$ can adaptively query $\mathcal{O}_\mathcal{X}$ and $\mathcal{O}_\mathcal{Y}$ with $x \in \mathcal{X}_\kappa$ and $y \in \mathcal{Y}_\kappa$ such that $\mathsf{P}_\kappa(x, y) = 0$, respectively. $\mathcal{A}$ is allowed to query each oracle at most once. Then, for all $\eta \in \{1, 2\}$, we have $\mathsf{G}_0^{(\zeta,\ell)\text{-}\mathsf{KE\text{-}ind}} \approx_c \mathsf{G}_1^{(\zeta,\ell)\text{-}\mathsf{KE\text{-}ind}}$.

Note that we can omit the terms that correspond to $g_{[1,i]}, h_{[1,i]}$ of the composite-order variant in the introduction by giving $\mathbf{a}_i^*, \mathbf{b}_i^*$ as $\mathbb{Z}_p$ elements to $\mathcal{A}$.

The following theorem says that all PESs with single-variable PMH satisfy (ζ, ℓ)-$\mathsf{KE\text{-}ind}$ for all $\zeta, \ell \in \mathbb{N}$. We defer its proof to the full version.

$\mathsf{G}_{\beta}^{(\zeta,\ell)\text{-KE-ind}}$

$\omega \leftarrow \mathsf{Param}(\mathsf{par}),\ \mathbb{G} \leftarrow \mathcal{G}_{\mathsf{BG}}(1^{\lambda})$

$\overline{\mathbf{A}}, \overline{\mathbf{B}} \leftarrow \mathbb{Z}_p^{(k+\zeta)\times(k+\zeta)},\ \mathbb{W} = (\mathbf{W}_1, \ldots, \mathbf{W}_{\omega}) \leftarrow (\mathbb{Z}_p^{(k+\zeta)\times(k+\zeta)})^{\omega}$

$P = (\mathbb{G}, [\mathbf{A}]_{\eta}, [\mathbf{B}]_{3-\eta}, \{\mathbf{a}_i^*\}_{i\in[\ell,\zeta]}, \{\mathbf{b}_i^*\}_{i\in[\ell+1,\zeta]}, \{[\mathbf{W}_i^{\top}\mathbf{A}]_{\eta}, [\mathbf{W}_i\mathbf{B}]_{3-\eta}\}_{i\in[\omega]})$

$\beta' \leftarrow \mathcal{A}^{\mathcal{O}_{\mathcal{X}}(\cdot), \mathcal{O}_{\mathcal{Y}}(\cdot,\cdot)}(P)$

$\mathcal{O}_{\mathcal{X}}(\cdot)$

Input: $x \in \mathcal{X}_{\kappa}$

$(n_1, n_2, \mathbf{c}(\mathbf{s}, \hat{\mathbf{s}}, \mathbf{w})) \leftarrow \mathsf{EncCt}(x)$

$\mathbf{c}_0 \leftarrow \mathsf{span}(\mathbf{A}, \mathbf{a}_1, \ldots, \mathbf{a}_{\ell}),\ \mathbf{s}_1, \ldots, \mathbf{s}_{n_1} \leftarrow \mathbb{Z}_p^k,\ \hat{\mathbf{s}}_1, \ldots, \hat{\mathbf{s}}_{n_2} \leftarrow \mathbb{Z}_p^{k+\zeta}$

$\mathbf{S} = (\mathbf{c}_0, \mathbf{A}\mathbf{s}_1, \ldots, \mathbf{A}\mathbf{s}_{n_1}),\ \widehat{\mathbf{S}} = (\hat{\mathbf{s}}_1, \ldots, \hat{\mathbf{s}}_{n_2})$

Output: $([\mathbf{S}]_{\eta}, [\mathbf{c}(\mathbf{S}, \widehat{\mathbf{S}}, \mathbb{W})]_{\eta})$

$\mathcal{O}_{\mathcal{Y}}(\cdot,\cdot)$

Input: $y \in \mathcal{Y}_{\kappa}$ and $\mathbf{h} \in \mathbb{Z}_p^{k+\zeta}$

$(m_1, m_2, \mathbf{k}(\mathbf{r}, \hat{\mathbf{r}}, \mathbf{w})) \leftarrow \mathsf{EncKey}(y),\ \mu \leftarrow \mathbb{Z}_p,\ \mathbf{r}_1, \ldots, \mathbf{r}_{m_1} \leftarrow \mathbb{Z}_p^k,\ \hat{\mathbf{r}}_1, \ldots, \hat{\mathbf{r}}_{m_2} \leftarrow \mathbb{Z}_p^{k+\zeta}$

$\mathbf{R} = (\mathbf{B}\mathbf{r}_1, \ldots, \mathbf{B}\mathbf{r}_{m_1}),\ \widehat{\mathbf{R}} = (\mathbf{h} + \boxed{\beta\mu\mathbf{a}_{\ell}^*}, \hat{\mathbf{r}}_1, \ldots, \hat{\mathbf{r}}_{m_2})$

Output: $([\mathbf{R}]_{3-\eta}, [\mathbf{k}(\mathbf{R}, \widehat{\mathbf{R}}, \mathbb{W})]_{3-\eta})$

Fig. 1. (ζ, ℓ)-KE-ind game.

Theorem 4 ((ζ,ℓ)-KE-ind of PES with Single-Variable PMH). *Let Γ be a PES with single-variable PMH. Then, for all constants $\zeta, \ell \in \mathbb{N}$, Γ satisfies (ζ,ℓ)-KE-ind under the $\mathcal{D}_k$-MDDH assumption. More precisely, for all PPT adversaries $\mathcal{A}$, there exists a PPT adversary $\mathcal{B}$ such that*

$$\mathsf{Adv}_{\mathcal{A},\Gamma}^{(\zeta,\ell)\text{-KE-ind}}(\lambda) \leq 2\mathsf{Adv}_{\mathcal{B}}^{\mathcal{D}_k\text{-MDDH}}(\lambda) + 2^{-\Omega(\lambda)}.$$

4 Predicate Transformations

In this section, we present several transformations for predicates, which enable us to construct a more expressive predicate from simple predicates. As shown later in Sect. 6, these transformations are sufficiently powerful to construct ABE schemes whose constructions from standard assumptions are still unknown. Concretely, we introduce four transformations called the direct sum, dual transformation, KP augmentation, and CP augmentation. Because the CP augmentation is obtained from the dual transformation and KP augmentation, the former three transformations are sufficient for our framework. We also present the corresponding transformations of PESs for each predicate transformation and prove that these PES transformations preserve the (ζ,ℓ)-KE-ind property. Starting from PESs with the single-variable PMH, which already satisfy (ζ,ℓ)-KE-ind, we can obtain a PES for a expressive predicate that satisfies (ζ',ζ')-KE-ind for some constant ζ'. Finally, we show that we can use the PES with (ζ',ζ')-KE-ind to construct an adaptively secure ABE scheme in Sect. 5.

4.1 Direct Sum of Predicate Families

Definition 9 (Direct Sum [9]**).** Let $\mathsf{P}^{(i)}_{\kappa_i} : \mathcal{X}^{(i)}_{\kappa_i} \times \mathcal{Y}^{(i)}_{\kappa_i} \to \{0,1\}$ be a predicate family. Let $\kappa = (\kappa_1, \ldots, \kappa_d)$. A predicate family for the direct sum of a predicate family set $\mathcal{P}_\kappa = (\mathsf{P}^{(1)}_{\kappa_1}, \ldots, \mathsf{P}^{(d)}_{\kappa_d})$, denoted by $\mathsf{DS}[\mathcal{P}_\kappa] : \bar{\mathcal{X}}_\kappa \times \bar{\mathcal{Y}}_\kappa \to \{0,1\}$, is defined as follows: let $\bar{\mathcal{X}}_\kappa = \bigcup_{i\in[d]}(\{i\} \times \mathcal{X}^{(i)}_{\kappa_i})$, $\bar{\mathcal{Y}}_\kappa = \bigcup_{i\in[d]}(\{i\} \times \mathcal{Y}^{(i)}_{\kappa_i})$, and define

$$\mathsf{DS}[\mathcal{P}_\kappa]((i_x, x), (i_y, y)) \Leftrightarrow (i_x = i_y) \wedge (\mathsf{P}^{(i_y)}_{\kappa i_y}(x, y) = 1).$$

We sometimes use another notation, $\mathsf{P}^{(1)}_{\kappa_1} \odot \cdots \odot \mathsf{P}^{(d)}_{\kappa_d}$, to denotes $\mathsf{DS}[\mathcal{P}_\kappa]$.

PES for $\mathsf{DS}[\mathcal{P}_\kappa]$**.** Let $\Gamma_i = (\mathsf{Param}_i, \mathsf{EncCt}_i, \mathsf{EncKey}_i, \mathsf{Pair}_i)$ be a PES for $\mathsf{P}^{(i)}_{\kappa_i}$. We construct a PES for $\mathsf{DS}[\mathcal{P}_\kappa]$, denoted by $\mathsf{DS\text{-}Trans}(\mathbf{\Gamma}) = (\mathsf{Param}', \mathsf{EncCt}', \mathsf{EncKey}', \mathsf{Pair}')$, where $\mathbf{\Gamma} = (\Gamma_1, \ldots, \Gamma_d)$.

- $\mathsf{Param}'(\mathsf{par}) \to \omega'$: Run $\omega_i \leftarrow \mathsf{Param}_i(\mathsf{par})$ and output $\sum_{i\in[d]} \omega_i$. This specifies common variables $\mathbf{w}' = (\mathbf{w}^{(1)}, \ldots, \mathbf{w}^{(d)})$, where $\mathbf{w}^{(i)} = (w^{(i)}_1, \ldots, w^{(i)}_{\omega_i})$.
- $\mathsf{EncCt}'((i_x, x)) \to (n'_1, n'_2, \mathbf{c}'(\mathbf{s}', \hat{\mathbf{s}}', \mathbf{w}'))$:
  - Output $(n_1, n_2, \mathbf{c}(\mathbf{s}, \hat{\mathbf{s}}, \mathbf{w}^{(i_x)})) \leftarrow \mathsf{EncCt}_{i_x}(x)$.
  - Define $n'_1 = n_1$, $n'_2 = n_2$, $\mathbf{s}' = \mathbf{s}$, and $\hat{\mathbf{s}}' = \hat{\mathbf{s}}$.
- $\mathsf{EncKey}'((i_y, y)) \to (m'_1, m'_2, \mathbf{k}'(\mathbf{r}', \hat{\mathbf{r}}', \mathbf{w}'))$:
  - Output $(m_1, m_2, \mathbf{k}(\mathbf{r}, \hat{\mathbf{r}}, \mathbf{w}^{(i_y)})) \leftarrow \mathsf{EncKey}_{i_y}(y)$.
  - Define $m'_1 = m_1$, $m'_2 = m_2$, $\mathbf{r}' = \mathbf{r}$, and $\hat{\mathbf{r}}' = \hat{\mathbf{r}}$.
- $\mathsf{Pair}'((i_x, x), (i_y, y)) \to (\mathbf{E}', \bar{\mathbf{E}}')$ and correctness:
  - Output $(\mathbf{E}, \bar{\mathbf{E}}) \leftarrow \mathsf{Pair}_{i_y}(x, y)$.
  - Correctness of Pair' directly follows from that of Pair_{i_y}.

Theorem 5 **((ζ, ℓ)-KE-ind** ***of*** **DS-Trans($\mathbf{\Gamma}$)).** *If Γ_i satisfies (ζ, ℓ)-KE-ind for all $i \in [d]$, then $\mathsf{DS\text{-}Trans}(\mathbf{\Gamma})$ satisfies (ζ, ℓ)-KE-ind. More precisely, for all PPT adversaries $\mathcal{A}$, there exist PPT adversary $\mathcal{B}$ such that*

$$\mathsf{Adv}^{(\zeta,\ell)\text{-KE-ind}}_{\mathcal{A},\mathsf{DS\text{-}Trans}(\mathbf{\Gamma})}(\lambda) \leq d \max_{i\in[d]} \mathsf{Adv}^{(\zeta,\ell)\text{-KE-ind}}_{\mathcal{B},\Gamma_i}(\lambda).$$

Proof. For $\beta \in \{0,1\}$, we can describe the (ζ, ℓ)-KE-ind game $\mathsf{G}^{(\zeta,\ell)\text{-KE-ind}}_\beta$ for $\mathsf{DS\text{-}Trans}(\mathbf{\Gamma})$ as shown in Fig. 2. To prove the theorem, we consider an adversary $\mathcal{B}$, which samples $t \leftarrow [d]$ and interacts with $\mathcal{O}_{\mathcal{X}^{(t)}}$ and $\mathcal{O}_{\mathcal{Y}^{(t)}}$ of the (ζ, ℓ)-KE-ind game for Γ_t. $\mathcal{B}$ internally runs an adversary $\mathcal{A}$ against (ζ, ℓ)-KE-ind of $\mathsf{DS\text{-}Trans}(\mathbf{\Gamma})$ and interacts with it as follows:

1. Let $\omega_i \leftarrow \mathsf{Param}_i(\mathsf{par})$. $\mathcal{B}$ is given $(\mathbb{G}, [\mathbf{A}]_\eta, [\mathbf{B}]_{3-\eta}, \{\mathbf{a}^*_i\}_{i\in[\ell,\zeta]}, \{\mathbf{b}^*_i\}_{i\in[\ell+1,\zeta]}, \{[\mathbf{W}^\top_{t,j}\mathbf{A}]_\eta, [\mathbf{W}_{t,j}\mathbf{B}]_{3-\eta}\}_{j\in[\omega_t]})$. It then samples $\mathbb{W}_i = (\mathbf{W}_{i,1}, \ldots, \mathbf{W}_{i,\omega_i}) \leftarrow (\mathbb{Z}^{(k+\zeta)\times(k+\zeta)}_p)^{\omega_i}$ for $i \in [d] \backslash t$.
2. $\mathcal{B}$ gives to $\mathcal{A}$ the following elements: $\mathbb{G}, [\mathbf{A}]_\eta, [\mathbf{B}]_{3-\eta}, \{\mathbf{a}^*_i\}_{i\in[\ell,\zeta]}, \{\mathbf{b}^*_i\}_{i\in[\ell+1,\zeta]}$, together with $\{[\mathbf{W}^\top_{i,j}\mathbf{A}]_\eta, [\mathbf{W}_{i,j}\mathbf{B}]_{3-\eta}\}_{i\in[d],j\in[\omega_i]}$
3. For $\mathcal{A}$'s query to $\mathcal{O}_{\bar{\mathcal{X}}}$ on (i_x, x), $\mathcal{B}$ replies as follows:

$\mathsf{G}_{\beta}^{(\zeta,\ell)\text{-KE-ind}}$

$\omega_i \leftarrow \mathsf{Param}_i(\mathsf{par}),\ \mathbb{G} \leftarrow \mathcal{G}_{\mathsf{BG}}(1^\lambda)$
$\overline{\mathbf{A}}, \overline{\mathbf{B}} \leftarrow \mathbb{Z}_p^{(k+\zeta)\times(k+\zeta)},\ \mathbb{W}_i = (\mathbf{W}_{i,1},\ldots,\mathbf{W}_{i,\omega_i}) \leftarrow (\mathbb{Z}_p^{(k+\zeta)\times(k+\zeta)})^{\omega_i}$
$P = (\mathbb{G}, [\mathbf{A}]_\eta, [\mathbf{B}]_{3-\eta}, \{\mathbf{a}_i^*\}_{i\in[\ell,\zeta]}, \{\mathbf{b}_i^*\}_{i\in[\ell+1,\zeta]}, \{[\mathbf{W}_{i,j}^\top \mathbf{A}]_\eta, [\mathbf{W}_{i,j}\mathbf{B}]_{3-\eta}\}_{i\in[d],j\in[\omega_i]})$
$\beta' \leftarrow \mathcal{A}^{\mathcal{O}_{\bar{\mathcal{X}}}(\cdot),\mathcal{O}_{\bar{\mathcal{Y}}}(\cdot,\cdot)}(P)$

$\mathcal{O}_{\bar{\mathcal{X}}}(\cdot)$

Input: $(i_x, x) \in \bar{\mathcal{X}}_\kappa$
$(n_1, n_2, \mathbf{c}(\mathbf{s}, \hat{\mathbf{s}}, \mathbf{w}^{(i_x)})) \leftarrow \mathsf{EncCt}_{i_x}(x)$
$\mathbf{c}_0 \leftarrow \mathsf{span}(\mathbf{A}, \mathbf{a}_1,\ldots,\mathbf{a}_\ell),\ \mathbf{s}_1,\ldots,\mathbf{s}_{n_1} \leftarrow \mathbb{Z}_p^k,\ \hat{\mathbf{s}}_1,\ldots,\hat{\mathbf{s}}_{n_2} \leftarrow \mathbb{Z}_p^{k+\zeta}$
$\mathbf{S} = (\mathbf{c}_0, \mathbf{A}\mathbf{s}_1,\ldots,\mathbf{A}\mathbf{s}_{n_1}),\ \widehat{\mathbf{S}} = (\hat{\mathbf{s}}_1,\ldots,\hat{\mathbf{s}}_{n_2})$
Output: $([\mathbf{S}]_\eta, [\mathbf{c}(\mathbf{S}, \widehat{\mathbf{S}}, \mathbb{W}_{i_x})]_\eta)$

$\mathcal{O}_{\bar{\mathcal{Y}}}(\cdot,\cdot)$

Input: $(i_y, y) \in \bar{\mathcal{Y}}_\kappa$ and $\mathbf{h} \in \mathbb{Z}_p^{k+\zeta}$
$(m_1, m_2, \mathbf{k}(\mathbf{r}, \hat{\mathbf{r}}, \mathbf{w}^{(i_y)})) \leftarrow \mathsf{EncKey}_{i_y}(y)$
$\mu \leftarrow \mathbb{Z}_p,\ \mathbf{r}_1,\ldots,\mathbf{r}_{m_1} \leftarrow \mathbb{Z}_p^k,\ \hat{\mathbf{r}}_1,\ldots,\hat{\mathbf{r}}_{m_2} \leftarrow \mathbb{Z}_p^{k+\zeta}$
$\mathbf{R} = (\mathbf{B}\mathbf{r}_1,\ldots,\mathbf{B}\mathbf{r}_{m_1}),\ \widehat{\mathbf{R}} = (\mathbf{h} + \boxed{\beta\mu\mathbf{a}_\ell^*}, \hat{\mathbf{r}}_1,\ldots,\hat{\mathbf{r}}_{m_2})$
Output: $([\mathbf{R}]_{3-\eta}, [\mathbf{k}(\mathbf{R}, \widehat{\mathbf{R}}, \mathbb{W}_{i_y})]_{3-\eta})$

Fig. 2. (ζ,ℓ)-KE-ind game for DS-Trans($\mathbf{\Gamma}$).

- If $i_x = t$, $\mathcal{B}$ queries its own oracle $\mathcal{O}_{\mathcal{X}^{(t)}}$ on x and gives the reply, which is $([\mathbf{S}]_\eta, [\mathbf{c}(\mathbf{S}, \widehat{\mathbf{S}}, \mathbb{W}_t)]_\eta)$, to $\mathcal{A}$.
- If $i_x \neq t$, $\mathcal{B}$ computes $\mathbf{c}(\mathbf{s}, \hat{\mathbf{s}}, \mathbf{w}^{(i_x)}), \mathbf{S}$, and $\widehat{\mathbf{S}}$ as show below, and gives $([\mathbf{S}]_\eta, [\mathbf{c}(\mathbf{S}, \widehat{\mathbf{S}}, \mathbb{W}_{i_x})]_\eta)$ to $\mathcal{A}$:

$$(n_1, n_2, \mathbf{c}(\mathbf{s}, \hat{\mathbf{s}}, \mathbf{w}^{(i_x)})) \leftarrow \mathsf{EncCt}_{i_x}(x),\ \mathbf{c}_0 \leftarrow \mathsf{Ker}(\mathbf{a}_{\ell+1}^*,\ldots,\mathbf{a}_\zeta^*),$$
$$\mathbf{s}_1,\ldots,\mathbf{s}_{n_1} \leftarrow \mathbb{Z}_p^k,\ \hat{\mathbf{s}}_1,\ldots,\hat{\mathbf{s}}_{n_2} \leftarrow \mathbb{Z}_p^{k+\zeta}$$
$$\mathbf{S} = (\mathbf{c}_0, \mathbf{A}\mathbf{s}_1,\ldots,\mathbf{A}\mathbf{s}_{n_1}),\ \widehat{\mathbf{S}} = (\hat{\mathbf{s}}_1,\ldots,\hat{\mathbf{s}}_{n_2}).$$

  Note that $\mathsf{span}(\mathbf{A}, \mathbf{a}_1,\ldots,\mathbf{a}_\ell) = \mathsf{Ker}(\mathbf{a}_{\ell+1}^*,\ldots,\mathbf{a}_\zeta^*)$.

4. For $\mathcal{A}$'s query to $\mathcal{O}_{\bar{\mathcal{Y}}}$ on (i_y, y), $\mathcal{B}$ replies as follows:
   - If $i_y = t$, $\mathcal{B}$ queries its own oracle $\mathcal{O}_{\mathcal{Y}^{(t)}}$ on y and gives the reply, which is $([\mathbf{R}]_{3-\eta}, [\mathbf{k}(\mathbf{R}, \widehat{\mathbf{R}}, \mathbb{W}_t)]_{3-\eta})$, to $\mathcal{A}$. Note that the first element of $\widehat{\mathbf{R}}$ is $\mathbf{h}$ (if $\beta = 0$) or $\mathbf{h} + \mu\mathbf{a}_\ell^*$ (if $\beta = 1$).
   - If $i_y \neq t$, $\mathcal{B}$ aborts the interaction with $\mathcal{A}$ and outputs a random bit β'
5. $\mathcal{B}$ outputs $\mathcal{A}$'s output as it is.

In the above experiment, $\mathcal{B}$ correctly simulates $\mathcal{O}_{\bar{\mathcal{X}}}$. Since $\mathcal{B}$ aborts the experiment if $i_y \neq t$, we focus on the case of $i_y = t$, which occurs with probability $1/d$. Note that since $i_x = t \Rightarrow \mathsf{P}^{(t)}(x, y) = 0$ from the game condition for DS-Trans($\mathbf{\Gamma}$), $\mathcal{B}$ follow the game condition for Γ_t. If $\beta = 0$ in the KE-ind game for Γ_t, $\mathcal{A}$'s view corresponds to that in $\mathsf{G}_0^{(\zeta,\ell)\text{-KE-ind}}$, and it corresponds to $\mathsf{G}_1^{(\zeta,\ell)\text{-KE-ind}}$ otherwise. Thus, we have $\Pr[i_y = t] \cdot \mathsf{Adv}_{\mathcal{A},\mathsf{DS\text{-}Trans}(\mathbf{\Gamma})}^{(\zeta,\ell)\text{-KE-ind}}(\lambda) + \Pr[i_y \neq t] \cdot 0 \leq \mathsf{Adv}_{\mathcal{B},\Gamma_t}^{(\zeta,\ell)\text{-KE-ind}}(\lambda) \leq \max_{i\in[d]} \mathsf{Adv}_{\mathcal{B},\Gamma_i}^{(\zeta,\ell)\text{-KE-ind}}(\lambda)$. This concludes the proof. □

4.2 Dual Predicates

Recall that the dual of $\mathsf{P}_\kappa : \mathcal{X}_\kappa \times \mathcal{Y}_\kappa \to \{0,1\}$ is $\mathsf{Dual}[\mathsf{P}_\kappa] : \bar{\mathcal{X}}_\kappa \times \bar{\mathcal{Y}}_\kappa \to \{0,1\}$ where $\bar{\mathcal{X}}_\kappa = \mathcal{Y}_\kappa$ and $\bar{\mathcal{Y}}_\kappa = \mathcal{X}_\kappa$, and $\mathsf{Dual}[\mathsf{P}_\kappa](x,y) = \mathsf{P}_\kappa(y,x)$.

PES for $\mathsf{Dual}[\mathsf{P}_\kappa]$. Let $\Gamma = (\mathsf{Param}, \mathsf{EncCt}, \mathsf{EncKey}, \mathsf{Pair})$ be a PES for P_κ. We construct a PES for $\mathsf{Dual}[\mathsf{P}_\kappa]$, denoted by $\mathsf{Dual\text{-}Trans}(\Gamma)$ as follows.

- $\mathsf{Param}'(\mathsf{par}) \to \omega'$: Run $\omega \leftarrow \mathsf{Param}(\mathsf{par})$ and output $\omega + 1$. This specifies common variables $\mathbf{w}' = (w_0, w_1, \ldots, w_\omega)$, where w_0 is a new common variable.
- $\mathsf{EncCt}'(x) \to (n_1', n_2', \mathbf{c}'(\mathbf{s}', \hat{\mathbf{s}}', \mathbf{w}'))$:
  - Run $(m_1, m_2, \mathbf{k}(\mathbf{r}, \hat{\mathbf{r}}, \mathbf{w})) \leftarrow \mathsf{EncKey}(x)$. Let s_{new} be a new special non-lone variable. Polynomials $\mathbf{c}'(\mathbf{s}', \hat{\mathbf{s}}', \mathbf{w}')$ are defined the same as $\mathbf{k}(\mathbf{r}, \hat{\mathbf{r}}, \mathbf{w})$ except that α is replaced with $s_{\mathsf{new}} w_0$.
  - Define $n_1' = m_1$, $n_2' = m_2$, $\mathbf{s}' = (s_{\mathsf{new}}, \mathbf{r})$, and $\hat{\mathbf{s}}' = \hat{\mathbf{r}}_{-\alpha}$.
- $\mathsf{EncKey}'(y) \to (m_1', m_2', \mathbf{k}'(\mathbf{r}', \hat{\mathbf{r}}', \mathbf{w}))$:
  - Run $(n_1, n_2, \mathbf{c}(\mathbf{s}, \hat{\mathbf{s}}, \mathbf{w})) \leftarrow \mathsf{EncCt}(y)$. Let α_{new} be a new special lone variable. Polynomials $\mathbf{k}'(\mathbf{r}', \hat{\mathbf{r}}', \mathbf{w}')$ are defined the same as $\mathbf{c}(\mathbf{s}, \hat{\mathbf{s}}, \mathbf{w})$ except that a polynomial $\alpha_{\mathsf{new}} - s_0 w_0$ is added as the first element of $\mathbf{k}'(\mathbf{r}', \hat{\mathbf{r}}', \mathbf{w}')$.
  - Define $m_1' = n_1 + 1$, $m_2' = n_2$, $\mathbf{r}' = \mathbf{s}$, and $\hat{\mathbf{r}}' = (\alpha_{\mathsf{new}}, \hat{\mathbf{s}})$.
- $\mathsf{Pair}'(x,y) \to (\mathbf{E}', \bar{\mathbf{E}}')$ and correctness:
  - Run $(\mathbf{E}, \bar{\mathbf{E}}) \leftarrow \mathsf{Pair}(y,x)$. Define $\mathbf{E}' = \begin{pmatrix} 1 & \\ & \bar{\mathbf{E}}^\top \end{pmatrix}$ and $\bar{\mathbf{E}}' = \mathbf{E}^\top$.
  - For correctness, we have

$$\mathbf{s}'\mathbf{E}'\mathbf{k}'^\top + \mathbf{c}'\bar{\mathbf{E}}'\mathbf{r}'^\top = (s_{\mathsf{new}}, \mathbf{r}) \begin{pmatrix} 1 & \\ & \bar{\mathbf{E}}^\top \end{pmatrix} (\alpha_{\mathsf{new}} - s_0 w_0, \mathbf{c})^\top + \mathbf{k}|_{\alpha \mapsto s_{\mathsf{new}} w_0} \mathbf{E}^\top \mathbf{s}^\top$$
$$= s_{\mathsf{new}}\alpha_{\mathsf{new}} - s_{\mathsf{new}} s_0 w_0 + s_{\mathsf{new}} s_0 w_0 = s_{\mathsf{new}} \alpha_{\mathsf{new}}.$$

Theorem 6 (((ζ,ℓ)-KE-ind *of* $\mathsf{Dual\text{-}Trans}(\Gamma)$)). *Let* $2 \le \ell \le \zeta$. *If* Γ *satisfies* $(\zeta, \ell-1)$-KE-ind, *then* $\mathsf{Dual\text{-}Trans}(\Gamma)$ *satisfies* (ζ,ℓ)-KE-ind *under the* $\mathcal{D}_k$*-MDDH assumption. More precisely, for all PPT adversaries* $\mathcal{A}$*, there exist PPT adversaries* $\mathcal{B}_1$ *and* $\mathcal{B}_2$ *such that*

$$\mathsf{Adv}^{(\zeta,\ell)\text{-KE-ind}}_{\mathcal{A},\mathsf{Dual\text{-}Trans}(\Gamma)}(\lambda) \le \mathsf{Adv}^{(\zeta,\ell-1)\text{-KE-ind}}_{\mathcal{B}_1,\Gamma}(\lambda) + 2\mathsf{Adv}^{\mathcal{D}_k\text{-MDDH}}_{\mathcal{B}_2}(\lambda) + 2^{-\Omega(\lambda)}.$$

Proof. For $\beta \in \{0,1\}$, we can describe the (ζ,ℓ)-KE-ind game $\mathsf{G}_\beta^{(\zeta,\ell)\text{-KE-ind}}$ for $\mathsf{Dual\text{-}Trans}(\Gamma)$ as shown in Fig. 3. To show this theorem, we consider two intermediate hybrids H_1 and H_2, which are also described in Fig. 3. That is, H_1 (resp. H_2) is defined the same as $\mathsf{G}_0^{(\zeta,\ell)\text{-KE-ind}}$ (resp. $\mathsf{G}_1^{(\zeta,\ell)\text{-KE-ind}}$) except that $\mathbf{d}_0$, the first elements of $\mathbf{R}$ generated in $\mathcal{O}_{\bar{\mathcal{Y}}}$, is set as $\mathbf{d}_0 \leftarrow \mathsf{span}(\mathbf{B}, \mathbf{b}_1, \ldots, \mathbf{b}_{\ell-1})$ instead of $\mathbf{B}\mathbf{r}_0$ where $\mathbf{r}_0 \leftarrow \mathbb{Z}_p^k$. From Lemma 1,2,3 below, we have $\mathsf{G}_0^{(\zeta,\ell)\text{-KE-ind}} \approx_c \mathsf{H}_1 \approx_c \mathsf{H}_2 \approx_c \mathsf{G}_1^{(\zeta,\ell)\text{-KE-ind}}$. This concludes the proof. □

Lemma 1. *For all PPT adversaries* $\mathcal{A}$*, there exists a PPT adversary* $\mathcal{B}$ *such that* $|\Pr[\langle \mathcal{A}, \mathsf{G}_0^{(\zeta,\ell)\text{-KE-ind}} \rangle = 1] - \Pr[\langle \mathcal{A}, \mathsf{H}_1 \rangle = 1]| \le \mathsf{Adv}^{\mathcal{D}_k\text{-MDDH}}_{\mathcal{B}}(\lambda)$.

$$\mathsf{G} \in \left\{ \mathsf{G}_0^{(\zeta,\ell)\text{-KE-ind}}, \boxed{\mathsf{H}_1}, \boxed{\boxed{\mathsf{H}_2}, \mathsf{G}_1^{(\zeta,\ell)\text{-KE-ind}}} \right\}$$

$\underline{\mathsf{G}}$ $\omega \leftarrow \mathsf{Param}(\mathsf{par}),\ \mathbb{G} \leftarrow \mathcal{G}_{\mathsf{BG}}(1^\lambda)$ $\overline{\mathbf{A}}, \overline{\mathbf{B}} \leftarrow \mathbb{Z}_p^{(k+\zeta)\times(k+\zeta)},\ \mathbb{W} = (\mathbf{W}_0^\top, \mathbf{W}_1^\top, \ldots, \mathbf{W}_\omega^\top) \leftarrow (\mathbb{Z}_p^{(k+\zeta)\times(k+\zeta)})^{\omega+1}$ $P = (\mathbb{G}, [\mathbf{A}]_\eta, [\mathbf{B}]_{3-\eta}, \{\mathbf{a}_i^*\}_{i\in[\ell,\zeta]}, \{\mathbf{b}_i^*\}_{i\in[\ell+1,\zeta]}, \{[\mathbf{W}_i^\top \mathbf{A}]_\eta, [\mathbf{W}_i \mathbf{B}]_{3-\eta}\}_{i\in[\omega]^+})$ $\beta' \leftarrow \mathcal{A}^{\mathcal{O}_{\bar{\mathcal{X}}}(\cdot), \mathcal{O}_{\bar{\mathcal{Y}}}(\cdot,\cdot)}(P)$
$\underline{\mathcal{O}_{\bar{\mathcal{X}}}(\cdot)}$ Input: $x \in \mathcal{X}_\kappa$ $(m_1, m_2, \mathbf{k}(\mathbf{r}, \hat{\mathbf{r}}, \mathbf{w})) \leftarrow \mathsf{EncKey}(x)$ $\mathbf{c}_0 \leftarrow \mathsf{span}(\mathbf{A}, \mathbf{a}_1, \ldots, \mathbf{a}_\ell),\ \mathbf{s}_1, \ldots, \mathbf{s}_{m_1} \leftarrow \mathbb{Z}_p^k,\ \hat{\mathbf{s}}_1, \ldots, \hat{\mathbf{s}}_{m_2} \leftarrow \mathbb{Z}_p^{k+\zeta}$ $\mathbf{S} = (\mathbf{A}\mathbf{s}_1, \ldots, \mathbf{A}\mathbf{s}_{m_1}),\ \widehat{\mathbf{S}} = (\mathbf{W}_0^\top \mathbf{c}_0, \hat{\mathbf{s}}_1, \ldots, \hat{\mathbf{s}}_{m_2})$ Output: $([\mathbf{c}_0]_\eta, [\mathbf{S}]_\eta, [\mathbf{k}(\mathbf{S}, \widehat{\mathbf{S}}, \mathbb{W})]_\eta)$
$\underline{\mathcal{O}_{\bar{\mathcal{Y}}}(\cdot,\cdot)}$ Input: $y \in \bar{\mathcal{Y}}_\kappa$ and $\mathbf{h} \in \mathbb{Z}_p^{k+\zeta}$ $(n_1, n_2, \mathbf{c}(\mathbf{s}, \hat{\mathbf{s}}, \mathbf{w})) \leftarrow \mathsf{EncCt}(y),\ \mu \leftarrow \mathbb{Z}_p,\ \mathbf{r}_0, \mathbf{r}_1, \ldots, \mathbf{r}_{n_1} \leftarrow \mathbb{Z}_p^k,\ \hat{\mathbf{r}}_1, \ldots, \hat{\mathbf{r}}_{n_2} \leftarrow \mathbb{Z}_p^{k+\zeta}$ $\mathbf{d}_0 = \mathbf{B}\mathbf{r}_0,\ \boxed{\mathbf{d}_0 \leftarrow \mathsf{span}(\mathbf{B}, \mathbf{b}_1, \ldots, \mathbf{b}_{\ell-1})}$ $\mathbf{R} = (\mathbf{d}_0, \mathbf{B}\mathbf{r}_1, \ldots, \mathbf{B}\mathbf{r}_{n_1}),\ \widehat{\mathbf{R}} = (\hat{\mathbf{r}}_1, \ldots, \hat{\mathbf{r}}_{n_2})$ Output: $([\mathbf{h} + \boxed{\mu \mathbf{a}_\ell^*} - \mathbf{W}_0 \mathbf{d}_0]_{3-\eta}, [\mathbf{R}]_{3-\eta}, [\mathbf{c}(\mathbf{R}, \widehat{\mathbf{R}}, \mathbb{W})]_{3-\eta})$

Fig. 3. (ζ,ℓ)-KE-ind game for Dual-Trans(Γ).

Proof. We describe the reduction algorithm $\mathcal{B}$. $\mathcal{B}$ is given an instance of $\mathcal{U}_{k+\ell-1,k}$ problem, $(\mathbb{G}, [\mathbf{M}]_{3-\eta}, [\mathbf{t}_\beta]_{3-\eta})$ where $\mathbf{t}_0 = \mathbf{M}\mathbf{u}$ and $\mathbf{t}_1 = \mathbf{v}$, where $\mathbf{u} \leftarrow \mathbb{Z}_p^k$ and $\mathbf{v} \leftarrow \mathbb{Z}_p^{k+\ell-1}$. Then, $\mathcal{B}$ chooses $\mathbf{X} \leftarrow \mathsf{GL}_{k+\zeta}(\mathbb{Z}_p)$ and sets

$$\overline{\mathbf{B}} = \mathbf{X}\begin{pmatrix} \widehat{\mathbf{M}} & & \\ \underline{\mathbf{M}} & \mathbf{I}_{\ell-1} & \\ & & \mathbf{I}_{\zeta-\ell+1} \end{pmatrix},\quad (\overline{\mathbf{B}}^\top)^{-1} = (\mathbf{X}^\top)^{-1}\begin{pmatrix} (\widehat{\mathbf{M}}^\top)^{-1} & -(\widehat{\mathbf{M}}^\top)^{-1}\underline{\mathbf{M}}^\top & \\ & \mathbf{I}_{\ell-1} & \\ & & \mathbf{I}_{\zeta-\ell+1} \end{pmatrix},$$

where $\widehat{\mathbf{M}}$ is the matrix consisting of the first k rows of $\mathbf{M}$, and $\underline{\mathbf{M}}$ is that consisting of the last $\ell-1$ rows of $\mathbf{M}$. Then, $\mathcal{B}$ can compute

$$[\mathbf{B}]_{3-\eta} = \left[\mathbf{X}\begin{pmatrix} \mathbf{M} \\ \mathbf{O} \end{pmatrix}\right]_{3-\eta},\quad (\mathbf{b}_{\ell+1}^* \| \ldots \| \mathbf{b}_\zeta^*) = (\mathbf{X}^\top)^{-1}\begin{pmatrix} \mathbf{O} \\ \mathbf{I}_{\zeta-\ell} \end{pmatrix}.$$

$\mathcal{B}$ generates $\overline{\mathbf{A}}$ and $\mathbb{W}$ by itself and computes the input P for $\mathcal{A}$ from them. When $\mathcal{A}$ queries $\mathcal{O}_{\bar{\mathcal{X}}}$, $\mathcal{B}$ replies honestly as shown in Fig. 3. When $\mathcal{A}$ queries $\mathcal{O}_{\bar{\mathcal{Y}}}$, $\mathcal{B}$ replies honestly except that it sets

$$[\mathbf{d}_0]_{3-\eta} = \left[\mathbf{X}\begin{pmatrix} \mathbf{t}_\beta \\ \mathbf{0} \end{pmatrix}\right]_{3-\eta},\quad [\mathbf{R}]_{3-\eta} = [(\mathbf{d}_0, \mathbf{B}\mathbf{r}_1, \ldots, \mathbf{B}\mathbf{r}_{m_1})]_{3-\eta}.$$

Now since we can write $\mathbf{t}_\beta = \begin{pmatrix} \widehat{\mathbf{M}} \\ \underline{\mathbf{M}} \end{pmatrix}\mathbf{u}_1 + \beta\begin{pmatrix} \mathbf{O} \\ \mathbf{I}_{\ell-1} \end{pmatrix}\mathbf{u}_2$, where $\mathbf{u}_1 \leftarrow \mathbb{Z}_p^k$ and $\mathbf{u}_2 \leftarrow \mathbb{Z}_p^{\ell-1}$, we have that $\mathbf{d}_0$ is uniformly distributed in $\mathsf{span}(\mathbf{B})$ if $\beta = 0$, and in $\mathsf{span}(\mathbf{B}, \mathbf{b}_1, \ldots, \mathbf{b}_{\ell-1})$ otherwise. Thus, the view of $\mathcal{A}$ corresponds to $\mathsf{G}_0^{(\zeta,\ell)\text{-KE-ind}}$ if $\beta = 0$, and H_1 otherwise. This concludes the proof. □

Lemma 2. *For all PPT adversaries $\mathcal{A}$, there exists a PPT adversary $\mathcal{B}$ such that* $|\Pr[\langle\mathcal{A},\mathsf{H}_1\rangle=1]-\Pr[\langle\mathcal{A},\mathsf{H}_2\rangle=1]|\le\mathsf{Adv}^{(\zeta,\ell-1)\text{-KE-ind}}_{\mathcal{B},\Gamma}(\lambda)+2^{-\Omega(\lambda)}$.

Proof. We show that the outputs of $\mathcal{O}_{\bar{\mathcal{Y}}}$ in H_1 and H_2 are computationally indistinguishable if the PES Γ for P_κ satisfies $(\zeta,\ell-1)$-KE-ind. We construct a PPT adversary $\mathcal{B}$ against $(\zeta,\ell-1)$-KE-ind of Γ that internally runs a PPT distinguisher $\mathcal{A}$ between H_1 and H_2. $\mathcal{B}$ behaves as follows.

1. $\mathcal{B}$ is given an input of $(\zeta,\ell-1)$-KE-ind game for Γ, $(\mathbb{G},[\mathbf{M}]_{3-\eta},[\mathbf{N}]_\eta,\{\mathbf{m}_i^*\}_{i\in[\ell-1,\zeta]},\{\mathbf{n}_i^*\}_{i\in[\ell,\zeta]},\{[\mathbf{V}_i^\top\mathbf{M}]_{3-\eta},[\mathbf{V}_i\mathbf{N}]_\eta\}_{i\in[\omega]})$. $\mathcal{B}$ implicitly defines that $\mathbf{A}=\mathbf{N}$, $\mathbf{B}=\mathbf{M}$, and $\mathbf{W}_i=\mathbf{V}_i^\top$ for $i\in[\omega]$.
2. $\mathcal{B}$ samples $\mathbf{W}_0\leftarrow\mathbb{Z}_p^{(k+\zeta)\times(k+\zeta)}$ and gives $P=(\mathbb{G},[\mathbf{A}]_\eta,[\mathbf{B}]_{3-\eta},\{\mathbf{a}_i^*\}_{i\in[\ell,\zeta]},\{\mathbf{b}_i^*\}_{i\in[\ell+1,\zeta]},\{[\mathbf{W}_i^\top\mathbf{A}]_\eta,[\mathbf{W}_i\mathbf{B}]_{3-\eta}\}_{i\in[\omega]^+})$ to $\mathcal{A}$.
3. For $\mathcal{A}$'s query to $\mathcal{O}_{\bar{\mathcal{X}}}$ on x, $\mathcal{B}$ samples $\mathbf{c}_0\leftarrow\mathsf{Ker}(\mathbf{a}_{\ell+1}^*,\ldots,\mathbf{a}_\zeta^*)$ and queries its own oracle $\mathcal{O}_{\mathcal{Y}}$ on $(x,\mathbf{W}_0^\top\mathbf{c}_0)$ to obtain $([\mathbf{T}]_\eta,[\mathbf{k}(\mathbf{T},\widehat{\mathbf{T}},\mathbb{V})]_\eta)$, where

   $$\mathbf{T}=(\mathbf{N}\mathbf{t}_0,\mathbf{N}\mathbf{t}_1,\ldots,\mathbf{N}\mathbf{t}_{m_1})=(\mathbf{A}\mathbf{t}_0,\mathbf{A}\mathbf{t}_1,\ldots,\mathbf{A}\mathbf{t}_{m_1}),$$
   $$\widehat{\mathbf{T}}=(\mathbf{W}_0^\top\mathbf{c}_0+\beta\hat{\mu}\mathbf{m}_{\ell-1}^*,\hat{\mathbf{t}}_1,\ldots,\hat{\mathbf{t}}_{m_2})=(\mathbf{W}_0^\top\mathbf{c}_0+\beta\hat{\mu}\mathbf{b}_{\ell-1}^*,\hat{\mathbf{t}}_1,\ldots,\hat{\mathbf{t}}_{m_2}),$$
   $$\mathbb{V}=(\mathbf{V}_1,\ldots,\mathbf{V}_\omega)=(\mathbf{W}_1^\top,\ldots,\mathbf{W}_\omega^\top).$$

   Note that $\hat{\mu}$ is a random value in $\mathbb{Z}_p$ chosen by $\mathcal{O}_{\mathcal{Y}}$. $\mathcal{B}$ implicitly defines that $\mathbf{s}_i=\mathbf{t}_i$ for $i\in[m_1]^+$, $\hat{\mathbf{s}}_i=\hat{\mathbf{t}}_i$ for $i\in[m_2]$, $\mathbf{S}=\mathbf{T}$, $\widehat{\mathbf{S}}=\widehat{\mathbf{T}}$, and $\mathbb{W}=\mathbb{V}$. $\mathcal{B}$ replies $([\mathbf{c}_0]_\eta,[\mathbf{S}]_\eta,[\mathbf{k}(\mathbf{S},\widehat{\mathbf{S}},\mathbb{W})]_\eta)$ to $\mathcal{A}$. Note that $\mathsf{span}(\mathbf{A},\mathbf{a}_1,\ldots,\mathbf{a}_\ell)=\mathsf{Ker}(\mathbf{a}_{\ell+1}^*,\ldots,\mathbf{a}_\zeta^*)$.
4. For $\mathcal{A}$'s query to $\mathcal{O}_{\bar{\mathcal{Y}}}$ with y and $\mathbf{h}$, $\mathcal{B}$ queries its own oracle $\mathcal{O}_{\mathcal{X}}$ on y to obtain $([\mathbf{U}]_{3-\eta},[\mathbf{c}(\mathbf{U},\widehat{\mathbf{U}},\mathbb{V})]_{3-\eta})$, where

   $$\mathbf{U}=(\mathbf{o}_0,\mathbf{M}\mathbf{u}_1,\ldots,\mathbf{M}\mathbf{u}_{n_1})=(\mathbf{o}_0,\mathbf{B}\mathbf{u}_1,\ldots,\mathbf{B}\mathbf{u}_{n_1}),\ \ \widehat{\mathbf{U}}=(\hat{\mathbf{u}}_1,\ldots,\hat{\mathbf{u}}_{n_2}).$$

   Note that $\mathbf{o}_0$ is randomly distributed in $\mathsf{span}(\mathbf{M},\mathbf{m}_1,\ldots,\mathbf{m}_{\ell-1})$, which equals to $\mathsf{span}(\mathbf{B},\mathbf{b}_1,\ldots,\mathbf{b}_{\ell-1})$. $\mathcal{B}$ implicitly defines that $\mathbf{r}_i=\mathbf{u}_i$ for $i\in[n_1]$, $\hat{\mathbf{r}}_i=\hat{\mathbf{u}}_i$ for $i\in[n_2]$, $\mathbf{R}=\mathbf{U}$, $\widehat{\mathbf{R}}=\widehat{\mathbf{U}}$, and $\mathbf{d}_0=\mathbf{o}_0$. $\mathcal{B}$ replies $([\mathbf{h}-\mathbf{W}_0\mathbf{d}_0]_{3-\eta},[\mathbf{R}]_{3-\eta},[\mathbf{c}(\mathbf{R},\widehat{\mathbf{R}},\mathbb{W})]_{3-\eta})$ to $\mathcal{A}$.
5. $\mathcal{B}$ outputs $\mathcal{A}$'s output as it is.

At a glance, this simulation seems that the distribution of the reply from $\mathcal{O}_{\bar{\mathcal{X}}}$ is changed. However, entire views of $\mathcal{A}$ correspond to H_1 and H_2. To see this, we redefine $\mathbf{W}_0$ as $\mathbf{W}_0=\widetilde{\mathbf{W}}_0-\frac{\beta\hat{\mu}}{\mathbf{a}_\ell^{*\top}\mathbf{c}_0}\mathbf{a}_\ell^*\mathbf{b}_{\ell-1}^{*\top}$ where $\widetilde{\mathbf{W}}_0\leftarrow\mathbb{Z}_p^{(k+\zeta)\times(k+\zeta)}$. Clearly, this does not change the distribution of $\mathbf{W}_0$. This affects $\mathcal{A}$'s view as follows:

$$P:\ \mathbf{W}_0^\top\mathbf{A}=\widetilde{\mathbf{W}}_0^\top\mathbf{A},\ \ \mathbf{W}_0\mathbf{B}=\widetilde{\mathbf{W}}_0\mathbf{B}.$$

$$\mathcal{O}_{\bar{\mathcal{X}}}:\ \mathbf{W}_0^\top\mathbf{c}_0+\beta\hat{\mu}\mathbf{b}_{\ell-1}^*=\widetilde{\mathbf{W}}_0^\top\mathbf{c}_0.$$

$$\mathcal{O}_{\bar{\mathcal{Y}}}:\ \mathbf{h}-\mathbf{W}_0\mathbf{d}_0=\mathbf{h}-\widetilde{\mathbf{W}}_0\mathbf{d}_0+\frac{\beta\hat{\mu}\mathbf{b}_{\ell-1}^{*\top}\mathbf{d}_0}{\mathbf{a}_\ell^{*\top}\mathbf{c}_0}\mathbf{a}_\ell^*=\mathbf{h}-\widetilde{\mathbf{W}}_0\mathbf{d}_0+\beta\mu\mathbf{a}_\ell^*.$$

Because $\hat{\mu}$ is randomly distributed in $\mathbb{Z}_p$, we can set $\mu = \frac{\hat{\mu}\mathbf{b}_{\ell-1}^{*\top}\mathbf{d}_0}{\mathbf{a}_\ell^{*\top}\mathbf{c}_0}$ if $\mathbf{b}_{\ell-1}^{*\top}\mathbf{d}_0 \neq 0$ and $\mathbf{a}_\ell^{*\top}\mathbf{c}_0 \neq 0$. Since $\mathbf{c}_0$ and $\mathbf{d}_0$ are randomly distributed in $\mathsf{span}(\mathbf{A}, \mathbf{a}_1, \ldots, \mathbf{a}_\ell)$ and $\mathsf{span}(\mathbf{B}, \mathbf{b}_1, \ldots, \mathbf{b}_{\ell-1})$, respectively, this is the case with an overwhelming probability. Thus, $\mathcal{A}$'s view corresponds to H_1 if $\beta = 0$ in the (ζ, ℓ)-KE-ind game of Γ, and it corresponds to H_2 otherwise. This concludes the proof. □

Lemma 3. *For all PPT adversaries $\mathcal{A}$, there exists a PPT adversary $\mathcal{B}$ such that* $|\Pr[\langle \mathcal{A}, \mathsf{H}_2\rangle = 1] - \Pr[\langle \mathcal{A}, \mathsf{G}_1^{(\zeta,\ell)\text{-KE-ind}}\rangle = 1]| \leq \mathsf{Adv}_{\mathcal{B}}^{\mathcal{D}_k\text{-MDDH}}(\lambda)$.

The proof of Lemma 3 is similar to Lemma 1, and hence we omit it here.

4.3 Key-Policy Augmentation

Definition 10 (Key-Policy Augmentation). A predicate family for key-policy Boolean formula augmentation over a single predicate family $\mathsf{P}_\kappa : \mathcal{X}_\kappa \times \mathcal{Y}_\kappa \to \{0,1\}$, denoted by $\mathsf{KBF1}[\mathsf{P}_\kappa] : \bar{\mathcal{X}}_\kappa \times \bar{\mathcal{Y}}_\kappa \to \{0,1\}$, where $\bar{\mathcal{X}}_\kappa = \mathcal{X}_\kappa$ and $\bar{\mathcal{Y}}_\kappa = \bigcup_{i\in\mathbb{N}}(\mathcal{Y}_\kappa^i \times \mathcal{F}_i)$, where $\mathcal{F}_i$ consists of all monotone Boolean formulae with input length i, is defined as follows. For $x \in \bar{\mathcal{X}}_\kappa$ and $y = ((y_1, \ldots, y_n), f) \in \bar{\mathcal{Y}}_\kappa$ where $f : \{0,1\}^n \to \{0,1\}$, we define

$$\mathsf{KBF1}[\mathsf{P}_\kappa](x, y) = f\big(\mathsf{P}_\kappa(x, y_1), \ldots, \mathsf{P}_\kappa(x, y_n)\big).$$

We use $\mathsf{KBF1}_{\mathsf{OR}}[\mathsf{P}_\kappa]$ (resp. $\mathsf{KBF1}_{\mathsf{AND}}[\mathsf{P}_\kappa]$) to denote a predicate family that is the same as $\mathsf{KBF1}[\mathsf{P}_\kappa]$ except that $\mathcal{F}_i$ in $\bar{\mathcal{Y}}_\kappa$ consists of monotone Boolean formulae whose all gates are OR (resp. AND) gates. The "1" in KBF1 refers to the property that the augmentation is over *one* predicate family. An augmentation over a *set* of predicate families follows analogously to [9], and we defer to Sect. 6 (and more details in the full version). In *dynamic* compositions, f can be chosen freely (as opposed to static ones, where f is fixed). *Unbounded* compositions mean n is unbounded.

PES for $\mathsf{KBF1}[\mathsf{P}_\kappa]$**.** Let $\Gamma = (\mathsf{Param}, \mathsf{EncCt}, \mathsf{EncKey}, \mathsf{Pair})$ be a PES for P_κ. We construct a PES for $\mathsf{KBF1}[\mathsf{P}_\kappa]$, denoted by $\mathsf{KBF1\text{-}Trans}(\Gamma)$ as follows. Let $\mathsf{Share_p}$ be the linear secret sharing algorithm on polynomials defined in Fig. 4.

- $\mathsf{Param}'(\mathsf{par}) = \mathsf{Param}(\mathsf{par})$ and $\mathsf{EncCt}'(x) = \mathsf{EncCt}(x)$
- $\mathsf{EncKey}'((y_1, \ldots, y_n), f) \to (m_1', m_2', \mathbf{k}'(\mathbf{r}', \hat{\mathbf{r}}', \mathbf{w}))$:
  - For $i \in [n]$, run $\mathsf{EncKey}(y_i)$ to obtain n sets of polynomials $\mathbf{k}^{(1)}, \ldots, \mathbf{k}^{(n)}$, where $\mathbf{k}^{(i)} = \mathbf{k}(\mathbf{r}^{(i)}, \hat{\mathbf{r}}^{(i)}, \mathbf{w})$.
  - Let τ be a number of AND gates in f. Let α_{new} be a new special lone variable and $\mathbf{u} = (u_1, \ldots, u_\tau)$ be new lone variables. Let $\sigma_1, \ldots, \sigma_n$ be polynomials that are an output of $\mathsf{Share_p}(f, \alpha_{\mathsf{new}}, \mathbf{u})$. A new set of polynomials $\mathbf{k}'^{(i)}$ is defined the same as $\mathbf{k}^{(i)}$ except that the variable $\alpha^{(i)}$ in each polynomial is replaced with σ_i.
  - Define $m_1' = nm_1$, $m_2' = \tau + nm_2$, and $\mathbf{k}'(\mathbf{r}', \hat{\mathbf{r}}', \mathbf{w}) = (\mathbf{k}'^{(1)}, \ldots, \mathbf{k}'^{(n)})$. Note that $\mathbf{r}' = (\mathbf{r}^{(1)}, \ldots, \mathbf{r}^{(n)})$ and $\hat{\mathbf{r}}' = (\alpha_{\mathsf{new}}, \mathbf{u}, \hat{\mathbf{r}}_{-\alpha^{(1)}}^{(1)}, \ldots, \hat{\mathbf{r}}_{-\alpha^{(n)}}^{(n)})$.

$\mathsf{Share_p}(f, \alpha, \mathbf{u})$

Input: A monotone Boolean formula $f = (n, w, m, G)$ with τ AND gates, a variable α, and τ variables $\mathbf{u} = (u_1, \ldots, u_\tau)$.

1. **Set a variable $\sigma_{\mathsf{out}} = \alpha$ on the output wire.**
2. **Let $\phi : [m] \to [\tau]$ be a function such that $\phi(i) = |\{j \mid j \le i \wedge G_1(j) = \mathrm{AND}\}|$, where $G_1(j)$ denotes the first element of $G(j)$. For each AND gate g with incoming wires a, b and an outgoing wire c where a polynomial σ_c is set on c, set new polynomials $\sigma_a = \sigma_c - u_{\phi(g)}$ and $\sigma_b = u_{\phi(g)}$ on a and b, respectively.**
3. **For each OR gate g with incoming wires a, b and an outgoing wire c where a vector σ_c is set on c, set new polynomials $\sigma_a = \sigma_c$, $\sigma_b = \sigma_c$ on a, b, respectively.**
4. **Output polynomials $\sigma_1, \ldots, \sigma_n$, which are set on the input wires $1, \ldots, n$.**

Fig. 4. Linear secret sharing scheme for Boolean formulae on polynomials.

- $\mathsf{Pair}'(x, y) \to (\mathbf{E}', \bar{\mathbf{E}}')$ and correctness:
  - Let polynomials $\sigma_1, \ldots, \sigma_n$ be an output of $\mathsf{Share_p}(f, \alpha_{\mathsf{new}}, \mathbf{u})$. It is not hard to see that, for all $b = (b_1, \ldots, b_n) \in \{0,1\}^n$ such that $f(b) = 1$, there exists a set $S \subseteq \{i \mid b_i = 1\}$ such that $\sum_{i \in S} \sigma_i = \alpha_{\mathsf{new}}$. Thus, if x and $y = ((y_1, \ldots, y_n), f)$ satisfy $\mathsf{KBF1}[\mathsf{P}_\kappa](x, y) = 1$, there exists $S \subseteq \{i \mid \mathsf{P}_\kappa(x, y_i) = 1\}$ such that $\sum_{i \in S} \sigma_i = \alpha_{\mathsf{new}}$.
  - For $i \in S$, run $\mathsf{Pair}(x, y_i) \to (\mathbf{E}^{(i)}, \bar{\mathbf{E}}^{(i)})$, satisfying $\mathbf{s}\mathbf{E}^{(i)}\mathbf{k}^{(i)\top} + \mathbf{c}\bar{\mathbf{E}}^{(i)}\mathbf{r}^{(i)\top} = \sigma_i s_0$. Then, we can obtain $\sum_{i \in S} \sigma_i s_0 = \alpha_{\mathsf{new}} s_0$ by the linear combination.

Theorem 7 ((ζ,ℓ)-KE-ind *of* KBF1-Trans(Γ)). *Let B be the maximum depth of f chosen by $\mathcal{A}$ in the (ζ,ℓ)-KE-ind game for* KBF1-Trans(Γ). *If Γ satisfies (ζ,ℓ)-KE-ind, then* KBF1-Trans(Γ) *satisfies (ζ,ℓ)-KE-ind as long as $B = O(\log \lambda)$. That is, for all PPT adversaries $\mathcal{A}$, there exists a PPT adversary $\mathcal{B}$ such that*

$$\mathsf{Adv}^{(\zeta,\ell)\text{-KE-ind}}_{\mathcal{A},\mathsf{KBF1\text{-}Trans}(\Gamma)}(\lambda) \le 2^{9B+1}\mathsf{Adv}^{(\zeta,\ell)\text{-KE-ind}}_{\mathcal{B},\Gamma}(\lambda).$$

We prove Lemma 7 by extending the techniques regarding pebbling arguments that Kowalczyk-Wee [26] have introduced in proving adaptive security of their ABE schemes for formulae with multi-use. We defer the proof to the full version.

Ciphertext-Policy Augmentation. Analogously to [9], for a predicate family P, we define its CP augmentation predicate—denoted as $\mathsf{CBF1}[\mathsf{P}]$—as the dual of $\mathsf{KBF1}[\mathsf{P}']$ where P' is the dual of P. Therefore, we can use the dual conversion—applying two times–sandwiching KBF1-Trans, to obtain a PES conversion for $\mathsf{CBF1}[\mathsf{P}]$. See the full version for more details.

4.4 Conforming PES for ABE

We can apply our transformations, namely, direct sum, dual, and key-policy augmentation, to a predicate family set $\mathcal{P}_\kappa$ multiple times to obtain a new predicate family P_κ. When we apply a PES to construct an ABE scheme, (ζ', ζ')-KE-ind for some constant ζ' implies the adaptive security of the resulting ABE scheme. The following theorem says that if we have predicate families $\mathcal{P}_\kappa = (\mathsf{P}^{(1)}_{\kappa_1}, \ldots, \mathsf{P}^{(d)}_{\kappa_d})$ that satisfy (ζ, ℓ)-KE-ind for all constants $\ell, \zeta \in \mathbb{N}$, we can construct an ABE scheme for a predicate family P_κ obtained by applying the above transformations to $\mathcal{P}_\kappa$ arbitrarily many times.

To state the theorem formally, we define a composed predicate set $f_c(\mathcal{P}_\kappa)$ for a predicate family set $\mathcal{P}_\kappa = (\mathsf{P}^{(1)}_{\kappa_1}, \ldots, \mathsf{P}^{(d)}_{\kappa_d})$. Let $\bar{\mathcal{P}}_\kappa$ be a predicate family set that consists of all predicate families obtained by applying one of transformations, $(\mathsf{DS}, \mathsf{Dual}, \mathsf{KBF1})$, to $\mathcal{P}_\kappa$. That is, $\bar{\mathcal{P}}_\kappa = (\mathsf{DS}[\mathcal{P}_\kappa], \{\mathsf{Dual}[\mathsf{P}^{(i)}_{\kappa_i}]\}_{i\in[d]}, \{\mathsf{KBF1}[\mathsf{P}^{(i)}_{\kappa_i}]\}_{i\in[d]})$ (we do not consider DS for a subset of $\mathcal{P}_\kappa$, because it can be embedded into $\mathsf{DS}[\mathcal{P}_\kappa]$). Let f be a deterministic procedure defined as $f(\mathcal{P}_\kappa) = \mathcal{P}_\kappa \cup \bar{\mathcal{P}}_\kappa$. Denote $f \circ \ldots \circ f(\mathcal{P}_\kappa)$ where f appears c times by $f_c(\mathcal{P}_\kappa)$. Then, we have the following theorem.

Theorem 8. *For all constant c and predicate family sets $\mathcal{P}_\kappa = (\mathsf{P}^{(1)}_{\kappa_1}, \ldots, \mathsf{P}^{(d)}_{\kappa_d})$, each of whose elements has a corresponding PES with (ζ, ℓ)-KE-ind for all constants $\zeta, \ell \in \mathbb{N}$, there exists a constant ζ' such that $\mathsf{P}_\kappa \in f_c(\mathcal{P}_\kappa)$ has a PES that satisfies (ζ', ζ')-KE-ind under the $\mathcal{D}_k$-MDDH assumption.*

Proof. Let $\mathbf{\Gamma} = (\Gamma_1, \ldots, \Gamma_d)$ be PESs for $(\mathsf{P}^{(1)}_{\kappa_1}, \ldots, \mathsf{P}^{(d)}_{\kappa_d})$, respectively. We can construct a PES Γ for P by applying PES transformations in Sects. 4.1, 4.2 and 4.3 to $\mathbf{\Gamma}$ multiple times. Let δ be the maximum number of Dual-Trans that is applied to each single PES Γ_i to obtain Γ. For instance, δ in the following PES is 2 because the first Γ_2 is transformed by Dual-Trans twice, and the others are transformed by Dual-Trans less that twice.

$$\mathsf{KBF1\text{-}Trans}\left(\mathsf{DS\text{-}Trans}\left(\mathsf{Dual\text{-}Trans}\left(\mathsf{DS\text{-}Trans}\left(\Gamma_1, \mathsf{Dual\text{-}Trans}\left(\Gamma_2\right)\right)\right), \Gamma_2, \Gamma_3\right)\right).$$

Then, it is not hard to see that we can construct Γ with (ζ', ζ')-KE-ind for $\zeta' = \delta + 1$. This directly follows from Theorems 5 to 7. □

Corollary 2. *Let $\mathcal{P}_\kappa = (\mathsf{P}^{(1)}_{\kappa_1}, \ldots, \mathsf{P}^{(d)}_{\kappa_d})$ be predicate families that have a PES with single-variable PMH. Then, we have a PES for $\mathsf{P}_\kappa \in f_c(\mathcal{P}_\kappa)$ with (ζ', ζ')-KE-ind for a constant ζ' under the $\mathcal{D}_k$-MDDH assumption, where $\zeta' - 1$ is the maximum number of Dual applied to each single predicate $\mathsf{P}^{(i)}_{\kappa_i}$ to obtain P_κ.*

This corollary directly follows from Theorems 4 and 8.

5 ABE from PES

In this section, we present our ABE scheme. We can construct an ABE scheme for any predicate family P_κ and a corresponding PES obtained in our framework if the PES satisfies (ζ, ζ)-KE-ind for some constant $\zeta \in \mathbb{N}$.

Construction. Let $\Gamma = (\mathsf{Param}, \mathsf{EncCt}, \mathsf{EncKey}, \mathsf{Pair})$ be a PES with (ζ, ζ)-KE-ind for a predicate family $\mathsf{P}_\kappa : \mathcal{X}_\kappa \times \mathcal{Y}_\kappa \to \{0, 1\}$. Then, we can construct an ABE scheme for predicate P_κ as follows.

$\mathsf{Setup}(1^\lambda, \kappa)$: Parse par from κ. It outputs pk and msk as follows.

$$\omega \leftarrow \mathsf{Param}(\mathsf{par}),\ \mathbb{G} \leftarrow \mathcal{G}_{\mathsf{BG}}(1^\lambda),\ \overline{\mathbf{A}}, \overline{\mathbf{B}} \leftarrow \mathbb{Z}_p^{(k+\zeta)\times(k+\zeta)},\ \mathbf{h} \leftarrow \mathbb{Z}_p^{k+\zeta},$$
$$\mathbb{W} = (\mathbf{W}_1, \ldots, \mathbf{W}_\omega) \leftarrow (\mathbb{Z}_p^{(k+\zeta)\times(k+\zeta)})^\omega,$$
$$\mathsf{pk}{=}(\mathbb{G}, [\mathbf{A}]_1, [\mathbf{W}_1^\top \mathbf{A}]_1, \ldots, [\mathbf{W}_\omega^\top \mathbf{A}]_1, [\mathbf{A}^\top \mathbf{h}]_\mathrm{T}),\ \mathsf{msk}{=}(\mathbf{B}, \mathbf{h}, \mathbf{W}_1, \ldots, \mathbf{W}_\omega).$$

$\mathsf{Enc}(\mathsf{pk}, x, M)$: It takes pk, $x \in \mathcal{X}_\kappa$, and $M \in G_\mathrm{T}$ as inputs, and outputs ct_x by computing as follows.

$$(n_1, n_2, \mathbf{c}(\mathbf{s}, \hat{\mathbf{s}}, \mathbf{w})) \leftarrow \mathsf{EncCt}(x),\ \mathbf{s}_0, \mathbf{s}_1, \ldots, \mathbf{s}_{n_1} \leftarrow \mathbb{Z}_p^k,\ \hat{\mathbf{s}}_1, \ldots, \hat{\mathbf{s}}_{n_2} \leftarrow \mathbb{Z}_p^{k+\zeta}$$
$$\mathbf{S} = (\mathbf{A}\mathbf{s}_0, \mathbf{A}\mathbf{s}_1, \ldots, \mathbf{A}\mathbf{s}_{n_1}),\ \widehat{\mathbf{S}} = (\hat{\mathbf{s}}_1, \ldots, \hat{\mathbf{s}}_{n_2})$$
$$\mathsf{ct}_x = (\mathsf{ct}_1, \mathsf{ct}_2, \mathsf{ct}_3) = ([\mathbf{S}]_1, [\mathbf{c}(\mathbf{S}, \widehat{\mathbf{S}}, \mathbb{W})]_1, [\mathbf{s}_0^\top \mathbf{A}^\top \mathbf{h}]_\mathrm{T} M).$$

$\mathsf{KeyGen}(\mathsf{pk}, \mathsf{msk}, y)$: It takes pk, msk, and $y \in \mathcal{Y}_\kappa$ as inputs, and outputs sk_y by computing as follows.

$$(m_1, m_2, \mathbf{k}(\mathbf{r}, \hat{\mathbf{r}}, \mathbf{w})) \leftarrow \mathsf{EncKey}(y),\ \mathbf{r}_1, \ldots, \mathbf{r}_{m_1} \leftarrow \mathbb{Z}_p^k,\ \hat{\mathbf{r}}_1, \ldots, \hat{\mathbf{r}}_{m_2} \leftarrow \mathbb{Z}_p^{k+\zeta}$$
$$\mathbf{R} = (\mathbf{B}\mathbf{r}_1, \ldots, \mathbf{B}\mathbf{r}_{m_1}),\ \widehat{\mathbf{R}} = (\mathbf{h}, \hat{\mathbf{r}}_1, \ldots, \hat{\mathbf{r}}_{m_2})$$
$$\mathsf{sk}_y = (\mathsf{sk}_1, \mathsf{sk}_2) = ([\mathbf{R}]_2, [\mathbf{k}(\mathbf{R}, \widehat{\mathbf{R}}, \mathbb{W})]_2).$$

$\mathsf{Dec}(\mathsf{pk}, \mathsf{ct}_x, \mathsf{sk}_y)$: It takes pk, $\mathsf{ct}_x = (\mathsf{ct}_1, \mathsf{ct}_2, \mathsf{ct}_3)$, and $\mathsf{sk}_y = (\mathsf{sk}_1, \mathsf{sk}_2)$ such that $\mathsf{P}_\kappa(x, y) = 1$. Let $(\mathbf{E}, \bar{\mathbf{E}}) \leftarrow \mathsf{Pair}(x, y)$. It outputs $M' = \mathsf{ct}_3/\Omega$ where

$$\Omega = \prod_{\substack{i\in[n_1+1]\\ j\in[m_3]}} e(\mathsf{ct}_{1,i}, \mathsf{sk}_{2,j})^{e_{i,j}} \cdot \prod_{\substack{i\in[n_3]\\ j\in[m_1]}} e(\mathsf{ct}_{2,i}, \mathsf{sk}_{1,j})^{\bar{e}_{i,j}}, \qquad (3)$$

and where $\mathsf{ct}_{i,j}$ and $\mathsf{sk}_{i,j}$ refer to the j-th element of ct_i and sk_i, respectively, and $e_{i,j}$ and $\bar{e}_{i,j}$ refer to the (i,j)-th element of $\mathbf{E}$ and $\bar{\mathbf{E}}$, respectively.

Correctness. In defining $\mathsf{ct}_x, \mathsf{sk}_y$, we effectively map variables of PES to vectors/matrice as $s_i \mapsto \mathbf{s}_i^\top \mathbf{A}^\top$, $\hat{s}_j \mapsto \hat{\mathbf{s}}_j^\top$, $r_v \mapsto \mathbf{B}\mathbf{r}_v$, $\hat{r}_u \mapsto \hat{\mathbf{r}}_u$, $\alpha \mapsto \mathbf{h}$, and $w_n \mapsto \mathbf{W}_n$. Therefore, intuitively, the correctness of PES, which we recall that it is the relation: $\sum_{i\in[n_1+1], j\in[m_3]} e_{i,j} s_{i-1} k_j + \sum_{i\in[n_3], j\in[m_1]} \bar{e}_{i,j} c_i r_j = \alpha s_0$, will preserve to exactly the relation $\Omega = [\mathbf{s}_0^\top \mathbf{A}^\top \mathbf{h}]_\mathrm{T}$, where Ω is defined in Eq. (3).

Theorem 9. *Suppose Γ satisfies (ζ,ζ)-*KE-ind. *Then, our ABE scheme is adaptively secure under the $\mathcal{D}_k$-MDDH assumption. Let q_{sk} be the maximum number of $\mathcal{A}$'s queries to* KeyGen. *For any PPT adversary $\mathcal{A}$, there exist PPT adversaries $\mathcal{B}_1$ and $\mathcal{B}_2$ such that*

$$\mathsf{Adv}_{\mathcal{A}}^{\mathsf{ABE}}(\lambda) \leq \mathsf{Adv}_{\mathcal{B}_1}^{\mathcal{D}_k\text{-}\mathsf{MDDH}}(\lambda) + q_{\mathsf{sk}} \mathsf{Adv}_{\mathcal{B}_2, \Gamma}^{(\zeta,\zeta)\text{-}\mathsf{KE}\text{-}\mathsf{ind}}(\lambda).$$

Proof. The proof follows the dual system methodology [36]. We consider a series of hybrids H_1 and $\mathsf{H}_{2,j}$ for $j \in [q_{\mathsf{sk}}]$. To define each hybrid, we introduce a so-called semi-functional (SF) ciphertext and secret key, which are generated differently from normal ones. Specifically, an SF-ciphertext is generated as

$$(n_1, n_2, \mathbf{c}(\mathbf{s}, \hat{\mathbf{s}}, \mathbf{w})) \leftarrow \mathsf{EncCt}(x),\ \mathbf{s}_1, \ldots, \mathbf{s}_{n_1} \leftarrow \mathbb{Z}_p^k,\ \boxed{\mathbf{c}_0}, \hat{\mathbf{s}}_1, \ldots, \hat{\mathbf{s}}_{n_2} \leftarrow \mathbb{Z}_p^{k+\zeta},$$
$$\mathbf{S} = (\boxed{\mathbf{c}_0}, \mathbf{A}\mathbf{s}_1, \ldots, \mathbf{A}\mathbf{s}_{n_1}),\ \widehat{\mathbf{S}} = (\hat{\mathbf{s}}_1, \ldots, \hat{\mathbf{s}}_{n_2}),$$
$$\mathsf{ct}_x = (\mathsf{ct}_1, \mathsf{ct}_2, \mathsf{ct}_3) = ([\mathbf{S}]_1, [\mathbf{c}(\mathbf{S}, \widehat{\mathbf{S}}, \mathbb{W})]_1, [\boxed{\mathbf{c}_0^\top}\mathbf{h}]_\mathsf{T} M).$$

An SF-secret key is generated as

$$(m_1, m_2, \mathbf{k}(\mathbf{r}, \hat{\mathbf{r}}, \mathbf{w})) \leftarrow \mathsf{EncKey}(y),\ \mathbf{r}_1, \ldots, \mathbf{r}_{m_1} \leftarrow \mathbb{Z}_p^k,\ \hat{\mathbf{r}}_1, \ldots, \hat{\mathbf{r}}_{m_2} \leftarrow \mathbb{Z}_p^{k+\zeta},$$
$$\boxed{\mu \leftarrow \mathbb{Z}_p},\ \mathbf{R} = (\mathbf{B}\mathbf{r}_1, \ldots, \mathbf{B}\mathbf{r}_{m_1}),\ \widehat{\mathbf{R}} = (\mathbf{h} + \boxed{\mu \mathbf{a}_\zeta^*}, \hat{\mathbf{r}}_1, \ldots, \hat{\mathbf{r}}_{m_2}),$$
$$\mathsf{sk}_y = (\mathsf{sk}_1, \mathsf{sk}_2) = ([\mathbf{R}]_2, [\mathbf{k}(\mathbf{R}, \widehat{\mathbf{R}}, \mathbb{W})]_2). \tag{4}$$

In the hybrids, the distribution of secret keys and the challenge ciphertext are modified as follows:

H_1: Same as the original game G except that the challenge ciphertext is SF.
$\mathsf{H}_{2,j}(j \in [q_{\mathsf{sk}}])$: Same as H_1 except that the first j secret keys given to $\mathcal{A}$ are SF.

We prove (in the full version) that $\mathsf{G} \approx_c \mathsf{H}_1 \approx_c \mathsf{H}_{2,1} \approx_c, \ldots, \approx_c \mathsf{H}_{2,q_{\mathsf{sk}}}$ and $\mathcal{A}$'s advantage in $\mathsf{H}_{2,q_{\mathsf{sk}}}$ is statistically close to 0. From these and the fact $\mathsf{Adv}_{\mathcal{A}}^{\mathsf{ABE}}(\lambda) = |\Pr[\langle \mathcal{A}, \mathsf{G}\rangle = \beta] - 1/2|$, we have that Theorem 9 holds. □

6 Extensions, Instantiations, and Applications

We obtain many applications in an analogous manner to the applications in [9].

Extended Framework. On the framework level, we obtain key-policy augmentation over *a set of predicate families*, denoted KBF, which is more powerful than the augmentation over a *single* predicate family (KBF1), as done in Sect. 4.3. This follows exactly the same modular approach as in [9]. That is, in our context, we can show that KBF is implied by KBF1 together with the direct sum and $\mathsf{CBF1}_{\mathsf{OR}}$. We defer the details to the full version. Moreover, more applications such as nested-policy ABE can also be obtained analogously to [9].

New Instantiations. On the instantiation level, we have showed the result overview in the introduction. Here, we briefly describe how to obtain such instantiations. The full details are deferred to the full version.

- Completely unbounded ABE for monotone Boolean formulae. Analogously to [9], we have that this predicate (in the key-policy flavor) is exactly $\mathsf{KBF1}[\mathsf{P}^{\mathsf{IBBE}}]$, where $\mathsf{P}^{\mathsf{IBBE}}$ is the predicate for ID-based broadcast encryption. IBBE can then be augmented from IBE, of which we know a PMH-secure PES from *e.g.*, [7]. The CP flavor is obtained by the dual conversion.

– Completely unbounded ABE for non-monotone Boolean formulae (the OSW type). This is also analogous to [9], where we consider two-mode IBBE (TIBBE), which can be then obtained by IBE and its negated predicate.
– Non-monotone KP-ABE with constant-size ciphertexts. A monotone variant is obtained by simply using the PMH-secure PES for IBBE with constant-size ciphertext encodings. Such a PES can be extracted from the PES for doubly spatial predicate in [7]. Since our KBF1-Trans preserves ciphertext encoding sizes, the converted scheme also obtains constant-size ciphertext encodings. For the non-monotone case, such a PES for TIBBE can be obtained by the disjunction of IBBE and negated IBBE (NIBBE). The latter can be viewed as a special case of negated doubly spatial predicate in [7], of which PES with constant-size encodings was reported. We directly construct a new TIBBE, which is two times efficient than the generic one from the disjunction (see the full version).
– CP-ABE with constant-size ciphertexts. First note that we consider schemes with some bound on the size of policies (Boolean formulae), which the same requirement as CP-ABE with constant-size ciphertexts of [1,9,10]. We obtain this by two steps. First we show that, when considering small-universe, KP-ABE implies CP-ABE (for Boolean formulae, with the bounded condition). We use the depth-universal circuit [18] in this conversion. Second we show that CP-ABE with small universe implies CP-ABE with large universe (again for Boolean formulae, with the bounded condition). To the best of our knowledge, these conversions were not known and can be of an independent interest, as they are applied to ABE in general (not necessarily to PES). Note that we cannot do that as Attrapadung *et al.* [10] did, who considered similar implications in the case of more powerful *span programs*.
– ABE with constant-size keys. CP/KP-ABE with constant-size keys is obtained by the dual of KP/CP-ABE with constant-size ciphertexts, respectively.

New Applications. As a new application, we provide a new unified predicate related to *non-monotone* ABE. Previously, there are two types of non-monotone ABE: the OSW type (Ostrovsky, Sahai, and Waters [31]) and the OT type (Okamoto and Takashima [30]). In the OSW type, a sub-predicate $P(y, X)$ amounts to check if an attribute is not in a set, *e.g.*, if $y \notin X$, while the OT type, a label tag is also attached, but a sub-predicate $P'((\text{tag}, y), (\overline{\text{tag}}, x))$ only checks the inequality on the same tag, *e.g.*, if $\text{tag} = \overline{\text{tag}} \wedge y \neq x$. Intuitively, the OSW type has a disadvantage in that the non-membership test takes the complement over the *whole universe* and this may be too much for some applications, where we would like to consider multiple sub-universe and confine the complement to only in the related sub-universe. On the other hand, the OT type confines the non-membership to those with the same tag, but the non-membership test is enabled only with the set of single element, *e.g.*, $\{x\}$. We unify both types to overcome both disadvantages; that is, a sub-predicate $P'((\text{tag}, y), (\overline{\text{tag}}, X))$ would check if $\text{tag} = \overline{\text{tag}} \wedge y \notin X$. We remark that when considering large-universe *monotone* ABE, there is no benefit to consider multiple spaces, since

$\mathbb{Z}_p$ is already exponentially large, and we can just treat a hashed value $H(\text{tag}, y)$ as an attribute in $\mathbb{Z}_p$. In non-monotone ABE, we have to check the equality (of tags) and the non-membership at once, and the approach by hashing does not work. We motivate more on the unified non-monotone ABE, and provide definitions and constructions in the full version.

Acknowledgement. Nuttapong Attrapadung was partly supported by JST CREST Grant Number JPMJCR19F6, and by JSPS KAKENHI Kiban-A Grant Number 19H01109.

References

1. Agrawal, S., Chase, M.: A study of pair encodings: predicate encryption in prime order groups. In: Kushilevitz, E., Malkin, T. (eds.) TCC 2016. LNCS, vol. 9563, pp. 259–288. Springer, Heidelberg (2016). https://doi.org/10.1007/978-3-662-49099-0_10
2. Agrawal, S., Chase, M.: FAME: fast attribute-based message encryption. In: ACM CCS 2017, pp. 665–682 (2017)
3. Agrawal, S., Chase, M.: Simplifying design and analysis of complex predicate encryption schemes. In: Coron, J.-S., Nielsen, J.B. (eds.) EUROCRYPT 2017. LNCS, vol. 10210, pp. 627–656. Springer, Cham (2017). https://doi.org/10.1007/978-3-319-56620-7_22
4. Agrawal, S., Maitra, M., Yamada, S.: Attribute based encryption (and more) for nondeterministic finite automata from LWE. In: Boldyreva, A., Micciancio, D. (eds.) CRYPTO 2019. LNCS, vol. 11693, pp. 765–797. Springer, Cham (2019). https://doi.org/10.1007/978-3-030-26951-7_26
5. Agrawal, S., Maitra, M., Yamada, S.: Attribute based encryption for deterministic finite automata from DLIN. In: Hofheinz, D., Rosen, A. (eds.) TCC 2019. LNCS, vol. 11892, pp. 91–117. Springer, Cham (2019). https://doi.org/10.1007/978-3-030-36033-7_4
6. Ambrona, M., Barthe, G., Schmidt, B.: Generic transformations of predicate encodings: constructions and applications. In: Katz, J., Shacham, H. (eds.) CRYPTO 2017. LNCS, vol. 10401, pp. 36–66. Springer, Cham (2017). https://doi.org/10.1007/978-3-319-63688-7_2
7. Attrapadung, N.: Dual system encryption via doubly selective security: framework, fully secure functional encryption for regular languages, and more. In: Nguyen, P.Q., Oswald, E. (eds.) EUROCRYPT 2014. LNCS, vol. 8441, pp. 557–577. Springer, Heidelberg (2014). https://doi.org/10.1007/978-3-642-55220-5_31
8. Attrapadung, N.: Dual system encryption framework in prime-order groups via computational pair encodings. In: Cheon, J.H., Takagi, T. (eds.) ASIACRYPT 2016. LNCS, vol. 10032, pp. 591–623. Springer, Heidelberg (2016). https://doi.org/10.1007/978-3-662-53890-6_20
9. Attrapadung, N.: Unbounded dynamic predicate compositions in attribute-based encryption. In: Ishai, Y., Rijmen, V. (eds.) EUROCRYPT 2019. LNCS, vol. 11476, pp. 34–67. Springer, Cham (2019). https://doi.org/10.1007/978-3-030-17653-2_2
10. Attrapadung, N., Hanaoka, G., Yamada, S.: Conversions among several classes of predicate encryption and applications to ABE with various compactness tradeoffs. In: Iwata, T., Cheon, J.H. (eds.) ASIACRYPT 2015. LNCS, vol. 9452, pp. 575–601. Springer, Heidelberg (2015). https://doi.org/10.1007/978-3-662-48797-6_24

11. Attrapadung, N., Libert, B., de Panafieu, E.: Expressive key-policy attribute-based encryption with constant-size ciphertexts. In: Catalano, D., Fazio, N., Gennaro, R., Nicolosi, A. (eds.) PKC 2011. LNCS, vol. 6571, pp. 90–108. Springer, Heidelberg (2011). https://doi.org/10.1007/978-3-642-19379-8_6
12. Attrapadung, N., Tomida, J.: Unbounded Dynamic Predicate Compositions in ABE from Standard Assumptions. Cryptology ePrint Archive, Report 2020/231 (2020). https://eprint.iacr.org/2020/231. (The full version of this paper)
13. Attrapadung, N., Yamada, S.: Duality in ABE: converting attribute based encryption for dual predicate and dual policy via computational encodings. In: Nyberg, K. (ed.) CT-RSA 2015. LNCS, vol. 9048, pp. 87–105. Springer, Cham (2015). https://doi.org/10.1007/978-3-319-16715-2_5
14. Boneh, D., Franklin, M.: Identity-based encryption from the weil pairing. In: Kilian, J. (ed.) CRYPTO 2001. LNCS, vol. 2139, pp. 213–229. Springer, Heidelberg (2001). https://doi.org/10.1007/3-540-44647-8_13
15. Chen, J., Gay, R., Wee, H.: Improved dual system ABE in prime-order groups via predicate encodings. In: Oswald, E., Fischlin, M. (eds.) EUROCRYPT 2015. LNCS, vol. 9057, pp. 595–624. Springer, Heidelberg (2015). https://doi.org/10.1007/978-3-662-46803-6_20
16. Chen, J., Gong, J., Kowalczyk, L., Wee, H.: Unbounded ABE via bilinear entropy expansion, revisited. In: Nielsen, J.B., Rijmen, V. (eds.) EUROCRYPT 2018. LNCS, vol. 10820, pp. 503–534. Springer, Cham (2018). https://doi.org/10.1007/978-3-319-78381-9_19
17. Chen, J., Wee, H.: Semi-adaptive attribute-based encryption and improved delegation for boolean formula. In: Abdalla, M., De Prisco, R. (eds.) SCN 2014. LNCS, vol. 8642, pp. 277–297. Springer, Cham (2014). https://doi.org/10.1007/978-3-319-10879-7_16
18. Cook, S., Hoover, H.: A depth-universal circuit. SIAM J. Comp. **14**, 4 (1985)
19. Escala, A., Herold, G., Kiltz, E., Ràfols, C., Villar, J.L.: An algebraic framework for Diffie-Hellman assumptions. J. Cryptol. **30**(1), 242–288 (2017)
20. Gong, J., Dong, X., Chen, J., Cao, Z.: Efficient IBE with tight reduction to standard assumption in the multi-challenge setting. In: Cheon, J.H., Takagi, T. (eds.) ASIACRYPT 2016. LNCS, vol. 10032, pp. 624–654. Springer, Heidelberg (2016). https://doi.org/10.1007/978-3-662-53890-6_21
21. Gong, J., Waters, B., Wee, H.: ABE for DFA from k-Lin. In: Boldyreva, A., Micciancio, D. (eds.) CRYPTO 2019. LNCS, vol. 11693, pp. 732–764. Springer, Cham (2019). https://doi.org/10.1007/978-3-030-26951-7_25
22. Gong, J., Wee, H.: Adaptively secure ABE for DFA from k-Lin and more. In: Canteaut, A., Ishai, Y. (eds.) EUROCRYPT 2020. LNCS, vol. 12107, pp. 278–308. Springer, Cham (2020). https://doi.org/10.1007/978-3-030-45727-3_10
23. Gorbunov, S., Vaikuntanathan, V., Wee, H.: Attribute-based encryption for circuits. In: ACM STOC 2013, pp. 545–554 (2013)
24. Goyal, V., Pandey, O., Sahai, A., Waters, B.: Attribute-based encryption for fine-grained access control of encrypted data. In: ACM CCS 2006, pp. 89–98 (2006)
25. Katz, J., Sahai, A., Waters, B.: Predicate encryption supporting disjunctions, polynomial equations, and inner products. In: Smart, N. (ed.) EUROCRYPT 2008. LNCS, vol. 4965, pp. 146–162. Springer, Heidelberg (2008). https://doi.org/10.1007/978-3-540-78967-3_9
26. Kowalczyk, L., Wee, H.: Compact adaptively secure ABE for NCs^1 from k-lin. J. Cryptol. **33**(3), 954–1002 (2019). https://doi.org/10.1007/s00145-019-09335-x

27. Lewko, A., Waters, B.: Unbounded HIBE and attribute-based encryption. In: Paterson, K.G. (ed.) EUROCRYPT 2011. LNCS, vol. 6632, pp. 547–567. Springer, Heidelberg (2011). https://doi.org/10.1007/978-3-642-20465-4_30
28. Lin, H., Luo, J.: Compact adaptively secure ABE from k-lin: Beyond NC^1 and towards NL. In: Canteaut, A., Ishai, Y. (eds.) EUROCRYPT 2020. LNCS, vol. 12107, pp. 247–277. Springer, Cham (2020). https://doi.org/10.1007/978-3-030-45727-3_9
29. Okamoto, T., Takashima, K.: Fully secure functional encryption with general relations from the decisional linear assumption. In: Rabin, T. (ed.) CRYPTO 2010. LNCS, vol. 6223, pp. 191–208. Springer, Heidelberg (2010). https://doi.org/10.1007/978-3-642-14623-7_11
30. Okamoto, T., Takashima, K.: Fully secure unbounded inner-product and attribute-based encryption. In: Wang, X., Sako, K. (eds.) ASIACRYPT 2012. LNCS, vol. 7658, pp. 349–366. Springer, Heidelberg (2012). https://doi.org/10.1007/978-3-642-34961-4_22
31. Ostrovsky, R., Sahai, A., Water, B.: Attribute-based encryption with non-monotonic access structures. In: ACM CCS 2007, pp. 195–203 (2007)
32. Rouselakis, Y., Waters, B.: Practical constructions and new proof methods for large universe attribute-based encryption. In: ACM CCS 2013, pp. 463–474 (2013)
33. Wang, X., Yu, H.: How to break MD5 and other hash functions. In: Cramer, R. (ed.) EUROCRYPT 2005. LNCS, vol. 3494, pp. 19–35. Springer, Heidelberg (2005). https://doi.org/10.1007/11426639_2
34. Takashima, K.: Expressive attribute-based encryption with constant-size ciphertexts from the decisional linear assumption. In: Abdalla, M., De Prisco, R. (eds.) SCN 2014. LNCS, vol. 8642, pp. 298–317. Springer, Cham (2014). https://doi.org/10.1007/978-3-319-10879-7_17
35. Tomida, J., Kawahara, Y., Nishimaki, R.: Fast, compact, and expressive attribute-based encryption. In: Kiayias, A., Kohlweiss, M., Wallden, P., Zikas, V. (eds.) PKC 2020. LNCS, vol. 12110, pp. 3–33. Springer, Cham (2020). https://doi.org/10.1007/978-3-030-45374-9_1
36. Waters, B.: Dual system encryption: realizing fully secure IBE and HIBE under simple assumptions. In: Halevi, S. (ed.) CRYPTO 2009. LNCS, vol. 5677, pp. 619–636. Springer, Heidelberg (2009). https://doi.org/10.1007/978-3-642-03356-8_36
37. Waters, B.: Functional encryption for regular languages. In: Safavi-Naini, R., Canetti, R. (eds.) CRYPTO 2012. LNCS, vol. 7417, pp. 218–235. Springer, Heidelberg (2012). https://doi.org/10.1007/978-3-642-32009-5_14
38. Wee, H.: Dual system encryption via predicate encodings. In: Lindell, Y. (ed.) TCC 2014. LNCS, vol. 8349, pp. 616–637. Springer, Heidelberg (2014). https://doi.org/10.1007/978-3-642-54242-8_26
39. Yamada, S., Attrapadung, N., Hanaoka, G., Kunihiro, N.: A framework and compact constructions for non-monotonic attribute-based encryption. In: Krawczyk, H. (ed.) PKC 2014. LNCS, vol. 8383, pp. 275–292. Springer, Heidelberg (2014). https://doi.org/10.1007/978-3-642-54631-0_16

Succinct and Adaptively Secure ABE for ABP from k-Lin

Huijia Lin(✉) and Ji Luo(✉)

University of Washington, Seattle, USA
{rachel,luoji}@cs.washington.edu

Abstract. We present *succinct* and *adaptively secure* attribute-based encryption (ABE) schemes for *arithmetic branching programs*, based on k-Lin in pairing groups. Our key-policy ABE scheme has ciphertexts of *constant size*, independent of the length of the attributes, and our ciphertext-policy ABE scheme has secret keys of *constant size*. Our schemes improve upon the recent succinct ABE schemes in [Tomida and Attrapadung, ePrint '20], which only handles Boolean formulae. All other prior succinct ABE schemes either achieve only selective security or rely on q-type assumptions.

Our schemes are obtained through a general and modular approach that combines a public-key inner product functional encryption satisfying a new security notion called gradual simulation security and an information-theoretic randomized encoding scheme called arithmetic key garbling scheme.

1 Introduction

Attribute-based encryption (ABE) [21] is an advanced form of public-key encryption for enforcing fine-grained access control. In the key-policy version, an authority generates a pair of master public and secret keys $\mathsf{mpk}, \mathsf{msk}$. Given mpk, everyone can encrypt a message m with an attribute x to get a ciphertext $\mathsf{ct}_x(m)$. Using the master secret key msk, the authority can issue a secret key sk_y tied to a policy y. Decrypting a ciphertext $\mathsf{ct}_x(m)$ using sk_y recovers the encrypted message m if the attribute x satisfies the policy y. Otherwise, no information about m is revealed. The security requirement of ABE mandates collusion resistance—no information of m should be revealed, even when multiple secret keys are issued, as long as none of them individually decrypts the ciphertext (i.e., the attribute satisfies none of the associated policies).

Over the past decade, a plethora of ABE schemes have been proposed for different expressive classes of policies, achieving different trade-offs between efficiency, security, and assumptions. Meanwhile, ABE has found numerous cryptographic and security applications. A primary desirata of ABE schemes is efficiency, in particular, having fast encryption algorithms and small ciphertexts. It turns out that the size of ABE ciphertexts can be *independent* of the length of the attribute x, and dependent only on the length of the message m and security parameter—we say such ciphertexts are *succinct* or have *constant size* (in

S. Moriai and H. Wang (Eds.): ASIACRYPT 2020, LNCS 12493, pp. 437–466, 2020.
https://doi.org/10.1007/978-3-030-64840-4_15

attribute length). Proposed first in [11] as a goal, succinct ciphertexts are possible because ABE does not require hiding the attribute x, and the decryption algorithm can take x as input in the clear. Consequently, ciphertexts only need to contain enough information of x to enforce the *integrity* of computation on x, which does not necessitate encoding the entire x.

Succinct ABE are highly desirable. For practical applications of ABE where long attributes are involved for sophisticated access control, succinct ciphertexts are much more preferable. From a theoretical point of view, succinct ciphertexts have (asymptotically) *optimal* size, as dependency on the message length and security parameter is inevitable. From a technical point of view, succinct ABE provides interesting mechanism for enforcing the integrity of computation without encoding the input. So far, several succinct ABE schemes have been proposed [5–7,22,23,27,28], but almost all schemes either rely on non-standard assumption or provide only weak security, as summarized in Tables 1 and 2.

Our Results. In this work, we first construct a *succinct* key-policy ABE (KP-ABE) simultaneously satisfying the following properties.

(1) *Expressiveness.* Support policies expressed as arithmetic branching programs (ABPs).
(2) *Security.* Satisfy adaptive security, as opposed to selective or semi-adaptive security.
(3) *Assumption.* Based on the standard assumptions as opposed to, e.g., q-type assumptions. Specifically, our scheme relies on the matrix decisional Diffie–Hellman (MDDH) assumption over pairing groups.
(4) *Efficiency.* Has succinct ciphertext.
    Concretely, each ciphertext consists of 5 group elements when assuming SXDH, and $2k + 3$ elements for MDDH_k (implied by k-Lin). Decryption involves the same number of pairing operations. Additionally, our scheme can work with the more efficient asymmetric prime-order pairing groups.

Next, we construct ciphertext-policy ABE (CP-ABE) with the same properties. Here, the secret keys are tied to attributes and ciphertexts to policies, and succinctness refers to having constant-size secret keys. Our scheme has keys consisting of 7 group elements based on SXDH and $3k + 4$ based on MDDH_k.

Besides succinctness (4), achieving the strong notion of adaptive security (2) based on standard assumptions (3) is also highly desirable from both a practical and a theoretical point of view. Prior to this work, only the recent construction of (KP and CP) ABE schemes by Tomida and Attrapadung [23] simultaneously achieves (2)–(4), and their scheme handles policies expressed as Boolean formulae. Our construction expands the class of policies to *arithmetic* branching programs, which is a more expressive model of computation. Our succinct ABE is also the first scheme natively supporting *arithmetic* computation over large fields,[1] whereas all prior succinct ABE schemes (even ones relying on q-type

[1] One can always convert an arithmetic computation into a Boolean one, which we consider non-native.

Table 1. KP-ABE schemes with succinct ciphertext.

Reference	Policy	Assumption	Adaptive	|mpk|	|sk|	|ct|	Dec
ALP [7]	MSP	q-type		$2n+1$	$m(n+1)$	3	3
YAHK [27]	MSP	q-type		$n+2$	$m(n+1)$	2	2
Tak [22]	MSP	2-Lin ✓		$18(2n+1)$	$6m(n+1)$	17	17
Att [5]	MSP	q-type	✓	$6n+42$	$3m(n+3)+9$	18	18
ZGT$^+$ [28]	MSP	k-Lin ✓		$2k^2(n+1)$	$2km(n+1)$	$4k$	$4k$
TA [23]	NC^1	$MDDH_k$ ✓	✓	$k(k+1)(n+3)$	$(k+1)m(n+2)$	$2k+2$	$2k+2$
Sect. 5	ABP	$MDDH_k$ ✓	✓	$k(k+2)(n+2)$	$(k+1)m(n+2)$ $+m$	$2k+3$	$2k+3$

MSP: monotone span programs. NC^1: Boolean formulae. ABP: arithmetic branching programs.
n = attribute length, m = policy size, p = group order.
\|mpk\|, \|sk\|, \|ct\| counts non-generator elements in source groups.
Dec counts the number of pairing operations in decryption.
Schemes based on k-Lin can be based on $MDDH_k$ at the cost of a few more elements in mpk.
ABE for arithmetic span programs can be obtained by reduction to MSP [6].

Table 2. CP-ABE schemes with succinct secret key.

Reference	Policy	Assumption	Adaptive	|mpk|	|sk|	|ct|	Dec
Att [5]	MSP	q-type	✓	$6n+54$	24	$3m(n+3)+15$	24
AHY [6]	ASP	q-type	✓	$O(n \log p)$	$O(1)$	$O(mn \log p)$	$O(1)$
TA [23]	NC^1	$MDDH_k$ ✓	✓	$O(k^2 n)$	$O(k)$	$O(kmn)$	$O(k)$
Ours [18]	ABP	$MDDH_k$ ✓	✓	$k(k+1)(n+4)$ $+k$	$3k+4$	$(k+1)m(n+2)$ $+m+k+1$	$3k+4$

assumptions and/or achieving only selective security) only work natively with Boolean computation. Lastly, we note that even when relaxing the efficiency requirement from having succinct ciphertext to *compact* ciphertext, whose size grows linearly with the length of the attribute, only a few schemes [13,15,17] simultaneously achieve (2)–(4), and the most expressive class of policies supported is also ABP, due to [17].

Our Techniques. The recent work of [17] presented a general framework for constructing *compact* adaptively secure ABE from MDDH. In this work, we improve their general framework to achieve *succinctness.* The framework of [17] yields linear-size ciphertexts because it crucially relies on *function-hiding* inner-product functional encryption (IPFE) [10,19]. IPFE allows issuing secret keys and ciphertexts tied to vectors $\mathbf{v}, \mathbf{u}$ respectively, and decryption reveals their inner product $\langle \mathbf{u}, \mathbf{v} \rangle$. The function-hiding property guarantees that nothing about $\mathbf{u}, \mathbf{v}$ beyond the inner product is revealed, which entails that ciphertexts and secret keys must have size linear in the length of the vectors.

Towards succinctness, our key idea is relaxing function-hiding to a *new and weaker* guarantee, called *gradual simulation security,* where only the vectors encrypted in the ciphertexts are hidden. Such IPFE can have succinct (constant-size) secret keys and can be public-key. We use new ideas to modify the framework of [17] to work with the weaker gradual simulation security and obtain succinct ciphertexts. Furthermore, we extend the framework to construct ciphertext-policy ABE, which is not handled in [17]. In summary, our techniques give a general and modular approach for constructing succinct and adaptively secure (KP and CP) ABE from MDDH.

Organization. In Sect. 1.1, we give an overview of how we construct our ABE schemes using inner-product functional encryption (IPFE) schemes with gradual simulation security and dual system encryption. We discuss related works in Sect. 1.2. After introducing the preliminaries in Sect. 2, we define gradual simulation security of IPFE and construct such an IPFE scheme in Sect. 3. In Sect. 4, we define 1-ABE and construct CP-1-ABE for ABP with succinct keys from gradually simulation-secure IPFE with succinct keys. In Sect. 5, we show how to construct KP-ABE with succinct ciphertexts using our CP-1-ABE and dual system encryption. Due to the lack of space, we refer the reader to the full version [18] for our construction of CP-ABE with succinct keys similarly to our KP-ABE construction.

1.1 Technical Overview

In this section, we give an overview of our construction of succinct ABE schemes, following the roadmap shown in Fig. 1.

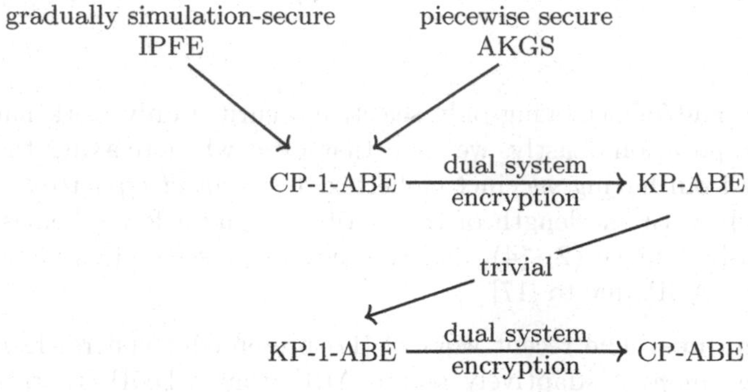

Fig. 1. The roadmap of our constructions.

1-ABE. The core of many ABE schemes is a 1-key 1-ciphertext secure secret-key ABE, or 1-ABE for short. Our construction improves the recent 1-ABE scheme for ABP by Lin and Luo (LL) [17], which achieves adaptive security but not succinctness.

Suppose we want decryption to recover the message $\mu \in \mathbb{Z}_p$ if (and only if) $f(\mathbf{x}) \neq 0$ for policy function $f : \mathbb{Z}_p^n \to \mathbb{Z}_p$ and attribute $\mathbf{x} \in \mathbb{Z}_p^n$. This is equivalent to computing $\mu f(\mathbf{x})$ upon decryption. The basic idea of the LL 1-ABE is that when a key (tied to f, μ)[2] and a ciphertext (tied to $\mathbf{x}$) are put together, one can compute a randomized encoding of $\mu f(\mathbf{x})$, denoted by $\widehat{\mu f(\mathbf{x})}$, which reveals $\mu f(\mathbf{x})$ and hence μ if $f(\mathbf{x}) \neq 0$. Since in ABE, we do not try to hide f or $\mathbf{x}$, the randomized encoding only needs to hide μ beyond the output $\mu f(\mathbf{x})$, referred to as the partially hiding property, first introduced by [14]. Due to the weak security guarantee, partially hiding randomized encoding can have extremely simple structure. In particular, LL defined a refined version of such randomized encoding, called arithmetic key garbling scheme (AKGS), with the following properties:

Linear Encoding. The encoding is in the form of

$$\widehat{\mu f(\mathbf{x})} = (L_1(\mathbf{x}), \ldots, L_m(\mathbf{x})),$$

where L_j's are *affine* functions of $\mathbf{x}$ and the coefficients of L_j's are *linear* in the message μ and the garbling randomness. L_j's are called *label functions* and $\ell_j = L_j(\mathbf{x})$ are called *labels*.

Linear Evaluation. There is a procedure Eval that can compute $\mu f(\mathbf{x})$ from $f, \mathbf{x}$ and the labels:

$$\mathsf{Eval}(f, \mathbf{x}, \ell_1, \ldots, \ell_m) = \mu f(\mathbf{x}).$$

Importantly, Eval is linear in the labels.[3]

The basic security of AKGS is simulation security. There needs to be an efficient simulator Sim that can perfectly simulate the labels given $f, \mathbf{x}, \mu f(\mathbf{x})$:

$$\mathsf{Sim}(f, \mathbf{x}, \mu f(\mathbf{x})) \to (\ell_1, \ldots, \ell_m) \equiv (L_1(\mathbf{x}), \ldots, L_m(\mathbf{x})).$$

Since the label functions are affine in $\mathbf{x}$ thus linear in $(1, \mathbf{x})$, the labels $\ell_j = L_j(\mathbf{x})$ can be securely computed using a *function-hiding* IPFE. In IPFE, keys $\mathsf{isk}(\mathbf{v})$ and ciphertexts $\mathsf{ict}(\mathbf{u})$ are generated for vectors $\mathbf{v}, \mathbf{u}$, and decryption yields their inner product $\langle \mathbf{u}, \mathbf{v} \rangle$ but nothing else. More precisely, function-hiding says two sets of keys and ciphertexts encoding different vectors are indistinguishable as long as they yield identical inner products:

$$(\{\mathsf{isk}_j(\mathbf{v}_j)\}, \{\mathsf{ict}_i(\mathbf{u}_i)\}) \approx (\{\mathsf{isk}_j(\mathbf{v}'_j)\}, \{\mathsf{ict}_i(\mathbf{u}'_i)\}) \text{ if } \langle \mathbf{u}_i, \mathbf{v}_j \rangle = \langle \mathbf{u}'_i, \mathbf{v}'_j \rangle \text{ for all } i, j.$$

That is, all vectors no matter encoded in keys or ciphertexts are protected. Moreover, function-hiding should hold even when these vectors are chosen adaptively by the adversary, depending on previously observed keys and ciphertexts.

In the LL 1-ABE scheme, an ABE key consists of many IPFE keys encoding the coefficients of the label functions (also denoted by L_j), and an ABE

---

[2] The reason why we put the message μ in the key will become clear later in the overview.

[3] In contrast, linear evaluation is impossible for fully hiding randomized encoding that hides $\mathbf{x}$ and f.

ciphertext is an IPFE ciphertext encrypting $(1, \mathbf{x})$, as illustrated below in Real Algorithms. When they are put together, IPFE decryption recovers exactly the labels $\ell_j = L_j(\mathbf{x}) = \langle L_j, (1, \mathbf{x})\rangle$, from which we can recover $\mu f(\mathbf{x})$ using the evaluation procedure. A technicality is that known IPFE are built from pairing groups, and decryption only reveals $\mu f(\mathbf{x})$ in the exponent of the target group. Nevertheless, one can recover $\mu f(\mathbf{x})$ also in the exponent, thanks to the linearity of AKGS evaluation.

Intuitively, the LL scheme is secure since IPFE only reveals the labels, and AKGS security guarantees only $\mu f(\mathbf{x})$ is revealed, given the labels. It is simple to formalize this idea in the selective setting, where $\mathbf{x}$ is chosen before querying the key for f. By the function-hiding property, it is indistinguishable to hardwire the labels in the IPFE keys as follows.

$$\begin{array}{ccc} \text{REAL ALGORITHMS} & & \text{HYBRID} \\ \left\{ \begin{array}{l} \mathsf{ct}_{\mathbf{x}}\text{: } \mathsf{ict}\ (\ 1, \mathbf{x}\ ) \\ \mathsf{sk}_{f,\mu}\text{: } \{\mathsf{isk}_j(\ L_j\ )\}_{j\in[m]} \end{array} \right\} & \approx & \left\{ \begin{array}{l} \mathsf{ct}_{\mathbf{x}}\text{: } \mathsf{ict}\ (\ \ 1\ \ , \mathbf{x}\ ) \\ \mathsf{sk}_{f,\mu}\text{: } \{\mathsf{isk}_j(\ L_j(\mathbf{x})\ , \mathbf{0}\ )\}_{j\in[m]} \end{array} \right\} \end{array}$$

After labels $L_j(\mathbf{x})$ are hardwired and label functions removed, AKGS security guarantees that the labels only reveal $\mu f(\mathbf{x})$, and μ is hidden if $f(\mathbf{x}) = 0$. Observe that for selective security, we only need hiding in the keys and not the ciphertext.

The above proof fails for adaptive security, in particular in the case where the secret key is queried before the ciphertext (we will focus on this harder case below). At key generation time, $\mathbf{x}$ is unknown and consequently the labels $L_j(\mathbf{x})$ are unknown. We also do not want to hardwire all the labels in the ciphertext as that would make the ciphertext as large as the policy. LL solves this problem by relying on a stronger security notion of AKGS called *piecewise security*:

- The marginal distribution of $\ell_2, \ldots, \ell_m$ is uniformly random, and ℓ_1 can be *reversely computed* from these other labels $\ell_2, \ldots, \ell_m$ and $f, \mathbf{x}$, by finding the unique ℓ_1 satisfying the constraint of evaluation correctness.[4]
- The other labels are *marginally random* even given the coefficients of all subsequent label functions, i.e.,

$$\big(L_j(\mathbf{x}), L_{j+1}, \ldots, L_m\big) \equiv \big(z, L_{j+1}, \ldots, L_m\big) \quad \text{for } z \xleftarrow{\$} \mathbb{Z}_p, \quad \text{for all } j > 1.$$

The first property implies a specific simulation strategy: Simply sample $\ell_2, \ldots, \ell_m$ as random, then solve for ℓ_1 from the correctness constraint. This strategy is particularly suitable for the adaptive setting, as only the simulation of ℓ_1 depends on the input $\mathbf{x}$. Thus, a conceivable simulation strategy for 1-ABE is to hardwire $\ell_2, \ldots, \ell_m$ in the secret key and ℓ_1 in the ciphertext. This would not hurt the compactness of the ciphertext.

---

[4] The original definition only requires ℓ_1 to be reversely *sampleable*. In [17], it is shown that the two are equivalent for piecewise security, and we stick to the simpler definition in this overview. In the full definition, ℓ_1 also depends on the computation result. For the purpose of this overview, the result is always $\mu f(\mathbf{x}) = 0$ as the adversary is restricted to non-decrypting queries.

Proving the indistinguishability of the real and the simulated worlds takes two steps. In the first step, the first label $\ell_1 = L_1(\mathbf{x})$ is hardwired into the IPFE ciphertext ict, and then changed to be reversely computed from the other labels and $f, \mathbf{x}$, which is possible since by the time we generate ict, we know both f and $\mathbf{x}$. In the second step, each isk_j for $j > 1$ is, one by one, switched from encoding the label function to encoding a random label. To do so, the jth label $\ell_j = L_j(\mathbf{x})$ is first hardwired into ict, after which it is switched to random relying on piecewise security, and lastly moved back to isk_j. Observe that the proof uses two extra slots in the vectors (one for ℓ_1, the other for each ℓ_j temporarily) and relies on hiding in both the keys and the ciphertext.

Lightweight Alternative to Function-Hiding. In a function-hiding IPFE, keys and ciphertexts must be of size at least linear in the vector dimension. This means the resulting ABE scheme can never be succinct. Our first observation is that function-hiding IPFE is an overkill. Since in ABE, $\mathbf{x}$ is not required to be hidden, it is quite wasteful to protect it inside an IPFE ciphertext. Indeed, selective security of the LL scheme does not rely on hiding in the ciphertext.

Our idea to achieve succinctness is to use a non-function-hiding IPFE scheme instead, e.g., public-key IPFE. Usually the vector in the key is included verbatim as part of the key, and the "essence" of the key (excluding the vector itself) could be significantly shorter than the vector. Indeed, many known public-key IPFE schemes [1,3] have succinct keys.

Since the coefficients of the label functions (which contains information about μ and the garbling randomness) *must* be hidden for the 1-ABE to be secure, and $\mathbf{x}$ is public, we should encrypt the coefficients of the label functions in IPFE *ciphertexts* and use an IPFE *key* for $(1, \mathbf{x})$ to compute the garbling. Since the message μ is together with f and the generation of IPFE ciphertexts is public-key, the 1-ABE scheme is more like a *public-key ciphertext-policy* ABE than a secret-key ABE, except we only consider security given a single key for some attribute $\mathbf{x}$. Therefore, we redefine 1-ABE as 1-key secure public-key CP-ABE,[5] and the idea is to construct it from a public key IPFE and AKGS as follows:

$$\left.\begin{array}{l}\mathsf{sk}_{\mathbf{x}}\colon\ \mathsf{isk}\ (\ 1, \mathbf{x}\ )\\ \mathsf{ct}_{f,\mu}\colon \{\mathsf{ict}_j(\ L_j\ )\}_{j\in[m]}\end{array}\right\}\xrightarrow[\mathsf{Dec}]{\text{IPFE}}\{\langle L_j, (1,\mathbf{x})\rangle = L_j(\mathbf{x}) = \ell_j\}_{j\in[m]}\xrightarrow[\mathsf{Eval}]{\text{AKGS}}\mu f(\mathbf{x}).$$

Our CP-1-ABE is $\mathbf{x}$-selectively secure if the underlying IPFE is indistinguishability-secure, similar to the selective security of LL scheme.

However, it is not immediate that we can prove adaptive security of this new scheme. The LL adaptive security proof requires hardwiring ℓ_1 and one of ℓ_j's with $\mathbf{x}$, which is now encoded in the secret key without hiding property. Taking a step back, hardwiring a label is really about removing its label function and only using the label, which is the inner product yielded by IPFE decryption. Our idea is to use simulation security to achieve this goal. A simulator for a

[5] This definition has the advantage of automatically being multi-ciphertext secure (if secure at all) over the secret-key definition. It is also more convenient to use in reductions for full ABE.

public-key IPFE can simulate the master public key, the secret keys, and one (or a few) ciphertext, using only the inner products, and the simulator can do so adaptively. Let us take simulating one ciphertext as an example.

$$\begin{array}{ccc} \text{REAL} & & \text{SIMULATION} \\ \left\{\begin{array}{c} \mathsf{mpk} \\ \{\mathsf{isk}_j(\ \mathbf{v}_j\ )\}_{j\le J^*} \\ \mathsf{ict}\ (\ \mathbf{u}\ ) \\ \{\mathsf{isk}_j(\ \mathbf{v}_j\ )\}_{j>J^*} \end{array}\right\} & \approx & \left\{\begin{array}{lll} & \widetilde{\mathsf{mpk}} & \\ \{\widetilde{\mathsf{isk}}_j(\ \mathbf{v}_j\ | & \varnothing &)\}_{j\le J^*} \\ \widetilde{\mathsf{ict}}\ (\ \varnothing\ | & \{\langle \mathbf{u},\mathbf{v}_j\rangle\}_{j\le J^*} &) \\ \{\widetilde{\mathsf{isk}}_j(\ \mathbf{v}_j\ | & \langle \mathbf{u},\mathbf{v}_j\rangle &)\}_{j>J^*} \end{array}\right\} \end{array} \quad (\star)$$

J^* is the number of keys issued before ciphertext generation. On the left are the honestly generated master public key, secret keys, and ciphertext. On the right is their simulation. The vertical bar separates what the real algorithms use and what the simulator (additionally) use. Since public-key IPFE completely reveals the key vectors,[6] they are always provided to the simulator. As for the other values:

- Before ciphertext simulation, there is no additional information supplied.
- When the ciphertext is simulated, the vector $\mathbf{u}$ is *not* provided, but its inner products with already simulated keys are provided to the simulator.[7]
- After ciphertext simulation, when simulating a key for $\mathbf{v}_j$, the inner product $\langle \mathbf{u}, \mathbf{v}_j \rangle$ is provided with $\mathbf{v}_j$.

Observe that the values after the vertical bar are exactly those computable using the functionality of IPFE *at that time*, so in simulation, anything about the encrypted vector *not yet* computable by the functionality of IPFE, simply does not exist (information-theoretically) at all. In the setting of our CP-1-ABE, we will simulate an IPFE ciphertext to remove its corresponding label function and only retain the label. Looking from the perspective of hardwiring, when we issue $\mathsf{sk}_{\mathbf{x}} = \mathsf{isk}(1, \mathbf{x})$ after we have created the ciphertext $\mathsf{ct}_{f,\mu}$ (in which ict_j has been simulated), the inner product ℓ_j is supplied to the simulator when we simulate isk, after the simulation of ict_j. This means the label ℓ_j is hardwired into isk.

Let us exemplify the proof of adaptive security in the more difficult case where $\mathsf{sk}_{\mathbf{x}}$ is queried after $\mathsf{ct}_{f,\mu}$. First, we simulate ict_1 so that the first label is hardwired into isk.

$$\begin{array}{ccc} \text{REAL ALGORITHMS} & & \ell_1 \text{ HARDWIRED} \\ \left\{\begin{array}{rl} \mathsf{ct}_{f,\mu}\colon & \mathsf{ict}_1(\ L_1\ ) \\ & \{\mathsf{ict}_j(\ L_j\ )\}_{j>1} \\ \mathsf{sk}_{\mathbf{x}}\colon & \mathsf{isk}\ (\ 1,\mathbf{x}\ ) \end{array}\right\} & \approx & \left\{\begin{array}{rl} \mathsf{ct}_{f,\mu}\colon & \widetilde{\mathsf{ict}}_1(\ \varnothing\ |\quad \varnothing\ ) \\ & \{\mathsf{ict}_j(\ L_j\ )\}_{j>1} \\ \mathsf{sk}_{\mathbf{x}}\colon & \widetilde{\mathsf{isk}}\ (\ 1,\mathbf{x}\ |\ \ell_1 = L_1(\mathbf{x})\ ) \end{array}\right\} \end{array}$$

[6] Anyone can encrypt the standard basis vectors using mpk, and use decryption algorithm to obtain each component of the vector in a secret key.

[7] Though the number J^* of inner products with already simulated keys is unbounded, since the vectors $\{\mathbf{v}_j\}_{j\le J^*}$ in the keys are public, these inner products are determined by those with any maximal subset of linearly independent $\mathbf{v}_j$'s, the number of which will not exceed the dimension. As such, the simulated ciphertext can still be compact.

(We omitted the master public key for brevity.) Note that ict_j's for $j > 1$ do not use *ciphertext* simulation but are created using the master public key (honest or simulated). Once ℓ_1 is hardwired, we can instead solve for it from the correctness equation.

The second step is to switch $\mathsf{ict}_j(L_j)$ to $\mathsf{ict}_j(\ell_j, \mathbf{0})$ for $\ell_j \xleftarrow{\$} \mathbb{Z}_p$ one by one, i.e., to simulate ℓ_j as random. To do so, we first simulate ict_j (hardwiring $\ell_j = L_j(\mathbf{x})$ into isk), then switch ℓ_j to random (via piecewise security), and lastly revert ict_j back to encryption (not simulated), but encrypting $(\ell_j, \mathbf{0})$ instead.

$$
\begin{array}{cc}
\text{BEFORE/AFTER SIMULATING } \ell_j & \ell_1, \ell_j \text{ HARDWIRED} \\
\left\{\begin{array}{ll}
\mathsf{ct}_{f,\mu}: & \widetilde{\mathsf{ict}}_1(\ \varnothing \mid \varnothing\ ) \\
 & \{\mathsf{ict}_{j'}(\ell_{j'}, \mathbf{0}\ )\}_{1<j'<j} \\
 & \mathsf{ict}_j\ (L_j \,/\, (\ell_j, \mathbf{0})\ ) \\
 & \{\mathsf{ict}_{j'}(\ L_{j'}\ )\}_{j'>j} \\
\mathsf{sk}_{\mathbf{x}}: & \widetilde{\mathsf{isk}}\ (\ 1, \mathbf{x} \mid \ell_1\ )
\end{array}\right\}
\rightleftharpoons
&
\left\{\begin{array}{ll}
\mathsf{ct}_{f,\mu}: & \widetilde{\mathsf{ict}}_1(\ \varnothing \mid \varnothing\ ) \\
 & \{\mathsf{ict}_{j'}(\ell_{j'}, \mathbf{0}\ )\}_{1<j'<j} \\
 & \widetilde{\mathsf{ict}}_j(\ \varnothing \mid \varnothing\ ) \\
 & \{\mathsf{ict}_{j'}(\ L_{j'}\ )\}_{j'>j} \\
\mathsf{sk}_{\mathbf{x}}: & \widetilde{\mathsf{isk}}\ (\ 1, \mathbf{x} \mid \ell_1, \ell_j\ )
\end{array}\right\} \\
\ell_2, \ldots, \ell_{j-1}, \ell_j \xleftarrow{\$} \mathbb{Z}_p, \text{ SOLVE FOR } \ell_1 & \ell_j = L_j(\mathbf{x}) \text{ OR } \ell_j \xleftarrow{\$} \mathbb{Z}_p
\end{array}
$$

During the proof, there are at most two simulated ciphertexts at any time, so it appears that we can just use a simulation-secure IPFE capable of simulating at most two ciphertexts. This is *not* the case. The tricky part is that the usual definition of simulation security in ($\star$) only requires the *real world* to be indistinguishable from *simulation*. However, in the step of simulating ℓ_j as random, we need to switch ict_j to simulation when ict_1 is already simulated (and symmetrically, reverting $\widetilde{\mathsf{ict}}_j$ back to encryption while keeping $\widetilde{\mathsf{ict}}_1$ simulated). It is unclear whether this transition is indistinguishable just via simulation security, because the definition says nothing about the indistinguishability of simulating *one more* ciphertext when there is already one simulated ciphertext, i.e.,

$$
(\widetilde{\mathsf{mpk}}, \widetilde{\mathsf{ict}}_1, \mathsf{ict}_2, \{\widetilde{\mathsf{isk}}_j\}_j) \approx (\widetilde{\mathsf{mpk}}, \widetilde{\mathsf{ict}}_1, \widetilde{\mathsf{ict}}_2, \{\widetilde{\mathsf{isk}}_j\}_j)\,?
$$

Note that when we want to simulate ℓ_j, the computation of ℓ_1 has complicated dependency on $\mathbf{x}$,[8] and we cannot hope to get around the issue by first reverting $\widetilde{\mathsf{ict}}_1$ back to normal encryption then simultaneously simulating $\mathsf{ict}_1, \mathsf{ict}_j$, because we do not know what to encrypt in ict_1.

Gradually Simulation-Secure IPFE. To solve the problem above, we define a stronger notion of simulation security, called *gradual simulation security.* It bridges the gap by capturing the idea that it is indistinguishable to simulate more ciphertexts even when some ciphertexts (and all the keys) are already simulated, as long as the total number of simulated ciphertexts does not exceed a preselected threshold. We show that the IPFE scheme in [3] can be adapted for gradual simulation security. The length of secret keys grows linearly in the maximum number of simulated ciphertexts, but not in the vector dimension. Plugging it into our CP-1-ABE construction, we obtain a CP-1-ABE with succinct keys.

[8] In fact, the computation is as complex as the computation of $f(\mathbf{x})$.

We remark that another way to get around the issue of simulation security is to notice that there are at most two ciphertexts simulated at any time and one of them is ict_1. Therefore, we can simply prepare two instances of IPFE (with independently generated master public and secret keys), one dedicated to ict_1 and the other to ict_j's (for $j > 1$). During the proof, the instance for ict_1 is always simulated, and the other instance is switched between simulation and normal. The downside of this method is that using two instances doubles 1-ABE key size. In contrast, the solution using gradually simulation-secure IPFE only needs one more $\mathbb{Z}_p$ element in CP-1-ABE key.

Comparison with Previous Techniques. Previous works constructing succinct ABE only natively support Boolean computations, whereas our method natively supports *arithmetic* computations. In [5–7,22,27], succinct ABE schemes are constructed from a special succinct ABE for set-membership policies (keys are tied to a set S and ciphertexts are tied to an element x; decryption succeeds if $x \in S$). Based on ABE for set-membership policies, one can obtain ABE for monotone span programs, or policies admitting linear secret sharing schemes. Those ingredients (the special ABE, MSP, LSS) are inherently only native to Boolean computations. Among them, the work of [6] constructs succinct ABE for arithmetic span programs by reduction to MSP at the cost of a $\Theta(\log p)$ blow-up in key sizes.

In [23,28], succinct ABE schemes are implicitly based on IPFE with succinct keys. The IPFE is only used to compute linear secret sharing schemes, and is used in a non-black-box way. In contrast, our 1-ABE can be constructed from any IPFE in a modular and black-box fashion, and we use it for arithmetic branching programs.

Dual System Encryption for Full ABE. To lift our CP-1-ABE to full KP-ABE, we need to flip the position of attributes and policies. Our idea is to use CP-1-ABE as a key encapsulation mechanism. More specifically, a KP-ABE key for policy f is a CP-1-ABE ciphertext $\mathsf{cpct}(f, \mu)$, where μ is the message in CP-1-ABE and encapsulated key in KP-ABE. A KP-ABE ciphertext for attribute $\mathbf{x}$ and message m consists of a CP-1-ABE key $\mathsf{cpsk}(\mathbf{x})$ and the masked message $\mu + m$. If decryption is authorized, CP-1-ABE decryption will give us μ, which can be used to unmask the message. Observe that the security of KP-ABE aligns with the security of CP-1-ABE, namely, in the KP-ABE security game:

- We only need to handle one ciphertext, for which we rely on 1-key security of CP-1-ABE.
- We need to handle multiple keys, which corresponds to multi-ciphertext security of CP-1-ABE. Since our CP-1-ABE is public-key, it indeed satisfies multi-ciphertext security given only one key.

However, we need to resolve the issue that encryption of KP-ABE is now secret-key, since we need to know both the master secret key of CP-1-ABE and μ (part of the master secret key of KP-ABE) to generate KP-ABE ciphertext.

We observe that our CP-1-ABE is linear, i.e., the spaces of cpmsk, cpsk, cpct, messages are vector spaces over $\mathbb{Z}_p$, and[9]

$$\begin{aligned} k_1\mathsf{cpsk}(\mathsf{cpmsk}_1, \mathbf{x}) \quad +k_2\mathsf{cpsk}(\mathsf{cpmsk}_2, \mathbf{x}) \quad &= \mathsf{cpsk}(k_1\mathsf{cpmsk}_1 + k_2\mathsf{cpmsk}_2, \mathbf{x}), \\ k_1\mathsf{cpct}(\mathsf{cpmsk}_1, f, \mu_1) + k_2\mathsf{cpct}(\mathsf{cpmsk}_1, f, \mu_2) & \\ &= \mathsf{cpct}(k_1\mathsf{cpmsk}_1 + k_2\mathsf{cpmsk}_2, f, k_1\mu_1 + k_2\mu_2). \end{aligned}$$

Here, $\mathsf{cpsk}(\mathsf{cpmsk}, \mathbf{x})$ and $\mathsf{cpct}(\mathsf{cpmsk}, f, \mu)$ represent that they are generated in the CP-1-ABE instance whose master secret key is cpmsk. We instantiate our CP-1-ABE with an IPFE such that the keys are linear in the master secret key and the ciphertexts are linear in both the master secret key and the encrypted vector. CP-1-ABE master secret key and keys are IPFE master secret key and keys, so cpsk's are linear in cpmsk. CP-1-ABE ciphertexts are IPFE ciphertexts for the label functions of AKGS, and AKGS is linear with respect to the message μ, so cpct's are linear in msk, μ.

Let G be an additive prime-order group generated by P and write $[\![a]\!] = aP$. Concretely, cpmsk and cpsk's will be $\mathbb{Z}_p$ elements. Now if we encode cpmsk in G, by linearity we can compute cpsk in G, and we denote this fact by

$$[\![\mathsf{cpsk}(\mathsf{cpmsk}, \mathbf{x})]\!] = \mathsf{cpsk}([\![\mathsf{cpmsk}]\!], \mathbf{x}).$$

Assume for the moment that this can also be done for cpct's and decryption still works.[10] Given the linearity, we can employ dual system encryption [24] to make the scheme public-key. In prime-order groups, the classic dual system encryption can be regarded as hash proof systems based on MDDH_k [9,12].[11]

Take MDDH_1 (DDH assumption) for example. KP-ABE prepares two instances of CP-1-ABE and two messages, and publishes the projection of them along a randomly sampled vector (b_1, b_2) in the exponent:

$$\begin{aligned} \mathsf{kpmpk} &= [\![b_1, b_2, b_1\mathsf{cpmsk}_1 + b_2\mathsf{cpmsk}_2, b_1\mu_1 + b_2\mu_2]\!] \quad \text{for } b_1, b_2 \xleftarrow{\$} \mathbb{Z}_p, \\ \mathsf{kpmsk} &= (\mathsf{cpmpk}_1, \mathsf{cpmpk}_2, \mathsf{cpmsk}_1, \mathsf{cpmsk}_2, \mu_1, \mu_2). \end{aligned}$$

Encryption is now public-key. A KP-ABE ciphertext simply uses a random CP-1-ABE master secret key in the projected space (a.k.a. *normal* space in dual system encryption) and use the projected μ to mask the message. A KP-ABE key consists of two CP-1-ABE ciphertexts, one in each instance encrypting the corresponding encapsulated key.

$$\begin{aligned} \mathsf{kpct}(\mathbf{x}, m) &= \big(s[\![b_1, b_2]\!], \mathsf{cpsk}(s[\![b_1\mathsf{cpmsk}_1 + b_2\mathsf{cpmsk}_2]\!], \mathbf{x}), m + s[\![b_1\mu_1 + b_2\mu_2]\!]\big) \\ &\qquad\qquad\qquad\qquad\qquad\qquad\qquad\qquad\qquad\qquad \text{for } s \xleftarrow{\$} \mathbb{Z}_p, \\ \mathsf{kpsk}(f) &= \big(\mathsf{cpct}(\mathsf{cpmsk}_1, f, \mu_1), \mathsf{cpct}(\mathsf{cpmsk}_2, f, \mu_2)\big). \end{aligned}$$

[9] The randomness in key generation/encryption should also take part in the linear homomorphism, but we omit it in this overview for brevity.

[10] In our case, cpct's are already group-encoded, and this is where pairing comes in.

[11] A few examples are [3,13,15,26]. Wee [25] also notices that certain usage of dual system encryption in composite-order groups is reminiscent of hash proof systems. There are other ways to use dual system encryption that are not captured by hash proof systems.

To decrypt, we first use linearity to combine the two CP-1-ABE ciphertexts into

$$\begin{aligned}&\mathsf{cpct}([\![sb_1\mathsf{cpmsk}_1 + sb_2\mathsf{cpmsk}_2]\!], f, [\![sb_1\mu_1 + sb_2\mu_2]\!])\\ &= [\![sb_1]\!]\mathsf{cpct}(\mathsf{cpmsk}_1, f, \mu_1) + [\![sb_2]\!]\mathsf{cpct}(\mathsf{cpmsk}_2, f, \mu_2).\end{aligned}$$

The master secret key of the combined cpct matches that of the cpsk in the KP-ABE ciphertext, and CP-1-ABE decryption will recover $[\![sb_1\mu_1 + sb_2\mu_2]\!]$, using which we can unmask to obtain the message m.

To argue security, we first replace $[\![sb_1, sb_2]\!]$ used in the challenge ciphertext by $[\![a_1, a_2]\!]$ for random $a_1, a_2 \xleftarrow{\$} \mathbb{Z}_p$ (using DDH), which is not co-linear with (b_1, b_2) with overwhelming probability. Ciphertexts in this form are said to be *semi-functional* in dual system encryption.

By the linearity, we can look at the ABE scheme from a new basis, namely $(b_1, b_2), (a_1, a_2)$. We denote the CP-1-ABE components and μ's in this basis with prime, e.g., $\mathsf{cpmsk}'_1 = b_1\mathsf{cpmsk}_1 + b_2\mathsf{cpmsk}_2$ and $\mathsf{cpmsk}'_2 = a_1\mathsf{cpmsk}_1 + a_2\mathsf{cpmsk}_2$. The KP-ABE master public key reveals cpmsk'_1 but not cpmsk'_2. A KP-ABE secret key for policy f is essentially $\mathsf{cpct}(\mathsf{cpmsk}'_1, f, \mu'_1)$ and $\mathsf{cpct}(\mathsf{cpmsk}'_2, f, \mu'_2)$. The challenge ciphertext has $\mathsf{cpsk}(\mathsf{cpmsk}'_2, \mathbf{x})$, and the message is masked by μ'_2. By CP-1-ABE security, μ'_2 (in cpct's) should be hidden, which means the message in the challenge ciphertext is hidden by μ'_2.

The proof completes by replacing μ'_2 in all the KP-ABE keys by random. ABE keys in this form are said to be *semi-functional* in dual system encryption.

Lastly, to base the scheme on MDDH_k, we use $k+1$ instances of CP-1-ABE, publish a k-dimensional projection (*normal* space), and reserve the unpublished dimension for the security proof (*semi-functional* space).

CP-ABE from KP-1-ABE. By symmetry, we can apply the transformation to obtain CP-ABE from KP-1-ABE. Moreover, our KP-ABE trivially serves as a KP-1-ABE. Therefore, the scheme is (ignoring group encoding)

$$\begin{aligned}\mathsf{cpmpk} &= (d_1, d_2, d_1\mathsf{kpmsk}_1 + d_2\mathsf{kpmsk}_2, d_1\nu_1 + d_2\nu_2) \quad \text{for } d_1, d_2 \xleftarrow{\$} \mathbb{Z}_p,\\ \mathsf{cpmsk} &= (\mathsf{kpmpk}_1, \mathsf{kpmpk}_2, \mathsf{kpmsk}_1, \mathsf{kpmsk}_2, \nu_1, \nu_2),\\ \mathsf{cpsk} &= \big(\mathsf{kpct}(\mathsf{kpmsk}_1, \mathbf{x}, \nu_1), \mathsf{kpct}(\mathsf{kpmsk}_2, \mathbf{x}, \nu_2)\big),\\ \mathsf{cpct} &= \big(td_1, td_2, \mathsf{kpsk}(t(d_1\mathsf{msk}_1 + d_2\mathsf{msk}_2), f), m + t(d_1\nu_1 + d_2\nu_2)\big) \text{ for } t \xleftarrow{\$} \mathbb{Z}_p.\end{aligned}$$

Again, KP-1-ABE is used to encapsulate keys ν_1, ν_2, whose projection masks the message in CP-ABE. Dual system encryption or hash proof system is used to obtain public-key encryption by publishing a random projection of KP-1-ABE master secret keys (in this case, along (d_1, d_2)).

One final observation is that only μ_1, μ_2 in KP-(1-)ABE need to be duplicated and projected, yielding only a small overhead in CP-ABE compared to KP-ABE. We leave the details to the full version [18].

We note that once we obtain KP-ABE from CP-1-ABE, going to CP-ABE using the same method is natural and simple.

1.2 Related Works

Succinct ABE. We compare our scheme with previous KP-ABE schemes with constant-size ciphertexts in Table 1 and CP-ABE schemes with constant-size secret keys in Table 2.

Compact ABE. Previous schemes achieving compactness (linear-size keys and ciphertexts, also known as "unbounded multi-use of attributes") and adaptive security based on standard assumptions are [15,23] for Boolean formulae, [13] for Boolean branching programs, and [17] for arithmetic branching programs. Among them, only [23] achieves succinctness.

ABE with Succinct f-Part. From pairing, we know several ABE schemes with succinct $\mathbf{x}$-part (ciphertexts in KP-ABE and keys in CP-ABE) and compact f-part (linear in the size of f), including ones in this work. One can also investigate succinctness in f-part (keys in KP-ABE and ciphertexts in CP-ABE). So far, the only schemes with succinct f-part are KP-ABE for polynomial-sized circuits based on LWE [8] and CP-ABE schemes for NC^1 based on LWE and pairing [4], in which the size of f-part depends on the depth but not the size of the circuit. Yet these schemes have compact but non-succinct $\mathbf{x}$-part.

Unbounded ABE. Our succinct ABE schemes have master public key of size linear in the attribute length. In general, one can further improve the size of master keys to be a constant, which requires the scheme to be able to handle attributes of any polynomial length. Such schemes are called unbounded ABE. So far, there are unbounded and compact ABE schemes (e.g., [15] for NC^1). It remains an interesting open problem to construct unbounded succinct schemes.

In summary, to the best of our knowledge, our schemes achieve one of the currently best trade-offs in terms of master key/secret key/ciphertext sizes.

2 Preliminaries

For two matrices $\mathbf{A}, \mathbf{B}$, their tensor product is denoted by $\mathbf{A} \otimes \mathbf{B}$. An affine function $f : \mathbb{Z}_p^n \to \mathbb{Z}_p$ over prime field $\mathbb{Z}_p$ is conveniently associated with its coefficient vector $\mathbf{f} \in \mathbb{Z}_p^{n+1}$ (the same letter in boldface) such that $f(\mathbf{x}) = \mathbf{f}^{\mathsf{T}} \begin{pmatrix} 1 \\ \mathbf{x} \end{pmatrix}$.

2.1 Arithmetic Branching Programs and Arithmetic Key Garbling

In this paper, we consider the class of decryption policies defined by arithmetic branching programs [20].

Definition 1 (ABP). *An arithmetic branching program (ABP) $f = (V, E, s, t, p, n, w)$ consists of a directed acyclic graph (V, E), two distinguished vertices $s, t \in V$, a prime field order p, an arity n, and a weight function*

$w : E \times \mathbb{Z}_p^n \to \mathbb{Z}_p$ that is affine in the second input. It computes the function $f : \mathbb{Z}_p^n \to \mathbb{Z}_p$ (written as the same letter) defined by

$$f(\mathbf{x}) = \sum_{\substack{s\text{-}t \text{ path} \\ e_1 \cdots e_i}} \prod_{j=1}^{i} w(e_j, \mathbf{x}).$$

Its size (denoted by $|f|$) is $|V|$. It induces two zero-test predicates*:*

$$f_{\neq 0}(\mathbf{x}) = \begin{cases} 0, & \text{if } f(\mathbf{x}) = 0; \\ 1, & \text{if } f(\mathbf{x}) \neq 0; \end{cases} \qquad f_{=0}(\mathbf{x}) = \neg f_{\neq 0}(\mathbf{x}).$$

Denote by ABP (resp. ABP_p^n) the class of all ABPs (resp. of field order p and arity n), and by ztABP_p^n the set of zero-test predicates induced by ABPs in ABP_p^n.

We rely on an arithmetic key garbling scheme for ABP.

Definition 2 (AKGS). *Let $\mathcal{F} = \{f\}$ be a class of functions $f : \mathbb{Z}_p^n \to \mathbb{Z}_p$. An* arithmetic key garbling scheme (AKGS) *for $\mathcal{F}$ consists of two efficient algorithms:*

- $\mathsf{Garble}(f, \alpha, \beta; \mathbf{r})$ *takes a function $f : \mathbb{Z}_p^n \to \mathbb{Z}_p \in \mathcal{F}$ and two secrets $\alpha, \beta \in \mathbb{Z}_p$ as input, and uses* uniform *randomness $\mathbf{r} \in \mathbb{Z}_p^{m'}$. It outputs coefficient vectors $\mathbf{L}_1, \ldots, \mathbf{L}_m \in \mathbb{Z}_p^{n+1}$ of m affine functions $L_1, \ldots, L_m : \mathbb{Z}_p^n \to \mathbb{Z}_p$ (called* label functions*). The vectors $\mathbf{L}_j$ are* linear *in $(\alpha, \beta, \mathbf{r})$. The amount of randomness m' and the number m of label functions are solely determined by f, and m is called the* garbling size *of f.*
- $\mathsf{Eval}(f, \mathbf{x}, \ell_1, \ldots, \ell_m)$ *takes as input a function $f : \mathbb{Z}_p^n \to \mathbb{Z}_p \in \mathcal{F}$, an input $\mathbf{x} \in \mathbb{Z}_p^n$, and m labels $\ell_1, \ldots, \ell_m \in \mathbb{Z}_p$. It outputs $\gamma \in \mathbb{Z}_p$ that is* linear *in $\ell_1, \ldots, \ell_m$.*

The scheme is required to be correct*, i.e., for all $f : \mathbb{Z}_p^n \to \mathbb{Z}_p \in \mathcal{F}, \alpha, \beta \in \mathbb{Z}_p$, $\mathbf{x} \in \mathbb{Z}_p^n$, it holds that*

$$\Pr\left[\begin{array}{l} (\mathbf{L}_1, \ldots, \mathbf{L}_m) \xleftarrow{\$} \mathsf{Garble}(f, \alpha, \beta) \\ \forall j \in [m],\ \ell_j \leftarrow L_j(\mathbf{x}) \end{array} : \mathsf{Eval}(f, \mathbf{x}, \ell_1, \ldots, \ell_m) = \alpha f(\mathbf{x}) + \beta \right] = 1.$$

We rely on the strong notion of piecewise security recently introduced in [17].

Definition 3 (piecewise security). *Let $(\mathsf{Garble}, \mathsf{Eval})$ be an AKGS for some function class $\mathcal{F}$. The scheme is* piecewise secure *if it satisfies the following two properties:*

- *The first label is* reversely sampleable *given the input, the output, and the other labels. That is, there is an efficient algorithm $\mathsf{RevSamp}$ such that for all $f : \mathbb{Z}_p^n \to \mathbb{Z}_p \in \mathcal{F}, \alpha, \beta \in \mathbb{Z}_p, \mathbf{x} \in \mathbb{Z}_p^n$, the following distributions are identical:*

$$\left\{\begin{array}{c}(\mathbf{L}_1,\ldots,\mathbf{L}_m)\xleftarrow{\$}\mathsf{Garble}(f,\alpha,\beta)\\ \ell_1\leftarrow L_1(\mathbf{x})\end{array} : (\ell_1,\mathbf{L}_2,\ldots,\mathbf{L}_m)\right\}$$

$$\equiv\left\{\begin{array}{c}(\mathbf{L}_1,\ldots,\mathbf{L}_m)\xleftarrow{\$}\mathsf{Garble}(f,\alpha,\beta)\\ \ell_j\leftarrow L_j(\mathbf{x})\text{ for } j\in[m], j>1\\ \ell_1\leftarrow\mathsf{RevSamp}(f,\mathbf{x},\alpha f(\mathbf{x})+\beta,\ell_2,\ldots,\ell_m)\end{array} : (\ell_1,\mathbf{L}_2,\ldots,\mathbf{L}_m)\right\}.$$

– *The other labels are* marginally random *even given all the subsequent label functions. That is, for all $f:\mathbb{Z}_p^n\to\mathbb{Z}_p\in\mathcal{F},\alpha,\beta\in\mathbb{Z}_p,\mathbf{x}\in\mathbb{Z}_p^n$, suppose the garbling size of f is m, then for all $j\in[m], j>1$, the following distributions are identical:*

$$\left\{\begin{array}{c}(\mathbf{L}_1,\ldots,\mathbf{L}_m)\xleftarrow{\$}\mathsf{Garble}(f,\alpha,\beta)\\ \ell_j\leftarrow L_j(\mathbf{x})\end{array} : (\ell_j,\mathbf{L}_{j+1},\ldots,\mathbf{L}_m)\right\}$$

$$\equiv\left\{\begin{array}{c}(\mathbf{L}_1,\ldots,\mathbf{L}_m)\xleftarrow{\$}\mathsf{Garble}(f,\alpha,\beta)\\ \ell_j\xleftarrow{\$}\mathbb{Z}_p\end{array} : (\ell_j,\mathbf{L}_{j+1},\ldots,\mathbf{L}_m)\right\}.$$

A piecewise secure AKGS is known for ABPs:

Lemma 4 ([14,17]). *There exists a piecewise secure AKGS for* ABP, *for which the garbling size of an ABP is the same as its size.*

Throughout the paper, we will use a vectorized version of the garbling algorithm. Let $\boldsymbol{\alpha},\boldsymbol{\beta}\in\mathbb{Z}_p^k$, then $\mathsf{Garble}(f,\boldsymbol{\alpha},\boldsymbol{\beta})$ is executed component-wise with independent randomness and the output are concatenated:

$$\text{for } t\in[k]:\quad (\mathbf{L}_1^{(t)},\ldots,\mathbf{L}_m^{(t)})\xleftarrow{\$}\mathsf{Garble}(f,\boldsymbol{\alpha}[t],\boldsymbol{\beta}[t]);$$

$$\text{for } j\in[m]:\qquad \mathbf{L}_j=\begin{pmatrix}\mathbf{L}_j^{(1)}\\ \vdots\\ \mathbf{L}_j^{(k)}\end{pmatrix}=\sum_{t=1}^{k}\mathbf{e}_j\otimes\mathbf{L}_j^{(t)};$$

$$\text{output}(\mathbf{L}_1,\ldots,\mathbf{L}_m).$$

Here, $\mathbf{e}_j\in\mathbb{Z}_p^k$ are the standard basis vectors and $\mathbf{L}_j$'s are column vectors of length $k(n+1)$. In the vectorized version, the randomness is a matrix and each row of the matrix is used for one invocation of the non-vectorized garbling. This notation is compatible with tensor products:

Lemma 5 (mixing and stitching). *Suppose $f:\mathbb{Z}_p^n\to\mathbb{Z}_p$.*

Let $\boldsymbol{\alpha},\boldsymbol{\beta}\in\mathbb{Z}_p^k,\mathbf{R}\in\mathbb{Z}_p^{k\times m'},\mathbf{c}\in\mathbb{Z}_p^k$, and define

$$(\mathbf{L}_1,\ldots,\mathbf{L}_m)\leftarrow\mathsf{Garble}(f,\boldsymbol{\alpha},\boldsymbol{\beta};\mathbf{R}),\quad (\mathbf{L}'_1,\ldots,\mathbf{L}'_m)\leftarrow\mathsf{Garble}(f,\mathbf{c}^{\mathsf{T}}\boldsymbol{\alpha},\mathbf{c}^{\mathsf{T}}\boldsymbol{\beta};\mathbf{c}^{\mathsf{T}}\mathbf{R}),$$

then $\mathbf{L}_j^{\mathsf{T}}(\mathbf{c}\otimes\mathbf{I}_{n+1})=(\mathbf{L}'_j)^{\mathsf{T}}$ for all $j\in[m]$.

Now let $\alpha,\beta\in\mathbb{Z}_p,\mathbf{r}\in\mathbb{Z}_p^{m'},\mathbf{d}\in\mathbb{Z}_p^k$, and define

$$(\mathbf{L}'_1,\ldots,\mathbf{L}'_j)\leftarrow\mathsf{Garble}(f,\alpha,\beta;\mathbf{r}),\quad (\mathbf{L}_1,\ldots,\mathbf{L}_j)\leftarrow\mathsf{Garble}(f,\alpha\mathbf{d},\beta\mathbf{d};\mathbf{d}\mathbf{r}^{\mathsf{T}}),$$

then $\mathbf{d}\otimes\mathbf{L}'_j=\mathbf{L}_j$ for all $j\in[m]$.

2.2 Attribute-Based Encryption

In the definition below, we explicitly take the description of policy/attribute out of the secret key/ciphertext so that we can characterize succinctness.

Definition 6 (ABE). *Let $\mathcal{M} = \{M_\lambda\}_{\lambda\in\mathbb{N}}$ be a sequence of message sets and $\mathcal{P} = \{\mathcal{P}_\lambda\}_{\lambda\in\mathbb{N}}$ a sequence of predicate families with $\mathcal{P}_\lambda = \{P : X_P \times Y_P \to \{0,1\}\}$. An* attribute-based encryption (ABE) *scheme for message space $\mathcal{M}$ and predicate space $\mathcal{P}$ consists of four efficient algorithms:*

- $\mathsf{Setup}(1^\lambda, P)$ *takes as input the security parameter 1^λ and a predicate $P \in \mathcal{P}_\lambda$, and outputs a pair of master public/secret keys* $(\mathsf{mpk}, \mathsf{msk})$.
- $\mathsf{KeyGen}(\mathsf{msk}, y)$ *takes as input a policy $y \in Y_P$ and outputs a secret key* sk.
- $\mathsf{Enc}(\mathsf{mpk}, x, g)$ *takes as input an attribute $x \in X_P$ and a message $g \in M_\lambda$, and outputs a ciphertext* ct.
- $\mathsf{Dec}(\mathsf{sk}, y, \mathsf{ct}, x)$ *takes as input a secret key, the policy of the key, a ciphertext, and the attribute of the ciphertext, and is supposed to recover the message if $P(x, y) = 1$.*

The scheme is required to be correct*, i.e., for all $\lambda \in \mathbb{N}, g \in M_\lambda, P \in \mathcal{P}_\lambda, x \in X_P$, $y \in Y_P$ such that $P(x, y) = 1$,*

$$\Pr\left[\begin{array}{r} (\mathsf{mpk},\mathsf{msk}) \xleftarrow{\$} \mathsf{Setup}(1^\lambda, P) \\ \mathsf{sk} \xleftarrow{\$} \mathsf{KeyGen}(\mathsf{msk}, y) \\ \mathsf{ct} \xleftarrow{\$} \mathsf{Enc}(\mathsf{mpk}, x, g) \end{array} : \mathsf{Dec}(\mathsf{sk}, y, \mathsf{ct}, x) = g\right] = 1.$$

Definition 7 (ABE for ABP). *Let $p = p(\lambda)$ be a sequence of prime numbers. A* key-policy ABE (KP-ABE) for ABP *over $\mathbb{Z}_{p(\lambda)}$ is defined for the following predicate family:*

$$\mathcal{P} = \{\mathcal{P}_\lambda\}, \quad \mathcal{P}_\lambda = \{P_{\lambda,n} : \mathbb{Z}_{p(\lambda)}^n \times \mathsf{ztABP}_{p(\lambda)}^n \to \{0,1\}\}, \quad P_{\lambda,n}(\mathbf{x}, y) = y(\mathbf{x}).$$

In a ciphertext-policy ABE (CP-ABE) for ABP *over $\mathbb{Z}_{p(\lambda)}$, the predicates are*

$$P_{\lambda,n} : \mathsf{ztABP}_{p(\lambda)}^n \times \mathbb{Z}_{p(\lambda)}^n \to \{0,1\}, \quad (y, \mathbf{x}) \mapsto y(\mathbf{x}).$$

Definition 8 (succinct ABE). *An ABE scheme has* succinct *ciphertext if the length of* ct *is a fixed polynomial in security parameter λ (independent of the length of x, y and the choice of P). Similarly, the scheme has* succinct *secret key if the length of* sk *is a fixed polynomial in λ.*

The above definition does not rule out trivially succinct schemes, e.g., one only supporting x, y of length at most λ. In this work, we construct KP-ABE for ABP with succinct ciphertexts and CP-ABE for ABP with succinct secret keys. These constructions are non-trivial because Setup can be run with any predicate $P_{\lambda,n}$ for attribute length n, the scheme works with policies of arbitrary size, and the ciphertexts in KP-ABE and the secret keys in CP-ABE have fixed size $\mathrm{poly}(\lambda)$, independent of n.

Security. We consider the standard IND-CPA security of ABE.

Definition 9 (IND-CPA of ABE [16]). *Adopt the notations in Definition 6. The scheme is* IND-CPA secure *if* $\mathsf{Exp}^0_{CPA} \approx \mathsf{Exp}^1_{CPA}$, *where* Exp^b_{CPA} *with adversary* $\mathcal{A}$ *proceeds as follows:*

- **Setup.** Launch $\mathcal{A}(1^\lambda)$ and receive from it a predicate $P \in \mathcal{P}_\lambda$. Run $(\mathsf{mpk}, \mathsf{msk}) \xleftarrow{\$} \mathsf{Setup}(1^\lambda, P)$ and send mpk to $\mathcal{A}$.
- **Query I.** Repeat the following for arbitrarily many rounds determined by $\mathcal{A}$: In each round, $\mathcal{A}$ submits a policy $y_q \in Y_P$ for a secret key. Upon this query, run $\mathsf{sk}_q \xleftarrow{\$} \mathsf{KeyGen}(\mathsf{msk}, y)$ and send sk_q to $\mathcal{A}$.
- **Challenge.** The adversary submits the challenge attribute $x^* \in X_P$ and two messages $g_0, g_1 \in M_\lambda$. Run $\mathsf{ct} \xleftarrow{\$} \mathsf{Enc}(\mathsf{mpk}, x, g_b)$ and return ct to $\mathcal{A}$.
- **Query II.** Same as Query I.
- **Guess.** The adversary outputs a bit b'. The outcome of the experiment is b' if $P(x^*, y_q) = 0$ for all y_q queried in Query I/II. Otherwise, the outcome is set to 0.

2.3 Pairing Groups and Matrix Diffie–Hellman Assumption

Throughout the paper, we use a sequence of pairing groups

$$\mathcal{G} = \{(G_{\lambda,1}, G_{\lambda,2}, G_{\lambda,\mathrm{T}}, g_{\lambda,1}, g_{\lambda,2}, e_\lambda)\}_{\lambda\in\mathbb{N}},$$

where $G_{\lambda,1}, G_{\lambda,2}, G_{\lambda,\mathrm{T}}$ are groups of prime order $p = p(\lambda)$, and $G_{\lambda,1}$ (resp. $G_{\lambda,2}$) is generated by $g_{\lambda,1}$ (resp. $g_{\lambda,2}$). The maps $e_\lambda : G_{\lambda,1} \times G_{\lambda,2} \to G_{\lambda,\mathrm{T}}$ are

- *bilinear:* $e_\lambda(g^a_{\lambda,1}, g^b_{\lambda,2}) = \big(e_\lambda(g_{\lambda,1}, g_{\lambda,2})\big)^{ab}$ for all $a, b \in \mathbb{Z}_{p(\lambda)}$; and
- *non-degenerate:* $g_{\lambda,\mathrm{T}} \overset{\mathrm{def}}{=\!=} e_\lambda(g_{\lambda,1}, g_{\lambda,2})$ generates $G_{\lambda,\mathrm{T}}$.

The group operations as well as the pairing e_λ must be efficiently computable.

When we talk about one group without thinking about pairing, the subscripts $1, 2, \mathrm{T}$ are dropped.

Bracket Notation. Fix a security parameter, for $i = 1, 2, \mathrm{T}$, we write $[\![\mathbf{A}]\!]_i$ for $g^{\mathbf{A}}_{\lambda,i}$, where the exponentiation is element-wise. When bracket notation is used, group operations are written additively and pairing is written multiplicatively, so that $[\![\mathbf{A}]\!]_i + [\![\mathbf{B}]\!]_i = [\![\mathbf{A}+\mathbf{B}]\!]_i$ and $[\![\mathbf{A}]\!]_1[\![\mathbf{B}]\!]_2 = [\![\mathbf{A}]\!]_2[\![\mathbf{B}]\!]_1 = [\![\mathbf{AB}]\!]_\mathrm{T}$. Furthermore, numbers can always operate with group elements, e.g., $\mathbf{A}[\![\mathbf{B}]\!]_1 = [\![\mathbf{AB}]\!]_1$.

Matrix Diffie–Hellman Assumption. In this paper, we rely on the MDDH assumptions.

Definition 10 (MDDH [12]). *Let* $G = \{(G_\lambda, g_\lambda)\}_{\lambda\in\mathbb{N}}$ *be a sequence of groups of prime order* $p = p(\lambda)$ *with their generators, and* $\ell = \ell(\lambda), q = q(\lambda)$ *polynomials. The* $MDDH^q_{k,\ell}$ assumption holds in G *if*

$$\{[\![\mathbf{A}, \mathbf{S}^\mathsf{T}\mathbf{A}]\!]\}_{\lambda\in\mathbb{N}} \approx \{[\![\mathbf{A}, \mathbf{C}^\mathsf{T}]\!]\}_{\lambda\in\mathbb{N}} \text{ for } \mathbf{A} \xleftarrow{\$} \mathbb{Z}^{k\times\ell(\lambda)}_{p(\lambda)}, \mathbf{S} \xleftarrow{\$} \mathbb{Z}^{k\times q(\lambda)}_{p(\lambda)}, \mathbf{C} \xleftarrow{\$} \mathbb{Z}^{\ell(\lambda)\times q(\lambda)}_{p(\lambda)}.$$

By default, $\ell = k + 1$ and $q = 1$. It is known [12] that k-Lin implies MDDH_k, which further implies $\mathrm{MDDH}^q_{k,\ell}$ for any polynomial ℓ, q.

3 IPFE with Gradual Simulation Security

In this work, we consider IPFE schemes based on MDDH-hard groups (potentially without pairing), where the ciphertext encodes the encrypted vector in the exponent of the group, and decryption computes the inner product in the exponent. In our definition below, we directly define such group-based IPFE. The definition can be easily modified for IPFE that are not group-based.

Definition 11 (IPFE). *Let $G = \{(G_\lambda, g_\lambda)\}_{\lambda \in \mathbb{N}}$ be a sequence of groups of prime order $p = p(\lambda)$ with their generators. A G-encoded public-key* inner-product functional encryption (IPFE) *scheme consists of four efficient algorithms:*

- $\mathsf{Setup}(1^\lambda, 1^n, 1^T)$ *takes as input the security parameter 1^λ, the dimension 1^n of the vectors, and an additional parameter 1^T (see Definition 12). It outputs a pair of master public/secret keys* $(\mathsf{mpk}, \mathsf{msk})$.
- $\mathsf{KeyGen}(\mathsf{msk}, \mathbf{v})$ *takes the master secret key and a vector as input, and outputs a secret key* sk.
- $\mathsf{Enc}(\mathsf{mpk}, [\![\mathbf{u}]\!])$ *takes the master public key and a vector (encoded in G) as input, and outputs a ciphertext* ct.
- $\mathsf{Dec}(\mathsf{sk}, \mathbf{v}, \mathsf{ct})$ *takes a secret key, the vector in the secret key, and a ciphertext as input, and is supposed to compute the inner product in the exponent.*

The scheme is required to be correct, *meaning that for all $\lambda, n, T \in \mathbb{N}$, $\mathbf{u}, \mathbf{v} \in \mathbb{Z}^n_{p(\lambda)}$, it holds that*

$$\Pr\left[\begin{array}{r} (\mathsf{mpk}, \mathsf{msk}) \xleftarrow{\$} \mathsf{Setup}(1^\lambda, 1^n, 1^T) \\ \mathsf{sk} \xleftarrow{\$} \mathsf{KeyGen}(\mathsf{msk}, \mathbf{v}) \\ \mathsf{ct} \xleftarrow{\$} \mathsf{Enc}(\mathsf{msk}, [\![\mathbf{u}]\!]) \end{array} : \mathsf{Dec}(\mathsf{sk}, \mathbf{v}, \mathsf{ct}) = [\![\mathbf{u}^\mathsf{T}\mathbf{v}]\!]\right] = 1.$$

The scheme is succinct *if the length of* sk *is independent of n and only depends on λ, T.*

Setup algorithm in the above definition takes an additional input 1^T specifying the desired level of simulation security, which we define next.

Gradual Simulation Security. When building the 1-ABE scheme, we rely on the notion of gradual simulation security, which is stronger than the usual simulation security (see [2]). Roughly speaking, on top of the requirement that simulation should be indistinguishable from the real scheme, the notion stipulates that even when some ciphertexts are already simulated, whether another ciphertext is honest or simulated should be indistinguishable. The parameter T specifies the maximum number of ciphertexts that can be simulated.

To navigate around the many indices involved in the definition, it is the easiest to keep in mind that i (hence I, I^*, I_t) always counts the ciphertexts, and that j (hence J, J^*, J_t) always counts the keys.

Definition 12 (gradual simulation security). *Adopt the notations in Definition 11. A* simulator *consists of three efficient algorithms:*

- $\mathsf{SimSetup}(1^\lambda, 1^n, 1^T)$ *takes the same input as* Setup, *and outputs a simulated master public key* mpk *and an internal state* st.[12]
- $\mathsf{SimKeyGen}(\mathsf{st}, \mathbf{v}, z_1, \ldots, z_I)$ *takes as input the internal state* st, *a vector* $\mathbf{v}$, *and a list* $z_1, \ldots, z_I$ *of inner products in* $\mathbb{Z}_{p(\lambda)}$ *(which are the intended inner products between this simulated key and all previously simulated ciphertexts). It outputs a simulated secret key* sk *and a new state* st′.
- $\mathsf{SimEnc}(\mathsf{st}, z_1, \ldots, z_J)$ *takes as input the internal state* st *and a list* $z_1, \ldots, z_J$ *of inner products in* $\mathbb{Z}_{p(\lambda)}$ *(which are the intended inner products between this simulated ciphertext and all previously simulated keys). It outputs a simulated ciphertext* ct *and a new state* st′.

The simulator gradually T-simulates *the scheme if it satisfies both* key simulation security *and* T-ciphertext simulation security *defined below.*

An IPFE scheme is gradually T-simulation-secure *if it can be gradually T-simulated by some simulator. The scheme is* gradually simulation-secure *if there exists a simulator such that the simulator gradually T-simulates the scheme for all $T = \mathrm{poly}(\lambda)$.*

Key Simulation Security. Roughly speaking, this captures the idea that it is indistinguishable to interact with the real authority (who generates and distributes mpk and sk's) versus the simulator issuing simulated mpk and sk's (without simulating any ciphertext). We require $\mathsf{Exp}_{\mathrm{real}} \approx \mathsf{Exp}_{\mathrm{sim}}$, which proceed as follows when run with an adversary $\mathcal{A}$:

- **Setup.** Launch $\mathcal{A}(1^\lambda)$ and receive from it $(1^n, 1^T)$. Run

$$\text{in } \mathsf{Exp}_{\mathrm{real}}: \quad (\mathsf{mpk}, \mathsf{msk}) \xleftarrow{\$} \mathsf{Setup}(1^\lambda, 1^n, 1^T)$$
$$\text{in } \mathsf{Exp}_{\mathrm{sim}}: \quad (\mathsf{mpk}, \mathsf{st}) \xleftarrow{\$} \mathsf{SimSetup}(1^\lambda, 1^n, 1^T)$$

  and send mpk to $\mathcal{A}$.
- **Challenge.** Repeat the following for arbitrarily many rounds determined by $\mathcal{A}$: In each round, $\mathcal{A}$ submits a vector $\mathbf{v}_j$. Upon this challenge, run

$$\text{in } \mathsf{Exp}_{\mathrm{real}}: \quad \mathsf{sk}_j \xleftarrow{\$} \mathsf{KeyGen}(\mathsf{msk}, \mathbf{v}_j)$$
$$\text{in } \mathsf{Exp}_{\mathrm{sim}}: \quad (\mathsf{sk}_j, \mathsf{st}') \xleftarrow{\$} \mathsf{SimKeyGen}(\mathsf{st}, \mathbf{v}_j) \quad \mathsf{st} \leftarrow \mathsf{st}'$$

  and send sk_j to $\mathcal{A}$.
- **Guess.** The adversary outputs a bit b', the outcome of the experiment.

We emphasize that there is no ciphertext challenge in the experiments. The adversary can generate ciphertexts on its own using mpk.

T-Ciphertext Simulation Security. Roughly speaking, this captures the idea that when interacting with the simulator, it is indistinguishable whether any subset of

12 It is understood that the state is maintained by one instance of simulator, and except in definitions, its creation, persistence, and update are suppressed when there is no danger of ambiguity.

ciphertexts are normally generated or simulated, as long as at most T ciphertexts are simulated. In the experiments below, we denote by $z_{i,j} \in \mathbb{Z}_p$ the decryption outcome (inner product) between the jth simulated secret key (ordered temporally among all queried secret keys) and the ith simulated ciphertext (ordered temporally among all queried ciphertexts, excluding the challenge ciphertext). We also let I_t, J_t be the number of simulated ciphertexts (excluding the challenge ciphertext) and secret keys at any time t. $\mathsf{Exp}^b_{T\text{-GS}}$ ($b \in \{0,1\}$) with adversary $\mathcal{A}$ proceeds as follows:

- **Setup.** Launch $\mathcal{A}(1^\lambda)$ and receive from it $(1^n, 1^T)$. Run

$$(\mathsf{mpk}, \mathsf{st}) \xleftarrow{\$} \mathsf{SimSetup}(1^\lambda, 1^n, 1^T)$$

  and send mpk to $\mathcal{A}$.
- **Query I.** Repeat the following for arbitrarily many rounds determined by $\mathcal{A}$: In each round, $\mathcal{A}$ has 2 options.
  - *Key Simulation Query*: $\mathcal{A}$ can submit a vector $\mathbf{v}_j$ with a list $z_{\leq I_t,j}$ of inner products for a secret key sk_j. The list $z_{\leq I_t,j}$ consists of $z_{1,j}, \ldots, z_{I_t,j}$, all the decryption outcomes between sk_j and the simulated ciphertexts queried up to this point. Upon this query, run

$$(\mathsf{sk}_j, \mathsf{st}') \xleftarrow{\$} \mathsf{SimKeyGen}(\mathsf{st}, \mathbf{v}_j, z_{1,j}, \ldots, z_{I_t,j}) \qquad \mathsf{st} \leftarrow \mathsf{st}'$$

    and send sk_j to $\mathcal{A}$.
  - *Ciphertext Simulation Query*: $\mathcal{A}$ can submit a list $z_{i,\leq J_t}$ of inner products for a simulated ciphertext ct_i. The list $z_{i,\leq J_t}$ consists of $z_{i,1}, \ldots, z_{i,J_t}$, all the decryption outcomes between ct_i and the simulated secret keys queried up to this point. Upon this query, run

$$(\mathsf{ct}_i, \mathsf{st}') \xleftarrow{\$} \mathsf{SimEnc}(\mathsf{st}, z_{i,1}, \ldots, z_{i,J_t}) \qquad \mathsf{st} \leftarrow \mathsf{st}'$$

    and send ct_i to $\mathcal{A}$.
- **Challenge.** The adversary submits a vector $\mathbf{u}^*$. Upon the challenge, let the total number of secret key queries in Query I be J^* and the total number of ciphertext queries in Query I be I^*, run

$$b = 0: \quad \mathsf{ct}^* \xleftarrow{\$} \mathsf{Enc}(\mathsf{mpk}, [\![\mathbf{u}^*]\!])$$
$$b = 1: \quad \mathsf{ct}^* \xleftarrow{\$} \mathsf{SimEnc}(\mathsf{st}, (\mathbf{u}^*)^\mathsf{T}\mathbf{v}_1, \ldots, (\mathbf{u}^*)^\mathsf{T}\mathbf{v}_{J^*}) \qquad \mathsf{st} \leftarrow \mathsf{st}'$$

  and send ct^* to $\mathcal{A}$.
- **Query II.** Same as Query I, except that in $\mathsf{Exp}^1_{T\text{-GS}}$, for each secret key query $\mathbf{v}_j$, we put $(\mathbf{u}^*)^\mathsf{T}\mathbf{v}_j$ immediately after $z_{I^*,j}$ in the argument list of $\mathsf{SimKeyGen}$ so that the simulator gets the correct list of inner products:

$$b = 0: \quad (\mathsf{sk}_j, \mathsf{st}') \xleftarrow{\$} \mathsf{SimKeyGen}(\mathsf{st}, \mathbf{v}_j, z_{1,j}, \ldots, z_{I^*,j}, \qquad z_{I^*+1,j}, \ldots, z_{I_t,j});$$
$$b = 1: \quad (\mathsf{sk}_j, \mathsf{st}') \xleftarrow{\$} \mathsf{SimKeyGen}(\mathsf{st}, \mathbf{v}_j, z_{1,j}, \ldots, z_{I^*,j}, (\mathbf{u}^*)^\mathsf{T}\mathbf{v}_j, z_{I^*+1,j}, \ldots, z_{I_t,j});$$
$$\mathsf{st} \leftarrow \mathsf{st}' \quad \text{(in either case)}.$$

- **Guess.** The adversary outputs a bit b'. The outcome of the experiment is b' if both constraints are satisfied:
  - the total number of ciphertext simulation queries in Query I/II is less than T;
  - the equation $\{\mathbf{u}_i^\top \mathbf{v}_j = z_{i,j} \quad \forall i, j\}$ (about $\mathbf{u}_i$'s) has a solution.

  Otherwise, the outcome is set to 0.

Remarks. In $\mathsf{Exp}^1_{T\text{-GS}}$, the challenge ciphertext ct^* is generated in the same way as the other simulated ciphertexts, and in Query II the inner products between sk_j and ct^* are appropriately positioned. From the simulator's perspective, there is no indication which ciphertext is the challenge ciphertext. This definition ensures that the simulator *cannot behave differently depending on whether a particular ciphertext is the challenge or not*, and simplifies the application of gradual simulation security in our construction of ABE.

Note that the simulator receives inner products $z_{i,j}$ in the clear and the adversary submits challenge $\mathbf{u}^*$ in $\mathsf{Exp}^b_{T\text{-GS}}$ in the clear, though the input to encryption and the output of decryption are group-encoded. This is necessary as otherwise, the simulator must solve discrete logarithm in G.

We note that when $T = 1$, gradual simulation security becomes the standard notion of simulation security. On the other hand, simulation security does not imply gradual simulation security. So this definition is a strict generalization of simulation security.

3.1 Construction of Gradually Simulation-Secure IPFE

The IPFE scheme in [3] has been proven simulation-secure [2]. We show that it can be adapted for gradual simulation security. The scheme has succinct keys, whose length grows linearly in T and polynomially in λ, and is independent of n, which eventually translates into the succinctness of our ABE scheme.

Construction 13 ([3]). The construction is described for a fixed value of λ, and λ is suppressed for brevity. Let G be a group (with generator g) of prime order p such that MDDH_k holds in G. Our G-encoded IPFE works as follows:

- $\mathsf{Setup}(1^n, 1^T)$ takes as input the dimension n and the maximum number T of simulated ciphertexts. It samples $\mathbf{A} \xleftarrow{\$} \mathbb{Z}_p^{k\times(k+T)}, \mathbf{W} \xleftarrow{\$} \mathbb{Z}_p^{(k+T)\times n}$ and outputs $\mathsf{mpk} = [\![\mathbf{A}, \mathbf{AW}]\!], \mathsf{msk} = \mathbf{W}$.
- $\mathsf{KeyGen}(\mathsf{msk}, \mathbf{v})$ outputs $\mathsf{sk} = \mathbf{Wv}$.
- $\mathsf{Enc}(\mathsf{mpk}, [\![\mathbf{u}]\!])$ samples $\mathbf{s} \xleftarrow{\$} \mathbb{Z}_p^k$ and outputs $\mathsf{ct} = (\mathbf{s}^\top[\![\mathbf{A}]\!], \mathbf{s}^\top[\![\mathbf{AW}]\!] + [\![\mathbf{u}^\top]\!])$.
- $\mathsf{Dec}(\mathsf{sk}, \mathbf{v}, \mathsf{ct})$ parses ct as $([\![\mathbf{c}^\top]\!], [\![\mathbf{t}^\top]\!])$ and outputs $-[\![\mathbf{c}^\top]\!]\mathsf{sk} + [\![\mathbf{t}^\top]\!]\mathbf{v}$.

The correctness is readily verified by

$$-[\![\mathbf{c}^\top]\!]\mathsf{sk} + [\![\mathbf{t}^\top]\!]\mathbf{v} = [\![-(\mathbf{s}^\top\mathbf{A})(\mathbf{Wv}) + (\mathbf{s}^\top\mathbf{AW} + \mathbf{u}^\top)\mathbf{v}]\!] = [\![\mathbf{u}^\top\mathbf{v}]\!].$$

The scheme is succinct as sk consists of $k + T$ elements in $\mathbb{Z}_p$, independent of n.

Theorem 14. *Suppose in Construction 13, the MDDH_k assumption holds in G, then the constructed scheme is gradually simulation-secure, and the T in the security definition is the T as input of* Setup.

The simulator for our scheme is built modularly upon that for the one-time pad IPFE scheme, which we sketc.h below. We refer the readers to the full version for a more detailed exposition.

One-Time Pad IPFE. OTP-IPFE is a secret-key IPFE:

- $\mathsf{Setup}(p, 1^n)$ samples the master secret key $\mathsf{msk} = \mathbf{w} \xleftarrow{\$} \mathbb{Z}_p^n$.
- $\mathsf{KeyGen}(\mathsf{msk}, \mathbf{v})$ outputs the secret key $\mathsf{sk} = \mathbf{w}^\mathsf{T}\mathbf{v}$ for $\mathbf{v} \in \mathbb{Z}_p^n$.
- $\mathsf{Enc}(\mathsf{msk}, \mathbf{u})$ outputs the ciphertext $\mathsf{ct} = (\mathbf{w} + \mathbf{u})^\mathsf{T}$.
- $\mathsf{Dec}(\mathsf{sk}, \mathbf{v}, \mathsf{ct})$ outputs $-\mathsf{sk} + \mathsf{ct}\mathbf{v}$ as the inner product.

Correctness is readily verified by $-\mathsf{sk} + \mathsf{ct}\mathbf{v} = -\mathbf{w}^\mathsf{T}\mathbf{v} + (\mathbf{w} + \mathbf{u})^\mathsf{T}\mathbf{v} = \mathbf{u}^\mathsf{T}\mathbf{v}$.

The scheme satisfies perfect simulation security for one ciphertext (defined similarly to the usual simulation security). The simulator works as follows:

- $\mathsf{SimSetup}(p, 1^n)$ samples the internal state as $\mathsf{st} = (\widetilde{\mathbf{w}}, \perp)$ with $\widetilde{\mathbf{w}} \xleftarrow{\$} \mathbb{Z}_p^n$. (Here, $\perp$ means that the ciphertext has not been simulated.)
- $\mathsf{SimKeyGen}(\mathsf{st}, \mathbf{v}_j)$ simulates a *pre*-challenge key for $\mathbf{v}_j$ as $\mathsf{sk}_j = \widetilde{\mathbf{w}}^\mathsf{T}\mathbf{v}_j$ and updates the state to $\mathsf{st}' = (\mathsf{st}, \mathbf{v}_j)$.
- $\mathsf{SimEnc}(\mathsf{st}, z_1, \ldots, z_{J^*})$ simulates the challenge ciphertext as a uniformly random solution ct^* of

$$-\widetilde{\mathbf{w}}^\mathsf{T}\mathbf{v}_j + \mathsf{ct}^*\mathbf{v}_j = z_j \quad \forall j \in [J^*],$$

  and updates the state to $\mathsf{st}' = (\perp, \mathsf{ct}^*)$ so that it knows the ciphertext has been simulated. (Here, J^* is the number of keys queried before ciphertext simulation, and z_j is the intended inner product between the ciphertext and the jth key.)
- $\mathsf{SimKeyGen}(\mathsf{st}, \mathbf{v}_j, z_j)$ simulates a *post*-challenge key for $\mathbf{v}_j$ as $\mathsf{sk}_j = \mathsf{ct}^*\mathbf{v}_j - z_j$ and does not update the state.

Dual System Encryption and Simulator. Construction 13 can be seen as dual system encryption applied to OTP-IPFE. There are $k + T$ instances of OTP-IPFE with the master secret keys being $\mathbf{W} \in \mathbb{Z}_p^{(k+T)\times n}$. We publish k projections of them (the *normal* space) in the master public key (i.e., $\mathbf{AW}$ with $\mathbf{A} \in \mathbb{Z}_p^{k\times(k+T)}$), and reserve T instances (the *semi-functional* space) for the simulator.

To simulate, we first switch the ciphertext into the semi-functional form, which means it uses an OTP-IPFE instance independent of the master public key. Then, we employ a change of variable to explicitly separate out *the* instance (also known as using the *parameter hiding* property). Lastly, the simulation can be delegated to OTP-IPFE simulator.

Let us take $T = 1$ for example. The first step is

$$\mathsf{ct}^* = ([\![\mathbf{s}^\mathsf{T}\mathbf{A}]\!], [\![\mathbf{s}^\mathsf{T}\mathbf{A}\mathbf{W} + \mathbf{u}^\mathsf{T}]\!]) \overset{\mathrm{MDDH}_k}{\approx} ([\![\mathbf{c}^\mathsf{T}]\!], [\![\mathbf{c}^\mathsf{T}\mathbf{W} + \mathbf{u}^\mathsf{T}]\!]) \quad \text{for } \mathbf{c} \xleftarrow{\$} \mathbb{Z}_p^{k+1}.$$

The second step is to perform a change of variable $\mathbf{W} = \widetilde{\mathbf{W}} + \mathbf{a}^\perp\mathbf{w}^\mathsf{T}$, where $\mathbf{W}, \mathbf{w}$ are random and $\mathbf{a}^\perp$ is the vector such that $\mathbf{A}\mathbf{a}^\perp = \mathbf{0}$ and $\mathbf{c}^\mathsf{T}\mathbf{a}^\perp = 1$ (which uniquely exists with overwhelming probability). With this change of variable, the keys and the challenge ciphertext become

$$\mathsf{mpk} = ([\![\mathbf{A}]\!], [\![\mathbf{A}\widetilde{\mathbf{W}}]\!]),$$
$$\mathsf{sk}_j = \widetilde{\mathbf{W}}\mathbf{v}_j + \mathbf{a}^\perp \boxed{\mathbf{w}^\mathsf{T}\mathbf{v}_j},$$
$$\mathsf{ct}^* = ([\![\mathbf{c}^\mathsf{T}]\!], [\![\mathbf{c}^\mathsf{T}\widetilde{\mathbf{W}} + \boxed{(\mathbf{w} + \mathbf{u})^\mathsf{T}}]\!]).$$

The terms highlighted in the boxes are exactly the keys and ciphertexts of OTP-IPFE with master secret key $\mathbf{w}$, and the last step is to use OTP-IPFE simulator to simulate these terms.

For general T, we simply prepare uniformly random $\mathbf{c}_1, \ldots, \mathbf{c}_T$ for each simulated ciphertext, and set $\mathbf{W} = \widetilde{\mathbf{W}} + \mathbf{a}_1^\perp\mathbf{w}_1^\mathsf{T} + \cdots + \mathbf{a}_T^\perp\mathbf{w}_T^\mathsf{T}$, where $\mathbf{a}_1^\perp, \ldots, \mathbf{a}_T^\perp$ are the solution to $\mathbf{A}\mathbf{a}_i^\perp = \mathbf{0}$, $\mathbf{c}_i^\mathsf{T}\mathbf{a}_i^\perp = 1$, and $\mathbf{c}_i^\mathsf{T}\mathbf{a}_{i'}^\perp = 0$ for all $i \neq i'$, so that the T instances for simulation do not "interfere" with each other. The keys and ciphertexts after replacing OTP-IPFE by simulation are

$$\mathsf{mpk} = ([\![\mathbf{A}]\!], [\![\mathbf{A}\widetilde{\mathbf{W}}]\!]),$$
$$\mathsf{sk}_j = \widetilde{\mathbf{W}}\mathbf{v}_j + \mathbf{a}_1^\perp\mathsf{SimKeyGen}(\mathsf{st}_1, \mathbf{v}_j, z_{1,j}) + \cdots + \mathbf{a}_T^\perp\mathsf{SimKeyGen}(\mathsf{st}_T, \mathbf{v}_j, z_{T,j}),$$
$$\mathsf{ct}_i^* = ([\![\mathbf{c}_i^\mathsf{T}]\!], [\![\mathbf{c}_i^\mathsf{T}\widetilde{\mathbf{W}} + \mathsf{SimEnc}(\mathsf{st}_i, z_{i,1}, \ldots, z_{i,J_t})]\!]),$$

which is how our simulator for Construction 13 works. Here, $\mathsf{st}_1, \ldots, \mathsf{st}_T$ track T independent instances of OTP-IPFE simulator. We refer the reader to the full version for the security proof.

4 Ciphertext-Policy 1-ABE for ABP

In this section, we construct the core component of our adaptively secure ABE, called *1-ABE*, from any gradually 2-simulation-secure IPFE. A 1-ABE has the same syntax as an ABE, except that

- The message space is $\mathbb{Z}_p$ for some p and decryption only needs to recover the message encoded in (another) group.
- In the security definition, the adversary is allowed to query at most one secret key.
- In the security definition, the adversary only chooses the attribute but not the message. The message is 0 in one experiment ($\mathsf{Exp}^0_{\text{1-ABE}}$), and is uniformly random in the other experiment ($\mathsf{Exp}^1_{\text{1-ABE}}$).[13]

[13] The adversary also does not receive the potential random message.

The relaxation of decryption correctness and the change of messages in the security definition are because 1-ABE will be used to encapsulate keys for full ABE. In full ABE, the group-encoded decryption result of 1-ABE is used to mask the message, and we argue security by replacing the encapsulated key by random.

ABE constructions in some previous works such as [15,17] go through an intermediate step of building a *secret-key* 1-ABE that is 1-key *1-ciphertext* secure. In the secret-key setting, keys and ciphertexts are symmetric, and consequently there is no distinction between ciphertext-policy and key-policy 1-ABE. In contrast, our 1-ABE is *public-key* and *1-key* secure. This asymmetry separates CP-1-ABE and KP-1-ABE. We remark that 1-ABE in [15,17] can be easily modified to fit our definition as CP-1-ABE. We will see that our definition is easier to use in reductions for full ABE.

Construction 15 (CP-1-ABE)**.** The construction is described for a fixed value of λ, and λ is suppressed for brevity. Let G be a group (with generator g) of prime order p, ($\mathsf{IPFE.Setup}, \mathsf{IPFE.KeyGen}, \mathsf{IPFE.Enc}, \mathsf{IPFE.Dec}$) a G-encoded IPFE, and ($\mathsf{Garble}, \mathsf{Eval}$) be an AKGS for ABP. We construct a 1-ABE for predicate space

$$\mathcal{P} = \{P_n \mid n \in \mathbb{N}\}, \quad P_n(y, \mathbf{x}) = y(\mathbf{x}) \text{ for } y \in \mathsf{ztABP}_p^n, \mathbf{x} \in \mathbb{Z}_p^n.$$

The scheme works as follows:

- $\mathsf{Setup}(1^n)$ takes as input the attribute length (i.e., P_n is represented by 1^n) and outputs $(\mathsf{mpk}, \mathsf{msk}) \xleftarrow{\$} \mathsf{IPFE.Setup}(1^{n+1})$.
- $\mathsf{KeyGen}(\mathsf{msk}, \mathbf{x})$ outputs $\mathsf{sk} \xleftarrow{\$} \mathsf{IPFE.KeyGen}(\mathsf{msk}, (1, \mathbf{x}))$.
  Note: *If the underlying IPFE has succinct secret keys, so does this scheme. For instance, when instantiated with Construction* 13 *with* $T = 2$ *under DDH, each secret key consists of just three group elements.*
- $\mathsf{Enc}(\mathsf{mpk}, y, \mu)$ garbles y with μ and encrypts the label functions in IPFE ciphertexts as follows:

$$\begin{aligned}
\text{if } y = f_{\neq 0}\text{:} \quad & \alpha \leftarrow \mu, \beta \leftarrow 0; \\
\text{if } y = f_{=0}\text{:} \quad & \alpha \xleftarrow{\$} \mathbb{Z}_p, \beta \leftarrow \mu; \\
(\mathbf{L}_1, \ldots, \mathbf{L}_m) & \xleftarrow{\$} \mathsf{Garble}(f, \alpha, \beta), \\
\text{for } j \in [m]\text{:} \quad & \mathsf{ict}_j \xleftarrow{\$} \mathsf{IPFE.Enc}(\mathsf{mpk}, [\![\mathbf{L}_j]\!]).
\end{aligned}$$

  The algorithm outputs $\mathsf{ct} = (\mathsf{ict}_1, \ldots, \mathsf{ict}_m)$.
- $\mathsf{Dec}(\mathsf{sk}, \mathbf{x}, \mathsf{ct}, y)$ takes as input a secret key sk for $\mathbf{x}$ and a ciphertext ct for y. If $y(\mathbf{x}) = 0$, the algorithm outputs $\perp$ and stops. Otherwise, it computes

$$\text{for } j \in [m]\text{:} \quad [\![\ell_j]\!] \leftarrow \mathsf{IPFE.Dec}(\mathsf{sk}, \mathsf{ict}_j)$$

$$[\![\mu']\!] \leftarrow \begin{cases} \frac{1}{f(\mathbf{x})}\mathsf{Eval}(f, \mathbf{x}, [\![\ell_1, \ldots, \ell_m]\!]), & \text{if } y = f_{\neq 0}; \\ \mathsf{Eval}(f, \mathbf{x}, [\![\ell_1, \ldots, \ell_m]\!]), & \text{if } y = f_{=0}; \end{cases}$$

  and outputs $[\![\mu']\!]$ as the message.

Note: *We show that the scheme is correct. By the correctness of IPFE, we have*

$$\ell_j = \mathbf{L}_j^{\mathsf{T}} \begin{pmatrix} 1 \\ \mathbf{x} \end{pmatrix} = L_j(\mathbf{x}),$$

where L_j's are the label functions defined by Garble. *Since* Eval *is linear in the labels, it can be performed in the exponent. By the correctness of AKGS,*

$$\begin{aligned} &\text{if } y = f_{\neq 0}, f(\mathbf{x}) \neq 0\text{:} \quad \mu' = \tfrac{1}{f(\mathbf{x})}(\alpha f(\mathbf{x}) + \beta) = \tfrac{1}{f(\mathbf{x})}(\mu f(\mathbf{x}) + 0) = \mu; \\ &\text{if } y = f_{=0}, f(\mathbf{x}) = 0\text{:} \quad \mu' = \alpha f(\mathbf{x}) + \beta = \alpha \cdot 0 + \mu = \mu. \end{aligned}$$

Theorem 16. *Suppose in Construction 15, the IPFE is gradually 2-simulation-secure and the AKGS is piecewise secure, then the constructed 1-ABE is secure.*

We refer the reader to the full version for the proof.

5 Key-Policy ABE for ABP

In this section, we apply the classic dual system encryption to obtain full KP-ABE from CP-1-ABE instantiated with the IPFE in Sect. 3.1.

Construction 17 (KP-ABE). The construction is described for a fixed value of λ, and λ is suppressed for brevity. Let G_1, G_2, G_{T} be pairing groups of prime order p for which MDDH_k holds in G_1, G_2, and let (Garble, Eval) be an AKGS for ABP. We construct an ABE for message space G_{T} and predicate space

$$\mathcal{P} = \{P_n \mid n \in \mathbb{N}\}, \quad P_n(\mathbf{x}, y) = y(\mathbf{x}) \text{ for } \mathbf{x} \in \mathbb{Z}_p^n, y \in \mathsf{ztABP}_p^n.$$

The scheme works as follows:

- $\mathsf{Setup}(1^n)$ takes as input the attribute length (i.e., P_n is represented by 1^n). It samples and sets

$$\begin{aligned} &\mathbf{A} \xleftarrow{\$} \mathbb{Z}_p^{k\times(k+2)}, \mathbf{B} \xleftarrow{\$} \mathbb{Z}_p^{k\times(k+1)}, \quad \mathbf{W} \xleftarrow{\$} \mathbb{Z}_p^{(k+2)\times(k+1)(n+1)}, \boldsymbol{\mu} \xleftarrow{\$} \mathbb{Z}_p^{k+1}, \\ &\mathsf{xpk} = ([\![\mathbf{B}^{\mathsf{T}}]\!]_1, [\![\mathbf{W}(\mathbf{B}^{\mathsf{T}} \otimes \mathbf{I}_{n+1})]\!]_1), \quad \mathsf{fpk} = ([\![\mathbf{A}]\!]_2, [\![\mathbf{AW}]\!]_2), \\ &\mathsf{mpk} = ([\![\boldsymbol{\mu}^{\mathsf{T}}\mathbf{B}^{\mathsf{T}}]\!]_{\mathrm{T}}, \mathsf{xpk}), \quad \mathsf{msk} = (\mathsf{fpk}, \boldsymbol{\mu}). \end{aligned}$$

Note: *We explain the connection with CP-1-ABE and dual system encryption (as demonstrated in Sect. 1.1). The matrix $\mathbf{W} = (\mathbf{W}_1 \cdots \mathbf{W}_{k+1})$ consists of $k+1$ master secret keys of CP-1-ABE concatenated by columns, each of shape $(k+2) \times (n+1)$. Its projection along a vector $\mathbf{b} = (b_1, \ldots, b_{k+1})^{\mathsf{T}}$ is*

$$\begin{aligned} b_1\mathbf{W}_1 + \cdots + b_{k+1}\mathbf{W}_{k+1} &= \mathbf{W}_1 \cdot b_1\mathbf{I}_{n+1} + \cdots + \mathbf{W}_{k+1} \cdot b_{k+1}\mathbf{I}_{n+1} \\ &= (\mathbf{W}_1 \cdots \mathbf{W}_{k+1}) \begin{pmatrix} b_1\mathbf{I}_{n+1} \\ \vdots \\ b_{k+1}\mathbf{I}_{n+1} \end{pmatrix} = \mathbf{W}(\mathbf{b} \otimes \mathbf{I}_{n+1}). \end{aligned}$$

The matrix $\mathbf{B} = (\mathbf{b}_1^{\mathsf{T}} \cdots \mathbf{b}_k^{\mathsf{T}})^{\mathsf{T}}$ consists of all the projection vectors, and $\mathbf{W}(\mathbf{B}^{\mathsf{T}} \otimes \mathbf{I}_{n+1})$ is the projections of $\mathbf{W}$ along $\mathbf{B}$ concatenated by columns.

– $\mathsf{KeyGen}(\mathsf{msk}, y)$ garbles y with $\boldsymbol{\mu}$ as follows:

$$\text{if } y = f_{\neq 0}\text{:} \quad \boldsymbol{\alpha} \leftarrow \boldsymbol{\mu}, \qquad \boldsymbol{\beta} \leftarrow \mathbf{0};$$
$$\text{if } y = f_{=0}\text{:} \quad \boldsymbol{\alpha} \xleftarrow{\$} \mathbb{Z}_p^{k+1}, \quad \boldsymbol{\beta} \leftarrow \boldsymbol{\mu};$$
$$(\mathbf{L}_1, \ldots, \mathbf{L}_m) \xleftarrow{\$} \mathsf{Garble}(f, \boldsymbol{\alpha}, \boldsymbol{\beta}).$$

It samples $\mathbf{s}_j \xleftarrow{\$} \mathbb{Z}_p^k$ for $j \in [m]$ and sets

$$\mathsf{sk}_{j,1} = \mathbf{s}_j^\mathsf{T} [\![\mathbf{A}]\!]_2, \quad \mathsf{sk}_{j,2} = \mathbf{s}_j^\mathsf{T} [\![\mathbf{AW}]\!]_2 + [\![\mathbf{L}_j^\mathsf{T}]\!]_2.$$

The algorithm outputs $\mathsf{sk} = (\mathsf{sk}_{1,1}, \mathsf{sk}_{1,2}, \ldots, \mathsf{sk}_{m,1}, \mathsf{sk}_{m,2})$.
Note: *Generating a key in KP-ABE means encrypting* $\boldsymbol{\mu}$ *in each CP-1-ABE instance, which boils down to generating IPFE ciphertexts, as shown above.*

– $\mathsf{Enc}(\mathsf{mpk}, \mathbf{x}, g)$ samples $\mathbf{r} \xleftarrow{\$} \mathbb{Z}_p^k$ and sets

$$\mathsf{ct}_1 = [\![\mathbf{B}^\mathsf{T}]\!]_1 \mathbf{r}, \quad \mathsf{ct}_2 = [\![\mathbf{W}(\mathbf{B}^\mathsf{T} \otimes \mathbf{I}_{n+1})]\!]_1 \left(\mathbf{r} \otimes \begin{pmatrix} 1 \\ \mathbf{x} \end{pmatrix}\right), \quad \mathsf{ct}_3 = [\![\boldsymbol{\mu}^\mathsf{T} \mathbf{B}^\mathsf{T}]\!]_\mathrm{T} \mathbf{r} + g.$$

The algorithms outputs $\mathsf{ct} = (\mathsf{ct}_1, \mathsf{ct}_2, \mathsf{ct}_3)$.
Note: *We remark that* $\mathbf{r}$ (resp. $\mathbf{B}^\mathsf{T}\mathbf{r}$) *is the coefficients of random linear combination w.r.t. the projections* (resp. the CP-1-ABE instances). *Here,* ct_2 *corresponds to a CP-1-ABE key w.r.t. randomly combined master secret key* $\mathbf{W}(\mathbf{B}^\mathsf{T}\mathbf{r} \otimes \mathbf{I}_{n+1})$*, which is an IPFE secret key for* $\binom{1}{\mathbf{x}}$*, i.e.,*

$$\mathsf{ct}_2 = [\![\mathbf{W}(\mathbf{B}^\mathsf{T}\mathbf{r} \otimes \mathbf{I}_{n+1}) \begin{pmatrix} 1 \\ \mathbf{x} \end{pmatrix}]\!]_1.$$

The ciphertext consists of $2k + 3$ *elements in* G_1 *and one element in* G_T*, hence is succinct.*

– $\mathsf{Dec}(\mathsf{sk}, y, \mathsf{ct}, \mathbf{x})$ first checks whether $y(\mathbf{x}) = 1$. If not, it outputs $\perp$ and terminates. Otherwise, it parses sk, ct as defined in $\mathsf{KeyGen}, \mathsf{Enc}$, computes

$$\text{for } j \in [m]\text{:} \quad [\![\ell_j]\!]_\mathrm{T} = -\mathsf{sk}_{j,1}\mathsf{ct}_2 + \mathsf{sk}_{j,2}\left(\mathsf{ct}_1 \otimes \begin{pmatrix} 1 \\ \mathbf{x} \end{pmatrix}\right);$$
$$[\![\mu']\!]_\mathrm{T} \leftarrow \begin{cases} \frac{1}{f(\mathbf{x})} \mathsf{Eval}(f, \mathbf{x}, [\![\ell_1, \ldots, \ell_m]\!]_\mathrm{T}), & \text{if } y = f_{\neq 0}; \\ \mathsf{Eval}(f, \mathbf{x}, [\![\ell_1, \ldots, \ell_m]\!]_\mathrm{T}), & \text{if } y = f_{=0}; \end{cases}$$

and outputs $\mathsf{ct}_3 - [\![\mu']\!]_\mathrm{T}$ as the recovered message.
Note: *We show that the scheme is correct. By definition (also cf. Construction* 13*),*

$$\ell_j = -\mathbf{s}_j^\mathsf{T}\mathbf{AW}(\mathbf{B}^\mathsf{T} \otimes \mathbf{I}_{n+1})\left(\mathbf{r} \otimes \begin{pmatrix} 1 \\ \mathbf{x} \end{pmatrix}\right) + (\mathbf{s}_j^\mathsf{T}\mathbf{AW} + \mathbf{L}_j^\mathsf{T})\left(\mathbf{B}^\mathsf{T}\mathbf{r} \otimes \begin{pmatrix} 1 \\ \mathbf{x} \end{pmatrix}\right)$$
$$= \mathbf{L}_j^\mathsf{T}\left(\mathbf{B}^\mathsf{T}\mathbf{r} \otimes \begin{pmatrix} 1 \\ \mathbf{x} \end{pmatrix}\right) = \mathbf{L}_j^\mathsf{T}(\mathbf{B}^\mathsf{T}\mathbf{r} \otimes \mathbf{I}_{n+1})\begin{pmatrix} 1 \\ \mathbf{x} \end{pmatrix}.$$

By Lemma 5, if we define $(\mathbf{L}'_1, \ldots, \mathbf{L}'_m) \leftarrow \mathsf{Garble}(f, \mathbf{r}^\mathsf{T}\mathbf{B}\boldsymbol{\alpha}, \mathbf{r}^\mathsf{T}\mathbf{B}\boldsymbol{\beta}; \mathbf{r}^\mathsf{T}\mathbf{B}\mathbf{R})$, *where* $\mathbf{R}$ *is the randomness used to generate* $\mathbf{L}_j$*'s, then*

$$\ell_j = \mathbf{L}_j^\mathsf{T}\left(\mathbf{B}^\mathsf{T}\mathbf{r} \otimes \mathbf{I}_{n+1}\right)\begin{pmatrix}1\\ \mathbf{x}\end{pmatrix} = (\mathbf{L}'_j)^\mathsf{T}\begin{pmatrix}1\\ \mathbf{x}\end{pmatrix} = L'_j(\mathbf{x}).$$

By the correctness of AKGS, we have

$$\mathsf{Eval}(f, \mathbf{x}, \ell_1, \ldots, \ell_m) = \mathbf{r}^\mathsf{T}\mathbf{B}\boldsymbol{\alpha} f(\mathbf{x}) + \mathbf{r}^\mathsf{T}\mathbf{B}\boldsymbol{\beta}.$$

In the two cases where decryption should succeed,

$$\text{if } y = f_{\neq 0}, f(\mathbf{x}) \neq 0\text{:}\quad \mu' = \tfrac{1}{f(\mathbf{x})}(\mathbf{r}^\mathsf{T}\mathbf{B}\boldsymbol{\mu} f(\mathbf{x}) + \mathbf{r}^\mathsf{T}\mathbf{B}\mathbf{0}) = \mathbf{r}^\mathsf{T}\mathbf{B}\boldsymbol{\mu};$$
$$\text{if } y = f_{=0}, f(\mathbf{x}) = 0\text{:}\quad \mu' = \mathbf{r}^\mathsf{T}\mathbf{B}\boldsymbol{\alpha} f(\mathbf{x}) + \mathbf{r}^\mathsf{T}\mathbf{B}\boldsymbol{\mu} = \mathbf{r}^\mathsf{T}\mathbf{B}\boldsymbol{\mu}.$$

Therefore, in both cases, we have $\mathsf{ct}_3 - [\![\mu']\!]_\mathrm{T} = [\![\boldsymbol{\mu}^\mathsf{T}\mathbf{B}^\mathsf{T}\mathbf{r}]\!]_T + g - [\![\mathbf{r}^\mathsf{T}\mathbf{B}\boldsymbol{\mu}]\!]_T = g.$

Minimizing Pairing Operations. The number of pairing operations in the decryption algorithm appears to depend on the garbling size of the policy and the attribute length. It can be reduced to $2k+3$ as follows.[14] Since Eval is linear in the labels, the decryption algorithm can first find $\gamma_1, \ldots, \gamma_m \in \mathbb{Z}_p$ such that

$$\mathsf{Eval}(f, \mathbf{x}, \ell_1, \ldots, \ell_m) = \sum_{j=1}^{m} \gamma_j \ell_j.$$

The computation of $[\![\mu']\!]_\mathrm{T}$ can be rewritten as

$$[\![\mu']\!]_\mathrm{T} = \sum_{j=1}^{m} \gamma_j [\![\ell_j]\!]_\mathrm{T} = \sum_{j=1}^{m} \gamma_j \left(-\mathsf{sk}_{j,1}\mathsf{ct}_2 + \mathsf{sk}_{j,2}\left(\mathsf{ct}_1 \otimes \begin{pmatrix}1\\ \mathbf{x}\end{pmatrix}\right)\right)$$
$$= -\left(\sum_{j=1}^{m} \gamma_j \mathsf{sk}_{j,1}\right)\mathsf{ct}_2 + \left(\sum_{j=1}^{m} \gamma_j \mathsf{sk}_{j,2}\right)\left(\mathbf{I}_{k+1} \otimes \begin{pmatrix}1\\ \mathbf{x}\end{pmatrix}\right)\mathsf{ct}_1.$$

Note that $\mathsf{ct}_1, \mathsf{ct}_2$ consist of $k+1, k+2$ group elements and only these elements (in G_1) take part in pairing. Therefore, the formula above only uses $2k+3$ pairing operations.

There are further optimizations possible, such as appropriately choosing which group of the two source groups to use for the secret key to reduce the cost of exponentiation in decryption. Next, we proceed to the security of our scheme.

---

[14] Syntactically, we use the pairing groups in black box, and there are only $2k+3$ elements in G_1 in a ciphertext and no element in G_1 in a secret key, so the operations can always be regrouped to use at most $2k+3$ pairing operations. The content below provides the concrete regrouping method.

Theorem 18. *Suppose in Construction 17, $MDDH_k$ holds in both G_1 and G_2, and the AKGS is piecewise secure, then the constructed scheme is IND-CPA secure.*

We refer the reader to the full version for the proof.

Acknowledgments. The authors were supported by NSF grants CNS-1528178, CNS-1929901, CNS-1936825 (CAREER), CNS-2026774, a Hellman Fellowship, a JP Morgan AI Research Award, the Defense Advanced Research Projects Agency (DARPA) and Army Research Office (ARO) under Contract No. W911NF-15-C-0236, and a subcontract No. 2017-002 through Galois. The views expressed are those of the authors and do not reflect the official policy or position of the Department of Defense, the National Science Foundation, or the U.S. Government. The authors thank the anonymous reviewers for their valuable comments.

References

1. Abdalla, M., Bourse, F., De Caro, A., Pointcheval, D.: Simple functional encryption schemes for inner products. In: Katz, J. (ed.) PKC 2015. LNCS, vol. 9020, pp. 733–751. Springer, Heidelberg (2015). https://doi.org/10.1007/978-3-662-46447-2_33
2. Agrawal, S., Libert, B., Maitra, M., Titiu, R.: Adaptive simulation security for inner product functional encryption. In: Kiayias, A., Kohlweiss, M., Wallden, P., Zikas, V. (eds.) PKC 2020. LNCS, vol. 12110, pp. 34–64. Springer, Cham (2020). https://doi.org/10.1007/978-3-030-45374-9_2
3. Agrawal, S., Libert, B., Stehlé, D.: Fully secure functional encryption for inner products, from standard assumptions. In: Robshaw, M., Katz, J. (eds.) CRYPTO 2016. LNCS, vol. 9816, pp. 333–362. Springer, Heidelberg (2016). https://doi.org/10.1007/978-3-662-53015-3_12
4. Agrawal, S., Yamada, S.: Optimal broadcast encryption from pairings and LWE. In: Canteaut, A., Ishai, Y. (eds.) EUROCRYPT 2020. LNCS, vol. 12105, pp. 13–43. Springer, Cham (2020). https://doi.org/10.1007/978-3-030-45721-1_2
5. Attrapadung, N.: Dual system encryption framework in prime-order groups via computational pair encodings. In: Cheon, J.H., Takagi, T. (eds.) ASIACRYPT 2016. LNCS, vol. 10032, pp. 591–623. Springer, Heidelberg (2016). https://doi.org/10.1007/978-3-662-53890-6_20
6. Attrapadung, N., Hanaoka, G., Yamada, S.: Conversions among several classes of predicate encryption and applications to ABE with various compactness tradeoffs. In: Iwata, T., Cheon, J.H. (eds.) ASIACRYPT 2015. LNCS, vol. 9452, pp. 575–601. Springer, Heidelberg (2015). https://doi.org/10.1007/978-3-662-48797-6_24
7. Attrapadung, N., Libert, B., de Panafieu, E.: Expressive key-policy attribute-based encryption with constant-size ciphertexts. In: Catalano, D., Fazio, N., Gennaro, R., Nicolosi, A. (eds.) PKC 2011. LNCS, vol. 6571, pp. 90–108. Springer, Heidelberg (2011). https://doi.org/10.1007/978-3-642-19379-8_6
8. Boneh, D., et al.: Fully key-homomorphic encryption, arithmetic circuit ABE and compact garbled circuits. In: Nguyen, P.Q., Oswald, E. (eds.) EUROCRYPT 2014. LNCS, vol. 8441, pp. 533–556. Springer, Heidelberg (2014). https://doi.org/10.1007/978-3-642-55220-5_30

9. Cramer, R., Shoup, V.: Universal hash proofs and a paradigm for adaptive chosen ciphertext secure public-key encryption. In: Knudsen, L.R. (ed.) EUROCRYPT 2002. LNCS, vol. 2332, pp. 45–64. Springer, Heidelberg (2002). https://doi.org/10.1007/3-540-46035-7_4
10. Datta, P., Dutta, R., Mukhopadhyay, S.: Functional encryption for inner product with full function privacy. In: Cheng, C.-M., Chung, K.-M., Persiano, G., Yang, B.-Y. (eds.) PKC 2016. LNCS, vol. 9614, pp. 164–195. Springer, Heidelberg (2016). https://doi.org/10.1007/978-3-662-49384-7_7
11. Emura, K., Miyaji, A., Nomura, A., Omote, K., Soshi, M.: A ciphertext-policy attribute-based encryption scheme with constant ciphertext length. In: Bao, F., Li, H., Wang, G. (eds.) ISPEC 2009. LNCS, vol. 5451, pp. 13–23. Springer, Heidelberg (2009). https://doi.org/10.1007/978-3-642-00843-6_2
12. Escala, A., Herold, G., Kiltz, E., Ràfols, C., Villar, J.: An algebraic framework for Diffie-Hellman assumptions. In: Canetti, R., Garay, J.A. (eds.) CRYPTO 2013. LNCS, vol. 8043, pp. 129–147. Springer, Heidelberg (2013). https://doi.org/10.1007/978-3-642-40084-1_8
13. Gong, J., Wee, H.: Adaptively secure ABE for DFA from k-Lin and more. In: Canteaut, A., Ishai, Y. (eds.) EUROCRYPT 2020. LNCS, vol. 12107, pp. 278–308. Springer, Cham (2020). https://doi.org/10.1007/978-3-030-45727-3_10
14. Ishai, Y., Wee, H.: Partial garbling schemes and their applications. In: Esparza, J., Fraigniaud, P., Husfeldt, T., Koutsoupias, E. (eds.) ICALP 2014. LNCS, vol. 8572, pp. 650–662. Springer, Heidelberg (2014). https://doi.org/10.1007/978-3-662-43948-7_54
15. Kowalczyk, L., Wee, H.: Compact adaptively secure ABE for NC^1 from k-Lin. In: Ishai, Y., Rijmen, V. (eds.) EUROCRYPT 2019. LNCS, vol. 11476, pp. 3–33. Springer, Cham (2019). https://doi.org/10.1007/978-3-030-17653-2_1
16. Lewko, A., Okamoto, T., Sahai, A., Takashima, K., Waters, B.: Fully secure functional encryption: attribute based encryption and (hierarchical) inner product encryption. In: Gilbert, H. (ed.) EUROCRYPT 2010. LNCS, vol. 6110, pp. 62–91. Springer, Heidelberg (2010). https://doi.org/10.1007/978-3-642-13190-5_4
17. Lin, H., Luo, J.: Compact adaptively secure ABE from k-Lin: beyond NC^1 and towards NL. In: Canteaut, A., Ishai, Y. (eds.) EUROCRYPT 2020. LNCS, vol. 12107, pp. 247–277. Springer, Cham (2020). https://doi.org/10.1007/978-3-030-45727-3_9
18. Lin, H., Luo, J.: Succinct and adaptively secure ABE for arithmetic branching programs from k-Lin. Cryptology ePrint Archive (2020). (to appear)
19. Lin, H., Vaikuntanathan, V.: Indistinguishability obfuscation from DDH-like assumptions on constant-degree graded encodings. In: Dinur, I. (ed.) 57th FOCS, pp. 11–20. IEEE Computer Society Press, October 2016. https://doi.org/10.1109/FOCS.2016.11
20. Nisan, N.: Lower bounds for non-commutative computation (extended abstract). In: 23rd ACM STOC, pp. 410–418. ACM Press, May 1991. https://doi.org/10.1145/103418.103462
21. Sahai, A., Waters, B.: Fuzzy identity-based encryption. In: Cramer, R. (ed.) EUROCRYPT 2005. LNCS, vol. 3494, pp. 457–473. Springer, Heidelberg (2005). https://doi.org/10.1007/11426639_27
22. Takashima, K.: Expressive attribute-based encryption with constant-size ciphertexts from the decisional linear assumption. In: Abdalla, M., De Prisco, R. (eds.) SCN 2014. LNCS, vol. 8642, pp. 298–317. Springer, Cham (2014). https://doi.org/10.1007/978-3-319-10879-7_17

23. Tomida, J., Attrapadung, N.: Unbounded dynamic predicate compositions in ABE from standard assumptions. Cryptology ePrint Archive, Report 2020/231 (2020). https://eprint.iacr.org/2020/231
24. Waters, B.: Dual system encryption: realizing fully secure IBE and HIBE under simple assumptions. In: Halevi, S. (ed.) CRYPTO 2009. LNCS, vol. 5677, pp. 619–636. Springer, Heidelberg (2009). https://doi.org/10.1007/978-3-642-03356-8_36
25. Wee, H.: Dual system encryption via predicate encodings. In: Lindell, Y. (ed.) TCC 2014. LNCS, vol. 8349, pp. 616–637. Springer, Heidelberg (2014). https://doi.org/10.1007/978-3-642-54242-8_26
26. Wee, H.: Attribute-hiding predicate encryption in bilinear groups, revisited. In: Kalai, Y., Reyzin, L. (eds.) TCC 2017. LNCS, vol. 10677, pp. 206–233. Springer, Cham (2017). https://doi.org/10.1007/978-3-319-70500-2_8
27. Yamada, S., Attrapadung, N., Hanaoka, G., Kunihiro, N.: A framework and compact constructions for non-monotonic attribute-based encryption. In: Krawczyk, H. (ed.) PKC 2014. LNCS, vol. 8383, pp. 275–292. Springer, Heidelberg (2014). https://doi.org/10.1007/978-3-642-54631-0_16
28. Zhang, K., et al.: Practical and efficient attribute-based encryption with constant-size ciphertexts in outsourced verifiable computation. In: Chen, X., Wang, X., Huang, X. (eds.) ASIACCS 2016, pp. 269–279. ACM Press, May/Jun 2016

Inner-Product Functional Encryption with Fine-Grained Access Control

Michel Abdalla[1,2](✉), Dario Catalano[3], Romain Gay[4], and Bogdan Ursu[5]

[1] DIENS, École normale supérieure, CNRS, PSL University, Paris, France
michel.abdalla@ens.fr
[2] Inria, Paris, France
[3] Dipartimento di Matematica e Informatica, Università di Catania, Catania, Italy
catalano@dmi.unict.it
[4] IBM Zurich, Zurich, Switzerland
romain.rgay@gmail.com
[5] Department of Computer Science, ETH Zurich, Zurich, Switzerland
bogdan.ursu@inf.ethz.ch

Abstract. We construct new functional encryption schemes that combine the access control functionality of attribute-based encryption with the possibility of performing linear operations on the encrypted data. While such a primitive could be easily realized from fully fledged functional encryption schemes, what makes our result interesting is the fact that our schemes simultaneously achieve all the following properties. They are public-key, efficient and can be proved secure under standard and well established assumptions (such as LWE or pairings). Furthermore, security is guaranteed in the setting where adversaries are allowed to get functional keys that decrypt the challenge ciphertext. Our first results are two functional encryption schemes for the family of functions that allow users to embed policies (expressed by monotone span programs) in the encrypted data, so that one can generate functional keys to compute weighted sums on the latter. Both schemes are pairing-based and quite generic: they combine the ALS functional encryption scheme for inner products from Crypto 2016 with any attribute-based encryption schemes relying on the dual-system encryption methodology. As an additional bonus, they yield simple and elegant multi-input extensions essentially for free, thereby broadening the set of applications for such schemes. Multi-input is a particularly desirable feature in our setting, since it gives a finer access control over the encrypted data, by allowing users to associate different access policies to different parts of the encrypted data. Our second result builds identity-based functional encryption for inner products from lattices. This is achieved by carefully combining existing IBE schemes from lattices with adapted, LWE-based, variants of ALS. We point out to intrinsic technical bottlenecks to obtain richer forms of access control from lattices. From a conceptual point of view, all our results can be seen as further evidence that more expressive forms of functional encryption can be realized under standard assumptions and with little computational overhead.

S. Moriai and H. Wang (Eds.): ASIACRYPT 2020, LNCS 12493, pp. 467–497, 2020.
https://doi.org/10.1007/978-3-030-64840-4_16

1 Introduction

Public-key encryption allows the owner of a secret key sk to decrypt any ciphertext created with respect to a corresponding public key pk. At the same time, without sk, one should not be able to extract any information whatsoever about the encrypted plaintext. This all-or-nothing feature is becoming restrictive nowadays as, in many applications, a much more fine grained access control to data is required. Functional encryption addresses this need by providing an encryption mechanism where decryption keys are associated with functions. Specifically, given a ciphertext $\mathsf{Enc}(m)$ and a secret key sk_f associated to some function f, the holder of sk_f learns $f(m)$ and nothing else.

Security for functional encryption is formalized via a variant of the standard indistinguishability notion. In a nutshell, this notion states that an adversary who is allowed to see secret keys corresponding to functions $f_1, \dots f_n$ should not be able to say which of the challenge messages m_0 or m_1 has been encrypted, as long as $f_i(m_0) = f_i(m_1)$, for all i. This indistinguishability notion has been proposed in [25,50] and shown inadequate for certain, somewhat complex, functionalities. These authors also suggested an alternative, simulation based, security notion that however turns out to be impossible to achieve for general functionalities without introducing additional restrictions. See [25,50] for details.

Since its introduction, functional encryption has attracted a lot of interest. Known results can be broadly categorized as focusing on (1) feasibility results for general functionalities, and on (2) concrete, efficient realizations for restricted functionalities of practical interest. Constructions of the first type are all horrendously inefficient. Also, they either rely on quite unstable assumptions (e.g. indistinguishability obfuscation) or impose severe restrictions on the number of secret keys that can be issued. Constructions of the second type, on the other hand, are known only for the case of linear functions and quadratic functions. Over the last few years, significant research efforts have been devoted to the quest of improving these constructions along different directions. For the case of the inner-product functionality (IPFE) [3], this meant, for instance, improved security guarantees (e.g. [4,11,20,26]), function hiding realizations (e.g. [22,32,33]), multi-input extensions (e.g. [5,7]), decentralized schemes (e.g. [1,2,30,46]), unbounded-size vectors (e.g. [34,54]) and specialized variants (e.g. [19]). For the case of quadratic functions, current schemes are limited to [18,35] in the public-key setting. Note that FE for inner products, which is the focus of this work, can be used a building block to obtain FE for quadratic functions. This fact, implicit in [18], is made explicit in [35] and in the private-key variants [14,47].

In spite of these efforts, only a few convincing practical applications of the primitive have been proposed so far. Notable examples include the recent non interactive protocol for hidden-weight coin flips from [31], a practical construction of function-hiding inner product FE with applications such as in biometric authentication, nearest-neighbor search on encrypted data in [45], an application of functional encryption for quadratic functions for performing private inference on encrypted data in [51].

A possible explanation for this is that, behind its charming theoretical appearance, functional encryption hides a fragile and potentially dangerous nature: each new released secret key inherently leaks information. This becomes particularly painful for the case of inner products, as, when encrypting plaintexts of length, say, n, holding n secret keys allows, in general, to recover the full plaintext completely. While this might seem inherent in the nature of IPFE, one might wonder if additional measures might be put in place to reduce leakage and make the primitive more appealing for applications. Think for instance of the case of a medical database. To preserve privacy while maintaining the possibility of performing simple descriptive statistics (such as the weighted mean) on the data, one might decide to encrypt the database using IPFE. A drawback of this solution, however, is that the confidentiality of the whole database is compromised if a sufficiently large number of different keys is released. This is problematic since this threshold might be easy to reach when many users access the database.

A natural way to limit the inherent information leakage of existing IPFE schemes would be to use FE primitives with more sophisticated functionalities. Ideally, this primitive should allow to embed access policies in the (encrypted) data while allowing to compute weighted sums on the latter. More precisely, each key should allow to obtain the desired inner product only when some appropriate access policy is satisfied. Going back to our medical example, this means that the confidentiality of a *particular* database entry would be compromised only if sufficiently many different keys satisfying the ciphertext policy associated with that entry are released.

Another way to look at the question, is providing additional security guarantees with respect to basic identity or attribute based encryption schemes. These typically control who is authorized to decrypt the data. Still, once the data is accessed, no additional control is possible: authorized users get the full information, while others get nothing. In this sense, it is natural to consider encryption primitives that, beyond access control, also permit to more carefully tune the information leakage.

Notice that the mechanisms above are easy to realize if one is willing to resort to functional encryption schemes for general functionalities. The trouble with this is that such a solution would be of little (if any) practical interest. Our goal, on the other hand, is to develop a scheme that implements the features above while retaining as much as possible all the nice properties of currently known IPFEs.

This motivates the following question.

Is it possible to develop an efficient, public-key, functional encryption scheme that allows users both to embed access policies in the encrypted data and to generate decryption keys to compute inner products on the data?

A Trivial Generic Approach. Since ABE and IPFE are both well-studied primitives, the first natural question is whether we can easily combine existing schemes to achieve our target notion. In the target scheme, each ciphertext is associated with a predicate P and encrypts a vector $\boldsymbol{x}$. Each functional decryption key $\mathsf{sk}_{\boldsymbol{y},\mathsf{att}}$ is associated with an attribute att and a vector $\boldsymbol{y}$. Decryption recovers $\langle \boldsymbol{x}, \boldsymbol{y} \rangle$ if $\mathsf{P}(\mathsf{att}) = 1$. If it is not the case, no information about $\boldsymbol{x}$ should be revealed.

Now, consider the approach of encrypting a plaintext via an IPFE and then encrypting the resulting ciphertext via the ABE. This is not secure against collusions as, once the outer ciphertext is decrypted, the inner one becomes completely independent from the ABE. To see why, assume we have keys for $\mathsf{sk}_{\boldsymbol{y}_0,\mathsf{att}_0}$ and $\mathsf{sk}_{\boldsymbol{y}_1,\mathsf{att}_0}$ and a ciphertext ct, encrypting a vector $\boldsymbol{x}$ under the predicate P such that $\mathsf{P}(\mathsf{att}_0) = 1$ and $\mathsf{P}(\mathsf{att}_1) = 0$. The trivial solution allows to use $\mathsf{sk}_{\boldsymbol{y}_0,\mathsf{att}_0}$ to obtain the original IPFE ciphertext, which can then be used with $\mathsf{sk}_{\boldsymbol{y}_1,\mathsf{att}_1}$ to obtain $\langle \boldsymbol{x}, \boldsymbol{y}_1 \rangle$ (even though we should only have been able to compute $\langle \boldsymbol{x}, \boldsymbol{y}_0 \rangle$). This means that mix-and-match attacks are possible. In fact, there seems to be no trivial solution to this problem.

Another Trivial Generic Approach. One other approach to limit the leakage is by encrypting various databases under a different IPFE public key for every recipient. Apart from the fact that this leads to a prohibitive blow-up in size, it would not be possible to aggregate data between different databases. Our solution has neither of these limitations and ensures that the ciphertext size is independent of the number of potential recipients.

Our Contributions. In this paper, we construct schemes for inner-product functional encryption with fine-grained access control. Our realizations are both efficient and provably secure under standard and well-established assumptions.

The key distinguishing feature of our constructions is that they can be proved secure in the, technically more challenging, setting where the adversary is allowed to (get keys to) decrypt the challenge ciphertext. Let us explain this more in detail. Popular specializations of functional encryption (such as identity-based encryption (IBE) [23,53] and attribute-based encryption [42,52]) are ones where the message is interpreted as a pair (I, m), where m is the actual message (often called the "payload") and I is a string, referred to as the index (or in the context of ciphertext-policy ABE [21], a predicate), that can be either public or private. For these schemes, confidentiality of the payload is guaranteed as long as no decryption keys associated with attributes that satisfy the predicate are issued. In our case, we still guarantee a meaningful security notion when keys which allow users to decrypt the payload are issued.

Private-index schemes also provide meaningful security guarantees when keys that decrypt are leaked, namely, they still hide the index in that case. However, as opposed to public-index schemes, for which we have constructions for all circuits from standard assumptions [24,40], such schemes can only handle restrictive policies, that are expressed by orthogonality testing (also referred to as inner-product encryption [44]), or assume a weaker security property, called *weak attribute hiding*, which limits the set of keys that the adversary can get. Namely, this property dictates that the adversary is only allowed to ask secret keys corresponding to functions that cannot be used to decrypt the challenge ciphertext. As observed in [41], a fully attribute-hiding predicate encryption for circuits would bring us tantalizing close to getting indistinguishability obfuscation, which explains why they are much harder to realize in practice.

We consider both public-index schemes where policies are expressive (they can be expressed by monotone span programs, which capture Boolean formulas), and private-index schemes for orthogonality testing (which captures constant depth Boolean formulas). In both settings, we permit a fine-tuned access to the payload, which, from a technical point of view, involve providing security even when the adversary obtains keys that decrypt the challenge ciphertext (even in the public-index case).

IP-FE WITH FINE-GRAINED ACCESS CONTROL FROM PAIRINGS. Our first main result is the construction of functional encryption schemes for the family of functions that allows users to embed policies on the encrypted data, so that one can generate decryption keys that computes weighted sums on the latter. More precisely, in our schemes, each ciphertext is associated with a predicate P and encrypts a (small norm) vector $\boldsymbol{x}$. Each functional decryption key is associated with an attribute att and a (small norm) vector $\boldsymbol{y}$. Decryption recovers $\langle \boldsymbol{x}, \boldsymbol{y} \rangle$ if att satisfies P. If this is not the case, security guarantees that no information about $\boldsymbol{x}$ is revealed.

Our constructions are quite generic and show that it is possible to combine existing pairing-based attribute-based encryption with the IPFE from [11]. Our construction relies on any attribute-based encryption that uses the dual-system encryption methodology [56]. In particular, we provide a modular framework that turns any ABE that supports the class of predicates $\mathcal{P}$ into a functional encryption scheme for the functions described by an attribute $\mathsf{att} \in \mathcal{U}$ and a vector $\boldsymbol{y}$, that given as input a vector $\boldsymbol{x}$ and a predicate $\mathsf{P} \in \mathcal{P}$, outputs $\langle \boldsymbol{x}, \boldsymbol{y} \rangle$ if $\mathsf{P}(\mathsf{att}) - 1$ and $\perp$ otherwise. For correctness to hold we require that both $\boldsymbol{x}$ and $\boldsymbol{y}$ are vectors of polynomially-bounded dimension and norm. We consider both the case where the policy P associated with a ciphertext is public, or at the contrary, remains hidden. As explained previously, leveraging state of the art pairing-based ABE, we obtain an FE for $\mathcal{P}$ described by monotone span programs, and an FE for $\mathcal{P}$ for any constant depth formula, where the formula itself remains hidden.

From a technical point of view, our first realization combines the IPFE from [11] with any predicate encoding for prime-order pairing groups. In a nutshell, predicate encodings [16,57] are a one-time secure, private key, statistical variant of ABE that are much simpler to construct and to deal with. The resulting construction achieves simulation security, but only in a selective sense, and unfortunately this happens to be the case even if the underlying building blocks achieve adaptive security. Informally, this comes from the fact that our security model explicitly allows the adversary to (get keys to) decrypt the challenge ciphertext. Technically, this means that, throughout the security proof, only functional decryption keys associated with pairs $(\mathsf{att}, \boldsymbol{y})$ for which $\mathcal{P}^*(\mathsf{att}) = 0$ can be turned into semi-functional ones (here $\mathcal{P}^*$ denotes the predicate chosen by the adversary for the challenge ciphertext). Following the dual-system encryption methodology, semi-functional keys refer to keys that cannot decrypt successfully the challenge ciphertext, but can decrypt correctly any other honestly generated ciphertext. Keys for which $\mathcal{P}^*(\mathsf{att}) = 1$ cannot be turned semi-functional as otherwise they would fail to (correctly) decrypt the challenge ciphertext. Such a decryption issue does not arise in typical ABE settings, as their security model explicitly prevents the adversary to decrypt the challenge ciphertext.

Our second construction circumvents this difficulty and obtains adaptive security by generalizing the techniques introduced in [49], later improved in [28] in the context of fully-hiding predicate encryption for inner product testing. Indeed, in fully-hiding predicate encryption, the proof also has to explicitly deal with the decryption issue sketched above. To do so, we introduce the notion of function encoding, which is the analogue of predicate encoding for functional encryption. Recall that predicate encodings, introduced in [16,57], are a "dumbed-down" version of ABE, and provide a framework to extend the dual system encryption methodology introduced by [56] in the context of adaptively-secure IBE to a broad class of ABE, including inner product testing, or Boolean formulas. In our case, we use the abstraction of function encoding to generalize the information-theoretic argument from [28] to capture a broad class of functional encryption, including inner-product FE with access control expressed by inner-product testing, Boolean formulas, and more.

Similarly to predicate encoding, which has received significant interest (particularly as its more general form referred to as Conditional-Disclosure of Secret, e.g. [15,37,39,48]), we believe the notion of function encoding could be interesting on its own.

In a nutshell, functional encodings enhance a more sophisticated information theoretic argument than traditional Dual System Encryption, where secret keys are switched to a semi-functional mode that still allows them to decrypt the challenge ciphertext, but yield different information than normally generated secret keys. Indeed, in the security proof, the ciphertext will encode the original message $\boldsymbol{x}_0$, but also the message $\boldsymbol{x}_1$, where the pair $(\boldsymbol{x}_0, \boldsymbol{x}_1)$ is chosen by the adversary during the indistinguishability game. Normal keys will decrypt with respect to the message $\boldsymbol{x}_0$, whereas the semi-functional keys will decrypt with respect to the message $\boldsymbol{x}_1$, thereby successfully proving security.

Identity-Based inner-product FE from lattices. Our second main result is the construction of two identity-based inner-product FE (IB-IPFE) from the LWE assumption[1]. Both schemes combine existing LWE-based IBE with the LWE-based inner-product FE from [11]. The first one uses the IBE from [38], where the public key described a trapdoor function for which it is hard to sample short preimage. Given the trapdoor—the master key of the IBE—it is possible to efficiently compute a short preimage of any target image. Each identity id yielding a different image, the corresponding preimage, a matrix of short coefficients $\boldsymbol{M}_{\mathsf{id}}$, defines the user secret key for id. As it turns out, to produce functional decryption keys associated with identity id and vector $\boldsymbol{y}$, we can simply give a projection $\boldsymbol{M}_{\mathsf{id}}\boldsymbol{y}$. We prove this remarkably simple scheme adaptively-secure in

[1] We stress that both schemes support exponentially large input domains, as for existing LWE-based inner-product FE schemes.

the random oracle model using the security argument of [38] to handle all functional decryption keys that do not decrypt the challenge ciphertext, whereas we use the proof techniques of [11] to take care of all keys that decrypt the challenge ciphertexts.

Our second constructions relies on the IBE from [10], where the public key can be used to derive an identity-based public key $\mathsf{pk}_{\mathsf{id}}$ for any identity id. The public key $\mathsf{pk}_{\mathsf{id}}$ describes a trapdoor function, for which, as in [38], it is hard to compute short preimages. A fixed target image, which belongs to the range of all the trapdoor functions $\mathsf{pk}_{\mathsf{id}}$ is made public. The user secret key for id is a short preimage of the fixed target image, for the function $\mathsf{pk}_{\mathsf{id}}$. Once again, user secret keys happen to be matrices, which can be projected to obtain functional decryption keys $\mathsf{sk}_{\mathsf{id},\boldsymbol{y}}$ and get an IB-IPFE.

As a bonus, our schemes inherit the anonymity property of the underlying IBE, that is, the identity associated with a ciphertext remains hidden as long as no functional decryption key that decrypts is issued.

Richer access control from lattices. The puncturing technique that is used in the security proof of [10] has been generalized to obtain ABE for all circuits in [24]. However, there are intrinsic technical limitations in our proof strategy which prevent from extending our scheme to the ABE case. In particular, to use the security argument of the IPFE from [11] as part of our own security proof, we rely on a lazy sampling argument: to obtain a functional decryption key $\mathsf{sk}_{\mathsf{id}^\star,\boldsymbol{y}}$ where $\mathsf{id}^\star$ is the identity of the challenge ciphertext, we first sample a matrix with short coefficients $\boldsymbol{M}_{\mathsf{id}^\star}$ and set the fixed public target image such that this short matrix is a preimage of the target image by the function described by the public key $\mathsf{pk}_{\mathsf{id}^\star}$. Concretely, the target image is a matrix $\boldsymbol{T}$, the public key $\mathsf{pk}_{\mathsf{id}} = \boldsymbol{A}_{\mathsf{id}^\star}$ is also a matrix, and we want $\boldsymbol{A}_{\mathsf{id}^\star}\boldsymbol{M}_{\mathsf{id}^\star} = \boldsymbol{T}$, where the matrices have matching dimensions. We can first sample $\boldsymbol{T}$, then use the trapdoor to compute $\boldsymbol{M}_{\mathsf{id}^\star}$ satisfying the previous equation, but we can also first sample a short $\boldsymbol{M}_{\mathsf{id}^\star}$, and then set $\boldsymbol{T} = \boldsymbol{A}_{\mathsf{id}^\star}\boldsymbol{M}_{\mathsf{id}^\star}$. This produces identically distributed matrices, and in the latter case, we can produce $\boldsymbol{M}_{\mathsf{id}^\star}$ without knowing the trapdoor, which is necessary in the security proof. The matrix $\boldsymbol{M}_{\mathsf{id}^\star}$ will actually correspond to the master secret key of the IPFE of [11]. The key $\mathsf{sk}_{\mathsf{id}^\star,\boldsymbol{y}}$ is $\boldsymbol{M}_{\mathsf{id}^\star}\boldsymbol{y}$, as described above, which corresponds to a functional decryption key for $\boldsymbol{y}$ in the scheme from [11]. However, this lazy sampling argument is inherently limited to the case where only one attribute (here, identity) satisfies the predicate (here, identity) of the challenge ciphertext. In the case of ABE, there can be multiple such attributes for a given predicate. We leave combining ABE for circuits with inner-product FE as a challenging open problem.

Multi-input extensions. As a final contribution, we show how to generalize our pairing-based IP-FE scheme to the multi input setting. Our realization is rather generic in the sense that it converts any single input construction of the primitive, satisfying few additional properties, into a multi input scheme supporting the same class of functionalities. Specifically, the required properties are that (1) the underlying IP-FE is pairings-based (2) its encryption and key generation algorithms can take as input large norm vectors and (3) its encryption algorithm enjoys linearly homomorphic properties. Recall that, to guarantee efficient decryption, our parings based constructions require that both the plaintext vectors $\boldsymbol{x}$ and the function vector $\boldsymbol{y}$ have small norm. What we require now is that, if one is willing to give up efficient decryption, the small norm condition can be relaxed (i.e. decryption returns an encoding of the output rather than the output itself).

On a technical level the transformation follows very closely the generic single-input to multi-input IP-FE transform by Abdalla *et al.* [5,7]. In this sense, we believe that the interesting contribution is the primitive itself. Indeed, information leakage is even more problematic in the multi input setting, as here users can combine their inputs with many different ciphertexts coming from other users. In the case of n users this easily leads to an information leakage that completely destroys security. While countermeasures could be put in place to limit the encryption and key queries that the adversary is allowed to ask, by resorting for instance, to the notion of multi-client IPFE, where ciphertexts are associated with time-stamps, and only ciphertext with matching time-stamps can be combined (e.g. [30]) we believe that our proposed primitive provides a more general and versatile solution to the problem.

Our construction allows users to compute weighted sums on encrypted vectors each associated with a possibly *different* access structure. In our medical example above, this might be used to add even more granularity to the access control of data. That is, some users may obtain keys that can compute statistics on some, but not all, the encrypted data. For instance, doctors in a hospital may be able to compute on a different set of encrypted data then employees of a health insurance company. Moreover, multi-input allows users to aggregate data coming from different sources.

Related Works. We emphasize that the primitive considered in this paper is natural, and as such, it has also been considered in previous works, either implicitly or explicitly.

In [34], Dufour-Sans and Pointcheval describe an identity-based functional encryption scheme for inner products as a byproduct of their realization of unbounded IPFE with succinct keys. Their construction is proven selectively secure in the random-oracle model based on the standard decisional bilinear Diffie-Hellman assumption. Compared to their construction, our pairing-based schemes provide support for significantly richer functionalities and are proven secure in the standard model.

In prior works [13,43], the authors define a so-called partially-hiding FE allowing for the computation on two inputs (x, y), where the input x is seen as a public attribute and the other one, y, remains hidden. The construction of [13] supports degree-2 computation on the private input y, and degree-1 computation on the public input x. Its security rely on the generic bilinear group model. In [43], functional secret keys support the computation of degree-2 polynomials on the private input, as in [13], but it supports NC_0 computation on the public input. As an additional benefit, the security of their construction rely on a standard assumption on pairing groups (namely, SXDH). In an early version of their eprint

[36] dating back to 2019, Jain, Lin and Sahai provided a partially-hiding FE allowing for degree-2 computation on the private input, and NC_1 computation on the public inputs; relying on the SXDH assumption. All of these schemes are in the secret-key setting. Our scheme has the advantage to be public-key, although our techniques inherently rely on the linearity of the inner-product functionality. All of those works focus on simulation, selective security, and use partially-hiding FE in the context of providing indistinguishability obfuscation.

In [29], Chen, Zang and Yiu propose a construction of attribute-based functional encryption for inner products. Like ours, their construction is pairing-based, but it is less generic, and relies on three decisional assumptions on bilinear groups of composite order $N = p_1 p_2 p_3$ (p_1, p_2, p_3 distinct primes), which are less efficient than prime-order groups. Our realizations, on the other hand, build generically from any dual system encryption-based ABE. In terms of security, their construction guarantees indistinguishability against adaptive adversaries in the standard model, but only in the weaker setting discussed above, where keys that decrypt cannot be leaked to the adversary, which does not capture the essence of the notion that we achieve, since it does not offer any additional security guarantees with respect to standard ABE schemes. We recall that all our schemes explicitly allow the adversary to get functional keys to decrypt the challenge ciphertext. Also, while our first scheme is only selectively secure, it achieves this in the stronger simulation setting. Finally, no extensions to the multi-input case are considered in [29].

In [58], Wee builds partially hiding predicate encryption schemes which *simultaneously* generalize existing attribute-based and inner-product predicate encryption schemes. Although his constructions support a larger class of policies than our constructions, the decryptor still has access to the payload message (a KEM key in this case) once the access policy is satisfied or to a uniformly random value otherwise. We see it as an interesting open problem to extend his work to also permit selective computations over the payload message when the access policy is satisfied.

Organization. Section 2 recalls some standard notation together with the syntax and security definitions for functional encryption schemes. Section 3 presents our constructions of inner-product FE with fine-grained access control from pairings. Section 4 describes our first lattice-based construction of identity-based functional encryption in the random-oracle model. In the full version [6], we also describe a lattice-based standard-model construction of identity-based functional encryption and present a multi-input extension of our schemes.

2 Preliminaries

Notation. We denote with $\lambda \in \mathbb{N}$ a security parameter. A *probabilistic polynomial time* (PPT) algorithm $\mathcal{A}$ is a randomized algorithm for which there exists a polynomial $p(\cdot)$ such that for every input x the running time of $\mathcal{A}(x)$ is bounded by $p(|x|)$. We say that a function $\varepsilon : \mathbb{N} \rightarrow \mathbb{R}^+$ is *negligible* if for every positive polynomial $p(\lambda)$ there exists $\lambda_0 \in \mathbb{N}$ such that for all $\lambda > \lambda_0$: $\varepsilon(\lambda) < 1/p(\lambda)$.

If S is a set, $x \leftarrow_{\mathrm{R}} S$ denotes the process of selecting x uniformly at random in S. If $\mathcal{A}$ is a probabilistic algorithm, $y \leftarrow_{\mathrm{R}} \mathcal{A}(\cdot)$ denotes the process of running $\mathcal{A}$ on some appropriate input and assigning its output to y. For a positive integer n, we denote by $[n]$ the set $\{1, \ldots, n\}$. We denote vectors $\boldsymbol{x} = (x_i)$ and matrices $\mathbf{A} = (a_{i,j})$ in bold. For a set S (resp. vector $\boldsymbol{x}$) $|S|$ (resp. $|\boldsymbol{x}|$) denotes its cardinality (resp. number of entries). Also, given two vectors $\boldsymbol{x}$ and $\boldsymbol{x}'$ we denote by $\boldsymbol{x} \| \boldsymbol{x}'$ their concatenation. By $\equiv$, we denote the equality of statistical distributions, and for any $\varepsilon > 0$, we denote by $\approx_\varepsilon$ the ε-statistical difference of two distributions. For any $x \in \mathbb{R}$, we denote by $\lfloor x \rfloor$ the largest integer less than or equal to x, while for any $z \in [0, 1]$, we denote by $\lfloor z \rceil$ the closest integer to z. For all $\boldsymbol{a}_i \in \mathbb{Z}_p^{n_i}$ for $i \in [n]$, we denote by $(\boldsymbol{a}_1, \ldots, \boldsymbol{a}_n) \in \mathbb{Z}_p^{\sum_{i \in [n]} n_i}$ a column vector, and by $(\boldsymbol{a}_1^\top | \cdots | \boldsymbol{a}_n^\top) \in \mathbb{Z}_p^{1 \times \sum_{i \in [n]} n_i}$ a row vector.

2.1 Pairing Groups

Let PGGen be a PPT algorithm that on input the security parameter 1^λ, returns a description $\mathcal{PG} = (\mathbb{G}_1, \mathbb{G}_2, \mathbb{G}_T, p, P_1, P_2, e)$ where for all $s \in \{1, 2, T\}$, $\mathbb{G}_s$ is an additive cyclic group of order p for a 2λ-bit prime p. $\mathbb{G}_1$ and $\mathbb{G}_2$ are generated by P_1 and P_2 respectively, and $e : \mathbb{G}_1 \times \mathbb{G}_2 \to \mathbb{G}_T$ is an efficiently computable (non-degenerate) bilinear map. Define $P_T := e(P_1, P_2)$, which is a generator of $\mathbb{G}_T$, of order p. We use implicit representation of group elements. For $s \in \{1, 2, T\}$ and $a \in \mathbb{Z}_p$, define $[a]_s = a \cdot P_s \in \mathbb{G}_s$ as the implicit representation of a in $\mathbb{G}_s$. More generally, for a matrix $\mathbf{A} = (a_{ij}) \in \mathbb{Z}_p^{n \times m}$ we define $[\mathbf{A}]_s$ as the implicit representation of $\mathbf{A}$ in $\mathbb{G}_s$:

$$[\mathbf{A}]_s := \begin{pmatrix} a_{11} \cdot P_s \ldots a_{1m} \cdot P_s \\ \\ a_{n1} \cdot P_s \ldots a_{nm} \cdot P_s \end{pmatrix} \in \mathbb{G}_s^{n \times m}.$$

Given $[a]_1$ and $[b]_2$, one can efficiently compute $[a \cdot b]_T$ using the pairing e. For matrices $\mathbf{A}$ and $\mathbf{B}$ of matching dimensions, define $e([\mathbf{A}]_1, [\mathbf{B}]_2) := [\mathbf{AB}]_T$. For any matrix $\mathbf{A}, \mathbf{B} \in \mathbb{Z}_p^{n \times m}$, any group $s \in \{1, 2, T\}$, we denote by $[\mathbf{A}]_s + [\mathbf{B}]_s = [\mathbf{A} + \mathbf{B}]_s$.

For any prime p, we define the following distributions. The DDH distribution over $\mathbb{Z}_p^2$: $a \leftarrow_{\mathrm{R}} \mathbb{Z}_p$, outputs $\boldsymbol{a} := \binom{1}{a}$. The DLIN distribution over $\mathbb{Z}_p^{3 \times 2}$: $a, b \leftarrow_{\mathrm{R}} \mathbb{Z}_p$, outputs $\mathbf{A} := \begin{pmatrix} a & 0 \\ 0 & b \\ 1 & 1 \end{pmatrix}$.

Definition 2.1 (DDH assumption). *For any adversary $\mathcal{A}$, any group $s \in \{1, 2, T\}$ and any security parameter λ, let*

$$\mathsf{Adv}^{\mathsf{DDH}}_{\mathbb{G}_s, \mathcal{A}}(\lambda) := |\Pr[1 \leftarrow \mathcal{A}(\mathcal{PG}, [\boldsymbol{a}]_s, [\boldsymbol{a}r]_s)] - \Pr[1 \leftarrow \mathcal{A}(\mathcal{PG}, [\boldsymbol{a}]_s, [\boldsymbol{u}]_s)]|,$$

where the probabilities are taken over $\mathcal{PG} \leftarrow_{\mathrm{R}} \mathsf{GGen}(1^\lambda, d)$, $\boldsymbol{a} \leftarrow_{\mathrm{R}} \mathsf{DDH}$, $r \leftarrow_{\mathrm{R}} \mathbb{Z}_p$, $\boldsymbol{u} \leftarrow_{\mathrm{R}} \mathbb{Z}_p^2$, and the random coins of $\mathcal{A}$. We say DDH holds in $\mathbb{G}_s$ if for all PPT adversaries $\mathcal{A}$, $\mathsf{Adv}^{\mathsf{DDH}}_{\mathbb{G}_s, \mathcal{A}}(\lambda)$ is a negligible function of λ.

Definition 2.2 (SXDH assumption). *For any security parameter λ and any pairing group $\mathcal{PG} = (\mathbb{G}_1, \mathbb{G}_2, \mathbb{G}_T, p, P_1, P_2, e) \leftarrow_{\text{R}} \mathsf{PGGen}(1^\lambda)$, we say SXDH holds in $\mathcal{PG}$ if DDH holds in $\mathbb{G}_1$ and $\mathbb{G}_2$.*

2.2 Functional Encryption

Definition 2.3 (Functional Encryption [25,50]**).** *Let $\mathcal{F}$ be a family of functions, with $f \in \mathcal{F}$ defined as $f : \mathcal{X} \to \mathcal{Y}$. A functional encryption scheme for $\mathcal{F}$ consists of the following algorithms:*

- $\mathsf{Setup}(1^\lambda, \mathcal{F})$*: takes as input the security parameter λ and a description of the function family $\mathcal{F}$, and outputs a master public key* mpk *and a master secret key* msk*. The master public key* mpk *is assumed to be part of the input of all the remaining algorithms.*
- $\mathsf{Enc}(x \in \mathcal{X})$*: takes as input the master public key* mpk *and a message $x \in \mathcal{X}$, and it outputs a ciphertext* ct.
- $\mathsf{KeyGen}(\mathsf{msk}, f \in \mathcal{F})$*: takes as input the master secret key* msk*, a function $f \in \mathcal{F}$, and it outputs a decryption key* sk_f.
- $\mathsf{Dec}(\mathsf{sk}_f, \mathsf{ct})$*: takes as input a decryption key* sk_f *along with a ciphertext* ct*, and it outputs a value $y \in \mathcal{Y}$ or the special symbol $\perp$ if it fails.*

A scheme as defined above is correct if for all security parameter λ, $x \in \mathcal{X}$, and $f \in \mathcal{F}$, we have: $\Pr[\mathsf{Dec}(\mathsf{sk}_f, \mathsf{ct}_x) = f(x)] = 1]$ *where the probability is taken over* $(\mathsf{mpk}, \mathsf{msk}) \leftarrow \mathsf{Setup}(1^\lambda, \mathcal{F})$, $\mathsf{sk}_f \leftarrow \mathsf{KeyGen}(\mathsf{msk}, f)$, $\mathsf{ct}_x \leftarrow \mathsf{Enc}(x)$.

Partial Information. For the rest of this paper, it is convenient to split the output of the function in two parts: $(f(x), \mathsf{part}(x))$, where $\mathsf{part}(x)$ is some partial information on x that is independent from f. For instance, we will consider the case of $x := (\mathsf{P}, \boldsymbol{x})$, where P is a predicate, and $\boldsymbol{x} \in \mathbb{Z}^d$ is a vector of dimension d; each function is described by a pair $(\mathsf{att}, \boldsymbol{y})$ where att is an attribute, and $\boldsymbol{y} \in \mathbb{Z}^d$. The output $f(x)$ reveals $\boldsymbol{x}^\top \boldsymbol{y}$ and P if $\mathsf{P}(\mathsf{att}) = 1$; only P otherwise. Note that the information P is always revealed, no matter the function. Considering this part of the input separately will be helpful later.

Security Notions. We first recall the selective indistinguishability variant for the security of functional encryption here.

Definition 2.4 (SEL-IND security). *For every functional encryption $\mathcal{FE}$, every security parameter λ, every stateful adversary $\mathcal{A}$, we define the following experiments for $\beta \in \{0,1\}$:*

<u>*Experiment*</u> $\mathbf{SEL\text{-}IND}_\beta^{\mathcal{FE}}(1^\lambda, \mathcal{A})$:
$(x_0, x_1) \leftarrow \mathcal{A}(1^\lambda, \mathcal{F})$
$(\mathsf{mpk}, \mathsf{msk}) \leftarrow \mathsf{Setup}(1^\lambda, \mathcal{F})$
$\mathsf{ct}^\star \leftarrow \mathsf{Enc}(x_\beta)$
$\beta' \leftarrow \mathcal{A}^{\mathsf{OKeyGen}(\cdot)}(\mathsf{mpk}, \mathsf{ct}^\star)$
Output: β'

where $\mathsf{OKeyGen}(\cdot)$ *is an oracle that on input* $f \in \mathcal{F}$*, outputs* $\mathsf{KeyGen}(\mathsf{msk}, f)$*. Additionally, if* $\mathcal{A}$ *ever calls the oracle* KeyGen *on an input* $f \in \mathcal{F}$*, the challenge queries* x_0, x_1 *must satisfy:* $f(x_0) = f(x_1)$ *and* $\mathsf{part}(x_0) = \mathsf{part}(x_1)$*.*

A functional encryption scheme $\mathcal{FE}$ *is SEL-IND-secure if for every PPT adversary* $\mathcal{A}$*, the following advantage is a negligible function of* λ*:*

$$\mathsf{Adv}^{\mathsf{SEL\text{-}IND}}_{\mathcal{FE},\mathcal{A}}(\lambda) = \left|\Pr\left[\mathbf{SEL\text{-}IND}^{\mathcal{FE}}_0(1^\lambda, \mathcal{A}) = 1\right] - \Pr\left[\mathbf{SEL\text{-}IND}^{\mathcal{FE}}_1(1^\lambda, \mathcal{A}) = 1\right]\right|$$

Now we give the adaptive, indistinguishability based variant of security for FE. It is the same as the previous definition, except the challenge (x^0, x^1) can be chosen adaptively, after seeing the public key and querying functional decryption keys.

Definition 2.5 (AD-IND security). *For every functional encryption* $\mathcal{FE}$*, every security parameter* λ*, every stateful adversary* $\mathcal{A}$*, we define the following experiments for* $\beta \in \{0, 1\}$*:*

Experiment $\mathbf{AD\text{-}IND}^{\mathcal{FE}}_\beta(1^\lambda, \mathcal{A})$:
$(\mathsf{mpk}, \mathsf{msk}) \leftarrow \mathsf{Setup}(1^\lambda, \mathcal{F})$
$(x_0, x_1) \leftarrow \mathcal{A}^{\mathsf{OKeyGen}(\cdot)}(1^\lambda, \mathcal{F})$
$\mathsf{ct}^\star \leftarrow \mathsf{Enc}(x_\beta)$
$\beta' \leftarrow \mathcal{A}^{\mathsf{OKeyGen}(\cdot)}(\mathsf{mpk}, \mathsf{ct}^\star)$
Output: β'

where $\mathsf{OKeyGen}(\cdot)$ *is an oracle that on input* $f \in \mathcal{F}$*, outputs* $\mathsf{KeyGen}(\mathsf{msk}, f)$*. Additionally, if* $\mathcal{A}$ *ever calls the oracle* KeyGen *on an input* $f \in \mathcal{F}$*, the challenge queries* x_0, x_1 *must satisfy:* $f(x_0) = f(x_1)$ *and* $\mathsf{part}(x_0) = \mathsf{part}(x_1)$*.*

A functional encryption scheme $\mathcal{FE}$ *is AD-IND-secure if for every PPT adversary* $\mathcal{A}$*, the following advantage is a negligible function of* λ*:*

$$\mathsf{Adv}^{\mathsf{AD\text{-}IND}}_{\mathcal{FE},\mathcal{A}}(\lambda) = \left|\Pr\left[\mathbf{AD\text{-}IND}^{\mathcal{FE}}_0(1^\lambda, \mathcal{A}) = 1\right] - \Pr\left[\mathbf{AD\text{-}IND}^{\mathcal{FE}}_1(1^\lambda, \mathcal{A}) = 1\right]\right|$$

We now give the simulation-based, selective security. Note that simulation security straightforwardly implies indistinguishable security.

Definition 2.6 (SEL-SIM security). *For any FE scheme* $\mathcal{FE}$ *for functionality* $\mathcal{F}$*, any security parameter* λ*, any PPT stateful adversary* $\mathcal{A}$*, and any PPT simulator* $\mathcal{S} := (\widetilde{\mathsf{Setup}}, \widetilde{\mathsf{Enc}}, \widetilde{\mathsf{KeyGen}})$*, we define the following two experiments.*

$\mathsf{Real}^{\mathcal{FE}}_{\mathcal{A}}(1^\lambda)$:	$\mathsf{Ideal}^{\mathcal{FE}}_{\mathcal{A},\mathcal{S}}(1^\lambda)$:
$x^\star \leftarrow \mathcal{A}(1^\lambda)$	$x^\star \leftarrow \mathcal{A}(1^\lambda)$
$(\mathsf{mpk}, \mathsf{msk}) \leftarrow \mathsf{Setup}(1^\lambda, \mathcal{F})$	$(\widetilde{\mathsf{mpk}}, \widetilde{\mathsf{msk}}) \leftarrow \widetilde{\mathsf{Setup}}(1^\lambda, \mathcal{F})$
$\mathsf{ct}^\star \leftarrow \mathsf{Enc}(x^\star)$	$\mathsf{ct}^\star \leftarrow \widetilde{\mathsf{Enc}}(\widetilde{\mathsf{msk}}, \mathsf{part}(x^\star))$
$\alpha \leftarrow \mathcal{A}^{\mathsf{OKeyGen}(\cdot)}(\mathsf{mpk}, \mathsf{ct}^\star)$	$\alpha \leftarrow \mathcal{A}^{\mathsf{OKeyGen}(\cdot)}(\widetilde{\mathsf{mpk}}, \mathsf{ct}^\star)$

In the real experiment, the key generation oracle OKeyGen, *when given as input* $f \in \mathcal{F}$, *returns* KeyGen(msk, f). *In the ideal experiment, the key generation oracle* OKeyGen, *when given as input* $f \in \mathcal{F}$, *computes* $f(x^\star)$, *and returns* $\widetilde{\mathsf{KeyGen}}(\widetilde{\mathsf{msk}}, \mathsf{part}(x^\star), f, f(x^\star))$, *where* $\mathsf{part}(x^\star)$ *denotes the partial information on* $x^\star$.

We say an FE scheme is SEL-SIM secure if for all PPT adversaries $\mathcal{A}$, *there exists a PPT simulator* $\mathcal{S} := (\widetilde{\mathsf{Setup}}, \widetilde{\mathsf{Enc}}, \widetilde{\mathsf{KeyGen}})$ *such that*

$$\mathsf{Adv}^{\mathsf{SEL\text{-}SIM}}_{\mathcal{FE},\mathcal{A}}(\lambda) := |\Pr[1 \leftarrow \mathsf{Real}^{\mathcal{FE}}_{\mathcal{A}}(1^\lambda)] - \Pr[1 \leftarrow \mathsf{Ideal}^{\mathcal{FE}}_{\mathcal{A},\mathcal{S}}(1^\lambda)]| = \mathsf{negl}(\lambda).$$

3 Inner-Product FE with Fine-Grained Access Control

In this section, we present functional encryption schemes for the family of functions that allows users to embed access policies in the encrypted data, and generate functional decryption keys that compute weighted sum on the latter. Namely, each ciphertext is associated with a predicate P, and encrypts a vector $\boldsymbol{x} \in [0, B]^d$ for some dimension d and some bound B. Each functional decryption key is associated with an attribute att and a vector $\boldsymbol{y} \in [0, B]^d$. Decryption recovers the inner product $\boldsymbol{x}^\top \boldsymbol{y} \in [0, dB^2]$ together with P if the attribute att satisfies the predicate P. Otherwise, it only recovers the predicate P, but no information about the encrypted vector $\boldsymbol{x}$ is revealed.

We show it is possible to combine existing pairing-based ABE together with the inner-product FE from [11]. Our generic construction works on any ABE that relies on the dual system encryption methodology, originally put forth by [56]. Namely, any such ABE that supports the class of predicates $\mathcal{P}$, can be turned into an FE scheme for the family $\mathcal{F}_{\mathsf{ipfe}(d,B),\mathcal{P}} := \mathcal{U} \times [0, B]^d$ of functions described by an attribute att $\in \mathcal{U}$ and a vector $\boldsymbol{y} \in [0, B]^d$, that given as input a predicate $\mathsf{P} \in \mathcal{P}$ where $\mathsf{P} : \mathcal{U} \rightarrow \{0, 1\}$ and a vector $\boldsymbol{x} \in [0, B]^d$, returns $\boldsymbol{x}^\top \boldsymbol{y} \in [0, dB^2]$ if P(att) = 1, 0 otherwise. Note that this can be compactly written as $\mathsf{P}(\mathsf{att}) \cdot \boldsymbol{x}^\top \boldsymbol{y}$. We will consider the case where the partial information that is leaked about $(\mathsf{P}, \boldsymbol{x})$ is P, which corresponds to the case of ABE with public indices, but also the case where the predicate itself is hidden, which corresponding to the case of predicate encryption, also referred to as ABE with private indices. For correctness, we require the bound B and the dimension d to be polynomially bounded.

We first give a scheme that builds upon any predicate encoding, a one-time secure, private-key, statistical variant of ABE, introduced in [16,57], later refined in [8,9,12,17] for prime-order pairing groups. Building a predicate encoding is much easier than directly building an attribute based encryption, since the heavy machinery that is being used to prove security of the resulting ABE is taken care of by these modular frameworks. We follow this line of work by giving a definition of predicate encoding which is essentially that of [27]. For simplicity, we leave the question of using more general predicate encodings, such as those from [9], which capture a larger class of ABE, as future work. Our modular construction is general enough to capture identity-based encryption, inner-product predicate encryption, and monotone span programs. A description of the corresponding concrete predicate encodings can be found in the full version of this paper [6].

3.1 FE with Simulation, Selective Security

First, we recall the definition of predicate encodings.

Definition 3.1 (predicate encoding). *Let $\mathcal{P}$ be a family of predicates and p be a prime. A predicate encoding for $(\mathcal{P}, \mathbb{Z}_p)$ is given by the following polynomial-time deterministic algorithms:*

- $\mathsf{Param}(\mathcal{P})$: *takes as input the family of predicates $\mathcal{P}$, and returns the parameters $(n, |\mathsf{ct}|, |\mathsf{sk}|) \in \mathbb{N}^3$.*
- $\mathsf{EncCt}(\mathsf{P})$: *takes as input a predicate $\mathsf{P} \in \mathcal{P}$, and returns a matrix $\mathbf{C} \in \mathbb{Z}_p^{n \times |\mathsf{ct}|}$.*
- $\mathsf{EncKey}(\mathsf{att})$: *takes as input an attribute $\mathsf{att} \in \mathcal{U}$, and returns a matrix $\mathbf{K} \in \mathbb{Z}_p^{(n+1) \times |\mathsf{sk}|}$.*
- $\mathsf{Decode}(\mathsf{P}, \mathsf{att})$: *takes as input a predicate $\mathsf{P} \in \mathcal{P}$, an attribute $\mathsf{att} \in \mathcal{U}$, and returns a vector $\boldsymbol{d} \in \mathbb{Z}_p^{|\mathsf{ct}|+|\mathsf{sk}|}$.*

We require the following properties.

Correctness. *If $\mathsf{P} \in \mathcal{P}$ and $\mathsf{att} \in \mathcal{U}$ such that $\mathsf{P}(\mathsf{att}) = 1$, $\mathbf{C} := \mathsf{EncCt}(\mathsf{P}) \in \mathbb{Z}_p^{n \times |\mathsf{ct}|}$, $\mathbf{K} := \mathsf{EncKey}(\mathsf{att}) \in \mathbb{Z}_p^{(n+1) \times |\mathsf{sk}|}$, $\boldsymbol{d} := \mathsf{Decode}(\mathsf{P}, \mathsf{att})$, then $\left(\begin{array}{c|c} \mathbf{0} & \multirow{2}{*}{$\mathbf{K}$} \\ \hline \mathbf{C} & \end{array}\right) \boldsymbol{d} = (1, 0, \ldots, 0) \in \mathbb{Z}_p^{n+1}$, where $\mathbf{0} \in \mathbb{Z}_p^{1 \times |\mathsf{ct}|}$.*

Security. *If $\mathsf{P} \in \mathcal{P}$ and $\mathsf{att} \in \mathcal{U}$ such that $\mathsf{P}(\mathsf{att}) = 0$, then the following are identically distributed:*

$$(\alpha | v_1 | \cdots | v_n) \left(\begin{array}{c|c} \mathbf{0} & \mathbf{K} \\ \hline \mathbf{C} & \end{array}\right) \quad \text{and} \quad (0 | v_1 | \cdots | v_n) \left(\begin{array}{c|c} \mathbf{0} & \mathbf{K} \\ \hline \mathbf{C} & \end{array}\right),$$

where $\alpha, v_1, \ldots, v_n \leftarrow_{\mathrm{R}} \mathbb{Z}_p$.

Example: Identity-Based Encryption.

- $\mathsf{Param}(\mathsf{IBE})$: takes as input the family of predicates $\mathcal{I}$, where each predicate is described by an identity $\mathsf{id} \in \mathcal{I}$, and returns 1 when given as an input an identity id' such that $\mathsf{id}' = \mathsf{id}$, returns 0 otherwise. It returns the parameters $(n = 2, |\mathsf{ct}| = 1, |\mathsf{sk}| = 1) \in \mathbb{N}^3$.
- $\mathsf{EncCt}(\mathsf{id})$: given $\mathsf{id} \in \mathcal{I}$, returns a matrix $\mathbf{C} = (1, \mathsf{id}) \in \mathbb{Z}_p^{2 \times 1}$ such that $(v_1 | v_2)\mathbf{C} = v_1 + \mathsf{id} v_2 \in \mathbb{Z}_p$.
- $\mathsf{EncKey}(\mathsf{id})$: given $\mathsf{id} \in \mathcal{I}$, returns a matrix $\mathbf{K} = (1, 1, \mathsf{id}) \in \mathbb{Z}_p^{3 \times 1}$ such that $(\alpha | v_1 | v_2)\mathbf{K} = \alpha + v_1 + \mathsf{id} v_2 \in \mathbb{Z}_p$.
- $\mathsf{Decode}(\mathsf{id}, \mathsf{id}')$: if $\mathsf{id} = \mathsf{id}'$, it returns the vector $\boldsymbol{d} := \binom{-1}{1} \in \mathbb{Z}_p^2$.

Our simulation, selectively secure FE is described in Fig. 1.

Correctness. Observe that for all predicates $\mathsf{P} \in \mathcal{P}$, the vector $[(\mathbf{W}_1^\top \boldsymbol{c}_1|\ldots|\mathbf{W}_n^\top \boldsymbol{c}_1)]_1 \in \mathbb{G}_1^{2\times n}$ can be computed from mpk and the randomness $s \leftarrow_{\mathrm{R}} \mathbb{Z}_p$ used by the encryption algorithm to compute $[\boldsymbol{c}_1]_1 := [\boldsymbol{a}s]_1$. Then, the encryption algorithm multiplies the resulting vector by the matrix $\mathbf{C} := \mathsf{EncCt}(\mathsf{P}) \in \mathbb{Z}_p^{n\times|\mathsf{ct}|}$ to obtain $[\mathbf{C}_2]_1 \in \mathbb{G}_1^{2\times|\mathsf{ct}|}$. Similarly, for all attributes $\mathsf{att} \in \mathcal{U}$, the vector $[(\mathbf{U}\boldsymbol{y}|\mathbf{W}_1\boldsymbol{k}_1|\ldots|\mathbf{W}_n\boldsymbol{k}_1)]_2 \in \mathbb{G}_2^{2\times(n+1)}$ can be computed from mpk, msk, and the randomness $r \leftarrow_{\mathrm{R}} \mathbb{Z}_p$ used by the key generation algorithm to compute $[\boldsymbol{k}_1]_2 := [\boldsymbol{b}r]_2$. Then, the key generation algorithm multiplies the resulting vector by the matrix $\mathbf{K} := \mathsf{EncKey}(\mathsf{att}) \in \mathbb{Z}_p^{(n+1)\times|\mathsf{sk}|}$ to obtain $[\mathbf{K}_2]_1 \in \mathbb{G}_2^{2\times|\mathsf{sk}|}$.

Let $\mathsf{P} \in \mathcal{P}$ and $\mathsf{att} \in \mathcal{U}$ such that $\mathsf{P}(\mathsf{att}) = 1$, $\boldsymbol{x}, \boldsymbol{y} \in [0,B]^d$, $(\mathsf{P}, [\boldsymbol{c}_1]_1, [\mathbf{C}_2]_1, [\boldsymbol{c}_3]_1) \leftarrow_{\mathrm{R}} \mathsf{Enc}(\mathsf{mpk}, \mathsf{P}, \boldsymbol{x})$, and $(\mathsf{att}, \boldsymbol{y}, [\boldsymbol{k}_1]_2, [\mathbf{K}_2]_2) \leftarrow_{\mathrm{R}} \mathsf{KeyGen}(\mathsf{msk}, \mathsf{att}, \boldsymbol{y})$. The values computed by the decryption algorithm are such that $[\boldsymbol{d}_1^\top]_T := [(\boldsymbol{c}_1^\top \mathbf{W}_1\boldsymbol{k}_1|\ldots|\boldsymbol{c}_1^\top \mathbf{W}_n\boldsymbol{k}_1)\mathbf{C}]_T \in \mathbb{G}_T^{1\times|\mathsf{ct}|}$, where $\mathbf{C} := \mathsf{EncCt}(\mathsf{P}) \in \mathbb{Z}_p^{n\times|\mathsf{ct}|}$, and $[\boldsymbol{d}_2^\top]_T := [(\boldsymbol{c}_1^\top \mathbf{U}\boldsymbol{y}|\boldsymbol{c}_1^\top \mathbf{W}_1\boldsymbol{k}_1|\ldots|\boldsymbol{c}_1^\top \mathbf{W}_n\boldsymbol{k}_1)\mathbf{K}]_T \in \mathbb{G}_T^{1\times|\mathsf{sk}|}$, where $\mathbf{K} := \mathsf{EncKey}(\mathsf{att}) \in \mathbb{Z}_p^{(n+1)\times|\mathsf{sk}|}$. Thus, by correctness of the predicate encoding $(\mathsf{Param}, \mathsf{EncCt}, \mathsf{EncKey}, \mathsf{Decode})$, we have $[\gamma]_T := [\boldsymbol{c}_1^\top \mathbf{U}\boldsymbol{y}]_T \in \mathbb{G}_T$. To see why, please note that, since $\boldsymbol{d}_1^\top = (\boldsymbol{c}_1^\top \mathbf{W}_1\boldsymbol{k}_1|\ldots|\boldsymbol{c}_1^\top \mathbf{W}_n\boldsymbol{k}_1)\mathbf{C} = (\boldsymbol{c}_1^\top \mathbf{U}\boldsymbol{y}|\boldsymbol{c}_1^\top \mathbf{W}_1\boldsymbol{k}_1|\ldots|\boldsymbol{c}_1^\top \mathbf{W}_n\boldsymbol{k}_1)\begin{pmatrix}\mathbf{0}\\ \mathbf{C}\end{pmatrix}$, $\gamma = (\boldsymbol{d}_1^\top|\boldsymbol{d}_2^\top)\boldsymbol{d} = (\boldsymbol{c}_1^\top \mathbf{U}\boldsymbol{y}|\boldsymbol{c}_1^\top \mathbf{W}_1\boldsymbol{k}_1|\ldots| \boldsymbol{c}_1^\top \mathbf{W}_n\boldsymbol{k}_1)\left(\begin{matrix}\mathbf{0}\\ \mathbf{C}\end{matrix}\middle|\mathbf{K}\right)\boldsymbol{d} = (\boldsymbol{c}_1^\top \mathbf{U}\boldsymbol{y}|\boldsymbol{c}_1^\top \mathbf{W}_1\boldsymbol{k}_1|\ldots|\boldsymbol{c}_1^\top \mathbf{W}_n\boldsymbol{k}_1)\cdot(1|0|\ldots|0])^\top = \boldsymbol{c}_1^\top \mathbf{U}\boldsymbol{y}$. Therefore, $[\mathsf{out}]_T = [\boldsymbol{x}^\top\boldsymbol{y}]_T$. Finally, assuming the value $B^2 d$ is polynomial in the security parameter, the decryption can efficiently recover the discrete logarithm out from $[\mathsf{out}]_T$.

Theorem 3.2 (SEL-SIM security). *If the underlying predicate encoding is secure, then the FE scheme from Fig. 1 is SEL-SIM secure. Namely, for any PPT adversary $\mathcal{A}$, there exist PPT adversaries $\mathcal{B}_1$ and $\mathcal{B}_2$ such that:*

$$\mathsf{Adv}^{\mathsf{SEL\text{-}IND}}_{\mathcal{FE},\mathcal{A}}(\lambda) \leq \mathsf{Adv}^{\mathsf{DDH}}_{\mathbb{G}_1,\mathcal{B}_1}(\lambda) + 2Q\cdot\mathsf{Adv}^{\mathsf{DDH}}_{\mathbb{G}_2,\mathcal{B}_2}(\lambda) + \tfrac{1}{p},$$

where Q denotes the number of queries to $\mathsf{OKeyGen}$.

Proof. The proof goes over a series of hybrid games, defined in Fig. 4. Let $\mathcal{A}$ be a PPT adversary. For any such game G, we denote by $\mathsf{Adv}_{\mathsf{G}}(\mathcal{A})$ the probability $\Pr[1 \leftarrow_{\mathrm{R}} \mathsf{G}(\mathcal{A})]$, that is, the probability that the game outputs 1 when interacting with $\mathcal{A}$. The probability is taken over the random coins of $\mathcal{A}$ and the game G itself. For an overview of the ciphertext and key distributions in the proof, see Figs. 2 and 3.

Game G_0: is the same as $\mathsf{Real}^{\mathcal{FE}}_{\mathcal{A}}(1^\lambda)$ from Definition 2.6.

Game G_1: in this game, the challenge ciphertext is switched to the semi-functional distribution (see Fig. 2). Namely, the vector $[\boldsymbol{c}_1]_1$ contained in the challenge ciphertext is switched to uniformly random over $\mathbb{G}_1^2$, using the DDH

Setup($1^\lambda, \mathcal{F}_{\mathsf{ipfe}(d,B),\mathcal{P}}$):

$\mathcal{PG} = (\mathbb{G}_1, \mathbb{G}_2, \mathbb{G}_T, p, P_1, P_2, e) \leftarrow \mathsf{PGGen}(1^\lambda)$, $\boldsymbol{a}, \boldsymbol{b} \leftarrow_{\mathrm{R}} \mathsf{DDH}$, $\mathbf{U} \leftarrow_{\mathrm{R}} \mathbb{Z}_p^{2\times d}$, $(n, |\mathsf{ct}|, |\mathsf{sk}|) \leftarrow \mathsf{Param}(\mathcal{P})$, for all $i \in [n]$, $\mathbf{W}_i \leftarrow_{\mathrm{R}} \mathbb{Z}_p^{2\times 2}$, $\mathsf{mpk} := ([\boldsymbol{a}]_1, [\boldsymbol{b}]_2, [\mathbf{U}^\top \boldsymbol{a}]_1, \{[\mathbf{W}_i^\top \boldsymbol{a}]_1, [\mathbf{W}_i \boldsymbol{b}]_2\}_{i\in[n]})$, $\mathsf{msk} := \mathbf{U}$. Return (mpk, msk).

Enc(mpk, P, $\boldsymbol{x}$):

$s \leftarrow_{\mathrm{R}} \mathbb{Z}_p$, $[\boldsymbol{c}_1]_1 := [\boldsymbol{a}s]_1$, $\mathbf{C} := \mathsf{EncCt}(\mathsf{P}) \in \mathbb{Z}_p^{n\times|\mathsf{ct}|}$, $[\mathbf{C}_2]_1 := [(\mathbf{W}_1^\top \boldsymbol{c}_1| \dots |\mathbf{W}_n^\top \boldsymbol{c}_1)\mathbf{C}]_1$, $[\boldsymbol{c}_3]_1 := [\boldsymbol{x} + \mathbf{U}^\top \boldsymbol{c}_1]_1$. Return $(\mathsf{P}, [\boldsymbol{c}_1]_1, [\mathbf{C}_2]_1, [\boldsymbol{c}_3]_1) \in \mathcal{P} \times \mathbb{G}_1^2 \times \mathbb{G}_1^{2\times|\mathsf{ct}|} \times \mathbb{G}_1^d$

KeyGen(msk, att, $\boldsymbol{y}$):

$r \leftarrow_{\mathrm{R}} \mathbb{Z}_p$, $[\boldsymbol{k}_1]_2 := [\boldsymbol{b}r]_2$, $\mathbf{K} := \mathsf{EncKey}(\mathsf{att}) \in \mathbb{Z}_p^{(n+1)\times|\mathsf{sk}|}$, $[\mathbf{K}_2]_2 := [(\mathbf{U}\boldsymbol{y}|\mathbf{W}_1\boldsymbol{k}_1| \dots |\mathbf{W}_n\boldsymbol{k}_1)\mathbf{K}]_2$, Return $(\mathsf{att}, \boldsymbol{y}, [\boldsymbol{k}_1]_2, [\mathbf{K}_2]_2) \in \mathcal{U} \times [0, B]^d \times \mathbb{G}_2 \times \mathbb{G}_2^{2\times|\mathsf{sk}|}$

Dec$\Big((\mathsf{P}, [\boldsymbol{c}_1]_1, [\mathbf{C}_2]_1, [\boldsymbol{c}_3]_1), (\mathsf{att}, \boldsymbol{y}, [\boldsymbol{k}_1]_2, [\mathbf{K}_2]_2)\Big)$:

$[\boldsymbol{d}_1]_T := e([\mathbf{C}_2]_1^\top, [\boldsymbol{k}_1]_2) \in \mathbb{G}_T^{|\mathsf{ct}|}$, $[\boldsymbol{d}_2^\top]_T := e([\boldsymbol{c}_1]_1^\top, [\mathbf{K}_2]_2) \in \mathbb{G}_T^{1\times|\mathsf{sk}|}$, $\boldsymbol{d} := \mathsf{Decode}(\mathsf{P}, \mathsf{att})$, $[\gamma]_T := [(\boldsymbol{d}_1^\top|\boldsymbol{d}_2^\top)\boldsymbol{d}]_T \in \mathbb{G}_T$, $[\mathsf{out}]_T := e([\boldsymbol{c}_3]_1^\top, [\boldsymbol{y}]_2) - [\gamma]_T$. Return out.

Fig. 1. A selectively-secure FE from pairings, for the function family $\mathcal{F}_{\mathsf{ipfe}(d,B),\mathcal{P}}$.

Ciphertext	$[\boldsymbol{c}_1]_1$	$[\mathbf{C}_2]_1$	$[\boldsymbol{c}_3]_1$	Hybrid
Normal	$[\boldsymbol{a}s]_1$, $s \leftarrow_{\mathrm{R}} \mathbb{Z}_p$	$[(\mathbf{W}_1^\top \boldsymbol{c}_1\| \dots \|\mathbf{W}_n^\top \boldsymbol{c}_1)\mathbf{C}]_1$	$[\boldsymbol{x}^\star + \mathbf{U}^\top \boldsymbol{c}_1]_1$	G_0
SF	$[\boldsymbol{c}_1]_1 \leftarrow_{\mathrm{R}} \mathbb{G}_1^2$	$[(\mathbf{W}_1^\top \boldsymbol{c}_1\| \dots \|\mathbf{W}_n^\top \boldsymbol{c}_1)\mathbf{C}]_1$	$[\boldsymbol{x}^\star + \mathbf{U}^\top \boldsymbol{c}_1]_1$	G_1
Simulated	$\boldsymbol{c}_1 \leftarrow_{\mathrm{R}} \mathbb{Z}_p^2 \setminus \mathrm{span}(\boldsymbol{a})$	$[(\mathbf{W}_1^\top \boldsymbol{c}_1\| \cdots \|\mathbf{W}_n^\top \boldsymbol{c}_1)\mathbf{C}]_1$	$[\mathbf{U}^\top \boldsymbol{c}_1]_1$	$\mathsf{Ideal}_{\mathcal{A},\mathcal{S}}^{\mathcal{FE}}(1^\lambda)$

Fig. 2. Overview of ciphertext distributions appearing in the proof of Theorem 3.2, with changes between hybrids highlighted with a gray background. SF stands for semi-functional. Here, $\mathbf{C} := \mathsf{EncCt}(\mathsf{P}^\star)$.

assumption. The game is described fully in Fig. 4 and is indistinguishable from G_0 by Lemma 3.3.

Lemma 3.3. *There exists a* PPT *adversary* $\mathcal{B}_1$*, such that:*

$$|\mathsf{Adv}_{\mathsf{G}_1}(\mathcal{A}) - \mathsf{Adv}_{\mathsf{G}_0}(\mathcal{A})| \le \mathsf{Adv}_{\mathbb{G}_1,\mathcal{B}_1}^{\mathsf{DDH}}(\lambda).$$

Proof. The PPT adversary $\mathcal{B}_1$ receives the DDH challenge $([\boldsymbol{a}]_1, [\boldsymbol{z}]_1)$ where $\boldsymbol{a} \leftarrow_{\mathrm{R}} \mathsf{DDH}$, $[\boldsymbol{z}]_1 := [\boldsymbol{a}s]_1$ with $s \leftarrow_{\mathrm{R}} \mathbb{Z}_p$ or $[\boldsymbol{z}]_1 \leftarrow_{\mathrm{R}} \mathbb{G}_1^2$, then samples $\mathbf{W}_i \leftarrow_{\mathrm{R}} \mathbb{Z}_p^{2\times 2}$, $\mathbf{U} \leftarrow_{\mathrm{R}} \mathbb{Z}_p^{2\times d}$, $\boldsymbol{b} \leftarrow_{\mathrm{R}} \mathsf{DDH}$ and simulates the experiment for $\mathcal{A}$ in the following way:

Simulation of the Master Public Key: Since $\mathcal{B}_1$ samples $\mathbf{U}$ and $\mathbf{W}_i$ himself, he can use the encoding $[\boldsymbol{a}]_1$ to compute $[\mathbf{U}^\top \boldsymbol{a}]_1$ and $\{[\mathbf{W}_i^\top \boldsymbol{a}]_1\}_{i\in[n]}$). Then $\mathcal{B}_1$, computes $(\{[\mathbf{W}_i \boldsymbol{b}]_2\}_{i\in[n]})$ and outputs $\mathsf{mpk} := ([\boldsymbol{a}]_1, [\boldsymbol{b}]_2, [\mathbf{U}^\top \boldsymbol{a}]_1, \{[\mathbf{W}_i^\top \boldsymbol{a}]_1, [\mathbf{W}_i \boldsymbol{b}]_2\}_{i\in[n]})$.

Type of jth Key	Remark	$[\boldsymbol{k}_1]_2$	$[\mathbf{K}_2]_2$	Hybrid
Normal	$r \leftarrow_R \mathbb{Z}_p$	$[\boldsymbol{b}r]_2$	$[(\mathbf{U}\boldsymbol{y}\|\mathbf{W}_1\boldsymbol{k}_1\|\cdots\|\mathbf{W}_n\boldsymbol{k}_1)\mathbf{K}]_2$	G_0
Pseudo	if $\mathsf{P}^\star(\mathsf{att}) = 0$	$[\boldsymbol{k}_1]_2 \leftarrow_R \mathbb{G}_1^2$	$[(\mathbf{U}\boldsymbol{y}\|\mathbf{W}_1\boldsymbol{k}_1\|\cdots\|\mathbf{W}_n\boldsymbol{k}_1)\mathbf{K}]_2$	$\mathsf{H}_{j-1.2}$
Pseudo SF	if $\mathsf{P}^\star(\mathsf{att}) = 0$	$[\boldsymbol{k}_1]_2 \leftarrow_R \mathbb{G}_1^2$	$[(\widetilde{\mathbf{U}}\boldsymbol{y}\|\mathbf{W}_1\boldsymbol{k}_1\|\cdots\|\mathbf{W}_n\boldsymbol{k}_1)\mathbf{K}]_2$	$\mathsf{H}_{j-1.7}$
SF	if $\mathsf{P}^\star(\mathsf{att}) = 0$	$[\boldsymbol{b}r]_2$	$[(\widetilde{\mathbf{U}}\boldsymbol{y}\|\mathbf{W}_1\boldsymbol{k}_1\|\cdots\|\mathbf{W}_n\boldsymbol{k}_1)\mathbf{K}]_2$	H_{j+1}
Simulated	if $\mathsf{P}^\star(\mathsf{att})=0$	$[\boldsymbol{b}r]_2$	$[(\widetilde{\mathbf{U}}\boldsymbol{y}\|\mathbf{W}_1\boldsymbol{k}_1\|\cdots\|\mathbf{W}_n\boldsymbol{k}_1)\mathbf{K}]_2$	$\mathsf{Ideal}_{\mathcal{A},\mathcal{S}}^{\mathcal{FE}}(1^\lambda)$
Simulated	if $\mathsf{P}^\star(\mathsf{att})=1$	$[\boldsymbol{b}r]_2$	$[(-\boldsymbol{y}^\top\boldsymbol{x}^\star \cdot \boldsymbol{a}^\perp + \mathbf{U}\boldsymbol{y}\|\mathbf{W}_1\boldsymbol{k}_1\|\cdots\|\mathbf{W}_n\boldsymbol{k}_1)\mathbf{K}]_2$	$\mathsf{Ideal}_{\mathcal{A},\mathcal{S}}^{\mathcal{FE}}(1^\lambda)$

Fig. 3. Overview of key distributions appearing in the proof of Theorem 3.2, with changes between hybrids highlighted with a gray background. SF stands for semi-functional. Throughout the figure, $\mathbf{K} = \mathsf{EncKey}(\mathsf{att})$.

Simulation of the Encryption Challenge: Adversary $\mathcal{B}_1$ sets $[\boldsymbol{c}_1]_1 := [\boldsymbol{z}]_1$, $\mathbf{C} := \mathsf{EncCt}(\mathsf{P})$, $[\mathbf{C}_2]_1 := [(\mathbf{W}_1^\top \boldsymbol{z}|\ldots|\mathbf{W}_n^\top \boldsymbol{z})\mathbf{C}]_1$, $[\boldsymbol{c}_3]_1 := [\boldsymbol{x}^\star + \mathbf{U}^\top \boldsymbol{z}]_1$, and returns $(\mathsf{P}, [\boldsymbol{c}_1]_1, [\mathbf{C}_2]_1, [\boldsymbol{c}_3]_1)$. When $\mathcal{B}_1$ gets a DDH challenge of the form $[\boldsymbol{z}]_1 := [\boldsymbol{a}s]_1$ with $s \leftarrow_R \mathbb{Z}_p$, it simulates G_1, whereas it simulates G_2 when $[\boldsymbol{z}]_1$ is uniformly random over $\mathbb{G}_1$.

Simulation of the Functional Keys: $\mathcal{B}_1$ generates the keys straightforwardly as described in G_0, using the matrix $\mathbf{U}$, $\{\mathbf{W}_i\}_{i\in[n]}$, and $\boldsymbol{b}$. □

Game G_2: in this game, all the functional decryption keys associated with an attribute att such that $\mathsf{P}^\star(\mathsf{att}) = 0$ are switched to semi-functional (see Fig. 3). That is, for these keys, the matrix $\widetilde{\mathbf{U}}$ (defined in Fig. 4) is used in place of the master secret key $\mathbf{U}$. Note that the matrix $\widetilde{\mathbf{U}}$, as opposed to the master secret key $\mathbf{U}$, can be computed (information theoretically) from mpk only. These semi-functional keys decrypt successfully normal ciphertexts (which can be produced from mpk), but fail to decrypt semi-functional ciphertexts. To switch keys from normal to semi-functional, we use a hybrid argument across keys, where each key is first switched to a high entropy distribution, typically referred to as pseudo mode in the dual system methodology [56], where the vector $[\boldsymbol{k}_1]_2$ contained in the key is switched to uniformly random over $\mathbb{G}_2^2$, using the DDH assumption. At this point, the proof relies on the security of the predicate encoding to switch the key a semi-functional distribution. After this statistical transition, the vector $[\boldsymbol{k}_1]_2$ is switched back to its original distribution, and the proof proceeds to the next key. Details of the transition from game G_1 to game G_2 are given in the full version of this paper [6].

Even though the hybrid argument used here is standard in the context of dual system encryption, the crucial difference is that only the keys associated with att such that $\mathsf{P}^\star(\mathsf{att}) = 0$ can be switched to semi-functional. The other keys should actually decrypt the challenge ciphertext properly. This is the reason the experiment needs to know in advance the value $\mathsf{P}^\star$, so as to determine which key can be switched. For the keys that cannot be switched, we use a security argument similar to that used in [11] instead.

G_0, $\boxed{\mathsf{G}_1, \boxed{\mathsf{G}_2}}$:

$(\mathsf{P}^\star, \boldsymbol{x}^\star) \leftarrow \mathcal{A}(1^\lambda)$

$\mathcal{PG} \leftarrow \mathsf{PGGen}(1^\lambda)$, $\boldsymbol{a}, \boldsymbol{b} \leftarrow_{\mathrm{R}} \mathsf{DDH}$, $\mathbf{U} \leftarrow_{\mathrm{R}} \mathbb{Z}_p^{2\times d}$, $(n, |\mathsf{ct}|, |\mathsf{sk}|) \leftarrow \mathsf{Param}(\mathcal{P})$, for all $i \in [n]$, $\mathbf{W}_i \leftarrow_{\mathrm{R}} \mathbb{Z}_p^{2\times 2}$, $\mathsf{mpk} := \big([\boldsymbol{a}]_1, [\boldsymbol{b}]_2, [\mathbf{U}^\top \boldsymbol{a}]_1, \{[\mathbf{W}_i^\top \boldsymbol{a}]_1, [\mathbf{W}_i \boldsymbol{b}]_2\}_{i\in[n]}\big)$

$\boxed{\boldsymbol{u}_0 := \frac{\mathbf{U}^\top \boldsymbol{a}}{\|\boldsymbol{a}\|_2^2} \in \mathbb{Z}_p^d, \widetilde{\mathbf{U}} := \boldsymbol{a}\boldsymbol{u}_0^\top \in \mathbb{Z}_p^{2\times d}}$

$\mathsf{ct}^\star \leftarrow \mathsf{OEnc}(\mathsf{P}^\star, \boldsymbol{x}^\star)$

$b \leftarrow \mathcal{A}^{\mathsf{OKeyGen}(\cdot)}(\mathsf{mpk}, \mathsf{ct}^\star)$

$\mathsf{OEnc}(\mathsf{P}^\star, \boldsymbol{x}^\star)$:

$s \leftarrow_{\mathrm{R}} \mathbb{Z}_p$, $[\boldsymbol{c}_1]_1 := [\boldsymbol{a}s]_1$, $\boxed{[\boldsymbol{c}_1]_1 \leftarrow_{\mathrm{R}} \mathbb{G}_1^2}$, $\mathbf{C} := \mathsf{EncCt}(\mathsf{P}^\star)$, $[\mathbf{C}_2]_1 := [(\mathbf{W}_1^\top \boldsymbol{c}_1|\ldots|\mathbf{W}_n^\top \boldsymbol{c}_1)\mathbf{C}]_1$, $[\boldsymbol{c}_3]_1 := [\boldsymbol{x}^\star + \mathbf{U}^\top \boldsymbol{c}_1]_1$. Return $(\mathsf{P}^\star, [\boldsymbol{c}_1]_1, [\mathbf{C}_2]_1, [\boldsymbol{c}_3]_1)$

$\mathsf{OKeyGen}(\mathsf{att}, \boldsymbol{y})$:

$r \leftarrow_{\mathrm{R}} \mathbb{Z}_p$, $[\boldsymbol{k}_1]_2 := [\boldsymbol{b}r]_2$, $\mathbf{K} := \mathsf{EncKey}(\mathsf{att})$, $[\mathbf{K}_2]_2 := [(\mathbf{U}\boldsymbol{y}|\mathbf{W}_1\boldsymbol{k}_1|\cdots|\mathbf{W}_n\boldsymbol{k}_1)\mathbf{K}]_2$, $\boxed{\text{If } \mathsf{P}^\star(\mathsf{att}) = 0, \text{ then } [\mathbf{K}_2]_2 := [(\widetilde{\mathbf{U}}\boldsymbol{y}|\mathbf{W}_1\boldsymbol{k}_1|\cdots|\mathbf{W}_n\boldsymbol{k}_1)\mathbf{K}]_2}$. Return $(\mathsf{att}, \boldsymbol{y}, [\boldsymbol{k}_1]_2, [\mathbf{K}_2]_2)$

Fig. 4. Hybrid games for the proof of Theorem 3.2.

Game $\mathsf{Ideal}_{\mathcal{A},\mathcal{S}}^{\mathcal{FE}}(1^\lambda)$: we show this game is statistically close to G_2. The simulator $\mathcal{S} := (\widetilde{\mathsf{Setup}}, \widetilde{\mathsf{Enc}}, \widetilde{\mathsf{KeyGen}})$ is described in Fig. 5. First, we use the fact that for all $\boldsymbol{a} \in \mathbb{Z}_p^2$, the following distributions are within $1/p$ statistical distance:

$$\boldsymbol{c}_1 \leftarrow_{\mathrm{R}} \mathbb{Z}_p^2 \text{ and } \boldsymbol{c}_1 \leftarrow_{\mathrm{R}} \mathbb{Z}_p^2 \setminus \mathsf{span}(\boldsymbol{a}).$$

The leftmost distribution corresponds to G_2, whereas the rightmost distribution corresponds to $\mathsf{Ideal}_{\mathcal{A},\mathcal{S}}^{\mathcal{FE}}(1^\lambda)$.

Then, we use the fact that for all $\boldsymbol{x}^\star \in \mathbb{Z}^d$, the following distributions are identical:

$$(\boldsymbol{a}, \boldsymbol{c}_1, \widetilde{\mathbf{U}}, \mathbf{U}) \text{ and } (\boldsymbol{a}, \boldsymbol{c}_1, \widetilde{\mathbf{U}}, \mathbf{U} - \boldsymbol{a}^\perp(\boldsymbol{x}^\star)^\top),$$

where $\boldsymbol{a} \leftarrow_{\mathrm{R}} \mathsf{DDH}$, $\boldsymbol{c}_1 \leftarrow_{\mathrm{R}} \mathbb{Z}_p^2 \setminus \mathsf{span}(\boldsymbol{a})$, $\mathbf{U} \leftarrow_{\mathrm{R}} \mathbb{Z}_p^{2\times d}$, $\boldsymbol{u}_0 := \frac{\mathbf{U}^\top \boldsymbol{a}}{\|\boldsymbol{a}\|_2^2}$, $\widetilde{\mathbf{U}} := \boldsymbol{a}\boldsymbol{u}_0^\top$, and $\boldsymbol{a}^\perp \in \mathbb{Z}_p^2$ such that $\boldsymbol{a}^\top \boldsymbol{a}^\perp = 0$ and $\boldsymbol{c}_1^\top \boldsymbol{a}^\perp = 1$. This is because $\mathbf{U}$ is a uniformly random matrix, so adding an offset $-\boldsymbol{a}^\perp(\boldsymbol{x}^\star)^\top$ does not change its distribution. This extra offset doesn't appear in $\widetilde{\mathbf{U}}$ since $\boldsymbol{a}^\top \boldsymbol{a}^\perp = 0$. The leftmost distribution corresponds to G_2, whereas the rightmost distribution corresponds to $\mathsf{Ideal}_{\mathcal{A},\mathcal{S}}^{\mathcal{FE}}(1^\lambda)$.

Putting everything together, we obtain:

$$|\mathsf{Adv}_{\mathsf{G}_2}(\mathcal{A}) - \Pr[1 \leftarrow_{\mathrm{R}} \mathsf{Ideal}_{\mathcal{A},\mathcal{S}}^{\mathcal{FE}}(1^\lambda)]| \leq \tfrac{1}{p}.$$

□

$\widetilde{\mathsf{Setup}}(1^\lambda, \mathcal{F}_{\mathsf{ipfe}(d,B),\mathcal{P}})$:
$\mathcal{PG} \leftarrow \mathsf{GGen}(1^\lambda)$, $\boldsymbol{a}, \boldsymbol{b} \leftarrow_{\mathrm{R}} \mathsf{DDH}$, $\boldsymbol{c}_1 \leftarrow_{\mathrm{R}} \mathbb{Z}_p^2 \setminus \mathsf{span}(\boldsymbol{a})$, $\boldsymbol{a}^\perp \leftarrow_{\mathrm{R}} \mathbb{Z}_p^2$ such that $\boldsymbol{c}_1^\top \boldsymbol{a}^\perp = 1$ and $\boldsymbol{a}^\top \boldsymbol{a}^\perp = 0, \mathbf{U} \leftarrow_{\mathrm{R}} \mathbb{Z}_p^{2 \times d}$, $\boldsymbol{u}_0 := \frac{\mathbf{U}^\top \boldsymbol{a}}{\|\boldsymbol{a}\|_2^2}$, $\widetilde{\mathbf{U}} := \boldsymbol{a}\boldsymbol{u}_0^\top$,
$(n, |\mathsf{ct}|, |\mathsf{sk}|) \leftarrow \mathsf{Param}(\mathcal{P})$, for all $i \in [n]$, $\mathbf{W}_i \leftarrow_{\mathrm{R}} \mathbb{Z}_p^{2\times 2}$
Return $\widetilde{\mathsf{pk}} := ([\boldsymbol{a}]_1, [\boldsymbol{b}]_2, [\mathbf{U}^\top \boldsymbol{a}]_1, \{[\mathbf{W}_i^\top \boldsymbol{a}]_1, [\mathbf{W}_i \boldsymbol{b}]_2\}_{i \in [n]})$, $\widetilde{\mathsf{msk}} := \left(\widetilde{\mathbf{U}}, \mathbf{U}, \boldsymbol{a}^\perp\right)$

$\widetilde{\mathsf{Enc}}(\widetilde{\mathsf{msk}}, \mathsf{P}^\star)$:
$\mathbf{C} := \mathsf{EncCt}(\mathsf{P})$, $[\mathbf{C}_2]_1 := [(\mathbf{W}_1^\top \boldsymbol{c}_1 | \cdots | \mathbf{W}_n^\top \boldsymbol{c}_1)\mathbf{C}]_1$, $[\boldsymbol{c}_3]_1 := [\mathbf{U}^\top \boldsymbol{c}_1]_1$. Return $(\mathsf{P}^\star, [\boldsymbol{c}_1]_1, [\mathbf{C}_2]_1, [\boldsymbol{c}_3]_1)$

$\widetilde{\mathsf{KeyGen}}(\widetilde{\mathsf{msk}}, \mathsf{P}^\star, \boldsymbol{y}, \mathsf{att}, \mathsf{P}^\star(\mathsf{att}) \cdot \boldsymbol{y}^\top \boldsymbol{x}^\star)$:
$r \leftarrow_{\mathrm{R}} \mathbb{Z}_p$, $[\boldsymbol{k}_1]_2 := [\boldsymbol{b}r]_2$, $\mathbf{K} := \mathsf{EncKey}(\mathsf{att})$.
If $\mathsf{P}^\star(\mathsf{att}) = 0$, then $[\mathbf{K}_2]_2 := [(\widetilde{\mathbf{U}}\boldsymbol{y} | \mathbf{W}_1 \boldsymbol{k}_1 | \cdots | \mathbf{W}_n \boldsymbol{k}_1)\mathbf{K}]_2$.
If $\mathsf{P}^\star(\mathsf{att}) = 1$, then $[\mathbf{K}_2]_2 := [(-\boldsymbol{y}^\top \boldsymbol{x}^\star \cdot \boldsymbol{a}^\perp + \mathbf{U}\boldsymbol{y} | \mathbf{W}_1 \boldsymbol{k}_1 | \cdots | \mathbf{W}_n \boldsymbol{k}_1)\mathbf{K}]_2$.
Return $(\mathsf{att}, \boldsymbol{y}, [\boldsymbol{k}_1]_2, [\mathbf{K}_2]_2)$

Fig. 5. PPT simulator for the security proof of the FE scheme from Fig. 4.

3.2 FE with Adaptive, Indistinguishability Based Security

In this section, we build FE schemes for the family of functions $\mathcal{F}_{\mathsf{ipfe}(d,B),\mathcal{P}}$, where $\mathcal{P}$ corresponds to identity-based encryption, inner-product predicate encryption, or even monotone span programs. Similarly to the selective construction in Sect. 3.1, we give a modular construction that builds upon a simple, information-theoretic, one-time secure object, that generalizes the notion of predicate encoding to functions, hence called function encoding. Namely, a function encoding is a private-key version of functional encryption that only satisfies a one-time security notion.

Recall that our construction from Sect. 3.1 fails to achieve adaptive security, even if the underlying building blocks are adaptively secure. The reason is that, throughout the security proof, only the functional decryption keys associated with a pair $(\mathsf{att}, \boldsymbol{y})$ such that $\mathsf{P}^\star(\mathsf{att}) = 0$ can be turned to semi-functional, where $\mathsf{P}^\star$ is the predicate chosen by the adversary for the challenge ciphertext. In fact, the other keys cannot be turned semi-functional, since they must decrypt correctly the challenge ciphertext, and not just ciphertexts that can be generated from the public key. This challenge does not arise in the typical dual system encryption methodology used for ABE, since none of the queried keys can decrypt.

A similar situation arose in the context of fully-hiding predicate encryption for inner products, where ciphertexts are associated with a vector $\widetilde{\boldsymbol{x}} \in \mathbb{Z}_p^n$, functional decryption keys are associated with $\widetilde{\boldsymbol{y}} \in \mathbb{Z}_p^n$, and decryption successfully recovers the plaintext if $\widetilde{\boldsymbol{x}}^\top \widetilde{\boldsymbol{y}} = 0$, whereas no information about that plaintext is revealed otherwise. As opposed to regular inner-product encryption, the vector $\widetilde{\boldsymbol{x}}$ is also hidden, the only bit of information that leaks is whether $\widetilde{\boldsymbol{x}}^\top \widetilde{\boldsymbol{y}} = 0$ or not. In this context, the adversary can query functional decryption keys that decrypt the challenge ciphertext. This is still a meaningful security notion since $\widetilde{\boldsymbol{x}}$ remains hidden even when such keys are queried.

We show that the techniques introduced by [49], later improved in [28] for adaptively secure fully-hiding predicate encryption for inner products are also relevant to obtain adaptively secure inner-product FE with fine-grained access control (even when the predicate is not hidden). In fact, using function encodings, a new notion we introduce that subsumes the notion of predicate encoding introduced in [16,57] in the context of adaptively-secure ABE, we generalize the approach of [28,49] to a large class of functional encryption schemes, whereas their scheme corresponds to the special case of inner-product encryption. Namely, we compile any function encoding for the function family $\mathcal{F}$ into an adaptively secure FE for the same class of functions from the SXDH assumption in asymmetric pairings. In the full version of this paper [6], we give concrete function encodings that correspond to identity-based encryption, inner-product predicate encryption, fully-hiding inner-product predicate encryption and monotone span programs.

Definition 3.4 (function encoding). *Let $\mathcal{F}$ be a family of functions where each function $f \in \mathcal{F}$ is of the form $f : \mathcal{X} \to \mathbb{Z}_p$, and p be a prime. A function encoding for $(\mathcal{F}, \mathbb{Z}_p)$ is given by the following polynomial-time deterministic algorithms:*

- $\mathsf{Param}(\mathcal{F})$*: takes as input the family of functions $\mathcal{F}$, and returns the parameters $(n, |\mathsf{ct}|, |\mathsf{sk}|) \in \mathbb{N}^3$.*
- $\mathsf{EncCt}(x)$*: takes as input $x \in \mathcal{X}$, and returns a matrix $\mathbf{C} \in \mathbb{Z}_p^{(n+1)\times|\mathsf{ct}|}$.*
- $\mathsf{EncKey}(f)$*: takes as input a function $f \in \mathcal{F}$, and returns a matrix $\mathbf{K} \in \mathbb{Z}_p^{(n+1)\times|\mathsf{sk}|}$.*
- $\mathsf{Decode}(f, \mathsf{part}(x))$*: takes as input the partial information $\mathsf{part}(x)$ of $x \in \mathcal{X}$ and $f \in \mathcal{F}$. It returns a vector $\boldsymbol{d} \in \mathbb{Z}_p^{|\mathsf{ct}|+|\mathsf{sk}|}$. (See Sect. 2.2 for a discussion on the partial information).*

We require the following properties.

Correctness. *For all $x \in \mathcal{X}$ and $f \in \mathcal{F}$, $\mathbf{C} := \mathsf{EncCt}(x) \in \mathbb{Z}_p^{(n+1)\times|\mathsf{ct}|}$, $\mathbf{K} := \mathsf{EncKey}(f) \in \mathbb{Z}_p^{(n+1)\times|\mathsf{sk}|}$, $\boldsymbol{d} := \mathsf{Decode}(f, \mathsf{part}(x))$, we have: $(\mathbf{C}|\mathbf{K})\boldsymbol{d} = (f(x), 0, \ldots, 0) \in \mathbb{Z}_p^{n+1}$.*

Security. *For any $x^0, x^1 \in \mathcal{X}$ and $f \in \mathcal{F}$ such that $f(x^0) = f(x^1)$ and $\mathsf{part}(x^0) = \mathsf{part}(x^1)$, the following are identically distributed:*

$$\boldsymbol{v}^\top(\mathbf{C}|\mathbf{K}) \text{ with } \mathbf{C} := \mathsf{EncCt}(x^0), \mathbf{K} := \mathsf{EncKey}(f)$$

and

$$\boldsymbol{v}^\top(\mathbf{C}|\mathbf{K}) \text{ with } \mathbf{C} := \mathsf{EncCt}(x^1), \mathbf{K} := \mathsf{EncKey}(f),$$

where $\boldsymbol{v} \leftarrow_{\mathrm{R}} \mathbb{Z}_p^{n+1}$.

$\mathsf{Setup}(1^\lambda, \mathcal{F}_{\mathsf{ipfe}(d,B),\mathcal{P}})$:

$\mathcal{PG} = (\mathbb{G}_1, \mathbb{G}_2, \mathbb{G}_T, p, P_1, P_2, e) \leftarrow \mathsf{PGGen}(1^\lambda)$, $\boldsymbol{a} \leftarrow_{\mathrm{R}} \mathsf{DDH}$, $\boldsymbol{b} \leftarrow_{\mathrm{R}} \mathbb{Z}_p^3$, $(n, |\mathsf{ct}|, |\mathsf{sk}|) \leftarrow \mathsf{Param}(\mathcal{F}_{\mathsf{ipfe}(d,B),\mathcal{P}})$, for all $i \in [0,n]$, $\mathbf{W}_i \leftarrow_{\mathrm{R}} \mathbb{Z}_p^{2\times 3}$, $\mathsf{mpk} := ([\boldsymbol{a}]_1, \{[\mathbf{W}_i^\top \boldsymbol{a}]_1\}_{i\in[n]})$, $\mathsf{msk} := ([\boldsymbol{b}]_2, \{[\mathbf{W}_i \boldsymbol{b}]_2\}_{i\in[n]})$. Return $(\mathsf{mpk}, \mathsf{msk})$

$\mathsf{Enc}(\mathsf{mpk}, \mathsf{P}, \boldsymbol{x})$:

$s \leftarrow_{\mathrm{R}} \mathbb{Z}_p$, $[\boldsymbol{c}_1]_1 := [\boldsymbol{a}s]_1 \in \mathbb{G}_1^2$, $\mathbf{C} := \mathsf{EncCt}(\mathsf{P}, \boldsymbol{x}) \in \mathbb{Z}_p^{(n+1)\times|\mathsf{ct}|}$, $[\mathbf{C}_2]_1 := [(\mathbf{W}_0^\top \boldsymbol{c}_1|\ldots|\mathbf{W}_n^\top \boldsymbol{c}_1)\mathbf{C}]_1 \in \mathbb{G}_1^{3\times|\mathsf{ct}|}$. Return $(\mathsf{part}(\mathsf{P}, \boldsymbol{x}), [\boldsymbol{c}_1]_1, [\mathbf{C}_2]_1)$.

$\mathsf{KeyGen}(\mathsf{msk}, \mathsf{att}, \boldsymbol{y})$:

$r \leftarrow_{\mathrm{R}} \mathbb{Z}_p$, $[\boldsymbol{k}_1]_2 := [\boldsymbol{b}r]_2 \in \mathbb{G}_2^3$, $\mathbf{K} := \mathsf{EncKey}(\mathsf{att}, \boldsymbol{y}) \in \mathbb{Z}_p^{(n+1)\times|\mathsf{sk}|}$, $[\mathbf{K}_2]_2 := [(\mathbf{W}_0 \boldsymbol{k}_1|\ldots|\mathbf{W}_n \boldsymbol{k}_1)\mathbf{K}]_2 \in \mathbb{G}_2^{2\times|\mathsf{sk}|}$, $[\boldsymbol{k}_3]_2 := [\mathbf{W}_0 \boldsymbol{k}_1]_2 \in \mathbb{G}_2^2$. Return $(\mathsf{att}, \boldsymbol{y}, [\boldsymbol{k}_1]_2, [\mathbf{K}_2]_2, [\boldsymbol{k}_3]_2)$.

$\mathsf{Dec}(\mathsf{part}(\mathsf{P}, \boldsymbol{x}), [\boldsymbol{c}_1]_1, [\mathbf{C}_2]_1, \boldsymbol{y}, [\boldsymbol{k}_1]_2, [\mathbf{K}_2]_2, [\boldsymbol{k}_3]_2)$:

$[\boldsymbol{d}_1]_T := e([\mathbf{C}_2]_1^\top, [\boldsymbol{k}_1]_2) \in \mathbb{G}_T^{|\mathsf{ct}|}$, $[\boldsymbol{d}_2^\top]_T := e([\boldsymbol{c}_1]_1^\top, [\mathbf{K}_2]_2) \in \mathbb{G}_T^{1\times|\mathsf{sk}|}$, $\boldsymbol{d} := \mathsf{Decode}(\mathsf{part}(\mathsf{P}, \boldsymbol{x}), \mathsf{att})$, $[\gamma]_T := [(\boldsymbol{d}_1, \boldsymbol{d}_2)^\top \boldsymbol{d}]_T \in \mathbb{G}_T$, Return $\mathsf{out} \in [0, dB^2]$ such that $[\gamma]_T = [\boldsymbol{c}_1^\top \boldsymbol{k}_3 \cdot \mathsf{out}]_T$. If there isn't such out, return $\perp$.

Fig. 6. An adaptively-secure FE from pairings, for the function family $\mathcal{F}_{\mathsf{ipfe}(d,B),\mathcal{P}}$.

Example: Identity-Based Encryption. Each function is described by an identity $\mathsf{id} \in \mathbb{Z}_p$ and a vector $\boldsymbol{y} \in [0,B]^d$, takes as input another identity $\mathsf{id}' \in \mathbb{Z}_p$ and a vector $\boldsymbol{x} \in [0,B]^d$, and outputs $\boldsymbol{x}^\top \boldsymbol{y}$ if $\mathsf{id} = \mathsf{id}'$, 0 otherwise. The partial information $\mathsf{part}(\boldsymbol{x}, \mathsf{id}) = \mathsf{id}$.

- Param: returns the parameters $(2d, |\mathsf{ct}| = d, |\mathsf{sk}| = n+1)$.
- $\mathsf{EncCt}(\boldsymbol{x}, \mathsf{id})$: given $\boldsymbol{x} \in \mathbb{Z}_p^n$ and $\mathsf{id} \in \mathbb{Z}_p$, returns a matrix $\mathbf{C} \in \mathbb{Z}_p^{(2d+1)\times d}$ such that $\mathbf{C}^\top(w_0, \boldsymbol{w}_1, \boldsymbol{w}_2) = (w_0 \boldsymbol{x} + \boldsymbol{w}_1 + \mathsf{id}\boldsymbol{w}_2) \in \mathbb{Z}_p^d$.
- $\mathsf{EncKey}(\boldsymbol{y}, \mathsf{id}')$: given $\boldsymbol{y} \in \mathbb{Z}_p^n$ and $\mathsf{id}' \in \mathbb{Z}_p$, returns a matrix $\mathbf{K} \in \mathbb{Z}_p^{(2d+1)\times 1}$ such that $\mathbf{K}^\top(w_0, \boldsymbol{w}_1, \boldsymbol{w}_2) = \boldsymbol{y}^\top(\boldsymbol{w}_1 + \mathsf{id}'\boldsymbol{w}_2) \in \mathbb{Z}_p$.
- $\mathsf{Decode}(\mathsf{id}, \mathsf{id}', \boldsymbol{y})$: if $\boldsymbol{x}^\top \boldsymbol{y} = 0$, it returns the vector $\boldsymbol{d} := (\boldsymbol{y}, -1) \in \mathbb{Z}_p^{d+1}$.

Our modular construction is presented in Fig. 6. Proofs of correctness and security are given below.

Correctness. Observe that for all predicates $\mathsf{P} \in \mathcal{P}$ and vectors $\boldsymbol{x} \in [0,B]^d$, the vector $[(\mathbf{W}_0^\top \boldsymbol{c}_1|\mathbf{W}_1^\top \boldsymbol{c}_1|\ldots|\mathbf{W}_n^\top \boldsymbol{c}_1)]_1 \in \mathbb{G}_1^{3\times n}$ can be computed from mpk and the randomness $s \leftarrow_{\mathrm{R}} \mathbb{Z}_p$ used by the encryption algorithm to compute $[\boldsymbol{c}_1]_1 := [\boldsymbol{a}s]_1$. Then, the encryption algorithm multiplies by the matrix $\mathbf{C} := \mathsf{EncCt}(\mathsf{P}, \boldsymbol{x}) \in \mathbb{Z}_p^{(n+1)\times|\mathsf{ct}|}$ to obtain $[\mathbf{C}_2]_1 \in \mathbb{G}_1^{3\times|\mathsf{ct}|}$. Similarly, for all attributes $\mathsf{att} \in \mathcal{U}$, the vector $[(\mathbf{W}_0 \boldsymbol{k}_1|\mathbf{W}_1 \boldsymbol{k}_1|\ldots|\mathbf{W}_n \boldsymbol{k}_1)]_2 \in \mathbb{G}_2^{2\times n}$ can be computed from mpk, msk, and the randomness $r \leftarrow_{\mathrm{R}} \mathbb{Z}_p$ used by the key generation algorithm

G_0, $\boxed{\mathsf{G}_1, \boxed{\mathsf{G}_2}}$:

$\beta \leftarrow_{\mathrm{R}} \{0,1\}$, $\mathcal{PG} \leftarrow \mathsf{PGGen}(1^\lambda)$, $\boldsymbol{a} \leftarrow_{\mathrm{R}} \mathrm{DDH}$, $\boldsymbol{b} \leftarrow_{\mathrm{R}} \mathbb{Z}_p^3$, $(n, |\mathsf{ct}|, |\mathsf{sk}|) \leftarrow \mathsf{Param}(\mathcal{F}_{\mathsf{ipfe}(d,B)}, \mathcal{P})$, for all $i \in [0,n]$, $\mathbf{W}_i \leftarrow_{\mathrm{R}} \mathbb{Z}_p^{2\times 3}$, $\mathsf{mpk} := \big([\boldsymbol{a}]_1, \{[\mathbf{W}_i^\top \boldsymbol{a}]_1,\}_{i\in[n]}\big)$
$\Big((\mathsf{P}^0, \boldsymbol{x}^0), (\mathsf{P}^1, \boldsymbol{x}^1)\Big) \leftarrow \mathcal{A}^{\mathsf{OKeyGen}(\cdot)}(1^\lambda, \mathsf{mpk})$
$\mathsf{ct}^\star \leftarrow_{\mathrm{R}} \mathsf{OEnc}\Big((\mathsf{P}^0, \boldsymbol{x}^0), (\mathsf{P}^1, \boldsymbol{x}^1)\Big)$
$\beta' \leftarrow \mathcal{A}^{\mathsf{OKeyGen}(\cdot)}(\mathsf{mpk}, \mathsf{ct}^\star)$
Return 1 if $\beta' = \beta$, 0 otherwise.

$\mathsf{OEnc}\Big((\mathsf{P}^0, \boldsymbol{x}^0), (\mathsf{P}^1, \boldsymbol{x}^1)\Big)$:

$s \leftarrow_{\mathrm{R}} \mathbb{Z}_p$, $[\boldsymbol{c}_1]_1 := [\boldsymbol{a}s]_1$, $\boxed{[\boldsymbol{c}_1]_1 \leftarrow_{\mathrm{R}} \mathbb{G}_1^2}$ $\mathbf{C} := \mathsf{EncCt}(\mathsf{P}^\beta, \boldsymbol{x}^\beta)$, $\boxed{\mathbf{C} := \mathsf{EncCt}(\mathsf{P}^0, \boldsymbol{x}^0)}$, $[\mathbf{C}_2]_1 := [(\mathbf{W}_0^\top \boldsymbol{c}_1 | \mathbf{W}_1^\top \boldsymbol{c}_1 | \ldots | \mathbf{W}_n^\top \boldsymbol{c}_1)\mathbf{C}]_T$, Return $\mathsf{ct}^\star := (\mathsf{part}(\mathsf{P}^\beta, \boldsymbol{x}^\beta), [\boldsymbol{c}_1]_1, [\mathbf{C}_2]_1)$

$\mathsf{OKeyGen}(\mathsf{att}, \boldsymbol{y})$:

$r \leftarrow_{\mathrm{R}} \mathbb{Z}_p$, $[\boldsymbol{k}_1]_2 := [\boldsymbol{b}r]_1$, $\mathbf{K} := \mathsf{EncKey}(\mathsf{att}, \boldsymbol{y})$, $[\mathbf{K}_2]_2 := [(\mathbf{W}_0\boldsymbol{k}_1 | \mathbf{W}_1\boldsymbol{k}_1 | \cdots | \mathbf{W}\boldsymbol{k}_1)\mathbf{K}]_2$, $[\boldsymbol{k}_3]_2 := [\mathbf{W}_0\boldsymbol{k}_1]_2$. Return $(\mathsf{att}, \boldsymbol{y}, [\boldsymbol{k}_1]_2, [\mathbf{K}_2]_2, [\boldsymbol{k}_3]_2)$

Fig. 7. Hybrid games for the proof of Theorem 3.5.

to compute $[\boldsymbol{k}_1]_2 := [\boldsymbol{b}r]_2$. Then, the key generation algorithm multiplies by the matrix $\mathbf{K} := \mathsf{EncKey}(\mathsf{att}, \boldsymbol{y}) \in \mathbb{Z}_p^{(n+1)\times|\mathsf{sk}|}$ to obtain $[\mathbf{K}_2]_1 \in \mathbb{G}_2^{2\times|\mathsf{sk}|}$.

Let $\mathsf{P} \in \mathcal{P}$ and $\mathsf{att} \in \mathcal{U}$ such that $\mathsf{P}(\mathsf{att}) = 1$, $\boldsymbol{x}, \boldsymbol{y} \in [0,B]^d$, $(\mathsf{part}(\mathsf{P}, \boldsymbol{x}), [\boldsymbol{c}_1]_1, [\mathbf{C}_2]_1) \leftarrow_{\mathrm{R}} \mathsf{Enc}(\mathsf{mpk}, \mathsf{P}, \boldsymbol{x})$, and $(\mathsf{att}, \boldsymbol{y}, [\boldsymbol{k}_1]_2, [\mathbf{K}_2]_2, [\boldsymbol{k}_3]_2) \leftarrow_{\mathrm{R}} \mathsf{KeyGen}(\mathsf{msk}, \mathsf{att}, \boldsymbol{y})$. The values computed by the decryption algorithm are such that $[\boldsymbol{d}_1]_T := \left[\mathbf{C}^\top \begin{pmatrix} \boldsymbol{c}_1^\top \mathbf{W}_0 \boldsymbol{k}_1 \\ \vdots \\ \boldsymbol{c}_1^\top \mathbf{W}_n \boldsymbol{k}_1 \end{pmatrix}\right]_T$, which implies that $[\boldsymbol{d}_1^\top]_T = [(\boldsymbol{c}_1^\top \mathbf{W}_0 \boldsymbol{k}_1 | \boldsymbol{c}_1^\top \mathbf{W}_1 \boldsymbol{k}_1 | \ldots | \boldsymbol{c}_1^\top \mathbf{W}_n \boldsymbol{k}_1)\mathbf{C}]_T \in \mathbb{G}_T^{1\times|\mathsf{ct}|}$, where $\mathbf{C} := \mathsf{EncCt}(\mathsf{P}, \boldsymbol{x}) \in \mathbb{Z}_p^{(n+1)\times|\mathsf{ct}|}$, and the second equality holds because $\boldsymbol{c}_1^\top \mathbf{W}_i \boldsymbol{k}_1 \in \mathbb{Z}_p$, for every $i \in \{0 \ldots n\}$. Also, $[\boldsymbol{d}_2^\top]_T := [(\boldsymbol{c}_1^\top \mathbf{W}_0 \boldsymbol{k}_1 | \boldsymbol{c}_1^\top \mathbf{W}_1 \boldsymbol{k}_1 | \ldots | \boldsymbol{c}_1^\top \mathbf{W}_n \boldsymbol{k}_1)\mathbf{K}]_T \in \mathbb{G}_T^{1\times|\mathsf{sk}|}$, where $\mathbf{K} := \mathsf{EncKey}(\mathsf{att}, \boldsymbol{y}) \in \mathbb{Z}_p^{(n+1)\times|\mathsf{sk}|}$. Thus, by correctness of the function encoding $(\mathsf{Param}, \mathsf{EncCt}, \mathsf{EncKey}, \mathsf{Decode})$, we have $[\gamma]_T := [\boldsymbol{c}_1^\top \mathbf{W}_0 \boldsymbol{k}_1 \cdot \boldsymbol{x}^\top \boldsymbol{y}]_T = [\boldsymbol{c}_1^\top \boldsymbol{k}_3 \cdot \boldsymbol{x}^\top \boldsymbol{y}] \in \mathbb{G}_T$. Therefore, assuming the value $B^2 d$ is polynomial in the security parameter, the decryption can efficiently recover $\mathsf{out} = \boldsymbol{x}^\top \boldsymbol{y} \in [0, B^2 d]$.

Theorem 3.5 (AD-IND security). *If the underlying function encoding is secure, then the FE scheme from Fig. 6 is AD-IND secure. Namely, for any PPT adversary $\mathcal{A}$, there exist PPT adversaries $\mathcal{B}_1$ and $\mathcal{B}_2$ such that:*

$$\mathsf{Adv}^{\mathsf{AD\text{-}IND}}_{\mathcal{FE},\mathcal{A}}(\lambda) \leq \mathsf{Adv}^{\mathsf{DDH}}_{\mathbb{G}_1,\mathcal{B}_1}(\lambda) + 4Q\mathsf{Adv}^{\mathsf{DDH}}_{\mathbb{G}_2,\mathcal{B}_2}(\lambda),$$

where Q denotes the number of queries to $\mathsf{OKeyGen}$.

Proof. The proof uses a series of hybrid games, described in Fig. 7. For each game G, we define by $\mathsf{Adv}_{\mathsf{G}}(\mathcal{A})$ the advantage of $\mathcal{A}$ in G, that is: $2 \cdot |\Pr[1 \leftarrow_{\mathrm{R}} \mathsf{G}(\mathcal{A})] - 1/2|$.

Game G_0: is defined such that $\mathsf{Adv}_{\mathsf{G}_0}(\mathcal{A}) = \mathsf{Adv}^{\mathsf{AD\text{-}IND}}_{\mathcal{FE},\mathcal{A}}(\lambda)$.

Game G_1: here we change the distribution of the vector $[\boldsymbol{c}_1]_1$ that is part of the challenge ciphertext to uniformly random over $\mathbb{G}_1^2$, using the DDH assumption in $\mathbb{G}_1$. Namely, we build a PPT adversary $\mathcal{B}_1$ such that:

$$|\mathsf{Adv}_{\mathsf{G}_0}(\mathcal{A}) - \mathsf{Adv}_{\mathsf{G}_1}(\mathcal{A})| \leq \mathsf{Adv}^{\mathsf{DDH}}_{\mathbb{G}_1,\mathcal{B}_1}(\lambda).$$

Upon receiving a challenge $(\mathcal{PG}, [\boldsymbol{a}]_1, [\boldsymbol{z}]_1)$, where $[\boldsymbol{z}]_1 := [\boldsymbol{a}s]_1$ for $s \leftarrow_{\mathrm{R}} \mathbb{Z}_p$, or $[\boldsymbol{z}]_1 \leftarrow_{\mathrm{R}} \mathbb{G}_1^2$, the adversary $\mathcal{B}_1$ samples $(n, |\mathsf{ct}|, |\mathsf{sk}|) \leftarrow \mathsf{Param}(\mathcal{F}_{\mathsf{ipfe}(d,B)}, \mathcal{P})$, for all $i \in [0,n]$, $\mathbf{W}_i \leftarrow_{\mathrm{R}} \mathbb{Z}_p^{2\times 3}$, and simulate $\mathcal{A}$'s view in a straightforward way, setting $[\boldsymbol{c}_1]_1 := [\boldsymbol{z}]_1$ in the challenge ciphertext.

Game G_2: here we change the distribution of the challenge ciphertext so that it doesn't depend on the random bit $\beta \leftarrow_{\mathrm{R}} \{0,1\}$ anymore. Clearly,

$$\mathsf{Adv}_{\mathsf{G}_2}(\mathcal{A}) = 0.$$

We show that G_1 and G_2 are computationally indistinguishable using the security of a private-key variant of our scheme. Namely, we exhibit a PPT adversary $\mathcal{B}_2$ such that:

$$|\mathbf{Adv}_{\mathsf{G}_1}(\mathcal{A}) - \mathbf{Adv}_{\mathsf{G}_2}(\mathcal{A})| \leq \mathsf{Adv}_{\mathsf{H}_0}(\mathcal{B}_2),$$

where $\mathsf{Adv}_{\mathsf{H}_0}(\mathcal{B}_2)$ denotes the advantage of $\mathcal{B}_2$ in game H_0, which is the private-key analogue of game G_0 (see Fig. 8). We use the fact that for any $i \in [0,n]$: $(\mathbf{W}_i^\top \boldsymbol{a}, \mathbf{W}_i^\top \boldsymbol{c}_1)$ with $\mathbf{W}_i \leftarrow_{\mathrm{R}} \mathbb{Z}_p^{2\times 3}$, $\boldsymbol{a} \leftarrow_{\mathrm{R}} \mathsf{DDH}$, $\boldsymbol{c}_1 \leftarrow_{\mathrm{R}} \mathbb{Z}_p^3$, is within negligible statistical distance from $(\mathbf{W}_i^\top \boldsymbol{a}, \boldsymbol{w}_i)$ with $\boldsymbol{w}_i \leftarrow_{\mathrm{R}} \mathbb{Z}_p^3$. Roughly speaking, the vectors $\boldsymbol{w}_i$ can be used as a fresh private-key, independent of the public key $\{[\mathbf{W}_i^\top \boldsymbol{a}]_1\}$. Note that when $\boldsymbol{a} \leftarrow_{\mathrm{R}} \mathsf{DDH}$ and $\boldsymbol{a}^\perp \leftarrow_{\mathrm{R}} \mathbb{Z}_p^2 \setminus \{\mathbf{0}\}$ such that $\boldsymbol{a}^\top \boldsymbol{a}^\perp = 0$, we have that the vectors $(\boldsymbol{a}|\boldsymbol{a}^\perp)$ form a basis of $\mathbb{Z}_p^2$. Thus we can write $\mathbf{W}_i^\top := \widetilde{\boldsymbol{w}}_i \boldsymbol{a}^\top + \boldsymbol{w}_i(\boldsymbol{a}^\perp)^\top$, where $\widetilde{\boldsymbol{w}}_i, \boldsymbol{w}_i \leftarrow_{\mathrm{R}} \mathbb{Z}_p^3$, and $\boldsymbol{a}^\perp \in \mathbb{Z}_p^2$ is such that $\boldsymbol{a}^\top \boldsymbol{a}^\perp = 0$ and $\boldsymbol{c}_1^\top \boldsymbol{a}^\perp = 1$. This way, the public key can be written as:

$$\mathsf{mpk} := \left([\boldsymbol{a}]_1, \{[\widetilde{\boldsymbol{w}}_i \boldsymbol{a}^\top \boldsymbol{a}]_1\}_{i\in[n]}\right),$$

the challenge ciphertext can be written as:

$$(\mathsf{part}(\mathsf{P}^\beta, \boldsymbol{x}^\beta), [\boldsymbol{c}_1]_1, [\mathbf{C}_2]_1), \text{ with } [\boldsymbol{c}_1]_1 \leftarrow_{\mathrm{R}} \mathbb{G}_1^2,$$
$$\mathbf{C} := \mathsf{EncCt}(\mathsf{P}^\beta, \boldsymbol{x}^\beta),$$
$$[\mathbf{C}_2]_1 := [(\boldsymbol{w}_0^\top | \boldsymbol{w}_1^\top | \ldots | \boldsymbol{w}_n^\top)\mathbf{C}]_1,$$

which corresponds exactly to game H_0. The functional decryption keys can be written as:

$$r \leftarrow_{\mathrm{R}} \mathbb{Z}_p, [\boldsymbol{k}_1]_2 := [\boldsymbol{b}r]_1, \mathbf{K} := \mathsf{EncKey}(\mathsf{att}, \boldsymbol{y}),$$
$$[\mathbf{K}_2]_2 := [(\boldsymbol{a}\widetilde{\boldsymbol{w}_0}^\top + \boldsymbol{a}^\perp \boldsymbol{w}_0^\top)\boldsymbol{k}_1 | \cdots |(\boldsymbol{a}\widetilde{\boldsymbol{w}_n}^\top + \boldsymbol{a}^\perp \boldsymbol{w}_n^\top)\boldsymbol{k}_1)\mathbf{K}]_2,$$
$$[\boldsymbol{k}_3]_2 := [(\boldsymbol{a}\widetilde{\boldsymbol{w}_0}^\top + \boldsymbol{a}^\perp \boldsymbol{w}_0^\top)\boldsymbol{k}_1]_2.$$

$\boxed{\mathsf{H}_0, \boxed{\mathsf{H}_1}}$:

$\beta \leftarrow_{\mathrm{R}} \{0,1\}$, $\mathcal{PG} \leftarrow \mathsf{PGGen}(1^\lambda)$, $(n, |\mathsf{ct}|, |\mathsf{sk}|) \leftarrow \mathsf{Param}(\mathcal{F}_{\mathsf{ipfe}(d,B)}, \mathcal{P})$, let $(\boldsymbol{b}|\boldsymbol{b}_2|\boldsymbol{b}_3)$ and $(\boldsymbol{b}^*|\boldsymbol{b}_2^*|\boldsymbol{b}_3^*)$ be two random dual basis of $\mathbb{Z}_p^3$. For all $i \in [0,n]$, $\boldsymbol{w}_i \leftarrow_{\mathrm{R}} \mathbb{Z}_p^3$. We write $\boldsymbol{w}_i := w_i^1\boldsymbol{b}^* + w_i^2\boldsymbol{b}_1^* + w_i^3\boldsymbol{b}_3^*$, with $w_i^1, w_i^2, w_i^3 \leftarrow_{\mathrm{R}} \mathbb{Z}_p$

$\Big((\mathsf{P}^0, \boldsymbol{x}^0), (\mathsf{P}^1, \boldsymbol{x}^1)\Big) \leftarrow \mathcal{A}(1^\lambda)$

$\mathsf{ct}^\star \leftarrow_{\mathrm{R}} \mathsf{OEnc}\Big((\mathsf{P}^0, \boldsymbol{x}^0), (\mathsf{P}^1, \boldsymbol{x}^1)\Big)$

$\beta' \leftarrow \mathcal{A}^{\mathsf{OKeyGen}(\cdot)}(\mathsf{ct}^\star)$

Return 1 if $\beta' = \beta$, 0 otherwise.

$\underline{\mathsf{OEnc}\Big((\mathsf{P}^0, \boldsymbol{x}^0), (\mathsf{P}^1, \boldsymbol{x}^1)\Big)}$:

$\mathbf{C}^\beta := \mathsf{EncCt}(\mathsf{P}^\beta, \boldsymbol{x}^\beta)$, $\mathbf{C}^0 := \mathsf{EncCt}(\mathsf{P}^0, \boldsymbol{x}^0)$,

$\boldsymbol{c}_2^{\beta\top} := (\boldsymbol{w}_0^\top|\ldots|\boldsymbol{w}_n^\top)\mathbf{C}^\beta$, $\boxed{\boldsymbol{c}_2^{\beta\top} := (\boldsymbol{b}^{*\top}w_0^1 + \boldsymbol{b}_2^{*\top}w_0^2|\ldots|\boldsymbol{b}^{*\top}w_n^1 + \boldsymbol{b}_2^{*\top}w_n^2)\mathbf{C}^\beta}$,

$\boldsymbol{c}_2^{0\top} := \mathbf{0}^\top$, $\boxed{\boldsymbol{c}_2^{0\top} := (\boldsymbol{b}_3^{*\top}w_0^3|\ldots|\boldsymbol{b}_3^{*\top}w_n^3)\mathbf{C}^0}$,

$\boldsymbol{c}_2 := \boldsymbol{c}_2^\beta + \boldsymbol{c}_2^0$.

Return $\mathsf{ct}^\star := (\mathsf{part}(\mathsf{P}^\beta, \boldsymbol{x}^\beta), \boldsymbol{c}_2)$

$\underline{\mathsf{OKeyGen}(\mathsf{att}, \boldsymbol{y})}$:

$\boldsymbol{k}_1 \leftarrow_{\mathrm{R}} \mathsf{span}(\boldsymbol{b})$, $\mathbf{K} := \mathsf{EncKey}(\mathsf{att}, \boldsymbol{y})$, $[\boldsymbol{k}_2^\top]_2 := [(\boldsymbol{w}_0^\top\boldsymbol{k}_1|\boldsymbol{w}_1^\top\boldsymbol{k}_1|\cdots|\boldsymbol{w}_n^\top\boldsymbol{k}_1)\mathbf{K}]_2$, $[k_3]_2 := [\boldsymbol{w}_0^\top\boldsymbol{k}_1]_2$. Return $(\mathsf{att}, \boldsymbol{y}, [\boldsymbol{k}_1]_2, [\boldsymbol{k}_2]_2, [k_3]_2)$

Fig. 8. Hybrid games for the proofs of adaptive security.

The adversary $\mathcal{B}_2$ samples $\widetilde{\boldsymbol{w}_i} \leftarrow_{\mathrm{R}} \mathbb{Z}_p^3$ for all $i \in [0,n]$ and $\boldsymbol{a} \leftarrow_{\mathrm{R}} \mathsf{DDH}$, $\boldsymbol{a}^\perp \leftarrow_{\mathrm{R}} \mathbb{Z}_p^2$ such that $\boldsymbol{a}^\top\boldsymbol{a}^\perp = 0$, thanks to which it can simulate the public key to $\mathcal{A}$. To generate the challenge ciphertext, $\mathcal{B}_2$ forwards the query $\Big((\mathsf{P}^0, \boldsymbol{x}^0), (\mathsf{P}^1, \boldsymbol{x}^1)\Big)$ to its own encryption oracle, and forwards its challenge ciphertext to $\mathcal{A}$. When $\mathcal{A}$ queries $\mathsf{OKeyGen}(\mathsf{att}, \boldsymbol{y})$, $\mathcal{B}_2$ queries its own oracle to get $\mathsf{sk}_{\mathsf{att},\boldsymbol{y}} := (\mathsf{att}, \boldsymbol{y}, [\boldsymbol{k}_1]_2, [\boldsymbol{k}_2]_2, [k_3]_2)$, where $[\boldsymbol{k}_2^\top]_2 := [(\boldsymbol{w}_0^\top\boldsymbol{k}_1|\ldots|\boldsymbol{w}_n^\top\boldsymbol{k}_1)\mathbf{K}]_2$ for $\mathbf{K} := \mathsf{EncKey}(\mathsf{att}, \boldsymbol{y})$, and $[k_3]_2 := [\boldsymbol{w}_0^\top\boldsymbol{k}_1]_2$. $\mathcal{B}_2$ computes $[\mathbf{K}_2']_2 := [\boldsymbol{a}^\perp\boldsymbol{k}_2^\top]_2 + [\boldsymbol{a}(\widetilde{\boldsymbol{w}_0}^\top|\ldots|\widetilde{\boldsymbol{w}_n}^\top)\mathbf{K}]_2$, and $[\boldsymbol{k}_3']_2 := [\boldsymbol{a}^\perp k_3]_2 + [\boldsymbol{a}\widetilde{\boldsymbol{w}_0}^\top\boldsymbol{k}_1]_2$, and returns $([\boldsymbol{k}_1]_2, [\mathbf{K}_2']_2, [\boldsymbol{k}_3']_2)$ to $\mathcal{A}$. In the full version [6], we show that $\mathsf{Adv}_{\mathsf{H}_0}(\mathcal{B}_2)$ is negligible.

□

4 A Lattice-Based Identity-Based Functional Encryption in the Random-Oracle Model

In this section, we give an overview of an identity-based functional encryption (IFE) for the inner-product functionality from LWE in the random-oracle model. In the full version [6], we provide a lattice-based scheme that is proven secure in the standard model, as well as more background on lattices.

$\mathsf{Setup}(1^\lambda, \mathcal{X}, \mathcal{Y})$:

$(\mathbf{A}, \mathbf{T}) \leftarrow_{\mathrm{R}} \mathsf{TrapGen}(1^n, 1^m)$

$\mathsf{mpk} \leftarrow \mathbf{A}, \mathsf{msk} \leftarrow \mathbf{T}$

$\mathsf{Enc}(\mathsf{mpk}, \mathsf{id}, \boldsymbol{x})$:

$\mathbf{U}_{\mathsf{id}} \leftarrow H(\mathsf{id})$

$\boldsymbol{s} \leftarrow_{\mathrm{R}} \mathbb{Z}_q^n$

$\boldsymbol{f}_1 \leftarrow_{\mathrm{R}} \mathcal{D}_{\mathbb{Z}^m,\sigma}$

$\boldsymbol{f}_2 \leftarrow_{\mathrm{R}} \mathcal{D}_{\mathbb{Z}^\ell,\sigma}$

$\mathsf{ct}_1 \leftarrow \mathbf{A}\boldsymbol{s} + \boldsymbol{f}_1$

$\mathsf{ct}_2 = \mathbf{U}_{\mathsf{id}}\boldsymbol{s} + \boldsymbol{f}_2 + \left\lfloor \frac{q}{K} \right\rfloor \cdot \boldsymbol{x}$

Return $(\mathsf{ct}_1, \mathsf{ct}_2)$

$\mathsf{KeyGen}(\mathsf{id}, \boldsymbol{y})$:

$\mathbf{U}_{\mathsf{id}} \leftarrow H(\mathsf{id})$

$\mathbf{Z}_{\mathsf{id}} \leftarrow_{\mathrm{R}} \mathsf{SamplePre}(\mathbf{A}, \mathbf{T}, \rho, \mathbf{U}_{\mathsf{id}})$

Return $(\boldsymbol{y}, \mathsf{sk}_{\mathsf{id},\boldsymbol{y}} := (\boldsymbol{y}^\top \cdot \mathbf{Z}_{\mathsf{id}}))$

$\mathsf{Dec}(\mathsf{ct}_1, \mathsf{ct}_2, \mathsf{sk}_{\mathsf{id},\boldsymbol{y}}, \boldsymbol{y})$:

$\mu = \boldsymbol{y}^\top \cdot \mathsf{ct}_2 - \mathsf{sk}_{\mathsf{id},\boldsymbol{y}} \cdot \mathsf{ct}_1$

$\mu' = \arg\min_{\mu' \in \{0 \ldots K+1\}} \left| \left\lfloor \frac{q}{K} \right\rfloor \cdot \mu - \mu' \right|$

Return μ'

Fig. 9. An identity-based inner-product functional encryption scheme $\mathcal{IFE}$ in the random-oracle model, where H denotes the random oracle. For descriptions of the algorithms TrapGen and SamplePre, please consult the full version of this paper [6]. Distribution $\mathcal{D}_{\mathbb{Z}^m,\sigma}$ denotes the discrete Gaussian distribution on $\mathbb{Z}^m$, of standard deviation σ, for more details see the full version [6].

4.1 Our Construction

In this section, we describe how to obtain an identity-based inner-product functional encryption scheme based on the hardness of LWE in the random-oracle model. Our idea is to start with a modification of the ALS functional encryption scheme for inner-products [11], proposed by [55] and which we recall in the full version of this paper [6]. We modify the identity-based encryption scheme of [38] in such a way as to support functional key generation queries, as in ALS. Our construction is described in Fig. 9. Ciphertexts encode vectors $\boldsymbol{x} \in \mathcal{X} := \{0, \ldots, P-1\}^\ell$ under an identity id. Secret keys correspond to an identity id and a vector $\boldsymbol{y} \in \mathcal{Y} := \{0, \ldots, V-1\}^\ell$. When the identities match, our scheme decrypts the bounded inner-product $\langle \boldsymbol{x}, \boldsymbol{y} \rangle \in \{0, \ldots, K-1\}$ where $K = \ell P V$.

Since our construction achieves anonymity and the size of input vectors $\boldsymbol{x}$ are fixed, no partial information about the input is leaked. That is, $\mathsf{part}(\boldsymbol{x}, \mathsf{id}) = \perp$.

Lemma 4.1 (Correctness). *For* $q \geq 2K\ell\sqrt{\ell}V\omega(\log^2 n)$, $\sigma = 2C\alpha q(\sqrt{m} + \sqrt{n} + \sqrt{\ell})$, $\rho \geq \omega(\sqrt{\log n})$, $m = 2n \log q$, *the scheme from Fig. 9 is correct.*

Proof. When identities match, observe that decryption yields $\boldsymbol{y}^\top \mathbf{U}\boldsymbol{s} + \boldsymbol{y}^\top \boldsymbol{f}_2 + \boldsymbol{y}^\top \mathbf{Z}\mathbf{A}\boldsymbol{s} + \boldsymbol{y}^\top \mathbf{Z}\boldsymbol{f}_1 + \left\lfloor \frac{q}{K} \right\rfloor \langle \boldsymbol{x}, \boldsymbol{y} \rangle$, which is equal to:

$$\underbrace{\boldsymbol{y}^\top \boldsymbol{f}_2 + \boldsymbol{y}^\top \mathbf{Z}\boldsymbol{f}_1}_{\text{error terms}} + \left\lfloor \frac{q}{K} \right\rfloor \langle \boldsymbol{x}, \boldsymbol{y} \rangle$$

This decrypts correctly as long as the error terms are small. As explained in the full version, we know that every entry of $\mathbf{Z}$ is with overwhelming probability bounded by $\omega(\log n)$, so $\|\mathbf{Z}\| \leq \sqrt{\ell} \cdot \omega(\log n)$, as long as $\rho \geq \omega(\sqrt{\log n})$. We can bound $\|\boldsymbol{y}^\top \mathbf{Z} \boldsymbol{e}_1\| \leq \ell\sqrt{\ell} V \omega(\log^2 n)$ and $\|\boldsymbol{y}\boldsymbol{e}_2\| \leq \ell V \omega(\sqrt{\log n})$, as long as $\sigma \geq \omega(\sqrt{\log n})$. For decryption to succeed, we want that the error terms are smaller than $\frac{q}{2K}$, which implies: $q \geq 2K\ell\sqrt{\ell}V\omega(\log^2 n)$, which is the case for our choice of parameters. □

Remark 4.2 (No smudging noise). We remark that in our setup, we rely on efficient lattice parameters and require no smudging or superpolynomial modulus.

Theorem 4.3 (Security). *Let n be the security parameter, $q \geq 2K\ell\sqrt{\ell}V\omega(\log^2 n)$, $\sigma = 2C\alpha q(\sqrt{m} + \sqrt{n} + \sqrt{\ell})$, $\rho \geq \omega(\sqrt{\log n})$, $m = 2n \log q$, $\alpha \leq \frac{\sigma}{2C\alpha q(\sqrt{m}+\sqrt{n}+\sqrt{\ell})}$, then the scheme from Fig. 9 is AD-IND-secure in the random-oracle model, assuming that $\mathsf{LWE}_{q,\alpha,n}$ is hard.*

The full proof of security can be found in the full version [6]. In the following, we give an overview of the security proof. We achieve adaptive security in the random-oracle model, where the proof closely follows that of [38], while making several changes to adapt the proof techniques to functional encryption.

In the security game, the adversary will be able to ask for functional keys $\mathsf{sk}_{\mathsf{id},\boldsymbol{y}}$, associated to any identity id and vector $\boldsymbol{y}$. Then, it will have to decide on two pairs (identity, plaintext) for the challenges $(\mathsf{id}_0^*, \boldsymbol{x}_0^*)$ and $(\mathsf{id}_1^*, \boldsymbol{x}_1^*)$. In the proof, we leverage the ROM to guess what identities id_0^* and id_1^* will be used for the challenge messages. Then we make the following observation: if the adversary obtained secret keys for either $\mathsf{id}_0^* \| \boldsymbol{y}$ or $\mathsf{id}_1^* \| \boldsymbol{y}$, for any $\boldsymbol{y}$, then it could trivially distinguish between encryptions of $\boldsymbol{x}_0$ under id_0^* and encryptions of $\boldsymbol{x}_1$ under id_1^*. However, this type of trivial attack should be excluded by the AD-IND definition, therefore the adversary cannot obtain decryption key queries for neither id_0^* or id_1^*.

Then, the proof distinguishes the two cases:

1. When $\mathsf{id}_0^* \neq \mathsf{id}_1^*$, security will be inherited from the security of the underlying IBE scheme of [38] through a direct reduction to LWE.
2. When $\mathsf{id}_0^* = \mathsf{id}_1^*$, functional decryption keys are allowed to be issued to the adversary and the proof will make use of the security of ALS [11]. This is only possible due to the compatibility of ALS with the IBE of [38].

Please consult the full version of this paper for the full proof of security [6]. In the latter, we also show how to construct an identity-based functional encryption scheme for inner-products in the *standard model*, by building upon [10].

Acknowledgment. The first author was supported in part by the European Union's Horizon 2020 Research and Innovation Programme under grant agreement 780108 (FENTEC), by the ERC Project aSCEND (H2020 639554), and by the French FUI project ANBLIC. The third author was partially supported by a Google PhD Fellowship in Privacy and Security. The fourth author was partially supported by the ERC Project PREP-CRYPTO (H2020 724307). Part of this work was done while the third author was at École normale supérieure, Paris, France, at UC Berkeley, California, USA, and at Cornell Tech, NY, USA.

References

1. Abdalla, M., Benhamouda, F., Gay, R.: From single-input to multi-client inner-product functional encryption. In: Galbraith, S.D., Moriai, S. (eds.) ASIACRYPT 2019, Part III. LNCS, vol. 11923, pp. 552–582. Springer, Cham (2019). https://doi.org/10.1007/978-3-030-34618-8_19
2. Abdalla, M., Benhamouda, F., Kohlweiss, M., Waldner, H.: Decentralizing inner-product functional encryption. In: Lin, D., Sako, K. (eds.) PKC 2019, Part II. LNCS, vol. 11443, pp. 128–157. Springer, Cham (2019). https://doi.org/10.1007/978-3-030-17259-6_5
3. Abdalla, M., Bourse, F., De Caro, A., Pointcheval, D.: Simple functional encryption schemes for inner products. In: Katz, J. (ed.) PKC 2015. LNCS, vol. 9020, pp. 733–751. Springer, Heidelberg (2015). https://doi.org/10.1007/978-3-662-46447-2_33
4. Abdalla, M., Bourse, F., De Caro, A., Pointcheval, D.: Better security for functional encryption for inner product evaluations. Cryptology ePrint Archive, Report 2016/011 (2016). http://eprint.iacr.org/2016/011
5. Abdalla, M., Catalano, D., Fiore, D., Gay, R., Ursu, B.: Multi-input functional encryption for inner products: function-hiding realizations and constructions without pairings. In: Shacham, H., Boldyreva, A. (eds.) CRYPTO 2018, Part I. LNCS, vol. 10991, pp. 597–627. Springer, Cham (2018). https://doi.org/10.1007/978-3-319-96884-1_20
6. Abdalla, M., Catalano, D., Gay, R., Ursu, B.: Inner-product functional encryption with fine-grained access control. Cryptology ePrint Archive, Report 2020/577 (2020). https://eprint.iacr.org/2020/577
7. Abdalla, M., Gay, R., Raykova, M., Wee, H.: Multi-input inner-product functional encryption from pairings. In: Coron, J.-S., Nielsen, J.B. (eds.) EUROCRYPT 2017, Part I. LNCS, vol. 10210, pp. 601–626. Springer, Cham (2017). https://doi.org/10.1007/978-3-319-56620-7_21
8. Agrawal, S., Chase, M.: A study of pair encodings: predicate encryption in prime order groups. In: Kushilevitz, E., Malkin, T. (eds.) TCC 2016, Part II. LNCS, vol. 9563, pp. 259–288. Springer, Heidelberg (2016). https://doi.org/10.1007/978-3-662-49099-0_10
9. Agrawal, S., Chase, M.: Simplifying design and analysis of complex predicate encryption schemes. In: Coron, J.-S., Nielsen, J.B. (eds.) EUROCRYPT 2017, Part I. LNCS, vol. 10210, pp. 627–656. Springer, Cham (2017). https://doi.org/10.1007/978-3-319-56620-7_22
10. Agrawal, S., Boneh, D., Boyen, X.: Efficient lattice (H)IBE in the standard model. In: Gilbert, H. (ed.) EUROCRYPT 2010. LNCS, vol. 6110, pp. 553–572. Springer, Heidelberg (2010). https://doi.org/10.1007/978-3-642-13190-5_28
11. Agrawal, S., Libert, B., Stehlé, D.: Fully secure functional encryption for inner products, from standard assumptions. In: Robshaw, M., Katz, J. (eds.) CRYPTO 2016, Part III. LNCS, vol. 9816, pp. 333–362. Springer, Heidelberg (2016). https://doi.org/10.1007/978-3-662-53015-3_12
12. Ambrona, M., Barthe, G., Schmidt, B.: Generic transformations of predicate encodings: constructions and applications. In: Katz, J., Shacham, H. (eds.) CRYPTO 2017, Part I. LNCS, vol. 10401, pp. 36–66. Springer, Cham (2017). https://doi.org/10.1007/978-3-319-63688-7_2
13. Ananth, P., Jain, A., Sahai, A.: Indistinguishability obfuscation without multilinear maps: iO from LWE, bilinear maps, and weak pseudorandomness. Technical report, Cryptology ePrint Archive, Report 2018/615 (2018). https://eprint.iacr.org/2018/615

14. Ananth, P., Sahai, A.: Projective arithmetic functional encryption and indistinguishability obfuscation from degree-5 multilinear maps. In: Coron, J.-S., Nielsen, J.B. (eds.) EUROCRYPT 2017, Part I. LNCS, vol. 10210, pp. 152–181. Springer, Cham (2017). https://doi.org/10.1007/978-3-319-56620-7_6
15. Applebaum, B., Arkis, B., Raykov, P., Vasudevan, P.N.: Conditional disclosure of secrets: amplification, closure, amortization, lower-bounds, and separations. In: Katz, J., Shacham, H. (eds.) CRYPTO 2017, Part I. LNCS, vol. 10401, pp. 727–757. Springer, Cham (2017). https://doi.org/10.1007/978-3-319-63688-7_24
16. Attrapadung, N.: Dual system encryption via doubly selective security: framework, fully secure functional encryption for regular languages, and more. In: Nguyen, P.Q., Oswald, E. (eds.) EUROCRYPT 2014. LNCS, vol. 8441, pp. 557–577. Springer, Heidelberg (2014). https://doi.org/10.1007/978-3-642-55220-5_31
17. Attrapadung, N.: Dual system encryption framework in prime-order groups via computational pair encodings. In: Cheon, J.H., Takagi, T. (eds.) ASIACRYPT 2016, Part II. LNCS, vol. 10032, pp. 591–623. Springer, Heidelberg (2016). https://doi.org/10.1007/978-3-662-53890-6_20
18. Baltico, C.E.Z., Catalano, D., Fiore, D., Gay, R.: Practical functional encryption for quadratic functions with applications to predicate encryption. In: Katz, J., Shacham, H. (eds.) CRYPTO 2017, Part I. LNCS, vol. 10401, pp. 67–98. Springer, Cham (2017). https://doi.org/10.1007/978-3-319-63688-7_3
19. Barbosa, M., Catalano, D., Soleimanian, A., Warinschi, B.: Efficient function-hiding functional encryption: from inner-products to orthogonality. In: Matsui, M. (ed.) CT-RSA 2019. LNCS, vol. 11405, pp. 127–148. Springer, Cham (2019). https://doi.org/10.1007/978-3-030-12612-4_7
20. Benhamouda, F., Bourse, F., Lipmaa, H.: CCA-secure inner-product functional encryption from projective hash functions. In: Fehr, S. (ed.) PKC 2017, Part II. LNCS, vol. 10175, pp. 36–66. Springer, Heidelberg (2017). https://doi.org/10.1007/978-3-662-54388-7_2
21. Bethencourt, J., Sahai, A., Waters, B.: Ciphertext-policy attribute-based encryption. In: 2007 IEEE Symposium on Security and Privacy, pp. 321–334. IEEE Computer Society Press, May 2007. https://doi.org/10.1109/SP.2007.11
22. Bishop, A., Jain, A., Kowalczyk, L.: Function-hiding inner product encryption. In: Iwata, T., Cheon, J.H. (eds.) ASIACRYPT 2015, Part I. LNCS, vol. 9452, pp. 470–491. Springer, Heidelberg (2015). https://doi.org/10.1007/978-3-662-48797-6_20
23. Boneh, D., Franklin, M.: Identity-based encryption from the Weil pairing. In: Kilian, J. (ed.) CRYPTO 2001. LNCS, vol. 2139, pp. 213–229. Springer, Heidelberg (2001). https://doi.org/10.1007/3-540-44647-8_13
24. Boneh, D., et al.: Fully key-homomorphic encryption, arithmetic circuit ABE and compact garbled circuits. In: Nguyen, P.Q., Oswald, E. (eds.) EUROCRYPT 2014. LNCS, vol. 8441, pp. 533–556. Springer, Heidelberg (2014). https://doi.org/10.1007/978-3-642-55220-5_30
25. Boneh, D., Sahai, A., Waters, B.: Functional encryption: definitions and challenges. In: Ishai, Y. (ed.) TCC 2011. LNCS, vol. 6597, pp. 253–273. Springer, Heidelberg (2011). https://doi.org/10.1007/978-3-642-19571-6_16
26. Castagnos, G., Laguillaumie, F., Tucker, I.: Practical fully secure unrestricted inner product functional encryption modulo p. In: Peyrin, T., Galbraith, S. (eds.) ASIACRYPT 2018, Part II. LNCS, vol. 11273, pp. 733–764. Springer, Cham (2018). https://doi.org/10.1007/978-3-030-03329-3_25

27. Chen, J., Gay, R., Wee, H.: Improved dual system ABE in prime-order groups via predicate encodings. In: Oswald, E., Fischlin, M. (eds.) EUROCRYPT 2015, Part II. LNCS, vol. 9057, pp. 595–624. Springer, Heidelberg (2015). https://doi.org/10.1007/978-3-662-46803-6_20
28. Chen, J., Gong, J., Wee, H.: Improved inner-product encryption with adaptive security and full attribute-hiding. In: Peyrin, T., Galbraith, S. (eds.) ASIACRYPT 2018, Part II. LNCS, vol. 11273, pp. 673–702. Springer, Cham (2018). https://doi.org/10.1007/978-3-030-03329-3_23
29. Chen, Y., Zhang, L., Yiu, S.M.: Practical attribute based inner product functional encryption from simple assumptions. Cryptology ePrint Archive, Report 2019/846 (2019). https://eprint.iacr.org/2019/846
30. Chotard, J., Dufour Sans, E., Gay, R., Phan, D.H., Pointcheval, D.: Decentralized multi-client functional encryption for inner product. In: Peyrin, T., Galbraith, S. (eds.) ASIACRYPT 2018, Part II. LNCS, vol. 11273, pp. 703–732. Springer, Cham (2018). https://doi.org/10.1007/978-3-030-03329-3_24
31. Connor, R.J., Schuchard, M.: Blind Bernoulli trials: a noninteractive protocol for hidden-weight coin flips. In: Heninger, N., Traynor, P. (eds.) USENIX Security 2019, pp. 1483–1500. USENIX Association, Berkeley (2019)
32. Datta, P., Dutta, R., Mukhopadhyay, S.: Functional encryption for inner product with full function privacy. In: Cheng, C.-M., Chung, K.-M., Persiano, G., Yang, B.-Y. (eds.) PKC 2016, Part I. LNCS, vol. 9614, pp. 164–195. Springer, Heidelberg (2016). https://doi.org/10.1007/978-3-662-49384-7_7
33. Datta, P., Okamoto, T., Tomida, J.: Full-hiding (unbounded) multi-input inner product functional encryption from the k-linear assumption. In: Abdalla, M., Dahab, R. (eds.) PKC 2018, Part II. LNCS, vol. 10770, pp. 245–277. Springer, Cham (2018). https://doi.org/10.1007/978-3-319-76581-5_9
34. Dufour-Sans, E., Pointcheval, D.: Unbounded inner-product functional encryption with succinct keys. In: Deng, R.H., Gauthier-Umaña, V., Ochoa, M., Yung, M. (eds.) ACNS 2019. LNCS, vol. 11464, pp. 426–441. Springer, Cham (2019). https://doi.org/10.1007/978-3-030-21568-2_21
35. Gay, R.: A new paradigm for public-key functional encryption for degree-2 polynomials. In: Kiayias, A., Kohlweiss, M., Wallden, P., Zikas, V. (eds.) PKC 2020, Part I. LNCS, vol. 12110, pp. 95–120. Springer, Cham (2020). https://doi.org/10.1007/978-3-030-45374-9_4
36. Jain, A., Lin, H., Sahai, A.: Simplifying constructions and assumptions for iO. Technical report, Cryptology ePrint Archive, Report 2019/1252 (2019). https://eprint.iacr.org/2019/1252
37. Gay, R., Kerenidis, I., Wee, H.: Communication complexity of conditional disclosure of secrets and attribute-based encryption. In: Gennaro, R., Robshaw, M. (eds.) CRYPTO 2015, Part II. LNCS, vol. 9216, pp. 485–502. Springer, Heidelberg (2015). https://doi.org/10.1007/978-3-662-48000-7_24
38. Gentry, C., Peikert, C., Vaikuntanathan, V.: Trapdoors for hard lattices and new cryptographic constructions. In: Ladner, R.E., Dwork, C. (eds.) 40th ACM STOC, pp. 197–206. ACM Press, May 2008. https://doi.org/10.1145/1374376.1374407
39. Gertner, Y., Ishai, Y., Kushilevitz, E., Malkin, T.: Protecting data privacy in private information retrieval schemes. J. Comput. Syst. Sci. **60**(3), 592–629 (2000)
40. Gorbunov, S., Vaikuntanathan, V., Wee, H.: Attribute-based encryption for circuits. In: Boneh, D., Roughgarden, T., Feigenbaum, J. (eds.) 45th ACM STOC, pp. 545–554. ACM Press, June 2013. https://doi.org/10.1145/2488608.2488677

41. Gorbunov, S., Vaikuntanathan, V., Wee, H.: Predicate encryption for circuits from LWE. In: Gennaro, R., Robshaw, M. (eds.) CRYPTO 2015, Part II. LNCS, vol. 9216, pp. 503–523. Springer, Heidelberg (2015). https://doi.org/10.1007/978-3-662-48000-7_25
42. Goyal, V., Pandey, O., Sahai, A., Waters, B.: Attribute-based encryption for fine-grained access control of encrypted data. In: Juels, A., Wright, R.N., De Capitani di Vimercati, S. (eds.) ACM CCS 2006, pp. 89–98. ACM Press, October/November 2006. https://doi.org/10.1145/1180405.1180418. Available as Cryptology ePrint Archive Report 2006/309
43. Jain, A., Lin, H., Matt, C., Sahai, A.: How to leverage hardness of constant-degree expanding polynomials over $\mathbb{R}$ to build $i\mathcal{O}$. In: Ishai, Y., Rijmen, V. (eds.) EUROCRYPT 2019, Part I. LNCS, vol. 11476, pp. 251–281. Springer, Cham (2019). https://doi.org/10.1007/978-3-030-17653-2_9
44. Katz, J., Sahai, A., Waters, B.: Predicate encryption supporting disjunctions, polynomial equations, and inner products. In: Smart, N. (ed.) EUROCRYPT 2008. LNCS, vol. 4965, pp. 146–162. Springer, Heidelberg (2008). https://doi.org/10.1007/978-3-540-78967-3_9
45. Kim, S., Lewi, K., Mandal, A., Montgomery, H., Roy, A., Wu, D.J.: Function-hiding inner product encryption is practical. In: Catalano, D., De Prisco, R. (eds.) SCN 2018. LNCS, vol. 11035, pp. 544–562. Springer, Cham (2018). https://doi.org/10.1007/978-3-319-98113-0_29
46. Libert, B., Ţiţiu, R.: Multi-client functional encryption for linear functions in the standard model from LWE. In: Galbraith, S.D., Moriai, S. (eds.) ASIACRYPT 2019, Part III. LNCS, vol. 11923, pp. 520–551. Springer, Cham (2019). https://doi.org/10.1007/978-3-030-34618-8_18
47. Lin, H.: Indistinguishability obfuscation from SXDH on 5-linear maps and locality-5 PRGs. In: Katz, J., Shacham, H. (eds.) CRYPTO 2017, Part I. LNCS, vol. 10401, pp. 599–629. Springer, Cham (2017). https://doi.org/10.1007/978-3-319-63688-7_20
48. Liu, T., Vaikuntanathan, V., Wee, H.: Conditional disclosure of secrets via non-linear reconstruction. In: Katz, J., Shacham, H. (eds.) CRYPTO 2017, Part I. LNCS, vol. 10401, pp. 758–790. Springer, Cham (2017). https://doi.org/10.1007/978-3-319-63688-7_25
49. Okamoto, T., Takashima, K.: Adaptively attribute-hiding (hierarchical) inner product encryption. In: Pointcheval, D., Johansson, T. (eds.) EUROCRYPT 2012. LNCS, vol. 7237, pp. 591–608. Springer, Heidelberg (2012). https://doi.org/10.1007/978-3-642-29011-4_35
50. O'Neill, A.: Definitional issues in functional encryption. Cryptology ePrint Archive, Report 2010/556 (2010). http://eprint.iacr.org/2010/556
51. Ryffel, T., Pointcheval, D., Bach, F., Dufour-Sans, E., Gay, R.: Partially encrypted deep learning using functional encryption. In: Wallach, H., Larochelle, H., Beygelzimer, A., d'Alché-Buc, F., Fox, E., Garnett, R. (eds.) Advances in Neural Information Processing Systems 32, pp. 4519–4530. Curran Associates, Inc. (2019). http://papers.nips.cc/paper/8701-partially-encrypted-deep-learning-using-functional-encryption.pdf
52. Sahai, A., Waters, B.: Fuzzy identity-based encryption. In: Cramer, R. (ed.) EUROCRYPT 2005. LNCS, vol. 3494, pp. 457–473. Springer, Heidelberg (2005). https://doi.org/10.1007/11426639_27
53. Shamir, A.: Identity-based cryptosystems and signature schemes. In: Blakley, G.R., Chaum, D. (eds.) CRYPTO 1984. LNCS, vol. 196, pp. 47–53. Springer, Heidelberg (1985). https://doi.org/10.1007/3-540-39568-7_5

54. Tomida, J., Takashima, K.: Unbounded inner product functional encryption from bilinear maps. In: Peyrin, T., Galbraith, S. (eds.) ASIACRYPT 2018, Part II. LNCS, vol. 11273, pp. 609–639. Springer, Cham (2018). https://doi.org/10.1007/978-3-030-03329-3_21
55. Wang, Z., Fan, X., Liu, F.-H.: FE for inner products and its application to decentralized ABE. In: Lin, D., Sako, K. (eds.) PKC 2019, Part II. LNCS, vol. 11443, pp. 97–127. Springer, Cham (2019). https://doi.org/10.1007/978-3-030-17259-6_4
56. Waters, B.: Dual system encryption: realizing fully secure IBE and HIBE under simple assumptions. In: Halevi, S. (ed.) CRYPTO 2009. LNCS, vol. 5677, pp. 619–636. Springer, Heidelberg (2009). https://doi.org/10.1007/978-3-642-03356-8_36
57. Wee, H.: Dual system encryption via predicate encodings. In: Lindell, Y. (ed.) TCC 2014. LNCS, vol. 8349, pp. 616–637. Springer, Heidelberg (2014). https://doi.org/10.1007/978-3-642-54242-8_26
58. Wee, H.: Attribute-hiding predicate encryption in bilinear groups, revisited. In: Kalai, Y., Reyzin, L. (eds.) TCC 2017, Part I. LNCS, vol. 10677, pp. 206–233. Springer, Cham (2017). https://doi.org/10.1007/978-3-319-70500-2_8

MoniPoly—An Expressive q-SDH-Based Anonymous Attribute-Based Credential System

Syh-Yuan Tan(✉) and Thomas Groß

School of Computing, Newcastle University, Newcastle upon Tyne, UK
{syh-yuan.tan,thomas.gross}@newcastle.ac.uk

Abstract. Modern attribute-based anonymous credential (ABC) systems benefit from special encodings that yield expressive and highly efficient show proofs on logical statements. The technique was first proposed by Camenisch and Groß, who constructed an SRSA-based ABC system with prime-encoded attributes that offers efficient AND, OR and NOT proofs. While other ABC frameworks have adopted constructions in the same vein, the Camenisch-Groß ABC has been the most expressive and asymptotically most efficient proof system to date, even if it was constrained by the requirement of a trusted message-space setup and an inherent restriction to finite-set attributes encoded as primes. In this paper, combining a new set commitment scheme and an SDH-based signature scheme, we present a provably secure ABC system that supports show proofs for complex statements. This construction is not only more expressive than existing approaches, but it is also highly efficient under unrestricted attribute space due to its ECC protocols only requiring a constant number of bilinear pairings by the verifier; none by the prover. Furthermore, we introduce strong security models for impersonation and unlinkability under adaptive active and concurrent attacks to allow for the expressiveness of our ABC as well as for a systematic comparison to existing schemes. Given this foundation, we are the first to comprehensively formally prove the security of an ABC with expressive show proofs. Specifically, building upon the q-(co-)SDH assumption, we prove the security against impersonation with a tight reduction. Besides the set commitment scheme, which may be of independent interest, our security models can serve as a foundation for the design of future ABC systems.

1 Introduction

An anonymous attribute-based credential (ABC) system allows a user to obtain credentials, that is, certified attribute set A from issuers and to anonymously

This work was supported in part by the European Research Council Starting Grant "Confidentiality-Preserving Security Assurance (CASCAde)" under Grant GA n°716980.

S. Moriai and H. Wang (Eds.): ASIACRYPT 2020, LNCS 12493, pp. 498–526, 2020.
https://doi.org/10.1007/978-3-030-64840-4_17

prove the possession of these credentials as well as properties of A. Anonymous credentials were first proposed by Chaum [25] but it does not draw much attention until Brands [12] constructed a pragmatic single-show ABC system and Camenisch and Lysyanskaya (CL) [21] presented a practical multi-show ABC system. CL-ABC system uses the signer's signature on a committed, and therefore blinded, attribute as the user credential. The proof of possession of a valid credential is a zero-knowledge proof of knowledge on the validity of the signature and the wellformedness of the commitment. This commit-and-sign technique has been employed by ABC systems from RSA-based signature scheme [22] and pairing-based signature schemes [4,5,7,9,15,19,20,23,24,42] on blocks of messages in which the i-th attribute is fixed as the exponent to the i-th base. Therefore, the show proofs have a computational complexity linear to the number of attributes in the credential, in terms of the modular exponentiations and scalar multiplications, respectively.

In contrast to the technique above which is termed as *traditional encoding* by Camenisch and Groß [17,18], they suggested a *prime encoding* for the SRSA-CL signature scheme [22] to offer show proofs on AND, OR and NOT statements with constant complexity for the prime-encoded attributes. Specifically, the Camenisch-Groß (CG) construction separates the unrestricted attribute space $\mathcal{S}$ into string attributes space and finite-set attributes space such that $\mathcal{S} = \mathcal{S}_S \cup \mathcal{S}_F$. The CG encoding uses a product of prime numbers to represent a finite-set attribute set $A_F \in \mathcal{S}_F$ in a single exponent, a technique subsequently applied to graphs as complex data structures [32,33]. Prime encoding results in highly efficient show proofs: each execution only requires a constant number of modular exponentiations. However, the construction constrains $\mathcal{S}_F$ to a set of pre-certified prime numbers and increases the public key size[1]. Furthermore, the security of the CG ABC system was only established on the properties of its show proofs and not formally on the overall properties of the ABC system. Despite these drawbacks, to the best of our knowledge, CG ABC system [18,32] is the only ABC system in the standard model that has show proof for AND, OR, and NOT statements with constant complexity.

Related Works. The SDH-CL signature scheme [19,23,44] is a popular candidate for the ABC system based on the traditional encoding. It is also referred as the BBS+ signature scheme [1,4,5,11,45,48] or the Okamoto signature scheme [2,39]. Au et al. [4] and Akagi et al. [2] constructed provably secure ABC systems on this foundation while Camenisch et al. [19] integrated a pairing-based accumulator to yield an ABC system that supports revocation. Later, Sudarsono et al. [45] applied the accumulator on $\mathcal{S}_F$ as in prime encoding and showed that the resulting ABC system can support show proofs for AND and OR statements with constant complexity. Yet, the accumulator requires a large public key size: $|\mathcal{S}_F|$ finite-set attributes plus the corresponding $|\mathcal{S}_F|$ signatures. Inspired by the concept of attribute-based signature, Zhang and Feng [48] solved the large

[1] If the prime numbers are not pre-certified by a signature each, the show proofs have to include expensive interval proofs.

public key problem, while additionally supporting threshold statements (ANY) in show proofs, at the cost of having the credential size linear to $|A_F|$. Comparing the traditional encoding-based ABC systems to the accumulator-based ABC systems, the latter require more bilinear pairing operations in the show proofs, and having either large public key or credential sizes.

There were some attempts to apply Camenisch et al.'s accumulator [19] and its variants on P-signatures [35], LRSW-CL signature [34] and structure preserving signatures [6,40,43] to support complex non-interactive zero-knowledge (NIZK) show proofs. Among all, Sadiah et al.'s ABC system [43] offers the most expressive show proofs. Considering only $\mathcal{S} = \mathcal{S}_F$, their ABC system allows constant-size and constant-complexity NIZK show proofs for monotone formulas at the cost of issuing $|\mathcal{P}(A_F)|$ credentials to every user where $\mathcal{P}(A_F)$ is the power set of the user attribute set A_F. Instead of performing this expensive process during the issuing protocol, Okishima and Nakanishi's ABC system [40] generates $\mathcal{P}(S_F)$ during key generation and inflates the public key size with $|\mathcal{P}(S_F)|$ signatures to enable constant-size non-interactive witness-indistinguishable (NIWI) show proofs for conjunctive composite formulas. There are also ABC systems [7,9] that were built on Pointcheval and Sanders' signature [41]. The ABC system proposed by Bemmann et al. [7] combines both traditional encoding and accumulator [38] to support monotone formulas under the non-interactive proof of partial knowledge protocol [3]. Although it has significantly shorter credential and supports unrestricted attribute space compared to that of Sadiah et al.'s [43], its show proofs complexity is linear to the number of literals in the monotone formula.

The findings on the use of accumulator in constructing ABC system correspond to the observations in the ABC transformation framework proposed by Camenisch et al. [16]. They discovered that the CL signatures are not able to achieve constant-size NIZK show proofs without random oracle. The framework takes in a structure-preserving signature scheme and a vector commitment scheme to produce an UC-secure ABC system. Their instantiation supports constant-size NIZK show proofs on subset statements and provably secure under the common reference string model. Using the similar ingredients, Fuchsbauer et al. [31] constructed an ABC system that offers constant-size NIZK show proofs on subset statement. The security models in the two works, however, are not designed to cover expressive show proofs. Other frameworks [9,20] that formalized the commit-and-sign technique and even those [7,40,43] support show proofs on complex statements also fall short in this aspect.

Research Gap. Existing constructions yield considerable restrictions when expressive show proofs are concerned: The SRSA-based CG scheme [17] as well as accumulator-based schemes [6,34,35,40,43,45] constrain the attribute space to finite-set attributes ($A_F \in \mathcal{S}_F$) and require a trusted setup that inflates either the public-key size or the credential size. Their expressiveness and the computational complexity are no better than the pairing-based constructions [2,4,7,31,48] and the general ABC frameworks [9,16,20] alike, when only string attributes ($A_S \in \mathcal{S}_S$) are considered. Expressive proofs for large attribute set are desirable in privacy-preserving applications such as direct anonymous attestation [13,14,26–29]. Also, we observe a need for a systematic canonicalization of security models for all mentioned schemes. In short, an ideal ABC system should have:

1. strong security assurance, and
2. appropriate public key size, and
3. expressive show proofs with low complexity regardless of the attribute space.

Our Contribution. We present a perfectly hiding and computationally binding set commitment scheme, called MoniPoly, which supports set membership proofs and disjointness proofs on the committed messages. Following the commit-and-sign methodology, we combine the MoniPoly commitment scheme tracing back to Kate et al.'s work [36] with SDH-based Camenisch-Lysyanskaya signature scheme [23,44] to present an efficient ABC system that support expressive show proofs for AND, OR and k-out-of-n threshold (ANY) clauses as well as their respective complements (NAND, NOR and NANY). Our ABC system is the most efficient construction for the unrestricted attribute space to-date. And it is at least as expressive as the existing constructions specially crafted for the restricted attribute space.

To the best of our knowledge, neither the constructions nor security models of existing ABC systems allow for complex interactive show proofs. As an immediate contribution, we rigorously define the necessary and stronger security notions for ABC systems. Our notions for security of impersonation resilience and unlinkability under adaptive active and concurrent attacks are stronger than those of the state-of-the-art ABC systems [16,20,31,40]. We prove the security of our construction with respect to the security against impersonation and linkability in the standard model, especially offering a tight reduction for impersonation resilience under the q-(co-)SDH assumption.

Organization. We organize the paper as follows. In Sect. 2, we briefly introduce the underlying SDH-based CL signature scheme. In Sect. 3, we present the MoniPoly commitment scheme. We present our ABC system which is a combination of the MoniPoly commitment scheme with SDH-based CL signatures [23,44] in Sect. 4. Section 5 offers an evaluation of the MoniPoly ABC in terms of security properties, expressivity as well as computational complexity in comparison to other schemes in the field.

2 Preliminaries

The MoniPoly commitment and ABC schemes are based on standard mathematical foundations in elliptic curves and bilinear maps as well as notions on signature schemes and proof systems. Readers may refer to the full version [46] for this information.

2.1 The SDH-Based CL Signature Scheme

Camenisch and Lysyanskaya [23] introduced a technique to construct secure pairing-based signature schemes which support signing on committed messages. They also showed that their technique can extract an efficient SDH-based signature scheme from Boneh et al.'s group signature [11] scheme but no security proof was provided. This scheme was later proven to be seuf-cma-secure with a tight reduction [44] to the SDH assumption in the standard model. We describe the SDH-CL signature scheme [19,23,44] as follows:

$\mathsf{KeyGen}(1^k)$: Construct three cyclic groups $\mathbb{G}_1, \mathbb{G}_2, \mathbb{G}_T$ of order p based on an elliptic curve whose bilinear pairing is $\mathsf{e} : \mathbb{G}_1 \times \mathbb{G}_2 \to \mathbb{G}_T$. Select random generators $a, b, c \in \mathbb{G}_1$, $g_2 \in \mathbb{G}_2$ and a secret value $x \in \mathbb{Z}_p^*$. Output the public key $pk = (\mathsf{e}, \mathbb{G}_1, \mathbb{G}_2, \mathbb{G}_T, p, a, b, c, g_2, X = g_2^x)$ and the secret key $sk = x$.

$\mathsf{Sign}(m, pk, sk)$: On input m, choose the random values $s, t \in \mathbb{Z}_p^*$ to compute $v = (a^m b^s c)^{\frac{1}{x+t}}$. In the unlikely case in which $x + t = 0 \mod p$ occurs, reselect a random t. Output the signature as $sig = (t, s, v)$.

$\mathsf{Verify}(m, sig, pk)$: Given $sig = (t, s, v)$, output 1 if the equation:

$$\begin{aligned} \mathsf{e}(v, X g_2^t) &= \mathsf{e}((a^m b^s c)^{\frac{1}{x+t}}, g_2^{x+t}) \\ &= \mathsf{e}(a^m b^s c, g_2). \end{aligned}$$

holds and output 0 otherwise.

Theorem 1. *[44] SDH-based CL signature scheme is* seuf-cma-*secure in the standard model if the Strong Diffie-Hellman problem is* $(t_{\mathsf{sdh}}, \varepsilon_{\mathsf{sdh}})$*-hard.*

3 MoniPoly Set Commitment Scheme

The key idea of set commitment scheme traces back to the polynomial commitment scheme [36] which can commit to a polynomial and support opening at indexes of the polynomial. Inheriting this nature, our MoniPoly set commitment scheme and similar ones [16,31] transform a message $m \in \mathbb{Z}_p$ into $(x' + m)$ where $x' \in \mathbb{Z}_p$ is not known to the user and multiple messages form a *monic polynomial* $f(x') = \prod_{i=1}^{n}(x' + m_i)$. This monic polynomial, in turn, can be rewritten as $f(x') = \sum_{i=0}^{n} \mathsf{m}_i x'^i$. Its coefficients $\mathsf{m}_i \in \mathbb{Z}_p^*$ can be efficiently computed, for instance, using the encoding algorithm $\mathsf{MPEncode}() : \mathbb{Z}_p^n \to \mathbb{Z}_p^{n+1}$ described in the full version [46].

Our commitment scheme's unique property is that it treats the opening value as one of the roots in the monic polynomial. Hence, the name *MoniPoly*. Folding the opening value into the monic polynomial yields compelling advantages, especially, enabling a greater design space for presentation proofs.

While related schemes [16,31,36] realize subset opening, our scheme supports the opening of intersection sets and difference sets, in addition. Thus, MoniPoly is more expressive. Furthermore, the presentation proofs created on MoniPoly are more efficient than other commitment-based frameworks. Finally, treating the opening value as a root of the monic polynomial yields a scheme that is closely aligned with well-established commitment scheme paradigms, which, in turn, fits into a range of popular signature schemes and enables signing committed messages.

3.1 Interface

We define the MoniPoly set commitment scheme as the following algorithms:

$$\mathsf{MoniPoly} = (\mathsf{Setup}, \mathsf{Commit}, \mathsf{Open}, \mathsf{OpenIntersection}, \mathsf{VerifyIntersection}, \mathsf{OpenDifference}, \mathsf{VerifyDifference})$$

1. $\mathsf{Setup}(1^k, n) \rightarrow (pk, sk)$. A pair of public and secret keys (pk, sk) are generated by a trusted authority based on the security parameter input 1^k. The message domain $\mathcal{D}$ is defined and $n-1$ is the maximum messages allowed. If n is fixed, sk is not required in the rest of the scheme.
2. $\mathsf{Commit}(pk, A, o) \rightarrow (C)$. On the input of pk, a message set $A \in \mathcal{D}^{n-1}$ and a random opening value $o \in \mathcal{D}$, output the commitment C.
3. $\mathsf{Open}(pk, C, A, o) \rightarrow b$. Return $b = 1$ if C is a valid commitment to A with the opening value o under pk, and return $b = 0$ otherwise.
4. $\mathsf{OpenIntersection}(pk, C, A, o, (A', l)) \rightarrow (I, W)$ or $\perp$. If $|A' \cap A| \geq l$ holds, return an intersection set $I = A' \cap A$ of length l with the corresponding witness W, and return an error $\perp$ otherwise.
5. $\mathsf{VerifyIntersection}(pk, C, (I, W), (A', l)) \rightarrow b$. Return $b = 1$ if W is a witness for S being the intersection set of length l for A' and the set committed to in C, and return $b = 0$ otherwise.
6. $\mathsf{OpenDifference}(pk, C, A, o, (A', \bar{l})) \rightarrow (D, W)$. If $|A' - A| \geq \bar{l}$ holds, return the difference set $D = A' - A$ of length $\bar{l}$ with the corresponding witness W, and return $\perp$ otherwise.
7. $\mathsf{VerifyDifference}(pk, C, (D, W), (A', \bar{l})) \rightarrow b$. Return $b = 1$ if W is the witness for D being the difference set of length $\bar{l}$ for A' and the set committed to in C, and return $b = 0$ otherwise.

3.2 Security Requirements

Definition 1. *A set commitment scheme is perfectly hiding if every commitment* $C = \mathsf{Commit}(pk, A, o)$ *is uniformly distributed such that there exists an* $o' \neq o$ *for all* $A' \neq A$ *where* $\mathsf{Open}(pk, C, A', o') = 1$.

Definition 2. *An adversary* $\mathcal{A}$ *is said to* $(t_{\mathsf{bind}}, \varepsilon_{\mathsf{bind}})$*-break the binding security of a set commitment scheme if* $\mathcal{A}$ *runs in time at most* t_{bind} *and furthermore:*

$$\Pr[\mathsf{Open}(pk, C, A_1, o_1) = \mathsf{Open}(pk, C, A_2, o_2) = 1] \geq \varepsilon_{\mathsf{bind}}.$$

for a negligible probability $\varepsilon_{\mathsf{bind}}$ *and any two pairs* $(A_1, o_1), (A_2, o_2)$ *output by* $\mathcal{A}$. *We say that a set commitment scheme is* $(t_{\mathsf{bind}}, \varepsilon_{\mathsf{bind}})$*-secure wrt. binding if no adversary* $(t_{\mathsf{bind}}, \varepsilon_{\mathsf{bind}})$*-breaks the binding security of the set commitment scheme.*

3.3 Construction

We describe the MoniPoly commitment scheme as follows:

$\mathsf{Setup}(1^k)$. Construct three cyclic groups $\mathbb{G}_1, \mathbb{G}_2, \mathbb{G}_T$ of order p based on an elliptic curve whose bilinear pairing is $e : \mathbb{G}_1 \times \mathbb{G}_2 \to \mathbb{G}_T$. Select random generators $a \in \mathbb{G}_1$, $g_2 \in \mathbb{G}_2$ and a secret values $x' \in \mathbb{Z}_p^*$. Compute the values $a_0 = a, a_1 = a^{x'}, \ldots, a_n = a^{x'^n}, X_0 = g_2, X_1 = g_2^{x'}, \ldots, X_n = g_2^{x'^n}$ to output the public key $pk = (\mathsf{e}, \mathbb{G}_1, \mathbb{G}_2, \mathbb{G}_T, p, \{a_i, X_i\}_{0 \le i \le n})$ and the secret key $sk = (x')$. Note that sk can be discarded by the authority if the parameter n is fixed.

$\mathsf{Commit}(pk, A, o)$. Taking as input a message set $A = \{m_1, \ldots, m_{n-1}\} \in \mathbb{Z}_p^*$ and the random opening value $o \in \mathbb{Z}_p^*$, output the commitment as

$$C = a_0^{(x'+o)\prod_{j=1}^{n-1}(x'+m_j)} = \prod_{j=0}^{n} a_j^{\mathsf{m}_j}$$

where $\{\mathsf{m}_j\} = \mathsf{MPEncode}(A \cup \{o\})$.

$\mathsf{Open}(pk, C, A, o)$. Return 1 if $C = \prod_{j=0}^{n} a_j^{\mathsf{m}_j}$ holds where $\{\mathsf{m}_j\} = \mathsf{MPEncode}(A \cup \{o\})$ and return 0 otherwise.

$\mathsf{OpenIntersection}(pk, C, A, o, (A', l))$. If $|A' \cap A| \geq l$ holds, return an intersection set $I = A' \cap A$ of length l and a witness such that:

$$\begin{aligned} W &= a_0^{(x'+o)\prod_{m_j \in (A-I)}(x'+m_j)} \\ &= \prod_{j=0}^{n-l} a_j^{\mathsf{w}_j} \end{aligned}$$

where $\{\mathsf{w}_j\} = \mathsf{MPEncode}((A \cup \{o\}) - I)$. Otherwise, return a null value $\perp$. The correctness can be verified as follows:

$$\begin{aligned} C &= W^{\prod_{m_j \in I}(x'+m_j)} \\ &= \left(a_0^{(x'+o)\prod_{m_j \in (A-I)}(x'+m_j)}\right)^{\prod_{m_j \in I}(x'+m_j)} \\ &= a_0^{(x'+o)\prod_{m_j \in A}(x'+m_j)} . \end{aligned}$$

$\mathsf{VerifyIntersection}(pk, C, I, W, (A', l))$. Return 1 if

$$\mathsf{e}\left(C \prod_{j=0}^{|A'|} a_j^{\mathsf{m}_{1,j}}, X_0\right) = \mathsf{e}\left(W \prod_{j=0}^{|A'|-l} a_j^{\mathsf{m}_{2,j}}, \prod_{j=0}^{l} X_j^{\mathsf{i}_j}\right)$$

holds and return 0 otherwise, where $\{\mathsf{i}_j\} = \mathsf{MPEncode}(I)$, $\{\mathsf{m}_{1,j}\} = \mathsf{MPEncode}(A')$ and $\{\mathsf{m}_{2,j}\} = \mathsf{MPEncode}(A' - I)$. The correctness is as follows:

$$\begin{aligned}
&\mathsf{e}\left(C \prod_{j=0}^{|A'|} a_j^{\mathsf{m}_{1,j}}, X_0\right) \\
&= \mathsf{e}(C, X_0)\, \mathsf{e}\left(\prod_{j=0}^{|A'|} a_j^{\mathsf{m}_{1,j}}, X_0\right) \\
&= \mathsf{e}\left(a_0^{(x'+o)\prod_{m_j \in A}(x'+m_j)}, X_0\right) \mathsf{e}\left(a_0^{\prod_{m_j \in A'}(x'+m_j)}, X_0\right) \\
&= \mathsf{e}\left(a_0^{(x'+o)\prod_{m_j \in (A-I)}(x'+m_j)}, X_0^{\prod_{m_j \in I}(x'+m_j)}\right) \\
&\quad \mathsf{e}\left(a_0^{\prod_{m_j \in (A'-I)}(x'+m_j)}, X_0^{\prod_{m_j \in I}(x'+m_j)}\right) \\
&= \mathsf{e}\left(W, \prod_{j=0}^{l} X_j^{\mathsf{i}_j}\right) \mathsf{e}\left(\prod_{j=0}^{|A'|-l} a_j^{\mathsf{m}_{2,j}}, \prod_{j=0}^{l} X_j^{\mathsf{i}_j}\right) \\
&= \mathsf{e}\left(W \prod_{j=0}^{|A'|-l} a_j^{\mathsf{m}_{2,j}}, \prod_{j=0}^{l} X_j^{\mathsf{i}_j}\right)
\end{aligned}$$

$\mathsf{OpenDifference}(pk, C, A, o, (A', \bar{l}))$. If $|A' \cap A| \geq \bar{l}$ holds, return a difference set $D = A' - A$ of length $\bar{l}$ and the witness $(W = \prod_{j=0}^{n-\bar{l}} a_j^{\mathsf{w}_j}, \{\mathsf{r}_j\}_{j=0}^{\bar{l}-1})$. The values $(\{\mathsf{w}_j\}, \{\mathsf{r}_j\}) = \mathsf{MPEncode}(A)/\mathsf{MPEncode}(D)$ are computed using expanded synthetic division such that $\{\mathsf{w}_j\}$ are the coefficients of quotient $q(x')$ and $\{\mathsf{r}_j\}$ are the coefficients of remainder $r(x')$. Specifically, let the polynomial divisor be $d(x') = \sum_j^{\bar{l}} \mathsf{d}_j x'^j$ where $\{\mathsf{d}_j\} = \mathsf{MPEncode}(D)$, the monic polynomial $f(x')$ in the commitment $C = a_0^{f(x')}$ can be rewritten as $f(x') = d(x')q(x') + r(x')$. Note that $\prod_{j=0}^{\bar{l}-1} a_j^{\mathsf{r}_j} \neq 1_{\mathbb{G}_1}$ whenever $d(x')$ cannot divide $f(x')$, i.e., the sets A and D are disjoint. The correctness can be verified from the following:

$$\begin{aligned}
C &= a_0^{(x'+o)\prod_{m_j \in A}(x'+m_j)} \\
&= a_0^{q(x')\prod_{m_j \in D}(x'+m_j)}\, a_0^{r(x')} \\
&= \left(\prod_{j=0}^{n-\bar{l}} a_j^{\mathsf{w}_j}\right)^{d(x')} a_0^{r(x')} \\
&= W^{d(x')} \prod_{j=0}^{\bar{l}-1} a_j^{\mathsf{r}_j}.
\end{aligned}$$

$\mathsf{VerifyDifference}(pk, C, D, (W, \{\mathsf{r}_j\}_{j=0}^{\bar{l}-1}), (A', \bar{l}))$. Return 1, if the following holds:

$$\mathsf{e}\left(C\prod_{j=0}^{\bar{l}-1} a_j^{-\mathsf{r}_j}\prod_{j=0}^{|A'|} a_j^{\mathsf{m}_{1,j}}, X_0\right) = \mathsf{e}\left(W\prod_{j=0}^{|A'|-\bar{l}} a_j^{\mathsf{m}_{2,j}}, \prod_{j=0}^{\bar{l}} X_j^{\mathsf{d}_j}\right), \prod_{j=0}^{\bar{l}-1} a_j^{\mathsf{r}_j} \neq 1_{\mathbb{G}_1}$$

and return 0 otherwise, where $\{\mathsf{d}_j\} = \mathsf{MPEncode}(D)$, $\{\mathsf{m}_{1,j}\} = \mathsf{MPEncode}(A')$ and $\{\mathsf{m}_{2,j}\} = \mathsf{MPEncode}(A' - D)$. The correctness is as follows:

$$\begin{aligned}
&\mathsf{e}\left(C\prod_{j=0}^{\bar{l}-1} a_j^{-\mathsf{r}_j}\prod_{j=0}^{|A'|} a_j^{\mathsf{m}_{1,j}}, X_0\right)\\
&= \mathsf{e}\left(C\prod_{j=0}^{\bar{l}-1} a_j^{-\mathsf{r}_j}, X_0\right)\mathsf{e}\left(\prod_{j=0}^{|A'|} a_j^{\mathsf{m}_{1,j}}, X_0\right)\\
&= \mathsf{e}\left(a_0^{d(x')q(x')+r(x')}a_0^{-r(x')}, X_0\right)\mathsf{e}\left(a_0^{\prod_{m_j\in A'}(x'+m_j)}, X_0\right)\\
&= \mathsf{e}\left(a_0^{d(x')q(x')}, X_0\right)\mathsf{e}\left(a_0^{\prod_{m_j\in(A'-D)}(x'+m_j)}, X_0^{\prod_{m_j\in D}(x'+m_j)}\right)\\
&= \mathsf{e}\left(a_0^{\sum_{j=0}^{n-\bar{l}} \mathsf{w}_{1,j}x'^j}, X_0^{d(x')}\right)\mathsf{e}\left(\prod_{j=0}^{|A'|-\bar{l}} a_j^{\mathsf{m}_{2,j}}, X_0^{d(x')}\right)\\
&= \mathsf{e}\left(W\prod_{j=0}^{|A'|-\bar{l}} a_j^{\mathsf{m}_{2,j}}, \prod_{j=0}^{\bar{l}} X_j^{\mathsf{d}_j}\right).
\end{aligned}$$

Remark 1. In the security analysis of MoniPoly, we will take a different approach compared to the previous constructions [16,31,36]. We consider the perfectly hiding property and the conventional computational binding property [30] that only requires an adversary cannot present two pairs (A_1, o_1) and (A_2, o_2) such that $\mathsf{Commit}(pk, A_1, o_1) = \mathsf{Commit}(pk, A_2, o_2)$. We will show in Section 3.4 that this conventional binding property is a superset of formers' subset binding properties.

3.4 Security Analysis

Theorem 2. *The MoniPoly commitment scheme is perfectly hiding.*

Proof. Given a commitment $C = a_0^{(x'+o)\prod_{j=1}^{n-1}(x'+m_j)}$, there are $|\mathbb{Z}_p^*| - 1$ possible pairs of $((m'_1, \ldots, m'_{n-1}), o') \neq ((m_1, \ldots, m_{n-1}), o)$ which can result in the same C. Furthermore, for every committed message set $\{m_1, \ldots, m_{n-1}\}$, there is a unique o such that:

$$\mathsf{dlog}_{a_0}(C) = (x' + o)\prod_{j=1}^{n-1}(x' + m_j) \mod p$$

$$o = \frac{\mathsf{dlog}_{a_0}(C)}{\prod_{j=1}^{n-1}(x' + m_j)} - x' \mod p$$

Since o is chosen independently of the committed messages $\{m_1, \ldots, m_{n-1}\}$, the latter are perfectly hidden. □

The following theorem considers an adversary which breaks the binding property by finding two different message sets A and A^* which can be of different lengths such that $|A| \geq |A^*|$. The proof is in the full version [46].

Theorem 3. *The MoniPoly commitment scheme is $(t_{\mathsf{bind}}, \varepsilon_{\mathsf{bind}})$-secure wrt. the binding security if the co-SDH problem is $(t_{\mathsf{cosdh}}, \varepsilon_{\mathsf{cosdh}})$-hard such that:*

$$\varepsilon_{\mathsf{bind}} = \varepsilon_{\mathsf{cosdh}}, t_{\mathsf{bind}} = t_{\mathsf{cosdh}} + T(n)$$

where $T(n)$ is the time for dominant group operations in $\mathbb{G}_1$ to extract a co-SDH solution where n is the total of committed messages plus the opening value.

4 Attribute-Based Anonymous Credential System

Table 1. Syntax and semantics for an access policy ϕ.

(a) BNF grammar.

BNF
attr ::= <attribute>=<value>
set ::= attr,set | attr
con ::= AND | NAND | OR | NOR
cont ::= ANY | NANY
clause ::= con(set) | cont(l,set)
stmt ::= clause $\wedge$ stmt | clause
policy ::= stmt(set) | $\perp$

(b)Truth table with respect to input A

Clause	Truth Condition
OR(A')	$\lvert A' \cap A\rvert > 0$
ANY($1 < l < \lvert A'\rvert, A'$)	$\lvert A' \cap A\rvert \geq l$
AND(A')	$\lvert A' \cap A\rvert = \lvert A'\rvert$
NOR(A')	$\lvert A' \cap \bar{A}\rvert > 0$
NANY($1 < l < \lvert A'\rvert, A'$)	$\lvert A' \cap \bar{A}\rvert \geq l$
NAND(A')	$\lvert A' \cap \bar{A}\rvert = \lvert A'\rvert$

Note: con = connective, cont = connective with threshold

Before presenting the formal definition of ABC system, we briefly define the attribute set A and the access policy ϕ in our proposed ABC system which are closely related to MoniPoly's opening algorithms. Informally, we view a relation between two attribute sets as a clause. Clauses can be accumulated using the logical $\wedge$ operator in building the composite statement for an access policy.

Attribute. We view a descriptive attribute set $A = \{m_1, \ldots, m_n\}$ as a user's identity. To be precise, an attribute m is an attribute-value pair in the format attribute=value and A is a set of attributes. For instance, the identity of a user can be described as: A = {"gender = male", "name = bob", "ID = 123456", "role = manager", "branch = Y"}.

Access Policy. An access policy ϕ as defined by the BNF grammar in Table 1 expresses the relationship between two attribute sets A and A'. An access policy ϕ is formed by an attribute set A as well as a statement stmt that specifies the relation between A and A'. We have some additional rules for the ϕ where we require $|A| = n > 1$ and $|A'| \leq n$. Besides, in the special case of $|A'| = 1$, the connective must be either AND or NAND. An access policy ϕ outputs 1 if the underlying statement is evaluated to true and outputs 0 otherwise. Taking the attribute set A above as an example, we have $\phi_{\mathsf{stmt}}(A) = \phi_{\mathsf{AND}(A'_1) \wedge \mathsf{OR}(A'_2)}(A) = 1$ for the attribute sets $A'_1 = \{\text{"role = manager"}\}$ and $A'_2 = \{\text{"branch = X", "branch = Y", "branch = Z"}\}$. Note that the attribute set A' has been implicitly defined by stmt and we simply write ϕ_{stmt} in the subsequent sections when the reference to the attribute set A' is clear.

4.1 Interface

We define an attribute-based anonymous credential system by five algorithms $\mathsf{ABC} = \{\mathsf{KeyGen}, \mathsf{Obtain}, \mathsf{Issue}, \mathsf{Prove}, \mathsf{Verify}\}$ as follows:

1. $\mathsf{KeyGen}(1^k, 1^n) \rightarrow (pk, sk)$: This algorithm is executed by the issuer. On the input of the security parameter k and the attributes upper bound n, it generates a key pair (pk, sk).
2. $(\mathsf{Obtain}(pk, A), \mathsf{Issue}(pk, sk)) \rightarrow (cred \text{ or } \perp)$: These two algorithms form the credential issuing protocol. The first algorithm is executed by the user with the input of the issuer's public key pk and an attribute set A. The second algorithm is executed by the issuer and takes as input the issuer's public key pk and secret key sk. At the end of the protocol, Obtain outputs a valid credential $cred$ produced by Issue or a null value $\perp$ otherwise.
3. $(\mathsf{Prove}(pk, cred, \phi_{\mathsf{stmt}}), \mathsf{Verify}(pk, \phi_{\mathsf{stmt}})) \rightarrow b$: These two algorithms form the credential presentation protocol. The second algorithm is executed by the credential verifier which takes as input the issuer's public key pk and has the right to decide the access policy ϕ_{stmt}. The first algorithm is executed by the credential prover which takes as input the issuer's public key pk, user's credential $cred$ and an access policy ϕ_{stmt} such that $\phi_{\mathsf{stmt}}(A) = 1$. If $\phi_{\mathsf{stmt}}(A) = 0$, the credential holder aborts and Verify outputs $b = 0$. If $\phi = \perp$, prover and verifier complete a proof of possession which proves the validity of credential only instead of a show proof which additionally proves the relation between A and A'. At the end of the protocol, Verify outputs $b = 1$ if it accepts prover and outputs $b = 0$ otherwise.

In the following, we define the key security requirements for an anonymous credential system in the form of *impersonation resilience* and *unlinkability.*

4.2 Security Requirements

4.2.1 Impersonation Resilience

The security goal of an ABC system requires that it is infeasible for an adversary to get accepted by the verifier in the show proof. The security against impersonation under active and concurrent attacks is described in the following game between an adversary $\mathcal{A}$ and a challenger $\mathcal{C}$.

Game 1 $(\mathsf{imp}-\mathsf{aca}(\mathcal{A},\mathcal{C}))$

1. ***Setup:*** *$\mathcal{C}$ runs $\mathsf{KeyGen}(1^k, 1^n)$ and sends pk to $\mathcal{A}$.*
2. ***Phase 1:*** *$\mathcal{A}$ is able to issue concurrent queries to the* Obtain, Prove *and* Verify *oracles where he plays the role of user, prover and verifier, respectively, on any attribute set A_i of his choice in the i-th query. $\mathcal{A}$ can also issue queries to the* IssueTranscript *oracle which takes in A_i and returns the corresponding transcripts of issuing protocol.*
3. ***Challenge:*** *$\mathcal{A}$ outputs the challenge attribute set A^* and its corresponding access policy ϕ^*_{stmt} such that $\phi^*_{\mathsf{stmt}}(A_i) = 0$ and $\phi^*_{\mathsf{stmt}}(A^*) = 1$ for every A_i queried to the* Obtain *oracle during Phase 1.*
4. ***Phase 2:*** *$\mathcal{A}$ can continue to query the oracles as in Phase 1 with the restriction that it cannot query an attribute set A_i to* Obtain *such that $\phi^*_{\mathsf{stmt}}(A_i) = 1$.*
5. ***Impersonate:*** *$\mathcal{A}$ completes a show proof as the prover with $\mathcal{C}$ as the verifier for the access policy $\phi^*_{\mathsf{stmt}}(A^*) = 1$. $\mathcal{A}$ wins the game if $\mathcal{C}$ outputs 1.*

Definition 3. *An adversary $\mathcal{A}$ is said to $(t_{\mathsf{imp}}, \varepsilon_{\mathsf{imp}})$-break the imp-aca security of an ABC system if $\mathcal{A}$ runs in time at most t_{imp} and wins in Game 1 such that:*

$$\Pr[(\mathcal{A}, \mathsf{Verify}(pk, \phi^*_{\mathsf{stmt}})) = 1] \geq \varepsilon_{\mathsf{imp}}$$

for a negligible probability $\varepsilon_{\mathsf{imp}}$. We say that an ABC system is imp-aca-secure *if no adversary $(t_{\mathsf{imp}}, \varepsilon_{\mathsf{imp}})$-wins Game 1.*

Note that we reserve the term *unforgeability* of the signature scheme in contrast to some contributions in the literature [2,9,16,20,31,42]. One can view our *impersonation resilience* notion as the stronger version of the *misauthentication resistance* from the ABC systems with expressive show proofs [6,40,43] which does not cover the active and concurrent adversary besides disallowing adaptive queries. We also introduce a new oracle, namely, IssueTranscript that covers the passive adversary for the issuing protocol. This makes our security definition more comprehensive than that by related works [9,16,20,31].

4.2.2 Unlinkability

Unlinkability requires that an adversary cannot link the attributes or instances among the issuing protocols and the presentation protocols. We consider two types of unlinkability notions, namely, *full attribute unlinkability* and *full protocol unlinkability.* We require that an adversary, after being involved in the generation of a list of credentials, cannot differentiate the sequence of two attribute sets in the full attribute unlinkability. The security model for full attribute unlinkability under active and concurrent attacks (aunl-aca) is defined as a game between an adversary $\mathcal{A}$ and a challenger $\mathcal{C}$.

Game 2 (aunl − aca($\mathcal{A}$,$\mathcal{C}$))

1. ***Setup:*** *$\mathcal{C}$ runs* KeyGen *and sends pk, sk to $\mathcal{A}$.*
2. ***Phase 1:*** *$\mathcal{A}$ is able to issue concurrent queries to the* Obtain*,* Issue*,* Prove *and* Verify *oracles where he plays the role of user, issuer, prover and verifier, respectively, on any attribute set A_i of his choice in the i-th query. $\mathcal{A}$ can also issue queries to an additional oracle, namely,* Corrupt *which takes in a transcript of issuing protocol or show proofs whose user or prover, respectively, is $\mathcal{C}$ and returns the entire internal state, including the random seed used by $\mathcal{C}$ in the transcript.*
3. ***Challenge:*** *$\mathcal{A}$ decides the two equal-length, non-empty attribute sets A_0, A_1 and the access policy ϕ^*_{stmt} which he wishes to challenge such that $\phi^*_{\mathsf{stmt}}(A_0) = \phi^*_{\mathsf{stmt}}(A_1) = 1$. $\mathcal{A}$ is allowed to select A_0, A_1 from the existing queries to* Obtain *in Phase 1. $\mathcal{C}$ responds by randomly choosing a challenge bit $b \in \{0,1\}$ and interacts as the user with $\mathcal{A}$ as the issuer to complete the protocols:*
$$(\mathsf{Obtain}(pk, A_b), \mathsf{Issue}(pk, sk)) \rightarrow cred_b,$$
$$(\mathsf{Obtain}(pk, A_{1-b}), \mathsf{Issue}(pk, sk)) \rightarrow cred_{1-b}.$$
Subsequently, $\mathcal{C}$ interacts as the prover with $\mathcal{A}$ as the verifier for polynomially many times as requested by $\mathcal{A}$ to complete the protocols in the same order:
$$(\mathsf{Prove}(pk, cred_b, \phi^*_{\mathsf{stmt}}), \mathsf{Verify}(pk, \phi^*_{\mathsf{stmt}})) \rightarrow 1,$$
$$(\mathsf{Prove}(pk, cred_{1-b}, \phi^*_{\mathsf{stmt}}), \mathsf{Verify}(pk, \phi^*_{\mathsf{stmt}})) \rightarrow 1.$$
4. ***Phase 2:*** *$\mathcal{A}$ can continue to query the oracles as in Phase 1 except querying the transcripts of the challenged issuing and show proofs to* Corrupt*.*
5. ***Guess:*** *$\mathcal{A}$ outputs a guess b' and wins the game if $b' = b$.*

Definition 4. *An adversary $\mathcal{A}$ is said to $(t_{\mathsf{aunl}}, \varepsilon_{\mathsf{aunl}})$-break the* aunl-aca-security *of an ABC system if $\mathcal{A}$ runs in time at most t_{aunl} and wins in Game 2 such that:*

$$|\Pr[b = b'] - \frac{1}{2}| \geq \varepsilon_{\mathsf{aunl}}$$

for a negligible probability $\varepsilon_{\mathsf{aunl}}$. We say that an ABC system is aunl-aca-secure *if no adversary $(t_{\mathsf{aunl}}, \varepsilon_{\mathsf{aunl}})$-wins Game 2.*

Our full attribute unlinkability is more generic than that in Camenisch et al.'s ABC transformation frameworks [16] where we assume the challenged attribute sets A_0, A_1 are not equivalent such that $A_0 \neq A_1$. Besides, unlike Ringers et al.'s unlinkability notion [42], ours covers both issuing and show proofs as in Camenisch et al.'s privacy notions [20], though the latter does not have a Corrupt oracle while the former does.

On the other hand, as far as we know, the full protocol unlinkability has not been considered before. This notion requires that an adversary, after being involved in the generation of a list of credentials, cannot link an instance of issuing protocol and an instance of a show proof that are under the same credential. The full protocol unlinkability under active and concurrent attacks (punl-aca) is defined as a game between an adversary $\mathcal{A}$ and a challenger $\mathcal{C}$:

Game 3 $(\mathsf{punl-aca}(\mathcal{A}, \mathcal{C}))$.

1. ***Setup:*** *Same to that of Game 2.*
2. ***Phase 1:*** *Same to that of Game 2.*
3. ***Challenge:*** *$\mathcal{A}$ decides the two equal-length, non-empty attribute sets A_0, A_1 and the access policy ϕ^*_{stmt} which he wishes to challenge such that $\phi^*_{\mathsf{stmt}}(A_0) = \phi^*_{\mathsf{stmt}}(A_1) = 1$. $\mathcal{A}$ is allowed to select A_0, A_1 from the existing queries to* Obtain *in Phase 1. $\mathcal{C}$ responds by randomly choosing two challenge bits $b_1, b_2 \in \{0, 1\}$ and interacts as the user with $\mathcal{A}$ as the issuer to complete the protocols in the order*
$$(\mathsf{Obtain}(pk, A_{b_1}), \mathsf{Issue}(pk, sk)) \rightarrow cred_{b_1},$$
$$(\mathsf{Obtain}(pk, A_{1-b_1}), \mathsf{Issue}(pk, sk)) \rightarrow cred_{1-b_1}.$$
Subsequently, $\mathcal{C}$ interacts as the prover with $\mathcal{A}$ as the verifier for polynomially many times as requested by $\mathcal{A}$ to complete the protocols in the order
$$(\mathsf{Prove}(pk, cred_{b_2}, \phi^*_{\mathsf{stmt}}), \mathsf{Verify}(pk, \phi^*_{\mathsf{stmt}})) \rightarrow 1,$$
$$(\mathsf{Prove}(pk, cred_{1-b_2}, \phi^*_{\mathsf{stmt}}), \mathsf{Verify}(pk, \phi^*_{\mathsf{stmt}})) \rightarrow 1.$$
4. ***Phase 2:*** *Same to that of full attribute unlinkability game.*
5. ***Guess:*** *$\mathcal{A}$ outputs a guessed pair of issuing protocol transcript $\pi_{(O,I)}$ and show proof transcript $\pi_{(P,V)}$ and wins the game if the pair is under the same credential such that $cred_{\pi_{(O,I)}} = cred_{\pi_{(P,V)}}$.*

Definition 5. *An adversary $\mathcal{A}$ is said to $(t_{\mathsf{punl}}, \varepsilon_{\mathsf{punl}})$-break the* punl-aca*-security of an ABC system if $\mathcal{A}$ runs in time at most t_{punl} and wins in Game 3 such that:*
$$|\Pr[cred_{\pi_{(O,I)}} = cred_{\pi_{(P,V)}}] - \frac{1}{2}| \geq \varepsilon_{\mathsf{punl}}$$
for a negligible probability $\varepsilon_{\mathsf{punl}}$. We say that an ABC system is punl-aca-secure *if no adversary $(t_{\mathsf{punl}}, \varepsilon_{\mathsf{punl}})$-wins Game 3.*

For the completeness of the security notion, we define a security notion weaker than unlinkability, namely, full anonymity in the full version [46] and show that Fuchsbauer et al.'s ABC system [31] cannot achieve this weaker security notion. Furthermore, we prove that the full attribute unlinkability implies full anonymity in an ABC system but the opposite does not hold. We also show that there is no reduction between full attribute unlinkability and full protocol unlinkability. Therefore, we only prove the security against the full attribute unlinkability and the full protocol unlinkability for our proposed ABC system.

4.3 Construction

Concisely, a user credential *cred* is an SDH-CL signature *sig* on the MoniPoly commitment C of his attribute set A. Next, the show proofs of our ABC system is proving the validity of *sig* and C such that:

$$PK\{(\cdots) : 1 = \mathsf{SDH\text{-}CL.Verify}(C, sig, pk) \wedge \\ 1 = \mathsf{MoniPoly.Verify}Pred(pk, C, A, W, (A', l))\}$$

where $Pred = \{\mathsf{Intersection}, \mathsf{Difference}\}$. The commitment verification algorithms are the main ingredient that form the access policy for our ABC system. We describe the proposed ABC system as follows:

$\mathsf{KeyGen}(1^k)$: Construct three cyclic groups $\mathbb{G}_1, \mathbb{G}_2, \mathbb{G}_T$ of order p based on an elliptic curve whose bilinear pairing is $e : \mathbb{G}_1 \times \mathbb{G}_2 \rightarrow \mathbb{G}_T$. Select random generators $a, b, c \in \mathbb{G}_1$, $g_2 \in \mathbb{G}_2$ and two secret values $x, x' \in \mathbb{Z}_p^*$. Compute the values $a_0 = a, a_1 = a^{x'}, \ldots, a_n = a^{x'^n}, X = g_2^x, X_0 = g_2, X_1 = g_2^{x'}, \ldots, X_n = g_2^{x'^n}$ to output the public key $pk = (\mathsf{e}, \mathbb{G}_1, \mathbb{G}_2, \mathbb{G}_T, p, b, c, \{a_i, X_i\}_{0 \leq i \leq n}, X)$ and the secret key $sk = (x, x')$.

$(\mathsf{Obtain}(pk, A), \mathsf{Issue}(pk, sk))$: User interacts with verifier as follows to generate a user credential *cred* on an attribute set $A = \{m_1, \ldots, m_{n-1}\}$.

1. User chooses a random opening value $o \in \mathbb{Z}_p^*$ to compute $C = \prod_{j=0}^{n} a_j^{\mathsf{m}_j} = \mathsf{Commit}(pk, A, o)$. Subsequently, user selects random $s_1 \in \mathbb{Z}_p^*$ to initialize the issuing protocol by completing the protocol with the issuer:

$$PK\left\{(\alpha_0, \ldots, \alpha_n, \sigma) : M = \prod_{j=0}^{n} a_j^{\alpha_j} b^{\sigma}\right\}$$

   where $\sigma = s_1$ and $\{\alpha_0, \ldots, \alpha_n\} = \{\mathsf{m}_0, \ldots, \mathsf{m}_n\}$.
2. Issuer proceeds to the next step if the protocol is verified. Else, issuer outputs $\perp$ and stops.
3. Issuer generates the SDH-CL signature for M as $sig = (t, s_2, v = (Mb^{s_2}c)^{1/(x+t)})$.
4. If *sig* is not a valid signature on $A \cup \{o\}$, user outputs $\perp$ and stops. Else, user outputs the credential as $cred = (t, s, v, A = A \cup \{o\})$ where:

$$s = s_1 + s_2, v = \left(a_0^{\prod_{j=1}^{n}(x' + m_j)} b^s c\right)^{1/(x+t)}.$$

4.3.1 Proof of Possession

This protocol proves the ownership of a valid credential *cred* and the wellformedness of the committed attribute set $A = \{m_1, \ldots, m_n\}$ without disclosing any attribute. The Prove and Verify algorithms interact as follows.
$(\mathsf{Prove}(pk, cred, \perp), \mathsf{Verify}(pk, \perp))$:

1. Verifier requests for a proof of possessions protocol by sending an empty access policy $\phi = \perp$.
2. Prover chooses random $r, y \in \mathbb{Z}_p^*$ to randomize the credential as $cred' = (t' = ty, s' = sr^2, v' = v^{r^2 y^{-1}})$.
3. Setting $v', W = \prod_{j=0}^{n-1} a_j^{\mathsf{w}'_j}$ as the public input where $\{\mathsf{w}'_j\}_{0 \leq j \leq n-1} = r \times \mathsf{MPEncode}(A - \{o\})$, prover runs the zero-knowledge protocol below with the verifier:

$$PK\Big\{(\rho, \tau, \gamma, \alpha_0, \alpha_1, \sigma) : \mathsf{e}(C^\rho b^\sigma c^\rho v'^{-\tau}, X_0) = \mathsf{e}(v'^\gamma, X) \wedge$$

$$\mathsf{e}(C^\rho, X_0) = \mathsf{e}(W, X_1^{\alpha_1} X_0^{\alpha_0})\Big\}$$

where $\rho = r^2, \tau = t', \gamma = y, \{\alpha_j\} = r \times \mathsf{MPEncode}(\{o\}), \sigma = s'$. The protocol above can be compressed as:

$$PK\Big\{(\rho, \tau, \gamma, \alpha_0, \alpha_1, \sigma) : \mathsf{e}(W, X_1^{\alpha_1} X_0^{\alpha_0})\mathsf{e}\left(b^\sigma c^\rho v'^{-\tau}, X_0\right) = \mathsf{e}(v'^\gamma, X)\Big\}$$

to realize a more efficient proof.
4. Verifier outputs 1 if the protocol is verified and 0 otherwise.

4.3.2 Show Proofs

A show proof proves the relation between the attribute set A in *cred* and the queried set A' chosen by the verifier. Using the same compression technique from the proof of possession, we describe the single clause show proofs by the following presentation protocols.

AND Proof. This protocol allows prover to disclose an attribute set $A' = \{m_1, \ldots, m_k\} \subseteq A$ upon the request from verifier and proves that his credential *cred* contains A'. The showing protocol for AND proof is as follows.

$(\mathsf{Prove}(pk, cred, \phi_{\mathsf{AND}(A')}), \mathsf{Verify}(pk, \phi_{\mathsf{AND}(A')}))$:

1. Verifier requests an AND proof for the attribute set $A' = \{m_1, \ldots, m_k\}$.
2. If $A' \nsubseteq A$, prover aborts and the verifier outputs 0.
3. Else, prover chooses random $r, y \in \mathbb{Z}_p^*$ to randomize the credential as $cred' = (t' = ty, s' = sr, v' = v^{ry^{-1}}, \{\mathsf{w}'_j\}_{0 \leq j \leq n-k} = r \times \mathsf{MPEncode}(A - A'))$.
4. Setting $v', W = \prod_{j=0}^{n-k} a_j^{\mathsf{w}'_j}$ as the public input, prover runs the zero-knowledge protocol below with the verifier:

$$PK\left\{(\rho, \tau, \gamma, \sigma) : \mathsf{e}\left(W, \prod_{j=0}^{k} X_j^{\mathsf{m}_j}\right) \mathsf{e}(b^\sigma c^\rho v'^{-\tau}, X_0) = \mathsf{e}(v'^\gamma, X)\right\}$$

where $\prod_{j=0}^{k} X_j^{\mathsf{m}_j}$ and $\{\mathsf{m}_j\} = \mathsf{MPEncode}(A')$ are computed by the verifier and $\rho = r, \tau = t', \gamma = y, \sigma = s'$.
5. Verifier outputs 1 if the protocol is verified and 0 otherwise.

ANY and OR Proofs. This is the show proof for the threshold statement, and it is an OR proof when the threshold is equal to one. Consider the scenario where the prover is given an attribute set $A' = \{m_1, \ldots, m_k\}$ and he needs to prove that he has l attributes $\{m_j\}_{1 \leq j \leq l} \in (A' \cap A)$ without the verifier knowing which attributes he is proving. The showing protocol for the ANY statement is as follows.

$(\mathsf{Prove}(pk, cred, \phi_{\mathsf{ANY}(l,A')}), \mathsf{Verify}(pk, \phi_{\mathsf{ANY}(l,A')}))$:

1. Verifier requests an $\mathsf{ANY}(l, A')$ proof for the attribute set $A' = \{m_1, \ldots, m_k\}$.
2. Prover randomly selects l-attribute intersection set $I \subseteq (A' \cap A)$. If no such I can be formed, the prover aborts and the verifier outputs 0.
3. Else, prover chooses random $r, y \in \mathbb{Z}_p^*$ to randomize the credential as $cred' = (t' = ty, s' = sr^2, v' = v^{r^2 y^{-1}}, \{\mathsf{w}'_j\}_{0 \leq j \leq n-l} = r \times \mathsf{MPEncode}(A - I))$.
4. Setting $v', W = \prod_{j=0}^{n-l} a_j^{\mathsf{w}'_j}, W' = \left(\prod_{j=0}^{k-l} a_j^{\mathsf{m}_{2,j}}\right)^{r^{-1}}$ as the public input where $\{\mathsf{m}_{2,j}\}_{0 \leq j \leq k-l} = \mathsf{MPEncode}(A' - I)$, prover runs the zero-knowledge protocol below with the verifier:

$$PK\Bigg\{(\rho, \tau, \gamma, \iota_0, \ldots, \iota_l, \sigma) :$$
$$\mathsf{e}\left(W'W, \prod_{j=0}^{l} X_j^{\iota_j}\right) \mathsf{e}\left(\prod_{j=0}^{k} a_j^{-\mathsf{m}_{1,j}} b^{\sigma} c^{\rho} v'^{-\tau}, X_0\right) = \mathsf{e}(v'^{\gamma}, X)\Bigg\}$$

where $\prod_{j=0}^{k} a_j^{-\mathsf{m}_{1,j}}$ and $\{\mathsf{m}_{1,j}\}_{0 \leq j \leq k} = \mathsf{MPEncode}(A')$ are computed by the verifier and $\rho = r^2, \tau = t', \gamma = y, \{\iota_j\}_{0 \leq j \leq l} = r \times \mathsf{MPEncode}(I), \sigma = s'$.
5. Verifier outputs 1 if the protocol is verified and 0 otherwise.

NAND and NOT Proofs. This is the showing protocol for the NAND statement which allows a prover to show that an attribute set $A' = \{m_1, \ldots, m_k\}$ is disjoint with the set A in his credential. Note that it is a NOT proof when $|A'| = 1$. The showing protocol on the NAND statement is as below.

$(\mathsf{Prove}(pk, cred, \phi_{\mathsf{NAND}(A')}), \mathsf{Verify}(pk, \phi_{\mathsf{NAND}(A')}))$:

1. Verifier requests a NAND proof for the attribute set $A' = \{m_1, \ldots, m_k\}$.
2. If $|A' - A| < k$, prover aborts and the verifier outputs 0.
3. Else, prover chooses random $r, y \in \mathbb{Z}_p^*$ to randomize the credential as $cred' = (t' = ty, s' = sr, v' = v^{ry^{-1}}, \{\mathsf{w}'_j = r\mathsf{w}_j\}_{0 \leq j \leq n-k}, \{\mathsf{r}'_j = r\mathsf{r}_j\}_{0 \leq j \leq k-1})$ where $(\{\mathsf{w}_j\}_{0 \leq j \leq n-k}, \{\mathsf{r}_j\}_{0 \leq j \leq k-1}) = \mathsf{MPEncode}(A)/\mathsf{MPEncode}(A')$.
4. Setting $v', W = \prod_{j=0}^{n-k} a_j^{\mathsf{w}'_j}$ as the public input, prover runs the zero-knowledge protocol with the verifier:

$$PK\Bigg\{(\rho, \tau, \gamma, \mu_0, \ldots, \mu_{k-1}, \sigma) : \prod_{j=0}^{k-1} a_j^{\mu_j} \neq \mathbb{G}_1 \wedge$$

$$\mathsf{e}\left(W, \prod_{j=0}^{k} X_j^{\mathsf{m}_j}\right) \mathsf{e}\left(\prod_{j=0}^{k-1} a_j^{\mu_j} b^{\sigma} c^{\rho} v'^{-\tau}, X_0\right) = \mathsf{e}(v'^{\gamma}, X)\Bigg\}$$

where $\prod_{j=0}^{k} X_j^{\mathsf{m}_j}$ and $\{\mathsf{m}_j\} = \mathsf{MPEncode}(A')$ are computed by the verifier and $\{\mu_j\} = \{\mathsf{r}'_j\}, \rho = r, \tau = t', \gamma = y, \sigma = s'$.
5. Verifier outputs 1 if the protocol is verified and 0 otherwise.

NANY Proof. This is the showing protocol for the negated threshold statement. Consider the scenario where the prover is given an attribute set $A' = \{m_1, \ldots, m_k\}$ and he needs to prove that an l-attribute set $D \subseteq (A' - A)$ are not in the credential without the verifier knowing which attributes he is proving. The showing protocol on the NANY statement is as below.

$(\mathsf{Prove}(pk, cred, \phi_{\mathsf{NANY}(\bar{l}, A')}), \mathsf{Verify}(pk, \phi_{\mathsf{NANY}(\bar{l}, A')}))$:

1. Verifier requests a NANY proof for the attributes $A' = \{m_1, \ldots, m_k\}$.
2. Prover randomly selects an $\bar{l}$-attribute difference set $D \in (A' - A)$. If no such D can be formed, prover aborts and the verifier outputs 0.
3. Else, prover chooses random $r, y \in \mathbb{Z}_p^*$ to randomize the credential as $cred' = (t' = ty, s' = sr^2, v' = v^{r^2 y^{-1}}, \{\mathsf{w}'_j = r\mathsf{w}_j\}_{0 \le j \le n-\bar{l}}, \{\mathsf{r}'_j = r^2 \mathsf{w}_j\}_{0 \le j \le \bar{l}-1})$ where $(\{\mathsf{w}_j\}_{0 \le j \le n-\bar{l}}, \{\mathsf{r}_j\}_{0 \le j \le \bar{l}-1}) = \mathsf{MPEncode}(A)/\mathsf{MPEncode}(D)$.
4. Setting $v', W = \prod_{j=0}^{n-\bar{l}} a_j^{\mathsf{w}'_j}, W' = \left(\prod_{j=0}^{k-\bar{l}} a_j^{\mathsf{m}_{2,j}}\right)^{r^{-1}}$ as the public input where $\{\mathsf{m}_{2,j}\}_{0 \le j \le k-\bar{l}} = \mathsf{MPEncode}(A' - D)$, prover runs the zero-knowledge protocol with the verifier:

$$PK\Bigg\{(\rho, \tau, \gamma, \delta_0, \ldots, \delta_{\bar{l}}, \mu_0, \ldots, \mu_{\bar{l}-1}, \sigma) : \prod_{j=0}^{\bar{l}-1} a_j^{\mu_j} \neq \mathbb{G}_1 \wedge$$

$$\mathsf{e}\left(W'W, \prod_{j=0}^{\bar{l}} X_j^{\delta_j}\right) \mathsf{e}\left(\prod_{j=0}^{k} a_j^{-\mathsf{m}_{1,j}} \prod_{j=0}^{\bar{l}-1} a_j^{\mu_j} b^{\sigma} c^{\rho} v'^{-\tau}, X_0\right) = \mathsf{e}(v'^{\gamma}, X)\Bigg\}$$

where $\prod_{j=0}^{k} a_j^{-\mathsf{m}_{1,j}}$ and $\{\mathsf{m}_{1,j}\}_{0 \le j \le k} = \mathsf{MPEncode}(A')$ are computed by the verifier and $\{\mu_j\} = \{\mathsf{r}'_j\}, \rho = r^2, \tau = t', \gamma = y, \{\delta_j\}_{0 \le j \le \bar{l}} = r \times \mathsf{MPEncode}(D), \sigma = s'$.
5. Verifier outputs 1 if the protocol is verified and 0 otherwise.

4.4 Efficiently Enabling Composite Statements

Composite statements, such as, composed of multiple high-level conjunctions, can be realized with MoniPoly efficiently. For that, we propose an efficient strategy instead of naively repeating the show proofs multiple times for an access policy with a composite statement.

The prover runs a proof of possession protocol followed by a proof to show that the committed attributes from every clause in the composite statement is part of the committed attributes in the credential. For instance, given the composite statement $\mathsf{stmt} = \mathsf{AND}(A'_1) \wedge \mathsf{ANY}(l, A'_2)$ where $k_1 = |A'_1|, k_2 = |A'_2|$, a prover can run the showing protocol as follows. Let $W_{A'_1} = \prod_{j=0}^{n-k_1} a_j^{\mathsf{w}'_{A'_1,j}}, W_{A'_2} = \prod_{j=0}^{n-l} a_j^{\mathsf{w}'_{A'_2,j}}, W'_{A'_2} = \prod_{j=0}^{k_2-l} a_j^{\mathsf{m}'_{A'_2,2,j}}$ where $\{\mathsf{w}'_{A'_1,j}\}_{0\leq j\leq n-k_1} = r^2 \times \mathsf{MPEncode}(A - A'_1)$, $\{\mathsf{w}'_{A'_2,j}\}_{0\leq j\leq n-l} = r \times \mathsf{MPEncode}(A - I)$, $\{\mathsf{m}'_{A'_2,2,j}\}_{0\leq j\leq k_{2-l}} = r^{-1} \times \mathsf{MPEncode}(A'_2 - I)$ for a randomly selected $r \in \mathbb{Z}_p^*$. Setting $v', W_{A'_1}, W_{A'_2}, W'_{A'_1}$ as public inputs, the prover runs the showing protocol on ϕ_{stmt} as follows:

$$PK\Bigg\{(\rho,\tau,\gamma,\iota_0,\ldots,\iota_l,\sigma):$$
$$\mathsf{e}\left(W_{A'_1}, \prod_{j=0}^{k-1} X_j^{\mathsf{m}_{A'_1,j}}\right)\mathsf{e}\left(W'_{A'_2}W_{A'_2}, \prod_{j=0}^{l} X_j^{\iota_j}\right)\mathsf{e}\left(\prod_{j=0}^{k_2} a_j^{-\mathsf{m}_{A'_2,1,j}}(b^\sigma c^\rho v'^{-\tau})^2, X_0\right)$$
$$= \mathsf{e}(v'^{2\gamma}, X)\Bigg\}$$

where $\prod_{j=0}^{k_1} X_j^{\mathsf{m}_{A'_1,j}}, \prod_{j=0}^{k_2} a_j^{\mathsf{m}_{A'_2,2,j}}, \{\mathsf{m}_{A'_1,1,j}\}_{0\leq j\leq k_1} = \mathsf{MPEncode}(A'_1)$, $\{\mathsf{m}_{A'_2,1,j}\}_{0\leq j\leq k_2} = \mathsf{MPEncode}(A'_2)$ are computed by the verifier and $\rho = r^2, \tau = t', \gamma = y, \{\iota_j\}_{0\leq j\leq l} = r \times \mathsf{MPEncode}(I), \sigma = s'$. It is thus obvious that for any composite statement of k clauses, we can run the protocol above in a similar way using $k+2$ pairings. In precise, the $k+1$ pairings on the left-hand side correspond to the k clauses and a credential. Lastly, the corresponding credential elements in the pairings at the left-hand side and right-hand side are brought up to the power of k, respectively. Note that the complexity of $k+2$ parings does not change even when negation clauses are involved.

4.5 Security Analysis

4.5.1 Impersonation Resilience

We establish the security of the *MoniPoly* ABC system by constructing a reduction to the (co-)SDH problem. To achieve tight security reduction, we make use of Multi-Instance Reset Lemma [37] as the knowledge extractor which requires the adversary $\mathcal{A}$ to run N parallel instances of impersonation under active and concurrent attacks. The challenger $\mathcal{C}$ can fulfill this requirement by simulating the $N-1$ instances from its given SDH instance which is random self-reducible [10]. Since this is obvious, we describe only the simulation for a single instance of impersonation under active and concurrent attacks in the security proofs.

Theorem 4. *If an adversary $\mathcal{A}$ $(t_{\mathsf{imp}}, \varepsilon_{\mathsf{imp}})$-breaks the* imp-aca-*security of the proposed anonymous credential system, then there exists an algorithm $\mathcal{C}$ which $(t_{\mathsf{cosdh}}, \varepsilon_{\mathsf{cosdh}})$-breaks the co-SDH problem such that:*

$$\frac{\varepsilon_{\mathsf{cosdh}}}{t_{\mathsf{cosdh}}} = \frac{\varepsilon_{\mathsf{imp}}}{t_{\mathsf{imp}}},$$

or an algorithm $\mathcal{C}$ *which* $(t_{\mathsf{sdh}}, \varepsilon_{\mathsf{sdh}})$*-breaks the SDH problem such that:*

$$\varepsilon_{\mathsf{imp}} \le \sqrt[N]{\sqrt{\varepsilon_{\mathsf{sdh}}} - 1 + \frac{1 + (q-1)!/p^{q-2}}{p}} + 1,$$
$$t_{\mathsf{imp}} \le t_{\mathsf{sdh}}/2N - T(q^2).$$

where N *is the total adversary instance,* $q = Q_{(O,I)} + Q_{(P,V)}$ *is the total query made to the* Obtain *and* Verify *oracles, while* $T(q^2)$ *is the time parameterized by* q *to setup the simulation environment and to extract the SDH solution. Consider the dominant time elements* t_{imp} *and* t_{sdh} *only, we have:*

$$\left(1 - \left(1 - \varepsilon_{\mathsf{imp}} + \frac{1 + (q-1)!/p^{q-2}}{p}\right)^N\right)^2 \le \varepsilon_{\mathsf{sdh}}, 2Nt_{\mathsf{imp}} \approx t_{\mathsf{sdh}}.$$

Let $N = (\varepsilon_{\mathsf{imp}} - \frac{1+(q-1)!/p^{q-2}}{p})^{-1}$*, we get* $\varepsilon_{\mathsf{sdh}} \ge (1 - e^{-1})^2 \ge 1/3$ *and the success ratio is:*

$$\frac{\varepsilon_{\mathsf{sdh}}}{t_{\mathsf{sdh}}} \ge \frac{1}{3 \cdot 2Nt_{\mathsf{imp}}}$$
$$\frac{6\varepsilon_{\mathsf{sdh}}}{t_{\mathsf{sdh}}} \ge \frac{\varepsilon_{\mathsf{imp}}}{t_{\mathsf{imp}}} - \frac{1 + (q-1)!/p^{q-2}}{t_{\mathsf{imp}}p}$$

which gives a tight reduction.

To modularize the proof for Theorem 4, we categorize the way an adversary impersonates in Table 2. This is like the approach in the tight reduction proof for the SDH-CL signature scheme proposed by Schäge [44]. Subsequently, we differentiate $\mathcal{A}$ into $\mathcal{A} = \{\mathcal{A}_{bind}, \mathcal{A}_1, \mathcal{A}_2, \mathcal{A}_3\}$ corresponding to four different simulation strategies by $\mathcal{C}$. We omit the proof for the binding property of MoniPoly commitment scheme $\mathcal{A}_{bind}$ which has been described in Theorem 3 and can be trivially applied here.

In each of the simulation strategy, we consider only the success probability of breaking the SDH problem which is weaker than the DLOG problem such that $\varepsilon_{\mathsf{sdh}} \ge \varepsilon_{\mathsf{dlog}}$. Let $M^* = \prod_{j=1}^n (x' + m_j^*)$ and $M_i = \prod_{j=1}^n (x' + m_{i,j})$ where $A^* = \{m_j^*\}$ and $A_i = \{m_j\}$, respectively, the DLOG problem can be solved whenever the forgery v^* produced by $\mathcal{A}$ equals to a v_i which has been generated by $\mathcal{C}$ such that:

$$\because v^* \equiv v_i$$
$$(a_0^{M^*} b^{s^*} c)^{\frac{1}{x+t^*}} \equiv (a_0^{M_i} b^{s_i} c)^{\frac{1}{x+t_i}}$$
$$(a_0^{M^* + s^*\beta + \gamma})^{\frac{1}{x+t^*}} \equiv (a_0^{M_i + s_i\beta + \gamma})^{\frac{1}{x+t_i}}$$
$$\therefore \frac{M^* + s^*\beta + \gamma}{x + t^*} \equiv \frac{M_i + s_i\beta + \gamma}{x + t_i} \mod p$$

Table 2. Types of impersonation and the corresponding assumptions.

Type	A	MPEncode(A)	s	t	v	Adversary	Assumption	Lemmas
0	0	1	*	*	*	$\mathcal{A}_{bind}$	co-SDH	Theorem 3
1	0	0	0	0	0	$\mathcal{A}_1$	SDH	1
2	0	0	0	0	1	$\mathcal{A}_1$	DLOG	1
3	0	0	0	1	0	$\mathcal{A}_2$	SDH	2
4	0	0	0	1	1	$\mathcal{A}_2$	DLOG	2
5	0	0	1	0	0	$\mathcal{A}_1$	SDH	1
6	0	0	1	0	1	$\mathcal{A}_1$	DLOG	1
7	0	0	1	1	0	$\mathcal{A}_3$	SDH	3
8	0	0	1	1	1	$\mathcal{A}_3$	DLOG	3
9	1	1	0	0	0	$\mathcal{A}_1$	SDH	1
10	1	1	0	0	1	$\mathcal{A}_1$	DLOG	1
11	1	1	0	1	0	$\mathcal{A}_2$	SDH	2
12	1	1	0	1	1	$\mathcal{A}_2$	DLOG	2
13	1	1	1	0	0	$\mathcal{A}_1$	SDH	1
14	1	1	1	0	1	$\mathcal{A}_1$	N/A	1
15	1	1	1	1	0	$\mathcal{A}_3$	SDH	3
16	1	1	1	1	1	$\mathcal{A}_3$	N/A	3

Note: * = 1 or 0, 1 = equal, 0 = unequal, N/A = not available

which leads to:

$$x \equiv \frac{t^* M_i - t_i M^* + \beta(t^* s_i - t_i s^*) + \gamma(t^* - t_i)}{M^* - M_i + \beta(s^* - s_i)} \mod p$$

where $\mathcal{C}$ can solve the SDH problem using x. Following the equation, the Type 14 impersonation $(A^*, v^*, s^*) = (A_i, v_i, s_i)$ will not happen as it causes a division by zero. On the other hand, Type 16 represents the impersonation using the uncorrupted *cred* generated by $\mathcal{C}$ when it answers $\mathcal{A}$'s IssueTranscript queries or Verify queries. If $\mathcal{A}$'s view is independent of $\mathcal{C}$'s choice of (t_i, s_i), we have $(t^*, s^*) \neq (t_i, s_i)$ with probability $1 - 1/p$. This causes Type 16 impersonation to happen with a negligible probability of $1/p$ at which point our simulation fails.

We present Lemmas 1, 2 and 3 corresponding to the adversaries $\mathcal{A}_1$, $\mathcal{A}_2$ and $\mathcal{A}_3$ as follows. The proofs for the lemmas are in the full version [46].

Lemma 1. *If an adversary $\mathcal{A}_1$ $(t_{\mathsf{imp}}, \varepsilon_{\mathsf{imp}})$-breaks the imp-aca-security of the proposed anonymous credential system, then there exists an algorithm $\mathcal{C}$ which $(t_{\mathsf{sdh}}, \varepsilon_{\mathsf{sdh}})$-solves the SDH problem such that:*

$$\varepsilon_{\mathsf{imp}} \leq \sqrt[N]{\sqrt{\varepsilon_{\mathsf{sdh}}} - 1} + \frac{1 + (q-1)!/p^{q-2}}{p} + 1,$$
$$t_{\mathsf{imp}} \leq t_{\mathsf{sdh}}/2N - T(q^2).$$

where N is the total of adversary instances, $q = Q_{(O,I)} + Q_{(P,V)}$ is the number of queries made to the Obtain *and* Verify *oracles, while $T(q^2)$ is the time parameterized by q to setup the simulation environment and to extract the SDH solution.*

Lemma 2. *If an adversary $\mathcal{A}_2$ $(t_{\mathsf{imp}}, \varepsilon_{\mathsf{imp}})$-breaks the imp-aca-security of the proposed anonymous credential system, then there exists an algorithm $\mathcal{C}$ which $(t_{\mathsf{sdh}}, \varepsilon_{\mathsf{sdh}})$-solves the SDH problem such that:*

$$\varepsilon_{\mathsf{imp}} \leq \sqrt[N]{\sqrt{\varepsilon_{\mathsf{sdh}}} - 1 + \frac{1 + (q-1)!/p^{q-2}}{p}} + 1,$$
$$t_{\mathsf{imp}} \leq t_{\mathsf{sdh}}/2N - T(q^2).$$

where N is the total of adversary instances, $q = Q_{(O,I)} + Q_{(P,V)}$ is the number of queries made to the Obtain *and* Verify *oracles, while $T(q^2)$ is the time parameterized by q to setup the simulation environment and to extract the SDH solution.*

Lemma 3. *If an adversary $\mathcal{A}_3$ $(t_{\mathsf{imp}}, \varepsilon_{\mathsf{imp}})$-breaks the imp-aca-security of the proposed anonymous credential system, then there exists an algorithm $\mathcal{C}$ which $(t_{\mathsf{sdh}}, \varepsilon_{\mathsf{sdh}})$-solves the SDH problem such that:*

$$\varepsilon_{\mathsf{imp}} \leq \sqrt[N]{\sqrt{\varepsilon_{\mathsf{sdh}}} - 1 + \frac{(q-1)!/p^{q-2}}{p}} + 1,$$
$$t_{\mathsf{imp}} \leq t_{\mathsf{sdh}}/2N - T(q^2).$$

where N is the total of adversary instances, $q = Q_{(O,I)} + Q_{(P,V)}$ is the number of queries made to the Obtain *and* Verify *oracles, while $T(q^2)$ is the time parameterized by q to setup the simulation environment and to extract the SDH solution.*

Combining Theorem 3, Lemmas 1, 2, and 3 gives Theorem 4 as required.

4.5.2 Unlinkability

Next, we prove the unlinkability of the proposed ABC system. It is sufficient to show that the witnesses, the committed attributes and the randomized credential in the issuing protocol and presentation protocol, respectively, are perfectly hiding. Then, we demonstrate that every instance of the protocols is uniformly distributed due to the random self-reducibility property. This implies that even when $\mathcal{A}$ is given access to the Obtain, Issue, Prove, Verify and Corrupt oracles, it does not has advantage in guessing the challenged attribute sets. The proofs for Lemma 5 and 7 are in the full version [46].

Lemma 4. *The committed attributes and the corresponding witness in the issuing protocol of the ABC system are perfectly hiding.*

Proof. By Theorem 2, the MoniPoly commitment $C = \prod_{j=0}^{n} a_j^{\mathsf{m}_j}$ in the issuing protocol is perfectly hiding. Subsequently, the value $M = Cb^{s_1}$ is a Pedersen commitment which is also perfectly hiding. The same reasoning is applicable on the commitment value in the zero-knowledge protocol $R = \prod_{j=0}^{n} a_j^{\tilde{\mathsf{m}}_j} b^{\tilde{s}_1}$ which has the same structure as that of M. □

Lemma 5. *The initialization of the issuing protocol in the ABC system has random self-reducibility.*

Lemma 6. *The randomized credential in the presentation protocol of the ABC system are perfectly hiding.*

Proof. Given a user's randomized credential $v' = v^{ry^{-1}}$ in the show proof, there are $|\mathbb{Z}_p^*| - 1$ possible pairs of $(r', y') \neq (r, y)$ which can result in the same v'. Besides, for each r, there is a unique y such that:

$$\mathsf{dlog}_{a_0}(v') = \mathsf{dlog}_{a_0}(v) r y^{-1}$$

$$y = \frac{\mathsf{dlog}_{a_0}(v)}{\mathsf{dlog}_{a_0}(v')} \cdot r$$

Since r, y are chosen independently from each other, and of the credential element v, the latter is perfectly hidden. The same reasoning applies on the randomized credential $v' = v^{r^2 y^{-1}}$. □

Lemma 7. *The presentation protocol of the ABC system offers random self-reducibility.*

Theorem 5. *If the initialization of the issuing protocol and the presentation protocol have random self-reducibility, and their witnesses, committed attributes as well as the randomized credential are perfectly hiding, the ABC system is* aunl-aca-secure*.*

Using the similar approach, we show that the security of full protocol unlinkability also holds for the proposed ABC system.

Theorem 6. *If the initialization of the issuing protocol and the presentation protocol have random self-reducibility, and their witnesses, committed attributes as well as randomized credential are perfectly hiding, the ABC system is* punl-aca-secure*.*

5 Evaluation

5.1 Security

We offer a general overview of security properties in comparison with other schemes here and offer the tightness analysis of our own scheme in the full version [46].

We summarize the security properties of ABC systems in either SDH or alternative paradigms in Table 3. The table shows that the relevant schemes vary significantly in their fulfilled security requirements. MoniPoly is the only ABC system that achieves the full range of security requirements. At the same time, it is proven secure in the standard model with a tight security reduction.

Table 3. Security properties of related ABC systems.

ABC System	Impersonation Resilience	Anonymity		Unlinkability			Security Model	Hard Problem	Tight Reduction
		I	P	I	P	I↔P			
ASM [4]	●	●	●	○	○	○	RO	SDH, DDHI	○
TAKS [47]	●	○	●	○	○	○	RO	SDH, DDH	○
AMO [2]	●	○	●	○	●	○	Standard	SDH, DLIN	○
CKS [19]	●	○	○	○	○	○	Standard	DHE, HSDHE	○
SNF [45]	●	○	○	○	○	○	Standard	SDH, DHE, HSDH, TDH	○
ZF [48]	●	○	●	○	●	○	Standard	SDH, HPDH, HSDH, TDH	○
BNF [6]	◐	○	◐	○	○	○	Standard	DLIN, SFP, DHE	○
CKLMNP [20]	●	○	○	●	●	○	Standard	SRSA, DLOG	○
BBDT [5]	●	○	●	○	○	○	Standard	SDH	○
RVH [42]	●	○	○	○	●	○	Standard	whLRSW	○
SNBF [43]	●	○	●	○	○	○	Standard	DLIN, SFP, DHE	○
ON [40]	◐	○	◐	○	○	○	Standard	DLIN, SFP, DHE	○
CDDH [15]	●	○	●	○	○	○	Standard	SCDHI	○
BB [8]	●	○	●	○	○	○	Generic	SDH, MSDH-1	○
BBBB+ [7]	●	◐	◐	○	○	○	RO	SDH, MSDH-1	○
BBDE [9]	●	●	●	○	○	○	Standard	SDH, MSDH-1	○
CG [17,18]	●	○	○	○	○	○	Standard	SRSA	○
CDHK [16]	●	○	○	●	●	○	CRS	SXDH, RootDH, BSDH, SDH, XDLIN, co-CDH, DBP	○
FHS [31]	●	●	●	○	◐	○	Generic	DDH, co-DLOG, co-SDH	○
This Work	●	●	●	●	●	●	Standard	SDH, co-SDH	●

Note: ●: proof provided, ◐: claim provided, ○: no claim, I: Issuing, P: Presentation
○ in Issuing: only weak anonymity or unlinkability/trusted issuer/no blind issuing

5.2 Expressivity and Computational Complexity

In Table 4, we compare the MoniPoly ABC system to relevant popular ABC systems with respect to their realized show proofs and asymptotic computational complexities. Table 4 is normalized in that it considers only the asymptotic complexity for the most expensive operations (e.g., the scalar multiplication, modular exponentiation, or pairing).

5.2.1 Expressivity over Unrestricted Attribute Space

The MoniPoly ABC system is the first scheme that can efficiently support all logical statements in the show proofs regardless of the types of attribute space (cf. Table 4). That is, MoniPoly operates on arbitrary attributes while offering a wide range of statements in its expressiveness.

We note that the traditional encoding can achieve the same expressiveness, in principle, in an unrestricted attribute space $\mathcal{S}$ as well as string attribute space $\mathcal{S}_S$. However, traditional encoding will yield inefficient proofs.

5.2.2 Expressivity over Finite-Set Attribute Space

Let us now consider the comparison with schemes with only finite-set attribute space $\mathcal{S}_F$. Most of the accumulator-based ABC systems [43,45] are restricted to finite-set attributes only. While MoniPoly supports negation statements in terms of expressivity, their show proofs do not. The restriction to finite-set attributes and monotone (non-negative) formula affords them a low asymptotic complexity in show proofs. However, their setup and issuing protocols are prohibitively expensive with exponential computational and space complexity ($O(2^{n_F})$ [40]

Table 4. Asymptotic complexity for show proofs in related ABC systems.

Property		ABC System							
Attribute Space		$\mathcal{S}_F$			$\mathcal{S}_S + \mathcal{S}_F$		$\mathcal{S}$		
Technique		Accumulator		Trad. Encd.	Accumulator	Prime Encd.	Trad. Encd.	Comm.	MoniPoly
Setup		$O(n_F)$	$O(2^{n_F})$	$O(n)$	$O(n)$	$O(n)$	$O(n)$	$O(n)$	$O(n)$
Issuing Protocol	Prover	$O(1)$	$O(1)$	$O(1)$	$O(n_S)$	$O(n)$	$O(n)$	$O(n)$	$O(n)$
	Verifier	$O(2^{\sqrt{n_F}})$	$O(n_F)$	$O(n)$	$O(n_S)$	$O(n)$	$O(n)$	$O(n)$	$O(n)$
Show Proofs: Possession	Prover	$O(n_F)$	$O(L)$	$O(n_S)+O(N)$	$O(n_S)+O(1)$	$O(n)+O(1)$	$O(n)$	$O(n)$	$O(n)$
	Verifier	$O(n_F)$	$O(L)$	$O(n_S)+O(N)$	$O(n_S)+O(1)$	$O(n)+O(1)$	$O(n)$	$O(n)$	$O(1)$
$\mathsf{AND}(A')$	Prover	$O(k_F)$	$O(L)$	$O(n_S-k_S)+O(N)$	$O(n_S-k_S)+O(1)$	$O(n_S-k_S)+O(1)$	$O(n-k)$	$O(n-k)$	$O(n-k)$
	Verifier	$O(k_F)$	$O(L)$	$O(n_S)+O(N)$	$O(n_S)+O(1)$	$O(n_S)+O(1)$	$O(n)$	$O(k)$	$O(k)$
$\mathsf{OR}(A')$	Prover	$O(k_F)$	$O(L)$	$O(n_Sk_S)+O(N)$	$O(n_Sk_S)+O(1)$	$O(n_Sk_S)+O(1)$	✗	✗	$O(n+k)$
	Verifier	$O(k_F)$	$O(L)$	$O(n_Sk_S)+O(N)$	$O(n_Sk_S)+O(1)$	$O(n_Sk_S)+O(1)$	✗	✗	$O(k)$
$\mathsf{ANY}(l, A')$	Prover	$O(k_F)$	$O(L)$	$O(n_S!)+O(N)$	✗	✗	✗	✗	$O(n-l+k)$
	Verifier	$O(k_F)$	$O(L)$	$O(n_S!)+O(N)$	✗	✗	✗	✗	$O(k+l)$
$\mathsf{NAND}(A')$	Prover	✗	$O(L)$	✗	✗	$O(n_S-k_S)+O(1)$	✗	✗	$O(n)$
	Verifier	✗	$O(L)$	✗	✗	$O(n_S)+O(1)$	✗	✗	$O(2k)$
$\mathsf{NOR}(A')$	Prover	✗	$O(L)$	✗	✗	✗	✗	✗	$O(n+k)$
	Verifier	✗	$O(L)$	✗	✗	✗	✗	✗	$O(k)$
$\mathsf{NANY}(\bar{l}, A')$	Prover	✗	$O(L)$	✗	✗	✗	✗	✗	$O(n+k)$
	Verifier	✗	$O(L)$	✗	✗	✗	✗	✗	$O(k+2\bar{l})$
Constant Size Proofs		✓	✓	✗	✓	✓	✗	✓	✓
Flexible Attribute Indexing		✗	✗	✗	✗	✗	✗	✓	✓
Schemes		[43]	[40]	[48]	[45]	[18]	[4,7–9,19]	[16,31]	This Work

Note: $\mathcal{S}$: attribute space, $k = |A'| \leq n = |A| = n_S + n_F$, S: string attributes, F: finite-attributes, L: maximum allowed $\wedge$ in CNF,
N: maximum attributes allowed in a statement, ✓: realized, ✗: not realized

and $O(2^{\sqrt{n_F}})$ [43]), in turn, restricting the number of attributes that can be feasibly encoded.

The latest ABC system in this line of work [40] proposes a workaround on the negated forms of attributes separately. In this scheme, each of its show proof has $O(L)$ complexity where L is the maximum number of $\wedge$ operators permitted in a composite conjunctive formulae. Moreover, the additional negated finite-set attributes double the credential size and the already massive public key size.

5.2.3 Comparison to Commitment-Based Schemes

MoniPoly bears similarities in terms of computational and communication complexity to other commitment-based ABC systems [16,31]. Although MoniPoly does not have constant asymptotic complexity, the verifier is required to compute only three pairings for a single-clause show proof. This makes our scheme the most efficient construction of its kind in this comparison. At the same time, apart from having constant-size AND proof similarly to the relevant commitment-based schemes [16,31], MoniPoly has constant-size possession proof.

5.2.4 Parametric Complexity Analysis

We estimate the computational complexity of the schemes listed in Table 4 and present in Fig. 1 the complexity for each ABC system at 128-bit security level. While schemes especially crafted for a restricted finite-set attribute space are the fastest schemes in the field, Monipoly is the most efficient ABC system based

(a) Proof of possession (128-bit). (b) AND proof (128-bit).

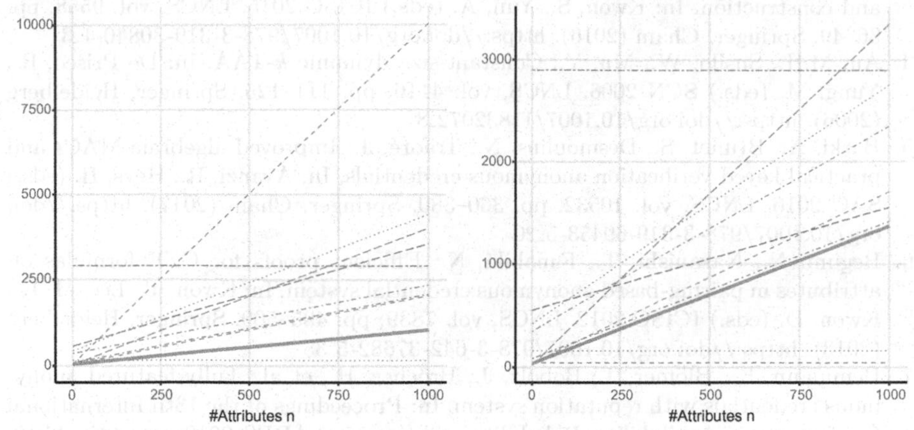

(c) Scheme

Fig. 1. Asymptotic complexity of ABC systems (scalar multiplications in $\mathbb{G}_1$)

on commitment schemes and outperforms most schemes in the field, overall. If strength in terms of security properties is a prerequisite, our ABC system outperforms all listed in Table 4 while having efficient constant size show proofs.

This estimation is based on the following relative computation costs in equivalents of scalar multiplications in $\mathbb{G}_1$:

BLS-12 curve at 128-bit security: for a scalar multiplication in $\mathbb{G}_2$, an exponentiation in $\mathbb{G}_T$ and a pairing, respectively, is about the same as computing 2, 6 and 9 scalar multiplications (M_1) in $\mathbb{G}_1$. The modular exponentiation of RSA-3072 on the other hand is equivalent to $5M_1$.

We also assume the computational cost in Type-1 pairing friendly curve is equivalent to that of Type-3 as well as $L = 1$ and $N = 1$. The details of the estimation can be found in the full version [46].

References

1. Abe, M., Fuchsbauer, G., Groth, J., Haralambiev, K., Ohkubo, M.: Structure-preserving signatures and commitments to group elements. In: Rabin, T. (ed.) CRYPTO 2010. LNCS, vol. 6223, pp. 209–236. Springer, Heidelberg (2010). https://doi.org/10.1007/978-3-642-14623-7_12
2. Akagi, N., Manabe, Y., Okamoto, T.: An efficient anonymous credential system. In: Tsudik, G. (ed.) FC 2008. LNCS, vol. 5143, pp. 272–286. Springer, Heidelberg (2008). https://doi.org/10.1007/978-3-540-85230-8_25

3. Anada, H., Arita, S., Sakurai, K.: Attribute-based two-tier signatures: definition and construction. In: Kwon, S., Yun, A. (eds.) ICISC 2015. LNCS, vol. 9558, pp. 36–49. Springer, Cham (2016). https://doi.org/10.1007/978-3-319-30840-1_3
4. Au, M.H., Susilo, W., Mu, Y.: Constant-size dynamic k-TAA. In: De Prisco, R., Yung, M. (eds.) SCN 2006. LNCS, vol. 4116, pp. 111–125. Springer, Heidelberg (2006). https://doi.org/10.1007/11832072_8
5. Barki, A., Brunet, S., Desmoulins, N., Traoré, J.: Improved algebraic MACs and practical keyed-verification anonymous credentials. In: Avanzi, R., Heys, H. (eds.) SAC 2016. LNCS, vol. 10532, pp. 360–380. Springer, Cham (2017). https://doi.org/10.1007/978-3-319-69453-5_20
6. Begum, N., Nakanishi, T., Funabiki, N.: Efficient proofs for CNF formulas on attributes in pairing-based anonymous credential system. In: Kwon, T., Lee, M.-K., Kwon, D. (eds.) ICISC 2012. LNCS, vol. 7839, pp. 495–509. Springer, Heidelberg (2013). https://doi.org/10.1007/978-3-642-37682-5_35
7. Bemmann, K., Blömer, J., Bobolz, J., Bröcher, H., et al.: Fully-featured anonymous credentials with reputation system. In: Proceedings of the 13th International Conference on Availability, Reliability and Security, ARES 2018, pp. 42:1–42:10. ACM (2018)
8. Blömer, J., Bobolz, J.: Delegatable attribute-based anonymous credentials from dynamically malleable signatures. In: Preneel, B., Vercauteren, F. (eds.) ACNS 2018. LNCS, vol. 10892, pp. 221–239. Springer, Cham (2018). https://doi.org/10.1007/978-3-319-93387-0_12
9. Blömer, J., Bobolz, J., Diemert, D., Eidens, F.: Updatable anonymous credentials and applications to incentive systems. In: Proceedings of the 2019 ACM SIGSAC Conference on Computer and Communications Security, CCS 2019, pp. 1671–1685. Association for Computing Machinery (2019)
10. Boneh, D., Boyen, X.: Short signatures without random oracles and the SDH assumption in bilinear groups. J. Cryptology **21**(2), 149–177 (2008)
11. Boneh, D., Boyen, X., Shacham, H.: Short group signatures. In: Franklin, M. (ed.) CRYPTO 2004. LNCS, vol. 3152, pp. 41–55. Springer, Heidelberg (2004). https://doi.org/10.1007/978-3-540-28628-8_3
12. Brands, S.A.: Rethinking Public Key Infrastructures and Digital Certificates: Building in Privacy. MIT Press, Cambridge (2000)
13. Brickell, E., Li, J.: Enhanced privacy id from bilinear pairing for hardware authentication and attestation. In: 2010 IEEE Second International Conference on Social Computing, pp. 768–775, August 2010
14. Brickell, E., Li, J.: A pairing-based DAA scheme further reducing TPM resources. In: Acquisti, A., Smith, S.W., Sadeghi, A.-R. (eds.) Trust 2010. LNCS, vol. 6101, pp. 181–195. Springer, Heidelberg (2010). https://doi.org/10.1007/978-3-642-13869-0_12
15. Camenisch, J., Drijvers, M., Dzurenda, P., Hajny, J.: Fast keyed-verification anonymous credentials on standard smart cards. In: Dhillon, G., Karlsson, F., Hedström, K., Zúquete, A. (eds.) SEC 2019. IAICT, vol. 562, pp. 286–298. Springer, Cham (2019). https://doi.org/10.1007/978-3-030-22312-0_20
16. Camenisch, J., Dubovitskaya, M., Haralambiev, K., Kohlweiss, M.: Composable and modular anonymous credentials: definitions and practical constructions. In: Iwata, T., Cheon, J.H. (eds.) ASIACRYPT 2015. LNCS, vol. 9453, pp. 262–288. Springer, Heidelberg (2015). https://doi.org/10.1007/978-3-662-48800-3_11
17. Camenisch, J., Groß, T.: Efficient attributes for anonymous credentials. In: Proceedings of the 15th ACM Conference on Computer and Communications Security, pp. 345–356. ACM (2008)

18. Camenisch, J., Groß, T.: Efficient attributes for anonymous credentials. ACM Trans. Inf. Syst. Secur. **15**(1), 4:1–4:30 (2012)
19. Camenisch, J., Kohlweiss, M., Soriente, C.: An accumulator based on bilinear maps and efficient revocation for anonymous credentials. In: Jarecki, S., Tsudik, G. (eds.) PKC 2009. LNCS, vol. 5443, pp. 481–500. Springer, Heidelberg (2009). https://doi.org/10.1007/978-3-642-00468-1_27
20. Camenisch, J., Krenn, S., Lehmann, A., Mikkelsen, G.L., Neven, G., Pedersen, M.Ø.: Formal treatment of privacy-enhancing credential systems. In: Dunkelman, O., Keliher, L. (eds.) SAC 2015. LNCS, vol. 9566, pp. 3–24. Springer, Cham (2016). https://doi.org/10.1007/978-3-319-31301-6_1
21. Camenisch, J., Lysyanskaya, A.: An efficient system for non-transferable anonymous credentials with optional anonymity revocation. In: Pfitzmann, B. (ed.) EUROCRYPT 2001. LNCS, vol. 2045, pp. 93–118. Springer, Heidelberg (2001). https://doi.org/10.1007/3-540-44987-6_7
22. Camenisch, J., Lysyanskaya, A.: A signature scheme with efficient protocols. In: Cimato, S., Persiano, G., Galdi, C. (eds.) SCN 2002. LNCS, vol. 2576, pp. 268–289. Springer, Heidelberg (2003). https://doi.org/10.1007/3-540-36413-7_20
23. Camenisch, J., Lysyanskaya, A.: Signature schemes and anonymous credentials from bilinear maps. In: Franklin, M. (ed.) CRYPTO 2004. LNCS, vol. 3152, pp. 56–72. Springer, Heidelberg (2004). https://doi.org/10.1007/978-3-540-28628-8_4
24. Chase, M., Meiklejohn, S., Zaverucha, G.: Algebraic macs and keyed-verification anonymous credentials. In: Proceedings of the 2014 ACM SIGSAC Conference on Computer and Communications Security, CCS 2014, pp. 1205–1216. ACM (2014)
25. Chaum, D.: Security without identification: transaction systems to make big brother obsolete. Commun. ACM **28**(10), 1030–1044 (1985)
26. Chen, L.: A DAA scheme requiring less TPM resources. In: Bao, F., Yung, M., Lin, D., Jing, J. (eds.) Inscrypt 2009. LNCS, vol. 6151, pp. 350–365. Springer, Heidelberg (2010). https://doi.org/10.1007/978-3-642-16342-5_26
27. Chen, L., Li, J.: Flexible and scalable digital signatures in TPM 2.0. In: Proceedings of the Conference on Computer & Communications Security (CCS), CCS 2013, pp. 37–48. ACM (2013)
28. Chen, X., Feng, D.: Direct anonymous attestation for next generation TPM (2008)
29. Chu, X., Yu, Q.: A new efficient property-based attestation protocol based on elliptic curves. In: 2012 IEEE 11th International Conference on Trust, Security and Privacy in Computing and Communications, pp. 730–736, June 2012
30. Damgård, I.: Commitment schemes and zero-knowledge protocols. In: Damgård, I.B. (ed.) EEF School 1998. LNCS, vol. 1561, pp. 63–86. Springer, Heidelberg (1999). https://doi.org/10.1007/3-540-48969-X_3
31. Fuchsbauer, G., Hanser, C., Slamanig, D.: Structure-preserving signatures on equivalence classes and constant-size anonymous credentials. J. Cryptology **32**(2), 498–546 (2019)
32. Groß, T.: Signatures and efficient proofs on committed graphs and NP-statements. In: Böhme, R., Okamoto, T. (eds.) FC 2015. LNCS, vol. 8975, pp. 293–314. Springer, Heidelberg (2015). https://doi.org/10.1007/978-3-662-47854-7_18
33. Groß, T.R.: Efficient certification and zero-knowledge proofs of knowledge on infrastructure topology graphs. In: Proceedings of the 6th Edition of the ACM Workshop on Cloud Computing Security, CCSW 2014, pp. 69–80. Association for Computing Machinery, New York (2014)
34. Guo, N., Gao, T., Wang, J.: Privacy-preserving and efficient attributes proof based on selective aggregate CL-signature scheme. Int. J. Comput. Math. **93**(2), 273–288 (2016)

35. Izabachène, M., Libert, B., Vergnaud, D.: Block-wise P-signatures and non-interactive anonymous credentials with efficient attributes. In: Chen, L. (ed.) IMACC 2011. LNCS, vol. 7089, pp. 431–450. Springer, Heidelberg (2011). https://doi.org/10.1007/978-3-642-25516-8_26
36. Kate, A., Zaverucha, G.M., Goldberg, I.: Constant-size commitments to polynomials and their applications. In: Abe, M. (ed.) ASIACRYPT 2010. LNCS, vol. 6477, pp. 177–194. Springer, Heidelberg (2010). https://doi.org/10.1007/978-3-642-17373-8_11
37. Kiltz, E., Masny, D., Pan, J.: Optimal security proofs for signatures from identification schemes. In: Robshaw, M., Katz, J. (eds.) CRYPTO 2016. LNCS, vol. 9815, pp. 33–61. Springer, Heidelberg (2016). https://doi.org/10.1007/978-3-662-53008-5_2
38. Nguyen, L.: Accumulators from bilinear pairings and applications. In: Menezes, A. (ed.) CT-RSA 2005. LNCS, vol. 3376, pp. 275–292. Springer, Heidelberg (2005). https://doi.org/10.1007/978-3-540-30574-3_19
39. Okamoto, T.: Efficient blind and partially blind signatures without random Oracles. In: Halevi, S., Rabin, T. (eds.) TCC 2006. LNCS, vol. 3876, pp. 80–99. Springer, Heidelberg (2006). https://doi.org/10.1007/11681878_5
40. Okishima, R., Nakanishi, T.: An anonymous credential system with constant-size attribute proofs for CNF formulas with negations. In: Attrapadung, N., Yagi, T. (eds.) IWSEC 2019. LNCS, vol. 11689, pp. 89–106. Springer, Cham (2019). https://doi.org/10.1007/978-3-030-26834-3_6
41. Pointcheval, D., Sanders, O.: Short randomizable signatures. In: Sako, K. (ed.) CT-RSA 2016. LNCS, vol. 9610, pp. 111–126. Springer, Cham (2016). https://doi.org/10.1007/978-3-319-29485-8_7
42. Ringers, S., Verheul, E., Hoepman, J.-H.: An efficient self-blindable attribute-based credential scheme. In: Kiayias, A. (ed.) FC 2017. LNCS, vol. 10322, pp. 3–20. Springer, Cham (2017). https://doi.org/10.1007/978-3-319-70972-7_1
43. Sadiah, S., Nakanishi, T., Begum, N., Funabiki, N.: Accumulator for monotone formulas and its application to anonymous credential system. J. Inf. Process. **25**, 949–961 (2017)
44. Schäge, S.: Tight proofs for signature schemes without random Oracles. In: Paterson, K.G. (ed.) EUROCRYPT 2011. LNCS, vol. 6632, pp. 189–206. Springer, Heidelberg (2011). https://doi.org/10.1007/978-3-642-20465-4_12
45. Sudarsono, A., Nakanishi, T., Funabiki, N.: Efficient proofs of attributes in pairing-based anonymous credential system. In: Fischer-Hübner, S., Hopper, N. (eds.) PETS 2011. LNCS, vol. 6794, pp. 246–263. Springer, Heidelberg (2011). https://doi.org/10.1007/978-3-642-22263-4_14
46. Tan, S.-Y., Groß, T.: Monipoly–an expressive q-SDH-based anonymous attribute-based credential system [extended version]. Cryptology ePrint Archive Report 2020/587 (ia.cr/2020/587), IACR, May 2020
47. Tsang, P.P., Au, M.H., Kapadia, A., Smith, S.W.: Blacklistable anonymous credentials: blocking misbehaving users without TTPS. In: Proceedings of the 14th ACM Conference on Computer and Communications Security, CCS 207, pp. 72–81. ACM (2007)
48. Zhang, Y., Feng, D.: Efficient attribute proofs in anonymous credential using attribute-based cryptography. In: Chim, T.W., Yuen, T.H. (eds.) ICICS 2012. LNCS, vol. 7618, pp. 408–415. Springer, Heidelberg (2012). https://doi.org/10.1007/978-3-642-34129-8_39

Updatable Encryption

The Direction of Updatable Encryption Does Not Matter Much

Yao Jiang(✉)

Norwegian University of Science and Technology, NTNU, Trondheim, Norway
yao.jiang@ntnu.no

Abstract. Updatable encryption schemes allow for key rotation on ciphertexts. A client outsourcing storage of encrypted data to a cloud server can change its encryption key. The cloud server can update the stored ciphertexts to the new key using only a token provided by the client.

This paper solves two open problems in updatable encryption, that of uni-directional vs. bi-directional updates, and post-quantum security.

The main result in this paper is to analyze the security notions based on uni- and bi-directional updates. Surprisingly, we prove that uni- and bi-directional variants of each security notion are equivalent.

The second result in this paper is to provide a new and efficient updatable encryption scheme based on the Decisional Learning with Error assumption. This gives us post-quantum security. Our scheme is bi-directional, but because of our main result, this is sufficient.

Keywords: Updatable encryption · Cloud storage · Key rotation · Lattice-based cryptography · Post-quantum cryptography

1 Introduction

Consider the following scenario: a client wishes to outsource data to a cloud storage provider with a cryptoperiod (client key lifetime). The cryptoperiod is decided by the client or the cloud storage provider or both. If the key lifetime is expired, the old key is no longer available for either encryption or decryption, a new key must be used in the new cryptoperiod. However, the client might still want to keep the data in the cloud storage in the new cryptoperiod and needs to update the data. The above requirement implies a need to update ciphertexts from the old key to the new key. During this process, it is also reasonable to expect that no information of plaintexts are leaked while updating. Another benefit to consider in such a scenario is that it can be used to protect the data and reduce the risk of key compromise over time.

Key rotation is the process of generating a new key and altering ciphertexts from the old key to the new key without changing the underlying massage.

Key rotation can be done by downloading the old ciphertext, decrypting with the old key, re-encrypting with a new key and reuploading the new ciphertext.

S. Moriai and H. Wang (Eds.): ASIACRYPT 2020, LNCS 12493, pp. 529–558, 2020.
https://doi.org/10.1007/978-3-030-64840-4_18

However, this is expensive. *Updatable encryption* (UE) [5,6,8,11,14,15] provides a better solution for key rotation. A client generates an *update token* and sends it to the cloud server, the cloud server can use this update token to update the ciphertexts from the old key to the new key. In recent years there has been considerable interest in understanding UE, including defining the security notions for UE and constructing UE schemes (we make a detailed comparison of related work in Sect. 1.1).

Consider the following two variants of UE schemes: *ciphertext-dependent* schemes and *ciphertext-independent* schemes. If the generation of update token depends on the ciphertext to be updated then the UE scheme is ciphertext-dependent. In ciphertext-dependent schemes, the updating process of a ciphertext requires a specific token which forces the client to download the old ciphertext before this token can be generated. Therefore, ciphertext-dependent schemes are less practical. If the token is independent of the old ciphertext then the UE scheme is ciphertext-independent. Hence, a single token can be used to update all ciphertexts a client owns. As ciphertext-independent schemes are considerably more efficient than ciphertext-dependent schemes, in terms of bandwidth, most recent works [7,8,14,15] focus on ciphertext-independent schemes. In this paper, we will focus on such schemes.

Consider the following four variants of updates for ciphertext-independent UE schemes: *uni-directional ciphertext* updates, *bi-directional ciphertext* updates, *uni-directional key* updates and *bi-directional key* updates. If the update token can only move ciphertexts from the old key to the new key then ciphertext updates in such UE schemes are uni-directional. If the update token can additionally downgrade ciphertexts from the new key to the old key then ciphertext updates in such UE schemes are bi-directional. On the other hand, the update token can potentially be used to derive keys from other keys. In the uni-directional key update setting, the update token can only infer the new key from the old key. While in the bi-directional key update setting, the update token can both upgrade and downgrade keys. Prior works [7,8,14,15] focus on UE schemes with bi-directional updates, and no security notion was introduced in uni-directional update setting. We close this gap. Intuitively, UE schemes with uni-directional updates are desirable, such schemes leak less ciphertext/key information to an adversary compared to schemes with bi-directional updates. In this paper, we analyze the relationship between security notions with uni- and bi-directional updates. We show that the (confidentiality and integrity) security of UE schemes are not influenced by uni- or bi-directional updates.

No-directional key updates is another key update setting to consider, where the update token cannot be used to derive keys. A UE scheme with optimal leakage, discussed in [15], is a scheme where no token inference (no token can be inferred via keys), keys cannot be updated via a token, and ciphertext updates are only uni-directional. We do not consider no token inference, instead in this work an update token can be computed via two consecutive epoch keys. We show that the no-directional key update variant of a security notion is strictly stronger than the uni- and bi-directional update variant of the same security notion.

While the study of security notions appears promising, existing ciphertext-independent UE schemes are either vulnerable to quantum computers or only achieve weak security. The schemes of Lehmann and Tackmann [15], Klooß et al. [14] and Boyd et al. [8] base their security on the DDH problem, and thus are only secure in the classical setting. Boneh et al. [6] constructed key homomorphic PRFs, based on the learning with errors (LWE) problem, and it can be used to construct UE schemes. However, all of these schemes of Boneh et al. [6] cannot achieve IND-UPD security (introduced in [15]).

In this work, we construct a post-quantum secure UE scheme and the security of our construction is based on hard lattice problems. In particular, our scheme provides the randIND-UE-CPA security (introduced in [8], stronger than IND-UPD and IND-ENC security).

Efficiency. All of the previous known ciphertext-independent UE schemes with security proofs (RISE, E&M, NYUE (NYUAE), SHINE) have computation cost that are comparable to PKE schemes that rely on the DDH problem, while our scheme has a computation cost that is comparable to PKE schemes that rely on lattice problems.

1.1 Related Work

Security Notions. Boneh et al. [6] introduced a security definition for UE, however, this notion is less adaptive than the later works [8,14,15] which allows the adversary to adaptively corrupt epoch keys and update tokens at any point in the game.

In the ciphertext-dependent setting, Everspaugh et al. [11] provided two security notions, a weak form of ciphertext integrity and re-encryption indistinguishability, that strengthen the security notion in [6]. Recently, Boneh et al. [5] introduced new definitions for updatable encryption in the ciphertext-dependent setting to further strengthen the confidentiality property and the integrity definition in [11]. Boneh et al. [5] stated that for authenticated updatable encryption schemes it is necessary to expect that ciphertexts will not reveal how many times they have been updated, which was a desired property independently presented in [8].

Lehmann and Tackmann [15] introduced two notions to achieve CPA security for ciphertext-independent UE schemes. Their IND-ENC notion requires that ciphertexts output by the encryption algorithm are indistinguishable from each other. Their IND-UPD notion ensures ciphertexts output by the update algorithm are indistinguishable from each other.

Klooß et al. [14] attempted to provide stronger security notions for ciphertext-independent UE than LT18, specifically, CCA security and integrity protection.

Boyd et al. [8] provided a new notion IND-UE which states that a ciphertext output by the encryption algorithm is indistinguishable from a ciphertext output by the update algorithm. They showed that the new notion is strictly stronger than any combinations of prior notions, both under CPA and CCA. They also tweaked the CTXT and CCA notions in [14] and showed the following generic composition result: CPA + CTXT $\Longrightarrow$ CCA.

Constructing Ciphertext-Independent Updatable Encryption Schemes. The UE scheme BLMR in [6] is an application of key homomorphic PRFs, however, the encrypted nonce in the ciphertext can be decrypted by an update token which makes it impossible for BLMR to achieve IND-UPD security.

In the classical setting, RISE in [15] is built from (public-key) ElGamal encryption, which only uses the public key in the update token. The security of RISE is based on the DDH assumption. Klooß et al. [14] provided two generic constructions, based on encrypt-and-MAC (E&M) and the Naor-Yung paradigm (NYUE and NYUAE). The security of E&M is based on the DDH assumption, and the security of NYUE and NYUAE are based on the SXDH assumption. Boyd et al. [8] constructed three permutation-based UE schemes, SHINE, which achieves strong security notions based on DDH.

Post-Quantum Secure Schemes. In the past decade, much work has been done on constructing lattice-based post-quantum secure PKE schemes, specifically the NIST Post-Quantum Standardization Project, round 2, submissions: CRYSTALS-KYBER [3], FrodoKEM [1], LAC [16], NewHope [2], NTRU [4,9], Round5 [18], SABER [10] and Three Bears [12]. A natural question is if we can turn a PKE scheme into a UE scheme, where the security of the UE follows from the PKE. We provide a specific UE scheme that is built form an LWE-based PKE scheme, and prove the security. The LWE-based scheme we use is in some sense very similar to RISE (which is based on ElGamal), however, as with most lattice-based constructions, there are significant technical problems in turning it into a UE scheme (see Sect. 5.2). Our LWE-based UE construction suggests that there is a limit to how generic any efficient construction can be, a generic construction that abstracts both our construction and RISE remains to be done.

1.2 Our Contributions

Our first contribution is defining six variants of security notions (a combination of three versions of key updates and two versions of ciphertext updates) for updatable encryption and analyzing the relations among these six variants of the same notion.

Our main result is that we demonstrate that our security notions with uni- and bi-directional updates are equivalent. When we analyze the security, we can treat UE schemes with uni-directional updates as with bi-directional updates, the security will not be influenced by the update direction. This means that UE schemes with uni-directional updates will not provide more security than

UE schemes with bi-directional updates. This is a surprising result.[1] This result implies that the search for uni-directional updatable encryption scheme seems less important.

Furthermore, we show that security notions with no-directional key updates are strictly stronger than uni- and bi- directional update variants of the corresponding notions. Finding UE schemes with no-directional key updates would be good, but it is much more challenge than finding UE schemes with uni-directional key updates (which is already believed to be difficult). We leave this as an open problem.

Our second major contribution is constructing an efficient post-quantum secure UE scheme. We analyze how to construct LWE-based updatable encryption schemes and provide one construction. Our construction follows the re-randomization idea of RISE, using public key in the update token to update ciphertexts. We build a suitable post-quantum secure PKE scheme to construct our UE scheme so that the encryption and update algorithms can use a public key as input instead of the secret key. We also show the difficulties of turning a PKE scheme into a UE scheme.

We show that our LWE-based UE scheme is randIND-UE-CPA secure under the DLWE assumption. In the randomized update setting, we show the difference between previous work (RISE, NYUE, NYUAE) and our scheme, and state that the method used in proving the security of LWE-based updatable encryption scheme is different from the previous approach.

1.3 Open Problems

Ideally we want UE schemes with no-directional key updates, no such UE schemes have been constructed so far. Whether such UE schemes exist and how to construct such UE schemes are still open problems.

Furthermore, not that many efficient UE schemes with strong security exist so far. It remains an open challenge to construct UE schemes with chosen ciphertext[2] post-quantum security.

[1] It is possible to construct a scenario where this result will not be true. Let's assume there exists a UE scheme with a leakage function that helps the adversary win the security game. This leakage function could, for example, give the adversary information about plaintexts when it knows enough keys. In this scenario, a UE scheme with uni-directional updates has better security than a UE scheme with bi-directional updates. Because the scheme with uni-directional updates has less key leakage and the leakage function provides less data to the adversary. However, this and similar constructions cannot capture the security we wish to have for UE schemes. In terms of the security expectation of key rotation, the keys used in the past should not reveal any data.

For constructions that do follow the security model and update mechanism for UE schemes, we have this surprising result.

[2] It is ideal to achieve detIND-UE-CCA security for UE schemes with deterministic updates and to achieve INT-PTXT and randIND-UE-CCA security for UE schemes with randomized updates.

2 Preliminaries

In this section we describe the notation used in this paper and present the necessary background material of updatable encryption. In the full version [13], we provide the real or random variant of indistinguishability under chosen-plaintext attack (IND\$-CPA) for encryption schemes and the background of hard lattice problems.

2.1 Notations

Let λ be the security parameter throughout the paper. Let negl denote as a negligible function. Let $\mathcal{U}(S)$ denote the uniform distribution over set S.

2.2 Updatable Encryption

Updatable encryption (UE) scheme is parameterized by a tuple of algorithms {UE.KG, UE.TG, UE.Enc, UE.Dec, UE.Upd} that operate in epochs, the epoch starts at 0. The key generation algorithm UE.KG outputs an epoch key $\mathbf{k}_\mathsf{e}$. The token generation algorithm UE.TG takes as input two epoch keys $\mathbf{k}_\mathsf{e}$ and $\mathbf{k}_{\mathsf{e}+1}$ and outputs an update token $\Delta_{\mathsf{e}+1}$, the update token can be used to move ciphertexts from epoch e to $\mathsf{e}+1$. The encryption algorithm UE.Enc takes as input an epoch key $\mathbf{k}_\mathsf{e}$ and a message $\mathbf{m}$ and outputs a ciphertext $\mathbf{c}_\mathsf{e}$. The decryption algorithm UE.Dec takes as input an epoch key $\mathbf{k}_\mathsf{e}$ and a ciphertext $\mathbf{c}_\mathsf{e}$ and outputs a message $\mathbf{m}'$. The update algorithm UE.Upd takes as input an update token $\Delta_{\mathsf{e}+1}$ and a ciphertext $\mathbf{c}_\mathsf{e}$ from epoch e and outputs an updated ciphertext $\mathbf{c}_{\mathsf{e}+1}$.

We stress that an update token can be computed via two consecutive epoch keys by token generation algorithm in this paper.

2.3 Existing Security Notions for Updatable Encryption

Klooß et al. [14] and Boyd et al. [8] defined the confidentiality and the integrity notions for updatable encryption schemes using experiments that are running between an adversary and a challenger. In each experiment, the adversary may send a number of oracle queries. The main differences between an experiment running the confidentiality game and one running the integrity game are the challenge and win condition. In the confidentiality game, the adversary tries to distinguish a fresh encryption from an updated ciphertext. In the integrity game, the adversary attempts to provide a valid forgery. At the end of an experiment the challenger evaluates whether or not the adversary wins, if a trivial win condition was triggered the adversary will always lose.

We follow the notation of security notions from Boyd et al. [8]. An overview of the oracles the adversary has access to in each security game is given in Fig. 1. A generic description of all confidentiality experiments and integrity experiments described in this paper is detailed in Fig. 2 and Fig. 3, resp.. Our oracle algorithms, see Fig. 4, are stated differently than in [8] and [14], however, conceptually they are the same. The oracles we use in our security games are as

Notions	$\mathcal{O}$.Enc	$\mathcal{O}$.Dec	$\mathcal{O}$.Next	$\mathcal{O}$.Upd	$\mathcal{O}$.Corr	$\mathcal{O}$.Chall	$\mathcal{O}$.Upd$\tilde{\mathsf{C}}$	$\mathcal{O}$.Try
detIND-UE-CPA	✓	×	✓	✓	✓	✓	✓	×
randIND-UE-CPA	✓	×	✓	✓	✓	✓	✓	×
detIND-UE-CCA	✓	✓	✓	✓	✓	✓	✓	×
randIND-UE-CCA	✓	✓	✓	✓	✓	✓	✓	×
INT-CTXT	✓	×	✓	✓	✓	×	×	✓
INT-PTXT	✓	×	✓	✓	✓	×	×	✓

Fig. 1. Oracles given to the adversary in different security games for updatable encryption schemes. × indicates the adversary does not have access to the corresponding oracle, ✓ indicates the adversary has access to the corresponding oracle.

follows, encrypt $\mathcal{O}$.Enc, decrypt $\mathcal{O}$.Dec, move to the next epoch $\mathcal{O}$.Next, update ciphertext $\mathcal{O}$.Upd, corrupt key or token $\mathcal{O}$.Corr, ask for the challenge ciphertext $\mathcal{O}$.Chall, get an updated version of the challenge ciphertext $\mathcal{O}.\mathsf{Upd}\tilde{\mathsf{C}}$, or test if a ciphertext is a valid forgery $\mathcal{O}$.Try. The detailed discussion of trivial win conditions are discussed in Sect. 2.6.

For the confidentiality game we have the following additional definitions that we will frequently use. While the security game is running, the adversary may query $\mathcal{O}$.Enc or $\mathcal{O}$.Upd oracles or corrupt tokens to know some (updated) versions of ciphertexts, we call them *non-challenge ciphertexts*. In addition, the adversary may query $\mathcal{O}$.Chall or $\mathcal{O}.\mathsf{Upd}\tilde{\mathsf{C}}$ oracles or corrupt tokens to infer some (updated) versions of the challenge ciphertext, we call them *challenge-equal ciphertexts*.

Definition 1. *Let* UE = {UE.KG, UE.TG, UE.Enc, UE.Dec, UE.Upd} *be an updatable encryption scheme. Then the* notion *advantage, for* notion ∈ {detIND-UE-CPA, randIND-UE-CPA, detIND-UE-CCA, randIND-UE-CCA}*, of an adversary* $\mathcal{A}$ *against* UE *is defined as*

$$\mathbf{Adv}_{\mathsf{UE},\ \mathcal{A}}^{\mathsf{notion}}(1^\lambda) = \left|\mathbf{Pr}[\mathbf{Exp}_{\mathsf{UE},\ \mathcal{A}}^{\mathsf{notion\text{-}1}} = 1] - \mathbf{Pr}[\mathbf{Exp}_{\mathsf{UE},\ \mathcal{A}}^{\mathsf{notion\text{-}0}} = 1]\right|,$$

where the experiment $\mathbf{Exp}_{\mathsf{UE},\ \mathcal{A}}^{\mathsf{notion\text{-}b}}$ *is given in Fig. 2 and Fig. 4.*

Definition 2. *Let* UE = {UE.KG, UE.TG, UE.Enc, UE.Dec, UE.Upd} *be an updatable encryption scheme. Then the* notion *advantage, for* notion ∈ {INT-CTXT, INT-PTXT}*, of an adversary* $\mathcal{A}$ *against* UE *is defined as*

$$\mathbf{Adv}_{\mathsf{UE},\ \mathcal{A}}^{\mathsf{notion}}(1^\lambda) = \mathbf{Pr}[\mathbf{Exp}_{\mathsf{UE},\ \mathcal{A}}^{\mathsf{notion}} = 1],$$

where the experiment $\mathbf{Exp}_{\mathsf{UE},\ \mathcal{A}}^{\mathsf{notion}}$ *is given in Fig. 3 and Fig. 4.*

2.4 Notations of the Leakage Sets

In this section, we describe the definition of leakage sets given by [15] and [14], these sets will later be used to check whether the leaked information will allow the adversary trivially win the security game. We analyze some properties of leakage sets and trivial win conditions in Sect. 3.1.

$\mathbf{Exp}_{\mathsf{UE},\ \mathcal{A}}^{\mathsf{xxIND\text{-}UE\text{-}atk\text{-}b}}$:
do Setup; phase $\leftarrow 0$
b$' \leftarrow \mathcal{A}^{oracles}(1^\lambda)$
if $\Big((\mathcal{K}^* \cap \mathcal{C}^* \neq \emptyset)$ **or** (xx$=$det **and**
$(\tilde{\mathsf{e}} \in \mathcal{T}^*$ **or** $\mathcal{O}$.Upd$(\bar{\mathsf{c}})$ is queried$))\Big)$ **then**
twf $\leftarrow 1$
if twf $= 1$ **then**
b$' \xleftarrow{\$} \{0,1\}$
return b$'$

Fig. 2. Generic description of the confidentiality experiment $\mathbf{Exp}_{\mathsf{UE},\ \mathcal{A}}^{\mathsf{xxIND\text{-}UE\text{-}atk\text{-}b}}$ for updatable encryption scheme UE and adversary $\mathcal{A}$, for xx $\in$ {det, rand} and atk $\in$ {CPA, CCA}. The flag phase tracks whether or not $\mathcal{A}$ has queried the $\mathcal{O}$.Chall oracle, $\tilde{\mathsf{e}}$ denotes the epoch in which the $\mathcal{O}$.Chall oracle happens, and twf tracks if the trivial win conditions are triggered. Figure 1 shows the oracles the adversary have access to in a specific security game. How to compute the leakage sets $\mathcal{K}^*, \mathcal{T}^*, \mathcal{C}^*$ are discussed in Sect. 2.5.

$\mathbf{Exp}_{\mathsf{UE},\ \mathcal{A}}^{\mathsf{INT\text{-}atk}}$
do Setup; win $\leftarrow 0$
$\mathcal{A}^{oracles}(1^\lambda)$
if twf $= 1$ **then**
win $\leftarrow 0$
return win

Fig. 3. Generic description of the integrity experiment $\mathbf{Exp}_{\mathsf{UE},\ \mathcal{A}}^{\mathsf{INT\text{-}atk}}$ for updatable encryption scheme UE and adversary $\mathcal{A}$, for atk $\in$ {CTXT, PTXT}. The flag win tracks whether or not the adversary provided a valid forgery and twf tracks if the trivial win conditions are triggered. Figure 1 shows the oracles the adversary have access to in a specific security game.

Epoch Leakage Sets. We use the following sets that track epochs in which the adversary corrupted a key or a token, or learned a version of challenge-ciphertext.

- $\mathcal{K}$: Set of epochs in which the adversary corrupted the epoch key (from $\mathcal{O}$.Corr).
- $\mathcal{T}$: Set of epochs in which the adversary corrupted the update token (from $\mathcal{O}$.Corr).
- $\mathcal{C}$: Set of epochs in which the adversary learned a challenge-equal ciphertext (from $\mathcal{O}$.Chall or $\mathcal{O}$.Upd$\tilde{\mathsf{C}}$).

We use $\mathcal{K}^*, \mathcal{T}^*$ and $\mathcal{C}^*$ as the extended sets of $\mathcal{K}$, $\mathcal{T}$ and $\mathcal{C}$ in which the adversary has learned or inferred information via its known tokens. We show how to compute $\mathcal{K}^*, \mathcal{T}^*$ and $\mathcal{C}^*$ in Sect. 2.5.

Information Leakage Sets. We use the following sets to track ciphertexts and their updates that can be known to the adversary.

- $\mathcal{L}$: Set of non-challenge ciphertexts (c, **c**, e; **m**), where query identifier c is a counter incremented with each new $\mathcal{O}$.Enc query. The adversary learned these ciphertexts from $\mathcal{O}$.Enc or $\mathcal{O}$.Upd.
- $\tilde{\mathcal{L}}$: Set of challenge-equal ciphertexts $(\tilde{\mathbf{c}}_{\mathsf{e}}, \mathsf{e})$. The adversary learned these ciphertexts from $\mathcal{O}$.Chall or $\mathcal{O}$.Upd$\tilde{\mathsf{C}}$.

Setup(1^λ)
$\mathsf{k}_0 \xleftarrow{\$} \mathsf{UE.KG}(1^\lambda)$
$\Delta_0 \leftarrow \perp; \mathsf{e}, \mathsf{c}, \mathsf{twf} \leftarrow 0$
$\mathcal{L}, \tilde{\mathcal{L}}, \mathcal{C}, \mathcal{K}, \mathcal{T} \leftarrow \emptyset$

$\mathcal{O}.\mathsf{Enc}(\mathbf{m})$:
$\mathsf{c} \leftarrow \mathsf{c} + 1$
$\mathbf{c} \xleftarrow{\$} \mathsf{UE.Enc}(\mathbf{k}_\mathsf{e}, \mathbf{m})$
$\mathcal{L} \leftarrow \mathcal{L} \cup \{(\mathsf{c}, \mathbf{c}, \mathsf{e}; \mathbf{m})\}$
return $\mathbf{c}$

$\mathcal{O}.\mathsf{Dec}(\mathbf{c})$:
$\mathbf{m}'$ or $\perp \leftarrow \mathsf{UE.Dec}(\mathbf{k}_\mathsf{e}, \mathbf{c})$
if $\Big((\mathsf{xx} = \mathsf{det}$ **and** $(\mathbf{c}, \mathsf{e}) \in \tilde{\mathcal{L}}^*)$ **or**
$(\mathsf{xx} = \mathsf{rand}$ **and** $(\mathbf{m}', \mathsf{e}) \in \tilde{\mathcal{Q}}^*)\Big)$ **then**
$\mathsf{twf} \leftarrow 1$
return $\mathbf{m}'$ or $\perp$

$\mathcal{O}.\mathsf{Next}()$:
$\mathsf{e} \leftarrow \mathsf{e} + 1$
$\mathbf{k}_\mathsf{e} \xleftarrow{\$} \mathsf{UE.KG}(1^n)$
$\Delta_\mathsf{e} \leftarrow \mathsf{UE.TG}(\mathbf{k}_{\mathsf{e}-1}, \mathbf{k}_\mathsf{e})$
if $\mathsf{phase} = 1$ **then**
$\tilde{\mathbf{c}}_\mathsf{e} \leftarrow \mathsf{UE.Upd}(\Delta_\mathsf{e}, \tilde{\mathbf{c}}_{\mathsf{e}-1})$

$\mathcal{O}.\mathsf{Upd}(\mathbf{c}_{\mathsf{e}-1})$:
if $(j, \mathbf{c}_{\mathsf{e}-1}, \mathsf{e} - 1; \mathbf{m}) \notin \mathcal{L}$ **then**
return $\perp$
$\mathbf{c}_\mathsf{e} \leftarrow \mathsf{UE.Upd}(\Delta_\mathsf{e}, \mathbf{c}_{\mathsf{e}-1})$
$\mathcal{L} \leftarrow \mathcal{L} \cup \{(j, \mathbf{c}_\mathsf{e}, \mathsf{e}; \mathbf{m})\}$
return $\mathbf{c}_\mathsf{e}$

$\mathcal{O}.\mathsf{Corr}(\mathsf{inp}, \hat{\mathsf{e}})$:
if $\hat{\mathsf{e}} > \mathsf{e}$ **then**
return $\perp$
if $\mathsf{inp} = \mathsf{key}$ **then**
$\mathcal{K} \leftarrow \mathcal{K} \cup \{\hat{\mathsf{e}}\}$
return $\mathbf{k}_{\hat{\mathsf{e}}}$
if $\mathsf{inp} = \mathsf{token}$ **then**
$\mathcal{T} \leftarrow \mathcal{T} \cup \{\hat{\mathsf{e}}\}$
return $\Delta_{\hat{\mathsf{e}}}$

$\mathcal{O}.\mathsf{Chall}(\bar{\mathbf{m}}, \bar{\mathbf{c}})$:
if $\mathsf{phase} = 1$ **then**
return $\perp$
$\mathsf{phase} \leftarrow 1; \tilde{\mathsf{e}} \leftarrow \mathsf{e}$
if $(\cdot, \bar{\mathbf{c}}, \tilde{\mathsf{e}} - 1; \bar{\mathbf{m}}_1) \notin \mathcal{L}$ **then**
return $\perp$
if $\mathsf{b} = 0$ **then**
$\tilde{\mathbf{c}}_{\tilde{\mathsf{e}}} \leftarrow \mathsf{UE.Enc}(\mathbf{k}_{\tilde{\mathsf{e}}}, \bar{\mathbf{m}})$
else
$\tilde{\mathbf{c}}_{\tilde{\mathsf{e}}} \leftarrow \mathsf{UE.Upd}(\Delta_{\tilde{\mathsf{e}}}, \bar{\mathbf{c}})$
$\mathcal{C} \leftarrow \mathcal{C} \cup \{\tilde{\mathsf{e}}\}$
$\tilde{\mathcal{L}} \leftarrow \tilde{\mathcal{L}} \cup \{(\tilde{\mathbf{c}}_{\tilde{\mathsf{e}}}, \tilde{\mathsf{e}})\}$
return $\tilde{\mathbf{c}}_{\tilde{\mathsf{e}}}$

$\mathcal{O}.\mathsf{Upd}\tilde{\mathsf{C}}$:
if $\mathsf{phase} \neq 1$ **then**
return $\perp$
$\mathcal{C} \leftarrow \mathcal{C} \cup \{\mathsf{e}\}$
$\tilde{\mathcal{L}} \leftarrow \tilde{\mathcal{L}} \cup \{(\tilde{\mathbf{c}}_\mathsf{e}, \mathsf{e})\}$
return $\tilde{\mathbf{c}}_\mathsf{e}$

$\mathcal{O}.\mathsf{Try}(\tilde{\mathbf{c}})$:
$\mathbf{m}'$ or $\perp \leftarrow \mathsf{UE.Dec}(\mathbf{k}_\mathsf{e}, \tilde{\mathbf{c}})$
if $\Big((\mathsf{atk} = \mathsf{CTXT}$ **and** $(\tilde{\mathbf{c}}, \mathsf{e}) \in \mathcal{L}^*)$ **or**
$(\mathsf{atk} = \mathsf{PTXT}$ **and** $(\mathbf{m}', \mathsf{e}) \in \mathcal{Q}^*)$ **or**
$\mathsf{e} \in \mathcal{K}^*\Big)$ **then**
$\mathsf{twf} \leftarrow 1$
if $\mathbf{m}' \neq \perp$ **then**
$\mathsf{win} \leftarrow 1$

Fig. 4. Oracles in security games for updatable encryption. How to compute the leakage sets $\mathcal{K}^*, \mathcal{T}^*, \mathcal{C}^*, \tilde{\mathcal{L}}^*, \tilde{\mathcal{Q}}^*, \mathcal{L}^*, \mathcal{Q}^*$ are discussed in Sect. 2.5 and Sect. 2.6.

In the deterministic update setting, we use $\mathcal{L}^*$ and $\tilde{\mathcal{L}}^*$ as the extended (ciphertext) sets of $\mathcal{L}$ and $\tilde{\mathcal{L}}$ in which the adversary has learned or inferred ciphertexts via its known tokens. In particular, we only use partial information of $\mathcal{L}^*$: the ciphertext and the epoch. Hence, we only track the set $\mathcal{L}^* = \{(\mathbf{c}, \mathsf{e})\}$.

In the randomized update setting, we use $\mathcal{Q}^*$ and $\tilde{\mathcal{Q}}^*$ as the extended (plaintext) sets of $\mathcal{L}$ and $\tilde{\mathcal{L}}$, that contain messages that the adversary can provide a ciphertext of - i.e. a forgery. Similarly, only partial information is needed: the plaintext and the epoch. Hence, we track sets $\mathcal{Q}^*$ and $\tilde{\mathcal{Q}}^*$ as follows.

- $\mathcal{Q}^*$: Set of plaintexts $(\mathbf{m}, \mathsf{e})$. The adversary learned or was able to create a ciphertext in epoch e with the underlying message $\mathbf{m}$.
- $\tilde{\mathcal{Q}}^*$: Set of challenge plaintexts $\{(\bar{\mathbf{m}}, \mathsf{e}), (\bar{\mathbf{m}}_1, \mathsf{e})\}$, where $(\bar{\mathbf{m}}, \bar{\mathbf{c}})$ is the input of challenge query $\mathcal{O}.\mathsf{Chall}$ and $\bar{\mathbf{m}}_1$ is the underlying message of $\bar{\mathbf{c}}$. The adversary learned or was able to create a challenge-equal ciphertext in epoch e with the underlying message $\bar{\mathbf{m}}$ or $\bar{\mathbf{m}}_1$.

Remark 1. Based on the definition of these sets, we observe that

a. $(\tilde{\mathbf{c}}_\mathsf{e}, \mathsf{e}) \in \tilde{\mathcal{L}} \iff \mathsf{e} \in \mathcal{C}$,
b. $(\tilde{\mathbf{c}}_\mathsf{e}, \mathsf{e}) \in \tilde{\mathcal{L}}^* \iff \mathsf{e} \in \mathcal{C}^* \iff (\bar{\mathbf{m}}, \mathsf{e}), (\bar{\mathbf{m}}_1, \mathsf{e}) \in \tilde{\mathcal{Q}}^*$.

We will use this remark to discuss how to compute $\mathcal{L}^*$, $\tilde{\mathcal{L}}^*$, $\mathcal{Q}^*$ and $\tilde{\mathcal{Q}}^*$ in Sect. 2.6.

2.5 Epoch Leakage Sets of Keys, Tokens and Ciphertexts

We follow the bookkeeping techniques and base our notations of the work of Lehmann and Tackmann [15], where we further analyze the epoch leakage sets. Specifically, we add a no-directional key update setting. Suppose a security game ends at epoch l, then, for any sets $\mathcal{K}, \mathcal{T}, \mathcal{C} \subseteq \{0, ..., l\}$, the following algorithms show how to compute the extended sets $\mathcal{K}^*, \mathcal{T}^*$ and $\mathcal{C}^*$ in different update settings.

Key Leakage. The adversary learned all keys in epochs in $\mathcal{K}$. In the no-directional key update setting, the adversary does not have more information about keys except for this set. In the uni-directional key update setting, if the adversary knows a key $\mathbf{k}_\mathsf{e}$ and an update token $\Delta_{\mathsf{e}+1}$ then it can infer the next key $\mathbf{k}_{\mathsf{e}+1}$. In the bi-directional key update setting, the adversary can additionally downgrade a key by a known token. In the kk-directional key update setting, for $\mathsf{kk} \in \{\mathsf{no}, \mathsf{uni}, \mathsf{bi}\}$, we denote the set $\mathcal{K}^*_{\mathsf{kk}}$ as the extended set of corrupted key epochs. We compute these sets as follows.

No-directional key updates: $\mathcal{K}^*_{\mathsf{no}} = \mathcal{K}$.

Uni-directional key updates:

$$\mathcal{K}^*_{\mathsf{uni}} \leftarrow \{\mathsf{e} \in \{0, ..., l\} | \mathsf{CorrK}(\mathsf{e}) = \mathsf{true}\}$$
$$\mathsf{true} \leftarrow \mathsf{CorrK}(\mathsf{e}) \iff (\mathsf{e} \in \mathcal{K}) \vee (\mathsf{CorrK}(\mathsf{e}\text{-}1) \wedge \mathsf{e} \in \mathcal{T}). \quad (1)$$

Bi-directional key updates:

$$\mathcal{K}^*_{\mathsf{bi}} \leftarrow \{\mathsf{e} \in \{0, ..., l\} | \mathsf{CorrK}(\mathsf{e}) = \mathsf{true}\}$$
$$\mathsf{true} \leftarrow \mathsf{CorrK}(\mathsf{e}) \iff$$
$$(\mathsf{e} \in \mathcal{K}) \vee (\mathsf{CorrK}(\mathsf{e}\text{-}1) \wedge \mathsf{e} \in \mathcal{T}) \vee (\mathsf{CorrK}(\mathsf{e}\text{+}1) \wedge \mathsf{e}\text{+}1 \in \mathcal{T}). \quad (2)$$

Token Leakage. A token is known to the adversary is either a corrupted token or a token inferred from two consecutive epoch keys, so the extended set of corrupted token epochs is computed by information in set $\mathcal{T}$ and set $\mathcal{K}^*_{\mathsf{kk}}$. The set $\mathcal{K}^*_{\mathsf{kk}}$ is computed as above depending on the key updates is no- or uni- or bi-directional. Hence, we denote $\mathcal{T}^*_{\mathsf{kk}}$ as the extended set of corrupted token epochs.

$$\mathcal{T}^*_{\mathsf{kk}} \leftarrow \{\mathsf{e} \in \{0, ..., l\} | (\mathsf{e} \in \mathcal{T}) \vee (\mathsf{e} \in \mathcal{K}^*_{\mathsf{kk}} \wedge \mathsf{e}\text{-}1 \in \mathcal{K}^*_{\mathsf{kk}})\}. \quad (3)$$

Challenge-Equal Ciphertext Leakage. The adversary learned all challenge-equal ciphertexts in epochs in $\mathcal{C}$. Additionally, the adversary can infer challenge-equal ciphertexts via tokens. In the uni-directional ciphertext update setting, the adversary can upgrade ciphertexts. In the bi-directional ciphertext update setting, the adversary can additionally downgrade ciphertexts.

We compute the extended set of challenge-equal epochs using the information contained in $\mathcal{C}$ and $\mathcal{T}^*_{\mathsf{kk}}$. The set $\mathcal{T}^*_{\mathsf{kk}}$ is computed as above depending on the key updates is no- or uni- or bi-directional. In the cc-directional ciphertext update setting, for $\mathsf{cc} \in \{\mathsf{uni}, \mathsf{bi}\}$, denote the set $\mathcal{C}^*_{\mathsf{kk,cc}}$ as the extended set of challenge-equal epochs. We compute these sets as follows.

Uni-directional ciphertext updates:

$$\mathcal{C}^*_{\mathsf{kk,uni}} \leftarrow \{\mathsf{e} \in \{0, ..., l\} | \mathsf{ChallEq}(\mathsf{e}) = \mathsf{true}\}$$
$$\mathsf{true} \leftarrow \mathsf{ChallEq}(\mathsf{e}) \iff (\mathsf{e} \in \mathcal{C}) \vee (\mathsf{ChallEq}(\mathsf{e}\text{-}1) \wedge \mathsf{e} \in \mathcal{T}^*_{\mathsf{kk}}). \quad (4)$$

Bi-directional ciphertext updates:

$$\mathcal{C}^*_{\mathsf{kk,bi}} \leftarrow \{\mathsf{e} \in \{0, ..., l\} | \mathsf{ChallEq}(\mathsf{e}) = \mathsf{true}\}$$
$$\mathsf{true} \leftarrow \mathsf{ChallEq}(\mathsf{e}) \iff$$
$$(\mathsf{e} \in \mathcal{C}) \vee (\mathsf{ChallEq}(\mathsf{e}\text{-}1) \wedge \mathsf{e} \in \mathcal{T}^*_{\mathsf{kk}}) \vee (\mathsf{ChallEq}(\mathsf{e}+1) \wedge \mathsf{e}+1 \in \mathcal{T}^*_{\mathsf{kk}}). \quad (5)$$

2.6 Trivial Win Conditions

The main benefit of using ciphertext-independent updatable encryption scheme is that it offers an efficient way for key rotation, where a single token can be used to update all ciphertexts. However, this property provides the adversary more power, the tokens can be used to gain more information, and gives the adversary more chances to win the security games. We again follow the trivial win analysis in [8,14,15] and exclude these trivial win conditions in the security games for UE. An overview of the trivial win conditions the challenger will check in each security game is given in Fig. 5.

Checking Trivial Win Conditions at the End of a Game

Trivial Wins via Keys and Ciphertexts. The following is used for analyzing all confidentiality games. If there exists an epoch $\mathsf{e} \in \mathcal{K}^* \cap \mathcal{C}^*$ in which the adversary knows the epoch key $\mathbf{k}_\mathsf{e}$ and a valid update of the challenge ciphertext $\tilde{\mathbf{c}}_\mathsf{e}$, then the adversary can use this epoch key to decrypt the challenge-equal ciphertext and know the underlying plaintext to win the confidentiality game. The trivial win condition "$\mathcal{K}^* \cap \mathcal{C}^* \neq \emptyset$" is checked in the end of a confidentiality game.

Notions	"$\mathcal{K}^* \cap \mathcal{C}^* \neq \emptyset$"	"$\tilde{e} \in \mathcal{T}^*$ or $\mathcal{O}.\mathsf{Upd}(\bar{c})$ is queried"	"$(c, e) \in \tilde{\mathcal{L}}^*$"	"$(m', e) \in \tilde{\mathcal{Q}}^*$"	"$e \in \mathcal{K}^*$"	"$(c, e) \in \mathcal{L}^*$"	"$(m', e) \in \mathcal{Q}^*$"
detIND-UE-CPA	✓	✓	×	×	×	×	×
randIND-UE-CPA	✓	×	×	×	×	×	×
detIND-UE-CCA	✓	✓	✓	×	×	×	×
randIND-UE-CCA	✓	×	×	✓	×	×	×
INT-CTXT	×	×	×	×	✓	✓	×
INT-PTXT	×	×	×	×	✓	×	✓

Fig. 5. Trivial win conditions considered in different security games for updatable encryption schemes. × indicates the security notion does not consider the corresponding trivial win condition, ✓ indicates the security notion considers the corresponding trivial win condition.

Trivial Wins via Direct Updates. The following is used for analyzing all confidentiality games with deterministic updates. If the adversary knows the update token $\Delta_{\tilde{e}}$ in the challenge epoch $\tilde{e}$ or the adversary queried an update oracle on the challenge input ciphertext $\mathcal{O}.\mathsf{Upd}(\bar{c})$ in epoch $\tilde{e}$, then it knows the updated ciphertext of $\bar{c}$ in epoch $\tilde{e}$ and it can compare the updated ciphertext with the challenge ciphertext to win the confidentiality game. The trivial win condition "$\tilde{e} \in \mathcal{T}^*$ or $\mathcal{O}.\mathsf{Upd}(\bar{c})$ is queried" is checked in the end of a confidentiality game.

Checking Trivial Win Conditions While Running a Game. The following overview of trivial win conditions are checked by an oracle. The sets $\tilde{\mathcal{L}}^*, \tilde{\mathcal{Q}}^*, \mathcal{K}^*, \mathcal{L}^*$ and $\mathcal{Q}^*$ are defined in Sect. 2.4.

- "$(\mathbf{c}, \mathsf{e}) \in \tilde{\mathcal{L}}^*$" are checked by $\mathcal{O}.\mathsf{Dec}$ oracles in the detIND-UE-CCA game,
- "$(\mathbf{m}', \mathsf{e}) \in \tilde{\mathcal{Q}}^*$" are checked by $\mathcal{O}.\mathsf{Dec}$ oracles in the randIND-UE-CCA game,
- "$\mathsf{e} \in \mathcal{K}^*$" are checked by $\mathcal{O}.\mathsf{Try}$ oracles in the INT-CTXT game or the INT-PTXT game,
- "$(\mathbf{c}, \mathsf{e}) \in \mathcal{L}^*$" are checked by $\mathcal{O}.\mathsf{Try}$ oracles in the INT-CTXT game
- "$(\mathbf{m}', \mathsf{e}) \in \mathcal{Q}^*$" are checked by $\mathcal{O}.\mathsf{Try}$ oracles in the INT-PTXT game.

General Idea. At the moment when the adversary queries a decryption query $\mathcal{O}.\mathsf{Dec}$ or a try query $\mathcal{O}.\mathsf{Try}$, the challenger computes the knowledge the adversary currently has, which is used to check if the adversary can trivially win a security game. More precisely, the challenger uses information in the sets $\mathcal{L}, \tilde{\mathcal{L}}, \mathcal{C}, \mathcal{K}, \mathcal{T}$ to compute the leakage sets $\tilde{\mathcal{L}}^*, \tilde{\mathcal{Q}}^*, \mathcal{K}^*, \mathcal{L}^*$ and $\mathcal{Q}^*$. Note that the sets $\mathcal{L}, \tilde{\mathcal{L}}, \mathcal{C}, \mathcal{K}, \mathcal{T}$ contains information the adversary learns at such a moment.

Trivial Wins via Decryptions in the Deterministic Update Setting. The following is used for analyzing the detIND-UE-CCA security notion. In the deterministic

for $i \in \{0, ..., \mathsf{e}\}$ **do**
  if $i \in \mathcal{C}^*_{\mathsf{kk,cc}}$ **then**
    $\tilde{\mathcal{L}}^*_{\mathsf{kk,cc}} \leftarrow \tilde{\mathcal{L}}^*_{\mathsf{kk,cc}} \cup \{(\tilde{\mathbf{c}}_i, i)\}$

Fig. 6. Algorithm for computing the set $\tilde{\mathcal{L}}^*_{\mathsf{kk,cc}}$, where $\mathsf{kk} \in \{\mathsf{no}, \mathsf{uni}, \mathsf{bi}\}$ and $\mathsf{cc} \in \{\mathsf{uni}, \mathsf{bi}\}$.

for $i \in \{0, ..., \mathsf{e}\}$ **do**
  if $i \in \mathcal{C}^*_{\mathsf{kk,cc}}$ **then**
    $\tilde{\mathcal{Q}}^*_{\mathsf{kk,cc}} \leftarrow \tilde{\mathcal{Q}}^*_{\mathsf{kk,cc}} \cup \{(\bar{\mathbf{m}}, i)\} \cup \{(\bar{\mathbf{m}}_1, i)\}$

Fig. 7. Algorithm for computing the set $\tilde{\mathcal{Q}}^*_{\mathsf{kk,cc}}$, where $\mathsf{kk} \in \{\mathsf{no}, \mathsf{uni}, \mathsf{bi}\}$ and $\mathsf{cc} \in \{\mathsf{uni}, \mathsf{bi}\}$.

update setting, if the adversary knows a challenge-equal ciphertext $(\tilde{\mathbf{c}}_{\mathsf{e}_0}, \mathsf{e}_0) \in \tilde{\mathcal{L}}$ and tokens from epoch $\mathsf{e}_0 + 1$ to epoch e, then the adversary can compute the updated challenge-equal ciphertext $\tilde{\mathbf{c}}_{\mathsf{e}}$ and send it to the decryption oracle to get the underlying message. Eventually, the adversary compares the received message with the challenge plaintexts to trivially win the security game.

We use the set $\tilde{\mathcal{L}}^*$ to check this trivial win condition, recall that $\tilde{\mathcal{L}}^*$ includes all challenge-equal ciphertexts the adversary has learned or inferred. Suppose the adversary queries a decryption oracle $\mathcal{O}.\mathsf{Dec}(\mathbf{c})$ in epoch e, if $(\mathbf{c}, \mathsf{e}) \in \tilde{\mathcal{L}}^*$ then the response of the decryption oracle leads to a trivial win to the adversary, hence, the challenger will set the trivial win flag to be 1.

By Remark 1, we have $(\tilde{\mathbf{c}}_{\mathsf{e}}, \mathsf{e}) \in \tilde{\mathcal{L}}^* \iff \mathsf{e} \in \mathcal{C}^*$, using this method we can easily compute the set $\tilde{\mathcal{L}}^*$. In Fig. 6 we show how the set $\tilde{\mathcal{L}}^*$ is computed, where the set $\mathcal{C}^*$ is computed by the algorithms discussed in Sect. 2.5.

Trivial Wins via Decryptions in the Randomized Update Setting. The following is used for analyzing the randIND-UE-CCA security notion. In the randomized update setting, if the adversary knows a challenge-equal ciphertext $(\tilde{\mathbf{c}}_{\mathsf{e}_0}, \mathsf{e}_0) \in \tilde{\mathcal{L}}$ and tokens from epoch $\mathsf{e}_0 + 1$ to epoch e, then the adversary can create arbitrary number of ciphertexts by updating $\tilde{\mathbf{c}}_{\mathsf{e}_0}$ from epoch e_0 to epoch e. Let $\mathbf{c}_{\mathsf{e}}$ denote a ciphertext generated in such a way. Notice that the ciphertext $\mathbf{c}_{\mathsf{e}}$ has the same underlying message as the challenge-equal ciphertext $\tilde{\mathbf{c}}_{\mathsf{e}_0}$. The adversary can send the computed ciphertext $\mathbf{c}_{\mathsf{e}}$ to the decryption oracle to get the underlying message and trivially win the security game.

We use the set $\tilde{\mathcal{Q}}^*$ to check this trivial win condition, recall that $\tilde{\mathcal{Q}}^*$ includes information about challenge plaintexts that the adversary has learned or can create challenge-equal ciphertexts of. Suppose the adversary queries a decryption oracle $\mathcal{O}.\mathsf{Dec}(\mathbf{c})$ in epoch e, if $\mathsf{UE.Dec}(\mathbf{k}_{\mathsf{e}}, \mathbf{c}) = \mathbf{m}'$ and $(\mathbf{m}', \mathsf{e}) \in \tilde{\mathcal{Q}}^*$ then the response of the decryption oracle leads to a trivial win to the adversary, hence, the challenger will set the trivial win flag to be 1.

By Remark 1, we have $(\mathbf{m}', \mathsf{e}) \in \tilde{\mathcal{Q}}^* \iff \mathsf{e} \in \mathcal{C}^*$, using this method we can easily compute the set $\tilde{\mathcal{Q}}^*$. Suppose the challenge input is $(\bar{\mathbf{m}}, \bar{\mathbf{c}})$ and the underlying message of $\bar{\mathbf{c}}$ is $\bar{\mathbf{m}}_1$. In Fig. 7 we show how the set $\tilde{\mathcal{Q}}^*$ is computed.

Remark 2. Our definition of this trivial win restriction is more generous than that of [14], they disallow the decryption of any ciphertext that decrypts to either of the two challenge plaintexts. We allow the decryption of a ciphertext

$$
\begin{array}{l}
\textbf{for } i \in \{0, ..., \mathsf{e}\} \textbf{ do} \\
\quad \textbf{for } (\cdot, \mathbf{c}, i; \cdot) \in \mathcal{L} \textbf{ do} \\
\quad\quad \mathcal{L}^*_{\mathsf{kk,cc}} \leftarrow \mathcal{L}^*_{\mathsf{kk,cc}} \cup \{(\mathbf{c}, i)\} \\
\quad \textbf{if } i \in \mathcal{T}^*_{\mathsf{kk}} \textbf{ then} \\
\quad\quad \textbf{for } (\mathbf{c}_{i-1}, i-1) \in \mathcal{L}^*_{\mathsf{kk,cc}} \textbf{ do} \\
\quad\quad\quad \mathbf{c}_i \leftarrow \mathsf{UE.Upd}(\Delta_i, \mathbf{c}_{i-1}) \\
\quad\quad\quad \mathcal{L}^*_{\mathsf{kk,cc}} \leftarrow \mathcal{L}^*_{\mathsf{kk,cc}} \cup \{(\mathbf{c}_i, i)\} \\
\quad\quad \textbf{if } \mathsf{cc} = \mathsf{bi} \textbf{ then} \\
\quad\quad\quad \textbf{for } (\mathbf{c}_i, i) \in \mathcal{L}^*_{\mathsf{kk,cc}} \textbf{ do} \\
\quad\quad\quad\quad \mathbf{c}_{i-1} \leftarrow \mathsf{UE.Upd}^{-1}(\Delta_i, \mathbf{c}_i) \\
\quad\quad\quad\quad \mathcal{L}^*_{\mathsf{kk,cc}} \leftarrow \mathcal{L}^*_{\mathsf{kk,cc}} \cup \{(\mathbf{c}_{i-1}, i-1)\}
\end{array}
$$

Fig. 8. Algorithm for computing the set $\mathcal{L}^*_{\mathsf{kk,cc}}$, where $\mathsf{kk} \in \{\mathsf{no}, \mathsf{uni}, \mathsf{bi}\}$ and $\mathsf{cc} \in \{\mathsf{uni}, \mathsf{bi}\}$.

$$
\begin{array}{l}
\textbf{for } i \in \{0, ..., \mathsf{e}\} \textbf{ do} \\
\quad \textbf{for } (\cdot, \cdot, i; \mathbf{m}) \in \mathcal{L} \textbf{ do} \\
\quad\quad \mathcal{Q}^*_{\mathsf{kk,cc}} \leftarrow \mathcal{Q}^*_{\mathsf{kk,cc}} \cup \{(\mathbf{m}, i)\} \\
\quad \textbf{if } i \in \mathcal{T}^*_{\mathsf{kk}} \textbf{ then} \\
\quad\quad \textbf{for } (\mathbf{m}, i-1) \in \mathcal{Q}^*_{\mathsf{kk,cc}} \textbf{ do} \\
\quad\quad\quad \mathcal{Q}^*_{\mathsf{kk,cc}} \leftarrow \mathcal{Q}^*_{\mathsf{kk,cc}} \cup \{(\mathbf{m}, i)\} \\
\quad\quad \textbf{if } \mathsf{cc} = \mathsf{bi} \textbf{ then} \\
\quad\quad\quad \textbf{for } (\mathbf{m}, i) \in \mathcal{Q}^*_{\mathsf{kk,cc}} \textbf{ do} \\
\quad\quad\quad\quad \mathcal{Q}^*_{\mathsf{kk,cc}} \leftarrow \mathcal{Q}^*_{\mathsf{kk,cc}} \cup \{(\mathbf{m}, i-1)\}
\end{array}
$$

Fig. 9. Algorithm for computing the set $\mathcal{Q}^*_{\mathsf{kk,cc}}$, where $\mathsf{kk} \in \{\mathsf{no}, \mathsf{uni}, \mathsf{bi}\}$ and $\mathsf{cc} \in \{\mathsf{uni}, \mathsf{bi}\}$.

that decrypts to a challenge plaintext as long as the adversary cannot learn (from $\mathcal{O}.\mathsf{Chall}$ or $\mathcal{O}.\mathsf{Upd}\tilde{\mathsf{C}}$) or infer (from tokens) a valid ciphertext of challenge plaintext in that epoch.

Trivial Forgeries by Keys. The following is used for analyzing all integrity games. If the adversary knows an epoch key $\mathbf{k}_\mathsf{e}$, then the adversary can create arbitrary number of valid forgeries of arbitrary messages under this epoch key $\mathbf{k}_\mathsf{e}$.

We use the set $\mathcal{K}^*$ to check this trivial win condition, recall that $\mathcal{K}^*$ includes all epochs the adversary learned or inferred an epoch key. Suppose the adversary queries a try oracle $\mathcal{O}.\mathsf{Try}(\mathbf{c})$ in epoch e, if $\mathsf{e} \in \mathcal{K}^*$ then the challenger will set the trivial win flag to be 1. We use algorithms discussed in Sect. 2.5 to compute the set $\mathcal{K}^*$.

Trivial Ciphertext Forgeries by Tokens. The following is used for analyzing the $\mathsf{INT\text{-}CTXT}$ security notion. From [14] we know that only UE schemes with deterministic updates can possibly achieve $\mathsf{INT\text{-}CTXT}$ security. In the deterministic update setting, if the adversary knows a ciphertext $(\mathrm{c}, \mathbf{c}, \mathsf{e}_0; \mathbf{m}) \in \mathcal{L}$ and tokens from epoch $\mathsf{e}_0 + 1$ to epoch e, then the adversary can create a valid updated ciphertext by updating $\mathbf{c}$ from epoch e_0 to epoch e.

We use the set $\mathcal{L}^*$ to check this trivial win condition, recall that $\mathcal{L}^*$ includes all ciphertexts that can be known or inferred to the adversary. Suppose the adversary queries a try oracle $\mathcal{O}.\mathsf{Try}(\mathbf{c})$ in epoch e, if $(\mathbf{c}, \mathsf{e}) \in \mathcal{L}^*$ then the challenger will set the trivial win flag to be 1. In Fig. 8 we show how the set $\mathcal{L}^*$ is computed.

Trivial Plaintext Forgeries by Tokens. The following is used for analyzing the $\mathsf{INT\text{-}PTXT}$ security notion. In the randomized update setting, if the adversary knows a ciphertext $(\mathrm{c}, \mathbf{c}, \mathsf{e}_0; \mathbf{m}) \in \mathcal{L}$ and tokens from epoch $\mathsf{e}_0 + 1$ to epoch e, then the adversary can create arbitrary number of valid forgeries of message $\mathbf{m}$ by updating $\mathbf{c}$ from epoch e_0 to epoch e.

We use the set $\mathcal{Q}^*$ to check this trivial win condition, recall that $\mathcal{Q}^*$ includes information about plaintexts that the adversary has learned or can create ciphertexts of. Suppose the adversary queries a try oracle $\mathcal{O}.\mathsf{Try}(\mathbf{c})$ in epoch e, if $\mathsf{UE.Dec}(\mathbf{k}_\mathsf{e}, \mathbf{c}) = \mathbf{m}'$ and $(\mathbf{m}', \mathsf{e}) \in \mathcal{Q}^*$ then the challenger will set the trivial win flag to be 1. In Fig. 9 we show how the set $\mathcal{Q}^*$ is computed.

3 Six Variants of Security Notions

In this section we first define six variants of security notions for updatable encryption schemes. In the end of this section, we compare the relationship among all these variants of each security notion.

For $\mathsf{kk} \in \{\mathsf{no}, \mathsf{uni}, \mathsf{bi}\}$ and $\mathsf{cc} \in \{\mathsf{uni}, \mathsf{bi}\}$, we define $(\mathsf{kk}, \mathsf{cc})$- variants of security notions, where kk refers to UE schemes with kk-directional key updates and cc to cc-directional ciphertext updates.

Definition 3 (The $(\mathsf{kk}, \mathsf{cc})$- variant of confidentiality notions). *Let* $\mathsf{UE} = \{\mathsf{UE.KG}, \mathsf{UE.TG}, \mathsf{UE.Enc}, \mathsf{UE.Dec}, \mathsf{UE.Upd}\}$ *be an updatable encryption scheme. Then the* $(\mathsf{kk}, \mathsf{cc})$-notion *advantage, for* $\mathsf{kk} \in \{\mathsf{no}, \mathsf{uni}, \mathsf{bi}\}$, $\mathsf{cc} \in \{\mathsf{uni}, \mathsf{bi}\}$ *and* $\mathsf{notion} \in \{\mathsf{detIND\text{-}UE\text{-}CPA}, \mathsf{randIND\text{-}UE\text{-}CPA}, \mathsf{detIND\text{-}UE\text{-}CCA}, \mathsf{randIND\text{-}UE\text{-}CCA}\}$, *of an adversary* $\mathcal{A}$ *against* UE *is defined as*

$$\mathbf{Adv}_{\mathsf{UE},\,\mathcal{A}}^{(\mathsf{kk},\mathsf{cc})\text{-}\mathsf{notion}}(1^\lambda) = \left|\mathbf{Pr}[\mathbf{Exp}_{\mathsf{UE},\,\mathcal{A}}^{(\mathsf{kk},\mathsf{cc})\text{-}\mathsf{notion}\text{-}1} = 1] - \mathbf{Pr}[\mathbf{Exp}_{\mathsf{UE},\,\mathcal{A}}^{(\mathsf{kk},\mathsf{cc})\text{-}\mathsf{notion}\text{-}0} = 1]\right|,$$

where the experiment $\mathbf{Exp}_{\mathsf{UE},\,\mathcal{A}}^{(\mathsf{kk},\mathsf{cc})\text{-}\mathsf{notion}\text{-}\mathsf{b}}$ *is the same as the experiment* $\mathbf{Exp}_{\mathsf{UE},\,\mathcal{A}}^{\mathsf{notion}\text{-}\mathsf{b}}$ *(see Fig. 2 and Fig. 4) except for all leakage sets are both in the* kk*-directional key update setting and* cc*-directional ciphertext update setting.*

Remark 3. Recall that we compute all leakage sets with kk-directional key updates and cc-directional ciphertext updates in Sect. 2.5 and Sect. 2.6.

Remark 4. The security notion RCCA, which we denote as randIND-UE-CCA, is from [14]. In our definition of this notion is stronger - the adversary has fewer trivial win restrictions - we discuss this difference in Remark 2.

Definition 4 (The $(\mathsf{kk}, \mathsf{cc})$- variant of integrity notions). *Let* $\mathsf{UE} = \{\mathsf{UE.KG}, \mathsf{UE.TG}, \mathsf{UE.Enc}, \mathsf{UE.Dec}, \mathsf{UE.Upd}\}$ *be an updatable encryption scheme. Then the* $(\mathsf{kk}, \mathsf{cc})$-notion *advantage, for* $\mathsf{kk} \in \{\mathsf{no}, \mathsf{uni}, \mathsf{bi}\}$, $\mathsf{cc} \in \{\mathsf{uni}, \mathsf{bi}\}$ *and* $\mathsf{notion} \in \{\mathsf{INT\text{-}CTXT}, \mathsf{INT\text{-}PTXT}\}$, *of an adversary* $\mathcal{A}$ *against* UE *is defined as*

$$\mathbf{Adv}_{\mathsf{UE},\,\mathcal{A}}^{(\mathsf{kk},\mathsf{cc})\text{-}\mathsf{notion}}(1^\lambda) = \mathbf{Pr}[\mathbf{Exp}_{\mathsf{UE},\,\mathcal{A}}^{(\mathsf{kk},\mathsf{cc})\text{-}\mathsf{notion}} = 1],$$

where the experiment $\mathbf{Exp}_{\mathsf{UE},\,\mathcal{A}}^{(\mathsf{kk},\mathsf{cc})\text{-}\mathsf{notion}}$ *is the same as the experiment* $\mathbf{Exp}_{\mathsf{UE},\,\mathcal{A}}^{\mathsf{notion}}$ *(see Fig. 3 and Fig. 4) except for all leakage sets are both in the* kk*-directional key update setting and* cc*-directional ciphertext update setting.*

3.1 Properties of Leakage Sets and Trivial Win Conditions

In this section, we prove some essential properties of key leakage, which will be used to analyze the trivial win conditions. We will use these trivial win properties to prove the relations among six variants of the same security notion in Sect. 3.2.

Properties of Key Updates. Here we look at some properties of sets $\mathcal{K}, \mathcal{T}, \mathcal{K}^*$ and $\mathcal{T}^*$ in terms of uni- and bi-directional key updates.

Firewall and Insulated Region. We first describe the definition of firewall and insulated region, which will be widely used in this paper. Firewall technique (see [8,14,15]) is used for doing cryptographic seperation. We follow the firewall definition in [8] and use firewall set $\mathcal{FW}$ (defined in [8]) to track each insulated region and its firewalls.

Definition 5. *An* insulated region *with* firewalls fwl *and* fwr *is a consecutive sequence of epochs* $(\mathsf{fwl}, \ldots, \mathsf{fwr})$ *for which:*

- $\{\mathsf{fwl}, \ldots, \mathsf{fwr}\} \cap \mathcal{K} = \emptyset$;
- $\mathsf{fwl}, \mathsf{fwr}+1 \notin \mathcal{T}$;
- $\{\mathsf{fwl}+1, \ldots, \mathsf{fwr}\} \subseteq \mathcal{T}$.

Remark 5. Based on Definition 5, we notice that all firewalls or all insulated regions (in other words, set $\mathcal{FW}$) are uniquely determined by $\mathcal{K}$ and $\mathcal{T}$. In particular, we denote the union of all insulated regions as set $\mathcal{IR}$, i.e. $\mathcal{IR} = \cup_{(\mathsf{fwl},\mathsf{fwr})\in\mathcal{FW}}\{\mathsf{fwl}, ..., \mathsf{fwr}\}$.

Then we look at the structure of the set $\mathcal{IR}$. Lemma 1 states that $\mathcal{IR}$ is the complementary set of $\mathcal{K}^*_{\mathsf{bi}}$. Furthermore, Lemma 3 shows that the complementary set of $\mathcal{IR}$ is the union of two types of epoch sets (see Definition 6 and Definition 7).

Lemma 1. *For any sets* $\mathcal{K}, \mathcal{T} \subseteq \{0, ..., l\}$, *we have* $\mathcal{K}^*_{\mathsf{bi}} = \{0, ..., l\} \setminus \mathcal{IR}$.

Proof. Note that Δ_0 and Δ_{l+1} do not exist, however, 0 and l can possibly be firewalls. For convenience, we just assume Δ_0 and Δ_{l+1} exist and the adversary is not allowed to corrupt these two tokens. Thus the set of epochs in which the adversary never corrupted the update token is: $\{0, ..., l+1\} \setminus \mathcal{T} = \{\bar{\mathsf{e}}_0 := 0, \bar{\mathsf{e}}_1, ..., \bar{\mathsf{e}}_t, \bar{\mathsf{e}}_{t+1} := l+1\}$, where $t \geq 0$.

In the bi-directional key update setting, if the adversary has corrupted a key in an epoch e, where $\mathsf{e} \in \{\bar{\mathsf{e}}_{i-1}, ..., \bar{\mathsf{e}}_i - 1\}$, then the adversary can infer all keys from epoch $\bar{\mathsf{e}}_{i-1}$ to epoch $\bar{\mathsf{e}}_i - 1$, that is $\{\bar{\mathsf{e}}_{i-1}, ..., \bar{\mathsf{e}}_i - 1\} \subseteq \mathcal{K}^*_{\mathsf{bi}}$, because all tokens from epoch $\bar{\mathsf{e}}_{i-1}+1$ to epoch $\bar{\mathsf{e}}_i - 1$ are corrupted. Otherwise, when no key in the sequence of epochs $\{\bar{\mathsf{e}}_{i-1}, ..., \bar{\mathsf{e}}_i - 1\}$ is corrupted, then $\{\bar{\mathsf{e}}_{i-1}, ..., \bar{\mathsf{e}}_i - 1\}$ is an insulated region . Therefore, for any i, $\{\bar{\mathsf{e}}_{i-1}, ..., \bar{\mathsf{e}}_i - 1\}$ is either an insulated region or a subset of $\mathcal{K}^*_{\mathsf{bi}}$.

Epoch	e_{start}	$e_{start}+1\ldots$		e_{end-1}	e_{end}
$\mathcal{K}$	×	×	...	×	✓
$\mathcal{T}$	✓	✓	...	✓	✓

Epoch	e_{start}	$e_{start}+1\ldots$		e_{end}
$\mathcal{K}^*_{uni}$	✓	✓	...	✓
$\mathcal{T}^*_{uni}$	✓	✓	...	✓

Fig. 10. Type 1 set of epochs (left), type 2 set of epochs (right). × indicates the keys/tokens are not revealed to the adversary, ✓ indicates the keys/tokens are revealed to the adversary.

We define two types of epoch sets in Definition 6 and Definition 7, which will later be used to analyze the structure of $\mathcal{IR}$. An overview of the corruption model of these two epoch sets are shown in Fig. 10.

Definition 6. *A set of* type1 *epochs is a consecutive sequence of epochs* $(e_{start}, \ldots, e_{end})$ *for which:*

- $\{e_{start}, \ldots, e_{end} - 1\} \cap \mathcal{K} = \emptyset$;
- $e_{end} \in \mathcal{K}$;
- $\{e_{start} + 1, \ldots, e_{end}\} \subseteq \mathcal{T}$.

Definition 7. *A set of* type2 *epochs is a consecutive sequence of epochs* $(e_{start}, \ldots, e_{end})$ *for which:*

- $\{e_{start}, \ldots, e_{end}\} \subseteq \mathcal{K}^*_{uni}$;
- $\{e_{start} + 1, \ldots, e_{end}\} \subseteq \mathcal{T}^*_{uni}$.

The following Lemma explains that if a key is revealed in the bi-directional key update setting but not in the uni-directional key update setting then the revealed key epoch can stretch to a type 1 epoch set. We use this property to prove Lemma 3.

Lemma 2. *If* $e \in \mathcal{K}^*_{bi} \setminus \mathcal{K}^*_{uni}$, *then there exists an epoch (say* e_u*) after* e *such that* $e_u \in \mathcal{K}$, $\{e, \ldots, e_u - 1\} \cap \mathcal{K} = \emptyset$ *and* $\{e + 1, ..., e_u\} \subseteq \mathcal{T}$.

Proof. As the assumption and Eqs. (1, 2), we have $e \in \mathcal{K}^*_{bi}$ is inferred from the next epoch key $\mathbf{k}_{e+1}$ via token Δ_{e+1}. That is $e + 1 \in \mathcal{K}^*_{bi}$ and $e + 1 \in \mathcal{T}$. If $e + 1 \notin \mathcal{K}^*_{uni}$, then $e + 2 \in \mathcal{K}^*_{bi}$ and $e + 2 \in \mathcal{T}$. Iteratively, we know that there exists an epoch after e, say e_u, such that $\{e, \ldots, e_u - 1\} \cap \mathcal{K}^*_{uni} = \emptyset$, $e_u \in \mathcal{K}^*_{uni}$ and $e + 1, ..., e_u \in \mathcal{T}$. Hence, $\{e, \ldots, e_u - 1\} \cap \mathcal{K} \subseteq \{e, \ldots, e_u - 1\} \cap \mathcal{K}^*_{uni} = \emptyset$. In particular, we know that $e_u \in \mathcal{K}$ since $e_u - 1 \notin \mathcal{K}^*_{uni}$.

Lemma 3. *For any sets* $\mathcal{K}, \mathcal{T} \subseteq \{0, ..., l\}$, *we have* $\{0, ..., l\} \setminus \mathcal{IR} = (\cup_{type\ 1}\{e_{start}, ..., e_{end}\}) \cup (\cup_{type\ 2}\{e_{start}, ..., e_{end}\})$, *where the two types of epoch sets are defined in Definition 6 and Definition 7.*

Proof. Suppose $e \in \{0, ..., l\} \setminus \mathcal{IR}$, by Lemma 1, we have $e \in \mathcal{K}^*_{bi}$. If $e \notin \mathcal{K}^*_{uni}$, we can apply Lemma 2 and have a set of type 1 epochs, assume $\{e, ..., e_u\}$. For all $e \in \mathcal{K}^*_{bi} \setminus \mathcal{K}^*_{uni}$, we can find a set of type 1 epochs. Hence, the rest epochs are in the type 2 epoch sets.

Remark 6. As a conclusion of Lemma 1 and Lemma 3, we have the sequence of all epochs are a union of three types of epoch sets, that are insulated regions, type 1 epochs and type 2 epochs. $\{0,...,l\} = (\cup_{(\mathsf{fwl},\mathsf{fwr})\in\mathcal{FW}}\{\mathsf{fwl},...,\mathsf{fwr}\}) \cup (\cup_{\mathsf{type\ 1}}\{\mathsf{e}_{\mathsf{start}},...,\mathsf{e}_{\mathsf{end}}\}) \cup (\cup_{\mathsf{type\ 2}}\{\mathsf{e}_{\mathsf{start}},...,\mathsf{e}_{\mathsf{end}}\})$.

Trivial Win Equivalences in the Uni- and Bi-Directional Update Setting. We now prove seven equivalences of the trivial win conditions. As a result, we have that in any security game if the trivial win conditions in the uni-directional update setting are triggered then the same trivial win conditions in the bi-directional update setting would be triggered as well. We will use these trivial win equivalences to prove the relation between uni- and bi-directional variants of security notions in Theorem 2.

The following two lemmas show that UE schemes with uni-directional updates has less leakage than UE schemes with bi-directional updates.

Lemma 4. *For any sets* $\mathcal{K},\mathcal{T},\mathcal{C}$ *and any* $\mathsf{kk}\in\{\mathsf{uni},\mathsf{bi}\}$, *we have* $\mathcal{C}^*_{\mathsf{kk,uni}}\subseteq\mathcal{C}^*_{\mathsf{kk,bi}}$, $\tilde{\mathcal{L}}^*_{\mathsf{kk,uni}}\subseteq\tilde{\mathcal{L}}^*_{\mathsf{kk,bi}}$, $\tilde{\mathcal{Q}}^*_{\mathsf{kk,uni}}\subseteq\tilde{\mathcal{Q}}^*_{\mathsf{kk,bi}}$, $\mathcal{L}^*_{\mathsf{kk,uni}}\subseteq\mathcal{L}^*_{\mathsf{kk,bi}}$, *and* $\mathcal{Q}^*_{\mathsf{kk,uni}}\subseteq\mathcal{Q}^*_{\mathsf{kk,bi}}$.

Proof. For any fixed kk-directional key updates, uni-directional ciphertext updates has less leakage than bi-directional ciphertext updates. More precisely, for any $\mathcal{K},\mathcal{T},\mathcal{C}$ and a fixed kk, we compute $\mathcal{K}^*_{\mathsf{kk}}$, $\mathcal{T}^*_{\mathsf{kk}}$, $\mathcal{C}^*_{\mathsf{kk,uni}}$ and $\mathcal{C}^*_{\mathsf{kk,bi}}$ using Eqs. (1, 2, 3, 4, 5). Then we have $\mathcal{C}^*_{\mathsf{kk,uni}}\subseteq\mathcal{C}^*_{\mathsf{kk,bi}}$. Furthermore, we use algorithms discussed in Sect. 2.6 to compute ciphertext/message leakage sets $\tilde{\mathcal{L}}^*,\tilde{\mathcal{Q}}^*,\mathcal{L}^*,\mathcal{Q}^*$. Similarly we get $\tilde{\mathcal{L}}^*_{\mathsf{kk,uni}}\subseteq\tilde{\mathcal{L}}^*_{\mathsf{kk,bi}}$, $\tilde{\mathcal{Q}}^*_{\mathsf{kk,uni}}\subseteq\tilde{\mathcal{Q}}^*_{\mathsf{kk,bi}}$, $\mathcal{L}^*_{\mathsf{kk,uni}}\subseteq\mathcal{L}^*_{\mathsf{kk,bi}}$, and $\mathcal{Q}^*_{\mathsf{kk,uni}}\subseteq\mathcal{Q}^*_{\mathsf{kk,bi}}$.

Lemma 5. *For any sets* $\mathcal{K},\mathcal{T},\mathcal{C}$ *and any* $\mathsf{cc}\in\{\mathsf{uni},\mathsf{bi}\}$, *we have* $\mathcal{K}^*_{\mathsf{uni}}\subseteq\mathcal{K}^*_{\mathsf{bi}}$, $\mathcal{T}^*_{\mathsf{uni}}\subseteq\mathcal{T}^*_{\mathsf{bi}}$, $\mathcal{C}^*_{\mathsf{uni,cc}}\subseteq\mathcal{C}^*_{\mathsf{bi,cc}}$, $\tilde{\mathcal{L}}^*_{\mathsf{uni,cc}}\subseteq\tilde{\mathcal{L}}^*_{\mathsf{bi,cc}}$, $\tilde{\mathcal{Q}}^*_{\mathsf{uni,cc}}\subseteq\tilde{\mathcal{Q}}^*_{\mathsf{bi,cc}}$, $\mathcal{L}^*_{\mathsf{uni,cc}}\subseteq\mathcal{L}^*_{\mathsf{bi,cc}}$ *and* $\mathcal{Q}^*_{\mathsf{uni,cc}}\subseteq\mathcal{Q}^*_{\mathsf{bi,cc}}$.

Proof. The proof is similar to the proof of Lemma 4. For any fixed cc-directional ciphertext updates, uni-directional key updates has less leakage than bi-directional key updates. More precisely, for any $\mathcal{K},\mathcal{T},\mathcal{C}$ and a fixed cc, we compute $\mathcal{K}^*_{\mathsf{uni}}$, $\mathcal{K}^*_{\mathsf{bi}}$, $\mathcal{T}^*_{\mathsf{uni}}$, $\mathcal{T}^*_{\mathsf{bi}}$, $\mathcal{C}^*_{\mathsf{uni,cc}}$ and $\mathcal{C}^*_{\mathsf{bi,cc}}$ using Eqs. (1, 2, 3, 4, 5). Then we have $\mathcal{K}^*_{\mathsf{uni}}\subseteq\mathcal{K}^*_{\mathsf{bi}}$, $\mathcal{T}^*_{\mathsf{uni}}\subseteq\mathcal{T}^*_{\mathsf{bi}}$, and therefore $\mathcal{C}^*_{\mathsf{uni,cc}}\subseteq\mathcal{C}^*_{\mathsf{bi,cc}}$. Furthermore, we use algorithms discussed in Sect. 2.6 to compute ciphertext/message leakage sets $\tilde{\mathcal{L}}^*,\tilde{\mathcal{Q}}^*,\mathcal{L}^*,\mathcal{Q}^*$. Similarly we get $\tilde{\mathcal{L}}^*_{\mathsf{uni,cc}}\subseteq\tilde{\mathcal{L}}^*_{\mathsf{bi,cc}}$, $\tilde{\mathcal{Q}}^*_{\mathsf{uni,cc}}\subseteq\tilde{\mathcal{Q}}^*_{\mathsf{bi,cc}}$, $\mathcal{L}^*_{\mathsf{uni,cc}}\subseteq\mathcal{L}^*_{\mathsf{bi,cc}}$ and $\mathcal{Q}^*_{\mathsf{uni,cc}}\subseteq\mathcal{Q}^*_{\mathsf{bi,cc}}$.

Equivalence for Trivial Win Condition " $\mathcal{K}^*\cap\mathcal{C}^*\neq\emptyset$*".*

Lemma 6. *For any sets* $\mathcal{K},\mathcal{T},\mathcal{C}\subseteq\{0,...,l\}$, *we have* $\mathcal{K}^*_{\mathsf{uni}}\cap\mathcal{C}^*_{\mathsf{uni,uni}}\neq\emptyset \iff \mathcal{K}^*_{\mathsf{bi}}\cap\mathcal{C}^*_{\mathsf{bi,bi}}\neq\emptyset$.

Proof. For any $\mathcal{K},\mathcal{T},\mathcal{C}$, we compute $\mathcal{K}^*_{\mathsf{uni}},\mathcal{C}^*_{\mathsf{uni,uni}},\mathcal{K}^*_{\mathsf{bi}}$ and $\mathcal{C}^*_{\mathsf{bi,bi}}$ using Eqs. (1, 2, 4, 5).

Note that $\mathcal{K}^*_{\mathsf{uni}} \subseteq \mathcal{K}^*_{\mathsf{bi}}$ and $\mathcal{C}^*_{\mathsf{uni,uni}} \subseteq \mathcal{C}^*_{\mathsf{bi,bi}}$, so $\mathcal{K}^*_{\mathsf{uni}} \cap \mathcal{C}^*_{\mathsf{uni,uni}} \subseteq \mathcal{K}^*_{\mathsf{bi}} \cap \mathcal{C}^*_{\mathsf{bi,bi}}$. It suffices to prove

$$\mathcal{K}^*_{\mathsf{bi}} \cap \mathcal{C}^*_{\mathsf{bi,bi}} \neq \emptyset \Rightarrow \mathcal{K}^*_{\mathsf{uni}} \cap \mathcal{C}^*_{\mathsf{uni,uni}} \neq \emptyset.$$

Suppose $\mathcal{K}^*_{\mathsf{bi}} \cap \mathcal{C}^*_{\mathsf{bi,bi}} \neq \emptyset$. We know that firewalls provide cryptographic separation, which make sure insulated regions are isolated from other insulated regions and the complementary set of all insulated regions. If the adversary never asks for any challenge-equal ciphertext in an epoch in the set $\{0, ..., l\} \setminus \mathcal{IR}$, then the adversary cannot infer any challenge-equal ciphertext in this set even in the bi-directional update setting. That is, $\mathcal{C}^*_{\mathsf{bi,bi}} \cap (\{0, ..., l\} \setminus \mathcal{IR}) = \emptyset$. However, $\{0, ..., l\} \setminus \mathcal{IR} \overset{\text{Lemma 1}}{=} \mathcal{K}^*_{\mathsf{bi}}$, then $\mathcal{K}^*_{\mathsf{bi}} \cap \mathcal{C}^*_{\mathsf{bi,bi}} = \emptyset$, which contradicts with the assumption. Therefore, there exists an epoch $\mathsf{e}' \in \{0, ..., l\} \setminus \mathcal{IR}$ such that the adversary has asked for a challenge-equal ciphertext in this epoch, that is $\mathsf{e}' \in \mathcal{C}$.

By Lemma 3, we know that e' is located in an epoch set which is either type 1 or type 2. Suppose $\mathsf{e}' \in \{\mathsf{e}_{\mathsf{start}}, ..., \mathsf{e}_{\mathsf{end}}\}$, we know that the epoch key $\mathbf{k}_{\mathsf{e}_{\mathsf{end}}}$ is known to the adversary even in the uni-directional key update setting, i.e. $\mathsf{e}_{\mathsf{end}} \in \mathcal{K}^*_{\mathsf{uni}}$. Furthermore, all tokens $\Delta_{\mathsf{e}'+1}, ..., \Delta_{\mathsf{e}_{\mathsf{end}}}$ are known to the adversary even in the uni-directional key update setting. Hence, the adversary can update the challenge-equal ciphertext $\tilde{\mathbf{c}}_{\mathsf{e}'}$ from epoch e' to epoch $\mathsf{e}_{\mathsf{end}}$ to know $\tilde{\mathbf{c}}_{\mathsf{e}_{\mathsf{end}}}$. Which means $\mathsf{e}_{\mathsf{end}} \in \mathcal{K}^*_{\mathsf{uni}} \cap \mathcal{C}^*_{\mathsf{uni,uni}}$, we have $\mathcal{K}^*_{\mathsf{uni}} \cap \mathcal{C}^*_{\mathsf{uni,uni}} \neq \emptyset$.

As a corollary of Lemma 4 to 6, we have the following equivalence. We only provide Corollary 1 with a fully detailed proof, since we will use similar proof techniques for Corollary 2 to 5.

Corollary 1. *For any sets* $\mathcal{K}, \mathcal{T}, \mathcal{C} \subseteq \{0, ..., l\}$, *we have* $\mathcal{K}^*_{\mathsf{uni}} \cap \mathcal{C}^*_{\mathsf{uni,uni}} \neq \emptyset \iff \mathcal{K}^*_{\mathsf{uni}} \cap \mathcal{C}^*_{\mathsf{uni,bi}} \neq \emptyset \iff \mathcal{K}^*_{\mathsf{bi}} \cap \mathcal{C}^*_{\mathsf{bi,uni}} \neq \emptyset \iff \mathcal{K}^*_{\mathsf{bi}} \cap \mathcal{C}^*_{\mathsf{bi,bi}} \neq \emptyset$.

Proof. By Lemma 4, we have $\mathcal{C}^*_{\mathsf{uni,uni}} \subseteq \mathcal{C}^*_{\mathsf{uni,bi}}$. By Lemma 5, we have $\mathcal{C}^*_{\mathsf{uni,bi}} \subseteq \mathcal{C}^*_{\mathsf{bi,bi}}$. Hence, $\mathcal{K}^*_{\mathsf{uni}} \cap \mathcal{C}^*_{\mathsf{uni,uni}} \subseteq \mathcal{K}^*_{\mathsf{uni}} \cap \mathcal{C}^*_{\mathsf{uni,bi}} \subseteq \mathcal{K}^*_{\mathsf{bi}} \cap \mathcal{C}^*_{\mathsf{bi,bi}}$. By Lemma 6, we have $\mathcal{K}^*_{\mathsf{uni}} \cap \mathcal{C}^*_{\mathsf{uni,uni}} \neq \emptyset \iff \mathcal{K}^*_{\mathsf{bi}} \cap \mathcal{C}^*_{\mathsf{bi,bi}} \neq \emptyset \iff \mathcal{K}^*_{\mathsf{uni}} \cap \mathcal{C}^*_{\mathsf{uni,bi}} \neq \emptyset$.

Similarly, we have $\mathcal{K}^*_{\mathsf{uni}} \cap \mathcal{C}^*_{\mathsf{uni,uni}} \overset{\text{Lemma 5}}{\subseteq} \mathcal{K}^*_{\mathsf{bi}} \cap \mathcal{C}^*_{\mathsf{bi,uni}} \overset{\text{Lemma 4}}{\subseteq} \mathcal{K}^*_{\mathsf{bi}} \cap \mathcal{C}^*_{\mathsf{bi,bi}}$ and therefore $\mathcal{K}^*_{\mathsf{uni}} \cap \mathcal{C}^*_{\mathsf{uni,uni}} \neq \emptyset \iff \mathcal{K}^*_{\mathsf{bi}} \cap \mathcal{C}^*_{\mathsf{bi,bi}} \neq \emptyset \iff \mathcal{K}^*_{\mathsf{bi}} \cap \mathcal{C}^*_{\mathsf{bi,uni}} \neq \emptyset$.

Remark 7. If the trivial win condition "$\mathcal{K}^* \cap \mathcal{C}^* \neq \emptyset$" is never triggered in the uni- or bi-directional update setting, then by Corollary 1 we have $\mathcal{K}^*_{\mathsf{bi}} \cap \mathcal{C}^*_{\mathsf{bi,bi}} = \emptyset$. By Lemma 1, we have $\{0, ..., l\} \setminus \mathcal{K}^*_{\mathsf{bi}} = \mathcal{IR}$. Therefore, $\mathcal{C}^*_{\mathsf{uni,uni}} \subseteq \mathcal{C}^*_{\mathsf{bi,bi}} \subseteq \{0, ..., l\} \setminus \mathcal{K}^*_{\mathsf{bi}} = \mathcal{IR}$. The relationship among the sets $\mathcal{C}^*_{\mathsf{uni,uni}}, \mathcal{C}^*_{\mathsf{bi,bi}}, \mathcal{IR}, \mathcal{K}^*_{\mathsf{uni}}, \mathcal{K}^*_{\mathsf{bi}}$ is shown in Fig. 11.

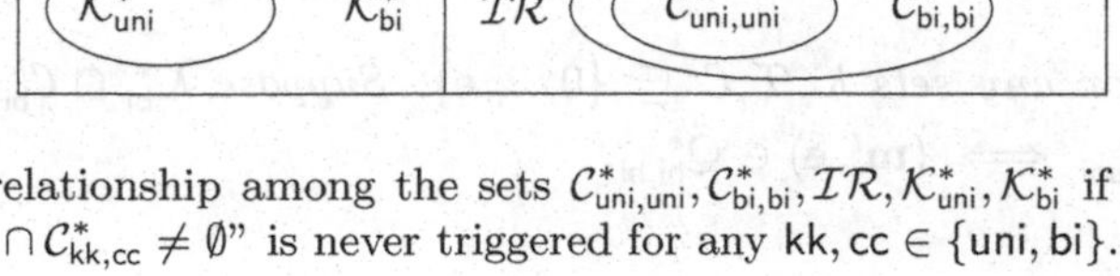

Fig. 11. The relationship among the sets $\mathcal{C}^*_{\mathsf{uni,uni}}, \mathcal{C}^*_{\mathsf{bi,bi}}, \mathcal{IR}, \mathcal{K}^*_{\mathsf{uni}}, \mathcal{K}^*_{\mathsf{bi}}$ if the trivial win condition "$\mathcal{K}^*_{\mathsf{kk}} \cap \mathcal{C}^*_{\mathsf{kk,cc}} \neq \emptyset$" is never triggered for any $\mathsf{kk}, \mathsf{cc} \in \{\mathsf{uni}, \mathsf{bi}\}$.

Equivalence for Trivial Win Condition " $\tilde{\mathsf{e}} \in \mathcal{T}^*$ ***or*** $\mathcal{O}.\mathsf{Upd}(\bar{\mathbf{c}})$ *is queried".* The event "$\mathcal{O}.\mathsf{Upd}(\bar{\mathbf{c}})$ is queried" is independent of the key and ciphertext updates, so this trivial win condition is either triggered or not triggered in all variants of a security notion. The following Lemma shows that if the challenge token is known to the adversary in the bi-directional key update setting, then it is also known to the adversary in the uni-directional key update setting.

Lemma 7. *For any* $\mathcal{K}, \mathcal{T}, \mathcal{C}$. *Suppose* $\mathcal{K}^*_{\mathsf{kk}} \cap \mathcal{C}^*_{\mathsf{kk},\mathsf{cc}} = \emptyset$, *where* $\mathsf{kk}, \mathsf{cc} \in \{\mathsf{uni}, \mathsf{bi}\}$, *then* $\tilde{\mathsf{e}} \in \mathcal{T}^*_{\mathsf{no}} \iff \tilde{\mathsf{e}} \in \mathcal{T}^*_{\mathsf{uni}} \iff \tilde{\mathsf{e}} \in \mathcal{T}^*_{\mathsf{bi}}$

Proof. We know that the challenge epoch $\tilde{\mathsf{e}} \in \mathcal{C}$, so $\tilde{\mathsf{e}} \notin \mathcal{K}^*_{\mathsf{kk}}$ for any kk-key updates, where $\mathsf{kk} \in \{\mathsf{uni}, \mathsf{bi}\}$. Since the adversary does not know the key $\mathbf{k}_{\tilde{\mathsf{e}}}$, which is needed to infer the update token $\Delta_{\tilde{\mathsf{e}}}$, so token $\Delta_{\tilde{\mathsf{e}}}$ cannot be inferred by the adversary. Therefore, $\tilde{\mathsf{e}} \in \mathcal{T}^*_{\mathsf{kk}}$ if and only if $\tilde{\mathsf{e}} \in \mathcal{T}$. Hence $\tilde{\mathsf{e}} \in \mathcal{T} \iff \tilde{\mathsf{e}} \in \mathcal{T}^*_{\mathsf{no}} \iff \tilde{\mathsf{e}} \in \mathcal{T}^*_{\mathsf{uni}} \iff \tilde{\mathsf{e}} \in \mathcal{T}^*_{\mathsf{bi}}$.

From now on until the end of this section, we assume the adversary queries a decryption oracle $\mathcal{O}.\mathsf{Dec}(\mathbf{c})$ or a try oracle $\mathcal{O}.\mathsf{Try}(\mathbf{c})$ in epoch e. We consider trivial win conditions which are checked in these oracles.

Equivalence for Trivial Win Condition " $(\mathbf{c}, \mathsf{e}) \in \tilde{\mathcal{L}}^*$ *".*

Lemma 8. *For any sets* $\mathcal{K}, \mathcal{T}, \mathcal{C} \subseteq \{0, ..., \mathsf{e}\}$. *Suppose* $\mathcal{K}^*_{\mathsf{bi}} \cap \mathcal{C}^*_{\mathsf{bi},\mathsf{bi}} = \emptyset$, *then* $(\mathbf{c}, \mathsf{e}) \in \tilde{\mathcal{L}}^*_{\mathsf{uni},\mathsf{uni}} \iff (\mathbf{c}, \mathsf{e}) \in \tilde{\mathcal{L}}^*_{\mathsf{bi},\mathsf{bi}}$.

Proof. By Remark 7 we have $\mathcal{C}^*_{\mathsf{uni},\mathsf{uni}} \subseteq \mathcal{C}^*_{\mathsf{bi},\mathsf{bi}} \subseteq \mathcal{IR}$. By Remark 1 we have $(\tilde{\mathbf{c}}_{\mathsf{e}}, \mathsf{e}) \in \tilde{\mathcal{L}}^* \iff \mathsf{e} \in \mathcal{C}^*$. Therefore, if $(\mathbf{c}, \mathsf{e}) \in \tilde{\mathcal{L}}^*_{\mathsf{uni},\mathsf{uni}}$ we have $\mathsf{e} \in \mathcal{C}^*_{\mathsf{uni},\mathsf{uni}} \subseteq \mathcal{C}^*_{\mathsf{bi},\mathsf{bi}}$ and $(\mathbf{c}, \mathsf{e}) \in \tilde{\mathcal{L}}^*_{\mathsf{bi},\mathsf{bi}}$.

If $(\mathbf{c}, \mathsf{e}) \in \tilde{\mathcal{L}}^*_{\mathsf{bi},\mathsf{bi}}$, then $\mathsf{e} \in \mathcal{C}^*_{\mathsf{bi},\mathsf{bi}} \subseteq \mathcal{IR}$. Suppose $\{\mathsf{fwl}, ..., \mathsf{e}\}$ is the last insulated region. If the adversary never asks for any challenge-equal ciphertext in this region, then $\{\mathsf{fwl}, ..., \mathsf{e}\} \cap \mathcal{C}^*_{\mathsf{bi},\mathsf{bi}} = \emptyset$, which contradicts with $\mathsf{e} \in \mathcal{C}^*_{\mathsf{bi},\mathsf{bi}} \cap \{\mathsf{fwl}, ..., \mathsf{e}\}$. Hence, $\{\mathsf{fwl}, ..., \mathsf{e}\} \cap \mathcal{C} \neq \emptyset$, and we can assume $\mathsf{e}' \in \{\mathsf{fwl}, ..., \mathsf{e}\} \cap \mathcal{C}$. By the definition of insulated region we have $\{\mathsf{fwl}+1, ..., \mathsf{e}\} \subseteq \mathcal{T}$, and the adversary can update the challenge-equal ciphertext $\tilde{\mathbf{c}}_{\mathsf{e}'}$ from epoch e' to epoch e to know $\tilde{\mathbf{c}}_{\mathsf{e}}$, i.e. $\mathsf{e} \in \mathcal{C}^*_{\mathsf{uni},\mathsf{uni}}$. Therefore, $(\mathbf{c}, \mathsf{e}) \in \tilde{\mathcal{L}}^*_{\mathsf{uni},\mathsf{uni}}$ as well.

As a corollary of Lemma 4, Lemma 5 and Lemma 8, we have the following result. The proof is similar to the proof of Corollary 1.

Corollary 2. *For any sets* $\mathcal{K}, \mathcal{T}, \mathcal{C} \subseteq \{0, ..., \mathsf{e}\}$. *Suppose* $\mathcal{K}^*_{\mathsf{bi}} \cap \mathcal{C}^*_{\mathsf{bi},\mathsf{bi}} = \emptyset$, *then* $(\mathbf{c}, \mathsf{e}) \in \tilde{\mathcal{L}}^*_{\mathsf{uni},\mathsf{uni}} \iff (\mathbf{c}, \mathsf{e}) \in \tilde{\mathcal{L}}^*_{\mathsf{uni},\mathsf{bi}} \iff (\mathbf{c}, \mathsf{e}) \in \tilde{\mathcal{L}}^*_{\mathsf{bi},\mathsf{uni}} \iff (\mathbf{c}, \mathsf{e}) \in \tilde{\mathcal{L}}^*_{\mathsf{bi},\mathsf{bi}}$.

Equivalence for Trivial Win Condition " $(\mathbf{m}', \mathsf{e}) \in \tilde{\mathcal{Q}}^*$ *".*

Lemma 9. *For any sets* $\mathcal{K}, \mathcal{T}, \mathcal{C} \subseteq \{0, ..., \mathsf{e}\}$. *Suppose* $\mathcal{K}^*_{\mathsf{bi}} \cap \mathcal{C}^*_{\mathsf{bi},\mathsf{bi}} = \emptyset$, *then* $(\mathbf{m}', \mathsf{e}) \in \tilde{\mathcal{Q}}^*_{\mathsf{uni},\mathsf{uni}} \iff (\mathbf{m}', \mathsf{e}) \in \tilde{\mathcal{Q}}^*_{\mathsf{bi},\mathsf{bi}}$.

Proof. The proof is similar to the proof of Lemma 8. We use the property that $(\mathbf{m}', \mathsf{e}) \in \tilde{\mathcal{Q}}^* \iff \mathsf{e} \in \mathcal{C}^*$.

As a corollary of Lemma 4, Lemma 5 and Lemma 9, we have the following result. The proof is similar to the proof of Corollary 1.

Corollary 3. *For any sets* $\mathcal{K}, \mathcal{T}, \mathcal{C} \subseteq \{0, ..., \mathsf{e}\}$. *Suppose* $\mathcal{K}^*_{\mathsf{bi}} \cap \mathcal{C}^*_{\mathsf{bi,bi}} = \emptyset$, *then* $(\mathbf{m}', \mathsf{e}) \in \tilde{\mathcal{Q}}^*_{\mathsf{uni,uni}} \iff (\mathbf{m}', \mathsf{e}) \in \tilde{\mathcal{Q}}^*_{\mathsf{uni,bi}} \iff (\mathbf{m}', \mathsf{e}) \in \tilde{\mathcal{Q}}^*_{\mathsf{bi,uni}} \iff (\mathbf{m}', \mathsf{e}) \in \tilde{\mathcal{Q}}^*_{\mathsf{bi,bi}}$.

Equivalence for Trivial Win Condition " $\mathsf{e} \in \mathcal{K}^*$ ".

Lemma 10. *For any sets* $\mathcal{K}, \mathcal{T}, \mathcal{C} \subseteq \{0, ..., \mathsf{e}\}$, *we have* $\mathsf{e} \in \mathcal{K}^*_{\mathsf{uni}} \iff \mathsf{e} \in \mathcal{K}^*_{\mathsf{bi}}$.

Proof. The adversary never knows any information in the future, that is, the adversary does not know a key in an epoch $\hat{\mathsf{e}} > \mathsf{e}$. If the adversary knows the current epoch key $\mathbf{k}_{\mathsf{e}}$, then it is either a corrupted key or a key inferred from prior epoch key, thus $\mathsf{e} \in \mathcal{K}^*_{\mathsf{uni}} \iff \mathsf{e} \in \mathcal{K}^*_{\mathsf{bi}}$.

Equivalence for Trivial Win Condition " $(\mathbf{c}, \mathsf{e}) \in \mathcal{L}^*$ ".

Lemma 11. *For any sets* $\mathcal{K}, \mathcal{T}, \mathcal{C} \subseteq \{0, ..., \mathsf{e}\}$. *Suppose* $\mathsf{e} \notin \mathcal{K}^*_{\mathsf{bi}}$, *then* $(\mathbf{c}, \mathsf{e}) \in \mathcal{L}^*_{\mathsf{uni,uni}} \iff (\mathbf{c}, \mathsf{e}) \in \mathcal{L}^*_{\mathsf{bi,bi}}$.

Proof. By assumption and Lemma 10 the current epoch $\mathsf{e} \notin \mathcal{K}^*_{\mathsf{kk}}$ for any $\mathsf{kk} \in \{\mathsf{uni}, \mathsf{bi}\}$. We know that, by Remark 6, e is located in an insulated region, assume it is in $\{\mathsf{fwl}, ..., \mathsf{e}\}$. Thus tokens $\Delta_{\mathsf{fwl}+1}, ..., \Delta_{\mathsf{e}}$ are known to the adversary in any update setting, that is, $\{\mathsf{fwl}+1, ..., \mathsf{e}\} \subseteq \mathcal{T} \subseteq \mathcal{T}^*_{\mathsf{uni}} \subseteq \mathcal{T}^*_{\mathsf{bi}}$. If the adversary never asks for any ciphertext in this region, then there is no ciphertext in epoch e located in the set $\mathcal{L}^*_{\mathsf{kk,cc}}$ for any $(\mathsf{kk}, \mathsf{cc})$. For all ciphertexts the adversary learns in an epoch i with $i \in \{\mathsf{fwl}, ..., \mathsf{e}\}$, the adversary can update them to epoch e using tokens. Hence, we have $(\mathbf{c}, \mathsf{e}) \in \mathcal{L}^*_{\mathsf{uni,uni}} \iff (\mathbf{c}, \mathsf{e}) \in \mathcal{L}^*_{\mathsf{bi,bi}}$.

As a corollary of Lemma 4, Lemma 5 and Lemma 11, we have the following result. The proof is similar to the proof of Corollary 1.

Corollary 4. *For any sets* $\mathcal{K}, \mathcal{T}, \mathcal{C} \subseteq \{0, ..., \mathsf{e}\}$. *Suppose* $\mathsf{e} \notin \mathcal{K}^*_{\mathsf{bi}}$, *then* $(\mathbf{c}, \mathsf{e}) \in \mathcal{L}^*_{\mathsf{uni,uni}} \iff (\mathbf{c}, \mathsf{e}) \in \mathcal{L}^*_{\mathsf{uni,bi}} \iff (\mathbf{c}, \mathsf{e}) \in \mathcal{L}^*_{\mathsf{bi,uni}} \iff (\mathbf{c}, \mathsf{e}) \in \mathcal{L}^*_{\mathsf{bi,bi}}$.

Equivalence for Trivial Win Condition " $(\mathbf{m}', \mathsf{e}) \in \mathcal{Q}^*$ ".

Lemma 12. *For any sets* $\mathcal{K}, \mathcal{T}, \mathcal{C} \subseteq \{0, ..., \mathsf{e}\}$. *Suppose* $\mathsf{e} \notin \mathcal{K}^*_{\mathsf{bi}}$, *then* $(\mathbf{m}', \mathsf{e}) \in \mathcal{Q}^*_{\mathsf{uni,uni}} \iff (\mathbf{m}', \mathsf{e}) \in \mathcal{Q}^*_{\mathsf{bi,bi}}$.

Proof. The proof is similar to the proof of Lemma 11. As $\mathsf{e} \notin \mathcal{K}^*_{\mathsf{kk}}$ for any $\mathsf{kk} \in \{\mathsf{uni}, \mathsf{bi}\}$, we know that e is located in an insulated region. Assume it is in $\{\mathsf{fwl}, ..., \mathsf{e}\}$, then the adversary has corrupted the tokens $\Delta_{\mathsf{fwl}+1}, ..., \Delta_{\mathsf{e}}$. If the adversary never asks for any ciphertext with the underlying message $\mathbf{m}'$ in this region, then $(\mathbf{m}', \mathsf{e}) \notin \mathcal{Q}^*_{\mathsf{kk,cc}}$ for any $(\mathsf{kk}, \mathsf{cc})$. Otherwise, suppose $(\cdot, \mathbf{c}_i, i; \mathbf{m}') \in \mathcal{L}$ with $i \in \{\mathsf{fwl}, ..., \mathsf{e}\}$, then the adversary can update $\mathbf{c}_i$, via tokens $\Delta_{i+1}, ..., \Delta_{\mathsf{e}}$, to a ciphertext in epoch e with the underlying message $\mathbf{m}'$ and we have $(\mathbf{m}', \mathsf{e}) \in \mathcal{Q}^*_{\mathsf{kk,cc}}$ for any $(\mathsf{kk}, \mathsf{cc})$.

As a corollary of Lemma 4, Lemma 5 and Lemma 12, we have the following result. The proof is similar to the proof of Corollary 1.

Corollary 5. *For any sets* $\mathcal{K}, \mathcal{T}, \mathcal{C} \subseteq \{0, ..., \mathsf{e}\}$*. Suppose* $\mathsf{e} \notin \mathcal{K}^*_{\mathsf{bi}}$*, then* $(\mathbf{m}', \mathsf{e}) \in \mathcal{Q}^*_{\mathsf{uni,uni}} \iff (\mathbf{m}', \mathsf{e}) \in \mathcal{Q}^*_{\mathsf{uni,bi}} \iff (\mathbf{m}', \mathsf{e}) \in \mathcal{Q}^*_{\mathsf{bi,uni}} \iff (\mathbf{m}', \mathsf{e}) \in \mathcal{Q}^*_{\mathsf{bi,bi}}$.

3.2 Relations Among Security Notions

In Fig. 12, Fig. 13 and Fig. 14, we show the relationship among six variants of the same security notion for UE schemes.

Figure 12 demonstrates that the uni- and bi-directional update variants of the same security notion are equivalent, which means that the security notions (confidentiality and integrity) in the uni-directional update setting are not strictly stronger than the corresponding security notions in the bi-directional update setting. Hence, the security of a UE scheme is not influenced if the update setting is uni- or bi-directional. In terms of confidentiality and integrity, when we analyze the security of a UE scheme we can analyze the security based on the UE scheme with bi-directional updates.

The six variants of confidentiality notions have the relationship shown in Fig. 13, where we present that the (no, uni)- variant of any confidentiality notion is strictly stronger than the other five variants of the corresponding confidentiality notion.

The six variants of integrity notions have the relationship shown in Fig. 14. No-directional key update variants of the same integrity notion is strictly stronger than the uni- or bi-directional key update variants. However, the two variants of no-directional key update notions are equivalent, that is, for the integrity notions uni- or bi-directional ciphertext update setting (with no-directional key updates) does not matter much.

It is ideal to construct an efficient UE scheme with no-directional key updates and uni-directional ciphertext updates. However, whether such a scheme exists is an open problem.

Theorem 1 (Informal Theorem). *The relations among the six variants of the same security notion are as in Fig. 12, Fig. 13 and Fig. 14. The precise results are stated and proven in the full version [13] and due to space constraints we only show Theorem 2.*

$$(\mathsf{bi},\mathsf{bi})\text{-}\mathsf{notion} \overset{\text{Thm. 2}}{\iff} (\mathsf{bi},\mathsf{uni})\text{-}\mathsf{notion} \overset{\text{Thm. 2}}{\iff} (\mathsf{uni},\mathsf{bi})\text{-}\mathsf{notion} \overset{\text{Thm. 2}}{\iff} (\mathsf{uni},\mathsf{uni})\text{-}\mathsf{notion}$$

Fig. 12. Relations among the uni- and bi-directional update variants of the same security notion, where notion $\in$ {INT-CTXT, INT-PTXT, detIND-UE-CPA, randIND-UE-CPA, detIND-UE-CCA, randIND-UE-CCA}.

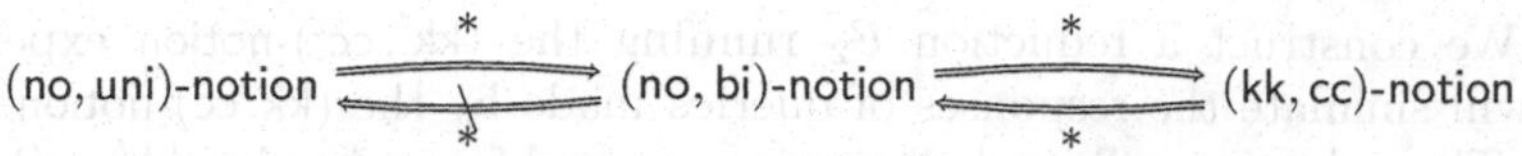

Fig. 13. Relations among the six variants of the same confidentiality notion, where kk, cc ∈ {uni, bi} and notion ∈ {detIND-UE-CPA, randIND-UE-CPA, detIND-UE-CCA, randIND-UE-CCA}. Results that are given only in the full version [13] are marked with ∗.

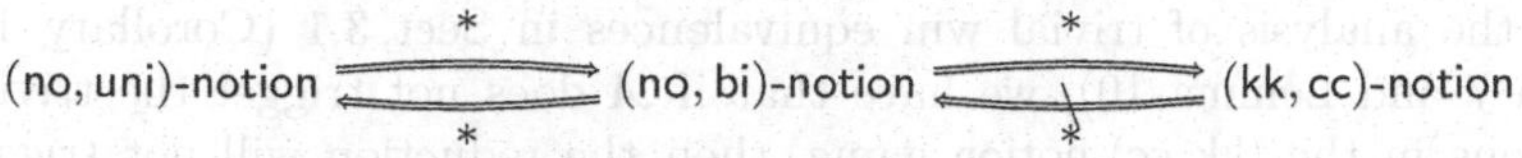

Fig. 14. Relations among the six variants of the same integrity notion, where kk, cc ∈ {uni, bi} and notion ∈ {INT-CTXT, INT-PTXT}. Results that are given only in the full version [13] are marked with ∗.

Remark 8 (Informal intuition of these relations). Consider the following confidentiality game, where we have an adversary against some variant of the confidentiality game for a UE scheme. The adversary corrupts a key $\mathbf{k}_1$ and a token Δ_2, and asks for a challenge ciphertext in epoch 2. For both uni- and bi-directional key update settings, the adversary can move the key $\mathbf{k}_1$ to epoch 2 and decrypt the challenge ciphertext to trivially win the confidentiality game. If the UE scheme has no-directional key updates and bi-directional ciphertext updates, the adversary can move the challenge ciphertext back to epoch 1 and decrypt it to trivially win the confidentiality game. However, if the UE scheme has no-directional key updates and uni-directional ciphertext updates, the adversary cannot trivially win the confidentiality game in this action.

Similarly, we consider the following integrity game, where we have an adversary against some variant of the integrity game for a UE scheme. The adversary corrupts a key $\mathbf{k}_1$ and a token Δ_2, and queries a try oracle in epoch 2. For both uni- and bi-directional key update settings, the adversary can move the key $\mathbf{k}_1$ to epoch 2 and provide forgeries in epoch 2 to trivially win the integrity game. However, if the UE scheme has no-directional key updates the adversary does not know $\mathbf{k}_2$, and cannot trivially win the integrity game.

The following Theorem shows that for any kk, cc, kk′, cc′ ∈ {uni, bi}, (kk′, cc′)-notion implies (kk, cc)-notion. Consequently, all four uni- and bi-directional update variants of the same notion are equivalent.

Theorem 2. *Let* UE = {UE.KG, UE.TG, UE.Enc, UE.Dec, UE.Upd} *be an updatable encryption scheme and* notion ∈ {INT-CTXT, INT-PTXT, detIND-UE-CPA, randIND-UE-CPA, detIND-UE-CCA, randIND-UE-CCA}. *For any* kk, cc, kk′, cc′ ∈ {uni, bi} *and any* (kk, cc)-notion *adversary* $\mathcal{A}$ *against* UE, *there exists a* (kk′, cc′)-notion *adversary* $\mathcal{B}_2$ *against* UE *such that*

$$\mathbf{Adv}_{\mathsf{UE},\ \mathcal{A}}^{(\mathsf{kk},\mathsf{cc})\text{-}\mathsf{notion}}(1^{\lambda}) = \mathbf{Adv}_{\mathsf{UE},\ \mathcal{B}_2}^{(\mathsf{kk}',\mathsf{cc}')\text{-}\mathsf{notion}}(1^{\lambda}).$$

Proof. We construct a reduction $\mathcal{B}_2$ running the (kk′, cc′)-notion experiment which will simulate the responses of queries made by the (kk, cc)-notion adversary $\mathcal{A}$. The reduction will send all queries received from $\mathcal{A}$ to its (kk′, cc′)-notion challenger, and forwarding the responses to $\mathcal{A}$. Eventually, the reduction receives a guess from $\mathcal{A}$ and forwards it to its own challenger. In the end, the (kk′, cc′)-notion challenger evaluates whether or not the reduction wins, if a trivial win condition was triggered the reduction is considered as losing the game. This final win evaluation will be passed to the adversary $\mathcal{A}$.

By the analysis of trivial win equivalences in Sect. 3.1 (Corollary 1 to 5, Lemma 7 and Lemma 10), we have that if $\mathcal{A}$ does not trigger the trivial win conditions in the (kk, cc)-notion game, then the reduction will not trigger the trivial win conditions in the (kk′, cc′)-notion game either. Similarly, if $\mathcal{A}$ does trigger the trivial win conditions in the (kk, cc)-notion game, then the reduction will also trigger the trivial win conditions in the (kk′, cc′)-notion game. Hence, the reduction perfectly simulates the (kk, cc)-notion game to adversary $\mathcal{A}$. And we have $\mathbf{Adv}_{\mathsf{UE},\ \mathcal{B}_2}^{(\mathsf{kk}',\mathsf{cc}')\text{-}\mathsf{notion}}(1^\lambda) = \mathbf{Adv}_{\mathsf{UE},\ \mathcal{A}}^{(\mathsf{kk},\mathsf{cc})\text{-}\mathsf{notion}}(1^\lambda)$.

Remark 9. For any notion $\in$ {detIND-UE-CPA, randIND-UE-CPA, detIND-UE-CCA, randIND-UE-CCA, INT-CTXT, INT-PTXT}, all four uni- and bi-directional update variants of the same notion are equivalent. We will use the (bi, bi)-notion variant to prove notion security for a specific UE schemes. For simplicity, we will denote the notion (bi, bi)-notion as notion.

4 LWE-based PKE Scheme

In this section, we look at an LWE-based PKE scheme LWEPKE, which is detailed in Fig. 15. We prove that LWEPKE is IND\$-CPA-secure, if the underlying LWE problem is hard. We will later use this PKE scheme to construct an updatable encryption scheme in Sect. 5.

4.1 PKE Construction

In the setup phase, the scheme LWEPKE randomly chooses a matrix $\mathbf{A} \xleftarrow{\$} \mathbb{Z}_q^{m\times n}$. The key generation algorithm samples a secret $\mathbf{s}$ from the uniform distribution $\mathcal{U}(\mathbb{Z}_q^n)$ and computes $\mathbf{p} = \mathbf{A}\cdot\mathbf{s}+\mathbf{e}$, where the error $\mathbf{e}$ is chosen from the discrete Gaussian distribution $D_{\mathbb{Z},\alpha}^m$. The matrix $\mathbf{A}$ and the vector $\mathbf{p}$ form the public key. Encryption takes a bit string $\mathbf{m} \in \{0,1\}^{1\times t}$ as input, and outputs a ciphertext $(\mathbf{A}^\intercal\cdot\mathbf{R}, \mathbf{p}^\intercal\cdot\mathbf{R}+\mathbf{e}'+\frac{q}{2}\mathbf{m} \mod q)$. Decryption is performed by computing $\mathbf{d} = \mathbf{c}_2 - \mathbf{s}^\intercal\cdot\mathbf{C}_1$. For each entry d_i of $\mathbf{d}$, the decryption algorithm outputs 0 if d_i is close to $0 \mod q$, and outputs 1 if d_i is close to $\frac{q}{2} \mod q$.

Parameter Setting. The parameter setting of the scheme LWEPKE is as follows:

– $n = \lambda$ is the security parameter,

$\underline{\mathsf{LWEPKE.Setup}(1^\lambda):}$
$\mathbf{A} \xleftarrow{\$} \mathbb{Z}_q^{m\times n}$

$\underline{\mathsf{LWEPKE.KG}(1^\lambda):}$
$\mathbf{s} \leftarrow \mathcal{U}(\mathbb{Z}_q^n)$
$\mathbf{e} \leftarrow D_{\mathbb{Z},\alpha}^m$
$\mathbf{p} \leftarrow \mathbf{A}\cdot\mathbf{s}+\mathbf{e} \mod q$
return $(\mathbf{s},\mathbf{p})$

$\underline{\mathsf{LWEPKE.Enc}(\mathbf{p},\mathbf{m}):}$
$\mathbf{R} \leftarrow \mathcal{D}_r^t$
$\mathbf{e}' \leftarrow D_{\mathbb{Z},\beta}^{1\times t}$
$\mathbf{C}_1 \leftarrow \mathbf{A}^\intercal\cdot\mathbf{R}$
$\mathbf{c}_2 \leftarrow \mathbf{p}^\intercal\cdot\mathbf{R}+\mathbf{e}'+\frac{q}{2}\mathbf{m} \mod q$
return $(\mathbf{C}_1,\mathbf{c}_2)$

$\underline{\mathsf{LWEPKE.Dec}(\mathbf{s},\mathbf{c}):}$
parse $\mathbf{c}=(\mathbf{C}_1,\mathbf{c}_2)$
$\mathbf{d} \leftarrow \mathbf{c}_2-\mathbf{s}^\intercal\cdot\mathbf{C}_1$
parse $\mathbf{d}=(d_1,\dots,d_t)$
for $i\in\{1,2,\dots,t\}$ **do**
  if $d_i\in(\frac{3q}{8},\frac{5q}{8})$ **then**
    $m_i'\leftarrow 1$
  else if $d_i\in(-\frac{q}{8},\frac{q}{8})$ **then**
    $m_i'\leftarrow 0$
  else
    return $\perp$
$\mathbf{m}'\leftarrow(m_1',\dots,m_t')$
return $\mathbf{m}'$

Fig. 15. The algorithms of the LWE-based LWEPKE scheme. The randomness distribution $\mathcal{D}_r$ is defined over $\mathbb{Z}_q^m$. $D_{\mathbb{Z},\alpha}, D_{\mathbb{Z},\beta}$ are discrete Gaussian distributions. The message $\mathbf{m}$ lies in $\{0,1\}^{1\times t}$.

- $q=q(n)\geq 2$ be a prime,
- $m=\mathsf{poly}(n)$ and $t=\mathsf{poly}(n)$ be two integers,
- $\mathcal{D}_r$ be a distribution over $\mathbb{Z}_q^m$ with min-entropy k such that $n\leq(k-2\log(1/\epsilon)-O(1))/\log(q)$ for negligible $\epsilon>0$, the infinite norm of the vector outputted by this distribution is at most $B=\mathsf{poly}(n)$ with overwhelming probability,
- $\alpha,\beta>0$ be two numbers such that $\beta\leq\frac{q}{8}$ and $\alpha B/\beta=\mathsf{negl}(n)$.
- $D_{\mathbb{Z},\alpha}$ and $D_{\mathbb{Z},\beta}$ be two discrete Gaussian distributions.

Remark 10. We specify that all operations in this paper are done in field $\mathbb{Z}_q$, and stop writing $\mod q$ for the rest of this paper.

4.2 Correctness and Security

Correctness. We claim that LWEPKE.Dec decrypts correctly with overwhelming probability. The decryption algorithm computes $\mathbf{d}=\mathbf{c}_2-\mathbf{s}^\intercal\cdot\mathbf{C}_1=\mathbf{e}^\intercal\cdot\mathbf{R}+\mathbf{e}'+\frac{q}{2}\mathbf{m}$, and outputs $\mathbf{m}$ if $\mathbf{e}^\intercal\cdot\mathbf{R}+\mathbf{e}'$ has distance at most $\frac{q}{8}$ from $\mathbf{0}$ mod q. The detailed analysis of the correctness is provided in the full version [13].

Security. We now show that LWEPKE is IND\$-CPA-secure under the assumption that the $\mathsf{DLWE}_{n,q,\alpha}$ problem is hard.

Theorem 3. *Let* LWEPKE *be the public key encryption described in Fig. 15, using the parameter setting described in Sect. 4.1. Then for any adversary* IND\$-CPA $\mathcal{A}$ *against* LWEPKE, *there exists an adversary* $\mathcal{B}$ *against* $\mathsf{DLWE}_{n,q,\alpha}$ *such that*

$$\mathbf{Adv}_{\mathsf{LWEPKE},\ \mathcal{A}}^{\mathsf{IND\$\text{-}CPA}}(1^\lambda)\leq t\epsilon+\mathbf{Adv}_{n,q,\alpha}^{\mathsf{DLWE}}(\mathcal{B})+\mathsf{negl}(n).$$

Proof sketch. We sketch the main idea of the proof and provide the full details in the full version [13]. We claim that the real challenge ciphertext $(\mathbf{C}_1, \mathbf{c}_2)$ is statistically close to the ciphertext generated as $(\mathbf{C}_1, \mathbf{s}^\mathsf{T} \cdot \mathbf{C}_1 + \mathbf{e}')$. Then first entry $\mathbf{C}_1$ is statistically close to a random element because of the leftover hash lemma, and therefore the whole ciphertext $(\mathbf{C}_1, \mathbf{s}^\mathsf{T} \cdot \mathbf{C}_1 + \mathbf{e}')$ is computationally indistinguishable from a random ciphertext based on the hardness of the learning with error.

5 LWE-based Updatable Encryption Scheme

We construct an LWE-based updatable encryption scheme LWEUE and prove that it is randIND-UE-CPA secure if the underlying LWE problem is hard.

5.1 UE Construction

We now introduce our updatable encryption scheme LWEUE, which is parameterized by an LWE-based PKE scheme LWEPKE (see Fig. 15). LWEUE uses algorithms from LWEPKE to do key generation, encryption and decryption. To generate a new key from an old key in the next algorithm, our UE scheme uses the homomorphic property of the LWE pairs. In particular, suppose the old key is $(\mathbf{s}_\mathsf{e}, \mathbf{p}_\mathsf{e})$, LWEUE.KG samples a new pair of LWE pairs $(\Delta^\mathbf{s}_{\mathsf{e}+1}, \Delta^\mathbf{p}_{\mathsf{e}+1})$ and sets $(\mathbf{s}_\mathsf{e}+\Delta^\mathbf{s}_{\mathsf{e}+1}, \mathbf{p}_\mathsf{e}+\Delta^\mathbf{p}_{\mathsf{e}+1})$ as the new epoch key, where $(\Delta^\mathbf{s}_{\mathsf{e}+1}, \mathbf{p}_\mathsf{e}+\Delta^\mathbf{p}_{\mathsf{e}+1})$ is the update token. To update ciphertexts, LWEUE uses the re-randomization idea that was similar to the idea from RISE in the work by Lehmann and Tackmann [15]. As the ciphertext can be re-randomized by the update token, the update algorithm uses the update token to update ciphertext from an old one to a new one. More precisely, the scheme LWEUE is described in Fig. 16.

Parameter Setting We use the parameter setting of the scheme LWEPKE, described in Sect. 4.1. Additionally, we require $\beta \leq \frac{q}{8\sqrt{l}}$, where $l = \mathsf{poly}(n)$ is an upper bound on the last epoch.

5.2 Construction Challenges in LWE-based UE Schemes

In this section, we discuss leakage from tokens due to bad UE construction and show how to solve this leakage problems.

Secret Key Distribution. We first state that a binary secret does not work in the UE scheme, as an update token might reveal the secret information. Suppose an entry of the update token $\Delta^\mathbf{s}_{\mathsf{e}+1} (= \mathbf{s}_{\mathsf{e}+1} - \mathbf{s}_\mathsf{e})$ is -1 (1, resp.), then we can conclude the corresponding entry of the previous secret $\mathbf{s}_\mathsf{e}$ is 1 (0, resp.) and the corresponding entry of the new secret $\mathbf{s}_{\mathsf{e}+1}$ is 0 (1, resp.).

We choose that secret keys and update tokens are sampled from the uniform distribution over $\mathbb{Z}_q^n$, which ensures that any corrupted token will not reveal any information about the relevant secret keys.

$\underline{\mathsf{Setup}(1^\lambda):}$
$\quad \mathbf{A} \leftarrow \mathsf{LWEPKE.Setup}(1^\lambda)$

$\underline{\mathsf{LWEUE.KG}(1^\lambda):}$
$\quad$ **if** $\mathsf{e} = 0$ **then**
$\qquad (\mathbf{s}_0, \mathbf{p}_0) \leftarrow \mathsf{LWEPKE.KG}(1^\lambda)$
$\quad$ **else**
$\qquad$ parse $\mathbf{k}_{\mathsf{e}-1} = (\mathbf{s}_{\mathsf{e}-1}, \mathbf{p}_{\mathsf{e}-1})$
$\qquad (\Delta_{\mathsf{e}}^{\mathbf{s}}, \Delta_{\mathsf{e}}^{\mathbf{p}}) \leftarrow \mathsf{LWEPKE.KG}(1^\lambda)$
$\qquad \mathbf{s}_{\mathsf{e}} \leftarrow \mathbf{s}_{\mathsf{e}-1} + \Delta_{\mathsf{e}}^{\mathbf{s}}$
$\qquad \mathbf{p}_{\mathsf{e}} \leftarrow \mathbf{p}_{\mathsf{e}-1} + \Delta_{\mathsf{e}}^{\mathbf{p}}$
$\qquad \mathbf{k}_{\mathsf{e}} \leftarrow (\mathbf{s}_{\mathsf{e}}, \mathbf{p}_{\mathsf{e}})$
$\quad$ **return** $\mathbf{k}_{\mathsf{e}}$

$\underline{\mathsf{LWEUE.TG}(\mathbf{k}_{\mathsf{e}}, \mathbf{k}_{\mathsf{e}+1}):}$
$\quad$ parse $\mathbf{k}_{\mathsf{e}} = (\mathbf{s}_{\mathsf{e}}, \mathbf{p}_{\mathsf{e}})$
$\quad$ parse $\mathbf{k}_{\mathsf{e}+1} = (\mathbf{s}_{\mathsf{e}+1}, \mathbf{p}_{\mathsf{e}+1})$
$\quad \Delta_{\mathsf{e}+1}^{\mathbf{s}} \leftarrow \mathbf{s}_{\mathsf{e}+1} - \mathbf{s}_{\mathsf{e}}$
$\quad \Delta_{\mathsf{e}+1} \leftarrow (\Delta_{\mathsf{e}+1}^{\mathbf{s}}, \mathbf{p}_{\mathsf{e}+1})$
$\quad$ **return** $\Delta_{\mathsf{e}+1}$

$\underline{\mathsf{LWEUE.Enc}(\mathbf{k}_{\mathsf{e}}, \mathbf{m}):}$
$\quad$ parse $\mathbf{k}_{\mathsf{e}} = (\mathbf{s}_{\mathsf{e}}, \mathbf{p}_{\mathsf{e}})$
$\quad \mathbf{c}_{\mathsf{e}} \leftarrow \mathsf{LWEPKE.Enc}(\mathbf{p}_{\mathsf{e}}, \mathbf{m})$
$\quad$ **return** $\mathbf{c}_{\mathsf{e}}$

$\underline{\mathsf{LWEUE.Dec}(\mathbf{k}_{\mathsf{e}}, \mathbf{c}_{\mathsf{e}}):}$
$\quad$ parse $\mathbf{k}_{\mathsf{e}} = (\mathbf{s}_{\mathsf{e}}, \mathbf{p}_{\mathsf{e}})$
$\quad \mathbf{m}' \leftarrow \mathsf{LWEPKE.Dec}(\mathbf{s}_{\mathsf{e}}, \mathbf{c}_{\mathsf{e}})$
$\quad$ **return** $\mathbf{m}'$

$\underline{\mathsf{LWEUE.Upd}(\Delta_{\mathsf{e}+1}, \mathbf{c}_{\mathsf{e}}):}$
$\quad$ parse $\Delta_{\mathsf{e}+1} = (\Delta_{\mathsf{e}+1}^{\mathbf{s}}, \mathbf{p}_{\mathsf{e}+1})$
$\quad$ parse $\mathbf{c}_{\mathsf{e}} = (\mathbf{C}_{\mathsf{e}}^1, \mathbf{c}_{\mathsf{e}}^2)$
$\quad (\mathbf{C}^1, \mathbf{c}^2) \xleftarrow{\$} \mathsf{LWEPKE.Enc}(\mathbf{p}_{\mathsf{e}+1}, \mathbf{0})$
$\quad \mathbf{C}_{\mathsf{e}+1}^1 \leftarrow \mathbf{C}_{\mathsf{e}}^1 + \mathbf{C}^1$
$\quad \mathbf{c}_{\mathsf{e}+1}^2 \leftarrow \mathbf{c}_{\mathsf{e}}^2 + (\Delta_{\mathsf{e}+1}^{\mathbf{s}})^\intercal \cdot \mathbf{C}_{\mathsf{e}}^1 + \mathbf{c}^2$
$\quad \mathbf{c}_{\mathsf{e}+1} \leftarrow (\mathbf{C}_{\mathsf{e}+1}^1, \mathbf{c}_{\mathsf{e}+1}^2)$
$\quad$ **return** $\mathbf{c}_{\mathsf{e}+1}$

Fig. 16. The algorithms of LWE-based updatable encryption scheme LWEUE, which is parameterized by an LWE-based PKE scheme LWEPKE.

Epoch Key Generation. Intuitively, it is natural to consider generating the epoch keys by sampling a secret $\mathbf{s}_i \leftarrow \mathcal{U}(\mathbb{Z}_q^n)$ and setting the public key to be $\mathbf{p}_i = \mathbf{A} \cdot \mathbf{s}_i + \mathbf{e}_i$, where $\mathbf{e}_i \leftarrow D_{\mathbb{Z},\alpha}^m$. Then the update token is set as $\Delta_i = (\mathbf{s}_i - \mathbf{s}_{i-1}, \mathbf{p}_i)$.

In a confidentiality game for such UE schemes, suppose the adversary knows two consecutive tokens Δ_{i-1} and Δ_i. Using these tokens the adversary can compute $\mathbf{p}_i - \mathbf{p}_{i-1} - \mathbf{A} \cdot \Delta_i^{\mathbf{s}} = \mathbf{e}_i - \mathbf{e}_{i-1}$, and knows $\mathbf{e}_i - \mathbf{e}_{i-1}$. Which means if the adversary knows a set of consecutive tokens $\Delta_i, \Delta_{i+1}, ..., \Delta_{i+j}$ then it will also know $\{\mathbf{e}_{i+1} - \mathbf{e}_i, \mathbf{e}_{i+2} - \mathbf{e}_i, ..., \mathbf{e}_{i+j} - \mathbf{e}_i\}$, the values in this set are sampled from a discrete Gaussian distribution centered at $\mathbf{e}_i$. Through evaluating these errors the adversary can possibly find the error value $\mathbf{e}_i$ and therefore knows the secret value $\mathbf{s}_i$. Furthermore, the adversary is allowed to ask for a challenge-equal ciphertext in epoch i, which will not trigger the trivial win condition, and can therefore break this confidentiality game. The above attack shows that this epoch key generation approach is not safe, it might leak the secret epoch key information.

We choose to generate a fresh pair $(\Delta_{\mathsf{e}+1}^{\mathbf{s}}, \Delta_{\mathsf{e}+1}^{\mathbf{p}})$ to compute the new epoch key and the update token, which makes sure the update token $\Delta_{\mathsf{e}+1} = (\Delta_{\mathsf{e}+1}^{\mathbf{s}}, \mathbf{p}_{\mathsf{e}+1})$ is independent from the previous epoch key. Additionally, this pair is computationally indistinguishable from a uniformly random pair as long as the underlying LWE problem is hard.

5.3 Correctness

Errors in updated ciphertexts increase when they are updated. Since the total number of epochs is bounded with a comparatively small integer l, the UE scheme supports a limited number of ciphertext updates. As a result, errors in updated ciphertexts will not grow too big and the decryption will be correct with overwhelming probability for some parameter setting. The correctness analysis is discussed in the full version [13].

5.4 Challenges of the Security Proof in LWE-based UE Schemes

In this section we highlight the difficulties when proving that LWEUE is a secure UE scheme, specifically, our UE scheme has a randomized update algorithm. Lehmann and Tackmann [15] and Klooß et al. [14] both described a method, similar to each other, to prove that updatable encryption schemes with randomized update algorithms are secure. Their technique can be seen when they prove that RISE and NYUE (NYUAE) are secure, resp. However, this method can not be directly used to prove that LWEUE is secure. The method introduced requires that UE schemes have perfect re-encryption, which means the distribution of updated ciphertexts has the same distribution as fresh encryptions. In their proof, they replace updated ciphertexts by fresh encryptions of the underlying messages. However, in the LWEUE scheme, we cannot simply replace updated ciphertexts by a fresh encryption because the randomness terms and the error terms grow while updating and an updated ciphertext does not have the same distribution as a fresh encryption.

5.5 Security

If LWEPKE is IND\$-CPA-secure then the output of the encryption algorithm is computationally indistinguishable from a pair of uniformly random elements. Hence, the fresh encryption in the LWEUE scheme is computationally indistinguishable from a pair of uniformly random elements as well. Furthermore, the update algorithm LWEUE.Upd runs the encryption algorithm of LWEPKE to re-randomize the old ciphertext to a new ciphertext, therefore, the updated ciphertext is also computationally indistinguishable from a pair of uniformly random elements. So, a fresh encryption is computationally indistinguishable from an updated ciphertext and LWEUE is randIND-UE-CPA secure (see Definition 1). This provides the underlying intuition for the security proof.

The full proof of Theorem 4 is given in the full version [13].

Theorem 4 (LWEUE is randIND-UE-CPA). *Let* LWEUE *be the updatable encryption scheme described in Fig. 16, using parameter setting described in Sect. 5.1. For any* randIND-UE-CPA *adversary* $\mathcal{A}$ *against* LWEUE, *there exists an adversary* $\mathcal{B}_4$ *against* $\mathsf{DLWE}_{n,q,\alpha}$ *such that*

$$\mathbf{Adv}^{\mathsf{randIND\text{-}UE\text{-}CPA}}_{\mathsf{LWEUE},\ \mathcal{A}}(1^\lambda) \leq 2(l+1)^3 \cdot \left(t\epsilon + 3\mathbf{Adv}^{\mathsf{DLWE}}_{n,q,\alpha}(\mathcal{B}_4) + \mathsf{negl}(n)\right).$$

Remark 11. Klooß et al. [14] introduced a generic construction of transforming CPA-secure UE schemes to UE schemes with PTXT and RCCA security. The main idea is to use the extended Naor-Yung (NY) CCA-transform [17] (for public-key schemes). The NY approach is to encrypt a message under two (public) keys of a CPA-secure encryption scheme. The extended NY approach additionally includes a proof that shows the owner knows a valid signature that contains the NY ciphertext pair and the underlying message. A potential future work would be to incorporate LWEUE to their construction to create a UE scheme that achieves PTXT and RCCA security.

Acknowledgements. We would like to thank Gareth T. Davies, Herman Galteland and Kristian Gjøsteen for fruitful discussions, and the anonymous reviewers for a number of valuable suggestions.

References

1. Alkim, E., et al.: FrodoKEM: learning with errors key encapsulation. https://frodokem.org/files/FrodoKEM-specification-20190330.pdf. Submission to the NIST Post-Quantum Standardization project, round 2
2. Alkim, E., Ducas, L., Pöppelmann, T., Schwabe, P.: Post-quantum Key exchange - a new hope. In: USENIX Security Symposium, pp. 327–343. USENIX Association (2016)
3. Avanzi, R., et al.: CRYSTALS-Kyber (version 2.0). https://pq-crystals.org/kyber/data/kyber-specification-round2.pdf. Submission to the NIST Post-Quantum Standardization project, round 2
4. Bernstein, D.J., Chuengsatiansup, C., Lange, T., van Vredendaal, C.: NTRU prime: reducing attack surface at low cost. In: Adams, C., Camenisch, J. (eds.) SAC 2017. LNCS, vol. 10719, pp. 235–260. Springer, Cham (2018). https://doi.org/10.1007/978-3-319-72565-9_12
5. Boneh, D., Eskandarian, S., Kim, S., Shih, M.: Improving speed and security in updatable encryption schemes. IACR Cryptol. ePrint Arch. **2020**, 222 (2020). https://eprint.iacr.org/2020/222
6. Boneh, D., Lewi, K., Montgomery, H., Raghunathan, A.: Key homomorphic PRFs and their applications. In: Canetti, R., Garay, J.A. (eds.) CRYPTO 2013. LNCS, vol. 8042, pp. 410–428. Springer, Heidelberg (2013). https://doi.org/10.1007/978-3-642-40041-4_23
7. Boneh, D., Lewi, K., Montgomery, H.W., Raghunathan, A.: Key homomorphic PRFs and their applications. IACR Cryptol. ePrint Arch. **2015**, 220 (2015). http://eprint.iacr.org/2015/220
8. Boyd, C., Davies, G.T., Gjøsteen, K., Jiang, Y.: Fast and secure updatable encryption. In: Micciancio, D., Ristenpart, T. (eds.) CRYPTO 2020. LNCS, vol. 12170, pp. 464–493. Springer, Cham (2020). https://doi.org/10.1007/978-3-030-56784-2_16
9. Chen, C., et al.: NTRU. https://ntru.org/f/ntru-20190330.pdf. Submission to the NIST Post-Quantum Standardization project, round 2
10. D'Anvers, J.-P., Karmakar, A., Sinha Roy, S., Vercauteren, F.: Saber: module-LWR based key exchange, CPA-secure encryption and CCA-secure KEM. In: Joux, A., Nitaj, A., Rachidi, T. (eds.) AFRICACRYPT 2018. LNCS, vol. 10831, pp. 282–305. Springer, Cham (2018). https://doi.org/10.1007/978-3-319-89339-6_16

11. Everspaugh, A., Paterson, K., Ristenpart, T., Scott, S.: Key rotation for authenticated encryption. In: Katz, J., Shacham, H. (eds.) CRYPTO 2017. LNCS, vol. 10403, pp. 98–129. Springer, Cham (2017). https://doi.org/10.1007/978-3-319-63697-9_4
12. Hamburg, M.: Three Bears. https://sourceforge.net/projects/threebears/. Submission to the NIST Post-Quantum Standardization project, round 2
13. Jiang, Y.: The direction of updatable encryption does not matter much. Cryptology ePrint Archive, Report 2020/622 (2020). https://eprint.iacr.org/2020/622
14. Klooß, M., Lehmann, A., Rupp, A.: (R)CCA secure updatable encryption with integrity protection. In: Ishai, Y., Rijmen, V. (eds.) EUROCRYPT 2019. LNCS, vol. 11476, pp. 68–99. Springer, Cham (2019). https://doi.org/10.1007/978-3-030-17653-2_3
15. Lehmann, A., Tackmann, B.: Updatable encryption with post-compromise security. In: Nielsen, J.B., Rijmen, V. (eds.) EUROCRYPT 2018. LNCS, vol. 10822, pp. 685–716. Springer, Cham (2018). https://doi.org/10.1007/978-3-319-78372-7_22
16. Lu, X., et al.: LAC Lattice-based Cryptosystems. Submission to the NIST Post-Quantum Standardization project, round 2 (2018)
17. Naor, M., Yung, M.: Public-key cryptosystems provably secure against chosen ciphertext attacks. In: Ortiz, H. (ed.) Proceedings of the 22nd Annual ACM Symposium on Theory of Computing, 13–17 May 1990, Baltimore, Maryland, USA, pp. 427–437. ACM (1990). https://doi.org/10.1145/100216.100273
18. Oscar, G.M., et al.: Round5. https://round5.org. Submission to the NIST Post-Quantum Standardization project, round 2

Improving Speed and Security in Updatable Encryption Schemes

Dan Boneh[1], Saba Eskandarian[1(✉)], Sam Kim[1,2], and Maurice Shih[3]

[1] Stanford University, Stanford, CA, USA
saba@cs.stanford.edu
[2] Simons Institute for the Theory of Computing, Berkeley, CA, USA
[3] Cisco Systems, San Jose, CA, USA

Abstract. Periodic key rotation is a common practice designed to limit the long-term power of cryptographic keys. Key rotation refers to the process of re-encrypting encrypted content under a fresh key, and overwriting the old ciphertext with the new one. When encrypted data is stored in the cloud, key rotation can be very costly: it may require downloading the entire encrypted content from the cloud, re-encrypting it on the client's machine, and uploading the new ciphertext back to the cloud.

An *updatable encryption scheme* is a symmetric-key encryption scheme designed to support efficient key rotation in the cloud. The data owner sends a short *update token* to the cloud. This update token lets the cloud rotate the ciphertext from the old key to the new key, without learning any information about the plaintext. Recent work on updatable encryption has led to several security definitions and proposed constructions. However, existing constructions are not yet efficient enough for practical adoption, and the existing security definitions can be strengthened.

In this work we make three contributions. First, we introduce stronger security definitions for updatable encryption (in the *ciphertext-dependent* setting) that capture desirable security properties not covered in prior work. Second, we construct two new updatable encryption schemes. The first construction relies only on symmetric cryptographic primitives, but only supports a bounded number of key rotations. The second construction supports a (nearly) unbounded number of updates, and is built from the Ring Learning with Errors (RLWE) assumption. Due to complexities of using RLWE, this scheme achieves a slightly weaker notion of integrity compared to the first. Finally, we implement both constructions and compare their performance to prior work. Our RLWE-based construction is 200× faster than a prior proposal for an updatable encryption scheme based on the hardness of elliptic curve DDH. Our first construction, based entirely on symmetric primitives, has the highest encryption throughput, approaching the performance of AES, and the highest decryption throughput on ciphertexts that were re-encrypted fewer than fifty times. For ciphertexts re-encrypted over fifty times, the RLWE construction dominates it in decryption speed.

The full version of this paper is available at https://eprint.iacr.org/2020/222.pdf.

S. Moriai and H. Wang (Eds.): ASIACRYPT 2020, LNCS 12493, pp. 559–589, 2020.
https://doi.org/10.1007/978-3-030-64840-4_19

1 Introduction

Consider a ciphertext ct that is a symmetric encryption of some data using key k. Key rotation is the process of decrypting ct using k, and re-encrypting the result using a fresh key k′ to obtain a new ciphertext ct′. One then stores ct′ and discards ct. Periodic key rotation is recommended, and even required, in several security standards and documents, including NIST publication 800-57 [7], the Payment Card Industry Data Security Standard (PCI DSS) [25], and Google's cloud security recommendations [17].

Key rotation can be expensive when the ciphertext is stored in the cloud, and the cloud does not have access to the keys. Key rotation requires the client to retrieve all the encrypted data from the cloud, re-encrypt it by decrypting with the old key and re-encrypting with the new key, and then upload the resulting ciphertext back to the cloud. The traffic to and from the cloud can incur significant networking costs when large amounts of data are involved. Alternatively, the client can send the old and the new key to the cloud, and have the cloud re-encrypt in place, but this gives the cloud full access to the data in the clear. We note that either way, the cloud must be trusted to discard the old ciphertext.

Updatable encryption [11,12,15,20,21] is a much better approach to key rotation for encrypted data stored in the cloud. Updatable encryption is a symmetric encryption scheme that supports the standard key-generation, encryption, and decryption algorithms, along with two additional algorithms called ReKeyGen and ReEncrypt used for key rotation. The re-key generation algorithm is invoked as $\mathsf{ReKeyGen}(\mathsf{k}, \mathsf{k}') \rightarrow \Delta$, taking as input a pair of keys, k and k′, and outputting a short "update token" Δ, also called a re-encryption key. The re-encryption algorithm is invoked as $\mathsf{ReEncrypt}(\Delta, \mathsf{ct}) \rightarrow \mathsf{ct}'$, taking as input a short Δ and a ciphertext ct encrypted under k, and outputting an updated ciphertext ct′ that is the encryption of the same data as in ct, but encrypted under k′.

If the client's data is encrypted using an updatable encryption scheme, then the client can use the re-key generation algorithm ReKeyGen to generate a short update token Δ to send the cloud. The cloud then runs the re-encryption algorithm ReEncrypt to update all the client's ciphertexts. As before, the cloud must be trusted to discard the old ciphertexts.

Defining Security. Intuitively, the update token Δ must not reveal any "useful" information to the cloud. This was formalized by Boneh et al. [11] against passive adversaries, and was improved and extended to provide security against active adversaries by Everspaugh et al. [15].

However, we show in Sect. 3 that these existing elegant definitions can be insufficient, and may not prevent some undesirable information leakage. In particular, we give a simple construction that satisfies the existing definitions, and yet an observer can easily learn the age of a ciphertext, namely the number of times that the ciphertext was re-encrypted since it was initially created. Ideally, this information should not leak to an observer who only sees the ciphertext. This issue was recently independently pointed out in [12].

The age of a ciphertext (i.e., the number of times that the ciphertext was re-encrypted) can leak sensitive private information about the plaintext in many real-world situations. We give two illustrative examples assuming an annual key rotation policy is in use:

- Consider a national database managed in the cloud where information about each individual is stored in a single fixed-size encrypted record. Suppose a newborn is recorded in the database at birth. If an annual key rotation policy is used, and records are encrypted using a scheme that leaks the number of key rotations, then an adversary (or a cloud administrator), who examines the stored ciphertexts will learn every person's age, even though age is regarded as personal identifiable information (PII) and must be protected.
- Consider a dating app, like Tinder or Match.com, that maintains customer information in an encrypted cloud storage. The number of key-updates on a person's file can indicate how long the person has been a customer, which is sensitive information that should be protected.

To address this definitional shortcoming, we define a stronger confidentiality property that requires that a re-encrypted ciphertext is always computationally indistinguishable from a freshly generated ciphertext, no matter how many times it was re-encrypted (Sects. 3.2 and 3.3). This ensures that an observer who sees the encrypted content at a particular point in time, cannot tell the ciphertext age. We also strengthen the integrity definition of [15] to cover additional tampering attacks, as discussed in Sect. 3.4.

Constructing Updatable Encryption. Next, we look for efficient constructions that satisfy our definitions. We give two new constructions: one based on nested authenticated encryption and another based on the Ring Learning With Errors (RLWE) problem [23,26].

Our first construction, presented in Sect. 4, makes use of carefully designed nested encryption, and can be built from any authenticated encryption cipher. It satisfies our strong confidentiality and integrity requirements, so that an adversary cannot learn the age of a ciphertext. However, the scheme only supports a bounded number of re-encryptions, where the bound is set when the initial ciphertext is created. Another limitation of this scheme is that decryption time grows linearly with the age of the ciphertext. Hence, the scheme is practical as long as the maximum number of re-encryptions is not too large. Our implementation and experiments, discussed below, make this precise.

Our second construction, presented in Sect. 5, makes use of an almost key-homomorphic PRF (KH-PRF) built from the RLWE problem. Recall that a key-homomorphic PRF (KH-PRF) [11,24] is a secure PRF $F : \mathcal{K} \times \mathcal{X} \to \mathcal{Y}$, where $(\mathcal{K}, +)$ and $(\mathcal{Y}, +)$ are finite groups, and the PRF is homomorphic with respect to its key, namely $F(k_1, x)+F(k_2, x) = F(k_1+k_2, x)$ for all $k_1, k_2 \in \mathcal{K}$ and $x \in \mathcal{X}$. We say that the PRF is an *almost* KH-PRF if the equality above holds up to a small additive error (see Definition 2.1). To see why a KH-PRF is useful for updatable encryption, consider a single message block $m_i \in \mathcal{Y}$ that is encrypted using counter mode as $\mathsf{ct}_i \leftarrow \mathsf{m}_i + F(\mathsf{k}, i)$, for some $i \in \mathcal{X}$ and $\mathsf{k} \in \mathcal{K}$. To rotate the key, the client chooses a new key $\mathsf{k}' \leftarrow \mathcal{K}$ and sends $\Delta = \mathsf{k}' - \mathsf{k} \in \mathcal{K}$ to the cloud. The cloud computes $\mathsf{ct}_i' = \mathsf{ct}_i + F(\Delta, i)$, which by the key-homomorphic property satisfies $\mathsf{ct}_i' = \mathsf{m}_i + F(\mathsf{k}', i)$, as required.

It remains an open challenge to construct a secure KH-PRF whose performance is comparable to AES. However, there are several known algebraic constructions. In the random oracle model [8,16], there is a simple KH-PRF based on the Decision Diffie-Hellman (DDH) assumption [24], and a simple almost KH-PRF based on the Learning With Rounding (LWR) problem [11]. There are also several KH-PRFs whose security does not depend on random oracles, as discussed in the related work section.

Everspaugh et al. [15] construct an updatable encryption scheme that supports unbounded key updates by combining a key-homomorphic PRF with authenticated encryption and a collision-resistant hash function. They evaluate their construction using the KH-PRF derived from DDH, in the random oracle model, instantiated in the 256-bit elliptic curve Curve25519 [9]. We show that the Everspaugh et al. [15] construction satisfies our new confidentiality security definitions for updatable encryption. However, compared to our first nested encryption construction that relies only on generic authenticated encryption, the implementation of the Everspaugh et al. construction is much slower as it uses expensive group operations.

In our second updatable encryption scheme, we significantly improve on the performance of the Everspaugh et al. [15] construction by extending it to work with an *almost* key-homomorphic PRF. Our construction supports nearly unbounded key-updates, and outperforms the Everspaugh et al. construction by 200× in speed. The high performance of the scheme is, in part, due to a new almost KH-PRF construction from the RLWE assumption. Almost KH-PRFs can already be constructed from the (Ring-) Learning with Rounding (RLWR) assumption [6,11]. However, we observe that for the specific setting of updatable encryption, the parameters of the PRF can be further optimized by modifying the existing PRF constructions to base security directly on the standard RLWE assumption. We provide the details of our construction in Sect. 6.

The use of an *almost* key-homomorphic PRF leads to some complications. First, there is a small ciphertext expansion to handle the noise that arises from the imperfection of the KH-PRF key-homomorphism. More importantly, due to the noisy nature of the ciphertext, we show that an adversary may gain information about the age of the corresponding plaintext using a chosen ciphertext attack, which violates our new security definition. Therefore, while this construction is attractive due to its performance, it can only be used in settings where revealing the age of a ciphertext is acceptable. In Sect. 5.3 we capture this security property using a relaxed notion of ciphertext integrity, and show that the scheme is secure in this model.

Implementation and Experiments. In Sect. 7, we experiment with our two updatable encryption schemes and measure their performance. For our first construction based on authenticated encryption, we measure the trade-off between its efficiency and the number of key rotations it can support. Based on our evaluation, our first construction performs better than the other schemes in both speed and ciphertext size, as long as any given ciphertext is to be re-encrypted at most twenty times over the course of its lifetime. It outperforms the other schemes in speed (but not in ciphertext size) as long as ciphertexts are re-encrypted at most fifty times.

For our second construction, which uses an almost key-homomorphic PRF based on RLWE, we compare its performance with that of Everspaugh et al. [15], which uses a key-homomorphic PRF over Curve25519. Since we use an almost key-homomorphic PRF that is inherently noisy, any message to be encrypted must be padded on the right to counteract the noise. Therefore, compared to the elliptic-curve based construction of Everspaugh et al., our construction produces larger ciphertexts (32% larger than those of Everspaugh et al.). However, in terms of speed, our implementation shows that our construction outperforms that of Everspaugh et al. by over 200×. We provide a more detailed analysis in Sect. 7. Implementations of both our constructions are open source and available at [1].

Summary of Our Contributions. Our contributions are threefold. First, we strengthen the definition of updatable encryption to provide stronger confidentiality and integrity guarantees. Second, we propose two new constructions. Finally, we experiment with both constructions and report on their real world performance and ciphertext expansion. Encryption throughput of our first construction, while allowing only a bounded number of key rotations, is close to the performance of AES. Our second construction, based on a key-homomorphic PRF from RLWE, is considerably faster than the previous construction of Everspaugh et al. [15], which is based on elliptic curves.

1.1 Related Work

Two Flavors of Updatable Encryption. There are two flavors of updatable encryption: *ciphertext-dependent* schemes [11,15] and *ciphertext-independent* schemes [12,20,21]. In a ciphertext-dependent updatable encryption scheme, the client can re-download a tiny fraction of the ciphertext that is stored by the server before generating the update tokens. In a ciphertext-independent updatable encryption scheme, the client generates its update token without needing to download any components of its ciphertext. In this work, we focus on the ciphertext-dependent setting, where constructions are considerably more efficient. We provide a detailed comparison of the two settings in the full version [10]. Additional discussion of the two models can be found in [21].

Key-Homomorphic PRFs. The concept of key-homomorphic PRFs was introduced by Naor, Pinkas, and Reingold [24], and was first formalized as a cryptographic primitive by Boneh et al. [11], who construct two KH-PRFs secure without random oracles: one from LWE, and another from multilinear maps. They also observe that any seed homomorphic PRG $G : \mathcal{S} \to \mathcal{S}^2$ gives a key-homomorphic PRF. More constructions for key-homomorphic PRFs from LWE include [5,13,19].

2 Preliminaries

Basic Notation. For an integer $n \geq 1$, we write $[n]$ to denote the set of integers $\{1, \ldots, n\}$. For a distribution $\mathcal{D}$, we write $x \leftarrow \mathcal{D}$ to denote that x is sampled from $\mathcal{D}$; for a finite set S, we write $x \xleftarrow{\text{R}} S$ to denote that x is sampled uniformly from S. We say that a family of distributions $\mathcal{D} = \{\mathcal{D}_\lambda\}_{\lambda \in \mathbb{N}}$ is *B-bounded* if the support of $\mathcal{D}$ is $\{-B, \ldots, B-1, B\}$ with probability 1.

Unless specified otherwise, we use λ to denote the security parameter. We say a function $f(\lambda)$ is negligible in λ, denoted by $\mathsf{negl}(\lambda)$, if $f(\lambda) = o(1/\lambda^c)$ for all $c \in \mathbb{N}$. We say an algorithm is efficient if it runs in probabilistic polynomial time in the length of its input. We use $\mathsf{poly}(\lambda)$ to denote a quantity whose value is bounded by a fixed polynomial in λ.

To analyze the exact security of our constructions in Sects. 4 and 5, we parameterize the security of these notions with respect to *advantage functions* $\varepsilon : \mathbb{N} \to \mathbb{R}$ that bound the probability of an efficient adversary breaking the security of the primitive.

Basic Cryptographic Primitives. We use a number of standard cryptographic tools throughout the paper, including collision-resistant hash functions, PRGs, PRFs, and authenticated encryption, definitions of which we provide in the full version of this work [10].

Key-Homomorphic PRFs. In this work, we use a special family of pseudorandom functions called *key-homomorphic PRFs* (KH-PRFs) that satisfy additional algebraic properties. Specifically, the key space $\mathcal{K}$ and the range $\mathcal{Y}$ of the PRF exhibit certain group structures such that evaluation of the PRF on any fixed input $x \in \mathcal{X}$ is homomorphic with respect to these group structures. We formally define a key-homomorphic PRF in the full version [10].

We also work with a slight relaxation of the notion of key-homomorphic PRFs. Namely, instead of requiring that the PRF outputs are perfectly homomorphic with respect to the PRF keys, we require that they are "almost" homomorphic in that $F(k_1, x) \otimes F(k_2, x) \approx F(k_1 \oplus k_2, x)$. Formally, we define an almost key-homomorphic PRF as follows.

Definition 2.1 (Almost Key-Homomorphic PRFs [11]). *Let $(\mathcal{K}, \oplus)$ be a group and let m and q be positive integers. Then, an efficiently computable deterministic function $F : \mathcal{K} \times \mathcal{X} \to \mathbb{Z}_q^m$ is a γ-almost key-homomorphic PRF if*

- *F is a secure PRF [10].*
- *For every key $k_1, k_2 \in \mathcal{K}$ and every $x \in \mathcal{X}$, there exists a vector $\mathbf{e} \in [0, \gamma]^m$ such that*

$$F(k_1, x) + F(k_2, x) = F(k_1 \oplus k_2, x) + \mathbf{e} \pmod{q}.$$

Authenticated Encryption. For our updatable encryption scheme in Sect. 4, we make use of authenticated encryption schemes that satisfy a stronger confidentiality requirement than the standard security requirement. Namely, we rely on authenticated encryption schemes that satisfy *ciphertext pseudorandomness*, which requires that an encryption of any message is computationally indistinguishable from a random string of suitable length. We provide the formal definitions in the full version [10]. Authenticated encryption schemes that satisfy ciphertext pseudorandomness can be constructed from pseudorandom functions or blockciphers in a standard way. Widely-used modes for authenticated encryption such as AES-GCM also satisfy ciphertext pseudorandomness.

3 New Definitions for Updatable Encryption

In this section, we present new security definitions for updatable encryption in the ciphertext dependent setting. Our definitions build upon and strengthen the confidentiality and integrity definitions for an updatable authenticated encryption scheme from Everspaugh et al. [15]. We start by defining the syntax for an updatable encryption scheme and its compactness and correctness conditions in Sect. 3.1. We then present security definitions for confidentiality and integrity, comparing each to prior definitions as we present them.

3.1 Updatable Encryption Syntax

For ciphertext-dependent updatable encryption schemes, it is useful to denote ciphertexts as consisting of two parts: a short ciphertext header $\hat{\mathsf{ct}}$, which the client can download to generate its update token, and a ciphertext body ct that encrypts the actual plaintext.

Formally, we define the syntax for an updatable encryption scheme as follows. To emphasize the ciphertext integrity properties of our constructions in Sect. 4 and Sect. 5, we refer to an updatable encryption scheme as an *updatable authenticated encryption* scheme in our definitions.

Definition 3.1 (Updatable Authenticated Encryption). *An* updatable authenticated encryption *(UAE) scheme for a message space* $\mathcal{M} = (\mathcal{M}_\lambda)_{\lambda\in\mathbb{N}}$ *is a tuple of efficient algorithms* $\Pi_{\mathsf{UAE}} =$ (KeyGen, Encrypt, ReKeyGen, ReEncrypt, Decrypt) *that have the following syntax:*

- $\mathsf{KeyGen}(1^\lambda) \to \mathsf{k}$*: On input a security parameter* λ*, the key generation algorithm returns a secret key* k.
- $\mathsf{Encrypt}(\mathsf{k}, \mathsf{m}) \to (\hat{\mathsf{ct}}, \mathsf{ct})$*: On input a key* k *and a message* $\mathsf{m} \in \mathcal{M}_\lambda$*, the encryption algorithm returns a ciphertext header* $\hat{\mathsf{ct}}$ *and a ciphertext body* ct.
- $\mathsf{ReKeyGen}(\mathsf{k}_1, \mathsf{k}_2, \hat{\mathsf{ct}}) \to \Delta_{1,2,\hat{\mathsf{ct}}}/\perp$*: On input two keys* $\mathsf{k}_1, \mathsf{k}_2$*, and a ciphertext header* $\hat{\mathsf{ct}}$*, the re-encryption key generation algorithm returns an update token* $\Delta_{1,2,\hat{\mathsf{ct}}}$ *or* $\perp$.
- $\mathsf{ReEncrypt}(\Delta, (\hat{\mathsf{ct}}, \mathsf{ct})) \to (\hat{\mathsf{ct}}', \mathsf{ct}')/\perp$*: On input an update token* Δ*, and a ciphertext* $(\hat{\mathsf{ct}}, \mathsf{ct})$*, the re-encryption algorithm returns a new ciphertext* $(\hat{\mathsf{ct}}', \mathsf{ct}')$ *or* $\perp$.
- $\mathsf{Decrypt}(\mathsf{k}, (\hat{\mathsf{ct}}, \mathsf{ct})) \to \mathsf{m}/\perp$*: On input a key* k*, and a ciphertext* $(\hat{\mathsf{ct}}, \mathsf{ct})$*, the decryption algorithm returns a message* m *or* $\perp$.

A trivial way of achieving an updatable authenticated encryption scheme is to allow a client to re-download the entire ciphertext, re-encrypt it, and send it back to the server. Therefore, for a UAE scheme to be useful and meaningful, we require that communication between the client and server be bounded and independent of the size of the message encrypted in the ciphertext to be updated. This is captured by the compactness property, which requires that any ciphertext header and update token have lengths that depend only on the security parameter.

Definition 3.2 (Compactness). *We say that an updatable authenticated encryption scheme* $\Pi_{\mathsf{UAE}} = (\mathsf{KeyGen}, \mathsf{Encrypt}, \mathsf{ReKeyGen}, \mathsf{ReEncrypt}, \mathsf{Decrypt})$ *for a message space* $\mathcal{M} = (\mathcal{M}_\lambda)_{\lambda \in \mathbb{N}}$ *is* compact *if there exist polynomials* $f_1(\cdot), f_2(\cdot)$ *such that for any* $\lambda \in \mathbb{N}$ *and message* $\mathsf{m} \in \mathcal{M}_\lambda$*, we have (with probability 1)*

$$|\hat{\mathsf{ct}}| \leq f_1(\lambda), \qquad |\Delta_{1,2,\hat{\mathsf{ct}}}| \leq f_2(\lambda),$$

where $\mathsf{k}_1, \mathsf{k}_2 \leftarrow \mathsf{KeyGen}(1^\lambda)$, $(\hat{\mathsf{ct}}, \mathsf{ct}) \leftarrow \mathsf{Encrypt}(\mathsf{k}_1, \mathsf{m})$, *and* $\Delta_{1,2,\hat{\mathsf{ct}}} \leftarrow \mathsf{ReKeyGen}(\mathsf{k}_1, \mathsf{k}_2, \hat{\mathsf{ct}})$. *That is, the lengths of the ciphertext header and update token are independent of the message length.*

The correctness condition for an updatable encryption scheme is defined in a natural way.

Definition 3.3 (Correctness). *We say that an updatable authenticated encryption scheme* $\Pi_{\mathsf{UAE}} = (\mathsf{KeyGen}, \mathsf{Encrypt}, \mathsf{ReKeyGen}, \mathsf{ReEncrypt}, \mathsf{Decrypt})$ *for a message space* $\mathcal{M} = (\mathcal{M}_\lambda)_{\lambda \in \mathbb{N}}$ *is* correct *if for any* $\lambda \in \mathbb{N}$, $N \in \mathbb{N}$ *and* $\mathsf{m} \in \mathcal{M}_\lambda$*, we have*

$$\Pr\left[\mathsf{Decrypt}(\mathsf{k}_N, (\hat{\mathsf{ct}}_N, \mathsf{ct}_N)) = \mathsf{m}\right] = 1,$$

where $\mathsf{k}_1, \ldots, \mathsf{k}_N \leftarrow \mathsf{KeyGen}(1^\lambda)$, $(\hat{\mathsf{ct}}_1, \mathsf{ct}_1) \leftarrow \mathsf{Encrypt}(\mathsf{k}_1, \mathsf{m})$, *and*

$$(\hat{\mathsf{ct}}_{i+1}, \mathsf{ct}_{i+1}) \leftarrow \mathsf{ReEncrypt}\big(\mathsf{ReKeyGen}(\mathsf{k}_i, \mathsf{k}_{i+1}, \hat{\mathsf{ct}}_i), (\hat{\mathsf{ct}}_i, \mathsf{ct}_i)\big),$$

for $i = 1, \ldots, N-1$.

We note that the definition above requires that the correctness of decryption to hold even after *unbounded* number of key updates. In Definition 4.1, we define a relaxation of this definition that requires correctness of decryption for a bounded number of updates.

3.2 Prior Notions of Confidentiality

Standard semantic security for a symmetric encryption scheme requires that an encryption of a message does not reveal any information about the message. In a regular symmetric encryption scheme, there exists only one way to produce a ciphertext: via the encryption algorithm. In an updatable authenticated encryption scheme, there exist two ways of producing a ciphertext: the encryption algorithm Encrypt that generates *fresh* ciphertexts and the re-encryption algorithm ReEncrypt that generates *re-encrypted* ciphertexts. Previous formulations of updatable encryption security capture the security of these algorithms in two separate security experiments. The security of the regular encryption algorithm Encrypt is captured by the notion of *message confidentiality* [11,15] while the security of the re-encryption algorithm ReEncrypt is captured by the notion of *re-encryption indistinguishability* [15].

Both security experiments are divided into three phases, and are parameterized by h, the number of *honest* keys, and d, the number of *dishonest* keys. During the *setup phase* of the security experiment, the challenger generates h keys $\mathsf{k}_1, \ldots, \mathsf{k}_h \leftarrow \mathsf{KeyGen}(1^\lambda)$ that are the game kept private from the adversary, and d keys $\mathsf{k}_{h+1}, \ldots, \mathsf{k}_{h+d}$ that are provided to the adversary. During the *query phase* of the experiment, the adversary is given access to a set of oracles that evaluate the algorithms Encrypt, ReKeyGen, and ReEncrypt, allowing the adversary to obtain ciphertexts under honest keys and rekey them.

The only distinction between the message-confidentiality and re-encryption indistinguishability experiments is in the way we define the final *challenge* oracle. In the message confidentiality experiment, the adversary is given access to a challenge oracle where it can submit a pair of messages $(\mathsf{m}_0, \mathsf{m}_1)$. As in a standard semantic security definition, the challenge oracle provides the adversary with an encryption of either m_0 or m_1 under a specified honest key, and the adversary's goal is to guess which of the messages was encrypted. In the re-encryption indistinguishability experiment, on the other hand, the adversary submits a pair of *ciphertexts* $\big((\hat{\mathsf{ct}}_0, \mathsf{ct}_0), (\hat{\mathsf{ct}}_1, \mathsf{ct}_1)\big)$ of the same length to the challenge oracle and receives a *re-encryption* of one of the ciphertexts. The adversary's goal in the re-encryption indistinguishability experiment is to guess which of the two ciphertexts was *re-encrypted.*

During the query phase of the experiment, the adversary can make queries to all four oracles as long as their evaluations do not allow the adversary to "trivially" learn which messages are encrypted by the challenge oracle. In particular, this means that no oracle will be allowed to rekey a challenge ciphertext from an honest key to a dishonest key. To this end, the challenger in each experiment keeps a table of challenge ciphertexts generated under each honest key and their re-encryptions. Much of the apparent complexity of formalizing the definition arises from enforcing this straightforward check. We provide the full definitions of Everspaugh et al. [15] in the full version [10].

3.3 Improving Confidentiality

One property that is not captured by the combination of message confidentiality and re-encryption indistinguishability is the indistinguishability of fresh ciphertexts from re-encrypted ciphertexts. In particular, an encryption scheme in which fresh ciphertexts have a completely different structure than those of re-encrypted ciphertexts can still separately satisfy message confidentiality for fresh encryptions and re-encryption indistinguishability for re-encryptions. In many situations, an adversary that learns whether a ciphertext is a fresh encryption or a re-encryption can deduce information about the underlying plaintext of a message.

Furthermore, in the re-encryption indistinguishability experiment, an adversary is required to submit two ciphertexts $\mathsf{ct}_0, \mathsf{ct}_1$ that have the *same* size $|\mathsf{ct}_0| = |\mathsf{ct}_1|$. If we consider the re-encryption algorithm ReEncrypt to be another form of fresh encryption, this admissibility condition on the adversary is quite intuitive. However, equal length plaintexts do not necessarily result in equal-length ciphertexts after different numbers of re-encryptions. This means existing definitions permit schemes that have a different structure for every possible number of re-encryptions.

Thus, the existing confidentiality definitions for an authenticated updatable encryption scheme fail to enforce the following properties:

- **Property 1**: Freshly generated ciphertexts are indistinguishable from ciphertexts that are generated via re-encryption.
- **Property 2**: Ciphertexts do not reveal how many times a re-encryption algorithm was performed on a given ciphertext.

We state the two properties separately because ciphertexts in our experiment comparing freshly-generated and re-encrypted ciphertexts must be of the same length to prevent trivial wins, which does not rule out the possibility of ciphertext length leaking information about age.

We now augment the confidentiality security definitions of Everspaugh et al. [15] to enforce these two properties.

Enforcing Property 1. A natural way to enforce that fresh ciphertexts are indistinguishable from re-encrypted ciphertexts is to define a security experiment analogous to the definitions of message confidentiality and re-encryption indistinguishability, but with respect to a challenge oracle that takes in either a message m or a ciphertext $(\hat{\mathsf{ct}}, \mathsf{ct})$ and either *encrypts* m or *re-encrypts* $(\hat{\mathsf{ct}}, \mathsf{ct})$.

We present the full definition of confidentiality below. The various checks included in the description of the oracles only serve to ensure that an adversary cannot take a challenge ciphertext under an honest key and obtain its re-encryption under a dishonest key, as this would result in a trivial win.

Definition 3.4 (Confidentiality). *Let* $\Pi_{\mathsf{UAE}} = (\mathsf{KeyGen}, \mathsf{Encrypt}, \mathsf{ReKeyGen}, \mathsf{ReEncrypt}, \mathsf{Decrypt})$ *be an updatable authenticated encryption scheme for a message space* $\mathcal{M} = (\mathcal{M}_\lambda)_{\lambda \in \mathbb{N}}$. *Then, for a security parameter* λ, *positive integers* $h, d \in \mathbb{N}$, *an adversary* $\mathcal{A}$, *and a binary bit* $b \in \{0,1\}$, *we define the confidentiality experiment* $\mathsf{Expt}^{\mathsf{conf}}_{\Pi_{\mathsf{UAE}}}(\lambda, h, d, \mathcal{A}, b)$ *and oracles* $\mathcal{O} = (\mathcal{O}_{\mathsf{Encrypt}}, \mathcal{O}_{\mathsf{ReKeyGen}}, \mathcal{O}_{\mathsf{ReEncrypt}}, \mathcal{O}_{\mathsf{Challenge}})$ *in Fig. 1. The experiment maintains a look-up table* T, *accessible by all the oracles, that maps* key index *and* ciphertext header *pairs to* ciphertext bodies.

$\underline{\mathsf{Expt}^{\mathsf{conf}}_{\Pi_{\mathsf{UAE}}}(\lambda, h, d, \mathcal{A}, b)}$:

$\mathsf{k}_1, \ldots, \mathsf{k}_{h+d} \leftarrow \mathsf{KeyGen}(1^\lambda)$

$b' \leftarrow \mathcal{A}^{\mathcal{O}}(k_{h+1}, \ldots, k_{h+d})$

Output $b' = b$

$\underline{\mathcal{O}_{\mathsf{Encrypt}}(i, \mathsf{m})}$:

Output $\mathsf{Encrypt}(\mathsf{k}_i, \mathsf{m})$

$\underline{\mathcal{O}_{\mathsf{Challenge}}(i, j, \mathsf{m}, (\hat{\mathsf{ct}}, \mathsf{ct}))}$:

if $j > h$:

  Output $\perp$

$(\hat{\mathsf{ct}}_0', \mathsf{ct}_0') \leftarrow \mathsf{Encrypt}(\mathsf{k}_j, \mathsf{m})$

$\Delta_{i,j,\hat{\mathsf{ct}}} \leftarrow \mathsf{ReKeyGen}(\mathsf{k}_i, \mathsf{k}_j, \hat{\mathsf{ct}})$

$(\hat{\mathsf{ct}}_1', \mathsf{ct}_1') \leftarrow \mathsf{ReEncrypt}(\Delta_{i,j,\hat{\mathsf{ct}}}, (\hat{\mathsf{ct}}, \mathsf{ct}))$

if $(\hat{\mathsf{ct}}_0', \mathsf{ct}_0') = \perp$ or $(\hat{\mathsf{ct}}_1', \mathsf{ct}_1') = \perp$:

  Output $\perp$

if $|\hat{\mathsf{ct}}_0'| \neq |\hat{\mathsf{ct}}_1'|$ or $|\mathsf{ct}_0'| \neq |\mathsf{ct}_1'|$:

  Output $\perp$

$\mathsf{T}[j, \hat{\mathsf{ct}}_b'] \leftarrow \mathsf{ct}_b'$

Output $(\hat{\mathsf{ct}}_b', \mathsf{ct}_b')$

$\underline{\mathcal{O}_{\mathsf{ReKeyGen}}(i, j, \hat{\mathsf{ct}})}$:

if $j > h$ and $T[i, \hat{\mathsf{ct}}] \neq \perp$:

  Output $\perp$

$\Delta_{i,j,\hat{\mathsf{ct}}} \leftarrow \mathsf{ReKeyGen}(\mathsf{k}_i, \mathsf{k}_j, \hat{\mathsf{ct}})$

if $T[i, \hat{\mathsf{ct}}] \neq \perp$:

  $(\hat{\mathsf{ct}}', \mathsf{ct}') \leftarrow \mathsf{ReEncrypt}(\Delta_{i,j,\hat{\mathsf{ct}}}, (\hat{\mathsf{ct}}, \mathsf{T}[i, \hat{\mathsf{ct}}]))$

  $\mathsf{T}[j, \hat{\mathsf{ct}}'] \leftarrow \mathsf{ct}'$

Output $\Delta_{i,j,\hat{\mathsf{ct}}}$

$\underline{\mathcal{O}_{\mathsf{ReEncrypt}}(i, j, (\hat{\mathsf{ct}}, \mathsf{ct}))}$:

$\Delta_{i,j,\hat{\mathsf{ct}}} \leftarrow \mathsf{ReKeyGen}(\mathsf{k}_i, \mathsf{k}_j, \hat{\mathsf{ct}})$

$(\hat{\mathsf{ct}}', \mathsf{ct}') \leftarrow \mathsf{ReEncrypt}(\Delta_{i,j,\hat{\mathsf{ct}}}, (\hat{\mathsf{ct}}, \mathsf{ct}))$

if $j > h$ and $\mathsf{T}[i, \hat{\mathsf{ct}}] \neq \perp$:

  Output $\perp$

if $j \leq h$ and $\mathsf{T}[i, \hat{\mathsf{ct}}] \neq \perp$:

  $\mathsf{T}[j, \hat{\mathsf{ct}}'] \leftarrow \mathsf{ct}'$

Output $(\hat{\mathsf{ct}}', \mathsf{ct}')$

Fig. 1. Security experiment for confidentiality (Definition 3.4) and update independence (Definition 3.6)

We say that an updatable authenticated encryption scheme Π_{UAE} *satisfies* confidentiality *if there exists a negligible function* $\mathsf{negl}(\cdot)$ *such that for all* $h, d \leq \mathsf{poly}(\lambda)$ *and efficient adversaries* $\mathcal{A}$*, we have*

$$\left| \Pr\left[\mathsf{Expt}^{\mathsf{conf}}_{\Pi_{\mathsf{UAE}}}(\lambda, h, d, \mathcal{A}, 0) = 1\right] - \Pr\left[\mathsf{Expt}^{\mathsf{conf}}_{\Pi_{\mathsf{UAE}}}(\lambda, h, d, \mathcal{A}, 1) = 1\right] \right| \leq \mathsf{negl}(\lambda).$$

Although our original goal in defining the confidentiality experiment above is to enforce the condition that fresh ciphertexts are indistinguishable from re-encrypted ciphertexts, the experiment captures a much wider class of confidentiality properties for an updatable authenticated encryption scheme. In fact, it is straightforward to show that a UAE scheme that satisfies the single confidentiality definition above automatically satisfies both message confidentiality and re-encryption indistinguishability. Specifically, since the confidentiality definition above implies that an encryption of a message is indistinguishable from a re-encryption of a ciphertext (given that the resulting ciphertexts are of the same length), this implies that for any two messages $\mathsf{m}_0, \mathsf{m}_1$ such that $|\mathsf{m}_0| = |\mathsf{m}_1|$, we have

$$\mathsf{Encrypt}(\mathsf{k}, \mathsf{m}_0) \approx_c (\hat{\mathsf{ct}}', \mathsf{ct}') \approx_c \mathsf{Encrypt}(\mathsf{k}, \mathsf{m}_1),$$

for any key k that is hidden from an adversary and any re-encrypted ciphertext $(\hat{\mathsf{ct}}', \mathsf{ct}')$ of appropriate length. Similarly, the confidentiality definition above implies that for two ciphertexts $(\hat{\mathsf{ct}}_0, \mathsf{ct}_0)$ and $(\hat{\mathsf{ct}}_1, \mathsf{ct}_1)$ of the same length,

$$\begin{aligned}\mathsf{ReEncrypt}(\mathsf{ReKeyGen}(\mathsf{k}, \mathsf{k}', \hat{\mathsf{ct}}_0), (\hat{\mathsf{ct}}_0, \mathsf{ct}_0)) \\ \approx_c (\hat{\mathsf{ct}}', \mathsf{ct}') \approx_c \\ \mathsf{ReEncrypt}(\mathsf{ReKeyGen}(\mathsf{k}, \mathsf{k}', \hat{\mathsf{ct}}_1), (\hat{\mathsf{ct}}_1, \mathsf{ct}_1)),\end{aligned}$$

for an appropriate key k' that is hidden from an adversary and any fresh ciphertext $(\hat{\mathsf{ct}}', \mathsf{ct}')$ of appropriate length.

In combination with our new strong compactness requirement (which we introduce in Definition 3.5), the security experiment in Definition 3.4 captures all the confidentiality properties we expect from an updatable encryption scheme. This is why we refer to the experiment in Definition 3.4 simply as the "confidentiality" experiment.

Enforcing Property 2. Enforcing that an updatable encryption ciphertext hides the number of key updates is less straightforward. Perhaps the most natural and general way to enforce this property is to modify the challenge oracle in Definition 3.4 as follows:

- $\mathcal{O}_{\mathsf{Challenge}}(\mathcal{I}, (\hat{\mathsf{ct}}_{0,0}, \mathsf{ct}_{0,0}), \mathcal{J}, (\hat{\mathsf{ct}}_{1,0}, \mathsf{ct}_{1,0}))$: A query consists of two sequences of indices $\mathcal{I} = (i_1, \ldots, i_\tau)$, $\mathcal{J} = (j_1, \ldots, j_{\tau'})$ for $\tau, \tau' \in \mathbb{N}$ such that $i_\tau = j_{\tau'}$ are honest keys, and $|\mathsf{ct}_{0,0}| = |\mathsf{ct}_{1,0}|$. The challenger computes two sequences of ciphertexts

$$\begin{aligned}&\Delta_{i_{\gamma-1}, i_\gamma} \leftarrow \mathsf{ReKeyGen}(\mathsf{k}_{i_{\gamma-1}}, \mathsf{k}_{i_\gamma}, \hat{\mathsf{ct}}_{0,i_\gamma}) \\ &(\hat{\mathsf{ct}}_{0,i_\gamma}, \mathsf{ct}_{0,i_\gamma}) \leftarrow \mathsf{ReEncrypt}(\Delta_{i_{\gamma-1}, i_\gamma}, \hat{\mathsf{ct}}_{0,i_{\gamma-1}}, \mathsf{ct}_{0,i_{\gamma-1}}) \quad \forall \gamma \in [\tau],\end{aligned}$$

and

$$\begin{aligned}&\Delta'_{j_{\gamma-1}, j_\gamma} \leftarrow \mathsf{ReKeyGen}(\mathsf{k}_{j_{\gamma-1}}, \mathsf{k}_{j_\gamma}, \hat{\mathsf{ct}}_{1,j_\gamma}) \\ &(\hat{\mathsf{ct}}_{1,j_\gamma}, \mathsf{ct}_{1,j_\gamma}) \leftarrow \mathsf{ReEncrypt}(\Delta'_{j_{\gamma-1}, j_\gamma}, \hat{\mathsf{ct}}_{1,j_{\gamma-1}}, \mathsf{ct}_{1,j_{\gamma-1}}) \quad \forall \gamma \in [\tau'].\end{aligned}$$

It returns either $(\hat{\mathsf{ct}}_{0,j_\tau}, \mathsf{ct}_{0,j_\tau})$ or $(\hat{\mathsf{ct}}_{1,j_{\tau'}}, \mathsf{ct}_{1,j_{\tau'}})$.

The challenge oracle above takes in two sequences of indices $\mathcal{I}$, $\mathcal{J}$, and re-encrypts either the ciphertext $(\hat{\mathsf{ct}}_{0,0}, \mathsf{ct}_{0,0})$ according to the sequence of keys specified by $\mathcal{I}$ or the ciphertext $(\hat{\mathsf{ct}}_{1,0}, \mathsf{ct}_{1,0})$ according to $\mathcal{J}$. Since the two sequences $\mathcal{I}$ and $\mathcal{J}$ can have differing lengths, an updatable encryption scheme that satisfies a security experiment with respect to such a challenge oracle must hide the number of times the re-encryption algorithm was applied to a ciphertext.

However, a security experiment that is defined with respect to the challenge oracle above is generally difficult to work with and requires notationally complicated proofs. Hence, instead of using the challenge oracle as defined above, we define a stronger *compactness* requirement on the ciphertexts of an updatable encryption scheme. Specifically, in addition to the compactness requirement as specified in Definition 3.2, we require that the size of a ciphertext always remains fixed no matter how many times the re-encryption algorithm is performed on a ciphertext.

Definition 3.5 (Strong Compactness). *We say that an updatable authenticated encryption scheme* $\Pi_{\mathsf{UAE}} = (\mathsf{KeyGen}, \mathsf{Encrypt}, \mathsf{ReKeyGen}, \mathsf{ReEncrypt}, \mathsf{Decrypt})$ *for a message space* $\mathcal{M} = (\mathcal{M}_\lambda)_{\lambda\in\mathbb{N}}$ *is* strongly compact *if for any* $\lambda \in \mathbb{N}$ *and any message* $\mathsf{m} \in \mathcal{M}_\lambda$, *it satisfies the* header compactness *and* body compactness *(with probability 1) after the following operations.*

- $\mathsf{k}_0, \mathsf{k}_1, \ldots, \mathsf{k}_N \leftarrow \mathsf{KeyGen}(1^\lambda)$
- $(\hat{\mathsf{ct}}_0, \mathsf{ct}_0) \leftarrow \mathsf{Encrypt}(\mathsf{k}_0, \mathsf{m})$
- *for* $i \in [N]$:
- $\Delta_{i,i-1,\hat{\mathsf{ct}}_{i-1}} \leftarrow \mathsf{ReKeyGen}(\mathsf{k}_{i-1}, \mathsf{k}_i, \hat{\mathsf{ct}}_{i-1})$
- $(\hat{\mathsf{ct}}_i, \mathsf{ct}_i) \leftarrow \mathsf{ReEncrypt}(\Delta_{i,i-1,\hat{\mathsf{ct}}_{i-1}}, (\hat{\mathsf{ct}}_{i-1}, \mathsf{ct}_{i-1}))$

- Header compactness*: There exist polynomials* $f_1(\cdot)$, $f_2(\cdot)$ *such that* $|\hat{\mathsf{ct}}_i| \le f_1(\lambda)$ *and* $|\Delta_{i,i-1,\hat{\mathsf{ct}}_{i-1}}| \le f_2(\lambda)$ *for all* $i \in [N]$, *i.e., header and update token lengths do not depend on the message length or the number of re-encryptions.*
- Body compactness*: We have* $|\mathsf{ct}_i| = |\mathsf{ct}_j|$ *for all* $0 \le i, j \le N$.

In combination with Definition 3.4, the strong compactness property implies that ciphertexts do not reveal how many times a re-encryption algorithm was performed on a given ciphertext. The confidentiality property of Definition 3.4 implies that the re-encryption of any two ciphertexts of the *same size* must be indistinguishable to an adversary. The strong compactness property requires that no matter how many re-encryption operations are performed on a given ciphertext, its length always *remains* the same size, thereby complementing Definition 3.4.

Update independence. In Construction 4.2, we present a UAE scheme that satisfies the strong compactness property of Definition 3.5 as well as message confidentiality and re-encryption indistinguishability, but does not fully satisfy the stronger notion of confidentiality as defined in Definition 3.4. Therefore, we define a slight relaxation of the confidentiality requirement as formulated in Definition 3.4 that we call *update independence* and show that Construction 4.2 satisfies this security definition. An update independence security experiment is defined identically to the confidentiality security experiment but without the re-encryption key generation oracle $\mathcal{O}_{\mathsf{ReKeyGen}}$. Since this oracle is removed, update independence does not suffice to imply message confidentiality and re-encryption indistinguishability. However, it still suffices to guarantee that fresh ciphertexts are indistinguishable from re-encrypted ciphertexts as long as update tokens are hidden from an adversary.

Definition 3.6 (Update Independence). *Let* $\Pi_{\mathsf{UAE}} = (\mathsf{KeyGen}, \mathsf{Encrypt}, \mathsf{ReKeyGen}, \mathsf{ReEncrypt}, \mathsf{Decrypt})$ *be an updatable authenticated encryption scheme for a message space* $\mathcal{M} = (\mathcal{M}_\lambda)_{\lambda\in\mathbb{N}}$. *Then, for a security parameter* λ, *positive integers* $h, d \in \mathbb{N}$, *an adversary* $\mathcal{A}$, *and a binary bit* $b \in \{0,1\}$, *we* *define the update independence experiment* $\mathsf{Expt}^{\mathsf{upd\text{-}ind}}_{\Pi_{\mathsf{UAE}}}(\lambda, h, d, \mathcal{A}, b)$ *and oracles* $\mathcal{O} = (\mathcal{O}_{\mathsf{Encrypt}}, \mathcal{O}_{\mathsf{ReEncrypt}}, \mathcal{O}_{\mathsf{Challenge}})$ *as in Fig. 1 with the* $\mathcal{O}_{\mathsf{ReKeyGen}}$ *oracle omitted. The experiment maintains a look-up table* T*, accessible by all the oracles, that maps* key index *and* ciphertext header *pairs to* ciphertext bodies.

We say that an updatable authenticated encryption scheme Π_{UAE} *satisfies* update independence *if there exists a negligible function* $\mathsf{negl}(\cdot)$ *such that for all* $h, d \leq \mathsf{poly}(\lambda)$ *and efficient adversaries* $\mathcal{A}$*, we have*

$$\left| \Pr\left[\mathsf{Expt}^{\mathsf{upd\text{-}ind}}_{\Pi_{\mathsf{UAE}}}(\lambda, h, d, \mathcal{A}, 0) = 1\right] - \Pr\left[\mathsf{Expt}^{\mathsf{upd\text{-}ind}}_{\Pi_{\mathsf{UAE}}}(\lambda, h, d, \mathcal{A}, 1) = 1\right] \right| \leq \mathsf{negl}(\lambda).$$

In combination with the message confidentiality and re-encryption indistinguishability properties, this relaxed requirement of update independence suffices for many practical scenarios. Since update tokens are generally sent over secure channels (e.g. TLS connection) from a client to a server, no malicious eavesdropper can gain access to them. For malicious servers that have access to update tokens, on the other hand, hiding how many times a re-encryption operation was previously applied on a ciphertext is less useful since the storage metadata of the ciphertexts already reveal this information to the server. In essence, update independence, when combined with message confidentiality and re-encryption indistinguishability, seems to satisfy the two properties we wanted from our new confidentiality definition without the convenient benefit of a single unified definition.

3.4 Integrity

The final security property that an updatable authenticated encryption scheme must provide is *ciphertext integrity*. The ciphertext integrity experiment for UAE is analogous to the standard ciphertext integrity experiment of an authenticated encryption scheme. As in the confidentiality experiment, the challenger starts the experiment by generating a set of honest keys, which are kept private from the adversary, and dishonest keys, which are provided to the adversary. Then, given oracle access to $\mathcal{O}_{\mathsf{Encrypt}}$, $\mathcal{O}_{\mathsf{ReEncrypt}}$, and $\mathcal{O}_{\mathsf{ReKeyGen}}$, the adversary's goal is to generate a new valid ciphertext that was not (1) previously output by $\mathcal{O}_{\mathsf{Encrypt}}$ or $\mathcal{O}_{\mathsf{ReEncrypt}}$, and (2) cannot be trivially derived via update tokens output by $\mathcal{O}_{\mathsf{ReKeyGen}}$.

Our integrity definition is similar to that of Everspaugh et al. [15], except the previous definition does not include the re-encryption oracle $\mathcal{O}_{\mathsf{ReEncrypt}}$, which we add. Giving the adversary access to a re-encryption oracle captures scenarios that are not covered by the previous definition. For instance, security with respect to our stronger integrity experiment guarantees that an adversary who compromises the key for a ciphertext cannot tamper with the data after the key has been rotated and the data re-encrypted.

Definition 3.7 (Integrity). *Let* $\Pi_{\mathsf{UAE}} = (\mathsf{KeyGen}, \mathsf{Encrypt}, \mathsf{ReKeyGen}, \mathsf{ReEncrypt}, \mathsf{Decrypt})$ *be an updatable authenticated encryption scheme for a message space* $\mathcal{M} = (\mathcal{M}_\lambda)_{\lambda \in \mathbb{N}}$*. Then, for a security parameter* λ*, positive integers*

$\mathsf{Expt}^{\mathsf{int}}_{\Pi_{\mathsf{UAE}}}(\lambda, h, d, \mathcal{A})$:

$\mathsf{k}_1, \ldots, \mathsf{k}_{h+d} \leftarrow \mathsf{KeyGen}(1^\lambda)$

$(i, (\hat{\mathsf{ct}}, \mathsf{ct})) \leftarrow \mathcal{A}^{\mathcal{O}}(k_{h+1}, \ldots, k_{h+d})$

if $i > h$:

  Output 0

$\mathsf{m} \leftarrow \mathsf{Decrypt}(\mathsf{k}_i, (\hat{\mathsf{ct}}, \mathsf{ct}))$

if $\mathsf{m} = \perp$ or $\mathsf{T}[i, \hat{\mathsf{ct}}] = \mathsf{ct}$:

  Output 0

else:

  Output 1

$\underline{\mathcal{O}_{\mathsf{Encrypt}}(i, \mathsf{m})}$:

$(\hat{\mathsf{ct}}, \mathsf{ct}) \leftarrow \mathsf{Encrypt}(\mathsf{k}_i, \mathsf{m})$

$\mathsf{T}[i, \hat{\mathsf{ct}}] \leftarrow \mathsf{ct}$

Output $(\hat{\mathsf{ct}}, \mathsf{ct})$

$\underline{\mathcal{O}_{\mathsf{ReEncrypt}}(i, j, (\hat{\mathsf{ct}}, \mathsf{ct}))}$:

$\Delta_{i,j,\hat{\mathsf{ct}}} \leftarrow \mathsf{ReKeyGen}(\mathsf{k}_i, \mathsf{k}_j, \hat{\mathsf{ct}})$

$(\hat{\mathsf{ct}}', \mathsf{ct}') \leftarrow \mathsf{ReEncrypt}(\Delta_{i,j,\hat{\mathsf{ct}}}, (\hat{\mathsf{ct}}, \mathsf{ct}))$

if $j \leq h$:

  $\mathsf{T}[j, \hat{\mathsf{ct}}'] \leftarrow \mathsf{ct}'$

Output $(\hat{\mathsf{ct}}', \mathsf{ct}')$

$\underline{\mathcal{O}_{\mathsf{ReKeyGen}}(i, j, \hat{\mathsf{ct}})}$:

if $i > h$ and $j \leq h$:

  Output $\perp$

$\Delta_{i,j,\hat{\mathsf{ct}}} \leftarrow \mathsf{ReKeyGen}(\mathsf{k}_i, \mathsf{k}_j, \hat{\mathsf{ct}})$

if $\mathsf{T}[i, \hat{\mathsf{ct}}] \neq \perp$:

  $(\hat{\mathsf{ct}}', \mathsf{ct}') \leftarrow \mathsf{ReEncrypt}(\Delta_{i,j,\hat{\mathsf{ct}}}, (\hat{\mathsf{ct}}, \mathsf{T}[i, \hat{\mathsf{ct}}]))$

  $\mathsf{T}[j, \hat{\mathsf{ct}}'] \leftarrow \mathsf{ct}'$

Output $\Delta_{i,j,\hat{\mathsf{ct}}}$

Fig. 2. Security experient for integrity (Definition 3.7)

$h, d \in \mathbb{N}$, and an adversary $\mathcal{A}$, we define the re-encryption integrity experiment $\mathsf{Expt}^{\mathsf{int}}_{\Pi_{\mathsf{UAE}}}(\lambda, h, d, \mathcal{A})$ *and oracles* $\mathcal{O} = (\mathcal{O}_{\mathsf{Encrypt}}, \mathcal{O}_{\mathsf{ReKeyGen}}, \mathcal{O}_{\mathsf{ReEncrypt}})$ *in Fig. 2. The experiment maintains a look-up table* T, *accessible by all the oracles, that maps* key index *and* ciphertext header *pairs to* ciphertext bodies.

We say that an updatable authenticated encryption scheme Π_{UAE} *satisfies* re-encryption integrity *if there exists a negligible function* $\mathsf{negl}(\cdot)$ *such that for all* $h, d \leq \mathsf{poly}(\lambda)$ *and any efficient adversary* $\mathcal{A}$, *we have*

$$\Pr\left[\mathsf{Expt}^{\mathsf{int}}_{\Pi_{\mathsf{UAE}}}(\lambda, h, d, \mathcal{A}) = 1\right] \leq \mathsf{negl}(\lambda).$$

Although our UAE construction in Sect. 4 can be shown to satisfy the strong notion of integrity formulated above, the construction in Sect. 5 that relies on almost key-homomorphic PRFs is not sufficient to satisfy the stronger notion. In Sect. 5, we formulate a relaxation of the notion of integrity that we call *relaxed integrity* and show that Construction 5.2 satisfies this weaker variant.

4 UAE with Bounded Updates

We begin this section by presenting an *insecure* UAE scheme that demonstrates the importance of the new definitions presented in Sect. 3. This scheme leaks the age of ciphertexts but nonetheless satisfies all security definitions for ciphertext-dependent UAE from prior work.

Next, we extend the insecure scheme to hide the age of ciphertexts, thereby satisfying the definition of update independence (Sect. 3.3, Definition 3.6). This upgrade comes at the cost of relaxing the correctness requirement of an updatable encryption scheme: the correctness of decryption is guaranteed only for an a priori bounded number of key updates.

4.1 A Simple Nested Construction

In this section, we provide a simple updatable authenticated encryption scheme using any authenticated encryption scheme. Our simple construction inherently leaks information about the message; namely, the construction leaks how many re-encryption operations were previously performed on a given ciphertext, thereby leaking information about the age of the encrypted message. Despite this information leakage, the construction satisfies all the UAE security definitions of Everspaugh et al. [15]. Hence, this construction demonstrates that prior security definitions did not yet capture all the necessary security properties that an updatable encryption scheme must provide.

The construction uses an authenticated encryption (AE) scheme. A key for this UAE scheme is a standard AE key $\hat{\mathsf{k}}$, which we call the *header key*. The UAE encryption algorithm implements standard chained encryption. To encrypt m using $\hat{\mathsf{k}}$, first generate a fresh *body key* $\mathsf{k_{ae}}$ and then encrypt the plaintext $\mathsf{ct} \leftarrow \mathsf{AE.Encrypt}(\mathsf{k_{ae}}, \mathsf{m})$. Next, the body key $\mathsf{k_{ae}}$ is encrypted under the header key $\hat{\mathsf{ct}} \leftarrow \mathsf{AE.Encrypt}(\hat{\mathsf{k}}, \mathsf{k_{ae}})$ to form the ciphertext header. Finally, output the UAE ciphertext $(\hat{\mathsf{ct}}, \mathsf{ct})$.

To update a ciphertext, the client and server proceed as follows:

- *Client*: The client downloads the ciphertext header $\hat{\mathsf{ct}}$ to recover the body key $\mathsf{k_{ae}}$. It then generates fresh header and body keys $\hat{\mathsf{k}}'$ and $\mathsf{k}'_{\mathsf{ae}}$, and sends a new ciphertext header $\hat{\mathsf{ct}}' \leftarrow \mathsf{AE.Encrypt}(\hat{\mathsf{k}}', (\mathsf{k}'_{\mathsf{ae}}, \mathsf{k_{ae}}))$ along with $\mathsf{k}'_{\mathsf{ae}}$ to the server.
- *Server*: The server replaces the old ciphertext header $\hat{\mathsf{ct}}$ with the new header $\hat{\mathsf{ct}}'$. It also generates a new ciphertext body by encrypting the original ciphertext as $\mathsf{ct}' \leftarrow \mathsf{AE.Encrypt}(\mathsf{k}'_{\mathsf{ae}}, (\hat{\mathsf{ct}}, \mathsf{ct}))$.

Now, even with many such key updates, the client can still recover the original ciphertext. Specifically, the client can first use its current header key $\hat{\mathsf{k}}$ to decrypt the ciphertext header and recover a body key $\mathsf{k_{ae}}$ *and* the old header key $\hat{\mathsf{k}}'$. It uses $\mathsf{k_{ae}}$ to remove the outer layer of encryption and recover the old ciphertext $(\hat{\mathsf{ct}}', \mathsf{ct}')$. The client repeats the same procedure with the old header key $\hat{\mathsf{k}}'$ and the old ciphertext $(\hat{\mathsf{ct}}', \mathsf{ct}')$. Note that decryption time grows linearly in the number of re-encryption operations.

To prove security, we must introduce an additional step during a ciphertext update. Namely, instead of setting the new ciphertext body as the encryption of the old ciphertext header and body $\mathsf{ct}' \leftarrow \mathsf{AE.Encrypt}(\mathsf{k}'_{\mathsf{ae}}, (\hat{\mathsf{ct}}, \mathsf{ct}))$, the server replaces $\hat{\mathsf{ct}}$ with a new ciphertext header $\hat{\mathsf{ct}}_{\mathsf{history}}$ that the client provides to the server encrypted under a new key $\hat{\mathsf{k}}_{\mathsf{history}}$. The main intuition of the construction, however, remains unchanged from the description above. Since the construction is a simpler form of the one formalized in Construction 4.2, we defer the formal statement of the construction and its associated security theorems for compactness, correctness, update independence, message confidentiality, re-encryption indistinguishability, and ciphertext integrity to the full version [10].

4.2 Bounded Correctness

We now define a variation of correctness that we call *bounded correctness.* The bounded correctness condition is defined in a natural way and analogously to Definition 3.3 (correctness). However, we do modify the syntax of the key generation algorithm KeyGen to additionally take in a parameter $t \in \mathbb{N}$ that specifies an upper bound on the number of key updates that a scheme can support. This allows the key generator to flexibly set this parameter according to its needs.

Definition 4.1 (Bounded Correctness). *We say that an updatable authenticated encryption scheme* $\Pi_{\mathsf{UAE}} = (\mathsf{KeyGen}, \mathsf{Encrypt}, \mathsf{ReKeyGen}, \mathsf{ReEncrypt}, \mathsf{Decrypt})$ *for a message space* $\mathcal{M} = (\mathcal{M}_\lambda)_{\lambda \in \mathbb{N}}$ *satisfies* bounded correctness *if for any* $\lambda, t \in \mathbb{N}$*, and* $\mathsf{m} \in \mathcal{M}_\lambda$*, we have (with probability 1)*

$$\Pr\left[\mathsf{Decrypt}(\mathsf{k}_t, (\hat{\mathsf{ct}}_t, \mathsf{ct}_t)) = \mathsf{m}\right] \geq 1 - \mathsf{negl}(\lambda),$$

where $\mathsf{k}_1, \ldots, \mathsf{k}_t \leftarrow \mathsf{KeyGen}(1^\lambda, 1^t)$, $(\hat{\mathsf{ct}}_1, \mathsf{ct}_1) \leftarrow \mathsf{Encrypt}(\mathsf{k}_1, \mathsf{m})$, *and*

$$(\hat{\mathsf{ct}}_{i+1}, \mathsf{ct}_{i+1}) \leftarrow \mathsf{ReEncrypt}\big(\mathsf{ReKeyGen}(\mathsf{k}_i, \mathsf{k}_{i+1}, \hat{\mathsf{ct}}_i), (\hat{\mathsf{ct}}_i, \mathsf{ct}_i)\big),$$

for $i = 1, \ldots, t-1$.

4.3 Nested Construction with Padding

Our modification of the nested construction is straightforward: we pad the ciphertexts such that as long as the number of key updates is bounded, their lengths are independent of the number of key updates that are performed on the ciphertexts. However, executing this simple idea requires some care. First, padding the (original) ciphertexts with structured strings reveals information about how many updates were previously performed on the ciphertexts. Therefore, we modify the encryption algorithm such that it pads the ciphertexts with random strings. If the underlying authenticated encryption scheme satisfies ciphertext pseudorandomness [10], an adversary cannot determine which component of a ciphertext corresponds to the original ciphertext and which component corresponds to a pad.[1]

However, simply padding the (original) ciphertexts with random strings also makes them highly malleable and easy to forge. To achieve integrity, we modify the encryption and re-encryption algorithms to additionally sample a pseudorandom generator (PRG) seed and include it as part of the UAE ciphertext header.

[1] As discussed in Sect. 2, authenticated encryption schemes that satisfy pseudorandomness can be constructed from pseudorandom functions or blockciphers in a standard way. Widely-used modes for authenticated encryption such as AES-GCM also satisfy pseudorandomness.

The encryption and re-encryption algorithms then generate the ciphertext pads from an evaluation of the PRG. By PRG security, the original ciphertext components and the pads are still computationally indistinguishable to an adversary, but now the adversary cannot easily forge ciphertexts as the decryption algorithm can verify the validity of a pad using the PRG seed.

The only remaining issue is correctness. Since the ciphertexts of our UAE scheme are pseudorandom, the re-encryption algorithm also does not have information about where the original ciphertext ends and padding begins. Therefore, we include this information as part of the re-encryption key (update token). This is the reason why this scheme satisfies update independence instead of our full confidentiality definition – even though ciphertexts fully hide their age, update tokens reveal information about the age of the ciphertext they are updating. The re-encryptor can now apply the re-encryption on the original ciphertext and adjust the padding length accordingly. We formalize the construction below.

Construction 4.2 (Nested Authenticated Encryption). *Our construction uses the following building blocks:*

- *An authenticated encryption scheme* $\Pi_{\mathsf{AE}} = (\mathsf{KeyGen}, \mathsf{Encrypt}, \mathsf{Decrypt})$ *with message space* $\mathcal{M} = (\mathcal{M}_\lambda)_{\lambda \in \mathbb{N}}$*. We additionally assume that* AE.Encrypt *satisfies* $\varepsilon_{\mathsf{ae}}^{\mathsf{rand}}$*-ciphertext pseudorandomness, i.e., that encryptions under* AE *are indistinguishable from random strings.*
  For the construction description below, we let $\rho = \rho_\lambda$ *denote the maximum size of an authenticated encryption key and we let* $\nu = \mathsf{poly}(\lambda)$ *be an additive overhead incurred by the encryption algorithm. For any key* $\mathsf{k_{ae}} \leftarrow \mathsf{AE.KeyGen}(1^\lambda)$ *and any message* $\mathsf{m} \in \mathcal{M}_\lambda$*, we have* $|\mathsf{k_{ae}}| = \rho$ *and* $|\mathsf{ct}| \leq |\mathsf{m}| + \nu$*, where* $\mathsf{ct} \leftarrow \mathsf{AE.Encrypt}(\mathsf{k_{ae}}, \mathsf{m})$.
- *A pseudorandom generator* $G : \{0,1\}^\lambda \to \{0,1\}^*$*. To simplify the presentation of the construction, we assume that* G *has unbounded output that is truncated to the required length on each invocation.*

We construct an updatable authenticated encryption scheme $\Pi_{\mathsf{UAE}} = (\mathsf{KeyGen}, \mathsf{Encrypt}, \mathsf{ReKeyGen}, \mathsf{ReEncrypt}, \mathsf{Decrypt})$ *for message space* $\mathcal{M} = (\mathcal{M}_\lambda)_{\lambda \in \mathbb{N}}$ *in Fig. 3.*

We formally state the compactness, correctness, and security properties of Construction 4.2 in the following theorem. We provide the formal proof in the full version [10].

Theorem 4.3. *Suppose the authenticated encryption scheme* Π_{AE} *satisfies correctness,* $\varepsilon_{\mathsf{ae}}^{\mathsf{conf}}$*-confidentiality,* $\varepsilon_{\mathsf{ae}}^{\mathsf{int}}$*-integrity, and* $\varepsilon_{\mathsf{ae}}^{\mathsf{rand}}$*-ciphertext pseudorandomness, and* G *satisfies* $\varepsilon_{\mathsf{prg}}$ *PRG security. Then the updatable authenticated encryption scheme* Π_{UAE} *in Construction 4.2 satisfies strong compactness, correctness, update independence, message confidentiality, and re-encryption indistinguishability.*

$\underline{\mathsf{KeyGen}(1^\lambda, 1^t)}$:
$\hat{\mathsf{k}} \leftarrow \mathsf{AE.KeyGen}(1^\lambda)$
$\mathsf{k} \leftarrow (\hat{\mathsf{k}}, t)$
Output k

$\underline{\mathsf{Encrypt}(\mathsf{k}, \mathsf{m})}$
$(\hat{\mathsf{k}}, t) \leftarrow \mathsf{k}$
$\mathsf{k_{ae}} \leftarrow \mathsf{AE.KeyGen}(1^\lambda)$
$s \xleftarrow{R} \{0,1\}^\lambda$
$\mathsf{ct_{payload}} \leftarrow \mathsf{AE.Encrypt}(\mathsf{k_{ae}}, \mathsf{m})$
$\mathsf{ct_{pad}} \leftarrow G(s)$ such that $\mathsf{ct_{pad}} \in \{0,1\}^{t \cdot (2\rho+\nu)}$
$\hat{\mathsf{ct}} \leftarrow \mathsf{AE.Encrypt}(\hat{\mathsf{k}}, (s, |\mathsf{ct_{payload}}|, \mathsf{k_{ae}}, \perp))$
$\mathsf{ct} \leftarrow (\mathsf{ct_{payload}}, \mathsf{ct_{pad}})$
Output $(\hat{\mathsf{ct}}, \mathsf{ct})$

$\underline{\mathsf{ReKeyGen}(\mathsf{k}_1, \mathsf{k}_2, \hat{\mathsf{ct}})}$:
$(\hat{\mathsf{k}}_1, t) \leftarrow \mathsf{k}_1$
$(\hat{\mathsf{k}}_2, t) \leftarrow \mathsf{k}_2$
$(s, \ell, \mathsf{k_{ae}}, \hat{\mathsf{k}}_{\mathsf{history}}) \leftarrow \mathsf{AE.Decrypt}(\mathsf{k}_1, \hat{\mathsf{ct}})$
if $(s, \ell, \mathsf{k_{ae}}, \hat{\mathsf{k}}_{\mathsf{history}}) = \perp$, output $\perp$
$\hat{\mathsf{k}}'_{\mathsf{history}} \leftarrow \mathsf{AE.KeyGen}(1^\lambda)$
$\hat{\mathsf{ct}}_{\mathsf{history}} \leftarrow \mathsf{AE.Encrypt}(\hat{\mathsf{k}}'_{\mathsf{history}}, (\mathsf{k_{ae}}, \hat{\mathsf{k}}_{\mathsf{history}}))$
$\mathsf{k}'_{\mathsf{ae}} \leftarrow \mathsf{AE.KeyGen}(1^\lambda)$
$s' \xleftarrow{R} \{0,1\}^\lambda$
$\ell' \leftarrow \ell + |\hat{\mathsf{ct}}_{\mathsf{history}}|$
$\hat{\mathsf{ct}}' \leftarrow \mathsf{AE.Encrypt}(\hat{\mathsf{k}}_2, (s', \ell', \mathsf{k}'_{\mathsf{ae}}, \hat{\mathsf{k}}'_{\mathsf{history}}))$
$\Delta_{1,2,\hat{\mathsf{ct}}} \leftarrow (\hat{\mathsf{ct}}', \hat{\mathsf{ct}}_{\mathsf{history}}, \ell, \mathsf{k}'_{\mathsf{ae}}, s')$
Output $\Delta_{1,2,\hat{\mathsf{ct}}}$

$\underline{\mathsf{ReEncrypt}(\Delta_{1,2,\hat{\mathsf{ct}}}, (\hat{\mathsf{ct}}, \mathsf{ct}))}$:
$(\hat{\mathsf{ct}}', \hat{\mathsf{ct}}_{\mathsf{history}}, \ell, \mathsf{k}'_{\mathsf{ae}}, s') \leftarrow \Delta_{1,2,\hat{\mathsf{ct}}}$
$(\mathsf{ct_{payload}}, \mathsf{ct_{pad}}) \leftarrow \mathsf{ct} \in \{0,1\}^\ell \times \{0,1\}^{|\mathsf{ct}|-\ell}$
if $|\mathsf{ct}| < \ell$, output $\perp$
$\mathsf{ct}'_{\mathsf{payload}} \leftarrow \mathsf{AE.Encrypt}(\mathsf{k}'_{\mathsf{ae}}, (\mathsf{ct_{payload}}, \hat{\mathsf{ct}}_{\mathsf{history}}))$
if $|\mathsf{ct}'_{\mathsf{payload}}| > |\mathsf{ct}|$, output $\perp$
$\mathsf{ct}'_{\mathsf{pad}} \leftarrow G(s')[1, \ldots, |\mathsf{ct}| - |\mathsf{ct}'_{\mathsf{payload}}|]$
$\mathsf{ct}' \leftarrow (\mathsf{ct}'_{\mathsf{payload}}, \mathsf{ct}'_{\mathsf{pad}}) \in \{0,1\}^{|\mathsf{ct}|}$
Output $(\hat{\mathsf{ct}}', \mathsf{ct}')$

$\underline{\mathsf{Decrypt}(\mathsf{k}, (\hat{\mathsf{ct}}, \mathsf{ct}))}$:
$(\hat{\mathsf{k}}, t) \leftarrow \mathsf{k}$
$(s, \ell, \mathsf{k}'_{\mathsf{ae}}, \hat{\mathsf{k}}'_{\mathsf{history}}) \leftarrow \mathsf{AE.Decrypt}(\hat{\mathsf{k}}, \hat{\mathsf{ct}})$
if $(s, \ell, \mathsf{k}'_{\mathsf{ae}}, \hat{\mathsf{k}}'_{\mathsf{history}}) = \perp$, output $\perp$
if $|\mathsf{ct}| < \ell$, output $\perp$
$(\mathsf{ct_{payload}}, \mathsf{ct_{pad}}) \leftarrow \mathsf{ct} \in \{0,1\}^\ell \times \{0,1\}^{|\mathsf{ct}|-\ell}$
$\mathsf{ct}'_{\mathsf{pad}} \leftarrow G(s)$ such that $|\mathsf{ct}'_{\mathsf{pad}}| = |\mathsf{ct_{pad}}|$
if $\mathsf{ct}'_{\mathsf{pad}} \neq \mathsf{ct_{pad}}$, output $\perp$
$(\mathsf{ct}', \hat{\mathsf{ct}}'_{\mathsf{history}}) \leftarrow \mathsf{AE.Decrypt}(\mathsf{k}'_{\mathsf{ae}}, \mathsf{ct_{payload}})$
if $(\mathsf{ct}', \hat{\mathsf{ct}}'_{\mathsf{history}}) = \perp$, output $\perp$
while $\hat{\mathsf{k}}'_{\mathsf{history}} \neq \perp$:
  $\mathsf{k_{ae}} \leftarrow \mathsf{k}'_{\mathsf{ae}}$
  $\hat{\mathsf{k}}_{\mathsf{history}} \leftarrow \hat{\mathsf{k}}'_{\mathsf{history}}$
  $\mathsf{ct} \leftarrow \mathsf{ct}'$
  $\hat{\mathsf{ct}}_{\mathsf{history}} \leftarrow \hat{\mathsf{ct}}'_{\mathsf{history}}$
  $(\mathsf{k}'_{\mathsf{ae}}, \hat{\mathsf{k}}'_{\mathsf{history}}) \leftarrow \mathsf{AE.Decrypt}(\hat{\mathsf{k}}_{\mathsf{history}}, \hat{\mathsf{ct}}_{\mathsf{history}})$
  if $(\mathsf{k}'_{\mathsf{ae}}, \hat{\mathsf{k}}'_{\mathsf{history}}) = \perp$, output $\perp$
  $(\mathsf{ct}', \hat{\mathsf{ct}}'_{\mathsf{history}}) \leftarrow \mathsf{AE.Decrypt}(\mathsf{k_{ae}}, \mathsf{ct})$
  if $(\mathsf{ct}', \hat{\mathsf{ct}}'_{\mathsf{history}}) = \perp$, output $\perp$
$\mathsf{m} \leftarrow \mathsf{AE.Decrypt}(\mathsf{k}'_{\mathsf{ae}}, \mathsf{ct}')$
Output m

Fig. 3. Our nested scheme.

For confidentiality, we have the following concrete security bounds for all $h, d = \mathsf{poly}(\lambda)$ *and efficient adversaries* $\mathcal{A}$ *that make at most* Q *oracle queries:*

$$\left| \Pr\left[\mathsf{Expt}^{\mathsf{upd\text{-}ind}}_{\Pi_{\mathsf{UAE}}}(\lambda, h, d, \mathcal{A}, 0) = 1\right] - \Pr\left[\mathsf{Expt}^{\mathsf{upd\text{-}ind}}_{\Pi_{\mathsf{UAE}}}(\lambda, h, d, \mathcal{A}, 1) = 1\right] \right| \\ \leq 2h \cdot \varepsilon^{\mathsf{conf}}_{\mathsf{ae}}(\lambda) + 2h \cdot \varepsilon^{\mathsf{int}}_{\mathsf{ae}}(\lambda) + 2Q \cdot \varepsilon_{\mathsf{prg}}(\lambda) + 4Q \cdot \varepsilon^{\mathsf{rand}}_{\mathsf{ae}}(\lambda)$$

$$\left| \Pr\left[\mathsf{Expt}^{\mathsf{msg\text{-}conf}}_{\Pi_{\mathsf{UAE}}}(\lambda, h, d, \mathcal{A}, 0) = 1\right] - \Pr\left[\mathsf{Expt}^{\mathsf{msg\text{-}conf}}_{\Pi_{\mathsf{UAE}}}(\lambda, h, d, \mathcal{A}, 1) = 1\right] \right| \\ \leq (2h + 4Q) \cdot \varepsilon^{\mathsf{conf}}_{\mathsf{ae}}(\lambda) + 2h \cdot \varepsilon^{\mathsf{int}}_{\mathsf{ae}}(\lambda)$$

$$\left| \Pr\left[\mathsf{Expt}^{\mathsf{re\text{-}enc\text{-}ind}}_{\Pi_{\mathsf{UAE}}}(\lambda, h, d, \mathcal{A}, 0) = 1\right] - \Pr\left[\mathsf{Expt}^{\mathsf{re\text{-}enc\text{-}ind}}_{\Pi_{\mathsf{UAE}}}(\lambda, h, d, \mathcal{A}, 1) = 1\right] \right| \\ \leq (2h + 4Q) \cdot \varepsilon^{\mathsf{conf}}_{\mathsf{ae}}(\lambda) + 2h \cdot \varepsilon^{\mathsf{int}}_{\mathsf{ae}}(\lambda)$$

For integrity, we have the following bound for all $h, d = \mathsf{poly}(\lambda)$ and efficient adversaries $\mathcal{A}$ that make at most Q challenge, ReKeyGen, *or* ReEncrypt *queries:*

$$\Pr\left[\mathsf{Expt}^{\mathsf{int}}_{\Pi_{\mathsf{UAE}}}(\lambda, h, d, \mathcal{A}) = 1\right] \leq (h + Q) \cdot \varepsilon^{\mathsf{int}}_{\mathsf{ae}}(\lambda) + (h + Q) \cdot \varepsilon^{\mathsf{conf}}_{\mathsf{ae}}(\lambda) + Q/2^{\lambda}$$

5 UAE from Key-Homomorphic PRFs

In this section, we generalize the updatable authenticated encryption construction of Everspaugh et al. [15] that is built from a perfectly key-homomorphic PRF, to also work using an almost key-homomorphic PRF. We do this by incorporating a plaintext encoding scheme into the construction such that encrypted messages can still be decrypted correctly after noisy key rotations. We show that this generalized UAE construction satisfies our notion of confidentiality (Definition 3.4), but only satisfies a relaxed integrity property. We first describe the construction in Sect. 5.2, and then analyze and prove its security in Sect. 5.3.

5.1 Encoding Scheme

Our construction of an updatable authenticated encryption scheme relies on an *almost* key-homomorphic PRF for which key-homomorphism holds under small noise. To cope with the noise in our updatable encryption scheme in Sect. 5.2, we must encode messages prior to encrypting them such that they can be fully recovered during decryption. A simple way of encoding the messages is to pad them with additional least-significant bits. However, more sophisticated ways of encoding the messages are possible with general error-correcting codes. In our construction description in Sect. 5.2, we use the syntax of a general encoding scheme that is described in Fact 5.1 below. In Sect. 7, we test the performance of our construction in Sect. 5.2 with simple padding.

Fact 5.1. *Let n, q, γ be positive integers such that $\gamma < q/4$, $\mu = \mu(\lambda)$ be a polynomial in λ, and $\mathcal{M} = \left(\{0,1\}^{\mu(\lambda)}\right)_{\lambda \in \mathbb{N}}$ be a message space. Then there exists a set of algorithms* (Encode, Decode) *with the following syntax:*

- $\mathsf{Encode}(\mathsf{m}) \to (\mathsf{m}_1, \ldots, \mathsf{m}_\ell)$: *On input a message $\mathsf{m} \in \mathcal{M}_\lambda$, the encoding algorithm returns a set of vectors $\mathsf{m}_1, \ldots, \mathsf{m}_\ell \in \mathbb{Z}_q^n$ for some $\ell \in \mathbb{N}$.*
- $\mathsf{Decode}(\mathsf{m}_1, \ldots, \mathsf{m}_\ell) \to \mathsf{m}$: *On input a set of vectors $\mathsf{m}_1, \ldots, \mathsf{m}_\ell \in \mathbb{Z}_q^n$, the decoding algorithm returns a message $\mathsf{m} \in \mathcal{M}_\lambda$.*

The algorithms (Encode, Decode) *satisfy the following property: for all strings* $\mathsf{m} \in \mathcal{M}_\lambda$ *and any error vectors* $\mathbf{e} = \mathbf{e}_1, \ldots, \mathbf{e}_\ell \in [\gamma]^n$*, if we set* $(\mathsf{m}_1, \ldots, \mathsf{m}_\ell) \leftarrow \mathsf{Encode}(\mathsf{m})$*, we have*

$$\mathsf{Decode}(\mathsf{m}_1 + \mathbf{e}_1, \ldots, \mathsf{m}_\ell + \mathbf{e}_\ell) = \mathsf{m}.$$

Due to the use of an encoding scheme, our construction can be viewed as supporting only a bounded number of updates – the encoding can only support so much noise before decoding fails. However, for our almost key-homomorphic PRF construction in Sect. 5.2, a simple padding scheme can be used as the encoding scheme. In this case, the bound on the number of updates grows exponentially in the size of the parameters of the scheme and therefore, the construction can be interpreted as permitting unbounded updates.

5.2 Construction

We next present our UAE scheme from an almost key-homomorphic PRF. We analyze its security in the next two subsections.

$\underline{\mathsf{KeyGen}(1^\lambda, 1^t)}$:
$\mathsf{k} \leftarrow \mathsf{AE.KeyGen}(1^\lambda)$
Output k

$\underline{\mathsf{ReKeyGen}(\mathsf{k}_1, \mathsf{k}_2, \hat{\mathsf{ct}})}$:
$\mu \leftarrow \mathsf{AE.Decrypt}(\mathsf{k}_1, \hat{\mathsf{ct}})$
if $\mu = \perp$, output $\perp$
$(\mathsf{k}_{\mathsf{prf}}, \mathsf{h}) \leftarrow \mu$
$\mathsf{k}'_{\mathsf{prf}} \xleftarrow{\mathrm{R}} \mathcal{K}_{\mathsf{PRF}}$
$\mathsf{k}^{\mathsf{up}}_{\mathsf{prf}} \leftarrow \mathsf{k}'_{\mathsf{prf}} - \mathsf{k}_{\mathsf{prf}}$
$\hat{\mathsf{ct}}' \leftarrow \mathsf{AE.Encrypt}(\mathsf{k}_2, (\mathsf{k}'_{\mathsf{prf}}, \mathsf{h}))$
$\Delta_{1,2,\hat{\mathsf{ct}}} \leftarrow (\hat{\mathsf{ct}}', \mathsf{k}^{\mathsf{up}}_{\mathsf{prf}})$

$\underline{\mathsf{ReEncrypt}(\Delta_{1,2,\hat{\mathsf{ct}}}, (\hat{\mathsf{ct}}, \mathsf{ct}))}$:
$(\hat{\mathsf{ct}}', \mathsf{k}^{\mathsf{up}}_{\mathsf{prf}}) \leftarrow \Delta_{1,2,\hat{\mathsf{ct}}}$
$(\mathsf{ct}_1, \ldots, \mathsf{ct}_\ell) \leftarrow \mathsf{ct}$
for $i \in [\ell]$:
  $\mathsf{ct}'_i \leftarrow \mathsf{ct}_i + F(\mathsf{k}^{\mathsf{up}}_{\mathsf{prf}}, i)$
$\mathsf{ct}' \leftarrow (\mathsf{ct}'_1, \ldots, \mathsf{ct}'_\ell)$
Output $(\hat{\mathsf{ct}}', \mathsf{ct}')$

$\underline{\mathsf{Encrypt}(\mathsf{k}, \mathsf{m})}$
$(\mathsf{m}_1, \ldots, \mathsf{m}_\ell) \leftarrow \mathsf{Encode}(\mathsf{m})$
$\mathsf{k}_{\mathsf{prf}} \xleftarrow{\mathrm{R}} \mathcal{K}_{\mathsf{PRF}}$
$\mathsf{h} \leftarrow H(\mathsf{m})$
$\hat{\mathsf{ct}} \leftarrow \mathsf{AE.Encrypt}(\mathsf{k}_{\mathsf{ae}}, (\mathsf{k}_{\mathsf{prf}}, \mathsf{h}))$
for $i \in [\ell]$:
  $\mathsf{ct}_i \leftarrow \mathsf{m}_i + F(\mathsf{k}_{\mathsf{prf}}, i)$
$\mathsf{ct} = (\mathsf{ct}_1, \ldots, \mathsf{ct}_\ell)$
Output $(\hat{\mathsf{ct}}, \mathsf{ct})$

$\underline{\mathsf{Decrypt}(\mathsf{k}, (\hat{\mathsf{ct}}, \mathsf{ct}))}$:
$\mu \leftarrow \mathsf{AE.Decrypt}(\mathsf{k}, \hat{\mathsf{ct}})$
if $\mu = \perp$, output $\perp$
$(\mathsf{k}_{\mathsf{prf}}, \mathsf{h}) \leftarrow \mu$
$(\mathsf{ct}_1, \ldots, \mathsf{ct}_\ell) \leftarrow \mathsf{ct}$
for $i \in [\ell]$:
  $\mathsf{m}_i \leftarrow \mathsf{ct}_i - F(\mathsf{k}_{\mathsf{prf}}, i)$
$\mathsf{m}' \leftarrow \mathsf{Decode}(\mathsf{m}_1, \ldots, \mathsf{m}_\ell)$
if $H(\mathsf{m}') = \mathsf{h}$, output m'
else, output $\perp$

Fig. 4. Our UAE from almost Key-Homomorphic PRFs.

Construction 5.2 (UAE from almost Key-Homomorphic PRFs). *Let n, q, γ, and β be positive integers. Our construction uses the following:*

- *A standard authenticated encryption scheme* $\Pi_{\mathsf{AE}} = (\mathsf{AE.KeyGen}, \mathsf{AE.Encrypt}, \mathsf{AE.Decrypt})$ *with message space* $\mathcal{M} = (\mathcal{M}_\lambda)_{\lambda \in \mathbb{N}}$.
- *A β-almost key-homomorphic PRF* $F : \mathcal{K}_{\mathsf{PRF}} \times \{0,1\}^* \to \mathbb{Z}_q^n$ *where* $(\mathcal{K}_{\mathsf{PRF}}, +)$ *and* $(\mathbb{Z}_q^n, +)$ *form groups.*
- *A collision resistant hash family* $\mathcal{H} = \{H : \mathcal{M}_\lambda \to \{0,1\}^\lambda\}$. *To simplify the construction, we assume that a description of a concrete hash function* $H \xleftarrow{R} \mathcal{H}$ *is included in each algorithm as part of a global set of parameters.*
- *An encoding scheme* (Encode, Decode) *that encodes messages in* $(\mathcal{M}, \lambda)_{\lambda \in \mathbb{N}}$ *as elements in* $\mathbb{Z}_q^n$. *The* Decode *algorithm decodes any error vectors* $\mathbf{e} \in [\gamma]^n$ *as in Fact 5.1 for any fixed* $\gamma = \beta \cdot \lambda^{\omega(1)}$.

We construct an updatable authenticated encryption scheme $\Pi_{\mathsf{UAE}} = (\mathsf{KeyGen}, \mathsf{Encrypt}, \mathsf{ReKeyGen}, \mathsf{ReEncrypt}, \mathsf{Decrypt})$ *for message space* $(\mathcal{M}_\lambda)_{\lambda \in \mathbb{N}}$ *in Fig. 4.*

5.3 Security Under Relaxed Integrity

We will show in the next subsection that neither Construction 5.2 nor the construction of Everspaugh et al. [15] satisfy our integrity definition. To prove security of either scheme we must relax the notion of integrity in Definition 3.7 to obtain what we call *relaxed integrity*. In this section we define relaxed integrity and then prove security of Construction 5.2. In the next subsection we discuss the implications of relaxed integrity to the security of the scheme in practice.

The relaxed integrity experiment modifies Definition 3.7 (integrity) in two ways. First, we require that an adversary's queries to the re-encryption oracle are well-formed ciphertexts that do not decrypt to "$\perp$". Without this restriction, there is an attack on both Construction 5.2 and the Everspaugh et al. [15] scheme, as we will discuss below.

Second, we modify the adversary's winning condition in the integrity game. When we use an *almost* key-homomorphic PRFs to instantiate Construction 5.2, any re-encryption incurs a small error that affects the low-order bits of the ciphertext. Therefore, to achieve correctness, we encrypt an encoding of a message (Fact 5.1) such that the decryption algorithm can still recover the full message even if the low-ordered bits are corrupted. This forces the construction to violate traditional ciphertext integrity as an adversary can forge new ciphertexts by adding noise to the low-order bits of a ciphertext. Our construction still guarantees that an adversary cannot generate new ciphertexts by modifying plaintexts or the high-order bits of ciphertexts. To capture this formally, we require that the ciphertext space $\mathcal{CT}$ associated with the UAE has a corresponding metric function $d : \mathcal{CT} \times \mathcal{CT} \to \mathbb{Z}$ (e.g., Euclidean distance) that gives a distance between any two ciphertexts. Then, in our relaxed integrity definition that is parameterized with a positive integer $\gamma \in \mathbb{N}$, an adversary wins the security experiment only if it produces a valid ciphertext that differs from any of the ciphertexts that it is given by more than γ.

The rest of the definition of relaxed integrity exactly matches Definition 3.7. We present the formal definition of relaxed integrity in the full version [10].

Security. The following theorem states the compactness, correctness, and security properties of Construction 5.2. The proof is presented in the full version [10].

Theorem 5.3. *Let Π_{UAE} be the updatable authenticated encryption scheme in Construction 5.2. If the authenticated encryption scheme Π_{AE} satisfies correctness, $\varepsilon_{\mathsf{ae}}^{\mathsf{conf}}$-confidentiality and $\varepsilon_{\mathsf{ae}}^{\mathsf{int}}$-integrity, $F : \mathcal{K}_{\mathsf{PRF}} \times \{0,1\}^* \rightarrow \mathcal{Y}$ satisfies $\varepsilon_{\mathsf{prf}}$-security, and $H : \mathcal{M}_\lambda \rightarrow \{0,1\}^\lambda$ is a $\varepsilon_{\mathsf{cr}}$-secure collision resistant hash function, then Π_{UAE} satisfies strong compactness, correctness, confidentiality, and γ-relaxed integrity.*

For confidentiality, we have the following concrete security bounds for all $h, d = \mathsf{poly}(\lambda)$ and efficient adversaries $\mathcal{A}$ that make at most Q challenge queries:

$$\left| \Pr\left[\mathsf{Expt}_{\Pi_{\mathsf{UAE}}}^{\mathsf{conf}}(\lambda, h, d, \mathcal{A}, 0) = 1\right] - \Pr\left[\mathsf{Expt}_{\Pi_{\mathsf{UAE}}}^{\mathsf{conf}}(\lambda, h, d, \mathcal{A}, 1) = 1\right] \right|$$
$$\leq 2h \cdot \varepsilon_{\mathsf{ae}}^{\mathsf{conf}}(\lambda) + 2h \cdot \varepsilon_{\mathsf{ae}}^{\mathsf{int}}(\lambda) + 2Q \cdot \varepsilon_{\mathsf{prf}}(\lambda)$$

For integrity, we have the following bound for all $h, d = \mathsf{poly}(\lambda)$ and efficient adversaries $\mathcal{A}$:

$$\Pr\left[\mathsf{Expt}_{\Pi_{\mathsf{UAE}}}^{\mathsf{relaxed\text{-}int}}(\lambda, h, d, \gamma, \mathcal{A}) = 1\right] \leq h \cdot \varepsilon_{\mathsf{ae}}^{\mathsf{int}}(\lambda) + \varepsilon_{\mathsf{cr}}(\lambda)$$

We note that when we instantiate Construction 5.2 with a perfect key-homomorphic PRF, we can use the trivial encoding scheme for $\gamma = 0$. In this case, the relaxed integrity experiment $\mathsf{Expt}_{\Pi_{\mathsf{UAE}}}^{\mathsf{relaxed\text{-}int}}(\lambda, h, d, 0, \mathcal{A})$ is comparable to the ciphertext integrity notion in [15].

5.4 Consequences of Relaxed Integrity

The relaxed integrity definition from Sect. 5.3 places two restrictions on the adversary relative to our full integrity definition (Definition 3.7). We discuss these two restrictions and their implications below.

Weakened Re-encryption Oracle. The first restriction of relaxed integrity is the weakened re-encryption oracle, which only re-encrypts well-formed ciphertexts. This relaxation of the definition is necessary to prove security of Construction 5.2 as there exists a simple adversary that breaks the integrity experiment when it is provided arbitrary access to the re-encryption oracle $\mathcal{O}_{\mathsf{ReEncrypt}}$. This attack applies equally well to the construction of Everspaugh et al. [15].

To carry out the attack, the adversary does the following:

1. Uses encryption oracle $\mathcal{O}_{\mathsf{Encrypt}}$ to receive a ciphertext $(\hat{\mathsf{ct}}, \mathsf{ct}) \leftarrow \mathcal{O}_{\mathsf{Encrypt}}(i, \mathsf{m})$ for a message $\mathsf{m} \in \mathcal{M}_\lambda$ and an honest key index i. For simplicity, suppose that the message m is encoded as a single vector in $\mathbb{Z}_q^n$: $\mathsf{Encode}(\mathsf{m}) \in \mathbb{Z}_q^n$ and therefore, $\mathsf{ct} \in \mathbb{Z}_q^n$.

2. Subtracts an arbitrary vector m' from the ciphertext body $\tilde{\mathsf{ct}} \leftarrow \mathsf{ct} - \mathsf{m}'$.
3. Submits the ciphertext $(\hat{\mathsf{ct}}, \tilde{\mathsf{ct}})$ to the re-encryption oracle $\mathcal{O}_{\mathsf{ReEncrypt}}$ to receive a new ciphertext $(\hat{\mathsf{ct}}', \tilde{\mathsf{ct}}') \leftarrow \mathcal{O}_{\mathsf{ReEncrypt}}(i, j, (\hat{\mathsf{ct}}, \tilde{\mathsf{ct}}))$ for an honest key index j.
4. Returns $(\hat{\mathsf{ct}}', \tilde{\mathsf{ct}}' + \mathsf{m}')$ as the ciphertext forgery.

Since the re-encryption algorithm is homomorphic, we have

$$\mathcal{O}_{\mathsf{ReEncrypt}}(i, j, \hat{\mathsf{ct}}, \tilde{\mathsf{ct}} - \mathsf{m}') + \mathsf{m}' = \mathcal{O}_{\mathsf{ReEncrypt}}(i, j, \hat{\mathsf{ct}}, \tilde{\mathsf{ct}}).$$

Therefore, the ciphertext $(\hat{\mathsf{ct}}', \tilde{\mathsf{ct}}' + \mathsf{m})$ is a valid forgery. This attack is ruled out in the relaxed integrity experiment, where the re-encryption oracle $\mathcal{O}_{\mathsf{ReEncrypt}}$ outputs a re-encrypted ciphertext only when the input ciphertexts are well-formed.

To carry out the attack above, an adversary must have arbitrary access to a re-encryption oracle. Therefore, Construction 5.2 still provides security against any active adversary that has arbitrary access to the decryption oracle, but only observes key rotations on well-formed ciphertexts. For applications where an adversary (e.g. a corrupted server) gains arbitrary access to the re-encryption oracle, Construction 5.2 provides passive security as opposed to active security. This also applies to [15].

Handling Noise. The second restriction imposed on the adversary is needed due to the noise allowed in Construction 5.2. In particular, the encoding scheme used in the construction allows an adversary to create new ciphertexts by adding small amounts of noise to an existing ciphertext. In combination with the decryption oracle, an adversary can take advantage of this property to gain information about the age of a ciphertext using a chosen ciphertext attack. Namely, an adversary can take a ciphertext and incrementally add noise to it before submitting the ciphertext to the decryption oracle. Based on how much noise an adversary can add to the ciphertext before the decryption oracle returns $\perp$, the adversary can approximate the relative size of the noise in the ciphertext. Since each key rotation in increases the noise associated with a ciphertext by a fixed amount, an adversary can gain information about the age of the ciphertext by learning the size of the noise in the ciphertext. Hence, the age of a ciphertext can be exposed using a chosen ciphertext attack.

For applications where the age of a ciphertext is not sensitive information, Construction 5.2 can be used as an efficient alternative to existing UAE schemes. When combined with confidentiality (Definition 3.4), the relaxed integrity definition provides an "approximate" analogue of the traditional chosen-ciphertext security. To see this, take any CCA-secure encryption scheme Π_{Enc} and modify it into a scheme Π'_{Enc} that is identical to Π_{Enc}, but the encryption algorithm appends a bit 0 to every resulting ciphertext, and the decryption algorithm discards the last bit of the ciphertext before decrypting. The scheme Π'_{Enc} is no longer CCA-secure as an adversary can take any ciphertext and flip its last bit to produce different valid ciphertext. However, the introduction of the last bit does not cause the scheme Π'_{Enc} to be susceptible to any concrete attack that violates security. Similarly, Construction 5.2 does not satisfy full ciphertext integrity due to its noisy nature; however, it still suffices to guarantee CCA security in practice.

These variants of CCA security were previously explored under the name of *Replayable CCA* and *Detectable CCA* [14,18], where it was argued that they are sufficient to provide security against an active attacker in practice.

6 Almost Key-Homomorphic PRFs from Lattices

In this section, we construct an almost key-homomorphic PRF from the Learning with Errors (LWE) assumption [26]. There are a number of standard variants of the LWE assumption in the literature that give rise to efficient PRF constructions. For instance, using the Learning with Rounding (LWR) [6,11] assumption, one can construct an almost key-homomorphic PRF in both the random-oracle and standard models. However, any LWR-based PRF involves a modular rounding step [6] that forces the output space of the PRF to be quite small compared to the key space. Hence, these PRFs are less optimal for the application of updatable encryption as the noise that is incurred by each key updates grows faster in the smaller output space. In this work, we modify the existing LWR-based KH-PRF constructions to work over the ring variant of the LWE problem called the Ring Learning with Errors (RLWE) problem [22]. We provide the precise definition in the full version [10]. The use of RLWE as opposed to LWR (or Ring-LWR) allows us to construct almost KH-PRFs that can support more key updates when applied to Construction 5.2.

We construct an almost key-homomorphic PRF from the hardness of the Ring Learning with Errors problem as follows.

Construction 6.1. *Let n, q, B, r, ℓ be positive integers, $\mathcal{R} = \mathbb{Z}[X]/(\phi)$ a polynomial ring for $\phi \in \mathbb{Z}[X]$, $\mathcal{R}_q = \mathbb{Z}_q[X]/(\phi)$, and χ an error distribution over $\mathcal{E}_B \subseteq \mathcal{R}$. We let $\mathsf{Samp}_\chi : \{0,1\}^r \rightarrow \mathcal{E}_B$ be a sampler for the error distribution χ that takes in a uniformly random string in $\{0,1\}^r$ and produces a ring element in $\mathcal{E}_B$ according to the distribution χ. For our construction, we set $\mathcal{X} = \{0,1\}^\ell$ to be the domain of the PRF and use two hash functions that are modeled as random oracles:*

- $H_0 : \{0,1\}^\ell \rightarrow \mathcal{R}_q$,
- $H_1 : \mathcal{R}_q \times \{0,1\}^\ell \rightarrow \{0,1\}^r$.

We define our pseudorandom function $F : \mathcal{R}_q \times \{0,1\}^\ell \rightarrow \mathcal{R}_q$ as follows:

$F(s, x)$:

1. *Evaluate $a \leftarrow H_0(x)$, $\rho \leftarrow H_1(s, x)$.*
2. *Sample $e \leftarrow \mathsf{Samp}_\chi(\rho)$.*
3. *Output $y \leftarrow a \cdot s + e$.*

We summarize the security and homomorphic properties of the PRF construction above in the following theorem. We provide its proof in the full version [10].

Theorem 6.2. *Let n, q, B, r, ℓ be positive integers, $\mathcal{R} = \mathbb{Z}[X]/(\phi)$ a polynomial ring for $\phi \in \mathbb{Z}[X]$, $\mathcal{R}_q = \mathbb{Z}_q[X]/(\phi)$, and χ an error distribution over $\mathcal{E}_B \subseteq \mathcal{R}_q$. Then, assuming that $\mathsf{RLWE}_{n,q,\chi}$ [10] is $\varepsilon_{\mathsf{RLWE}}$-secure, the pseudorandom function in Construction 6.1 is a $\varepsilon_{\mathsf{prf}}$-secure $2B$-almost key-homomorphic PRF (Definition 2.1) with key space and range $(\mathcal{R}_q, +)$ such that $\varepsilon_{\mathsf{prf}}(\lambda) = \varepsilon_{\mathsf{RLWE}}(\lambda)$.*

7 Evaluation

In this section we evaluate the performance of our nested and KH-PRF based UAE constructions (Constructions 4.2 and 5.2), comparing their performance to that of the ReCrypt scheme of Everspaugh et al. [15] both in terms of running time and ciphertext size. We find that our constructions dramatically improve on the running time of the Everspaugh et al. [15] UAE at the cost of an increase in ciphertext size (albeit our ciphertext sizes are still considerably smaller than those of ciphertext-independent schemes [12,20,21]).

RLWE Parameters

	$\lvert q\rvert = 28$	$\lvert q\rvert = 60$	$\lvert q\rvert = 120$	$\lvert q\rvert = 128$
n	1024	2048	4096	4096
B	352	498	704	704

Fig. 5. RLWE parameters for each value of $|q|$ used in our evaluation.

We implemented our constructions in C and evaluated their performance on an 8-core Ubuntu virtual machine with 4 GB of RAM running on a Windows 10 computer with 64 GB and a 12-core AMD 1920x processor @3.8 GHz. We use AES-NI instructions to accelerate AES and AVX instructions for applicable choices of lattice parameters. Our implementation is single-threaded and does not take advantage of opportunities for parallelism beyond a single core. We rely on OpenSSL for standard cryptographic primitives and rely on prior implementations of NTT and the SHAKE hash function [4,27]. All numbers reported are averages taken over at least 1,000 trials. Our choice of lattice parameters for each modulus size $|q|$ (the length of q in bits) is based on the best known attacks on RLWE [3], as shown in Fig. 5. We discuss some aspects of our KH-PRF implementation in the full version [10]. Our implementation is open source and available at [1].

Encryption and Re-encryption Costs. Figure 6 shows encryption and re-encryption times for our KH-PRF based UAE construction for various block sizes of the underlying KH-PRF as well as the ReCrypt scheme [15] and our nested construction with padding configured to support up to 128 re-encryptions. Our lattice-based KH-PRF scheme, when run with the best parameters, has from 250× to over 500× higher encryption throughput than ReCrypt as the message size increases from 4 kB to 100 kB. We note that, since KH-PRFs imply

Encrypt and ReEncrypt Throughput (MB/sec)							
	KH-PRF UAE					ReCrypt	Nested
	$\lvert q\rvert = 28$	$\lvert q\rvert = 28$ (AVX)	$\lvert q\rvert = 60$	$\lvert q\rvert = 120$	$\lvert q\rvert = 128$	[15]	$t = 128$
4KB Messages							
Encrypt	24.85	**31.97**	20.32	0.76	0.70	0.12	406.69
ReEncrypt	29.80	**41.03**	32.13	0.82	0.74	0.14	706.37
32KB Messages							
Encrypt	29.85	39.89	**61.90**	5.94	5.50	0.12	1836.9
ReEncrypt	32.33	44.51	**83.06**	6.43	5.85	0.15	2606.8
100KB Messages							
Encrypt	31.03	41.63	**65.11**	9.42	9.12	0.12	3029.5
ReEncrypt	33.30	45.77	**79.63**	9.92	8.70	0.14	3766.2

Fig. 6. Comparing the throughput of our KH-PRF, ReCrypt, and our nested construction configured to allow 128 re-encryptions, for messages of length 4 kB, 32 kB, and 100 kB. Higher numbers are better. Our KH-PRF is evaluated with four choices of q. The AVX column refers to an implementation that takes advantage of Intel's AVX vector instructions.

key exchange [2], we should not expect to be able to instantiate the KH-PRF approach with performance any better than that of public key primitives. The nested AES construction, on the other hand, has 13–47× the encryption throughput of our KHPRF-based construction. The nested AES scheme approaches the machine's peak AES throughput of 4.45 GB/s as the message size increases.

We find that for small messages (4 kB), our KH-PRF with 28 bit output space (and accelerated with AVX instructions) performs the best, but as messages grow larger the KH-PRF with 60 bit output space outperforms other categories. Larger block sizes tend to perform worse because the output of the PRF no longer fits into compiler provided primitive types, causing arithmetic operations to become less efficient. Increasing the message size improves performance because the proportion of total time occupied by fixed-cost operations decreases, e.g.,

KeyGen and ReKeyGen Time (µsecs)			
	KH-PRF UAE	ReCrypt	Nested
	$\lvert q\rvert = 60$	[15]	$t = 128$
32KB Messages			
KeyGen	3.0	1.0	2.6
ReKeyGen	72.7	308.8	10.1

Fig. 7. KeyGen and ReKeyGen costs. The main differences in performance are caused by whether the ReKeyGen algorithm needs to sample only AES keys or also KH-PRF keys, the type of KH-PRF used, and the number of ciphertexts contained in the update token.

due to the large blocks in which the KH-PRF output is generated. We run our remaining experiments with $|q| = 60$ because it has the overall best performance.

Key Generation. Key generation is a faster and less time-sensitive operation than encryption, re-encryption, and decryption because it only occurs once for a small ciphertext header before an entire ciphertext is encrypted or re-encrypted. We show the performance of our KH-PRF based UAE as well as ReCrypt and nested encryption on KeyGen and ReKeyGen operations in Fig. 7. Generating a key in all three schemes is very fast because it only requires generating a random 128-bit symmetric key. The cost of rekeying depends on the underlying tool used to re-encrypt. ReKeyGen runs very quickly in the nested construction because it only consists of a couple AES-GCM encryptions of a fixed-size ciphertext header. The other two constructions rely on different types of KH-PRFs and incur most of their costs in generating the update keys for those PRFs.

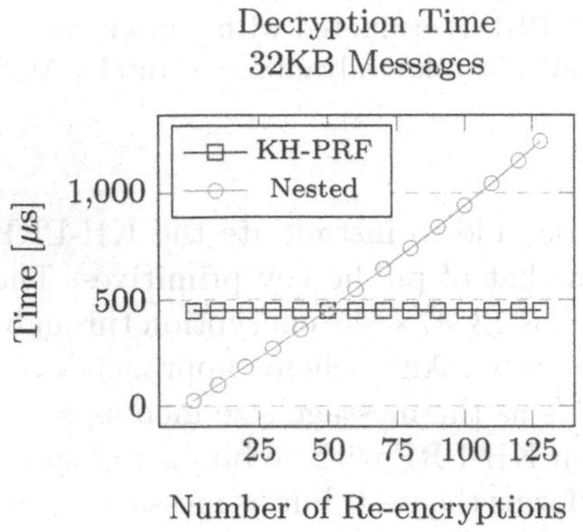

Fig. 8. KH-PRF based UAE ($|q| = 60$) and nested UAE ($t = 128$) decryption times. The KH-PRF construction decrypts faster than nested AES when there are more than 50 re-encryptions. ReCrypt is not depicted as it takes 500× longer than our KH-PRF based UAE to decrypt.

Ciphertext Expansion
32KB Messages

KH-PRF UAE	
$\|q\| = 28$	133%
$\|q\| = 60$	36%
$\|q\| = 120$	20%
$\|q\| = 128$	19%
Nested UAE	
$t = 20$	3%
$t = 128$	19%
ReCrypt [15]	3%

Fig. 9. Ciphertext body expansion for the KH-PRF based UAE, Nested UAE, and ReCrypt. Our constructions generally have larger ciphertext expansion than ReCrypt, although the Nested UAE matches ReCrypt for some settings, e.g., annually re-keying data for 20 years.

Decryption Costs. Figure 8 shows decryption costs for our two main constructions and the tradeoffs between them. We omit the decryption performance of ReCrypt from this graph because it is 500× slower than our KH-PRF based construction and is strictly dominated by both schemes for the range of parameters we measured. Decryption time for the nested AES construction depends linearly on the number of re-encryptions that have occurred because decryption needs to remove each layer of encryption to reach the plaintext. As such, it begins much faster than the KH-PRF construction, as it only requires standard symmetric primitives for which hardware acceleration is available, but becomes slower after about 50 re-encryptions. The KH-PRF construction could also vary its performance slightly based on the number of expected re-encryptions by varying the amount of padding applied in the message encoding process. However, we chose to evaluate the scheme with a fixed amount of padding that is enough to support about 128 re-encryptions.

Ciphertext Size. The ciphertext size of a ciphertext-dependent UAE scheme consists of two parts: a fixed-size header and the body, whose size depends on the plaintext. Figure 9 compares ciphertext body expansion between our constructions and ReCrypt. Our KH-PRF based scheme and ReCrypt have 80-Byte headers, while our nested construction has a 116-Byte header. Our KH-PRF based construction is implemented with padding on each block depending on the size $|q|$. For example, a 60-bit block contains 44 bits of plaintext and 16 bits of padding. This corresponds to a 36% ciphertext size expansion. The lowest ciphertext expansion for our evaluation of the KH-PRF based scheme occure when $|q| = 128$, with 19% expansion. ReCrypt has lower ciphertext expansion, at 3%. The ciphertext size of our nested construction depends on the expected number of encryptions. It has a constant 32-Byte overhead on top of the plaintext, followed by another 48 Bytes for each re-encryption. For a 32 kB message, a ReCrypt ciphertext takes 33 kB and a ciphertext under our KH-PRF scheme takes 43.6 kB. A ciphertext under our nested construction will match the size of a ReCrypt ciphertext after 19 re-encryptions. This fits well with a ciphertext that is re-encrypted once a year over a 20-year lifetime. Supporting 128 re-encryptions still only requires a 38.3 kB ciphertext, matching the expansion of the KH-PRF based PRF when $|q| = 128$.

Conclusions. Based on the performance of the schemes we evaluated, we can make the following recommendations:

- If the ciphertext is to be re-encrypted only 10 or 20 times over the course of its lifetime, say once a year for twenty years to satisfy NIST recommendations [7] and PCI DSS [25] requirements, then one should use the nested construction, as it will provide the best performance and ciphertext size. This is especially true of ciphertexts that are decrypted infrequently.
- If the ciphertext is to be re-encrypted more frequently and its age is sensitive information, then Recrypt [15] should be used.
- If the ciphertext is to be re-encrypted frequently, but its age is less sensitive, then our almost KH-PRF based scheme can be used for high performance.

Future Work. We have constructed a performant updatable encryption scheme based on RLWE, but it remains an open problem to construct a UAE scheme from RLWE that satisfies our strongest integrity definition with decryption time independent of ciphertext age. We hope that future work will result in such a construction.

Acknowledgments. This work was funded by NSF, DARPA, a grant from ONR, and the Simons Foundation. Opinions, findings and conclusions or recommendations expressed in this material are those of the authors and do not necessarily reflect the views of DARPA. Part of this work was done while the third author was visiting the Simons Institute for the Theory of Computing as a Ripple Research Fellow.

References

1. Source code repository. https://github.com/moshih/UpdateableEncryption_Code
2. Alamati, N., Montgomery, H., Patranabis, S.: Symmetric primitives with structured secrets. In: Boldyreva, A., Micciancio, D. (eds.) CRYPTO 2019. LNCS, vol. 11692, pp. 650–679. Springer, Cham (2019). https://doi.org/10.1007/978-3-030-26948-7_23
3. Albrecht, M.R., Player, R., Scott, S.: On the concrete hardness of learning with errors. J. Math. Cryptol. **9**(3), 169–203 (2015)
4. Alkim, E., Ducas, L., Pöppelmann, T., Schwabe, P.: Post-quantum key exchange - a new hope. In: USENIX Security (2016)
5. Banerjee, A., Peikert, C.: New and improved key-homomorphic pseudorandom functions. In: Garay, J.A., Gennaro, R. (eds.) CRYPTO 2014. LNCS, vol. 8616, pp. 353–370. Springer, Heidelberg (2014). https://doi.org/10.1007/978-3-662-44371-2_20
6. Banerjee, A., Peikert, C., Rosen, A.: Pseudorandom functions and lattices. In: Pointcheval, D., Johansson, T. (eds.) EUROCRYPT 2012. LNCS, vol. 7237, pp. 719–737. Springer, Heidelberg (2012). https://doi.org/10.1007/978-3-642-29011-4_42
7. Barker, E.: NIST special publication 800–57 part 1 revision 4: recommendation for key management (2016)
8. Bellare, M., Rogaway, P.: Random oracles are practical: a paradigm for designing efficient protocols. In: CCS (1993)
9. Bernstein, D.J.: Curve25519: new Diffie-Hellman speed records. In: Yung, M., Dodis, Y., Kiayias, A., Malkin, T. (eds.) PKC 2006. LNCS, vol. 3958, pp. 207–228. Springer, Heidelberg (2006). https://doi.org/10.1007/11745853_14
10. Boneh, D., Eskandarian, S., Kim, S., Shih, M.: Improving speed and security in updatable encryption schemes. Cryptology ePrint Archive, Report 2020/222 (2020). https://eprint.iacr.org/2020/222
11. Boneh, D., Lewi, K., Montgomery, H., Raghunathan, A.: Key homomorphic PRFs and their applications. In: Canetti, R., Garay, J.A. (eds.) CRYPTO 2013. LNCS, vol. 8042, pp. 410–428. Springer, Heidelberg (2013). https://doi.org/10.1007/978-3-642-40041-4_23
12. Boyd, C., Davies, G.T., Gjøsteen, K., Jiang, Y.: Fast and secure updatable encryption. In: Micciancio, D., Ristenpart, T. (eds.) CRYPTO 2020. LNCS, vol. 12170, pp. 464–493. Springer, Cham (2020). https://doi.org/10.1007/978-3-030-56784-2_16
13. Brakerski, Z., Vaikuntanathan, V.: Constrained key-homomorphic PRFs from standard lattice assumptions. In: Dodis, Y., Nielsen, J.B. (eds.) TCC 2015. LNCS, vol. 9015, pp. 1–30. Springer, Heidelberg (2015). https://doi.org/10.1007/978-3-662-46497-7_1
14. Canetti, R., Krawczyk, H., Nielsen, J.B.: Relaxing chosen-ciphertext security. In: Boneh, D. (ed.) CRYPTO 2003. LNCS, vol. 2729, pp. 565–582. Springer, Heidelberg (2003). https://doi.org/10.1007/978-3-540-45146-4_33

15. Everspaugh, A., Paterson, K., Ristenpart, T., Scott, S.: Key rotation for authenticated encryption. In: Katz, J., Shacham, H. (eds.) CRYPTO 2017. LNCS, vol. 10403, pp. 98–129. Springer, Cham (2017). https://doi.org/10.1007/978-3-319-63697-9_4
16. Fiat, A., Shamir, A.: How to prove yourself: practical solutions to identification and signature problems. In: Odlyzko, A.M. (ed.) CRYPTO 1986. LNCS, vol. 263, pp. 186–194. Springer, Heidelberg (1987). https://doi.org/10.1007/3-540-47721-7_12
17. Google. Key rotation. https://cloud.google.com/kms/docs/key-rotation
18. Hohenberger, S., Lewko, A., Waters, B.: Detecting dangerous queries: a new approach for chosen ciphertext security. In: Pointcheval, D., Johansson, T. (eds.) EUROCRYPT 2012. LNCS, vol. 7237, pp. 663–681. Springer, Heidelberg (2012). https://doi.org/10.1007/978-3-642-29011-4_39
19. Kim, S.: Key-homomorphic pseudorandom functions from LWE with small modulus. In: Canteaut, A., Ishai, Y. (eds.) EUROCRYPT 2020. LNCS, vol. 12106, pp. 576–607. Springer, Cham (2020). https://doi.org/10.1007/978-3-030-45724-2_20
20. Klooß, M., Lehmann, A., Rupp, A.: (R)CCA secure updatable encryption with integrity protection. In: Ishai, Y., Rijmen, V. (eds.) EUROCRYPT 2019. LNCS, vol. 11476, pp. 68–99. Springer, Cham (2019). https://doi.org/10.1007/978-3-030-17653-2_3
21. Lehmann, A., Tackmann, B.: Updatable encryption with post-compromise security. In: Nielsen, J.B., Rijmen, V. (eds.) EUROCRYPT 2018. LNCS, vol. 10822, pp. 685–716. Springer, Cham (2018). https://doi.org/10.1007/978-3-319-78372-7_22
22. Lyubashevsky, V., Peikert, C., Regev, O.: On ideal lattices and learning with errors over rings. In: Gilbert, H. (ed.) EUROCRYPT 2010. LNCS, vol. 6110, pp. 1–23. Springer, Heidelberg (2010). https://doi.org/10.1007/978-3-642-13190-5_1
23. Lyubashevsky, V., Peikert, C., Regev, O.: A toolkit for ring-LWE cryptography. In: Johansson, T., Nguyen, P.Q. (eds.) EUROCRYPT 2013. LNCS, vol. 7881, pp. 35–54. Springer, Heidelberg (2013). https://doi.org/10.1007/978-3-642-38348-9_3
24. Naor, M., Pinkas, B., Reingold, O.: Distributed pseudo-random functions and KDCs. In: Stern, J. (ed.) EUROCRYPT 1999. LNCS, vol. 1592, pp. 327–346. Springer, Heidelberg (1999). https://doi.org/10.1007/3-540-48910-X_23
25. PCI Security Standards Council. Payment card industry data security standard (2018)
26. Regev, O.: On lattices, learning with errors, random linear codes, and cryptography. In: STOC (2005)
27. Seiler, G.: Faster AVX2 optimized NTT multiplication for Ring-LWE lattice cryptography. IACR Cryptology ePrint Archive 2018:39 (2018)

CCA Updatable Encryption Against Malicious Re-encryption Attacks

Long Chen(✉), Yanan Li, and Qiang Tang

New Jersey Institute of Technology, Newark, NJ 07102, USA
{longchen,ly252,qiang}@njit.edu

Abstract. Updatable encryption (UE) is an attractive primitive, which allows the secret key of the outsourced encrypted data to be updated to a fresh one periodically. Several elegant works exist studying various security properties. We notice several major issues in existing security models of (ciphertext dependent) updatable encryption, in particular, integrity and CCA security. The adversary in the models is only allowed to request the server to re-encrypt *honestly* generated ciphertext, while in practice, an attacker could try to inject arbitrary ciphertexts into the server as she wishes. Those malformed ciphertext could be updated and leveraged by the adversary and cause serious security issues.

In this paper, we fill the gap and strengthen the security definitions in multiple aspects: most importantly our integrity and CCA security models remove the restriction in previous models and achieve standard notions of integrity and CCA security in the setting of updatable encryption. Along the way, we refine the security model to capture post-compromise security and enhance the re-encryption indistinguishability to the CCA style. Guided by the new models, we provide a novel construction **ReCrypt**$^+$, which satisfies our strengthened security definitions. The technical building block of homomorphic hash from a group may be of independent interests. We also study the relations among security notions; and a bit surprisingly, the folklore result in authenticated encryption that IND-CPA plus ciphertext integrity imply IND-CCA security does *not* hold for ciphertext dependent updatable encryption.

1 Introduction

Increasingly number of companies, government bodies and personal users choose to store their data on the cloud instead of their local devices. As a public infrastructure, frequent data breaches from the cloud were reported. One potential mitigation is to let the user to upload encrypted data and keep the decryption key locally. However, even if these data are protected by encryption mechanisms, there are still risks that the users' decryption keys get compromised, especially after the key has been in use for a while. It is widely acknowledged (and implemented in industry) that a wiser strategy is to let the user periodically refresh the secret key which is used to protect the data (and update the corresponding ciphertext in the cloud). For instance, the Payment Card Industry Data Security Standard (PCI DSS) [6,13] requires that the credit card data must be stored

S. Moriai and H. Wang (Eds.): ASIACRYPT 2020, LNCS 12493, pp. 590–620, 2020.
https://doi.org/10.1007/978-3-030-64840-4_20

in encrypted form and mandates key rotation, i.e., encrypted data is regularly refreshed from an old to a newly generated key. The similar strategy has also been adopted by many cloud storage providers, such as Google and Amazon [10].

Though we have many standardized encryption tools to use, facilitating key rotation requires care. A naive solution is to let the client download all encrypted data, decrypt, choose a new key, encrypt the data, and upload the new ciphertext to the cloud server. This is obviously too inefficient (e.g.., large communication for big data) to be useful. To efficiently and securely execute the key rotation, Boneh et al. [4] proposed a new primitive called updatable encryption (UE) for efficiently updating ciphertexts with a new key. In such a scheme, a client only needs to retrieve a very *short* piece (called header) of information, and generates a *short* update token that allows the server to re-encrypt the data himself from existing ciphertext, while preserving the security of the encryption. Everspaugh et al. [10] gave a systematic study of UE, especially on the key rotation on *authenticated encryption*, which is the standard practice for encryption. The seemingly paradoxical feature of modifying ciphertext while maintaining integrity is both necessary and conceptually intriguing; more importantly, integrity is as indispensable as confidentiality in secure storage. Very recently, Boneh et al. [3] proposed strengthening on confidentiality and improved the efficiency of [10].

Security of Updatable Encryption in a Nutshell. The security models of updatable encryption mimic those of authenticated encryption (AE) to capture both the confidentiality and integrity of the massage. But a critical difference is that UE wishes to capture the survivability of the system after the server is briefly breached or the client is temporarily hacked. To characterize these attack scenarios, the adversary in the UE model is allowed to view the secret keys in the previous epochs and the current version of the continuously updating ciphertext. And also, other related information generated during the key rotations, such as the update tokens, headers, will also be leaked to the adversary. The only restriction is to rule out the trivial impossibility that the secret key and the ciphertext are both obtained by the attacker simultaneously. Since adversary's strategy could be very diverse, clearly defining the boundary so that the strategies leading to trivial break of the system are disallowed is complex.

In the pioneer work [10], Everspaugh et al. defined an IND-CPA analogous security called UP-IND and a ciphertext integrity (CTXT) analogous security called UP-INT-CTXT. CCA security was not considered at all in [3,10], as in a standard AE scheme, it is well-known that IND-CPA and CTXT imply IND-CCA security. However, given that those security models are fairly complex, we first ask a question *whether such implication still holds in the general ciphertext dependent updatable encryption.*[1]

[1] A very recent work [5] demonstrates this relationship still holds for UE in the ciphertext independent setting, which is a special case for updatable encryption that headers are not needed for update, Both settings have pros and cons [3], which we will discuss in detail in the section of related works. In this paper, we focus on the general ciphertext dependent UE, as [3,4,10].

The Security After the Server Being Compromised. A more serious issue is related to those existing definitions themselves. Compared to the models for AE schemes, the UE models should fully consider the content security when the server is occasionally compromised. As noticed by [14], the previous integrity model UP-INT-CTXT is only against restricted attackers: the attacker is not allowed to ask the server to re-encrypt a *maliciously* formed ciphertexts that is of her choice. Instead, she can only query the re-encryption oracle with honestly generated ciphertext that was received from the challenger via related oracles (e.g.., (re)encryption oracle). Clearly, an adversary could try to inject all kinds of ciphertext into the server and eventually got updated and mixed into the user-supplied ciphertext. Indeed, as Klooß, et al. concluded, both the confidentiality and integrity protections in [10] "*are only guaranteed against passive adversaries*".

Indeed, existing constructions of updatable encryption will become insecure if we allow the *malicious re-encryption queries.* In the full version [9], we provide a concrete example to show an active "attack" on the integrity of the KSS scheme proposed by Everspaugh et al. [10]. It follows that the constructions are vulnerable against active adversaries who try to inject malformed ciphertext, which immediately violates the integrity; and what's worse, such capability could be leveraged to break confidentiality. The situation is the same in [3].

Having noticed the problem, some partial progresses have been made in the ciphertext independent setting [14].[2] In their first construction, they also have the same restriction in both ciphertext integrity and CCA security. In their second construction, they remove the restriction partially, that achieved plaintext integrity and RCCA security (Replayable CCA [7]). It is widely believed that PTXT does not provide a strong enough integrity guarantee for secure storage [20], as the adversary may still be able to generate a ciphertext that was mauled from a target ciphertext. While RCCA has another restriction that a ciphertext generated by re-randomizing a challenge ciphertext is not allowed to query decryption oracle, thus clearly not CCA.

The Security After the Key Being Compromised. Besides characterizing the server breach scenario, how to precisely define the security when the breach occurs on the client side also needs to be crystal clear. The main motivation of updatable encryption is to enable the outsourced storage to "regain" security even the client got temporarily hacked, so long as the system later executes the update process (updating both secret key and ciphertext). However, it has been pointed out in [18] that the security model of [10] is ambiguous regarding whether the adversary is allowed to see a certain version of the challenge ciphertext, which is updated from a ciphertext that was encrypted under a leaked key.

If we look at the example for the model of UP-IND [10] in more detail: the keys are all generated once and there are no clearly defined epochs. Suppose the

[2] As mentioned above and we will discuss further in related work, the security of ciphertext dependent UE are even more involved due to the extra headers and flexible generation of update tokens.

challenge ciphertext c_1^* is first encrypted under k_1. When the adversary queries c_1^*'s update under k_3 after the adversary queries k_2, the challenger will directly re-encrypt the challenge ciphertext c_1^* under k_1 to a ciphertext c_3^* under k_3. During this procedure, the challenge ciphertext has never been updated to some version under the key k_2. More generally, in the model of [10], for all the versions of exposed challenge ciphertext, their previous version were always encrypted under a safe key which has never been exposed. (This is the same in [3]).

But in reality, the server updates sequentially, all ciphertext have been updated from a previous version whose key may be leaked (that's why it is related to post-compromise security). It is possible that the updated ciphertext contains some private information accessible to the key of the prior ciphertext version. Also, the adversary likely pretends as the client to query the header she wants, even including that of challenge ciphertext encrypted under breached keys.

For those reasons, a model that aims to precisely capture post-compromise security was proposed in [18] for the ciphertext independent setting, in which the client generates one update token for all ciphertext. However, it is unclear whether we can adapt straightforwardly the security from ciphertext independent setting to the more general ciphertext dependent setting. In the former, there was no headers involved, and one update token will be used to update all ciphertext; while in the latter, a more careful treatment is needed to deal with those headers and ciphertext specific update tokens.

1.1 Our Contributions

In this paper, we give a systematic study of standard ciphertext integrity and security notions against CCA attacks, in the general setting of ciphertext dependent updatable encryption (CDUE). We summarize our results with comparison with previous work in Table 1.

Table 1. Comparison of properties of existing UE schemes. CD/CI means ciphertext dependent/independent respectively; CCA^- and CTXT^- means the models that disallow malicious re-encryption queries.

Scheme	Update Manner	Conf.	Integrity	ReEnc IND
BLMR [4]	CD	CPA	No	CPA
KSS [10]	CD	CPA	CTXT^-	$\perp$
ReCrypt [10]	CD	CPA	CTXT^-	CPA
Nested UAE[3]	CD	CPA	CTXT^-	CPA
KH-PRF UAE [3]	CD	CPA	CTXT^-	CPA
RISE [18]	CI	CPA	No	CPA
E& M [14]	CI	CCA^-	CTXT^-	CPA
NYUE [14]	CI	RCCA	PTXT	CPA
SHINE [5]	CI	CCA^-	CTXT^-	CCA^-
ReCrypt$^+$	CD	CCA	CTXT	CCA

Security Models and Relations. We provide a new model combination *strengthened* UP-IND-CCA (sUP-IND-CCA) and *strengthened* UP-INT-CTXT (sUP-INT-CTXT) to characterize both the confidentiality and the integrity of CDUE. Comparing the combination of UP-IND and UP-INT suggested in [3,10], our model strengthens the security in following aspects.

- We capture the active adversary who can query the re-encryption oracle with maliciously generated ciphertexts in confidentiality and ciphertext integrity models (CPA, CCA and CTXT). To demonstrate the practical security improvement in our models, we also show an "attack" on the KSS scheme [10] when facing malicious re-encryption in the full version [9].
- We use the notion of epoch from [18] in both the confidentiality and integrity models, to capture the post-compromise security. As noted before, we need to carefully deal with the headers, and flexibly generated update tokens in ciphertext dependent setting. We added two more oracles to give a more fine-grained characterization. $\mathcal{O}_{\mathsf{Next}}(\cdot)$ is used to force the challenger to update, and $\mathcal{O}_{\mathsf{Header}}(i)$ is used to respond with the header of challenge ciphertext in epoch i (updated from previous epoches). In the full version [9], we provide a variation of KSS scheme from [10] which fails to achieve post-compromise security, but was proven secure in the existing model.
- Interestingly, after clearly defining the CPA, CCA and CTXT securities, we show that in contrast with the conventional wisdom in AE, IND-CPA security + CTXT security do *not* imply IND-CCA security in the setting of ciphertext dependent UE. Note that the CCA attack on our counter example holds with or without malicious re-encryption. That means we have to study both IND-CCA security and CTXT security in ciphertext dependent UE.
- As a byproduct, we also consider CCA style of re-encryption indistinguishability, which is to capture update unlinkability. We defer details regarding this part to the full version [9].

Construction. With the strengthened security models at hand, we set force to construct a (ciphertext dependent) updatable encryption named **ReCrypt**$^+$, which can be proven secure under our sUP-IND-CCA, sUP-INT-CTXT and sUP-REENC-CCA models. Our starting point is the **Recrypt** scheme in [10], which already has the basic confidentiality and integrity. The existing attacks reminded us several main challenges: first we need to ensure that the update procedure is as "independent" as possible so that post-compromise security can be achieved; next major challenge is how to mute the malicious re-encryption attacks. Intuitively, the validity of ciphertexts must be checked before updating. Here is the dilemma: the server does not have the secret key, thus have to rely on the assistance of the client to do the checking. But the client only sees the short header during the key rotation.

Let us walk through the subtleties and our ideas. **ReCrypt** follows the standard Key Encapsulation Mechanism (KEM) + Data Encapsulation Mechanism (DEM) with secret sharing. Specifically, its header is a KEM $\mathsf{Kem}(k, x)$ for the DEM key share x under the master key k, and the body is with the form $(y, \mathsf{Dem}(x \oplus y, m))$ for the DEM key share y and the DEM of the message m. During the key rotation, the header (i.e. $\mathsf{Kem}(k, x)$) will be sent back to the client. We can instantiate the KEM via an authenticated encryption. Hence the validity of the header part can be directly verified by the client who holds the master key. However, the main challenge remains as validity check of the ciphertext body still has to be carried out on the server side.

A Naive Attempt. A naive suggestion is to hash all the ciphertext body can include the digest into the header plaintext. The client will use the AE to check whether the header is intact, and include the digest in the update token, so that the server can check the body. This has two major problems: first, it immediately kills the possibility for efficient update; moreover, such a method may not be sure: when the server notices the invalidity of the ciphertext after receiving the decrypted digest from the client, the update token has already been sent out. The server may stop re-encryption, but the adversary who obtains the update token may already be able to infer useful information.

Enable Validity Checking. To facilitate efficient update and checking, we would need a "hash" that satisfies the following: (1) it compresses the ciphertext body, otherwise the header would be too long; (2) it is "binding", so that the server can check the digest and ciphertext body; (3) it is partially hiding: as the secret key of previous epoch might be leaked, combining with part of the ciphertext may lead to the exposure of some master key; (4) it satisfies certain key homomorphism so that efficient update could be facilitated. Using a commitment scheme will not be compressing; while using a collision resistant hash may not be hiding. We proceeds in two steps: the key share y needs to be protected, thus it will be committed to c_y using a homomorphic commitment scheme; while the payload carrying the actual encrypted data will be compressed into a short digest h with a homomorphic collision resistant hash. $c_y||h$ will be the derived digest.

Avoid Dangerous Update Token. Regarding the second problem, either the server or the client should be able to detect the invalidity of ciphertext *before* the update token has been generated! To facilitate such verifiability, we put $c_y||h$ as the associated data to encrypt them together with the key share in the header using authenticated encryption with associated data. We emphasize that encrypting the digest using AE directly (without putting them in plain as well) will be problematic, as now the server cannot check first, adversary may inject a header which is not bound to the ciphertext body, e.g., taking from a previous ciphertext. Now the client cannot detect and will generate the update token.

Homomorphically Hash from a Group. One more subtlety remains, as the above verification ideas have not considered how to be compatible with the re-encryption. Specifically, **ReCrypt** updates the DEM part via the key homomorphic pseudorandom functions (KH-PHF) [4]. When the DEM part is updated by adding new KH-PRF values, we wish that the hash value of the DEM part, which is included in the header, can be updated by the client conveniently according to those KH-PRF values. Therefore, we design a new homomorphic collision resistant hash function, whose domain needs to match the range of the KH-PRF which is some particular groups instead of binary strings. Specifically, we construct such homomorphic hash functions from the asymmetric bilinear maps $e : \mathbb{G}_1 \times \mathbb{G}_2 \to \mathbb{G}_T$. The KH-PRF could be constructed over $\mathbb{G}_1$, where the DDH problem is hard.

1.2 Related Works

Two Flavors of Updatable Encryption. As we briefly mentioned above, in many of the updatable encryption schemes, during the key rotation, the client would first retrieve a small piece of the ciphertext (called header), and then generates a update token. Such kind of UE is called ciphertext dependent UE [3, 4, 10], (CDUE in short). On the other hand, one may insist that the client directly generates the update token. Such a UE scheme is called ciphertext independent UE [5,14,18] (CIUE in short).

Though ciphertext independent UE saves one round of communication, the header is normally extremely short in ciphertext dependent UE. More importantly, since in a ciphertext dependent UE, the client can generate update token based on each ciphertext header, this gives a fine-grained control over updating procedure and security: the client could choose to update only part of the ciphertext, and leakage of some token does not influence other ciphertext.

As discussed in detail in previous work [3], there are both pros and cons for these two flavors of UE, and the different updating paradigms yield different security definitions, applications and construction strategies. In this article, we focus on ciphertext dependent schemes, and fill the gap exists in integrity and CCA security. We also refer to the full version [9] for more detailed comparisons.

Other Related Works. The first updatable encryption scheme (**BLMR**) is proposed by Boneh et al. [4]. However, only the confidentiality is considered in this work, and the other security notions have not been formalized. Later, Everspaugh et al.[10] provided a systematic study of updatable encryption in the ciphertext dependent setting, as we discussed, they did not allow malicious re-encryption in integrity and CPA notions, which are the main objective of this paper. Very recently, Boneh et al. [3] revisit the results of Everspaugh et al. about CDUE. Their security notion is similar to [10], and they did not consider the post-compromise security and the malicious update resistance. Moreover, **Nested UAE** can only proceed the key rotation with bounded number of times.

Lehmann and Tackmann [18] point out the models UP-IND and UP-REENC in [10] are hard to capture the post compromise security. So they provide the models (IND-ENC and IND-UPD) and the construction (**RISE**) with the post-compromise security. Recently, Klooß et al. [14] add the integrity considerations to [18], and provide two constructions (**E&M** without malicious update resistance and **NYUE** with only plaintext integrity and the weaker RCCA security).

Boy et al. [5] first formally prove that for CIUE without malicious update, the folklore relationship in authenticated encryption that the combination of CPA and CTXT security yields CCA security still holds. However, the relationship for CDUE remains open.

2 Preliminary

Here we describe several primitives that will be used in our construction.

Authenticated-Encryption with Associated-Data Authenticated encryption with associated-data (AEAD) is a variant of authenticated encryption (AE) that allows a recipient to check the integrity of both the encrypted and unencrypted information in a message. AEAD binds associated data (AD) to the ciphertext and to the context where it is supposed to appear so that attempts to "cut-and-paste" a valid ciphertext into a different context are detected and rejected. Specifically, an AEAD scheme consists of following three algorithms:

- $\mathsf{KeyGen}(1^\lambda)$ takes the security parameter λ as input, and outputs the secret key k.
- $\mathsf{Enc}(k, m, ad)$ takes the secret key k, a message m and the associated data ad as inputs, and outputs the ciphertext c.
- $\mathsf{Dec}(k, c, ad)$: take the secret key k, a ciphertext c and the associate data ad as inputs, and outputs the decrypted message m or the symbol $\perp$ to denote the decryption failure.

For the detailed security definition, we refer to the full version [9].

Commitment. A commitment scheme $\mathbf{Com} = \{\mathsf{Init}, \mathsf{Com}, \mathsf{Open}\}$ consists of three following algorithms: Init is used to generate the public parameter; Com outputs a commitment value *com* from a message m, while Open will check whether the commitment *com* is bound to the message m. A commitment scheme should satisfy both the *hiding* and *binding* properties. The hiding property requires the distributions of the commitment values for different messages can not be distinguished by the adversary, while the binding property requires the commitment value can not be opened to two different messages.

Some commitment schemes, such as the Pederson commitment [22], also satisfy the homomorphic property, which are called the homomorphic commitment. Specifically, the message space, the randomness opening space and the commitment values are all defined over additives group $\mathbb{G}_1$, $\mathbb{G}_2$ and $\mathbb{G}_3$ respect to the operations $\oplus$, $\odot$ and $\otimes$. The commitment scheme satisfies $\mathsf{Com}(m_1, open_1) \otimes \mathsf{Com}(m_2, open_2) = \mathsf{Com}(m_1 \oplus m_2, open_1 \odot open_2)$.

Key-Homomorphic Pusedorandom Function. The notion of key-homomorphic PRFs was proposed by Boneh et al. [4], and used in the UE constructions [10,18]. Specifically, a key-homomorphic PRF $F : \mathcal{K} \times \mathcal{X} \rightarrow \mathcal{Y}$ is a secure psedorandom function which satisfy the following property: for every $k_1, k_2 \in \mathcal{K}$, and every $x \in \mathcal{X}$: $\mathsf{F}(k_1, x) \otimes \mathsf{F}(k_2, x) = \mathsf{F}((k_1 \oplus k_2), x)$ where $\otimes$ and $\oplus$ are group operations respect to $\mathcal{K}$ and $\mathcal{Y}$. One example construction is to define as $y = H(x)^x$ where $H(\cdot)$ is a random oracle from a bit string to a group element.

3 Formalization

In this section, we formalize the syntax of the ciphertext dependent updatable encryption scheme following [10].

Intuitively, the data flow of the outsource storage from CDUE can be seen in Fig. 1. With loss of generality, we divide the whole storage period into multiple time epochs. At the beginning of the storage, the client generates a secret key k_0 for the epoch 0, encrypts his file m with the key k_0, and outsources the initial ciphertext $C_0 = \left(\tilde{C}_0, \bar{C}_0\right)$ to the server. Here $\tilde{C}_0$ is the header and $\bar{C}_0$ is the body. After a specific epoch e, the serve will send back the header $\tilde{C}_e$. The client will generate a new key k_{e+1}, compute a token $\Delta_{e,\tilde{C}_e}$ and send it back to the server. The server will update the old ciphertext C_e to the new one C_{e+1} with the token $\Delta_{e,\tilde{C}_e}$. Formally, we have the following definition.

Definition 1 (Updatable Encryption). *The ciphertext dependent updatable encryption (CDUE) consists of the following six algorithms*

$$\textbf{\textit{CDUE}} = (\textsf{Setup}, \textsf{KeyGen}, \textsf{Encrypt}, \textsf{Decrypt}, \textsf{ReKeyGen}, \textsf{Recrypt}).$$

- $\textsf{Setup}(1^\lambda)$ *is a randomized algorithm run by the client. It takes the security parameter* λ *as input and outputs the public parameter pp which will be shared with the server. Later all algorithms take pp as input implicitly.*
- $\textsf{KeyGen}(e)$ *is a randomized algorithm run by the client. It takes the epoch index* e *as input and outputs a secret key* k_e *for the epoch* e.
- $\textsf{Encrypt}(k_e, m)$ *is a randomized algorithm run by the client. It takes the secret key* k_e *and the message* m *as inputs, and outputs the ciphertext* $C_e = (\tilde{C}_e, \bar{C}_e)$ *which consists of two parts, i.e., the header* $\tilde{C}_e$ *and the body* $\bar{C}_e$.
- $\textsf{Decrypt}(k_e, C_e)$ *is a deterministic algorithm run by the client. It takes the secret key* k_e *and the ciphertext* C_e *as inputs, and outputs the message* m *or the symbol* $\perp$.
- $\textsf{ReKeyGen}\ (k_e, k_{e+1}, \tilde{C}_e)$ *is a randomized algorithm run by the client. It takes the header* $\tilde{C}_e$*, the old secret key* k_e *of the last epoch and the new secret key* k_{e+1} *of the current epoch as inputs, and generates a re-encrypt token* $\Delta_{e,\tilde{C}}$ *or outputs the symbol* $\perp$.
- $\textsf{Recrypt}(\Delta_{e,\tilde{C}_e}, C_e)$ *is a deterministic algorithm run by the server. It takes the re-encrypt token* $\Delta_{e,\tilde{C}_e}$ *and the ciphertext* $C_e = (\tilde{C}_e, \bar{C}_e)$ *as inputs, and*

outputs a new ciphertext $C_{e+1} = \left(\tilde{C}_{e+1}, \bar{C}_{e+1}\right)$ *under the secret key* k_{e+1} *or the symbol* $\perp$.

Note that the above formalization is tailored to our ciphertext integrity definition. Particularly, here we require the algorithm Recrypt to be deterministic. It is because, if the server is allowed to randomly re-encrypt the ciphertext given the token and the header, a malicious server may run this procedure more than one time, and get multiple (maybe exponentially large number of) versions of the updated ciphertext. Consequently, this makes the challenger to track the trivially obtained ciphertext in the CTXT game extremely difficult. Moreover, such a restriction of the syntax has little impact on the construction, since the algorithm Recrypt is deterministic for almost all existing CDUE schemes [3,10].

Besides, the syntax of the CIUE scheme can be viewed as a special case of the ciphertext dependent scheme in Definition 1 when choosing a dummy header, although its security definition may be different. In this case, the server has no need to send the header back, and the update token is generated from the old and new keys directly.

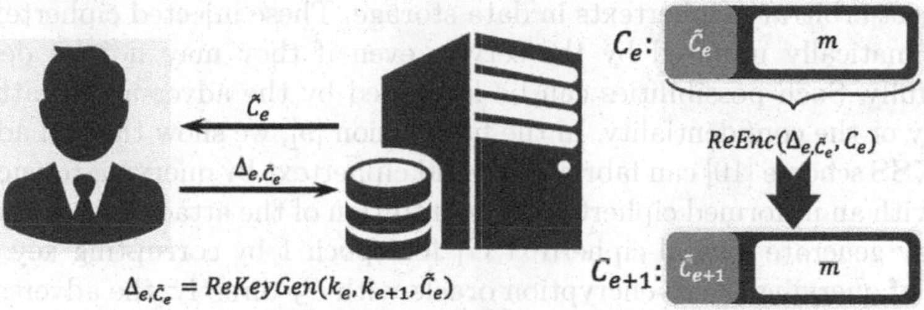

Fig. 1. The data flow between client and cloud during the key update of the ciphertext $C_e = \left(\tilde{C}_e, \bar{C}_e\right)$ for the epoch e. The client receives a small ciphertext header $\tilde{C}_e$, and runs ReKeyGen to produce a compact update token $\Delta_{e,\tilde{C}_e}$. The server uses this token to re-encrypt the ciphertext C_e to C_{e+1}.

Correctness. We define the correctness of CDUE if the ciphertext can still be correctly decrypted after arbitrary times of key update. Specifically, we have the following formal defintion.

Definition 2 (Correctness). *For an updatable encryption scheme* **CDUE**, *each epoch key* k_i *is generated by* **CDUE**.KeyGen(i) *for epoches from* 0 *to* e. *For a message* m *and any integer* i *such that* $0 \le i \le e$, *let* $c_i \leftarrow$ **CDUE**.Encrypt(k_i, m) *and recursively define for* $i < j \le e$,

$$\Delta_{j-1,\tilde{C}_{j-1}} \leftarrow \mathsf{ReKeyGen}\left(k_{j-1}, k_j, \tilde{C}_{j-1}\right),$$

$$C_j \leftarrow \mathsf{Recrypt}\left(\Delta_{j-1,\tilde{C}_{j-1}}, C_{j-1}\right).$$

Then ***CDUE*** *is correct if* $\Pr[\boldsymbol{CDUE}.\mathit{Decrypt}(k_e, C_e) = m] = 1$ *for any message* m*, any integer* e *and any integer* i *such that* $0 \leq i \leq e$.

Compactness. We say that a CDUE scheme is compact if the size of total communications between client and server during update is independent of the length of the plaintext. In practice, the compactness guarantees that the communication cost for the key update procedure is efficient.

4 Strengthened Security Models

In this section, we systematically study the security definitions of the CDUE. As we explained in the introduction, the previous model combination UP-IND + UP-INT [3,10] needs to be strengthened in multiple aspects.

Malicious Re-encryption Attack. All previous CDUE definitions [3,10] did not consider malicious re-encryption threats, particularly for integrity, i.e. the adversary may query *maliciously generated* ciphertexts to the re-encryption oracle. However, a real-world adversary who can temporarily compromise the server may inject arbitrary ciphertexts in data storage. These injected ciphertexts may be automatically updated by the server, even if they may not be decrypted successfully. Such possibilities can be leveraged by the adversary to attack the integrity or the confidentiality. In the full version [9], we show that an adversary of the **KSS** scheme [10] can fabricate a valid ciphertext by querying re-encryption oracle with an ill-formed ciphertext. The intuition of the attack is that the adversary may generate a valid ciphertext C_1 for epoch 1 by corrupting key k_1. But instead of querying the re-encryption oracle with C_1 directly, the adversary may query with a invalid ciphertext $C_1' = f(C_1)$ which is a modification of C_1' via certain operation f. After getting an updated ciphertext C_2' (which is still invalid), the adversary can recover a valid ciphertext C_2 from C_2' though an inverse operation f^{-1}. More importantly, since C_2 is not directly generated via querying the re-encryption oracle or the encryption oracle, and the epoch key k_2 has not been corrupted, C_2 will be considered as a legitimate forgery in the CTXT game!

Post-compromise Security. The security model in [3,10], as discussed in [18], is hard to capture the post compromise security. More precisely, the UP-IND model is ambiguous that whether the adversary is allowed to view certain version of the challenge ciphertext updated from a key corrupt epoch. We gave exemplary explanations in the introduction. and we will give a concrete example in [9] to show a scheme proved secure under UP-IND model, but can be attacked by a real world adversary. As pointed by Lehmann and Tackmann in [18], this ambiguity is caused by the missing of the epoch notion in UP-IND. The integrity model UP-INT has a similar problem. Of course, the definition is more involved as we also need to consider the leaked headers, and flexible generation of tokens.

Chosen Ciphertext Attack. The chosen ciphertext attack is a real threat to a UE system. One the one hand, a malicious server may choose an arbitrary ciphertext to answer the retrieve query of the client, and learn the information about the decryption result later on from side channels (e.g.. the server may easily learn whether the decryption is successful according the response of the client.); on the other hand, temporary breaches of the client's device may happen occasionally. Although the secret key may not be easy to steal due to the limit of time, the adversary may use the compromised device as an decryption oracle. Nevertheless, the previous models for CDUE in [3,10] have not considered the chosen ciphertext attack. One may hope that UP-IND plus UP-INT can imply a CCA style security analogous to the AE setting, but such a relation have never been proved for UE. We will show soon that it turns out to be false!

In the following, we formally define our strengthened security models for CDUE: for confidentiality, we provide the sUP-IND-CCA model; for integrity, we provide the sUP-INT-CTXT model; for re-encryption indistinguishability, we provide the sUP-REENC-CCA model in the full version [9]. Moreover, we also provide the sUP-IND-CPA model without the decryption oracle for completeness, and show a counter example where a CDUE scheme is sUP-IND-CPA and sUP-INT-CTXT but not sUP-IND-CCA secure. That inspires us that the corresponding model relation is different with the case for authenticated encryption.

4.1 Confidentiality

Now we start from the confidentiality, and describe models strengthened UP-IND-CPA and strengthened UP-IND-CCA (sUP-IND-CPA and sUP-IND-CCA for short) which mimic the standard CPA and CCA model of AE. In these models, the key is evolving with the epochs. Beside the challenge ciphertext and the encryption/decryption oracle, the adversary is additionally allowed to obtain keys of some epochs. This captures that the client's keys are leaked. Also the adversary has the ability to get some previous versions of the challenge ciphertexts and update tokens. This captures that previous storage in the server may not be securely erased in time. To exclude the trivial impossibility, we disallow the adversary to learn a version of the challenge ciphertext and corrupt the key *within the same epoch.* However, the adversary is always allowed to see the header of any updated version of the original challenge ciphertext, even getting its body is forbidden. This is because the adversary may pretend the client in front of the server and ask the header[3].

Note that our models sUP-IND-CPA and sUP-IND-CCA have fully considered that the cases that the adversary may compromise the server during some epoch and read its memory or tamper some ciphertexts. So we allow the adversary to query the re-encryption oracle with maliciously generated ciphertexts. However, the key update procedure should follow the instructions of the UE

[3] In the real world, the communication between a client and a server is typically via TLS without the user authentication [16], since the client does not have a PKI certificate. Therefore pretending the client in front of the server is not difficult.

scheme, i.e., the server will recover at the end of the epoch and *honestly execute the key rotation instructions*. The assumption is inevitable for UE, since no UE scheme can achieve the basic security if a fully malicious server refuses to execute the update operation. In practice, a benign server can quickly detect the invasion by the intrusion detection systems (IDSs), recover from the breach in time before the next key rotation with a high probability.

Experiment Structure. We first describe the structure of the confidentiality game in Fig. 2, and explain in detail how the oracles are defined right after Definition 3. As mentioned above, we also introduce the epoch notion to denote the time sequence following [18]. We index every epoch in the experiments according to its order from 0, and record the index of the current epoch with variable e. Note that in our game the challenge ciphertexts are automatically updated when moving to the next epoch. This enables us to provide to the adversary some updated versions of the challenge ciphertext which are indeed updated from an epoch in which the key is corrupted, as well as the header of the version of the challenge ciphertext in the key corrupted epoch, thus our model easily captures the post-compromise security (which was ambiguous in existing models).

sUP-IND-ATK $Exp^{\mathcal{A}}_{\mathsf{sUP\text{-}IND\text{-}ATK}}(\lambda)$

$pp \leftarrow_{\$} \mathsf{Setup}(\lambda)$, Initialize $e, \mathbb{K}, \mathbb{IC}, \mathbb{KC}, \mathbb{TO}, \mathbb{CE}$

$k_0 \leftarrow \mathsf{KeyGen}(pp)$, $\mathbb{K}(0) \leftarrow k_0$

$(m_0, m_1, state) \leftarrow_{\$} \mathcal{A}^{\mathcal{O}_1}$

Procced only if $|m_0| = |m_1|$

$b \leftarrow_{\$} \{0,1\}$, $C^* \leftarrow \mathsf{Encrypt}(k_e, m_b)$, Set $\mathbb{CE}(e) \leftarrow C^*$

$b' \leftarrow_{\$} \mathcal{A}^{\mathcal{O}_2}(state)$

for $i = 1$ *to* e

  if $\mathbb{KC}(i) = \mathsf{true} \wedge \mathbb{IC}(i) = \mathsf{true}$ **then return** $\perp$

return $(b' == b)$

Fig. 2. The sUP-IND-ATK experiment, where ATK could be CPA or CCA. When ATK is CPA, $\mathcal{O}_1 := (\mathcal{O}_{\mathsf{Enc}}, \mathcal{O}_{\mathsf{Next}}, \mathcal{O}_{\mathsf{KeyCorrupt}}, \mathcal{O}_{\mathsf{ReEnc}}, \mathcal{O}_{\mathsf{Token}})$ and $\mathcal{O}_2 := (\mathcal{O}_{\mathsf{Enc}}, \mathcal{O}_{\mathsf{Next}}, \mathcal{O}_{\mathsf{KeyCorrupt}}, \mathcal{O}_{\mathsf{ReEnc}}, \mathcal{O}_{\mathsf{Token}}, \mathcal{O}_{\mathsf{Header}}, \mathcal{O}_{\mathsf{ChallengeCT}})$. When ATK is CCA, $\mathcal{O}_1$ additionally includes $\mathcal{O}_{\mathsf{Dec}}$ and $\mathcal{O}_2$ additionally includes $\mathcal{O}_{\mathsf{Dec}}$.

Definition 3 (sUP-IND-CPA(CCA)). *Define the sUP-IND-CPA(CCA) experiment as Fig. 2 where ATK is CPA(CCA). An updatable encryption scheme is called sUP-IND-CPA(CCA) secure if for any P.P.T adversary $\mathcal{A}$ the advantage*

$$Adv_{\mathcal{A}}^{sUP\text{-}IND\text{-}CPA(CCA)} := \left| \Pr[Exp^{\mathcal{A}}_{\mathit{Adaptive\ UE\text{-}CPA}}(\lambda) \Rightarrow 1] - \frac{1}{2} \right|$$

is negligible for the security parameter λ.

As explained before, our sUP-IND-CPA(CCA) strengthen previous confidentiality model in aspects of the malicious update resistance and the post-compromise security. Also. the sUP-IND-CCA strengthens the security against chosen ciphertext attack. To more clearly elaborate this claim, next we will describe the behaviour of the challenger during the game in detail. Especially, we will show how the challenge to maintain his internal states and answer each queries of the adversary.

The Internal State of the Challenger. During the games, with respect to the adversary's behaviour and the key evolution, the challenger will maintain and update the following tables to keep track of the overall state, which will be used to rule out the trivial impossibility. The rows of each table are indexed by the epoch indices.

Special cares are needed for those tables related to challenge ciphertexts. To explain, we call the ciphertexts that are updated from the challenge ciphertext *challenge-equal* ciphertexts. There is at least one challenge-equal ciphertext for every epoch since the challenge epoch. And the adversary can choose to view the challenge-equal ciphertext in any key-uncorrupted epoch and the header of the challenge-equal ciphertext in any key-corrupted epoch (via concrete oracles defined below). Note that our model does not limit to repeat querying the $\mathcal{O}_{\mathsf{ReEnc}}$ oracle with the challenge ciphertext and the challenge-equal ciphertext. Since the ReKeyGen algorithm (hence the ciphertext update procedure) could be randomize, the adversary can acquire multiple the challenge-equal ciphertexts of the same epoch.

As previous models [3,10], we also consider static key corruption, which means that the adversary is required to commit whether he will corrupt the key of the current epoch in advance before the challenger generating this epoch key, computing the tokens and updating all the ciphertexts to this epoch.

- Table $\mathbb{K}$ is used to record the secret key of every epoch, each entry is the secret key k_i of epoch i. All entries of $\mathbb{K}$ are initialized as $\perp$.
- Table $\mathbb{KC}$ is used to keep track of the adversary's commitments about the key corruption. Each entry is one Boolean value $b \in \{\mathsf{true}, \mathsf{false}\}$. When an epoch i begins, the static adversary needs to set $\mathbb{KC}(i)$ as true or false, which denotes her commitment about whether the secret key of that epoch i can be corrupted in the game.
- Table $\mathbb{CE}$ is used to record all the challenge-equal ciphertexts during the experiment. Specifically, each entry $\mathbb{CE}(i)$ contains all the challenge-equal ciphertexts of the corresponding epoch. All the ciphertexts are updated to the current epoch automatically with key update. All entries will be initially set as $\perp$ during the experiment.
- Table $\mathbb{TO}$ is used to keep track of the event that a token related to challenge-equal ciphertext is corrupted. Specifically, the i-th entry is one Boolean value $b \in \{\mathsf{true}, \mathsf{false}\}$. Here $\mathbb{TO}(i+1) = \mathsf{true}$ denotes that the following event has happened during the game: a valid token updating *any* one challenge-equal

ciphertext from epoch i to epoch $i+1$ has been queried by the adversary. All entries will be initially set as false during the experiment.
- Table $\mathbb{IC}$ is used to keep track of the event of the adversary's corruption of the challenge-equal ciphertexts. Specifically, each entry i contains one Boolean value $b \in \{\mathsf{true}, \mathsf{false}\}$. Here $\mathbb{IC}(i) = \mathsf{true}$ means the following event has happened during the game: there are certain challenge-equal ciphertext in the epoch i has been learned by adversary via different oracles (to be defined below) directly or indirectly. Note that there may be multiple challenge-equal ciphertexts for one epoch due the randomized key update procedure. Here we make $\mathbb{IC}(i) = \mathsf{true}$ if *anyone* of the challenge-equal ciphertexts for epoch i is leaked to the adversary. All entries will be set false when the game starts.

Oracles of the Adversary. We now formally define the queries that adversary is allowed to ask. Note that the epoch variable e will automatically increase during the game, and the key and the challenge-equal ciphertexts are automatically updated accordingly. This procedure is triggered by the oracle $\mathcal{O}_{\mathsf{Next}}$. Hence the challenge-equal ciphertexts will be updated to the key-corrupted epochs, and the adversary can see their headers but not bodies. This feature helps us to go beyond the restriction of the models in [10], and capture post compromise security. Also note that we allow the adversary to query $\mathcal{O}_{\mathsf{ReEnc}}$ with maliciously generated ciphertexts, and $\mathcal{O}_{\mathsf{ReEnc}}$ may return $\perp$ if the ReKeyGen and Recrypt algorithms include a invalid ciphertext detection mechanism. Similarly, $\mathcal{O}_{\mathsf{Token}}$ may reply $\perp$ when queried with an invalid header.

- *Turn to next epoch oracle* $\mathcal{O}_{\mathsf{Next}}(b)$: This oracle is to used to inform the challenger to evolve to the next epoch $e+1$, and update all challenge-equal ciphertexts in table $\mathbb{CE}(e)$ to the epoch $e+1$. Specifically, the input of the oracle $\mathcal{O}_{\mathsf{Next}}$ is a bit b which denotes whether the epoch key k_{e+1} will be corrupted later on, the challenger will record $\mathbb{KC}(e+1) = b$ in the key corruption table. Moreover, the challenger runs $\mathsf{KeyGen}(pp)$ to produce a new key k_{e+1} for the new epoch $e+1$ and sets $\mathbb{K}(e+1) = k$ in the key record table. For each challenge-equal ciphertext $C_e = (\tilde{c}_e, \bar{c}_e) \in \mathbb{CE}(e)$ (if the challenge-equal ciphertext table $\mathbb{CE}(e)$ is not empty), run the token generation algorithm $\Delta_{e,e+1,\tilde{c}} \leftarrow_\$ \mathsf{ReKeyGen}(k_e, k_{e+1}, \tilde{c}_e)$ and the update algorithm $C' \leftarrow \mathsf{Recrypt}(\Delta_{e,e+1,\tilde{c}_e}, C_e)$ for each ciphertext and import all the updated ciphertexts to the row $\mathbb{CE}(e)$. Finally, the challenger updates the current epoch variable e by adding one as $e \leftarrow e+1$.
- *Encrypt oracle* $\mathcal{O}_{\mathsf{Enc}}(m)$: This oracle is used to ask the challenger to encrypt a message m under the current epoch key. The challenger will run $C \leftarrow \mathsf{Encrypt}(k_e, m)$ and return the ciphertext C to the adversary.
- *Decrypt oracle* $\mathcal{O}_{\mathsf{Dec}}(C)$: This oracle is to ask the challenger to decrypt ciphertext C under the current epoch key. When queried with a ciphertext C, the challenger will check the table $\mathbb{CE}$ to identify whether C could be a challenge-equal ciphertext. If $C \notin \mathbb{CE}(i)$ for i from 0 to e, the challenger will run the algorithm $m \leftarrow \mathsf{Decrypt}(k_e, C)$ to decrypt C with current key k_e and return

m to the adversary; otherwise, return $\perp$. This is to avoid the trivial attack that the adversary may query $\mathcal{O}_{\mathsf{Dec}}$ on a challenge-equal ciphertext.

- *Key corrupt oracle* $\mathcal{O}_{\mathsf{KeyCorrupt}}(i)$: This oracle is used to corrupt the keys for previous epochs. Note that in our static model the adversary is only allowed to corrupt the key that he has committed before. When queried the epoch index i, the challenger checks the key corruption commit table $\mathbb{KC}(i)$ at first. If $\mathbb{KC}(i) = \mathsf{true}$, the challenger returns the secret key k_i of the epoch i. Otherwise, he returns $\perp$.
- *Token corrupt oracle* $\mathcal{O}_{\mathsf{Token}}(i, \tilde{c})$: The adversary is allowed to query this oracle to obtain update tokens. When queried with an epoch index i and the corresponding ciphertext header $\tilde{c}$, the challenger will run the token generation algorithm $\Delta_{i,i+1,\tilde{c}} \leftarrow\!\!\$\ \mathsf{ReKeyGen}(k_i, k_{i+1}, \tilde{c})$, and return the token $\Delta_{i,i+1,\tilde{c}}$ to the adversary. If $\Delta_{i,i+1,\tilde{c}} \neq \perp$ and the header $\tilde{c}$ has even appeared in $\mathbb{CE}(i)$, the challenger will update the token corruption table $\mathbb{TO}$, the challenge-equal ciphertext table $\mathbb{CE}$ and the challenge-equal ciphertext corruption table $\mathbb{IC}$ accordingly.
  - The challenger sets $\mathbb{TO}(i+1)$ as true to mark the event that some update token of certain challenge-equal ciphertexts for epoch i has been leaked to the adversary.
  - The challenger automatically updates all the challenge-equal ciphertexts with header same to $\tilde{c}$ in $\mathbb{CE}(i)$ from epoch i to the current epoch e. Particularly, the challenger iteratively runs $\mathsf{ReKeyGen}$ and $\mathsf{Recrypt}$ algorithm to update these ciphertexts by epoch, while archiving all generated challenge-equal ciphertexts along the way to the corresponding rows of $\mathbb{CE}$.
  - Update the table $\mathbb{IC}$ to mark the epochs in which the adversary may see challenge-equal ciphertexts as follows: for each ℓ from i to e, if $\mathbb{IC}(\ell) \wedge \mathbb{TO}(\ell+1) = \mathsf{true}$, then set $\mathbb{IC}(\ell+1)$ set as true. Moreover, for most existing CDUE schemes [3,10], given the updated ciphertext in the second epoch, the corresponding token from the first epoch to the second epoch, and the header of ciphertext in the first epoch, it is not difficult to recover the complete ciphertext in the second epoch. This property is called the *bi-directional update* by Everspauph et al., which also should be taken into consideration for the game winning condition. Hence for any ℓ decreasing from $i+1$ to 0, if $\mathbb{IC}(\ell) \wedge \mathbb{TO}(\ell) = \mathsf{true}$, we let the challenger set $\mathbb{IC}(\ell-1)$ as true.
- *Challenge-equal ciphertexts' header oracle* $\mathcal{O}_{\mathsf{Header}}\,(i)$: This oracle is used to acquire the header of the challenge-equal ciphertext in the key corrupted epoch i. When queried with the epoch index i, the challenger will return all the headers of the challenge-equal ciphertexts in $\mathbb{CE}$.
- *Challenge-equal ciphertexts oracle* $\mathcal{O}_{\mathsf{ChallengeCT}}(i)$: This oracle is used to acquire the existing challenge-equal ciphertexts in the epoch i. When queried with the epoch index i, the challenger will return all the challenge-equal ciphertexts in the row $\mathbb{CE}(i)$ and update the challenge-equal ciphertext corruption table $\mathbb{IC}$ to mark the leakage of challenge-equal ciphertexts as following:

- Set $\mathbb{IC}(i)$ as true to mark the leakage of challenge-equal ciphertexts in epoch i.
- For any ℓ from $i+1$ to e, if $\mathbb{IC}(\ell-1) = \mathsf{true} \wedge \mathbb{TO}(\ell) = \mathsf{true}$, then set $\mathbb{IC}(\ell)$ as true to mark the leakage of the challenge-equal ciphertexts that may be updated by the adversary herself via leaked tokens.
- For any ℓ from i to 1, if $\mathbb{IC}(\ell) \wedge \mathbb{TO}(\ell) = \mathsf{true}$, then set $\mathbb{IC}(\ell-1)$ as true to mark the leakage of former challenge-equal ciphertexts that may be recovered by the adversary herself via leaked tokens and the bi-directional update property.[4]

– *Re-encryption oracle* $\mathcal{O}_{\mathsf{ReEnc}}(i, C)$: This oracle is used to update any ciphertexts of the epoch i to the current epoch. As considering the adversary may query the oracle $\mathcal{O}_{\mathsf{ReEnc}}$ with maliciously generated ciphertexts, the oracle $\mathcal{O}_{\mathsf{ReEnc}}$ is allowed to return $\perp$ according to the scheme specification, which is different with the previous works [10,14,18]. Specifically, when $\mathcal{O}_{\mathsf{ReEnc}}$ is queried with a ciphertext C and an epoch index i, the challenger defines $C_i = (\tilde{c}_i, \bar{c}_i)$ as $C = (\tilde{c}, \bar{c})$, and iteratively runs token generation algorithm $\Delta_{k_i,k_{i+1},\tilde{c}_l} \leftarrow_{\$} \mathsf{ReKeyGen}(k_l, k_{l+1}, \tilde{c}_l)$ and the re-encryption algorithm $C_{l+1} \leftarrow \mathsf{Recrypt}(\Delta_{k_i,k_{i+1},\tilde{c}_l}, C_l)$ for all integers $l \in [i, e)$. If all $\mathsf{Recrypt}$ procedures are carried out successfully, the challenger will return the generated C_e to the adversary. Moreover, if the queried ciphertext $C \in \mathbb{CE}$ (i.e., it is the challenge-equal ciphertext), the challenger will update the tables $\mathbb{IC}$ and $\mathbb{CE}$ accordingly:
  - For all $l \in [i, e)$, the challenger archives the newly generated challenge-equal ciphertext C_l in $\mathbb{CE}(l)$.
  - The challenger sets $\mathbb{IC}(e)$ as true to mark the leakage of the challenge-equal ciphertext in epoch e.
  - Additionally, the challenger may have to go backward and update the entry $\mathbb{IC}(l)$ for the epochs before e. This is because given the challenge-equal ciphertext of the epoch e, the adversary may recover the former challenge-equal ciphertext via the leaked tokens and the bi-directional update property. Specifically, for l start decreasing from e, the challenger sets $\mathbb{IC}(l-1) = \mathsf{true}$ until he finds $\mathbb{IC}(l) \wedge \mathbb{TO}(l) = \mathsf{false}$.

sUP-IND-CPA v.s. UP-IND. Note that even our sUP-IND-CPA security is stronger than UP-IND [10] in following aspects. Firstly, sUP-IND-CPA can characterize the post-compromise security which is ignored in UP-IND. Although the constructions in [3,10] is post-compromise secure, there do exist constructions (see in the full version [9]) which are UP-IND secure but without the post-compromise security. Secondly, unlike sUP-IND-CPA, UP-IND does not allow the adversary to query the re-encryption oracle with malformed ciphertexts with the same header as the challenge ciphertext. Therefore, the KSS scheme in [10] is proved secure under UP-IND, but can be attacked by maliciously re-encrypting

---

[4] For simplicity, we assume that if the adversary can acquire one of the challenge-equal ciphertext in the epoch e, she can automatically get all other challenge-equal ciphertexts in the same epoch.

a forged ciphertext with the same header of the challenge ciphertext to a key corrupted epoch. In this way, the adversary can somehow compute the challenge-equal ciphertext that he is not supposed to see in a key corrupted epoch. The detailed attack is shown in the full version [9].

Bi-Directional Update. Given the previous update token and the former ciphertext header, we assume that one can reversely downgrade a ciphertext to a previous epoch. This property is naturally satisfied by the two constructions **KSS** and **ReCrypt** in [10]. Therefore, for fully capturing the challenge-equal ciphertext corruption to avoid trivial win, the challenger needs to update the challenge-equal ciphertext corruption table $\mathbb{IC}$ forward and backward whenever a challenge-equal ciphertext or token is corrupted. This backward inference should have appeared in the model of [10], but due to the inherent limitation of their model, the challenge-equal ciphertext that the adversary can see is always directly updated from a key-uncorrupted epoch. So this negligence has not been fully reflected in their paper.

4.2 Integrity

Then we describe our model sUP-INT-CTXT for CDUE. Like our sUP-IND-CCA model, our integrity model strengthens the UP-INT model in [10] in the sense that allowing the adversary to query the ReEnc oracle with maliciously generated ciphertexts and introducing the epoch notion to capture the post-compromise security. Similar to our confidential models, the challenger needs to maintain table $\mathbb{K}$ to record generated secret keys, and table $\mathbb{KC}$ to keep track of the adversary's key corruption commitment. Besides, the challenger also needs to maintain the following trivially obtained ciphertexts table $\mathbb{T}$ especially for the sUP-INT-CTXT model.

- Table $\mathbb{T}$ is used to keep track of ciphertexts that the adversary can trivially obtain. These ciphertexts are acquired by adversary from three sources: 1) directly response from the $\mathcal{O}_{\mathsf{Enc}}$ oracle, 2) response from the $\mathcal{O}_{\mathsf{ReEnc}}$ oracle, and 3) derived by the adversary herself from querying ciphertexts and update tokens. Specifically, its rows are indexed by the epoch index and ciphertext header pairs $(i, \tilde{c})$, and entries are the header'associated ciphertext body $\bar{c}$. To make the definition more general, we allow $\mathbb{T}(i, \tilde{c})$ to include multiple ciphertext bodies $\bar{c}$ associated to the same header. All entries will be set $\perp$ when the game start.

Specifically, we define the sUP-INT-CTXT experiment as Fig. 3. Similar to [14], we only accept forgeries that the adversary makes in the current and final epoch e_{end}, but not in the past. This matches the concept of UE where the secret keys and update tokens of old epochs will (ideally) be deleted, and thus a forgery for an old key is meaningless anyway. The experiment requests the adversary, after engaging with the oracles $\mathcal{O}_{\mathsf{Enc}'}$, $\mathcal{O}_{\mathsf{Dec}}$, $\mathcal{O}_{\mathsf{Token}'}$, $\mathcal{O}_{\mathsf{Next}}$, $\mathcal{O}_{\mathsf{KeyCorrupt}}$ and $\mathcal{O}_{\mathsf{ReEnc}'}$, to generate a new legal ciphertext C^* for the current epoch. The adversary wins if the two requirements hold simultaneously. One is the new ciphertext C^* can be successfully decrypted by the current epoch key k_e. The other is that C^* is not a trivial win, i.e. the ciphertext C^* is not in the trivially obtained table ciphertext table $\mathbb{T}$ and the current epoch key k_e has not been corrupted.

During the sUP-INT-CTXT experiment, the challenger's behaviours to response the oracles $\mathcal{O}_{\mathsf{Dec}}$, $\mathcal{O}_{\mathsf{Next}}$ and $\mathcal{O}_{\mathsf{KeyCorrupt}}$ are similar to the sUP-IND-CCA experiment. However, there are three different oracles $\mathcal{O}_{\mathsf{Enc}'}$, $\mathcal{O}_{\mathsf{Token}'}$ and $\mathcal{O}_{\mathsf{ReEnc}'}$ in sUP-INT-CTXT that require the challenger to update the table $\mathbb{T}$ accordingly.

- *Encryption oracle* $\mathcal{O}_{\mathsf{Enc}'}(m)$: This oracle is used to query the encryption of the message m under the current epoch key k_e. Specifically, the challenger will return $\mathsf{Enc}(k_e, m)$ to the adversary. Also he will parse the ciphertext $\mathsf{Enc}(k_e, m) = (\tilde{c}, \bar{c})$ and update the table $\mathbb{T}$ as $\mathbb{T}(e, \tilde{c}) \leftarrow \bar{c}$.
- *Re-encryption oracle* $\mathcal{O}_{\mathsf{ReEnc}'}(i, C)$: This oracle is used to update any ciphertexts of the epoch i to the current epoch like $\mathcal{O}_{\mathsf{ReEnc}}$ in sUP-IND-CCA. When the oracle $\mathcal{O}_{\mathsf{ReEnc}'}$ is queried with an epoch index i and a ciphertext C, if the challenger can successfully update C to $C' = (\tilde{c}', \bar{c}')$ of the current epoch e, he will return C' to the adversary. Additionally, $\bar{c}'$ will be added to $\mathbb{T}(e, \hat{c'})$.
- *Token corrupt oracle* $\mathcal{O}_{\mathsf{Token}'}(i, \bar{c})$: When the oracle $\mathcal{O}_{\mathsf{Token}'}$ is queried with an epoch index i and a ciphertext header $\tilde{c}$ during the sUP-INT-CTXT experiment, the challenger will return $\perp$ if $\mathbb{KC}(i) = \mathsf{true}$, otherwise the challenger will run the token generation algorithm $\Delta_{i,i+1,\tilde{c}} \leftarrow_{\$} \mathsf{ReKeyGen}(k_i, k_{i+1}, \tilde{c})$ and return the token $\Delta_{i,i+1,\tilde{c}}$ to adversary $\mathcal{A}$. If $\Delta_{i,i+1,\tilde{c}}$ is not $\perp$, the challenger will updates the trivially obtained ciphertext $\mathbb{T}$ accordingly: for all ciphertext bodies $\bar{c} \in \mathbb{T}(i, \tilde{c})$, the challenger will automatically generate the corresponding ciphertext $C' \leftarrow \mathsf{Recrypt}(\Delta_{k_i, k_{i+1}, \tilde{c}}, (\tilde{c}, \bar{c}))$ for next epoch, parse $C' = (\tilde{c}', \bar{c}')$ and record them in the row $\mathbb{T}(i, \tilde{c}')$.

Definition 4 (sUP-INT-CTXT). *Define the sUP-INT-CTXT experiment as Fig. 3. An updatable encryption scheme is called sUP-INT-CTXT secure if for any P.P.T. adversary $\mathcal{A}$ the following advantage*

$$\mathsf{Adv}_{\mathcal{A}}^{sUP\text{-}INT\text{-}CTXT} := \Pr[Exp_{sUP\text{-}INT\text{-}CTXT}^{\mathcal{A}}(\lambda) \Rightarrow 1]$$

is negligible in the security parameter λ.

Note that any token corruption is disallowed from a key corrupted epoch to a key uncorrupted epoch in the sUP-INT-CTXT model, as well as in the existing models [3,10] for ciphertext integrity. Since in a key corrupted epoch, the adversary can generate any ciphertext, and the challenger does not know which ciphertexts the header used to query the $\mathcal{O}_{\mathsf{Token}}$ oracle is corresponding to. Thus, such attack should be restricted in the ciphertext integrity game. We also know that in the message confidentiality models, sUP-IND-CPA and sUP-IND-CCA, the adversary is allowed to query any token except for the challenge-equal ciphertext from the key corrupted epoch to the key uncorrupted epoch in which the challenge-equal ciphertext is corrupted. Such a difference also cause

$Exp^{\mathcal{A}}_{\mathsf{sUP\text{-}INT\text{-}CTXT}}(\lambda)$

$pp \leftarrow_{\$} \mathsf{Setup}(\lambda)$
Initialize $e, \mathbb{K}, \mathbb{T}, \mathbb{KC}$
$k_0 \leftarrow \mathsf{KeyGen}(pp);\ \mathbb{K}(0) \leftarrow k_0$
$C^* = (\tilde{c}^*, \bar{c}^*) \leftarrow_{\$} \mathcal{A}^{\mathcal{O}_{\mathsf{Enc'}}, \mathcal{O}_{\mathsf{Next}}, \mathcal{O}_{\mathsf{KeyCorrupt}}, \mathcal{O}_{\mathsf{ReEnc'}}, \mathcal{O}_{\mathsf{Token'}}}$
if $(\mathsf{Decrypt}(k_e, C^*) \neq \perp) \wedge (\bar{c}^* \notin \mathbb{T}(e, \tilde{c}^*)) \wedge (\mathbb{KC}(e) \neq \mathsf{true})$
  return 1
else return 0

Fig. 3. The sUP-INT-CTXT experiment.

that the combination of sUP-IND-CPA security and sUP-INT-CTXT security is not sufficient to imply the sUP-IND-CCA security, which we will discuss in the next subsection.

4.3 sUP-IND-CPA + sUP-INT-CTXT $\not\Rightarrow$ sUP-IND-CCA

It is widely known that for the authenticated encryption, the IND-CPA security plus the INT-CTXT security imply the IND-CCA security [1]. This implication still holds for CIUE [5]. However, the case for CDUE is different. More interestingly, we find this particularity is inherent for general CDUE, since even under weaker security models, this implication does not work either, including under a weaken version of our models without malicious update and under existing models in [3,10] which do not capture post-compromise security or malicious update security. In the following, we will show a special CDUE scheme which is sUP-IND-CPA and sUP-INT-CTXT secure but not sUP-IND-CCA secure. Our counter example is inspired by our own construction **ReCrypt**$^+$, but we believe it can be generalized to a large class of CDUE schemes.

This counterintuitive gap comes from the fact that querying $\mathcal{O}_{\mathsf{Token}}$ from a key-corrupted epoch to a key-uncorrupted epoch is forbidden during the sUP-INT-CTXT game, but the adversary in the sUP-IND-CCA game has the ability to acquire that kind of tokens for non-challenge-equal ciphertexts. Such token queries in sUP-INT-CTXT are forbidden, since in a key corrupted epoch the header used to query the $\mathcal{O}_{\mathsf{Token}}$ oracle is unknown to the challenger. Thus an sUP-IND-CCA adversary can leverage such tokens and the decryption oracle to launch attacks.

Intuitively, if an updating token contains secret information which can be leveraged by the adversary who knows the previous epoch key, the adversary may be able to modify the challenge-equal ciphertext and use the result to query the decryption oracle to get more information about the challenge ciphertext. More precisely, we add the ciphertext header of the new scheme with a redundant MAC, and make the encryption of the MAC key contained in the token. If the adversary corrupt the key of the former epoch and query a token for a non-challenge-equal ciphertext from that epoch, she can learn the MAC key and modify the MAC in the next epoch challenge-equal ciphertext. After that, she may query the modified challenge-equal ciphertext to the decryption oracle. Note that this attack even does not leverage the malicious re-encryption ability!

Suppose the **CDUE** is the CDUE scheme which is both sUP-IND-CPA and sUP-INT-CTXT secure. Moreover, CDUE has a special property: the update token $\Delta_{i,\tilde{c}_i}$ must explicitly contain the header $\tilde{c}_{i+1}$ of the new ciphertext in epoch $i+1$. Such a property is satisfied by most CDUE schemes, say **KSS** and **ReCrypt** in [10] and our **ReCrypt**$^+$in Sect. 5.

Let **SKE** = (KeyGen, Enc, Dec) be an IND-CPA secure symmetric key encryption. Let **MAC** = (KeyGen, Tag, Verify) be a deterministic MAC scheme which is unforgerable under chosen message attack (e.g.. hash-based MACs). Note that the deterministic property guarantees that there is only one valid MAC for each message under one secret key. Then we construct the scheme **CDUE**′ as follows:

- **CDUE**′.Setup(1^λ): Generate the public parameter pp via **CDUE**.Setup.
- **CDUE**′.KeyGen(pp): Use **CDUE**.KeyGen to generate an epoch key k_e of **CDUE** and use **MAC**.KeyGen to generate a MAC key mk_e. The new epoch key k'_e of **CDUE**′ is (k_e, mk_e).
- **CDUE**′.Encrypt(k'_e, m): Parse the secret key $k'_e = (k_e, mk_e)$. Given the plaintext m, firstly use **CDUE**.Enc to encrypt m under the secret key k_e and generate the ciphertext $C_e = (\tilde{c}_e, \bar{c}_e)$. Secondly, concatenate the header $\tilde{c}_e$ with one bit 1 and compute a MAC $\tau_e =$ **MAC**.Tag$(mk_e, \tilde{c}_e \| 1)$. Finally, output the ciphertext $C'_e = (\tilde{c}'_e, \bar{c}_e)$ where the new header $\tilde{c}'_e = (\tilde{c}_e, \tau_e)$.
- **CDUE**′.Decrypt(k'_e, C'_e): Parse $C'_e = (\tilde{c}'_e, \bar{c}_e)$ where $\tilde{c}'_e = (\tilde{c}_e, \tau_e)$. Verify whether **MAC**.Verify$(mk_e, \tau_e, \tilde{c}_e \| 1) = 1$ or **MAC**.Verify$(mk_e, \tau_e, \tilde{c}_e \| 0) = 1$. If one of above two cases is true, use the **CDUE**.Decrypt to decrypt the ciphertext $C_e = (\tilde{c}_e, \bar{c}_e)$ and return the decryption result.
- **CDUE**′.ReKeyGen($k'_e, k'_{e+1}, \tilde{c}'_e$): Parse $\tilde{c}'_e = (\tilde{c}_e, \tau_e)$, $k'_e = (k_e, mk_e)$ and $k'_{e+1} = (k_{e+1}, mk_{e+1})$. Firstly, verify whether **MAC**.Verify$(\tau_e, \tilde{c}_e \| 1) = 1$. If it is true, invoke **CDUE**.ReKeyGen$(k_e, k_{e+1}, \tilde{c}_e)$ to generate the token $\Delta_{e,\tilde{c}_e}$. Note that according to our assumption about **CDUE**, $\Delta_{e,\tilde{c}_e}$ has the form $(\tilde{c}_{e+1}, \delta_{e,\tilde{c}_e})$ where $\tilde{c}_{e+1}$ is the new header and $\delta_{e,\tilde{c}_e}$ denotes the other information. Secondly, compute the new MAC $\tau_{e+1} =$ **MAC**.Tag$(mk_{e+1}, \tilde{c}_{e+1} \| 1)$ and the new header $\tilde{c}'_{e+1} = (\tilde{c}_{e+1}, \tau_{e+1})$. Finally, encrypt mk_{e+1} under the key k_e as **SKE**.Enc$_{k_e}(mk_{e+1})$, and output the update token $\Delta'_{e,\tilde{c}'_e} = (\tilde{c}'_{e+1}, \delta_{e,\tilde{c}_e},$ **SKE**.Enc$_{k_e}(mk_{e+1}))$ for **CDUE**′.
- **CDUE**′.ReEncrypt($\Delta'_{e,\tilde{c}'_e}, C'_e$): First parse the token $\Delta'_{e,\tilde{c}'_e} = (\tilde{c}'_{e+1}, \delta_{e,\tilde{c}_e},$ **SKE**.Enc$_{k_e}(mk_{e+1}))$ and the ciphertext $C'_e = (\tilde{c}'_e, \bar{c}_e) = ((\tilde{c}_e, \tau_e), \bar{c}_e)$. Then derive the **CDUE** token $\Delta_{e,\tilde{c}_e} = (\tilde{c}_{e+1}, \delta_{e,\tilde{c}_e})$ from $\Delta'_{e,\tilde{c}'_e}$, and $C_e = (\tilde{c}_e, \bar{c}_e)$ from C'_e. Invoke **CDUE**.ReEncrypt$(\Delta_{e,\tilde{c}_e}, C_e)$ to get $C_{e+1} = (\tilde{c}_{e+1}, \bar{c}_{e+1})$. Finally output $C'_{e+1} = (\tilde{c}'_{e+1}, \bar{c}_{e+1})$ by replacing $\tilde{c}_{e+1}$ with the new header $\tilde{c}'_{e+1}$ in the token $\Delta'_{e,\tilde{c}'_e}$.

In the following two lemmas, we show that the above $\mathbf{CDUE}'$ is sUP-IND-CPA and sUP-INT-CTXT secure when **MAC** is deterministic (like HMAC [15]). The sUP-IND-CPA is obvious since the augmented MAC will not leak any information about the plaintext. Since the CTXT model disallows the adversary to see the token from a key-corrupted epoch to a key-uncorrupted epoch, the MAC key will never be leaked. The sUP-INT-CTXT comes from the MAC's unforgerability. We put the formal proof in the full version [9].

Lemma 1. *If* **CDUE** *is sUP-IND-CPA secure and* **MAC** *is deterministic (i.e. there is only one valid MAC for each message under one secret key),* $\mathbf{CDUE}'$ *is sUP-IND-CPA secure.*

Lemma 2. *If* **CDUE** *is sUP-INT-CTXT secure,* **SKE** *is IND-CPA secure and* **MAC** *is multi-user CMA unforgerable, then* $\mathbf{CDUE}'$ *is sUP-INT-CTXT secure.*

The CCA Attack. We provide a CCA attack as follows. The adversary commits to corrupt the key of the epoch e, but will not corrupt the key of the epoch $e+1$. Then the adversary queries a token of non-challenge ciphertext header $\tilde{c}_{e,0}$, and she will get a token $\Delta'_{e,\tilde{c}'_{e,0}} = (\tilde{c}'_{e+1,0}, \delta_{e,\tilde{c}_{e,0}}, \mathbf{SKE}.\mathsf{Enc}_{k_e}(mk_{e+1}))$. Since the key $k'_e = (k_e, mk_e)$ has been corrupted by the adversary, she can recover mk_{e+1} for $\mathbf{SKE}.\mathsf{Enc}_{k_e}(mk_{e+1})$ easily. Then the adversary acquires the challenge-equal ciphertext $C'_{e+1,1} = ((\tilde{c}_{e+1,1}, \tau_{e+1,1}), \bar{c}_{e+1,1})$ in the epoch $e+1$, where $\tau_{e+1,1} = \mathbf{MAC}_{mk_{e+1}}(\tilde{c}_{e+1,1}\|1)$. Since the adversary knows mk_{e+1}, she can modify $C'_{e+1,1}$ into a new ciphertext $C'_{e+1,2} = ((\tilde{c}_{e+1,1}, \tau'_{e+1}), \bar{c}_{e+1,,1})$ by shifting the attached bit in the MAC message and acquiring $\tau'_{e+1} = \mathbf{MAC}_{mk_{e+1}}(\tilde{c}_{e+1,1}\|0)$. According to the design of our decryption algorithm, τ'_{e+1} still can pass the verification even the attached bit is 0 but not 1. So $C'_{e+1,2}$ is still a valid ciphertext of the epoch $e+1$, and it will not be recognized as a challenge-equal ciphertext by the sUP-IND-CCA challenger. The adversary can query $\mathcal{O}_{\mathsf{Dec}}$ with $C'_{e+1,2}$ in the epoch $e+1$, and learn the challenge bit. Therefore, we have the following theorem.

Theorem 1. *For* **CDUE**, *the security combination of sUP-IND-CPA and sUP-INT-CTXT cannot imply sUP-IND-CCA security.*

The Gap is Inherent. One may be curious about whether the counter-intuitive gap is caused by the malicious update resistance or the post-compromise security. However, we find that the gap between the CPA+CTXT and CCA is inherent for general CDUE. To note that, firstly we show the implication does not hold for a weaker collection of our models (we define UP-IND-CPA, UP-INT-CTXT and UP-IND-CCA in the full version [9] following the former paradigm but adding a restriction to the re-encryption oracle), which only capture the post-compromise security but not malicious update security. Then we have the following Theorem 2. The intuition comes from that the CCA attack on our artificially designed $\mathbf{CDUE}'$ scheme does not need to query malicious ciphertexts on the re-encryption oracle. Moreover, the security gap holds even for the weakest models[5] in [3,10] without the post-compromise security or the malicious update resistance. Indeed, it is not hard to see that the above **CDUE**$'$ is also UP-IND and UP-INT secure, while the CCA attack can still apply.

Theorem 2. *For a ciphertext dependent UE, the security combination of UP-IND-CPA and UP-INT-CTXT do not imply UP-IND-CCA security.*

5 UE Construction with Strengthened Integrity

Next we describe our new CDUAE construction **ReCrypt**$^+$. Comparing with previous CDUAE constructions [3,10], our scheme not only naturally inherits their advantage that the plaintext space could be a bit string with arbitrary length, but also has the strengthened security to resist the malicious re-encryption attack. During the security analysis, we prove our scheme secure under sUP-IND-CCA and sUP-INT-CTXT as above mentioned. So our scheme has a strengthened security in aspects of the post-compromise security, the malicious re-encryption resistance and the chosen ciphertexts attack resistance.

5.1 Construction Framework

Our construction **ReCrypt**$^+$ follows the paradigm of the **ReCrypt** scheme proposed by Everspauph et al. The original **ReCrypt** in [10] not only follows the KEM + DEM with the secret sharing structure, but also involves the key-homomophic PRF to achieve the re-encryption indistinguishability. However, as pointed by in the introduction, **ReCrypt** in [10] suffers the malicious re-encryption attack.

The key to resist the malicious re-encryption attack is to verify the validity of the ciphertext before re-encryption. Therefore our scheme not only involves the AEAD to enable the client to verify the header of the ciphertext, but also uses the collision-resistant homomorphic hash function and homomorphic commitment to help the server to check the consistency of the body with the header. These measures guarantee that the adversary always learns nothing when querying the ReEnc oracle with a forged ciphertexts. In the meantime, the homomorphic properties of the hash function and the commitment scheme make that the update operations to apply smoothly. The detailed construction is as follows, and also shown in Fig. 4.

Let **HomHash**.Setup and **HomHash**.Eval be the algorithms of a homomorphic collision-resistant hash function with the following syntax.

Definition 5. *A homomorphic hash function* H_{hom} *is a linear function that maps vectors of starting group elements* $\mathbf{v} = (v_1, \ldots, v_n) \in \mathbb{G}_{HS}^n$ *into one target group element* $u \in \mathbb{G}_{HT}$ *which is defined by the following two algorithms:*

[5] The similar CCA model can be trivially obtained by adding an additional decryption oracle for ciphertexts decryption except for the challenge-equal ciphertexts.

$\mathsf{Setup}(\lambda)$

$hk \leftarrow_\$ \mathbf{HomHash}.\mathsf{Setup}(\lambda), \mathsf{hcom}.pp \leftarrow_\$ \mathbf{HCOM}.\mathsf{Init}(\lambda)$
return $(hk, \mathsf{hcom}.pp)$

$\mathsf{KeyGen}(\lambda)$

$k \leftarrow_\$ \mathbf{AEAD}.\mathsf{KeyGen}(1^\lambda)$, **return** k

$\mathsf{Encrypt}(k, m)$

Map $m \rightarrow (m_1, m_2, \ldots, m_n) \in \mathbb{G}^n_{PRF}, z \leftarrow_\$ \mathbb{K}_{PRF}$
$d_i \leftarrow m_i + \mathsf{F}(z, i), d = (d_1, d_2, \ldots, d_n) \in \mathbb{G}^n_{PRF}, h \leftarrow \mathbf{HomHash}.\mathsf{Eval}(hk, d)$
$y \leftarrow_\$ \mathbb{K}_{PRF}, hcom \leftarrow \mathbf{HCOM}.\mathsf{com}(y; hopen), x = z - y$
$ct \leftarrow_\$ \mathbf{AEAD}.\mathsf{Enc}(k, x, (h, hcom))$
$\tilde{c} = (ct, h, hcom)$// *Ciphertext header*
$\bar{c} = (y, hopen, d)$// *Ciphertext body*
return $C = (\tilde{c}, \bar{c})$

$\mathsf{Decrypt}(k, C)$

Parse $C = ((ct, h, hcom), (y, hopen, d))$
if $h == \mathbf{HomHash}.\mathsf{Eval}(hk, d) \wedge \mathbf{HCom}.\mathsf{Open}(hcom, y, hopen) == 1$ **then**
// *Check the body is consistent with the header.*
$x^\star \leftarrow \mathbf{AEAD}.\mathsf{Dec}(k, \tilde{c}^1, (h, hcom))$
for $1 \leq i \leq n$ **do** $m_i^\star \leftarrow d_i - \mathsf{F}(x^\star - y, d_i)$ **return** $m^\star = m_1^\star, \ldots, m_n^\star$
return $\perp$

$\mathsf{ReKeygen}(k, k', \tilde{c})$

Parse $\tilde{c} = (ct, h, hcom), m' \leftarrow \mathbf{AEAD}.\mathsf{Dec}(k, ct, (h, hcom))$
if $m' \neq \perp$ **then**// *Check the returned header is valid.*
$\Delta z \leftarrow_\$ \mathbb{K}_{PRF}, \ \Delta d_i \leftarrow \mathsf{F}(\Delta z, i), \Delta d = \Delta d_1, \Delta d_2, \ldots, \Delta d_n$
$h' \leftarrow h + \mathbf{HomHash}.\mathsf{Eval}(hk, \Delta d), \ \Delta y \leftarrow_\$ \{0,1\}^*$
$hcom' \leftarrow hcom + \mathbf{HCom}.\mathsf{Com}(\Delta y, hopen_\Delta), \ x' = x + \Delta z - \Delta y,$
$ct' \leftarrow_\$ \mathbf{AEAD}.\mathsf{Enc}(k', x', (h', hcom')), \ \tilde{c}' = (ct', h', hcom')$
return $\Delta = (\tilde{c}', \Delta y, hopen_\Delta, \Delta z)$
else **return** $\perp$

$\mathsf{ReEncrypt}(C, \Delta)$

Parse $C = ((ct, h, hcom), (y, hopen, d)), \Delta = (\tilde{c}', (\Delta y, hopen_\Delta, \Delta z))$
if $\mathbf{HCOM}.\mathsf{Open}(hcom, y, r) == 1 \wedge h == \mathbf{HomHash}.\mathsf{Eval}(hk, d)$ **then**
// *Check the body is consistent with the header.*
$y' = y + \Delta y, \quad r' = r + \Delta r, \quad$ Parse $d = (d_1, d_2, \ldots, d_n)$
$d_i' \leftarrow d_i + \mathcal{F}(\Delta z, i), \quad d' = (d_1', d_2', \ldots, d_n')$
$hopen' = hopen + hopen_\Delta, \quad y' = y + \Delta y, \quad \bar{c}' = (y', hopen', d')$
return $C' = (\tilde{c}', \bar{c}')$
return $\perp$

Fig. 4. Construction for ReCrypt$^+$

- ***HomHash***.*Setup*(1^λ) : *On input the security parameter* λ, *output an evaluation key hk;*
- ***HomHash***.*Eval*$(hk, \boldsymbol{v})$: *On input the evaluation key hk and a vector of starting group elements* $\mathbf{v} = (v_1, \ldots, v_n) \in \mathbb{G}_{HS}^n$, *output one target group element* $u \in \mathbb{G}_{HT}$.

Fixed the evaluation key hk, we can write as $H_{hom}(\boldsymbol{v})$ = ***HomHash***.*Eval* $(hk, \boldsymbol{v}) = u$. *Specifically, it should satisfies the following properties:*

- Collision resistance: *The probability for any P.P.T adversary to generate the two vectors* $\boldsymbol{v}$ *and* $\boldsymbol{v}'$ *in* $\mathbb{G}_{HS}^n$ *which satisfy* $H_{hom}(\boldsymbol{v}) = H_{hom}(\boldsymbol{v}')$ *is negligible.*
- Homomorphism: *We have* $H_{hom}(\boldsymbol{v}) + H_{hom}(\boldsymbol{v}') = H_{hom}(\boldsymbol{v} + \boldsymbol{v}')$.

Let $\mathsf{F} : \mathbb{K}_{PRF} \times \mathcal{M}_{PRF} \rightarrow \mathbb{G}_{PRF}$ be the key homomorphic PRF as described in Subsect. 2, whose codomain is a cyclic group $\mathbb{G}_{PRF} \subseteq \mathbb{G}_{HS}$ and key space $\mathbb{K}_{PRF}$ is also an additive group. Let **HCOM**.Init, **HCOM**.Com and **HCOM**.Open be the algorithms for the homomorphic commitment scheme described in Subsect. 2, whose message space, opening randomness space and commitment value are $\mathbb{M}_{COM}$, $\mathbb{O}_{COM}$ and $\mathbb{C}_{COM}$, respectively. Specifically, we require that the message space $\mathbb{M}_{COM}$ contains the PRF key space $\mathbb{K}_{PRF}$. Let the **AEAD**.KeyGen, **AEAD**.Enc and **AEAD**.Dec be the algorithms for AEAD as described in Subsect. 2, whose key space, message space and ciphertext space are $\mathbb{K}_{AEAD}$, $\mathbb{M}_{AEAD}$ and $\mathbb{C}_{AEAD}$.

- **ReCrypt**$^+$.Setup(λ): Run the **HomHash**.Setup algorithm to generate the parameter hk for the homomorphic collision-resistant hash function. Also run the **HCOM**.Init to generate the parameter hcom.pp for the homomorphic commitment. The public parameter **ReCrypt**$^+$.pp=(hk, hcom.pp) will be taken as the implicit input of the following algorithm.
- **ReCrypt**$^+$.KeyGen(λ): Run the **AEAD**.KeyGen(λ) to generate the key of AEAD $k \in \mathbb{K}_{AEAD}$.
- **ReCrypt**$^+$.Encrypt(k, m): The algorithm proceeds as follows.
  1. Map the message m into n group elements $m_1, m_2, \ldots, m_n \in \mathbb{G}_{PRF}^n$.
  2. Use the key-homomorphic PRF to encrypt each block m_i. Specifically, sample a PRF key $z \in \mathbb{K}_{PRF}$ and then mask each message m_i as $d_i = m_i + \mathsf{F}(z, i) \in \mathbb{G}_{PRF}$.
  3. Let $d = (d_1, d_2, \ldots, d_n) \in \mathbb{G}_{PRF}^n$. Since $d \in \mathbb{G}_{PRF}^n \subseteq \mathbb{G}_{HS}^n$, one can compute the homomorphic hash function on d and derive **HomHash**.Eval$(hk, d) = h \in \mathbb{G}$.
  4. Randomly choose two shares $x, y \in \mathbb{K}_{PRF}$ of z such that $x + y = z$.
  5. Use the homomorphic commitment scheme to commit the share y, and generate the commitment **HCom**.Com$(y, hopen)$ = $hcom \in \mathbb{C}_{COM}$, where $hopen \in \mathbb{O}_{COM}$ is the corresponding opening randomness.
  6. Use the AEAD to encrypt the key share $x \in \mathbb{K}_{PRF} \subseteq \{0,1\}^\lambda$ with the auxiliary data the HCRH value $h \in \mathbb{G}_{HT} \subseteq \{0,1\}^\lambda$ and the homomorphic commitment $hcom \in \mathbb{C}_{COM} \subseteq \{0,1\}^\lambda$. Get the ciphertext $ct \in \mathbb{C}_{AEAD}$.

7. The header of the UE ciphertext is $\tilde{c} = (ct, h, hcom) \in \mathbb{C}_{AEAD} \times \mathbb{G}_{HT} \times \mathbb{C}_{COM}$, and the body of the UE ciphertext $\bar{c} = (y, hopen, d) \in \mathbb{K}_{PRF} \times \mathbb{O}_{COM} \times \mathbb{G}^n_{PRF}$.

- **ReCrypt**$^+$.Decrypt(k, C): Given $k \in \mathbb{K}_{PRF}$ and the ciphertext $C = (\tilde{c}, \bar{c})$, the UE decryption algorithm first parses the ciphertext C as the header $\tilde{c} = (ct, h, hcom) \in \mathbb{C}_{AEAD} \times \mathbb{G}_{HT} \times \mathbb{C}_{COM}$ and the body $\bar{c} = (y, hopen, d) \in \mathbb{K}_{PRF} \times \mathbb{O}_{COM} \times \mathbb{G}^n_{PRF}$, and proceeds as follows:
  1. Verify **HomHash**.Eval$(hk, d) \stackrel{?}{=} h \in \mathbb{G}_{HT}$ for $d \in \mathbb{G}^n_{PRF} \subseteq \mathbb{G}^n_{HS}$,
  2. Verify whether $hcom \in \mathbb{C}_{COM}$ is a valid commitment of $y \in \mathbb{K}_{PRF} \subseteq \mathbb{M}_{COM}$, so one invokes the homomorphic commitment opening algorithm **HCom**.Open$(hcom, y, hopen)$ and check the results whether equals to 1.
  3. Decrypt the AEAD ciphertext ct with the current epoch key k and the auxiliary data h and $hcom$.
  4. If above verification passes and the AEAD decryption algorithm successfully outputs $x \in \mathbb{K}_{PRF}$, the UE decryption algorithm will recover all $m_i \in \mathbb{G}_{PRF}$ by computing $m_i = d_i - \mathsf{F}(x - y, i)$, otherwise it returns $\perp$.
- **ReCrypt**$^+$.ReKeyGen $(k, \tilde{c})$: The algorithm parses the header $\tilde{c} = (ct, h, hcom) \in \mathbb{C}_{AEAD} \times \mathbb{G}_{HT} \times \mathbb{C}_{COM}$, and proceeds as follows:
  1. Use the currency secret key $k \in \mathbb{K}_{AEAD}$ to decrypt ct with the auxiliary data $(h, hcom)$. If the AEAD decryption successfully return $x \in \mathbb{K}_{PRF}$, execute following steps, otherwise return $\perp$.
  2. Choose a random $\Delta z \in \mathbb{K}_{PRF}$, and compute $\Delta d_i = \mathsf{F}(\Delta z, i) \in \mathbb{G}_{PRF}$.
  3. Let $\Delta d = (\Delta d_1, \ldots, \Delta d_n) \in \mathbb{G}^n_{PRF} \subseteq \mathbb{G}^n_{HS}$. Compute the new hash value $h' = h + $ **HomHash**.Eval$(hk, \Delta d) \in \mathbb{G}_{HT}$.
  4. Generate a new group element $\Delta y \in \mathbb{K}_{PRF}$ and its homomorphic commitment **HCom**.com$(\Delta y, hopen_\Delta) = hcom_\Delta \in \mathbb{G}_{COM}$. So the new commitment is $hcom' = hcom + hcom_\Delta$.
  5. Compute $x' = x + \Delta z - \Delta y \in \mathbb{K}_{PRF}$. Encrypt x' with the new master key k' and auxiliary data $(h', hcom')$, and get the AEAD ciphertext $ct' =$ **AEAD**.Enc$(k', x', (h', hcom'))$.
  6. Let the new header $\tilde{c}' = (ct', h', hcom') \in \mathbb{C}_{AEAD} \times \mathbb{G}_{HT} \times \mathbb{C}_{COM}$. Return the update token $\Delta = (\tilde{c}', \Delta y, hopen_\Delta, \Delta z)$.
- **ReCrypt**$^+$.ReEncrypt(C, Δ): The algorithm will first parse the ciphertext header $\tilde{c} = (ct, (h, hcom))$, the ciphertext body $\bar{c} = (y, hopen, d)$ and the update token $\Delta = (\tilde{c}', \Delta y, hopen_\Delta, \Delta z)$, then proceeds as follows.
  1. Verify whether **HomHash**.Eval$(hk, d) = h \in \mathbb{G}_{HT}$ for $d \in \mathbb{G}^n_{HS}$,
  2. Verify whether $hcom \in \mathbb{G}_{COM}$ is a valid commitment of $y \in \mathbb{K}_{PRF}$, i.e., invoke the opening algorithm **HCom**.Open$(hcom, y, hopen)$ and check the result whether equals to 1.
  3. If above verification can be passed, compute $d' = (d'_1, d'_2, \ldots, d'_n) \in \mathbb{G}_{PRF} \subseteq R^n$ where $d'_i = d_i + \mathsf{F}(\Delta z, i) \in \mathbb{G}_{PRF}$.
  4. Compute the new commitment opening $hopen' = hopen + hopen_\Delta$.
  5. Compute $y' = y + \Delta y$.
  6. Generate new ciphertext $C' = (\tilde{c}', \bar{c})'$ by taking $\tilde{c}'$ from the token Δ as the new header and setting $\bar{c}' = (y', hopen', d') \in \mathbb{K}_{PRF} \times \mathbb{O}_{COM} \times \mathbb{G}^n_{PRF}$.

5.2 Homomorphic Hash Functions from DDH Groups

To make the following **ReCrypt**$^+$framework works, we should construct a homomorphic embedding from the range of the key homomorphic PRF into the domain of the collision-resistant hash function (i.e, $\mathbb{G}_{PRF} \rightarrow \mathbb{G}_{HS}$). Note that trivial dictionary maps do not work here, since we should make those homomorphic properties still hold. To handle this issue, we will involve a critical primitive named *the homomorphic hash function from DDH groups.* Previous homomorphic hash function schemes only allow the messages to be exponents [8,11,17] or short ring elements [19]. In contrast, we hope the message can be chosen from a group where the decisional Diffie-Hellman (DDH) problem is hard, since the domain of the hash function will be the range of the key-homomorphic PRF.

If there is not requirement for the message group $\mathbb{G}$, a homomorphic hash scheme is not hard to obtain. Chaum et al. have shown a homomorphic collision-resistant hash function can be constructed from an *exponential homomorphic hash* scheme [8,17]. In their construction, $\mathbb{G}'$ is a finite cyclic group of order p. The public key hk contain $h_1, \ldots, h_n$ as generators of $\mathbb{G}'$. Let $\mathbb{G} = \mathbb{Z}_p$ be a group of exponents for $\mathbb{G}'$. For any positive integer n, $\mathsf{H}_{Hom} : \mathbb{G}^n \rightarrow \mathbb{G}'$ is defined as $\mathsf{H}_{hom}(v_1, \ldots, v_n) = \prod_{j=1}^{n} h_j^{v_j}$. The homomorphic property is easily verified, and collision resistance is implied by the discrete logarithm assumption in $\mathbb{G}'$.

However, in our construction **ReCrypt**$^+$, the DDH problem is required to be hard over $\mathbb{G}$, since $\mathbb{G}$ will be the range of the key-homomorphic pseudorandom function. The above exponential homomorphic hash construction does not trivially satisfy this requirement, since the operation over $\mathbb{G} = \mathbb{Z}_p$ is the *addition* but not the *multiplication*. To find the relation between a random element and a generator is easy in $\mathbb{G}$.

Our homomorphic hash function from DDH groups is based on a bilinear map over elliptic curves where the external Diffie-Hellman (XDH) assumption is hard. Specifically, the homomorphic function works on a bilinear group $(p, \mathbb{G}_1, \mathbb{G}_2, \mathbb{G}_T, e)$ where p is a k-bit prime, $\mathbb{G}_1, \mathbb{G}_2, \mathbb{G}_T$ are cyclic groups of order p and $e : \mathbb{G}_1 \times \mathbb{G}_2 \leftarrow \mathbb{G}_T$ is a non-degenerate bilinear map. The XDH assumption states that the Decisional Diffie Hellman (DDH) assumption is hard in the group $\mathbb{G}_1$ (not necessarily hard in $\mathbb{G}_2$). The XDH is believed to be true in asymmetric pairings generated using special MNT curves [2,21].

So the message are chosen from the group $\mathbb{G}_1^n$, the algorithms of the homomorphic hash function are defined as follows.

- **HomHash**.$\mathsf{Setup}(\mathbb{G}, n)$: Randomly pick $g \leftarrow_{\$} \mathbb{G}_2 \backslash \{1\}$ and elements $x_1, \ldots, x_n \leftarrow_{\$} \mathbb{Z}_p$. Define $h_1 = g^{x_1}, \ldots, h_n = g^{x_n}$. Output $hk = (h_1, \ldots, h_n) \in \mathbb{G}_2^n$.
- **HomHash**.Eval $(hk, \mathbf{v})$: Given a key $hk = (h_1, \ldots, h_n) \in \mathbb{G}_2^n$ and a vector $\mathbf{v} = (v_1, \ldots, v_n) \in \mathbb{G}_1^n$, output $\prod_{j=1}^{n} e(v_j, h_j) \in \mathbb{G}_T$.

For a fixed hk, $\mathsf{H}_{hom} : \mathbb{G}_1^n \rightarrow \mathbb{G}_T$ is defined as $\mathsf{H}_{hom}(\mathbf{v}) = $ **HomHash**.$\mathsf{Eval}(hk, \mathbf{v})$.

The homomorphism can be easily verified. Suppose $\mathsf{H}_{hom}(\mathbf{v}) = \prod_{j=1}^{n} e(v_j, h_j)$ and $\mathsf{H}_{hom}(\mathbf{v}') = \prod_{j=1}^{n} e(v'_j, h_j)$, and we have

$$\mathsf{H}_{hom}(\mathbf{v}) \cdot \mathsf{H}_{hom}(\mathbf{v}') = \prod_{j=1}^{n} e(v_j, h_j) \cdot \prod_{j=1}^{n} e(v'_j, h_j) = \prod_{j=1}^{n} e(v_j v'_j, h_j).$$

The collision resistance is based on the double pairing assumption whose hardness is shown by Groth in [12]. The double pairing problem is given random elements $g_r, g_t \in \mathbb{G}_2$ to find a non-trivial couple $(r, t) \in \mathbb{G}_1^2$ such that $e(r, g_r)e(t, g_t) = 1$. The proof could be found in the full version [9].

Lemma 3 (Collision resistance). *The double pairing assumption holds for the bilinear group $(p, \mathbb{G}_1, \mathbb{G}_2, \mathbb{G}_T, e)$. The homomorphic hash function H_{hom} defined as above is collision resistant.*

5.3 Instantiation

To make the above framework works, we should construct a homomorphic embedding from the range of the key homomorphic PRF into the domain of the collision-resistant hash function (i.e, $\mathbb{G}_{PRF} \to \mathbb{G}_{HS}$), as well as a homomorphism from the key space of $\mathbb{K}_{PRF}$ to the commitment message space $\mathbb{M}_{COM}$.

ReCrypt$^+$can be instantiated over a bilinear group $(p, \mathbb{G}_1, \mathbb{G}_2, \mathbb{G}_T, e)$ over elliptic curves where the external Diffie-Hellman (XDH) assumption and the double pairing assumption are hard. To handle the homomorphic embedding from $\mathbb{G}_{PRF}$ to $\mathbb{G}_{HS}$, we adopt the DDH based key-homomorphic PRF described in Subsect. 2 over $\mathbb{G}_{PRF} = \mathbb{G}_1$ and $\mathbb{K}_{PRF} = \mathbb{Z}_p$, and the homomorphic hash function described in Subsect. 5.2 over $(p, \mathbb{G}_1, \mathbb{G}_2, \mathbb{G}_T, e)$.

To handle the homomorphism from $\mathbb{K}_{PRF}$ to $\mathbb{M}_{COM}$, we adopt the Pedersen commitment over the group $\mathbb{G}_1$. The commitment scheme is specified with two random public group generators g and h in $\mathbb{G}_1$. The opening randomness *hopen* is randomly chosen from $\mathbb{Z}_p$ and the commitment message m is also from $\mathbb{Z}_p$. The commitment is $\mathsf{Com}(m, hopen) = h^{hopen} g^m \in \mathbb{G}_1$. Since the PRF key space $\mathbb{K}_{PRF}$ and the commitment message $\mathbb{M}_{COM}$ are both $\mathbb{Z}_p^*$, the homomorphism is naturally inherent.

5.4 Security Analysis

Now we show that our construction **ReCrypt**$^+$ is secure under the models sUP-IND-CCA, sUP-INT-CTXT and sUP-REENC-CCA. Due to page limitation, we will provide detailed proofs in the full version [9].

sUP-IND-CCA. We are now ready to state the sUP-IND-CCA security of our **ReCrypt**$^+$ scheme. Our security proof is similar to the **ReCrypt** except that 1) sUP-IND-CCA has $\mathcal{O}_{\mathsf{Dec}}$, 2) and allow to query malicious generated ciphertext to $\mathcal{O}_{\mathsf{ReEnc}}$ and malicious header to $\mathcal{O}_{\mathsf{Token}}$. Besides, 3) we put the commitment of the secret share of DEM key in the head. So the intuition of the security proof comes from: First of all, the authenticity of AEAD, the binding property of the commitment and the collision-resistance of the hash function guarantee that all ciphertexts that could be successful decrypted or reencrypted is honestly generated. Secondly, the authenticity of AEAD guarantee that all token is generated from honest generated ciphertext headers. Thirdly, the hiding property of the commitment can hide the secret share of DEM key y. Formally, we have the following theorem and give the formal proof in [9].

Theorem 3 (sUP-IND-CCA Security of ReCrypt$^+$). *Let **ReCrypt$^+$** be an updatable encryption scheme as defined in Sect. 5.1. **ReCrypt$^+$** is sUP-IND-CCA secure if **AEAD** is MU-RoR-AE secure (Sect. 2), the homomorphic commitment **HCOM** is statistic hiding and computation binding, and the key homomorphic PRF is pseudorandom.*

sUP-INT-CTXT. We first provide the analysis result for sUP-INT-CTXT. Intuitively, we first assume that **ReCrypt$^+$** is not sUP-INT-CTXT secure, and then construct contradictions with the existing conditions to prove the lemma. As a ciphertext contains a ciphertext header and a ciphertext body, a successful forgery can forge the ciphertext header or the ciphertext body. we make a reduction from the ciphertext header forgery to the break of ciphertext integrity of AEAD scheme, and make reductions from the ciphertext body forgery to the break of binding of commitment scheme **HCom** or the break of collision resistance of homomorphic hash function **HomHash**. Formally, we have the following theorem and give the formal proof in [9].

Theorem 4 (sUP-INT-CTXT Security of ReCrypt$^+$). *Let **ReCrypt$^+$** be an updatable encryption scheme as defined in Sect. 5.1. **ReCrypt$^+$** is sUP-INT-CTXT secure, if **AEAD** scheme is CTXT scheme, **HCom** scheme has computational binding property, and **HomHash** scheme is collision resistant.*

sUP-REENC-CCA. To demonstrate that our **ReCrypt$^+$** scheme is sUP-REENC-CCA secure, we introduce a property called *perfect re-encryption* proposed in [14]. Perfect re-encryption assures that for any ciphertext of updatable encryption, decrypt-then-encrypt has the same distribution with re-encryption. We give a formal definition of perfect re-encryption for UE setting defined in the full version [9]. We notice that **ReCrypt$^+$**naturally satisfy the perfect re-encryption property. As pointed by [14], the perfect re-encryption property plus the sUP-IND-CCA security imply the sUP-REENC-CCA security. So we have the following theorem whose formal proof is in [9].

Theorem 5 (sUP-REENC-CCA Security). *Since **ReCrypt$^+$** as defined in Sect. 5.1 has the perfect re-encryption property and satisfy the sUP-IND-CCA security, **ReCrypt$^+$** is sUP-REENC-CCA secure.*

Acknowledgement. We thank anonymous reviewers from ASIACRYPT 20 for valuable comments. Qiang and Ya-Nan are supported in part by NSF grant CNS #1801492. Qiang is also supported in part by a Google Faculty Award.

References

1. Bellare, M., Namprempre, C.: Authenticated encryption: relations among notions and analysis of the generic composition paradigm. J. Cryptol. **21**(4), 469–491 (2008). https://doi.org/10.1007/s00145-008-9026-x
2. Boneh, D., Boyen, X., Shacham, H.: Short group signatures. In: Franklin, M. (ed.) CRYPTO 2004. LNCS, vol. 3152, pp. 41–55. Springer, Heidelberg (2004). https://doi.org/10.1007/978-3-540-28628-8_3
3. Boneh, D., Eskandarian, S., Kim, S., Shih, M.: Improving speed and security in updatable encryption schemes. Cryptology ePrint Archive, Report 2020/222 (2020). https://eprint.iacr.org/2020/222
4. Boneh, D., Lewi, K., Montgomery, H., Raghunathan, A.: Key homomorphic PRFs and their applications. In: Canetti, R., Garay, J.A. (eds.) CRYPTO 2013. LNCS, vol. 8042, pp. 410–428. Springer, Heidelberg (2013). https://doi.org/10.1007/978-3-642-40041-4_23
5. Boyd, C., Davies, G.T., Gjøsteen, K., Jiang, Y.: Fast and secure updatable encryption. In: Micciancio, D., Ristenpart, T. (eds.) CRYPTO 2020. LNCS, vol. 12170, pp. 464–493. Springer, Cham (2020). https://doi.org/10.1007/978-3-030-56784-2_16
6. Morse, E.A., Raval, V.: PCI DSS: payment card industry data security standards in context. Comput. Law Secur. Rev. **24**(6), 540–554 (2008)
7. Canetti, R., Krawczyk, H., Nielsen, J.B.: Relaxing chosen-ciphertext security. In: Boneh, D. (ed.) CRYPTO 2003. LNCS, vol. 2729, pp. 565–582. Springer, Heidelberg (2003). https://doi.org/10.1007/978-3-540-45146-4_33
8. Chaum, D., van Heijst, E., Pfitzmann, B.: Cryptographically strong undeniable signatures, unconditionally secure for the signer. In: Feigenbaum, J. (ed.) CRYPTO 1991. LNCS, vol. 576, pp. 470–484. Springer, Heidelberg (1992). https://doi.org/10.1007/3-540-46766-1_38
9. Chen, L., Li, Y.-N., Tang, Q.: CCA updatable encryption against malicious re-encryption attacks (full version). Cryptology ePrint Archive, Report 2020/XXX (2020)
10. Everspaugh, A., Paterson, K., Ristenpart, T., Scott, S.: Key rotation for authenticated encryption. In: Katz, J., Shacham, H. (eds.) CRYPTO 2017. LNCS, vol. 10403, pp. 98–129. Springer, Cham (2017). https://doi.org/10.1007/978-3-319-63697-9_4
11. Gennaro, R., Katz, J., Krawczyk, H., Rabin, T.: Secure network coding over the integers. In: Nguyen, P.Q., Pointcheval, D. (eds.) PKC 2010. LNCS, vol. 6056, pp. 142–160. Springer, Heidelberg (2010). https://doi.org/10.1007/978-3-642-13013-7_9
12. Groth, J.: Homomorphic trapdoor commitments to group elements. IACR Cryptol. ePrint Archive **2009**, 7 (2009)
13. Payment Card Industry. Data Security Standard. Requirements and Security Assessment Procedures. Version 3.2 PCI Security Standards Council (2016)
14. Klooß, M., Lehmann, A., Rupp, A.: (R)CCA secure updatable encryption with integrity protection. In: Ishai, Y., Rijmen, V. (eds.) EUROCRYPT 2019. LNCS, vol. 11476, pp. 68–99. Springer, Cham (2019). https://doi.org/10.1007/978-3-030-17653-2_3

15. Krawczyk, H., Bellare, M., Canetti, R.: HMAC: Keyed-hashing for message authentication (1997)
16. Krawczyk, H., Paterson, K.G., Wee, H.: On the security of the TLS protocol: a systematic analysis. In: Canetti, R., Garay, J.A. (eds.) CRYPTO 2013. LNCS, vol. 8042, pp. 429–448. Springer, Heidelberg (2013). https://doi.org/10.1007/978-3-642-40041-4_24
17. Krohn, M.N., Freedman, M.J., Mazieres, D.: On-the-fly verification of rateless erasure codes for efficient content distribution. In: Proceedings of IEEE Symposium on Security and Privacy, pp. 226–240. IEEE (2004)
18. Lehmann, A., Tackmann, B.: Updatable encryption with post-compromise security. In: Nielsen, J.B., Rijmen, V. (eds.) EUROCRYPT 2018. LNCS, vol. 10822, pp. 685–716. Springer, Cham (2018). https://doi.org/10.1007/978-3-319-78372-7_22
19. Lyubashevsky, V., Micciancio, D., Peikert, C., Rosen, A.: SWIFFT: a modest proposal for FFT hashing. In: Nyberg, K. (ed.) FSE 2008. LNCS, vol. 5086, pp. 54–72. Springer, Heidelberg (2008). https://doi.org/10.1007/978-3-540-71039-4_4
20. Maurer, U., Rüedlinger, A., Tackmann, B.: Confidentiality and integrity: a constructive perspective. In: Cramer, R. (ed.) TCC 2012. LNCS, vol. 7194, pp. 209–229. Springer, Heidelberg (2012). https://doi.org/10.1007/978-3-642-28914-9_12
21. Miyaji, A., Nakabayashi, M., Takano, S.: Characterization of elliptic curve traces under FR-reduction. In: Won, D. (ed.) ICISC 2000. LNCS, vol. 2015, pp. 90–108. Springer, Heidelberg (2001). https://doi.org/10.1007/3-540-45247-8_8
22. Pedersen, T.P.: Non-interactive and information-theoretic secure verifiable secret sharing. In: Feigenbaum, J. (ed.) CRYPTO 1991. LNCS, vol. 576, pp. 129–140. Springer, Heidelberg (1992). https://doi.org/10.1007/3-540-46766-1_9

Determining the Core Primitive for Optimally Secure Ratcheting

Fatih Balli[1], Paul Rösler[2(✉)], and Serge Vaudenay[1]

[1] LASEC, École polytechnique fédérale de Lausanne, Ecublens, Switzerland
{fatih.balli,serge.vaudenay}@epfl.ch

[2] Chair for Network and Data Security, Ruhr University Bochum, Bochum, Germany
paul.roesler@rub.de

Abstract. After ratcheting attracted attention mostly due to practical real-world protocols, recently a line of work studied ratcheting as a primitive from a theoretic point of view. Literature in this line, pursuing the strongest security of ratcheting one can hope for, utilized for constructions strong, yet inefficient key-updatable primitives – based on hierarchical identity based encryption (HIBE). As none of these works formally justified utilizing these building blocks, we answer the yet open question under which conditions their use is actually *necessary*.

We revisit these strong notions of ratcheted key exchange (RKE), and propose a more realistic (slightly stronger) security definition. In this security definition, both exposure of participants' local secrets and attacks against executions' randomness are considered. While these two attacks were partially considered in previous work, we are the first to unify them cleanly in a natural game based notion.

Our definitions are based on the systematic RKE notion by Poettering and Rösler (CRYPTO 2018). Due to slight (but meaningful) changes to regard attacks against randomness, we are ultimately able to show that, in order to fulfill strong security for RKE, public key cryptography with (independently) updatable key pairs is a necessary building block. Surprisingly, this implication already holds for the simplest RKE variant.

Hence, (1) we model optimally secure RKE under randomness manipulation to cover realistic attacks, (2) we (provably) extract the core primitive that is necessary to realize strongly secure RKE, and (3) our results indicate which relaxations in security allow for constructions that only rely on standard public key cryptography.

1 Introduction

The term "ratcheting" as well as the underlying concept of continuously updating session secrets for secure long-term communication settings originates from real-world messaging protocols [13–15]. In these protocols, first forward-secrecy [15]

The full version [2] of this article is available as entry 2020/148 in the IACR eprint archive.

S. Moriai and H. Wang (Eds.): ASIACRYPT 2020, LNCS 12493, pp. 621–650, 2020.
https://doi.org/10.1007/978-3-030-64840-4_21

and later security after state exposures [14] (also known as future secrecy, backward secrecy, or post-compromise security) were aimed to be achieved as the exposure of the devices' local states was considered a practical threat. The main motivation behind this consideration is the typical lifetime of sessions in messaging apps. As messaging apps are nowadays usually run on smartphones, the lifetime of messaging sessions is proportional to the ownership duration of a smartphone (typically several years). Due to the long lifetime of sessions and the mobile use of smartphones, scenarios, in which the local storage – containing the messaging apps' secret state – can be exposed to an attacker, are extended in comparison to use cases of other cryptographic protocols.

Practical Relevance of Randomness Manipulation
In addition to exposures of locally stored state secrets, randomness for generating (new) secrets is often considered vulnerable. This is motivated by numerous attacks in practice against randomness sources (e.g., [9]), randomness generators (e.g., [5,19]), or exposures of random coins (e.g., [18]). Most theoretic approaches try to model this threat by allowing an adversary to *reveal* attacked random coins of a protocol execution (as it was also conducted in related work on ratcheting). This, however, assumes that the attacked protocol honestly and uniformly samples its random coins (either from a high-entropy source or using a random oracle) and that these coins are only afterwards leaked to the attacker. In contrast, practically relevant attacks against bad randomness generators or low-entropy sources (e.g., [5,9,19]) change the distribution from which random coins are sampled. Consequently, this threat is only covered by a security model if considered adversaries are also allowed to *influence* the execution's (distribution of) random coins. Thus, it is important to consider randomness *manipulation* (instead of reveal), if attacks against randomness are regarded practically relevant.

The overall goal of ratcheting protocols is to reduce the effect of any such non-permanent and/or non-fatal attack to a minimum. For example, an ongoing communication under a non-fatal attack should become secure as soon as the adversary ends this attack or countermeasures become effective. Examples for countermeasures are replacing bad randomness generators via software updates, eliminating state exposing viruses, etc. Motivated by this, most widely used messaging apps are equipped with mechanisms to regularly update the local secrets such that only a short time frame of communication is compromised if an adversary was successful due to obtaining local secrets and/or attacking random coins.

Real-World Protocols
The most prominent and most widely deployed real-world ratcheting protocol is the Signal protocol (used by WhatsApp, Skype, and others). The analysis of this protocol in a multi-stage key agreement model [6] was the first theoretic treatment of ratcheting in the literature. Cohn-Gordon et al. [6], however, focus on grasping the precise security that Signal offers rather than generically defining ratcheting as an independent primitive. While the security provided by Signal

is sufficient in most real-world scenarios, we focus in this work on the theoretic analysis of the (optimally secure) primitive ratcheting.

GENERIC TREATMENT OF RATCHETING AS A PRIMITIVE
In the following we shortly introduce and review previous modeling approaches for strongly secure ratcheting. We thereby abstractly highlight modeling choices that crucially affect the constructions, secure according to these models respectively. Specifically, we indicate why some models can be instantiated with only public key cryptography (PKC) – bypassing our implication result – and others cannot. In Table 1 we summarize this overview.

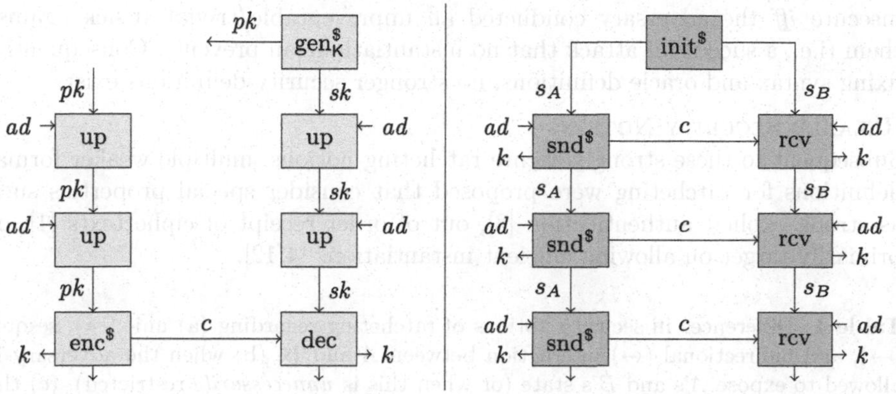

Fig. 1. Conceptual depiction of kuKEM* (on the left) and unidirectional RKE (on the right). '$' in the upper index of an algorithm name denotes that the algorithm runs probabilistically and *ad* is associated data.

The initial generic work that considers ratcheted key exchange (RKE) as a primitive and defines its syntax, correctness, and security (in a yet impractical variant) is by Bellare et al. [3]. Abstractly, their concept of ratcheted key exchange, depicted in the right part of Fig. 1, consist of an initialization that provides two session participants A and B with a state that can then be used by them to repeatedly compute new keys in this session (e.g., for use in higher level protocols). In their restricted communication model, A is allowed to compute new keys with her state and accordingly send ciphertexts to B who can then compute (the same) keys with his state. During these key computations, A's and B's states are updated respectively (to minimize the effect of state exposures). As B can only comprehend key computations from A (on receipt of a ciphertext) but cannot actively initiate the computation of new keys, this variant was later called unidirectional RKE [17]. Beyond this restriction of the communication model, the security definition by Bellare et al. only allows the adversary to expose A's temporary local state secrets, while B's state cannot be exposed (which in turn requires no forward-secrecy with respect to state updates by B). Following Bellare et al., Poettering and Rösler [16,17]propose a revised security definition of unidirectional RKE (URKE: allowing also the exposure of B's state) and extend the communication model to define syntax, correctness, and security of *sesqui*directional RKE (SRKE: additionally allows B to only send special update ciphertexts to A that do not trigger a new key computation but help him to recover from state exposures) and *bi*directional RKE (BRKE: defines A and B to participate equivalently in the communication). With a similar instantiation as Poettering and Rösler, Jaeger and Stepanovs [10] define security for bidirectional channels under state exposures and randomness reveal.

All of the above mentioned works define security *optimally* with respect to their syntax definition and the adversary's access to the primitive execution (modeled via oracles in the security game). This is reached by declaring secrets insecure *iff* the adversary conducted an unpreventable/trivial attack against them (i.e., a successful attack that no instantiation can prevent). Consequently, fixing syntax and oracle definitions, no stronger security definitions exist.

Relaxed Security Notions
Subsequent to these strongly secure ratcheting notions, multiple weaker formal definitions for ratcheting were proposed that consider special properties such as strong explicit authentication [8], out of order receipt of ciphertexts [1], or primarily target on allowing efficient instantiations [4,12].

Table 1. Differences in security notions of ratcheting regarding (a) uni- ($\rightarrow$), sesqui- ($\mapsto$), and bidirectional ($\leftrightarrow$) interaction between A and B, (b) when the adversary is allowed to expose A's and B's state (or when this is *unnecessarily* restricted), (c) the adversary's ability to reveal or manipulate algorithm invocations' random coins, and (d) how soon and how complete recovery from these two attacks into a secure state is required of *secure* constructions (or if *unnecessary* delays or exceptions for recovery are permitted). ('*Unnecessary*' refers to restrictions beyond those that are immediately implied by optimal security definitions (that only restrict the adversary with respect to unpreventable/trivial attacks).) Recovery from attacks required by Jost et al. [12] is *immediate* in so far as their restrictions of state exposures introduce delays implicitly. Gray marked cells indicate the reason (i.e., relaxations in security) why respective instantiations can rely on standard PKC only (circumventing our implication result). Rows without gray marked cells have no construction based on pure PKC.

	(a) Interaction	(b) State Exposure	(c) Bad Randomness	(d) Recovery
C+ [6]	$\leftrightarrow$	Always allowed	Reveal	Delayed
B+ [3]	$\rightarrow$	Only allowed for A	Reveal	Immediate
PR [17]	$\rightarrow$	Always allowed	Not considered	Immediate
	$\mapsto$	Always allowed	Not considered	Immediate
	$\leftrightarrow$	Always allowed	Not considered	Immediate
JS [10]	$\leftrightarrow$	Always allowed	Reveal	Immediate
DV [8]	$\leftrightarrow$	Always allowed	Not considered	Partial
JMM [12]	$\rightarrow$	Partially restricted	Reveal	(Immediate)
	$\mapsto$	Partially restricted	Reveal	(Immediate)
	$\leftrightarrow$	Partially restricted	Reveal	(Immediate)
ACD [1]	$\leftrightarrow$	Always allowed	Manipulation	Delayed
CDV [4]	$\leftrightarrow$	Always allowed	Not considered	Delayed
This work	$\rightarrow$	Always allowed	Manipulation	Immediate

While these works are syntactically similar, we shortly sketch their different relaxations regarding security – making their security notions sub-optimal. Durak and Vaudenay [8] and Caforio et al. [4] forbid the adversary to perform impersonation attacks against the communication between A and B during the establishment of a *secure* key. Thus, they do not require recovery from state exposures – which are a part of impersonation attacks – in all possible cases, which we denote as "partial recovery" (see Table 1). Furthermore, both works neglect bad randomness as an attack vector. In the security experiments by Jost et al. [12] and Alwen et al. [1] constructions can delay the recovery from attacks longer than necessary (Jost et al. therefore temporarily forbid the exposure of the local state). Additionally, they do not require the participants' states to become incompatible (immediately) on active attacks against the communication.

Instantiations of Ratcheting
Interestingly, both mentioned *uni*directional RKE instantiations that were defined to depict optimal security [3,17] as well as bidirectional real-world examples such as the Signal protocol (analyzed in [6]), and instantiations of the above named relaxed security notions [1,4,8,12] only rely on standard PKC (cf. rows in Table 1 with gray cells).

In contrast, both mentioned optimally secure bidirectional ratcheting variants (i.e., sesquidirectional and bidirectional RKE [17], and bidirectional strongly secure channel [10]) are based on a strong cryptographic building block, called *key-updatable public key encryption*, which can be built from hierarchical identity based encryption (HIBE). Intuitively, key-updatable public key encryption is standard public key encryption that additionally allows to update public key and secret key independently with respect to some associated data (a conceptual depiction of this is on the left side of Fig. 1). Thereby an updated secret key cannot be used to decrypt ciphertexts that were encrypted to previous (or different) versions of this secret key (where versions are defined over the associated data used for updates).

We emphasize a significant difference between key-updatable public key encryption and HkuPke (introduced in [12]): in HkuPke key updates rely on interactive communication between holders of public key and secret key, and associated data for key updates is not fully adversary-controlled. These differences make it strictly weaker, insufficient for optimal security of RKE (on which we further elaborate in Sect. 3).

Necessity for Strong Building Blocks
Natural questions that arise from this line of work are, whether and under which conditions such strong (HIBE-like) building blocks are not only sufficient but also necessary to instantiate the strong security of (bidirectional) RKE. In order to answer these questions, we build key-updatable public key cryptography from ratcheted key exchange. Consequently we affirm the necessity and provide (sufficient) conditions for relying on these strong building blocks. We therefore minimally adjust the syntax of key-updatable key encapsulation

mechanism (kuKEM) [17] and consider the manipulation of algorithm invocations' random coins in our security definitions of kuKEM and RKE.

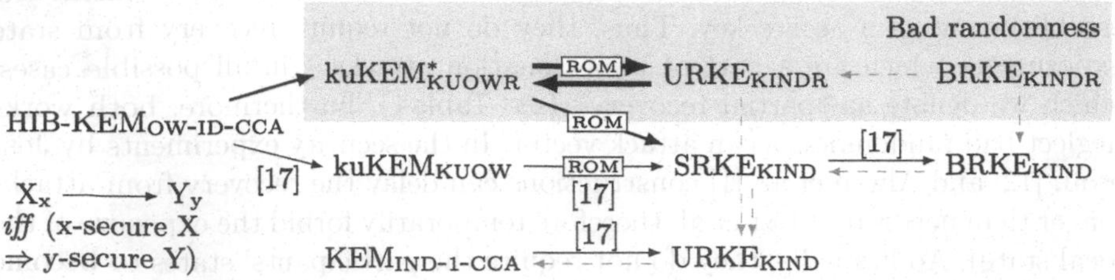

Fig. 2. The contributions of this paper (bold arrows) and their connection to previous work (thin arrows) involving RKE (uni-, sesqui-, and bidirectional) and KEM (standard, hierarchical-identity-based, and key-updatable) primitives. ROM indicates that the proof holds in the random oracle model. $\text{kuKEM}^*_{\text{KUOWR}} \Rightarrow_{\text{ROM}} \text{SRKE}_{\text{KIND}}$ is not formally proven in this paper, but we point out that the proof of $\text{kuKEM}_{\text{KUOW}} \Rightarrow_{\text{ROM}} \text{SRKE}_{\text{KIND}}$ from [17] can be rewound. Gray dashed connections indicate trivial implications (due to strictly weaker syntax or security definitions).

As a result we show that (see Fig. 2):

- kuKEM* (with one-way security under manipulation of randomness)[1] $\Rightarrow_{\text{ROM}}$ Unidirectional RKE (with key indistinguishability under manipulation of randomness),
- Unidirectional RKE (with key indistinguishability under manipulation of randomness) ⇒ kuKEM* (with one-way security under manipulation of randomness).

Given the security notions established in honest randomness setting and their connections to each other, one would also expect Group RKE ⇒ Bidirectional RKE ⇒ Sesquidirectional RKE ⇒ Unidirectional RKE to follow. Hence, our results indicate that stronger RKE variants also likely require building blocks as hard as kuKEM*. Furthermore, our results show that: One-way security under manipulation of randomness of kuKEM* $\Rightarrow_{\text{ROM}}$ Key indistinguishability of *sesquidirectional* RKE. Interestingly, these results induce that (when considering strong security) ratcheted key exchange requires these strong (HIBE-like) building blocks not only for bidirectional communication settings, but already for the unidirectional case. Both mentioned previous unidirectional RKE schemes can bypass our implication because they forbid exposures of B's state [3] or assume secure randomness [17] (see Table 1). We describe attacks against each of both constructions in our security definition in the full version [2]. Similarly,

[1] The asterisk at kuKEM* indicates the minimal adjustment to the kuKEM syntax definition from [17]. For the kuKEM* we consider one-way security as it suffices to achieve strong security for RKE.

the discussed relaxed security definitions of ratcheting [1,4,6,8,12] allow for efficient constructions because they restrict the adversary more than necessary (see Table 1). Although our analysis was partially motivated by the use of kuKEM in [10,17], we do not ultimately answer whether these particular constructions necessarily relied on it. Rather we provide a clean set of conditions under which RKE and kuKEM clearly imply each other as we do not consider the justification of previous constructions but a clear relation for future work important.

Thus, we show that sufficient conditions for necessarily relying on kuKEM as a building block of RKE are: (a) unrestricted exposure of both parties' local states, (b) consideration of attacks against algorithm invocations' random coins, and (c) required immediate recovery from these two attacks into a secure state by the security definition (i.e., the adversary is only restricted with respect to unpreventable/trivial attacks).[2]

Contributions

The contributions of our work can be summarized as follows:

- We are the first who systematically define optimal security of key-updatable KEM and unidirectional RKE under randomness manipulation (in Sects. 3 and 4) and thereby consider this practical threat in addition to state exposures in an instantiation-independent notion of RKE. Thereby we substantially enhance the respective models by Poettering and Rösler [17].
- In Sect. 5, we construct unidirectional RKE generically from a kuKEM* to show that the latter suffices as a building block for the former under manipulation of randomness.
- To show that kuKEM* is not only sufficient but also necessary to build unidirectional RKE (under randomness manipulation), we provide a construction of kuKEM* from a generic unidirectional RKE scheme in Sect. 6.

With our results we distill the core building block of strongly secure ratcheted key exchange down to its syntax and security definition. This allows further research to be directed towards instantiating kuKEM* schemes that are more familiar and easier in terms of security requirements, rather than attempting to construct seemingly more complex RKE primitives.[3] Simultaneously, our results

[2] Note that there may exist further sets of sufficient conditions for relying on kuKEMs since, for example, sesqui- and bidirectional RKE by Poettering and Rösler [16,17] violate condition (b) but base on kuKEMs as well. We refer the reader to Appendix B.2 in [16] for a detailed explanation of why their scheme presumably also must rely on a kuKEM. We leave the identification of further sets of conditions as future work.

[3] For example, the bidirectional channel construction in the proceedings version of [10] is not secure according to the security definition (but a corrected version is published as [11]), in the acknowledgments of [16] it is mentioned that an early submitted version of their construction was also flawed, and for an earlier version of [8] we detected during our work (and informed the authors) that the construction was insecure under bad randomness such that the updated proceedings version (also available as [7]) disregards attacks against randomness entirely. Finally, we detected and reported that the construction of HkuPke in [12] is not even correct.

indicate the cryptographic hardness of ratcheted key exchange and thereby help to systematize and comprehend the security definitions and different dimensions of ratcheting in the literature. As a consequence, our results contribute to a fact-based trade-off between security and efficiency for RKE by providing requirements for relying on heavy building blocks and thereby revealing respective bypasses.

2 Preliminaries

2.1 Notation

By $x \leftarrow y$ we define the assignment of the value of variable y to variable x and thus for a function X, $x \leftarrow \mathrm{X}(y)$ means that x is assigned with the evaluation output of X on input y. We define $\mathtt{T}, \mathtt{F}$ as Boolean values for true and false. The shortcut notion $w \leftarrow x\ ?\ y : z$ means that 'if $x = \mathtt{T}$, then $w \leftarrow y$, otherwise $w \leftarrow z$'. For a probabilistic algorithm Y, $x \leftarrow_{\$} \mathrm{Y}(y)$ denotes the probabilistic evaluation of Y on input y with output x and $x \leftarrow \mathrm{Y}(y; r)$ denotes the deterministic evaluation of Y on y with output x where the evaluation's randomness is fixed to r. For a set $\mathcal{X}$, $x \leftarrow_{\$} \mathcal{X}$ is the uniform random sampling of value x from $\mathcal{X}$. We use the shortcut notion $\mathcal{X} \xleftarrow{\cup} \mathcal{Y}$ to denote the union $\mathcal{X} \leftarrow \mathcal{X} \cup \mathcal{Y}$ of sets $\mathcal{X}$ and $\mathcal{Y}$.

Symbol 'ϵ' denotes an empty string and symbol '$\perp$' denotes an undefined element or an output that indicates rejections (thus it is not an element of explicitly defined sets).

By $\mathcal{X}^*$, we denote the set of all lists of arbitrary size whose elements belong to $\mathcal{X}$. We abuse the notation of empty string 'ϵ' by writing $L = \epsilon$ for an empty list L. If an element $x \in \mathcal{X}$ is appended to list L then we denote this by $L \leftarrow L \| x$ (or simply $L \xleftarrow{\|} x$). Thus, '$\|$' denotes a special concatenation symbol that is not an element of any of the explicitly defined sets. We define relations prefix-or-equal $\preceq$ and strictly-prefix $\prec$ over two lists. For instance, for lists $L, L_0 = L\|x, L_1 = L\|y$ where $x, y \in \mathcal{X}, x \neq y$ we have that $L \preceq L, L \nprec L, L \prec L_0, L \prec L_1, L_0 \npreceq L_1, L_1 \npreceq L_0$ meaning that L is a prefix of L_0 and L_1 but neither of L_0, L_1 is a prefix of the other. By $X[\cdot]$ we denote an associative array.

In our security experiments, that we denote with **Game**, we invoke adversaries via instruction 'Invoke'. These adversaries are denoted by $\mathcal{A}, \mathcal{B}$. Adversaries have access to the security experiment's interface, which is defined by oracles that are denoted by the term **Oracle**. Games are terminated via instructions 'Stop with x' (meaning that x is returned by the game) or 'Reward b' (meaning that the game terminates and returns 1 if $b = \mathtt{T}$). In procedures that we denote by **Proc** and in oracles, we use the shortcut notion 'Require x'. Depending on the procedure's or oracle's number of return values n, that means 'If $x = \mathtt{F}$, then return $\perp^n$'.

2.2 Message Authentication Code

We define a message authentication code to be a set of algorithms $\mathsf{M} = (\mathrm{tag}, \mathrm{vfy}_\mathsf{M})$ over a set of symmetric keys $\mathcal{K}$, a message space $\mathcal{M}$, and a tag space $\mathcal{T}$. The syntax is defined as:

$$\mathcal{K} \times \mathcal{M} \to \mathrm{tag} \to \mathcal{T}$$
$$\mathcal{K} \times \mathcal{M} \times \mathcal{T} \to \mathrm{vfy}_\mathsf{M} \to \{\mathtt{T}, \bot\}$$

Please note that we define the tag algorithm explicitly deterministic.

For correctness of a MAC we define that for all $k \in \mathcal{K}$ and all $m \in \mathcal{M}$ it is required that $\mathrm{vfy}_\mathsf{M}(k, m, \mathrm{tag}(k, m)) = \mathtt{T}$.

We define a one-time multi-instance strong unforgeability notion SUF for MAC security – that is equivalent with standard strong unforgeability – for which the formal security game is depicted in the full version [2]. That is, for a game in which an adversary can generate instances i (with independent uniformly random keys $k_i \leftarrow_\$ \mathcal{K}$) via an oracle Gen, the adversary can query a Tag oracle on a message m from message space $\mathcal{M}$ for each instance at most once to obtain the respective MAC tag. Additionally, the adversary can verify MAC tags for specified messages and instances via oracle Vfy and obtain an instance's key by querying an Expose oracle for this instance. The adversary wins by providing a forgery (m, τ) for an instance i to the Vfy oracle if there was no $\mathrm{Tag}(i, m)$ query before with output τ and if i's key was not exposed via oracle Expose. We define the advantage of winning the SUF game against a MAC scheme M as $\mathrm{Adv}^{\mathrm{suf}}_{\mathsf{M}}(\mathcal{A}) = \Pr[\mathrm{SUF}_\mathsf{M}(\mathcal{A}) \to 1]$.

3 Sufficient Security for Key-Updatable KEM

A key-updatable key encapsulation mechanism (kuKEM) is a key encapsulation mechanism that provides update algorithms for public key and secret key with respect to some associated data respectively. Prior to our work, this primitive was used to instantiate sesquidirectional RKE. In order to allow for our equivalence result, we minimally adjust the original kuKEM notion by Poettering and Rösler [17] and call it kuKEM*. The small, yet crucial changes comprise allowed updates of public and secret key during encapsulation and decapsulation (in our syntax definition) as well as the adversary's ability to manipulate utilized randomness of encapsulations (in our security definition). In Sect. 6 the rationales behind these changes are clarified. In order to provide a coherent definition, we not only describe alterations towards previous work but define kuKEM* entirely (as we consider our changes to be a significant contribution and believe that this strengthens comprehensibility).

Syntax. A kuKEM* is a set of algorithms $\mathsf{K} = (\mathrm{gen}_\mathsf{K}, \mathrm{up}, \mathrm{enc}, \mathrm{dec})$ with sets of public keys $\mathcal{PK}$ and secret keys $\mathcal{SK}$, a set of associated data $\mathcal{AD}$ for updating the keys, a set of ciphertexts $\mathcal{C}$ (with $\mathcal{AD} \cap \mathcal{C} = \emptyset$), and a set of encapsulated keys $\mathcal{K}$. Furthermore we define $\mathcal{R}$ as the set of random coins used during the encapsulation:

$\text{gen}_K \to_{\$} \mathcal{PK} \times \mathcal{SK}$
$\mathcal{PK} \times \mathcal{AD} \to \text{up} \to \mathcal{PK}$
$\mathcal{SK} \times \mathcal{AD} \to \text{up} \to \mathcal{SK}$
$\mathcal{PK} \times \mathcal{R} \to \text{enc} \to \mathcal{PK} \times \mathcal{K} \times \mathcal{C}$ or $\mathcal{PK} \to \text{enc} \to_{\$} \mathcal{PK} \times \mathcal{K} \times \mathcal{C}$
$\mathcal{SK} \times \mathcal{C} \to \text{dec} \to (\mathcal{SK} \times \mathcal{K}) \cup \{(\bot, \bot)\}$

Please note that the encapsulation and decapsulation may modify the public key and the secret key respectively – as a result, the kuKEM* is stateful (where the public key is a public state).[4]

Correctness. The correctness for kuKEM* is (for simplicity) defined through game CORR$_K$ (see Fig. 3), in which an adversary $\mathcal{A}$ can query encapsulation, decapsulation, and update oracles. The adversary (against correctness) wins if different keys are computed during decapsulation and the corresponding encapsulation even though compatible key updates were conducted and ciphertexts from encapsulations were directly forwarded to the decapsulation oracle.

Definition 1 (kuKEM* correctness). *A kuKEM* scheme K is correct if for every $\mathcal{A}$, the probability of winning game CORR$_K$ from Fig. 3 is* $\Pr[\text{CORR}_K(\mathcal{A}) \to 1] = 0$.

Game CORR$_K(\mathcal{A})$	**Oracle** Up$_R(ad)$	**Oracle** Dec(c)
00 $(pk, sk) \leftarrow_{\$} \text{gen}_K$	09 Require $ad \in \mathcal{AD}$	17 Require $c \in \mathcal{C}$
01 $key[\cdot] \leftarrow \bot$	10 $sk \leftarrow \text{up}(sk, ad)$	18 $(sk, k) \leftarrow \text{dec}(sk, c)$
02 $trs \leftarrow \epsilon; trr \leftarrow \epsilon$	11 $trr \xleftarrow{"} ad$	19 $trr \xleftarrow{"} c$
03 Invoke $\mathcal{A}$	12 Return	20 If $trr \preceq trs$:
04 Stop with 0		21 Reward $k \neq key[trr]$
	Oracle Enc()	22 Return
Oracle Up$_S(ad)$	13 $(pk, k, c) \leftarrow_{\$} \text{enc}(pk)$	
05 Require $ad \in \mathcal{AD}$	14 $trs \xleftarrow{"} c$	
06 $pk \leftarrow \text{up}(pk, ad)$	15 $key[trs] \leftarrow k$	
07 $trs \xleftarrow{"} ad$	16 Return (pk, c)	
08 Return		

Fig. 3. The correctness notion of kuKEM* captured through game CORR.

Security. Here we describe KUOWR security of kuKEM* as formally depicted in Fig. 4. KUOWR defines one-way security of kuKEM* under randomness manipulation in a multi-instance/multi-challenge setting.

Intuitively, the KUOWR game requires that a secret key can only be used for decapsulation of a ciphertext if prior to this decapsulation all updates of this

---

[4] As kuKEM* naturally provides no security for encapsulated keys if the adversary can manipulate the randomness for gen$_K$ already, we only consider the manipulation of random coins for enc.

Game $\text{KUOWR}_{\mathsf{K}}(\mathcal{A})$
00 $n \leftarrow 0$
01 Invoke $\mathcal{A}$
02 Stop with 0

Oracle Gen
03 $n \leftarrow n+1$
04 $(pk_n, sk_n) \leftarrow_{\$} \text{gen}_{\mathsf{K}}$
05 $\text{CK}_n[\cdot] \leftarrow \bot$; $\text{XP}_n \leftarrow \emptyset$
06 $trs_n \leftarrow \epsilon$; $trr_n \leftarrow \epsilon$
07 $SK_n[\cdot] \leftarrow \bot$
08 $SK_n[trr_n] \leftarrow sk_n$
09 Return pk_n

Oracle $\text{Up}_S(i, ad)$
10 Require $1 \le i \le n \wedge ad \in \mathcal{AD}$
11 $pk_i \leftarrow \text{up}(pk_i, ad)$
12 $trs_i \xleftarrow{\shortparallel} ad$
13 Return pk_i

Oracle $\text{Enc}(i, rc)$
14 Require $1 \le i \le n$
15 · Require $rc \in \mathcal{R} \cup \{\epsilon\}$
16 · If $rc = \epsilon$: $mr \leftarrow \text{F}$; $rc \leftarrow_{\$} \mathcal{R}$
17 · Else: $mr \leftarrow \text{T}$
18 · $(pk_i, k, c) \leftarrow \text{enc}(pk_i; rc)$
19 · $trs_i \xleftarrow{\shortparallel} c$
20 · If $mr = \text{F}$: $\text{CK}_i[trs_i] \leftarrow k$
21 · Return (pk_i, c)

Oracle $\text{Solve}(i, tr, k)$
22 Require $1 \le i \le n$
23 Require $tr \notin \text{XP}_i$
24 Require $\text{CK}_i[tr] \ne \bot$
25 Reward $k = \text{CK}_i[tr]$
26 Return

Oracle $\text{Up}_R(i, ad)$
27 Require $1 \le i \le n \wedge ad \in \mathcal{AD}$
28 $sk_i \leftarrow \text{up}(sk_i, ad)$
29 $trr_i \xleftarrow{\shortparallel} ad$
30 $SK_i[trr_i] \leftarrow sk_i$
31 Return

Oracle $\text{Dec}(i, c)$
32 Require $1 \le i \le n \wedge c \in \mathcal{C}$
33 · $(sk_i, k) \leftarrow \text{dec}(sk_i, c)$
34 · $trr_i \xleftarrow{\shortparallel} c$
35 · $SK_i[trr_i] \leftarrow sk_i$
36 · If $\text{CK}_i[trr_i] \ne \bot$:
37 · Return
38 · Return k

Oracle $\text{Expose}(i, tr)$
39 Require $1 \le i \le n$
40 · Require $SK_i[tr] \in \mathcal{SK}$
41 · $\text{XP}_i \xleftarrow{\cup} \{tr^* \in (\mathcal{AD} \cup \mathcal{C})^* : tr \preceq tr^*\}$
42 Return $SK_i[tr]$

Fig. 4. Security experiment KUOWR, modeling one-way security of key-updatable KEM in a multi-instance/multi-challenge setting under randomness manipulation. Lines of code tagged with '·' are (substantially) modified with respect to KUOW security in [16]. Line 41 is a shortcut notion that can be implemented efficiently. CK: challenge keys, XP: exposed secret keys, *trs*, *trr*: transcripts.

secret key and all decapsulations with this secret key were consistent with the updates of and encapsulations with the respective public key. This is reflected by using the transcript (of public key updates and encapsulations or secret key updates and decapsulations) as a reference to encapsulated "challenge keys" and secret keys.

In order to let the adversary play with the kuKEM*'s algorithms, the game provides oracles Gen, Up_S, Up_R, Enc, and Dec. Thereby instances (i.e., key pairs) can be generated via oracle Gen and are referenced in the remaining oracles by a counter that refers to when the respective instance was generated.

For encapsulation via oracle Enc, the adversary can either choose the invocation's random coins by setting rc to some value that is not the empty string ϵ or let the encapsulation be called on fresh randomness by setting $rc = \epsilon$ (line 16).

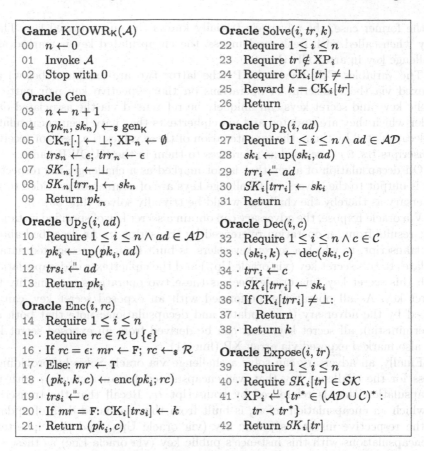

In the former case, the adversary trivially knows the encapsulated key. Thus, only when called with fresh randomness, the encapsulated key is marked as a challenge key in array CK (line 20).

The variables CK, SK, and XP (the latter two are explained below) are indexed via the transcript of operations on the respective key pair part. As public keys and secret keys can uniquely be referenced via the associated data under which they are updated and via ciphertexts that have been encapsulated or decapsulated by them, the concatenation of these values (i.e., sent or received transcripts trs, trr) are used as references to them in the KUOWR game.

On decapsulation of a key that is not marked as a challenge, the respective key is output to the adversary. Challenge keys are of course not provided to the adversary as thereby the challenge would be trivially solved (line 36).

Via oracle Expose, the adversary can obtain a secret key of specified instance i that results from an operation referenced by transcript tr. As described above, the transcript, to which a secret key refers, is built from the associated data of updates to this secret key (via oracle Up_R) and the ciphertexts of decapsulations with this secret key (via oracle Dec) as these two operations may modify the secret key. As all operations, performed with an exposed secret key, can be traced by the adversary (i.e., updates and decapsulations; note that both are deterministic), all secret keys that can be derived from an exposed secret key are also marked exposed via array XP (line 41).

Finally, an adversary can solve a challenge via oracle Solve by providing a guess for the challenge key that was encapsulated for an instance i with the encapsulation that is referenced by transcript tr. Recall that the transcript, to which an encapsulation refers, is built from the associated data of updates to the respective instance's public key (via oracle Up_S) and the ciphertexts of encapsulations with this instance's public key (via oracle Enc) as these two operations may modify the public key for encapsulation. If the secret key for decapsulating the referenced challenge key is not marked exposed (line 23) and the guess for the challenge key is correct (line 24), then game KUOWR stops with '1' (via 'Reward') meaning that the adversary wins.

Definition 2 (KUOWR **Advantage**). *The advantage of an adversary $\mathcal{A}$ against a* kuKEM* *scheme* K *in game* KUOWR *from Fig. 4 is defined as* $\text{Adv}_{\mathsf{K}}^{\text{kuowr}}(\mathcal{A}) = \Pr[\text{KUOWR}_{\mathsf{K}}(\mathcal{A}) \rightarrow 1]$.

We chose to consider one-way security as opposed to key indistinguishability for the kuKEM* as it suffices to show equivalence with key indistinguishability of RKE (in the ROM).

Differences Compared to Previous Security Definition. In Fig. 4 we denote changes from KUOW security (cf., Figure 1 [16]) by adding '·' at the beginning of lines. Below we elaborate on these differences.

The main difference in our definition of KUOWR security compared to KUOW security is that we allow the adversary to manipulate the execution's random coins. As we define encapsulation and decapsulation to (potentially) update the used public key or secret key, another conceptual difference is that we only allow the adversary to encapsulate and decapsulate once under each public and secret key. Thus, we assume that public and secret keys are overwritten on encapsulation and decapsulation respectively. In contrast to our security definition, in the KUOW security game only the current secret key of an instance can be exposed. Even though we assume the secret key to be replaced by its newer versions on updates or decapsulations, there might be, for example, backups that store older secret key versions. As a result we view the restriction of only allowing exposures of the current secret key artificial.[5] An important notational choice is that we index the variables with transcripts *trs*, *trr* instead of integer counters. This notation reflects the idea that public key and secret key only stay compatible as long as they are used correspondingly and immediately diverge on different associated data or tampered ciphertexts.

We further highlight the fundamental difference towards HkuPke by Jost et al. [12]. Their notion of HkuPke does not allow (fully adversary-controlled) associated data on public and secret key updates and additionally requires (authenticated) interaction between the holders of the key parts thereby. Looking ahead, this makes this primitive insufficient for diverging the public key from the secret key (in the states) of users A and B during an impersonation of A towards B in (U)RKE (especially under randomness manipulation). This is, however, required in an optimal security definition but explicitly excluded in the sub-optimal RKE notion by Jost et al. [12]. Since the syntax of HkuPke is already inadequate to reflect this security property, we cannot provide a separating attack. Nevertheless, we further expound this weakness in the full version [2].

Instantiation. A kuKEM* scheme, secure in the KUOWR game, can be generically constructed from an OW-CCA adaptively secure hierarchical identity based key encapsulation mechanism (HIB-KEM). The construction – the same as in [16] – is provided for completeness in Fig. 5. The update of public keys is the concatenation of associated data (interpreted as identities in the HIB-KEM) and the update of secret keys is the delegation to lower level secret keys in the identity hierarchy. The reduction is immediate: After guessing for which public key and after how many updates the challenge encapsulation that is solved by the adversary is queried, the challenge from the OW-CCA game is embedded into the respective KUOWR challenge.

Sufficiency of KUOWR *for SRKE.* Before proving equivalence between security of key-updatable KEM and ratcheted key exchange, we shed a light on implications due to the differences between our notion of kuKEM* and its KUOWR security and the notion of kuKEM and its KUOW security in [16].

[5] It is important to note that the equivalence between KUOWR security of kuKEM* and KINDR security of URKE is independent of this definitional choice – if either both definitions allow or both definitions forbid the exposure of also past secret keys or states respectively, equivalence can be shown.

```
Proc gen_K
(pk_ID, sk_ID) ←$ gen_ID
id ← ε
pk ← (pk_ID, id)
sk ← sk_ID
Return (pk, sk)

Proc enc(pk)
(pk_ID, id) ← pk
(c, k) ←$ enc_ID(pk_ID, id)
id ←∥ c
pk ← (pk_ID, id)
Return (pk, k, c)

Proc up(sk, ad)
sk ← del_ID(sk, ad)
Return sk

Proc up(pk, ad)
(pk_ID, id) ← pk
id ←∥ ad
pk ← (pk_ID, id)
Return pk

Proc dec(sk, c)
k ← dec_ID(sk, c)
sk ← del_ID(sk, c)
Return (sk, k)
```

Fig. 5. Generic construction of a kuKEM* from a hierarchical identity based KEM $\mathsf{HK} = (\mathrm{gen_{ID}}, \mathrm{del_{ID}}, \mathrm{enc_{ID}}, \mathrm{dec_{ID}})$ (slightly differing from construction in [16] Fig. 2 by adding an internal key update in encapsulation and decapsulation respectively).

Remark 1. Even though the KUOWR game provides more power to the adversary in comparison to the KUOW game by allowing manipulation of random coins, exposures of past secret keys, and providing an explicit decapsulation oracle (instead of an oracle that only allows for checks of ciphertext-key pairs; cf., Figure 1 [16]), the game also restricts the adversary's power by only allowing decapsulations under the current secret key of an instance (as opposed to also checking ciphertext-key pairs for past secret keys of an instance as in the KUOW game). One can exploit this and define protocols that are secure with respect to one game definition but allow for attacks in the other game. Consequently, neither of both security definitions implies the other one.

Despite the above described distinction between both security definitions, KUOWR security suffices to build sesquidirectional RKE according to the KIND definition in [17] – which was yet the weakest notion of security of RKE for which a construction was built from a key-updatable public key primitive. The ability to check ciphertext-key pairs under past versions of secret keys of an instance is actually never used in the proof of Poettering and Rösler [16]. The only case in which this Check oracle is used in their proof is B's receipt of a manipulated ciphertext from the adversary. Checking whether a ciphertext-key pair for the current version of a secret key of an instance is valid, can of course be conducted by using the Dec oracle of our KUOWR notion. For full details on their proof we refer the reader to Appendix C in [16].

Consequently, for the construction of KIND secure sesquidirectional RKE (according to [17] Figure 18) from Poettering and Rösler [17], the used kuKEM must either be KUOW secure (see [17] Figure 1) or KUOWR secure (see Fig. 4), which is formally depicted in the following observation. Thus, even though these notions are not equivalent, they both suffice for constructing KIND secure sesquidirectional RKE.

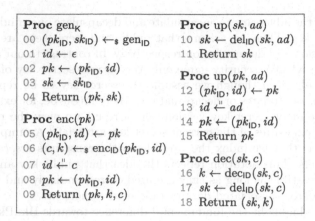

Observation 1. *The sesquidirectional RKE protocol* R *from [17] Fig. 6 offers* key indistinguishability *according to [17] Fig. 8 if function* H *is modeled as a random oracle, the* kuKEM* *provides* KUOWR *security according to Fig. 4, the one-time signature scheme provides* SUF *security according to [16] Fig. 22, the* MAC *scheme* M *provides* SUF *security according to Sect. 2.2, and the symmetric-key space of the* kuKEM* *is sufficiently large.*

4 Unidirectional RKE Under Randomness Manipulation

Unidirectional RKE (URKE) is the simplest variant of ratcheted key exchange. After a common initialization of a session between two parties A and B, it enables the continuous establishment of keys within this session. In this unidirectional setting, A can initiate the computation of keys repeatedly. With each computation, a ciphertext is generated that is sent to B, who can then comprehend the computation and output (the same) key. Restricting A and B to this unidirectional communication setting, in which B cannot respond, allows to understand the basic principles of ratcheted key exchange. For the same reasons we provided the whole definition of kuKEM* before (i.e., we see our changes as a significant contribution and aim for a coherent depiction), we fully define URKE under randomness manipulation below.

Syntax. We recall that URKE is a set of algorithms $\mathsf{UR} = (\text{init}, \text{snd}, \text{rcv})$ defined over sets of A's and B's states $\mathcal{S}_A$ and $\mathcal{S}_B$ respectively, a set of associated data $\mathcal{AD}$, a set of ciphertexts $\mathcal{C}$, and a set of keys $\mathcal{K}$ established between A and B. We extend the syntax of URKE by explicitly regarding the utilized randomness of the snd algorithm. Consequently we define $\mathcal{R}$ as the set of random coins $rc \in \mathcal{R}$ used in snd. To highlight that A only sends and B only receives in URKE, we may add 'A' and 'B' as handles to the index of snd, and rcv respectively.

$$\text{init} \to_{\$} \mathcal{S}_A \times \mathcal{S}_B$$
$$\mathcal{S}_A \times \mathcal{AD} \times \mathcal{R} \to \text{snd} \to \mathcal{S}_A \times \mathcal{K} \times \mathcal{C} \text{ or } \mathcal{S}_A \times \mathcal{AD} \to \text{snd} \to_{\$} \mathcal{S}_A \times \mathcal{K} \times \mathcal{C}$$
$$\mathcal{S}_B \times \mathcal{AD} \times \mathcal{C} \to \text{rcv} \to \mathcal{S}_B \times \mathcal{K} \cup \{(\bot, \bot)\}$$

Please note that de-randomizing (or explicitly considering the randomness of) the initialization of URKE is of little value since an adversary, when controlling the random coins of init, obtains all information necessary to compute all keys between A and B.

Correctness. Below we define correctness for URKE. Intuitively a URKE scheme is correct, if all keys produced with send operations of A can also be obtained with the resulting ciphertext by the respective receive operations of B.

Definition 3 (**URKE Correctness**). *Let* $\{ad_i \in \mathcal{AD}\}_{i \geq 1}$ *be a sequence of associated data. Let* $\{s_{A,i}\}_{i \geq 0}, \{s_{B,i}\}_{i \geq 0}$ *denote the sequences of* A*'s and* B*'s states generated by applying* $\text{snd}(\cdot, ad_i)$ *and* $\text{rcv}(\cdot, ad_i, \cdot)$ *operations iteratively for* $i \geq 1$, *that is,* $(s_{A,i}, k_i, c_i) \leftarrow_{\$} \text{snd}(s_{A,i-1}, ad_i)$ *and* $(s_{B,i}, k'_i) \leftarrow \text{rcv}(s_{B,i-1}, ad_i, c_i)$. *We say* URKE *scheme* $\mathsf{UR} = (\text{init}, \text{snd}, \text{rcv})$ *is correct if for all* $s_{A,0}, s_{B,0} \leftarrow_{\$}$ init, *for all associated data sequences* $\{ad_i\}_{i\geq 1}$, *and for all random coins used for* snd *calls, the key sequences* $\{k_i\}_{i\geq 1}$ *and* $\{k'_i\}_{i\geq 1}$ *generated as above are equal.*

Security. For security, we provide the KINDR game for defining key indistinguishability under randomness manipulation of URKE in Fig. 6. In this game, the adversary can let the session participants A and B send and receive ciphertexts via SndA and RcvB oracle queries respectively to establish keys between them. By querying the Reveal or Challenge oracles, the adversary can obtain these established keys or receive a challenge key (that is either the real established key or a randomly sampled element from the key space) respectively. Finally, the adversary can expose A's and B's state as the output of a specified send or receive operation respectively via oracles ExposeA or ExposeB.

When querying the SndA oracle, the adversary can specify the random coins for the invocation of the snd algorithm from the set $\mathcal{R}$ or indicate that it wants the random coins to be sampled uniformly at random by letting $rc = \epsilon$. By allowing the adversary to set the randomness for the invocations of the snd algorithm and exposing past states (which was not permitted in the definition of Poettering and Rösler [17]), new trivial attacks arise.

Below we review and explain the trivial attacks of the original URKE KIND game, map them to our version, and then introduce new trivial attacks that arise due to randomness manipulation.

A conceptual difference between our game definition and the games by Poettering and Rösler [17] is the way variables (especially arrays) are indexed. While the KIND games of [17] make use of counters (of send and receive operations) to index computed keys and adversarial events, we use the communicated transcripts, sent and received by A and B respectively, as indices. We thereby heavily exploit the fact that synchronicity (and divergence) of the communication between A and B are defined over these transcripts, which results in a more comprehensible (but equivalent) game notation. Please note that, due to our indexing scheme, it suffices for our game definition to maintain a common key array $key[\cdot]$ and common sets of known keys KN and challenged keys CH for A and B (as opposed to arrays and sets for each party).[6]

The lines marked with '$\cdot$' in Fig. 6 denote the handling of trivial attacks without randomness manipulation (as in [17]). Lines marked with '$\circ$' introduce modifications that become necessary due the new trivial attacks based on manipulation of randomness.

Trivial attacks without randomness manipulations are:

(a) If the adversary reveals a key via oracle Reveal, then challenging this key via oracle Challenge is trivial. In order to prevent reveal and challenge of the same key, sets KN and CH trace which keys have been revealed (line 23)

[6] This is because a key, computed during the sending of A and the corresponding receiving of B, only differs between A and B if the received transcript of B diverged from the sent transcript of A.

```
Game KINDR^b_UR(A)
00   XP_A ← ∅; MR ← ∅
01   KN ← ∅; CH ← ∅
02   trs ← ε; trr ← ε
03   S_A[·] ← ⊥; S_B[·] ← ⊥
04   key[·] ← ⊥;
05   (s_A, s_B) ←$ init
06   S_A[trs] ← s_A; S_B[trr] ← s_B
07   b' ←$ A
08 · Require KN ∩ CH = ∅
09   Stop with b'

Oracle SndA(ad, rc)
10   Require ad ∈ AD ∧ rc ∈ R ∪ {ε}
11   If rc = ε:
12     (s_A, k, c) ←$ snd(s_A, ad)
13   Else:
14     (s_A, k, c) ← snd(s_A, ad; rc)
15 ∘   MR ←∪ {trs||(ad, c)}
16 ∘   If trs ∈ XP_A:
17 ∘     KN ←∪ {trs||(ad, c)}
18 ∘     XP_A ←∪ {trs||(ad, c)}
19   trs ←|| (ad, c)
20   key[trs] ← k; S_A[trs] ← s_A
21   Return c

Oracle Reveal(tr)
22   Require key[tr] ∈ K
23 · KN ←∪ {tr}
24   Return key[tr]

Oracle RcvB(ad, c)
25   Require ad ∈ AD ∧ c ∈ C ∧ s_B ≠ ⊥
26 · If trr||(ad, c) ⋠ trs
       ∧LCP(trs, trr) ∈ XP_A:
27 ·   KN ←∪ {trr||(ad, c)}
28   (s_B, k) ← rcv(s_B, ad, c)
29   If k = ⊥: Return ⊥
30   trr ←|| (ad, c)
31   key[trr] ← k; S_B[trr] ← s_B
32   Return

Oracle ExposeA(tr)
33   Require S_A[tr] ∈ S_A
34 · XP_A ←∪ {tr}
35 ∘ trace ← {tr* ∈ TR* : ∀tr' ∈ TR*
       (tr ≺ tr' ⪯ tr* ⟹ tr' ∈ MR)}
36 ∘ KN ←∪ trace; XP_A ←∪ trace
37   Return S_A[tr]

Oracle ExposeB(tr)
38   Require S_B[tr] ∈ S_B
39 · KN ←∪ {tr* ∈ TR* : tr ≺ tr*}
40   Return S_B[tr]

Oracle Challenge(tr)
41   Require key[tr] ∈ K
42 · Require tr ∉ CH
43   k ← b ? key[tr] : $(K)
44 · CH ←∪ {tr}
45   Return k
```

Fig. 6. Games KINDR^b, $b \in \{0, 1\}$, for URKE scheme UR. Lines of code tagged with a '·' denote mechanisms to prevent or detect trivial attacks without randomness manipulation; trivial attacks caused by randomness manipulation are detected and prevented by lines tagged with '∘'. We define $\mathrm{LCP}(X, Y)$ to return the longest common prefix between X and Y, which are lists of atomic elements $z_i \in (\mathcal{AD} \times \mathcal{C})$. By longest common prefix we mean the longest list $Z = z_0 \| \ldots \| z_n$ for which $Z \preceq X \wedge Z \preceq Y$. We further define $\mathcal{TR} = \mathcal{AD} \times \mathcal{C}$. Line 39 is a shortcut notion that can be implemented efficiently. XP: exposed states, MR: states and keys affected by manipulated randomness, KN: known keys, CH: challenge keys, *trs*, *trr*: transcripts.

and challenged (line 44). The adversary only wins, if the intersection of both sets is empty (line 08). Additionally, a key must only be challenged once as otherwise bit b can be obtained trivially (line 42).
Example: $c \leftarrow \mathrm{SndA}(\epsilon, \epsilon)$; $k \leftarrow \mathrm{Reveal}((\epsilon, c))$; Return $k = \mathrm{Challenge}((\epsilon, c))$

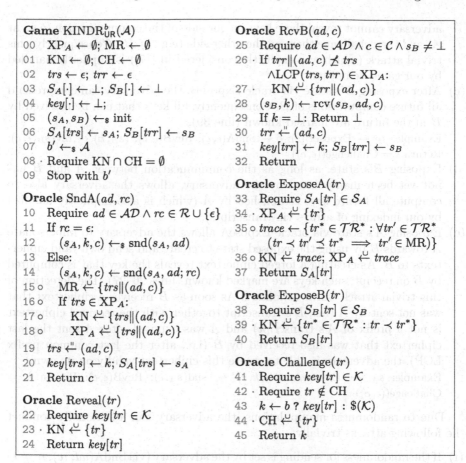

(b) As keys, that are computed by both parties (because ciphertexts between them have not been manipulated yet), are stored only once in array *key* (due to the indexing of arrays with transcripts instead of pure counters), the adversary cannot reveal these keys on one side of the communication (e.g., at A) and then challenge them on the other side (e.g., at B). Consequently, this trivial attack (which was explicitly considered in [17]) is implicitly handled by our game definition.

(c) After exposing B's state via oracle ExposeB, the adversary can comprehend all future computations of B. Consequently, all keys that can be received by B in the future are marked known (line 39).
Example: $s_B \leftarrow \text{ExposeB}(\epsilon)$; $c \leftarrow \text{SndA}(\epsilon, \epsilon)$; $\text{RcvB}(\epsilon, c)$; $(s_B, k) \leftarrow \text{rcv}(s_B, \epsilon, c)$; Return $k = \text{Challenge}((\epsilon, c))$

(d) Exposing B's state, as long as the communication between A and B has not yet been manipulated by the adversary, allows the adversary also to compute all future keys established by A (which is also implicitly handled by our indexing of arrays via transcripts).

(e) Exposing A's state via oracle ExposeA allows the adversary to impersonate A towards B by using the exposed state to create and send own valid ciphertexts to B. As creating a forged ciphertext reveals the key that is computed by B on receipt, such keys are marked known (lines 26–27). The detection of this trivial attack works as follows: As soon as B receives a ciphertext that was not sent by A (i.e., B's transcript together with the received ciphertext is not a prefix of A's transcript) and A was exposed after A sent the last ciphertext that was also received by B (i.e., after the last common prefix LCP), the adversary is able to create this ciphertext validly on its own.[7]
Example: $s_A \leftarrow \text{ExposeA}$; $(s_A, k, c) \leftarrow \text{snd}(s_A, \epsilon)$; $\text{RcvB}(\epsilon, c)$; Return $k = \text{Challenge}((\epsilon, c))$

Due to randomness manipulations, the adversary can additionally conduct the following attacks trivially:

(f) If the randomness for sending is set by the adversary (via $\text{SndA}(ad, rc)$, $rc \neq \epsilon$) and the state, used for this sending, is exposed (via ExposeA), then also the next state of A, output by this send operation, will be known (and marked as exposed) as sending is thereby deterministically computed on inputs that are known by the adversary (lines 16, 18). Since the adversary can also retrospectively expose A's state, all computations that can be traced, due to continuous manipulated randomness of subsequent SndA oracle queries (unified in set MR) after such an exposure, are also marked as exposed (lines 35–36).
Example: $rc \leftarrow_{\$} \mathcal{R}$; $c' \leftarrow \text{SndA}(\epsilon, rc)$; $\text{RcvB}(\epsilon, c')$; $s_A \leftarrow \text{ExposeA}(\epsilon)$; $(s_A, k', c') \leftarrow \text{snd}(s_A, \epsilon; rc)$; $(s_A, k, c) \leftarrow_{\$} \text{snd}(s_A, \epsilon)$; $\text{RcvB}(\epsilon, c)$; Return $k = \text{Challenge}((\epsilon, c') \| (\epsilon, c))$

(g) Similarly, if the randomness for sending is set by the adversary and the state that A uses during this send operation is exposed, then the key, computed

[7] Please note that we need to detect this trivial attack this way (in contrast to the game in [17]) because the adversary can forge ciphertexts to B without letting the communication between A and B actually diverge. It can do so by creating an own valid ciphertext which it sends to B (via $s_A \leftarrow \text{ExposeA}(\epsilon)$; $rc \leftarrow_{\$} \mathcal{R}$; $(s_A, k, c) \leftarrow \text{snd}(s_A, \epsilon; rc)$; $\text{RcvB}(\epsilon, c)$) but then it lets A compute the same ciphertext (via $\text{SndA}(\epsilon, rc)$). As a result, A and B are still in sync.

during sending, is known by the adversary since its computation is thereby deterministic (lines 16–17, 35–36).
Example: $rc \leftarrow_{\$} \mathcal{R}$; $c \leftarrow$ SndA(ϵ, rc); $s_A \leftarrow$ ExposeA(ϵ); $(s_A, k, c) \leftarrow$ snd$(s_A, \epsilon; rc)$; Return $k =$ Challenge$((\epsilon, c))$

Based on this game, we define the advantage of an adversary in breaking the security of an URKE scheme as follows.

Definition 4 (KINDR **Advantage).** *The advantage of an adversary $\mathcal{A}$ against a* URKE *scheme* UR *in game* KINDR *from Fig. 6 is defined as* $\mathrm{Adv}^{\mathrm{kindr}}_{\mathsf{UR}}(\mathcal{A}) = \left|\Pr[\mathrm{KINDR}^0_{\mathsf{UR}}(\mathcal{A}) = 1] - \Pr[\mathrm{KINDR}^1_{\mathsf{UR}}(\mathcal{A}) = 1]\right|$.

We say that an URKE scheme UR is secure if the advantage is negligible for all probabilistic polynomial time adversaries $\mathcal{A}$.

Please note that KINDR security of URKE is strictly stronger than both KIND security notions of URKE, defined by Bellare et al. [3] and Poettering and Rösler [17] (which themselves are incomparable among each other).

5 KuKEM* to URKE

Since our ultimate goal is to show that existence of a kuKEM* primitive is a necessary and sufficient condition to construct a URKE primitive – albeit requiring the help of other common cryptographic primitives such as hash functions (modeled as random oracle) and message authentication codes –, we dedicate this section to proving the latter of these implications.

Construction of URKE *from* kuKEM*. We give a generic way to construct a URKE scheme UR from a kuKEM* scheme K with the help of random oracle H and MAC scheme M. This transformation K → UR is fully depicted in Fig. 7. Below we briefly describe the algorithms of URKE scheme UR = (init, snd, rcv).

During the state initiation algorithm init, a kuKEM* key pair (sk, pk) is generated such that the encapsulation key pk is embedded into the sender state s_A, and the decapsulation key sk into the receiver state s_B. The remaining state variables are exactly same for A and B. More specifically, two further keys are generated during initialization: the symmetric state key K and a MAC key $k.m$. Furthermore the sent or received transcript (initialized with an empty string ϵ) is stored in each state. For brevity, we assume that K, $k.m$, and the update key $k.u$ (used during sending and receiving; see below) all belong to the same key domain $\mathcal{K}$ that is sufficiently large.

On sending, public key pk in A's state is used by the encapsulation algorithm to generate key k and ciphertext c. Then, MAC key $k.m$, contained in the current state of A, is used to issue a tag τ over the tuple of associated data ad and encapsulation ciphertext c. The finally sent ciphertext, denoted by C, is a concatenation of c and τ. The output key $k.o$, as well as the symmetric keys of the next state of A are obtained from the random oracle, on input of the symmetric state key K, the freshly encapsulated key k, and the history of sent

Proc init
$(pk, sk) \leftarrow_{\$} \text{gen}_{\mathsf{K}}$
$K \leftarrow_{\$} \mathcal{K};\ k.m \leftarrow_{\$} \mathcal{K}$
$t \leftarrow \epsilon$
$S_A \leftarrow (pk, K, k.m, t)$
$S_B \leftarrow (sk, K, k.m, t)$
Return (S_A, S_B)

Proc $\text{snd}(S_A, ad)$
$(pk, K, k.m, t) \leftarrow S_A$
$(pk, k, c) \leftarrow_{\$} \text{enc}(pk)$
$\tau \leftarrow \text{tag}(k.m, (ad, c))$
$C \leftarrow (c, \tau)$
$t \xleftarrow{\Vert} (ad, c)$
$(k.o, K, k.m, k.u) \leftarrow \text{H}(K, k, t)$
$pk \leftarrow \text{up}(pk, k.u)$
$S_A \leftarrow (pk, K, k.m, t)$
Return $(S_A, k.o, C)$

Proc $\text{rcv}(S_B, ad, C)$
$(sk, K, k.m, t) \leftarrow S_B$
$(c, \tau) \leftarrow C$
Require $\text{vfy}_{\mathsf{M}}(k.m, (ad, c), \tau)$
$(sk, k) \leftarrow \text{dec}(sk, c)$
Require $k \neq \perp$
$t \xleftarrow{\Vert} (ad, c)$
$(k.o, K, k.m, k.u) \leftarrow \text{H}(K, k, t)$
$sk \leftarrow \text{up}(sk, k.u)$
$S_B \leftarrow (sk, K, k.m, t)$
Return $(S_B, k.o)$

Fig. 7. Construction of a URKE scheme from a kuKEM* scheme $\mathsf{K} = (\text{gen}_{\mathsf{K}}, \text{up}, \text{enc}, \text{dec})$, a message authentication code $\mathsf{M} = (\text{tag}, \text{vfy}_{\mathsf{M}})$, and a random oracle H. For simplicity we denote the key space of the MAC and the space of the symmetric key K in s_A with the same symbol $\mathcal{K}$.

transcript t. Finally, a kuKEM* update is applied on pk under associated data that is derived from the random oracle output (denoted by $k.u$). Please note that the encapsulation algorithm is the only randomized operation inside snd. Hence the random coins of the latter are only used by the encapsulation.

On receiving, the operations are on par with the sending algorithm. Namely, the received ciphertext C is parsed as the encapsulation ciphertext c and the MAC tag τ. The latter is verified with regards to the MAC key $k.m$, stored in the state of B. After the key k is decapsulated, the same input to the random oracle H is composed. The symmetric components of the next state and $k.o$ are derived from the random oracle's output. Finally, the secret key sk is updated with $k.u$, so that it is in-sync with the update of pk.

We remark that our construction in Fig. 7 differs from the unidirectional RKE scheme by Poettering and Rösler [17] only in the output of the random oracle and in the subsequent use of the kuKEM*'s update algorithm (instead they freshly generated a new KEM key pair from the random oracle output). These changes are, nevertheless, significant as their scheme is insecure when the adversary is able to (reveal or) manipulate the random coins for invocations of the snd algorithm. We give a detailed attack description against their scheme in our model in the full version [2].

Theorem 1. *If* kuKEM* *scheme* K *is* KUOWR *secure according to Fig. 4,* MAC *scheme* M *is* SUF *secure according to Sect. 2.2, and* H *is a hash function modeled as random oracle, then* URKE *scheme* UR *from Fig. 7 is* KINDR *secure according to Fig. 6 with*

$$\text{Adv}^{\text{kindr}}_{\mathsf{UR}}(\mathcal{A}) \leq \text{Adv}^{\text{kuowr}}_{\mathsf{K}}(\mathcal{B}_{\mathsf{K}}) + \text{Adv}^{\text{suf}}_{\mathsf{M}}(\mathcal{B}_{\mathsf{M}}) + \frac{q_{\text{H}} \cdot (q_{\text{SndA}} + q_{\text{RcvB}})}{|\mathcal{K}|}$$

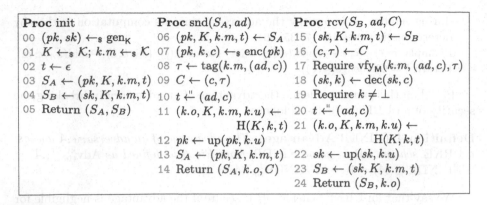

where $\mathcal{A}$ is an adversary against KINDR *security,* $\mathcal{B}_{\mathsf{K}}$ *is an adversary against* KUOWR *security,* $\mathcal{B}_{\mathsf{M}}$ *is an adversary against* SUF *security,* $\mathcal{K}$ *is the key domain in the construction* UR, q_{SndA}, q_{RcvB}, *and* q_{H} *are the number of* SndA, RcvB *and* H *queries respectively by* $\mathcal{A}$, *and the running time of* $\mathcal{A}$ *is approximately the running time of* $\mathcal{B}_{\mathsf{K}}$ *and* $\mathcal{B}_{\mathsf{M}}$.

Proof (Sketch, Theorem 1). We here give the sketch of the full proof that is in the full version [2]. Our idea is to design a series of games **Game 0-5**, in which differences between subsequent games are only syntactical and the advantage of the adversary $\mathcal{A}$ remains same. From this fifth game we are then ultimately able to reduce either of the following cases, that are explained below, to one of the hardness assumptions.

Consider the following scenarios which lead to a win for the adversary $\mathcal{A}$. Since the challenged keys are derived from the random oracle, we argue that, if $\mathcal{A}$ does not make a random oracle query $\mathrm{H}(K, k, t)$ for any of the challenged keys, then its advantage in guessing the challenge bit correctly remains negligible. We do not consider random oracle queries to keys that are trivially revealed to the adversary, as they do not lead to a win in the KINDR game (e.g., if the exposed state of B helps the adversary to trivially query H). Therefore, we regard the following three events in which $\mathcal{A}$ makes such *special* random oracle queries:

- The random oracle query $\mathrm{H}(K, k, t)$ belongs to one of the keys derived by the sender, in which fresh random coins, unknown to the adversary, are used for sending (and hence for encapsulation). In this case, we can give a reduction to the KUOWR game with respect to kuKEM* scheme K, in which the reduction wins the KUOWR game by using the encapsulated key k as the solution.
- The random oracle query $\mathrm{H}(K, k, t)$ belongs to one of the keys, derived from the sender where the used random coins are chosen by the adversary. We know that $\mathcal{A}$ did not expose the respectively used states of A or B as this leads to a trivial win. Therefore, we can show that the symmetric state keys K in these cases are independent from the view of $\mathcal{A}$. This implies that making such special $\mathrm{H}(K, k, t)$ query requires a collision in the key domain $\mathcal{K}$, whose probability is bounded by $q_{\mathrm{H}} \cdot (q_{\mathrm{SndA}} + q_{\mathrm{RcvB}})/|\mathcal{K}|$.
- The random oracle query $\mathrm{H}(K, k, t)$ belongs to one of the keys, derived by the receiver B, who reaches to an out-of-sync status (if B is still in-sync with A, then one of the two cases above are relevant). Since each received ciphertext contains a MAC tag, we can show that the first received ciphertext by B that is different from the sent ciphertext by A either corresponds to a trivial impersonation or can be used to reduce this event to a forgery in the SUF game with respect to MAC scheme M.

Therefore, by bounding the probability of these three cases, we can deduce the adversary's advantage (which is negligible under the named assumptions). □

6 URKE to kuKEM*

In order to show that public key encryption with independently updatable key pairs (in our case kuKEM*) is a necessary building block for ratcheted key exchange, we build the former from the latter. The major obstacle is that the updates of public key and secret key of a kuKEM* are conducted independently – consequently no communication between holder of the public key and holder of the secret key can be assumed for updates. In contrast, all actions in ratcheted key exchange are based on communication (i.e., sent or received ciphertexts). Another property that public key updates for kuKEM* must fulfill – in contrast to state updates in KIND secure unidirectional RKE as in [17] – is that they must not leak any information on the according secret key during the update computation. In the following we describe how we solve these two issues and present a reduction of KUOWR security to KINDR security of a generic URKE scheme.

Construction of kuKEM* *from* URKE. The weaker KIND security of URKE (as in [17]) already allows that the sender's state s_A can always be exposed without affecting the security of any established keys (as long as this exposed state is not used to impersonate A towards B). Consequently, A's pure state reveals no information on encapsulated keys nor on B's secret key(s). KIND security of URKE further implies that B's state only reveals information on keys that have not yet been computed by B (while earlier computed keys stay secure). One can imagine A's state consequently as the public part of a (stateful) key pair and B's state as the secret counterpart.

The two above mentioned crucial properties of KUOW(R) security are, however, not implied by KIND security when using s_A as the public key and s_B as the secret key of a kuKEM. Firstly, updating s_B (as part of receiving a ciphertext) requires that the ciphertext, generated during sending of A (and updating of s_A), is known by B but the syntax of kuKEM does not allow an interaction between public key holder and secret key holder. This issue can be solved by de-randomizing the snd algorithm. If A's state as part of the public key is updated via a de-randomized invocation of snd, the secret key holder can also obtain the ciphertext that A would produce for the same update (by invoking the de-randomized/deterministic snd) and then update s_B with this ciphertext via rcv. A conceptional depiction of this is in Fig. 8. Thereby the secret key is defined to contain s_A in addition to s_B.

Secondly, in the URKE construction of Poettering and Rösler [17] A temporarily computes secrets of B that match A's updated values during sending. As a result, normal KIND security allows that a de-randomized snd invocation reveals the secrets of B to an adversary if s_A is known (see the full version [2] for a detailed description of this attack). In order to solve this issue, the security definition of URKE must ensure that future encapsulated keys' security is not compromised if snd is invoked under a known state s_A and with random coins that are chosen by an adversary (i.e., KINDR security).

Our generic construction of a KUOWR secure kuKEM* from a generic KINDR secure URKE scheme is depicted in Fig. 9. As described before, the public key contains state s_A and the secret key contains both states (s_A, s_B) that are derived from the init algorithm. In order to update the public key, the snd algorithm is invoked on state s_A, with the update associated data, and fixed

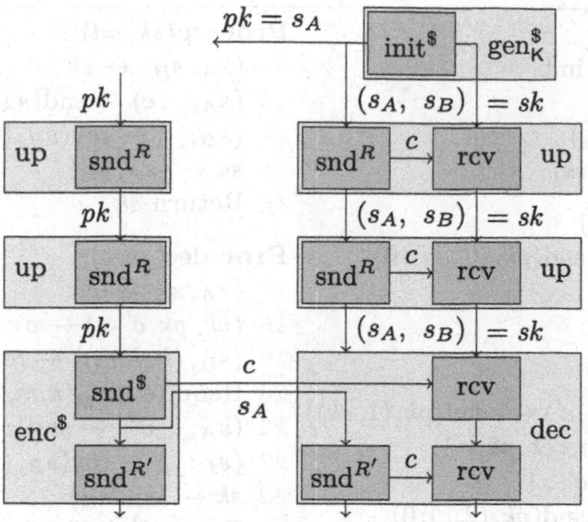

Fig. 8. Conceptual depiction of kuKEM* construction from generic URKE scheme. The symbol in the upper index of an algorithm name denotes the source of random coins ('\$' indicates uniformly sampled). R is a fixed value. For clarity we omit *ad* inputs and k outputs (cf. Fig. 1).

randomness. The output key and ciphertext are thereby ignored. Accordingly, the secret key is updated by first invoking the snd algorithm on state s_A with the same fixed randomness and the update associated data. This time the respective ciphertext from A to B is not omitted but used as input to rcv algorithm with the same associated data under s_B.

Encapsulation and decapsulation are conducted by invoking snd probabilistically and rcv respectively. In order to separate updates from en-/decapsulation, a '0' or '1' is prepended to the associated data input of snd and rcv respectively. For bounding the probability of a ciphertext collision in the proof, a randomly sampled 'collision key' *ck* is attached to the associated data of the snd invocation in encapsulation. In order to accordingly add *ck* to the associated data of rcv as part of the decapsulation, *ck* is appended to the ciphertext. Since state s_A, output by the snd algorithm during the encapsulation, is computed probabilistically, it is also attached to the encapsulation ciphertext, so that (the other) s_A, embedded in the secret key, can be kept compatible with the public key holder's. To bind *ck* and s_A to the ciphertext, both are integrity protected by a message authentication code (MAC) that takes one part of the key from the snd invocation as MAC key (only the remaining key bytes are output as the encapsulated kuKEM* key). Additionally the whole ciphertext (i.e., URKE ciphertext, collision key, state s_A, and MAC tag) is used as associated data for an additional 'internal update' of the public key and the secret key in encapsulation and decapsulation respectively. This is done to escalate manipulations of collision key, state s_A, or MAC tag (as part of the ciphertext) back into the URKE states s_A and s_B (as part of public key and secret key). For full details on the rationales behind these two *binding* steps we refer the reader to the proof.

```
Proc gen_K
(s_A, s_B) ←$ init
pk ← s_A
sk ← (s_A, s_B)
Return (pk, sk)

Proc up(pk, ad)
(pk, _, _) ← snd(pk, (0, ad); 0)
Return pk

Proc enc(pk)
ck ←$ 𝒦
(pk, (k, k.m), c') ←$ snd(pk, (1, ck))
τ ← tag(k.m, (ck, pk, c'))
c ← (ck, pk, c', τ)
(pk, _, _) ← snd(pk, (2, c); 0)
Return (pk, k, c)

Proc up(sk, ad)
(s_A, s_B) ← sk
(s_A, _, c) ← snd(s_A, (0, ad); 0)
(s_B, _) ← rcv(s_B, (0, ad), c)
sk ← (s_A, s_B)
Return sk

Proc dec(sk, c)
(s_A, s_B) ← sk
(ck, pk, c', τ) ← c
(s_B, (k, k.m)) ← rcv(s_B, (1, ck), c')
Require vfy_M(k.m, (ck, pk, c'), τ)
(s_A, _, c'') ← snd(pk, (2, c); 0)
(s_B, _) ← rcv(s_B, (2, c), c'')
sk ← (s_A, s_B)
Return (sk, k)
```

Fig. 9. Construction of a key-updatable KEM from a generic URKE scheme $\mathsf{UR} = (\text{init}, \text{snd}, \text{rcv})$ and one-time message authentication code $\mathsf{M} = (\text{tag}, \text{vfy}_{\mathsf{M}})$.

Interestingly, the public key holder can postpone the de-randomized snd invocation for public key updates until encapsulation and instead only remember the updates' associated data without compromising security. However, the updates of the secret key must be performed immediately as otherwise an exposure of the current secret key reveals also information on its past versions. Thereby the computation of snd in the up algorithm must be conducted during the secret key update without interaction between public key holder and secret key holder.

Theorem 2. *If* URKE *scheme* UR *is* KINDR *secure according to Fig. 6, one-time* MAC M *is* SUF *secure according to Sect. 2.2, and for all* $(k, k.m) \in \mathcal{K}_{\mathsf{UR}}$ *it holds that* $k \in \mathcal{K}_{\mathsf{K}}$ *and* $k.m \in \mathcal{K}_{\mathsf{M}}$, *then* kuKEM* *scheme* K *from Fig. 9 is* KUOWR *secure according to Fig. 4 with*

$$\mathrm{Adv}_{\mathsf{K}}^{\mathrm{kuowr}}(\mathcal{A}) \leq q_{\mathrm{Gen}} q_{\mathrm{Enc}} \cdot \left(\mathrm{Adv}_{\mathsf{UR}}^{\mathrm{kindr}}(\mathcal{B}_{\mathsf{UR}}) + \mathrm{Adv}_{\mathsf{M}}^{\mathrm{suf}}(\mathcal{B}_{\mathsf{M}}) + \frac{1}{|\mathcal{K}|} \right),$$

$$\text{with } \mathrm{Adv}_{\mathsf{M}}^{\mathrm{suf}}(\mathcal{B}_{\mathsf{M}}) \leq \mathrm{Adv}_{\mathsf{UR}}^{\mathrm{kindr}}(\mathcal{B}_{\mathsf{UR}})$$

where $\mathcal{A}$ *is an adversary against* KUOWR *security,* $\mathcal{B}_{\mathsf{UR}}$ *is an adversary against* KINDR *security of* UR, $\mathcal{B}_{\mathsf{M}}$ *is an adversary against* SUF *security of* M, q_{Gen} *and* q_{Enc} *are the number of* Gen *and* Enc *queries by* $\mathcal{A}$ *respectively,* $\mathcal{K}$ *is the space from which ck is sampled, and the running time of* $\mathcal{A}$ *is approximately the running time of* $\mathcal{B}_{\mathsf{UR}}$ *and* $\mathcal{B}_{\mathsf{M}}$.

In the full version [2] we show how to construct an SUF secure one-time MAC from a generic KINDR secure URKE scheme, which implies the second term in Theorem 2. We prove Theorem 2 below and provide a formal pseudo-code version of the simulation's game hops in the full version [2].

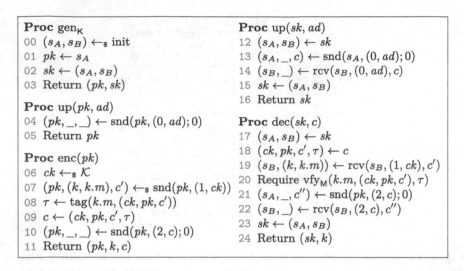

Proof (Theorem 2). We conduct the proof in four game hops: In the first game hop we guess for which instance the first valid Solve oracle query is provided by the adversary; in the second game hop, we guess for which Enc oracle query of the previously guessed instance the first valid Solve oracle query is provided; additionally the simulation aborts in this game hop if the adversary crafts this first valid ciphertext and provides it to the Dec oracle before it is output by the Enc oracle; in the third game hop, we replace the key, output by the first snd invocation in this guessed Enc oracle query by a randomly sampled key (which is reduced to KINDR security of UR); in the final game hop, we abort on a MAC forgery, provided to the Dec oracle, that belongs to the ciphertext that is output by the guessed Enc oracle query (which is reduced to the SUF security of M).

Game 0. This game is equivalent to the original KUOWR game.

Game 1. The simulation guesses for which instance n_{Gen} the first key k^* is provided to the Solve oracle such that the secret key for decapsulation is not marked exposed (i.e., $tr^* \notin \text{XP}_{n_{\text{Gen}}}$) and the provided key equals the indicated challenge key (i.e., $k^* = \text{CK}_{n_{\text{Gen}}}[tr^*]$). Therefore n_{Gen} is randomly sampled from $[q_{\text{Gen}}]$, where q_{Gen} is the number of Gen oracle queries by the adversary. The reduction aborts if n_{Gen} is not the instance for which the first valid Solve oracle query is provided.

Consequently we have $\text{Adv}^{G_0} = q_{\text{Gen}} \cdot \text{Adv}^{G_1}$.

Game 2. The simulation guesses in which of n_{Gen}'s Enc queries the challenge is created, that is the first valid query to the Solve oracle by the adversary. Therefore n_{Enc} is randomly sampled from $[q_{\text{Enc}}]$ and the simulation aborts if either the randomness for the n_{Enc}'s Enc query is manipulated as thereby no challenge would be created, or the first valid query to the Solve oracle is for another challenge than the one created by n_{Gen}'s n_{Enc}th Enc query, or a secret key that helps to trivially solve the challenge from n_{Gen}'s n_{Enc}th Enc query is exposed.

In addition, the simulation aborts if, before the n_{Gen}'s n_{Enc}th Enc query was made, Dec was queried on a ciphertext (with the same preceding transcript) that contains the same URKE ciphertext and 'collision key' ck as n_{Gen}'s n_{Enc}th Enc query. As the probability of a collision in the URKE transcript (i.e., associated data and ciphertext of the first snd invocation of n_{Gen}'s n_{Enc}th Enc query were previously already provided to n_{Gen}'s n_{Enc}th Dec query under the same preceding transcript) is bounded by a collision in the the key space $\mathcal{K}$ (as thereby ck as associated data must collide), we have $\text{Adv}^{G_1} = q_{\text{Enc}} \cdot \left(\text{Adv}^{G_2} + \frac{1}{|\mathcal{K}|}\right)$.

Game 3. The simulation replaces the output $(k, k.m)$ from the first snd invocation of n_{Gen}'s n_{Enc}th Enc query by values randomly sampled.

An adversary that can distinguish between **Game 2** and **Game 3** can be turned into an adversary that breaks KINDR security of URKE scheme UR. We describe the reduction below: The reduction obtains n_{Gen}'s public key in oracle Gen via oracle ExposeA from the KINDR game. Invocations of snd in Up_S to n_{Gen} are replaced by SndA and ExposeA queries. Invocations of snd in Up_R to

n_{Gen} are processed by the reduction itself and the subsequent rcv invocations are replaced by RcvB queries. The state s_B in queries to Expose for n_{Gen} is obtained via ExposeB queries to the KINDR game. For all queries to Enc of n_{Gen} the snd invocations are replaced by SndA and ExposeA queries. kuKEM* key and MAC key $(k, k.m)$ for n_{Gen}'s Enc oracle queries are obtained via Reveal – except for n_{Gen}'s n_{Enc}th Enc query, in which these two keys are obtained from the Challenge oracle in the KINDR game. Invocations of rcv in the Dec oracle for n_{Gen} are replaced by RcvB queries and Reveal queries (in case the respective key was not already computed in the Enc oracle). The snd invocation in oracle Dec is directly computed by the reduction.

In order to show that manipulations of transcripts in the KUOWR game manipulate equivalently the transcripts in the KINDR game (such that the state s_A in the public key diverges from state s_B in the secret key iff the transcripts $trs_{n_{\mathsf{Gen}}}$ and $trr_{n_{\mathsf{Gen}}}$ diverge), we define the translation array TR[·] that maps the transcript of n_{Gen} in the KUOWR game to the according transcripts in the KINDR game.

As **Game 2** aborts if n_{Gen}'s n_{Enc}th Enc query entails no valid KINDR challenge, or if the respective ciphertext was already crafted by the adversary (and provided to the Dec oracle), an adversary, distinguishing the real key pair $(k, k.m)$ from the randomly sampled one, breaks KINDR security. Formally, the solution for n_{Gen}'s n_{Enc}th Enc query to the Solve oracle is compared with the challenge key k from the KINDR Challenge oracle (which is obtained during n_{Gen}'s n_{Enc}th Enc query): If the keys equal, the reduction terminates with $b' = 0$ (as thereby the KINDR game's challenge entailed the real key), otherwise it terminates with $b' = 1$.

Consequently we have $\mathrm{Adv}^{G_2} \leq \mathrm{Adv}^{G_3} + \mathrm{Adv}^{\mathrm{kindr}}_{\mathsf{UR}}(\mathcal{B}_{\mathsf{UR}})$.

Game 4. The only way, the adversary can win in **Game 3**, is to keep secret key and public key of n_{Gen} compatible (by updating them equivalently and forwarding all Enc queries to the Dec oracle) and then forwarding only the URKE ciphertext c' of n_{Gen}'s n_{Enc}th Enc query to the Dec oracle while manipulating parts of the remaining challenge ciphertext. Thereby the Dec oracle outputs the correct challenge key such that the adversary trivially wins.[8]

We therefore define **Game 4** to let the simulation abort if a forgery of the MAC tag for the challenge ciphertext is provided to the Dec oracle. Distinguishing between **Game 3** and **Game 4** can hence be reduced to the SUF security of the one-time MAC M. We describe the reduction below: Instead of sampling $k.m$ randomly, the MAC tag for n_{Gen}'s n_{Enc}th Enc query is derived from the Tag oracle of the SUF game. Since an abort requires that the URKE challenge ciphertext c' is indeed received in oracle Dec (and also the transcripts prior to this ciphertext equal for $trs_{n_{\mathsf{Gen}}}$ and $trr_{n_{\mathsf{Gen}}}$), the URKE key (containing $k.m$)

[8] Please note that after this manipulation, the states s_A and s_B in the public key and secret key respectively diverge, but the key, output by the Dec oracle, still equals the challenge key. In case, the URKE ciphertext c' from the challenge ciphertext is already provided manipulately to the Dec oracle, the challenge key is already independent from the key, computed in the Dec oracle.

equals. As a consequence, a crafted ciphertext (pk, c', τ), provided to the Dec oracle, is a forgery τ for message (pk, c') in the SUF game.

Consequently we have $\mathrm{Adv}^{G_3} \leq \mathrm{Adv}^{G_4} + \mathrm{Adv}^{\mathrm{suf}}_{\mathsf{M}}(\mathcal{B}_{\mathsf{M}})$.

As the challenge key from n_{Gen}'s n_{Enc}th Enc query is randomly sampled and cannot be derived from any other oracle, the advantage of winning in **Game 4** is $\mathrm{Adv}^{G_4} = 0$.

Summing up the advantages above, we have:

$$\mathrm{Adv}^{\mathrm{kuowr}}_{\mathsf{K}}(\mathcal{A}) \leq q_{\mathrm{Gen}} q_{\mathrm{Enc}} \cdot \left(\mathrm{Adv}^{\mathrm{kindr}}_{\mathsf{UR}}(\mathcal{B}_{\mathsf{UR}}) + \mathrm{Adv}^{\mathrm{suf}}_{\mathsf{M}}(\mathcal{B}_{\mathsf{M}}) + \frac{1}{|\mathcal{K}|} \right)$$

where $\mathrm{Adv}^{\mathrm{suf}}_{\mathsf{M}}(\mathcal{B}_{\mathsf{M}}) \leq \mathrm{Adv}^{\mathrm{kindr}}_{\mathsf{UR}}(\mathcal{B}_{\mathsf{UR}})$ follows from an SUF secure one-time MAC construction from a generic KINDR secure URKE scheme UR (which is described in the full version [2]). □

7 Discussion

Our results clearly show that key-updatable key encapsulation is a necessary building block for optimally secure ratcheted key exchange, if the security definition of the latter regards manipulation of the algorithm invocations' random coins. As unidirectional RKE can naturally be built from sesquidirectional RKE, which in turn can be built from bidirectional RKE (which can be derived from optimally secure group RKE), our results are expected to hold also for the according security definitions under these extended communication settings. In contrast, security definitions of ratcheting that restrict the adversary more than necessary in exposing the local state or in solving embedded game challenges (i.e., by excluding more than unpreventable attacks) allow for instantiations that can dispense with these inefficient building blocks.

However, the two previous security definitions fulfilled by constructions that use kuKEM as a building block (cf. Table 1) consider only *randomness reveal* [10] or even *secure randomness* [17]. This raises the question whether using kuKEM in these cases was indeed necessary (or not). The resulting gap between the notions of ratcheting that can be built from only standard PKC and our optimally secure URKE definition with *randomness manipulation*, implying kuKEM, will be discussed in the following.

Implications under Randomness Reveal. The core of our proof (showing that URKE implies kuKEM under randomness manipulation) is to utilize URKE's state update in algorithms snd and rcv for realizing public key and secret key updates in kuKEM's up algorithm. In order to remove the otherwise necessary communication between snd and rcv algorithms of RKE, snd is de-randomized by fixing its random coins to a static value. While this de-randomization *trick* is not immediately possible if the reduction to URKE KIND security cannot manipulate the randomness of snd invocations, one can utilize a programmable random oracle to emulate it: instead of fixing the (input) random coins of snd invocations to a static value, one could derive these coins from the output of a random oracle on input of the respective update's associated data (i.e., *ad* input of algorithm up). Additionally, instead of directly forwarding the update's associated data to the associated data input of snd, another random oracle could be interposed between them. The reduction then simply pre-computes all kuKEM up invocations independent of associated data inputs by querying the SndA oracle in the URKE KIND game on random associated data strings. Then the reduction reveals all used random coins in the URKE KIND game and programs them as output into the random oracle lazily (i.e., as soon as the adversary queries the random oracle on update associated data strings). By correctly guessing, which of the adversary's random oracle queries fit its queried kuKEM update invocations, the reduction can perform the same de-randomization trick as in our proof. The probability of guessing correctly is, however, exponential in the number of queried kuKEM updates such that a useful implication may only be derivable for a constant number of queried updates.

In conclusion, we conjecture that URKE under randomness reveal already requires the use of a kuKEM-like building block with a constantly bounded number of public key and secret key updates. Thereby we argue that our proof approach partially carries over to the case of randomness reveal. This would indicate that the use of a kuKEM-like building block in the construction of Jaeger and Stepanovs [10] is indeed necessary. The formal analysis of this conjecture is left as an open question for future work.

Implications Under Secure Randomness. For optimal security under secure randomness, Poettering and Rösler [17] show that URKE can be instantiated from standard PKC only (cf. Table 1). In contrast, their construction for sesquidirectional RKE (SRKE: a restricted interactive RKE variant) uses kuKEM for satisfying optimal security under secure randomness. Since a reduction towards SRKE (under KIND security with secure randomness) has no access to random coins respectively used in the RKE algorithms, our de-randomization trick seems inapplicable. Furthermore, while the RKE algorithms snd and rcv can use exchanged ciphertexts for their state updates, generically transforming this state update to realize a 'silent', non-interactive key update needed for kuKEM without our trick appears (at least) problematic.

Nevertheless, it is likely that SRKE KIND security under secure randomness requires kuKEM-like building blocks. This intuition is based on an example attack by Poettering and Rösler [16, Appendix B.2]. It illustrates that a key k^*, computed by any secure SRKE construction under the following attack, needs to be indistinguishable from a random key according to this security notion. The attack proceeds as follows: 1. Alice's and Bob's states are exposed ($s_A \leftarrow \mathrm{ExposeA}(\epsilon)$; $s_B \leftarrow \mathrm{ExposeB}(\epsilon)$), 2. Bob sends update information to Alice (which is possible in SRKE) to recover from his exposure ($c \leftarrow \mathrm{SndB}(\epsilon, \epsilon)$; $\mathrm{RcvA}(\epsilon, c)$). Keys established by Alice after receiving the update information are required to be secure again. Translated to the kuKEM setting, this step corresponds to Bob generating a new key pair and publishing the respective public key. 3. Simultaneously Alice is impersonated towards Bob ($(s'_A, k', c') \leftarrow_\$ \mathrm{snd}_A(s_A, \epsilon)$; $\mathrm{RcvB}(\epsilon, c')$). This requires Bob's state to become incompatible with Alice's state. In the kuKEM setting, this corresponds to the secret key being updated with c' as associated data. Note that c' can be independent of Bob's state update from step 2 via c, and the computation of c' is controlled by the adversary. 4. Afterwards Bob's state is again exposed ($s'_B \leftarrow \text{ExposeB}((\epsilon, c)\|(\epsilon, c'))$). 5. Finally, Alice sends and establishes key k^* which is required to be secure ($c'' \leftarrow \text{SndA}(\epsilon, \epsilon)$). 6. Exposing Alice's state thereafter should not harm security of k^* ($s''_A \leftarrow \text{ExposeA}((\epsilon, c''))$).

We observe that, as with a kuKEM public key, Alice's state is publicly known during the entire attack. Only Alice's random coins when establishing k^* and updating her state, and Bob's random coins when sending, as well as his resulting state until he receives c' are hidden towards the adversary. We furthermore note that, by computing ciphertext c', the adversary controls Bob's state update. As a consequence, Bob's state update must reach forward-secrecy for key k^* with respect to adversarially chosen associated update data c' and Bob's resulting (diverged) state s'_B.

All in all, the security requirements highlighted by this attack emphasize the similarity of kuKEM's and SRKE's security. Nevertheless, we note that all our attempts to apply our proof technique for this case failed due to the above mentioned problems. Therefore, formally substantiating or disproving the intuition conveyed by this attack remains an open question for future work.

Open Questions and Impact. With our work we aim to motivate research on another remaining open problem: can key-updatable KEM be instantiated more efficiently than generically from HIBE? It is, in contrast, evident that equivalence between HIBE and RKE is unlikely as constructions of the latter only utilize "one identity path" of the whole "identity tree" of the former.

Conclusively, we note that defining security for, and constructing schemes of interactive ratcheted key exchange variants (i.e., under bidirectional communication) is highly complicated and consequently error-prone.(See footnote 3) By providing generic constructions (instead of ad-hoc designs) and grasping core components and concepts of ratcheted key exchange, complexity is reduced and sources of errors are eliminated. Additionally, our equivalence result serves as a benchmark for current and future designs of ratcheted key exchange – especially group RKE. For future constructions that only rely on standard public key cryptography either of the following questions may arise: how far is the adversary restricted such that our implication is circumvented, or how far is the construction secure under the respective security definition?

References

1. Alwen, J., Coretti, S., Dodis, Y.: The double ratchet: security notions, proofs, and modularization for the signal protocol. In: Ishai, Y., Rijmen, V. (eds.) EUROCRYPT 2019. LNCS, vol. 11476, pp. 129–158. Springer, Cham (2019). https://doi.org/10.1007/978-3-030-17653-2_5
2. Balli, F., Rösler, P., Vaudenay, S.: Determining the core primitive for optimally secure ratcheting. Cryptology ePrint Archive, Report 2020/148 (2020). full version of this article. Available at https://eprint.iacr.org/2020/148

3. Bellare, M., Singh, A.C., Jaeger, J., Nyayapati, M., Stepanovs, I.: Ratcheted encryption and key exchange: the security of messaging. In: Katz, J., Shacham, H. (eds.) CRYPTO 2017. LNCS, vol. 10403, pp. 619–650. Springer, Cham (2017). https://doi.org/10.1007/978-3-319-63697-9_21
4. Caforio, A., Durak, F.B., Vaudenay, S.: On-demand ratcheting with security awareness. Cryptology ePrint Archive, Report 2019/965 (2019). https://eprint.iacr.org/2019/965
5. Checkoway, S., et al.: On the practical exploitability of dual EC in TLS implementations. In: Fu, K., Jung, J. (eds.) USENIX Security 2014, pp. 319–335. USENIX Association (2014)
6. Cohn-Gordon, K., Cremers, C.J.F., Dowling, B., Garratt, L., Stebila, D.: A formal security analysis of the signal messaging protocol. In: 2017 IEEE European Symposium on Security and Privacy, EuroS&P 2017, Paris, France, 26–28 April 2017, pp. 451–466 (2017)
7. Durak, F.B., Vaudenay, S.: Bidirectional asynchronous ratcheted key agreement with linear complexity. Cryptology ePrint Archive, Report 2018/889 (2018). https://eprint.iacr.org/2018/889
8. Durak, F.B., Vaudenay, S.: Bidirectional asynchronous ratcheted key agreement with linear complexity. In: Attrapadung, N., Yagi, T. (eds.) IWSEC 2019. LNCS, vol. 11689, pp. 343–362. Springer, Cham (2019). https://doi.org/10.1007/978-3-030-26834-3_20
9. Heninger, N., Durumeric, Z., Wustrow, E., Halderman, J.A.: Mining your PS and QS: detection of widespread weak keys in network devices. In: Kohno, T. (ed.) USENIX Security 2012, pp. 205–220. USENIX Association (2012)
10. Jaeger, J., Stepanovs, I.: Optimal channel security against fine-grained state compromise: the safety of messaging. In: Shacham, H., Boldyreva, A. (eds.) CRYPTO 2018. LNCS, vol. 10991, pp. 33–62. Springer, Cham (2018). https://doi.org/10.1007/978-3-319-96884-1_2
11. Jaeger, J., Stepanovs, I.: Optimal channel security against fine-grained state compromise: The safety of messaging. Cryptology ePrint Archive, Report 2018/553 (2018). https://eprint.iacr.org/2018/553
12. Jost, D., Maurer, U., Mularczyk, M.: Efficient ratcheting: almost-optimal guarantees for secure messaging. In: Ishai, Y., Rijmen, V. (eds.) EUROCRYPT 2019. LNCS, vol. 11476, pp. 159–188. Springer, Cham (2019). https://doi.org/10.1007/978-3-030-17653-2_6
13. Langley, A.: Source code of Pond (2016). https://github.com/agl/pond
14. Marlinspike, M., Perrin, T.: The double ratchet algorithm (2016). https://whispersystems.org/docs/specifications/doubleratchet/doubleratchet.pdf
15. Off-the-Record Messaging (2016). http://otr.cypherpunks.ca
16. Poettering, B., Rösler, P.: Asynchronous ratcheted key exchange. Cryptology ePrint Archive, Report 2018/296 (2018). https://eprint.iacr.org/2018/296
17. Poettering, B., Rösler, P.: Towards bidirectional ratcheted key exchange. In: Shacham, H., Boldyreva, A. (eds.) CRYPTO 2018. LNCS, vol. 10991, pp. 3–32. Springer, Cham (2018). https://doi.org/10.1007/978-3-319-96884-1_1
18. Rescorla, E., Salter, M.: Extended random values for TLS (2009). https://tools.ietf.org/html/draft-rescorla-tls-extended-random-02
19. Yilek, S., Rescorla, E., Shacham, H., Enright, B., Savage, S.: When private keys are public: results from the 2008 Debian OpenSSL vulnerability. In: Proceedings of the 9th ACM SIGCOMM Internet Measurement Conference, IMC 2009, Chicago, Illinois, USA, 4–6 November 2009, pp. 15–27 (2009)

Zero Knowledge

Cryptography from One-Way Communication: On Completeness of Finite Channels

Shweta Agrawal[1], Yuval Ishai[2], Eyal Kushilevitz[2], Varun Narayanan[3](✉), Manoj Prabhakaran[4], Vinod Prabhakaran[3], and Alon Rosen[5]

[1] Indian Institute of Technology Madras, Chennai, India
shweta@iitm.ac.in
[2] Technion, Haifa, Israel
{yuvali,eyalk}@cs.technion.ac.il
[3] Tata Institute of Fundamental Research, Mumbai, India
varunnkv@gmail.com, vinodmp@tifr.res.in
[4] Indian Institute of Technology Bombay, Mumbai, India
mp@cse.iitb.ac.in
[5] IDC Herzliya, Herzliya, Israel
alon.rosen@idc.ac.il

Abstract. Garg et al. (Crypto 2015) initiated the study of cryptographic protocols over noisy channels in the non-interactive setting, namely when only one party speaks. A major question left open by this work is the completeness of *finite* channels, whose input and output alphabets do not grow with the desired level of security. In this work, we address this question by obtaining the following results:

1. **Completeness of Bit-ROT with Inverse Polynomial Error.** We show that bit-ROT (i.e., Randomized Oblivious Transfer channel, where each of the two messages is a single bit) can be used to realize general randomized functionalities with inverse polynomial error. Towards this, we provide a construction of string-ROT from bit-ROT with inverse polynomial error.

2. **No Finite Channel is Complete with Negligible Error.** To complement the above, we show that *no* finite channel can be used to realize string-ROT with negligible error, implying that the inverse polynomial error in the completeness of bit-ROT is inherent. This holds even with semi-honest parties and for computational security, and is contrasted with the (negligible-error) completeness of string-ROT shown by Garg et al.

3. **Characterization of Finite Channels Enabling Zero-Knowledge Proofs.** An important instance of secure computation is zero-knowledge proofs. Noisy channels can potentially be used to realize *truly non-interactive* zero-knowledge proofs, without trusted common randomness, and with non-transferability and deniability features that cannot be realized in the plain model. Garg et al. obtain such zero-knowledge proofs from the binary erasure channel (BEC)

S. Moriai and H. Wang (Eds.): ASIACRYPT 2020, LNCS 12493, pp. 653–685, 2020.
https://doi.org/10.1007/978-3-030-64840-4_22

and the binary symmetric channel (BSC). We complete the picture by showing that in fact *any non-trivial channel* suffices.

1 Introduction

A noisy communication channel is a probabilistic function $\mathcal{C} : \mathcal{X} \to \mathcal{Y}$, mapping a sent symbol x to a received symbol y. Standard examples include the *binary symmetric channel* (BSC), which flips a bit $x \in \{0, 1\}$ with probability $0 < p < 1/2$, and the *binary erasure channel* (BEC), which erases x with probability p. A fundamental question in information-theoretic cryptography is – what cryptographic protocols can be constructed from noisy communication channels? This question has been studied extensively, with respect to various cryptographic tasks and a variety of channels, and has uncovered a rich landscape of structural relationships. Starting with the pioneering work of Wyner [30] who showed that the wiretap channel can be used for secure communication, many works studied the usefulness of noisy channels for additional cryptographic tasks (e.g., [5,6,14,23,25,28,29]). This culminated in a complete characterization of the channels on which oblivious transfer, and hence general secure two-party computation, can be based [12,13].

Most cryptographic constructions from noisy channels crucially require interaction. While this is not a barrier for some applications, there are several useful settings which are inherently non-interactive. A natural question that arises is what cryptographic tasks can be realized using only *one-way* noisy channels, namely by protocols over noisy channels in which only one party speaks. The question of realizing *secure communication* in this setting was the topic of Wyner's work, and is a central theme in the big body of work on "physical layer security" [8,24].

A clean way to capture tasks that can potentially be realized using one-way noisy communication is via a *sender-receiver* functionality, which takes an input from a *sender* S and delivers a (possibly) randomized output to a *receiver* R. In more detail, such a sender-receiver functionality is a deterministic or randomized mapping $f : \mathcal{A} \to \mathcal{B}$ that takes an input $a \in \mathcal{A}$ from a sender S and delivers an output $b = f(a)$ to a receiver R. In the randomized case, the randomness is internal to the functionality; neither S nor R learn it or can influence its choice.

Useful Instances. Several important cryptographic tasks can be captured as sender-receiver functionalities. For instance, a foundational primitive in cryptography is non-interactive zero-knowledge (NIZK) [9,15], which is typically constructed in the common random string (CRS) model. NIZK proofs can be captured in the sender-receiver framework by a deterministic function that takes an NP-statement and a witness from the sender and outputs the statement along with the output of the verification predicate to the receiver. As noted by Garg et al. [17], secure implementation of this function over a one-way channel provides the first *truly* non-interactive solution to zero knowledge proofs, where no trusted common randomness is available to the parties. Moreover, this solution can achieve useful properties of interactive zero-knowledge protocols such as non-transferability and deniability, which are impossible to achieve in the standard non-interactive setting. Another example from [17] is that of randomly generating "puzzles" without giving any of the parties an advantage in solving them. For instance, the sender can transmit to a receiver a random Sudoku challenge, or a random image of a one-way function, while the receiver is guaranteed that the sender has no advantage in solving the puzzle and can only general a puzzle of the level of difficulty prescribed by the randomized algorithm that generates it. A third example of a useful sender-receiver functionality is randomized blind signatures, which can be used for applications such as e-cash [3,10,11]. Blind signatures are captured by a randomized function that takes a message and a signing key from the sender and delivers a signature on some randomized function of the message to the receiver (for instance by adding a random serial number to a given dollar amount).[1] Another use-case for such randomized blind signatures is a non-interactive certified PKI generation, where an authority can issue to a user signed public keys, while only the users learn the corresponding secret keys. Applications notwithstanding, understanding the cryptographic power of noisy channels with one-way communication is a fundamental question from the theoretical standpoint.

Prior Work. A large body of theoretical and applied work studied how to leverage one-way communication to construct secure message transmission (see, e.g., [4,24] and references therein). More recently, Garg et al. [17] broadened the scope of this study to include more general cryptographic functionalities. Notably, they showed that one-way communication over the standard BEC or BSC channels suffices for realizing NIZK, or equivalently any *deterministic* sender-receiver functionality. Moreover, for general (possibly randomized) functionalities, a randomized *string-OT* channel or (string-ROT for short) is complete. A string-ROT channel takes a pair of random ℓ-bit strings from the sender and delivers only one of them, chosen at random by the channel, to the receiver. This completeness result was extended in [17] to other channels. However, in all of these general completeness results, the input and alphabet size of the channel grow (super-polynomially) with both the desired level of security and the complexity of the functionality being realized. On the negative side, it was shown in [17] that standard BEC/BSC channels are *not* complete. A major question that was left open is the existence of a complete *finite* channel, whose input and output alphabets do not grow with the security parameter or the complexity of the functionality. Furthermore, for the special case of deterministic functionalities (equivalently, NIZK), it was not known whether completeness holds for *all* non-trivial finite channels.

---

[1] In more detail, the sender can generate an anonymous \$100 bill by letting the input be $m =$ (Sender-name, 100) and the transmitted message be (m, id) for a random identifier *id* picked by the functionality. Consider the scenario where multiple \$100 bills are sent to different receivers. The id is needed to prevent double spending. Anonymity comes from the fact that the sender doesn't learn *id*, so it cannot associate a particular \$100 bill with the receiver to whom it was sent.

Next, we describe our framework in a bit more detail, followed by a summary of our results, which essentially settle the above mentioned questions.

Our Framework. Let $\mathcal{C}$ be a finite channel. We define a one-way secure computation protocol (OWSC) for a functionality f over channel $\mathcal{C}$ as a randomized encoder that maps the sender's input a into a sequence $\boldsymbol{x}$ of channel inputs, and a decoder that maps the sequence of receiver's channel outputs $\boldsymbol{y}$ into an output b. Given an error parameter ϵ, the protocol should satisfy the following security requirements: (i) given the sender's view, which consists of its input a and the message $\boldsymbol{x}$ that it fed into the channel, the receiver's output should be distributed as $f(a)$, and (ii) the view of the receiver, namely the message $\boldsymbol{y}$ it received from the channel, can be simulated from $f(a)$. Note that (i) captures receiver security against a corrupt sender as well as correctness, while (ii) captures sender security against a corrupt receiver.

We will construct OWSC protocols for various functionalities over various finite channels. Of particular interest to us is the randomized ℓ-bit string-ROT channel discussed above, which we denote by $\mathcal{C}^{\ell}_{\mathsf{ROT}}$, and its finite instance $\mathcal{C}^{1}_{\mathsf{ROT}}$ that we refer to as the *bit-ROT* channel.

1.1 Our Results

We are ready to state our results:

1. **Completeness of Bit-ROT with Inverse Polynomial Error.** We show that bit-ROT is complete for randomized functionalities with *inverse polynomial* simulation error. Towards this, we provide a construction of string-ROT from bit-ROT with inverse polynomial error, and appeal to the completeness of string-ROT. This is captured by the following (formal statement in Theorem 7):

Theorem 1. *(Informal) The bit-ROT channel ($\mathcal{C}^{1}_{\mathsf{ROT}}$) is complete for one-way secure computation, with* inverse-polynomial error. *This holds for both semi-honest and malicious parties. The protocol establishing completeness can either be efficient in the circuit size, in which case it is computationally secure using any pseudorandom generator, or efficient in the branching program size, in which case is it information-theoretically secure.*

2. **No Finite Channel is Complete with Negligible Error.** To complement the above positive result, we show that *no* finite channel is complete for randomized functionalities with negligible error. This is contrasted with the completeness of string-ROT discussed above. In more detail, we prove the following theorem (formal statement in Theorem 9):

Theorem 2. *(Informal): No finite channel is complete for one-way secure computation, with negligible error, even with semi-honest parties and for computational security. More concretely, string-ROT cannot be implemented in this setting.*

3. **Every Non-trivial Finite Channel is Complete for Zero-Knowledge.** As discussed above, a particularly compelling use case for one-way communication over noisy channels is *truly non-interactive* zero-knowledge proofs, without a trusted common randomness setup and with desirable features such as non-transferability and deniability. The results of Garg et al. [17] obtain such NIZK proofs from the binary erasure channel (BEC) and the binary symmetric channel (BSC). This raises the question whether *all* non-trivial channels enable NIZK.
   We show that this is indeed the case if we define a "trivial" channel to be one that either does not enable communication at all, or is essentially equivalent to a noiseless channel, when used by malicious senders. In more detail, we prove the following theorem (see Sect. 5 for a formal statement):

Theorem 3. *(Informal): Given a language $L \in \mathrm{NP} \setminus \mathrm{BPP}$, a one-way secure computation protocol over channel $\mathcal{C}$ for zero-knowledge for L exists if and only if $\mathcal{C}$ is non-trivial.*

1.2 Our Techniques

In this section we provide an overview of our techniques.

Completeness of Bit-ROT with Inverse Polynomial Error. We show that bit-ROT is complete for randomized functionalities with inverse polynomial error. Towards this, we show, in Theorem 6, that (ℓ-bit) string-ROT can be realized with polynomially many invocations of bit-ROT channel with inverse-polynomial error. The OWSC protocol is efficient in ℓ and is secure even against malicious adversaries.

In more detail, we use *average case secret sharing*, which is a weak version of ramp secret sharing, where both the reconstruction and privacy conditions are to be satisfied for a random set of r players and t players respectively, where r and t are the reconstruction and privacy thresholds, respectively. Theorem 4 provides a construction of OWSC protocol for string-ROT using bit-ROT given an average case secret sharing schemes (Avg-SSS) with sufficiently small gap parameter. The analysis of this theorem crucially uses the *anti-concentration bound* for Bernoulli sums for a small window around the mean. In Theorem 5, we construct efficient Avg-SSS for N players in which the gap between r and t is inverse polynomial in N and which have inverse polynomial privacy guarantee. The scheme we construct and its analysis build on techniques for secret sharing with binary shares that were recently introduced by Lin et al. [22] (for a different goal). Our result on efficient realization of string-ROT from bit-ROT directly follows from combining the above two results.

Impossibility of String-ROT from Finite Channel with Negligible Error. Next, we show that string-ROT cannot be constructed from bit-ROT with negligible error. We establish our result in two steps. Our first negative result in Theorem 8 shows that string-ROT cannot be realized with polynomially many invocations of bit-ROT channel while guaranteeing negligible error.

Our proof is inspired by [17]. In more detail, we use an isoperimetric inequality for Boolean hypercubes (Harper's theorem), to show the existence of strategies that can efficiently guess both input strings in any implementation of string-ROT with polynomially bounded number of bit-ROT invocations, which is a violation of the ROT security. The machine we describe for guessing the two input strings is computationally efficient, hence our impossibility result applies to computationally bounded semi-honest adversaries.

We then extend this result in Theorem 9 to show that no finite channel can be used to realize string-ROT using polynomially many invocations of the channel while guaranteeing negligible error. To show this, we model a channel as a function from the input of the channel and its internal randomness to the output of the channel. We then proceed to prove the impossibility in a manner similar to the impossibility for the bit-ROT channel.

Impossibility of Completeness of Finite Channels with Negligible Error. Theorem 9 shows that string-ROT cannot be realized over any finite channel efficiently (in terms of the number of channel invocations) and with negligible error, even in the computational setting. Since string-ROT is a simple functionality which has a small description in many functional representation classes, we obtain an impossibility result that strikes off the possibility of a complete channel with negligible error for most function representation classes of interest.

Characterization of Finite Channels Enabling Zero-Knowledge Proofs. It is a fundamental question to understand which channels enable ZK proofs. We give a complete characterization of all finite channels over which a OWSC protocol for zero-knowledge (proof of knowledge) functionality is possible. In fact, we show that the only channels which do not enable zero-knowledge proofs are "trivial" channels (a proof over a trivial channel translates to a proof over a plain one-way communication channel which is possible only for languages in BPP). Over any other finite channel, we build a statistical zero-knowledge proof of knowledge, which is unconditionally secure. Our result generalizes a result of [17], which gave OWSC zero-knowledge proof protocols over Binary Erasure Channels (BEC) and Binary Symmetric Channels (BSC) only. Extending this result to all non-trivial channels requires new ideas, exploiting a geometric view of channels.

2 Preliminaries

To begin, we define some notation that we will use throughout the paper.

Notation 1. *A member of a finite set $\mathcal{X}$ is represented by x and sampling an independent uniform sample from $\mathcal{X}$ is denoted by $x \xleftarrow{\$} \mathcal{X}$. A vector in $\mathcal{X}^n$ is represented by $\boldsymbol{x} \in \mathcal{X}^n$, whose coordinate $i \in [n]$ is represented by either x_i or $\boldsymbol{x}(i)$.*

For a vector $x \in \mathcal{X}^n$ and a set $A \subseteq [n]$, the restriction of x to the set A, represented by $x|_A$ is the vector with all the coordinates outside of A replaced by an erasure symbol $\perp$ which is not a member of $\mathcal{X}$. That is, $x|_A(i) = x(i)$ if $i \in A$ and $x|_A(i) = \perp$ otherwise. Finally, $\Delta(\mu_0, \mu_1)$ denotes the total variation distance between distributions μ_0 and μ_1.

2.1 Sender-Receiver Functionalities and Channels

This work addresses secure computation tasks that are made possible by one-way communication over a noisy channel. Such tasks can be captured by *sender-receiver* functionalities, that take an input from a *sender* S and deliver a (possibly) randomized output to a *receiver* R. More precisely, a sender-receiver functionality is a randomized mapping $f : \mathcal{A} \to \mathcal{B}$ that takes an input $a \in \mathcal{A}$ from a sender S and delivers an output $b = f(a)$ to a receiver R. We will sometimes refer to f simply as a *function* and write $f(a; \rho)$ when we want to make the internal randomness of f explicit.

In order to realize f, we assume that S and R are given parallel access to a *channel* $\mathcal{C} : \mathcal{X} \to \mathcal{Y}$, which is a sender-receiver functionality that is typically much simpler than the target function f. We will typically view $\mathcal{C}$ as being *finite* whereas f will come from an infinite class of functions. We will be interested in the number of invocations of $\mathcal{C}$ required for realizing f with a given error ϵ (if possible at all).

We will be particularly interested in the following channel.

Definition 1 (ROT channel). *The ℓ-bit randomized string oblivious transfer channel (or ℓ-bit string-ROT for short), denoted by $\mathcal{C}^{\ell}_{\mathsf{ROT}}$, takes from S a pair of strings $a_0, a_1 \in \{0,1\}^{\ell}$, and delivers to R*

$$\mathcal{C}^{\ell}_{\mathsf{ROT}}(a_0, a_1) = \begin{cases} (a_0, \perp) & w.p.\ \frac{1}{2}, \\ (\perp, a_1) & w.p.\ \frac{1}{2}. \end{cases}$$

Finally, it is sometimes convenient to assume that a sender-receiver functionality f can additionally take a *public input* that is known to both parties. For instance, in a zero-knowledge proof such a public input can include the NP-statement, or in blind signatures it can include the receiver's public verification key (allowing f to check the validity of the secret key). All of our definitions and results can be easily extended to this more general setting.

2.2 Secure Computation with One-Way Communication

A secure protocol for $f : \mathcal{A} \to \mathcal{B}$ over a channel $\mathcal{C}$ is formalized via the standard definitional framework of reductions in secure computation. Our default setting shall be that of *information-theoretic* security against *semi-honest* parties, with extensions to the setting of computational security and malicious parties. All our negative results in fact hold for the weakest setting of computational security against semi-honest parties. All our positive results hold for (either information-theoretic or computational) security against malicious parties.

OWSC Protocols. A one-way secure computation protocol for f over $\mathcal{C}$ specifies a randomized encoder that maps the sender's input a into a sequence of channel inputs $\boldsymbol{x}$, and a decoder that maps the receiver's channel outputs $\boldsymbol{y}$ into an output b. Given an error parameter ϵ, the protocol should satisfy the following security requirements: (i) given the sender's view, which consists of an input a and the message $\boldsymbol{x}$ that it fed into the channel, the receiver's output should be distributed as $f(a)$, and (ii) the view of the receiver, namely the message $\boldsymbol{y}$ it received from the channel, can be simulated from $f(a)$. Note that (i) captures receiver security against a corrupt sender as well as correctness, while (ii) captures sender security against a corrupt receiver. We formalize this below.

Definition 2 (One-way secure computation). *Given a randomized function $f : \mathcal{A} \to \mathcal{B}$ and a channel $\mathcal{C} : \mathcal{X} \to \mathcal{Y}$, a pair of randomized functions $\langle \mathsf{S}, \mathsf{R} \rangle$, where $\mathsf{S} : \mathcal{A} \to \mathcal{X}^N$ and $\mathsf{R} : \mathcal{Y}^N \to \mathcal{B}$ is said to be an (N, ϵ)* OWSC protocol for *f* over *$\mathcal{C}$ if there exists a simulator $\mathsf{Sim}_\mathsf{R} : \mathcal{B} \to \mathcal{Y}^N$, such that for all $a \in \mathcal{A}$,*

$$\Delta\left((\mathsf{S}(a), f(a)), (\mathsf{S}(a), \mathsf{R}(\mathcal{C}(\mathsf{S}(a))))\right) \le \epsilon$$

$$\Delta\left(\mathsf{Sim}_\mathsf{R}(f(a)), \mathcal{C}(\mathsf{S}(a))\right) \le \epsilon$$

OWSC for Malicious Parties. In this case, our security requirement coincides with UC security, but with simplifications implied by the communication model. Specifically, since a corrupt receiver has no input to the functionality nor any message in the protocol, UC security against a malicious receiver is the same as in the semi-honest setting. UC security against a malicious sender, on the other hand, requires that from any arbitrary strategy of the sender, a simulator is able to extract a valid input.

Formally, an OWSC protocol for f over $\mathcal{C}$ is secure against malicious parties if, in addition to the requirements in Definition 2, there exists a randomized simulator $\mathsf{Sim}_\mathsf{S} : \mathcal{X}^N \to \mathcal{A}$ such that for every $\boldsymbol{x} \in \mathcal{X}^N$,

$$\Delta\left(f(\mathsf{Sim}_\mathsf{S}(\boldsymbol{x})), \mathsf{R}(\mathcal{C}(\boldsymbol{x}))\right) \le \epsilon.$$

In our (positive) results in this setting, we shall require the simulator to be computationally efficient as well.

OWSC with Computational Security. We can naturally relax the above definition of (statistical) (N, ϵ) OWSC to *computational* (N, T, ϵ) OWSC, for a distinguisher size bound T, by replacing each statistical distance bound $\Delta(A, B) \le \epsilon$ by the condition that for all circuits C of size T, $|\Pr(C(A) = 1) - \Pr(C(B) = 1)| \le \epsilon$.

Complete Channels for OWSC. So far, we considered OWSC protocols for a concrete function f and with a concrete level of security ϵ. However, in a cryptographic context, one is typically interested in a single "universal" protocol that takes a description $\hat{f}$ of a function f and a security parameter λ as inputs and runs in polynomial time in its input length.

To meaningfully specify the goal of such a universal OWSC protocol, we need to fix a representation class $\mathcal{F}$ that defines an association between a bit-string $\hat{f}$ and the (deterministic or randomized) function f it represents. The representation classes $\mathcal{F}$ we will be interested in include *circuits* (capturing general polynomial-time computations) and *branching programs* (capturing logarithmic-space computations and logarithmic-depth circuits). The string-ROT channel $\mathcal{C}^{\ell}_{\mathsf{ROT}}$ can also be viewed as a degenerate function class $\mathcal{F}$ in which $\hat{f} = 1^{\ell}$ specifies the string length.

If a channel $\mathcal{C}$ enables a universal protocol for $\mathcal{F}$, we say that $\mathcal{C}$ is *OWSC-complete* for $\mathcal{F}$. We will distinguish between completeness with inverse-polynomial error and completeness with negligible error, depending on how fast the error vanishes with λ. We will also distinguish between completeness with statistical and computational security. We formalize this notion of completeness below.

Definition 3 (OWSC-complete channel). *Let $\mathcal{F}$ be a function representation class and $\mathcal{C}$ be a channel. We say that $\mathcal{C}$ is* OWSC-complete *for evaluating $\mathcal{F}$ with (statistical)* inverse-polynomial *error if for every positive integer c there is a polynomial-time protocol $\Pi = \langle \mathsf{S}, \mathsf{R} \rangle$ that, on common input $(1^{\lambda}, \hat{f})$, realizes (N, ϵ) OWSC of f over $\mathcal{C}$, where $\epsilon = \mathcal{O}(\frac{1}{\lambda^c})$ and $N = poly(\lambda, |\hat{f}|)$. We say that $\mathcal{C}$ is complete with* negligible *error if there is a single Π as above such that ϵ is negligible in λ. We similarly define the computational notions of completeness by requiring the above to hold with (N, T, ϵ) instead of (N, ϵ), for an arbitrary polynomial $T = T(\lambda)$.*

As discussed above, useful instances of $\mathcal{F}$ include circuits, branching programs, and string-ROT. We will assume statistical security against semi-honest parties by default, and will explicitly indicate when security is computational or against malicious parties.

2.3 OWSC Zero-Knowledge Proof of Knowledge

For a language L in NP, let R_L denote a polynomial time computable relation such that $x \in L$ if and only if for some w of length polynomial in the length of x, we have $R_L(x, w) = 1$. In the classic problem of *zero-knowledge proof*, given a common input $x \in L$, a polynomial time prover who has access to a w such that $R_L(x, w) = 1$ wants to convince a polynomial time verifier that $x \in L$, without revealing any additional information about w. On the other hand, if $x \notin L$, even a computationally unbounded prover should not be able to make the verifier accept the proof, except with negligible probability.

While classically, the prover and the verifier are allowed to interact with each other, or in the case of Non-Interactive Zero-Knowledge (NIZK), are given a common random string generated by a trusted third party, in a ZK protocol in the OWSC model, a single string is transmitted from the prover to the receiver, over a channel $\mathcal{C}$, with no other trusted set up. We shall require information-theoretic security, with both soundness and zero-knowledge properties defined via simulation. As simulation-based soundness corresponds to a proof of knowledge (PoK), we shall refer to this primitive as OWSC/$\mathcal{C}$ ZK-PoK.[2]

Definition 4 (OWSC Zero-knowledge Proof of Knowledge). *Given a channel $\mathcal{C}$, a pair of PPT algorithms $(\mathsf{P}_{ZK}, \mathsf{V}_{ZK})$ is a* OWSC/$\mathcal{C}$ zero-knowledge proof of knowledge (ZK-PoK) *for an* NP *language L with an associated relation R_L if the following hold:*

Completeness. *There is a negligible function* negl, *such that $\forall x \in L$ and w such that $R_L(x, w) = 1$,*

$$\Pr\left[\mathsf{V}_{ZK}(1^\lambda, x, \mathcal{C}(\mathsf{P}_{ZK}(1^\lambda, x, w))) \neq 1\right] = \text{negl}(\lambda)$$

(where the probability is over the randomness of P_{ZK} and V_{ZK} and that of the channel).

Soundness. *There exists a probabilistic polynomial time (PPT) extractor E such that, for all x and all collection of strings z_λ (collection indexed by λ)*

$$R_L\left(x, E(1^\lambda, x, z_\lambda)\right) = 0 \;\Rightarrow\; \Pr\left[\mathsf{V}_{ZK}(1^\lambda, x, \mathcal{C}(z_\lambda)) = 1\right] = \text{negl}(\lambda).$$

Zero-Knowledge. *There exists a PPT simulator S such that, for all $x \in L$, and w such that $R_L(x, w) = 1$,*

$$\mathcal{C}(\mathsf{P}_{ZK}(1^\lambda, x, w)) \approx_{\text{negl}(\lambda)} S(1^\lambda, x),$$

where $\approx$ represents computational indistinguishability.

In our construction we use the notion of oblivious zero-knowledge PCP, which was explicitly defined in [17]. In the problem of *oblivious zero-knowledge PCP*, a prover with access to $x \in L$ and w such that $R_L(x, w) = 1$ would like to publish a proof. The verifier's algorithm probes a constant number of random locations in the published proof and decides to accept or reject while guaranteeing correctness and soundness. The notion of oblivious zero-knowledge requires that the PCP is zero-knowledge when each bit in the proof is erased with finite probability.

Definition 5 (Oblivious ZK-PCP). *[17, Definition 1]* $(\mathsf{P}_{oZK}, \mathsf{V}_{oZK})$ *is a (c, ν)-oblivious ZK-PCP with knowledge soundness κ for an NP language L if, when λ is the security parameter, $\mathsf{P}_{oZK}, \mathsf{V}_{oZK}$ are probabilistic algorithms that run in polynomial time in λ and the length of the input x and satisfy the following conditions.*

Completeness. $\forall (x, w) \in R_L$ *when* $\pi \xleftarrow{\$} \mathsf{P}_{oZK}(x, w, \lambda)$, $\Pr(\mathsf{V}_{oZK}(x, \pi^*)) = 1$ *for all choices of π^* obtained by erasing arbitrary locations of π.*

[2] Indeed, an OWSC/$\mathcal{C}$ ZK-PoK protocol is equivalent to an information-theoretic UC-secure protocol for the ZK functionality in the $\mathcal{C}$-hybrid model, with an additional requirement that the protocol involves a single invocation of $\mathcal{C}$ and no other communication.

c-Soundness. *There exists a PPT extractor E such that, for all x and purported proofs π', if $(x, E(x, \pi')) \notin R_L$ then*

$$\Pr(\mathsf{V}_{oZK}(x, g(\pi')) = 0) \geq \kappa,$$

where the probability is taken over the random choices of g, where g is any function that replaces all but c locations of π' with $\perp$ (and leaves the other locations untouched).

ν-Zero-Knowledge. *There exists a PPT simulator S such that, for all $x \in L$, the following distributions are statistically indistinguishable:*

- *Sample $\pi \xleftarrow{\$} \mathsf{P}_{oZK}(\lambda, x, w)$, replace each bit in π with $\perp$ with probability $1 - \nu$ and output the resultant value.*
- *$S(x, \lambda)$.*

As described in [17], the following result is implied by a construction in [2]:

Proposition 1 *[17, Proposition 1]. For any constant $\nu \in (0, 1)$, there exists a $(3, \nu)$-oblivious ZK-PCP with a knowledge soundness $\kappa = 1 - \frac{1}{p(\lambda)}$, where $p(\lambda)$ is some polynomial in λ.*

3 String-ROT from Bit-ROT with Inverse Polynomial Error

In this section, we construct string-ROT from bit-ROT with inverse polynomial error, and apply this to show that bit-ROT is complete for general sender-receiver functionalities with inverse-polynomial error. Since the intuition was discussed in Sect. 1, we proceed directly with the construction.

3.1 Average Case Secret Sharing

An N player average case secret sharing scheme, for ℓ-bit secrets with reconstruction threshold r and privacy threshold t, consists of a sharing algorithm Share and a reconstruction algorithm Recst which guarantees that a random subset of t players learns nothing about the secret and that a random set of r players can reconstruct the secret with high probability. This is formalized by the next definition, where the following notation will be useful.

Notation 2. *For integers $1 \leq s \leq N$, we use the following families of subsets of $[N]$: $\mathcal{A}_s = \{A \subseteq [N] : |A| = s\}$, $\mathcal{A}_{\geq s} = \{A \subseteq [N] : |A| \geq s\}$, and $\mathcal{A}_{\leq s} = \{A \subseteq [N] : |A| \leq s\}$.*

Definition 6. *A $(\ell, N, t, r, \epsilon)$ average-case secret-sharing scheme (Avg-SSS, for short) is a pair of randomized algorithms $\langle \mathsf{Share}, \mathsf{Recst} \rangle$ such that,*

$$\mathsf{Share} : \{0,1\}^\ell \times \mathcal{R} \to \{0,1\}^N \quad \textit{and} \quad \mathsf{Recst} : \{0,1,\perp\}^N \to \{0,1\}^\ell,$$

where $\mathcal{R}$ is the private randomness, that satisfy the following properties.

Reconstruction Property: Recst *must be able to reconstruct any secret from a uniformly random set of r shares produced by* Share*, with at least $1-\epsilon$ probability. Formally, for all $\boldsymbol{s} \in \{0,1\}^\ell$,*

$$\Pr(\mathsf{Recst}(\mathsf{Share}(\boldsymbol{s})|_A) = \boldsymbol{s}) \geq 1 - \epsilon,$$

where the probability is over the randomness used by Share *and the choice of $A \xleftarrow{\$} \mathcal{A}_r$.*

Privacy Property: *t random shares of every pair of secrets are ϵ-close to each other in statistical distance. Formally, for all $\boldsymbol{s}, \boldsymbol{s}' \in \{0,1\}^\ell$, and $A \xleftarrow{\$} \mathcal{A}_t$,*

$$\Delta\left((\mathsf{Share}(\boldsymbol{s})|_A), (\mathsf{Share}(\boldsymbol{s}')|_A)\right) \leq \epsilon.$$

We will typically be interested in $(\ell, N, t, r, \epsilon)$-Avg-SSS where ℓ, t, r, ϵ are functions of N and require Share, Recst to be probabilistic algorithms with poly(N) complexity.

3.2 String-ROT from Bit-ROT and Average Case Secret Sharing

In this section, we show that an average case secret sharing scheme can be used to reduce string ROT to bit ROT. The following theorem demonstrates such a reduction.

Theorem 4. *For $\delta \in (0, \frac{1}{2})$ and for sufficiently large N, given a $(\ell, N, t, r, \epsilon)$-*Avg-SSS*, with $t = \lfloor \frac{N}{2} \rfloor - N^\delta$, $r = \lceil \frac{N}{2} \rceil + N^\delta$ and $\epsilon = N^{\delta - \frac{1}{2}}$, there exists a secure (even against malicious parties) $(N, 4N^{\delta-\frac{1}{2}})$ OWSC protocol for $\mathcal{C}^\ell_{\mathsf{ROT}}$ over $\mathcal{C}^1_{\mathsf{ROT}}$. If the* Avg-SSS *scheme is efficient in N, then so is our protocol.*

Proof: Let $\langle \mathsf{Share}, \mathsf{Recst} \rangle$ be an $(\ell, N, t, r, \epsilon)$-Avg-SSS. The protocol that realizes $\mathcal{C}^\ell_{\mathsf{ROT}}$ in the OWSC/$\mathcal{C}^1_{\mathsf{ROT}}$ model proceeds as follows.

Let $(\boldsymbol{a}_0, \boldsymbol{a}_1) \in \{0,1\}^\ell \times \{0,1\}^\ell$ be the input to the $\mathcal{C}^\ell_{\mathsf{ROT}}$. Sender computes $\boldsymbol{x}_0 = \mathsf{Share}(\boldsymbol{a}_0)$ and $\boldsymbol{x}_1 = \mathsf{Share}(\boldsymbol{a}_1)$. For $i = 1, \ldots, N$, sender sends $(\boldsymbol{x}_0(i), \boldsymbol{x}_1(i))$ in the i-th invocation of the $\mathcal{C}^1_{\mathsf{ROT}}$ channel.

The receiver gets $\boldsymbol{x}_0|_A, \boldsymbol{x}_1|_{[N]\setminus A}$, where A is a uniformly random subset of $[N]$. If $|A| \geq r$, it uniformly samples $A_0 \subseteq A$ such that $|A_0| = r$ and outputs $(\mathsf{Recst}(\boldsymbol{x}_0|_{A_0}), \perp)$, and if $|[N] \setminus A| \geq r$, it uniformly samples $A_1 \subseteq [N] \setminus A$ such that $|A_1| = r$ and outputs $(\perp, \mathsf{Recst}(\boldsymbol{x}_1|_{A_1}))$. If $|A| \in (t, r)$, R samples $\boldsymbol{a}_0, \boldsymbol{a}_1 \xleftarrow{\$} \{0,1\}^\ell$ and $i \xleftarrow{\$} \{0,1\}$ and outputs $(\boldsymbol{a}_0, \perp)$ if $i = 0$ and $(\perp, \boldsymbol{a}_1)$ if $i = 1$.

Complexity. The complexity of this reduction is N. If Avg-SSS is efficient, the protocol is efficient as well.

Security. We first show that the receiver's output is consistent with probability at least $1 - 3N^{\delta-\frac{1}{2}}$. That is, if the input to the sender is $(\boldsymbol{a}_0, \boldsymbol{a}_1)$, with probability $1 - 3N^{\delta-\frac{1}{2}}$, the receiver outputs either $(\perp, \boldsymbol{a}_1)$ or $(\boldsymbol{a}_0, \perp)$. To show this, we bound the probability of the event $|A| \in (t, r)$ using an anti-concentration bound on Bernoulli sums and then argue that conditioned on $|A| \notin (t, r)$, the receiver's output is consistent with probability $\geq 1 - \epsilon$.

Claim 1. *Let X_i be i.i.d Bernoulli$(\frac{1}{2})$ random variables for $i \in [N]$. Then, for all $\delta \in (0, 1/2)$,*

$$\Pr\left(\left|\sum_{i\in[N]} X_i - \left\lceil\frac{N}{2}\right\rceil\right| < N^{\delta}\right) \leq 2N^{\delta-\frac{1}{2}}.$$

Proof: This follows from the fact that,

$$\forall k \in [N],\ \Pr\left(\sum_{i\in[N]} X_i = k\right) \leq \Pr\left(\sum_{i\in[N]} X_i = \lceil N/2\rceil\right) \leq N^{-1/2}.$$

□

Denote the event $|A| \notin (t, r)$ by E. Since $r - t = 2N^{\delta}$, $\Pr(E) \geq 1 - 2N^{\delta-\frac{1}{2}}$ by the above claim. Conditioned on $|A| \geq r$, A is uniformly distributed in $\mathcal{A}_{\geq r}$. Hence, A_0 is uniformly distributed in $\mathcal{A}_r$. The receiver is correct if $\mathsf{Recst}(\mathsf{Share}(\boldsymbol{a}_0)|_{A_0}) = \boldsymbol{a}_0$. By the reconstruction property of $\langle\mathsf{Share}, \mathsf{Recst}\rangle$, for all $\boldsymbol{a}_0 \in \{0,1\}^{\ell}$, we have

$$\Pr(\mathsf{Recst}(\mathsf{Share}(\boldsymbol{a}_0)|_{A_0}) = \boldsymbol{a}_0) \geq 1 - \epsilon = 1 - N^{\delta-\frac{1}{2}},$$

where the probability is over the randomness used by Share and $A_0 \xleftarrow{\$} \mathcal{A}_r$. Similar bound applies for $\Pr(\mathsf{Recst}(\mathsf{Share}(\boldsymbol{a}_1)|_{A_1})$ conditioned on the event $|A| \leq t$. From these observations, the probability that the receiver outputs $(\boldsymbol{a}_0, \perp)$ or $(\perp, \boldsymbol{a}_1)$ when the sender's input is $(\boldsymbol{a}_0, \boldsymbol{a}_1)$ can be lower bounded as,

$$\Pr(E) \cdot \Pr(\text{Receiver outputs } (\boldsymbol{a}_0, \perp) \text{ or } (\perp, \boldsymbol{a}_1)|E) \geq (1 - 2N^{\delta-\frac{1}{2}})(1 - N^{\delta-\frac{1}{2}}) \geq 1 - 3N^{\delta-\frac{1}{2}}.$$

Furthermore, when $|A| \notin (t, r)$, the events $|A| \geq r$ and $N - |A| \geq r$ are equiprobable. That is, the index on which the receiver outputs $\perp$ is decided entirely by the randomness in the channel. Hence, for all $\boldsymbol{a}_0, \boldsymbol{a}_1 \in \{0,1\}^{\ell}$,

$$\Delta\Big((\boldsymbol{a}_0, \boldsymbol{a}_1, \mathsf{S}(\boldsymbol{a}_0, \boldsymbol{a}_1), \mathsf{R}(\mathcal{C}^{1}_{\mathsf{ROT}}(\mathsf{S}(\boldsymbol{a}_0, \boldsymbol{a}_1)))), \big(\boldsymbol{a}_0, \boldsymbol{a}_1, \mathsf{S}(\boldsymbol{a}_0, \boldsymbol{a}_1), \mathcal{C}^{\ell}_{\mathsf{ROT}}(\boldsymbol{a}_0, \boldsymbol{a}_1)\big)\Big) \leq 3N^{\delta-\frac{1}{2}}.$$

We now analyze security against the receiver. We claim that conditioned on the event $|A| \leq t$, for any $\boldsymbol{a}_0, \boldsymbol{a}'_0, \boldsymbol{a}_1 \in \{0,1\}^{\ell}$, the view of the receiver when the input to the sender is $(\boldsymbol{a}_0, \boldsymbol{a}_1)$ is sufficiently close to its view when the sender's input is $(\boldsymbol{a}'_0, \boldsymbol{a}_1)$. Note that conditioned on $|A| \leq t$, $|A|$ is a uniformly random set of size at most t. Our claim is that for all $\boldsymbol{a}_0, \boldsymbol{a}'_0 \in \{0,1\}^{\ell}$ and $A \xleftarrow{\$} \mathcal{A}_{\leq t}$,

$$\Delta\left(\mathsf{Share}(\boldsymbol{a}_0)|_A, \mathsf{Share}(\boldsymbol{a}'_0)|_A\right) \leq \epsilon = N^{\delta-\frac{1}{2}}.$$

To show this, note that the output distributions of the following two experiments are the same for every $\boldsymbol{a} \in \{0,1\}^{\ell}$:

(1) Choose $0 \leq k \leq t$ with probability $\Pr_{S \xleftarrow{\$} \mathcal{A}_{\leq t}}(|S| = k)$. When $A \xleftarrow{\$} \mathcal{A}_t$, let B be a uniformly random subset of A of size k. Output $\mathsf{Share}(\boldsymbol{a})|_B$.

(2) $A \xleftarrow{\$} \mathcal{A}_{\leq t}$, output $\mathsf{Share}(\boldsymbol{a})|_A$.
Hence, the distribution $\mathsf{Share}(\boldsymbol{a}_0)|_A$ where $A \xleftarrow{\$} \mathcal{A}_{\leq t}$ can be generated by post-processing the distribution $\mathsf{Share}(\boldsymbol{a}_0)|_A$ where $A \xleftarrow{\$} \mathcal{A}_t$. The claim now follows from the privacy guarantee of Avg-SSS and the fact that statistical distance only decreases on post-processing.

On input $(\perp, \boldsymbol{a}_1)$ the simulator Sim_R proceeds as follows: Sample $\boldsymbol{a} \xleftarrow{\$} \{0,1\}^\ell$ and run the algorithm of the sender with input $(\boldsymbol{a}, \boldsymbol{a}_1)$, to generate $(\boldsymbol{x}_0, \boldsymbol{x}_1)$. Sample $A \xleftarrow{\$} \mathcal{A}_{\leq t}$ and output $(\boldsymbol{x}_0|_A, \boldsymbol{x}_1|_{[N]\setminus A})$. The case for $(\boldsymbol{a}_0, \perp)$ is symmetric.

That Sim_R satisfies sender's privacy follows from the following observations: (a) The event $|A| \notin (t,r)$ happens with probability at least $1 - 2N^{\delta - \frac{1}{2}}$. (b) $\boldsymbol{a}_0$ (resp. $\boldsymbol{a}_1$) is decoded correctly with probability $1 - N^{\delta-\frac{1}{2}}$ when $|A| \geq r$ (resp. $|A| \leq t$). Furthermore, conditioned on both these events, the receiver's view for input $(\boldsymbol{a}_0, \boldsymbol{a}_1)$ and for input $(\boldsymbol{a}_0', \boldsymbol{a}_1)$ are at most $N^{\delta-\frac{1}{2}}$ far in statistical distance, for all $\boldsymbol{a}_0, \boldsymbol{a}_0' \in \{0,1\}^\ell$. Hence,

$$\Delta\left(\mathsf{Sim}_\mathsf{R}(\mathcal{C}^\ell_\mathsf{ROT}(\boldsymbol{a}_0, \boldsymbol{a}_1)), \mathcal{C}^1_\mathsf{ROT}(\mathsf{S}(\boldsymbol{a}_0, \boldsymbol{a}_1))\right) \leq 4N^{\delta-\frac{1}{2}}$$

UC-Security Against Malicious Adversaries. For any $\boldsymbol{x} \in \{0,1\}^N$, simulator Sim_S works as follows. Sample $A_{\geq r} \xleftarrow{\$} \mathcal{A}_{\geq r}$ and $A_{\leq t} \xleftarrow{\$} \mathcal{A}_{\leq t}$ (this can be done efficiently by rejection sampling). Let $(\boldsymbol{b}_0, \perp) = \mathsf{R}(\boldsymbol{x}|_{A_{\geq r}})$ and $(\perp, \boldsymbol{b}_1) = \mathsf{R}(\boldsymbol{x}|_{A_{\leq t}})$. Sample $A \xleftarrow{\$} [N]$, if $|A| \in (t,r)$, output $(\boldsymbol{s}_0, \boldsymbol{s}_1)$, where $\boldsymbol{s}_0, \boldsymbol{s}_1 \xleftarrow{\$} \{0,1\}^\ell$, else output $(\boldsymbol{b}_0, \boldsymbol{b}_1)$.

We claim that distribution $\mathcal{C}^1_\mathsf{ROT}(\mathsf{Sim}_\mathsf{S}(\boldsymbol{x}))$ is identical to the output distribution of the receiver when a malicious sender sends $\boldsymbol{x}$. In the event that $|A| \in (t,r)$, the output of the receiver is distributed as if the input to the string-ROT were a pair of random strings. In the events $A \in \mathcal{A}_{\leq t}$ and $A \in \mathcal{A}_{\geq r}$, R outputs according to a random erasure from $\mathcal{A}_{\leq t}$ and $\mathcal{A}_{\geq r}$ respectively. This is indeed the distribution generated by the simulator and so this proves the theorem. □

Remark 1. The OWSC protocol is said to be Las-Vegas if it either aborts after returning $\perp$ or is correct conditioned on not aborting, *i.e.*, outputs $(\boldsymbol{a}_0, \perp)$ or $(\perp, \boldsymbol{a}_1)$ with equal probability. Suppose the Avg-SSS is Las-Vegas in the following sense. For every $A \in \mathcal{A}_r$, Recst either reconstructs the secret correctly or aborts after returning $\perp$. We can tweak the above OWSC protocol to output $\perp$ whenever $|A| \in (t,r)$ and to return whatever the Recst outputs when $|A| \geq r$ makes the OWSC protocol also Las-Vegas. This guarantees that in Theorem 4, if Avg-SSS is Las-Vegas, then OWSC protocol is also Las-Vegas. In the next section, we will construct an Avg-SSS scheme which is Las-Vegas.

3.3 Construction of Average Case Secret Sharing

In this section, we construct an average case secret sharing scheme. Our construction is similar to the construction of constant rate secret sharing schemes in [22]. The only difference is that the reconstruction and privacy properties are with respect to random corruptions, hence we are able to use randomized erasure correcting codes with better error parameters. Before we describe the construction, we provide the following definitions.

Definition 7. *A function* $\mathsf{Ext} : \{0,1\}^d \times \{0,1\}^n \to \{0,1\}^\ell$ *is a* (k, ϵ) *strong seeded extractor if for every random variable* X*, with alphabet* $\{0,1\}^n$ *and min-entropy* k*, when* $\boldsymbol{z} \xleftarrow{\$} \{0,1\}^d$ *and* $\boldsymbol{r} \xleftarrow{\$} \{0,1\}^\ell$*,*

$$\Delta\left((\mathsf{Ext}(\boldsymbol{z}, X), \boldsymbol{z}), (\boldsymbol{r}, \boldsymbol{z})\right) \leq \epsilon.$$

A randomized map Ext^{-1} *is an inverter map of* Ext *if it maps* $\boldsymbol{z} \in \{0,1\}^d, \boldsymbol{s} \in \{0,1\}^\ell$ *to a sample from the uniform distribution over* $\{0,1\}^n$*, i.e.* U_n*, subject to* $(\mathsf{Ext}(\boldsymbol{z}, U^n) = \boldsymbol{s})$.

The following lemma describes an improvement of Trevisan's extractor [27] due to Raz *et al.* [26]. The statement itself is from [22].

Lemma 1 *[22, Lemma 4]. There is an explicit linear* (k, ϵ) *strong seeded extractor* $\mathsf{Ext} : \{0,1\}^d \times \{0,1\}^n \to \{0,1\}^\ell$ *with* $d = \mathcal{O}(\log^3 n/\epsilon)$ *and* $\ell = k - \mathcal{O}(d)$.

The other component in our construction is an erasure correcting code. Since Avg-SSS allows for shared randomness between the sharing algorithm Share and the reconstruction algorithm Recst, we could use randomized erasure correcting codes.

Definition 8. *An* (n, k, r, ϵ)*-linear erasure correcting scheme* (Enc, Dec) *consists of a linear encoder* $\mathsf{Enc} : \{0,1\}^k \to \{0,1\}^n$ *and a decoder* $\mathsf{Dec} : \{0,1\}^n \to \{0,1\}^k$ *such that, for all* $\boldsymbol{x} \in \{0,1\}^k$*,*

$$\Pr_{A \xleftarrow{\$} \mathcal{A}_r} \left(\mathsf{Dec}(\,\mathsf{Enc}(\boldsymbol{x})|_A) \neq \boldsymbol{x}\right) \leq \epsilon.$$

Lemma 2. *For all* $k \leq r \leq n$*, there exist efficient* (n, k, r, ϵ)*-linear erasure correcting schemes with* $\epsilon = 2^{k-r}$.

A proof of the lemma is provided in the full version [1], where we will also argue that the erasure correcting code we construct is Las-Vegas *i.e.*, the decoder either aborts or correctly decodes the message. It can be verified that the Avg-SSS scheme we construct is Las-Vegas whenever the erasure correcting scheme is Las-Vegas.

Theorem 5. *For parameters* $t < n < n + d < r < N$ *and* ℓ, ϵ*, let* $\mathsf{Ext} : \{0,1\}^d \times \{0,1\}^n \to \{0,1\}^\ell$ *be a linear* $(n - t, \epsilon)$ *strong seeded extractor with inverter map* Ext^{-1}*. Let* (Enc, Dec) *be a* $(N, n + d, r, \epsilon)$*-randomized linear erasure correcting code. Then,* ⟨Share, Recst⟩*, described below, is a* $(\ell, N, t, r, 8\epsilon)$*-Avg-SSS:*

$$\mathsf{Share}(\boldsymbol{s}) = \mathsf{Enc}(\boldsymbol{z}||\mathsf{Ext}^{-1}(\boldsymbol{z}, \boldsymbol{s})), \textit{where } \boldsymbol{z} \xleftarrow{\$} \{0,1\}^d,$$

$$\mathsf{Recst}(\boldsymbol{v}|_A) = \mathsf{Ext}(\boldsymbol{z}||\boldsymbol{x}), \textit{where } \boldsymbol{z}||\boldsymbol{x} = \mathsf{Dec}(\boldsymbol{v}|_A)$$

where $\boldsymbol{s} \in \{0,1\}^\ell$ *and* $A \subset [N]$*, when* $(\cdot||\cdot)$ *is the concatenation operator.*

Proof: We show that the scheme satisfies the reconstruction and privacy properties.

Reconstruction. By the performance guarantee of the error correcting code, for any $\boldsymbol{v} \in \{0,1\}^{n+d}$,

$$\Pr_{A \xleftarrow{\$} \mathcal{A}_r} (\mathsf{Dec}(\mathsf{Enc}(\boldsymbol{v})|_A) = \boldsymbol{v}) \geq 1 - \epsilon.$$

Hence, $\mathsf{Recst}(\boldsymbol{v}|_A) = \boldsymbol{s}$, for a random A, with probability $1 - \epsilon$.

Privacy. We use the following result from [22]:

Lemma 3 *[22, Lemma 13]. Let* $\mathsf{Ext} : \{0,1\}^d \times \{0,1\}^n \to \{0,1\}^\ell$ *be a linear* (k, ϵ) *strong extractor. Let* $f_A : \{0,1\}^{n+d} \to \{0,1\}^t$ *be an affine function with* $t \leq n - k$. *For any* $\boldsymbol{s}, \boldsymbol{s}' \in \{0,1\}^\ell$, *when* $(Z, X) = (U_d, U_n)|(\mathsf{Ext}(U_d, U_n) = \boldsymbol{s})$ *and* $(Z', X') = (U_d, U_n)|(\mathsf{Ext}(U_d, U_n) = \boldsymbol{s}')$, *we have*

$$\Delta(f_A(Z, X), f_A(Z', X')) \leq 8\epsilon.$$

Enc is a linear function and for any $A \subseteq [N]$ the restriction operator $(\cdot)|_A$ is a projection. Hence, for any $\boldsymbol{s} \in \{0,1\}^\ell$ and $A \subseteq [N]$ such that $|A| = t$, $\mathsf{Share}(\boldsymbol{s})|_A$ is an affine map with range $\{0,1\}^t$ applied to $(U_d, U_n)|(\mathsf{Ext}(U_d, U_n) = \boldsymbol{s})$. Ext used in the theorem is a $(n - t, \epsilon)$ extractor, hence the privacy follows directly from the above lemma. □

For any N and $\delta \in (0, 1/2)$, Lemma 1 guarantees an explicit linear $(N^\delta, \frac{1}{8N})$ strong seeded extractor $\mathsf{Ext} : \{0,1\}^d \times \{0,1\}^{\frac{N}{2}} \to \{0,1\}^\ell$ with $d = \mathcal{O}(\log^3 N)$ and $\ell = N^\delta - \mathcal{O}(\log^3 N)$. Furthermore, Lemma 2 guarantees a (N, k, r, ϵ)-linear erasure correcting code for $k = \frac{N}{2} + d$, $r = \frac{N}{2} + N^\delta$ and $\epsilon = \frac{1}{8N}$ (in fact, the lemma gives much better maximum error probability guarantees, but we would not need this). Note that both Ext^{-1} and $(\mathsf{Enc}, \mathsf{Dec})$ are efficient. Using this extractor and the erasure correcting scheme in Theorem 5, we obtain the following corollary.

Corollary 1. *For large enough* N *and* $\delta \in (0, \frac{1}{2})$, *when* $\ell = \frac{N^\delta}{2}, t = \frac{N}{2} - N^\delta, r = \frac{N}{2} + N^\delta$ *and* $\epsilon = \frac{1}{N}$, *there exists an efficient* $(\ell, N, t, r, \epsilon)$*-*$\mathsf{Avg\text{-}SSS}$.

Given such a $\mathsf{Avg\text{-}SSS}$, we appeal to the Theorem 4 to get the following theorem.

Theorem 6. *For* $\delta \in (0, \frac{1}{2})$, *there exists an efficient protocol that realizes* (N, ϵ) *secure OWSC for* $\mathcal{C}^\ell_{\mathsf{ROT}}$ *over* $\mathcal{C}^1_{\mathsf{ROT}}$, *with* $\epsilon = \mathcal{O}(N^{\delta - \frac{1}{2}})$, *and* $\ell = \frac{N^\delta}{2}$. *In particular, bit-ROT is complete for string-ROT with inverse-polynomial error.*

3.4 General Completeness of Bit-ROT with Inverse Polynomial Error

In the previous section, we showed that bit-ROT is complete for string-ROT with inverse-polynomial error. Garg *et al.* [17] (Theorem 11) showed that string-ROT is complete for arbitrary *finite* functionalities even for the case of malicious parties, where the (statistical) error is negligible in the ROT string length ℓ. Combined with our reduction from string-ROT to bit-ROT, this gives a similar completeness result for bit-ROT with inverse-polynomial error. Below we extend this to functions represented by branching programs and circuits, where in the latter case we need to settle for computational security using any (black-box) pseudorandom generator. Thus, assuming the existence of a one-way function, bit-ROT is complete with inverse-polynomial computational error for any polynomial-time computable functionality.

Theorem 7 (Bit-ROT is complete with inverse-polynomial error). *The bit-ROT channel* $\mathcal{C}^1_{\mathsf{ROT}}$ *is OWSC-complete, with* inverse-polynomial error, *for evaluating* circuits *with computational security against malicious parties, assuming a (black-box) pseudorandom generator. Moreover, replacing circuits by* branching programs, *the same holds* unconditionally *with inverse-polynomial* statistical *error.*

Proof: We start by addressing the simpler case of semi-honest parties. In this case, the computational variant follows by combining the reduction from string-ROT to bit-ROT with Yao's garbled circuit construction [31] in the following way. Given a randomized sender-receiver functionality $f(a;r)$, define a deterministic (two-way) functionality f' that takes (a, r_1) from the sender and r_2 from the receiver, and outputs $f(a; r_1 \oplus r_2)$ to the receiver. Using Yao's protocol to securely evaluate f' with uniformly random choices of r_1, r_2, we get a computationally secure reduction of f to (chosen-input) string-OT where the receiver's inputs are random. Replacing the random choices of the receiver by the use of a string-ROT channel, we get a computational OWSC protocol for f over string-ROT using any (black-box) PRG. Finally, applying the reduction from string-ROT to bit-ROT with a suitable choice of parameters, we get the inverse-polynomial completeness result for circuits with semi-honest parties. A similar result for branching programs with statistical (and unconditional) security can be obtained using information-theoretic analogues of garbled circuits [16,18,20].

To obtain similar protocols for malicious parties, we appeal to a result of [19], which obtains an analogue of Yao's protocol with security against *malicious* parties by only making a black-box use of a pseudorandom generator along with parallel calls to a string-OT oracle.[3] (This result too has an unconditional version for the case of branching programs.) Unlike Yao's protocol, the protocol from [19] encodes the receiver's input before feeding it into the parallel OTs. However, this encoding has the property that a random receiver input is mapped to random OT choice bits. Thus, the same reduction as before applies. □

The unconditional part of Theorem 7 implies polynomial-time statistically-secure protocols (with inverse-polynomial error) for the complexity classes $\mathbf{NC}^1$ and **Logspace**. This is a vast generalization of the positive result for $\mathcal{C}^\ell_{\mathsf{ROT}}$. In the result for general circuits, the use of a pseudorandom generator is inherent given the current state of the art on constant-round secure computation.

[3] Note that the conceptually simpler approach of applying NIZK proofs is not applicable here, since in the setting of secure computation over noisy channels there is no public transcript to which such a proof can apply.

$\langle \mathsf{S}, \mathsf{R} \rangle(\boldsymbol{a}_0, \boldsymbol{a}_1)$

1. $(\boldsymbol{x}_0, \boldsymbol{x}_1) = \mathsf{S}(\boldsymbol{a}_0, \boldsymbol{a}_1)$.
2. Sample $\boldsymbol{s} \xleftarrow{\$} \{0,1\}^N$ and let $(\boldsymbol{y}_0, \boldsymbol{y}_1) = f^N_{\mathcal{C}^1_{\mathsf{ROT}}}((\boldsymbol{x}_0, \boldsymbol{x}_1), \boldsymbol{s})$.
3. $(\boldsymbol{b}_0, \boldsymbol{b}_1) = \mathsf{R}(\boldsymbol{y}_0, \boldsymbol{y}_1)$.
4. Output $((\boldsymbol{a}_0, \boldsymbol{a}_1), (\boldsymbol{x}_0, \boldsymbol{x}_1), (\boldsymbol{y}_0, \boldsymbol{y}_1), (\boldsymbol{b}_0, \boldsymbol{b}_1))$.

Fig. 1. Execution of a protocol $\langle \mathsf{S}, \mathsf{R} \rangle$ for OWSC of $\mathcal{C}^\ell_{\mathsf{ROT}}$ over $\mathcal{C}^1_{\mathsf{ROT}}$ channel. Here $\boldsymbol{a}_0, \boldsymbol{a}_1$ are the ℓ-bit input strings for $\mathcal{C}^\ell_{\mathsf{ROT}}$, the N-bit strings $\boldsymbol{x}_0, \boldsymbol{x}_1$ are the inputs for the N invocations of the $\mathcal{C}^1_{\mathsf{ROT}}$ channel, $\boldsymbol{y}_0, \boldsymbol{y}_1$ are the outputs of these N invocations, and $\boldsymbol{b}_0, \boldsymbol{b}_1$ are the outputs of $\mathcal{C}^\ell_{\mathsf{ROT}}$.

4 Impossibility of String-ROT from Bit-ROT with Negligible Error

In this section we show that string-ROT with negligible error is impossible to achieve from bit-ROT. Moreover, this holds even against a computationally bounded semi-honest adversary.

Theorem 8. *For sufficiently large N and $\ell \geq 2\log N$, an $(N, \frac{1}{N^2})$ OWSC protocol for $\mathcal{C}^\ell_{\mathsf{ROT}}$ over $\mathcal{C}^1_{\mathsf{ROT}}$ is impossible even against semi-honest parties. In fact, the same holds even if one settles for OWSC with computational security. That is, there exists a polynomial $T = T(N)$ such that there is no computational $(N, T, \frac{1}{N^2})$ OWSC protocol for $\mathcal{C}^\ell_{\mathsf{ROT}}$ over $\mathcal{C}^1_{\mathsf{ROT}}$.*

Proof: $\mathcal{C}^1_{\mathsf{ROT}}$ may be equivalently described as a randomized function $f_{\mathcal{C}^1_{\mathsf{ROT}}}$ from the input of the channel and the internal randomness of the channel to the output of the channel. Formally, For $(x_0, x_1) \in \{0,1\} \times \{0,1\}$, and $s \in \{0,1\}$,

$$f_{\mathcal{C}^1_{\mathsf{ROT}}}((x_0, x_1), s) = \begin{cases} (x_0, \perp) & \text{if } s = 0, \\ (\perp, x_1) & \text{if } s = 1. \end{cases}$$

Observe that for all $(x_0, x_1) \in \{0,1\} \times \{0,1\}$, the following distributions are identical: (1) $\mathcal{C}^1_{\mathsf{ROT}}(x_0, x_1)$ and (2) Sample $s \xleftarrow{\$} \{0,1\}$ and output $f_{\mathcal{C}^1_{\mathsf{ROT}}}((x_0, x_1), s)$. Similarly, N invocations of $\mathcal{C}^1_{\mathsf{ROT}}$ are equivalent to the randomized function $f^N_{\mathcal{C}^1_{\mathsf{ROT}}}$ which on input $(\boldsymbol{x}_0, \boldsymbol{x}_1) \in \{0,1\}^N \times \{0,1\}^N$, samples $\boldsymbol{s} \xleftarrow{\$} \{0,1\}^N$ and outputs $(\boldsymbol{y}_0, \boldsymbol{y}_1)$, where $(\boldsymbol{y}_0(i), \boldsymbol{y}_1(i)) = f_{\mathcal{C}^1_{\mathsf{ROT}}}((\boldsymbol{x}_0(i), \boldsymbol{x}_1(i)), \boldsymbol{s}(i))$.

Suppose $\langle \mathsf{S}, \mathsf{R} \rangle$ is a $(N, \frac{1}{N^2})$ OWSC protocol for $\mathcal{C}^\ell_{\mathsf{ROT}}$ over $\mathcal{C}^1_{\mathsf{ROT}}$ channel. The joint distribution generated by this protocol for an input (pair of strings) $(\boldsymbol{a}_0, \boldsymbol{a}_1) \in \{0,1\}^\ell \times \{0,1\}^\ell$ is described in Fig. 1. The receiver's algorithm R can be assumed to be deterministic w.l.o.g. since we may fix the randomness in the decoder incurring only a constant hit to the $\epsilon = \frac{1}{N^2}$ parameter. This is because, for most values of $(\boldsymbol{y}_0, \boldsymbol{y}_1)$, R should decode one of the indices with low probability of error and should be almost entirely unsure of the other index. Refer to the full version [1] for a formal proof.

$\mathsf{M}(\boldsymbol{y}_0, \boldsymbol{y}_1)$

1. Compute $(\boldsymbol{b}_0, \boldsymbol{b}_1) = \mathsf{R}(\boldsymbol{y}_0, \boldsymbol{y}_1)$ (suppose $(\boldsymbol{b}_0, \boldsymbol{b}_1) = (\hat{\boldsymbol{a}}_0, \perp)$ w.l.o.g).
2. Compute $(\hat{\boldsymbol{y}}_0, \hat{\boldsymbol{y}}_1)$ as follows: Sample $j \xleftarrow{\$} [N]$. For $i \in \{0,1\}$ and $k \in [N] \setminus \{j\}$, set $\hat{\boldsymbol{y}}_i(k) = \boldsymbol{y}_i(k)$. If $\boldsymbol{y}_i(j) = \perp$, sample $\hat{\boldsymbol{y}}_i(j) \xleftarrow{\$} \{0,1\}$, and if $\boldsymbol{y}_i(j) \neq \perp$ then $\hat{\boldsymbol{y}}_i(j) = \perp$.
3. Compute $(\hat{\boldsymbol{b}}_0, \hat{\boldsymbol{b}}_1) = \mathsf{R}(\hat{\boldsymbol{y}}_0, \hat{\boldsymbol{y}}_1)$.
4. If $(\hat{\boldsymbol{b}}_0, \hat{\boldsymbol{b}}_1) = (\perp, \hat{\boldsymbol{a}}_1)$, then output $(\hat{\boldsymbol{a}}_0, \hat{\boldsymbol{a}}_1)$; else, abort.

Fig. 2. Execution of the machine M

In the sequel, for brevity, we would represent the tuples $(\boldsymbol{a}_0, \boldsymbol{a}_1), (\boldsymbol{x}_0, \boldsymbol{x}_1)$, $(\boldsymbol{y}_0, \boldsymbol{y}_1)$ and $(\boldsymbol{b}_0, \boldsymbol{b}_1)$ also by $\boldsymbol{a}, \boldsymbol{x}, \boldsymbol{y}$ and $\boldsymbol{b}$, respectively, whenever this does not cause confusion. For $(\boldsymbol{a}_0, \boldsymbol{a}_1) \in \{0,1\}^\ell \times \{0,1\}^\ell$, consider the joint distribution $\langle \mathsf{S}, R\rangle(\boldsymbol{a}_0, \boldsymbol{a}_1)$ described in Fig. 1. We now make some claims about this distribution.

Lemma 4. *There exists a set* $X \subseteq \{0,1\}^N \times \{0,1\}^N$ *such that* $\Pr(\boldsymbol{x} \in X) \geq 1 - \frac{2}{N}$ *and for all* $\boldsymbol{x} \in X$,

$$\Pr(\boldsymbol{b}_0 = \perp | \boldsymbol{x}) \geq \frac{1}{2} - \frac{1}{N} \quad \text{and} \quad \Pr(\boldsymbol{b}_1 = \perp | \boldsymbol{x}) \geq \frac{1}{2} - \frac{1}{N}.$$

The lemma is a consequence of computational $\frac{1}{N^2}$-security against sender. Intuitively, the sender can guess the index of the message output by the receiver with substantial probability if $\Pr(\boldsymbol{x} \in X) < 1 - \frac{2}{N}$. Refer to the full version [1] for a formal proof.

We now design a machine M that guesses both $\boldsymbol{a}_0$ and $\boldsymbol{a}_1$ from $(\boldsymbol{y}_0, \boldsymbol{y}_1)$ with substantial probability, contradicting sender's privacy. On receiving $\boldsymbol{y}$, machine M uses the receiver's strategy $\mathsf{R}(\boldsymbol{y})$ to decode one of the messages, say $\boldsymbol{a}_i$, where i is either 1 or 0. It then computes $\boldsymbol{a}_{1-i}$ by 'guessing' a random neighbor of $\boldsymbol{y}$, say $\hat{\boldsymbol{y}}$ and computing $\mathsf{R}(\hat{\boldsymbol{y}})$. We would show that with substantial probability, $\mathsf{R}(\hat{\boldsymbol{y}})$ yields $\boldsymbol{a}_{1-i}$, breaking sender's privacy property. M is formally described in Fig. 2.

Analysis of M: We show that M outputs $(\boldsymbol{a}_0, \boldsymbol{a}_1)$ with substantial probability. We would analyze the output of the machine M for a fixed $\boldsymbol{x} \in X$, where X is as guaranteed by Lemma 4. Define function $f_{\boldsymbol{x}} : \{0,1\}^N \to \{0,1\}$ such that when $\boldsymbol{y} = f^N_{\mathcal{C}^1_{\mathsf{ROT}}}(\boldsymbol{x}, \boldsymbol{s})$, $f_{\boldsymbol{x}}(\boldsymbol{s}) = 1$ if $\mathsf{R}(\boldsymbol{y}) = (\boldsymbol{b}_0, \boldsymbol{b}_1)$ such that $\boldsymbol{b}_0 = \perp$ and 0 otherwise. We next observe a property of $f_{\boldsymbol{x}}$ which is a consequence of an isoperimetric inequality on Boolean hypercubes (Harper's Lemma). For binary strings $\boldsymbol{u}, \boldsymbol{v} \in \{0,1\}^n$, denote the Hamming distance between them by $|\boldsymbol{u} - \boldsymbol{v}|$.

Lemma 5. *For any function* $f : \{0,1\}^n \to \{0,1\}$, *if* $\Pr_{\boldsymbol{v} \xleftarrow{\$} \{0,1\}^n} (f(\boldsymbol{v}) = i) \geq \frac{1}{2}(1 - \frac{1}{\sqrt{n}})$ *for each* $i \in \{0,1\}$, *then* $\Pr_{\boldsymbol{v} \xleftarrow{\$} \{0,1\}^n} (\exists \tilde{\boldsymbol{v}} : |\boldsymbol{v} - \tilde{\boldsymbol{v}}| = 1 \text{ and } f(\tilde{\boldsymbol{v}}) = 1 - f(\boldsymbol{v})) \geq \Omega(\frac{1}{\sqrt{n}})$.

In words, the lemma says that if f is a 2-coloring of the Boolean hypercube, where the colors are (almost) balanced, then a significant fraction of the nodes of the hypercube, have a neighbor of a different color.

By Harper's Lemma, Hamming balls have the smallest vertex boundary amongst all sets of the same probability. W.l.o.g, the probability of $f(\boldsymbol{v}) = 1$ is at most $\frac{1}{2}$ and at least $\frac{1}{2}(1 - \frac{1}{\sqrt{n}})$ and $\Pr_{\boldsymbol{v} \xleftarrow{\$} \{0,1\}^n}(|\boldsymbol{v} - \mathbf{0}| = \lfloor \frac{n}{2} \rfloor) \geq \frac{1}{2\sqrt{n}}$, where $\mathbf{0}$ is the all zero string. Hence the Hamming ball centered at $\mathbf{0}$ with probability at most $\frac{1}{2}$ and at least $\frac{1}{2}(1 - \frac{1}{\sqrt{n}})$ has strings with $\lfloor \frac{n}{2} \rfloor$ or $\lfloor \frac{n}{2} \rfloor - 1$ number of 1's in its boundary. Consequently, the size of this boundary is $\Omega(\frac{1}{\sqrt{n}})$.

For any $\boldsymbol{x} \in \{0,1\}^N \times \{0,1\}^N$, the input to M is $\boldsymbol{y} = f^N_{\mathcal{C}^1_{\mathsf{ROT}}}(\boldsymbol{x}, \boldsymbol{s})$, where $\boldsymbol{s} \xleftarrow{\$} \{0,1\}^N$. The process of generating $\hat{\boldsymbol{y}}$ in $M(\boldsymbol{y})$ is equivalent to the following process. Compute $(\hat{\boldsymbol{x}}_0, \hat{\boldsymbol{x}}_1)$ and $\hat{\boldsymbol{s}}$ as follows: Sample $j \leftarrow [N]$, set $\hat{\boldsymbol{s}}(j) = 1 - \boldsymbol{s}(j)$ and $(\hat{\boldsymbol{x}}_0(j), \hat{\boldsymbol{x}}_1(j)) \xleftarrow{\$} \{0,1\} \times \{0,1\}$. For all $k \neq j$, set $\hat{\boldsymbol{s}}(k) = \boldsymbol{s}(k)$ and $(\hat{\boldsymbol{x}}_0(k), \hat{\boldsymbol{x}}_1(k)) = (\boldsymbol{x}_0(k), \boldsymbol{x}_1(k))$. Compute $\hat{\boldsymbol{y}} = f^N_{\mathcal{C}^1_{\mathsf{ROT}}}(\hat{\boldsymbol{x}}, \hat{\boldsymbol{s}})$. We make the following observations about the above process.

(i.) $\hat{\boldsymbol{s}}$ is uniformly distributed over $\{0,1\}^N$ and $|\boldsymbol{s} - \hat{\boldsymbol{s}}| = 1$.
(ii.) $\hat{\boldsymbol{y}} = f^N_{\mathcal{C}^1_{\mathsf{ROT}}}(\boldsymbol{x}, \hat{\boldsymbol{s}})$ with probability $\frac{1}{2}$.
(iii.) For any $\boldsymbol{x} \in X$, $\Pr(f_{\boldsymbol{x}}(\boldsymbol{s}) = 1 - f_{\boldsymbol{x}}(\hat{\boldsymbol{s}})) \geq \Omega(\frac{1}{N\sqrt{N}})$.

(i) follows from $\boldsymbol{s}$ being uniform in $\{0,1\}^N$ and $\hat{\boldsymbol{s}}$ being obtained by flipping the value of a random coordinate of $\boldsymbol{s}$. (ii) can be verified easily from the process description. When $\boldsymbol{x} \in X$ and $\boldsymbol{s} \xleftarrow{\$} \{0,1\}^N$, $\Pr(f_{\boldsymbol{x}}(\boldsymbol{s}) = i) \geq \frac{1}{2}(1 - \frac{1}{\sqrt{N}})$ for $i \in \{0,1\}$, by Lemma 4. Hence, by Harper's Lemma,

$$\Pr\left(\exists \tilde{\boldsymbol{s}} : |\boldsymbol{s} - \tilde{\boldsymbol{s}}| = 1 \text{ and } f_{\boldsymbol{x}}(\tilde{\boldsymbol{s}}) = 1 - f_{\boldsymbol{x}}(\boldsymbol{s})\right) \geq \Omega(\frac{1}{\sqrt{N}}).$$

Conditioned on the event that such a $\tilde{\boldsymbol{s}}$ exists, $\hat{\boldsymbol{s}} = \tilde{\boldsymbol{s}}$ with probability at least $\frac{1}{N}$. This proves (iii).

$(\boldsymbol{b}_0, \boldsymbol{b}_1)$ is said to be correct if it is either $(\boldsymbol{a}_0, \perp)$ or $(\perp, \boldsymbol{a}_1)$. Let E_1 be the event '$\boldsymbol{b} = \mathsf{R}\left(f^N_{\mathcal{C}^1_{\mathsf{ROT}}}(\boldsymbol{x}, \boldsymbol{s})\right)$ is correct'. Since $\boldsymbol{s}$ is uniform in $\{0,1\}^N$, by the correctness property, E_1 happens with probability $1 - \frac{1}{N^2}$. Let E_2 be the event '$\boldsymbol{b} = \mathsf{R}(f^N_{\mathcal{C}^1_{\mathsf{ROT}}}(\boldsymbol{x}, \hat{\boldsymbol{s}})$ is correct'. By (i), $\hat{\boldsymbol{s}}$ is also uniform in $\{0,1\}^N$, hence E_2 happens with probability $1 - \frac{1}{N^2}$. From (ii) and (iii) we conclude that, when $\boldsymbol{x} \in X$, $M(\boldsymbol{y})$ outputs $(\hat{\boldsymbol{a}}_0, \hat{\boldsymbol{a}}_1)$ (instead of aborting) with probability $\Omega(\frac{1}{N\sqrt{N}})$. Since $\boldsymbol{x} \in X$ happens with probability $(1 - \frac{2}{N})$, we may conclude that with probability at least $(1 - \frac{2}{N})\Omega(\frac{1}{N\sqrt{N}})$, the following event E_3 occurs: $\hat{\boldsymbol{y}} = f^N_{\mathcal{C}^1_{\mathsf{ROT}}}(\boldsymbol{x}, \hat{\boldsymbol{s}})$ and M outputs $(\hat{\boldsymbol{a}}_0, \hat{\boldsymbol{a}}_1)$. In the event $E_1 \cap E_2 \cap E_3$, the machine M guesses the input correctly and outputs $(\boldsymbol{a}_0, \boldsymbol{a}_1)$. By a union bound, $E_1 \cap E_2 \cap E_3$ happens with probability $(1 - \frac{2}{N})\Omega(\frac{1}{N\sqrt{N}}) - \frac{2}{N^2}$. Hence, M predicts $(\boldsymbol{a}_0, \boldsymbol{a}_1)$ with probability $\Omega(\frac{1}{N\sqrt{N}})$. This is a contradiction since, when $\ell = 2\log N$ and the protocol is $\frac{1}{N^2}$-secure, the adversary can succeed in guessing both inputs with at most $2^{-2\log N} + \frac{1}{N^2} = \frac{2}{N^2}$ probability. This proves the theorem. □

4.1 Extending Impossibility to All Finite Channels

In this section we show that the negative result from the previous section applies not only to bit-ROT but, in fact, to all finite channels. W.l.o.g we consider channels with rational conditional probability matrices. We begin by modeling an arbitrary finite channel as a randomized function.

Definition 9. *Consider a channel $\mathcal{C} : \mathcal{X} \to \mathcal{Y}$ with rational conditional distribution matrix. We define the* states of $\mathcal{C}$ *as a finite set* $\mathcal{C}.\mathsf{states}$ *and the* channel function $f_{\mathcal{C}} : \mathcal{X} \times \mathcal{C}.\mathsf{states} \to \mathcal{Y}$*, such that for all $x \in \mathcal{X}$ and $y \in \mathcal{Y}$,*

$$\Pr(\mathcal{C}(x) = y) = \Pr_{s \xleftarrow{\$} \mathcal{C}.\mathsf{states}} (f(x, s) = y).$$

We emphasize that our channels are all memoryless, and that "states" in this context should be interpreted as the internal randomness of the channel used in each invocation (uniform distribution over the set $\mathcal{C}.\mathsf{states}$).

The existence of $\mathcal{C}.\mathsf{states}$ and $f_{\mathcal{C}}$ is proved in the full version [1]. For the convenience of modeling we have defined $f_{\mathcal{C}}$ in such a way that the state is chosen uniformly at random from $\mathcal{C}.\mathsf{states}$. Given the above definition, for a fixed input $x \in \mathcal{X}$, the channel $\mathcal{C}$ essentially samples a state uniformly from $\mathcal{C}.\mathsf{states}$ and deterministically maps x to the output y. This model motivates our next observation about multiple uses of the channel.

For a finite N, let $\boldsymbol{x} = (x_1, \ldots, x_N) \in \mathcal{X}^N$ and let $\boldsymbol{y} = (y_1, \ldots, y_N) \in \mathcal{Y}^N$ be the output of N independent uses of $\mathcal{C}$ with input $\boldsymbol{x}$. Then the distribution $(\boldsymbol{x}, \boldsymbol{y})$ can be thought to be generated by the following equivalent process: Sample $\boldsymbol{s} = (s_1, \ldots, s_N) \leftarrow (\mathcal{C}.\mathsf{states})^N$ and for $i = 1, \ldots, N$, compute $y_i = f_{\mathcal{C}}(x_i, s_i)$.

Before we state the next lemma, we set up some notation for generalizing distance between strings over finite alphabets. For $\boldsymbol{x}, \tilde{\boldsymbol{x}} \in \mathcal{X}^n$, $|\boldsymbol{x} - \tilde{\boldsymbol{x}}| = 1$ if they differ in exactly one of the n coordinates, *i.e.*, there exists $i \in [n]$ such that $x_i \neq \tilde{x}_i$ and $x_j = \tilde{x}_j$ for all $j \neq i$. The following lemma is an extension of the isoperimetric bound in Lemma 5 that we used for proving Theorem 8. The lemma is formally proved in the full version [1].

Lemma 6. *Let $\mathcal{X}$ be a finite set such that $|\mathcal{X}| = 2^k$ for some k. For any function $f : \mathcal{X}^n \to \{0, 1\}$, if $\Pr_{\boldsymbol{x} \xleftarrow{\$} \mathcal{X}^n}(f(\boldsymbol{x}) = i) \geq \frac{1}{2} - \frac{1}{\sqrt{k \cdot n}}$, for each $i \in \{0, 1\}$, then*

$$\Pr_{\boldsymbol{x} \xleftarrow{\$} \mathcal{X}^n} (\exists \tilde{\boldsymbol{x}} : |\boldsymbol{x} - \tilde{\boldsymbol{x}}| = 1 \text{ and } f(\tilde{\boldsymbol{x}}) = 1 - f(\boldsymbol{x})) \geq \Omega\left(\frac{1}{\sqrt{k \cdot n}}\right).$$

We are now ready to state the generalization of Theorem 8.

Theorem 9. *Let $\mathcal{C}$ be a finite channel. For sufficiently large N and $\ell \geq 2 \log N$, an $(N, \frac{1}{N^2})$ OWSC protocol for $\mathcal{C}^{\ell}_{\mathsf{ROT}}$ over $\mathcal{C}$ is impossible even against semi-honest parties. In fact, the same holds even if one settles for computational security.*

Proof: We proceed in the same way we showed the impossibility in Theorem 8. To prove a contradiction, suppose $\langle \mathsf{S}, \mathsf{R} \rangle$ is a $(N, \frac{1}{N^2})$ OWSC protocol for $\mathcal{C}^{\ell}_{\mathsf{ROT}}$

$\langle \mathsf{S}, \mathsf{R} \rangle(\boldsymbol{a}_0, \boldsymbol{a}_1)$

1. $\boldsymbol{x} \xleftarrow{\$} S(\boldsymbol{a}_0, \boldsymbol{a}_1)$.
2. Sample $\boldsymbol{r} \xleftarrow{\$} (\mathcal{C}.\mathsf{states})^N$.
3. Compute $\boldsymbol{y}$ where $y_i = f_{\mathcal{C}}(x_i, r_i)$.
4. $(\boldsymbol{b}_0, \boldsymbol{b}_1) = \mathsf{R}(\boldsymbol{y})$.
5. Output $((\boldsymbol{a}_0, \boldsymbol{a}_1), \boldsymbol{x}, \boldsymbol{y}, (\boldsymbol{b}_0, \boldsymbol{b}_1))$.

Fig. 3. Execution of a protocol $\langle \mathsf{S}, \mathsf{R} \rangle$ for OWSC of $\mathcal{C}^{\ell}_{\mathsf{ROT}}$ over channel $\mathcal{C} : \mathcal{X} \to \mathcal{Y}$. Here $\boldsymbol{a}_0, \boldsymbol{a}_1$ are the ℓ-bit input strings for $\mathcal{C}^{\ell}_{\mathsf{ROT}}$, the N-bit strings $\boldsymbol{x}_0, \boldsymbol{x}_1$ are the inputs for the N invocations of $\mathcal{C}$, $\boldsymbol{y}_0, \boldsymbol{y}_1$ are the outputs of these N invocations, and $\boldsymbol{b}_0, \boldsymbol{b}_1$ are the outputs of $\mathcal{C}^{\ell}_{\mathsf{ROT}}$.

$\mathsf{M}(\boldsymbol{y})$

1. Compute $(\boldsymbol{b}_0, \boldsymbol{b}_1) = \mathsf{R}(\boldsymbol{y})$.
2. Sample $i \xleftarrow{\$} [N], x \xleftarrow{\$} \mathcal{X}, r \xleftarrow{\$} \mathcal{C}.\mathsf{states}$.
3. Compute $\tilde{\boldsymbol{y}}$, where $\tilde{y}_i = f_{\mathcal{C}}(x, r)$ and $\tilde{y}_j = y_j$ for all $j \neq i$.
4. Compute $(\tilde{\boldsymbol{b}}_0, \tilde{\boldsymbol{b}}_1) = \mathsf{R}(\tilde{\boldsymbol{y}})$.
5. If $(\boldsymbol{b}_1, \tilde{\boldsymbol{b}}_0) = (\perp, \perp)$, output $(\boldsymbol{b}_0, \tilde{\boldsymbol{b}}_1)$ and if $(\boldsymbol{b}_0, \tilde{\boldsymbol{b}}_1) = (\perp, \perp)$, output $(\tilde{\boldsymbol{b}}_0, \boldsymbol{b}_1)$; else, abort.

Fig. 4. Execution of the machine M

over $\mathcal{C}$. The joint distribution, generated by the protocol for input $(\boldsymbol{a}_0, \boldsymbol{a}_1) \in \{0,1\}^{\ell} \times \{0,1\}^{\ell}$, is described in Fig. 3. We would use a machine M similar to the one used in the proof of Theorem 8 to guess both $\boldsymbol{a}_0$ and $\boldsymbol{a}_1$ from the received $\boldsymbol{y}$ with substantial probability, contradicting sender's privacy. The machine is described in Fig. 4. Intuitively, M tries to obtain one string from $\boldsymbol{y}$ (due to correctness of the ROT protocol) and the other string, by changing one item of $\boldsymbol{y}$, and hoping to get into a case where the receiver outputs the other string.

Analysis of M. We show that M outputs $(\boldsymbol{a}_0, \boldsymbol{a}_1)$ with substantial probability. As observed in Lemma 4, since the protocol is $\frac{1}{N^2}$-secure, due to the receiver's privacy property, there exists a set $X \subseteq \mathcal{X}^N$ such that $\Pr(\boldsymbol{x} \in X) \geq 1 - \frac{2}{N}$ and for all $\boldsymbol{x} \in X$,

$$P(\boldsymbol{b}_0 = \perp | \boldsymbol{x}) \geq \frac{1}{2} - \frac{1}{N} \quad \text{and} \quad P(\boldsymbol{b}_1 = \perp | \boldsymbol{x}) \geq \frac{1}{2} - \frac{1}{N}.$$

Fix an $\boldsymbol{x} \in X$. Recall that for a fixed $\boldsymbol{x} \in \mathcal{X}^N$, the output $\boldsymbol{y}$ of the channel is a deterministic function of the state of the channel $\boldsymbol{r}$, *i.e.*, $\boldsymbol{y} = f^N_{\mathcal{C}}(\boldsymbol{x}, \boldsymbol{r})$. Here $f^N_{\mathcal{C}}(\boldsymbol{x}, \boldsymbol{r})$ outputs $\boldsymbol{y}$ such that $y_i = f_{\mathcal{C}}(x_i, r_i)$. Define function $f_{\boldsymbol{x}} : (\mathcal{C}.\mathsf{states})^N \to \{0,1\}$ as follows: for $\boldsymbol{r} \in (\mathcal{C}.\mathsf{states})^N$, when $f^N_{\mathcal{C}}(\boldsymbol{x}, \boldsymbol{r}) = \boldsymbol{y}$ and $(\boldsymbol{b}_0, \boldsymbol{b}_1) = \mathsf{R}(\boldsymbol{y})$, then $f_{\boldsymbol{x}}(\boldsymbol{r}) = 0$ if $\boldsymbol{b}_0 = \perp$ and $f_{\boldsymbol{x}}(\boldsymbol{r}) = 1$ otherwise. Hence, for all $\boldsymbol{x} \in X$, function $f_{\boldsymbol{x}}$ is such that $\Pr_{\boldsymbol{r} \xleftarrow{\$} (\mathcal{C}.\mathsf{states})^N}(f(\boldsymbol{x}) = i) \geq \frac{1}{2} - \frac{1}{N}$ for $i = 0, 1$. When $\frac{1}{N^2} \leq \frac{1}{k \cdot N}$, invoking Lemma 6,

$$\Pr_{r \xleftarrow{\$} (\mathcal{C}.\mathsf{states})^N} \left(\exists \tilde{\boldsymbol{r}} : |\boldsymbol{r} - \tilde{\boldsymbol{r}}| = 1 \text{ and } f_{\boldsymbol{x}}(\boldsymbol{r}) = 1 - f_{\boldsymbol{x}}(\tilde{\boldsymbol{r}})\right) \geq \Omega\left(\frac{1}{\sqrt{k \cdot n}}\right).$$

Note that $\boldsymbol{y}$ is generated by $\boldsymbol{x}$ and a random state $\boldsymbol{r} \leftarrow (\mathcal{C}.\mathsf{states})^N$ (see Fig. 3). On input $\boldsymbol{y}$, machine M can be equivalently thought to be computing $\tilde{\boldsymbol{y}}$ as $f_{\mathcal{C}}^N(\tilde{\boldsymbol{x}}, \tilde{\boldsymbol{r}})$, where $\tilde{\boldsymbol{x}}$ and $\tilde{\boldsymbol{r}}$ can be described as follows: Choose a random coordinate $i \xleftarrow{\$} [N]$ (see Fig. 4) and $\tilde{\boldsymbol{x}}$ is computed as $\tilde{x}_i \xleftarrow{\$} \mathcal{X}$ and $\tilde{x}_j = x_j$ for $j \neq i$ and $\tilde{\boldsymbol{r}}$ is computed as $\tilde{r}_i \xleftarrow{\$} \mathcal{C}.\mathsf{states}$ and $\tilde{r}_j = r_j$ for $j \neq i$. We make the following simple observations.

(i). $\tilde{\boldsymbol{r}}$ is distributed uniformly in $(\mathcal{C}.\mathsf{states})^N$ and $|\boldsymbol{r} - \tilde{\boldsymbol{r}}| = 1$.
(ii). $\Pr(\tilde{\boldsymbol{x}} = \boldsymbol{x}) = \frac{1}{|\mathcal{X}|}$.
(iii). With probability $\Omega(\frac{1}{N\sqrt{N}})$, we have $f_{\boldsymbol{x}}(\tilde{\boldsymbol{r}}) = 1 - f_{\boldsymbol{x}}(\boldsymbol{r})$.

Here, (i) and (ii) are clear from the process. For any $\boldsymbol{s} \in \{0,1\}^N$ such that $|\boldsymbol{r} - \boldsymbol{s}| = 1$, $\tilde{\boldsymbol{r}} = \boldsymbol{s}$ with probability $\frac{1}{N \cdot |\mathcal{C}.\mathsf{states}|} = \frac{1}{2^k \cdot N}$. Hence, when $\boldsymbol{x} \in X$ and $\boldsymbol{r} \xleftarrow{\$} \{0,1\}^N$, the probability of the event '$f_{\boldsymbol{x}}(\boldsymbol{r}) = 1 - f_{\boldsymbol{x}}(\tilde{\boldsymbol{r}})$' is at least $\frac{1}{2^k \cdot N} \cdot \Omega(\frac{1}{\sqrt{k \cdot N}}) = \Omega(\frac{1}{N\sqrt{N}})$.

We are now ready to show that M outputs $\boldsymbol{a}_0, \boldsymbol{a}_1$ with substantial probability. Let E_1 be the event '$\tilde{\boldsymbol{x}} = \boldsymbol{x}$ and $f_{\boldsymbol{x}}(\tilde{\boldsymbol{r}}) = 1 - f_{\boldsymbol{x}}(\boldsymbol{r})$'. We have already established that conditioned on any $\boldsymbol{x} \in X$, the event E_1 occurs with probability $\Omega(\frac{1}{N\sqrt{N}})$. Since $\Pr(\boldsymbol{x} \in X) \geq 1 - \frac{2}{N}$, the probability of E_1 is at least $(1 - \frac{2}{N}) \cdot \Omega(\frac{1}{N\sqrt{N}})$. Let E_2 be the event '$\mathsf{R}(f_{\mathcal{C}}^N(\boldsymbol{x}, \boldsymbol{r}))$ is correct' and E_3 be the event '$\mathsf{R}(f_{\mathcal{C}}^N(\boldsymbol{x}, \tilde{\boldsymbol{r}}))$ is correct'. Since $\boldsymbol{r}$ and $\tilde{\boldsymbol{r}}$ are uniformly distributed in $\{0,1\}^N$, by the correctness of the protocol, E_2 and E_3 occur with probability at least $1 - \frac{1}{N^2}$. In the event $E_1 \cap E_2 \cap E_3$, the machine M guesses the input correctly and outputs $(\boldsymbol{a}_0, \boldsymbol{a}_1)$. By a union bound, $E_1 \cap E_2 \cap E_3$ happens with probability $(1 - \frac{2}{N})\Omega(\frac{1}{N\sqrt{N}}) - 2\frac{1}{N^2}$. Hence, M predicts $(\boldsymbol{a}_0, \boldsymbol{a}_1)$ with probability $\Omega(\frac{1}{N\sqrt{N}})$. Note that this is a contradiction since, when $\ell = 2\log N$, such a machine should not exist when the protocol is $\frac{1}{N^2}$-secure. This proves the theorem. □

5 Zero-Knowledge Proofs from Any Non-trivial Channel

In this section, we characterize finite channels that allow OWSC of zero-knowledge proofs of knowledge. Our result states that *zero-knowledge proofs of knowledge* (ZK PoK) can be realized with OWSC over a channel if and only if the channel is non-trivial. A trivial channel is one which is *essentially equivalent* (as formalized below) to a noiseless channel, when used by actively corrupt senders.

Theorem 10 (Informal). *Given a language $L \in$ NP\BPP, an $\mathsf{OWSC}/\mathcal{C}$ zero-knowledge protocol for L exists if and only if $\mathcal{C}$ is non-trivial.*

Previously, this result was known only for two special channels, namely, BEC and BSC [17]. To extend it to all non-trivial channels, we need to take a closer look at the properties of abstract channels. To understand what a non-trivial channel is, it is helpful to geometrically model a channel as we do below.

Redundant Inputs, Core and Trivial Channels. Given a channel $\mathcal{C} : \mathcal{X} \to \mathcal{Y}$, for each input $\alpha \in \mathcal{X}$, define a $|\mathcal{Y}|$-dimensional vector $\boldsymbol{\mu}_\alpha$ with coordinates indexed by elements of $\mathcal{Y}$, such that $\boldsymbol{\mu}_\alpha(\beta) = \Pr(\mathcal{C}(\alpha) = \beta)$ for each $\beta \in \mathcal{Y}$. We define the convex polytope $R_\mathcal{C}$ associated with $\mathcal{C}$ as the convex hull of the vectors $\{\boldsymbol{\mu}_\alpha | \alpha \in \mathcal{X}\}$.

Any $\alpha \in \mathcal{X}$ such that $\boldsymbol{\mu}_\alpha$ is a convex combination of $\{\boldsymbol{\mu}_{\alpha'} | \alpha' \in \mathcal{X} \setminus \{\alpha\}\}$ is a *redundant* input, because a sender could perfectly simulate the use of α with a linear combination of other inputs, without being detected (and possibly obtaining more information about the output at the receiver's end). Geometrically, a redundant input corresponds to a point in the interior of (possibly a face of) $R_\mathcal{C}$ (or multiple inputs that share the same vertex of the polytope). Consider a new channel $\widehat{\mathcal{C}}$ without any redundant inputs, obtained by restricting $\mathcal{C}$ to a subset of inputs, one for each vertex of the convex hull. $\widehat{\mathcal{C}}$ is called the *core* of $\mathcal{C}$.[4]

We note that $\mathcal{C} : \mathcal{X} \to \mathcal{Y}$ can be securely realized over $\widehat{\mathcal{C}} : \widehat{\mathcal{X}} \to \mathcal{Y}$, with security (in fact, UC security) against *active* adversaries. In this protocol, when the sender is given an input $\alpha \in \mathcal{X} \setminus \widehat{\mathcal{X}}$, it samples an input α' from $\widehat{\mathcal{X}}$ according to a distribution that results in the same channel output distribution as produced by α (this is always possible since $R_\mathcal{C}$ is the same as $R_{\widehat{\mathcal{C}}}$). Correctness (when both parties are honest) and security against a corrupt receiver are immediate from the fact that the output distribution is correct; security against a corrupt sender follows from the fact that its only action in the protocol - sending an input to $\widehat{\mathcal{C}}$– can be carried out as it is in the ideal world involving $\mathcal{C}$, with the same effect. This means that there is a secure OWSC protocol over $\mathcal{C}$ only if such a protocol exists over $\widehat{\mathcal{C}}$. In turn, since $\widehat{\mathcal{C}}$ has no redundant inputs, it suffices to characterize which channels among those without redundant inputs, admit ZK proofs.

A channel without any redundant inputs is *trivial* if the output distributions for each of its input symbols are disjoint from each other. Such a channel corresponds to a noiseless channel, as the receiver always learns exactly the symbol that was input to the channel. Over a noiseless channel, zero-knowledge proofs exist only for languages in BPP.

Our main goal then, is to show that if a channel $\mathcal{C}$ without redundant inputs is non-trivial, then every language in NP has an OWSC/$\mathcal{C}$ zero-knowledge protocol. We start by providing some intuition about how we achieve this.

5.1 Intuition Behind the Construction

The ZK protocol involves sending many independently generated copies of an Oblivious ZK-PCP over the channel, after encoding it appropriately; the verifier

[4] The notions of redundancy and core were defined more generally in [21], in the context of 2-party functionalities where both parties have inputs and outputs. Here we present simpler definitions that suffice for the case of channels.

tests the proof using a carefully designed scheme before accepting it. The encoding and testing are designed to ensure, on one hand, erasure of a large fraction of the bits in the proofs (to guarantee zero-knowledge) and, on the other hand, delivery of sufficiently many bits so that the verifier can detect if the transmitted proof is incorrect (for soundness). At a high-level, the transmission and testing of the proof takes place over three "layers": (i) an inner-most *binary channel layer* at the bottom, (ii) an *erasure layer* over it, and (iii) an outer *PCP layer*. The inner-most and outer-most layers are used to ensure soundness while the middle and outer-most layers work in tandem to obtain the zero-knowledge property.

Binary-Input Channel Layer. A given channel $\mathcal{C}$ (without redundant inputs) may have an arbitrary number of inputs, which may provide the prover with room for cheating in the protocol. The binary-input channel layer involves a mechanism to enforce that the prover (mostly) uses only a prescribed pair of distinct input symbols α_0 and α_1. We require that over several uses of the channel, if the sender uses a different symbol significantly often, then the receiver can detect this from the empirical distribution of the output symbols it received. This requires that the sender cannot simulate the effect of sending a combination of these two symbols by using a combination of some other symbols. Using the geometric interpretation of the channel, this corresponds to the requirement that the line segment connecting the two vertices $\boldsymbol{\mu}_{\alpha_0}$ and $\boldsymbol{\mu}_{\alpha_1}$ of the polytope $R_{\mathcal{C}}$ actually form an *edge* of the polytope. However, for the erasure layer (described below) to work we require that the output distributions of α_0 and α_1 have intersecting supports. In Lemma 7, we show that in any non-trivial channel $\mathcal{C}$ (without redundant inputs), there indeed exist α_0, α_1 which satisfy both these requirements simultaneously. Then, in Lemma 8, we show that there is a statistical test—whose parameters are determined by the geometry of the polytope $R_{\mathcal{C}}$—that can distinguish between a sender who sends a long sequence of these two symbols from a sender who uses other symbols in a significant fraction of positions.

Erasure Layer. We can obtain a non-zero probability of *perfect erasure* by encoding 0 as the pair (α_0, α_1) and 1 as the pair (α_1, α_0), to be transmitted over two independent uses of the channel $\mathcal{C}$. Since there is some symbol β such that both $q_0 := \Pr(\mathcal{C}(\alpha_0) = \beta) > 0$ and $q_1 := \Pr(\mathcal{C}(\alpha_1) = \beta) > 0$, the probability of the receiver obtaining (β, β) is the same positive value $q_0 q_1$, whether 0 or 1 is sent as above.[5] Hence, one can interpret the view of the receiver as obtained by post-processing the output of a BEC with erasure probability $q_0 q_1$, so that the erasure symbol is mapped to the outcome (β, β).

At the receiver's end, we use a maximum likelihood decoding, that always outputs a bit (rather than allowing an erasure symbol as well); if the likelihood of a received pair of symbols is the same for 0 and 1, it is decoded as a uniformly random bit. Note that if the sender sends a pair (α_0, α_0) or (α_1, α_1), then the decoding strategy will have the same effect as when the sender sends the encoding

[5] This is essentially identical to the Von Neumann extractor trick.

of a random bit – namely, it will be decoded to a uniformly random bit. Thus, the net effect of these two layers is that the prover communicates with the verifier using bits sent via a BSC, except for a few positions where the sender may arbitrarily control the channel characteristics. While the receiver's view includes more information than the output of the BSC, it can be entirely simulated from the output of a BEC.

PCP Layer. At the outer-most layer, our proof resembles the OWSC/*BSC* ZK protocol of [17], but is in fact somewhat simpler.[6] Here, the prover simply sends several independently generated copies of an Oblivious ZK-PCP (routed through the inner layers discussed above). As we noted above, the view of the receiver is obtained by post-processing the output of a BEC; hence, by choosing the parameters of the ZK-PCP appropriately, we can ensure that the receiver's view can be statistically simulated.

Ensuring soundness requires more work. The receiver, after obtaining the bits decoded from the inner layers (provided that no deviation was detected at the inner-most layer), can try to execute the PCP verification on each proof. However, it cannot reject the proof on encountering a single proof that fails the verification, because, even if the prover is honest, the channel can introduce errors in the received bits. As such, the verifier should be prepared to tolerate a certain probability of error. One may expect that if the proof was originally incorrect, then the probability of error would increase. However, this intuition is imprecise: it is plausible that a wrong proof can match or even surpass some honest proofs in the probability of passing the PCP verification.

To deal with this, we note that it is not necessary to carry out the original PCP verification test on the received bits, but rather one should design a statistical test that separates all correct proofs from incorrect proofs, *as received through the inner layers.* We show that for any predicate used by the original PCP verifier, there is an *error-score* one can assign to the bits decoded from the BSC, so that the *expected* error-score of the decoded bits is lower when they originally satisfy the PCP verifier's predicate. The verifier accepts or rejects the proof by computing the empirical average of the score across all repetitions of the proof, and thresholding it appropriately.

We remark that our scoring scheme and its analysis are more direct, and perhaps simpler, compared to the one in [17]. An additional subtlety that arises in our case is that there can be a few positions where the inner layers do not constitute the BSC that we try to enforce. Nevertheless, the above approach remains robust to such deviations, by ensuring that the scores come from a suitably bounded range.

[6] In [17], an encoding scheme was used to argue that with some probability, the bits sent through the BSC are "erased." But this encoding turns out to be redundant, as a BSC implicitly guarantees erasure: Concretely, a BSC with error probability p can be simulated by post-processing a BEC with erasure probability $2p$. The post-processing corresponds to decoding the erasure symbol as a uniformly random bit.

5.2 Properties of Non-trivial Channels

The following lemma shows that if $\mathcal{C}$ is non-trivial and without redundant inputs, there is a pair of input symbols α_0, α_1 with properties that we can use to enforce binary-input channel layer in Lemma 8 and to realize erasure channel layer in Lemma 9. Proofs of these lemmas are provided in the full version [1] (Fig. 5).

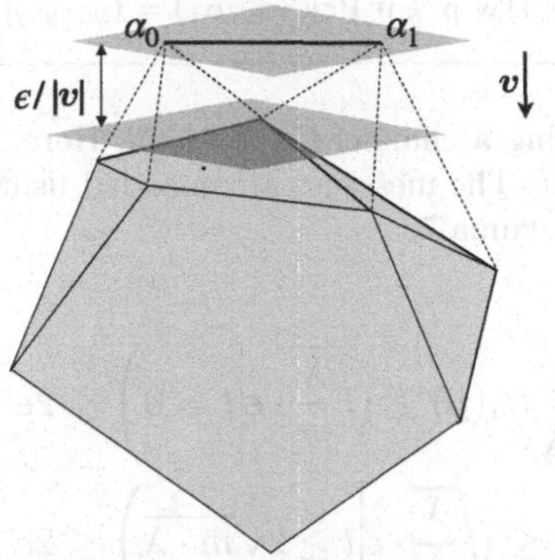

Fig. 5. Illustration of condition (ii) in Lemma 7. The polytope $R_\mathcal{C}$ is illustrated here. Since $\mathcal{C}$ has no redundant symbols, there is a bijection between vertices of $R_\mathcal{C}$ and the input symbols of the channel. The edge between $\boldsymbol{\mu}_{\alpha_0}$ and $\boldsymbol{\mu}_{\alpha_1}$ is highlighted. The solid part is the convex hull of the vertices other than $\boldsymbol{\mu}_{\alpha_0}$ and $\boldsymbol{\mu}_{\alpha_1}$. By the separating hyperplane theorem [7], there exists a vector $\boldsymbol{v} \in [-1,1]^{\mathcal{Y}}$ and $\epsilon > 0$ as illustrated. In Lemma 8, the existence of $\boldsymbol{v}, \epsilon$ is used to devise the statistical test that enforces the binary input channel layer. That $\boldsymbol{\mu}_{\alpha_0}$ and $\boldsymbol{\mu}_{\alpha_1}$ have intersecting support is used in realizing the erasure layer.

Lemma 7. *If $\mathcal{C} : \mathcal{X} \to \mathcal{Y}$ without redundant inputs is non-trivial, then there exist distinct symbols $\alpha_0, \alpha_1 \in \mathcal{X}$, $\boldsymbol{v} \in [-1,1]^{\mathcal{Y}}$ and $\epsilon > 0$ with the following properties:*

(i) $\exists y \in \mathcal{Y}$ such that $\boldsymbol{\mu}_{\alpha_0}(y), \boldsymbol{\mu}_{\alpha_1}(y) > 0$.
(ii) $\langle \boldsymbol{\mu}_{\alpha_0}, \boldsymbol{v} \rangle = \langle \boldsymbol{\mu}_{\alpha_1}, \boldsymbol{v} \rangle$, and for all $\alpha \in \mathcal{X} \setminus \{\alpha_0, \alpha_1\}$, $\langle \boldsymbol{\mu}_{\alpha}, \boldsymbol{v} \rangle - \langle \boldsymbol{\mu}_{\alpha_0}, \boldsymbol{v} \rangle \geq \epsilon$.

In the next lemma, we show that, over several uses of $\mathcal{C}$, a sender who uses only α_0, α_1 described in the previous lemma, can be distinguished from one that uses other symbols (different than α_0, α_1) significantly often, using the empirical distribution of the output symbols. Let histogram of a vector $\boldsymbol{y} \in \mathcal{Y}^m$ be defined as $\mathsf{hist}_{\boldsymbol{y}}(\beta) = \frac{1}{m}|\{i \in [m] : y_i = \beta\}|$ for all $\beta \in \mathcal{Y}$. The following function is a statistical test that achieves this: $f_m(\boldsymbol{y}) = \langle \mathsf{hist}_{\boldsymbol{y}}, \boldsymbol{v} \rangle - \langle \boldsymbol{\mu}_{\alpha_0}, \boldsymbol{v} \rangle$.

Lemma 8. *If a channel $\mathcal{C}$ without redundant inputs is non-trivial, then there exist $\alpha_0, \alpha_1 \in \mathcal{X}, \epsilon > 0$ and functions $f_m : \mathcal{Y}^m \to \mathbb{R}$, for $m \in \mathbb{N}$, such that, for all $\lambda > 0$, when $\boldsymbol{x} \in \mathcal{X}^m, t = |\{i \in [m] : x_i \notin \{\alpha_0, \alpha_1\}\}|$ and $\boldsymbol{y} = \mathcal{C}(\boldsymbol{x})$,*

$\langle \mathsf{Enc}, \mathsf{Dec} \rangle(a)$

For channel $\mathcal{C} : \mathcal{X} \to \mathcal{Y}$, choose $\alpha_0, \alpha_1 \in \mathcal{X}$ that satisfy the conditions in Lemma 7. When $a \in \{0,1\}$,

1. $\mathsf{Enc}(a) = (x_0, x_1)$ where $x_0 = \alpha_a$ and $x_1 = \alpha_{1-a}$.
2. $(y_0, y_1) = \mathcal{C}(x_0, x_1)$.
3. $\mathsf{Dec}(y_0, y_1) = \begin{cases} b \text{ if } \Pr[\mathcal{C}(\alpha_b, \alpha_{1-b}) = (y_0, y_1)] > \Pr[\mathcal{C}(\alpha_{1-b}, \alpha_b) = (y_0, y_1)], \\ 0 \text{ (resp. 1) w. p. } \frac{1}{2} \text{ if } \Pr[\mathcal{C}(\alpha_0, \alpha_1) = (y_0, y_1)] = \Pr[\mathcal{C}(\alpha_1, \alpha_0) = (y_0, y_1)]. \end{cases}$

Fig. 6. Realizing BSC using a channel $\mathcal{C} : \mathcal{X} \to \mathcal{Y}$. Here, a is the input bit to BSC channel and b is its output. The messages are encoded using symbols $\alpha_0, \alpha_1 \in \mathcal{X}$ that satisfy the conditions in Lemma 7.

$$\Pr\left(f_m(\boldsymbol{y}) \geq \sqrt{\frac{\lambda}{m}} \cdot \epsilon \,\middle|\, t = 0 \right) \leq 2e^{-\frac{\lambda \cdot \epsilon^2}{2}} \quad \textit{and}$$

$$\Pr\left(f_m(\boldsymbol{y}) \leq \sqrt{\frac{\lambda}{m}} \cdot \epsilon \,\middle|\, t \geq 2\sqrt{m \cdot \lambda} \right) \leq 2e^{-\frac{\lambda \cdot \epsilon^2}{2}}.$$

The following lemma analyzes the coding scheme in Fig. 6 that realizes erasure layer using α_0, α_1 described in Lemma 7. The fidelity of the scheme is a consequence of $\boldsymbol{\mu}_{\alpha_0}$ and $\boldsymbol{\mu}_{\alpha_1}$ being distinct. As we already observed, receiving (β, β) in this scheme is effectively the same as receiving an erasure. The lemma shows that since $\boldsymbol{\mu}_{\alpha_0}, \boldsymbol{\mu}_{\alpha_1}$ having intersecting supports, erasure happens with non-zero probability. The lemma also formalizes the observation that sending invalid encodings (α_i, α_i) for $i \in \{0,1\}$ is effectively the same as sending the valid encoding of a random bit.

Lemma 9. *The scheme* $\langle \mathsf{Enc}, \mathsf{Dec} \rangle$ *in Fig. 6 satisfies the following properties:*

(i). $\Pr[\mathsf{Dec}(\mathsf{Enc}(a)) = a] = p > \frac{1}{2}$ *for* $a \in \{0,1\}$*;*
(ii). $\Pr[\mathsf{Dec}(\mathcal{C}(\alpha_i, \alpha_i)) = 0] = \frac{1}{2}$ *for* $i = 0, 1$*;*
(iii). Let $\perp$ *be the event that the receiver gets* (β, β) *as output, where* β *is in the support of* $\boldsymbol{\mu}_{\alpha_0}$ *and* $\boldsymbol{\mu}_{\alpha_1}$*. Then* $\Pr(\perp | \mathsf{Enc}(a)) = \rho > 0$*, for all* $a \in \{0,1\}$*.*

The Binary Symmetric Channel (BSC), with parameter p, is defined as $\mathsf{BSC}^p : \{0,1\} \to \{0,1\}$ such that for $b \in \{0,1\}$, $\Pr(\mathsf{BSC}^p(b) = b) = p$. Consider the scenario where a configuration $\boldsymbol{x} \in \{0,1\}^k$ is sent through BSC^p amongst which $S \subset \{0,1\}^k$ is the set of acceptable configurations. The following lemma assigns scores $\{\gamma_{\boldsymbol{y}}^S\}_{\boldsymbol{y} \in \{0,1\}^k}$ to the received configurations in such a way that the expected score is 0 when an acceptable configuration $\boldsymbol{x} \in S$ is sent and the expected score is a strictly positive constant ϕ^S when an unacceptable configuration $\boldsymbol{x} \notin S$ in sent.

Lemma 10. *For $k \in \mathbb{N}$, let $U = \{0,1\}^k$ and $S \subseteq U$. For $\boldsymbol{x}, \boldsymbol{y} \in U$, define $p_{\boldsymbol{xy}} = \Pr(\mathsf{BSC}^p(\boldsymbol{x}) = \boldsymbol{y})$. There exists $\phi^S > 0$ and $\{\gamma_{\boldsymbol{y}}^S\}_{\boldsymbol{y}\in U} \in [-1,1]$ such that*

$$\sum_{\boldsymbol{y}\in U} p_{\boldsymbol{xy}}\gamma_{\boldsymbol{y}}^S = 0, \forall \boldsymbol{x} \in S \quad \textit{and} \quad \sum_{\boldsymbol{y}\in U} p_{\boldsymbol{xy}}\gamma_{\boldsymbol{y}}^S = \phi^S, \forall \boldsymbol{x} \notin S.$$

Proof: Consider the matrix $M \in \mathbb{R}^{U\times U}$ such that $M_{\boldsymbol{xy}} = p_{\boldsymbol{xy}}$. By the definition of BSC^p, when $|\boldsymbol{x} - \boldsymbol{y}|$ denotes the Hamming distance between $\boldsymbol{x}, \boldsymbol{y} \in U$, $p_{\boldsymbol{xy}} = (1-p)^{|\boldsymbol{x}-\boldsymbol{y}|} \cdot p^{k-|\boldsymbol{x}-\boldsymbol{y}|}$. It can be verified that, when $\otimes$ denotes the tensor operation,

$$M = H^{\otimes k}, \text{ where } H = \begin{bmatrix} p & 1-p \\ 1-p & p \end{bmatrix}.$$

Since H is invertible and tensor operation preserves non-singularity, M is an invertible matrix. The existence of $\phi^S > 0$ and $\{\gamma_{\boldsymbol{y}}^S\}_{\boldsymbol{y}\in U} \in [-1,1]$ follows directly from the invertibility of M. □

5.3 Construction and Analysis

The scheme $\langle \mathsf{P}_{ZK}, \mathsf{V}_{ZK}\rangle$ is given in Fig. 7. We now formally prove that this is a zero-knowledge proof of knowledge with negligible completeness and soundness error.

We first comment on the strategy of a malicious prover who encodes bits as (α_i, α_i) for $i = 0, 1$. Notice that the statistical test of thresholding $f_{2n\cdot\ell}(\boldsymbol{y})$ is insensitive to such a malicious strategy. But, by statement (ii) in Lemma 9, a bit that is encoded as (α_i, α_i) is decoded as 0 (resp. 1) with probability $\frac{1}{2}$. Hence, with respect to decoding, such a malicious strategy is effectively the same as encoding a random bit honestly using Enc. Consequently, every malicious prover strategy (including ones that encode bits incorrectly using (α_i, α_i)) can be thought of as a randomized strategy over a sub-class of strategies in which each bit is encoded as (α, α'), where $\alpha \neq \alpha'$. Hence, in the sequel, we analyze soundness only with respect to this class of strategies.

The proof proceeds by bounding the number of bad proofs a malicious sender can send without getting rejected by the tests performed by the verifier. We define B_{encoding} as the set of bad proofs in which at least one bit is encoded using symbols outside the set $\{\alpha_0, \alpha_1\}$. Also, define $B_{\text{incorrect}}$ as the set of proofs in which each bit is correctly encoded using Enc, but the proof itself is invalid. This is formalized as the proofs from which the extractor E for $\langle \mathsf{P}_{oZK}, \mathsf{V}_{oZK}\rangle$ cannot extract a valid witness. We would argue soundness by showing that if the sizes of B_{encoding} and $B_{\text{incorrect}}$ are substantial, then V_{ZK} rejects with all but negligible probability. Furthermore, completeness follows from the tests accepting an honest prover with all but negligible probability. These are established in the following claims; see the full version [1] for formal proofs. Formally, B_{encoding} and $B_{\text{incorrect}}$ are defined as follows.

$$B_{\text{encoding}} = \{i \in [n] : \exists (j,k) \in [\ell] \times \{0,1\} \text{ s.t. } x_k^{i,j} \notin \{\alpha_0, \alpha_1\}\},$$
$$B_{\text{incorrect}} = \{i \in [n] : i \notin B_{\text{encoding}} \text{ and } R_L(x, E(\pi_i, x)) = 0\}.$$

$\langle \mathsf{P}_{ZK}, \mathsf{V}_{ZK} \rangle$

Common input to prover and verifier $x \in L$.
Auxiliary input to prover w such that $R_L(x, w) = 1$.
For a non-trivial channel $\mathcal{C}$, without redundant symbols, consider symbols $\alpha_0, \alpha_1 \in \mathcal{X}$, functions f_m, for $m \in \mathbb{N}$, and $\epsilon > 0$ as described in Lemma 8. Let $\langle \mathsf{Enc}, \mathsf{Dec} \rangle$ be the encoding scheme described in Figure 6 w.r.t. α_0, α_1. Let p and ρ be as described in Lemma 9 for this encoding scheme. For $S \subset \{0,1\}^3$, consider $\gamma_{\boldsymbol{y}}^S$, for each $\boldsymbol{y} \in \{0,1\}^3$, and ϕ^S, from Lemma 10 with respect to BSC^p. Define $\phi = \min_{S \subset \{0,1\}^3} \phi^S$. For security parameter λ, let $(\mathsf{P}_{oZK}, \mathsf{V}_{oZK})$ be a $(3, 1-\rho)$-ZK-PCP with knowledge soundness κ. Finally, when $\ell = \mathrm{poly}(\lambda, |x|)$ is the length of proof output by P_{oZK}, let $n = \left(\frac{\ell\lambda}{\kappa}\right)^2$.

1. P_{ZK} samples $\pi_1, \ldots, \pi_n \xleftarrow{\$} \mathsf{P}_{oZK}(x, w, \lambda)$. For all $i \in [n], j \in [\ell]$, let the jth bit in the proof π_i be $b_{i,j}$, then encode $b_{i,j}$ using Enc to obtain $(x_0^{i,j}, x_1^{i,j})$.
2. For all $i \in [n], j \in [\ell]$, let $(y_0^{i,j}, y_1^{i,j}) = \mathcal{C}\left(x_0^{i,j}, x_1^{i,j}\right)$. Let $\boldsymbol{y}$ be the vector $\left(y_k^{i,j}\right)_{i \in [n], j \in [\ell], k \in \{0,1\}}$.
3. If $f_{2n\cdot\ell}(\boldsymbol{y}) \geq \sqrt{\frac{\lambda}{2n\ell}}$, then V_{ZK} aborts and rejects the proof. Otherwise, V_{ZK} decodes $\pi_1, \ldots, \pi_n$ as $\hat{\pi}_1, \ldots, \hat{\pi}_n$ such that, for $i \in [n]$ and $j \in [\ell]$, the bit $b_{i,j}$ is decoded as $\hat{b}_{i,j} = \mathsf{Dec}\left(y_0^{i,j}, y_1^{i,j}\right)$. For each $k \in [n]$, choose 3 random indices $a_1, a_2, a_3 \in [\ell]$ of $\hat{\pi}_k$. If S is the set of accepting configurations for the indices (a_1, a_2, a_3) w.r.t. $\mathsf{V}_{oZK}(x, \cdot)$, set $s_k = \gamma_{\hat{\boldsymbol{b}}_k}^S$, where $\hat{\boldsymbol{b}}_k = (\hat{b}_{k,a_1}, \hat{b}_{k,a_2}, \hat{b}_{k,a_3})$. If $\frac{1}{n}\sum_{k \in n} s_k < \frac{\kappa \cdot \phi}{12}$, then V_{ZK} accepts, else it rejects.

Fig. 7. Description of OWSC/$\mathcal{C}$ ZKPoK scheme for a non-trivial channel $\mathcal{C}$ without redundant input symbols.

Claim 2. *If $B_{encoding}$ is empty, then the probability with which $f_{2n\cdot\ell}(\boldsymbol{y}) \geq \sqrt{\frac{\lambda}{2n\ell}}$ is negligible in λ. If $|B_{encoding}| \geq \frac{n\kappa\phi}{6}$, then the probability with which $f_{2n\cdot\ell}(\boldsymbol{y}) < \sqrt{\frac{\lambda}{2n\ell}}$ is negligible in λ.*

Claim 3. *If $B_{encoding} = B_{incorrect} = \emptyset$, then $\frac{1}{n}\sum_{k=1}^{n} s_k \geq \frac{\kappa\cdot\phi}{12}$ with probability at most $2e^{-\frac{1}{2}\left(\frac{\ell\lambda\cdot\phi}{12}\right)^2}$. If $|B_{encoding}| \leq n\kappa\phi$ and $|B_{incorrect}| \geq \frac{n}{3}$, then $\frac{1}{n}\sum_{k=1}^{n} s_k < \frac{\kappa\cdot\phi}{12}$ with probability at most $2e^{-\frac{1}{2}\left(\frac{\ell\lambda\cdot\phi}{12}\right)^2}$.*

Below, we argue that $\langle \mathsf{P}_{ZK}, \mathsf{V}_{ZK} \rangle$ is a zero-knowledge proof using these claims.

Completeness. The above claims directly imply that if $\pi_1, \ldots, \pi_n$ are valid proofs which are correctly encoded, then V_{ZK} accepts with all but negligible probability.

Soundness. We build an extractor E' from E (the extractor for $\langle \mathsf{P}_{oZK}, \mathsf{V}_{oZK} \rangle$) as follows. For each $i \in [n]$, extractor E' tries to extract a proof π_i^* from the encoding of the purported proof π_i. Rejecting each purported proof π_i that is incorrectly encoded, *i.e.*, $i \in B_{\mathrm{encoding}}$. If for some i, we have

$R_L(x, E(\pi_i^*, x)) = 1$, output $E(\pi_i^*, x)$; else, output $\bot$. Clearly, E' aborts only if $B_{\text{encoding}} \cup B_{\text{incorrect}} = [n]$. But the above claims imply that V_{ZK} rejects with all but negligible probability, whenever $|B_{\text{encoding}} \cup B_{\text{incorrect}}| \geq \frac{2n}{3}$.

Zero-Knowledge. By Lemma 9, Enc induces an erasure ($\bot$ in the lemma) with probability $\rho > 0$. Recall that the proof uses a $(3, 1-\rho)$-ZK-PCP $\langle \mathsf{P}_{oZK}, \mathsf{V}_{oZK} \rangle$. Let S be a simulator for this ZK-PCP. The construction of simulator S' for $\langle \mathsf{P}_{ZK}, \mathsf{V}_{ZK} \rangle$, using the simulator S is quite straightforward: S' runs n independent executions of $S(x, \lambda)$ to get $\pi_1^*, \ldots, \pi_n^*$. It is easy to see that if S produced a perfect simulation of the ZK-PCP, then S' would also produce a perfect simulation of the verifier's view in the ZK proof. Since the simulation by S incurs a negligible error, so does the simulation by S'.

Acknowledgements. We thank the anonymous Asiacrypt reviewers for their careful reading and many helpful comments. This Research was supported by Ministry of Science and Technology, Israel and Department of Science and Technology, Government of India, and in part by the International Centre for Theoretical Sciences (ICTS) during a visit for participating in the program-Foundational Aspects of Blockchain Technology (ICTS/Prog-fabt2020/01). In addition, S. Agrawal was supported by the DST "Swarnajayanti" fellowship, and Indo-French CEFIPRA project; Y. Ishai was supported by ERC Project NTSC (742754), NSF-BSF grant 2015782, ISF grant 2774/20, and BSF grant 2018393; E. Kushilevitz was supported by ISF grant 2774/20, BSF grant 2018393, and NSF-BSF grant 2015782; V. Narayanan and V. Prabhakaran were supported by the Department of Atomic Energy, Government of India, under project no. RTI4001, DAE OM No. 1303/4/2019/R&D-II/DAE/1969 dated 7.2.2020; M. Prabhakaran was supported by the Dept. of Science and Technology, India via the Ramanujan Fellowship; A. Rosen was supported in part by ISF grant No. 1399/17 and Project PROMETHEUS (Grant 780701).

References

1. Agrawal, S., Ishai, Y., Kushilevitz, E., Narayanan, V., Prabhakaran, M., Prabhakaran, V., Rosen, A.: Cryptography from one-way communication: on completeness of finite channels. In: Cryptology ePrint Archive (2020)
2. Ajtai, M.: Oblivious rams without cryptogrpahic assumptions. In: STOC 2010, pp. 181–190 (2010)
3. Bellare, M., et al.: iKP - a family of secure electronic payment protocols. In: USENIX Workshop on Electronic Commerce (1995)
4. Bellare, M., Tessaro, S., Vardy, A.: Semantic security for the wiretap channel. In: Safavi-Naini, R., Canetti, R. (eds.) CRYPTO 2012. LNCS, vol. 7417, pp. 294–311. Springer, Heidelberg (2012). https://doi.org/10.1007/978-3-642-32009-5_18
5. Bennett, C.H., Brassard, G., Crepeau, C., Maurer, U.M.: Generalized privacy amplification. IEEE Trans. Inf. Theor. **41**(6), 1915–1923 (1995)
6. Bennett, C.H., Brassard, G., Robert, J.-M.: Privacy amplification by public discussion. SIAM J. Comput. **17**(2), 210–229 (1988)
7. Bertsimas, D., Tsitsiklis, J.N.: Introduction to Linear Optimization. Athena Scientific, Nashua (1997)
8. Bloch, M., Barros, J.: Physical-Layer Security: from Information Theory to Security Engineering. Cambridge University Press, Cambridge (2011)

9. Blum, M., Feldman, P., Micali, S.: Proving security against chosen ciphertext attacks. In: Goldwasser, S. (ed.) CRYPTO 1988. LNCS, vol. 403, pp. 256–268. Springer, New York (1990). https://doi.org/10.1007/0-387-34799-2_20
10. Chaum, D.: Blind signatures for untraceable payments. In: Chaum, D., Rivest, R.L., Sherman, A.T. (eds.) Advances in Cryptology, pp. 199–203. Springer, Boston, MA (1983). https://doi.org/10.1007/978-1-4757-0602-4_18
11. Chaum, D.: Online cash checks. In: Quisquater, J.-J., Vandewalle, J. (eds.) EUROCRYPT 1989. LNCS, vol. 434, pp. 288–293. Springer, Heidelberg (1990). https://doi.org/10.1007/3-540-46885-4_30
12. Crepeau, C., Kilian, J.: Achieving oblivious transfer using weakened security assumptions. In: FOCS, pp. 42–52 (1988)
13. Crépeau, C., Morozov, K., Wolf, S.: Efficient unconditional oblivious transfer from almost any noisy channel. In: Blundo, C., Cimato, S. (eds.) SCN 2004. LNCS, vol. 3352, pp. 47–59. Springer, Heidelberg (2005). https://doi.org/10.1007/978-3-540-30598-9_4
14. Damgård, I., Kilian, J., Salvail, L.: On the (Im)possibility of basing oblivious transfer and bit commitment on weakened security assumptions. In: Stern, J. (ed.) EUROCRYPT 1999. LNCS, vol. 1592, pp. 56–73. Springer, Heidelberg (1999). https://doi.org/10.1007/3-540-48910-X_5
15. Feige, U., Lapidot, D., Shamir, A.: Multiple non-interactive zero knowledge proofs based on a single random string. In: FOCS, vol. 1, pp. 308–317, October 1990
16. Feige, U., Kilian, J., Naor, M.: A minimal model for secure computation (extended abstract). In: STOC, pp. 554–563 (1994)
17. Garg, S., Ishai, Y., Kushilevitz, E., Ostrovsky, R., Sahai, A.: Cryptography with one-way communication. In: Gennaro, R., Robshaw, M. (eds.) CRYPTO 2015. LNCS, vol. 9216, pp. 191–208. Springer, Heidelberg (2015). https://doi.org/10.1007/978-3-662-48000-7_10
18. Ishai, Y., Kushilevitz, E.: Private simultaneous messages protocols with applications. In: ISTCS 1997, pp. 174–184. IEEE Computer Society (1997)
19. Ishai, Y., Kushilevitz, E., Ostrovsky, R., Prabhakaran, M., Sahai, A.: Efficient non-interactive secure computation. In: Paterson, K.G. (ed.) EUROCRYPT 2011. LNCS, vol. 6632, pp. 406–425. Springer, Heidelberg (2011). https://doi.org/10.1007/978-3-642-20465-4_23
20. Kilian, J.: Founding cryptography on oblivious transfer. In: STOC, pp. 20–31 (1988)
21. Kraschewski, D., Maji, H.K., Prabhakaran, M., Sahai, A.: A full characterization of completeness for two-party randomized function evaluation. In: Nguyen, P.Q., Oswald, E. (eds.) EUROCRYPT 2014. LNCS, vol. 8441, pp. 659–676. Springer, Heidelberg (2014). https://doi.org/10.1007/978-3-642-55220-5_36
22. Lin, F., Cheraghchi, M., Guruswami, V., Safavi-Naini, R., Wang, H.: Secret sharing with binary shares. In: ITCS, pp. 53:1–53:20 (2019)
23. Maurer, U.M.: Perfect cryptographic security from partially independent channels. In: STOC 1991, pp. 561–571 (1991)
24. Poor, H.V., Schaefer, R.F.: Wireless physical layer security. Proc. Natl. Acad. Sci. **114**(1), 19–26 (2017)
25. Ranellucci, S., Tapp, A., Winkler, S., Wullschleger, J.: On the efficiency of bit commitment reductions. In: Lee, D.H., Wang, X. (eds.) ASIACRYPT 2011. LNCS, vol. 7073, pp. 520–537. Springer, Heidelberg (2011). https://doi.org/10.1007/978-3-642-25385-0_28
26. Raz, R., Reingold, O., Vadhan, S.: Extracting all the randomness and reducing the error in trevisan's extractors. J. Comput. Syst. Sci. **65**, 97–128 (2002)

27. Trevisan, L.: Extractors and pseudorandom generators. J. ACM **48**(4), 860–879 (2001)
28. Winter, A., Nascimento, A.C.A., Imai, H.: Commitment capacity of discrete memoryless channels. In: Paterson, K.G. (ed.) Cryptography and Coding 2003. LNCS, vol. 2898, pp. 35–51. Springer, Heidelberg (2003). https://doi.org/10.1007/978-3-540-40974-8_4
29. Wullschleger, J.: Oblivious transfer from weak noisy channels. In: Reingold, O. (ed.) TCC 2009. LNCS, vol. 5444, pp. 332–349. Springer, Heidelberg (2009). https://doi.org/10.1007/978-3-642-00457-5_20
30. Wyner, A.D.: The wire-tap channel. Bell Syst. Tech. J. **54**(8), 1355–1387 (1975)
31. Yao, A.C.C.: How to generate and exchange secrets (extended abstract). In: FOCS 1986, pp. 162–167 (1986)

Succinct Functional Commitment for a Large Class of Arithmetic Circuits

Helger Lipmaa(✉) and Kateryna Pavlyk

Simula UiB, Bergen, Norway
{helger,kateryna}@simula.no

Abstract. A succinct functional commitment (SFC) scheme for a circuit class **CC** enables, for any circuit $\mathcal{C} \in \mathbf{CC}$, the committer to first succinctly commit to a vector $\boldsymbol{\alpha}$, and later succinctly open the commitment to $\mathcal{C}(\boldsymbol{\alpha}, \boldsymbol{\beta})$, where the verifier chooses $\boldsymbol{\beta}$ at the time of opening. Unfortunately, SFC commitment schemes are known only for severely limited function classes like the class of inner products. By making non-black-box use of SNARK-construction techniques, we propose a SFC scheme for the large class of semi-sparse polynomials. The new SFC scheme can be used to, say, efficiently (1) implement sparse polynomials, and (2) aggregate various interesting SFC (e.g., vector commitment and polynomial commitment) schemes. The new scheme is evaluation-binding under a new instantiation of the computational uber-assumption. We provide a thorough analysis of the new assumption.

Keywords: Aggregated functional commitment · Dejà Q · Functional commitment · SNARK · Uber-assumption · Vector commitment

1 Introduction

A succinct functional commitment (SFC) scheme [29] for a circuit class **CC** enables the committer, for any $\mathcal{C} \in \mathbf{CC}$, to first commit to a vector $\boldsymbol{\alpha}$, and later open the commitment to $\mathcal{C}(\boldsymbol{\alpha}, \boldsymbol{\beta})$, where the verifier chooses $\boldsymbol{\beta}$ at the time of opening. An SFC scheme must be evaluation-binding (given a commitment, it is intractable to open it to $\boldsymbol{\xi} = \mathcal{C}(\boldsymbol{\alpha}, \boldsymbol{\beta})$ and $\boldsymbol{\xi}' = \mathcal{C}(\boldsymbol{\alpha}, \boldsymbol{\beta})$ for $\boldsymbol{\xi} \neq \boldsymbol{\xi}'$) and hiding (a commitment and possibly many openings should not reveal any additional information about $\boldsymbol{\alpha}$). Succinctness means that both the commitment and the opening have length $\mathsf{polylog}(|\boldsymbol{\alpha}|, |\boldsymbol{\beta}|)$.

In particular, an SFC scheme for inner products (SIPFC) assumes that, $\mathcal{C}$ computes the inner product $(\boldsymbol{\alpha}, \boldsymbol{\beta}) \rightarrow \langle \boldsymbol{\alpha}, \boldsymbol{\beta} \rangle$ [25,29,30]. As explained in [29], one can use an SIPFC scheme to construct succinct vector commitment schemes [12], polynomial commitment schemes [27], and accumulators [5]. Each of these primitives has a large number of independent applications. Succinct polynomial commitment schemes have recently become very popular since they can be used to construct (updatable) SNARKs [15,35,40,41] (a direction somewhat opposite to the one we will pursue in the current paper). Since, in several applications (e.g.,

S. Moriai and H. Wang (Eds.): ASIACRYPT 2020, LNCS 12493, pp. 686–716, 2020.
https://doi.org/10.1007/978-3-030-64840-4_23

in cryptocurrencies, [38]), one has to run many instances of SFC in parallel, there is a recent surge of interest in aggregatable SFC schemes, [8,9,22,28,38]. All mentioned papers propose *succinct* FC schemes for limited functionalities.

Since there are no prior SFC schemes for broader classes of functions, there is a large gap between function classes for which an SFC scheme is known and the class of all efficiently (e.g., poly-size arithmetic circuits) verifiable functions. Filling a similar gap is notoriously hard in the case of related primitives like functional encryption, homomorphic encryption, and NIZK. A natural question to ask is whether something similar holds in the case of functional commitment.

It is easy to construct an SFC for all poly-size circuits under non-falsifiable assumptions: given a commitment to $\boldsymbol{\alpha}$, the opening consists of a SNARK argument [20,23,31] that $\mathcal{C}(\boldsymbol{\alpha}, \boldsymbol{\beta}) = \boldsymbol{\xi}$. However, while non-falsifiable assumptions are required to construct SNARKs [21], they are not needed in the case of SFC schemes. Thus, just using SNARK as a black-box is not a satisfactory solution.

Moreover, since one can construct non-succinct NIZK from falsifiable assumptions for NP, one can construct a non-succinct FC (nSFC) from a non-succinct NIZK. Bitansky [6] pursued this approach, proposing an nSFC, for all circuits, that uses NIZK as a black-box. By using NIWIs in a non-black-box manner, Bitansky proposed another, non-trivial, nSFC scheme that does not achieve zero-knowledge but does not require the CRS model. Alternatively, consider the FC scheme where the commitment consists of fully-homomorphic encryptions C_i of individual coefficients α_i, and the opening is the randomizer R of the evaluation of the circuit $\mathcal{C}$ on them. The verifier can re-evaluate the circuit on C_i and her input, and then check that the result is equal to $\mathsf{Enc}(\boldsymbol{\xi}; R)$. However, the resulting FC is not succinct since one has to encrypt all α_i individually.

Thus, the main question is to construct *succinct* FC schemes, under falsifiable assumptions, for a wide variety of functionalities.

Our Contributions. We propose a falsifiable SFC scheme $\mathsf{FC_{sn}}$ for the class of *semi-sparse polynomials* $\mathbf{CC} = \mathbf{CC}_{\Sigma\Pi\forall}$ whose correct computation can be verified by using an arbitrary polynomial-size arithmetic circuit that is "compilable" according to the definition, given in a few paragraphs. Notably, $\mathsf{FC_{sn}}$ allows efficiently aggregate various SFC schemes, e.g., vector commitments with inner-product commitments and polynomial commitments. We analyze the power of $\mathbf{CC}_{\Sigma\Pi\forall}$ by using techniques from algebraic complexity theory; the name of the class will be explain in Sect. 4.

We prove that $\mathsf{FC_{sn}}$ is secure under a new falsifiable assumption (computational span-uber-assumption in a group $\mathbb{G}_1$) that is reminiscent of the well-known computational uber-assumption in $\mathbb{G}_1$. We then thoroughly analyze the security of the new assumption.

Our Techniques. Next, we provide a high-level overview of our technical contributions. The construction of $\mathsf{FC_{sn}}$ consists of the following steps.

1. Compilation of the original circuit $\mathcal{C}$ computing the fixed function $\mathcal{F} \in \mathbf{CC}$ to a circuit $\mathcal{C}^*$ consisting of four public subcircuits.

2. Representation of $\mathcal{C}^*$ in the QAP language which SNARKs usually use.
3. Construction of SFC for the QAP representation, by using SNARK techniques in a non-black-box way.

Next we describe these steps in detail.

Circuit Compilation. Let $\mathcal{C} : \mathbb{Z}_p^{\mu_\alpha} \times \mathbb{Z}_p^{\mu_\beta} \to \mathbb{Z}_p^{\kappa}$ be a polynomial-size arithmetic circuit that, on input $(\boldsymbol{\alpha}, \boldsymbol{\beta})$, outputs $\boldsymbol{\xi} = \mathcal{F}(\boldsymbol{\alpha}, \boldsymbol{\beta}) = (\mathcal{F}_i(\boldsymbol{\alpha}, \boldsymbol{\beta}))_{i=1}^{\kappa}$. Here, the committer's input $\boldsymbol{\alpha}$ is secret, and the verifier's input is public. We modify the circuit $\mathcal{C}$ to a compiled circuit $\mathcal{C}^*$, see Fig. 1, that consists of the subcircuits $\mathcal{C}_\phi$, $\mathcal{C}_\psi$, $\mathcal{C}_\chi$, and $\mathcal{C}_\xi$. In the commitment phase, the committer uses the circuit $\mathcal{C}_\phi$ to compute several polynomials $\phi_i(\boldsymbol{\alpha})$ depending on only 1 (this allows the output polynomials to have a non-zero constant term) and $\boldsymbol{\alpha}$. In the opening phase, the verifier sends $\boldsymbol{\beta}$ to the committer, who uses the circuit $\mathcal{C}_\psi$ to compute several polynomials $\psi_i(\boldsymbol{\beta})$ depending on 1 and $\boldsymbol{\beta}$. The verifier can redo this part of the computation. After that, the committer uses the circuit $\mathcal{C}_\chi$ to compute several polynomials $\chi_i(\boldsymbol{\alpha}, \boldsymbol{\beta})$ from the inputs and outputs of $\mathcal{C}_\phi$ and $\mathcal{C}_\psi$. Finally, the committer uses $\mathcal{C}_\xi$ to compute the outputs $\mathcal{F}_i(\boldsymbol{\alpha}, \boldsymbol{\beta})$ of $\mathcal{C}^*$. We will explain more thoroughly this compilation in Sect. 3.

Intuitively, the compilation restricts the class of circuits in two ways. First, we add a small circuit $\mathcal{C}_\xi$ at the top of the compiled circuit to guarantee that the R1CS representation of $\mathcal{C}^*$ has several all-zero columns and rows, which helps us in the security reduction. This does, however, not restrict the circuit class for which the SFC is defined and it only increases the number of gates by κ. Second, $\mathcal{C}_\chi$ is restricted to have multiplicative depth 1, i.e., it sums up products of polynomials in $\boldsymbol{\alpha}$ with polynomials in $\boldsymbol{\beta}$. This guarantees that in a collision, the two accepted openings have a linear relation that does not depend on secret data $\boldsymbol{\alpha}$. The latter makes it possible for the reduction to break the underlying falsifiable assumption. Thus, we are restricted to the class $\mathbf{CC}_{\Sigma\Pi\forall}$ of circuits where each output can be written as $\sum_{i,j} \phi_i(\boldsymbol{\alpha})\psi_j(\boldsymbol{\beta})$, for efficiently computable polynomials ϕ_i and ψ_j, and the sum is taken over number $\mathsf{poly}(\lambda)$ products.

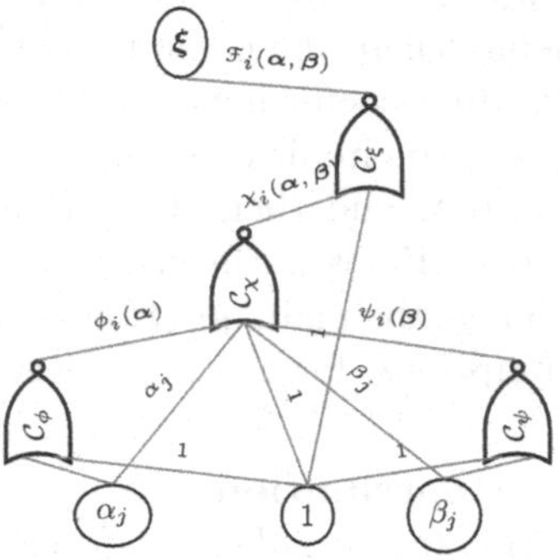

Fig. 1. The compiled circuit $\mathcal{C}^*$.

By employing tools from the algebraic complexity theory, in Sect. 4, we study the class $\mathbf{CC}_{\Sigma\Pi\forall}$ of "compilable" (according to the given definition) arithmetic circuits. We say that a polynomial $f \in \mathbf{CC}_{\Sigma\Pi\forall}$ if f has a circuit that belongs to $\mathbf{CC}_{\Sigma\Pi\forall}$. The new SFC scheme can implement f iff $f \in \mathbf{CC}_{\Sigma\Pi\forall}$. First, we show that any sparse polynomial (over indeterminates, chosen by both the committer and the verifier) f belongs to $\mathbf{CC}_{\Sigma\Pi\forall}$. Second, we construct a non-sparse polynomial $f \in \mathbf{CC}_{\Sigma\Pi\forall}$. This relies on a result of Ben-Or who constructed an $O(n^2)$-size arithmetic circuit that simultaneously computes the dth symmetric polynomial $\sigma_d(X_1, \ldots, X_n)$, for $d \in [1\,..\,n]$. Third, we construct a polynomial $f \in \mathbf{VP}$ such that $f \notin \mathbf{CC}_{\Sigma\Pi\forall}$, where **VP** is the class of poly-degree polynomials that have poly-size circuits, [39].

R1CS/QAP Representation. Let $\mathcal{C}$ be an arithmetic circuit, and $\mathcal{C}^*$ be its compilation. A circuit evaluation can be verified by verifying a matrix equation, where matrices define the circuit uniquely and reflect all the circuit constraints. SNARKs usually use QAP (Quadratic Arithmetic Program, [20]), a polynomial version of R1CS, which allows for better efficiency.

Constructing the Underlying SNARK. Intuitively, we start constructing a SNARK for $\mathcal{C}^*$ by following the approach of Groth [24] who proposed the most efficient known zk-SNARK, or more precisely, its recent modification by Lipmaa [33]. However, we modify this approach whenever it suits our goals. The new SFC inherits the efficiency of Groth's SNARK; this is the main reason why we chose Groth's SNARK; it may be the case that SFCs constructed from less efficient SNARKs have other desirable properties, but this is out of the scope of the current paper. We chose the modified version of [33] due to its versatility: [33] explains sufficiently well how to construct a SNARK for QAP so that it is feasible to modify its approach to suit the current paper.

The New SFC Scheme. In the SNARKs of [24,33], the argument consists of three group elements, $\pi = ([\mathsf{A}]_1, [\mathsf{B}]_2, [\mathsf{C}]_1)$. (We use the bracket additive notation, see Sect. 2.) Due to our restrictions on $\mathcal{C}^*$, both $[\mathsf{A}]_1$ and $[\mathsf{B}]_2$ can be written as sums of a non-functional commitment that depends on the secret data only and a non-functional commitment that depends on public data only. By the public data we mean $(\boldsymbol{\beta}, \mathcal{F}(\boldsymbol{\alpha}, \boldsymbol{\beta}))$; any other function of $\boldsymbol{\alpha}$ is a part of the secret data. E.g., $[\mathsf{A}]_1 = [\mathsf{A}_s]_1 + [\mathsf{A}_p]_1$, where $[\mathsf{A}_s]_1$ is computed by the committer before $\boldsymbol{\beta}$ becomes available, and $[\mathsf{A}_p]_1$ can be recomputed by the verifier since it only depends on the public data. However, $[\mathsf{C}]_1 = [\mathsf{C}_{sp}]_1 + [\mathsf{C}_p]_1$, where $[\mathsf{C}_p]_1$ depends only on public data but $[\mathsf{C}_{sp}]_1$ depends both on public and private data.

In the new SFC commitment scheme, the functional commitment is $C = ([\mathsf{A}_s]_1, [\mathsf{B}_s]_2)$ and the opening is $[\mathsf{C}_{sp}]_1$. After receiving the opening, the verifier recomputes $[\mathsf{A}_p]_1$, $[\mathsf{B}_p]_2$, and $[\mathsf{C}_p]_1$, and then runs the SNARK verifier on the argument $\pi = ([\mathsf{A}_s]_1 + [\mathsf{A}_p]_1, [\mathsf{B}_s]_2 + [\mathsf{B}_p]_2, [\mathsf{C}_{sp}]_1 + [\mathsf{C}_p]_1)$. However, as we will see later, the commitment also includes auxiliary elements $[\mathsf{B}_i^{\mathsf{aux}}]_1$ needed to obtain an efficient security reduction.

We will denote the new SFC commitment scheme by $\mathsf{FC}_{\mathsf{sn}}$. We denote by $\mathsf{FC}_{\mathsf{sn}}^{\mathcal{C}}$ its specialization to the circuit $\mathcal{C}$.

Applications. To demonstrate the usefulness of $\mathsf{FC}_{\mathsf{sn}}$, we will give several applications: some of them are well-known, and some are new. In all cases, the function of interest can be rewritten as a semi-sparse polynomial in $(\boldsymbol{\alpha}, \boldsymbol{\beta})$. Some of these examples are closely related to but still sufficiently different from IPFC. In particular, [29] showed how to use an efficient IPFC to construct SFC for polynomial commitments [27], accumulators [5], and vector commitments [12] (See the full version [34].). We use $\mathsf{FC}_{\mathsf{sn}}$ to construct subvector commitments [28], aggregated polynomial commitment [9,15] (one can commit to multiple polynomials at once, each of which can be opened at a different point), and multivariate polynomial commitments [10]. Also, we outline a few seemingly new applications like the aggregated inner product (that, in particular, can be used to implement subvector commitment) and evaluation-point commitment schemes. (See the full version [34].) All described commitment schemes are succinct.

Importantly, $\mathsf{FC}_{\mathsf{sn}}$ achieves easy aggregation in a more general sense. Let $\mathcal{C}_i$ be some circuits for which efficient SFC schemes exist. We can then construct an efficient SFC for the circuit that consists of the sequential composition of $\mathcal{C}_i$-s. In particular, we can aggregate multiple polynomial commitment schemes, some vector commitment schemes, and say an evaluation-point commitment scheme. Some of the referred papers [8,9,22,28,38] construct aggregated commitment schemes for a concrete circuit (e.g., an aggregated polynomial commitment scheme). Importantly, $\mathsf{FC}_{\mathsf{sn}}$ allows one to aggregate different SFC schemes.

Security. The correctness and perfect hiding proofs are straightforward. The main thing worthy of note here is that we have three definitions of hiding (com-hiding, open-hiding, and zero-knowledge, see Sect. 2). For the sake of completeness, we also give three different hiding proofs. The SFC schemes must work in the CRS model to obtain zero-knowledge. However, since zero-knowledge is stronger than the other two definitions, the proof of zero-knowledge, that follows roughly from the zero-knowledge of the related SNARK, suffices. Note that say [29] only considered the weakest hiding notion (com-hiding).

The evaluation-binding proof differs significantly from the knowledge-soundness proofs of SNARKs. The knowledge-soundness of SNARKs can only be proven under non-falsifiable assumptions [21]. In particular, Groth proved the knowledge-soundness of the SNARK from [24] in the generic group model while Lipmaa [33] proved it under HAK (hash-algebraic knowledge assumption, a tautological knowledge assumption) and a known computational assumption (namely, q-PDL [31]). Such assumptions have very little in common with assumptions we use. As expected, a knowledge-soundness proof that uses non-falsifiable assumptions has a very different flavor compared to an evaluation-binding proof that only uses falsifiable assumptions. We emphasize it is not clear a priori that an SFC constructed from SNARKs could rely on falsifiable assumptions.

We prove the evaluation-binding of $\mathsf{FC}_{\mathsf{sn}}$ under the new $(\mathcal{R}, \mathcal{S}, \{f_i\})$-*computational span-uber-assumption* in source group $\mathbb{G}_1$, where $\mathcal{R}, \mathcal{S} \subset \mathbb{Z}_p[X, Y]$ and $f_i \in \mathbb{Z}_p[X, Y]$ with $f_i \notin \operatorname{span}(\mathcal{R})$. This assumption states that given a commitment key $\mathsf{ck} = ([\varrho(\chi, y) : \varrho \in \mathcal{R}]_1, [\sigma(\chi, y) : \sigma \in \mathcal{S}]_2)$, where χ, y are random trapdoors, it is difficult to compute $(\boldsymbol{\Delta} \neq \mathbf{0}, \sum_{i=1}^{\kappa} \Delta_i [f_i(\chi, y)]_1)$, where $\boldsymbol{\Delta}$ is adversarially chosen. (See Definition 6 for a formal definition.) Importantly, if $\kappa = 1$ then we just have an uber-assumption in $\mathbb{G}_1$. We show that (see Theorem 2), for concrete $\mathcal{R}$ and f_i, $f_i(X, Y) \notin \operatorname{span}(\mathcal{R})$.

The full evaluation-binding proof is quite tricky and relies significantly on the structure of matrices U, V, W, and of the commitment key. Given a collision, we "almost" compute $(\boldsymbol{\Delta}, \sum \Delta_i [f_i(\chi, y)]_1)$, where $\boldsymbol{\Delta}$ is the componentwise difference between two claimed values of $\mathfrak{F}(\boldsymbol{\alpha}, \boldsymbol{\beta})$. To eliminate "almost" in the previous sentence, the committer outputs κ additional "helper" elements $[\mathsf{B}_i^{\mathsf{aux}}]_1$, where extra care has to be used to guarantee that the helper elements can be computed given the commitment key. In both cases, to succeed, we need to assume that the matrices (U, V, W) satisfy some natural restrictions stated in individual theorems. These restrictions are collected together in Theorem 1.

Analysis of the Span-Uber-Assumption. The span-uber-assumption is falsifiable and, thus, significantly more realistic than non-falsifiable (knowledge) assumptions needed to prove the adaptive soundness of SNARKs. Still, it is a new assumption and thus we have written down *three* different proofs that it follows from already known assumptions. (See Lemma 2 and Theorem 4, and another theorem in the full version).

In the full version [34], we prove that the span-uber-assumption in $\mathbb{G}_1$ holds under the known $(\mathcal{R}, \mathcal{S}, f_i')$-computational uber-assumption in the target group $\mathbb{G}_T$ [7]. Here, f_i' are different from but related to f_i. We also prove that $f_i' \notin \text{span}(\mathcal{RS})$. Since $f_i(X, Y) \notin \text{span}(\mathcal{R})$ and $f_i'(X, Y) \notin \text{span}(\mathcal{RS})$ (in the case of the uber-assumption in $\mathbb{G}_T$), we have an instantiation of the computational uber-assumption, known to be secure [7] in the generic group model.

Since the generic group model is very restrictive and has known weaknesses [16,17] not shared by well-chosen knowledge assumptions, we will use the newer methodology of [33]. In the full version [34], we prove that if $f_i \notin \text{span}(\mathcal{R})$ then the $(\mathcal{R}, \mathcal{S}, \{f_i\})$-computational span-uber-assumption in $\mathbb{G}_1$ holds under a HAK and a PDL assumption. Since uber-assumption in $\mathbb{G}_T$ is not secure under a HAK assumption (the latter only handles the case the adversary outputs elements in source groups since the target group is non generic), this result is orthogonal to the previous result. As a corollary of independent interest, we get that if $f_i(X, Y) \notin \text{span}(\mathcal{R})$ then uber-assumption in $\mathbb{G}_1$ holds under a HAK and a PDL assumption.

In composite-order bilinear groups, the computational uber-assumption in $\mathbb{G}_T$ holds under a subgroup hiding assumption [13]. Thus, due to Lemma 2, a composite-order group span-uber-assumption (and also the new SFC) is secure under a subgroup hiding assumption. In Theorem 4, we use the Déjà Q approach of [14] to prove that the span-uber-assumption in $\mathbb{G}_\iota$, $\iota \in \{1, 2\}$, is secure under a subgroup hiding assumption. This proof is more direct than the reduction through an uber-assumption in $\mathbb{G}_T$. Moreover, the Déjà Q approach is more applicable if one is working in the source group. Whether a similar reduction holds in the case of prime-order groups is an interesting open question.

Efficiency. It is difficult to provide a detailed efficiency comparison of our newly constructed scheme to all the abundant existing work in all applications. $\mathsf{FC}_{\mathsf{sn}}$ is *generic*, works for a large class of circuits, and can tackle scenarios, not possible with previous work, but at the same time, it can also be used to solve the much simpler case of, e.g., inner product. We stress that $\mathsf{FC}_{\mathsf{sn}}$, when straightforwardly specialized to the IPFC case, is nearly as efficient as the most efficient known prior IPFC, losing ground only in the CRS length. On the other hand, we are not aware of *any* previous aggregated IPFC schemes (See the full version [34].).

This paper uses heavily a yet unpublished paper [33] of the first author.

2 Preliminaries

If $\mathcal{R} = (\varrho_1(\boldsymbol{X}), \dots, \varrho_n(\boldsymbol{X}))$ is a tuple of polynomials over $\mathbb{Z}_p[\boldsymbol{X}]$ and $\boldsymbol{x}$ is a vector of integers then $\mathcal{R}(\boldsymbol{x}) := (\varrho_1(\boldsymbol{x}), \dots, \varrho_n(\boldsymbol{x}))$. Let $\mathbb{Z}_p^{(\leq d)}[X]$ be the set of degree-$\leq d$ polynomials over $\mathbb{Z}_p$. For a matrix U, let $\boldsymbol{U}_i$ be its ith row, $\boldsymbol{U}^{(j)}$ be its jth column. Let $\boldsymbol{a} \circ \boldsymbol{b}$ denote the component-wise product of two vectors $\boldsymbol{a}$ and $\boldsymbol{b}$, $(\boldsymbol{a} \circ \boldsymbol{b})_i = a_i b_i$. Let $\boldsymbol{a}_1 // \dots // \boldsymbol{a}_n = \begin{pmatrix} \boldsymbol{a}_1 \\ \dots \\ \boldsymbol{a}_n \end{pmatrix}$ denote the vertical concatenation of vectors $\boldsymbol{a}_i$. λ is the security parameter, and 1^λ denotes its unary representation. PPT denotes probabilistic polynomial-time. For an algorithm $\mathcal{A}$, range($\mathcal{A}$) is the range of $\mathcal{A}$, i.e., the set of valid outputs of $\mathcal{A}$, $\mathsf{RND}_\lambda(\mathcal{A})$ denotes the random tape of $\mathcal{A}$ (assuming the given value of λ), and $r \leftarrow_\$ \mathcal{S}$ denotes the uniformly random choice of a randomizer r from the set/distribution $\mathcal{S}$.

Interpolation. Assume ν is a power of two, and let ω be the νth primitive root of unity modulo p. Such ω exists, given that $\nu \mid (p-1)$. Then,

- $\ell(X) := \prod_{i=1}^{\nu}(X - \omega^{i-1}) = X^\nu - 1$ is the unique degree ν monic polynomial such that $\ell(\omega^{i-1}) = 0$ for all $i \in [1 \,..\, \nu]$.
- For $i \in [1 \,..\, \nu]$, $\ell_i(X)$ is the *ith Lagrange basis polynomial*, i.e., the unique degree $\nu - 1$ polynomial s.t. $\ell_i(\omega^{i-1}) = 1$ and $\ell_i(\omega^{j-1}) = 0$ for $i \neq j$. Clearly, $\ell_i(X) := \ell(X)/(\ell'(\omega^{i-1})(X - \omega^{i-1})) = (X^\nu - 1)\omega^{i-1}/(\nu(X - \omega^{i-1}))$.

Moreover, $(\ell_j(\omega^{i-1}))_{i=1}^{\nu} = \boldsymbol{e}_j$ (the jth unit vector) and $(\ell(\omega^{i-1}))_{i=1}^{\nu} = \boldsymbol{0}_\nu$.

Bilinear Pairings. Let ν be an integer parameter (the circuit size in our application). A bilinear group generator $\mathsf{Pgen}(1^\lambda, \nu)$ returns $(p, \mathbb{G}_1, \mathbb{G}_2, \mathbb{G}_T, \hat{e}, \mathsf{P}_1, \mathsf{P}_2)$, where $\mathbb{G}_1, \mathbb{G}_2, \mathbb{G}_T$ are three additive cyclic groups of prime order p, $\hat{e} : \mathbb{G}_1 \times \mathbb{G}_2 \rightarrow \mathbb{G}_T$ is a non-degenerate efficiently computable bilinear pairing, and P_ι is a fixed generator of $\mathbb{G}_\iota$. We assume $\mathsf{P}_T = \hat{e}(\mathsf{P}_1, \mathsf{P}_2)$. We require the bilinear pairing to be Type-3, i.e., there is no efficient isomorphism between $\mathbb{G}_1$ and $\mathbb{G}_2$. For efficient interpolation, we assume that p is such that $\nu \mid (p-1)$. When emphasizing efficiency is not important, we drop the parameter ν and just write $\mathsf{p} \leftarrow \mathsf{Pgen}(1^\lambda)$. We use additive notation together with the standard elliptic-curve "bracket" notation. Namely, we write $[a]_\iota$ to denote $a\mathsf{P}_\iota$, and $[a]_1 \bullet [b]_2$ to denote $\hat{e}([a]_1, [b]_2)$. We use freely the bracket notation together with matrix notation, e.g., if $AB = C$ as matrices then $[A]_1 \bullet [B]_2 = [C]_T$.

Uber-Assumption. The following assumption is a special case of the more general uber-assumption of [7,11].

Definition 1 ([7,11]). *Let* $\mathsf{p} \leftarrow \mathsf{Pgen}(1^\lambda)$. *Let* $\mathcal{R}$, $\mathcal{S}$, *and* $\mathcal{T}$ *be three tuples of bivariate polynomials from* $\mathbb{Z}_p[X, Y]$. *Let* f *be a bivariate polynomial from* $\mathbb{Z}_p[X, Y]$. *The* $(\mathcal{R}, \mathcal{S}, \mathcal{T}, f)$-computational uber-assumption *for* Pgen *in group* $\mathbb{G}_\iota$, *where* $\iota \in \{1, 2, T\}$, *states that for any PPT adversary* $\mathcal{A}$, $\mathsf{Adv}^{\mathsf{uber}}_{\mathsf{Pgen},\mathcal{R},\mathcal{S},\mathcal{T},f,\mathcal{A}}(\lambda) = \mathsf{negl}(\lambda)$, *where* $\mathsf{Adv}^{\mathsf{uber}}_{\mathsf{Pgen},\mathcal{R},\mathcal{S},\mathcal{T},f,\mathcal{A}}(\lambda) :=$

$$\Pr\left[\begin{array}{l}\mathsf{p} \leftarrow \mathsf{Pgen}(1^\lambda); \chi, y \leftarrow_\$ \mathbb{Z}_p^*; \mathsf{ck} \leftarrow ([\mathcal{R}(\chi, y)]_1, [\mathcal{S}(\chi, y)]_2, [\mathcal{T}(\chi, y)]_T) : \\ \mathcal{A}(\mathsf{ck}) = [f(\chi, y)]_\iota\end{array}\right].$$

[7,11] considered the general case of c-variate polynomials for any c. In our case, $\mathcal{T} = \emptyset$; then, we have an $(\mathcal{R}, \mathcal{S}, f)$-computational uber-assumption in $\mathbb{G}_\iota$.

Importantly [7,11], (i) if $f(X,Y)$ is not in the span of $\{\varrho(X,Y)\}$ then the $(\mathcal{R}, \mathcal{S}, \mathcal{T}, f)$-computational uber-assumption for $\mathbb{G}_1$ holds in the generic group model, and (ii) if $f(X,Y)$ is not in the span of $\{\varrho(X,Y)\sigma(X,Y)+\tau(X,Y)\}$ then the $(\mathcal{R}, \mathcal{S}, \mathcal{T}, f)$-computational uber-assumption for $\mathbb{G}_T$ is difficult in the generic group model. We will only invoke the uber-assumption in the case $f(X,Y)$ is not in the span of $\{\varrho(X,Y)\}$.

QAP. Let $\mathbf{R} = \{(\mathsf{z}, \mathsf{wit})\}$ be a relation between statements and witnesses. Quadratic Arithmetic Program (QAP) was introduced in [20] as a language where for an input z and witness wit, $(\mathsf{z}, \mathsf{wit}) \in \mathbf{R}$ can be verified by using a parallel quadratic check. QAP has an efficient reduction from the (either Boolean or Arithmetic) CIRCUIT-SAT. Thus, an efficient zk-SNARK for QAP results in an efficient zk-SNARK for CIRCUIT-SAT.

We consider arithmetic circuits that consist only of fan-in-2 multiplication gates, but either input of each multiplication gate can be any weighted sum of wire values, [20]. Let $\mu_0 < \mu$ be a non-negative integer. In the case of arithmetic circuits, ν is the number of multiplication gates, μ is the number of wires, and μ_0 is the number of public inputs.

Let $\mathbb{F} = \mathbb{Z}_p$, such that ω is the ν-th primitive root of unity modulo p. This requirement is needed for the sake of efficiency, and we will make it implicitly throughout the paper. However, it is not needed for the new SFC to work. Let U, V, and W be instance-dependent matrices and let a be a witness. A QAP is characterized by the constraint $U\mathsf{a} \circ V\mathsf{a} = W\mathsf{a}$. Let $L_{\boldsymbol{a}}(X) := \sum_{i=1}^{\nu} a_i \ell_i(X)$ be the interpolating polynomial of $\boldsymbol{a} = (a_1, \ldots, a_\nu)^\top$ at points ω^{i-1}, with $L_{\boldsymbol{a}}(\omega^{i-1}) = a_i$. For $j \in [1 \mathinner{..} \mu]$, define $u_j(X) := L_{\boldsymbol{U}^{(j)}}(X)$, $v_j(X) := L_{\boldsymbol{V}^{(j)}}(X)$, and $w_j(X) := L_{\boldsymbol{W}^{(j)}}(X)$ to be interpolating polynomials of the jth column of the corresponding matrix. Thus, $u_j, v_j, w_j \in \mathbb{Z}_p^{(\le \nu-1)}[X]$. Let $u(X) = \sum_{j=1}^{\mu} \mathsf{a}_j u_j(X)$, $v(X) = \sum_{j=1}^{\mu} \mathsf{a}_j v_j(X)$, and $w(X) = \sum_{j=1}^{\mu} \mathsf{a}_j w_j(X)$. Then $U\mathsf{a} \circ V\mathsf{a} = W\mathsf{a}$ iff $\ell(X) \mid u(X)v(X) - w(X)$ iff $u(X)v(X) \equiv w(X) \pmod{\ell(X)}$ iff there exists a polynomial $\mathcal{H}(X)$ such that $u(X)v(X) - w(X) = \mathcal{H}(X)\ell(X)$.

A QAP instance $\mathcal{I}_{\mathsf{qap}}$ is equal to $(\mathbb{Z}_p, \mu_0, \{u_j, v_j, w_j\}_{j=1}^{\mu})$. $\mathcal{I}_{\mathsf{qap}}$ defines the following relation:

$$\mathbf{R}_{\mathcal{I}_{\mathsf{qap}}} = \left\{ \begin{array}{l} (\mathsf{z}, \mathsf{wit})\colon \mathsf{z} = (\mathsf{a}_1, \ldots, \mathsf{a}_{\mu_0})^\top \wedge \mathsf{wit} = (\mathsf{a}_{\mu_0+1}, \ldots, \mathsf{a}_\mu)^\top \wedge \\ u(X)v(X) \equiv w(X) \pmod{\ell(X)} \end{array} \right\}, \quad (1)$$

where $u(X)$, $v(X)$, and $w(X)$ are as above. Alternatively, $(\mathsf{z}, \mathsf{wit}) \in \mathbf{R}$ if there exists a (degree $\le \nu - 2$) polynomial $\mathcal{H}(X)$, s.t. the following key equation holds:

$$\chi(X) := u(X)v(X) - w(X) - \mathcal{H}(X)\ell(X) = 0 \ . \quad (2)$$

On top of checking Eq. (2), the verifier also needs to check that $u(X)$, $v(X)$, and $w(X)$ are correctly computed: that is, (i) the first μ_0 coefficients a_j in $u(X)$

are equal to the public inputs, and (ii) $u(X)$, $v(X)$, and $w(X)$ are all computed by using the same coefficients a_j for $j \le \mu$.

Since both the committer and the verifier have inputs, we will use a variation of QAP that handles public inputs differently (see Sect. 3). In particular, we will use different parameters instead of μ_0.

SNARKs. Let $\mathcal{R}$ be a relation generator, such that $\mathcal{R}(1^\lambda)$ returns a polynomial-time decidable binary relation $\mathbf{R} = \{(\mathsf{z}, \mathsf{wit})\}$. Here, z is a statement, and wit is a witness. $\mathcal{R}$ also outputs the system parameters p that will be given to the honest parties and the adversary. A *non-interactive zero-knowledge (NIZK) argument system* $\Psi = (\mathsf{K_{crs}}, \mathsf{P}, \mathsf{V}, \mathsf{Sim})$ for $\mathcal{R}$ consists of four PPT algorithms:

CRS generator: $\mathsf{K_{crs}}$ is a probabilistic algorithm that, given $(\mathbf{R}, \mathsf{p}) \in \mathrm{range}(\mathcal{R}(1^\lambda))$, outputs $(\mathsf{crs}, \mathsf{td})$ where crs is a CRS and td is a simulation trapdoor. Otherwise, it outputs a special symbol $\perp$.

Prover: P is a probabilistic algorithm that, given $(\mathbf{R}, \mathsf{p}, \mathsf{crs}, \mathsf{z}, \mathsf{wit})$ for $(\mathsf{z}, \mathsf{wit}) \in \mathbf{R}$, outputs an argument π. Otherwise, it outputs $\perp$.

Verifier: V is a probabilistic algorithm that, given $(\mathbf{R}, \mathsf{p}, \mathsf{crs}, \mathsf{z}, \pi)$, returns either 0 (reject) or 1 (accept).

Simulator: Sim is a probabilistic algorithm that, given $(\mathbf{R}, \mathsf{p}, \mathsf{crs}, \mathsf{td}, \mathsf{z})$, outputs an argument π.

A NIZK argument system must satisfy completeness (an honest verifier accepts an honest prover), knowledge-soundness (if a prover makes an honest verifier accept, then one can extract from the prover a witness wit), and zero-knowledge (there exists a simulator that, knowing CRS trapdoor but not the witness, can produce accepting statements with the verifier's view being indistinguishable from the view when interacting with an honest prover). See the full version [34] for formal definitions. A *SNARK (succinct non-interactive argument of knowledge,* [20,23,24,31–33]*)* is a NIZK argument system where the argument is sublinear in the input size.

Functional Commitment Schemes. Let $\mathcal{D}$ be some domain. In a functional commitment scheme for a circuit $\mathcal{C} : \mathcal{D}^{\mu_\alpha} \times \mathcal{D}^{\mu_\beta} \to \mathcal{D}^\kappa$, one first commits to a vector $\boldsymbol{\alpha} \in \mathcal{D}^{\mu_\alpha}$, obtaining a functional commitment C. The goal is to allow the committer to later open C to $\boldsymbol{\xi} = \mathcal{C}(\boldsymbol{\alpha}, \boldsymbol{\beta}) \in \mathcal{D}^\kappa$, where $\boldsymbol{\beta} \in \mathcal{D}^{\mu_\beta}$ is a public input that is chosen by the verifier before the opening. We generalize the notion of functional commitment, given in [29], from inner products to arbitrary circuits. Compared to [29], we also provide a stronger hiding definition.

Let $\mathbf{CC}$ be a class of circuits $\mathcal{C} : \mathcal{D}^{\mu_\alpha} \times \mathcal{D}^{\mu_\beta} \to \mathcal{D}^\kappa$. A *functional commitment scheme* FC *for* $\mathbf{CC}$ is a tuple of four (possibly probabilistic) polynomial time algorithms $(\mathsf{KC}, \mathsf{com}, \mathsf{open}, \mathsf{V})$, where

Commitment-key generator: $\mathsf{KC}(1^\lambda, \mathcal{C})$ is a probabilistic algorithm that, given a security parameter $\lambda \in \mathbb{N}$ and a circuit $\mathcal{C} \in \mathbf{CC}$, outputs a commitment key ck and a trapdoor key tk. We implicitly assume 1^λ and $\mathcal{C}$ are described by ck.

Commitment: $\mathsf{com}(\mathsf{ck}, \boldsymbol{\alpha}; r)$ is a probabilistic algorithm that takes as input the commitment key ck, a message vector $\boldsymbol{\alpha} \in \mathcal{D}^{\mu_\alpha}$ and some randomizer r. It outputs (C, D), where C is a commitment to $\boldsymbol{\alpha}$ and D is a decommitment information. We denote the first output C of $\mathsf{com}(\mathsf{ck}; \boldsymbol{\alpha}; r)$ by $\mathsf{com}_1(\mathsf{ck}; \boldsymbol{\alpha}; r)$.

Opening: $\mathsf{open}(\mathsf{ck}, C, D, \boldsymbol{\beta})$ is a deterministic algorithm that takes as input the commitment key ck, a commitment C (to $\boldsymbol{\alpha}$), a decommitment information D, and a vector $\boldsymbol{\beta} \in \mathcal{D}^{\mu_\beta}$. Assume that the ith output value of the circuit $\mathcal{C}$ is $\mathcal{F}_i(\boldsymbol{\alpha}, \boldsymbol{\beta})$, where $\mathcal{F}_i$ is a public function. It computes an opening $\mathsf{op}_{\boldsymbol{\xi}}$ to $\boldsymbol{\xi} = \mathcal{F}(\boldsymbol{\alpha}, \boldsymbol{\beta}) := (\mathcal{F}_i(\boldsymbol{\alpha}, \boldsymbol{\beta}))_{i=1}^{\kappa}$.

Verification: $\mathsf{V}(\mathsf{ck}, C, \mathsf{op}_{\boldsymbol{\xi}}, \boldsymbol{\beta}, \boldsymbol{\xi})$ is a deterministic algorithm that takes as input the commitment key ck, a commitment C, an opening $\mathsf{op}_{\boldsymbol{\xi}}$, a vector $\boldsymbol{\beta} \in \mathcal{D}^{\mu_\beta}$, and $\boldsymbol{\xi} \in \mathcal{D}^{\kappa}$. It outputs 1 if $\mathsf{op}_{\boldsymbol{\xi}}$ is a valid opening for C being a commitment to some $\boldsymbol{\alpha} \in \mathcal{D}^{\mu_\alpha}$ such that $\mathcal{F}_i(\boldsymbol{\alpha}, \boldsymbol{\beta}) = \boldsymbol{\xi}$ and outputs 0 otherwise.

Security of FC. Next, we give three definitions of the hiding property for FC schemes of increasing strength. The first definition corresponds to the definition of hiding given in [29] and essentially states that commitments do not reveal any information about $\boldsymbol{\alpha}$. The other two definitions seem to be novel at least in the context of general FC. We provide all three definitions, since in some applications, a weaker definition might be sufficient. Moreover, the third definition (zero-knowledge) makes only sense in the CRS model; in a CRS-less model, one can rely on the open-hiding property.

Definition 2 (Perfect com-hiding). *A functional commitment scheme* $\mathsf{FC} = (\mathsf{KC}, \mathsf{com}, \mathsf{open}, \mathsf{V})$ *for circuit class* $\mathbf{CC}$ *is* perfectly hiding *if for any* λ, $\mathcal{C} \in \mathbf{CC}$, $(\mathsf{ck}, \mathsf{tk}) \leftarrow \mathsf{KC}(1^\lambda, \mathcal{C})$, *for all* $\boldsymbol{\alpha}_1, \boldsymbol{\alpha}_2 \in \mathcal{D}^{\mu_\alpha}$ *with* $\boldsymbol{\alpha}_1 \neq \boldsymbol{\alpha}_2$, *the two distributions* δ_1 *and* δ_2 *are identical, where*

$$\delta_b := \{(\mathsf{ck}, C_b) : r \leftarrow_{\$} \mathsf{RND}_\lambda(\mathsf{com}); (C_b, D_b) \leftarrow \mathsf{com}(\mathsf{ck}, \boldsymbol{\alpha}_b; r)\} \ .$$

The open-hiding property is considerably stronger, stating that the commitment and the openings together do not reveal more information on $\boldsymbol{\alpha}$ than the values $\mathcal{C}(\boldsymbol{\alpha}, \boldsymbol{\beta}_i)$ on queried values $\boldsymbol{\beta}_i$. Trivial non-succinct FC schemes, where one uses a perfectly-hiding commitment scheme to commit to $\boldsymbol{\beta}$, and then in the opening phase, opens the whole database, are com-hiding but not open-hiding.

Definition 3 (Perfect open-hiding). *A functional commitment scheme* $\mathsf{FC} = (\mathsf{KC}, \mathsf{com}, \mathsf{open}, \mathsf{V})$ *for circuit class* $\mathbf{CC}$ *is* perfectly open-hiding *if for any* λ, $\mathcal{C} \in \mathbf{CC}$, $(\mathsf{ck}, \mathsf{tk}) \leftarrow \mathsf{KC}(1^\lambda, \mathcal{C})$, *for all* $\boldsymbol{\alpha}_1, \boldsymbol{\alpha}_2 \in \mathcal{D}^{\mu_\alpha}$ *with* $\boldsymbol{\alpha}_1 \neq \boldsymbol{\alpha}_2$, *and* $Q = \mathsf{poly}(\lambda)$ *of* $\boldsymbol{\beta}_i$ *such that* $\mathcal{C}(\boldsymbol{\alpha}_1, \boldsymbol{\beta}_i) = \mathcal{C}(\boldsymbol{\alpha}_2, \boldsymbol{\beta}_i)$ *for all* $i \leq Q$, *the two distributions* δ_1 *and* δ_2 *are identical, where* $\delta_b :=$

$$\{(\mathsf{ck}, C_b, \{\mathsf{open}(\mathsf{ck}, C_b, D_b, \boldsymbol{\beta}_i)\}) : r \leftarrow_{\$} \mathsf{RND}_\lambda(\mathsf{com}); (C_b, D_b) \leftarrow \mathsf{com}(\mathsf{ck}, \boldsymbol{\alpha}_b; r)\} \ .$$

Finally, zero-knowledge FC schemes have simulation-based hiding. While simulation-based security is a gold standard in cryptography, it is usually more complicated to achieve than game-based security. In particular, one needs to have a trusted ck (and its trapdoor) to achieve zero-knowledge. We will leave it as an open problem whether one can use instead the much weaker bare public key (BPK) model, by using the techniques of [1,2,4,18]. Note that [33] showed that their SNARKs are all secure in the BPK model.

Definition 4 (Perfect zero-knowledge). *An FC scheme* $\mathsf{FC} = (\mathsf{KC}, \mathsf{com}, \mathsf{open}, \mathsf{V})$ *for* **CC** *is* perfectly zero-knowledge *if there exists a PPT simulator* Sim, *such that for all* λ, *all* $\mathcal{C} \in \mathbf{CC}$, $(\mathsf{ck}, \mathsf{tk}) \leftarrow \mathsf{KC}(1^\lambda, \mathcal{C})$, *for all* $\boldsymbol{\alpha} \in \mathcal{D}^{\mu_\alpha}$, *for any poly-size set of* $\boldsymbol{\beta}_i$, δ_0 *and* δ_1 *are identical, where*

$$\delta_0 := \{(\mathsf{ck}, C, \{\mathsf{open}(\mathsf{ck}, C, D, \boldsymbol{\beta}_i)\}) : r \leftarrow_{\$} \mathsf{RND}_\lambda(\mathsf{com}); (C, D) \leftarrow \mathsf{com}(\mathsf{ck}, \boldsymbol{\alpha}; r)\} \ ,$$
$$\delta_1 := \{(\mathsf{ck}, \mathsf{Sim}(\mathsf{ck}, \mathsf{td}, \{\boldsymbol{\beta}_i\}, \{\mathcal{C}(\boldsymbol{\alpha}, \boldsymbol{\beta}_i)\}))\} \ .$$

Next, we will define evaluation-binding. Evaluation-binding can be weaker than binding, but sometimes the two notions are equivalent. (Consider the case of the inner product when the adversary asks the committer to open a commitment for $\boldsymbol{\beta} = \boldsymbol{e}_i$ for each i). In the context of FC schemes, evaluation-binding is *the* distinguishing security notion.

Definition 5 (Computational evaluation-binding). *A functional commitment scheme* $\mathsf{FC} = (\mathsf{KC}, \mathsf{com}, \mathsf{open}, \mathsf{V})$ *for circuit class* **CC** *is* computationally evaluation-binding *if for any* λ, $\mathcal{C} \in \mathbf{CC}$, *and a non-uniform PPT adversary* $\mathcal{A}$, $\mathsf{Adv}^{\mathsf{bind}}_{\mathsf{FC},\lambda,\mathcal{C},\mathcal{A}}(\lambda) = \mathsf{negl}(\lambda)$, *where* $\mathsf{Adv}^{\mathsf{bind}}_{\mathsf{FC},\lambda,\mathcal{C},\mathcal{A}}(\lambda) :=$

$$\Pr\left[\begin{array}{l}(\mathsf{ck}, \mathsf{tk}) \leftarrow \mathsf{KC}(1^\lambda, \mathcal{C}); (C, \boldsymbol{\beta}, \boldsymbol{\xi}, \mathrm{op}_{\boldsymbol{\xi}}, \widetilde{\boldsymbol{\xi}}, \widetilde{\mathrm{op}}_{\boldsymbol{\xi}}) \leftarrow \mathcal{A}(\mathsf{ck}) : \boldsymbol{\beta} \in \mathcal{D}^{\mu_\beta} \wedge \\ \boldsymbol{\xi} \neq \widetilde{\boldsymbol{\xi}} \in \mathcal{D}^{\kappa} \wedge \mathsf{V}(\mathsf{ck}, C, \mathrm{op}_{\boldsymbol{\xi}}, \boldsymbol{\beta}, \boldsymbol{\xi}) = \mathsf{V}(\mathsf{ck}, C, \widetilde{\mathrm{op}}_{\boldsymbol{\xi}}, \boldsymbol{\beta}, \widetilde{\boldsymbol{\xi}}) = 1\end{array}\right] \ .$$

An FC scheme is *succinct* (SFC), if both the commitments and openings have length that is polylogarithmic in $|\boldsymbol{\alpha}|$ and $|\boldsymbol{\beta}|$.

3 The New SFC Scheme

In this section, we will construct a succinct functional commitment (SFC) scheme for (almost) all polynomial-size arithmetic circuits by mixing techniques from SNARKs with original ideas, needed to construct a SFC scheme. Let $\mathfrak{F}$ be a fixed vector function that takes inputs from two parties, the committer and the verifier. Let α_j be private inputs of the committer, used when committing. Let β_j be public inputs of the verifier, used when opening the commitment.

Let $\mathcal{C}$ be an arithmetic circuit that inputs α_j and β_j and computes $\mathfrak{F}(\boldsymbol{\alpha}, \boldsymbol{\beta}) = (\mathfrak{F}_i(\boldsymbol{\alpha}, \boldsymbol{\beta}))_{i=1}^{\kappa}$, where $\boldsymbol{\alpha}$ is the private input of the committer and $\boldsymbol{\beta}$ is chosen by the verifier, possibly only later. We compile $\mathcal{C}$ to a circuit $\mathcal{C}^*$ that consists of four subcircuits $\mathcal{C}_\phi$, $\mathcal{C}_\psi$, $\mathcal{C}_\chi$ and $\mathcal{C}_\xi$. We need the division to four subcircuits to prove evaluation-binding; we will give more details later.

After that, we use the QAP-representation [20] (more precisely, the approach of [33]) of arithmetic circuits, obtaining polynomials $\mathsf{A}(X, Y)$, $\mathsf{B}(X, Y)$ (the "commitment polynomials" to all left/right inputs of all gates of $\mathcal{C}^*$, correspondingly), and $\mathsf{C}(X, Y)$ (the "opening polynomial"), such that $\mathsf{C}(X, Y)$ is in the linear span of the "polynomial commitment key" $\mathsf{ck}_1 = (\varrho(X,Y) : \varrho \in \mathcal{R})$ if and only if the committer was honest. The circuit compilation allows us to divide the polynomials to "private" parts (transmitted during the commitment) and "public" parts (trasmitted during the opening), such that one can, given two different openings for the same commitment, break a computational assumption. We then use SNARK-based techniques to construct the SFC for $\mathcal{C}^*$ with succinct commitment and opening. We postpone security proofs to Sect. 5; we currently emphasize that the evaluation-binding proof is novel (in particular, not related to the knowledge-soundness proofs of SNARKs at all).

Circuit Compilation. Let $\mathcal{C}$ be a polynomial-size arithmetic circuit that, on input $(\boldsymbol{\alpha}, \boldsymbol{\beta})$, outputs $\boldsymbol{\xi} = \boldsymbol{\mathfrak{F}}(\boldsymbol{\alpha}, \boldsymbol{\beta}) = (\mathfrak{F}_i(\boldsymbol{\alpha}, \boldsymbol{\beta}))_{i=1}^{\kappa}$. We compile $\mathcal{C}$ to a *compiled circuit* $\mathcal{C}^*$, see Fig. 1, that consists of the public subcircuits $\mathcal{C}_\phi$, $\mathcal{C}_\psi$, $\mathcal{C}_\chi$, and $\mathcal{C}_\xi$ that are combined as follows. In the commitment phase, the committer uses the circuit $\mathcal{C}_\phi$ to compute a number of polynomials $\phi_i(\boldsymbol{\alpha})$ depending on only 1 and $\boldsymbol{\alpha}$. More precisely, $\boldsymbol{\phi}(\boldsymbol{\alpha}) = (\phi_1(\boldsymbol{\alpha}), \ldots, \phi_{\mu_\phi}(\boldsymbol{\alpha}))$ denotes the set of the outputs of all (including intermediate) gates in $\mathcal{C}_\phi$ (the same is the case of other circuits and corresponding polynomials). The commitment depends only on 1, $\boldsymbol{\alpha}$, and $\boldsymbol{\phi}(\boldsymbol{\alpha})$. In the opening phase, the verifier sends $\boldsymbol{\beta}$ to the committer, who uses the circuit $\mathcal{C}_\psi$ to compute some polynomials $\psi_i(\boldsymbol{\beta})$ depending on 1 and $\boldsymbol{\beta}$. This part of the computation is public and can be redone by the verifier.

After that, the committer uses the circuit $\mathcal{C}_\chi$ to compute a number of polynomials $\chi_i(\boldsymbol{\alpha}, \boldsymbol{\beta})$ from the inputs and outputs of $\mathcal{C}_\phi$ and $\mathcal{C}_\psi$, i.e., from $(1, \boldsymbol{\alpha}, \boldsymbol{\beta}, \boldsymbol{\phi}(\boldsymbol{\alpha}), \boldsymbol{\psi}(\boldsymbol{\beta}))$. $\mathcal{C}_\chi$ has multiplicative depth 1, and thus, w.l.o.g., each $\chi_i(\boldsymbol{\alpha}, \boldsymbol{\beta})$ is a product of some $\phi_j(\boldsymbol{\alpha})$ with some $\psi_k(\boldsymbol{\beta})$. Finally, the committer uses $\mathcal{C}_\xi$ to compute the outputs $\mathfrak{F}_i(\boldsymbol{\alpha}, \boldsymbol{\beta})$ of $\mathcal{C}^*$. We will explain the need for such compilation after Eqs. (7) and (8). We will summarize all actual restrictions on the circuits in Theorem 1. In the introduction, we gave an intuitive explanation of how this compilation reduces the circuit class that we can handle. See Sect. 4 for an additional discussion on the power of this circuit class.

Next, let $\mathbf{a} \in \mathbb{Z}_p^{\mu}$ be the value of all wires of $\mathcal{C}^*$. We write

$$\mathbf{a} = 1 // \boldsymbol{\alpha} // \boldsymbol{\phi}(\boldsymbol{\alpha}) // \boldsymbol{\beta} // \boldsymbol{\psi}(\boldsymbol{\beta}) // \boldsymbol{\chi}(\boldsymbol{\alpha}, \boldsymbol{\beta}) // \boldsymbol{\mathfrak{F}}(\boldsymbol{\alpha}, \boldsymbol{\beta}) \ . \tag{3}$$

Here, $\boldsymbol{\alpha} \in \mathbb{Z}_p^{\mu_\alpha}$, $\boldsymbol{\phi}(\boldsymbol{\alpha}) \in \mathbb{Z}_p^{\mu_\phi}$, $\boldsymbol{\beta} \in \mathbb{Z}_p^{\mu_\beta}$, $\boldsymbol{\psi}(\boldsymbol{\beta}) \in \mathbb{Z}_p^{\mu_\psi}$, $\boldsymbol{\chi}(\boldsymbol{\alpha}, \boldsymbol{\beta}) \in \mathbb{Z}_p^{\mu_\chi}$, and $\boldsymbol{\mathfrak{F}}(\boldsymbol{\alpha}, \boldsymbol{\beta}) \in \mathbb{Z}_p^{\kappa}$. Thus, $\mu = 1 + \mu_\alpha + \mu_\beta + \mu_\phi + \mu_\psi + \mu_\chi + \kappa$. To use the RC1S approach, we construct matrices U, V, and W, such that $U\mathbf{a} \circ V\mathbf{a} = W\mathbf{a}$ iff $\mathcal{C}^*$ is correctly computed. Let $\boldsymbol{\alpha}^* = (1 // \boldsymbol{\alpha} // \boldsymbol{\phi}(\boldsymbol{\alpha})) \in \mathbb{Z}_p^{1+\mu_\alpha+\mu_\phi}$ and $\boldsymbol{\beta}^* = (1 // \boldsymbol{\beta} // \boldsymbol{\psi}(\boldsymbol{\beta})) \in \mathbb{Z}_p^{1+\mu_\beta+\mu_\psi}$. First, we define R1CS-matrices $U_\phi, U_\psi, U_\chi, U_\xi, V_\phi, V_\psi, V_\chi$ such that (various subcircuits of) $\mathcal{C}^*$ are correctly computed iff

$$\begin{gathered} U_\phi \boldsymbol{\alpha}^* \circ V_\phi \boldsymbol{\alpha}^* = \boldsymbol{\phi}(\boldsymbol{\alpha}) \ , \quad U_\psi \boldsymbol{\beta}^* \circ V_\psi \boldsymbol{\beta}^* = \boldsymbol{\psi}(\boldsymbol{\beta}) \ , \\ U_\chi \begin{pmatrix} \boldsymbol{\alpha}^* \\ \boldsymbol{\beta} \\ \boldsymbol{\psi}(\boldsymbol{\beta}) \end{pmatrix} \circ V_\chi \begin{pmatrix} \boldsymbol{\alpha}^* \\ \boldsymbol{\beta} \\ \boldsymbol{\psi}(\boldsymbol{\beta}) \end{pmatrix} = \boldsymbol{\chi}(\boldsymbol{\alpha}, \boldsymbol{\beta}) \ , \quad U_\xi \boldsymbol{\chi}(\boldsymbol{\alpha}, \boldsymbol{\beta}) \circ \mathbf{1} = \boldsymbol{\mathfrak{F}}(\boldsymbol{\alpha}, \boldsymbol{\beta}) \ . \end{gathered} \tag{4}$$

Here, $U_\phi, V_\phi \in \mathbb{Z}_p^{\mu_\phi \times (1+\mu_\alpha+\mu_\phi)}$, $U_\psi, V_\psi \in \mathbb{Z}_p^{\mu_\psi \times (1+\mu_\beta+\mu_\psi)}$, $U_\chi, V_\chi \in \mathbb{Z}_p^{\mu_\chi \times (1+\mu_\alpha+\mu_\beta+\mu_\phi+\mu_\psi)}$, and $U_\xi \in \mathbb{Z}_p^{\kappa \times \mu_\chi}$. In particular,

$$\mathcal{F}_i(\boldsymbol{\alpha}, \boldsymbol{\beta}) = \sum_{j=1}^{\mu_\chi} U_{\xi ij} \chi_j(\boldsymbol{\alpha}, \boldsymbol{\beta}) \ , \quad i \in [1 \mathinner{..} \kappa] \ . \tag{5}$$

Next, we define $U, V, W \in \mathbb{Z}_p^{\nu \times \mu}$, as

$$\left(\begin{array}{c|c|c|c|c|c|c}
1 & \boldsymbol{\alpha} & \boldsymbol{\phi}(\boldsymbol{\alpha}) & \boldsymbol{\beta} & \boldsymbol{\psi}(\boldsymbol{\beta}) & \boldsymbol{\chi}(\boldsymbol{\alpha},\boldsymbol{\beta}) & \boldsymbol{\mathcal{F}}(\boldsymbol{\alpha},\boldsymbol{\beta}) \\ \hline\hline
\multicolumn{3}{c|}{U_\phi} & & & & \\ \hline
U_\psi & & & \multicolumn{2}{c|}{U_\psi} & & \\ \hline
\multicolumn{5}{c|}{U_\chi} & & \\ \hline
 & & & & & U_\xi & \\ \hline
\end{array}\right)
\left(\begin{array}{c|c|c|c|c|c|c}
1 & \boldsymbol{\alpha} & \boldsymbol{\phi}(\boldsymbol{\alpha}) & \boldsymbol{\beta} & \boldsymbol{\psi}(\boldsymbol{\beta}) & \boldsymbol{\chi}(\boldsymbol{\alpha},\boldsymbol{\beta}) & \boldsymbol{\mathcal{F}}(\boldsymbol{\alpha},\boldsymbol{\beta}) \\ \hline\hline
\multicolumn{3}{c|}{V_\phi} & & & & \\ \hline
V_\psi & & & \multicolumn{2}{c|}{V_\psi} & & \\ \hline
\multicolumn{5}{c|}{V_\chi} & & \\ \hline
\mathbf{1}_\kappa & & & & & & \\ \hline
\end{array}\right)
\left(\begin{array}{c|c|c|c|c|c|c}
1 & \boldsymbol{\alpha} & \boldsymbol{\phi}(\boldsymbol{\alpha}) & \boldsymbol{\beta} & \boldsymbol{\psi}(\boldsymbol{\beta}) & \boldsymbol{\chi}(\boldsymbol{\alpha},\boldsymbol{\beta}) & \boldsymbol{\mathcal{F}}(\boldsymbol{\alpha},\boldsymbol{\beta}) \\ \hline\hline
 & & I_{\mu_\phi} & & & & \\ \hline
 & & & & I_{\mu_\psi} & & \\ \hline
 & & & & & I_{\mu_\chi} & \\ \hline
 & & & & & & I_\kappa \\ \hline
\end{array}\right) \tag{6}$$

correspondingly. Clearly, $\nu := \mu_\phi + \mu_\psi + \mu_\chi + \kappa$. Here, we labeled vertically each column of each matrix by the supposed value of the corresponding coefficients of $\mathsf{a} = 1 // \boldsymbol{\alpha} // \dots // \boldsymbol{\mathcal{F}}(\boldsymbol{\alpha}, \boldsymbol{\beta})$. Some submatrices ($U_\psi$ and V_ψ) are divided between non-continuous areas. The empty submatrices are all-zero in the compiled instance. Clearly, $U\mathsf{a} \circ V\mathsf{a} = W\mathsf{a}$ iff Eq. (4) holds.

QAP Representation. Recall that $\ell_i(X) \in \mathbb{Z}_p^{(\leq \nu-1)}[X]$, $i \in [1 \mathinner{..} \nu]$, interpolates the ν-dimensional unit vector $\boldsymbol{e}_i$. To obtain a QAP representation of the equation $U\mathsf{a} \circ V\mathsf{a} = W\mathsf{a}$, we use interpolating polynomials; e.g., $u_j(X)$ interpolates the jth column of U. (See Sect. 2.) To simplify notation, we introduce polynomials like $u_{\phi j}(X)$ and $u_{\chi j}(X)$, where say $u_{\chi j}(X)$ interpolates (*all* ν *rows of the*) the jth column of the $\nu \times (1 + \mu_\alpha + \mu_\beta + \mu_\phi + \mu_\psi)$ submatrix of U that contains U_χ. E.g., $u_{\chi j}(X)$ interpolates the jth column of U_χ (preceded and followed by 0 rows), $u_{\chi j}(X) = \sum_{i=1}^{\mu_\chi} U_{\chi ij} \ell_{\mu_\phi+\mu_\psi+i}(X)$.

We divide the polynomials $u(X)$ and $v(X)$ into two addends: one polynomial (u_s, v_s, resp.) that depends on $\boldsymbol{\alpha}$ but not on $\boldsymbol{\beta}$, and another polynomial (u_p, v_p, resp.) that depends on public values ($\boldsymbol{\beta}$ and $\{\mathcal{F}_i(\boldsymbol{\alpha}, \boldsymbol{\beta})\}$) but not on $\boldsymbol{\alpha}$ otherwise. Such a division is possible due to the way $\mathcal{C}^*$ is composed from the subcircuits. Thus, $u(X) = \sum_{j=1}^{\mu} \mathsf{a}_j u_j(X) = u_s(X) + u_p(X)$ and $v(X) = \sum_{j=1}^{\mu} \mathsf{a}_j v_j(X) = v_s(X) + v_p(X)$, where

$$\begin{aligned}
u_s(X) &= \textstyle\sum_{j=2}^{\mu_\alpha+\mu_\phi+1} \mathsf{a}_j u_j(X) \\
&= \textstyle\sum_{j=1}^{\mu_\alpha} \alpha_j (u_{\phi,1+j}(X) + u_{\chi,1+j}(X)) + \\
&\quad \textstyle\sum_{j=1}^{\mu_\phi} \phi_j(\boldsymbol{\alpha})(u_{\phi,1+\mu_\alpha+j}(X) + u_{\chi,1+\mu_\alpha+j}(X)) \ , \\
u_p(X) &= u_1(X) + \textstyle\sum_{j=\mu_\alpha+\mu_\phi+2}^{\mu} \mathsf{a}_j u_j(X) \\
&= u_1(X) + \textstyle\sum_{j=1}^{\mu_\beta} \beta_j (u_{\psi,1+j}(X) + u_{\chi,1+\mu_\alpha+\mu_\phi+j}(X)) + \\
&\quad \textstyle\sum_{j=1}^{\mu_\psi} \psi_j(\boldsymbol{\beta})(u_{\psi,1+\mu_\beta+j}(X) + u_{\chi,1+\mu_\alpha+\mu_\phi+\mu_\beta+j}(X)) + \\
&\quad \underbrace{\textstyle\sum_{j=1}^{\mu_\chi} \chi_j(\boldsymbol{\alpha}, \boldsymbol{\beta}) u_{\xi,1+j}(X)}_{=\sum_{i=1}^{\kappa} \mathcal{F}_i(\boldsymbol{\alpha},\boldsymbol{\beta}) \ell_{\nu-\kappa+i}(X)} \ ,
\end{aligned} \tag{7}$$

and

$$\begin{aligned} v_s(X) &= \textstyle\sum_{j=2}^{\mu_\alpha+\mu_\phi+1} \mathsf{a}_j v_j(X) \\ &= \textstyle\sum_{j=1}^{\mu_\alpha} \alpha_j (v_{\phi,1+j}(X) + v_{\chi,1+j}(X)) + \\ &\quad \textstyle\sum_{j=1}^{\mu_\phi} \phi_j(\boldsymbol{\alpha})(v_{\phi,1+\mu_\alpha+j}(X) + v_{\chi,1+\mu_\alpha+j}(X)) , \\ v_p(X) &= \mathsf{a}_1 v_1(X) + \textstyle\sum_{j=\mu_\alpha+\mu_\phi+2}^{\mu} \mathsf{a}_j v_j(X) \\ &= v_1(X) + \textstyle\sum_{j=1}^{\mu_\beta} \beta_j \left(v_{\psi,1+j}(X) + v_{\chi,1+\mu_\alpha+\mu_\phi+j}(X)\right) + \\ &\quad \textstyle\sum_{j=1}^{\mu_\psi} \psi_j(\boldsymbol{\beta})(v_{\psi,1+\mu_\beta+j}(X) + v_{\chi,1+\mu_\alpha+\mu_\phi+\mu_\beta+j}(X)) . \end{aligned} \tag{8}$$

(In particular, recall that $\mathsf{a}_1 = 1$.) Here, $u_1(X) = u_{\phi 1}(X) + u_{\psi 1}(X) + u_{\chi 1}(X)$ and $v_1(X) = v_{\phi 1}(X) + v_{\psi 1}(X) + v_{\chi 1}(X) + \sum_{i=1}^{\kappa} \ell_{\nu-\kappa+i}(X)$. The concrete shape of all these polynomials follows from Eqs. (3) and (6).

In Theorems 2 and 3 (see their claims and proofs), we will need several conditions to hold. Next, we will state and prove that these conditions hold for $\mathcal{C}^*$. One can observe directly that most of the guarantees, given by $\mathcal{C}^*$ about the shape of U, V, W, are actually required by the following conditions. Since the addition of the circuit $\mathcal{C}_\xi$ is essentially for free (it only means the addition of κ gates), many of the following conditions are very easy to satisfy; we will denote such conditions by a superscript + as in (a)$^+$. *We emphasize that the only restrictive conditions are Items i and j that basically state that $\mathcal{C}_\chi$ can only have multiplicative depth* 1. (See Remark 1 for discussion.) That is, the new SFC scheme will work for all circuits $\mathcal{C}$ that have a polynomial-size compiled circuit $\mathcal{C}^*$, such that $\mathcal{C}_\chi$ has multiplicative depth 1.

Theorem 1. *Let $\mathcal{C}$ be an arithmetic circuit and let $\mathcal{C}^*$ be its compiled version, so that U, V, W are defined as in Eq.* (6). *Then the following holds.*

(a)$^+$ For $j \in [1 \mathinner{..} \mu - \kappa]$: if $\boldsymbol{W}^{(j)} = \mathbf{0}$ then $U_{\nu-\kappa+i,j} = 0$ for $i \in [1 \mathinner{..} \kappa]$.
(b)$^+$ For $I \in [1 \mathinner{..} \kappa]$ and $j \in [1 \mathinner{..} \mu - \kappa]$, $W_{\nu-\kappa+I,j} = 0$.
(c)$^+$ For $j \in [2 \mathinner{..} 1 + \mu_\alpha + \mu_\phi]$, $v_{\phi j}(X), v_{\chi j}(X)$ are in the span of $(\ell_i(X))_{i=1}^{\nu-\kappa}$.
(d)$^+$ For $j \in [2 + \mu_\alpha + \mu_\phi \mathinner{..} \mu]$, $v_1(X) - \sum_{i=1}^{\kappa} \ell_{\nu-\kappa+i}(X)$ and $v_j(X)$ are in the span of $(\ell_i(X))_{i=1}^{\nu-\kappa}$.
(e)$^+$ For $j \in [\mu - \kappa \mathinner{..} \mu]$, $\boldsymbol{U}^{(j)} = \mathbf{0}$.
(f)$^+$ For $j \in [\mu - \kappa \mathinner{..} \mu]$, $\boldsymbol{V}^{(j)} = \mathbf{0}$.
(g)$^+$ For $i \in [1 \mathinner{..} \kappa]$, $w_{\mu-\kappa+i}(X) = \ell_{\nu-\kappa+i}(X)$.
(h) The set of non-zero $\boldsymbol{W}^{(j)}$, $j \in [1 \mathinner{..} \mu - \kappa]$, is linearly independent.
(i) For $j \in [\mu - \mu_\chi - \kappa + 1 \mathinner{..} \mu - \kappa]$, $U_{ij} = 0$ if $i \leq \nu - \kappa$, while the last κ rows of this column range define a matrix U_ξ that satisfies Eq. (4).
(j) For $j \in [\mu - \mu_\chi - \kappa + 1 \mathinner{..} \mu - \kappa]$, $\boldsymbol{V}^{(j)} = \mathbf{0}$.

Proof. First, we summarize the requirements, denoting each submatrix of U, V, and W by the number of condition that ascertains that this submatrix is 0 (or has a well-defined non-zero form); moreover, Item h states that the columns of W, that contain identity matrices, are linearly independent. That is, $U, V, W =$

$$
\left(\begin{array}{c|c|c|c|c|c|c}
\mathbf{1} & \boldsymbol{\alpha} & \boldsymbol{\phi}(\boldsymbol{\alpha}) & \boldsymbol{\beta} & \boldsymbol{\psi}(\boldsymbol{\beta}) & \boldsymbol{\chi}(\boldsymbol{\alpha},\boldsymbol{\beta}) & \boldsymbol{\mathfrak{F}}(\boldsymbol{\alpha},\boldsymbol{\beta}) \\ \hline
\multicolumn{3}{c|}{U_\phi} & & & i & e \\ \hline
U_\psi & & & \multicolumn{2}{c|}{U_\psi} & i & e \\ \hline
\multicolumn{5}{c|}{U_\chi} & i & e \\ \hline
a & a & & a & & U_\xi i & e
\end{array}\right)
\left(\begin{array}{c|c|c|c|c|c|c}
\mathbf{1} & \boldsymbol{\alpha} & \boldsymbol{\phi}(\boldsymbol{\alpha}) & \boldsymbol{\beta} & \boldsymbol{\psi}(\boldsymbol{\beta}) & \boldsymbol{\chi}(\boldsymbol{\alpha},\boldsymbol{\beta}) & \boldsymbol{\mathfrak{F}}(\boldsymbol{\alpha},\boldsymbol{\beta}) \\ \hline
\multicolumn{3}{c|}{V_\phi} & & & j & f \\ \hline
V_\psi & & & \multicolumn{2}{c|}{V_\psi} & j & f \\ \hline
\multicolumn{5}{c|}{V_\chi} & j & f \\ \hline
\mathbf{1}_\kappa d & c & c & d & d & dj & df
\end{array}\right)
\left(\begin{array}{c|c|c|c|c|c|c}
\mathbf{1} & \boldsymbol{\alpha} & \boldsymbol{\phi}(\boldsymbol{\alpha}) & \boldsymbol{\beta} & \boldsymbol{\psi}(\boldsymbol{\beta}) & \boldsymbol{\chi}(\boldsymbol{\alpha},\boldsymbol{\beta}) & \boldsymbol{\mathfrak{F}}(\boldsymbol{\alpha},\boldsymbol{\beta}) \\ \hline
 & & I_{\mu_\phi} & & & & g \\ \hline
 & & & & I_{\mu_\psi} & & g \\ \hline
 & & & & & I_{\mu_\chi} & g \\ \hline
b & b & b & b & b & b & I_\kappa g
\end{array}\right)
$$

Item a: follows since $\boldsymbol{W}^{(j)} = \mathbf{0}$ in the columns labeled by 1, $\boldsymbol{\alpha}$ and $\boldsymbol{\beta}$, and the last rows of U in all these columns are equal to 0, according to Eq. (6).

Item b: obvious from W in Eq. (6).

Item c: follows since the last rows of V, corresponding to columns labeled by $\boldsymbol{\alpha}$ and $\boldsymbol{\beta}$, are equal to 0.

Item d: follows since the last rows of V, corresponding to columns labeled by $\boldsymbol{\beta}$, $\boldsymbol{\psi}(\boldsymbol{\beta})$, $\boldsymbol{\chi}(\boldsymbol{\alpha},\boldsymbol{\beta})$, and $\boldsymbol{\mathfrak{F}}(\boldsymbol{\alpha},\boldsymbol{\beta})$, are equal to 0, and the last rows of $\boldsymbol{V}^{(1)}$ are equal to $\mathbf{1}_\kappa$.

Items e **to g, i and j:** follows from direct observation.

Item h: follows from the fact that $\boldsymbol{W}^{(j)} = \mathbf{0}$ for some columns j, and the submatrix of W that consists of the rest of the columns is an identity matrix. □

Remark 1. The compiled circuit $\mathcal{C}^*$ satisfies some conditions, not required by Theorem 1. First, by Item h, the set of non-zero $\boldsymbol{W}^{(j)}$ has to be linearly independent (not necessarily an identity matrix), while in Eq. (6), the corresponding columns constitute an identity matrix. Second, by Item a, last rows of $\boldsymbol{U}^{(j)}$ need to be zero only if $\boldsymbol{W}^{(j)}$ is 0; one can insert dummy gates to $\mathcal{C}^*$ such that W has no zero columns. This essentially just corresponds to the fact that we start with an arithmetic circuit and each constraint is about a concrete gate being correctly evaluated. Third, several submatrices of U, V, W are all-zero in our template while there is no actual need for that. For example, U_ξ can be generalized, and U_ϕ and U_ψ can also both depend on $\boldsymbol{\alpha}$ and $\boldsymbol{\beta}$. For the sake of simplicity, we stick to the presented compilation process, and leave the possible generalizations to future work.

SNARK-Related Techniques. Next, we follow [33] to derive polynomials related to the SNARK, underlying the new SFC. We simplify the derivation a bit, and refer to [33] for full generality. Let $\mathsf{A}(X,Y) = r_a + u(X)Y$ and $\mathsf{B}(X,Y) = r_b + v(X)Y$ for $r_a, r_b \leftarrow_\$ \mathbb{Z}_p$. ([33] considered the general case where $\mathsf{A}(X,Y) = r_a Y^\alpha + u(X)Y^\beta$ and $\mathsf{B}(X,Y) = r_b Y^\alpha + v(X)Y^\beta$ for some small integers α, β to be fixed later). The addends r_a and r_b are needed to protect the secret information hidden by $\mathsf{A}(X,Y)$ and $\mathsf{B}(X,Y)$, and we use the indeterminate Y to simplify the security proofs. As with u and w, we divide the polynomials $\mathsf{A}, \mathsf{B}, \mathsf{C}$ into two addends: (i) a polynomial (A_s, B_s, C_{sp}), where A_s and B_s depend on $\boldsymbol{\alpha}$ but not on $\boldsymbol{\beta}$ while C_{sp} depends on both $\boldsymbol{\alpha}$ and $\boldsymbol{\beta}$, and (ii) a polynomial ($\mathsf{A}_p, \mathsf{B}_p, \mathsf{C}_p$, resp.) that depends on public values ($\boldsymbol{\beta}$ and $\{\mathfrak{F}_i(\boldsymbol{\alpha},\boldsymbol{\beta})\}$) but not on $\boldsymbol{\alpha}$ otherwise.

(Such a division was not possible in [33] since there one did not work with a compiled circuit $\mathcal{C}^*$.) Then,

$$\begin{aligned}\mathsf{A}_s(X,Y) &= r_a + u_s(X)Y\ , & \mathsf{A}_p(X,Y) &= u_p(X)Y\ ,\\ \mathsf{B}_s(X,Y) &= r_b + v_s(X)Y\ , & \mathsf{B}_p(X,Y) &= v_p(X)Y\ .\end{aligned} \tag{9}$$

For integer constants δ and η that we will fix later, define

$$\begin{aligned}\mathsf{C}(X,Y) &= (\mathsf{A}(X,Y) + Y^\delta)(\mathsf{B}(X,Y) + Y^\eta) - Y^{\delta+\eta}\\ &= (r_a + u(X)Y + Y^\delta)(r_b + v(X)Y + Y^\eta) - Y^{\delta+\eta}\\ &= r_a(v(X)Y + Y^\eta) + r_b(\mathsf{A}(X,Y) + Y^\delta) + (u(X)v(X) - w(X))Y^2 +\\ &\quad u(X)Y^{\eta+1} + v(X)Y^{\delta+1} + w(X)Y^2\\ &= r_a(v(X)Y + Y^\eta) + r_b(\mathsf{A}(X,Y) + Y^\delta) + \mathcal{H}(X)\ell(X)Y^2 +\\ &\quad u(X)Y^{\eta+1} + v(X)Y^{\delta+1} + w(X)Y^2\ ,\end{aligned}$$

where the last equation holds iff the committer is honest (see Eq. (2)). Intuitively, we want that a committer must be able to compute $\mathsf{C}(X,Y)$ iff he was honest.

Following [33], the inclusion of Y^δ and Y^η in the definition of $\mathsf{C}(X,Y)$ serves two goals. First, it introduces the addend $u(X)Y^{\eta+1} + v(X)Y^{\delta+1} + w(X)Y^2 = \sum_{j=1}^{\mu} \mathsf{a}_j(u_j(X)Y^{\eta+1} + v_j(X)Y^{\delta+1} + w_j(X)Y^2)$ that makes it easier to verify that P uses the same coefficients α_j when computing $[\mathsf{A}]_1$, $[\mathsf{B}]_2$, and $[\mathsf{C}]_1$. Second, the coefficient of Y^2 is $u(X)v(X) - w(X)$ that divides by $\ell(X)$ iff the committer is honest. That is, the coefficient of Y^2 is $\mathcal{H}(X)\ell(X)$ for some polynomial $\mathcal{H}(X)$ iff the prover is honest and thus $\boldsymbol{\xi} = \mathfrak{F}(\boldsymbol{\alpha}, \boldsymbol{\beta})$.

Let γ be another small integer, fixed later. Let $\mathsf{C}(X,Y) = \mathsf{C}_{sp}(X,Y) + \mathsf{C}_p(X,Y)Y^\gamma$, where $\mathsf{C}_p(X,Y)$ depends only on $\boldsymbol{\xi}$. (In [33], $\mathsf{C}_{sp}(X,Y)$ was multiplied with Y^α but here $\alpha = 0$.) The factor Y^γ is used to "separate" the public and the secret parts. In the honest case,

$$\begin{aligned}\mathsf{C}_{sp}(X,Y) &= r_a(v(X)Y + Y^\eta) + r_b(\mathsf{A}(X,Y)Y + Y^\delta) +\\ &\quad \mathcal{H}(X)\ell(X)Y^2 + \textstyle\sum_{j=1}^{\mu-\kappa} \mathsf{a}_j(u_j(X)Y^{\eta+1} + v_j(X)Y^{\delta+1} + w_j(X)Y^2)\ ,\\ \mathsf{C}_p(X,Y) &= \textstyle\sum_{j=\mu-\kappa+1}^{\mu} \mathsf{a}_j(u_j(X)Y^{\eta+1-\gamma} + v_j(X)Y^{\delta+1-\gamma} + w_j(X)Y^{2-\gamma})\\ &= \textstyle\sum_{i=1}^{\kappa} \mathcal{F}_i(\boldsymbol{\alpha}, \boldsymbol{\beta})(u_{\mu-\kappa+i}(X)Y^{\eta+1-\gamma} + v_{\mu-\kappa+i}(X)Y^{\delta+1-\gamma} + w_{\mu-\kappa+i}(X)Y^{2-\gamma})\ .\end{aligned}$$

Intuitively, the verifier checks that $\mathsf{C}_{sp}(X,Y)$ is correctly computed by checking that $\mathcal{V}(X,Y) = 0$, where

$$\begin{aligned}\mathcal{V}(X,Y) := &(\mathsf{A}_s(X,Y) + \mathsf{A}_p(X,Y) + Y^\delta)(\mathsf{B}_s(X,Y) + \mathsf{B}_p(X,Y) + Y^\eta)\\ &- (\mathsf{C}_{sp}(X,Y) + \mathsf{C}_p(X,Y)Y^\gamma) - Y^{\delta+\eta}\ .\end{aligned}$$

Here, $(\mathsf{A}_s, \mathsf{B}_s)$ (the part of (A, B) that only depends on private information) is the functional commitment, C_{sp} is the opening, and A_p, B_p, and C_p can be recomputed by the verifier given public information.

$\mathsf{KC}(1^\lambda, \mathcal{C})$: $\mathsf{p} \leftarrow \mathsf{Pgen}(1^\lambda, \nu)$; Let $\mathcal{C}^*$ be the compiled arithmetic circuit; $\mathcal{C}^*$ defines ν, μ, and other parameters. For $\mathsf{tk} = (\chi, y) \leftarrow_\$ (\mathbb{Z}_p^*)^2$ s.t. $\chi^\nu \neq 1$, $\mathsf{ck} =$

$$\begin{pmatrix} [1, (\chi^i y)_{i=0}^{\nu-1}, y^\eta, (\chi^i \ell(\chi) y^2)_{i=0}^{\nu-2}, (u_j(\chi) y^{\eta+1} + v_j(\chi) y^{\delta+1} + w_j(\chi) y^2)_{j=1}^{\mu-\kappa}]_1, \\ [(u_{\mu-\kappa+i}(\chi) y^{\eta+1-\gamma} + v_{\mu-\kappa+i}(\chi) y^{\delta+1-\gamma} + w_{\mu-\kappa+i}(\chi) y^{2-\gamma})_{i=1}^{\kappa}, y^\delta]_1, \\ [1, (\chi^i y)_{i=0}^{\nu-1}, y^\gamma, y^\eta]_2, [y^{\delta+\eta}]_T \end{pmatrix}.$$

Return $(\mathsf{ck}, \mathsf{tk})$;

$\mathsf{com}(\mathsf{ck}; \boldsymbol{\alpha}; r_a, r_b)$: // $r_a, r_b \leftarrow_\$ \mathbb{Z}_p$;
 Compute $(\mathsf{a}_j)_{j=2}^{\mu_\alpha+\mu_\phi+1}$ from $\boldsymbol{\alpha}$;
 Let $\mathsf{A}_s(X, Y) \leftarrow r_a + \sum_{i=0}^{\nu-1} A_i X^i Y$ be as in Eq. (9);
 Let $\mathsf{B}_s(X, Y) \leftarrow r_b + \sum_{i=0}^{\nu-1} B_i X^i Y$ be as in Eq. (9);
 For $i \in [1 \mathinner{..} \kappa]$: $\mathsf{B}_i^{\mathsf{aux}}(X, Y) \leftarrow \ell_{\nu-\kappa+i}(X) \mathsf{B}_s(X, Y) Y$;
 $[\mathsf{A}_s]_1 \leftarrow r_a[1]_1 + \sum_{i=0}^{\nu-1} A_i [\chi^i y]_1$; $[\mathsf{B}_s]_2 \leftarrow r_b[1]_2 + \sum_{i=0}^{\nu-1} B_i [\chi^i y]_2$;
 For $i \in [1 \mathinner{..} \kappa]$: $[\mathsf{B}_i^{\mathsf{aux}}]_1 \leftarrow [\mathsf{B}_i^{\mathsf{aux}}(\chi, y)]_1$;
 $C \leftarrow ([\mathsf{A}_s, \{\mathsf{B}_i^{\mathsf{aux}}\}_{i=1}^{\kappa}]_1, [\mathsf{B}_s]_2)$; $D \leftarrow (\boldsymbol{\alpha}, r_a, r_b)$; return (C, D);

$\mathsf{open}(\mathsf{ck}; C = ([\mathsf{A}_s, \{\mathsf{B}_i^{\mathsf{aux}}\}_{i=1}^{\kappa}]_1, [\mathsf{B}_s]_2), D = (\boldsymbol{\alpha}, r_a, r_b), \boldsymbol{\beta})$:
 Compute $\mathbf{a}$ from $\boldsymbol{\alpha}$ and $\boldsymbol{\beta}$;
 Compute $[(\ell_j(\chi) y)_{j=1}^{\nu}]_1$ from $[(\chi^i y)_{i=0}^{\nu-1}]_1$; // Needs to be done once
 Compute $[(u_j(\chi) y, v_j(\chi) y)_{j=1}^{\mu}]_1$ from $[(\chi^i y)_{i=0}^{\nu-1}]_1$; // Needs to be done once
 Compute $[(w_j(\chi) y)_{j=1}^{\mu}]_1$ from $[(\chi^i y)_{i=0}^{\nu-1}]_1$; // Needs to be done once
 $u(X) \leftarrow \sum_{j=1}^{\mu} \mathsf{a}_j u_j(X)$; $v(X) \leftarrow \sum_{j=1}^{\mu} \mathsf{a}_j v_j(X)$; $w(X) \leftarrow \sum_{j=1}^{\mu} \mathsf{a}_j w_j(X)$;
 $\mathcal{H}(X) \leftarrow (u(X) v(X) - w(X)) / \ell(X)$;
 $[\mathsf{A}_p]_1 \leftarrow [\mathsf{A}_p(\chi, y)]_1$ where $\mathsf{A}_p(X, Y)$ is as in Eq. (9);
 $[\mathsf{C}_{sp}]_1 \leftarrow r_a([v(\chi) y]_1 + [y^\eta]_1) + r_b([\mathsf{A}_s]_1 + [\mathsf{A}_p]_1 + [y^\delta]_1) +$
 $\sum_{i=0}^{\nu-2} \mathcal{H}_i [\chi^i \ell(\chi) y^2]_1 + \sum_{j=1}^{\mu-\kappa} \mathsf{a}_j [u_j(\chi) y^{\eta+1} + v_j(\chi) y^{\delta+1} + w_j(\chi) y^2]_1$;
 return $\mathsf{op}_{\boldsymbol{\xi}} \leftarrow [\mathsf{C}_{sp}]_1$;

$\mathsf{V}(\mathsf{ck}, C = ([\mathsf{A}_s, \{\mathsf{B}_i^{\mathsf{aux}}\}_{i=1}^{\kappa}]_1, [\mathsf{B}_s]_2), [\mathsf{C}_{sp}]_1, \boldsymbol{\beta}, \{\xi_i\}_{i=1}^{\kappa})$: // $\xi_i =^? \mathcal{F}_i(\boldsymbol{\alpha}, \boldsymbol{\beta})$
 Compute $[(\ell_{\nu-\kappa+i}(\chi) y)_{i=1}^{\kappa}]_1$ from $[(\chi^i y)_{i=0}^{\nu-1}]_1$; // Needs to be done once
 Compute $[(\ell_{\nu-\kappa+i}(\chi) y^{2-\gamma})_{i=1}^{\kappa}]_1$ from $[(\chi^i y^{2-\gamma})_{i=0}^{\nu-1}]_1$; // Needs to be done once
 Compute $[(\ell_{\nu-\kappa+i}(\chi) y)_{i=1}^{\kappa}]_2$ from $[(\chi^i y)_{i=0}^{\nu-1}]_2$; // Needs to be done once
 Compute needed $[u_j(\chi) y]_1$ from $[(\chi^i y)_{i=0}^{\nu-1}]_2$; // done once
 Compute needed $[v_j(\chi) y]_2$ from $[(\chi^i y)_{i=0}^{\nu-1}]_2$; // done once
 $[\mathsf{A}_p]_1 \leftarrow [\mathsf{A}_p(\chi, y)]_1$ where $\mathsf{A}_p(X, Y)$ is as in Eq. (9);
 $[\mathsf{B}_p]_2 \leftarrow [\mathsf{B}_p(\chi, y)]_2$ where $\mathsf{B}_p(X, Y)$ is as in Eq. (9);
 $[\mathsf{C}_p]_1 \leftarrow \sum_{i=1}^{\kappa} \xi_i [\ell_{\nu-\kappa+i}(\chi) y^{2-\gamma}]_1$;
 Check $([\mathsf{A}_s]_1 + [\mathsf{A}_p]_1 + [y^\delta]_1) \bullet ([\mathsf{B}_s]_2 + [\mathsf{B}_p]_2 + [y^\eta]_2) = [\mathsf{C}_{sp}]_1 \bullet [1]_2 + [\mathsf{C}_p]_1 \bullet [y^\gamma]_2 + [y^{\delta+\eta}]_T$;
 For $i \in [1 \mathinner{..} \kappa]$: check $[\ell_{\nu-\kappa+i}(\chi) y]_1 \bullet [\mathsf{B}_s]_2 = [\mathsf{B}_i^{\mathsf{aux}}]_1 \bullet [1]_2$;

Fig. 2. SNARK-based SFC scheme $\mathsf{FC}_{\mathsf{sn}}^{\mathcal{C}}$ for arithmetic circuit $\mathcal{C}$

The New SFC Scheme $\mathsf{FC}_{\mathsf{sn}}$: Details. We are now ready to describe the new succinct functional commitment scheme $\mathsf{FC}_{\mathsf{sn}}$, see Fig. 2. Here, instead of operating with bivariate polynomials like $\mathsf{A}(X, Y)$, one operates with their encodings like $[\mathsf{A}_s(\chi, y)]_\iota$ in the source groups, where χ and y are secret trapdoors. The commitment key of the SFC scheme contains the minimal amount of information needed to perform commitment, opening, and verification by honest parties. The expression of ck in KC has a generic form; one can replace the polynomials $u_j(X)$, $v_j(X)$, $w_j(X)$ with their values evident from Eq. (6). Finally, $\ell_j(X)$ (and thus also $u_j(X)$, $v_j(X)$, and $w_j(X)$) has degree $\nu - 1$ and can thus be computed from $(X^i)_{i=0}^{\nu-1}$, while $\ell(X)$ has degree ν. We explain in the correctness proof of Theorem 3 how to compute $[\mathsf{B}_i^{\mathsf{aux}}(\chi, y)]_1$.

Note that $\mathsf{FC}_{\mathsf{sn}}$ can also be seen as a SNARK proving that $\mathcal{F}(\boldsymbol{\alpha}, \boldsymbol{\beta}) = \boldsymbol{\xi}$, if we let the prover to compute $[\mathsf{A}_p]_1$, $[\mathsf{B}_p]_2$, and $[\mathsf{C}_p]_1$.

Instantiation. Let $\mathcal{C}$ be a fixed circuit. Let $\mathcal{R}$ and $\mathcal{S}$ be two sets of bivariate polynomials, such that the commitment key of $\mathsf{FC}_{\mathsf{sn}}^{\mathcal{C}}$ is equal to $\mathsf{ck} = ([\mathcal{R}(\chi, y)]_1, [\mathcal{S}(\chi, y)]_2)$. Similarly to [33], let

$$\mathsf{Mon}_1 = \{0, 1, 2, 2 - \gamma, \delta, \delta + 1, \delta + 1 - \gamma, \eta, \eta + 1, \eta + 1 - \gamma\} \tag{10}$$

be the set of exponents of Y in all polynomials from $\mathcal{R}$. Let $\mathsf{Crit} = \{2, \eta + 1\}$ and $\overline{\mathsf{Crit}} = \mathsf{Mon}_1 \setminus \mathsf{Crit}$. For the evaluation-binding proof to hold, we need to fix values of $\gamma, \delta, \eta \in \mathbb{Z}_p$, such that the coefficients from Crit are unique, i.e.,

$$2, \eta + 1 \notin \{0, 1, 2 - \gamma, \delta, \delta + 1, \delta + 1 - \gamma, \eta, \eta + 1 - \gamma\} \quad \text{and} \quad \eta + 1 \neq 2 \ . \tag{11}$$

That is, $\mathsf{Crit} \cap \overline{\mathsf{Crit}} = \emptyset$ and $|\mathsf{Crit}| = 2$. It follows from Theorem 1 that the polynomial $f_i(X, Y) := \ell_{\nu-\kappa+i}(X) Y^{\eta+1}$, $i \in [1 \mathinner{..} \kappa]$, does not belong to $\operatorname{span}(\mathcal{R})$.

We will later consider two different evaluations for γ, δ, and η. Replacing γ, δ, and η with 1, 0, and 3 guarantees that Eq. (11) holds (see Theorem 2, Item 1, for more). Then,

$$\mathsf{ck} = \begin{pmatrix} [1, (\chi^i y)_{i=0}^{\nu-1}, y^3, (\chi^i \ell(\chi) y^2)_{i=0}^{\nu-2}, (u_j(\chi) y^4 + v_j(\chi) y^1 + w_j(\chi) y^2)_{j=1}^{\mu-\kappa}]_1, \\ [(u_{\mu-\kappa+i}(\chi) y^3 + v_{\mu-\kappa+i}(\chi) y^0 + w_{\mu-\kappa+i}(\chi) y^1)_{i=1}^{\kappa}, y^0]_1, \\ [1, (\chi^i y)_{i=0}^{\nu-1}, y^1, y^3]_2, [y^3]_T \end{pmatrix} .$$

In this case, the ck has one element (namely, $[1]_1$) twice, and thus ck can be shortened by one element.

Alternatively, replacing γ, δ, and η with 4, 0, and 7 (this choice is sufficient for the evaluation-binding reduction to uber-assumption in $\mathbb{G}_T$ to work and will be explained in Theorem 2, Item 2), we get

$$\mathsf{ck} = \begin{pmatrix} [1, (\chi^i y)_{i=0}^{\nu-1}, y^7, (\chi^i \ell(\chi) y^2)_{i=0}^{\nu-2}, (u_j(\chi) y^8 + v_j(\chi) y^1 + w_j(\chi) y^2)_{j=1}^{\mu-\kappa}]_1, \\ [(u_{\mu-\kappa+i}(\chi) y^4 + v_{\mu-\kappa+i}(\chi) y^{-3} + w_{\mu-\kappa+i}(\chi) y^{-2})_{i=1}^{\kappa}, y^0]_1, \\ [1, (\chi^i y)_{i=0}^{\nu-1}, y^4, y^7]_2, [y^7]_T \end{pmatrix} .$$

Then, ck has one element ($[1]_1$) twice, and thus it can be shortened.

Efficiency. The CRS length is $1 + \nu + 1 + (\nu - 1) + (\mu - \kappa) + \kappa + 1 = 2\nu + \mu + 2$ elements from $\mathbb{G}_1$, $\nu + 3$ elements from $\mathbb{G}_2$, and 1 element from $\mathbb{G}_T$. In the case of fixed γ, δ and η in the previous two paragraphs, the CRS length will shorten by 1 element of $\mathbb{G}_1$.

The functional commitment takes $(\nu+1)+\kappa(\nu+1)=(\kappa+1)(\nu+1)$ exponentiations in $\mathbb{G}_1$ and $\nu+1$ exponentiations in $\mathbb{G}_2$. The length of the functional commitment is $\kappa+1$ elements of $\mathbb{G}_1$ and 1 element of $\mathbb{G}_2$.

The opening takes $\mu_\beta+\mu_\psi+\kappa$ (to compute $[\mathsf{A}_p]_1$; note that $u_1(X)$ and other simular polynomials are precomputed), $\mu_\alpha+\mu_\beta+\mu_\phi+\mu_\psi$ (to compute $[v(\chi)y]_1$) and $2+(\nu-1)+(\mu-\kappa)=\nu+\mu-\kappa+1$ (to compute $[\mathsf{C}_{sp}]_1$) exponentiations in $\mathbb{G}_1$, in total, $\nu+\mu+\mu_\alpha+2\mu_\beta+\mu_\phi+2\mu_\psi+1$ exponentiations. The length of the opening is 1 element of $\mathbb{G}_1$.

The verification takes $(\mu_\beta+\mu_\psi+\kappa)+\kappa=\mu_\beta+\mu_\psi+2\kappa$ (to compute $[\mathsf{A}_p,\mathsf{C}_p]_1$) exponentiations in $\mathbb{G}_1$, $\mu_\beta+\mu_\psi$ (to compute $[\mathsf{B}_p]_2$) exponentiations in $\mathbb{G}_2$, and $2\kappa+3$ pairings. Here, we do not count computations (e.g., computation of $[\ell_{\nu-\kappa+i}(\chi)y]_1$ from $[(\chi^i y)_{i=0}^{\nu-1}]_1$) that are only done once per the CRS.

The real efficiency depends of course significantly on the concrete application. We will give some detailed examples in the full version [34].

4 On the Circuit Class and Example Applications

Next, we study the power of the implementable circuit class $\mathbf{CC}_{\Sigma\Pi\forall}$, and we show that many known functional commitment scheme are for functionalities that belong to this class, and thus can be implemented by $\mathsf{FC}_{\mathsf{sn}}$.

In this section, we assume basic knowledge of the algebraic complexity theory. See [37] for necessary background. **VP** is the class of polynomial families $\{f_n\}$, where f_n is an univariate polynomial of $\mathsf{poly}(n)$ variables of $\mathsf{poly}(n)$ degree that has an arithmetic circuit of $\mathsf{poly}(n)$ size [39]. $\Sigma\Pi\Sigma$ (resp., $\Sigma\Pi\Sigma\Pi$) is the class of depth-3 (resp., depth-4) circuits composed of alternating levels of sum and product gates with a sum gate at the top [37, Sect. 3.5]. *Sparse polynomials* are n-variate polynomials that have $\mathsf{poly}(n)$ monomials.

Recall that a compiled circuit $\mathcal{C}^*$ can evaluate a vector polynomial $\boldsymbol{f}(\boldsymbol{\alpha},\boldsymbol{\beta})=(f_i(\boldsymbol{\alpha},\boldsymbol{\beta}))_{i=1}^{\kappa}$ iff $\kappa\in\mathsf{poly}(\lambda)$ and each f_i can be written as

$$f_i(\boldsymbol{\alpha},\boldsymbol{\beta})=\sum\phi_j(\boldsymbol{\alpha})\psi_k(\boldsymbol{\beta}) \ , \tag{12}$$

where all polynomials ϕ_j and ψ_k are in the complexity class **VP**, and there are a polynomial number of additions in the representation Eq. (12) (thus, also a polynomial number of polynomials ϕ_j and ψ_k). We call such representation an *efficient* $\Sigma\Pi\forall$*-representation* (here, $\forall$ denotes "any") of $\boldsymbol{f}$, and we denote by $\mathbf{CC}_{\Sigma\Pi\forall}$ the class of circuits (or vector polynomials) that have an efficient $\Sigma\Pi\forall$-presentation. Clearly, $\mathsf{FC}_{\mathsf{sn}}$ can implement $\boldsymbol{f}$ iff $\boldsymbol{f}\in\mathbf{CC}_{\Sigma\Pi\forall}$.

It is clear that all sparse polynomials in **VP** have an efficient $\Sigma\Pi\forall$-representation, and thus $\mathsf{FC}_{\mathsf{sn}}$ can implement all sparse polynomials. However, we can do more. For example, consider the polynomial $f'(\alpha,\boldsymbol{\beta})=\prod_{i=1}^{n}(\alpha+\beta_i)$ for $n=\mathsf{poly}(\lambda)$. Since f' has 2^n monomials, it is not sparse. However, we can rewrite f' as $f'(\alpha,\boldsymbol{\beta})=\sum_{d=0}^{n}\alpha^d\sigma_{n-d}(\boldsymbol{\beta})$, where $\sigma_{n-d}(\boldsymbol{\beta})=\sum_{T\subseteq[1\,..\,n],|T|=d}\prod_{i\in T}\beta_i$ is the $(n-d)$th symmetric polynomial. There exists a $\Sigma\Pi\Sigma$ circuit of size $O(n^2)$,

Table 1. Rewriting the functionalites of various SFC as sparse polynomials

Type	μ_α	μ_β	f_i
Inner-product commitment [25,29]	n	n	$\sum_{j=1}^{n} \alpha_j \beta_j$
Polynomial commitment [27]	n	n	$\sum_{j=0}^{n-1} \alpha_j \beta^j$
Vector commitment [12]	n	1	$\alpha_I = \sum_{j=1}^{n} \alpha_j e_{Ij}$
Accumulator [3,5]	1	n	$\sum_{j=0}^{\mu_\alpha - 1} \chi_{\alpha j} \beta^j$
Evaluation-point commitment	1	n	$\sum_{j=0}^{n-1} \alpha^j \beta_j$
c-variate polynomial commitment [10,36]	$\binom{n+c}{c}$	c	$\sum \alpha_j \prod_{k=1}^{c} \beta_k^{j_k}$

due to Ben-Or (see [37, Sect. 3.5]), that computes all n symmetric polynomials in parallel. Thus, f has an efficient $\Sigma\Pi\forall$ -representation, and thus $\mathsf{FC}_{\mathsf{sn}}$ can implement at least one non-sparse polynomial.

On the other hand, $\mathbf{CC}_{\Sigma\Pi\forall} \subseteq \mathbf{VP}$. To see that $\mathbf{CC}_{\Sigma\Pi\forall} \subsetneq \mathbf{VP}$, consider the polynomial $f''(\boldsymbol{\alpha}, \boldsymbol{\beta}) = \prod_{i=1}^{n} (\alpha_i + \beta_i)$ for $n = \mathsf{poly}(\lambda)$. Since f'' has 2^n monomials, it is not sparse. Considering β_i as coefficients, it also has 2^n monomials in $\boldsymbol{\alpha}$ (the case of considering α_i as coefficients is dual), and thus any $\Sigma\Pi\forall$-representation of f'' requires at least 2^n addition gates. Since f'' can be implemented by a $\Pi\Sigma$ circuit [37], it means $\Pi\Sigma \not\subset \mathbf{CC}_{\Sigma\Pi\forall}$; however, clearly, $\Pi\Sigma \not\subset \mathbf{CC}_{\Sigma\Pi\forall}$ so $\mathbf{CC}_{\Sigma\Pi\forall}$ is incomparable to $\Pi\Sigma$. Thus

$$\text{the class of sparse polynomials} \subsetneq \mathbf{CC}_{\Sigma\Pi\forall} \subsetneq \mathbf{VP} \ .$$

It is an interesting open problem to characterize $\mathbf{CC}_{\Sigma\Pi\forall}$. Motivated by our analysis of α'', it seems we can implement all polynomials $f(\boldsymbol{\alpha}, \boldsymbol{\beta})$, where either the dimension μ_α of $\boldsymbol{\alpha}$ or the dimension μ_β of $\boldsymbol{\beta}$ is logarithmic in λ. Really, if $\mu_\alpha = O(\log \lambda)$ then there are at most $2^{\mu}_{\alpha} = \mathsf{poly}(\lambda)$ possible monomials $\phi_i(\boldsymbol{\alpha})$ in $\boldsymbol{\alpha}$, and thus there exists an efficient $\Sigma\Pi\forall$-representation of f.

Known Types of SFCs as (Semi-)Sparse Polynomials. In Table 1, we write down the functionalities of several previous known types of SFCs. This shows that in all such cases, one has a sparse polynomial and thus can use $\mathsf{FC}_{\mathsf{sn}}$ to implement them. In none of these cases, one needs the power of non-sparse semi-sparse polynomials, and we leave it as another open question to find an application where such power is needed. In the case of the vector commitment scheme (resp., accumulator), one implements the inner-product scheme with $\boldsymbol{\beta} = \boldsymbol{e}_I$ (resp., $\chi_{\boldsymbol{\alpha}}(X) = \prod(X - \alpha_i)$). In the case of say the polynomial commitment scheme, $\boldsymbol{\beta} = (1, \beta, \ldots, \beta^{n-1})$ and thus $\mu_\beta = n$.

Aggregation. The next lemma is straightforward.

Lemma 1. *Assume that* $\mathcal{C}_i \in \mathbf{CC}_{\Sigma\Pi\forall}$*, where* $i \in [1\,..\,Q]$*, and* $Q = \mathsf{poly}(\lambda)$*. Then their parallel composition* $\mathcal{C}^{\|} = (\mathcal{C}_1 \| \ldots \| \mathcal{C}_Q) \in \mathbf{CC}_{\Sigma\Pi\forall}$.

Proof. Obvious since we can just "parallelize" the representation in Eq. (12). □

In practice, Lemma 1 is very important since it means that $\mathsf{FC}_{\mathsf{sn}}$ allows to aggregate a polynomial number of SFCs for which $\mathsf{FC}_{\mathsf{sn}}$ is efficient. It just results in a larger circuit $\mathcal{C}^{\|}$(and thus larger parameters like μ and κ. However, as the length of the commitment in $\mathsf{FC}_{\mathsf{sn}}$ depends on κ, it means that the commitment stays succinct when $Q < |\mathsf{wit}|$. On the other hand, the length of the opening will be one group element, independently of Q.

As a corollary of Lemma 1, we can construct succinct aggregated inner-product SFCs, accumulators, (multi-point / multi-polynomial) polynomial commitment schemes, vector commitment schemes (including subvector commitment schmes), but also aggregate all these SFC variants with each other. Due to the lack of space, we will give more details and examples in the full version [34].

Example: Succinct Aggregated Inner-Product Functional Commitment. In an aggregated SIPFC, the committer commits to $\boldsymbol{\alpha}$ and then opens it simultaneously to $\langle \boldsymbol{\alpha}, \boldsymbol{\beta}_i \rangle = \sum_{j=1}^{n} \alpha_j \beta_{ij}$ for κ different verifier-provided vectors $\boldsymbol{\beta}_i$, where $i \in [1 \mathinner{..} \kappa]$. Assume $\boldsymbol{\alpha}$ and each $\boldsymbol{\beta}_i$ are n-dimensional vectors. There is no circuit $\mathcal{C}_\phi$ or $\mathcal{C}_\psi$. Given $\boldsymbol{\alpha}$ and $\boldsymbol{\beta}_i$, $\mathcal{C}_\chi$ computes κn products $\chi_{ij}(\boldsymbol{\alpha}, \boldsymbol{\beta}) = \alpha_j \beta_{ij}$, $i \in [1 \mathinner{..} \kappa]$ and $j \in [1 \mathinner{..} n]$, and $\mathcal{C}_\xi$ sums them together to obtain κ outputs $\mathcal{F}_i(\boldsymbol{\alpha}, \boldsymbol{\beta}) = \sum_{j=1}^{n} \alpha_j \beta_{ij}$. Thus, $U_\chi = \mathbf{1}_\kappa \otimes I_n \in \mathbb{Z}_p^{\kappa n \times n}$, $V_\chi = I_{\kappa n}$, $U_\xi = I_n \otimes \mathbf{1}_\kappa^\top \in \mathbb{Z}_p^{n \times \kappa n}$ (note that $\mathcal{C}_\chi$ does not take 1 as an input), and

$$U = \left(\begin{array}{c|c|c|c|c} 1 & \boldsymbol{\alpha} & \boldsymbol{\beta} & \boldsymbol{\chi}(\boldsymbol{\alpha},\boldsymbol{\beta}) & \boldsymbol{\mathcal{F}}(\boldsymbol{\alpha},\boldsymbol{\beta}) \\ \hline & U_\chi & & & \\ \hline & & & U_\xi & \end{array}\right), \quad V = \left(\begin{array}{c|c|c|c|c} 1 & \boldsymbol{\alpha} & \boldsymbol{\beta} & \boldsymbol{\chi}(\boldsymbol{\alpha},\boldsymbol{\beta}) & \boldsymbol{\mathcal{F}}(\boldsymbol{\alpha},\boldsymbol{\beta}) \\ \hline & & V_\chi & & \\ \hline 1 & & & & \end{array}\right), \quad W = \left(\begin{array}{c|c|c|c|c} 1 & \boldsymbol{\alpha} & \boldsymbol{\beta} & \boldsymbol{\chi}(\boldsymbol{\alpha},\boldsymbol{\beta}) & \boldsymbol{\mathcal{F}}(\boldsymbol{\alpha},\boldsymbol{\beta}) \\ \hline & & & I_{\kappa n} & \\ \hline & & & & I_\kappa \end{array}\right).$$

Here, $\nu = \kappa(n+1)$, $\mu = 1 + n + \kappa n + \kappa n + \kappa = (\kappa+1)n + \kappa + 1$, $\mathsf{A}_s(X,Y) = r_a + \sum_{j=1}^{n} \alpha_j u_{\chi j}(X) Y$, $\mathsf{A}_p(X,Y) = \sum_{i=1}^{\kappa} \langle \boldsymbol{\alpha}, \boldsymbol{\beta}_i \rangle \ell_{\nu-\kappa+i}(X) Y$. Importantly, $\mathsf{B}_s(X,Y) = 0$ (since there is nothing to hide, one can set $r_b \leftarrow 0$; hence, also $\mathsf{B}_i^{\mathsf{aux}}(X,Y) = 0$; thus the commitment is only one group element, $[\mathsf{A}_s]_1$), and $\mathsf{B}_p(X,Y) = \sum_{i=1}^{\kappa} \ell_{\nu-\kappa+i}(X)Y + \sum_{i=1}^{\kappa} \sum_{j=1}^{n} \beta_{ij} v_{\chi, n(i-1)+j}(X) Y$. The verifier has to execute 2κ exponentiations in $\mathbb{G}_1$ to compute $[\mathsf{A}_p]_1$ and $[\mathsf{C}_p]_1$, κn exponentiations in $\mathbb{G}_2$ to compute $[\mathsf{B}_p]_2$, and 3 pairings. We emphasize that here, both the functional commitment and the opening will consist of a single group element. One obtains IPFC by setting $\kappa \leftarrow 1$; in this case, the verification executes 2 exponentiations in $\mathbb{G}_1$, n exponentiations in $\mathbb{G}_2$, and 3 pairings.

Let us briefly compare the resulting *non-aggregated* IPFC with the IPFC of [25]. Interestingly, while the presented IPFC is a simple specialization of the general SFC scheme, it is only slightly less efficient than [25]. Let g_ι denote the bitlength of an element of the group $\mathbb{G}_\iota$. The CRS length is $2ng_1 + (n+1)g_2$ in [25], and $(3(\kappa+1) + (4\kappa+1)n)g_1 + (\kappa + \kappa n + 3)g_2 + 1g_T$ (this shortens to $(5n+6)g_1 + (n+4)g_2 + 1g_T$ when $\kappa = 1$) in our case. The commitment takes $n+1$ exponentiations in [25], and $n + 2$ in our case. Interestingly, a straightforward [25] opening takes $\Theta(n^2)$ multiplications (this can be probably optimized), while in our case it takes $\Theta(n \log n)$ multiplications. The verifier takes n exponentiations in [25], and $n+3$ here. The commitment and opening are both 1 group elements in both schemes. Thus, our *generic, unoptimized* scheme is essentially as efficient as the most efficient known prior IPFC, losing ground only in the CRS length. On the other hand, we are not aware of *any* previous aggregated IPFC schemes.

5 Security of $\mathsf{FC_{sn}}$

Next, we prove the security of $\mathsf{FC_{sn}}$. While its correctness and hiding proofs are straightforward, evaluation-binding is far from it. As before, for a fixed $\mathcal{C}$, let $\mathcal{R}$ and $\mathcal{S}$ be two sets of bivariate polynomials, s.t. $\mathsf{ck} = ([\mathcal{R}(\chi, y)]_1, [\mathcal{S}(\chi, y)]_2)$. For a fixed $\mathcal{C}$, in Theorem 3, we will reduce evaluation-binding of $\mathsf{FC^{\mathcal{C}}_{sn}}$ to a $(\mathcal{R}, \mathcal{S}, \{f_i\})$-*span-uber-assumption* in $\mathbb{G}_1$, a new assumption that states that it is difficult to output an element $\sum \Delta_i [f_i(\chi, y)]_1$ together with the coefficient vector $\boldsymbol{\Delta} \neq \mathbf{0}$, where $f_i \notin \operatorname{span}(\mathcal{R})$. Thus, it is a generalization of the $(\mathcal{R}, \mathcal{S}, \cdot)$-computational uber-assumption in $\mathbb{G}_1$. Importantly, if $\kappa = 1$ then it is equivalent to the latter. To motivate the span-uber-assumption, we will show that it follows from the more conventional $(\mathcal{R}, \mathcal{S}, f'_I)$-computational uber-assumption (for a related set of polynomials f'_i) in $\mathbb{G}_T$ [7]; see Lemma 2. Thus, for the concrete parameters $\mathcal{R}, \mathcal{S}, \{f_i\}$, and $\{f'_i\}$,

uber-assumption in $\mathbb{G}_T \Rightarrow$ span-uber-assumption in $\mathbb{G}_1 \Rightarrow$ uber-assumption in $\mathbb{G}_1$

For the reduction to the PDL and HAK assumptions in the full version [34] to work, we also prove that $f_i \notin \operatorname{span}(\mathcal{R})$ and $f'_i \notin \operatorname{span}(\mathcal{RS})$; see Theorem 2. (Intuitively, this is needed for the span-uber-assumptions to be secure in the generic model.) Each concrete proof (e.g., the proof of correctness, the proof of evaluation-binding, and the proofs that $f_i \notin \operatorname{span}(\mathcal{R})$ and $f'_i \notin \operatorname{span}(\mathcal{RS})$) puts some simple restrictions on the matrices U, V, W. They can usually be satisfied by slightly modifying the underlying arithmetic circuit.

Definition 6. *Let $\mathcal{R}$, $\mathcal{S}$, and $\mathcal{T}$ be three tuples of bivariate polynomials over $\mathbb{Z}_p[X, Y]$. Let f_i be bivariate polynomial over $\mathbb{Z}_p[X, Y]$. The $(\mathcal{R}, \mathcal{S}, \mathcal{T}, \{f_i\}_{i=1}^{\kappa})$* computational span-uber-assumption *for* Pgen *in group $\mathbb{G}_\iota$, where $\iota \in \{1, 2, T\}$, states that for any PPT adversary $\mathcal{A}$, $\mathsf{Adv}^{\mathsf{setuber}}_{\mathsf{Pgen}, \mathcal{R}, \mathcal{S}, \mathcal{T}, \{f_i\}, \mathcal{A}}(\lambda) = \mathsf{negl}(\lambda)$, where* $\mathsf{Adv}^{\mathsf{setuber}}_{\mathsf{Pgen}, \mathcal{R}, \mathcal{S}, \mathcal{T}, \{f_i\}, \mathcal{A}}(\lambda) :=$

$$\Pr\left[\begin{array}{l} \mathsf{p} \leftarrow \mathsf{Pgen}(1^\lambda); \chi, y \leftarrow_\$ \mathbb{Z}_p^*; \\ \mathsf{ck} \leftarrow ([\mathcal{R}(\chi, y)]_1, [\mathcal{S}(\chi, y)]_2, [\mathcal{T}(\chi, y)]_T); \\ (\boldsymbol{\Delta} \in \mathbb{Z}_p^\kappa, [z]_\iota) \leftarrow \mathcal{A}(\mathsf{ck}) : \boldsymbol{\Delta} \neq \mathbf{0} \wedge [z]_\iota = \sum_{i=1}^{\kappa} \Delta_i [f_i(\chi, y)]_\iota \end{array}\right].$$

If $\kappa = 1$ then the $(\mathcal{R}, \mathcal{S}, \mathcal{T}, \{f\})$ span-uber-assumption is the same as the $(\mathcal{R}, \mathcal{S}, \mathcal{T}, f_1)$ uber-assumption: in this case the adversary is tasked to output $\mathbb{Z}_p \ni \Delta \neq 0$ and $\Delta [f_1(\chi, y)]_\iota$ which is equivalent to outputting $[f_1(\chi, y)]_\iota$.

We will now show that the used polynomials are linearly independent.

Theorem 2. *Write* $\mathsf{ck} = ([\varrho(X,Y) : \varrho \in \mathcal{R}]_1, [\sigma(X,Y) : \sigma \in \mathcal{S}]_2)$ *as in Fig. 2. For* $i \in [1 \mathinner{..} \kappa]$, *let* $f_i(X,Y) := \ell_{\nu-\kappa+i}(X)Y^{\eta+1}$ *and* $f'_i(X,Y) := (\ell_{\nu-\kappa+i}(X))^2 Y^{\eta+2}$.

1. *Assume* $\gamma = 1$, $\delta = 0$, *and* $\eta = 3$. *Assume Items a and h of Theorem 1 hold. Then* $f_i(X,Y) \notin \mathrm{span}(\mathcal{R})$ *for* $i \in [1 \mathinner{..} \kappa]$.
2. *Assume* $\gamma = 4$, $\delta = 0$, $\eta = 7$, *and that Items a, b and h of Theorem 1 hold. Then* $f'_i(X,Y) \notin \mathrm{span}(\mathcal{RS})$ *for* $i \in [1 \mathinner{..} \kappa]$.

Proof. **(1:** $f_I \notin \mathrm{span}(\mathcal{R})$**).** Let Mon_1 be as in Eq. (10) and $\mathsf{Crit} = \{2, \eta + 1\}$. For the rest of the proof to make sense, as we will see in a few paragraphs, we need to fix γ, δ, and η so that the coefficients in Mon_1 and in $\mathsf{Mon}_1 \setminus \mathsf{Crit}$ are different (in particular, the coefficients in Crit are different from each other). A small exhaustive search shows that one can define $\gamma = 1$, $\delta = 0$, $\eta = 3$, as in the claim. This setting can be easily manually verified, by noticing that $\mathsf{Mon}_1 = \{0, 1, 2, 3, 4\}$, $\mathsf{Crit} = \{2, 4\}$, and thus $\mathsf{Mon}_1 \setminus \mathsf{Crit} = \{0, 1, 3\}$.

Assume that, for some I, $f_I(X,Y) = \ell_{\nu-\kappa+I}(X)Y^{\eta+1}$ belongs to the span of $\mathcal{R}$. We consider the coefficients of Y^i, for $i \in \mathsf{Crit}$, in the resulting equality (for some unknown coefficients in front of the polynomials from $\mathcal{R}$), and derive a contradiction from this. Thus, we write down an arbitrary linear combination of polynomials in $\mathcal{R}$ as a linear combination of $u_j(X)Y^{\eta+1} + v_j(X)Y^{\delta+1} + w_j(X)Y^2$, $X^i \ell(X) Y^2$, and $T(X,Y)$, where $T(X,Y)$ is some polynomial with monomials that do not have Y^i for $i \in \mathsf{Crit}$. That is,

$$\begin{aligned}\ell_{\nu-\kappa+I}(X)Y^{\eta+1} = &\textstyle\sum_{j=1}^{\mu-\kappa} t'_j (u_j(X)Y^{\eta+1} + v_j(X)Y^{\delta+1} + w_j(X)Y^2) + \\ &t(X)\ell(X)Y^2 + T(X,Y)\end{aligned} \tag{13}$$

for some $t(X) \in \mathbb{Z}_p[X]$ (thus $t(X)\ell(X)Y^2$ encompasses all $X^i\ell(X)Y^2$) and integers t'_j.

First, considering only the coefficient of Y^2 in both the left-hand side and the right hand side of Eq. (13),

$$\textstyle\sum_{j=1}^{\mu-\kappa} t'_j w_j(X) + t(X)\ell(X) = 0 \enspace .$$

Due to Item h of Theorem 1, either $w_j(X) = 0$ or $t'_j = 0$ for $j \in [1 \mathinner{..} \mu - \kappa]$. Let $\mathcal{J} \subset [1 \mathinner{..} \mu - \kappa]$ be the set of indices $j \in [1 \mathinner{..} \mu - \kappa]$ so that $w_j(X) = 0$.

Second, considering only the coefficient of $Y^{\eta+1}$ in Eq. (13),

$$\ell_{\nu-\kappa+I}(X) = \textstyle\sum_{j=1}^{\mu-\kappa} t'_j u_j(X) = \sum_{j \in \mathcal{J}} t'_j u_j(X) \enspace .$$

Due to Item a of Theorem 1, $\ell_{\nu-\kappa+I}(X)$ is linearly independent of (the non-zero elements of) $\{u_j(X)\}_{j \in \mathcal{J}}$, a contradiction. Hence, $f_I(X,Y) \notin \mathrm{span}(\mathcal{R})$.

(Item 2: $f'_I \notin \mathrm{span}(\mathcal{RS})$**).** For the proof to make sense, as we will see in a few paragraphs, we need that the set of critical coefficients $\mathsf{Crit}' := \{3, \eta + 2\}$ (that is different from Crit above) is different from the set $\mathsf{Mon}' \setminus \mathsf{Crit}'$ all other coefficients in $\mathcal{RS}$, where $\mathsf{Mon}' :=$

$$\left\{\begin{array}{l} 0, 1, 2, 3, 2-\gamma, 3-\gamma, \gamma, \gamma+1, \gamma+2, \delta, 1+\delta, 2+\delta, 1-\gamma+\delta, 2-\gamma+\delta, \\ \gamma+\delta, 1+\gamma+\delta, \eta, 2\eta, \eta+1, \eta+2, -\gamma+\eta+1, -\gamma+\eta+2, \gamma+\eta, \\ \gamma+\eta+1, \delta+\eta, 1+\delta+\eta, 1-\gamma+\delta+\eta, 1+2\eta, 1-\gamma+2\eta \end{array}\right\} \enspace .$$

is defined by $\mathsf{Mon}' = \mathsf{Mon}_1 + \mathsf{Mon}_2$, where Mon_1 is as in Eq. (10) and $\mathsf{Mon}_2 = \{0, 1, \gamma, \eta\}$ is the set of exponents of Y in all polynomials from $\mathcal{S}$. A small exhaustive search, performed by using computer algebra, shows that one can define $\gamma = 4, \delta = 0, \eta = 7$, as in the claim. This setting can be easily manually verified, by noticing that $\mathsf{Mon}' \setminus \mathsf{Crit}' = \{-3, -2, -1, 0, 1, 2, 4, 5, 6, 7, 8, 11, 12, 14, 15\}$ and $\mathsf{Crit}' = \{3, 9\}$.

Assume now in contrary that $f'_I \in \operatorname{span}(\mathcal{RS})$. Then, as in Item 1, $(\ell_{\nu-\kappa+I}(X))^2 Y^{\eta+2}$ is in the span of some polynomials containing Y^i for $i \in \mathsf{Crit}'$ (and we need to quantify the coefficients of these polynomials) and of all other polynomials. Clearly, the first type of polynomials are in the span of $X^i \ell(X) Y^2$ times Y^η, $X^i \ell(X) Y^2$ times $X^k Y$, $u_j(X) Y^{\eta+1} + v_j(X) Y^{\delta+1} + w_j(X) Y^2$ times Y^η, and $u_j(X) Y^{\eta+1} + v_j(X) Y^{\delta+1} + w_j(X) Y^2$ times $X^k Y$, for properly chosen i, j, and k. Thus,

$$
\begin{aligned}
(\ell_{\nu-\kappa+I}(X))^2 Y^{\eta+2} = {} & t(X)\ell(X)Y^{\eta+2} + t''(X)\ell(X)Y^3 + \\
& \textstyle\sum_{j=1}^{\mu-\kappa} t'_j(X)(u_j(X)Y^{2\eta+1} + v_j(X)Y^{\delta+\eta+1} + w_j(X)Y^{\eta+2}) + \\
& \textstyle\sum_{j=1}^{\mu-\kappa} t^*_j(X)(u_j(X)Y^{\eta+2} + v_j(X)Y^{\delta+2} + w_j(X)Y^3) + T(X,Y)
\end{aligned}
$$

where $t'_j(X)$, $t^*_j(X)$, $t(X)$ and $t''(X)$ are univariate polynomials, and $T(X,Y)$ is a polynomial that does not contain monomials with Y^i, $i \in \mathsf{Crit}'$. We now consider separately the coefficients of Y^i in this equation for each $i \in \mathsf{Crit}'$ and derive a contradiction.

First, considering the coefficients of Y^3, we get $\sum_{j=1}^{\mu-\kappa} t^*_j(X) w_j(X) + t''(X)\ell(X) = 0$. Due to Item h of Theorem 1, either $t^*_j(X) = 0$ or $w_j(X) = 0$ for $1 \le j \le \mu - \kappa$. Let $\mathcal{J} \subset [1 \,..\, \mu - \kappa]$ be the set of indices j so that $w_j(X) = 0$.

Second, the coefficients of $Y^{\eta+2}$ give us

$$
\begin{aligned}
(\ell_{\nu-\kappa+I}(X))^2 &= \textstyle\sum_{j=1}^{\mu-\kappa} t^*_j(X)u_j(X) + \sum_{j=\mu_\alpha+2}^{\mu-\kappa} t'_j(X)w_j(X) + t(X)\ell(X) \\
&= \textstyle\sum_{j\in\mathcal{J}} t^*_j(X)u_j(X) + \sum_{j\notin\mathcal{J}} t'_j(X)w_j(X) + t(X)\ell(X) \enspace .
\end{aligned}
$$

Due to Items a, b and h of Theorem 1 (and of the fact that $(\ell_{\nu-\kappa+i}(X))^2$ has degree 2ν), $\{(\ell_{\nu-\kappa+I}(X))^2\} \cup \{u_j(X)\}_{j\in\mathcal{J}} \cup \{w_j(X)\}_{j\notin\mathcal{J}} \cup \{X^i\ell(X)\}_{i=0}^{\nu-2}$ is linearly independent. Contradiction, and thus $f'_I(X,Y) \notin \operatorname{span}(\mathcal{RS})$. □

Next, we show that for the concrete choice of the parameters $\mathcal{R}$, $\mathcal{S}$, f_i, and f'_i, the span-uber-assumption in $\mathbb{G}_1$ is at least as strong as the uber-assumption in $\mathbb{G}_T$. The new assumption may be weaker since the latter assumption argues about elements in $\mathbb{G}_T$, which may not always be possible [26]. However, the proof of Lemma 2 depends crucially on the concrete parameters.

Lemma 2. (Uber-assumption in $\mathbb{G}_T \Rightarrow$ span-uber-assumption). *Assume $\gamma = 4$, $\delta = 0$, and $\eta = 7$. Let $\mathsf{FC}^{\mathcal{C}}_{\mathsf{sn}}$ be the SFC scheme for arithmetic circuits in Fig. 2. Write $\mathsf{ck} = ([\varrho(X,Y) : \varrho \in \mathcal{R}]_1, [\sigma(X,Y) : \sigma \in \mathcal{S}]_2)$ as in Fig. 2. For $i \in [1 \,..\, \kappa]$, let $f_i(X,Y) := \ell_{\nu-\kappa+i}(X)Y^{\eta+1}$ and $f'_i(X,Y) := (\ell_{\nu-\kappa+i}(X))^2 Y^{\eta+2}$. If the $(\mathcal{R}, \mathcal{S}, f'_I)$ computational uber-assumption holds in $\mathbb{G}_T$ for each $I \in [1 \,..\, \kappa]$ then the $(\mathcal{R}, \mathcal{S}, \{f_i\}_{i=1}^{\kappa})$ computational span-uber-assumption holds in $\mathbb{G}_1$.*

Proof (Sketch). Assume $\mathcal{A}$ is an adversary against the $(\mathcal{R}, \mathcal{S}, \{f_i\}_{i=1}^{\kappa})$ computational span-uber-assumption that has successfully output $\boldsymbol{\Delta} \neq \mathbf{0}$ and $[z]_1 = \sum_{i=1}^{\kappa} \Delta_i [f_i(\chi, y)]_1 = \sum_{i=1}^{\kappa} \Delta_i [\ell_{\nu-\kappa+i}(X) Y^{\eta+1}]_1$.

Since $\boldsymbol{\Delta} \neq \mathbf{0}$, then there exists at least one coordinate I such that $\Delta_I \neq 0$. Let $\mathcal{B}$ be the following adversary against the $(\mathcal{R}, \mathcal{S}, f_I)$ computational uber-assumption in $\mathbb{G}_T$. Given ck and $[z]_1$, $\mathcal{B}$ computes

$$1/\Delta_I \cdot [z]_1 \bullet [\ell_{\nu-\kappa+I}(\chi) y]_2 = \textstyle\sum_{i=1}^{\kappa} \Delta_i/\Delta_I \cdot [\ell_{\nu-\kappa+i}(\chi) y^{\eta+1}]_1 \bullet [\ell_{\nu-\kappa+I}(\chi) y]_2 \ .$$

Let $d_i(X)$ be the rational function satisfying $d_i(X)\ell(X) = \ell_{\nu-\kappa+i}(X)\ell_{\nu-\kappa+I}(X)$. Clearly, $d_i(X)$ is a polynomial for $i \neq I$. Thus, $d(X) := \sum_{i \neq I} \Delta_i/\Delta_I \cdot d_i(X)$ is a polynomial of degree $\leq \nu - 2$. Since $[y^{\eta}]_2$ is a part of the commitment key, $\mathcal{B}$ can efficiently compute $\sum_{i \neq I} \Delta_i/\Delta_I \cdot [\ell_{\nu-\kappa+i}(\chi) y^{\eta+1}]_1 \bullet [\ell_{\nu-\kappa+I}(\chi) y]_2 = \sum_{i \neq I} \Delta_i/\Delta_I \cdot [d_i(\chi)\ell(\chi) y^2]_1 \bullet [y^{\eta}]_2 = [d(\chi)\ell(\chi)y^2]_1 \bullet [y^{\eta}]_2$. Thus, $\mathcal{B}$ can compute

$$\begin{aligned} [z^*]_T = [f_I(\chi, y)]_T &\leftarrow [\ell_{\nu-\kappa+I}(\chi) y^{\eta+1}]_1 \bullet [\ell_{\nu-\kappa+I}(\chi) y]_2 \\ &= 1/\Delta_I \cdot [z]_1 \bullet [\ell_{\nu-\kappa+I}(\chi) y]_2 - [d(\chi)\ell(\chi)y^2]_1 \bullet [y^{\eta}]_2 \end{aligned}$$

and break the $(\mathcal{R}, \mathcal{S}, f'_I)$-computational uber-assumption in $\mathbb{G}_T$. □

Theorem 3 (Security of $\mathsf{FC}_{\mathsf{sn}}$). *Let $\mathcal{C}$ be a fixed circuit and let $\mathsf{FC}_{\mathsf{sn}}^{\mathcal{C}}$ be the SFC scheme in Fig. 2. Let $\mathsf{ck} = ([\varrho(X, Y) : \varrho \in \mathcal{R}]_1, [\sigma(X, Y) : \sigma \in \mathcal{S}]_2)$ as in Fig. 2. For $i \in [1 \mathinner{..} \kappa]$, let $f_i(X, Y) := \ell_{\nu-\kappa+i}(X) Y^{\eta+1}$.*

1. *Assume Item c of Theorem 1 holds. Then $\mathsf{FC}_{\mathsf{sn}}^{\mathcal{C}}$ is correct.*
2. *$\mathsf{FC}_{\mathsf{sn}}^{\mathcal{C}}$ is perfectly com-hiding.*
3. *$\mathsf{FC}_{\mathsf{sn}}^{\mathcal{C}}$ is perfectly open-hiding.*
4. *$\mathsf{FC}_{\mathsf{sn}}^{\mathcal{C}}$ is perfectly zero-knowledge.*
5. *Assume that either $\gamma = 1$, $\delta = 0$, and $\eta = 3$ or $\gamma = 4$, $\delta = 0$, and $\eta = 7$. Assume that Items d to g, i and j of Theorem 1 hold. If the $(\mathcal{R}, \mathcal{S}, \{f_i\})$-computational span-uber-assumption holds in $\mathbb{G}_1$ then the SFC scheme $\mathsf{FC}_{\mathsf{sn}}^{\mathcal{C}}$ is computationally evaluation-binding.*

Proof **(1: correctness).** We first show that the prover can compute $\mathsf{B}_i^{\mathsf{aux}}(X, Y)$, and then that the verification equation holds. Recall that for $i \in [1 \mathinner{..} \kappa]$, $\mathsf{B}_i^{\mathsf{aux}}(X, Y) = \ell_{\nu-\kappa+i}(X)\mathsf{B}_s(X, Y)Y = \ell_{\nu-\kappa+i}(X)(r_b + v_s(X, Y)Y)Y$, where $v_s(X)$ is as in Eq. (8). First, the addend $r_b \ell_{\nu-\kappa+i}(X)Y$ belongs to the span of $(X^i Y)_{i=0}^{\nu-1} \subset \mathcal{R}$. Second, due to Item c of Theorem 1, for all $j \in [2 \mathinner{..} 1 + \mu_\alpha + \mu_\phi]$,

$$\ell(X) \mid \ell_{\nu-\kappa+i}(X) v_{\phi j}(X) \quad \text{and} \quad \ell(X) \mid \ell_{\nu-\kappa+i}(X) v_{\chi j}(X) \ ,$$

and thus $\mathsf{B}_i^{\mathsf{aux}}(X, Y) - r_b \ell_{\nu-\kappa+i}(X)Y$ is equal to $b'_i(X)\ell(X)Y^2$ for some polynomial $b'_i(X) \in \mathbb{Z}_p^{\leq(\nu-2)}[X]$. Thus, $\mathsf{B}_i^{\mathsf{aux}}(X) \in \mathrm{span}(\mathcal{R})$ and the committer can compute $[\ell_{\nu-\kappa+i}(\chi)\mathsf{B}_s y]_2 = [\mathsf{B}_i^{\mathsf{aux}}(\chi, y)]_2$.

Assume that $\mathsf{ck} \leftarrow \mathsf{KC}(1^\lambda, \mathcal{C})$, $([\mathsf{A}_s, \{\mathsf{B}_i^{\mathsf{aux}}\}_{i=1}^{\kappa}]_1, [\mathsf{B}_s]_2) \leftarrow \mathsf{com}(\mathsf{ck}; \boldsymbol{\alpha}; r_a, r_b)$ and $[\mathsf{C}_{sp}]_1 \leftarrow \mathsf{open}(\mathsf{ck}; ([\mathsf{A}_s, \{\mathsf{B}_i^{\mathsf{aux}}\}_{i=1}^{\kappa}]_1, [\mathsf{B}_s]_2), (\boldsymbol{\alpha}, r_a, r_b), \boldsymbol{\beta})$. It is clear that then the verifier accepts.

(2: perfect com-hiding). Follows from the fact that $([\mathsf{A}_s]_1, [\mathsf{B}_s]_2)$ is perfectly masked by uniformly random $r_a, r_b \leftarrow_\$ \mathbb{Z}_p$. Moreover, $[\mathsf{B}_i^{\mathsf{aux}}]_1$ are publicly verifiable functions of $[\mathsf{B}_s]_2$.

(3: perfect open-hiding). Due to com-hiding and the fact that $[\mathsf{A}_p]_1$, $[\mathsf{B}_p]_2$, and $[\mathsf{C}_p]_1$ only depend on $(\boldsymbol{\beta}, \{\mathcal{F}_i(\boldsymbol{\alpha}, \boldsymbol{\beta})\})$ (and not on $\boldsymbol{\alpha}$ otherwise), it means that the distribution of all elements in the opening (except possibly $[\mathsf{C}_{sp}]_1$) is the same for any two vectors $\boldsymbol{\alpha}_1$ and $\boldsymbol{\alpha}_2$ that satisfy $\mathcal{F}_i(\boldsymbol{\alpha}_1, \boldsymbol{\beta}) = \mathcal{F}_i(\boldsymbol{\alpha}_2, \boldsymbol{\beta})$ for all i, Since $[\mathsf{C}_{sp}]_1$ is the unique element that makes the verifier to accept, this means that the same claim holds for the whole opening, and $\mathsf{FC}_{\mathsf{sn}}^{\mathcal{C}}$ is open-hiding.

(4: perfect zero-knowledge). We construct Sim as follows. It has (χ, y) as the trapdoor. It samples random $\mathsf{A}_s, \mathsf{B}_s \leftarrow_\$ \mathbb{Z}_p$, and then sets $[\mathsf{B}_i^{\mathsf{aux}}]_1 \leftarrow [\ell_{\nu-\kappa+i}(\chi) y \mathsf{B}_s]_1$ for all i. It computes B_p (by using the trapdoors), $[\mathsf{A}_p]_1$, and $[\mathsf{C}_p]_1$. It then computes the unique $[\mathsf{C}_{sp}]_1$ that makes the verifier to accept,

$$[\mathsf{C}_{sp}]_1 \leftarrow ((\mathsf{A}_s + y^\delta)(\mathsf{B}_s + \mathsf{B}_p) + \mathsf{A}_s y^\eta)[1]_1 + (\mathsf{B}_s + \mathsf{B}_p + y^\eta)[\mathsf{A}_p]_1 - y^\gamma [\mathsf{C}_p]_1 .$$

(5: evaluation-binding). Assume that $\mathcal{A}$ is an evaluation-binding adversary that, with probability $\varepsilon_{\mathcal{A}}$ and in time $\tau_{\mathcal{A}}$, returns a collision $(([\mathsf{A}_s, \{\mathsf{B}_i^{\mathsf{aux}}\}_{i=1}^\kappa]_1, [\mathsf{B}_s]_2); \boldsymbol{\beta}; \{\xi_i\}, [\mathsf{C}_{sp}]_1, \{\tilde{\xi}_i\}, [\tilde{\mathsf{C}}_{sp}]_1)$ with $\boldsymbol{\xi} \neq \tilde{\boldsymbol{\xi}}$, such that (here, $[\mathsf{A}_p, \mathsf{C}_p]_1$ / $[\tilde{\mathsf{A}}_p, \tilde{\mathsf{C}}_p]_1$ is the opening in the collision),

$$[\mathsf{A}_s + \mathsf{A}_p + y^\delta]_1 \bullet [\mathsf{B}_s + \mathsf{B}_p + y^\eta]_2 = [\mathsf{C}_{sp}]_1 \bullet [1]_2 + [\mathsf{C}_p]_1 \bullet [y^\gamma]_2 + [y^{\delta+\eta}]_T ,$$
$$[\mathsf{A}_s + \tilde{\mathsf{A}}_p + y^\delta]_1 \bullet [\mathsf{B}_s + \mathsf{B}_p + y^\eta]_2 = [\tilde{\mathsf{C}}_{sp}]_1 \bullet [1]_2 + [\tilde{\mathsf{C}}_p]_1 \bullet [y^\gamma]_2 + [y^{\delta+\eta}]_T ,$$

and $[\ell_{\nu-\kappa+i}(\chi) y]_1 \bullet [\mathsf{B}_s]_2 = [\mathsf{B}_i^{\mathsf{aux}}]_1 \bullet [1]_2$ for $i \in [1 \,..\, \kappa]$. Here we used the fact that by Items f and j of Theorem 1 (see also the definition of $u_p(X)$ and $v_p(X)$ in Eqs. (7) and (8)), the value of $[\mathsf{B}_p]_2$ stays the same in both openings.

We now construct an adversary $\mathcal{B}$ against the computational uber-assumption in $\mathbb{G}_1$. From the collision, by subtracting the second equation from the first equation and then moving everything from $\mathbb{G}_T$ (the result of pairings) to $\mathbb{G}_1$,

$$[(\mathsf{A}_p - \tilde{\mathsf{A}}_p)(\mathsf{B}_s + \mathsf{B}_p + y^\eta)]_1 = [\mathsf{C}_{sp}]_1 - [\tilde{\mathsf{C}}_{sp}]_1 + [(\mathsf{C}_p - \tilde{\mathsf{C}}_p) y^\gamma]_1 \cdot \qquad (14)$$

Denote $\Delta_i := \xi_i - \tilde{\xi}_i$. Let $\mathbf{a}$ and $\tilde{\mathbf{a}}$ be witnesses, used by $\mathcal{A}$ when creating the collision. Without any further assumptions (see Eqs. (7) and (9)), $A_p(X) - \tilde{A}_p(X) = \sum_{j=\mu_\alpha+\mu_\phi+2}^{\mu} (\mathsf{a}_j - \tilde{\mathsf{a}}_j) u_j(X) Y = \sum_{j=\mu-\mu_\chi-\kappa}^{\mu-\kappa} (\mathsf{a}_j - \tilde{\mathsf{a}}_j) u_j(X) Y + \sum_{j=\mu-\kappa+1}^{\mu} \Delta_{j-(\mu-\kappa)} u_j(X) Y$. (This is since for $j \le \mu_\alpha + \mu_\phi + 1$, $\mathsf{a}_j = \tilde{\mathsf{a}}_j$ is either fixed by the commitment or can be recomputed by the verifier from $\boldsymbol{\beta}$ alone.) Thus, Eq. (14) is equivalent to

$$\begin{aligned}&\left(\sum_{j=1}^{\mu_\chi} (\mathsf{a}_{\mu-\mu_\chi-\kappa+j} - \tilde{\mathsf{a}}_{\mu-\mu_\chi-\kappa+j}) u_{\xi j}(\chi) y + \sum_{i=1}^{\kappa} \Delta_i u_{\mu-\kappa+i}(\chi) y\right)(\mathsf{B}_s + \mathsf{B}_p + y^\eta) \\ &\quad = (\mathsf{C}_{sp} - \tilde{\mathsf{C}}_{sp}) + \sum_{i=1}^{\kappa} \Delta_i \left(u_{\mu-\kappa+i}(\chi) y^{\eta+1} + v_{\mu-\kappa+i}(\chi) y^{\delta+1} + w_{\mu-\kappa+i}(\chi) y^2\right) .\end{aligned}$$

Assuming Items e to g of Theorem 1,

$$\sum_{i=1}^{\mu_\chi} (\mathsf{a}_{\mu-\mu_\chi-\kappa+i} - \tilde{\mathsf{a}}_{\mu-\mu_\chi-\kappa+i}) u_{\xi j}(\chi) y (\mathsf{B}_s + \mathsf{B}_p + y^\eta) = (\mathsf{C}_{sp} - \tilde{\mathsf{C}}_{sp}) + \sum_{i=1}^{\kappa} \Delta_i \ell_{\nu-\kappa+i}(\chi) y^2 .$$

Assuming additionally Item i of Theorem 1,

$$\sum_{i=1}^{\kappa} \Delta_i\,[\ell_{\nu-\kappa+i}(\chi)y(\mathsf{B}_s + \mathsf{B}_p + y^{\eta})]_1 = [\mathsf{C}_{sp}]_1 - [\tilde{\mathsf{C}}_{sp}]_1 + \sum_{i=1}^{\kappa} \Delta_i[\ell_{\nu-\kappa+i}(\chi)y^2]_1 \;.$$

Let $[z]_1 := \sum_{i=1}^{\kappa} \Delta_i[\ell_{\nu-\kappa+i}(\chi)y^{\eta+1}]_1 (= \sum \Delta_i[f_i(\chi, y)]_1)$. In what follows, we show that $\mathcal{B}$ can compute $[z]_1$ and thus break the span-uber-assumption. From the last displayed equation, we get

$$\begin{aligned}[z]_1 + \sum_{i=1}^{\kappa} \Delta_i[\ell_{\nu-\kappa+i}(\chi)(\mathsf{B}_p - y)y]_1 &= [\mathsf{C}_{sp}]_1 - [\tilde{\mathsf{C}}_{sp}]_1 - \sum_{i=1}^{\kappa} \Delta_i[\ell_{\nu-\kappa+i}(\chi)\mathsf{B}_s y]_1 \\ &= [\mathsf{C}_{sp}]_1 - [\tilde{\mathsf{C}}_{sp}]_1 - \sum_{i=1}^{\kappa} \Delta_i[\mathsf{B}_i^{\mathsf{aux}}]_1 \;.\end{aligned}$$

(The last equation is guaranteed by $[\ell_{\nu-\kappa+i}(\chi)y]_1 \bullet [\mathsf{B}_s]_2 = [\mathsf{B}_i^{\mathsf{aux}}]_1 \bullet [1]_2$.)

We now show how to efficiently compute $[\ell_{\nu-\kappa+i}(\chi)(\mathsf{B}_p - y)y]_1$. Let $t(X) = v_p(X) - \sum_{i=1}^{\kappa} \ell_{\nu-\kappa+i}(X)$. Let $h_i'(X)$ be the rational function that satisfies

$$\begin{aligned} h_i'(X)\ell(X) &= \ell_{\nu-\kappa+i}(X)\left(\mathsf{B}_p(X,Y)/Y - 1\right) \\ &= \ell_{\nu-\kappa+i}(X)\left(t(X) + \sum_{i=1}^{\kappa} \ell_{\nu-\kappa+i}(X) - 1\right) \\ &= \ell_{\nu-\kappa+i}(X)(t(X) + \sum_{j\neq i} \ell_{\nu-\kappa+j}(X)) + \ell_{\nu-\kappa+i}(X)(\ell_{\nu-\kappa+i}(X) - 1) \;. \end{aligned} \quad (15)$$

Due to Item d of Theorem 1 and the definition of $t(X)$ (see also Eqs. (7) and (8)),

$$\ell(X) \mid \ell_{\nu-\kappa+i}(X)t(X) \;.$$

Moreover, $\ell(X) \mid \ell_{\nu-\kappa+i}(X)\ell_{\nu-\kappa+j}(X)$, for $i \neq j$, and $\ell(X) \mid \ell_{\nu-\kappa+i}(X)(\ell_{\nu-\kappa+i}(X) - 1)$. Thus, the polynomial on the right-hand side of Eq. (15) divides by $\ell(X)$. Thus, $h_i'(X)$ is a polynomial of degree $\leq \nu - 2$ and thus $\mathcal{B}$ can compute efficiently

$$[\ell_{\nu-\kappa+i}(\chi)(\mathsf{B}_p - y)y]_1 = [\ell_{\nu-\kappa+i}(\chi)(\mathsf{B}_p/y - 1)y^2]_1 = [h_i'(\chi)\ell(\chi)y^2]_1 \;,$$

and then

$$\begin{aligned}[z]_1 = &\sum_{i=1}^{\kappa} \Delta_i[\ell_{\nu-\kappa+i}(\chi)y^{\eta+1}]_1 \\ &\leftarrow([\mathsf{C}_{sp}]_1 - [\tilde{\mathsf{C}}_{sp}]_1) - \sum_{i=1}^{\kappa} \Delta_i\left([\mathsf{B}_i^{\mathsf{aux}}]_1 + [h_i'(\chi)\ell(\chi)y^2]_1\right) \;.\end{aligned}$$

Thus, given the collision, $\mathcal{B}$ outputs $(\boldsymbol{\Delta}, [z]_1 = \sum \Delta_i[f_i(\chi, y)]_1)$ for $f_i(X, Y) \notin \mathrm{span}(\mathcal{R})$. Thus, $\mathcal{B}$ breaks (w.p. $\varepsilon_{\mathcal{A}}$ and time close to $t_{\mathcal{A}}$) the $(\mathcal{R}, \mathcal{S}, \{f_i\})$-computational span-uber-assumption in $\mathbb{G}_1$ in the case $f_i \notin \mathrm{span}(\mathcal{R})$. □

The following Corollary follows from Item 5 in Theorem 3 and Lemma 2.

Corollary 1. *Let $\mathcal{C}$ be a fixed circuit. Let $\gamma = 4$, $\delta = 0$, and $\eta = 7$. Let $f_i'(X,Y) := (\ell_{\nu-\kappa+i}(X))^2 Y^{\eta+2}$. If the $(\mathcal{R}, \mathcal{S}, f_I')$-computational uber-assumption holds in $\mathbb{G}_T$ for all $I \in [1 \mathinner{..} \kappa]$ then $\mathsf{FC}_{\mathsf{sn}}^{\mathcal{C}}$ is computationally evaluation-binding.*

Remark 2. Importantly, the indeterminate Y is crucial in establishing the independence of f_i from $\mathcal{R}$. Let $\mathcal{R}^* := \{(X^i)_{i=0}^{\nu-1}, (X^i\ell(X))_{i=0}^{\nu-2}\}$, $\mathcal{S}^* := \{(X^i)_{i=0}^{\nu-1}\}$, and $f_i^* := \ell_{\nu-\kappa+i}(X)$. One can establish that $\mathsf{FC}_{\mathsf{sn}}^{\mathcal{C}}$ is evaluation-binding under the $(\mathcal{R}^*, \mathcal{S}^*, \{f_i^*\})$-computational span-uber-assumption in $\mathbb{G}_1$. Really, consider the following $(\mathcal{R}^*, \mathcal{S}^*, \{f_i^*\})$-span-uber-assumption adversary $\mathcal{B}^*$ that will create y herself, generate a new ck based on her input and y, and then use $\mathcal{B}$ in Theorem 3 to break the $(\mathcal{R}^*, \mathcal{S}^*, \{f_i^*\})$-computational span-uber-assumption. $\mathcal{B}^*$ will have similar success as $\mathcal{B}$. However, $f_i^* \in \mathrm{span}(\mathcal{R}^*)$ and thus the $(\mathcal{R}^*, \mathcal{S}^*, \{f_i^*\})$-computational span-uber-assumption itself is not secure.

On the Security of the Span-Uber-Assumption. It is known that in composite-order bilinear groups, the computational uber-assumption in $\mathbb{G}_T$ holds under appropriate subgroup hiding assumptions [13]. Hence, a composite-order group version of the span-uber-assumption (and also of the new SFC) is secure under a subgroup hiding assumption. In the full version [34], we will use the Déjà Q approach of [14] directly to prove that the span-uber-assumption in $\mathbb{G}_\iota$, $\iota \in \{1, 2\}$, is secure under a subgroup hiding assumption. More precisely, we establish the following corollary. (See the full version [34] for the definition of subgroup hiding and extended adaptive parameter hiding.)

Theorem 4. *The $(\mathcal{R}, \mathcal{S}, \{f_i\}_{i=1}^{\kappa})$-computational span-uber-assumption holds in the source group $\mathbb{G}_1$ with all but negligible probability if*

1. *subgroup hiding holds in $\mathbb{G}_1$ with respect to $\mu = \{\mathsf{P}_1^2, \mathsf{P}_2^1\}$,*
2. *subgroup hiding holds in $\mathbb{G}_2$ with respect to $\mu = \{\mathsf{P}_1^1\}$,*
3. *extended adaptive parameter hiding holds with respect to $\mathcal{R} \cup \{f_i\}_{i=1}^{\kappa}$ and $\mathsf{aux} = \{\mathsf{P}_2^{1\sigma(\cdot)}\}_{\sigma \in \mathcal{S}}$ for any $\mathsf{P}_2^1 \in \mathbb{G}_2$.*
4. *the polynomials in $\mathcal{R}$ have maximum degree $\mathsf{poly}(\lambda)$.*

Here, $\mathbb{G}_1, \mathbb{G}_2, \mathbb{G}_T$ are additive groups of composite order $N = p_1 p_2$ ($p_1 \neq p_2$) and $\mathsf{P}_\iota^1 \in \mathbb{G}_{\iota,p_1}$, $\mathsf{P}_\iota^2 \in \mathbb{G}_{\iota,p_2}$ are randomly sampled subgroup generators, where $\mathbb{G}_{\iota,p_j}$ is the subgroup of $\mathbb{G}_\iota$ of order p_j and $\mathsf{P}_\iota \in \mathbb{G}_\iota = \mathbb{G}_{\iota,p_1} \oplus \mathbb{G}_{\iota,p_2}$.

The direct proof in the full version [34] is simpler than the mentioned two-step proof since it does not rely on the intermediate step of reducing the span-uber-assumption to a uber-assumption in $\mathbb{G}_T$. Moreover, the Déjà Q approach is more straightforward in case one works in the source group. We will leave it up to future work to reduce *prime-order* span-uber-assumption to a simpler assumption; there has been almost no prior work on reducing prime-order *assumptions.*

Finally, in the full version [34], by following [33], we will prove that the span-uber-assumption is secure under a hash algebraic knowledge (HAK) assumption and the well-known PDL assumption [31], from which it follows that is secure in the algebraic group model (with hashing) [19] under the PDL assumption.[1] Following the semi-generic-group model of [26], the HAK assumptions of [33] are defined only in the case when the adversary outputs elements in the source groups (but not in $\mathbb{G}_T$), and thus one cannot prove the security of the computational uber-assumption in $\mathbb{G}_T$ using the approach of [33]. Thus, in a well-defined sense, the span-uber-assumption is weaker than the uber-assumption in $\mathbb{G}_T$.

[1] As a corollary of independent interest, we also show in the full version [34] that if $f \notin \mathrm{span}(\mathcal{R})$ then the $(\mathcal{R}, \mathcal{S}, \mathcal{T})$-uber-assumption follows from HAK and PDL.

References

1. Abdolmaleki, B., Baghery, K., Lipmaa, H., Zając, M.: A subversion-resistant SNARK. In: Takagi, T., Peyrin, T. (eds.) ASIACRYPT 2017, Part III. LNCS, vol. 10626, pp. 3–33. Springer, Cham (2017). https://doi.org/10.1007/978-3-319-70700-6_1
2. Abdolmaleki, B., Lipmaa, H., Siim, J., Zając, M.: On QA-NIZK in the BPK model. In: Kiayias, A., Kohlweiss, M., Wallden, P., Zikas, V. (eds.) PKC 2020, Part I. LNCS, vol. 12110, pp. 590–620. Springer, Cham (2020). https://doi.org/10.1007/978-3-030-45374-9_20
3. Barić, N., Pfitzmann, B.: Collision-free accumulators and fail-stop signature schemes without trees. In: Fumy, W. (ed.) EUROCRYPT 1997. LNCS, vol. 1233, pp. 480–494. Springer, Heidelberg (1997). https://doi.org/10.1007/3-540-69053-0_33
4. Bellare, M., Fuchsbauer, G., Scafuro, A.: NIZKs with an untrusted CRS: security in the face of parameter subversion. In: Cheon, J.H., Takagi, T. (eds.) ASIACRYPT 2016, Part II. LNCS, vol. 10032, pp. 777–804. Springer, Heidelberg (2016). https://doi.org/10.1007/978-3-662-53890-6_26
5. Benaloh, J., de Mare, M.: One-way accumulators: a decentralized alternative to digital signatures. In: Helleseth, T. (ed.) EUROCRYPT 1993. LNCS, vol. 765, pp. 274–285. Springer, Heidelberg (1994). https://doi.org/10.1007/3-540-48285-7_24
6. Bitansky, N.: Verifiable random functions from non-interactive witness-indistinguishable proofs. In: Kalai, Y., Reyzin, L. (eds.) TCC 2017, Part II. LNCS, vol. 10678, pp. 567–594. Springer, Cham (2017). https://doi.org/10.1007/978-3-319-70503-3_19
7. Boneh, D., Boyen, X., Goh, E.-J.: Hierarchical identity based encryption with constant size ciphertext. In: Cramer, R. (ed.) EUROCRYPT 2005. LNCS, vol. 3494, pp. 440–456. Springer, Heidelberg (2005). https://doi.org/10.1007/11426639_26
8. Boneh, D., Bünz, B., Fisch, B.: Batching techniques for accumulators with applications to IOPs and stateless blockchains. In: Boldyreva, A., Micciancio, D. (eds.) CRYPTO 2019, Part I. LNCS, vol. 11692, pp. 561–586. Springer, Cham (2019). https://doi.org/10.1007/978-3-030-26948-7_20
9. Boneh, D., Drake, J., Fisch, B., Gabizon, A.: Efficient polynomial commitment schemes for multiple points and polynomials. Technical report 2020/081, IACR (2020)
10. Bowe, S., Grigg, J., Hopwood, D.: Halo: recursive proof composition without a trusted setup. Technical report (2019). https://electriccoin.co/wp-content/uploads/2019/09/Halo.pdf
11. Boyen, X.: The uber-assumption family. In: Galbraith, S.D., Paterson, K.G. (eds.) Pairing 2008. LNCS, vol. 5209, pp. 39–56. Springer, Heidelberg (2008). https://doi.org/10.1007/978-3-540-85538-5_3
12. Catalano, D., Fiore, D.: Vector commitments and their applications. In: Kurosawa, K., Hanaoka, G. (eds.) PKC 2013. LNCS, vol. 7778, pp. 55–72. Springer, Heidelberg (2013). https://doi.org/10.1007/978-3-642-36362-7_5
13. Chase, M., Maller, M., Meiklejohn, S.: Déjà Q all over again: tighter and broader reductions of q-type assumptions. In: Cheon, J.H., Takagi, T. (eds.) ASIACRYPT 2016, Part II. LNCS, vol. 10032, pp. 655–681. Springer, Heidelberg (2016). https://doi.org/10.1007/978-3-662-53890-6_22

14. Chase, M., Meiklejohn, S.: Déjà Q: using dual systems to revisit q-type assumptions. In: Nguyen, P.Q., Oswald, E. (eds.) EUROCRYPT 2014. LNCS, vol. 8441, pp. 622–639. Springer, Heidelberg (2014). https://doi.org/10.1007/978-3-642-55220-5_34
15. Chiesa, A., Hu, Y., Maller, M., Mishra, P., Vesely, N., Ward, N.: Marlin: preprocessing zkSNARKs with universal and updatable SRS. In: Canteaut, A., Ishai, Y. (eds.) EUROCRYPT 2020, Part I. LNCS, vol. 12105, pp. 738–768. Springer, Cham (2020). https://doi.org/10.1007/978-3-030-45721-1_26
16. Dent, A.W.: Adapting the weaknesses of the random oracle model to the generic group model. In: Zheng, Y. (ed.) ASIACRYPT 2002. LNCS, vol. 2501, pp. 100–109. Springer, Heidelberg (2002). https://doi.org/10.1007/3-540-36178-2_6
17. Fischlin, M.: A note on security proofs in the generic model. In: Okamoto, T. (ed.) ASIACRYPT 2000. LNCS, vol. 1976, pp. 458–469. Springer, Heidelberg (2000). https://doi.org/10.1007/3-540-44448-3_35
18. Fuchsbauer, G.: Subversion-zero-knowledge SNARKs. In: Abdalla, M., Dahab, R. (eds.) PKC 2018, Part I. LNCS, vol. 10769, pp. 315–347. Springer, Cham (2018). https://doi.org/10.1007/978-3-319-76578-5_11
19. Fuchsbauer, G., Kiltz, E., Loss, J.: The algebraic group model and its applications. In: Shacham, H., Boldyreva, A. (eds.) CRYPTO 2018, Part II. LNCS, vol. 10992, pp. 33–62. Springer, Cham (2018). https://doi.org/10.1007/978-3-319-96881-0_2
20. Gennaro, R., Gentry, C., Parno, B., Raykova, M.: Quadratic span programs and succinct NIZKs without PCPs. In: Johansson, T., Nguyen, P.Q. (eds.) EUROCRYPT 2013. LNCS, vol. 7881, pp. 626–645. Springer, Heidelberg (2013). https://doi.org/10.1007/978-3-642-38348-9_37
21. Gentry, C., Wichs, D.: Separating succinct non-interactive arguments from all falsifiable assumptions. In: 43rd ACM STOC, pp. 99–108 (2011)
22. Gorbunov, S., Reyzin, L., Wee, H., Zhang, Z.: PointProofs: aggregating proofs for multiple vector commitments. Technical report 2020/419, IACR (2020)
23. Groth, J.: Short pairing-based non-interactive zero-knowledge arguments. In: Abe, M. (ed.) ASIACRYPT 2010. LNCS, vol. 6477, pp. 321–340. Springer, Heidelberg (2010). https://doi.org/10.1007/978-3-642-17373-8_19
24. Groth, J.: On the size of pairing-based non-interactive arguments. In: Fischlin, M., Coron, J.-S. (eds.) EUROCRYPT 2016, Part II. LNCS, vol. 9666, pp. 305–326. Springer, Heidelberg (2016). https://doi.org/10.1007/978-3-662-49896-5_11
25. Izabachène, M., Libert, B., Vergnaud, D.: Block-wise P-signatures and non-interactive anonymous credentials with efficient attributes. In: Chen, L. (ed.) IMACC 2011. LNCS, vol. 7089, pp. 431–450. Springer, Heidelberg (2011). https://doi.org/10.1007/978-3-642-25516-8_26
26. Jager, T., Rupp, A.: The semi-generic group model and applications to pairing-based cryptography. In: Abe, M. (ed.) ASIACRYPT 2010. LNCS, vol. 6477, pp. 539–556. Springer, Heidelberg (2010). https://doi.org/10.1007/978-3-642-17373-8_31
27. Kate, A., Zaverucha, G.M., Goldberg, I.: Constant-size commitments to polynomials and their applications. In: Abe, M. (ed.) ASIACRYPT 2010. LNCS, vol. 6477, pp. 177–194. Springer, Heidelberg (2010). https://doi.org/10.1007/978-3-642-17373-8_11
28. Lai, R.W.F., Malavolta, G.: Subvector commitments with application to succinct arguments. In: Boldyreva, A., Micciancio, D. (eds.) CRYPTO 2019, Part I. LNCS, vol. 11692, pp. 530–560. Springer, Cham (2019). https://doi.org/10.1007/978-3-030-26948-7_19

29. Libert, B., Ramanna, S.C., Yung, M.: Functional commitment schemes: from polynomial commitments to pairing-based accumulators from simple assumptions. In: ICALP 2016. LIPIcs, vol. 55, pp. 30:1–30:14 (2016)
30. Libert, B., Yung, M.: Concise mercurial vector commitments and independent zero-knowledge sets with short proofs. In: Micciancio, D. (ed.) TCC 2010. LNCS, vol. 5978, pp. 499–517. Springer, Heidelberg (2010). https://doi.org/10.1007/978-3-642-11799-2_30
31. Lipmaa, H.: Progression-free sets and sublinear pairing-based non-interactive zero-knowledge arguments. In: Cramer, R. (ed.) TCC 2012. LNCS, vol. 7194, pp. 169–189. Springer, Heidelberg (2012). https://doi.org/10.1007/978-3-642-28914-9_10
32. Lipmaa, H.: Succinct non-interactive zero knowledge arguments from span programs and linear error-correcting codes. In: Sako, K., Sarkar, P. (eds.) ASIACRYPT 2013, Part I. LNCS, vol. 8269, pp. 41–60. Springer, Heidelberg (2013). https://doi.org/10.1007/978-3-642-42033-7_3
33. Lipmaa, H.: Simulation-extractable ZK-SNARKs revisited. Technical report 2019/612, IACR (2019) https://eprint.iacr.org/2019/612. Accessed 8 Feb 2020
34. Lipmaa, H., Pavlyk, K.: Succinct functional commitment for a large class of arithmetic circuits. Technical Report 2020/?, IACR (2020)
35. Maller, M., Bowe, S., Kohlweiss, M., Meiklejohn, S.: Sonic: zero-knowledge SNARKs from linear-size universal and updatable structured reference strings. In: ACM CCS 2019, pp. 2111–2128 (2019)
36. Papamanthou, C., Shi, E., Tamassia, R.: Signatures of correct computation. In: Sahai, A. (ed.) TCC 2013. LNCS, vol. 7785, pp. 222–242. Springer, Heidelberg (2013). https://doi.org/10.1007/978-3-642-36594-2_13
37. Shpilka, A., Yehudayoff, A.: Arithmetic circuits: a survey of recent results and open questions. In: Foundations and Trends in Theoretical Computer Science, vol. 5. Now Publishers Inc. (2010)
38. Tomescu, A., Abraham, I., Buterin, V., Drake, J., Feist, D., Khovratovich, D.: Aggregatable subvector commitments for stateless cryptocurrencies. Technical report 2020/527, IACR (2020)
39. Valiant, L.G.: Completeness classes in algebra. In: STOC 1979, pp. 249–261 (1979)
40. Wahby, R.S., Tzialla, I., Shelat, A., Thaler, J., Walfish, M.: Doubly-efficient zkSNARKs without trusted setup. In: IEEE SP 2018, pp. 926–943 (2018)
41. Zhang, Y., Genkin, D., Katz, J., Papadopoulos, D., Papamanthou, C.: vSQL: verifying arbitrary SQL queries over dynamic outsourced databases. In: IEEE SP 2017, pp. 863–880 (2017)

Crowd Verifiable Zero-Knowledge and End-to-End Verifiable Multiparty Computation

Foteini Baldimtsi[1], Aggelos Kiayias[2,3], Thomas Zacharias[2(✉)], and Bingsheng Zhang[4,5]

[1] George Mason University, Fairfax, USA
foteini@gmu.edu
[2] The University of Edinburgh, Edinburgh, UK
{akiayias,tzachari}@inf.ed.ac.uk
[3] IOHK, Hong Kong, China
[4] Zhejiang University, Hangzhou, China
bingsheng@zju.edu.cn
[5] Alibaba-Zhejiang University Joint Research Institute of Frontier Technologies, Hangzhou, China

Abstract. Auditing a secure multiparty computation (MPC) protocol entails the validation of the protocol transcript by a third party that is otherwise untrusted. In this work, we introduce the concept of *end-to-end verifiable* MPC (VMPC), that requires the validation to provide a correctness guarantee even in the setting that all servers, trusted setup primitives and all the client systems utilized by the input-providing users of the MPC protocol are subverted by an adversary. To instantiate VMPC, we introduce a new concept in the setting of zero-knowlegde protocols that we term *crowd verifiable zero-knowledge* (CVZK). A CVZK protocol enables a prover to convince a set of verifiers about a certain statement, even though each one individually contributes a small amount of entropy for verification and some of them are adversarially controlled. Given CVZK, we present a VMPC protocol that is based on discrete-logarithm related assumptions. At the high level of adversity that VMPC is meant to withstand, it is infeasible to ensure perfect correctness, thus we investigate the classes of functions and verifiability relations that are feasible in our framework, and present a number of possible applications the underlying functions of which can be implemented via VMPC.

Keywords: Multi-party computation · Zero-knowledge · Privacy · Verifiability

F. Baldimtsi—Supported by NSF grant 1717067.

A. Kiayias and T. Zacharias—Supported by Horizon 2020 project #780477 (PRIViLEDGE).

B. Zhang—Supported by the Leading Innovative and Entrepreneur Team Introduction Program of Zhejiang (Grant No. 2018R01005) and Zhejiang Key R&D Plan (Grant No. 2019C03133).

S. Moriai and H. Wang (Eds.): ASIACRYPT 2020, LNCS 12493, pp. 717–748, 2020.
https://doi.org/10.1007/978-3-030-64840-4_24

1 Introduction

Over the last 30 years, secure multiparty computation (MPC) has transitioned from theoretical feasibility results [32,57,58] to real-world implementations [12,24,26,27,43,55] that can be used for a number of different security critical operations including auctions [12], e-voting [1,23,41], and privacy preserving statistics [13,48]. An important paradigm for MPC that captures a large number of applications is the *client-server* model [6,25,30,33,38,49] where participants of the system are distinguished between clients and servers, with the clients contributing input for the computation and receiving the output, while the servers, operating in an oblivious fashion, are processing the data given by the clients.

The servers performing the MPC protocol collectively ensure the privacy preservation of the execution, up to the information that is leaked by the output itself. There do exist protocols that achieve this level of privacy provided that there exists *at least one server* that is not subverted by the adversary. The typical execution of such protocols involves the clients encoding their input suitably for processing by the servers (e.g., by performing secret-sharing [35]) and receiving the encoded output which they reconstruct to produce the final result. While the level of privacy achieved by such protocols is adequate for their intended applications and their performance has improved over time (e.g., protocols such as SPDZ [27] and [26,39] achieve very good performance for real world applications by utilizing an offline/online approach [5]), there are still crucial considerations for their deployment in the real-world especially if the outcome of the MPC protocol has important committing and actionable consequences (such as e.g., in e-voting, auctions and other protocols).

To address this consideration, Baum, Damgård and Orlandi [4] asked whether it is feasible to construct efficient *auditable* MPC protocols. In auditable MPC, an external observer who is given access to the protocol transcript, can verify that the protocol was executed correctly even if all the servers (but not client devices) were subverted by the adversary. The authors of [4] observe that this is theoretically feasible if a common reference string (CRS) is available to the participants and provide an efficient instantiation of such protocol by suitably amending the SPDZ protocol [27]. While the above constitutes a good step towards addressing real world considerations of deploying MPC protocols, there are serious issues that remain from the perspective of auditability. Specifically, the work of [4] does not provide any guarantees about the validity of the output in case, (i) the CRS is subverted, or (ii) the users' client devices get corrupted.

Verification of the correctness of the result by any party, even if all servers are corrupt (but not client devices), has also been studied by Schoenmakers and Veeningen [56] in the context of *universally verifiable* MPC. The security analysis in [56] is in the random oracle model and still, the case of corrupted client devices is not considered. Moreover, achieving universally verifiable (or publicly auditable) MPC in the standard model is stated as an open problem.

Unfortunately, the threat of malicious CRS and client byzantine behavior cannot be dismissed: in fact, it has been extensively studied in the context of e-voting systems, which are a very compelling use-case for MPC, and frequently invoked as one of the important considerations for real-world deployment. Specifically, the issue of malicious clients has been studied in the end-to-end verifiability model for e-voting, e.g., [44] while the issue of removing setup assumptions such as the CRS or random oracles has been also recently considered [40,41].

The fact that the concept of end-to-end verifiability has been so far thoroughly examined in the e-voting area comes not as surprise, since elections is a prominent example where auditing the correctness of the execution is a top integrity requirement. Nonetheless, transparency in terms of end-to-end verification can be a highly desirable feature in several other scenarios, such as auctions, demographic statistics, financial analysis, or profile matching where the (human) users contributing their inputs may have a keen interest in auditing the correctness of the computation (e.g., highest bid, unemployment rate, average salary, order book matching in trading). From a mathematical aspect, it appears that several other use-cases of MPC evaluation functions besides tallying that fall into the scope of end-to-end verification have not been examined.

To capture these considerations and instead of pursuing tailored-made studies for each use-case, in this work, we take a step forward and propose a unified treatment of the problem of end-to-end verifiability in MPC under a "human-client-server" setting. In particular, we separate human users from their client devices (e.g., smartphones) in the spirit of the "ceremony" concept [29,42] of voting protocols. While client devices can be thought of as stateful, probabilistic, interactive Turing machines, we model human users to be limited in two ways: (a) humans are bad sources of randomness; formally, the randomness of a user can be adversarially guessed with non-negligible probability, i.e. its min-entropy is up to logarithmic to the security parameter, and (b) humans cannot perform complicated calculations; i.e. humans' computational complexity is linear in the security parameter (i.e., the minimum for reading the input). Given this modeling we ask:

Is it possible to construct auditable MPC protocols, in the sense that everyone who has access to the transcript can verify that the output is correct, even if all servers, client devices and setup assumptions (e.g. a common reference string) are subverted by an adversary?

We answer this question by introducing the concept of *end-to-end verifiable multiparty computation* (VMPC) and presenting both feasibility and infeasibility results for different classes of functions. Some of the most promising applications of VMPC include e-voting, privacy preserving statistics and supervised learning of classifiers over private data.

1.1 Technical Overview and Contributions

VMPC Model. The security property of VMPC is modeled in the universal composability (UC) framework [15], aiming to unifying two lines of research on secure computing: end-to-end verifiable e-voting (which typically separates humans from their devices in security analysis) and client-server (auditable) MPC. More specifically, we define the VMPC ideal functionality as $\mathcal{F}_{\mathsf{vmpc}}^{f,R}(\mathcal{P})$, where $\mathcal{P}$ is a set of players, including users, client devices, servers and a verifier; f is the MPC function to be evaluated, and R is a relation that is used to measure the distance between the returned VMPC output and the correct (true) computation result. As will be explained later, when the VMPC output is verified, it is guaranteed that the output is not "far" from the truth.

The Distinction Between Users and Clients. In order to capture "end-to-end verifiability", we have to make a distinction between users and clients: the users are the humans with limited computation and entropy that interact with their client devices (e.g., smartphones or laptops) to provide input to the MPC. To accommodate this, our ideal functionality acknowledges these two roles and for this reason it departs from the previous formulation of auditable MPC [4]. A critical challenge in VMPC is the fact that the result should be verifiable even if *all* clients and servers are corrupted!

The Role of the Verifier. VMPC departs from the conventional UC definition of MPC since there should be a special entity, the verifier, that verifies the correctness of the output. The concept of the verifier in our modeling is an abstraction only. The verifier is invoked only for auditing and trusted only for verifiability, not privacy. It can be any device, organization, or computer system that the user trusts to do the audit. Moreover, it is straightforward to extend the model to involve multiple verifiers as discussed in Sect. 5 and hence only for simplicity we choose to model just a single entity. We note that the human user cannot perform auditing herself due to the fact that it requires cryptographic computations. As in e-voting, verification is delegatable, i.e., the verifier obtains users' individual audit data in an out-of-band manner.

EUC with a Super-Polynomial Helper. The astute readers may notice that a UC realization of the VMPC primitive in a setting where there is no trusted setup such as a CRS is infeasible. Indeed, it is well known [15] that non-trivial MPC functionalities cannot be UC-realized without a trusted setup. To go around these impossibility results and still provide a composable construction, we utilize the extended UC model with a helper $\mathcal{H}$, ($\mathcal{H}$-EUC security) [17]. This model, which can been seen as an adaptation of the super-polynomial simulation concept [54] in the UC setting, enables one to provide standard model constructions that are composable and at the same time real world secure, using a "complexity leveraging" argument that requires subexponential security for the underlying cryptographic primitives. In particular, in the setting of $\mathcal{H}$-EUC security, translating a real world attack to an ideal world attack requires a super-polynomial computation. More precisely, a polynomial-time operation that invokes a super-polynomial helper program $\mathcal{H}$. It follows that if the distance of the real world from the ideal is bounded by the distinguishing advantage of some underlying cryptographic distributions, assuming subexponential indistinguishability is sufficient to infer the security for the primitive.

System Architecture. We assume there exists a *consistent and public bulletin board*(BB) (modeled as the global functionality $\mathcal{G}_{\mathsf{BB}}$) that can be accessed by all the VMPC players except human users, i.e., by the client devices, the servers and the verifier. In addition, we assume there exists an authenticated channel (modeled as the functionality $\mathcal{F}_{\mathsf{auth}}$) between the human users and the verifier. Besides, we assume there exists a secure channel (modeled as the functionality $\mathcal{F}_{\mathsf{sc}}$) between the human users and their local client devices. A VMPC scheme consists of four sub-protocols: Initialize (setup phase among servers), Input (run by servers, users-clients), Compute (executed by the servers) and Verify (executed by the verifier and users). According to the e-voting and pre-processing MPC approach [11,26,27,52], we consider *minimal user interaction* - the users independently interact with the system once in order to submit their inputs. This limitation is challenging from a protocol design perspective.

The Breadth of VMPC Feasibility. We explore the class of functions that can be realized by VMPC, since in our setting, contrary to general MPC results, it is *infeasible* to compute any function with perfect correctness. To see this with a simple example, consider some function f that outputs the XOR of the input bits. It is easy to see that each user has too little entropy to challenge the set of malicious clients and servers about the proper encoding of her private input. However, even if a single input bit is incorrectly encoded by the user's client (which can be undetected with non-negligible probability) the output XOR value can be flipped. To accommodate for this natural deficiency, our VMPC functionality enforces a relation R between the reported output and the correct output. It is clear that depending on the function f, a different relation R may be achievable. We capture this interplay between correctness and the function to be computed by introducing the notion of a *spreading relation* R for a function $f : X \to Y$. Informally, given a certain metric over the input space, a spreading relation over the range of f, satisfies that whenever x, x' are close w.r.t. the metric, the images of x, x' are related. A typical case of a spreading relation can emerge when f is a Lipschitz function for a given metric. Based on the above, we show that one cannot hope to compute a function f with a relation over the range of f that is more "refined" than a spreading relation.

Building Blocks. VMPC is a complex primitive and we introduce *novel building blocks* to facilitate it. ZK proofs cannot be directly used for VMPC since we require a 3-round public-coin protocol to comply with our minimal interaction setting and this is infeasible, cf. [31,37], while we cannot utilize a subversion-sound NIZK either, cf. [7], since in this case, we can at best obtain witness indistinguishability which is insufficient for proving the simulation-based privacy needed for VMPC.

Crowd Verifiable Zero-Knowledge (CVZK). To overcome these issues we introduce a new cryptographic primitive that we call *crowd verifiable zero-knowledge* which may also be of independent interest. In CVZK, a single prover tries to convince a set of n verifiers (a "crowd") of the validity of a certain statement. Although the notion of multi-verifier zero-knowledge already exists in the literature, e.g. [14,47], the focus of CVZK is different. Namely, the challenge for CVZK is that each human verifier is restricted to contribute up to a logarithmic number of random bits and hence, if, say all but one verifiers are corrupted, there would be insufficient entropy available in order to achieve a low soundness error. Thus, the only way to go forward for the verifiers is to assume the relative honesty of the crowd, i.e., there is a sufficient number of them acting honestly and introduce enough randomness in the system so that the soundness error can be small. The notion of CVZK is critical towards realizing VMPC, since in the absence of reliable client systems, the users have no obvious way of challenging the system's operation; users, being humans, are assumed to be bad sources of entropy that cannot contribute individually a sufficient number of random bits to provide a sufficiently low soundness error.

Coalescence Functions and CVZK Instantiation. We introduce *coalescence functions* (Sect. 3.2) to typify the randomness extraction primitive that is at the core of our CVZK construction. In CVZK, it is not straightforward how to use the random bits that honest verifiers contribute. The reason is that the adversary, who is in control of the prover and a number of verifiers, may attempt to use the malicious verifiers' coins to "cancel" the entropy of the honest verifiers and assist the malicious prover to convince them of a wrong statement. Coalescence relates to collective coin flipping [8] and randomness condensers [28]. In particular, a coalescence function is a deterministic function that tries to make good use of the entropy of its input. Specifically, a coalescence function takes as an input a non-oblivious symbol fixing source and produces a series of blocks, one of which is guaranteed to be of high entropy; these blocks will be subsequently used in conjunction to form the challenge implementing CVZK. We construct coalescence functions using a one-round collective coin flipping protocol and the (strongly) resilient function defined in [50]. Then, we present a compiler that takes a fully input delayed Σ-protocol and leads to a CVZK construction that performs a parallel proof w.r.t. each block produced by the coalescence function. Our CVZK construction is secure for any number of corrupted users up to $O(n^c/\log^3 n)$, for some constant $c < 1$ and a set of n users.

VMPC Construction. Our VMPC construction is based on CVZK. It uses an offline / online approach (a.k.a. pre-processing mode) for computing the output (proposed by Beaver [5] and utilized numerous times [4,27]). In a nutshell, our construction follows the paradigm of SPDZ [27] and BDO [4]. Namely, the data are shared and committed on the BB. The underlying secret sharing scheme and the commitment scheme have compatible linearly homomorphic properties; therefore, the auditor can check the correctness of the protocol execution by performing the same operations over the committed data. In addition, to achieve crowd verifiability, all the ZK proofs need to be transformed to CVZK – (i) in the pre-processing phase, the servers post the first move of the CVZK on the BB; (ii) in the input phase, the (human) users collaboratively generate the challenge coins of the CVZK; (iii) in the output phase, the servers post the protocol output together with the third move of the CVZK, which completes the CVZK proofs.

We prove indistinguishability between real and ideal world for our construction under adaptive onewayness [53] of the discrete-logarithm function and the decisional Diffie-Hellman assumption. We infer that, by utilizing sub-exponential versions of those assumptions, our protocol realizes the ideal description of VMPC, in the $\mathcal{H}$-EUC model, for any (symmetric) function f with correctness up to a spreading relation R for f.

We note that an alternative but sub-optimal approach to VMPC would be to add the Benaloh challenge mechanism [9,10], that has been proposed in the context of e-voting to mitigate corrupted client devices, to the BDO protocol [4]. However, the resulting VMPC protocol would still require a trusted setup, e.g., CRS or Random Oracle (RO), and therefore it would fall short of our objective to realize VMPC in the plain model. Moreover, the Benaloh challenge mechanism requires the client to have a second trusted device that is capable of performing a cryptographic computation *prior to submitting her input* to the VMPC protocol and being able to communicate with it in an authenticated manner. Instead, the only requirement in our VMPC protocol is to have authenticated access to a verifier in the final step of the protocol.

Applications. As already mentioned, a main motivation for this work is the apparent connection of end-to-end verifiability to several practical MPC instantiations for real-world scenarios. Thus, we conclude by discussing possible applications of VMPC and examine how their underlying function can be combined with suitable spreading relations and implemented. We provide some interesting examples: (i) E-voting functions: where the final election tally aggregates the votes provided by the voters, (ii) privacy-preserving statistics: where the final outcome is a statistic that is calculated over uni-dimensional data, (iii) privacy-preserving processing of multi-dimensional data: where functions that correlate across different dimensions are calculated, (iv) supervised learning of classifiers: where the outcome is a model that results from training on private data.

2 Preliminaries

Notation. By λ we denote the security parameter and by $\mathsf{negl}(\cdot)$ the property that a function is negligible in some parameter. We write $\mathrm{poly}(x)$ to denote that a value is polynomial in x, PPT to denote probabilistic polynomial time, and $[n]$ as the abbreviation of the set $\{1, \dots, n\}$. $H_{\min}(\mathbb{D})$ denotes the min entropy of a distribution $\mathbb{D}$ and $\mathbb{U}_n$ denotes the uniform distribution over $\{0,1\}^n$. By $x \xleftarrow{\$} S$, we denote that x is sampled uniformly at random from set S, and by $X \sim \mathbb{D}$ that the random variable X follows the distribution $\mathbb{D}$.

Σ-Protocols. Let $R_{\mathcal{L}}$ be polynomial-time-decidable witness relation for an **NP**-language $\mathcal{L}$. A *Σ-protocol* is a 3-move public coin protocol between a prover, $\Sigma.\mathsf{Prv}$, and a verifier, $\Sigma.V$, where the goal of the prover, having a witness w, is to convince the verifier that some statement x is in language $\mathcal{L}$. We split the prover $\Sigma.\mathsf{Prv}$ into two algorithms $(\Sigma.\mathsf{Prv}_1, \Sigma.\mathsf{Prv}_2)$. A Σ-protocol for $(x, w) \in \mathcal{R}_{\mathcal{L}}$ consists of the following PPT algorithms:

- $\Sigma.\mathsf{Prv}_1(x, w)$: on input $x \in \mathcal{L}$ and w s.t. $(x, w) \in \mathcal{R}_{\mathcal{L}}$, it outputs the first message of the protocol, a, and a state $\mathsf{st}_P \in \{0,1\}^*$.
- $\Sigma.\mathsf{Prv}_2(\mathsf{st}_P, e)$: after receiving the challenge $e \in \{0,1\}^\lambda$ from $\Sigma.V$ and on input the state st_P, it outputs the prover's response z.
- $\Sigma.\mathsf{Verify}(x, a, e, z)$: on input a transcript (x, a, e, z), it outputs $b \in \{0,1\}$. A transcript is called *accepting* if $\Sigma.\mathsf{Verify}(x, a, e, z) = 1$.

We care about the following properties: (i) completeness, (ii) special soundness, and (iii) *special honest verifier zero-knowledge (sHVZK)*, i.e., if the challenge e is known in advance, then there is a PPT simulator $\Sigma.\mathsf{Sim}$ that simulates the transcript on input (x, e). In addition, we allow completeness of a Σ-protocol to be non-perfect, i.e. have a negligible error, and sHVZK to be computational.

One-Round Collective Coin Flipping and Resilient Functions. The core of our CVZK construction is similar to a *one-round collective coin flipping (1RCCF)* process: (1) each player generates and broadcasts a coin c within the same round, (2) a uniformly random string is produced (with high probability). The adversary can see the honest players' coins first and then decide the corrupted players' coins. The 1RCCF notion was introduced in [8] and is closely related to the notion of resilient functions which we recall below.

Definition 1 (Resilient function). *Let $f : \{0,1\}^m \longrightarrow \{0,1\}$ be a Boolean function on variables $x_1, \ldots, x_m$. The* influence *of a set $S \subseteq \{x_1, \ldots, x_m\}$ on f, denoted by $I_S(f)$, is defined as the probability that f is undetermined after fixing the variables outside S uniformly at random. Let $I_q(f) = \min_{S \subseteq \{x_1,\ldots,x_m\}, |S| \le q} I_S(f)$. We say that f is (q, ε)-*resilient *if $I_q(f) \le \varepsilon$. In addition, for $0 < \tau < 1$, we say f is τ-*strongly resilient *if for all $1 \le q \le n$, $I_q(f) \le \tau \cdot q$.*

We use the $(\Theta(\log^2 m/m))$-*strongly resilient* function defined in [50] (i.e., any coalition of q bits has influence at most $\Theta(q \cdot \log^2 m/m)$) which has a bias $1/2 \pm 1/10$. We note that it has been shown that for any Boolean function on $m^{O(1)}$ bits, even one bit can have influence $\Omega(\log m/m^{O(1)})$ [36]. Hence, it is not possible to get a single bit string with $\varepsilon = m^{-\Omega(1)}$.

Publicly Samplable Adaptive One-Way Functions. Adaptive one-way functions (adaptive OWFs, or AOWFs for short) were formally introduced by Pandey *et al.* [53]. In a nutshell, a family of AOWFs is indexed by a tag, $\mathsf{tag} \in \{0,1\}^\lambda$, such that for any tag, it is hard for any PPT adversary to invert $f_{\mathsf{tag}}(\cdot)$ for randomly sampled images, even when given access to the *inversion oracle* of $f_{\mathsf{tag}'}(\cdot)$ for any other $\mathsf{tag}' \neq \mathsf{tag}$. Here, we define a variant of AOWFs where the adversary is provided a *publicly sampled* image as inversion challenge.

Definition 2. *Let $\mathbf{F} = \left\{\{f_{\mathsf{tag}} : X_{\mathsf{tag}} \longrightarrow Y_{\mathsf{tag}}\}_{\mathsf{tag} \in \{0,1\}^\lambda}\right\}_{\lambda \in \mathbb{N}}$ be an AOWF family. We say that $\mathbf{F}$ is* publicly samplable adaptive one-way (PS-AOWF) *if:*

(1) There is an efficient deterministic image-mapping algorithm $\mathsf{IM}(\cdot,\cdot)$ such that for every $\mathsf{tag} \in \{0,1\}^\lambda$, it holds that

$$\Pr\left[\omega \leftarrow \mathbb{U}_\lambda : \mathsf{IM}(\mathsf{tag}, \omega) \in Y_{\mathsf{tag}}\right] = 1 - \mathsf{negl}(\lambda) .$$

(2) Let $\mathcal{O}(\mathsf{tag},\cdot,\cdot)$ *denote the* inversion oracle *(as in [53]) that, on input* tag' *and* y *outputs* $f^{-1}_{\mathsf{tag}'}(y)$ *if* $\mathsf{tag}' \neq \mathsf{tag}, |\mathsf{tag}'| = |\mathsf{tag}|$*, and* $\perp$ *otherwise. Then, for every PPT adversary* $\mathcal{A}$ *and every* $\mathsf{tag} \in \{0,1\}^\lambda$*, it holds that*

$$\Pr\left[\omega \leftarrow \mathbb{U}_\lambda : \mathcal{A}^{\mathcal{O}(\mathsf{tag},\cdot,\cdot)}(\mathsf{tag},\omega) = f^{-1}_{\mathsf{tag}}(\mathsf{IM}(\mathsf{tag},\omega))\right] = \mathsf{negl}(\lambda)\,.$$

For notation simplicity, in the rest of the paper we omit indexing by $\lambda \in \mathbb{N}$ and simply write $\mathbf{F} = \{f_{\mathsf{tag}} : X_{\mathsf{tag}} \longrightarrow Y_{\mathsf{tag}}\}_{\mathsf{tag}\in\{0,1\}^\lambda}$.

The main difference between PS-AOWFs and AOWFs, as used in [53], is *public samplability*: even if $\mathcal{A}$ is given the random coins, ω, used for the image mapping algorithm $\mathsf{IM}(\cdot,\cdot)$, it can only invert the OWF with negligible probability. In the full version of this paper [2], we provide an instantiation of a PS-AOWF based on the hardness of discrete logarithm problem (DLP) in the generic group model.

Externalized UC with Global Helper. Universal Composability (UC) is a widely accepted simulation-based model to analyze protocol security. In the UC framework, all the ideal functionalities are "subroutine respectful" in the sense that each protocol execution session has its own copy of the functionalities, which only interact with the single protocol session. This subroutine respecting feature does not always naturally reflect the real world scenarios; for instance, we typically want the trusted setup (e.g., CRS or PKI) to be deployed once and then used in multiple protocols. To handle global setups the generalized UC (GUC) framework was introduced [16]. However, as noted in the introduction, given that in this work we want to avoid the use of a trusted setup (beyond a consistent bulletin board), while still providing a composable construction, we revert to the extended UC model with super-polynomial time helpers, denoted by $\mathcal{H}$-EUC [17]. In this model both the simulator and the adversary can access a (externalized super-polynomial time) global *helper* functionality $\mathcal{H}$.

3 CVZK and Coalescence Functions

A *crowd verifiable zero-knowledge* (CVZK) argument for a language $\mathcal{L} \in \mathbf{NP}$ with a witness relation $R_\mathcal{L}$ is an interactive proof between a PPT prover, that consists of a pair of algorithms $\mathsf{CVZK}.P = (\mathsf{CVZK.Prv}_1, \mathsf{CVZK.Prv}_2)$, and a *collection of PPT verifiers* $(\mathsf{CVZK}.V_1, \ldots, \mathsf{CVZK}.V_n)$. The private input of the prover is some witness w s.t. $(x,w) \in R_\mathcal{L}$, where x is a public statement. In a CVZK argument execution, the interaction is in three moves as follows:

(1) The prover $\mathsf{CVZK.Prv}_1(x,w)$ outputs the statement x and a string a to all n verifiers and outputs a state st_P.
(2) For $\ell \in [n]$, each verifier $\mathsf{CVZK}.V_\ell(x,a)$ sends a challenge c_ℓ to the prover and keeps a private state st_ℓ (e.g., the coins of V_ℓ). Note that $\mathsf{CVZK}.V_\ell$ gets as input only (x,a), and computes her challenge independently from the other verifiers.
(3) After receiving c_ℓ for all $\ell = \{1,\ldots,n\}$, $\mathsf{CVZK.Prv}_2(x,w,a,\langle c_1,\ldots, c_n\rangle, \mathsf{st}_P)$ outputs its response, z.

Additionally, there is a verification algorithm CVZK.Verify that takes as input the execution transcript $\langle x, a, \langle c_\ell \rangle_{\ell \in [n]}, z \rangle$ and optionally, a state st_ℓ, $\ell \in [n]$ (if run by CVZK.V_ℓ), and outputs 0/1.

As discussed in the introduction, CVZK is particularly interesting when each verifier contributes limited (human-level) randomness individually, yet the randomness of all verifiers (seen as a crowd) provides enough entropy to support the protocol's soundness. This unique feature of CVZK will be in the core of the security analysis of our VMPC construction (Sect. 7). Nonetheless, from a mere definitional aspect, the verifiers need not to be limited, so for generality, we pose no restrictions on the entropy of their individual challenges in our definition.

3.1 CVZK Definition

We consider an adversary that statically corrupts up to a ratio of the verifier crowd. Let $\mathcal{I}_{\mathsf{corr}}$ be the set of indices of corrupted verifiers.

Definition 3. *Let n be a positive integer, $0 \leq t_1, t_2, t_3 \leq n$ be positive values and $\epsilon_1(\cdot), \epsilon_2(\cdot)$ be real functions. A tuple of PPT algorithms* $\langle$(CVZK.Prv$_1$, CVZK.Prv$_2$), (CVZK.$V_1, \ldots,$ CVZK.V_n), CVZK.Verify$\rangle$ *is a* $(t_1, t_2, t_3, \epsilon_1, \epsilon_2)$-crowd-verifiable zero-knowledge argument of membership (CVZK-AoM) *for a language $\mathcal{L} \in \mathbf{NP}$, if the following properties are satisfied:*

(i). (t_1, ϵ_1)***-Crowd-Verifiable Completeness:*** *For every $x \in \mathcal{L} \cap \{0,1\}^{\mathsf{poly}(\lambda)}$, $w \in R_{\mathcal{L}}(x)$, every PPT adversary $\mathcal{A}$ and every $\mathcal{I}_{\mathsf{corr}} \subseteq [n]$ such that $|\mathcal{I}_{\mathsf{corr}}| \leq t_1$, the probability that the following experiment returns 1 is less or equal to $\epsilon_1(\lambda)$.*

$\mathbf{Expt}^{\mathsf{CVCompl}}_{(t_1, \mathcal{A}, \mathcal{I}_{\mathsf{corr}})}(1^\lambda, x, w)$

1. CVZK.Prv$_1(x, w)$ *outputs the message a and state* st_P*;*
2. ***For*** $\ell \in [n] \setminus \mathcal{I}_{\mathsf{corr}}$, *run* CVZK.$V_\ell(x, a) \rightarrow (c_\ell, \mathsf{st}_\ell)$*;*
3. $\mathcal{A}(x, a, \langle c_\ell \rangle_{\ell \in [n] \setminus \mathcal{I}_{\mathsf{corr}}})$ *outputs* $\langle c'_1, \ldots, c'_n \rangle$*;*
4. CVZK.Prv$_2(x, w, a, \langle c'_1, \ldots, c'_n \rangle, \mathsf{st}_P)$ *outputs response z;*
5. ***If*** $(\forall \ell \in [n] \setminus \mathcal{I}_{\mathsf{corr}} : c'_\ell = c_\ell)$ AND ((CVZK.Verify$(x, a, \langle c'_1, \ldots, c'_n \rangle, z) = 0$) OR $(\exists \ell \in [n] \setminus \mathcal{I}_{\mathsf{corr}} :$ CVZK.Verify$(x, a, \langle c'_1, \ldots, c'_n \rangle, z, \mathsf{st}_\ell) = 0$)) ***then*** *return 1;* ***else*** *return* 0;

(ii). (t_2, ϵ_2)***-Crowd-Verifiable Soundness:*** *For every $x \in \{0,1\}^{\mathsf{poly}(\lambda)} \setminus \mathcal{L}$, every PPT adversary $\mathcal{A}$ and every $\mathcal{I}_{\mathsf{corr}} \subseteq [n]$ such that $|\mathcal{I}_{\mathsf{corr}}| \leq t_2$, the probability that the following experiment returns 1 is less or equal to $\epsilon_2(\lambda)$.*

$\mathbf{Expt}^{\mathsf{CVSound}}_{(t_2, \mathcal{A}, \mathcal{I}_{\mathsf{corr}})}(1^\lambda, x)$

1. $\mathcal{A}(x, \mathcal{I}_{\mathsf{corr}})$ *outputs a message a;*
2. ***For*** $\ell \in [n] \setminus \mathcal{I}_{\mathsf{corr}}$, *run* CVZK.$V_\ell(x, a) \rightarrow (c_\ell, \mathsf{st}_\ell)$*;*
3. $\mathcal{A}(x, a, \langle c_\ell \rangle_{\ell \in [n] \setminus \mathcal{I}_{\mathsf{corr}}})$ *outputs* $\langle c'_1, \ldots, c'_n \rangle$ *and response z;*
4. ***If*** $(\forall \ell \in [n] \setminus \mathcal{I}_{\mathsf{corr}} : c'_\ell = c_\ell)$ AND (CVZK.Verify$(x, a, \langle c'_1, \ldots, c'_n \rangle, z) = 1$) AND $(\forall \ell \in [n] \setminus \mathcal{I}_{\mathsf{corr}} :$ CVZK.Verify$(x, a, \langle c'_1, \ldots, c'_n \rangle, z, \mathsf{st}_\ell) = 1$) ***then*** *return 1* ***else*** *return* 0;

(iii). t_3**-Crowd-Verifiable Zero-Knowledge:** *For every* $x \in \mathcal{L} \cap \{0,1\}^{\mathrm{poly}(\lambda)}$, $w \in R_{\mathcal{L}}(x)$, *every PPT adversary* $\mathcal{A}$ *and every* $\mathcal{I}_{\mathsf{corr}} \subseteq [n]$ *such that* $|\mathcal{I}_{\mathsf{corr}}| \leq t_3$, *there is a PPT simulator* $\mathsf{CVZK.Sim} = (\mathsf{CVZK.Sim}_1, \mathsf{CVZK.Sim}_2)$ *such that the outputs of the following two experiments are computationally indistinguishable.*

$\mathbf{Expt}^{\mathsf{CVZK}}_{(\mathsf{Ideal},t_3,\mathcal{A},\mathcal{I}_{\mathsf{corr}})}(1^\lambda, x)$	$\mathbf{Expt}^{\mathsf{CVZK}}_{(\mathsf{Real},t_3,\mathcal{A},\mathcal{I}_{\mathsf{corr}})}(1^\lambda, x, w)$
1. $\mathsf{CVZK.Sim}_1(x, \mathcal{I}_{\mathsf{corr}})$ *outputs* a, $\mathsf{st}_{\mathsf{Sim}}$, *and* $\langle c_\ell \rangle_{\ell \in [n] \setminus \mathcal{I}_{\mathsf{corr}}}$;	1. $\mathsf{CVZK.Prv}_1(x, w)$ *outputs* a *and state* st_P;
2. $\mathcal{A}(x, a, \langle c_\ell \rangle_{\ell \in [n] \setminus \mathcal{I}_{\mathsf{corr}}})$ *outputs* $\langle c'_1, \ldots, c'_n \rangle$;	2. *For* $\ell \in [n] \setminus \mathcal{I}_{\mathsf{corr}}$, *run* $\mathsf{CVZK}.V_\ell(x, a) \to (c_\ell, \mathsf{st}_\ell)$;
3. $\mathsf{CVZK.Sim}_2(x, a, \langle c'_1, \ldots, c'_n \rangle, \mathsf{st}_{\mathsf{Sim}})$ *outputs* z;	3. $\mathcal{A}(x, a, \langle c_\ell \rangle_{\ell \in [n] \setminus \mathcal{I}_{\mathsf{corr}}})$ *outputs* $\langle c'_1, \ldots, c'_n \rangle$;
4. $b \leftarrow \mathcal{A}(x, z)$;	4. $\mathsf{CVZK.Prv}_2(x, w, a, \langle c'_1, \ldots, c'_n \rangle, \mathsf{st}_P)$ *outputs* z;
5. *If* $(\forall \ell \in [n] \setminus \mathcal{I}_{\mathsf{corr}} : c'_\ell = c_\ell)$, *then return* b; *else return* $\perp$;	5. $b \leftarrow \mathcal{A}(x, z)$;
	6. *If* $(\forall \ell \in [n] \setminus \mathcal{I}_{\mathsf{corr}} : c'_\ell = c_\ell)$, *then return* b; *else return* $\perp$;

Analogously, we can also define a CVZK argument of knowledge as follows. We say that $\langle(\mathsf{CVZK.Prv}_1, \mathsf{CVZK.Prv}_2), (\mathsf{CVZK}.V_1, \ldots, \mathsf{CVZK}.V_n), \mathsf{CVZK.Verify}\rangle$ *is a* $(t_1, t_2, t_3, \epsilon_1)$-crowd-verifiable zero-knowledge argument of knowledge (CVZK-AoK), *if it satisfies* (t_1, ϵ_1)*-Completeness and* t_3*-Crowd-Verifiable Zero-Knowledge as previously, and the following property:*

t_2**-Crowd-Verifiable Validity:** *There exists a PPT extractor* $\mathsf{CVZK.Ext}$ *such that for every* $x \in \{0,1\}^{\mathrm{poly}(\lambda)}$, *every PPT adversary* $\mathcal{A}$ *and every* $\mathcal{I}_{\mathsf{corr}} \subseteq [n]$ *such that* $|\mathcal{I}_{\mathsf{corr}}| \leq t_2$, *the following holds: if there is a non-negligible function* $\alpha(\cdot)$ *such that*

$$\Pr\left[\mathbf{Expt}^{\mathsf{CVSound}}_{(t_2,\mathcal{A},\mathcal{I}_{\mathsf{corr}})}(1^\lambda, x) = 1\right] \geq \alpha(\lambda),$$

then there is a non-negligible function $\beta(\cdot)$ *such that*

$$\Pr[w^* \leftarrow \mathsf{CVZK.Ext}^{\mathcal{A}}(x, \mathcal{I}_{\mathsf{corr}}) : (x, w^*) \in R_{\mathcal{L}}] \geq \beta(\lambda).$$

Remark 1 (Relativized CVZK security). Definition 3 specifies CVZK security against a PPT adversary $\mathcal{A}$ and a PPT simulator $\mathsf{CVZK.Sim}$. Note that the notions of crowd-verifiable completeness, soundness, validity, and zero-knowledge can be extended so that they hold even when $\mathcal{A}$, and maybe $\mathsf{CVZK.Sim}$, has also access to a (potentially super-polynomial) oracle $\mathcal{H}$.

3.2 Coalescence Functions

We introduce the notion of a *coalescence function*, which will be a core component of our CVZK construction (cf. Sect. 4). In particular, coalescence functions will be the key for exploiting the CVZK verifiers' randomness in the presence of an adversary (a malicious prover) that aims to "cancel" the entropy of the honest verifiers. Given the verifiers' coins, a coalescence function will produce a collection of (challenge) strings such that at least one of the strings has sufficient entropy to support CVZK soundness. At a high level, a function F achieves coalescence, if when provided as input an n-dimensional vector that is (i) sampled from a distribution $\mathbb{D}_\lambda$, and (ii) adversarially tampered at up to t-out-of-n vector components, it outputs a sequence of m k-bit strings so that with overwhelming probability, at least one of the m strings is statistically close to uniformly random. Our definition of F postulates the existence of "good" events $\mathsf{G}_1, \ldots \mathsf{G}_m$, defined over the input distribution, where conditional to G_i being true, the corresponding output string is statistically close to uniform. Coalescence is achieved if the probability that such a "good" event occurs is overwhelming.

Definition 4. *Let n, k, m be polynomial in λ and $\mathbf{In} = (in^{(1)}, \ldots, in^{(n)})$ be an n-dimensional vector sampled according to the distribution ensemble $\{\mathbb{D}_\lambda\}_\lambda$ so that the support of $\mathbb{D}_\lambda$ is Ω_λ. Let $F : \Omega_\lambda \longrightarrow (\{0,1\}^k)^m$ be a function. For any adversary $\mathcal{A}$, any $t \le n$, and any $\mathcal{I}_{\mathsf{corr}} \subseteq [n]$ such that $|\mathcal{I}_{\mathsf{corr}}| \le t$, we define the following experiment:*

$\mathbf{Expt}^{\mathsf{Coal}}_{(t,\mathcal{A},\mathcal{I}_{\mathsf{corr}})}(1^\lambda)$

1. *Set* $\mathbf{In} = (in^{(1)}, \ldots, in^{(n)}) \leftarrow \mathbb{D}_\lambda$;
2. $\mathcal{A}(\langle in^{(\ell)} \rangle_{\ell \in \mathcal{I}_{\mathsf{corr}}})$ *outputs* $\mathbf{In}' = (in'^{(1)}, \ldots, in'^{(n)})$ *s.t.* $\forall \ell \in [n] \setminus \mathcal{I}_{\mathsf{corr}} : in'^{(\ell)} = in^{(\ell)}$;
3. *Return* $(d_1, \ldots, d_m) \leftarrow F(\mathbf{In}')$;

*We say that the function $F : \Omega_\lambda \to (\{0,1\}^k)^m$ is a (k, m, t)-*coalescence function w.r.t. $\mathbb{D}_\lambda$, *if there exist events $\mathsf{G}_1, \ldots \mathsf{G}_m$ over Ω_λ such that the following two conditions hold:*

(1) $\Pr[\wedge_{i=1}^m \neg \mathsf{G}_i] = \mathsf{negl}(\lambda)$, *and*
(2) for every adversary $\mathcal{A}$ and every $\mathcal{I}_{\mathsf{corr}} \subseteq [n]$ such that $|\mathcal{I}_{\mathsf{corr}}| \le t$, it holds that for all $i \in [m]$, the random variable $(d_i|\mathsf{G}_i)$ is statistically $\mathsf{negl}(\lambda)$*-close to $\mathbb{U}_k$, where $(d_1, \ldots, d_m) \leftarrow \mathbf{Expt}^{\mathsf{Coal}}_{(t,\mathcal{A},\mathcal{I}_{\mathsf{corr}})}(1^\lambda)$. Note that $(X|\mathsf{A})$ denotes the random variable X conditional on the event* A.

Furthermore, we require that a (k, m, t)-coalescence function F w.r.t. $\mathbb{D}_\lambda$ satisfies the following two additional properties:

Completeness: *the output of F on inputs sampled from $\mathbb{D}_\lambda$, denoted by $F(\mathbb{D}_\lambda)$, is statistically* $\mathsf{negl}(\lambda)$*-close to the uniform distribution $(\mathbb{U}_k)^m$ over $(\{0,1\}^k)^m$.*

Efficient Samplability: *there exists a PPT algorithm* $\mathsf{Sample}(\cdot)$ *such that the following two conditions hold:*
(a) $\Pr_{(d_1,\ldots,d_m)\leftarrow(\mathbb{U}_k)^m}\left[\mathbf{In} \leftarrow \mathsf{Sample}(d_1, \ldots, d_m) : F(\mathbf{In}) = (d_1, \ldots, d_m)\right] = 1 - \mathsf{negl}(\lambda)$.
(b) The distribution $\mathsf{Sample}\big((\mathbb{U}_k)^m\big)$ *is statistically* $\mathsf{negl}(\lambda)$*-close to* $\mathbb{D}_\lambda$.

In Sect. 4.1, we present an implementation of a coalescence function w.r.t. $\mathbb{U}_n$ based on 1RCCF.

4 CVZK Construction

In this section, we show how to compile any Σ-protocol into a 3-move CVZK protocol. Our CVZK construction is a compiler that utilizes an explicit instantiation of a coalescence function from 1RCCF and a special class of protocols where both the prover and the simulator operate in an "input-delayed" manner, i.e., they do not need to know the statement in the first move. Our CVZK protocol will be a basic tool for the construction of our VMPC scheme (cf. Sect. 7). As noted in the introduction, the security of the VMPC scheme is in the extended UC model (EUC), where both the simulator and the adversary have access to a (externalized super-polynomial time) global helper functionality $\mathcal{H}$, denoted as $\mathcal{H}$-EUC security. Therefore, the CVZK protocol must also be secure against PPT adversaries with oracle access to some helper.

4.1 Coalescence Functions from 1RCCF

As mentioned in Sect. 2, it is not possible to produce a *single* random string via collective coin flipping and hope it has exponentially small statistical distance from a uniformly random string. Nevertheless, we show that it is possible to produce *several* random strings such that with overwhelming probability *one of them* is close to uniformly random, as dictated by the coalescence property.

Description. Let $n = \lambda^\gamma$ for a constant $\gamma > 1$ and assume $\lambda \log \lambda$ divides n. Let f_{res} denote the $(\Theta(\log^2 m/m))$-strongly resilient function over m bits proposed in [50]. We define the instantiation of the coalescence function $F : \{0,1\}^n \longrightarrow (\{0,1\}^{\frac{\lambda}{\log^2 \lambda}})^{\log \lambda}$ as follows:

Step 1. On input $C := (c_1, \ldots, c_n)$, F partitions the n-bit input C into $\lambda \log \lambda$ blocks $B_1, \ldots, B_{\lambda \log \lambda}$, with $\frac{n}{\lambda \log \lambda}$ bits each. Namely $B_j := (c_{\frac{(j-1)n}{\lambda \log \lambda}+1}, \ldots, c_{\frac{jn}{\lambda \log \lambda}})$, where $j \in [\lambda \log \lambda]$.

Step 2. Then, F groups every λ blocks together, resulting to $\log \lambda$ groups, denoted as $G_1, \ldots, G_{\log \lambda}$. Namely, $G_i := (B_{(i-1)\lambda+1}, \ldots, B_{i\lambda})$, where $i \in [\log \lambda]$. Within each group G_i, we apply the resilient function f_{res} on each block $B_{(i-1)\lambda+k}$, $k \in [\lambda]$, to output 1 bit; hence, for each group G_i, by sequentially running f_{res} we obtain a λ-bit string $(b_{i,1}, \ldots, b_{i,\lambda}) \leftarrow (f_{\mathsf{res}}(B_{(i-1)\lambda+1}), \ldots, f_{\mathsf{res}}(B_{i\lambda}))$, and $\log \lambda$ strings in total for all the groups G_i, $i \in [\log \lambda]$.

Step 3. The resilient function f_{res} in [50] has a bias $\frac{1}{10}$. Therefore, even if the input G_i is random, the output bits $(b_{i,1}, \ldots, b_{i,\lambda})$ are not a random sequence of $\lambda \log \lambda$ bits due to this bias. In order to make the output of F balanced (i.e., unbiased), for each group G_i, $i \in [\log \lambda]$, we execute the following process: on input $(b_{i,1}, \ldots, b_{i,\lambda})$, we perform a *sequential (von Neumann) rejection sampling* over pairs of bits until an unbiased string $d_i := (d_{i,1}, \ldots, d_{i,\frac{\lambda}{\log^2 \lambda}})$ is produced, with $\frac{\lambda}{\log^2 \lambda}$ bits length as described below:

1. Set two indices $j \leftarrow 1$ and $k \leftarrow 1$;
2. **While** $\left((j < \lambda) \wedge (k < \frac{\lambda}{\log^2 \lambda})\right)$:
   - **If** $b_{i,j} \neq b_{i,j+1}$, **then** set $d_{i,k} \leftarrow b_{i,j}$ and $k \leftarrow k + 1$;
   - Set $j \leftarrow j + 2$;
3. **If** $k = \frac{\lambda}{\log^2 \lambda}$, **then** return $d_i := (d_{i,1}, \ldots, d_{i,\frac{\lambda}{\log^2 \lambda}})$;
4. **else** return $d_i := (b_{i,1}, \ldots, b_{i,\frac{\lambda}{\log^2 \lambda}})$;

Finally, we define the output of $F(C)$ as the sequence $(d_1, \ldots, d_{\log \lambda})$.

Security. The security of $F(\cdot)$ is stated below and is proved in the full version of this paper [2].

Theorem 1. *Let $\gamma > 1$ be a constant and $n = \lambda^\gamma$. Then, the function $F : \{0,1\}^n \longrightarrow (\{0,1\}^{\frac{\lambda}{\log^2 \lambda}})^{\log \lambda}$ described in Sect. 4.1 is a $\left(\frac{\lambda}{\log^2 \lambda}, \log \lambda, \frac{n^{1-\frac{1}{\gamma}}}{\log^3 n}\right)$-coalescence function w.r.t. uniform distribution $\mathbb{U}_n$ that satisfies completeness and efficient samplability.*

By Theorem 1, for $n = \lambda^\gamma$, if the adversary can corrupt up to $\frac{n^{1-\frac{1}{\gamma}}}{\log^3 n}$ verifiers, then on input the n verifiers' coins, F outputs $\log \lambda$ strings of $\frac{\lambda}{\log^2 \lambda}$ bits, such that with probability $1 - \mathsf{negl}(\lambda)$, at least one of the $\log \lambda$ strings is statistically close to uniformly random.

4.2 A Helper Family for AOWF Inversion

Let $\mathbf{F} = \{f_{\mathsf{tag}} : X_{\mathsf{tag}} \longrightarrow Y_{\mathsf{tag}}\}_{\mathsf{tag} \in \{0,1\}^\lambda}$ be a (publicly samplable) AOWF family. In Fig. 1, we define the associated helper family $\mathbf{H} = \{\mathcal{H}_S\}_{S \subset \{0,1\}^\lambda}$ (we omit indexing by $\lambda \in \mathbb{N}$ for simplicity). Here, S refers to the subset of tags of entities controlled by an adversary. Namely, the adversary can only ask for preimages that are consistent with its corruption extent.

The helper $\mathcal{H}_S(\cdot,\cdot)$, where $S \subset \{0,1\}^\lambda$.
On query (tag, β), if $\mathsf{tag} \in S$, then it returns a value $\alpha \in X_{\mathsf{tag}}$ s.t. $f_{\mathsf{tag}}(\alpha) = \beta$. Otherwise, it returns $\bot$.

Fig. 1. The helper family $\mathbf{H} = \{\mathcal{H}_S\}_{S \subset \{0,1\}^\lambda}$ w.r.t. $\mathbf{F} = \{f_{\mathsf{tag}}\}_{\mathsf{tag} \in \{0,1\}^\lambda}$.

4.3 Fully Input-Delayed Σ-Protocols

In our CVZK construction, we utilize a special class of Σ-protocols where both the prover and the simulator do not need to know the proof statement in the first move. Such "input-delayed" protocols (at least for the prover side) have been studied in the literature (e.g., [19,20,34,46]). To stress the input-delayed property for both prover and simulator, we name these protocols *fully input-delayed* and provide their definition below.

Definition 5. *Let $\Sigma.\Pi := (\Sigma.\mathsf{Prv}_1, \Sigma.\mathsf{Prv}_2, \Sigma.\mathsf{Verify})$ be a Σ-protocol for a language $\mathcal{L} \in \mathbf{NP}$. We say that $\Sigma.\Pi$ is* fully input-delayed *if for every $x \in \mathcal{L}$, it satisfies the following two properties:*

(1) Input-delayed proving*: $\Sigma.\mathsf{Prv}_1$ takes as input only the length of x, $|x|$.*
(2) Input-delayed simulation*: there exists an sHVZK simulator $\Sigma.\mathsf{Sim} := (\Sigma.\mathsf{Sim}_1, \Sigma.\mathsf{Sim}_2)$ s.t. $\Sigma.\mathsf{Sim}_1$ takes as input only $|x|$ and the challenge c.*

As we will see in Sect. 4.4, CVZK can be built upon any fully input-delayed protocol (in a black-box manner) for a suitable "one-way" language that is secure against helper-aided PPT adversaries. Here, for generality, we propose an instantiation of such a protocol from the fully input-delayed proof for the Hamiltonian Cycle problem of Lapidot and Shamir (LS) [46]. By the LS protocol, we know that there exists a fully input-delayed Σ-protocol for every **NP** language. In the full version of this paper [2], we recall the LS protocol and show that it is secure against helper-aided PPT adversaries, when built upon a commitment scheme that is also secure against PPT adversaries with access to the same helper. In addition, we propose an instantiation of such a commitment scheme based on ElGamal, assuming an "adaptive" variant of the DDH problem in the spirit of AOWFs [53].

4.4 Generic CVZK Compiler

We present a generic CVZK compiler for any Σ-protocol $\Sigma.\Pi = (\Sigma.\mathsf{Prv}_1, \Sigma.\mathsf{Prv}_2, \Sigma.\mathsf{Verify})$ for an **NP** language $\mathcal{L}$ and $(x, w) \in \mathcal{R}_{\mathcal{L}}$. Let $\mathbf{F} = \{f_{\mathsf{tag}} : X_{\mathsf{tag}} \longrightarrow Y_{\mathsf{tag}}\}_{\mathsf{tag}\in\{0,1\}^{\lambda/\log^2\lambda}}$ be a PS-AOWF family (cf. Definition 2), and tag_ℓ be the identity of the verifier $\mathsf{CVZK}.V_\ell$ for $\ell \in [n]$. Let $|\mathsf{tag}_1| = \cdots = |\mathsf{tag}_n|$. For each $\ell \in [n]$, our compiler utilizes a fully input-delayed Σ-protocol $\mathsf{InD}.\Pi := (\mathsf{InD}.\mathsf{Prv}_1, \mathsf{InD}.\mathsf{Prv}_2, \mathsf{InD}.\mathsf{Verify})$ for the language $\mathcal{L}^*_{\mathsf{tag}_\ell}$ defined as:

$$\mathcal{L}^*_{\mathsf{tag}_\ell} = \left\{\beta \in Y_{\mathsf{tag}_\ell} \;\middle|\; \exists \alpha \in X_{\mathsf{tag}_\ell} : f_{\mathsf{tag}_\ell}(\alpha) = \beta\right\}. \tag{1}$$

For simplicity, we say that $\mathsf{InD}.\Pi$ is for the family $\left\{\mathcal{L}^*_{\mathsf{tag}_\ell}\right\}_{\ell\in[n]}$, without referring specifically to the family member.

Description. In terms of architecture, our CVZK compiler is in the spirit of disjunctive proofs [20,22]: the prover must show that either (i) *knows a witness* w for $x \in \mathcal{L}$ or (ii) *can invert a hard instance* of the PS-AOWF f_{tag}. However, several adaptations are required so that validity and ZK are preserved in the CVZK setting where multiple (individually weak) verifiers are present. First, the challenge C provided by the n verifiers is given as input to the coalescence function $F(\cdot)$ defined in Sect. 4.1 which outputs $\log\lambda$ strings $(d_1, \ldots, d_{\log\lambda})$, each $\frac{\lambda}{\log^2\lambda}$ bits long. In addition, the compiler maintains a fixed disjunctive mode so that the prover always (i) proves the knowledge of w for $x \in \mathcal{L}$ and (ii) simulates the knowledge of a collection of inversions to hard instances.

To prove the knowledge of w for $x \in \mathcal{L}$, the prover executes $\log\lambda$ parallel runs of the compiled Σ-protocol $\Sigma.\Pi$ for $(x, w) \in \mathcal{R}_{\mathcal{L}}$, where the challenge in the i-th run is the XOR operation of the i-th block of $\frac{n}{\log\lambda}$ verifiers' bits from C and some randomness provided by the prover in the first move. To simulate the inversions to hard instances, our compiler exploits the fully input-delayed property of $\mathsf{InD}.\Pi$. In particular, it runs $n \cdot \log\lambda$ parallel simulations of $\mathsf{InD}.\Pi$ where the (ℓ, j)-th run, $(\ell, j) \in [n]\times[\log\lambda]$, is for a hard instance (statement) $x^*_{\ell,j}$ associated with the identity tag_ℓ of $\mathsf{CVZK}.V_\ell$. The statement $x^*_{\ell,j}$ is created later on in the third move of the protocol by running the image-mapping algorithm of $\mathbf{F}$ on input tag_ℓ and the j-th string output by $F(C)$, d_j. The latter is feasible because the first move of the input-delayed simulator $\mathsf{InD.Sim}$ is executed obliviously to the statement.

By the coalescence property of $F(\cdot)$, the output $F(C)$ preserves enough entropy, so that any malicious CVZK prover corrupting less than $\frac{n^{1-\frac{1}{\gamma}}}{\log^3 n}$ verifiers is forced to be challenged on the knowledge of (i) w for $x \in \mathcal{L}$ or (ii) an inversion of a hard instance, in at least one of the corresponding parallel executions. Thus, by the adaptive one-way property of $\mathbf{F}$, the (potentially malicious) prover must simulate the knowledge of all inversions and *indeed prove* the knowledge of w for $x \in \mathcal{L}$, so CVZK validity is guaranteed.

The ZK property of our compiler relies on the sHVZK properties of $\Sigma.\Pi$ and $\mathsf{InD}.\Pi$, yet we remark that the CVZK simulation must be *straight-line* (no rewindings) so that our construction can be deployed in the $\mathcal{H}$-EUC setting of our VMPC scheme. For this reason, we do "complexity leveraging" along the lines of super-polynomial simulation introduced in [54], by allowing our simulator to have access to members of the helper family $\mathbf{H}$ defined in Fig. 1. Our CVZK compiler is presented in detail in Fig. 2.

Security. To prove the security of our CVZK generic compiler we use a simulator pair $(\mathsf{CVZK.Sim}_1, \mathsf{CVZK.Sim}_2)$, where $\mathsf{CVZK.Sim}_2$ is given oracle access to a member of the super-polynomial helper family $\mathbf{H} = \{\mathcal{H}_S\}_{S \subset \{0,1\}^{\lambda/\log^2\lambda}}$ defined in Fig. 1. We state our CVZK security theorem below and prove it in the full version of this paper [2].

Theorem 2. *Let* $\Sigma.\Pi = (\Sigma.\mathsf{Prv}_1, \Sigma.\mathsf{Prv}_2, \Sigma.\mathsf{Verify})$ *be a* Σ*-protocol for some language* $\mathcal{L} \in \mathbf{NP}$ *where the challenge is chosen uniformly at random. Let* $\mathbf{F} = \{f_{\mathsf{tag}} : X_{\mathsf{tag}} \longrightarrow Y_{\mathsf{tag}}\}_{\mathsf{tag} \in \{0,1\}^{\lambda/\log^2\lambda}}$ *be a PS-AOWF family (cf. Definition 2), and let* $\mathbf{H} = \{\mathcal{H}_S\}_{S \subset \{0,1\}^{\lambda/\log^2\lambda}}$ *be the associated helper family defined in Fig. 1. Let* $\mathsf{InD}.\Pi := (\mathsf{InD.Prv}_1, \mathsf{InD.Prv}_2, \mathsf{InD.Verify})$ *be a fully input-delayed* Σ*-protocol for the language family* $\{\mathcal{L}^*_{\mathsf{tag}_\ell}\}_{\ell \in [n]}$ *defined in Eq.(1).*
Let $\gamma > 1$ *be a constant and* $n = \lambda^\gamma$*. Let* $\mathsf{CVZK}.\Pi$ *be the CVZK compiler for the language* $\mathcal{L}$ *with* n *verifiers described in Fig. 2 over* $\Sigma.\Pi$, $\mathsf{InD}.\Pi$ *and* $\mathbf{F}$*. Then, against any adversary* $\mathcal{A}$*, it holds that:*

(1) If the image-mapping algorithm $\mathsf{IM}(\cdot,\cdot)$ *of* $\mathbf{F}$ *has error* $\epsilon(\cdot)$[1], $\Sigma.\Pi$ *has completeness error* $\delta(\cdot)$ *and* $\mathsf{InD}.\Pi$ *has perfect completeness, then for every* $t_1 \leq \frac{n^{1-\frac{1}{\gamma}}}{\log^2 n}$, $\mathsf{CVZK}.\Pi$ *satisfies* (t_1, ϵ_1)*-crowd verifiable completeness, where* $\epsilon_1(\lambda) := \delta(\lambda)\log\lambda + n\log\lambda\epsilon(\lambda)2^{\Theta(\log^2 n)} + \mathsf{negl}(\lambda)$.

(2) If $\Sigma.\Pi$ *and* $\mathsf{InD}.\Pi$ *are special sound, then for every* $t_2 \leq \frac{n^{1-\frac{1}{\gamma}}}{\log^3 n}$*, there is a negligible function* $\epsilon_2(\cdot)$ *s.t.* $\mathsf{CVZK}.\Pi$ *satisfies* (t_2, ϵ_2)*-crowd verifiable soundness and* t_2*-crowd verifiable validity.*

(3). Let $t_3 \leq n$ *and consider any subset of indices of corrupted verifiers* $\mathcal{I}_{\mathsf{corr}} \subseteq [n]$ *s.t.* $|\mathcal{I}_{\mathsf{corr}}| \leq t_3$*. Let* $\mathcal{A}$ *be PPT with access to a helper* $\mathcal{H}_S$ *from* $\mathbf{H}$*,*

[1] The PS-AOWF family instantiated in [2] has perfect samplability, i.e. $\epsilon(\lambda) = 0$.

1. $\mathsf{CVZK.Prv}_1(x, w)$:
   - For $i \in [\log \lambda]$, run $(a_i, \mathsf{st}_i) \leftarrow \Sigma.\mathsf{Prv}_1(x, w)$.
   - Pick random $R := (r_1, \ldots, r_n) \leftarrow \{0,1\}^n$.
   - For $\ell \in [n]$ and $j \in [\log \lambda]$, run $(a^*_{\ell,j}, \mathsf{st}^*_{\ell,j}) \leftarrow \mathsf{InD.Sim}_1(r_\ell, size)$, where $size = \log \lambda \cdot |M_{\frac{\lambda}{\log^2 \lambda}}(\mathsf{tag}_\ell, \cdot)|$ and $|M_{\frac{\lambda}{\log^2 \lambda}}(\mathsf{tag}_\ell, \cdot)|$ is the circuit size of $f_{\mathsf{tag}_\ell}(\cdot)$ as in Definition 2.
   - Output $A := \left(\{a_i\}_{i \in [\log \lambda]}, \{a^*_{\ell,j}\}_{\ell \in [n]}^{j \in [\log \lambda]}\right)$ and the state $\mathsf{st}_P := \left(R, \{\mathsf{st}_i\}_{i \in [\log \lambda]}, \{\mathsf{st}^*_{\ell,j}\}_{\ell \in [n]}^{j \in [\log \lambda]}\right)$.
2. The verifiers generate coins $C := (c_1, \ldots, c_n) \in \{0,1\}^n$. I.e., for $\ell \in [n]$, $\mathsf{CVZK}.V_\ell(x, a)$ outputs a random bit c_ℓ.
3. $\mathsf{CVZK.Prv}_2(x, w, A, C, \mathsf{st}_P)$:
   - Parse $\mathsf{st}_P := \left(R, \{\mathsf{st}_i\}_{i \in [\log \lambda]}, \{\mathsf{st}^*_{\ell,j}\}_{\ell \in [n]}^{j \in [\log \lambda]}\right)$.
   - Compute the coalescence function $F(\cdot)$ defined in Section 4.1 on input C to get $F(C) = (d_1, \ldots, d_{\log \lambda})$, where $d_j \in \{0,1\}^{\lambda/\log^2 \lambda}$, $j \in [\log \lambda]$.
   - Set $E := R \oplus C$, and parse E as $(e_1, \ldots, e_{\log \lambda})$, where $e_i \in \{0,1\}^{n/\log \lambda}$.
   - For $i \in [\log \lambda]$, run $z_i \leftarrow \Sigma.\mathsf{Prv}_2(\mathsf{st}_i, e_i)$.
   - For $\ell \in [n]$ and $j \in [\log \lambda]$:
     - Run $\beta_{\ell,j} \leftarrow \mathsf{IM}(\mathsf{tag}_\ell, d_j)$, where $\mathsf{IM}(\cdot, \cdot)$ is the image-mapping algorithm of the family $\mathbf{F}$, as in Definition 2.
     - Define the statement $x^*_{\ell,j} := \beta_{\ell,j}$ for $\mathcal{L}^*_{\mathsf{tag}_\ell}$.
     - Run $z^*_{\ell,j} \leftarrow \mathsf{InD.Sim}_2(\mathsf{st}^*_{\ell,j}, x^*_{\ell,j})$.
   - Output $Z := \left(E, \{z_i\}_{i \in [\log \lambda]}, \{z^*_{\ell,j}\}_{\ell \in [n]}^{j \in [\log \lambda]}\right)$.
4. $\mathsf{CVZK.Verify}(x, A, C, Z)$:
   - Parse $A := \left(\{a_i\}_{i \in [\log \lambda]}, \{a^*_{\ell,j}\}_{\ell \in [n]}^{j \in [\log \lambda]}\right)$.
   - Parse $Z := \left(E, \{z_i\}_{i \in [\log \lambda]}, \{z^*_{\ell,j}\}_{\ell \in [n]}^{j \in [\log \lambda]}\right)$.
   - Compute $(d_1, \ldots, d_{\log \lambda}) \leftarrow F(C)$.
   - Compute $R := (r_1, \ldots, r_n) = E \oplus C$ and parse E as $(e_1, \ldots, e_{\log \lambda})$.
   - For $i \in [\log \lambda]$, check that $\Sigma.\mathsf{Verify}(x, a_i, e_i, z_i) = 1$.
   - For $\ell \in [n]$ and $j \in [\log \lambda]$, run $\beta_{\ell,j} \leftarrow \mathsf{IM}(\mathsf{tag}_\ell, d_j)$ and define the statement $x^*_{\ell,j} = \beta_{\ell,j}$. Then, check that $\mathsf{InD.Verify}(x^*_{\ell,j}, a^*_{\ell,j}, r_\ell, z^*_{\ell,j}) = 1$.
   - Output 1 if all the checks are valid; output 0, otherwise.

Fig. 2. The generic CVZK compiler $\mathsf{CVZK}.\Pi$.

where (i) $\{\mathsf{tag}_\ell\}_{\ell \in \mathcal{I}_{\mathsf{corr}}} \subseteq S$ *and (ii)* $\{\mathsf{tag}_\ell\}_{\ell \in [n] \setminus \mathcal{I}_{\mathsf{corr}}} \cap S = \emptyset$. *If* $\Sigma.\Pi$ *and* $\mathsf{InD}.\Pi$ *are sHVZK against PPT distinguishers with access to* $\mathcal{H}_S$*, then there is a PPT simulator pair* $\left(\mathsf{CVZK.Sim}_1, \mathsf{CVZK.Sim}_2^{\mathcal{H}_S}\right)$ *s.t.* $\mathsf{CVZK}.\Pi$ *is* t_3*-crowd-verifiable zero-knowledge against PPT distinguishers with access to* $\mathcal{H}_S$.

5 End-to-End Verifiable MPC

We introduce *end-to-end verifiable multiparty computation (VMPC)*, which as we show in Sect. 7, can be realized with the use of CVZK. A VMPC scheme encompasses the interaction among sets of *users*, *clients* and *servers*, so that the correct computation of some fixed function f of the users' private inputs can be verified, while their privacy is preserved. End-to-end verifiability suggests that even when *all* servers and *all* users' clients are corrupted, verification is still possible (although, obviously, in an all-malicious setting, privacy is violated). Furthermore, a user's audit data do not leak information about her private input so the verification mechanism may be delegated to an external verifier.

5.1 VMPC Syntax

Let $\mathcal{U} = \{U_1, \ldots, U_n\}$ be a set of n users where every user has an associated client $\mathcal{C} = \{C_1, \ldots, C_n\}$. Let $\mathcal{S} = \{S_1, \ldots, S_k\}$ be a set of k servers. All clients and servers run in polynomial time. Every server has write permission to a consistent *bulletin board* (BB) to which all parties have read access. Each user U_ℓ receives her private input x_ℓ from some set X (which includes a special symbol "abstain") and is associated with a *client* C_ℓ for engaging in the VMPC execution. In addition, there exists an efficient *verifier* V responsible for auditing procedures. The *evaluation function* associated with the VMPC scheme is denoted by $f : X^n \longrightarrow Y$, where X^n is the set of vectors of length n, the coordinates of which are elements in X, and Y is the range set. All parameters and set sizes n, k are polynomial in the security parameter λ.

Note that we consider the concept of a single verifier that audits the VMPC execution on behalf of the users, in the spirit of delegatable receipt-free verification that is established in e-voting literature (e.g. [18,41,51]). Alternatively, we could involve multiple verifiers, e.g. one for each user, and require that all or a threshold of them verify successfully. This approach does not essentially affect the design and security analysis of a VMPC scheme, as (i) individual verifiability is captured in our description via the delegatable verification carried out by the single verifier and (ii) a threshold of collective user randomness is anyway needed. Which of the two directions is preferable, is mostly a matter of deployment and depends on the real world scenario where the VMPC is used.

Separating Users from Their Client Devices. The distinction between the user and her associated client is crucial for the analysis of VMPC security where end-to-end verifiability is preserved in an all-malicious setting, i.e., where the honest users are against a severe adversarial environment that controls the entire VMPC execution by corrupting all servers and all clients. In this setting, each user is an entity with limited "human level" power, unable of performing complex cryptographic operations which are outsourced to her associated client. A secure VMPC scheme should be designed in a way that withstands such attacks, based on the engagement of the honest users in the execution.

VMPC security relies on the *internal randomness* that each user generates during her interaction with the system. By r_ℓ we denote the randomness generated by the user U_ℓ and κ_ℓ is the min-entropy of r_ℓ. Let $\kappa := \min\{\kappa_\ell \mid \ell \in [n]\}$ be the min-entropy of all users' randomness, that we call the *user min-entropy* of a VMPC scheme. Given that we view U_ℓ as a "human entity", the values of κ are small and insufficient for secure implementation of cryptographic primitives. Namely, each individual user contributes randomness that can be guessed by an adversary with non-negligible probability. Formally, it should hold $\kappa = O(\log\lambda)$, i.e. $2^{-\kappa}$ is a non-negligible value and hence insufficient for any cryptographic operation. From a computational point of view, users cannot perform complicated calculations and their computational complexity is linear in λ (i.e., the minimum for reading the input).

Protocols. A VMPC scheme consists of the following protocols:

- **Initialize** (executed among the servers). At the end of the protocol each server S_i posts a public value Params_i in the BB and maintains private state st_i. By $\mathsf{Params} = \{\mathsf{Params}_i,\ i \in [k]\}$ we denote the execution's public parameters.
- **Input** (executed among the servers and the users along with their associated clients). We restrict the interaction in the simple setting where the users engage in the **Input** protocol *without interacting* with each other. Specifically, each user U_ℓ, provides her input x_ℓ to her client C_ℓ (e.g., smartphone or desktop PC) which in turn interacts with the servers. By her interaction with C_ℓ, the user U_ℓ obtains some string α_ℓ that will be used as *individual audit data*.
- **Compute** (executed among the servers). At the end of the protocol, the servers post an *output value* y and the *public audit data* τ on the BB. Then, everyone may obtain the output y from the BB.
- **Verify** (executed by the verifier V and the users). In particular, V requests the individual audit data α_ℓ from each user U_ℓ and reads y, τ from the BB. Subsequently it provides each user U_ℓ with a pair (y, v), where $v \in \{0, 1\}$ denotes the verification success or failure.

Remark 2. The **Initialize** protocol can operate as a setup service that is run ahead of time and is used for multiple executions, while the **Input** protocol represents the online interaction between a user, her client and the servers.

5.2 Security Framework

We define a functionality that captures the two fundamental properties that every VMPC should achieve: (i) standard *MPC security* and (ii) *end-to-end verifiability.* Our model for VMPC is in the spirit of $\mathcal{H}$-EUC security [17], which allows for the preservation of the said properties under arbitrary protocol compositions. Thus, VMPC security refers to indistinguishability between an ideal and a real world setting by any environment that schedules the execution. In our definition we assume the functionality of a *Bulletin Board* $\mathcal{G}_{\mathsf{BB}}$ (with consistent write/read operations) and a functionality $\mathcal{F}_{\mathsf{sc}}$ that models a *Secure Channel* between each user and her client (we recall $\mathcal{G}_{\mathsf{BB}}$ and $\mathcal{F}_{\mathsf{sc}}$ in the full version [2]).

Ideal World Setting. We formally describe the *ideal VMPC functionality* $\mathcal{F}^{f,R}_{\mathsf{vmpc}}(\mathcal{P})$ that is defined w.r.t. to an *evaluation function* $f : X^n \longrightarrow Y$ and a *binary relation* $R \subseteq \mathsf{Img[f]} \times \mathsf{Img}[f]$ over the image of f. The functionality $\mathcal{F}^{f,R}_{\mathsf{vmpc}}(\mathcal{P})$ operates with the parties in $\mathcal{P} = \mathcal{U} \cup \mathcal{C} \cup \mathcal{S} \cup \{V\}$, which include the users $\mathcal{U} = \{U_1, \ldots, U_n\}$ along with their associated clients $\mathcal{C} = \{C_1, \ldots, C_n\}$, the servers $\mathcal{S} = \{S_1, \ldots, S_k\}$, and the verifier V.

The relation R determines the level of security offered by $\mathcal{F}_{\mathsf{vmpc}}^{f,R}(\mathcal{P})$ in terms of adversarial manipulation of the output computed value. E.g., if R is the equality relation $\{(y,y) \mid y \in Y\}$, then no deviation from the actual intended evaluation will be permitted by the $\mathcal{F}_{\mathsf{vmpc}}^{f,R}(\mathcal{P})$. Finally, the environment $\mathcal{Z}$ provides the parties with their inputs and determines a subset $L_{\mathsf{corr}} \subset \mathcal{P}$ of statically corrupted parties. Along the lines of the $\mathcal{H}$-EUC model, we consider an externalized global *helper* functionality $\mathcal{H}$ in both the ideal and real world. The helper $\mathcal{H}$ can interact with parties in $\mathcal{P}$ and the environment $\mathcal{Z}$. Namely, $\mathcal{Z}$ sends L_{corr} to $\mathcal{H}$ at the beginning or the execution. In this work, we allow $\mathcal{H}$ to run in super-polynomial time w.r.t. the security parameter λ. At a high level, $\mathcal{F}_{\mathsf{vmpc}}^{f,R}(\mathcal{P})$ interacts with the ideal adversary Sim as follows:

- At the **Initialize** phase, it waits for the servers and clients to be ready for the VMPC execution.
- At the **Input** phase, it receives the user's inputs. It leaks the input of U_ℓ to the adversary only if (i) all servers are corrupted or (ii) the client C_ℓ of U_ℓ is corrupted. If neither (i) nor (ii) holds, then $\mathcal{F}_{\mathsf{vmpc}}^{f,R}(\mathcal{P})$ only reveals whether U_ℓ abstained from the execution.
- At the **Compute** phase, upon receiving all user's inputs denoted as vector $\mathbf{x} \in X^n$, it computes the output value $y = f(\mathbf{x})$.
- At the **Verify** phase, upon receiving a verification request from V (which is a dummy party here), the functionality is responsible for playing the role of an "ideal verifier" for every user U_ℓ. On the other hand, Sim sends to $\mathcal{F}_{\mathsf{vmpc}}^{f,R}(\mathcal{P})$ an adversarial (hence, not necessarily meaningful) output value $\tilde{y}$ for the VMPC execution for U_ℓ. Then, $\mathcal{F}_{\mathsf{vmpc}}^{f,R}(\mathcal{P})$'s verification verdict w.r.t. U_ℓ will depend on the interaction with Sim and potentially the relation of $y, \tilde{y}$ w.r.t. R. We stress that $\mathcal{F}_{\mathsf{vmpc}}^{f,R}(\mathcal{P})$ will consider $\tilde{y}$ only if (a) all servers are corrupted, or (b) an honest user's client is corrupted[2]. If this is not the case, then it will always send the actual computed value y to U_ℓ and its verification verdict will not depend on R, which is in line with the standard notion of MPC correctness. The functionality $\mathcal{F}_{\mathsf{vmpc}}^{f,R}(\mathcal{P})$ is presented in Fig. 3.

Real World Setting. In the real world setting, all the entities specified in the set $\mathcal{P}$ are involved in an execution of a VMPC scheme Π = (**Initialize, Input, Compute, Verify**) in the presence of functionalities $\mathcal{G}_{\mathsf{BB}}$ and $\mathcal{F}_{\mathsf{sc}}$. As in the ideal world, the environment $\mathcal{Z}$ provides the inputs and determines the corruption subset $L_{\mathsf{corr}} \subset \mathcal{P}$. $\mathcal{Z}$ will also send L_{corr} to $\mathcal{H}$ at the beginning of the execution. During **Initialize**, the servers interact with the users' clients. During the **Input** protocol, every honest user U_ℓ engages by providing her private input x_ℓ via C_ℓ and obtaining her individual audit data α_ℓ. The execution is run in the presence of a PPT adversary $\mathcal{A}$ that observes the network traffic and corrupts the parties specified in L_{corr}.

[2] In case an honest user's client is corrupted, an "input replacement" attack can take place which makes it impossible to deliver (the true output) y to the user.

VMPC Definition. As in the $\mathcal{H}$-EUC framework [17], we consider an environment $\mathcal{Z}$ that provides inputs to all parties, interacts with helper $\mathcal{H}$ and schedules the execution. In the ideal world setting, $\mathcal{Z}$ outputs the bit $\mathsf{EXEC}^{\mathcal{F}^{f,R}_{\mathsf{vmpc}}(\mathcal{P})}_{\mathsf{Sim},\mathcal{Z},\mathcal{H}}(\lambda)$, and in the real world the bit $\mathsf{EXEC}^{\mathcal{P},\Pi^{\mathcal{G}_{\mathsf{BB}},\mathcal{F}_{\mathsf{sc}}}}_{\mathcal{A},\mathcal{Z},\mathcal{H}}(\lambda)$. Security is defined as follows:

Definition 6. *Let* $f : X^n \longrightarrow Y$ *be an evaluation function and* $R \subseteq \mathsf{Img}[f] \times \mathsf{Img}[f]$ *be a binary relation. Let* $\mathcal{H}$ *be a helper functionality. We say that a VMPC scheme* $\Pi^{\mathcal{G}_{\mathsf{BB}},\mathcal{F}_{\mathsf{sc}}}$ *operating with the parties in* $\mathcal{P}$, $\mathcal{H}$-EUC realizes $\mathcal{F}^{f,R}_{\mathsf{vmpc}}(\mathcal{P})$ with error ϵ, *if for every PPT adversary* $\mathcal{A}$ *there is an ideal PPT simulator* Sim *such that for every PPT environment* $\mathcal{Z}$, *it holds that*

$$\left|\Pr\left[\mathsf{EXEC}^{\mathcal{F}^{f,R}_{\mathsf{vmpc}}(\mathcal{P})}_{\mathsf{Sim},\mathcal{Z},\mathcal{H}}(\lambda)=1\right]-\Pr\left[\mathsf{EXEC}^{\mathcal{P},\Pi^{\mathcal{G}_{\mathsf{BB}},\mathcal{F}_{\mathsf{sc}}}}_{\mathcal{A},\mathcal{Z},\mathcal{H}}(\lambda)=1\right]\right| < \epsilon\,.$$

Strength of Our VMPC Security Model. Based on the description of $\mathcal{F}^{f,R}_{\mathsf{vmpc}}$, the private input x_ℓ of an honest user U_ℓ is leaked if her client C_ℓ is corrupted, or if all servers are malicious, so in our VMPC model, the honest users' clients and at least one server must be non-corrupted for privacy. For integrity, we require that the verifier remains honest, while $\mathcal{G}_{\mathsf{BB}}$ captures the notion of a consistent and public bulletin board. We informally argue that these requirements are essential for VMPC feasibility, at least for meaningful cases of functions and relations. Clearly, since the users communicate with the servers only via their clients, the user has to provide her input to the client which has to be trusted for privacy. Besides, if the adversary can corrupt all the servers, then it can completely run the **Compute** protocol and along with the environment, schedule the evaluation of f that, in general, may leak information on individual inputs that Sim cannot infer just by receiving the evaluation of f on the entire input vector.

Furthermore, if the real world verifier is malicious, then it can provide arbitrary verdicts regardless of the "verification rules" imposed by R, which rules are respected by $\mathcal{F}^{f,R}_{\mathsf{vmpc}}(\mathcal{P})$ in the ideal world (the same would hold even we considered multiple verifiers per user). Finally, in case of no consistent BB, since the communication between parties is not assumed authenticated, an adversary can disconnect the parties separating them into disjoint groups, and provide partial and mutually inconsistent views of the VMPC execution per group. For more details, we refer to Barak *et al.* [3] and the full version of this paper [2], where we discuss the strength of our model w.r.t. the server, client, and verifier corruption.

6 Spreading Relations

In this section, we study the characteristics that a function $f : X^n \longrightarrow Y$ must have w.r.t. some relation $R \subseteq \mathsf{Img}[f] \times \mathsf{Img}[f]$ to be realized by a VMPC scheme. Recall that in our setting, all entities capable of performing cryptographic operations might be corrupted and only a subset of users is honest. This requirement poses limitations not present in other security models (e.g. [4]), where auditable/ verifiable MPC is feasible for a large class of functions (arithmetic circuits) given

The functionality operates with the following parties $\mathcal{P} = \mathcal{U} \cup \mathcal{C} \cup \mathcal{S} \cup \{V\}$. The set $L_{\mathsf{corr}} \subset \mathcal{P}$ contains all corrupted parties.

Initialize.

– It sets its status to 'init' and initializes four lists $L_{\mathsf{start}}, L_{\mathsf{comp}}, L_{\mathsf{cast}}$ and L_{ready} as empty and a list L_{in} as $\langle (U_\ell, \cdot) \rangle_{U_\ell \in \mathcal{U}}$.

– Upon receiving $(\textsc{Start}, \mathsf{sid})$ from $S_i \in \mathcal{S}$, if its status is 'init', then it updates $L_{\mathsf{start}} \leftarrow L_{\mathsf{start}} \cup \{S_i\}$. If $|L_{\mathsf{start}}| = k$, it sets the status to 'input'.

– Upon receiving $(\textsc{Ready}, \mathsf{sid})$ from C_ℓ, if its status is 'init', then it sends public delayed output $(\textsc{Ready}, \mathsf{sid})$ to Sim and adds C_ℓ to L_{ready}.

Input.

– Upon receiving $(\textsc{Cast}, \mathsf{sid}, x_\ell)$ from U_ℓ, if (i) the status is 'input', and (ii) $C_\ell \in L_{\mathsf{corr}}$ or $\{S_1, \ldots, S_k\} \subseteq L_{\mathsf{corr}}$, then it sends $(\textsc{Cast}, \mathsf{sid}, U_\ell, x_\ell)$ to Sim. Otherwise, it sends $(\textsc{Cast}, \mathsf{sid}, U_\ell, (x_\ell \stackrel{?}{=} \text{'abstain'}))$ to Sim. If the status is 'input' and the entry in L_{in} indexed by U_ℓ is $(U_\ell, \cdot)$, then it updates the entry as (U_ℓ, x_ℓ).

– Upon receiving $(\textsc{Record}, \mathsf{sid}, U_\ell, \tilde{x}_\ell)$ from Sim, if (i) the status is 'input', and (ii) $(U_\ell, \cdot) \notin L_{\mathsf{cast}}$, then

∘ If $C_\ell \in L_{\mathsf{corr}}$, then it adds $(U_\ell, \tilde{x}_\ell)$ to L_{cast}.

∘ If (a) $C_\ell \notin L_{\mathsf{corr}}$, (b) there is a record $(U_\ell, x_\ell) \in L_{\mathsf{in}}$ and (c) $C_\ell \in L_{\mathsf{ready}}$ or $x_\ell = \mathsf{abstain}$, then it adds (U_ℓ, x_ℓ) to L_{cast}.

– Upon receiving $(\textsc{Compute}, \mathsf{sid})$ from $S_i \in \mathcal{S}$, if its status is 'input', then it updates $L_{\mathsf{comp}} \leftarrow L_{\mathsf{comp}} \cup \{S_i\}$. If $|L_{\mathsf{comp}}| = k$, it sets the status to 'compute'. For every U_ℓ s.t. there is no record in L_{cast}, it adds $(U_\ell, \mathsf{abstain})$ to L_{cast}.

Compute.

– If status is 'compute' and L_{cast} contains records for all users $U_1, \ldots, U_n$, it computes $y \leftarrow f(\langle x_\ell \rangle_{(U_\ell, x_\ell) \in L_{\mathsf{cast}}})$ and sends $(\textsc{Output}, \mathsf{sid}, y)$ to Sim.

– Upon receiving $(\textsc{Audit}, \mathsf{sid})$ from Sim, it sets the status to 'audit'.

Verify.

– Upon receiving $(\textsc{Verify}, \mathsf{sid})$ from V, if the status is 'audit', then it sends $(\textsc{Verify}, \mathsf{sid})$ to Sim.

– Upon receiving $(\textsc{Verify\_Response}, \mathsf{sid}, U_\ell, \tilde{y}, \tilde{v})$ from Sim, if the status is 'audit':

(1) If (i) $\tilde{v} = 1$, and (ii) $V \notin L_{\mathsf{corr}}$ then

• If there exists an $S_i \notin L_{\mathsf{corr}}$ and for all ℓ' such that $U_{\ell'} \notin L_{\mathsf{corr}}$ it holds that $C_{\ell'} \notin L_{\mathsf{corr}}$, then it sends $(\textsc{Result}, \mathsf{sid}, y, 1)$ to U_ℓ.

• Else, (all servers are corrupted, or there is an honest $U_{\ell'}$ with a corrupted $C_{\ell'}$)

∘ If $(y, \tilde{y}) \in R$, then it sends $(\textsc{Result}, \mathsf{sid}, \tilde{y}, 1)$ to U_ℓ.

∘ If $(y, \tilde{y}) \notin R$, then it sends $(\textsc{Result}, \mathsf{sid}, \tilde{y}, 0)$ to U_ℓ.

(2) Else if (i) $\tilde{v} = 0$ or (ii) $V \in L_{\mathsf{corr}}$, then it sends $(\textsc{Result}, \mathsf{sid}, \tilde{y}, \tilde{v})$ to U_ℓ.

Fig. 3. The ideal VMPC functionality $\mathcal{F}_{\mathsf{vmpc}}^{f,R}(\mathcal{P})$.

(i) the existence of a trusted randomness source or a random oracle or (ii) the fact that both the honest user and her client are considered as one non-corrupted entity. As a consequence, for some evaluation function f and binary relation R, if VMPC realization is feasible, then this is due to the nature of the users' engagement in the VMPC execution. Namely, we consider that the users interact using some randomness that implies a level of *unpredictability* in the eyes of the attacker that prevents end-to-end verifiability (as determined by relation R) or secrecy from being breached. Naturally, this engagement results in a security error that strongly depends on (i) *the number of honest users* whose inputs are attacked by the adversary and (ii) *the user min entropy* κ. On the contrary, it is plausible that if an adversary controlling the entire execution can guess all the users' coins, then this execution is left defenseless against the adversary's attacks. As mentioned in Sect. 5, the possible values for κ remain at a "human level", in the sense that the randomness r_ℓ of U_ℓ can be guessed with good probability. Typically, we assume that $2^{-\kappa}$ is non-negligible in the security parameter λ by setting $\kappa = O(\log\lambda)$.

We view the sets X^n and Y as metric spaces equipped with metrics d_{X^n} and d_Y respectively. For the domain X^n, we select the metric that provides an estimation of the number of honest users that have been attacked, i.e. their inputs are modified by the real world adversary. So, we fix d_{X^n} as the metric Dcr_n that counts the number of vector elements that two inputs $\mathbf{x} = (x_1, \dots, x_n), \mathbf{x}' = (x'_1, \dots, x'_n)$ differ. Formally, $\mathsf{Dcr}_n(\mathbf{x}, \mathbf{x}') = \big|\{\ell \in [n] \mid x_\ell \neq x'_\ell\}\big|$.

We examine feasibility of realizing $\mathcal{F}^{f,R}_{\mathsf{vmpc}}$ w.r.t. f, R according to the following reasoning: assuming that cryptographic security holds, then an adversarial input that has some distance δ w.r.t. Dcr_n from the honest inputs cannot cause a significant divergence y' from the actual evaluation $y = f(\mathbf{x})$. Here, divergence is interpreted as the case where y, y' are not in some fixed relation R. For instance, if divergence means that the deviation from the actual evaluation is no more than δ, this can be expressed as y, y' not being in the *bounded distance relation* R_δ defined as follows:

$$R_\delta := \{(z, z') \in Y \times Y \mid \mathrm{d}_Y(z, z') \leq \delta\}\ . \tag{2}$$

An interesting class of evaluation functions that can be realized in an VMPC manner w.r.t. R_δ are the ones that satisfy some *relaxed isometric property*, thus inherently preventing evaluation from "large" deviation blow ups when the distance between honest and adversarial inputs is bounded, as specified by Eq. (2) for some positive value δ. One noticeable example are the *Lipschitz functions*; namely, for some $L > 0$, if the evaluation function $f : X^n \longrightarrow Y$ is *L-Lipschitz*, then for every $\mathbf{x}, \mathbf{x}' \in X^n$ it holds that $\mathrm{d}_Y\big(f(\mathbf{x}), f(\mathbf{x}')\big) \leq L \cdot \mathsf{Dcr}_n(\mathbf{x}, \mathbf{x}')$.

Thus, in the case of an L-Liptshitz function f and bounded distance relation R_δ, the following condition holds:

$$\forall \mathbf{x}, \mathbf{x}' \in X^n : \mathsf{Dcr}_n(\mathbf{x}, \mathbf{x}') \leq \delta/L \Rightarrow R_\delta\big(f(\mathbf{x}), f(\mathbf{x}')\big)\ .$$

In general, the above condition implies that the ideal functionality $\mathcal{F}^{f,R}_{\mathsf{vmpc}}(\mathcal{P})$ will accept a simulation when the adversarial value y' *can be derived by an input vector* that is no more than δ-far from the actual users' inputs. This interesting property fits perfectly with our intuition of VMPC realization and captures Lipschitz functions and bounded distance relations as special case. Based on the above, we introduce the notion of *spreading relations* as follows.

Definition 7 (Spreading relation). *Let* (X^n, Dcr_n) *and* (Y, d_Y) *be metric spaces,* $f : X^n \longrightarrow Y$ *be a function and* δ *be a non-negative real value. We say that* $R \subseteq \mathsf{Img}[f] \times \mathsf{Img}[f]$ *is a* δ-spreading relation over $\mathsf{Img}[f]$, *if for every* $\mathbf{x}, \mathbf{x}' \in X^n$ *it holds that*

$$\mathsf{Dcr}_n(\mathbf{x}, \mathbf{x}') \leq \delta \Rightarrow R(f(\mathbf{x}), f(\mathbf{x}')) .$$

The Breadth of VMPC Feasibility. Given Definition 7, we formally explore the boundaries of VMPC feasibility given some fixed values κ, δ. Intuitively, we show that if f is symmetric[3], then VMPC realization with a small (typically $\mathsf{negl}(\delta)$) error is infeasible when R is not a δ-spreading relation over $\mathsf{Img}[f]$, or if the users engage in the VMPC execution in a "deterministic way" (i.e., $\kappa = 0$). A detailed discussion and a proof sketch can be found in the full version of this paper [2].

Theorem 3. *Let* $f : X^n \longrightarrow Y$ *be a symmetric function,* $R \subseteq \mathsf{Img}[f] \times \mathsf{Img}[f]$ *be a binary relation and* κ, δ *be non-negative values, where* $\delta \leq \frac{n}{2}$. *Then, one of the following two conditions holds:*

(1) R is a δ*-spreading relation over* $\mathsf{Img}[f]$.
(2) For every VMPC scheme $\Pi^{\mathcal{G}_{\mathsf{BB}}, \mathcal{F}_{\mathsf{sc}}}$ *with parties in* $\mathcal{P} = \{U_1, \ldots, U_n\} \cup \{C_1, \ldots, C_n\} \cup \{S_1, \ldots, S_k\} \cup \{V\}$ *and user min entropy* κ*, and every helper* $\mathcal{H}$*, there is a negligible function* ϵ *and a non-negligible function* γ *such that* $\Pi^{\mathcal{G}_{\mathsf{BB}}, \mathcal{F}_{\mathsf{sc}}}$ *does not* $\mathcal{H}$*-EUC realize* $\mathcal{F}^{f,R}_{\mathsf{vmpc}}(\mathcal{P})$ *with error less than* $\min\{2^{-\kappa\delta} - \epsilon(\lambda), \gamma(\lambda)\}$.

7 Constructing VMPC from CVZK

A number of efficient practical MPC protocols [11,26,27,52] have been proposed in the pre-processing model. Such protocols consist of two phases: *offline* and *online*. During the *offline* phase, the MPC parties jointly compute authenticated correlated randomness, which typically is independent of the parties' inputs. During the *online* phase, the correlated randomness is consumed to securely evaluate the MPC function over the parties' inputs. Our VMPC construction follows the same paradigm as [4]. Our main challenge is to transform a publicly audible MPC to a VMPC *without* a trusted setup.

Our construction utilizes a number of tools that are presented in the full version of this paper [2]: (i) a perfectly binding homomorphic commitment that is secure against helper-aided PPT adversaries, (ii) a *dual-mode homomorphic commitment* DC, which allows for two ways to choose the commitment key s.t. the commitment is either perfectly binding or equivocal, (iii) a *Σ-protocol for Beaver triples*, and (iv) CVZK proofs that derive from compiling straight-line simulatable ZK proofs for **NP** languages via our CVZK construction from Sect. 4. Note that plain ZK does not comply with the VMPC corruption model, as all servers and clients can be corrupted and each user has limited entropy. Additionally, our

[3] $f(x_1, \ldots, x_n)$ is symmetric iff it is unchanged by any permutation of its variables.

protocol utilizes a secure channel functionality $\mathcal{F}_{\mathsf{sc}}$ between human users U_ℓ and their local clients C_ℓ; and an authenticated channel functionality $\mathcal{F}_{\mathsf{auth}}$ between human users U_ℓ and verifier V. Both channels can be instantiated from physical world, such as isolated rooms and trusted mailing service. To provide intuition, we first present a construction for the single-server setting.

Single-Server VMPC. As a warm-up, we present the simpler case of a single MPC server S. In this setting, no privacy can be guaranteed when S is corrupted, yet end-to-end verifiability should remain, since the property should hold even if *all servers* are corrupted. For simplicity, by using CVZK to prove a statement, we mean that the prover (server) runs $\mathsf{CVZK.Prv}_1$ to generate the first move of the CVZK proof and posts it on BB (formalized as $\mathcal{G}_{\mathsf{BB}}$ in [2]) during the **Initialize** phase. Each user then acts as a CVZK verifier to generate and post a coin on the BB at **Input** phase. The prover uses $\mathsf{CVZK.Prv}_2$ to complete the proof by posting the third move of the CVZK proof to the BB at the **Compute** phase. At **Verify**, anyone can check the CVZK transcripts posted on the BB.

- At the **Initialize** phase, S first generates a perfectly binding commitment key of the dual-mode homomorphic commitment as $\mathsf{ck} \leftarrow \mathsf{DC.Gen}(1^\lambda)$ which posts on the BB and shows that ck is a binding key using CVZK. Then, S generates and commits to two random numbers $r_\ell^{(0)}, r_\ell^{(1)} \in \mathbb{Z}_p$ to the BB for each user U_ℓ, $\ell \in [n]$. Denote the corresponding commitments as $c_\ell^{(0)}$ and $c_\ell^{(1)}$. Furthermore, S generates sufficiently many random Beaver triples (depending on the multiplication gates of the circuit to be evaluated), i.e., triples $(a, b, c) \in (\mathbb{Z}_p)^3$ such that $c = a \cdot b$, and then commits the triples to the BB by showing their correctness using the CVZK compiled from the Σ-protocol for Beaver triples. For each user U_ℓ, $\ell \in [n]$, S sends $r_\ell^{(0)}$ and $r_\ell^{(1)}$ to her client C_ℓ.
- At the **Input** phase, C_ℓ sends (displays) $r_\ell^{(0)}$ and $r_\ell^{(1)}$ to U_ℓ. Assume U_ℓ's input is x_ℓ. U_ℓ randomly picks $b_\ell \leftarrow \{0, 1\}$ and computes $\delta_\ell = x_\ell - r_\ell^{(b_\ell)}$[4]. Then, U_ℓ sends (b_ℓ, δ_ℓ) to C_ℓ, which in turn posts $(U_\ell, \delta_\ell, b_\ell)$ to the BB, where U_ℓ is the user ID. Finally, U_ℓ obtains $(b_\ell, \delta_\ell, r_\ell^{(1-b_\ell)})$ as her individual audit data α_ℓ.
- At the **Compute** phase, S fetches posted messages from the BB. For $\ell \in [n]$, S sets $c_\ell \leftarrow c_\ell^{(b_\ell)} \cdot \mathsf{DC.Com}_{\mathsf{ck}}(\delta_\ell; \mathbf{0})$ and opens $c_\ell^{(1-b_\ell)}$ to the BB (note that c_ℓ commits to x_ℓ). S follows the arithmetic circuit to evaluate $f(x_1, \ldots, x_n)$ using $(c_1, \ldots, c_n)$ as the input commitments. Specifically, (i) for addition gate $z = x + y$, S uses homomorphic property to set the commitment of z as $\mathsf{DC.Com}_{\mathsf{ck}}(x) \cdot \mathsf{DC.Com}_{\mathsf{ck}}(y)$; (ii) for multiplication gate $z = x \cdot y$, S needs to consume a pre-committed random Beaver triple. Denote the commitments of x and y as X and Y, respectively and the triple commitments as (A, B, C)

[4] Note that this step requires the "human" user to perform some linear operation in $\mathbb{Z}_p$. If we want to avoid *any* type of computation in the user side (apart from coin-flipping), then the client can also send a pre-computed lookup table for all δ_ℓ (assuming that the user input space is polynomial).

which commit to a, b, c s.t. $a \cdot b = c$. Then, S opens the commitment X/A as α and Y/B as β to the BB. It then sets the commitment of z as $C \cdot B^{\alpha} \cdot A^{\beta} \cdot \mathsf{DC.Com}_{\mathsf{ck}}(\alpha \cdot \beta)$. By homomorphic property, it is easy to see that $z = x \cdot y$. Finally, S opens the commitments corresponding to the output gate(s) of the arithmetic circuit as the final result.

- At the **Verify** phase, V requests and receives the individual audit data $\{\alpha_\ell\}_{\ell \in [n]}$ from each user U_ℓ, $\ell \in [n]$, via $\mathcal{F}_{\mathsf{auth}}$. First, V parses $\alpha_\ell = (b_\ell, \delta_\ell, r_\ell^{(1-b_\ell)})$, for $\ell \in [n]$. Next, V fetches all the transcript from the BB, and it executes the following steps: (1) it checks that the posted b_ℓ on the BB match the ones in α_ℓ; (2) it verifies that the openings of all the commitments are valid; (3) it verifies that all the CVZK proofs are valid; (4) it re-computes the arithmetic circuit using the commitments and openings posted on the BB to verify the computation correctness. If all checks are successful, V sets the verification bit $v := 1$, else it sets $v := 0$. Finally, it sends the opening of the result commitment (i.e., $f(x_1, \ldots, x_n)$) along with v to every user U_ℓ, $\ell \in [n]$.

Security Analysis. We provide an informal discussion on the security of the single-server construction in terms of privacy and end-to-end verifiability.

Privacy. The single-server VMPC construction preserves user U_ℓ's privacy when the server S and C_ℓ are honest. In particular, since the underlying commitment scheme is computationally hiding under the adaptively secure DDH assumption (cf. [2] for a definition), all the posted commitments to values X/A and Y/B leak no information (up to a $\mathsf{negl}(\lambda)$ error) about the users' inputs to a PPT adversary with access to the helper. Furthermore, while computing the multiplication gates, the openings have uniform distribution, as the plaintext is masked by a random group element.

End-to-End Verifiability. Let f be an evaluation function and R be a δ-spreading relation over $\mathsf{Img}[f]$ (cf. Definition 7), where $\delta \geq 0$ is an integer. We informally discuss how the single-server VMPC protocol achieves end-to-end verifiability w.r.t. R, with error that is negligible in λ and δ. Assume that the adversary $\mathcal{A}$ corrupts the MPC server, all users' clients and no more than $n^{1-\frac{1}{\gamma}}/\log^3 n$ users. First, we note that if $\mathcal{A}$ additionally corrupts the verifier V, we can construct a simple simulator that engages with $\mathcal{A}$ by playing the role of honest users and simply forwards the malicious response of V to $\mathcal{F}^{f,R}_{\mathsf{vmpc}}(\mathcal{P})$ along with the adversarial tally y'.

For the more interesting case where V is honest, we list the types of attacks that $\mathcal{A}$ may launch below:

- *Commitment attack:* $\mathcal{A}$ attempts to open some commitment c of a message m, to a value $m' \neq m$. By the perfect binding property of ElGamal commitment, this attack has zero success probability.
- *Soundness attack:* $\mathcal{A}$ attempts to convince the verifier of an invalid CVZK proof. By the $\left(n^{1-\frac{1}{\gamma}}/\log^3 n, \mathsf{negl}(\lambda)\right)$-crowd-verifiable soundness of our CVZK compiler (cf. Theorem 2), $\mathcal{A}$ has $\mathsf{negl}(\lambda)$ probability of success in such an attack.

- *Client attack:* by corrupting the client C_ℓ of U_ℓ, $\mathcal{A}$ provides U_ℓ with a pair of random values $(\hat{r}_\ell^{(0)}, \hat{r}_\ell^{(1)})$, where one component $\hat{r}_\ell^{(b^*)}$ is different than $r_\ell^{(b^*)}$ in the pair $(r_\ell^{(0)}, r_\ell^{(1)})$ committed to BB. Hence, if $\mathcal{A}^*$ guesses the coin of U_ℓ correctly (i.e. $b^* = b_\ell$), then it can perform the VMPC execution by replacing U_ℓ's input x_ℓ with input $x_\ell^* = x_\ell + (\hat{r}_\ell^{(b^*)} - r_\ell^{(b^*)})$ without being detected. Given that U_ℓ flips a fair coin, this attack has 1/2 success probability.

This list of attacks is complete; if none of the above attacks happen, then by the properties of the secret sharing scheme, $\mathcal{A}$ can not tamper the VMPC computation on the consistent BB without being detected.

Leaving aside the $\mathsf{negl}(\lambda)$ cryptographic error inserted by combinations of commitment and soundness attacks, the adversary's effectiveness relies on the scale of client attacks that it can execute. If it performs more than δ client attacks, then by the description of client attacks, V will detect and reject with at least $1 - 2^{-\delta}$ probability. So, with at least $1 - 2^{-\delta}$ probability, a simulator playing the role of the (honest) verifier will also send a reject message ($\tilde{v} = 0$) for every honest user to $\mathcal{F}_{\mathsf{vmpc}}^{f,R}(\mathcal{P})$ and indistinguishability is preserved.

On the other hand, if $\mathcal{A}$ performs less than δ client attacks, then the actual input $\mathbf{x}$ and the adversarial one $\mathbf{x}'$ are δ-close w.r.t. $\mathsf{Dcr}_n(\cdot,\cdot)$. Since the relation R is δ-spreading, we have that $(f(\mathbf{x}), f(\mathbf{x}')) \in R$ holds. So, when the simulator plays the role of the (honest) verifier that accepts, it sends an accept message ($\tilde{v} = 1$) for every honest user to $\mathcal{F}_{\mathsf{vmpc}}^{f,R}(\mathcal{P})$ which in turn will also accept (since $(f(\mathbf{x}), f(\mathbf{x}')) \in R$ holds). Besides, $\mathcal{F}_{\mathsf{vmpc}}^{f,R}(\mathcal{P})$ will reject whenever the simulator sends a reject message, hence, indistinguishability is again preserved.

We conclude that the single-server VMPC scheme achieves end-to-end verifiability with overall error $2^{-\delta} + \mathsf{negl}(\lambda)$.

Extension to Multi-server VMPC. The single-server VMPC can be naturally extended to a multi-server version by secret-sharing the server's state. The protocol is similar to BDO [4] and SPDZ [26,27]. However, all the underlying ZK proofs need to be compiled in CVZK. More specifically, we define an offline functionality $\mathcal{F}_{\mathsf{V.Offline}}$ to generate shared random Beaver triples and shared random values. The main differences between our $\mathcal{F}_{\mathsf{V.Offline}}$ and the ones used in SPDZ and its variants are (i) The MAC is removed from all the shares, and (ii) $\mathcal{F}_{\mathsf{V.Offline}}$ has to be crowd verifiable. Due to space limitations, we provide the formal description of $\mathcal{F}_{\mathsf{V.Offline}}$ and its realization in the $\mathcal{H}$-EUC model in the full version of this paper [2]. Moreover, in [2], we formally present the multi-server VMPC scheme $\Pi_{\mathsf{online}}^{\mathcal{G}_{\mathsf{BB}},\mathcal{F}_{\mathsf{sc}},\mathcal{F}_{\mathsf{auth}},\mathcal{F}_{\mathsf{V.Offline}}}$ in the $\{\mathcal{G}_{\mathsf{BB}}, \mathcal{F}_{\mathsf{sc}}, \mathcal{F}_{\mathsf{auth}}, \mathcal{F}_{\mathsf{V.Offline}}\}$-hybrid model along with a proof sketch of the following theorem.

Theorem 4. *Let $\Pi_{\mathsf{online}}^{\mathcal{G}_{\mathsf{BB}},\mathcal{F}_{\mathsf{sc}},\mathcal{F}_{\mathsf{auth}},\mathcal{F}_{\mathsf{V.Offline}}}$ be our VMPC scheme with n users. Let $\gamma > 1$ be a constant such that $n = \lambda^\gamma$. Let $f : X^n \longrightarrow Y$ be a symmetric function and $R \subseteq \mathsf{Img}[f] \times \mathsf{Img}[f]$ be a δ-spreading relation over $\mathsf{Img}[f]$. The scheme $\Pi_{\mathsf{online}}^{\mathcal{G}_{\mathsf{BB}},\mathcal{F}_{\mathsf{sc}},\mathcal{F}_{\mathsf{auth}},\mathcal{F}_{\mathsf{V.Offline}}}$ $\mathcal{H}$-EUC realizes $\mathcal{F}_{\mathsf{vmpc}}^{f,R}(\mathcal{P})$ in the $\{\mathcal{G}_{\mathsf{BB}}, \mathcal{F}_{\mathsf{sc}}, \mathcal{F}_{\mathsf{auth}}, \mathcal{F}_{\mathsf{V.Offline}}\}$-hybrid model with error $2^{-\delta} + \mathsf{negl}(\lambda)$ under the adaptive DDH assumption, against any PPT environment $\mathcal{Z}$ that statically corrupts at most $\frac{n^{1-\frac{1}{\gamma}}}{\log^3 n}$*

users, assuming the underlying CVZK is $(n, \mathsf{negl}(\lambda))$*-crowd verifiable complete,* $\left(\frac{n^{1-\frac{1}{\eta}}}{\log^3 n}, \mathsf{negl}(\lambda)\right)$*-crowd verifiable sound, and n-crowd verifiable zero-knowledge.*

Remark 3. When $\delta = \omega(\log \lambda)$, then $\Pi_{\mathsf{online}}^{\mathcal{G}_{\mathsf{BB}}, \mathcal{F}_{\mathsf{sc}}, \mathcal{F}_{\mathsf{auth}}, \mathcal{F}_{\mathsf{V.Offline}}}$ $\mathcal{H}$-EUC realizes $\mathcal{F}_{\mathsf{vmpc}}^{f,R}(\mathcal{P})$.

8 Applications of VMPC

Examples of interesting VMPC application scenarios may refer to e-voting, as well as any type of privacy-preserving data processing where for transparency reasons, it is important to provide evidence of the integrity of the outcome, e.g., demographic statistics or financial analysis. In our modeling, the most appealing cases - in terms of usability by a user with "human level" limitations - are the ones where the error is small for the lowest possible entropy, e.g. users contribute only 1 bit. Hence, for simplicity we set $\kappa = 1$. Following the reasoning in Sect. 6 and by Theorem 3, when $\kappa = 1$, a VMPC application can be feasible when it is w.r.t. to δ-spreading relations and with an error expected to be $\mathsf{negl}(\delta)$ (ignoring the $\mathsf{negl}(\lambda)$ cryptographic error). In general, we can calibrate the security error by designing VMPC schemes that support sufficiently large values of κ. We present a selection of interesting VMPC applications below.

e-Voting. The security analysis of several e-voting systems (e.g. [21,41,45]) is based on the claim that "assuming cryptographic security, by attacking one voter you change one vote, thus you add at most one to the total tally deviation". This claim can be seen as a special case of VMPC security for an evaluation (tally) function which is 1-Lipschitz and tally deviation is naturally captured by R_δ defined in Eq. (2). Thus, if the voters contribute min entropy of 1 bit, then we expect that e-voting security holds with error $\mathsf{negl}(\delta)$.

Privacy-Preserving Statistics. Let $X = [a, b]$ be a range of integer values, $Y = [a, b]$ and $f := \frac{\sum_{\ell=1}^{n} x_\ell}{n}$ be the average of all users' inputs. E.g., $[a, b]$ could be the number of unemployed adults or dependent members in a family, the range of the employees' salary in a company, or the household power consumption in a city measured by smart meters. If we set d_Y to the absolute value $|\cdot|$, then f is a $\frac{b-a}{n}$-Lipschitz function for Dcr_n and $|\cdot|$, so for user min entropy of 1 bit, we expect that (f, R_δ) can be realized with error $\mathsf{negl}(\frac{\delta n}{b-a})$. This also generalizes to other aggregate statistics such as calculating higher moments over the data set.

Privacy-Preserving Processing of Multidimensional Data (Profile Matching). A useful generalization of the privacy-preserving statistics case is when performing processing on multidimensional data collected from multiple sources. A simple two-dimensional example illustrating this follows. Let X_1, X_2 be two domains of attributes and $X := X_1 \times X_2$, i.e. each input x_ℓ is an attribute pair $(x_{\ell,1}, x_{\ell,2})$. Let $Y = [n]$, P_1, P_2 be predicates over X_1, X_2 respectively and let $f := \sum_{\ell=1}^{n} P_1(x_{\ell,1}) \cdot P_2(x_{\ell,2})$ be the function that counts the number of inputs that satisfy both P_1, P_2. E.g., X_1 could be the set of dates and X_2 be the locations, fragmented in area units. Then, f could count the number of people that are in a specific place and have their birthday. If we set d_Y to $|\cdot|$, then f is a 1-Lipschitz function for Dcr_n and $|\cdot|$. (f, R_δ) can be realized with error $\mathsf{negl}(\delta)$.

Supervised Learning of (binary) Classifiers. In many use cases, functions that operate as classifiers are being "trained" via a machine learning algorithm (e.g. Perceptron) on input a vector of training data. Here, we view the users' inputs as training data that are vectors of dimension m, i.e. $x_\ell = (x_{\ell,1}, \dots, x_{\ell,m}) \in [a_1, b_1] \times \cdots \times [a_m, b_m]$, where $[a_i, b_i]$, $i \in [m]$ are intervals. The evaluation function f outputs a hyperplane $HP(\mathbf{x}) := \{\mathbf{w} \cdot \mathbf{z} \mid \mathbf{z} \in \mathbb{R}^m\}$ that defines the decision's 0/1 output. If the adversary changes $\mathbf{x}$ with some $\mathbf{x}'$ s.t. $\mathsf{Dcr}_n(\mathbf{x}, \mathbf{x}') \leq \delta$, then the adversarially computed hyperplane $HP(\mathbf{x}') := \{\mathbf{w}' \cdot \mathbf{z} \mid \mathbf{z} \in \mathbb{R}^m\}$ must be close to $HP(\mathbf{x})$, otherwise the attack is detected. This could be expressed by having $\mathbf{w}, \mathbf{w}'$ be δ close w.r.t. the Euclidean distance. Assume now that for a set of new data points $\mathbf{z}_1, \dots, \mathbf{z}_t$ we set the relation as "$R\big(HP(\mathbf{x}), HP(\mathbf{x}')\big) \Leftrightarrow \forall j \in [t]$ the classifier makes the same decision for $\mathbf{z}_j$". Then, clearly R is a spreading relation w.r.t. to f, suggesting that the functionality of calculating classifier is resilient against attacks on less than δ of the training data.

References

1. Alwen, J., Ostrovsky, R., Zhou, H.-S., Zikas, V.: Incoercible multi-party computation and universally composable receipt-free voting. In: Gennaro, R., Robshaw, M. (eds.) CRYPTO 2015. LNCS, vol. 9216, pp. 763–780. Springer, Heidelberg (2015). https://doi.org/10.1007/978-3-662-48000-7_37
2. Baldimtsi, F., Kiayias, A., Zacharias, T., Zhang, B.: Crowd verifiable zero-knowledge and end-to-end verifiable multiparty computation. IACR Cryptology ePrint Archive 2020:711 (2020)
3. Barak, B., Canetti, R., Lindell, Y., Pass, R., Rabin, T.: Secure computation without authentication. In: Shoup, V. (ed.) CRYPTO 2005. LNCS, vol. 3621, pp. 361–377. Springer, Heidelberg (2005). https://doi.org/10.1007/11535218_22
4. Baum, C., Damgård, I., Orlandi, C.: Publicly auditable secure multi-party computation. In: Abdalla, M., De Prisco, R. (eds.) SCN 2014. LNCS, vol. 8642, pp. 175–196. Springer, Cham (2014). https://doi.org/10.1007/978-3-319-10879-7_11
5. Beaver, D.: Efficient multiparty protocols using circuit randomization. In: Feigenbaum, J. (ed.) CRYPTO 1991. LNCS, vol. 576, pp. 420–432. Springer, Heidelberg (1992). https://doi.org/10.1007/3-540-46766-1_34
6. Beaver, D.: Commodity-based cryptography (extended abstract). In: STOC (1997)
7. Bellare, M., Fuchsbauer, G., Scafuro, A.: NIZKs with an untrusted CRS: security in the face of parameter subversion. In: Cheon, J.H., Takagi, T. (eds.) ASIACRYPT 2016. LNCS, vol. 10032, pp. 777–804. Springer, Heidelberg (2016). https://doi.org/10.1007/978-3-662-53890-6_26
8. Ben-Or, M., Linial, N.: Collective coin flipping, robust voting schemes and minima of Banzhaf values. In: FOCS (1985)
9. Benaloh, J.: Simple verifiable elections. In: USENIX EVT. USENIX Association (2006)

10. Benaloh, J.: Ballot casting assurance via voter-initiated poll station auditing. In: EVT (2007)
11. Bendlin, R., Damgård, I., Orlandi, C., Zakarias, S.: Semi-homomorphic encryption and multiparty computation. In: Paterson, K.G. (ed.) EUROCRYPT 2011. LNCS, vol. 6632, pp. 169–188. Springer, Heidelberg (2011). https://doi.org/10.1007/978-3-642-20465-4_11
12. Bogetoft, P., et al.: Secure multiparty computation goes live. In: Dingledine, R., Golle, P. (eds.) FC 2009. LNCS, vol. 5628, pp. 325–343. Springer, Heidelberg (2009). https://doi.org/10.1007/978-3-642-03549-4_20
13. Bost, R., Popa, R.A., Tu, S., Goldwasser, S.: Machine learning classification over encrypted data. In: NDSS (2015)
14. Burmester, M., Desmedt, Y.: Broadcast interactive proofs. In: Davies, D.W. (ed.) EUROCRYPT 1991. LNCS, vol. 547, pp. 81–95. Springer, Heidelberg (1991). https://doi.org/10.1007/3-540-46416-6_7
15. Canetti, R.: Universally composable security: a new paradigm for cryptographic protocols. In: FOCS (2001)
16. Canetti, R., Dodis, Y., Pass, R., Walfish, S.: Universally composable security with global setup. In: Vadhan, S.P. (ed.) TCC 2007. LNCS, vol. 4392, pp. 61–85. Springer, Heidelberg (2007). https://doi.org/10.1007/978-3-540-70936-7_4
17. Canetti, R., Lin, H., Pass, R.: Adaptive hardness and composable security in the plain model from standard assumptions. In: FOCS (2010)
18. Chaum, D.: Secret-ballot receipts: true voter-verifiable elections. In: IEEE S&P (2004)
19. Ciampi, M., Persiano, G., Scafuro, A., Siniscalchi, L., Visconti, I.: Improved OR-Composition of sigma-protocols. In: TCC (2016)
20. Ciampi, M., Persiano, G., Scafuro, A., Siniscalchi, L., Visconti, I.: Online/Offline OR composition of sigma protocols. In: Fischlin, M., Coron, J.-S. (eds.) EUROCRYPT 2016. LNCS, vol. 9666, pp. 63–92. Springer, Heidelberg (2016). https://doi.org/10.1007/978-3-662-49896-5_3
21. Cortier, V., Galindo, D., Küsters, R., Mueller, J., Truderung, T.: SoK: verifiability notions for e-voting protocols. IEEE Security & Privacy (2016)
22. Cramer, R., Damgård, I., Schoenmakers, B.: Proofs of partial knowledge and simplified design of witness hiding protocols. In: Desmedt, Y.G. (ed.) CRYPTO 1994. LNCS, vol. 839, pp. 174–187. Springer, Heidelberg (1994). https://doi.org/10.1007/3-540-48658-5_19
23. Cramer, R., Gennaro, R., Schoenmakers, B.: A secure and optimally efficient multi-authority election scheme. In: Fumy, W. (ed.) EUROCRYPT 1997. LNCS, vol. 1233, pp. 103–118. Springer, Heidelberg (1997). https://doi.org/10.1007/3-540-69053-0_9
24. Damgård, I., Damgård, K., Nielsen, K., Nordholt, P.S., Toft, T.: Confidential benchmarking based on multiparty computation. In: Grossklags, J., Preneel, B. (eds.) FC 2016. LNCS, vol. 9603, pp. 169–187. Springer, Heidelberg (2017). https://doi.org/10.1007/978-3-662-54970-4_10
25. Damgård, I., Ishai, Y., Krøigaard, M., Nielsen, J.B., Smith, A.: Scalable multiparty computation with nearly optimal work and resilience. In: Wagner, D. (ed.) CRYPTO 2008. LNCS, vol. 5157, pp. 241–261. Springer, Heidelberg (2008). https://doi.org/10.1007/978-3-540-85174-5_14
26. Damgård, I., Keller, M., Larraia, E., Pastro, V., Scholl, P., Smart, N.P.: Practical covertly secure MPC for dishonest majority – Or: breaking the SPDZ limits. In: Crampton, J., Jajodia, S., Mayes, K. (eds.) ESORICS 2013. LNCS, vol. 8134, pp. 1–18. Springer, Heidelberg (2013). https://doi.org/10.1007/978-3-642-40203-6_1

27. Damgård, I., Pastro, V., Smart, N., Zakarias, S.: Multiparty computation from somewhat homomorphic encryption. In: Safavi-Naini, R., Canetti, R. (eds.) CRYPTO 2012. LNCS, vol. 7417, pp. 643–662. Springer, Heidelberg (2012). https://doi.org/10.1007/978-3-642-32009-5_38
28. Dodis, Y., Ristenpart, T., Vadhan, S.P.: Randomness condensers for efficiently samplable, seed-dependent sources. In: TCC (2012)
29. Ellison, C.: Ceremony design and analysis. IACR ePrint, Report 2007/399 (2007)
30. Feige, U., Kilian, J., Naor, M.: A minimal model for secure computation (extended abstract). In: STOC (1994)
31. Fleischhacker, N., Goyal, V., Jain, A.: On the existence of three round zero-knowledge proofs. In: Nielsen, J.B., Rijmen, V. (eds.) EUROCRYPT 2018. LNCS, vol. 10822, pp. 3–33. Springer, Cham (2018). https://doi.org/10.1007/978-3-319-78372-7_1
32. Goldreich, O., Micali, S., Wigderson, A.: How to play any mental game or A completeness theorem for protocols with honest majority. In: STOC (1987)
33. Halevi, S., Lindell, Y., Pinkas, B.: Secure computation on the web: computing without simultaneous interaction. In: Rogaway, P. (ed.) CRYPTO 2011. LNCS, vol. 6841, pp. 132–150. Springer, Heidelberg (2011). https://doi.org/10.1007/978-3-642-22792-9_8
34. Hazay, C., Venkitasubramaniam, M.: On the power of secure two-party computation. In: Robshaw, M., Katz, J. (eds.) CRYPTO 2016. LNCS, vol. 9815, pp. 397–429. Springer, Heidelberg (2016). https://doi.org/10.1007/978-3-662-53008-5_14
35. Ishai, Y., Kushilevitz, E., Paskin, A.: Secure multiparty computation with minimal interaction. In: Rabin, T. (ed.) CRYPTO 2010. LNCS, vol. 6223, pp. 577–594. Springer, Heidelberg (2010). https://doi.org/10.1007/978-3-642-14623-7_31
36. Kahn, J., Kalai, G., Linial, N.: The influence of variables on Boolean functions (extended abstract). In: FOCS (1988)
37. Kalai, Y.T., Rothblum, G.N., Rothblum, R.D.: From obfuscation to the security of fiat-Shamir for proofs. In: Katz, J., Shacham, H. (eds.) CRYPTO 2017. LNCS, vol. 10402, pp. 224–251. Springer, Cham (2017). https://doi.org/10.1007/978-3-319-63715-0_8
38. Kamara, S., Mohassel, P., Riva, B.: Salus: a system for server-aided secure function evaluation. In: CCS (2012)
39. Keller, M., Orsini, E., Scholl, P.: MASCOT: faster malicious arithmetic secure computation with oblivious transfer. In: CCS (2016)
40. Kiayias, A., Zacharias, T., Zhang, B.: DEMOS-2: scalable E2E verifiable elections without random oracles. In: CCS (2015)
41. Kiayias, A., Zacharias, T., Zhang, B.: End-to-end verifiable elections in the standard model. In: Oswald, E., Fischlin, M. (eds.) EUROCRYPT 2015. LNCS, vol. 9057, pp. 468–498. Springer, Heidelberg (2015). https://doi.org/10.1007/978-3-662-46803-6_16
42. Kiayias, A., Zacharias, T., Zhang, B.: Ceremonies for end-to-end verifiable elections. In: Fehr, S. (ed.) PKC 2017. LNCS, vol. 10175, pp. 305–334. Springer, Heidelberg (2017). https://doi.org/10.1007/978-3-662-54388-7_11
43. Kreuter, B., Shelat, A., Shen, C.: Billion-gate secure computation with malicious adversaries. In: USENIX (2012)
44. Küsters, R., Truderung, T., Vogt, A.: Accountability: definition and relationship to verifiability. In: CCS (2010)
45. Küsters, R., Truderung, T., Vogt, A.: Clash attacks on the verifiability of e-voting systems. IEEE Security & Privacy (2012)

46. Lapidot, D., Shamir, A.: Publicly verifiable non-interactive zero-knowledge proofs. In: Menezes, A.J., Vanstone, S.A. (eds.) CRYPTO 1990. LNCS, vol. 537, pp. 353–365. Springer, Heidelberg (1991). https://doi.org/10.1007/3-540-38424-3_26
47. Lepinski, M., Micali, S., Shelat, A.: Fair-zero knowledge. In: Kilian, J. (ed.) TCC 2005. LNCS, vol. 3378, pp. 245–263. Springer, Heidelberg (2005). https://doi.org/10.1007/978-3-540-30576-7_14
48. Lindell, Y., Pinkas, B.: Secure multiparty computation for privacy-preserving data mining. IACR ePrint 2008/197 (2008)
49. López-Alt, A., Tromer, E., Vaikuntanathan, V.: On-the-fly multiparty computation on the cloud via multikey fully homomorphic encryption. In: STOC (2012)
50. Meka, R.: Explicit resilient functions matching Ajtai-Linial. In: SODA (2017)
51. Neff, C.A.: Practical high certainty intent verification for encrypted votes. Inc. whitepaper, Votehere (2004)
52. Nielsen, J.B., Nordholt, P.S., Orlandi, C., Burra, S.S.: A new approach to practical active-secure two-party computation. In: Safavi-Naini, R., Canetti, R. (eds.) CRYPTO 2012. LNCS, vol. 7417, pp. 681–700. Springer, Heidelberg (2012). https://doi.org/10.1007/978-3-642-32009-5_40
53. Pandey, O., Pass, R., Vaikuntanathan, V.: Adaptive one-way functions and applications. In: Wagner, D. (ed.) CRYPTO 2008. LNCS, vol. 5157, pp. 57–74. Springer, Heidelberg (2008). https://doi.org/10.1007/978-3-540-85174-5_4
54. Pass, R.: Simulation in quasi-polynomial time, and its application to protocol composition. In: Biham, E. (ed.) EUROCRYPT 2003. LNCS, vol. 2656, pp. 160–176. Springer, Heidelberg (2003). https://doi.org/10.1007/3-540-39200-9_10
55. Pinkas, B., Schneider, T., Smart, N.P., Williams, S.C.: Secure two-party computation is practical. In: Matsui, M. (ed.) ASIACRYPT 2009. LNCS, vol. 5912, pp. 250–267. Springer, Heidelberg (2009). https://doi.org/10.1007/978-3-642-10366-7_15
56. Schoenmakers, B., Veeningen, M.: Universally verifiable multiparty computation from threshold homomorphic cryptosystems. In: Malkin, T., Kolesnikov, V., Lewko, A.B., Polychronakis, M. (eds.) ACNS 2015. LNCS, vol. 9092, pp. 3–22. Springer, Cham (2015). https://doi.org/10.1007/978-3-319-28166-7_1
57. Yao, A.C.: Protocols for secure computations (extended abstract). In: FOCS (1982)
58. Yao, A.C.: How to generate and exchange secrets (extended abstract). In: FOCS (1986)

Non-interactive Composition of Sigma-Protocols via Share-then-Hash

MasayukiAbe[1(✉)], Miguel Ambrona[1], Andrej Bogdanov[2], Miyako Ohkubo[3], and Alon Rosen[4]

[1] NTT Secure Platform Laboratories, Musashino, Japan
{masayuki.abe.cp,miguel.ambrona.fu}@hco.ntt.co.jp
[2] Chinese University of Hong Kong, Shatin, Hong Kong
andrejb@cse.cuhk.edu.hk
[3] Security Fundamentals Laboratory, CSR, NICT, Tokyo, Japan
m.ohkubo@nict.go.jp
[4] Herzliya Interdisciplinary Center, Herzliya, Israel
alon.rosen@idc.ac.il

Abstract. Proofs of partial knowledge demonstrate the possession of certain subsets of witnesses for a given collection of statements $x_1, \ldots, x_n$. Cramer, Damgård, and Schoenmakers (CDS), built proofs of partial knowledge, given "atomic" protocols for individual statements x_i, by having the prover randomly secret share the verifier's challenge and using the shares as challenges for the atomic protocols. This simple and highly-influential transformation has been used in numerous applications, ranging from anonymous credentials to ring signatures.

We consider what happens if, instead of using the shares directly as challenges, the prover first hashes them. We show that this elementary enhancement can result in significant benefits:

- the proof contains a *single* atomic transcript per statement x_i,
- it suffices that the atomic protocols are κ-special sound for $\kappa \geq 2$,
- when compiled to a signature scheme using the Fiat-Shamir heuristic, its unforgeability can be proved in the *non-programmable* random oracle model.

None of the above features is satisfied by the CDS transformation.

Keywords: Sigma-protocols · Random oracles · Proof of partial knowledge

1 Introduction

The focus of this paper is three-move public-coin proof systems. In such protocols, a prover sends an initial message, a, to the verifier who answers back with a random challenge, e. The prover finally replies with z, based on which the verifier accepts or rejects the proof. Σ-protocols [19] are a special class of 3PC protocols that have been used as building blocks in a wide variety of applications, and have been the subject of intensive study.

S. Moriai and H. Wang (Eds.): ASIACRYPT 2020, LNCS 12493, pp. 749–773, 2020.
https://doi.org/10.1007/978-3-030-64840-4_25

One property that makes a Σ-protocol easy to work with is the so-called *2-special soundness*: given any pair of "colliding" transcripts, (a, e, z) and (a, e', z') for $e \neq e'$, one can efficiently extract a witness w for the instance x being proved. The zero-knowledge property is exhibited using a specific type of simulator, which takes x and e as input, and outputs a and z that form an accepting transcript. Being public-coin, with a uniformly chosen challenge sent by the verifier, the protocol can be made non-interactive using the Fiat-Shamir heuristic [26], where the prover generates the challenge e on its own by applying a hash function modeled as a random oracle to the initial message a.

Several techniques for efficient composition of Σ-protocols can be found in the literature. Among them, the technique by Cramer, Damgård, and Schoenmakers (CDS for short) is the most popular and well-studied [21]. In its simplest form, the CDS technique is used for proving the *disjunction* of n statements $x_1, \dots, x_n$, convincing the verifier that the prover knows a witness w for at least one of the statements x_i. To this end, the prover shares a given challenge e into challenges $e_1, \dots, e_n$ under the constraint that $e = e_1 \oplus \cdots \oplus e_n$ and uses e_i as the challenge in an individual run of the Σ-protocol for statement x_i.

Since the prover can choose in advance all but one shared challenge e_{i^*} for which w_{i^*} is known, it may run the simulator on (x_i, e_i) for all $i \neq i^*$ and the prescribed prover algorithm on (x_{i^*}, w_{i^*}). This enables the prover to complete the protocol given a witness for at least one out of n instances. If the atomic protocols are 2-special sound, the compound protocol is 2-special sound as well.

The way in which the verifier challenge is secret-shared can be generalized to implement any composition predicate that is efficiently computable by a monotone span program [20]. Since the compound protocol remains a Σ-protocol, it can also be made non-interactive via the Fiat-Shamir heuristic. While security is proved in the random oracle model, it does not necessitate trusted setup which is often required by efficient non-interactive proofs.

1.1 Our Contribution

We propose a simple enhancement to the CDS composition method and show that it results in several desirable features. In simple terms, the modification can be described as follows:

"Hash each share before using it as a challenge".

As simple as it appears to be, this modification enjoys significant benefits over the original CDS transformation: (1) in computation and communication efficiency, (2) in allowing a wider variety of choices for the underlying atomic protocols, and (3) in the tightness of the analysis in the random oracle model. We now elaborate on each of these benefits separately.

Recycling of Transcripts for Repeated Statements. In the CDS transformation, the transcript of the compound protocol contains one instance of the atomic protocol for each occurrence of a statement x_i in the formula or monotone span program. In contrast, our proposed transformation allows to "recycle" transcripts of atomic protocols and let them have a *single* appearance per x_i. This may result in savings in prover computation and communication, whenever base statements x_i occur repeatedly, especially in cases where the monotone span program describing the compound statement cannot be simplified to have few occurrences of x_i.

Consider for example the following compound statement, described in disjunctive normal form: $(x_1 \wedge x_2) \vee (x_1 \wedge x_3) \vee (x_3 \wedge x_4)$. Notice that in this case the instance x_1 appears in two clauses (and so does x_3). When applying the CDS transformation, a prover (wishing to protect w_1 from leaking) must run independent executions of the atomic Σ-protocol for each appearance of x_1 in the formula. Otherwise, in case that the initial message a for proving x_1 is shared by two transcripts (a_1, e_1, z_1) and (a_1, e_1', z_1'), it may be the case that $e_1 \neq e_1'$ which would yield a colliding pair of transcripts, enabling, even an honest verifier, to extract the witness w_1 for x_1. In some cases one may be able to find an equivalent formula with fewer occurrences of specific variables. However, performing such simplifications in general is a non-trivial and potentially error-prone process. Furthermore, in some cases it may simply be not possible. Indeed, a recent implementation of compound statements [44] is aware of such issues and takes explicit care to refrain from merging the initial messages for the same statements in the formula. Their compiler halts when a repeated statement is detected and let the programmer decide what to do. Such issues were also explicitly considered in the original CDS protocol. When a share of a challenge exceeds the challenge space size, CDS explicitly require to repeat the atomic protocol for the same instance so that the joint challenge space covers the maximum length of the shared challenges.

By applying a hash function to the secret-shared challenges in all occurrences of x_i we compress and fit the challenge to the original challenge space size. Assuming that the hash function is modeled as a random oracle, soundness is guaranteed by the fact that hashed challenges are randomly and uniformly distributed. This allows us to run the atomic proof for a given instance x_i only once, independently of how many times it appears in the compound formula, hence simplifies the protocol. Furthermore, it improves both the running time of the prover and verifier, and reduces the size of the proof. Consider, for instance, the compound statement $(x_1 \wedge x_2) \vee (x_1 \wedge x_3) \vee (x_3 \wedge x_4)$ again. The CDS+FS combination would require six transcripts: one per literal. Ours leads to a proof with simply four transcripts: one per variable, regardless of the number of occurrences in the formula. More concretely, our proof consists of four transcripts $(a_1, e_1, z_1), ..., (a_4, e_4, z_4)$ together with secret shares (s_1, s_2, s_3, s_4) where each (a_i, e_i, z_i) is accepting with respect to the i-th Σ-protocol and $e_i = H(s_i)$. Furthermore, the shares are such that all qualified sets of shares (according to the *dual* access structure induced by formula) recover the secret $s := H(a_1, \ldots, a_4)$. In our example this could be enforced by setting $s_1 := \{d_1, d_2\}$, $s_2 := \{d_1\}$, $s_3 = \{d_2, d_3\}$, and $s_4 = \{d_3\}$ where $d_1 + d_2 + d_3 = s$. See Sect. 3.2 for a more detailed comparison between our scheme with previous work in terms of performance and proof size.

Wider Choice for Special Soundness of Atomic Protocols. Special soundness is, by definition, restricted to the case where two colliding transcripts are necessary and sufficient for extracting a witness. However, some protocols in the literature are only known to satisfy a more relaxed κ-special soundness requirement, in which $\kappa > 2$ colliding transcripts are necessary and sufficient for witness extraction.

The original CDS transformation was designed to only handle 2-special soundness, and indeed may totally lose soundness if applied to general κ-sound protocols for $\kappa > 2$ [25]. As an example of 3-special soundness, consider Stern's protocol [54], often used in the context of lattices and codes [25,39,40,47]. In its basic version, a challenge is chosen from $\{0, 1, 2\}$ and a cheating prover, or zero-knowledge simulator, having no witness can answer to two preliminary chosen challenge values out of the three. The original CDS technique for composing two runs of the protocol suggests to share challenge e as $e = e_1 + e_2 \bmod 3$ and use e_1 and e_2 as a challenge in each run. This is however totally insecure since a cheating prover may simulate on $e_1 \in \{0, 1\}$ and $e_2 \in \{1, 2\}$ and pick a proper combination of challenge values for e_1 and e_2 to fulfill the constraint $e = e_1 + e_2 \bmod 3$ for any challenge $e \in \{0, 1, 2\}$. Such an attack works even with parallel repetition of the protocol, with challenge space $\{0, 1, 2\}^\ell$ for polynomial ℓ, and even after applying the Fiat-Shamir transformation, as the adversary can similarly attack each coordinate individually and win with probability 1.

Applying an ideal hash function to e_1 and e_2 individually makes them uniformly distributed over the challenge space. With large enough challenge space, which can be obtained by parallel repetition of Stern's basic protocol, this virtually prevents a cheating prover from controlling the distribution of the challenges.

We prove that this intuition is valid in the random oracle model. As a result, our scheme is sound even for κ-special sound protocols with $\kappa > 2$. Other well-known examples of κ-special sound protocols ranges from the widely known GMW protocol for graph 3-colorability [31], and a useful protocol for a binary opening of Pedersen-like commitments (with 3-special soundness) [10], to a fun protocol for Sudoku puzzles [32].

Various Flavors of Soundness. We prove soundness in different flavors in the programmable and/or non-programmable random oracle models (NPROM) [48]. As shown in [18], when viewed as a non-interactive membership argument system, CDS composition with Fiat-Shamir (henceforth CDS+FS) is sound in NPROM provided that underlying protocols are optimally sound. Ours covers more relaxed statistically sound protocols.

If one of the two hash functions, one used for FS and the other used for hashing shares, is programmable random oracle, our construction provides simulation extractability [8], which is a strong form of knowledge soundness. If both are programmable, and the underlying protocol is unique response where z is unique for x, a, and e, it is strongly simulation extractable.

Unforgeability in Non-programmable Random Oracle Model. In a recent paper, Fischlin, Harasser, and Janson [28] show that when the CDS protocol is compiled into a signature scheme via the Fiat-Shamir transform, its unforgeability against adaptive chosen message attacks cannot be (black-box) proved in NPROM. They aregue that it contrasts to a *sequential* composition considered in [3].

The share-hashing in our construction circumvents this impossibility result. A key observation in the (im)possibility argument of [28] is that the sequential composition in [3] makes hash queries for each underlying protocol execution in some order, and the order of the queries reveals which instance the adversary is attacking. In contrast, CDS+FS makes a combined hash query for all underlying protocol executions at once, thus revealing no information which execution the adversary is attacking. This difference is precisely what renders the signature scheme via the sequential composition provably unforgeable in the NPROM, and CDS+FS not.

Since in our transformation hashing is applied for each execution of the underlying protocol, observing the order of the queries reveals which ones the adversary is attacking, just as in the example above. We are thus able to prove unforgeability in the NPROM, using the same proof strategy as developed in [28].

1.2 Applications

Our minor modification to the CDS+FS transformation means that it can serve as a plug-in replacement for most applications of the CDS protocol, with the only exceptions being the ones in which using a random oracle is not allowed.

In some cases the applicability of our transformation goes beyond what could have been achieved by CDS+FS. As a demonstration, consider a generic construction of a ring signature scheme [51] with the following added features: (1) it supports any monotone formula access structure, (2) it can be built from κ-special-sound Σ-protocols for hard languages, (3) it is unforgeable against chosen message and chosen ring attacks in the NPROM, and (4) it is setup-free in the sense that players do not need to interact to each other or to access public parameters (except for security parameter) to set up their public-keys.

The CDS+FS transformation is equipped with all the features mentioned above, and can be used to construct a secure signature scheme in a standard manner. However, we do not know how to prove its unforgeability in the NPROM, the main difficulty being that, unlike the case of a standard signature scheme, a ring-signature adversary is allowed to specify the access structure. Let us elaborate on this point further below.

In [28], it is shown that a non-interactive argument system for a simple cyclic graph representing a sequence of disjunctions can be turned into a secure signature scheme in the NPROM where the public key is a set of instances of a hard language. In the security argument, the reduction simulates signatures using a non-tight qualified set of instances, and, by observing queries to the random oracle, identifies which instance the adversary is attacking. It is then shown that replacing the target instance with an incorrect one that has no corresponding witness does not make much difference to the computationally limited adversary since those instances are supposed to be indistinguishable and signatures can still be simulated as the remaining correct instances form a qualified set.

In the attack scenario for ring signatures, however, it is the adversary who chooses the access structure. The adversary can ask a signature on a full set of instances so that the only qualified set is tight. Accordingly, signatures cannot be simulated if an instance is turned into an incorrect one.

Our solution is to form each key by a disjunctive relation over two instances, and combine them into a single monotone formula. This allows to simulate signatures even if one of the pairs is turned into incorrect, and just as in [28] enables us to argue that attacking the incorrect instance is unsuccessful in the NPROM. The resulting scheme yields signatures whose size is linear in the number of involved public keys.

While there exist more compact ring signature schemes, e.g., [7], with logarithmic-size signatures and without using random oracles, our construction is more flexible in the choice of underlying building blocks and in the number of instantiations. This is on top of being the first scheme provable in the NPROM.

1.3 Related Work

Composition of Proof Systems. The task of proving compound statements in a zero-knowledge manner can be in principle realized generically by reducing to some NP-complete language, and in some cases even a flexible and convenient one such as satisfiability of Quadratic Arithmetic Programs. This approach is flexible, as it allows to dynamically adjust the statement to be proved depending on the application at hand. A popular application that has seen prominence recently is that of proving possession of a preimage of a value under a specified hash function. Recent implementations demonstrate reasonable performance, though we are still in early stage of deployment, and further progress is required.

Composition is an active topic also in the context of NIZKs in the common reference string model. There are number of existing techniques in the literature, e.g., [2,13,29,33,35,45,50], to implement disjunctive relations for the Groth-Sahai proofs [36] and Quasi-Adaptive NIZKs [38]. One of the common ideas is to use arithmetic relations of the form $x(x-1) = 0$ that naturally translate to logical disjunctions: $(x = 1) \vee (x = 0)$. Another popular approach is to split a common reference string in two parts so that one of them can be used for simulation, whereas using a witness for the other part is unavoidable. In [5], Agrawal, Ganesh, and Mohassel studied efficient monotone composition of algebraic and non-algebraic statements combining both Σ-protocols and generic NIZKs for NP.

The composition technique most relevant to our work is that of ring-like sequential composition, introduced in [3] and revisited recently in [28], all of which admit soundness proofs in the NPROM. Recently, [1] consider a generalization of sequential composition to so-called *acyclicity programming* (a model that is closely related to branching programs), which in some cases goes beyond CDS composition, the latter being limited to monotone span programs in terms of expressibility. Still, generally speaking the two transformations are incomparable, and it should be mentioned that both CDS and our current transformation are able to easily handle the important case of threshold access structures. Precise proof sizes and computational costs are also incomparable as they depend on the structure of the compound relation.

Fiat-Shamir Transform in NPROM and the Standard Model. The issue of programmability of random oracles in the case the Fiat-Shamir transform is discussed in [18,42]. They present an efficient FS transformation for constructing NIZK in the common reference and random oracle models whose zero-knowledge property does not rely on random oracles and only the proof of soundness requires a NPROM. The proof for soundness in the NPROM in [18] demands optimal soundness from the underlying protocol: for every false statement and every first message, there exists at most one challenge that has a valid response satisfying the verification predicate.

Not relying on programmable random oracles in the soundness argument of Fiat-Shamir transform may allow to instantiate the hash function under milder assumptions such as key dependent message secure encryption [15] or lattice-based assumptions [14,49] through the notion of correlation intractability [16]. They require the underlying protocol optimally sound [18] and design the hash function used in the FS transform so that it hardly outputs the bad challenge for which a valid response exists. Unfortunately, the additional hashing for generating challenges in our construction makes it hard to follow their approach as the bad challenge function will depend on the hash function.

Ring Signatures. A fair number of papers devote themselves to improve and generalize the seminal work of ring signatures scheme in [51]. In [12], a general monotone access structure is supported for composition of signatures based on trapdoor permutations. A construction based on Σ-protocols is presented in [3] and extended in [43] with a simple mechanism for anonymity revocation, and in [4] with a support for threshold structures. These early works, followed by, e.g., [37], achieve the setup-free property in the *programmable* random oracle model. We note that the scheme in [4] hashes shared challenges to adjust the challenge size to incorporate RSA keys in a ring. When the ring consists only of the discrete-log type ones, it can be seen as a special case of our construction, a composition of Schnorr proofs with hashed shares, but none of the benefits claimed in this paper were considered.

There are number of schemes, e.g., [6,11,17,22,23,30,34,41,52,53], that require trusted setup but provide more flexible access structures and/or achieves high performance when instantiated with mathematically rich primitives such as pairings, lattices, and codes. A scheme in [7] is favorable in that the security is proven in the standard model, no trusted setup is needed, and the proof size is logarithmic in the number of involved public-keys limiting the access structure only to a ring.

2 Preliminaries

For a finite set S, we write $a \leftarrow S$ to denote that a is uniformly sampled from S. We denote the security parameter by $\lambda \in \mathbb{N}$. Given two functions $f, g : \mathbb{N} \rightarrow [0, 1]$, we write $f \approx g$ if the difference $|f(\lambda) - g(\lambda)|$ is asymptotically smaller than the inverse of any polynomial. A function f is said to be *negligible* if $f \approx 0$, whereas it is said to be *overwhelming* when $f \approx 1$. For integers m, n, such that $n \geq m$, we denote by $[m, n]$ the range $\{m, m+1, \ldots, n\}$. We denote by $[n]$ the range $[1, n]$. By $\mathbb{N}^*$ we denote the space of arbitrarily-long sequences of numbers in $\mathbb{N}$. When A is a probabilistic algorithm, we denote by $A(x; r)$ an execution of A on input x and random coin r taken from an appropriate domain defined for A. If the random coin is not important in the context, we simply write as $A(x)$.

Let $R : \mathcal{X} \times \mathcal{W} \to \{0,1\}$ be a binary relation defined over a set of instances $\mathcal{X}$ and a set of witnesses $\mathcal{W}$. We write $(x, w) \in R$ as a shorthand for (x, w) satisfying $R(x, w) = 1$. For convenience, we separate instances according to the security parameter. By R_λ, we mean relation R on instances of length λ. Let L_R be the language defined as $L_R := \{x \in \mathcal{X} \mid \exists w \in \mathcal{W} : R(x, w) = 1\}$. A statement is a relation on an instance, which is true if and only if the instance is in the language defined by the relation. We say that L_R is a hard language if $(x, w) \in R$ is efficiently and uniformly sampleable, and there exists $\tilde{L}$ that is efficiently sampleable, has no intersection with L_R, and is computationally indistinguishable from L_R. We abuse notation and write $(x, w) \leftarrow R$ to represent uniform sampling of (x, w) satisfying R. For a monotone access structure Γ over $[n]$ and a set of n relations $\boldsymbol{R} := (R_1, \ldots, R_n)$, we denote by $\Gamma_{\boldsymbol{R}}$ a relation obtained by composing relation $R_i \in \boldsymbol{R}$ following structure Γ.

2.1 Σ-protocols

A Σ-protocol for relation R is a three-round public-coin proof system that is special honest verifier zero-knowledge and 2-special sound as defined in the following. It is witness indistinguishable and statistically sound. We also introduce additional security notions on which we rely when proving stronger properties about our construction.

Definition 1 (Three-round public-coin proof system). *A* three-round public-coin proof system *for relation R consists of algorithms $(\mathcal{C}, \mathcal{Z}, \mathcal{V})$ where:*

- *$a \leftarrow \mathcal{C}(x, w\,; r)$ computes an initial message, a, for the given instance x and witness w with a random coin r uniformly taken from an appropriate domain.*
- *$z \leftarrow \mathcal{Z}(x, w, r, e)$ computes an answer, z, for the given challenge $e \in \{0,1\}^\mu$, and coin r used to generate a on x and w.*
- *$1/0 \leftarrow \mathcal{V}(x, a, e, z)$ outputs 1 or 0 for acceptance or rejection, respectively.*

We say a three-round public-coin proof system is complete *if for every $\lambda \geq 1$, every pair $(x, w) \in R$, where $|x| = \lambda$, for all $e \in \{0,1\}^\mu$, for all $a \leftarrow \mathcal{C}(x, w\,; r)$, and for all $z \leftarrow \mathcal{Z}(x, w, r, e)$, $\mathcal{V}(x, a, e, z) = 1$ holds.*

Definition 2 (Special Honest Verifier Zero-Knowledge). *A three-round public-coin proof system $(\mathcal{C}, \mathcal{Z}, \mathcal{V})$ is* special honest verifier zero knowledge *if there exists a probabilistic polynomial-time algorithm $\mathcal{S}$ such that, for every stateful PPT adversary $\mathcal{A}$,*

$$\begin{aligned} &\Pr\left[(x, e) \leftarrow \mathcal{A}(1^\lambda);\ a \leftarrow \mathcal{C}(x, w; r);\ z \leftarrow \mathcal{Z}(x, w, r, e) : \mathcal{A}(a, z) = 1\right] \\ \approx\ &\Pr\left[(x, e) \leftarrow \mathcal{A}(1^\lambda);\ (a, z) \leftarrow \mathcal{S}(x, e) \qquad\qquad\qquad\qquad : \mathcal{A}(a, z) = 1\right] \end{aligned}$$

where r is sampled form the corresponding distribution and $\mathcal{A}$ must output values such that $(x, w) \in R$ and e is in $\{0,1\}^\mu$.

Definition 3 (Witness Inidistinguishability). *A three-round public-coin proof system $(\mathcal{C}, \mathcal{Z}, \mathcal{V})$ is* witness indistinguishable *if for all $x \in L_R$, and all w_1, w_2 satisfying $R(x, w_1) = R(x, w_2) = 1$, transcripts (a_1, e, z_1) and (a_2, e, z_2) distribute identically, where $a_i \leftarrow \mathcal{C}(x, w_i; r_i)$, $e \leftarrow \{0,1\}^\mu$, $z \leftarrow \mathcal{Z}(x, w_i, r_i, e)$ for $i = 1, 2$.*

Special soundness [19] is a special form of knowledge soundness which guarantees that, given two colliding transcripts $(x, a, \{e_1, z_1\}, \{e_2, z_2\})$, a witness w (for x) can be extracted efficiently if $e_1 \neq e_2$. A generalized form of this notion appears in the literature, e.g., [9,10,34,55]. Intuitively, κ-special soundness states that given κ-colliding transcripts $(x, a, \{e_1, z_1\}, \dots, \{e_\kappa, z_\kappa\})$, a witness w can be extracted if all values $e_1, \dots, e_\kappa$ are distinct. A question is from which distribution the challenges should be sampled and with how much probability the extraction should succeed. In some literature it is asked to hold for any e_i and to succeed perfectly. This is however too strong for our purpose as we would like to capture a wide variety of protocols, including the parallel version of Stern's protocol where an exponential number (but still negligible compared to the size of the challenge space) of colliding transcripts can be prepared without knowing the witness; on the other hand, a small number of collision over uniformly chosen challenges is sufficient for successful extraction with high probability. Consequently, we adopt the following definition.

Definition 4 (κ-Special Soundness). *A three-round public-coin proof system is* κ-special sound *with knowledge error ϵ if, there exists a deterministic polynomial-time algorithm $\mathcal{E}$ such that, for any stateful probabilistic polynomial-time adversary $\mathcal{A}$, and for all t polynomial in λ, it holds:*

$$\Pr\left[\begin{array}{rl} (x,a) & \leftarrow \mathcal{A}(1^\lambda) \\ e_1,\dots,e_t & \leftarrow \{0,1\}^\mu \\ (z_1,\dots,z_t) & \leftarrow \mathcal{A}(e_1,\dots,e_t) \\ w \leftarrow & \mathcal{E}(x,a,\{e_1,z_1\},\dots,\{e_t,z_t\}) \end{array} : \begin{array}{c} \sum_{i=1}^t \mathcal{V}(x,a,e_i,z_i) \geq \kappa \\ \wedge \\ R(x,w) = 0 \end{array}\right] \leq \epsilon$$

where every e_i is distinct. It is special sound if ϵ is a negligible function and κ is polynomial in the security parameter. In particular, we say that it is perfectly special sound *if $\epsilon = 0$.*

There are different flavors of soundness as a proof of membership. An example is *optimal soundness*, which asserts that for any false instance x and any a, there exists at most one challenge e for which the transcript will pass the verification. In other words, for any $x \notin L_R$ and any a, and for all values $e \in \{0,1\}^\mu$ (except at most one), $\mathcal{V}(x, a, e, \cdot)$ is the zero function. We use more general statistical soundness allowing negligible error probability.

Definition 5 (Statistical Soundness). *A three-round public-coin proof system* $(\mathcal{C}, \mathcal{Z}, \mathcal{V})$ *is* statistically sound *with soundness error* ϵ_{st} *if for any (possibly unbounded) adversary* $\mathcal{A}$, *for all* $x \notin L_R$ *and all* $a \in \{0,1\}^*$,

$$\Pr[e \leftarrow \{0,1\}^{\mu};\ z \leftarrow \mathcal{A}(x,a,e)\ :\ \mathcal{V}(x,a,e,z) = 1] < \epsilon_{\mathsf{st}}\ .$$

We say it is statistically sound if ϵ_{st} *is negligible in* λ.

In other words, a three-round public-coin proof system is statistical sound with bound ϵ_{st} if and only if for every $x \notin L_R$ and any $a \in \{0,1\}^*$, at most a ϵ_{st} fraction of challenges has an answer that passes the verification.

In order to achieve stronger variant of simulation soundness, we require the uniqueness of z for (x, a, e). This is the so-called *unique response* property [24,27] and was stated in [34] in a general form as follows.

Definition 6 (Quasi-unique response). *A* Σ*-protocol has* quasi-unique responses *if for any security parameter* $\lambda \in \mathbb{N}$, *any polynomial-size* $\nu \in \{0,1\}^*$, *and for any PPT algorithm, the probability that, given* 1^{λ} *and* ν *as input, the adversary outputs* (x, a, e, z, z') *satisfying* $\mathcal{V}(x, a, e, z) = \mathcal{V}(x, a, e, z') = 1$ *and* $z \neq z'$ *is negligible in* λ.

2.2 Non-interactive Arguments

We define non-interactive argument systems in a way that captures Σ-protocols transformed by the Fiat-Shamir heuristics in the random oracle model. Let $\mathcal{R}$ be a random oracle that returns an independently and uniformly chosen value in an appropriate domain for every distinct input.

Definition 7 (Non-Interactive Argument System). *A* non-interactive argument system *for relation* R *in the random oracle model is a pair of polynomial-time oracle algorithms* (Prove, Verify) *that, for random oracle* $\mathcal{R}$:

- $\pi \leftarrow \mathsf{Prove}^{\mathcal{R}}(x, w)$ *is a probabilistic algorithm that takes an instance* x *and a witness* w *and outputs a proof* π.
- $0/1 \leftarrow \mathsf{Verify}^{\mathcal{R}}(x, \pi)$ *is a deterministic algorithm that takes* x *and* π, *and outputs either* 1 *or* 0 *representing acceptance or rejection, respectively.*

It is complete *if, for every sufficiently large* $\lambda \in \mathbb{N}$, *and every* $(x, w) \in R$, $\mathsf{Verify}^{\mathcal{R}}(x, \mathsf{Prove}^{\mathcal{R}}(x, w))$ *outputs* 1 *except with negligible probability in* λ. *The probability is taken over coins of* Prove *and* $\mathcal{R}$.

Definition 8 (Zero-Knowledge). *A non-interactive argument system* (Prove, Verify) *for relation* R *is zero-knowledge in the random oracle model if there exists a PPT stateful algorithm* Sim *that for all probabilistic polynomial-time distinguisher* D, $\Pr[1 \leftarrow D^{\mathcal{R},\mathcal{O}_1}(1^{\lambda})] - \Pr[1 \leftarrow D^{\mathcal{O}_2}(1^{\lambda})]$ *is negligible in* λ. $\mathcal{O}_1$ *is an oracle that, given* (x, w) *as input, returns* $\perp$ *if* $(x, w) \notin R$, *else returns the output of* $\mathsf{Prove}^{\mathcal{R}}(x, w)$. $\mathcal{O}_2$ *and* Sim *have two input interfaces.* $\mathcal{O}_2$ *forwards any string* *given through the first interface to the first interface of* Sim *and returns its output. Given* (x, w) *as input to the second interface,* $\mathcal{O}_2$ *returns* $\perp$ *if* $(x, w) \notin R$*, else forwards* x *to the second interface of* Sim *and returns the output. The probability is taken over coins of* D, $\mathcal{R}$, Prove, *and* Sim.

Definition 9 (Soundness). *A non-interactive argument system* (Prove, Verify) *for* L_R *is* sound *if for any PPT oracle algorithm* $\mathcal{A}$*, any* $x \notin L_R$, $\Pr[\pi \leftarrow \mathcal{A}^{\mathcal{R}}(x) : 1 = \mathsf{Verify}^{\mathcal{R}}(x, \pi)]$ *is negligible in* λ*. The probability is taken over coins of* $\mathcal{A}$ *and* $\mathcal{R}$.

Simulation extractability is a stronger notion of simulation soundness. Intuitively, it guarantees that even after having seen simulated proofs on arbitrary instances, the adversary cannot create a valid proof on a fresh instance for which the knowledge extraction fails. This notion was defined in the common reference string model in [33] and in the random oracle model in [8].

Definition 10 (Simulation Extractability). *A non-interactive zero-knowledge argument system* (Prove, Verify) *for relation* R *with zero-knowledge simulator* Sim *is simulation extractable in the random oracle model if, for any PPT oracle algorithm* $\mathcal{A}$*, there exists an expected polynomial-time algorithm* $\mathcal{E}$ *for which the following experiment returns* 1.

$\mathsf{Expr}^{\mathsf{se}}_{\mathcal{A}}(\lambda)$:
1. *Run* $(x, \pi) \leftarrow \mathcal{A}^{\mathsf{Sim}}(1^\lambda)$.
2. *Output* 1 *if* $0 \leftarrow \mathsf{Verify}^{\mathsf{Sim}}(x, \pi)$ *or* x *has been queried to the second interface of* Sim.
3. *Run* $w \leftarrow \mathcal{E}^{\mathcal{A}}(x, \pi, \sigma)$.
4. *Output* $b := R(x, w)$.

Parameter σ *is the view of* Sim*. It is strongly simulation extractable if the freshness condition in Step 2 is on* (x, π) *as a pair instead of just on* x.

The above definitions are for the programmable random oracle model. To cast non-programmable random oracles in the definitions, allow every entity direct access to the oracle [48].

3 The Share-then-Hash Technique

3.1 Construction

Let n be a polynomial in λ. Let SS be a perfect secret sharing scheme over $\{0,1\}^\mu$ for an access structure over $[n]$ of size polynomial in n. Let Share be the sharing algorithm of SS, and $D(s)$ be distribution of outputs from Share(s). For qualified set A and secret $s \in \{0,1\}^\mu$, we denote by $D_A(s)$ the joint distribution of shares in A. We denote by A^c the set $[n] \backslash A$ and by D_{A^c} the distribution of shares for the non-qualified set A^c of A, which is independent of the secret (due to SS being a perfect secret sharing scheme). For a set of shares $S := (s_1, \ldots, s_n)$

and a set $A \subseteq [n]$, we denote by S_A the set of shares indexed by A, i.e., $S_A := \{s_i \in S \mid i \in A\}$. For the sake of readability, we assume that S_A identifies A from its data structure. A perfect secret sharing scheme over secret space $\{0,1\}^\mu$ for polynomial μ in λ is *semi-smooth* [21] if on top of standard polynomial-time and space requirements it satisfies the following properties:

- There exists a polynomial-time algorithm, CheckShares that, given a full set of shares and a secret, returns 1 if all qualified sets of shares recover the secret. It returns 0, otherwise.
- There exists a polynomial-time algorithm, Complete that, for any secret s, any non-qualified set A^c, and any set of shares $S_{A^c} \in D_{A^c}$, outputs a set of shares in $D(s)$ that includes S_{A^c} as shares for A^c.

Note that the presence of CheckShares does not imply that SS is a verifiable secret sharing scheme where, given a share s_i and public parameters, one can assure consistency of the share. Semi-smooth secret sharing schemes exist for threshold and general monotone access structures represented by monotone span programs [20].

Let Γ be a monotone access structure over $[n]$, and Γ^* be the *dual* of Γ defined as $A \in \Gamma^* \Leftrightarrow A^c \notin \Gamma$ [46]. (Note that the dual operation is an involution, i.e., $(\Gamma^*)^* = \Gamma$.) Let SS = (Share, CheckShares, Complete) be a semi-smooth perfect secret sharing scheme over $\{0,1\}^\mu$ for Γ^*. Let $\boldsymbol{x} := (x_1, \ldots, x_n)$ be a set of instances and $\boldsymbol{w} := (w_1, \ldots, w_n)$ be a witness set where for a qualified set $A \in \Gamma$, let relation $R_i(x_i, w_i) = 1$ hold for all $i \in A$. Let $\Sigma_i = (\mathcal{C}_i, \mathcal{Z}_i, \mathcal{V}_i)$ be a sigma-protocol for relation R_i. We assume all Σ-protocols have a common challenge space $\{0,1\}^\mu$ for certain polynomial μ in security parameter λ. Let $H_e : \{0,1\}^* \to \{0,1\}^\mu$ and $H_c : \{0,1\}^* \to \{0,1\}^\mu$ be hash functions.

Theorem 1. *Figure 1 describes a non-interactive argument system for $\Gamma_{\boldsymbol{R}}$:*

- *It is complete and witness indistinguishable.*
- *It is zero-knowledge if H_c or H_e are modeled as programmable random oracles.*
- *It is a sound membership proof for language $L_{\Gamma_{\boldsymbol{R}}}$ if H_c and H_e are modeled as non-programmable random oracles and all Σ_i are statistically sound.*
- *It is simulation extractable if H_c and H_e are random oracles and at least one is programmable and if and all Σ_i are κ-special sound.*
- *It is strongly simulation extractable if both H_c and H_e are programmable random oracles, and all Σ_i are κ-special sound and unique response.*

Completeness and witness indistinguishability can be shown as in the original CDS+FS scheme. Zero-knowledge in the programmable random oracle model is assured by inspecting the simulators from Fig. 2. The first simulator is for the case where H_c is programmable and the second one is for the case where H_e is programmable. In the following, we focus on soundness in different flavors and present a proof sketch for them, without stating concrete bounds, but our arguments are detailed enough to derive full proofs. We use the following proposition taken from [21].

$\mathsf{Prove}_\Gamma(\boldsymbol{x}, \boldsymbol{w})$:

1. Set $A := \{ i \mid R_i(x_i, w_i) = 1 \, \forall i \in [n] \}$ and $A^c := [n] \setminus A$.
2. Sample $s' \leftarrow \{0,1\}^\mu$, and set $(s'_1, \ldots, s'_n) \leftarrow \mathsf{Share}_{\Gamma^*}(s')$, $S_{A^c} := \{s'_i \mid i \in A^c\}$.
3. For all $i \in A^c$, set $e_i := H_e(\Gamma, \boldsymbol{x}, i, s'_i)$, and run $(z_i, a_i) \leftarrow \mathcal{S}_i(x_i, e_i)$.
4. For all $i \in A$, set $a_i \leftarrow \mathcal{C}_i(x_i, w_i; r_i)$.
5. Set $s := H_c(\Gamma, \boldsymbol{x}, a_1, \ldots, a_n)$, and $(s_1, \ldots, s_n) \leftarrow \mathsf{Complete}_{\Gamma^*}(s, S_{A^c})$.
6. For all $i \in A$, set $e_i := H_e(\Gamma, \boldsymbol{x}, i, s_i)$, and run $z_i \leftarrow \mathcal{Z}_i(x_i, w_i, r_i, e_i)$.
7. Return $\pi := \{(a_i, z_i), s_i\}_{i \in [n]}$.

$\mathsf{Verify}_\Gamma(\boldsymbol{x}, \pi)$:

1. Parse π as $\{(a_i, z_i), s_i\}_{i \in [n]}$.
2. Set $s := H_c(\Gamma, \boldsymbol{x}, a_1, \ldots, a_n)$ and $e_i := H_e(\Gamma, \boldsymbol{x}, i, s_i) \, \forall i \in [n]$.
3. Return $\bigwedge_{i \in [n]} \mathcal{V}_i(x_i, a_i, e_i, z_i) \wedge \mathsf{CheckShares}_{\Gamma^*}(s, s_1, \ldots, s_n)$.

Fig. 1. Share-then-Hash CDS+FS for relation Γ_R.

Proposition 1. *Let Γ be monotone. A set is qualified in Γ if and only if it has a non-empty intersection with every qualified set in Γ^*.*

Proof (Of soundness as a membership proof system). Suppose that an adversary $\mathcal{A}$ outputs a valid proof $\hat{\pi} = \{(\hat{a}_i, \hat{z}_i), \hat{s}_i\}_{i \in [n]}$ on instance $\hat{\boldsymbol{x}} = (\hat{x}_1, \ldots, \hat{x}_n)$ and access structure Γ after making at most q queries to the random oracles. For the forged proof to be considered a valid forgery (in the soundness game), $\hat{\boldsymbol{x}}$ must be a false instance (with respect to Γ), i.e., for every qualified set $A \in \Gamma$, there must exist some $i \in A$ such that $x_i \notin L_{R_i}$. Furthermore, $\mathsf{CheckShares}_{\Gamma^*}(\hat{s}, \hat{s}_1, \ldots, \hat{s}_n)$ must be 1, for $\hat{s} := H_c(\Gamma, \hat{\boldsymbol{x}}, \hat{a}_1, \ldots, \hat{a}_n)$; and $\mathcal{V}_i(\hat{x}_i, \hat{a}_i, \hat{e}_i, \hat{z}_i)$ must be accepting for $\hat{e}_i := H_e(\Gamma, \hat{\boldsymbol{x}}, i, \hat{s}_i)$ and all $i \in [n]$.

If for some $i^* \in [n]$ such that $x_{i^*} \notin L_{R_{i^*}}$ the adversary did not make query $H_e(\Gamma, \hat{\boldsymbol{x}}, i^*, \hat{s}_i)$, since value $\hat{e}_{i^*}$ is assigned uniformly at random by H_e, the probability that $1 = \mathcal{V}_{i^*}(x_{i^*}, a_{i^*}, e_{i^*}, z_{i^*})$ for already fixed x_{i^*}, a_{i^*}, and z_{i^*} is at most $\epsilon_{\mathsf{st}} := \max_{i \in [n]}(\epsilon_{\mathsf{st}_i})$ where ϵ_{st_i} is the statistical soundness error of Σ_i. Similarly, if $H_c(\hat{\boldsymbol{x}}, \hat{a}_1, \ldots, \hat{a}_n)$ was not queried by the adversary, after the random assignemt of $\hat{s}$, by H_c, the probability that $\mathsf{CheckShares}_{\Gamma^*}(\hat{s}, \hat{s}_1, \ldots, \hat{s}_n)$ is successful is at most $2^{-\mu}$ ($\hat{s}$ must be equal to the value determined by $\hat{s}_1, \ldots, \hat{s}_n$).

Now, let Ω be the set of indices $i \in [n]$ where $x_i \notin L_{R_i}$ holds and $\hat{e}_i := H_e(\Gamma, \hat{\boldsymbol{x}}, i, \hat{s}_i)$ appears before $\hat{s} := H_c(\Gamma, \hat{\boldsymbol{x}}, \hat{a}_1, \ldots, \hat{a}_n)$ in the view of $\mathcal{A}$. First, assume that for all qualified sets $A \in \Gamma$, $A \cap \Omega$ is not empty. In virtue of Proposition 1, Ω must be a qualified set in Γ^* and thus, $\{\hat{s}_i\}_{i \in \Omega}$ uniquely determines a secret, s^*. Therefore, $\mathsf{CheckShares}_{\Gamma^*}(\hat{s}, \hat{s}_1, \ldots, \hat{s}_n) = 1$ will be satisfied only if $\hat{s}$ equals s^*, which happens with probability at most $2^{-\mu}$ since $\hat{s}$ is randomly assigned by H_c independently of $\{\hat{s}_i\}_{i \in \Omega}$.

$\mathsf{Sim1}_\Gamma(\boldsymbol{x})$:

1. Sample $s \leftarrow \{0,1\}^\mu$, and set $(s_1, \ldots, s_n) \leftarrow \mathsf{Share}_{\Gamma^*}(s)$.
2. For all $i \in [n]$, set $e_i := H_e(\Gamma, \boldsymbol{x}, i, s_i)$, and $(z_i, a_i) \leftarrow \mathcal{S}_i(x_i, e_i)$.
3. Program H_c to output s on input $(\Gamma, \boldsymbol{x}, a_1, \ldots, a_n)$.
4. Return $\pi := \{(a_i, z_i), s_i\}_{i\in[n]}$.

$\mathsf{Sim2}_\Gamma(\boldsymbol{x})$:

1. For all $i \in [n]$, set $e_i \leftarrow \{0,1\}^\mu$, and $(z_i, a_i) \leftarrow \mathcal{S}_i(x_i, e_i)$.
2. Set $s := H_c(\Gamma, \boldsymbol{x}, a_1, \ldots, a_n)$, and $(s_1, \ldots, s_n) \leftarrow \mathsf{Share}_{\Gamma^*}(s)$.
3. For all $i \in [n]$, program H_e to output e_i on input $(\Gamma, \boldsymbol{x}, i, s_i)$.
4. Return $\pi := \{(a_i, z_i), s_i\}_{i\in[n]}$.

Fig. 2. Zero-knowledge simulators.

Finally, suppose that there exists $A \in \Gamma$ with $A \cap \Omega = \emptyset$. In this case, there must exist $i^* \in A$ with $x_{i^*} \notin L_{R_{i^*}}$ (remember that $\hat{\boldsymbol{x}}$ is a false instance) and such that query $\hat{e}_{i^*} := H_e(\Gamma, \hat{\boldsymbol{x}}, i^*, \hat{s}_{i^*})$ appears after query $\hat{s} := H_c(\Gamma, \hat{\boldsymbol{x}}, \hat{a}_1, \ldots, \hat{a}_n)$ in the view of $\mathcal{A}$. Then, the probability that there exists a $\hat{z}_{i^*}$ that can satisfy $\mathcal{V}_{i^*}(\hat{x}_{i^*}, \hat{a}_{i^*}, \hat{e}_{i^*}, \hat{z}_{i^*}) = 1$ for fixed $(\hat{x}_{i^*}, \hat{a}_{i^*})$ is upper-bound by the statistical soundness error of Σ_{i^*}, which is upper-bounded by ϵ_{st}.

Accordingly, a valid proof on a false statement can be produced with probability at most $2\epsilon_{\mathsf{st}} + 2^{-\mu}$. □

Proof (Of simulation extractability). We first prove the case where H_c is programmable and H_e is non-programmable. Suppose that adversary $\mathcal{A}$ playing in the simulation extractability game, running in time t and performing at most q queries to the random oracle, outputs an instance $\hat{\boldsymbol{x}} = (\hat{x}_1, \ldots, \hat{x}_n)$ and a valid proof $\hat{\pi} = \{(\hat{a}_i, \hat{z}_i), \hat{s}_i\}_{i\in[n]}$ on $\hat{\boldsymbol{x}}$ with probability δ. For the output to be valid, it must hold that $\mathsf{CheckShares}_{\Gamma^*}(\hat{s}, \hat{s}_1, \ldots, \hat{s}_n) = 1$ for $\hat{s} := H_c(\Gamma, \hat{\boldsymbol{x}}, \hat{a}_1, \ldots, \hat{a}_n)$ and, additionally, for all $i \in [n]$, $\mathcal{V}_i(\hat{x}_i, \hat{a}_i, \hat{e}_i, \hat{z}_i) = 1$, where $\hat{e}_i := H_e(\Gamma, \hat{\boldsymbol{x}}, i, \hat{s}_i)$. Furthermore, $\hat{\boldsymbol{x}}$ must be different from any instance $\boldsymbol{x}$ observed by the simulation oracle.

The extractor runs the code of $\mathcal{A}$, simulating the proving oracle using $\mathsf{Sim1}$ in Fig. 2 until a valid proof $\hat{\pi} = \{(\hat{a}_i, \hat{z}_i), \hat{s}_i\}_{i\in[n]}$ on an instance $\boldsymbol{x}$ is produced. The extractor then identifies the query $H_c(\Gamma, \hat{\boldsymbol{x}}, \hat{a}_1, \ldots, \hat{a}_n)$ in the adversaries execution and forks the execution at this point by providing a different uniformly chosen value as an answer to this query. By repeating the above forking $2\tau/\delta$ times for $\tau := \kappa n$, the extractor obtains τ valid proofs with a constant probability. We now argue that, if τ random secrets $\hat{s}^{(i)}$ for $i = 1, \ldots, \tau$ are shared to n players in a way that they pass $\mathsf{CheckShares}$ consistency check, then, for every qualified set of players, there is a player who receives at least κ distinct shares. The following lemma states it formally.

Lemma 1. *For sufficiently large polynomial μ in λ, for any semi-smooth secret sharing scheme over $\{0,1\}^\mu$, for any small constant κ, for any constant $\tau \geq \kappa n - 2n + 2$, for any stateless unbound algorithm $\mathcal{B}$, the following experiment returns* 1 *with negligible probability in λ.*

1. For $i = 1$ to τ, do $s^{(i)} \leftarrow \{0,1\}^\mu$, and $(s_1^{(i)}, \ldots, s_n^{(i)}) \leftarrow \mathcal{B}(s^{(i)})$.
2. Return 1 if $1 = \mathsf{CheckShares}_{\Gamma^*}(s^{(i)}, s_1^{(i)}, \ldots, s_n^{(i)})$ for all $i = 1, \ldots, \tau$ and there exists a qualified set, A, such that, for each $j \in A$, number of distinct shares among $s_j^{(1)}, \ldots, s_j^{(\tau)}$ is less than κ. Return 0, otherwise.

We first prove the following claim.

Claim 1. Let A be a qualified set and assume $\tau \geq \kappa|A| - 2|A| + 2$. The probability that for all $j \in A$, the set $S_j^{(\tau)} = \{s_j^{(1)}, \ldots, s_j^{(\tau)}\}$ has size less than κ is at most $(\tau - 1)(\kappa - 1)^{|A|}2^{-\mu}$.

Proof (Of Lemma 1). Set $\tau = \kappa n - 2n + 2$. By Claim 1 and a union bound, the probability that there exists a qualified set A such that $|S_j^{(\tau)}| < \kappa$ for all $j \in A$ is at most $2^n \cdot (\tau - 1)(\kappa - 1)^n 2^{-\mu}$. If this is not the case, then the set A of all j such that $|S_j^{(\tau)}| < \kappa$ is not qualified. □

Proof (Of Claim 1). We will show that as long as all sets $S_j^{(i)}$, $j \in A$ have size less than κ, the probability that $\sum_{j \in A} |S_j^{(i+1)}| = \sum_{j \in A} |S_j^{(i)}|$ is at most $(\kappa - 1)^{|A|}2^{-\mu}$. Initially, $\sum_{j \in A} |S_j^{(1)}| = |A|$. By a union bound over $1 \leq i < \tau$, $\sum_{j \in A} |S_j^{(\tau)}| \geq |A| + \tau - 1$ with probability at least $1 - (\tau - 1)(\kappa - 1)^{|A|}2^{-\mu}$. By our choice of τ, this condition implies $|S_j^{(\tau)}| \geq \kappa$ for some $j \in A$. By the reconstruction property, there is an *injective* function R_A that maps valid sequences $(s_j : j \in A)$ of shares to secrets $s \in \{0,1\}^\mu$. Assuming $|S_j^{(i)}| < \kappa$ for all $j \in A$, the image of R_A evaluated on the product set $\prod_{j \in A} S_j^{(i)}$ can have size at most $(\kappa - 1)^{|A|}$. So if $s^{(i+1)}$ is chosen at random from $\{0,1\}^\mu$, then the probability it belongs to the image of $R_A(\prod_{j \in A} S_j^{(i)})$ is at most $(\kappa - 1)^{|A|}2^{-\mu}$. By the injectivity of R_A, for any sequence $(s_j^{(i+1)} : j \in A)$ that reconstructs to $s^{(i+1)}$, $s_j^{(i+1)}$ must reside outside $S_j^{(i)}$ for at least one party $j \in A$, so the sum $\sum_{j \in A} |S_j^{(i)}|$ grows as desired. □

According to Lemma 1, with non-negligible probability, it holds that, for every qualified set $A \in \Gamma^*$, there exists $i \in A$ that yields $(\hat{a}_i, (\hat{s}_i^{(1)}, \hat{z}_i^{(1)}), \ldots, (\hat{s}_i^{(\kappa)}, \hat{z}_i^{(\kappa)}))$ that satisfies $1 = \mathcal{V}_i(\hat{x}_i, \hat{a}_i, \hat{e}_i^{(j)}, \hat{z}_i^{(j)})$ for $\hat{e}_i^{(j)} := H_e(\Gamma, \hat{\mathbf{x}}, i, \hat{s}_i^{(j)})$. Since all $\hat{e}_i^{(j)}$ are distinct except for negligible probability due to the uniform output from H_e, we have κ-colliding transcript $(\hat{a}_i, (\hat{e}_i^{(1)}, \hat{z}_i^{(1)}), \ldots, (\hat{e}_i^{(\kappa)}, \hat{z}_i^{(\kappa)}))$ over uniformly chosen challenges, which allows to extract $\hat{w}_i$ with overwhelming probability. What remains is the same as the knowledge soundness proof of the original CDS scheme; according to Proposition 1, there exists a qualified set A in Γ for which $\hat{w}_i$ for all $i \in A$ are extracted.

We next sketch a proof for the case where H_c is non-programmable and H_e is programmable. This time we do not require Lemma 1. The extractor first runs the adversary until it obtains a valid forgery. Proof queries from the adversary is answered by executing Sim2 in Fig. 2, which programs at most n random points on H_e in each invocation. Then the extractor rewinds the adversary to the point where it first receives $\hat{s}$ for query $H_c(\Gamma, \hat{\boldsymbol{x}}, \hat{a}_1, \ldots, \hat{a}_n)$. The extractor then continues the simulation as well as the first run except that it answers every fresh query to H_e with an independently chosen random value. These queries to H_e made after receiving $\hat{s}$ from H_c are for a qualified set, $A \in \Gamma$, as we observed in the proof of soundness since otherwise $\mathsf{CheckShares}_{\Gamma^*}(\hat{s}, \hat{s}_1, \ldots, \hat{s}_n)$ in the verification returns 1 with probability at most $2^{-\mu}$. By repeating the above rewinding $2\kappa/\delta$ times, the extractor obtains κ valid forged proofs on $(\boldsymbol{x}, \hat{a}_1, \ldots, \hat{a}_n)$ with a constant probability. The forged proofs constitute κ colliding transcripts for each $x_{i \in A}$ unless random assignments to H_e collide by chance. Thus, by running the κ-special soundness extractor with the colliding transcripts as an input, a valid witness is obtained except for a negligible probability. We finally note that H_c must still be modeled as (non-programmable) random oracle to assure that $\hat{a}_i$ is fixed before $\hat{s}_i$ is queried to H_c. □

Proof (Of strong simulation extractability). This time, we relax the condition on $(\hat{\boldsymbol{x}}, \hat{\pi})$ so that it must be different from any pair $(\boldsymbol{x}, \pi)$ observed by the simulation oracle. As we have already proved the case of $\hat{\boldsymbol{x}} \neq \boldsymbol{x}$ in the above, we consider $\hat{\boldsymbol{x}} = \boldsymbol{x}$ and $\hat{\pi} \neq \pi$ happens for some $(\boldsymbol{x}, \pi)$ observed by the simulation oracle. Let $\pi = \{(a_i, z_i), s_i\}_{i \in [n]}$. If $(\hat{a}_1, \ldots, \hat{a}_n) \neq (a_1, \ldots, a_n)$, then we fork at query $H_c(\Gamma, \hat{\boldsymbol{x}}, \hat{a}_1, \ldots, \hat{a}_n)$ and do the same as done in the proof of simulation extractability. Otherwise, if $(\hat{a}_1, \ldots, \hat{a}_n) = (a_1, \ldots, a_n)$ and $(\hat{s}_1, \ldots, \hat{s}_n) \neq (s_1, \ldots, s_n)$, we again fork at query $H_c(\Gamma, \hat{\boldsymbol{x}}, \hat{a}_1, \ldots, \hat{a}_n)$. Observe that the query is made by zero-knowledge simulator. So we cannot answer to the newly assigned value with the same $\hat{a}_i$. We instead simulate by using the same (a_i, e_i, z_i) for every $i \in [n]$. It can be done by programming H_e with the same output $\hat{e}_i$ on a new input s_i in each fork. More precisely, for every new assignment of $s^{(j)}$ to $H_c(\Gamma, \hat{\boldsymbol{x}}, \hat{a}_1, \ldots, \hat{a}_n)$ in the j-th fork, compute $(s_1^{(j)}, \ldots, s_n^{(j)}) \leftarrow \mathsf{Share}_{\Gamma^*}(s^{(j)})$. Then define $H_e(\Gamma, \boldsymbol{x}, i, s_i^{(j)})$ by e_i used in the original run and answer with the same z_i. Accordingly, though shares s_i appear in the respective challenge round differ in every fork, simulated transcript (a_i, e_i, z_i) remains the same. Now, τ successful forks leads to extracting witness in a qualified set in Γ as before. Due to the quasi-unique response property, we are already done since $(\hat{x}_i, \hat{a}_i, \hat{s}_i) = (x_i^{(k)}, a_i^{(k)}, s_i^{(k)})$ cannot accommodate with restriction $(\hat{x}_i, \hat{a}_i, \hat{s}_i, \hat{z}_i) \neq (x_i^{(k)}, a_i^{(k)}, s_i^{(k)}, z_i^{(k)})$ except for negligible probability. □

3.2 Comparison with CDS

In order to illustrate the efficiency gain and the recycling technique of our new construction, consider the following general DNF formula on n-variables:

$$f(x_1, \ldots, x_n) = (x_{j_{\{1,1\}}} \wedge \ldots \wedge x_{j_{\{1,m_1\}}}) \vee \ldots \vee (x_{j_{\{\ell,1\}}} \wedge \ldots \wedge x_{j_{\{\ell,m_\ell\}}}) \ , \quad (1)$$

and let $N := \sum_{i=1}^{\ell} m_i$ be the total number of literals in f. Let Γ be the access structure over $[n]$ induced by f, and consider the following well-known and widely used perfect secret sharing of $s \in \mathbb{Z}_p$ (for some μ-bits prime p) under policy Γ^*:

$\mathsf{Share}_{\Gamma^*}(s)$:

sample $d_1, \ldots, d_\ell \leftarrow \mathbb{Z}_p$ uniformly restricted to $d_1 + \ldots + d_\ell = s$;
set $s_i := \{d_k \mid i \in \{j_{\{k,1\}}, \ldots, j_{\{k,m_k\}}\} \, \forall k \in [\ell]\} \;\; \forall i \in [n]$;
return $(s_1, \ldots, s_n)$.

Table 1. Comparison between previous work ([20,21]) and the Share-then-Hash CDS (this work). Values N, n and ℓ represent the number of literals, number of variables and number of clauses in the DNF formula (1) respectively. Value α (respectively ζ) represents the size in bits of the *first message* (respectively *last message*) of sigma protocols Σ_i. (Challenges are assumed to belong in $\{0,1\}^\mu$).

	Proof system	
Property	CDS+FS	Share-then-Hash CDS+FS
Proof size	$N(\alpha + \zeta) + \mu\ell$	$n(\alpha + \zeta) + \mu\ell$
Optimized proof size[†]	$N\zeta + \mu\ell$	$n\zeta + \mu\ell$
Support for ($\kappa > 2$)-special soundness	✗	✓
Unforgeability in NPROM[‡]	✗	✓

[†] When every a is uniquely identified and efficiently recoverable given (e, z).
[‡] When considered as a signature scheme. See Section 4.

The CDS+FS technique would yield a proof for Γ_R consisting of N transcripts where for all $k \in [\ell]$ and $k' \in [m_k]$, transcript $(a_{\{k,k'\}}, e_k, z_{\{k,k'\}})$ is accepting with respect to the $j_{\{k,k'\}}$-th Σ-protocol. Also, for $s := H(\Gamma, \boldsymbol{x}, a_{\{1,1\}}, \ldots, a_{\{\ell,m_\ell\}})$, it must hold $e_1 + \cdots + e_\ell = s$. This results in a total proof size in bits of:

$$\mu\ell + \textstyle\sum_{k\in[\ell]} \left(\sum_{k'\in[m_k]} |a_{\{k,k'\}}| + |z_{\{k,k'\}}|\right).$$

Instead, with our scheme from Fig. 1, the resulting proof consists of n transcripts $\{(a_i, z_i)\}_{i\in[n]}$ together with a set of shares $\{s_i\}_{i\in[n]}$ produced by the above Share algorithm. Transcript (a_i, e_i, z_i) is accepting with respect the i-th Σ-protocol, where $e_i := H(\Gamma, \boldsymbol{x}, i, s_i)$ for every $i \in [n]$ and for $s := H(\Gamma, \boldsymbol{x}, a_1, \ldots, a_n)$, $\mathsf{CheckShares}(s, s_1, \ldots, s_n) = 1$. In this case, the total proof size in bits results in[1]:

$$|(s_1, \ldots, s_n)| + \textstyle\sum_{i\in[n]} |a_i| + |z_i| \;\; = \mu\ell + \sum_{i\in[n]} |a_i| + |z_i|$$

We refer to Table 1 for a more detailed comparison between the two proof systems. For simplicity, we assume that all Σ-protocols require first messages

[1] Although the total length of secrets $(s_1, \ldots, s_n)$ is μN, as above it is enough to store the ℓ disjunction values $(d_1, \ldots, d_\ell)$ sampled by Share.

of similar length say $|a| = \alpha$, and also last messages of similar length $|z| = \zeta$. Some Σ-protocols are such that, given (e, z), there exists a unique value of a that makes the transcript accepting and that can be efficiently computed. In those cases, it is possible to optimize the proof size by not including the a value of any transcript. During verification, the omitted values are computed from the corresponding (e, z). Notice that this optimization can be applied to both schemes and it does not compromise soundness, since the prover has committed to the final share s (dependent of the a values) through the random oracle H. Further optimizations may be possible, e.g. reducing the number of shares that appear in the proof, depending on the access structure.

Observe that the size of proofs produced with the share-then-hash technique can be dramatically smaller than the size of proofs with standard CDS+FS since, in general, N can be much larger than n. This improvement comes from the fact that share-then-hash proofs include exactly 1 transcript per atomic statement, which is a notable improvement since many practical scenarios involve complex and heavy sigma protocols. Having to produce (and then verify) independent transcripts for the same statement would be undesirable. Finally, notice that this optimization also brings computational savings since fewer transcripts need to be produced.

4 Application

This section presents a general ring signature scheme that supports monotone structures and is unforgeable against chosen message and chosen ring attacks in the NPROM. Note that when $n = 1$ the syntax and unforgeability of ring signature schemes reduce to those for ordinary signature schemes.

Definition 11 (General Ring Signature Scheme). *A ring signature scheme* RS *is triple of polynomial-time algorithm, described by* $(\mathsf{KeyGen}, \mathsf{Sign}, \mathsf{Verify})$ *such that*

- $\mathsf{KeyGen}(1^\lambda)$: *It takes an input the security parameter* 1^λ *and outputs a pair* (vk, sk) *of verification and signing key. This execution is proceeded individually by each player.*
- $\mathsf{Sign}(\boldsymbol{vk}, \boldsymbol{sk}, msg, \Gamma)$: *It takes a set of verification keys* $\boldsymbol{vk} := (vk_1, \ldots, vk_n)$, *a monotone access structure* Γ *over* $[n]$, *a set of secret keys* $\boldsymbol{sk}$, *and a message* $msg \in \{0,1\}^*$ *and outputs a signature* σ.
- $\mathsf{Verify}(\boldsymbol{vk}, msg, \sigma, \Gamma)$: *It takes* $\boldsymbol{vk}, msg, \sigma$, *and* Γ, *and outputs either* 1 *for acceptance, or* 0 *for rejection.*

It is correct, if, for every $\lambda \in \mathbb{N}$, $n \geq 1$, *any monotone access structure* Γ *over* $[n]$, *any* $\boldsymbol{vk} := (vk_1, \ldots, vk_n)$ *and* $\boldsymbol{sk} := (sk_1, \ldots, sk_n)$ *that there exists* $A \in \Gamma$ *such that* $(vk_i, sk_i) \in \mathsf{KeyGen}(1^\lambda)$ *holds for all* $i \in A$, *for all* $msg \in \{0,1\}^*$, $\mathsf{RS.Verify}(\boldsymbol{vk}, msg, \mathsf{Sign}(\boldsymbol{vk}, \boldsymbol{sk}, msg, \Gamma), \Gamma) = 1$ *holds except for negligible probability.*

Definition 12 (Signer Anonymity). *A ring signature scheme is anonymous if, for any* $\lambda \in \mathbb{N}$, *any* $n \geq 1$, *any monotone structure* Γ *over* $[n]$, *any* $\boldsymbol{vk} = (vk_1, \cdots, vk_n)$, *and any* $\boldsymbol{sk}^{(b)} := (sk_1^{(b)}, \ldots, sk_n^{(b)})$ *for* $b = 0, 1$ *that there exists* $A \in \Gamma$ *such that* $(vk_i, sk_i^{(b)}) \in \mathsf{KeyGen}(1^\lambda)$ *holds for all* $i \in A$, *and for any* $msg \in \{0,1\}^*$, *two distributions* $(\boldsymbol{vk}, msg, \mathsf{Sign}(\boldsymbol{vk}, \boldsymbol{sk}^{(0)}, msg, \Gamma), \Gamma)$ *and* $(\boldsymbol{vk}, msg, \mathsf{Sign}(\boldsymbol{vk}, \boldsymbol{sk}^{(1)}, msg, \Gamma), \Gamma)$ *are statistically indistinguishable.*

Definition 13 (Unforgeability). *A ring signature scheme is unforgeable against adaptive chosen message and chosen ring attacks if for any sufficiently large* λ, *any* $n \geq 1$, *any polynomial-time adversary* $\mathcal{A}$, *the following experiment returns* 1 *only with negligible probability in* λ.

$\mathsf{Expr}^{\mathsf{euf}}_{\mathsf{RS},\mathcal{A}}(\lambda)$:

1. *Run* $(vk_i, sk_i) \leftarrow \mathsf{RS.KeyGen}(1^\lambda)$ *for* $i \in [n]$. *Initialize* U *with* $\emptyset$.
2. *Run* $(\hat{\boldsymbol{vk}}, \hat{msg}, \hat{\pi}, \hat{\Gamma}) \leftarrow \mathcal{A}^{\mathcal{S},\mathcal{C}}(\boldsymbol{vk})$ *where* $\mathcal{S}$ *and* $\mathcal{C}$ *are oracles that:*
   - $\mathcal{S}$: *Given* $(\boldsymbol{vk}', msg, \Gamma, A)$ *as input, if* $\boldsymbol{vk}' \subseteq \boldsymbol{vk}$, Γ *is a monotone structure over* $[n'] := [|\boldsymbol{vk}'|]$, *and* $A \in \Gamma$, *it returns* $\sigma \leftarrow \mathsf{RS.Sign}(\boldsymbol{vk}', \boldsymbol{sk}', msg, \Gamma)$ *where* $\boldsymbol{sk}' = (sk_1, \ldots, sk_{n'})$ *that* $(vk_i, sk_i) \in \mathsf{RS.KeyGen}(1^\lambda)$ *for all* $i \in A$ *and* $sk_i = \perp$ *for all* $i \in [n'] \setminus A$. *It returns* $\perp$, *otherwise.*
   - $\mathcal{C}$: *Given* $i \in [n]$, *it adds* vk_i *to* U, *and returns* sk_i.
3. *Output* 1 *if all the following conditions are met.*
   - $1 = \mathsf{RS.Verify}(\hat{\boldsymbol{vk}}, \hat{msg}, \hat{\pi}, \hat{\Gamma})$
   - $\hat{\boldsymbol{vk}} \subseteq \boldsymbol{vk}$
   - $\forall A \in \hat{\Gamma}, \{\hat{vk}_i \in \hat{\boldsymbol{vk}} \mid i \in A\} \not\subseteq U$
   - $(\hat{\boldsymbol{vk}}, \hat{msg}, \hat{\Gamma})$ *has never been submitted to* $\mathcal{S}$

   Otherwise output 0.

For binary relation R, let $R_\vee$ be disjunctive relation $R_\vee((x_1, x_2), (w_1, w_2)) := R(x_1, w_1) \vee R(x_2, w_2)$. Let $\mathsf{DecompOR}$ be an algorithm that, given a monotone access structure Γ over $[n]$ as input, outputs a monotone access structure Λ over $[2n]$ that $\Gamma_{\boldsymbol{R}_\vee} = \Lambda_{\boldsymbol{R}}$ holds for $\boldsymbol{R}_\vee := (R_\vee^{(1)}, \ldots, R_\vee^{(n)})$ and $\boldsymbol{R} := (R^{(1)}, \ldots, R^{(2n)})$. Let $\Sigma = (\mathcal{C}, \mathcal{Z}, \mathcal{V})$ be a Σ-protocol for R. Let $(\mathsf{Prove}, \mathsf{Verify})$ be a scheme in Fig. 1 using Σ. We present our construction of ring signature scheme for monotone access structure in Fig. 3.

Theorem 2. *The scheme in Fig. 3 is a ring signature scheme for monotone access structure. It is signer anonymous if* Σ *is witness indistinguishable. It is unforgeable against chosen message and ring attacks if* L_R *is a hard language,* Σ *is witness indistinguishable and statistically sound, and hash functions* H_c *and* H_e *are non-programmable random oracles for output space* 2^μ *for sufficiently large* μ.

RS.KeyGen(1^λ):

1. Sample $(x_1, w_1) \leftarrow R_\lambda$ and $(x_2, w_2) \leftarrow R_\lambda$ independently.
2. Output $vk := (x_1, x_2)$ and $sk := (w_1, w_2)$.

RS.Sign($\boldsymbol{vk}, \boldsymbol{sk}, msg, \Gamma$):

1. Parse $\boldsymbol{vk} = (vk^{(1)}, \ldots, vk^{(n)})$ as $\boldsymbol{x} = (x_1, \ldots, x_{2n})$, and $\boldsymbol{sk} = (sk^{(1)}, \ldots, sk^{(n)})$ as $\boldsymbol{w} = (w_1, \ldots, w_{2n})$. (Some $sk^{(i)}$ can be $\perp$. Then $w_{2j} = w_{2j+1} = \perp$.)
2. Run $\Lambda \leftarrow$ DecompOR(Γ).
3. Run $\pi \leftarrow \mathsf{Prove}_\Lambda(\boldsymbol{x}, \boldsymbol{w})$ including msg in all hashings as input.
4. Output π as a signature.

RS.Verify($\boldsymbol{vk}, msg, \pi, \Gamma$):

1. Parse $\boldsymbol{vk} = (vk^{(1)}, \ldots, vk^{(n)})$ as $\boldsymbol{x} = (x_1, \ldots, x_{2n})$.
2. Run $\Lambda \leftarrow$ DecompOR(Γ).
3. Run $b \leftarrow \mathsf{Verify}_\Lambda(\boldsymbol{x}, \pi)$ including msg in all hashings as input.
4. Output b

Fig. 3. Proposed ring signature scheme for access structure Γ.

Proof. Correctness and signer anonymity is almost directly from the completeness and witness indistinguishability of the underlying Σ respectively. Thus we focus on proving unforgeability. Outline of our proof follows that of [28].

Game 1: This is the same as the experiment for the chosen message and chosen ring attack. Let G_i be the event that the experiment in Game i outputs 1. We have $\Pr[G_1] = \Pr[\mathsf{Expr}^{\mathsf{euf}}_{\mathsf{RS},\mathcal{A}}(\lambda) = 1]$ by definition.

Let $C \subseteq [n]$ be the index of the corrupted verification keys in the game. Let $\hat{\boldsymbol{vk}}$, $\hat{msg}$, $\hat{\pi}$, and $\hat{\Gamma}$ be the final output from the adversary. Without loss of generality, we assume that $\hat{\boldsymbol{vk}} = \boldsymbol{vk}$ and $\hat{\Gamma}$ is over $[n]$. (The adversary can choose $\hat{\Gamma}$ over a subset of $[n]$. We can turn such an adversary to one that outputs $\hat{\Gamma}$ as we want.) Let $\hat{\pi}$ be parsed to $\hat{\pi} = \{(\hat{a}_i, \hat{z}_i), \hat{s}_i\}_{i \in [2n]}$. As a valid forgery, it satisfies $C \notin \hat{\Gamma}$. Furthermore, every $(\hat{a}_i, \hat{z}_i), \hat{s}_i$ verifies as $1 = \mathsf{CheckShares}_{\hat{\Lambda}^*}(\hat{s}, \hat{s}_1, \ldots, \hat{s}_{2n})$ for $\hat{s} := H_c(\hat{\Lambda}, \boldsymbol{x}, msg, \hat{a}_1, \ldots, \hat{a}_{2n})$, and $1 = \mathcal{V}_i(\hat{x}_i, \hat{a}_i, \hat{e}_i, \hat{z}_i)$ for $\hat{e}_i := H_e(\hat{\Lambda}, \boldsymbol{x}, msg, i, \hat{s}_i)$ for $i \in [2n]$.

Game 2: We clean up the game by halting at win-by-chance events. As we argued in the proof of soundness, the adversary must make relevant hash queries to the corresponding oracles by itself. As also shown in the same place, there must exist a qualified set A^* in $\hat{\Lambda}$ that, for all $i \in A^*$, $\hat{e}_i := H_e(\hat{\Lambda}, \boldsymbol{x}, msg, i, \hat{s}_i)$ appears after $\hat{s} := H_c(\hat{\Lambda}, \boldsymbol{x}, msg, \hat{a}_1, \ldots, \hat{a}_{2n})$ in the view of the adversary. If any of these are not the case at the end, we let the experiment output 0.

Since these events happen only by chance over the choices of H_c and H_e for large enough domain $\{0,1\}^\mu$, we have $|\Pr[G_2] - \Pr[G_1]| < O(q/2^\mu)$ for at most q times of queries to the random oracles throughout the game.

Game 3: Uniformly choose $i^* \leftarrow [2n]$ and select x_{i^*} as a no-instance, i.e., $x_{i^*} \leftarrow \tilde{L}(\lambda)$ where $\tilde{L}$ is a language that is indistinguishable from L_R and has no intersection with it.

Let $i^{*\mathsf{c}}$ denote $\lfloor i^*/2 \rfloor$, which is the index of the verification key containing x_{i^*}. For now, suppose that $i^{*\mathsf{c}} \notin C$ happens. Answering to the signing queries from the adversary can be done by using the remaining witnesses since they are in a qualified set of Λ. It is perfect due to the WI property of the underlying proofs. If the output distribution of the experiment changes noticeably from that in the previous game, we can construct a successful distinguisher for L_R and $\tilde{L}$. Let ϵ_{hd} denote the bound for indistinguishability of L_R. We have $|\Pr[G_3 \,|\, i^{*\mathsf{c}} \notin C] - \Pr[G_2]| \leq \epsilon_{\mathsf{hd}}$.

We now evaluate $\Pr[G_3 \,|\, i^{*\mathsf{c}} \notin C]$. Since $C \notin \hat{\Gamma}$, there exists $i^\dagger \in A^*$ that $i^{\dagger\mathsf{c}} \notin C$. We have $i^\dagger = i^*$ with probability $1/2n$ for uniform i^*. (Note that, for this case, $i^{*\mathsf{c}} \notin C$ holds as well.) For $x_{i^*} \notin L_R$ and fixed $\hat{a}_{i^*}$, probability that challenge $\hat{e}_{i^*}$ uniformly chosen by $H_e(\hat{\Lambda}, \boldsymbol{x}, msg, i^*, \hat{s}_{i^*})$ can have $\hat{z}_{i^*}$ that satisfies $1 = \mathcal{V}(x_{i^*}, \hat{a}_{i^*}, \hat{e}_{i^*}, \hat{z}_{i^*})$ is bound by the statistical soundness error, denoted by ϵ_{st}, of Σ. We thus have $\Pr[G_3 \,|\, i^{*\mathsf{c}} \notin C \wedge i^\dagger = i^*] = \frac{1}{2n} \cdot \Pr[G_3 \,|\, i^{*\mathsf{c}} \notin C] < \epsilon_{\mathsf{st}}$.

By accumulating the all above bounds, we have $\Pr[\mathsf{Expr}^{\mathsf{euf}}_{\mathsf{RS},\mathcal{A}}(\lambda) = 1] < O(q/2^{\mu}) + \epsilon_{\mathsf{hd}} + 2n\epsilon_{\mathsf{st}}$ which is negligible if q, n, and μ are polynomials in λ, and ϵ_{hd} and ϵ_{st} are negligible in λ as stated. □

5 Concluding Remarks

In this work, we have revisited the CDS composition technique and proposed a modification, that we coin the *share-then-hash* methodology. Our simple technique enhances the previous composition in several flavors, including *more compact* proofs (one single transcript per atomic statement), *better generality* (it is not limited to 2-special sound atomic protocols) and security proofs under *weaker assumptions* (soundness can be proven in the non-programmable random oracle model). Consequently, our results can lead to more efficient, general and secure cryptographic primitives that rely on proofs of partial knowledge.

Proving lower bounds on the proof size and communication complexity of partial proofs of knowledge is an appealing target for future work. In particular, it would be interesting to know if our construction is optimal under some measure or criteria. Another interesting direction for future work would be explore the application of our share-then-hash technique to other scenarios.

References

1. Abe, M., Ambrona, M., Bogdanov, A., Ohkubo, M., Rosen, A.: Acyclicity programming for sigma protocols. Unpublished manuscript, April 2020
2. Abe, M., Chase, M., David, B., Kohlweiss, M., Nishimaki, R., Ohkubo, M.: Constant-size structure-preserving signatures: generic constructions and simple assumptions. J. Cryptol. **29**(4), 833–878 (2016)

3. Abe, M., Ohkubo, M., Suzuki, K.: 1-out-of-n signatures from a variety of keys. In: Zheng, Y. (ed.) ASIACRYPT 2002. LNCS, vol. 2501, pp. 415–432. Springer, Heidelberg (2002). https://doi.org/10.1007/3-540-36178-2_26
4. Abe, M., Ohkubo, M., Suzuki, K.: Efficient threshold signer-ambiguous signatures from variety of keys. IEICE Trans. Fund. **E87–A**(2), 471–479 (2004)
5. Agrawal, S., Ganesh, C., Mohassel, P.: Non-interactive zero-knowledge proofs for composite statements. In: Shacham, H., Boldyreva, A. (eds.) CRYPTO 2018, Part III. LNCS, vol. 10993, pp. 643–673. Springer, Cham (2018). https://doi.org/10.1007/978-3-319-96878-0_22
6. Aguilar Melchor, C., Cayrel, P.-L., Gaborit, P.: A new efficient threshold ring signature scheme based on coding theory. In: Buchmann, J., Ding, J. (eds.) PQCrypto 2008. LNCS, vol. 5299, pp. 1–16. Springer, Heidelberg (2008). https://doi.org/10.1007/978-3-540-88403-3_1
7. Backes, M., Döttling, N., Hanzlik, L., Kluczniak, K., Schneider, J.: Ring signatures: logarithmic-size, no setup—from standard assumptions. In: Ishai, Y., Rijmen, V. (eds.) EUROCRYPT 2019, Part III. LNCS, vol. 11478, pp. 281–311. Springer, Cham (2019). https://doi.org/10.1007/978-3-030-17659-4_10
8. Bernhard, D., Pereira, O., Warinschi, B.: How not to prove yourself: pitfalls of the Fiat-Shamir heuristic and applications to helios. In: Wang, X., Sako, K. (eds.) ASIACRYPT 2012. LNCS, vol. 7658, pp. 626–643. Springer, Heidelberg (2012). https://doi.org/10.1007/978-3-642-34961-4_38
9. Beullens, W.: Sigma protocols for MQ, PKP and SIS, and fishy signature schemes. In: Canteaut, A., Ishai, Y. (eds.) EUROCRYPT 2020, Part III. LNCS, vol. 12107, pp. 183–211. Springer, Cham (2020). https://doi.org/10.1007/978-3-030-45727-3_7
10. Bootle, J., Cerulli, A., Chaidos, P., Ghadafi, E., Groth, J., Petit, C.: Short accountable ring signatures based on DDH. In: Pernul, G., Ryan, P.Y.A., Weippl, E. (eds.) ESORICS 2015, Part I. LNCS, vol. 9326, pp. 243–265. Springer, Cham (2015). https://doi.org/10.1007/978-3-319-24174-6_13
11. Boyen, X.: Mesh signatures. In: Naor, M. (ed.) EUROCRYPT 2007. LNCS, vol. 4515, pp. 210–227. Springer, Heidelberg (2007). https://doi.org/10.1007/978-3-540-72540-4_12
12. Bresson, E., Stern, J., Szydlo, M.: Threshold ring signatures and applications to ad-hoc groups. In: Yung, M. (ed.) CRYPTO 2002. LNCS, vol. 2442, pp. 465–480. Springer, Heidelberg (2002). https://doi.org/10.1007/3-540-45708-9_30
13. Camenisch, J., Chandran, N., Shoup, V.: A public key encryption scheme secure against key dependent chosen plaintext and adaptive chosen ciphertext attacks. In: Joux, A. (ed.) EUROCRYPT 2009. LNCS, vol. 5479, pp. 351–368. Springer, Heidelberg (2009). https://doi.org/10.1007/978-3-642-01001-9_20
14. Canetti, R., et al.: Fiat-Shamir: from practice to theory. In: Charikar, M., Cohen, E. (eds.) Proceedings of the 51st Annual ACM SIGACT Symposium on Theory of Computing, STOC 2019, Phoenix, AZ, USA, 23–26 June 2019, pp. 1082–1090. ACM (2019)
15. Canetti, R., Chen, Y., Reyzin, L., Rothblum, R.D.: Fiat-Shamir and correlation intractability from strong KDM-secure encryption. In: Nielsen, J.B., Rijmen, V. (eds.) EUROCRYPT 2018, Part I. LNCS, vol. 10820, pp. 91–122. Springer, Cham (2018). https://doi.org/10.1007/978-3-319-78381-9_4
16. Canetti, R., Goldreich, O., Halevi, S.: The random oracle methodology, revisited. J. ACM **51**(4), 557–594 (2004)

17. Chandran, N., Groth, J., Sahai, A.: Ring signatures of sub-linear size without random oracles. In: Arge, L., Cachin, C., Jurdziński, T., Tarlecki, A. (eds.) ICALP 2007. LNCS, vol. 4596, pp. 423–434. Springer, Heidelberg (2007). https://doi.org/10.1007/978-3-540-73420-8_38
18. Ciampi, M., Persiano, G., Siniscalchi, L., Visconti, I.: A transform for NIZK almost as efficient and general as the Fiat-Shamir transform without programmable random oracles. In: Kushilevitz, E., Malkin, T. (eds.) TCC 2016, Part II. LNCS, vol. 9563, pp. 83–111. Springer, Heidelberg (2016). https://doi.org/10.1007/978-3-662-49099-0_4
19. Cramer, R.: Modular design of secure yet practical cryptographic protocols. Ph.D. thesis, University of Amsterdam, January 1997
20. Cramer, R., Damgård, I., MacKenzie, P.: Efficient zero-knowledge proofs of knowledge without intractability assumptions. In: Imai, H., Zheng, Y. (eds.) PKC 2000. LNCS, vol. 1751, pp. 354–372. Springer, Heidelberg (2000). https://doi.org/10.1007/978-3-540-46588-1_24
21. Cramer, R., Damgård, I., Schoenmakers, B.: Proofs of partial knowledge and simplified design of witness hiding protocols. In: Desmedt, Y.G. (ed.) CRYPTO 1994. LNCS, vol. 839, pp. 174–187. Springer, Heidelberg (1994). https://doi.org/10.1007/3-540-48658-5_19
22. Dallot, L., Vergnaud, D.: Provably secure code-based threshold ring signatures. In: Parker, M.G. (ed.) IMACC 2009. LNCS, vol. 5921, pp. 222–235. Springer, Heidelberg (2009). https://doi.org/10.1007/978-3-642-10868-6_13
23. Dodis, Y., Kiayias, A., Nicolosi, A., Shoup, V.: Anonymous identification in ad hoc groups. In: Cachin, C., Camenisch, J.L. (eds.) EUROCRYPT 2004. LNCS, vol. 3027, pp. 609–626. Springer, Heidelberg (2004). https://doi.org/10.1007/978-3-540-24676-3_36
24. Faust, S., Kohlweiss, M., Marson, G.A., Venturi, D.: On the non-malleability of the Fiat-Shamir transform. In: Galbraith, S., Nandi, M. (eds.) INDOCRYPT 2012. LNCS, vol. 7668, pp. 60–79. Springer, Heidelberg (2012). https://doi.org/10.1007/978-3-642-34931-7_5
25. Feng, H., Liu, J., Wu, Q., Li, Y.-N.: Traceable ring signatures with post-quantum security. In: Jarecki, S. (ed.) CT-RSA 2020. LNCS, vol. 12006, pp. 442–468. Springer, Cham (2020). https://doi.org/10.1007/978-3-030-40186-3_19
26. Fiat, A., Shamir, A.: How to prove yourself: practical solutions to identification and signature problems. In: Odlyzko, A.M. (ed.) CRYPTO 1986. LNCS, vol. 263, pp. 186–194. Springer, Heidelberg (1987). https://doi.org/10.1007/3-540-47721-7_12
27. Fischlin, M.: Communication-efficient non-interactive proofs of knowledge with online extractors. In: Shoup, V. (ed.) CRYPTO 2005. LNCS, vol. 3621, pp. 152–168. Springer, Heidelberg (2005). https://doi.org/10.1007/11535218_10
28. Fischlin, M., Harasser, P., Janson, C.: Signatures from sequential-OR proofs. In: Canteaut, A., Ishai, Y. (eds.) EUROCRYPT 2020, Part III. LNCS, vol. 12107, pp. 212–244. Springer, Cham (2020). https://doi.org/10.1007/978-3-030-45727-3_8
29. Garg, S., Rao, V., Sahai, A., Schröder, D., Unruh, D.: Round optimal blind signatures. In: Rogaway, P. (ed.) CRYPTO 2011. LNCS, vol. 6841, pp. 630–648. Springer, Heidelberg (2011). https://doi.org/10.1007/978-3-642-22792-9_36
30. Ghadafi, E.M.: Sub-linear blind ring signatures without random oracles. In: Stam, M. (ed.) IMACC 2013. LNCS, vol. 8308, pp. 304–323. Springer, Heidelberg (2013). https://doi.org/10.1007/978-3-642-45239-0_18

31. Goldreich, O., Micali, S., Wigderson, A.: How to prove All NP statements in zero-knowledge and a methodology of cryptographic protocol design (extended abstract). In: Odlyzko, A.M. (ed.) CRYPTO 1986. LNCS, vol. 263, pp. 171–185. Springer, Heidelberg (1987). https://doi.org/10.1007/3-540-47721-7_11
32. Gradwohl, R., Naor, M., Pinkas, B., Rothblum, G.N.: Cryptographic and physical zero-knowledge proof systems for solutions of sudoku puzzles. TCS **44**(2), 245–268 (2009)
33. Groth, J.: Simulation-sound NIZK proofs for a practical language and constant size group signatures. In: Lai, X., Chen, K. (eds.) ASIACRYPT 2006. LNCS, vol. 4284, pp. 444–459. Springer, Heidelberg (2006). https://doi.org/10.1007/11935230_29
34. Groth, J., Kohlweiss, M.: One-out-of-many proofs: or how to leak a secret and spend a coin. In: Oswald, E., Fischlin, M. (eds.) EUROCRYPT 2015, Part II. LNCS, vol. 9057, pp. 253–280. Springer, Heidelberg (2015). https://doi.org/10.1007/978-3-662-46803-6_9
35. Groth, J., Ostrovsky, R., Sahai, A.: Perfect non-interactive zero knowledge for NP. In: Vaudenay, S. (ed.) EUROCRYPT 2006. LNCS, vol. 4004, pp. 339–358. Springer, Heidelberg (2006). https://doi.org/10.1007/11761679_21
36. Groth, J., Sahai, A.: Efficient noninteractive proof systems for bilinear groups. SIAM J. Comput. **41**(5), 1193–1232 (2012)
37. Herranz, J., Sáez, G.: Ring signature schemes for general ad-hoc access structures. In: Castelluccia, C., Hartenstein, H., Paar, C., Westhoff, D. (eds.) ESAS 2004. LNCS, vol. 3313, pp. 54–65. Springer, Heidelberg (2005). https://doi.org/10.1007/978-3-540-30496-8_6
38. Jutla, C.S., Roy, A.: Shorter quasi-adaptive NIZK proofs for linear subspaces. J. Cryptol. **30**(4), 1116–1156 (2017)
39. Libert, B., Ling, S., Nguyen, K., Wang, H.: Zero-knowledge arguments for lattice-based accumulators: logarithmic-size ring signatures and group signatures without trapdoors. In: Fischlin, M., Coron, J.-S. (eds.) EUROCRYPT 2016, Part II. LNCS, vol. 9666, pp. 1–31. Springer, Heidelberg (2016). https://doi.org/10.1007/978-3-662-49896-5_1
40. Libert, B., Ling, S., Nguyen, K., Wang, H.: Zero-knowledge arguments for lattice-based PRFs and applications to E-cash. In: Takagi, T., Peyrin, T. (eds.) ASIACRYPT 2017, Part III. LNCS, vol. 10626, pp. 304–335. Springer, Cham (2017). https://doi.org/10.1007/978-3-319-70700-6_11
41. Libert, B., Peters, T., Qian, C.: Logarithmic-size ring signatures with tight security from the DDH assumption. In: Lopez, J., Zhou, J., Soriano, M. (eds.) ESORICS 2018, Part II. LNCS, vol. 11099, pp. 288–308. Springer, Cham (2018). https://doi.org/10.1007/978-3-319-98989-1_15
42. Lindell, Y.: An efficient transform from sigma protocols to NIZK with a CRS and non-programmable random oracle. In: Dodis, Y., Nielsen, J.B. (eds.) TCC 2015, Part I. LNCS, vol. 9014, pp. 93–109. Springer, Heidelberg (2015). https://doi.org/10.1007/978-3-662-46494-6_5
43. Liu, J.K., Wei, V.K., Wong, D.S.: A separable threshold ring signature scheme. In: Lim, J.-I., Lee, D.-H. (eds.) ICISC 2003. LNCS, vol. 2971, pp. 12–26. Springer, Heidelberg (2004). https://doi.org/10.1007/978-3-540-24691-6_2
44. Lueks, W., Kulynych, B., Fasquelle, J., Bail-Collet, S.L., Troncoso, C.: zksk: a library for composable zero-knowledge proofs. In: Cavallaro, L., Kinder, J., Domingo-Ferrer, J. (eds.) Proceedings of the 18th ACM Workshop on Privacy in the Electronic Society, WPES@CCS 2019, London, UK, 11 November 2019, pp. 50–54. ACM (2019)

45. Malkin, T., Teranishi, I., Vahlis, Y., Yung, M.: Signatures resilient to continual leakage on memory and computation. In: Ishai, Y. (ed.) TCC 2011. LNCS, vol. 6597, pp. 89–106. Springer, Heidelberg (2011). https://doi.org/10.1007/978-3-642-19571-6_7
46. Martin, K.M., Simmons, G.J., Jackson, W.-A.: The geometry of shared secret schemes. Bull. ICA **1**, 71–88 (1991)
47. Nguyen, K., Tang, H., Wang, H., Zeng, N.: New code-based privacy-preserving cryptographic constructions. In: Galbraith, S.D., Moriai, S. (eds.) ASIACRYPT 2019, Part II. LNCS, vol. 11922, pp. 25–55. Springer, Cham (2019). https://doi.org/10.1007/978-3-030-34621-8_2
48. Nielsen, J.B.: Separating random oracle proofs from complexity theoretic proofs: the non-committing encryption case. In: Yung, M. (ed.) CRYPTO 2002. LNCS, vol. 2442, pp. 111–126. Springer, Heidelberg (2002). https://doi.org/10.1007/3-540-45708-9_8
49. Peikert, C., Shiehian, S.: Noninteractive zero knowledge for np from (plain) learning with errors. In: Boldyreva, A., Micciancio, D. (eds.) CRYPTO 2019, Part I. LNCS, vol. 11692, pp. 89–114. Springer, Cham (2019). https://doi.org/10.1007/978-3-030-26948-7_4
50. Ràfols, C.: Stretching groth-sahai: NIZK proofs of partial satisfiability. In: Dodis, Y., Nielsen, J.B. (eds.) TCC 2015, Part II. LNCS, vol. 9015, pp. 247–276. Springer, Heidelberg (2015). https://doi.org/10.1007/978-3-662-46497-7_10
51. Rivest, R.L., Shamir, A., Tauman, Y.: How to leak a secret. In: Boyd, C. (ed.) ASIACRYPT 2001. LNCS, vol. 2248, pp. 552–565. Springer, Heidelberg (2001). https://doi.org/10.1007/3-540-45682-1_32
52. Schäge, S., Schwenk, J.: A CDH-based ring signature scheme with short signatures and public keys. In: Sion, R. (ed.) FC 2010. LNCS, vol. 6052, pp. 129–142. Springer, Heidelberg (2010). https://doi.org/10.1007/978-3-642-14577-3_12
53. Shacham, H., Waters, B.: Efficient ring signatures without random oracles. In: Okamoto, T., Wang, X. (eds.) PKC 2007. LNCS, vol. 4450, pp. 166–180. Springer, Heidelberg (2007). https://doi.org/10.1007/978-3-540-71677-8_12
54. Stern, J.: A new paradigm for public key identification. IEEE Trans. Inf. Theory **42**(6), 1757–1768 (1996)
55. Wikström, D.: Special soundness revisited. IACR Cryptology ePrint Archive, 2018:1157 (2018)

Succinct Diophantine-Satisfiability Arguments

Patrick Towa[1,2,4](✉) and Damien Vergnaud[3,4]

[1] IBM Research, Zurich, Switzerland
patrick.towa@gmail.com
[2] DIENS, École Normale Supérieure, CNRS, PSL University, Paris, France
[3] Sorbonne Université, CNRS, LIP6, 75005 Paris, France
[4] Institut Universitaire de France, Paris, France

Abstract. A *Diophantine equation* is a multi-variate polynomial equation with integer coefficients, and it is satisfiable if it has a solution with all unknowns taking integer values. Davis, Putnam, Robinson and Matiyasevich showed that the general Diophantine satisfiability problem is undecidable (giving a negative answer to Hilbert's tenth problem) but it is nevertheless possible to argue in zero-knowledge the knowledge of a solution, if a solution is known to a prover.

We provide the first succinct honest-verifier zero-knowledge argument for the satisfiability of Diophantine equations with a communication complexity and a round complexity that grows logarithmically in the size of the polynomial equation. The security of our argument relies on standard assumptions on hidden-order groups. As the argument requires to commit to integers, we introduce a new integer-commitment scheme that has much smaller parameters than Damgård and Fujisaki's scheme. We finally show how to succinctly argue knowledge of solutions to several NP-complete problems and cryptographic problems by encoding them as Diophantine equations.

1 Introduction

A *Diophantine equation* is a multi-variate polynomial equation with integer coefficients, and it is satisfiable if it has a solution with all unknowns taking integer values. Davis, Putnam, Robinson and Matiyasevich [20] showed that any computational problem can be modeled as finding a solution to such equations, thereby proving that the general Diophantine-satisfiability problem is undecidable and giving a negative answer to Hilbert's tenth problem. For instance, several classical NP-problems such as 3-SAT, Graph 3-colorability or Integer Linear Programming can be readily encoded as Diophantine equations. Several cryptographic problems such as proving knowledge of an RSA signature, that a committed value is non-negative or that encrypted votes are honestly shuffled by a mix-net, can also be encoded as Diophantine equations.

S. Moriai and H. Wang (Eds.): ASIACRYPT 2020, LNCS 12493, pp. 774–804, 2020.
https://doi.org/10.1007/978-3-030-64840-4_26

Efficient zero-knowledge arguments of knowledge of solutions to Diophantine equations, if a solution is known to a party, can thus be useful for many practical cryptographic tasks; and doing so requires to do zero-knowledge proofs on committed integers.

1.1 Prior Work

Integer Commitments. Fujisaki and Okamoto [15] presented the first efficient integer commitment scheme and also suggested a zero-knowledge protocol for verifying multiplicative relations over committed values. Such a commitment scheme allows to commit to any $x \in \mathbb{Z}$ in a group of unknown order, with a Pedersen-like commitment scheme. This makes the security analysis more intricate since division modulo the unknown group order cannot be performed in general. As an evidence that this setting is error-prone, Michels showed that the Fujisaki–Okamoto proof system was flawed. Damgård and Fujisaki [11] later proposed a statistically hiding and computationally binding integer commitment scheme under standard assumptions in a hidden-order group $\mathbb{G}$ with an efficient argument of knowledge of openings to commitments, and arguments of multiplicative relations over committed values. This primitive gives rise to a (honest-verifier) zero-knowledge proof of satisfiability of a Diophantine equation with M multiplications over $\mathbb{Z}$ that requires $\Omega(M)$ integer commitments and $\Omega(M)$ proofs of multiplicative relations [11,19]. These complexities have not been improved since then.

Circuit Satisfiability over $\mathbb{Z}_p$. Similarly, it is possible to design a zero-knowledge proof of satisfiability of an arithmetic circuit over $\mathbb{Z}_p$ using Pedersen's commitment scheme [21] in a group $\mathbb{G}$ of public prime order p. An immediate solution is to use the additive homomorphic properties of Pedersen's commitment and zero-knowledge protocols for proving knowledge of the contents of commitments and for verifying multiplicative relations over committed values [8,22].

For an arithmetic circuit with M multiplication gates, this protocol requires $\Omega(M)$ commitments and $\Omega(M)$ arguments of multiplication consistency and has a communication complexity of $\Omega(M)$ group elements. In 2009, Groth [17] proposed a sub-linear size zero-knowledge arguments for statements involving linear algebra and used it to reduce this communication complexity to $O\left(\sqrt{M}\right)$ group elements. This breakthrough initiated a decade of progress for zero-knowledge proofs for various statements (see e.g., [3,5,6,18] and references therein). It culminated with the argument system "*Bulletproofs*" proposed by Bünz, Bootle, Boneh, Poelstra, Wuille and Maxwell [6] which permits to prove the satisfiability of such an arithmetic circuit with communication complexity $O(\log(M))$ and round complexity $O(\log(M))$. The corner stone of their protocol is an argument that two committed vectors satisfy an inner-product relation. It has logarithmic communication and round complexity in the vector length, and its security only relies on the discrete-logarithm assumption and does not require a trusted setup.

Circuit satisfiability over any finite field is an NP-complete problem so the "*Bulletproofs*" argument system has widespread applications. However, as mentioned above, in many cryptographic settings, it is desirable to prove statements such as "the committed value x is a valid RSA signature on a message m for an RSA public key (N, e)". In this case, the prover has to convince the verifier that $x^e = H(m) \bmod N$, or in other words that there exists an integer k such that $x^e + kN = H(m)$ where this equality holds over the integers for $|k| \leq N^{e-1}$ and H some cryptographic hash function. In order to use directly an argument of satisfiability of an arithmetic circuit to prove the knowledge of a pair (x, k) which satisfies this equation, one needs to use a group $\mathbb{G}$ a prime order p with $p > N^e$ (and to additionally prove that $x < N$ and $k < N^e$). For a large e, this approach results in a proof with prohibitive communication complexity.

Moreover, in various settings, such as the Integer-Linear-Programming problem, there is no *a priori* upper-bound on the sizes of the integer solutions during setup when p is defined. Being able to argue on integers instead of residue classes modulo a fixed prime integer then becomes necessary. Besides, generic reductions to circuit satisfiability over prime-order fields for some simple problems naturally defined over the integers may return circuits with a very large number of multiplication gates and even the "*Bulletproofs*" argument system could produce large proofs. Modeling computational problems using Diophantine equations is more versatile, and a succinct argument system for Diophantine satisfiability thus has many potential applications.

1.2 Contributions

We provide the first succinct argument for the satisfiability of Diophantine equations with a communication complexity and a round complexity that grows logarithmically in the size of the polynomial equation[1]. It is statistical honest-verifier zero-knowledge and is extractable under standard computational assumptions over hidden-order groups such as RSA groups or ideal-class groups.

Integer Commitments. Section 3 introduces a new computationally hiding and binding commitment scheme that allows to commit to vectors of integers. It is close to Damgård and Fujisaki's seminal proposal, but has much smaller parameters. Denoting by λ the security parameter and letting $2^{b_{\mathbb{G}}}$ be an upper bound on the group order, the version of our scheme which allows to commit to n integers at once has parameters consisting of $O(b_{\mathbb{G}} + \log n)$ bits instead of $\Omega(nb_{\mathbb{G}} \cdot \text{polylog}(\lambda))$ as with the generalized version of Damgård and Fujisaki's scheme.

Damgård and Fujisaki's commitment scheme, for $n = 1$, is a variant of Pedersen's commitment in a hidden-order group $\mathbb{G}$: given two group elements $g, h \in \mathbb{G}$,

[1] Our goals and techniques differ completely from those proposed by Bünz, Fisch and Szepieniec [7] where they used what they called *Diophantine Arguments of Knowledge (DARK)* to construct a commitment scheme for polynomials over prime finite fields (using the so-called *Kronecker substitution* for determining the coefficients of a polynomial by evaluating it at a single value, see e.g., [16, p. 245]).

the commitment to an integer value $x \in \mathbb{Z}$ is $C = g^x h^r$, where r is an integer of appropriate size. The hiding property of their scheme crucially relies on the fact that $g \in \langle h \rangle$, which is not always guaranteed as the group may not be cyclic. Damgård and Fujisaki's proposed a Schnorr-type [22] protocol to prove such statements, but their challenge set is restricted to $\{0, 1\}$ to guarantee soundness under the assumptions on the group. Their protocol must then be repeated logarithmically many times to achieve negligible soundness, and the resulting parameters are large. The situation is worse when n is large as commitments are computed as $g_1^{x_1} \cdots g_n^{x_n} h^r$ and a proof for each g_i must be computed.

Our scheme is based on the observation that proving that $g^2 \in \langle h^2 \rangle$ can be done more efficiently in a single protocol run under the assumptions on the group. Our commitments are thus computed as $(g^x h^r)^2 \in \mathbb{G}$. We further such how to aggregate the proofs of several such statements to reduce the size of our parameters when n is large.

Succinct Inner-Product Arguments on Integers. Section 4 presents a succinct argument that two integer vectors committed with our scheme satisfy an inner-product relation. That is, an argument of knowledge of vectors $\mathbf{a}$ and $\mathbf{b} \in \mathbb{Z}^n$ (and of a randomness $r \in \mathbb{Z}$) that open a commitment C and such that $\langle \mathbf{a}, \mathbf{b} \rangle = z$ given a public integer z. Succinct here means that the communication complexity of the prover is of order $O(\ell + \log(n) b_{\mathbb{G}})$, where ℓ is the bit length of the largest witness. The complexity is measured in bits as during the protocol, the prover sends logarithmically many group elements and three integers, but these latter could be arbitrarily large.

The argument of Bünz et al. [6] for inner-product relations over $\mathbb{Z}_p$ is not applicable to integers as their proof of extractability relies on the generalized discrete-logarithm assumption for which there is no equivalent in hidden-order groups that may not even be cyclic, and on the invertibility of elements in $\mathbb{Z}_p^*$ since it requires to solve linear systems over $\mathbb{Z}_p$. Besides, their argument is not zero-knowledge and is on vectors committed with the non-hiding version of Pedersen's scheme (i.e., with nil randomness). Therefore, whenever it is used as a sub-protocol of another one, techniques specific to the larger protocol must always be used to guarantee that it is zero-knowledge. del Pino, Seiler and Lyubashevsky [12] later solved this issue by adapting the argument of Bünz et al. in prime-order groups to make it perfectly honest-verifier zero-knowledge with the full-fledged Pedersen's scheme.

Our protocol uses halve-then-recurse techniques similar to those of Bünz et al. for the Sect. 3.2 commitment scheme in hidden-order groups and thus allows to succinctly argue on integers, but only uses the integrality of $\mathbb{Z}$ as a ring since one cannot invert modulo the unknown order. (Note that these techniques are themselves inspired by the recursive inner-product argument of Bootle et al. [5].) In particular, we prove that even though one cannot a priori solve in $\mathbb{Z}$ the linear system of Bünz et al. required to prove the extractability of their protocol, one can instead solve a "relaxed" system in $\mathbb{Z}$. Then, under the assumptions on the hidden-order group, we show that the solution to the relaxed system is enough to extract a representation of the commitment in the public bases. In groups with public prime orders, the assumption that discrete-logarithm relations are hard to compute allows to conclude that this representation of the commitment actually leads to a valid witness, but this assumption is not a priori translatable to hidden-order groups. Instead, we prove that a similar assumption in the subgroup generated by a randomly sampled element is weaker than the assumptions on the group, and that suffices to prove the extractability of the protocol. The details of these technical challenges are outlined in Sect. 4.1.

Furthermore, as the group order is unknown to all parties, the argument is only statistically honest-verifier zero-knowledge. To ensure this property, the randomness range of the prover is carefully[2] adapted to allow for simulatability without knowledge of a witness.

Succinct Arguments for Diophantine Equations. Section 5 presents our succinct protocol to argue satisfiability of Diophantine equations. Our approach is inspired by Skolem's method [23] which consists in reducing the degree of the polynomial by introducing new variables to obtain a new polynomial of degree at most 4, in such a way that the satisfiability of one polynomial implies that of the other. Tailoring Skolem's method to the problem of arguing satisfiability, we show how to reduce the satisfiability of any polynomial in $\mathbb{Z}[x_1, \ldots, x_\nu]$ of total degree δ with μ monomials to the existence of vectors $\mathbf{a}_L = [a_{L,1} \cdots a_{L,n}]$, $\mathbf{a}_R = [a_{R,1} \cdots a_{R,n}]$ and $\mathbf{a}_O = [a_{O,1} \cdots a_{O,n}]$ in $\mathbb{Z}^n$, for $n \leq \nu\lfloor \log \delta \rfloor + (\delta - 1)\mu$, such that $a_{O,i} = a_{L,i} a_{R,i}$ for all $i \in \{1, \ldots, n\}$, and that satisfy $1 \leq Q \leq 1 + 2\nu(\lfloor \log \delta \rfloor - 1) + (\delta - 2)\mu$ linear constraints of the form

$$\langle \mathbf{w}_{L,q}, \mathbf{a}_L \rangle + \langle \mathbf{w}_{R,q}, \mathbf{a}_R \rangle + \langle \mathbf{w}_{O,q}, \mathbf{a}_O \rangle = c_q,$$

where $\mathbf{w}_{L,q}, \mathbf{w}_{R,q}, \mathbf{w}_{O,q} \in \mathbb{Z}^n$ and $c_q \in \mathbb{Z}$ for all $q \in \{1, \ldots, Q\}$. Our reduction is constructive as it allows to infer the vectors and the constraints directly from the original polynomial.

Bootle et al. [5] then Bünz et al. [6] gave an argument system for proving knowledge of vectors in $\mathbb{Z}_p$ (instead of $\mathbb{Z}$) that satisfy such constraints. They use this protocol to argue for the satisfiability of arithmetic circuits over $\mathbb{Z}_p$. Our argument shares similarities with theirs, but again there are key technical differences that arise from the fact that $\mathbb{Z}$ is not a field. Indeed, as one cannot invert nor reduce integers modulo the unknown orders of the bases, we use different techniques notably to prevent the integers involved in the argument from increasing too much, and to ensure consistency between the variables in the entry-wise product and those in the linear constraints. Guaranteeing this latter consistency requires to construct new polynomials for the argument that do not involve inverting integers. Besides, one cannot use their commitment-key switching technique which consists in interpreting g^a as a commitment to xa to the base $g^{x^{-1}}$ in groups of public prime order. Finally, extra precaution must be taken to guarantee the zero-knowledge property as integers are not reduced

[2] As another evidence that cryptography in hidden-order groups is error prone, Fouque and Poupard [14] broke the RDSA signature from [4] for which this randomness range was not wisely selected.

modulo p and may carry information about the witness. These challenges and the ways we overcome them are described in details in the full version [24, Section 6.2].

As a result, the communication complexity of our Diophantine-satisfiability argument has a communication complexity of $O(\delta\ell + \min(\nu, \delta)\log(\nu + \delta)\, b_{\mathbb{G}} + H)$ bits, if the absolute value of all the polynomial coefficients is upper-bounded by 2^H for some integer H. In contrast, the overall communication complexity using Damgård and Fujisaki's multiplication argument is upper-bounded by $O\left(\binom{\nu+\delta}{\delta}\left(\delta\ell + \log\left(\binom{\nu+\delta}{\delta}\right) H + b_{\mathbb{G}}\right)\right)$ and lower-bounded by $\Omega\left(\binom{\nu+\delta}{\delta}(\ell + b_{\mathbb{G}})\right)$.

Applications. The full version [24] presents several applications of our Diophantine-satisfiability argument. We provide explicit reductions to Diophantine satisfiability for the following problems:

- argument of knowledge of a (possibly committed) RSA e-th root in $\mathbb{Z}_N$ of some public value with $O(\log(\log(e))b_{\mathbb{G}})$ bits. This has application to credential systems when combined with proofs of non-algebraic statements [9];
- argument of knowledge of $O(\log(\log p)b_{\mathbb{G}})$ bits for ECDSA signatures with a prime p, and of $O(\log(\log q)b_{\mathbb{G}} + \log(\log p))$ bits for DSA signatures with primes p and q. The signed message is public, but can be committed if the argument is combined with proofs of non-algebraic statements [9];
- argument that two committed lists of integers of length n are permutations of each other with $O(\ell + \log(n)b_{\mathbb{G}})$ bits
- argument of satisfiability of a 3-SAT Boolean formula with m clauses and n variables with $O(\log(n + m)b_{\mathbb{G}})$ bits;
- argument of satisfiability of an Integer-Linear-Programming problem of the form $\mathbf{x} \in \mathbb{N}^n$ and $\mathbf{A}\mathbf{x}^{\mathrm{T}} \geq \mathbf{b}^{\mathrm{T}}$, for $\mathbf{A} \in \mathbb{Z}^{m\times n}$ and $\mathbf{b} \in \mathbb{Z}^m$, with $O(\ell + \log(4n + 3m)$ $b_{\mathbb{G}} + \log\|\mathbf{A}\|_\infty + \log\|\mathbf{b}\|_\infty)$ bits.

2 Preliminaries

This section introduces the notation used throughout the paper, recalls standard assumptions on generators of hidden-order groups, and defines commitment schemes and argument systems.

2.1 Notation

For $x \in \mathbb{Z}$, $|x|$ denotes its absolute value. All logarithms are in base 2. For any two integers $a \leq b \in \mathbb{Z}$, $[\![a; b]\!]$ denotes the set $\{a\}$ if $a = b$ and $\{a, a+1, \ldots, b\}$ if $a < b$. For an integer $n \geq 1$, $[\![n]\!]$ stands for the set $[\![1; n]\!]$. Given a vector $\mathbf{a} \in \mathbb{Z}^n$, $\mathbf{a}X$ denotes the vector $\left[a_1X\ a_2X \cdots a_nX\right] \in \mathbb{Z}^n[X]$.

For a given group $(\mathbb{G}, \cdot)$, $T_{\mathbb{G}}$ denotes the binary complexity of computing group operations. For $h \in \mathbb{G}$, $\sqrt{\langle h^2 \rangle}$ denotes the subgroup $\left\{g \in \mathbb{G} \colon \exists \alpha \in \mathbb{Z}, g^2 = h^{2\alpha}\right\}$.

For $\mathbf{g} \in \mathbb{G}^n$, if n is even, set $\mathbf{g}_1 := [g_1 \cdots g_{n/2}]$ and $\mathbf{g}_2 := [g_{n/2+1} \cdots g_n]$, and if n is odd, set $\mathbf{g}_1 := [g_1 \cdots g_{\lfloor n/2 \rfloor} 1_{\mathbb{G}}]$ and $\mathbf{g}_2 := [g_{\lceil n/2 \rceil} \cdots g_n]$. For $\mathbf{a} \in \mathbb{Z}^n$, if n is even, set $\mathbf{a}_1 := [a_1 \cdots a_{n/2}]$ and $\mathbf{a}_2 := [a_{n/2+1} \cdots a_n]$, and if n is odd, set $\mathbf{a}_1 := [a_1 \cdots a_{\lfloor n/2 \rfloor} 0]$ and $\mathbf{a}_2 := [a_{\lceil n/2 \rceil} \cdots a_n]$.

For $n \in \mathbb{N}^*$, $z \in \mathbb{Z}$ and $\mathbf{g} = [g_1 \dots g_n] \in \mathbb{G}^n$, let $\mathbf{g}^z := [g_1^z \cdots g_n^z] \in \mathbb{G}^n$. For $\mathbf{a} = [a_1 \dots a_n] \in \mathbb{Z}^n$, define $\mathbf{g}^{\mathbf{a}} := \prod_{i=1}^n g_i^{a_i}$. For $\mathbf{g}$ and $\mathbf{h}$ in $\mathbb{G}^n$, $\mathbf{g} \circ \mathbf{h} \in \mathbb{G}^n$ denotes their Hadamard product, i.e., their component-wise product.

2.2 Hidden-Order-Group Generators and Hardness Assumptions

A hidden-order-group generator G is an algorithm which takes as input a security parameter 1^λ and returns the description of a finite Abelian group $(\mathbb{G}, \cdot)$ and an integer $P \geq 2$. Integer P is assumed to be smaller than the order of $\mathbb{G}$, but to still be a super-polynomial function of the security parameter. The role of P is mainly to adjust the soundness of the protocols herein, as their challenge spaces will typically be $[\![0; P^{\Omega(1)} - 1]\!]$.

It is also assumed that given the description of $\mathbb{G}$, the group law and the inversion of group elements can be efficiently computed, that group elements can be sampled uniformly at random and that an upper bound $2^{b_{\mathbb{G}}}$ on $\mathrm{ord}(\mathbb{G})$ can be efficiently computed, with $b_{\mathbb{G}} := b_{\mathbb{G}}(\lambda)$ polynomial in λ (it is further assumed that $b_{\mathbb{G}} = \Omega(\lambda)$). Recall that the bit complexity of an elementary operation in a group $\mathbb{G}$ is denoted $T_{\mathbb{G}}$.

The following assumptions are classical for hidden-order-group generators and were introduced by Damgård and Fujisaki [11]. They are best illustrated for P such that natural integers less than P are factorizable in polynomial time in λ (e.g., $\lambda^{\log^{\Omega(1)}(\lambda)}$ given current knowledge in computational number theory), and for $\mathbb{G}$ as the group $\mathbb{Z}_N^*$ for an RSA modulus N with prime factors p and q such that $p = q = 3 \mod 4$, $\gcd(p-1, q-1) = 2$ and the number of divisors of $p-1$ and $q-1$ with prime factors less than P is of magnitude $O(\lambda)$. However, these assumptions are believed to also hold over generators of ideal-class groups.

Definition 2.1 (Strong-Root Assumption). *A group generator* G *satisfies the* (T, ε)*-strong-root assumption if for all* $\lambda \in \mathbb{N}$, *for every adversary* $\mathcal{A}$ *that runs in time at most* $T(\lambda)$,

$$\Pr\left[g^n = h \wedge n > 1 : \begin{array}{c} (\mathbb{G}, P) \leftarrow \mathsf{G}(1^\lambda) \\ h \leftarrow_{\$} \mathbb{G} \\ (g, n) \leftarrow \mathcal{A}(\mathbb{G}, P, h) \end{array} \right] \leq \varepsilon(\lambda).$$

This assumption is simply a generalization of the strong RSA assumption [2,15] to hidden-order groups.

Definition 2.2 (Small-Order Assumption). *A group generator* G *satisfies the* (T, ε)*-small-order assumption if for all* $\lambda \in \mathbb{N}$, *for every adversary* $\mathcal{A}$ *that runs in time at most* $T(\lambda)$,

$$\Pr\left[\begin{array}{c} g^n = 1_{\mathbb{G}} \wedge g^2 \neq 1_{\mathbb{G}} \\ 0 < n < P \end{array} : \begin{array}{c} (\mathbb{G}, P) \leftarrow \mathsf{G}(1^\lambda) \\ (g, n) \leftarrow \mathcal{A}(\mathbb{G}, P) \end{array} \right] \leq \varepsilon(\lambda).$$

The small-order assumption simply states that it should be hard to find low-order elements in the group (different from $1_{\mathbb{G}}$), except for square roots of unity which may be easy to compute (e.g., -1 in RSA groups). In the group $\mathbb{Z}_N^*$ for $N = pq$ with p and q prime such that $\gcd(p-1, q-1) = 2$, Damgård and Fujisaki [11] showed that factoring N can be reduced to this problem in polynomial time if integers less than P are factorizable in polynomial time in λ.

Definition 2.3 (Orders with Low Dyadic Valuation). *A group generator* G *satisfies the low-dyadic-valuation assumption on orders if for all* $\lambda \in \mathbb{N}$, *for every* $(\mathbb{G}, P) \leftarrow \mathsf{G}(1^\lambda)$, *for every* $g \in \mathbb{G}$, $\operatorname{ord}(g)$ *is divisible by 2 at most once.*

Notice that in the group $\mathbb{Z}_N^*$ for $N = pq$ with p and q prime such that $p = q = 3 \bmod 4$, the order of any element is divisible by 2 at most once since 2 divides $p-1$ and $q-1$ exactly once.

Definition 2.4 (Many Rough-Order Elements or μ-Assumption). *An integer is said to be* P*-rough if all its prime factors are greater than or equal to* P. *A group generator* G *satisfies the* μ*-assumption that there are many rough-order elements in the groups generated by* G *(or simply the* μ*-assumption) if for all every parameter* $\lambda \in \mathbb{N}$,

$$\Pr\left[\operatorname{ord}(h) \textit{ is } P\textit{-rough} : \begin{array}{c}(\mathbb{G}, P) \leftarrow \mathsf{G}(1^\lambda) \\ h \leftarrow_\$ \mathbb{G}\end{array}\right] \geq \mu(\lambda).$$

2.3 Non-interactive Commitments

A (non-interactive) commitment scheme consists of an algorithm $\mathsf{Setup}(1^\lambda) \rightarrow pp$ which generates public parameters (implicit inputs to the other algorithms); a key-generation algorithm $\mathsf{KG}(pp) \rightarrow ck$; a probabilistic algorithm $\mathsf{Com}(ck, x) \rightarrow (C, d)$ that computes a commitment C to a value x and an opening or decommitment information d on the input of ck; and a deterministic algorithm $\mathsf{ComVf}(ck, C, x, d) \rightarrow b \in \{0, 1\}$ which returns a bit indicating whether the decommitment d is valid (bit 1) for C and x w.r.t. key ck, or not (bit 0). Formal definitions of the correctness, hiding and binding properties of commitment schemes are given in the full version [24].

Discussion. The syntax above separates the commitment-key generation algorithm from the setup algorithm although these are often tacitly combined, especially for commitments in public-order groups. The main reason is that doing so allows to define the hiding property for schemes even when the keys are possibly *invalid.* This question does not arise for schemes with keys that are elements of a prime-order group $\mathbb{G} = \langle g \rangle$ (e.g., Pedersen's scheme [21]) since any element $h \in \mathbb{G}^*$ is a valid commitment key. However, when the scheme is defined over an unknown-order group $\mathbb{G}$ which may not be cyclic, and that keys are elements of the *subgroup* generated by an element (as it is the case for Damgård–Fujisaki commitments recalled in Sect. 3.1), say h, there may not be an efficient way to test whether another element $g \in \mathbb{G}$ is in $\langle h \rangle$. Computing a commitment with an invalid key may then not guarantee that the commitment is hiding. That is why the scheme will be required to be hiding even if commitments are computed with a potentially invalid key.

2.4 Argument Systems

This section defines argument systems for families of languages. The languages are parametrized by public parameters and Common-Reference Strings (CRSs). As a simple example, given an Abelian group $\mathbb{G}$ (which could be non-cyclic) and an element $h \in \mathbb{G}$ (the parameters) and another element $g \in \langle h \rangle$ (the CRS), consider the language of group elements $C \in \mathbb{G}$ such that there exists $x, y \in \mathbb{Z}$ for which $C = g^x h^y$. This language is clearly parametrized by the parameters and the CRS, and one can give an argument system for this parametrized language in the same vein as what is subsequently done in the paper. However, to lighten the notation, arguments will be (abusively) referred to as arguments for languages rather than arguments for families of languages.

Formally, an argument system (or protocol) for a language $\mathcal{L} = \mathcal{L}_{pp,crs}$ (or equivalently, for the corresponding relation $\mathcal{R} = \mathcal{R}_{pp,crs}$) consists of a quadruple $\Pi = (\mathsf{Setup}, \mathsf{CRSGen}, \mathsf{Prove}, \mathsf{Vf})$ such that $\mathsf{Setup}(1^\lambda) \rightarrow pp$ returns public parameters on the input of a security parameter, $\mathsf{CRSGen}(pp) \rightarrow crs$ returns a CRS, and $\langle \mathsf{Prove}(crs, x, w) \rightleftharpoons \mathsf{Vf}(crs, x) \rangle \rightarrow (\tau, b) \in \{0,1\}^* \times \{0,1\}$ are interactive algorithms (τ denotes the transcript of the interaction and b the decision bit of Vf). The public parameters are assumed to be tacit inputs to algorithms Prove and Vf, even though they may at times be made explicit for instantiated protocols, especially when the CRS is the empty string (in which case the CRS is omitted from the syntax). The definitions of the (culpable) soundness, extractability and honest-verifier zero-knowledge properties of argument systems are given in the full version [24].

The non-interactive argument system derived from an interactive one Π via the Fiat–Shamir heuristic [13] with a random oracle $\mathcal{H}$ is denoted $FS.\Pi^{\mathcal{H}}$.

3 Integer Commitments

This section recalls a scheme due to Damgård and Fujisaki which allows to commit to integers[3]. Then comes a new integer-commitment scheme with parameters smaller than those of Damgård and Fujisaki's scheme, and which are also more efficient to compute. For the version of our scheme which allows to commit to n integers, the parameters are of $O(b_{\mathbb{G}} + \log n)$ bits instead of $\Omega(n b_{\mathbb{G}} \log P)$ as with the generalized version of Damgård and Fujisaki's scheme, where $2^{b_{\mathbb{G}}}$ is an upper bound on the group order.

[3] Couteau, Peters and Pointcheval [10] proved that in the case of RSA groups (with Blum integers), the security of Damgård and Fujisaki's scheme is provable under (a variant of) the RSA assumption instead of the strong RSA assumption. This also holds for our scheme. However, this result does not concern generic hidden-order groups.

3.1 Damgård–Fujisaki Commitments

The Damgård–Fujisaki commitment scheme [11,15], parameterized by a group generator G, consists of the following algorithms.

$\mathsf{Setup}(1^\lambda) \rightarrow pp$: run $(\mathbb{G}, P) \leftarrow \mathsf{G}(1^\lambda)$, generate $h \leftarrow_\$ \mathbb{G}$ and return $(\mathbb{G}, P, h)$.
Recall that these parameters are implicit inputs to all the other algorithms.

$\mathsf{KG}(pp) \rightarrow ck$: generate $\alpha \leftarrow_\$ [\![0; 2^{b_\mathbb{G}+\lambda}]\!]$ ($2^{b_\mathbb{G}}$ is an upper bound on $\mathrm{ord}(\mathbb{G})$), compute and return $g \leftarrow h^\alpha$.

$\mathsf{Com}(g, x \in \mathbb{Z}) \rightarrow (C, d)$: generate $r \leftarrow_\$ [\![0; 2^{b_\mathbb{G}+\lambda}]\!]$, compute $C \leftarrow g^x h^r$, set $d \leftarrow (r, 1_\mathbb{G})$ and return (C, d).

$\mathsf{ComVf}(g, C, x, d) \rightarrow b \in \{0, 1\}$: parse d as $(r, \tilde{g})$. If $C = g^x h^r \tilde{g}$ and $\tilde{g}^2 = 1_\mathbb{G}$, return 1, else return 0.

Equivalently, the commitment-algorithm could simply set the decommitment information d to r, and the commitment-verification would return 1 if the equality $C^2 = \left(g^x h^d\right)^2$ holds and 0 otherwise. The squaring in the verification is due to the fact that the small-order assumption does not exclude the possibility to efficiently compute square roots of unity, and they thus relaxed the verification equation to allow for sound argument of knowledge of openings to commitments. In other words, the scheme would still be binding without the squaring in the verification equation, and the relaxation is simply an artifact to allow for sound arguments.

More precisely, suppose that the verification were not relaxed, i.e., that it would only check that $C = g^x h^d$. Two accepting transcripts (D, e_1, z_1, t_1) and (D, e_2, z_2, t_2) of a standard Schnorr-type argument of knowledge of an opening would imply that $C^{e_1-e_2} = g^{z_2-z_1} h^{t_2-t_1}$. Assuming $e_1, e_2 \in [\![0; P-1]\!]$, $e_1 \neq e_2$, and that $e_1 - e_2$ divides $z_2 - z_1$ and $t_2 - t_1$ (Damgård and Fujisaki showed that this latter event occurs with probability negligibly close to 1/2 under the assumptions on the group generator), the previous equality would imply that $\left(g^{(z_2-z_1)/(e_1-e_2)} h^{(t_2-t_1)/(e_1-e_2)} C^{-1}\right)^{e_1-e_2} = 1_\mathbb{G}$, and the small-order assumption would only allow to conclude that $C^2 = \left(g^{(z_2-z_1)/(e_1-e_2)} h^{(t_2-t_1)/(e_1-e_2)}\right)^2$. The trivial attack in which an adversary computes C as $g^x h^d \tilde{g}$ with $\tilde{g} \in \mathbb{G}$ such that $\tilde{g}^2 = 1_\mathbb{G}$ would then not be excluded by the protocol.

Properties. Damgård and Fujisaki's scheme is correct, is computationally binding under the strong-root assumption and the μ-assumption, and is statistically hiding. Its hiding property crucially relies on the fact that $g \in \langle h \rangle$. To guarantee the statistical hiding property of the scheme *without trusted key generation*, the party which computes g is then also required to compute a non-interactive proof that $g \in \langle h \rangle$. The commitment algorithm would then verify the proof and proceed as above if it is valid, and otherwise return $\perp$. Damgård and Fujisaki proposed to compute such a proof with a Schnorr-type protocol with $\{0, 1\}$ as challenge set. To attain a soundness error of at most $1/P$, the proof must then be repeated at least $\lceil \log P \rceil$ times. With the Fiat–Shamir heuristic, each proof consists of (c, z), and the total proof in the public parameters then consists of $\lceil \log P \rceil (b_\mathbb{G} + 2\lambda + 2) = \Omega(b_\mathbb{G} \log P)$ bits (recall that P is super-polynomial in λ, e.g., $\lambda^{\log \lambda}$).

3.2 A New Integer-Commitment Scheme

This section introduces a novel integer-commitment scheme that is close to Damgård and Fujisaki's scheme, but with an argument (rather than a proof) of only $O(b_{\mathbb{G}})$ (with b such that $\mathrm{ord}(\mathbb{G}) \leq 2^{b_{\mathbb{G}}}$) bits in non-trusted keys, and the argument only requires a single protocol run to reach the same soundness error. As the soundness of the protocol relies on computational assumptions on the group generator, the scheme is only computationally hiding, whereas Damgård and Fujisaki's cut-and-choose protocol is perfectly sound (the prover is not assumed to be computationally bounded) but inefficient.

Formally, let G be a group generator and let $FS.\Pi^{\mathcal{H}}$ be a Fiat–Shamir non-interactive argument system with random oracle $\mathcal{H}$ for the language $\{g \in \mathbb{G}, \ell \in \mathbb{N}^* : \exists \alpha \in [\![0; 2^{\ell}]\!], g = h^{\alpha}\}$, given parameters $(\mathbb{G}, P, h, 1)$ (integer 1 is just to indicate that there is only one group element g in the word for which the proof is computed) and the empty string as CRS. The proof of the hiding property will require the protocol to satisfy culpable soundness w.r.t. the language $\sqrt{\langle h^2 \rangle}$. The scheme, parameterized by G and further denoted $\mathscr{C}$, consists of the following algorithms:

$\mathsf{Setup}(1^{\lambda}) \to pp$: run $(\mathbb{G}, P) \leftarrow \mathsf{G}(1^{\lambda})$, generate $h \leftarrow_{\$} \mathbb{G}$ and return $(\mathbb{G}, P, h)$. Recall that these parameters are implicit inputs to all the other algorithms.

$\mathsf{KG}(pp) \to ck$: generate $\alpha \leftarrow_{\$} [\![0; 2^{b_{\mathbb{G}}+\lambda}]\!]$, compute $g \leftarrow h^{\alpha}$ and a proof $\pi \leftarrow FS.\Pi^{\mathcal{H}}.\mathsf{Prove}((\mathbb{G}, P, h, 1), (g, b_{\mathbb{G}} + \lambda), \alpha)$, and return (g, π).

$\mathsf{Com}((g, \pi), x \in \mathbb{Z}) \to (C, d)$: if $FS.\Pi^{\mathcal{H}}.\mathsf{Vf}((\mathbb{G}, P, h, 1), (g, b_{\mathbb{G}}+\lambda), \pi) = 0$, then return $\perp$; else generate $r \leftarrow_{\$} [\![0; 2^{b_{\mathbb{G}}+\lambda}]\!]$, compute $C \leftarrow (g^x h^r)^2$, set $d \leftarrow r$ and return (C, d).

$\mathsf{ComVf}((g, \pi), C, x, d) \to b \in \{0, 1\}$: if $C^2 = \left(g^x h^d\right)^4$ return 1, else return 0.

See the full version [24] for the proofs of correctness and security of the scheme.

Comparison with Damgård–Fujisaki Commitments. As for Damgård and Fujisaki's commitments, the squaring in the verification equation (compared to the computation of commitments) is again to later allow for sound arguments of knowledge of openings. The main difference compared to Damgård and Fujisaki's commitments is that commitments are computed as $(g^x h^r)^2$ instead of $g^x h^r$. It is simply due to the fact that π only guarantees that $g^2 \in \langle h^2 \rangle$, not that $g \in \langle h \rangle$, hence the power 2 in the computation of commitments to ascertain that they are hiding. However, only requiring that $g^2 \in \langle h^2 \rangle$ instead of $g \in \langle h \rangle$ is precisely what allows to have much smaller arguments that can be computed in a single protocol run.

Argument System FS.$\Pi^{\mathcal{H}}$. It only remains to provide a protocol $FS.\Pi^{\mathcal{H}}$ to argue knowledge of an integer $\alpha \in \mathbb{Z}$ such that $g^2 = h^{2\alpha}$, which is sufficient for the commitment scheme to be computationally hiding. We first give an interactive protocol Π for the language $\{g \in \mathbb{G}, \ell \in \mathbb{N}^* : \exists \alpha \in [\![0; 2^{\ell}]\!], g = h^{\alpha}\}$ given parameters $(\mathbb{G}, P) \leftarrow \mathsf{G}(1^{\lambda})$ and that satisfies culpable soundness w.r.t. $\sqrt{\langle h^2 \rangle}$, and then apply the Fiat–Shamir heuristic to obtain $FS.\Pi^{\mathcal{H}}$.

In more detail, the (interactive) protocol Π is as follows: the prover generates $k \leftarrow_\$ [\![0; 2^{\ell+\lambda}P]\!]$, computes $t \leftarrow h^k$ and sends t to the verifier; the verifier chooses $c \leftarrow_\$ [\![0; P-1]\!]$ and sends it to the prover; the prover then replies with $r \leftarrow k - c\alpha$, and the verifier accepts if and only if $h^r g^c = t$. With the Fiat–Shamir heuristic, the proof consists of (c, r), i.e., $2\lfloor \log P \rfloor + \ell + \lambda + 3$ bits. For $\ell = b_{\mathbb{G}} + \lambda$, that is $2\lfloor \log P \rfloor + b_{\mathbb{G}} + 2\lambda + 3 = O(b_{\mathbb{G}})$ bits (recall that $P \leq 2^{b_{\mathbb{G}}}$ and $b_{\mathbb{G}} = \Omega(\lambda)$).

The completeness, statistical honest-verifier zero-knowledge and extractability properties of this protocol are proved in the full version [24].

Arguing Knowledge of Openings. As for Damgård and Fujisaki's commitments, one can efficiently argue knowledge of openings, i.e., of integers x and r such that a given commitment C satisfies $C^2 = (g^x h^r)^4$.

The protocol imposes an upper bound of ℓ on the bit length of the witness, with ℓ being part of the (public) word. It is simply to adapt the randomness range of the prover (and of the honest-verifier zero-knowledge simulator) to ensure that the protocol remains statistically honest-verifier zero-knowledge; and ℓ can be arbitrarily large. The protocol does *not* guarantee that the largest absolute value in the extracted witness is at most ℓ bits long[4]. In technical terms, the protocol is for the relation $\{(C \in \mathbb{G}, \ell \in \mathbb{N}^*; x, r \in [\![0; 2^\ell]\!]) : C^2 = (g^x h^r)^4\}$ that satisfies culpable extractability for the relation $\Sigma := \{(C \in \mathbb{G}, \ell \in \mathbb{N}^*; x, r \in \mathbb{Z}) : C^2 = (g^x h^r)^4\}$.

More precisely, consider the problem of arguing in zero-knowledge knowledge of integers x and r such that $C^2 = (g^x h^r)^4$ and $|x|, |r| \leq 2^\ell$, for a group element C chosen by the prover and public bases h and g, and a public proof π that $g \in \sqrt{\langle h^2 \rangle}$. The prover first verifies π and aborts if it is invalid. The prover generates $y, s \leftarrow_\$ [\![0; P2^{\ell+\lambda}]\!]$, computes and sends $D \leftarrow (g^y h^s)^2$ to the verifier. The verifier then chooses $e \leftarrow_\$ [\![0; P-1]\!]$, sends it to the prover, and this latter replies with $z \leftarrow y - ex$ and $t \leftarrow s - er$ (computed in $\mathbb{Z}$). The verifier then accepts if and only if $(g^z h^t)^2 C^e = D$.

The properties of this protocol are proved in the full version [24].

Multi-integer Commitments. The above commitments can be generalized to vectors of integers just like Damgård–Fujisaki commitments (as Couteau, Peters and Pointcheval did [10]). That is to say, the scheme can be extended to commit to several integers at once.

Formally, let G be a group generator and suppose that there exists a non-interactive argument system $FS.\Pi^{\mathcal{H}}$ with random oracle $\mathcal{H}$ for the language $\{g_1, \ldots, g_n \in \mathbb{G}, \ell \in \mathbb{N}^* : \exists \alpha_1, \ldots, \alpha_n \in [\![0; 2^\ell]\!], \forall i \in [\![n]\!]\ g_i = h^{\alpha_i}\}$ given parameters $(\mathbb{G}, P, h, n)$ and the empty string as CRS.

$\mathsf{Setup}(1^\lambda, n) \rightarrow pp$: run $(\mathbb{G}, P) \leftarrow \mathsf{G}(1^\lambda)$, generate $h \leftarrow_\$ \mathbb{G}$ and return $(\mathbb{G}, P, h, n)$.
$\mathsf{KG}(pp) \rightarrow ck$: generate $\alpha_i \leftarrow_\$ [\![0; 2^{b_{\mathbb{G}}+\lambda}]\!]$ for $i \in [\![n]\!]$, compute $g_i \leftarrow h^{\alpha_i}$ and $\pi \leftarrow FS.\Pi^{\mathcal{H}}.\mathsf{Prove}((\mathbb{G}, P, h, n), (\mathbf{g}, b_{\mathbb{G}} + \lambda), (\alpha_i)_{i=1}^n)$, and return $(\mathbf{g}, \pi)$.

[4] To prove such statements using hidden-order groups, Lipmaa's range argument [19], corrected by Couteau, Peters and Pointcheval [10], is suitable.

$\mathsf{Com}\left((\mathbf{g},\pi), x_1,\ldots,x_n \in \mathbb{Z}\right) \rightarrow (C,d)$: if $FS.\Pi^{\mathcal{H}}.\mathsf{Vf}((\mathbb{G},P,h,n),(\mathbf{g},b_{\mathbb{G}}+\lambda),\pi)=0$ return $\perp$; generate $r \leftarrow_{\$} [\![0;2^{b_{\mathbb{G}}+\lambda}]\!]$, compute $C \leftarrow \left(\prod_{i=1}^{n} g_i^{x_i} h^r\right)^2$, set $d \leftarrow r$ and return (C,d).

$\mathsf{ComVf}\left((\mathbf{g},\pi), C, x_1,\ldots,x_n, d\right) \rightarrow b \in \{0,1\}$: if $C^2 = \left(\prod_i g_i^{x_i} h^d\right)^4$ return 1, else return 0.

The only missing component is an interactive protocol Π that satisfies culpable soundness w.r.t. $\{g_1,\ldots,g_n \in \mathbb{G}\colon \exists \alpha_1,\ldots,\alpha_n \in \mathbb{Z}, \forall i \in [\![n]\!]\, g_i^2 = h^{2\alpha_i}\}$. A possible solution is to run n times in parallel the protocol from the case $n=1$ for each of the α_i values. However, they achieve an overall $2^{-\lambda}$ statistical distance from n simulated arguments, the range of the prover's randomness in the protocol must be multiplied by n so that each argument is $2^{-\lambda}n^{-1}$-zero-knowledge. A better solution is to use the protocol presented in the full version [24, Section 5.3], which results in arguments of $O(b_{\mathbb{G}}+\log n)$ bits. This should be compared to the $\Omega(nb_{\mathbb{G}}\log P)$-bit parameters of the generalized Damgård–Fujisaki commitments.

4 Succinct Inner-Product Arguments on Integers

This section gives a statistically honest-verifier zero-knowledge, logarithmic-size inner-product argument on integers committed in hidden-order groups with the scheme from Sect. 3.2. That is, an argument of knowledge of vectors $\mathbf{a}$ and $\mathbf{b} \in \mathbb{Z}^n$, and of a randomness $r \in \mathbb{Z}$ such that $C^2 = \left(\mathbf{g}^{\mathbf{a}}\mathbf{h}^{\mathbf{b}}f^r\right)^4$ and $\langle \mathbf{a},\mathbf{b}\rangle = z$ given public bases $\mathbf{g}$ and $\mathbf{h}$, a public commitment C and a public integer z; and the bit-communication complexity of the protocol is logarithmic in of order $O(\ell+\log nb_{\mathbb{G}})$ where ℓ is an upper-bound on the bit length of the largest integer witness and $2^{b_{\mathbb{G}}}$ an upper-bound on the order of the group.

4.1 Formal Description

This section formalizes the protocol and states the properties it satisfies.

Relations. The protocol is an honest-verifier zero-knowledge argument for

$$\mathcal{R} := \left\{(C \in \mathbb{G}, z \in \mathbb{Z}, \ell \in \mathbb{N}^*; \mathbf{a},\mathbf{b} \in \mathbb{Z}^n, r \in \mathbb{Z}) : C^2 = \left(\mathbf{g}^{\mathbf{a}}\mathbf{h}^{\mathbf{b}}f^r\right)^4 \wedge \langle \mathbf{a},\mathbf{b}\rangle = z \wedge \left\|[\mathbf{a}\ \mathbf{b}\ r]\right\|_\infty < 2^\ell\right\}$$

given parameters $(\mathbb{G},P,f,n)$ with $f \in \mathbb{G}$ and $n \in \mathbb{N}^*$, and $(\mathbf{g},\mathbf{h},\pi_{crs}) \in \mathbb{G}^{2n} \times \{0,1\}^*$ as CRS.

The relation imposes the largest value (in absolute value) in the witness $[\mathbf{a}\ \mathbf{b}\ r]$ to be at most ℓ bits long, with ℓ being part of the (public) word. As for the argument of knowledge of openings in Sect. 3.2, it is again to adapt the randomness range of the prover and of the honest-verifier zero-knowledge simulator to make sure that the protocol remains statistically honest-verifier zero-knowledge; and ℓ can be arbitrarily large. However, the protocol does not necessarily return a witness with integers of at most ℓ bits in absolute value. In other words, the protocol satisfies culpable extractability w.r.t. the relation

$$\Sigma := \left\{(C \in \mathbb{G}, z \in \mathbb{Z}, \ell \in \mathbb{N}^*; \mathbf{a}, \mathbf{b} \in \mathbb{Z}^n, r \in \mathbb{Z}) : C^2 = \left(\mathbf{g}^{\mathbf{a}}\mathbf{h}^{\mathbf{b}} f^r\right)^4 \wedge \langle \mathbf{a}, \mathbf{b} \rangle = z\right\}.$$

The argument for $\mathcal{R}$ is actually reduced to a logarithm-size argument (given on Fig. 2) for the following relation in which the inner product is also committed:

$$\mathcal{R}' := \left\{(C \in \mathbb{G}, \ell \in \mathbb{N}^*; \mathbf{a}, \mathbf{b} \in \mathbb{Z}^n, r \in \mathbb{Z}) : C^2 = \left(\mathbf{g}^{\mathbf{a}}\mathbf{h}^{\mathbf{b}} e^{\langle \mathbf{a}, \mathbf{b} \rangle} f^r\right)^4 \wedge \left\|[\mathbf{a}\ \mathbf{b}\ r]\right\|_\infty < 2^\ell\right\}$$

given parameters $(\mathbb{G}, P, f, n)$ with $f \in \mathbb{G}$ and $n \in \mathbb{N}^*$, and $(\mathbf{g}, \mathbf{h}, e, \pi_{crs}) \in \mathbb{G}^{2n+1} \times \{0,1\}^*$ as CRS. Again, the protocol does not guarantee that the extracted witness satisfies the bounds on its bit length – denote by Σ' the relation defined as $\mathcal{R}'$ without the restriction on the size of the witness.

During the reduction, the verifier chooses a base $e \in \langle f \rangle$ and proves to the prover that e is in $\sqrt{\langle f^2 \rangle}$, which guarantees to the prover that the commitment Ce^{2z} remains hiding. (As explained in Sect. 3, this precaution is not needed in groups of public prime orders.) However, since the protocol in Sect. 3.2 is only honest-verifier, and the extractability of the argument system partly relies on the fact that the prover does not know a discrete-logarithm relation between e and f, the verifier must compute a non-interactive argument with a random oracle. In other words, the extractability of the argument relies on the zero-knowledge property of the protocol in Sect. 3.2. Moreover, the CRS of the protocol includes a proof that $\mathbf{g}$ and $\mathbf{h}$ are in $\sqrt{\langle f^2 \rangle}^n$, and the argument is only guaranteed to be honest-verifier zero-knowledge if it is indeed the case; that is, the zero-knowledge property of the argument relies on the soundness of the protocol. This mirroring in the properties of two protocols is simply due to the fact that at the beginning of the inner-product argument, the prover becomes the verifier of the protocol for $\mathbf{g}, \mathbf{h} \in \sqrt{\langle f^2 \rangle}^n$.

Main Insights. The goal is to have a protocol for $\mathcal{R}'$ in which the prover sends only $2\lceil \log n \rceil + 2$ group elements and three integers of at most $O(\ell + b_\mathbb{G} + \log(n)\log(P))$ bits. The main idea is to have the prover first send a constant number of commitments that depend on the witness vectors (which are in $\mathbb{Z}^n$), so that the verifier can thereafter choose *integer* linear combinations (defined by an integer x) of the witness vectors that are of length $n/2$ (to ease the explanation, further assume n to be a power of 2 in this section). These new vectors then serve as witness for a new commitment derived from the original commitment on which the proof is computed, the commitments sent by the prover and x; in bases of length $n/2$ and determined by the original bases and x. The prover and the verifier can thus recursively run the protocol with vectors of length $n/2$. After $\log n$ recursive calls, the vectors are of length 1, and the parties run a protocol that two committed integers a and b satisfy $ab = z$ for a public z.

In more detail, given $\mathbf{a}, \mathbf{b} \in \mathbb{Z}^n$ and $r \in \mathbb{Z}$ such that $C^2 = \left(\mathbf{g}^{\mathbf{a}}\mathbf{h}^{\mathbf{b}}e^{\langle \mathbf{a},\mathbf{b}\rangle}f^r\right)^4$, the prover first sends commitments $U \leftarrow \left(\mathbf{g}_1{}^{\mathbf{a}_2}\mathbf{h}_2{}^{\mathbf{b}_1}e^{\langle \mathbf{a}_2,\mathbf{b}_1\rangle}f^{s_u}\right)^2$ and $V \leftarrow \left(\mathbf{g}_2{}^{\mathbf{a}_1}\mathbf{h}_1{}^{\mathbf{b}_2}\right.$ $\left.e^{\langle \mathbf{a}_1,\mathbf{b}_2\rangle}f^{s_v}\right)^2$, for s_u and s_v with uniform distribution over an integer set large enough for the commitments to be hiding. The verifier chooses $x \leftarrow_\$ [\![0; P-1]\!]$, sends it to the prover, and this latter computes $\mathbf{a}' \leftarrow \mathbf{a}_1 + x\mathbf{a}_2$, $\mathbf{b}' \leftarrow x\mathbf{b}_1 + \mathbf{b}_2$ and $t \leftarrow s_v + rx + s_u x^2$. Note that all these operations are performed in $\mathbb{Z}$ and do not require to invert any integer. Now note that

$$\left(\left(\mathbf{g}_1^x \circ \mathbf{g}_2\right)^{\mathbf{a}'}\left(\mathbf{h}_1 \circ \mathbf{h}_2^x\right)^{\mathbf{b}'} e^{\langle \mathbf{a}',\mathbf{b}'\rangle} f^t\right)^4 = \left(U^{x^2}C^xV\right)^2,$$

which means that the prover and verifier can run the protocol again with $\mathbf{g}_1^x \circ \mathbf{g}_2$ and $\mathbf{h}_1 \circ \mathbf{h}_2^x$ as bases and $\mathbf{a}'$ and $\mathbf{b}'$ (all of size $n/2$ instead of n) as witness for $U^{x^2}C^xV$.

To understand how a witness consisting of integer vectors can be extracted, suppose that one can obtain three transcripts $\left(U, V, x_j, \mathbf{a}'_j, \mathbf{b}'_j, t'_j\right)_{i=1}^3$ such that

$$\left(\left(\mathbf{g}_1{}^{x_j} \circ \mathbf{g}_2\right)^{\mathbf{a}'_j}\left(\mathbf{h}_1 \circ \mathbf{h}_2{}^{x_j}\right)^{\mathbf{b}'_j} e^{\left\langle \mathbf{a}'_j,\mathbf{b}'_j\right\rangle} f^{t_j}\right)^4 = \left(U^{x_j^2}C^{x_j}V\right)^2$$

for all $j \in [\![3]\!]$. The goal is to find a representation of C in the bases $\mathbf{g}$, $\mathbf{h}$, e and f. To do so, consider the linear system:

$$\mathbf{X}\begin{bmatrix} v_1 \\ v_2 \\ v_3 \end{bmatrix} = \begin{bmatrix} 0 \\ 1 \\ 0 \end{bmatrix} \text{ for } \mathbf{X} := \begin{bmatrix} 1 & 1 & 1 \\ x_1 & x_2 & x_3 \\ x_1^2 & x_2^2 & x_3^2 \end{bmatrix} \text{ and indeterminate } \begin{bmatrix} v_1 \\ v_2 \\ v_3 \end{bmatrix}.$$

It does not necessarily have a solution in $\mathbb{Z}^3$ (and this is the first major difference with Bulletproofs in groups with public prime orders). However, denoting by $\operatorname{adj}(\mathbf{X})$ the adjugate matrix of $\mathbf{X}$ (which is in $\mathbb{Z}^{3\times 3}$), the column vector

$$v_C := \operatorname{adj}(\mathbf{X})\begin{bmatrix} 0 \\ 1 \\ 0 \end{bmatrix} \text{ satisfies } \mathbf{X}v_C = \mathbf{X}\operatorname{adj}(\mathbf{X})\begin{bmatrix} 0 \\ 1 \\ 0 \end{bmatrix} = \begin{bmatrix} 0 \\ \det(\mathbf{X}) \\ 0 \end{bmatrix}$$

since $\mathbf{X}\operatorname{adj}(\mathbf{X}) = \det(\mathbf{X})\mathbf{I}_3$. Therefore, via linear combinations with coefficient determined by v_C, one can obtain $\mathbf{a}_C, \mathbf{b}_C \in \mathbb{Z}^n$ and $z_C, r_C \in \mathbb{Z}$ such that $U^{2\det \mathbf{X}} = \left(\mathbf{g}^{\mathbf{a}_C}\mathbf{h}^{\mathbf{b}_C}e^{z_C}f^{r_C}\right)^4$. If the challenges x_1, x_2, x_3 are pairwise distinct, then $\det \mathbf{X} \neq 0$, and Lemma 4.2 shows that under the assumptions on the group generator, $2\det \mathbf{X}$ must divide (with overwhelming probability) $4z_C$, $4r_C$ and each of the components of $4\mathbf{a}_C$, $4\mathbf{b}_C$. Therefore, up to a relabeling of $2\mathbf{a}_C/\det \mathbf{X}$ and so on, one can extract $\mathbf{a}_C, \mathbf{b}_C \in \mathbb{Z}^n$ and $z_C, r_C \in \mathbb{Z}$ such that $U = \left(\mathbf{g}^{\mathbf{a}_C}\mathbf{h}^{\mathbf{b}_C}e^{z_C}f^{r_C}\right)^2\tilde{g}_C$ for $\tilde{g}_C \in \mathbb{G}$ that satisfies $\tilde{g}_C^2 = 1_{\mathbb{G}}$.

Nonetheless, it is not yet certain that $z_C = \langle \mathbf{a}_C, \mathbf{b}_C \rangle$. To guarantee it, it suffices to extract similar representations for U and V, and replacing U, C and V by those representations in the equality $\left((\mathbf{g}_1^x \circ \mathbf{g}_2)^{\mathbf{a}'} (\mathbf{h}_1 \circ \mathbf{h}_2^x)^{\mathbf{b}'} e^{\langle \mathbf{a}', \mathbf{b}' \rangle} f^t\right)^4 = \left(U^{x^2} C^x V\right)^2$ for any $x \in \{x_1, x_2, x_3\}$. This leads to a discrete-logarithm relation $1_{\mathbb{G}} = \mathbf{g}_1{}^{p_{\mathbf{g}_1}(x)} \mathbf{g}_2{}^{p_{\mathbf{g}_2}(x)} \mathbf{h}_1{}^{p_{\mathbf{h}_1}(x)} \mathbf{h}_2{}^{p_{\mathbf{h}_2}(x)} e^{p_e(x)} f^{p_f(x)}$ with $p_{\mathbf{g}_1}, p_{\mathbf{g}_2}, p_{\mathbf{h}_1}, p_{\mathbf{h}_2}, p_e, p_f$ polynomials in $\mathbb{Z}[x]$ of degree at most 2. Lemma 4.3 essentially states that it is hard to find discrete-logarithm relations in the subgroup generated by a group element $f \leftarrow_\$ \mathbb{G}$ (this is the second main difference with Bulletproofs in groups with public prime orders). It thus implies that if the bases are all in $\langle f \rangle$ with exponents chosen uniformly at random over a large integer set, these polynomials must all be zero (with overwhelming probability) when evaluated at x; and $p_{\mathbf{g}_1}, p_{\mathbf{h}_2}$ and p_e together lead to an integer polynomial of degree 4, with leading coefficient $z_C - \langle \mathbf{a}_c, \mathbf{b}_C \rangle$, which must then be nil when evaluated at x. Therefore, starting with five accepting transcripts instead of three entails that this polynomial of degree 4 must be nil and thus $z_C = \langle \mathbf{a}_c, \mathbf{b}_C \rangle$, i.e., $\mathbf{a}_C, \mathbf{b}_C \in \mathbb{Z}^n, r_C \in \mathbb{Z}$ is a valid witness for C.

As for the zero-knowledge property of the scheme, the ranges of s_u and s_v at each of the $\log n$ recursion step are chosen so that the statistical distance of (U, V) to a pair of uniform values in $\langle f^2 \rangle$ is at most $\left(\log(n) 2^\lambda\right)^{-1}$. It then remains to compute an upper-bound on the bit length of the witness at the last step of the protocol so that the randomness of the prover can be chosen from a set of which the bit length is λ times larger. The calculation is detailed in the proof of the zero-knowledge property presented in the full version [24].

Protocol Algorithms. The argument system for relation $\mathcal{R}$ is further denoted Π. It uses as building blocks a group generator G and the Fiat–Shamir non-interactive variant $FS.\tilde{\Pi}^{\mathcal{H}}$ with a random oracle $\mathcal{H}$ of a protocol $\tilde{\Pi}$ for the language $\left\{(\mathbf{g}, \mathbf{h}) \in \mathbb{G}^{2n} : \exists \alpha, \beta \in \mathbb{Z}^{2n}, \forall i \in [\![n]\!]\, g_i = f^{\alpha_i} \wedge h_i = f^{\beta_i}\right\}$ given parameters $(\mathbb{G}, P, f, 2n)$ and the empty string as CRS. Protocol $\tilde{\Pi}^{\mathcal{H}}$ is later assumed to satisfy culpable soundness w.r.t. the language $\left\{(\mathbf{g}, \mathbf{h}) \in \mathbb{G}^{2n} : \exists \alpha, \beta \in \mathbb{Z}^{2n}, \forall i \in [\![n]\!]\, g_i^2 = f^{2\alpha_i} \wedge h_i^2 = f^{2\beta_i}\right\}$. The protocol algorithms are then as follows:

- Π.$\mathsf{Setup}\left(1^\lambda, n \in \mathbb{N}^*\right)$ runs $(\mathbb{G}, P') \leftarrow \mathsf{G}\left(1^\lambda\right)$, computes $P := \left\lfloor P'^{1/3} \right\rfloor$ (the power 1/3 is to ensure extractability under the assumptions on the group generator), generates $f \leftarrow_\$ \mathbb{G}$ and returns $pp \leftarrow (\mathbb{G}, P, n, f)$ as public parameters.
- Π.$\mathsf{CRSGen}(pp)$ generates $\alpha_i, \beta_i \leftarrow_\$ [\![0; 2^{b_{\mathbb{G}}+2\lambda}]\!]$ for $i \in [\![n]\!]$, computes $g_i \leftarrow f^{\alpha_i}$, $h_i \leftarrow f^{\beta_i}$ and $\pi_{crs} \leftarrow FS.\tilde{\Pi}^{\mathcal{H}}.\mathsf{Prove}((\mathbb{G}, P, f, 2n), (\mathbf{g}, \mathbf{h}), \alpha, \beta)$, and returns $(\mathbf{g}, \mathbf{h}, \pi_{crs})$.
- Π.Prove and Π.Vf are as on Fig. 1. They run as sub-routines the proving and verification algorithms of a protocol Π' for relation $\mathcal{R}'$. Algorithms Π'.Prove and Π'.Vf additionally take as input a variable i which keeps track of the recursion depth during the protocol execution to adjust the randomness of the prover.

$\mathcal{P}(n, f, \mathbf{g}, \mathbf{h}, \pi_{crs}, C, z, \ell; \mathbf{a}, \mathbf{b}, r)$		$\mathcal{V}(n, f, \mathbf{g}, \mathbf{h}, \pi_{crs}, C, z, \ell)$
	$C^2 = \left(\mathbf{g}^{\mathbf{a}}\mathbf{h}^{\mathbf{b}} f^r\right)^4 \wedge \langle \mathbf{a}, \mathbf{b}\rangle = z \wedge \left\|[\mathbf{a}\ \mathbf{b}\ r]\right\|_\infty < 2^\ell$	
		if $FS.\tilde{\Pi}^{\mathcal{H}}.\mathsf{Vf}((\mathbb{G}, P, f, 2n), (\mathbf{g}, \mathbf{h}), \pi_{crs}) = 0$ then return $\perp$
		$\alpha \leftarrow_\$ [\![0; 2^{b+2\lambda}]\!]$; $e \leftarrow f^\alpha$
		$\pi \leftarrow FS.\tilde{\Pi}^{\mathcal{H}}.\mathsf{Prove}((\mathbb{G}, P, f, 1), e, \alpha)$
	$\xleftarrow{e, \pi}$	
if $FS.\tilde{\Pi}^{\mathcal{H}}.\mathsf{Vf}((\mathbb{G}, P, f, 1), e, \pi) = 0$ then return $\perp$		
run the protocol on Figure 2 on input $(1, n, f, \mathbf{g}, \mathbf{h}, e, C_1 := Ce^{2z}, \ell; \mathbf{a}, \mathbf{b}, r)$		

Fig. 1. Inner-Product Argument on Integers.

Prover-Communication Complexity. Throughout the protocol, the prover sends $2n' + 2$ group elements (with $n' = \lceil \log n \rceil$), two integers ($a'$ and b') less than $2^\ell P^{n'}$ in absolute value and an integer (u) less than $\left(2n' 2^{b_{\mathbb{G}}+\lambda} P^{n'+3} + 2^\ell (P-1)^{n'+2}\right)\left(1 + 2^\lambda\right)$ in absolute value. The bit communication complexity of the prover is then of order $O\left(\ell + \log(n)(b_{\mathbb{G}} + \log P) + \lambda + \max\left(\log\log n + b_{\mathbb{G}} + \lambda, \ell\right)\right)$. Since $\log P \leq b_{\mathbb{G}} = \Omega(\lambda)$, that is $O\left(\ell + \log(n) b_{\mathbb{G}} + \max\left(\log\log n + b_{\mathbb{G}}, \ell\right)\right)$, or even $O\left(\ell + \log(n) b_{\mathbb{G}}\right)$ bits (n is here assumed to be greater than 1).

Verification via a Single Multi-exponentiation. As described on Fig. 2, the verifier computes a new commitment $U_i^{x_i^2} C_i^{x_i} V_i$, and new vectors $\mathbf{g}_1^{x_i} \circ \mathbf{g}_2$ and $\mathbf{h}_1 \circ \mathbf{h}_2^{x_i}$ at each recursion step i. In total, the verifier then has to compute $n' := \lceil \log n \rceil$ 3-exponentiations with exponents less than P^2 and two $\lceil n 2^{-i} \rceil$-exponentiations with exponents less than P for $i = 0, \ldots, n'-1$. At the last stage of the protocol, the verifier also has to check that $\left(g^{x_{n'+1} a'} h^{x_{n'+1} b'} e^{a'b'} f^u\right)^4 = \left(C_{n'+1}^{x_{n'+1}^2} \Gamma^{x_{n'+1}} \Delta\right)^2$, i.e., a 7-exponentiation with exponents (in absolute value) less than the bit length of the largest exponent.

Alternatively, the verifier could simply generate the challenges after receiving the U_i and V_i values, delay its verification to the last stage of the protocol and then do a single multi-exponentiation. As shown below, this multi-exponentiation is a $(2n + 2n' + 5)$-exponentiation, which results in computational savings in practice since computing a k-exponentiation with ℓ-bit exponents requires ℓ group operations with a pre-computed table of 2^k group elements following classical sliding-window methods [1], which is much faster than computing k separate single exponentiations with ℓ-bit exponents (which requires $k\ell$ group operations with a single group element in memory) and multiplying the result[5].

[5] If n is large, then the pre-computation might be prohibitively long with the standard multi-exponentiation method, in which case one would rather split the multi-exponentiation in small batches. In any case, delaying the verification until the last step already has the benefit of eliminating latency in the verification.

$\mathcal{P}(i, n, f, \mathbf{g}, \mathbf{h}, e, C_i, \ell; \mathbf{a}, \mathbf{b}, r)$		$\mathcal{V}(i, n, f, \mathbf{g}, \mathbf{h}, e, C_i, \ell)$

$$C_i^2 = \left(\mathbf{g}^{\mathbf{a}}\mathbf{h}^{\mathbf{b}} e^{\langle \mathbf{a},\mathbf{b}\rangle} f^r\right)^4 \wedge \|[\mathbf{a}\ \mathbf{b}\ r]\|_\infty < 2^\ell$$

if $n = 1$

$\alpha, \beta \leftarrow_\$ [\![0; 2^{\ell+\lambda} P^i]\!]$
$s \leftarrow_\$ [\![0; 2(i-1)2^{b_{\mathbb{G}}+\lambda}]\!]$
$t \leftarrow_\$ [\![0; 2(i-1)2^{b_{\mathbb{G}}+2\lambda} P^{i+2} + 2^{\ell+\lambda}(P-1)^{i+1}]\!]$
Replace $i-1$ by 1 if $i = 1$
$\Gamma \leftarrow \left(g^\alpha h^\beta e^{\alpha b + a\beta} f^s\right)^2$
$\Delta \leftarrow \left(e^{\alpha\beta} f^t\right)^2$

$\xrightarrow{\Gamma, \Delta}$

$x_i \leftarrow_\$ [\![0; P-1]\!]$

$\xleftarrow{x_i}$

$a' \leftarrow \alpha + a x_i$
$b' \leftarrow \beta + b x_i$
$u \leftarrow t + s x_i + r x_i^2$

$\xrightarrow{a', b', u}$

$$\left(g^{x_i a'} h^{x_i b'} e^{a'b'} f^u\right)^4 \stackrel{?}{=} \left(C_i^{x_i} \Gamma^{x_i} \Delta\right)^2$$

else

$s_u, s_v \leftarrow_\$ [\![0; 2(\lceil \log n \rceil + i - 1)\, 2^{b_{\mathbb{G}}+\lambda}]\!]$
$U_i \leftarrow \left(\mathbf{g_1}^{\mathbf{a}_2} \mathbf{h_2}^{\mathbf{b}_1} e^{\langle \mathbf{a}_2, \mathbf{b}_1 \rangle} f^{s_u}\right)^2$
$V_i \leftarrow \left(\mathbf{g_2}^{\mathbf{a}_1} \mathbf{h_1}^{\mathbf{b}_2} e^{\langle \mathbf{a}_1, \mathbf{b}_2 \rangle} f^{s_v}\right)^2$

$\xrightarrow{U_i, V_i}$

$x_i \leftarrow_\$ [\![0; P-1]\!]$

$\xleftarrow{x_i}$

$\mathbf{a}' \leftarrow \mathbf{a}_1 + x_i \mathbf{a}_2$
$\mathbf{b}' \leftarrow x_i \mathbf{b}_1 + \mathbf{b}_2$
$t \leftarrow s_v + r x_i + s_u x_i^2$

$$\text{recurse on } \left(i+1,\ \lceil n/2 \rceil,\ f,\ \mathbf{g}_1^{x_i} \circ \mathbf{g}_2,\ \mathbf{h}_1 \circ \mathbf{h}_2^{x_i},\ e,\ C_{i+1} := U_i^{x_i^2} C_i^{x_i} V_i,\ \ell; \mathbf{a}', \mathbf{b}', t\right)$$

Fig. 2. Argument for Relation $\mathcal{R}'$.

In the full version [24], we show that in case n is a power of 2, the verifier then only has to check that

$$\left(\prod_{i=1}^{n} g_i^{\prod_{j\in S_i} x_j}\right)^{4x_{n'+1}a'} \left(\prod_{i=1}^{n} h_i^{\prod_{j\in [\![n]\!]\setminus S_i} x_j}\right)^{4x_{n'+1}b'} e^{4a'b'} f^{4u}$$
$$= \left(U_{n'}^{x_{n'}} \prod_{i=1}^{n'-1} U_i^{x_i x_{i+1}\cdots x_{n'}} C^{x_1\cdots x_{n'}} \prod_{i=1}^{n'-1} V_i^{x_{i+1}\cdots x_{n'}} V_{n'}\right)^{2x_{n'+1}^2} \Gamma^{2x_{n'+1}} \Delta^2,$$

with $S_i := \{j \in [\![n']\!] : n' + 1 - j\text{th bit of } i - 1 \text{ is } 0\}$, i.e., do a $(2n + 2n' + 5)$-exponentiation with exponents (in absolute value) less than

$$4\max\left(2^{\ell} P^{2n'+1}, \overbrace{2^{2\ell} P^{2n'}}^{|a'b'|<}, \overbrace{\left(2n' 2^{b_{\mathbb{G}}+\lambda} P^{n'+1} + 2^{\ell}(P-1)^{n'+2}\right)\left(1+2^{\lambda}\right)}^{|u|<}\right).$$

Verification thus requires $O(\ell + b_{\mathbb{G}} + \log(n)\log(P))$ group operations ($n \geq 2$). We also show how to handle verification with a single multi-exponentiation in case n is not a power of 2 unlike previous work.

4.2 Completeness and Security

In the full version [24], we prove that the protocol is complete, honest-verifier zero-knowledge if $\tilde{\Pi}$ is sound, and that it is extractable under the assumptions on the group generator presented in Sect. 2.2. The proof of extractability is based on Lemma 4.3 and Lemma 4.2, and Lemma 4.2 relies on Lemma 4.1. The proof of Lemmas 4.2 and 4.3 are given in this section as they are the main ingredients of the proof of extractability which differ from those in the case of groups with public prime orders. The proof of Lemma 4.1 relies on elementary arithmetic and is given in full version.

Lemma 4.1. *Let n be a natural integer and let $a_0, \ldots, a_n, b$ and N be integers, with $N \geq 1$. Assuming that the a_i integers are not all nil modulo N, the number of tuples $(x_0, \ldots, x_n) \in \mathbb{Z}_N^{n+1}$ such that $a_0x_0 + \cdots + a_nx_n + b = 0 \bmod N$ is either 0 or $N^n \gcd(a_0, \ldots, a_n, N)$.*

Lemma 4.2. *Consider the problem (depending on λ) of computing, on input $(\mathbb{G}, P) \leftarrow \mathsf{G}(1^{\lambda})$ and $f \leftarrow_{\$} \mathbb{G}$ and $(f^{x_i})_{i=0}^{n}$ (for integers $x_i \leftarrow_{\$} [\![0; 2^{2b_{\mathbb{G}}+\lambda}(n+1)]\!]$) an element $C \in \mathbb{G}$ and integers $a_0, \ldots, a_n, b, \delta$ such that $1 < |\delta| < P$, δ does not divide b or at least one of the a_i integers, and $C^{\delta} = f_0^{a_0} \cdots f_n^{a_n} f^b$.*

Under the $(T^{\mathrm{strg}}, \varepsilon^{\mathrm{strg}})$-strong-root assumption, the $(T^{\mathrm{ord}}, \varepsilon^{\mathrm{ord}})$-small-order assumption, the low-dyadic-valuation assumption and the μ-assumption over G, the probability that any probabilistic algorithm running in time T solves this problem is at most $\left(1/2 - 2^{-\lambda} - (1-\mu)\right)^{-1}\left(\varepsilon^{\mathrm{ord}} + \varepsilon^{\mathrm{strg}} + 1 - \mu\right)$, if T is such that $(n+1)\max(\log(n+1), 1)\log(P) b_{\mathbb{G}} T T_{\mathbb{G}} \leq \Omega\left(\min\left(T^{\mathrm{strg}}, T^{\mathrm{ord}}\right)\right)$.

Proof. Let $\mathcal{A}$ be an algorithm as in the statement of the lemma and assume without loss of generality that $\delta > 0$ (if $\delta < 0$, raise the equality to the power -1). The equality $C^\delta = f_0^{a_0} \cdots f_n^{a_n} f^b$ implies that $C^\delta = f^{\sum_i a_i x_i + b}$. The goal is to show that in case δ does not divide $\sum_i a_i x_i + b$, algorithm $\mathcal{A}$ can be used to violate the assumptions on generator G; and to show that conditioned on the event in which $\mathcal{A}$ solves the problem, the probability that δ divides $\sum_i a_i x_i + b$ is at most $1/2 + 2^{-\lambda} + (1 - \mu)$.

More precisely, if δ does not divide $\sum_i a_i x_i + b$, let $d := \gcd(\delta, \sum_i a_i x_i + b)$ and $u, v \in \mathbb{Z}$ such that $d = u\delta + v(\sum_i a_i x_i + b)$. Then, $f^d = (f^u C^v)^\delta$, i.e., $\left((f^u C^v)^{\delta/d} f^{-1}\right)^d = 1_{\mathbb{G}}$. Since $1 \le d < \delta < P$ by assumption, the small-order assumption over G implies that the element $\tilde{g} := (f^u C^v)^{\delta/d} f^{-1}$ is such that $\tilde{g}^2 = 1_{\mathbb{G}}$ with probability at least $\varepsilon^{\mathrm{ord}}$. If $\tilde{g} = 1_{\mathbb{G}}$ and $d > 1$, then $\left((f^u C^v)^{\delta/d}, d\right)$ is a solution to the strong-root problem. Otherwise,

* if δ/d is odd, then $\tilde{g}^{\delta/d} = \tilde{g}$ and therefore, $(f^u C^v \tilde{g}, \delta/d)$ is a solution to the strong-root problem
* if δ/d is even, then the low-dyadic-valuation assumption on orders implies that $\mathrm{ord}\left((f^u C^v)^{\delta/d}\right)$ is odd, which is impossible if $\mathrm{ord}(f)$ is P-rough (and thus odd) since $\mathrm{ord}(f\tilde{g}) = 2\,\mathrm{ord}(f)$ in this case.

Consequently, δ does not divide $\sum_i a_i x_i + b$ with probability at most $\varepsilon^{\mathrm{ord}} + \varepsilon^{\mathrm{strg}} + 1 - \mu$.

Since $|a_i|, |b| \le 2^{O(T)}$, $\sum_i a_i x_i + b$ can be computed in time $O\left((n+1)T(b_{\mathbb{G}} + \log(n+1))\right)$. Then, u and v can be computed in time $O((T + b_{\mathbb{G}} + \log(n+1)) \log P)$ with the extended Euclidean algorithm as $|\sum_i a_i x_i + b| \le n(n+1)2^{O(T)} 2^{2b_{\mathbb{G}} + \lambda} + 2^{O(T)}$ and $|\delta| \le P$; and u and v are such that $|u|, |v| \le \max\left(|\delta|, |\sum_i a_i x_i + b|\right)/d$. Besides, computing δ/d can be done in time $O\left(\log^2 P\right)$ and then $f^u C^v \tilde{g}$ in $O\left(\max\left(T + b_{\mathbb{G}} + \log(n+1), \log P\right)\right) = O\left(T + b_{\mathbb{G}} + \log(n+1)\right)$ group operations since $P \le 2^{b_{\mathbb{G}}}$. The solution to the strong-root problem can thus be computed in time $O\left((n+1)(b_{\mathbb{G}} + \log(n+1))T + (T + b_{\mathbb{G}} + \log(n+1)) \log(P) T_{\mathbb{G}}\right)$, after the bases $f_0, \ldots, f_n$ have been computed in $O((n+1)\max(\log(n+1), 1) b_{\mathbb{G}})$ group operations.

It remains to show that δ divides $\sum_i a_i x_i + b$ with probability at most $1/2 + 2^{-\lambda} + 1 - \mu$ conditioned on the event in which $\mathcal{A}$ solves the problem. To do so, consider the event in which it occurs. Let p and j respectively be a prime and a positive integer such that p^j divides δ and p^j does not divide b or at least one of the a_i integers. Such p and j necessarily exist for an assumption of the lemma is that δ does not divide b or at least one of the a_i integers. Note that p^j cannot divide all the a_i integers as it would otherwise divide b as well, since it divides $\sum_i a_i x_i + b$. Moreover, if μ-assumption that there are many rough-order elements in the groups generated by G holds, p does not divide $\mathrm{ord}(f)$. Therefore, if the μ-assumption holds, p^j does not divide $a_i \,\mathrm{ord}(f)$ for some $i \in [\![0; n]\!]$.

For $i \in [\![0;n]\!]$, let $0 \leq \rho_i < \mathrm{ord}(f)$ be the unique integer such that $x_i = \mathrm{ord}(f)\lfloor x_i/\mathrm{ord}(f)\rfloor + \rho_i$, and note that $f^{x_i} = f^{\rho_i}$. Then, $\sum_i a_i x_i + b = \sum_i a_i \mathrm{ord}(f) \lfloor x_i/\mathrm{ord}(f)\rfloor + \sum_i a_i\rho_i + b = 0 \bmod p^j$ and $a_i \mathrm{ord}(f) \neq 0 \bmod p^j$ for some $i \in [\![0;n]\!]$. Lemma 4.1 shows that the equation $\sum_i A_i X_i + B = 0 \bmod p^j$ with $A_i := a_i \mathrm{ord}(f)$ and $B := \sum_i a_i\rho_i + b$ has at most $p^{jn}\gcd\left(a_0 \mathrm{ord}(f), \ldots, a_n \mathrm{ord}(f), p^j\right)$ solutions, and $\gcd\left(a_0 \mathrm{ord}(f), \ldots, a_n \mathrm{ord}(f), p^j\right)$ is at most p^{j-1} since $a_i \mathrm{ord}(f) \neq 0 \bmod p^j$ for some $i \in [\![0;n]\!]$. However, the variables $X_i := \lfloor x_i/\mathrm{ord}(f)\rfloor$ are identically distributed and independent of the values returned by $\mathcal{A}(\mathbb{G}, P, f, f^{\rho_0}, \ldots, f^{\rho_n})$; and their distribution is at a statistical distance of at most $\mathrm{ord}(f)2^{-2b_{\mathbb{G}}-\lambda}(n+1)^{-1} \leq 2^{-b_{\mathbb{G}}-\lambda}(n+1)^{-1}$ from the uniform distribution over $[\![0; \lfloor (n+1)2^{2b_{\mathbb{G}}+\lambda}/\mathrm{ord}(f)\rfloor]\!] \supseteq [\![0;(n+1)2^{b_{\mathbb{G}}+\lambda}]\!]$. Besides, if a variable X is uniformly distributed over the set $[\![0;(n+1)2^{b_{\mathbb{G}}+\lambda}]\!]$, then the distribution of $X \bmod p^j$ is at a statistical distance of at most $p^j 2^{-b_{\mathbb{G}}-\lambda}(n+1)^{-1} \leq (P-1)2^{-b_{\mathbb{G}}-\lambda}(n+1)^{-1}$ from the uniform distribution over $\mathbb{Z}_{p^j}$. The distribution of the random vector $\left[X_0 \bmod p^j \cdots X_n \bmod p^j\right]$ is then at a statistical distance of at most $P2^{-b_{\mathbb{G}}-\lambda} \leq 2^{-\lambda}$ from the uniform distribution over $\mathbb{Z}_{p^j}^{n+1}$. Consequently, the equation $\sum_i a_i x_i + b = 0 \bmod p^j$ can then be satisfied with probability at most $2^{-\lambda} + p^{j(n+1)-1}/\left(p^j\right)^{n+1} \leq 1/2 + 2^{-\lambda}$ and thus, δ divides $\sum_i a_i x_i + b$ with probability at most $1/2 + 2^{-\lambda} + 1 - \mu$.

In summary, denoting by ε the probability that $\mathcal{A}$ solves the problem of the statement of the lemma, $\varepsilon \leq \varepsilon^{\mathrm{ord}} + \varepsilon^{\mathrm{strg}} + 1 - \mu + \left(1/2 + 2^{-\lambda} + 1 - \mu\right)\varepsilon$, which is equivalent to $\varepsilon \leq \left(1/2 - 2^{-\lambda} - (1-\mu)\right)^{-1}\left(\varepsilon^{\mathrm{ord}} + \varepsilon^{\mathrm{strg}} + 1 - \mu\right)$. □

Lemma 4.3. (Discrete-Logarithm Relations). *Let n be a non-negative integer. Consider the problem (depending on λ) of computing, on the input of $(\mathbb{G}, P) \leftarrow \mathsf{G}(1^\lambda)$ and of group elements $f \leftarrow_\$ \mathbb{G}$ and $(f^{x_i})_{i=0}^n$ (for $x_i \leftarrow_\$ [\![0; 2^{2b_{\mathbb{G}}+\lambda}(n+1)]\!]$), integers $a_0, \ldots, a_n, b$ such that $f_0^{a_0} \cdots f_n^{a_n} f^b = 1_{\mathbb{G}}$ although at least one of $a_0, \ldots, a_n, b$ is non-zero. Under the $(T^{\mathrm{strg}}, \varepsilon^{\mathrm{strg}})$-strong-root assumption, the $(T^{\mathrm{ord}}, \varepsilon^{\mathrm{ord}})$-small-order assumption, the low-dyadic-valuation assumption and the μ-assumption over G, the probability that any probabilistic algorithm running in time at most T solves this problem is at most*

$$\varepsilon^{\mathrm{strg}} + \max\left(2^{-b_{\mathbb{G}}-\lambda+1}, \left(1/2 - 2^{-\lambda} - (1-\mu)\right)^{-1}\left(\varepsilon^{\mathrm{ord}} + \varepsilon^{\mathrm{strg}} + 1 - \mu\right)\right)$$

if T is such that $(n+1)\max(\log(n+1), 1)\log(P) b_{\mathbb{G}} T T_{\mathbb{G}} \leq \Omega\left(\min\left(T^{\mathrm{strg}}, T^{\mathrm{ord}}\right)\right)$.

Proof. Let $\mathcal{A}$ be an algorithm as in the statement of the lemma and denote the probability that it solves the problem by ε. If $a_0 = \cdots = a_n = 0$, then $b \neq 0$ by assumption and a lemma in the full version [24, Lemma 3.4] shows that since $f^b = 1_{\mathbb{G}}$, there exists an algorithm that solves the strong-root problem in time at most $T + O(\log b)$ with probability at least ε, and since $b = 2^{O(T)}$, $\varepsilon \leq \varepsilon^{\mathrm{strg}}$. Now turn to the case in which $a_i \neq 0$ for some $i \in [\![0;n]\!]$. If $n = 0$, then $f^{a_0 x_0 + b} = 1_{\mathbb{G}}$ by assumption. Writing x_0 as $x_0 = \mathrm{ord}(f)\lfloor x_0/\mathrm{ord}(f)\rfloor + \rho_0$ for $0 \leq \rho_0 < \mathrm{ord}(f)$, the random variable $X_0 := \lfloor x_0/\mathrm{ord}(f)\rfloor$ is independent of the values returned by $\mathcal{A}(\mathbb{G}, P, f, f^{\rho_0})$, and is at a statistical distance of at most $\mathrm{ord}(f)2^{-2b_{\mathbb{G}}-\lambda} \leq 2^{-b_{\mathbb{G}}-\lambda}$ from the uniform distribution over $[\![0; \lfloor 2^{2b_{\mathbb{G}}+\lambda}/\mathrm{ord}(f)\rfloor]\!] \supseteq [\![0; 2^{b_{\mathbb{G}}+\lambda}]\!]$. However, for $A_0 := a_0 \operatorname{ord}(f)$ and $B := a_0\rho_0 + b$, the equation $A_0 X_0 + B = 0$ in $\mathbb{Z}$ has no solution if $A_0 \nmid B$ and exactly one otherwise. Therefore, the probability that $a_0 x_0 + b = 0$ in $\mathbb{Z}$ is at most $2^{-b_{\mathbb{G}}-\lambda+1}$, and there exists an algorithm that solves the strong-root problem in time at most $O(T)$ with probability at least $\varepsilon - 2^{-b-\mathbb{G}-\lambda+1}$, so $\varepsilon \leq \varepsilon^{\text{strg}} + 2^{-b_{\mathbb{G}}-\lambda+1}$.

If $n > 0$, it suffices to prove that the probability that $f_0^{a_0} \cdots f_n^{a_n} f^b = 1_{\mathbb{G}}$ and $\sum_i a_i x_i + b = 0$ is at most $\left(1/2 - 2^{-\lambda} - (1-\mu)\right)^{-1} \left(\varepsilon^{\text{ord}} + \varepsilon^{\text{strg}} + 1 - \mu\right)$. Then, in case $f^{\sum_i a_i x_i + b} = 1_{\mathbb{G}}$ and $\sum_i a_i x_i + b \neq 0$, a lemma in the full version [24, Lemma 3.4] shows that this probability is at most $\varepsilon^{\text{strg}}$. This then would imply that

$$\varepsilon \leq \varepsilon^{\text{strg}} + \left(1/2 - 2^{-\lambda} - (1-\mu)\right)^{-1} \left(\varepsilon^{\text{ord}} + \varepsilon^{\text{strg}} + 1 - \mu\right).$$

Suppose that $\sum_i a_i x_i + b = 0$ (and $f_0^{a_0} \cdots f_n^{a_n} f^b = 1_{\mathbb{G}}$). Let $d := \gcd(a_0, \ldots, a_n)$ and note that d necessarily divides b. Besides, $\sum_i a_i x_i + b = 0$ if and only if $\sum_i (a_i/d) x_i + (b/d) = 0$ and therefore, we have $f_0^{a_0/d} \cdots f_n^{a_n/d} f^{b/d} = 1_{\mathbb{G}}$ with $\gcd(a_0/d, \ldots, a_n/d) = 1$. However, $1_{\mathbb{G}}^2 = 1_{\mathbb{G}} = f_0^{a_0/d} \cdots f_n^{a_n/d} f^{b/d}$ although the integers a_i/d cannot all be even as they are coprime. Lemma 4.2 then implies that $\sum_i a_i x_i + b = 0$ with probability at most $\left(1/2 - 2^{-\lambda} - (1-\mu)\right)^{-1} \left(\varepsilon^{\text{ord}} + \varepsilon^{\text{strg}} + 1 - \mu\right)$. □

5 Succinct Argument for Diophantine Equations

This section gives a succinct argument to argue satisfiability of Diophantine equations. Although Davis, Putnam, Robinson and Matiyasevich [20] showed that there does not exist an algorithm that can decide whether any Diophantine equation has a solution (thereby giving a negative answer to Hilbert's tenth problem), one can argue in zero-knowledge knowledge of a solution, if a solution is known to the prover, which convinces the verifier that the equation is satisfiable.

Damgård and Fujisaki gave [11, Section 4.2] a protocol to argue, given three commitments C_1, C_2, C_3 computed with their scheme, knowledge of openings x_1, x_2, x_3 such that $x_3 = x_1 x_2$. Therefore, to show the satisfiability of an ν-variate polynomial $\sum_{\mathbf{i} \in \mathbb{N}^\nu} a_{\mathbf{i}} x_1^{i_1} \cdots x_\nu^{i_\nu}$ of total degree δ using their scheme, if the polynomial can be computed in $M(\nu, \delta)$ multiplications, then one would have to compute $2M(\nu, \delta)+1$ integer commitments and compute $M(\nu, \delta)$ multiplication-consistency arguments. As Damgård and Fujisaki's scheme is additively homomorphic, the verifier can verify addition itself.

Computing a monomial $x_1^{i_1} \cdots x_\nu^{i_\nu}$ can be done in at most $\delta - 1$ multiplications since the polynomial is of total degree δ. Without any further restriction on the polynomial than its number of variables ν and its total degree δ, the best bound on the number of multiplications (between variables) one can give is $\delta - 1$ as δ could be less than ν, and all i_k at most 1. Evaluating an ν-variate polynomial of total degree δ thus *a priori* requires $(\delta - 1)\binom{\nu+\delta}{\delta}$ multiplications as such a polynomial has at most $\binom{\nu+\delta}{\delta}$ monomials. This can be improved to $\binom{\nu+\delta}{\delta} - \nu - 1 \leq \binom{\nu+\delta}{\delta}$ multiplications by evaluating all possible monomials (even those which may have coefficient 0) recursively by increasing degree and storing the previous evaluations. There exist more efficient methods for specific polynomials (e.g., recursive Horner's method for polynomials with a small numbers of monomials of large degree) but no better upper-bound on the number of multiplications is known for generic polynomials.

Consider a prover that wants to argue the satisfiability of a (generic) ν-variate polynomial of total degree δ with integer coefficients of absolute value upper-bounded by 2^H for some integer H. The communication complexity of the arguments of the first multiplication gates are of order $\Omega(\log P+\ell+b_{\mathbb{G}})$ if ℓ denotes the maximum bit length of any coordinate in the solution. Since the total degree of the polynomial is δ, the bit length of the witness at the maximum-depth multiplication gates can be as large as $\delta\ell+\log\left(\binom{\nu+\delta}{\delta}\right)H$ and the communication complexity of the argument of the satisfiability of the Diophantine equation (i.e., the proof that the polynomial actually evaluates to 0) is $\Omega\left(\delta\ell+\log\left(\binom{\nu+\delta}{\delta}\right)H+b_{\mathbb{G}}\right)$. The overall communication complexity with Damgård and Fujisaki's scheme is therefore upper-bounded by $O\left(\binom{\nu+\delta}{\delta}\left(\delta\ell+\log\left(\binom{\nu+\delta}{\delta}\right)H+b_{\mathbb{G}}\right)\right)$ and lower-bounded by $\Omega\left(\binom{\nu+\delta}{\delta}(\ell+b_{\mathbb{G}})\right)$ for generic polynomials.

This section shows how to argue the satisfiability of Diophantine equations with a communication complexity of order $O\left(\delta\ell+\min(\nu,\delta)\log(\nu+\delta)\,b_{\mathbb{G}}+H\right)$.

5.1 Arguments via Polynomial-Degree Reductions

Our approach to argue for Diophantine satisfiability is different and is inspired by Skolem's method [23]. The idea is to give a systematic method to turn any polynomial equation to another of degree at most 4 by increasing the number of variables so that the satisfiability of one polynomial implies that of the other. The resulting polynomial is such that its satisfiability is equivalent to the satisfiability (over the integers) of a Hadamard product of the form $\mathbf{a}_L \circ \mathbf{a}_R = \mathbf{a}_O$ and of linear equations with the entries of $\mathbf{a}_L$, $\mathbf{a}_R$ and $\mathbf{a}_O$ as indeterminate. The length of these latter vectors is the number of variables in the resulting polynomial, and if the original polynomial is ν-variate and of total degree at most δ, then the new polynomial has at most $\nu\lfloor\log\delta\rfloor+(\delta-1)\mu$ variables, where $\mu\leq\binom{\nu+\delta}{\delta}$ is the number of monomials in the original polynomial.

On this account, if one can argue for the satisfiability of such Hadamard products and linear constraints, then one can argue for the satisfiability of the original polynomial. In the protocol given in Sect. 5.2, the prover only sends logarithmically many group elements in the length of the vectors in the Hadamard product, and a constant number of integers. The bit length of those integers is upper-bounded by $O\left(\delta\ell+b_{\mathbb{G}}+\min(\nu,\delta)\log(\nu+\delta)\log P+H\right)$ if the bit length of the witness is upper-bounded by ℓ and the bit length of each coefficient of the polynomial is at most H.

Reducing Arbitrary Polynomials to Polynomials of Degree at Most 4. We now give a systematic procedure to reduce any Diophantine equation into an equation of degree at most 4 of which the satisfiability can be reduced to the satisfiability of a Hadamard product and linear constraints; and the Hadamard product and the constraints can be read immediately from the resulting polynomial. The presentation is gradual as it starts with ν-variate affine equations, proceeds with ν-variate Diophantine equations in which the degree in each variable is at most 1, further tackles univariate polynomials of arbitrary degree and then considers arbitrary Diophantine equations. The method applies to every multivariate integer polynomial, but for specific polynomials, more astute techniques could lead to a smaller number of new variables and/or constraints.

Step 1–Affine Equations. Given an integer polynomial $a_1x_1 + \cdots + a_\nu x_\nu + b \in \mathbb{Z}[x_1, \ldots, x_\nu]$, set $\mathbf{a}_O \leftarrow [x_1 \cdots x_\nu]$ and for all $i \in [\![\nu]\!]$, set $\mathbf{a}_{L,i} = 1$ and $\mathbf{a}_{R,i} = x_i$. The equation $a_1x_1 + \cdots + a_\nu x_\nu + b = 0$ is satisfied if and only if $\langle [a_1 \cdots a_\nu], \mathbf{a}_O \rangle = -b$ and $\mathbf{a}_L \circ \mathbf{a}_R = \mathbf{a}_O$. Note that no variable or linear constraint was added to the system of equations.

Step 2–Restricted Diophantine Equations. Consider an integer polynomial $\sum_{\mathbf{i}\in\mathbb{N}^\nu} a_{\mathbf{i}} x_1^{i_1} \cdots x_\nu^{i_\nu} \in \mathbb{Z}[x_1, \ldots, x_\nu]$ of total degree δ s.t. $a_{\mathbf{i}} \neq 0_{\mathbb{Z}} \implies \mathbf{i} \in \{0,1\}^\nu$, i.e., the polynomial is of degree at most 1 in each variable. For all $\mathbf{i} \in \mathbb{N}^\nu \setminus \{0_{\mathbb{N}^\nu}\}$ such that $a_{\mathbf{i}} \neq 0_{\mathbb{Z}}$, let $\{j_1, \ldots, j_{w(\mathbf{i})}\}$ be the subset of $[\![\nu]\!]$ such that $j_1 < \cdots < j_{w(\mathbf{i})}$ and $i_{j_1} = \cdots = i_{w(\mathbf{i})} = 1$, with $w(\mathbf{i})$ denoting the Hamming weight of $\mathbf{i}$ (which is necessarily less than δ). If $w(\mathbf{i}) > 1$, introduce new variables

$$u_{\mathbf{i},1} \leftarrow x_{j_1}x_{j_2}, \quad u_{\mathbf{i},2} \leftarrow u_{\mathbf{i},1}x_{j_3}, \quad \ldots, \quad u_{\mathbf{i},w(\mathbf{i})-1} \leftarrow u_{\mathbf{i},w(\mathbf{i})-2}x_{j_{w(\mathbf{i})}},$$

with the convention that $u_{\mathbf{i},0} := x_{j_1}$. Note that $\sum_{\mathbf{i}\in\mathbb{N}^\nu} a_{\mathbf{i}} x_1^{i_1} \cdots x_\nu^{i_\nu} = 0$ if and only if

$$\sum_{\substack{\mathbf{i}\in\mathbb{N}^\nu :\, a_{\mathbf{i}}\neq 0_{\mathbb{Z}} \\ w(\mathbf{i})>1}} \sum_{k=1}^{w(\mathbf{i})-1} \left(u_{\mathbf{i},k} - u_{\mathbf{i},k-1}x_{j_{k+1}}\right)^2 + \left(\sum_{\mathbf{i}\in\mathbb{N}^\nu} \mathbf{a}_{\mathbf{i}} u_{\mathbf{i},w(\mathbf{i})-1}\right)^2 = 0,$$

with the convention that $u_{0_{\mathbb{N}^\nu},-1} = 1$. This latter polynomial is of degree 4, and the equation is satisfied if and only if the linear equation $\sum_{\mathbf{i}\in\mathbb{N}^\nu} \mathbf{a}_{\mathbf{i}} u_{\mathbf{i},w(\mathbf{i})-1} = 0$ is as well as the constraints $u_{\mathbf{i},k} - u_{\mathbf{i},k-1}x_{j_{k+1}} = 0$. Set then

$$\mathbf{a}_L \leftarrow \left[x_{j_1}\ u_{\mathbf{i},1} \cdots u_{\mathbf{i},w(\mathbf{i})-2}\right]\ \mathbf{a}_R \leftarrow \left[x_{j_2}\ x_{j_3} \cdots x_{j_{w(\mathbf{i})}}\right]\ \mathbf{a}_O \leftarrow \left[u_{\mathbf{i},1}\ u_{\mathbf{i},2} \cdots u_{\mathbf{i},w(\mathbf{i})-1}\right],$$

and introduce the linear constraints $\mathbf{a}_{L,i+1} - \mathbf{a}_{O,i} = 0$ for $i \in \{1, \ldots, w(\mathbf{i}) - 2\}$. The procedure introduces at most $\delta - 1$ new variables and $\delta - 2$ new linear constraints per monomial, and since there are at most $\binom{\nu+\delta}{\delta}$ monomials in an ν-variate polynomial of total degree δ, that is at most $(\delta - 1)\binom{\nu+\delta}{\delta}$ variables and $(\delta - 2)\binom{\nu+\delta}{\delta}$ constraints.

Step 3–Univariate Polynomials. Given a polynomial $Z = a_0 + a_1 x + \cdots + a_\delta x^\delta \in \mathbb{Z}[x]$ of degree $\delta \geq 2$, introduce variables

$$u_1 \leftarrow x^2, \quad u_2 \leftarrow u_1^2, \quad \ldots, \quad u_{\lfloor \log \delta \rfloor} \leftarrow u_{\lfloor \log \delta \rfloor - 1}^2.$$

Now notice that $a_0 + a_1 x + \cdots + a_\delta x^\delta = 0$ if and only if

$$(u_1 - x^2)^2 + \sum_{i=2}^{\lfloor \log \delta \rfloor} (u_i - u_{i-1}^2)^2 + (Z'(x, u_1, \ldots, u_{\lfloor \log \delta \rfloor}))^2 = 0,$$

where $Z'(x, u_1, \ldots, u_{\lfloor \log \delta \rfloor})$ is $\lfloor \log \delta \rfloor + 1$-variate integer polynomial in which the degree of each variable is at most 1, i.e., if and only if $Z'(x, u_1, \ldots, u_{\lfloor \log \delta \rfloor}) = 0$ and the constraints $u_1 - x^2 = 0$ and $u_{i+1} - u_i^2 = 0$ are satisfied.
Since

$$\sum_{i=0}^{\delta} a_i x^i = a_0 + \sum_{k=0}^{\lfloor \log \delta \rfloor} \sum_{i=2^k}^{2^{k+1}-1} a_i x^i = a_0 + \sum_{k=0}^{\lfloor \log \delta \rfloor} \sum_{i=2^k}^{2^{k+1}-1} a_i x^{i_0} u_1^{i_1} \cdots u_{k-1}^{i_{k-1}} u_k,$$

where $i_0, \ldots, i_{k-1}$ is the binary decomposition of i and $a_i := 0$ for $i > \delta$, this give an explicit expression for Z'.

Set then $\mathbf{a}_L \leftarrow \mathbf{a}_R \leftarrow [x \; u_1 \cdots u_{\lfloor \log \delta \rfloor - 1}]$ and $\mathbf{a}_O \leftarrow [u_1 \; u_2 \cdots u_{\lfloor \log \delta \rfloor}]$, and introduce constraints

$$\mathbf{a}_{L,i+1} - \mathbf{a}_{O,i} = \mathbf{a}_{R,i+1} - \mathbf{a}_{O,i} = 0$$

for all $i \in [\![\lfloor \log \delta \rfloor - 1]\!]$.
As the second step shows that the satisfiability of Z' can be reduced to a Hadamard product and linear constraints, the satisfiability of Z can be reduced to a Hadamard product and linear constraints. This procedure introduces $\lfloor \log \delta \rfloor$ new variables and $2(\lfloor \log \delta \rfloor - 1)$ new linear constraints. It is important for Step 4 to remark that the number of monomial of Z' is at most the same as the number of monomials in Z.

Step 4–Arbitrary Diophantine Equations. For any integer polynomial $Z = \sum_{\mathbf{i} \in \mathbb{N}^\nu} a_\mathbf{i} x_1^{i_1} \cdots x_\nu^{i_\nu} \in \mathbb{Z}[x_1, \ldots, x_\nu]$ (for $\nu \geq 2$) of total degree δ, apply Step 3 to Z considering it as a polynomial in $\mathbb{Z}[x_2, \ldots, x_\nu][x_1]$, i.e., a polynomial in x_1 with coefficients in $\mathbb{Z}[x_2, \ldots, x_\nu]$. Let Z' be the resulting polynomial with coefficients in $\mathbb{Z}[x_2, \ldots, x_\nu]$ and of degree at most 1 in each variable as in Step 3. Repeat Step 3 with Z' and variable x_2. After Step 3 has been repeated for each $x_1, \ldots, x_\nu$, at most $\nu \lfloor \log \delta \rfloor$ new variables and $2\nu(\lfloor \log \delta \rfloor - 1)$ new linear constraints have been introduced, the resulting polynomial is of degree at most 1 in all variables and has coefficients in $\mathbb{Z}$. Concerning its total degree, note that during the process, for each monomial $x_1^{i_1} \cdots x_\nu^{i_\nu}$, the term $x_k^{i_k}$ is replaced by at most one variable if $i_k \leq 2$ and by the product of $\log i_k + 1 \leq i_k$ variables if ß$_k > 2$ for all $k \in [\![\nu]\!]$, so the total degree remains at most δ. Now apply then Step 2 to the resulting polynomial.

In summary, the procedure reduces the satisfiability of any polynomial in $\mathbb{Z}[x_1, \ldots, x_\nu]$ of total degree δ with μ monomials ($\mu \leq \binom{\nu+\delta}{\delta}$ necessarily) to the satisfiability of a Hadamard product $\mathbf{a}_L \circ \mathbf{a}_R = \mathbf{a}_O$, with $\mathbf{a}_L$, $\mathbf{a}_R$ and $\mathbf{a}_O$ integer vectors of length at most $\nu\lfloor\log\delta\rfloor + (\delta-1)\mu$, and Q linear constraints of the form

$$\langle \mathbf{w}_{L,q}, \mathbf{a}_L \rangle + \langle \mathbf{w}_{R,q}, \mathbf{a}_R \rangle + \langle \mathbf{w}_{O,q}, \mathbf{a}_O \rangle = c_q$$

for all $q \in [\![Q]\!]$ with $Q \leq 1 + 2\nu(\lfloor\log\delta\rfloor - 1) + (\delta - 2)\mu$ and with $\mathbf{w}_{L,q}, \mathbf{w}_{R,q}, \mathbf{w}_{O,q}$ integer vectors and $c_q \in \mathbb{Z}$. The coefficients of the linear constraints introduced by the procedure are in $\{-1, 0, 1\}$, except for one of which the coefficients are the coefficients of the original polynomial.

Example. As a simple illustration of the procedure, consider the polynomial $2x^3+xy-1$. The procedure introduces new variables $u \leftarrow x^2$, $v \leftarrow xy$ and $w \leftarrow ux$, and the equation $2x^3 + xy - 1 = 0$ is satisfiable if and only if $(u - x^2)^2 + (v - xy)^2 + (w - ux)^2 + (2w + v - 1)^2 = 0$ also is, which allows to write a Hadamard product and linear constraints which are satisfiable if and only if this latter equation is.

Diophantine Equations as Circuits. It is worth noting that any polynomial in $\mathbb{Z}[x_1, \ldots, x_\nu]$ can naturally be viewed as an arithmetic circuit with integer inputs, and addition gates correspond to addition between two integers and similarly for multiplication gates. One could then think of applying the procedure of Bootle et al. [5, Appendix A] to turn the polynomial in a system of linear constraints and a Hadamard product. However, their procedure a priori requires to put matrices in reduced Row-Echelon form, which is not always possible with integer matrices as one cannot divide in $\mathbb{Z}$. We explain how to overcome this obstacle in the full version [24].

In any case, the issue with using this procedure to argue for Diophantine satisfiability is that one cannot readily infer the constraints from the initial polynomial and one must always determine them on a case-by-case basis. Besides, if one uses the circuit directly inferred by the monomials of the polynomial without introducing new variables to decrease its degree (which would amount to modifying the circuit), computing x_1^δ for instance requires $\delta-1$ multiplications instead of $\lfloor\log\delta\rfloor$ as with our method.

5.2 Protocol

Section 5.1 shows how to reduce the satisfiability of any polynomial in $\mathbb{Z}[x_1, \ldots, x_\nu]$ of total degree δ with μ monomials ($\mu \leq \binom{\nu+\delta}{\delta}$ necessarily) to the satisfiability of a Hadamard product $\mathbf{a}_L \circ \mathbf{a}_R = \mathbf{a}_O$, with $\mathbf{a}_L$, $\mathbf{a}_R$ and $\mathbf{a}_O$ integer vectors of length at most $\nu\lfloor\log\delta\rfloor + (\delta - 1)\mu$, and $1 + 2\nu(\lfloor\log\delta\rfloor - 1) + (\delta - 2)\mu$ linear constraints of the form

$$\langle \mathbf{w}_{L,q}, \mathbf{a}_L \rangle + \langle \mathbf{w}_{R,q}, \mathbf{a}_R \rangle + \langle \mathbf{w}_{O,q}, \mathbf{a}_O \rangle = c_q$$

for all $q \in [\![Q]\!]$, with $\mathbf{w}_{L,q}, \mathbf{w}_{R,q}, \mathbf{w}_{O,q}$ integer vectors and $c_q \in \mathbb{Z}$.

To argue for Diophantine satisfiability, it thus suffices to give a protocol protocol such relations. The following protocol is actually for more general relations in which variables of the polynomial can be committed (with the scheme in Sect. 3), which allows to argue on committed values while saving the cost of encoding the commitment scheme as an integer polynomial. More precisely, the protocol is for the relation

$$\Big\{\Big(\mathbf{W}_L, \mathbf{W}_R, \mathbf{W}_O \in \mathbb{Z}^{Q\times n}, \mathbf{W}_V \in \mathbb{Z}^{Q\times m}, \mathbf{V} \in \mathbb{G}^m, \mathbf{c} \in \mathbb{Z}^Q, \ell \in \mathbb{N}^*; \mathbf{a}_L, \mathbf{a}_R, \mathbf{a}_O \in \mathbb{Z}^n, \mathbf{v}, \rho \in \mathbb{Z}^m\Big) :$$
$$\mathbf{a}_L \circ \mathbf{a}_R = \mathbf{a}_O \wedge \mathbf{W}_L \mathbf{a}_L^{\mathrm{T}} + \mathbf{W}_R \mathbf{a}_R^{\mathrm{T}} + \mathbf{W}_O \mathbf{a}_O^{\mathrm{T}} = \mathbf{W}_V \mathbf{v}^{\mathrm{T}} + \mathbf{c}^{\mathrm{T}} \wedge \forall i \in [\![m]\!]\ V_i^2 = \left(e^{v_i} f^{\rho_i}\right)^4\Big\}$$

given parameters $(\mathbb{G}, P, n, Q, m, f)$ such that $f \in \mathbb{G}$ and $n, Q, m \in \mathbb{N}^*$, and $(\mathbf{g}, \mathbf{h}, \pi_{crs}) \in \mathbb{G}^{2n} \times \{0,1\}^*$. For fixed parameters n, Q and m, Sect. 5.1 shows that the protocol allows to prove the satisfiability of any polynomial in $\mathbb{Z}[X_1, \ldots, X_\nu]$ of total degree δ and with μ monomials if $\nu\lfloor \log\delta \rfloor + (\delta-1)\mu \leq n$ and $1 + 2\nu(\lfloor\log\delta\rfloor - 1) + (\delta-2)\mu + m \leq Q$. The additional term m in the number of constraints compared to the previous section is to ensure the consistency between the committed variables $\mathbf{v}$ and the ones in the inner product.

Bünz et al. [6] gave a protocol for a similar relation in $\mathbb{Z}_p$ instead of $\mathbb{Z}$ to argue for the satisfiability of arithmetic circuits over $\mathbb{Z}_p$ (without the bounds related to integer polynomials as it was not their target) that is inspired by the one of Bootle et al. [5]. The general idea of our protocol for this relation is similar to the two previous ones, but there are key differences that arise from the fact that $\mathbb{Z}$ is not a field. The full version [24] gives details about the construction of the protocol. The main differences with that of Bünz et al. is that (1) one cannot send integers in the protocol as they may contain information about the witness (2) the polynomials $l(X)$ and $r(X)$ are different and of higher degree again because $\mathbb{Z}$ is not a field and (3) the commitment-key switching techniques used in their protocol is not applicable because the group order is unknown.

Building Blocks. The protocol builds mainly on the protocol on Fig. 2, and on three auxiliary protocols: a protocol Π_{crs} to prove that the CRS is well-formed [24, Section 5.3], a protocol Π' to aggregate arguments of opening to integer commitments [24, Section 5.2] and a protocol $\tilde{\Pi}$ to argue knowledge of an integer vector that opens to commitments in different bases [24, Section 5.4], i.e., a base-switching argument. These arguments may be in the random-oracle model with an oracle $\mathcal{H}$.

Protocol Algorithms. The protocol is denoted Π. The parameter-generation algorithm and the CRS generator are as in Sect. 4.1. The algorithms of the prover and the verifier are given on Fig. 3. On that figure, $\mathbf{W}$ denotes the matrix $\left[\mathbf{W}_L\ \mathbf{W}_R\ \mathbf{W}_O\ \mathbf{W}_V\right]$. The values ℓ', $\tilde{\ell}$ and ℓ_2 are given in Sect. 5.2.

Prover-Communication Complexity. In the full version [24], we show that the prover sends $O(\ell + \log(n)b_{\mathbb{G}} + \log Q + \log m + \log \|W\|_\infty)$ bits during the protocol (the term $\log m$ disappears in case $m = 0$). Therefore, for a polynomial in $\mathbb{Z}[X_1, \ldots, X_\nu]$ of total degree δ, with μ monomials and with coefficients less than 2^H in absolute value, assuming that $\nu\lfloor\log\delta\rfloor + (\delta-1)\mu \leq n$ and that $1 + 2\nu(\lfloor\log\delta\rfloor - 1) + (\delta-2)\mu + m \leq Q$, the

$\mathcal{P}\,(f, \mathbf{g}, \mathbf{h}, e, \pi_{crs}, \mathbf{W}, \mathbf{V}, \mathbf{c}, \ell; \mathbf{a}_L, \mathbf{a}_R, \mathbf{a}_O, \mathbf{v}, \rho)$ $\qquad\qquad$ $\mathcal{V}$

$$\mathbf{a}_L \circ \mathbf{a}_R = \mathbf{a}_O \wedge \mathbf{W}_L\mathbf{a}_L^{\mathrm{T}} + \mathbf{W}_R\mathbf{a}_R^{\mathrm{T}} + \mathbf{W}_O\mathbf{a}_O^{\mathrm{T}} = \mathbf{W}_V\mathbf{v}^{\mathrm{T}} + \mathbf{c}^{\mathrm{T}} \wedge \forall i \in [\![m]\!]\ V_i^2 = (e^{v_i} f^{\rho_i})^4$$
$$\left\|\left[\mathbf{a}_L\ \mathbf{a}_R\ \mathbf{a}_O\ \mathbf{v}\ \rho\right]\right\|_\infty < 2^\ell$$

---

return $\perp$ if $FS.\Pi^{\mathcal{H}}_{crs}.\mathsf{Vf}\left((\mathbb{G}, P, f, 2n+1), (\mathbf{g}, \mathbf{h}, e), \pi_{crs}\right) = 0$

$\rho_I, \rho_O \leftarrow_\$ [\![0; 2^{b_{\mathbb{G}}+\lambda+3}]\!]$

$C_I \leftarrow (\mathbf{g}^{\mathbf{a}_L}\mathbf{h}^{\mathbf{a}_R} f^{\rho_I})^2$

$C_O \leftarrow (\mathbf{g}^{\mathbf{a}_O} f^{\rho_O})^2$

$$\xrightarrow{C_I, C_O}$$

$\mathbf{y} \leftarrow_\$ [\![0; P-1]\!]^n$

$\mathbf{z} \leftarrow_\$ [\![0; P-1]\!]^Q$

$$\xleftarrow{\mathbf{y}, \mathbf{z}}$$

$l(X) \leftarrow (\mathbf{a}_L + \mathbf{z}\mathbf{W}_R)\,X + \mathbf{a}_O X^2 + \mathbf{a}_L X^3 - \mathbf{a}_O X^4$

$r(X) \leftarrow -\mathbf{1}^n + \mathbf{z}\mathbf{W}_O + (\mathbf{a}_R + \mathbf{z}\mathbf{W}_L)\,X + \mathbf{y}X^2 + \mathbf{y} \circ \mathbf{a}_R X^3$

$l(X), r(X) \in \mathbb{Z}^n[X]$ and $\mathbf{1}^n := [1\ 1 \cdots 1] \in \mathbb{Z}^n$

$t(X) \leftarrow \langle l(X), r(X) \rangle = \sum_{i=1}^{7} t_i X^i$

$t(X) \in \mathbb{Z}[X]$ and $t_6 = 0$

$\forall i \in [\![7]\!] \setminus \{2, 6\},\ s_i \leftarrow_\$ [\![0; 2^{b_{\mathbb{G}}+\lambda+3}]\!], T_i \leftarrow (e^{t_i} f^{s_i})^2$

Commit to the non-zero coefficients of $t(X)$ except for t_2

$\rho'_I \leftarrow_\$ [\![0; 2^{b_{\mathbb{G}}+\lambda+3}]\!],\ C'_I \leftarrow \left(\mathbf{g}^{\mathbf{a}_L}\mathbf{h}^{\mathbf{y}\circ\mathbf{a}_R} f^{\rho'_I}\right)^2$

Commit to the inputs in $(\mathbf{g}, \mathbf{h}')$ with $\mathbf{h}' := \left[h_1^{y_1}\ h_2^{y_2} \cdots h_n^{y_n}\right]$

$$\xrightarrow{\mathbf{T} := \left[T_1\ T_3\ T_4\ T_5\ T_7\right], C'_I}$$

$$\xleftrightarrow{(\tau', b') \leftarrow \langle \Pi'.\mathsf{Prove}(m+5, f, e, \mathbf{T}, \mathbf{V}, \ell'; \mathbf{t}, \mathbf{s}) \rightleftharpoons \Pi'.\mathsf{Vf}(m+5, f, e, \mathbf{T}, \mathbf{V}, \ell') \rangle}$$

Argue knowledge of representations of $(T_i)_{i \neq 2,6}$ and $(V_j)_{j=1}^m$ in (e, f)

if $b' = 0$ return $\perp$

$$\xleftrightarrow{\left(\tilde{\tau}, \tilde{b}\right) \leftarrow \left\langle \tilde{\Pi}.\mathsf{Prove}\left(2, f, (\mathbf{g}, \mathbf{h}), (\mathbf{g}, \mathbf{h}'), C_I, C'_I, \tilde{\ell}; \mathbf{a}_L, \mathbf{a}_R, \rho_I, \rho'_I\right) \rightleftharpoons \tilde{\Pi}.\mathsf{Vf}\left(2, f, (\mathbf{g}, \mathbf{h}), (\mathbf{g}, \mathbf{h}'), C_I, C'_I, \tilde{\ell}\right) \right\rangle}$$

Argue that C_I and C'_I are commitments to the same inputs in $(\mathbf{g}, \mathbf{h})$ and $(\mathbf{g}, \mathbf{h}')$

if $\tilde{b} = 0$ return $\perp$

$x \leftarrow_\$ [\![0; P-1]\!]$

$$\xleftarrow{x}$$

$\mathbf{l}, \mathbf{r} \leftarrow l(x), r(x) \in \mathbb{Z}^n$

$\sigma \leftarrow \rho_I x + \rho'_I x^3 + \rho_O\,(x^2 - x^4) + s_1 x + \langle \mathbf{z}\mathbf{W}_V, \rho \rangle\, x^2$

$+ \sum_{3 \leq i \neq 6 \leq 7} s_i x^i \ \ //\ \rho = [\rho_1 \cdots \rho_m]$

$$W_L, W_R, W_O \leftarrow \mathbf{h}^{\mathbf{z}\mathbf{W}_L}, \mathbf{g}^{\mathbf{z}\mathbf{W}_R}, \mathbf{h}^{\mathbf{z}\mathbf{W}_O}$$

$$C_{\mathbf{l},\mathbf{r}} \leftarrow C_I^x C_I'^{x^3} C_O^{(x^2-x^4)} \left(\mathbf{h}^{-\mathbf{1}^n} \mathbf{h}'^{x^2} W_L^x W_R^x W_O\right)^2$$

$C_{\mathbf{l},\mathbf{r}}$ is a commitment to $\mathbf{l}$ and $\mathbf{r}$ in $(\mathbf{g}, \mathbf{h})$

$$C = C(x) \leftarrow C_{\mathbf{l},\mathbf{r}} T_1^x \left(e^{2(\langle \mathbf{z}, \mathbf{c} \rangle + \delta(\mathbf{z}))} \mathbf{V}^{\mathbf{z}\mathbf{W}_V}\right)^{x^2} \prod_{3 \leq i \neq 6 \leq 7} T_i^{x^i}$$

$$C = \left(\mathbf{g}^{\mathbf{l}}\mathbf{h}^{\mathbf{r}} e^{\langle \mathbf{l}, \mathbf{r} \rangle} f^{\sigma}\right)^2$$

run the protocol on Figure 2 on input $(1, n, f, \mathbf{g}, \mathbf{h}, e, C, \ell_2; \mathbf{l}, \mathbf{r}, \sigma)$

Fig. 3. Succinct Argument of Diophantine-Equation Satisfiability.

communication complexity of the protocol is of order $O\left(\delta\ell'' + \log\left(\delta\binom{\nu+\delta}{\delta}\right) b_{\mathbb{G}} + H\right) = O\left(\delta\ell'' + \min(\nu,\delta)\log(\nu+\delta)\, b_{\mathbb{G}} + H\right)$, where ℓ'' is the maximum bit length of the integers in the solution. Here $H = \lfloor \log \|W\|_\infty \rfloor + 1$ as the procedure gives linear constraints determined by the coefficients of the polynomial.

Verification Efficiency. Similarly to Sect. 4.1, the verifications of Π', $\tilde{\Pi}$ and the protocol on Fig. 2 can each be done via single multi-exponentiations, with exponents of at most $O\left(\ell + b_{\mathbb{G}} + \log(n)\log(P) + \log Q + \log m + \log \|W\|_\infty\right)$ bits. For a polynomial in $\mathbb{Z}[X_1, \ldots, X_\nu]$ of total degree δ, with μ monomials and with coefficients less than 2^H in absolute value, that is $O\left(\delta\ell'' + b_{\mathbb{G}} + \min(\nu,\delta)\log(\nu+\delta)\, \log P + H\right)$ bits, where ℓ'' is the maximum bit length of the integers in the solution.

Completeness and Security. In the full version [24], we show that the protocol Π is complete, honest-verifier zero-knowledge, and extractable under the assumptions on the group generator.

Acknowledgements. This work was supported by the French ANR ALAMBIC Project (ANR-16-CE39-0006) and the EU H2020 Research and Innovation Program under Grant Agreement No. 786725 (OLYMPUS).

References

1. Avanzi, R.M.: The complexity of certain multi-exponentiation techniques in cryptography. J. Cryptol. **18**(4), 357–373 (2005). https://doi.org/10.1007/s00145-004-0229-5
2. Barić, N., Pfitzmann, B.: Collision-free accumulators and fail-stop signature schemes without trees. In: Fumy, W. (ed.) EUROCRYPT 1997. LNCS, vol. 1233, pp. 480–494. Springer, Heidelberg (1997). https://doi.org/10.1007/3-540-69053-0_33
3. Bayer, S., Groth, J.: Zero-knowledge argument for polynomial evaluation with application to blacklists. In: Johansson, T., Nguyen, P.Q. (eds.) EUROCRYPT 2013. LNCS, vol. 7881, pp. 646–663. Springer, Heidelberg (2013). https://doi.org/10.1007/978-3-642-38348-9_38
4. Biehl, I., Buchmann, J.A., Hamdy, S., Meyer, A.: A signature scheme based on the intractability of computing roots. Des. Codes Cryptogr. **25**(3), 223–236 (2002). https://doi.org/10.1023/A:1014927327846
5. Bootle, J., Cerulli, A., Chaidos, P., Groth, J., Petit, C.: Efficient zero-knowledge arguments for arithmetic circuits in the discrete log setting. In: Fischlin, M., Coron, J.-S. (eds.) EUROCRYPT 2016, Part II. LNCS, vol. 9666, pp. 327–357. Springer, Heidelberg (2016). https://doi.org/10.1007/978-3-662-49896-5_12
6. Bünz, B., Bootle, J., Boneh, D., Poelstra, A., Wuille, P., Maxwell, G.: Bulletproofs: short proofs for confidential transactions and more. In: 2018 IEEE Symposium on Security and Privacy, pp. 315–334. IEEE Computer Society Press (2018)
7. Bünz, B., Fisch, B., Szepieniec, A.: Transparent SNARKs from DARK compilers. In: Canteaut, A., Ishai, Y. (eds.) EUROCRYPT 2020, Part I. LNCS, vol. 12105, pp. 677–706. Springer, Cham (2020). https://doi.org/10.1007/978-3-030-45721-1_24

8. Camenisch, J., Stadler, M.: Efficient group signature schemes for large groups (extended abstract). In: Kaliski, B.S. (ed.) CRYPTO 1997. LNCS, vol. 1294, pp. 410–424. Springer, Heidelberg (1997). https://doi.org/10.1007/BFb0052252
9. Chase, M., Ganesh, C., Mohassel, P.: Efficient zero-knowledge proof of algebraic and non-algebraic statements with applications to privacy preserving credentials. In: Robshaw, M., Katz, J. (eds.) CRYPTO 2016, Part III. LNCS, vol. 9816, pp. 499–530. Springer, Heidelberg (2016). https://doi.org/10.1007/978-3-662-53015-3_18
10. Couteau, G., Peters, T., Pointcheval, D.: Removing the strong RSA assumption from arguments over the integers. In: Coron, J.-S., Nielsen, J.B. (eds.) EUROCRYPT 2017, Part II. LNCS, vol. 10211, pp. 321–350. Springer, Cham (2017). https://doi.org/10.1007/978-3-319-56614-6_11
11. Damgård, I., Fujisaki, E.: A statistically-hiding integer commitment scheme based on groups with hidden order. In: Zheng, Y. (ed.) ASIACRYPT 2002. LNCS, vol. 2501, pp. 125–142. Springer, Heidelberg (2002). https://doi.org/10.1007/3-540-36178-2_8
12. del Pino, R., Lyubashevsky, V., Seiler, G.: Short discrete log proofs for FHE and Ring-LWE ciphertexts. In: Lin, D., Sako, K. (eds.) PKC 2019, Part I. LNCS, vol. 11442, pp. 344–373. Springer, Cham (2019). https://doi.org/10.1007/978-3-030-17253-4_12
13. Fiat, A., Shamir, A.: How to prove yourself: practical solutions to identification and signature problems. In: Odlyzko, A.M. (ed.) CRYPTO 1986. LNCS, vol. 263, pp. 186–194. Springer, Heidelberg (1987). https://doi.org/10.1007/3-540-47721-7_12
14. Fouque, P.-A., Poupard, G.: On the security of RDSA. In: Biham, E. (ed.) EUROCRYPT 2003. LNCS, vol. 2656, pp. 462–476. Springer, Heidelberg (2003). https://doi.org/10.1007/3-540-39200-9_29
15. Fujisaki, E., Okamoto, T.: Statistical zero knowledge protocols to prove modular polynomial relations. In: Kaliski Jr., B.S. (ed.) CRYPTO 1997. LNCS, vol. 1294, pp. 16–30. Springer, Heidelberg (1997). https://doi.org/10.1007/BFb0052225
16. Gathen, J., von zur Gerhard, J.: Modern Computer Algebra, 3rd edn. Cambridge University Press, Cambridge (2013)
17. Groth, J.: Linear algebra with sub-linear zero-knowledge arguments. In: Halevi, S. (ed.) CRYPTO 2009. LNCS, vol. 5677, pp. 192–208. Springer, Heidelberg (2009). https://doi.org/10.1007/978-3-642-03356-8_12
18. Groth, J., Kohlweiss, M.: One-out-of-many proofs: or how to leak a secret and spend a coin. In: Oswald, E., Fischlin, M. (eds.) EUROCRYPT 2015, Part II. LNCS, vol. 9057, pp. 253–280. Springer, Heidelberg (2015). https://doi.org/10.1007/978-3-662-46803-6_9
19. Lipmaa, H.: On diophantine complexity and statistical zero-knowledge arguments. In: Laih, C.-S. (ed.) ASIACRYPT 2003. LNCS, vol. 2894, pp. 398–415. Springer, Heidelberg (2003). https://doi.org/10.1007/978-3-540-40061-5_26
20. Matiyasevich, Y.V.: Enumerable sets are diophantine. Sov. Math. Dokl. **11**, 354–358 (1970)
21. Pedersen, T.P.: Non-interactive and information-theoretic secure verifiable secret sharing. In: Feigenbaum, J. (ed.) CRYPTO 1991. LNCS, vol. 576, pp. 129–140. Springer, Heidelberg (1992). https://doi.org/10.1007/3-540-46766-1_9
22. Schnorr, C.P.: Efficient signature generation by smart cards. J. Cryptol. **4**(3), 161–174 (1991). https://doi.org/10.1007/BF00196725

23. Skolem, T.: Diophantische Gleichungen. Ergebnisse der Mathematik und ihrer Grenzgebiete. Chelsea Pub. Co., New York (1950)
24. Towa, P., Vergnaud, D.: Succinct diophantine-satisfiability arguments. Cryptology ePrint Archive, Report 2020/682 (2020). https://eprint.iacr.org/2020/682

Individual Simulations

Yi Deng[1,2,3](✉)

[1] State Key Laboratory of Information Security,
Institute of Information Engineering, Chinese Academy of Sciences, Beijing, China
deng@iie.ac.cn
[2] State Key Laboratory of Cryptology, Beijing, China
[3] School of Cyber Security, University of Chinese Academy of Sciences,
Beijing, China

Abstract. We develop an *individual* simulation technique that explicitly makes use of particular properties/structures of a given adversary's functionality. Using this simulation technique, we obtain the following results.

1. We construct the *first* protocols that *break previous black-box barriers* under the standard hardness of factoring, both of which are *polynomial time simulatable* against *all a-priori bounded polynomial size* distinguishers:
   - Two-round selective opening secure commitment scheme.
   - Three-round concurrent zero knowledge and concurrent witness hiding argument for NP in the bare public-key model.
2. We present a simpler two-round weak zero knowledge and witness hiding argument for NP in the plain model under the sub-exponential hardness of factoring. Our technique also yields a significantly simpler proof that existing distinguisher-dependent simulatable zero knowledge protocols are also polynomial time simulatable against all distinguishers of a-priori bounded polynomial size.

The core conceptual idea underlying our individual simulation technique is an observation of the *existence* of *nearly optimal extractors* for all hard distributions: For any NP-instance(s) sampling algorithm, there exists a polynomial-size witness extractor (depending on the sampler's functionality) that almost outperforms any circuit of a-priori bounded polynomial size in terms of the success probability.

1 Introduction

1.1 Background

The simulation paradigm [GMR89] plays a pivotal role in complexity-based cryptography, which takes the reductionist approach to prove the security of a given cryptosystem. In a typical security proof, we devise a reduction algorithm, which invokes as a subroutine the adversary that claims to break the target cryptosystem, to crack the underlying hard problem. In this process, the reduction algorithm needs to simulate the honest parties for the adversary in order to exploit its

S. Moriai and H. Wang (Eds.): ASIACRYPT 2020, LNCS 12493, pp. 805–836, 2020.
https://doi.org/10.1007/978-3-030-64840-4_27

power. For most interactive cryptographic protocols, simulating the adversary's view is actually the essential part of the reduction.

The most commonly used simulation strategy is black-box simulation, which appears very restrictive since the black-box simulator ignores the internal workings of the adversary completely. Indeed, starting from the seminal work of Impagliazzo and Rudich [IR89], a lot of impossibility results regarding black-box simulation were proved in a variety of settings. In the last two decades, several new simulation techniques, notably the PCP-based non-black-box simulation [Bar01] and the recently distinguisher-dependent simulation [JKKR17, BKP19] techniques, were developed to get around certain black-box barriers on the round-complexity of cryptographic protocols. However, for many basic protocols, it still remains unclear whether the known black-box impossibility results on their round-complexity might be overcome using new (non-black-box) reduction/simulation techniques. In this paper, we consider the round-complexity of several related fundamental protocols: selective opening secure commitments and zero knowledge protocols.

Commitment Scheme Secure Under the Selective Opening Attacks. In a selective opening attack against a commitment scheme, the receiver observes many commitments and is allowed to ask the committer to open some of them. Dwork et al. [DNRS03] put foward the notion of selective opening security and asked if we can construct such a commitment that the unopened commitments in the selective opening attack still stay hiding. As showed in [DNRS03], this problem has a deep connection with the existence of 3-round zero knowledge and the soundness of the Fiat-Shamir heuristics.

Bellare et al. [BHY09] constructed the first selective opening secure commitment. The high-level idea of their construction (and the follow-up from [ORSV13] by Ostrovsky et al.) is as follows. The receiver generates a trapdoor for an equivocal trapdoor commitment scheme, and proves of knowledge of the trapdoor via a cut-and-choose type protocol; the committer then uses this trapdoor commitment scheme to commit to a value. In simulation, the simulator first extracts the trapdoor by rewinding the receiver, and then can open a commitment to any value it wishes. So far, the best known construction of (simulation-based notion of) selective opening secure commitment requires three rounds [ORSV13].

There is an obstacle to further reduce the round-complexity of selective opening secure commitment. Note that in a two-round scheme[1] the receiver sends only one message and the standard black-box simulator/extractor that treats the (possibly malicious) receiver as a black-box would fail. Indeed, Xiao [Xia11, Xia13] proved that it is impossible to achieve selective opening security in 2 rounds with a black-box simulator.

---

[1] The round-complexity of a commitment scheme refers to the one of its committing phase. In this paper we focus on commitment schemes with a non-interactive opening phase.

Zero Knowledge Protocols in Two and Three Rounds. Early constructions of zero knowledge proofs (with statistical soundness) [GMR89] and arguments (with computational soundness) [BCC88] are quite simple and round-efficient: only three messages are exchanged in a session. However, this round efficiency is achieved at the cost of huge soundness error. The work [FLS99] provides a very popular method–the so-called FLS-paradigm– to construct four round zero knowledge argument with negligible soundness error. In the FLS-paradigm, a zero knowledge protocol for proving some NP statement $x \in L$ proceeds in two phases. In the first phase, the verifier generates two puzzles and proves to the prover that he knows a solution to one of these puzzles; In the second phase, the prover proves to the verifier that either the statement being proven is true or he knows a solution to one of puzzles. Both proofs are carried out using a witness indistinguishable proof of knowledge. In simulation, an efficient simulator is able to extract a solution to one of these puzzles from a malicious verifier and then carry out the second phase using the solution just extracted as a witness.

Whether there are 3-round zero knowledge protocols with negligible soundness error based on standard assumptions for non-trivial languages is still a widely open problem. On the negative side, the work [GK96] showed that it is impossible to achieve 3-round zero knowledge argument or proof via black-box simulation. Similar impossibility result [Pas11] hold even for a relaxed notion of zero knowledge–witness hiding protocol [FS90]. Recently, Fleischhacker et al. [FGJ18] and Canetti et al. [CCH+19] extended this impossibility result to non-black-box simulation technique, and gave very strong negative evidence against the existence of 3-round zero knowledge *proofs* for non-trivial languages.

In their recently work [JKKR17], Jain et al. observed that a good distinguisher may leak some useful secrets of the verifier in certain settings, which will enable a successful simulation of the verifier's view. They developed a distinguisher-dependent simulation technique and constructed three-round delayed-input *weak* ϵ-distributional zero knowledge [DNRS03] from standard assumptions in a model where the simulator is allowed to depend on the distinguisher. Very recently, Bitansky et al. [BKP19] introduced a homomorphic trapdoor paradigm and presented a three-round *weak* ϵ-zero knowledge argument in the same model, but their simulator works for any individual statement (rather than in the distributional setting). Both constructions of [JKKR17,BKP19] can be made into two rounds assuming certain *sub-exponential* hardness.

Concurrent Zero Knowledge Protocols and the Bare Public Key (BPK) Model. Dwork et al. [DNS98] formalized the notion of concurrent zero knowledge in a setting where multiple sessions of the same protocol take place, and a malicious verifier is allowed to fully control the message scheduling. A protocol is called concurrent zero knowledge if it preserves zero knowledge even in this concurrent setting. Prabhakaran et al. [PRS02] refined the analysis of the simulators of [KP01,RK99] and proved (almost) logarithmic ($\widetilde{O}(\log n)$) round-complexity is sufficient for concurrent zero knowledge protocol, which almost matches the black-box lower bound of [CKPR01]. In his breakthrough work [Bar01], Barak introduced a non-black-box simulation technique that makes use of the malicious verifier's code in simulation, and generated a long-line follow-up works (e.g., [DGS09,CLP13,BP15], just to name a few) to reduce the round-complexity of concurrent zero knowledge. However, despite decades of intensive research, the known constant-round constructions [CLP15a,FKP19] of concurrent zero knowledge still require non-standard assumptions.

Canetti et al. [CGGM00] introduced a very attracting model–the BPK model–to further reduce the round-complexity of stronger notions of zero knowledge, such as concurrent zero knowledge and resettable zero knowledge (which allows a verifier to reset the prover). In this model, each verifier deposits a public key in a public file and stores the associated secret key before any interaction with the prover begins. A huge advantage of this model is that, the trapdoors/secret keys useful for the simulator are fixed in advance, and if a simulator obtained all these trapdoors, it can simulate any session in a straight-line manner. Many constructions [YZ07,DFG+11,SV12] of concurrent/resettable zero knowledge in this model follows the FLS paradigm in which the verifier proves knowledge of his secret key in the first phase, and thus they require at least four rounds.

The question of whether we can achieve concurrent zero knowledge in fewer rounds in the BPK model is also subject to black-box limitations: As showed in [MR01,APV05], it is impossible to achieve concurrent *black-box* zero knowledge with concurrent (even sequential) soundness in three rounds in this model.

1.2 Motivation

In black-box simulations mentioned above, a simulator is usually to extract a piece of secret information from the adversary and then use it to mimic the honest parties (without knowing their private inputs). For such an extraction to go through, we usually design protocols so that the adversary is required to provide a proof of knowledge of such a piece of secret information. This incurs several additional rounds of interaction given the state-of-the-art constructions of proof of knowledge.

Indeed, Barak showed the adversary's code and internal workings allow us to break black-box barriers in certain settings. His non-black-box simulation technique relies on the PCP mechanism and often gives rise to complicated and (relatively) round-inefficient constructions. So far, for almost all known simulation techniques (including Barak's non-black-box simulation), the simulator is *universal* and is able to work for any adversary. This is in sharp contrast to the *individual* simulators, as required in most of security definitions, which switches the order of qualifiers $\exists\ \mathsf{Sim}\ \forall\ \mathcal{A}dv$:

- Universal Simulation: $\exists\ \mathsf{Sim}\ \forall\ \mathcal{A}dv$, Sim fools all efficient distinguishers.
- Individual Simulation: $\forall\ \mathcal{A}dv\ \exists\ \mathsf{Sim}$, Sim fools all efficient distinguishers.

Literally, an individual simulator is only required to work for a given *individual* adversary, thus we can assume that the simulator "knows/hardwires" any useful properties/structures (if exists) of this adversary's *functionality*, not just its code. This makes individual simulators more powerful than universal/black-box ones. Under the widely believed hardness of reverse engineering[2], we cannot expect an efficient universal simulator to be able to figure out some useful property/structure about the adversary's functionality from its code. A natural question arises:

Can we develop individual simulations to break the known black-box barriers?

A motivating example is the black-box lower bound on round-complexity of concurrent zero knowledge [CKPR01], in which Canetti et al. constructed an explicit concurrent verifier strategy (for an arbitrary almost logarithmic round proof system) whose view cannot be simulated by any efficient black-box simulator (unless the statement being proven is trivial). However, as already showed in [Den17], an individual simulator can simulate this adversary's view in a straightforward way when given as input a certain crucial subfunctionality of the adversary. This demonstrates the potential power of individual simulations, but does not give a proof of the concurrent zero knowledge of the underlying protocol, which requires us to show for *any* efficient verifier we can build a successful individual simulator.

1.3 Summary of Our Results

In this paper we develop an individual simulation technique that explicitly makes use of particular properties/structures of the adversary's functionality, and achieve several constructions for selective opening secure commitment and zero knowledge arguments that break the known black-box lower bounds on their round-complexity.

As our main conceptual contribution, we show that for any NP-instance(s) sampling algorithm, there exists a nearly optimal *individual* witness extractor (depending on the sampler's functionality) that almost outperforms any circuit of a-priori bounded size. Combining this extraction strategy with an algebraic technique for Blum's encryption scheme, we obtain the following results.

The First Protocols That Break Previous Black-Box Barriers. We construct the *first* protocols that *break black-box barriers* mentioned above under the standard hardness of factoring, both of which are *polynomial time simulatable* against *all a-priori bounded polynomial size* distinguishers:

- Two-round selective opening secure commitment scheme.
- Three-round concurrent zero knowledge and concurrent witness hiding argument for NP in the bare public-key model.

All these protocols are quasi-polynomial time simulatable against all polynomial-size distinguishers with a *negligible* distinguishing gap.

Simpler Construction and Analysis of Zero Knowledge Protocols. We present a construction of two-round weak zero knowledge and witness hiding

[2] Under this assumption, the work [DGL+16] showed a limitation of universal simulation in a particular setting.

argument for NP in the plain model under the sub-exponential hardness of factoring, which is much simpler than the constructions in [JKKR17, BKP19, DK18, BGI+17]. Our technique also yields a significantly simpler proof of the equivalence theorem of [CLP15b]) for existing distinguisher-dependent simulatable zero knowledge protocols in [JKKR17, BKP19], showing that these protocols are also polynomial time simulatable against all distinguishers of a-priori bounded polynomial size.

1.4 Individual Extractions and Simulations: An Overview

Recall that the standard simulation-based security definitions only require that for every adversary, there *exists* a simulator that can fool all efficient distinguishers. This means such an existential simulator, like distinguishers, can depend on any properties/structures of the *functionality* of a given specific verifier.

Imagine that we have a two-round FLS-type protocol (A, B) in which B sends an NP instance y in the first round, with these properties:

1. A solution to the instance y generated by a adversary $\mathcal{B}$ enables the simulator to efficiently generate $\mathcal{B}$'s view that is indistinguishable from the real interaction;
2. Distinguishing the honest A's message from even a dummy message is equivalent to extracting a solution to y from $\mathcal{B}$.

In this scenario, for a given adversary $\mathcal{B}$, there are only two cases in which an efficient simulator will win[3]: a) the simulator succeeds to extract a solution to y from $\mathcal{B}$, or, b) no efficient algorithm can extract a solution to y except for negligible probability. In the former case, by the first property of (A, B), regardless of whether the distinguisher knows the solution, the simulator can reconstruct $\mathcal{B}$'s view successfully; in the latter case, the distinguisher does not know the solution either, and thus by the second property of (A, B), a simulator can easily fool the distinguisher.

Nearly Optimal Extractors for Single-instance Samplers. Note that the above solution extraction algorithm– the key subroutine of the simulator–can also be *individual*: It can depend on any property/structure of the individual adversary $\mathcal{B}$, besides being given the same input as $\mathcal{B}$.

To simulate $\mathcal{B}$'s view, one naive approach is to apply the best possible extractor (in terms of success probability) to extract a solution then simulate. An issue with this approach is that the success probability of an extractor may increase with its size. This makes it hard to control the size of the extractor (and the simulator). In this paper, we consider a weak simulation security–(T, ϵ)-simulatability: The simulation is required only against distinguishers of size T with distinguishing gap less than ϵ. Note that this notion is stronger than the

[3] Here we are aiming to construct a normal simulator, not a distinguisher-dependent simulator like the ones in [JKKR17, BKP19].

distinguisher-dependent simulatability defined in [CLP15b, JKKR17], where the simulator depends on the specific distinguishing algorithm, not just its size.

We view $\mathcal{B}$ as a single-instance sampler, and show that for any $\mathcal{B}$ there exists of a good extractor that outperforms all circuits of size T (given the *same* input as the extractor) with at most gap ϵ. The basic proof strategy is to keep iterating to include new powerful circuits into the extractor until we have a desired one.

Subtleties. One should be careful when carrying out this proof strategy. First, the number of iterations in this process may depend on the security parameter n, and this may cause some difficulties in controlling the size of the final circuit family Ext; second, in the asymptotic setting, when we add a new circuit family to the extractor, this family may work only when the security parameter n is greater than a specific n_0. Thus, it is possible that the iterative procedure keeps increasing the number n_0, and therefore we are not able to specify any n_0' so that the final circuit family Ext works for all $n > n_0'$.

To get around these difficulties, we use the a-priori fixed T and ϵ as a *global* guideline, and do *local* iterations at each parameter n[4]: In each iteration of this process, we have an extractor Ext at the beginning and ask: Does there *exist* another instance solver C of size T, given the same input as Ext, such that

$$\Pr\left[y \leftarrow \mathcal{B} : C \text{ extractsasolutionto } y \textit{ but } \mathsf{Ext} \text{ fails}\right] > \epsilon?$$

If so, then we have a new extractor: On input y, it runs the Ext first, and if Ext fails then runs C to extract a solution to y. This will increase the success probability of the extractor by at least ϵ; otherwise, we return the current extractor Ext.

It is not hard to verify that, after at most $\frac{1}{\epsilon}$ steps, we will have an extractor Ext of size at most $O(T\frac{1}{\epsilon})$ such that, the event that Ext fails to extract a solution to y but some other circuit of size T succeeds happens with probability at most ϵ.

The Dependence on the Functionality of the Sampler. We give two examples to illustrate how the nearly optimal extractor Ext *intrinsically* depends on the functionality of the sampler. Consider the following two image-sampling algorithms for some one-way permutation g: (a) use randomness y and then generate an image $x = g(y)$, and (b) sample a random string x from the co-domain of g. Then, for the former sampler, there is a nearly optimal extractor (taking the sampler's randomness y) that can simply output the pre-image y of the given sampled image x with probability 1; for the latter, a dummy algorithm (with success probability 0) is also an optimal extractor (this is almost best possible since g is one-way).

With this nearly optimal extractor, we now have an *individual* simulator for $\mathcal{B}$: it first applies this nearly optimal individual extractor Ext to extract a solution to y generated by $\mathcal{B}$ and then simulates in a somewhat straightforward manner (see below). Note that this simulator inherently depends on the functionality of

---

[4] We would like to stress that one cannot expect this process to be constructive.

the adversary (instance sampler) since the nearly optimal extractor does, and that it will fool all distinguishers[5] of size T except for probability at most ϵ.

Now, if the protocol (A, B) satisfies the above two properties, we have a good individual simulator against all distinguishers of size T. Our remaining task is to construct protocols with such properties.

A suitable building block for such protocols is the well-known encryption scheme based on the hardness of factoring. The public key of the encryption scheme is a Blum integer N, and the secret key is a prime factor of N. A ciphertext of a bit b is given by $c = (f_N(s), h(s) \oplus b)$, where $f_N : QR_N \rightarrow QR_N$ defined by $f_N(s) = s^2 \bmod N$ and h is the hardcore of f_N. A key property (implied by [TW87]) of this encryption scheme we will make use of is the equivalence between distinguishing ciphertexts and extracting a secret key, even if the public key N is not a Blum integer[6].

Constructions. With these extraction and construction ideas in mind, we construct selective opening secure commitment and zero knowledge arguments as follows.

Two-Round Selective Opening Secure Commitment: In the committing phase, we have the receiver generate a Blum integer N for the committer; upon receiving N, the committer uses the trapdoor commitment scheme (a prime factor of N serves as a trapdoor) [FS89] to compute a commitment c, encrypts it bit-wise under the public-key N and sends these encryptions to the receiver; In the opening phase, the committer sends the opening of c to the receiver, and the latter decrypts the encryptions received in the first phase and accepts if the plaintext is c and the opening received is a valid opening of c. This construction relies on *polynomial hardness* of factoring.

Three-Round Weak Concurrent Zero Knowledge in the BPK Model: In the key registration phase, each verifier generates two Blum integers (N_0, N_1) as its public-key, and stores *two* prime factors (q_0, q_1), $q_i|N_i$ for $i \in \{0, 1\}$. In the proof phase, the prover and the verifier execute the three round parallel version of Blum's protocol (Let a session be of the form (a, e, z)) in which the prover proves "the statement to be proven is true or I know a prime factor of one of the two integers", and in addition, the prover encrypts the last message z bit-wise under each of verifier's public key. The verifier decrypts all these ciphertexts and obtains $\hat{z}$ and $\tilde{z}$, and accepts if $\hat{z} = \tilde{z}$ and the underlying transcript is accepting. This construction relies on *polynomial hardness* of factoring.

Two-Round Weak Zero Knowledge in the Plain Model: The verifier sends a Blum integer N (and stores one prime factor) to the prover, and the prover computes a commitment c to n zeros, sends back c together with ciphertexts (encrypted bit-wise under N) of a NIWI proof for "the statement to be proven is true or I know a prime factor of N". The verifier decrypts the ciphertexts, and accepts

[5] One can think of a distinguisher as a solution extractor since they are essentially equivalent because of the property 2. of (A, B).

[6] In this case, we view any prime factor of N as a secret key.

if the plaintexts forms an accepting NIWI proof. This construction relies on sub-exponential hardness of factoring.

A Difficulty in the Individual Simulations for Composable Protocols. At a high level, our simulation strategy for these protocols are quite simple: The simulator first applies the nearly optimal extractor to obtain the corresponding witness for each session, and if the extractor succeeds, then it can simulate this session in a straightforward manner; otherwise, it sends a dummy message in the last round of the protocol.

The Simulator for the Commitment Scheme. Suppose that a malicious receiver R^* initiates k sessions in parallel. In the committing phase, for each $i \in [k]$, the simulator first runs the nearly optimal extractor and tries to obtain a prime factor of N_i sent by R^*, and commits to 0 via the trapdoor commitment scheme and obtains a commitment c_i, then sends encryptions of c_i; In the opening phase, upon receiving $\{b_i\}_{i \in I}$ and the index set I, then the simulator opens c_i in the following way: If $b_i = 0$, open it in an honest way; if $b_i = 1$ and the extractor succeeds to extract a prime factor of N_i, then use it as trapdoor and open c_i to value 1; else send $(b_i = 1, dec')$ to R^*, where the decommiment $(b_i = 1, dec')$ is a valid opening of some commitment c_i'. (In other words, in the third case, the simulator pretends that the ciphertexts it sent in the committing phase is bit-wise encryptions of c_i').

The Simulators for zero knowledge protocols are much simpler. For concurrent zero knowledge protocol in the BPK model, after the key registration phase, for each pair (N_0, N_1) registered by a malicious V^*, the simulator first tries to extract a prime factor of one of (N_0, N_1) using the nearly optimal extractor; if this extraction is successful, then the simulator can simulate any session under (N_0, N_1) successfully; otherwise, the simulator simply computes encryptions of all zeros under both public keys in the last round. The same simulation strategy works also for the protocol in the plain model.

One must be careful in proving that these simulations are indistinguishable from the real interaction against any distinguisher of a-priori bounded size T except for small probability ϵ. A technical difficulty arises in such proofs due to the *composition* of the first two protocols. Let us take the example of the simulator for the commitment scheme. As usual, the proof of (T, ϵ)-simulatability is done by a hybrid argument. We construct a sequence of hybrid non-uniform simulators, gradually switching from the simulation to the real interaction, so that a consecutive pair of simulators, say the i-th and the $(i+1)$-th simulators, behave differently only in the i-th session in the case that the extractor fails to factor N_i, and then prove that any two consecutive simulations are indistinguishable except for a very small probability by contradiction: For any D_n of size T that distinguishes the i-th and the $(i+1)$-th simulations with a large distinguishing gap, we use D_n to construct a circuit A_n that contradicts the optimality of the nearly optimal extractor. However, to exploit the power of D_n, A_n needs also to simulate other sessions for D_n, which in turn requires A_n to know prime factors for some other N_j's $(j \neq i)$ obtained by the extractor. (otherwise A_n needs to run the extractor on its own, which results in the circuit A_n of size larger than the extractor and thus makes no sense).

Nearly Optimal Extractors for Multi-instance Samplers. We prove a stronger result of the existence of nearly optimal extractors for all multiple-instance sampling algorithms to address the above issue. Specifically, for any polynomial t and any t-instance sampler, we show there exists a nearly optimal extractor such that, for every $i \in [t]$, for any circuit C of a-prior bound size that is given *the output of the extractor*, the probability that C solves the i-th instance but the extractor fails is small. This result is proved by a similar argument as above, but a more delicate iterative procedure is requried.

Binding/Soundness: Trust the Adversary. At first glance, the binding and soundness properties of the first two protocols seem to be problematic. For the binding of our commitment scheme, a usual proof-by-contradiction approach is to construct a reduction with oracle access to the cheating committer to factor the public key N. A problem with this approach is that the reduction itself does not know the corresponding secret key (i.e., a prime factor of N), and as a consequence, it cannot decrypt the message from the committer to obtain the commitment c and determine whether the opening sent by the cheating committer is a valid decommitment of c. Here we use a "trust the adversary" trick to save the proof: Since the cheating committer can make the *honest* receiver (who knows the secret key) accept two different decommitments, these decommitments should be valid for the same commitment c. Hence, in reduction, the reduction algorithm can trust the committer and simply assume that the two decommitments are both valid for some unknown c.

A similar but more subtle problem occurs in the proof of soundness of the zero knowledge protocol in the BPK model. In this case, a usual reduction algorithm keeps one secret key of N_i (for a random $i \in \{0,1\}$) in the public key pair (N_0, N_1), and wants to use the power of the cheating prover to factor N_{1-i}. However, such a reduction seems to fail for the following cheating P^*: At the begining P^* somehow magically factors *both* N_0 and N_1 and obtains q_0 and q_1; in its last step, it compute z_0 and z_1 using witnesses q_0 and q_1 respectively, and sends to the verifier encryptions of z_0 and z_1 under the public keys N_0 and N_1 respectively. Note that the reduction can decrypt only the encryptions under public key N_i, and hence it can only obtain a prime factor of N_i by rewinding P^* (using the special soundness of Blum's protocol). However, this issue is taken care by the verification step in which the honest verifier decrypts *all* encryptions and check if the two last round messages z_0 and z_1 are equal and both acceptable. Thus, such a cheating P^* cannot make an honest verifier accept at all, and therefore is not a successful cheating prover. In other words, for a successful cheating prover, the reduction algorithm can trust that the two last round messages of Blum's protocol encrypted under both public keys are equal. This is the key to the proof of soundness.

1.5 Related Work and Discussion

On Upgrading the Distinguisher-Dependent Simulatable Zero Knowledge. As mentioned earlier, it is proved in [CLP15b] that, in the *plain* model, distinguisher-dependent simulatable zero knowledge protocols (such as [JKKR17, BKP19]) satisfy the stronger notion of (T, ϵ)-simulatabibility. However, this "distinguisher-dependent simulation then upgrade" approach to (T, ϵ)-simulatability seems to work only for *standalone* zero knowledge protocols in the *plain* model. Note that the equivalence theorem of [CLP15b] says nothing about zero knowledge in other models/settings, or other cryptographic primitives, like the commitment schemes under *parallel composition* and *concurrent* zero knowledge in the BPK model considered in this paper.

The equivalence theorem of [CLP15b] was proved via the minimax theorem, which leads to a complicated proof[7]. Our proof of existence of a nearly optimal extractor is quite simple and easy to understand, and it can also be used to upgrade existing constructions of [JKKR17, BKP19]. However, it is unclear if our technique could be used to prove the full version of the equivalence theorem of [CLP15b].

Other Notions of Selective Opening Security for Commitments. The work of [BHY09] also introduced the notion of selective opening security under *concurrent* composition, where a malicious receiver is allowed to interact with the committers concurrently. This notion is stronger than the selective opening security under *parallel* composition considered in this paper. However, as proved in [ORSV13], we cannot achieve such a security in the *full-fledged* concurrent setting if the simulator does not know the distribution of the message committed to by the honest committer. Another related notion is the indistinguishability-based selective opening security, which can be achieved by any statistical hiding (standalone) commitment scheme [BHY09].

Conditional Disclosure Schemes. A conditional disclosure scheme can be thought of as *interactive* version of witness encryption [AIR01, BP12, PA17]. It is a useful tool for constructing protocols of low round-complexity, such as the three round zero knowledge protocol of [BKP19], but the usage of such a scheme often requires an additional sub-protocol to make sure a (malicious) party indeed knows a relevant witness. The protocols in this paper do not need such an extra sub-protocol, and therefore is significantly simpler than previous constructions.

(T, ϵ)-Security in Practice. A silent feature of the notion of (T, ϵ)-simulatability is that the we need not embed the parameters T and ϵ into the protocol instructions. That is, we can have a *single* construction that achieves (T, ϵ)-simulatability for *any* polynomial T and *any* inverse polynomial ϵ, which stands in sharp contrast to Barak's n-bounded concurrent zero knowledge argument, whose construction depends on the a-priori upper-bound n on the number of total sessions allowed. From a practical point of view, we think the weak notion

[7] See https://eprint.iacr.org/2013/260.pdf for the detailed proof.

of (T, ϵ)-simulatability is good enough in practice: For any fixed security parameter λ, any constants κ and ε, it already achieves a *concrete* (κ, ε)-simulatability, since there always exist T and ϵ satisfying $T(\lambda) > \kappa$ and $\epsilon(\lambda) < \varepsilon$.

1.6 Organization

We present relevant definitions in Sect. 2. In Sect. 3, we prove the existence of nearly optimal extractors for all hard distributions. In Sect. 4, we give a formal proof of the equivalence between distinguishing ciphertexts and extracting a secret key for the factoring-based encryption scheme. In the last three sections, we give our main results on selective opening secure commitment, weak concurrent zero knowledge in the BPK model and the two-round weak zero knowledge respectively.

2 Preliminaries

Throughout the paper, we let n be the security parameter. We write the set $\{1, 2, ..., m\}$ as $[m]$, and the set $\{i, i+1, ..., j\}$ as $[i, j]$. We denote by $\bar{x} = \{x_i\}_{i \in [k]} \leftarrow \bar{D}^k$ the process of sampling k times x from D independently. A function $negl(n)$ is called negligible if it vanishes faster than any inverse polynomial. We write $\{X_n\}_{n \in \mathbb{N}} \stackrel{c}{\approx} \{Y_n\}_{n \in \mathbb{N}}$ to indicate that the two distribution ensembles $\{X_n\}_{n \in \mathbb{N}}$ and $\{Y_n\}_{n \in \mathbb{N}}$ are computationally indistinguishable. A Blum integer N is a product of two primes p, q satisfying $p, q \equiv 3 \bmod 4$. We denote by $\mathsf{Blum}(1^n)$ the algorithm that on input a security parameter n outputs a Blum integer N and one of its prime factors q, where the corresponding two prime factors are of length n. Due to space limitations, we refer readers to [Gol01] for definitions of witness indistinguishability, witness hiding.

Commitment and Trapdoor Commitment Schemes. Commitment schemes are "digital" safes. Formally, a commitment scheme (C, R) is a two-phase protocol between a committer C and a receiver R. To commit to a bit $b \in \{0, 1\}$, $C(b)$ and R execute the committing phase of (C, R) (denoted by $(C, R)_{\mathsf{Com}}$) and generate a commitment transcript $\mathsf{Com}(b)$; To decommit $\mathsf{Com}(b)$, C and R execute the opening phase of (C, R) (denoted by $(C, R)_{\mathsf{Open}}$) and reveal a decommitment (b, dec), and R accepts if the decommitment is valid.

Definition 1 (Commitment Scheme). *A two-phase protocol (C, R) is called a commitment scheme if it satisfies the following two properties:*

- *Binding: For every committer C^* of polynomial-size, the probability of the following event is negligible: C^* interacts with R and generates a commitment $\mathsf{Com}(b)$ in the committing phase, and then produces two decommitments (b, dec) and (b', dec') with $b \neq b'$ in two executions of the opening phase.*
- *Hiding: For every receiver R^* of polynomial size, the commitments $\mathsf{Com}(0)$ and $\mathsf{Com}(1)$ are computational indistinguishable.*

A trapdoor commitment scheme is a commitment scheme with an additional property: Given a trapdoor, C can later open a commitment to different values. In [FS89], Feige and Shamir showed how to transform Blum's 3-round interactive proof into a trapdoor commitment scheme. In our construction of selective opening secure commitment, we need a version of Feige-Shamir trapdoor commitment based on factoring. Using a standard commitment (built from the factoring assumption) Com as a building block, our trapdoor commitment scheme (TDGen, TDCom, Open, Fakeopen) proceeds as follows.

- TDGen: On input the security parameter n, TDGen generates $(N, q) \leftarrow \mathsf{Blum}(1^n)$. Define an NP relation $\{(N, q) : q|N\}$, and transform (N, q) into a graph G and an associated Hamiltonian cycle $H \subseteq G$. Output $((N, G), q)$.
- TDCom: On input G, a bit b and randomness r, if $b = 0$, pick a random permutation π and commit to the adjacency matrix of $\pi(G)$; if $b = 1$, pick a random cycle H' and commit to the adjacency matrix of H'. In both cases, we use commitment scheme Com when committing to the adjacency matrix.
- Open: On input $(G, \mathsf{TDCom}(G, b, r), b, r)$, if $b = 0$, send π and open the entire adjacency matrix of $\pi(G)$; if $b = 1$, open the non-zero entries in the adjacency matrix of H' (i.e., open the cycle H'). We denote by (b, dec) the decommitment of the commiment $\mathsf{TDCom}(G, b, r)$.
- Fakeopen: On input $(G, H, \mathsf{TDCom}(G, 0, r), b, r)$, open to b in the same way as Open by setting $H' = \pi(H)$. Note that only when TDCom commits to 0, the commitment can be opened to both 0 and 1.

A Crucial Property. Our construction of a selective opening secure commitment scheme relies on the following property of the above trapdoor commitment scheme, which can be easily proved by applying standard hybrid argument to the underlying commitment scheme Com:
$\{(c, (1, dec)) : c \leftarrow \mathsf{TDCom}(G, 1, r); (1, dec) \leftarrow \mathsf{Open}(G, \mathsf{TDCom}(G, 1, r), 1, r)\}$ and $\{(c, (1, dec)) : c \leftarrow \mathsf{TDCom}(G, 0, r); (1, dec) \leftarrow \mathsf{Fakeopen}(G, H, \mathsf{TDCom}(G, 0, r), 1, r)\}$ are indistinguishable.

(T, ϵ)-Secure Under Selective Opening Attacks. Consider a k-parallel composition of a commitment scheme (C, R). A committer C^k and a receiver R^* execute the committing phase k times in parallel and generate k commitments $\{\zeta^i\}_{i\in[k]}$ to $\bar{b} = b_1||b_2||\cdots||b_k$, each ζ^i is a commitment to b_i. In a selective opening attack, R^* chooses a set $I \in \mathcal{I}$ (possibly depending the commitments received) and asks the committer C^k to open the commitments $\{\zeta^i\}_{i\in I}$, where $\mathcal{I}$ is the family of subset of $[k]$. Informally, the commitment scheme (C, R) is said to be secure under selective opening attacks if the remaining unopened commitments still stay secret.

Definition 2 ((T, ϵ)-secure under selective opening attacks). *Let k be an arbitrary polynomial in n, and $\mathcal{B}$ be a distribution on $\{0, 1\}^k$, and $\mathcal{I}$ be the family of subset of $[k]$. A commitment scheme (C, R) is (T, ϵ)-secure under selective opening attacks if for any polynomial T, any inverse polynomial ϵ, any polynomial size $\mathcal{B}$, and any polynomial size R^*, there exists a polynomial size* Sim *such* *that for any distinguisher* D_n *of size* T, D_n *cannot tell apart the following two distributions*

- $(C^k(\bar{b}), R^*)$: $\bar{b} \leftarrow \mathcal{B}$; $\{\zeta^i\}_{i\in[k]} \leftarrow (C^k(\bar{b}), R^*)_{\mathsf{Com}}$; $I \leftarrow R^*(\{\zeta^i\}_{i\in[k]})$; $\{(b_i, dec_i)\}_{i\in I} \leftarrow (C^k(\bar{b}), R^*)_{\mathsf{Open}}$; $Out_{R^*} \leftarrow R^*(\{(b_i, dec_i)\}_{i\in I})$. *Output* $(\bar{b}, I, Out_{R^*})$;
- SIM: $\bar{b} \leftarrow \mathcal{B}$; $I \leftarrow \mathsf{Sim}$; $Out_{\mathsf{Sim}} \leftarrow \mathsf{Sim}(\{b_i\}_{i\in I}))$. *Output* $(\bar{b}, I, Out_{\mathsf{Sim}})$,

with probability greater than ϵ, *i.e.*,

$$|\Pr[\mathsf{D}_n((C^k(\bar{b}), R^*)) = 1] - \Pr[\mathsf{D}_n(\text{SIM}) = 1]| < \epsilon.$$

Delayed Input Argument and (T, ϵ)-ZK. Let L be an NP language and R_L be its associated relation. An interactive argument system (P, V) for L is a pair of parties of polynomial size, in which the prover P wants to convince the verifier V of some statement $x \in L$. We denote by $(P, V)(x)$ the output of V at the end of interaction on common input x, and by $\mathsf{View}_V^P(x)$ the view of the verifier in the real interaction. Without loss of generality, we have the verifier V outputs 1 (resp. 0) if V accepts (resp. rejects).

In this paper we consider *delayed-input* interactive arguments, in which the common input to both parties is the size of the statement x, and the verifier receives x only in the last round. Note that in a delayed-input interactive argument, a malicious prover may choose statement depending on the history, and thus such an argument needs to satisfy a stronger notion of adaptive soundness (cf. [JKKR17]).

A delayed-input argument system is zero knowledge if the view of the (even malicious) verifier in an interaction can be efficiently reconstructed. In this paper, we consider a weak version of zero knowledge–(T, ϵ)-zero knowledge [CLP15b], in which the indistinguishability gap between the real interaction and the simulation is at most ϵ against any T-size distinguisher.

Definition 3 (Delayed-input (T, ϵ)-zero knowledge). *We say that a delayed-input interactive argument* (P, V) *for language* L *is* (T, ϵ)*-zero-knowledge if for any polynomial* T, *any inverse polynomial* ϵ, *any polynomial-size* V^*, *there exists a circuit* Sim *of polynomial size such that for any* $x \in L$ *and any probabilistic* T*-size circuit* $\{D_n\}_{n\in\mathbb{N}}$ *and sufficiently large* n, *it holds that*

$$\left|\Pr[\mathsf{D}_n(\mathsf{View}_{V^*}^P(x)) = 1] - \Pr[\mathsf{D}_n(\mathsf{Sim}(x)) = 1]\right| < \epsilon.$$

Concurrent Zero Knowledge with Concurrent Soundness in the BPK Model. The bare public-key model (BPK model) simply works in two phases: the key-registration phase and the proof phase. In the key-registration phase, each verifier registers a public-key pk (the honest verifier is supposed to store the corresponding secret key sk) on a public-file F before the proof phase. In the proof phase, on a common input x, the prover and the verifier interact under the verifier's public key. The completeness of an interactive argument is normally defined.

Concurrent Soundness in the BPK Model. A malicious concurrent prover P^* is allowed to launch the following attack: In the proof phase, on input a pubic key pk, P^* initiates polynomially many sessions, in each of which it chooses a statement x adpatively (based on the history so far), and fully controls the message scheduling in the entire interaction with V.

Definition 4 (Concurrent Soundness in the BPK model). *An interactive argument (P, V) for a language L in the BPK model is called* concurrent sound *if for all malicious* concurrent *prover P^*, the probability that it makes V accept a false statement $x \notin L$ is negligible.*

Concurrent (T, ϵ)-Zero Knowledge in the BPK Model. A malicious concurrent verifier V^* is allowed to generate an arbitrary file F of polynomially many public keys in the key-registration phase. In the proof phase, it receives s (for some polynomial s) statements $\bar{x} = \{x_i\}_{i\in[s]}$, and initiates at most s sessions under public keys on F. During the entire interaction, V^* fully controls the message scheduling.

Definition 5 (Concurrent (T, ϵ)-zero knowledge In the BPK model). *An interactive argument (P, V) for language L is called concurrent (T, ϵ)-zero-knowledge if for any polynomial T, any inverse polynomial ϵ, any polynomial-size concurrent V^*, any polynomial s, there exists a circuit* Sim *of polynomial size such that for any Yes instances $\bar{x} = \{x_i\}_{i\in[s]}$, for any probabilistic T-size circuit $\{\mathsf{D}_n\}_{n\in\mathbb{N}}$ and sufficiently large n it holds that*

$$\left|\Pr[\mathsf{D}_n(\mathsf{View}_{V^*}^{P(F)}(\bar{x})) = 1] - \Pr[\mathsf{D}_n(\mathsf{Sim}(\bar{x})) = 1]\right| < \epsilon.$$

3 The Existence of Nearly Optimal Extractors for All Hard Distribution

In this section we prove the existence of nearly optimal extractors for all NP-instance(s) sampling algorithms. Essentially, we show that, for any NP-instance(s) sampler, any polynomial T, any inverse polynomial ϵ, and any circuit family C_n of size T, there exists an efficient extractor such that the probability that C_n extracts a witness for an instance generated by the sampler but the extractor fails is at most ϵ. Furthermore, if the extractor is allowed to be of quasi-polynomial size, then the same result holds with respect to *negligible* ϵ.

Let Samp be an arbitrarily sampling algorithm over an NP language L and $\{Y_n\}_{n\in\mathbb{N}}$ be its input distribution ensemble. Throughout this paper, we assume that the input $y \leftarrow Y_n$ to Samp includes its randomness. (Thus one can view Samp as a deterministic algorithm.)

Lemma 1 [nearly optimal (T, ϵ)-Extractor]**.** *Let* Samp *be as above. Let $f : \{0,1\}^* \rightarrow \{0,1\}^*$ be an arbitrary (not necessarily efficient-computable) function.*

1. *For every polynomial T, every inverse polynomial ϵ, there exists a probabilistic circuit family* $\mathsf{Ext} := \{\mathsf{Ext}_n\}_{n\in\mathbb{N}}$ *of polynomial size such that for every probabilistic circuit family* $\{C_n\}_{n\in\mathbb{N}}$ *of size T,*

$$\Pr\left[\begin{array}{c} y \leftarrow Y_n; x \leftarrow \mathsf{Samp}(y); \\ w \leftarrow \mathsf{Ext}_n(x, y, f(y)); \\ w' \leftarrow C_n(x, y, f(y)) \end{array} : \begin{array}{c} (x, w) \notin R_L \wedge \\ (x, w') \in R_L \end{array}\right] < \epsilon(n) \tag{1}$$

We call Ext *a (T, ϵ)-extractor.*
2. *There exists a probabilistic circuit family* $\mathsf{Ext} := \{\mathsf{Ext}_n\}_{n\in\mathbb{N}}$ *of quasi-polynomial size such that for every probabilistic circuit family* $\{C_n\}_{n\in\mathbb{N}}$ *of polynomial size, the above probability is negligible.*

Remark 1. Jumping ahead, in our protocols the receiver/verifier will play the role of the hard instance sampler. For all our constructions, we need not take the function f into account since they just compute a hard instance based solely on their random tape. However, when our protocols are used as a sub-protocol in some big protocols or in the settings of [JKKR17,BKP19], the receiver/verifier may compute a hard instance based on some history y, and the simulator may need certain secret information $f(y)$ (e.g., an opening of a commitment in history y) to go through. In such cases, it is more flexible to allow the extractor to take as additional input $f(y)$.

As mentioned in the introduction, the basic idea underlying the proof is to keep iterating to include new powerful circuits into the extractor until we have a desired one. For applications, we need a stronger and robust version of Lemma 1 for samplers that output multiple instances, which we prove below.

Fix a polynomial t and consider a t-instance sampler Samp that is given y as input and outputs t instances of NP language L, $(x_1, x_2, \cdot, \cdot, \cdot, x_t) \leftarrow \mathsf{Samp}(y)$, where y is drawn from distribution Y_n.

Lemma 2 [nearly optimal (T, ϵ)-Extractor for t-Instance Sampler]. *Let L be an NP language and poly be the size of the circuits for deciding the NP-relation R_L. Let* Samp *be an arbitrarily t-instance sampling algorithm over L with input distribution ensemble $\{Y_n\}_{n\in\mathbb{N}}$. Let $f : \{0,1\}^* \rightarrow \{0,1\}^*$ be an arbitrary (not necessarily efficient-computable) function.*

1. *For every polynomial T, every inverse polynomial ϵ, there exists a probabilistic circuit family* $\mathsf{Ext} := \{\mathsf{Ext}_n\}_{n\in\mathbb{N}}$ *of size $O(\frac{t}{\epsilon}(T + poly))$, such that for every $j \in [t]$, every probabilistic circuit family $\{C_n\}_{n\in\mathbb{N}}$ of size T,*

$$\Pr\left[\begin{array}{c} y \leftarrow Y_n; \{x_k\}_{k\in[t]} \leftarrow \mathsf{Samp}(y); \\ \{w_k\}_{k\in[t]} \leftarrow \mathsf{Ext}_n(\{x_k\}_{k\in[t]}, y, f(y)); \\ w'_j \leftarrow C_n(\{x_k\}_{k\in[t]}, \{w_k\}_{k\in[t]}, y, f(y)) \end{array} : \begin{array}{c} (x_j, w_j) \notin R_L \wedge \\ (x_j, w'_j) \in R_L \end{array}\right] < \epsilon(n), \tag{2}$$

where the probability takes over the randomness choice of y, and the random tapes for that for Ext_n *and C_n.*

2. *There exists a probabilistic circuit family* $\mathsf{Ext} := \{\mathsf{Ext}_n\}_{n \in \mathbb{N}}$ *of quasi-polynomial size such that for every* $j \in [t]$ *and every probabilistic circuit family* $\{C_n\}_{n \in \mathbb{N}}$ *of polynomial size, the above probability is negligible.*

Remark 2. Notice that in the above lemma we allow the circuit C_n to take the output of Ext_n as input. This does not matter for a single-instance sampler. However, as we shall see in Sect. 5 and 6, this property is critical for hybrid arguments to go through in the composable settings.

Lemma 2 says there is an extractor for the multi-instance sampler that is nearly optimal for solving instances in every coordinate $j \in [t]$. We argue the existence of such a nearly optimal extractor via the following delicate iterative procedure. In each *outer* iteration $i \in [\frac{t}{\epsilon}]$, for every $j \in [t]$ we ask if there is circuit $C_{n,j}^{(i)}$ that, *taking as input the output of the current* Ext_n, can be used to increase the success probability of solving the j-th instance x_j by (at least) ϵ, and if so, then we add $C_{n,j}$ to Ext_n.

Proof (of Lemma 2). For every $j \in [t]$, we define $\uplus_j$ composition of two circuits Ext_n and $C_{n,j}$ in the following way:

$\mathsf{Ext}_n \uplus_j C_{n,j}(\{x_k\}_{k \in [t]}, y, f(y))$:

1. Sampling a random tape for Ext_n, obtain $\{w_k\}_{k \in [t]} \leftarrow \mathsf{Ext}_n(\{x_k\}_{k \in [t]}, y, f(y))$;
2. If $(x_j, w_j) \in R_L$, return $\{w_k\}_{k \in [t]}$;
3. Sampling a random tape for $C_{n,j}$, obtain $w'_j \leftarrow C_{n,j}(\{x_k\}_{k \in [t]}, \{w_k\}_{k \in [t]}, y, f(y))$;
4. If $(x_j, w'_j) \in R_L$, then $w_j \leftarrow w'_j$ and return $\{w_k\}_{k \in [t]}$; otherwise, return $\{w_k\}_{k \in [t]}$.

Note that the order of executions of these two circuits matters here since we have the second circuit take as input the output of the first circuit. This applies to each iteration of the following construction, and the final circuit Ext_n will execute all these $C_{n,j}^i$ in the order of their appearance. Let $\mathsf{Ext}_n^{(0)}$ be a dummy circuit that outputs t zeros. For an arbitrary t-instance Samp, we construct a nearly optimal extractor Ext_n as follows[8].

Constructing circuit Ext_n for the t-instance Samp:

1. $\mathsf{Ext}_n \leftarrow \mathsf{Ext}_n^{(0)}$;
2. For $i = 1$ to $\frac{t}{\epsilon}$, do:
   2.1 For $j = 1$ to t, do:

[8] We would like to stress that in this construction the number of outer iterations may reach $\frac{t}{\epsilon}$. Notice that in each iteration, the quality of the current extractor may have impact on the answer to the question of whether or not there exists a new satisfactory circuit $C_{n,j}^{(i)}$ since the new target circuit is given the output of the current extractor. Thus, even if there does not exists a satisfactory $C_{n,j}^{(i)}$ in the i-th outer iteration, we cannot rule out the possibility that we will find a satisfactory $C_{n,j}^{(i+1)}$ in the $(i+1)$-th outer iteration, because the extractor would become more powerful as iterations proceed.

If $\exists$ a circuit $C_{n,j}^{(i)}$ of size T s.t.

$$\Pr\left[\begin{array}{c} y \leftarrow Y_n; \{x_k\}_{k\in[t]} \leftarrow \mathsf{Samp}(y); \\ \{w_k\}_{k\in[t]} \leftarrow \mathsf{Ext}_n(\{x_k\}_{k\in[t]}, y, f(y)); \\ w_j' \leftarrow C_{n,j}^{(i)}(\{x_k\}_{k\in[t]}, \{w_k\}_{k\in[t]}, y, f(y)) \end{array} : \begin{array}{c} (x_j, w_j) \notin R_L \wedge \\ (x_j, w_j') \in R_L \end{array}\right] \geq \epsilon(n), \tag{3}$$

then $\mathsf{Ext}_n \leftarrow \mathsf{Ext}_n \uplus_j C_{n,j}^{(i)}$;

2.2 If for any $j \in [t]$, $\nexists$ $C_{n,j}^{(i)}$ satisfying (3), then break and return Ext_n.

3. Return Ext_n

We now show that the Ext_n constructed above satisfies Lemma 2. We first make the following two observations:

1. For any $j' \neq j$, the circuit $\mathsf{Ext}_n \uplus_{j'} C_{n,j'}^{(i)}$ solves the j-th instance x_j with exactly the same probability of Ext_n. This is because in the above composition $C_{n,j}$ is only invoked to correct the witness w_j obtained by Ext_n.
2. For each new $C_{n,j}^{(i)}$, the circuit $\mathsf{Ext}_n \uplus_j C_{n,j}^{(i)}$ increases the success probability of solving the j-th instance x_j by (at least) ϵ.

Note that if in some outer iteration $i \leq \frac{t}{\epsilon}$, no new circuit is added to Ext_n in any inner iteration $j \in [t]$, then the iterative process will return a desirable circuit Ext_n as required in Lemma 2; otherwise, the following two events must happen during the entire iterative process: (a) There are (at least) $\frac{t}{\epsilon}$ circuits $C_{n,j}^{(i)}$ of size T that are added to Ext_n, and (b) For each $j \in [t]$ the number of circuits $C_{n,j}^{(i_m)}$ ($i_m \in [\frac{t}{\epsilon}]$) added to Ext_n is at most $\frac{1}{\epsilon}$. The latter event (b) holds because of the two observations mentioned above, which imply that adding more than $\frac{1}{\epsilon}$ circuits $C_{n,j}^{(i_m)}$ would yield an extractor with success probability of solving the j-th instance greater than 1.

Putting (a) and (b) together, we have that, for every j, exactly $\frac{1}{\epsilon}$ circuits $C_{n,j}^{(i_m)}$ are added to Ext_n, and the final circuit Ext_n returned solves the j-th instance with probability 1. It is easy to verify that the size of the final Ext_n is of at most $O(\frac{t}{\epsilon}(T + \text{poly}))$. This concludes Lemma 2.

For the second part of this lemma, one can set T and ϵ to be $n^{\omega(1)}$ and $\frac{1}{n^{\omega(1)}}$ respectively, construct the circuit family $\mathsf{Ext} = \{\mathsf{Ext}_n\}_{n\in\mathbb{N}}$ of size $n^{\omega(1)}$ in a similar way. $\square$

4 Extracting the Secret Key of a Variant of Rabin's Encryption Scheme

We are now going to apply Lemma 2 to a variant of a factoring-based encryption scheme, and show the existence of a nearly optimal secret-key extractor, such that the probability that an arbitrary bounded-size circuit family succeeds in distinguishing ciphertexts but the extractor fails to extract a secret key is very small.

We consider an encryption scheme based on Rabin's trapdoor one-way permutations. Let N be a Blum integer of length n, and QR_N be the set of quadratic residues (mod N). Rabin's trapdoor one way permutation $f_N : QR_N \to QR_N$ (with a prime factor of N as its trapdoor) is defined as $f_N(s) = s^2 \bmod N$. The one-wayness of f_N is based on the fact that different square roots lead to factor N. Specifically, given a circuit A of size T that inverts $f_N(s)$ with probability ε, by Lemma 10 in [TW87], we have a circuit of size $O(T\frac{1}{\varepsilon})$ that can factor N with probability negligibly close to 1.

Let $h(\cdot)$ be an arbitrary hard-core function of $f_N(\cdot)$[9]. We follow the classic approach and obtain the following semantically secure bit encryption scheme ($\mathsf{Gen} = \mathsf{Blum}, \mathsf{Enc}, \mathsf{Dec}$). The public key is a randomly generated Blum integer N, and the secret key is a prime factor of N:

- Enc_N: To encrypt a bit b, the encryption algorithm Enc selects a random $s \in QR_N$ (which can be done by selecting a random $t \in Z_N$ and then set s to be $t^2 \bmod N$), and computes $f_N(s)$ and $h(s) \oplus b$. Enc outputs the ciphertext $c = (f_N(s), h(s) \oplus b)$;
- Dec_N: To decrypt a ciphertext c, the decryption algorithm Dec uses the secret key to invert the first part of c, and then computes $h(s)$ and outputs b.

The semantic security follows from the hardness of factoring assumption: A good ciphertext distinguisher will give rise to an efficient algorithm that finds square roots modulo N, which can be used to factor N.

In our constructions of commitment and zero knowledge protocols, we will have one party generate one (or two) public key(s) of the above encryption scheme and use one secret key to decrypt the messages from the other party. We would like to stress that, in case that a malicious party generates a non-Blum integer as its public key, the function f_N in the encryption may no longer be a permutation. Fortunately, such a malicious behavior only causes difficulty for the malicious party to decrypt the ciphertext computed by the honest party, and does not affect the property –the equivalence between distinguishing ciphertexts and factoring– that is required to establish simulatability of our protocols.

We now give a formal statement of this property with respect to the encryption scheme above. Here we slightly abuse these notations, and define $f_N : QR_N \to QR_N$ and the "encryption" function $\mathsf{Enc}_N(b) := (f_N(s), h(s) \oplus b)$ over an arbitrary (positive) integer N.

Lemma 3 [Implied by [GL89, ACGS88, TW87]]. *For any positive integer N of length n and any inverse polynomial $\delta(n)$, if there exists a probabilistic circuit family $\{A_n\}_{n \in \mathbb{N}}$ of size T such that for any auxiliary input $\alpha \in \{0,1\}^*$,*

[9] The constructions of the hardcore of $f_N(\cdot)$ appeared in [ACGS88, GL89]. Note that, when using the Goldreich-Levin hardcore function [GL89], we need to change the description of our encryption scheme a little bit, since the Goldreich-Levin hardcore function is actually constructed for the permutation $f'_N(s,r) = (f_N(s), r)$ (where $|r| = |s|$). We ignore such changes in the description of our encryption scheme for the sake of simplifying the presentation.

$$\Pr[b \leftarrow \{0,1\}; c \leftarrow \mathsf{Enc}_N(b); A_n(c, N, \alpha) = b' : b = b'] \geq \frac{1}{2} + \delta(n)$$

then there exists a probabilistic circuit family $\{B_n\}_{n\in\mathbb{N}}$ *of size* $O(\frac{1}{\delta^5}n^3T)$ *that can factor* N *with probability*

$$\Pr[q \leftarrow B_n(N, \alpha) : q|N] \geq 1 - negl(n).$$

Proof Sketch. The hardcore theorems [GL89, ACGS88] state that, given a successful distinguisher A_n of size T for the "encryption" function Enc_N with advantage δ, we can construct a new circuit of size $O(\frac{1}{\delta^4}n^3T)$ that computes the square roots modulo N with roughly the same successful probability. If δ is an inverse polynomial, then by [TW87] such a square root circuit can be used to factor the integer N in size $O(\frac{1}{\delta^5}n^3T)$ with probability negligibly close to 1. □

Applying Lemma 2 to a t-integer sampler $\{N_i\}_{i\in[t]} \leftarrow \mathsf{Samp}$, we can show that there exists a nearly optimal extractor Ext for Samp such that for every j if Ext fails to extract a prime factor of N_j, then no circuit of a-prior bounded size can distinguish a ciphertext (except for small advantage). Formally, we obtain the following result (and defer the proof of this lemma to the full version).

Lemma 4. *Let t be a polynomial, and* Samp *be an arbitrarily t-integer sampling algorithm with input distribution ensemble* $\{Y_n\}_{n\in\mathbb{N}}$. *Let* $f : \{0,1\}^* \rightarrow \{0,1\}^*$ *be an arbitrary (not necessarily efficiently computable) function.*

1. *For any polynomial T, any inverse polynomial ϵ, there exists a probabilistic circuit family* $\mathsf{Ext} := \{\mathsf{Ext}_n\}_{n\in\mathbb{N}}$ *of polynomial-size such that for every probabilistic circuit family* $\{A_n\}_{n\in\mathbb{N}}$ *of size T, for every* $j \in [t]$, *we have*

$$\Pr\left[\begin{array}{r} y \leftarrow Y_n; \{N_i\}_{i\in[t]} \leftarrow \mathsf{Samp}(y); \\ \{q_i\}_{i\in[t]} \leftarrow \mathsf{Ext}_n(\{N_i\}_{i\in[t]}, y, f(y)); \\ b \leftarrow \{0,1\}; c \leftarrow \mathsf{Enc}_{N_j}(b); \\ b' \leftarrow A_n(c, \{q_i\}_{i\in[t]}, \{N_i\}_{i\in[t]}, j, y, f(y)) \end{array} : \begin{array}{c} b = b' \wedge \\ q_j \nmid N_j \end{array}\right]$$
$$< \frac{1}{2}\Pr\left[\begin{array}{r} y \leftarrow Y_n; \{N_i\}_{i\in[t]} \leftarrow \mathsf{Samp}(y); \\ \{q_i\}_{i\in[t]} \leftarrow \mathsf{Ext}_n(\{N_i\}_{i\in[t]}, y, f(y)) \end{array} : q_j \nmid N_j\right] + \epsilon(n)$$

2. *There exists a probabilistic circuit family* Ext *of quasi-polynomial size such that for every probabilistic circuit family* $\{C_n\}_{n\in\mathbb{N}}$ *of polynomial size, the above holds with respect to a negligible function* ϵ.

5 Selective Opening (T, ϵ)-Secure Commitment Scheme

We use the following ingredients in our construction of a selective opening secure commitment scheme:

- The trapdoor commitment (TDGen, TDCom, Open, Fakeopen) described in Sect. 2;

– The variant of Rabin's encryption scheme presented in Sect. 4.

With these two building blocks, we construct a selective opening secure commitment scheme as follows. In the committing phase, we have the receiver run the trapdoor generator and produce (N, q) $(q|N)$ and transform (N, q) into (G, H), then send N and the graph G to the committer; upon receiving N, the committer invokes TDCom and generates a commitment c, encrypts c bit-by-bit under the public key N, and sends all these encryptions to the receiver. In the opending phase, the committer simply sends the opening of c to the receiver, who decrypts the ciphertexts received in the committing phase using secret keys q and obtains c, and checks whether the opening received from the committer is a valid decommitment of c.

Formally, our selective opening secure commitment scheme proceeds as follows.

$\mathsf{Protocol}_{soa}$:

Committing phase:

$R \longrightarrow C$: $((N, G), q) \leftarrow \mathsf{TDGen}(1^n)$. Send (N, G).

$C \longrightarrow R$: $c = c_1||c_2||\cdots||c_\ell \leftarrow \mathsf{TDCom}(G, b, r)$, $\{\zeta_i \leftarrow \mathsf{Enc}_N(c_i)\}_{i\in[\ell]}$. Send $\{\zeta_i\}_{i\in[\ell]}$.

Opening Phase:

$C \longrightarrow R$: Send $(b, dec) \leftarrow \mathsf{Open}(G, \mathsf{TDCom}(G, b, r), b, r)$.

R: $c \leftarrow \{\mathsf{Dec}_N(\zeta_i, q)\}_{i\in[\ell]}$. Accept iff (b, dec) is a valid opening of c.

Theorem 1. *Assuming the standard hardness of factoring,* $\mathsf{Protocol}_{soa}$ *is a commitment scheme that satisfies the following properties:*

1. *(T, ϵ)-security under selective opening attacks.*
2. *Full security under selective opening attacks with a quasi-polynomial simulator.*

Proof. Note that the second property follows directly from the first property and the second part of Lemma 4. Here we just prove the first property.

Computational Binding Property. Suppose that there is a malicious adversary C^* that can open a random commitment to two different values with noticeable probability δ. We construct an efficient algorithm Factor, which uses C^* as a subroutine, to break the factoring assumption.

Factor plays the role of the honest receiver R, except that it doesn't check if a decommitment is consistent with the plaintext c encrypted in the ciphertexts received in the committing phase. More specifically, given a Blum integer N as input, Factor transforms it into a graph G, and sends (N, G) to C^* as its first message; upon receiving C^*'s committing phase message and two different decommitments (b, dec) and (b', dec') (with $b \neq b'$), Factor applies the standard extractor to these decommitments, and if it extracts a prime factor q of N, outputs it.

Note that a successful opening in a real interaction implies at least that the decommitment received by R is a valid opening of the plaintext c encrypted by C^* in the committing phase. That means, in case C^* successfully opens a commitment to two different decommitments (b, dec) and (b', dec') in the real world, one can alway extract a prime factor of N from only the two decommitments (without the need for knowledge of the plaintext c). Thus, the above algorithm Factor will output a prime factor of N with probability δ, breaking the factoring assumption.

(T, ϵ)-Security Under Selective Opening. Our simulation strategy for a k-parallel selective opening attacker R^* is quite simple in spirit. When receiving the first k integers $N_1, N_2, ..., N_k$, the simulator applies the nearly optimal extractor against T-size circuits and tries to extract a prime factor for each N_i, if it succeeds for some N_i, then the i-th commitment becomes equivocal and can be opened to different values; if it fails for N_i, then, in the eye of a T-size distinguisher, the i-th commitment is also "equivocal", since it is unable to extract a secret key of N_i either, and hence unable to tell whether the commitment c determined by the decommitment (b', dec') received is the very plaintext encrypted in the ciphertexts.

To give a formal description of the simulator, we introduce the following notations. (In what follows, we ignore the function f considered in Sect. 3 and 4.)

- $\{Y_n\}_{n\in\mathbb{N}}$: the distribution ensemble of the randomnesses for the k-parallel selective opening receiver R^*.
- Algorithm Samp is defined to be the committing phase of R^*: $y \leftarrow Y_n$, $\{N_i, G_i\}_{i\in[k]} \leftarrow R^*(y)$, output $\{N_i\}_{i\in[k]}$.
- $(T', \delta) := ((kT_c + T), \frac{\epsilon}{k\ell})$. Here T_c and T denote the size of the committer C and the distinguisher D_n respectively. ϵ is the advantage of the distinguisher that we tolerate. Note that our goal is to show that an arbitrary circuit of size T cannot distinguish a simulation from the real interaction with advantage greater than ϵ.

For the above sampling algorithm Samp, Lemma 4 guarantees that there exists a nearly optimal $(T', \delta = \frac{\epsilon}{k\ell})$-extractor $\mathsf{Ext} := \{\mathsf{Ext}_n\}_{n\in\mathbb{N}}$ against any plaintext-extractor of size T'. Let $\mathcal{B}$ be a k-bit message distribution.

Consider the following distribution SIM generated by Sim.

SIM:

1. $y \leftarrow Y_n$; $\{N_i, G_i\}_{i\in[k]} \leftarrow R^*$; $\bar{b} = b_1||b_2|| \cdots ||b_k \leftarrow \mathcal{B}$;
2. Sim runs $\mathsf{Ext}_n(\{N_i\}_{i\in[k]}, y)$ and obtains $\{q_i\}_{i\in[k]}$.
3. Sim computes k commitments to 0 independently, $c^i \leftarrow \mathsf{TDcom}(G_i, 0, r_i)$, $1 \le i \le k$, $\zeta^i \leftarrow \{\mathsf{Enc}_{N_i}(c^i_j)\}_{j\in[\ell]}$, and sends $\{\zeta^i\}_{i\in[k]}$ to R^*.

4. Upon receiving $I \leftarrow R^*(\{\zeta^i\}_{i\in[k]})$ and $\{b_i\}_{i\in I}$, Sim opens $\{\zeta^i\}_{i\in I}$ in the following way:
   (a) If $b_i = 0$, open ζ^i to $(b_i = 0, dec_i)$ in an honest way;
   (b) If $q_i|N_i$ and $b_i = 1$, run $\mathsf{Fakeopen}(G_i, H_i, c^i, 0, r_i)$ to open ζ^i to $(b_i = 1, dec_i)$, where H_i is a simple cycle of G_i, transformed from (N_i, q_i);
   (c) If $q_i \nmid N_i$ and $b_i = 1$, compute a commitment $\tilde{c}^i \leftarrow \mathsf{TDcom}(G_i, 1, \tilde{r}_i)$ to 1, and set the opening of ζ^i to be the decommitment $(1, dec_i)$ of $\tilde{c}^i$.
5. Run $Out_{\mathsf{Sim}} \leftarrow R^*(\{(b_i, dec_i))\}_{i\in I})$, and output $(\bar{b}, I, Out_{\mathsf{Sim}})$.

We use hybrid argument to prove that SIM is indistinguishable from the real interaction between R^* and C^k. Consider the following sequence of hybrid experiments, in each of which we allow Sim to take the message $\bar{b}$ as an auxiliary input.

Define SIM^0 be identical to SIM. For $1 \le m \le k$, SIM^m acts in the same way as SIM^{m-1} except that Sim in SIM^m computes the m-th commitment c^m to b_m in step 3 and opens it honestly in step 4 when $m \in I$.

Note that SIM^k is identical to the real interaction. To conclude the proof of Theorem 1, it remains to show that, for every distinguisher D_n of size T, for all $1 \le m \le k$,

$$|\Pr[\mathsf{D}_n(\mathrm{SIM}^{m-1}) = 1] - \Pr[\mathsf{D}_n(\mathrm{SIM}^m) = 1]| < \frac{\epsilon}{k}. \quad (4)$$

We now construct a sequence of sub-hybrids to establish the inequality (4). Fix an $m \in [k]$. For $0 \le t \le \ell$, consider the hybrid SIM_t^m:

SIM_t^m:

1. Run step 1 and 2 of SIM and obtain $\bar{b}$, $\{N_i, G_i\}_{i\in[k]}$ and $\{q_i\}_{i\in[k]}$.
2. On input $\bar{b}$, Sim runs TDcom and generates the first $m-1$ commitments to $b_1, b_2, ..., b_{m-1}$, and the last $k-m-1$ commitments to 0, and then encrypts these commitments bit-wise and obtains $\{\zeta^i\}_{i\in[k]\setminus m}$. Sim computes the m-th commitment in the following way:
   (a) If $q_m|N_m$ or $b_m = 0$, Sim computes a commitment c^m to 0 and generates ζ^m correspondingly.
   (b) If $q_m \nmid N_m$ and $b_m = 1$, it computes a commitment c^m to 0 and a commitment $\tilde{c}^m$ to 1, and the bit-wise encryptions ζ^m of $\hat{c}^m = c_1^m||\cdots||c_t^m||\tilde{c}_{t+1}^m||\cdots||\tilde{c}_\ell^m$, where c_j^m and $\tilde{c}_j^m$ are the j-th bit of c^m and $\tilde{c}^m$ respectively.

   Sim sends $\{\zeta^i\}_{i\in[k]}$ to R^*.
3. Upon receiving $I \leftarrow R^*(\{\zeta^i\}_{i\in[k]})$, Sim does the following: for $i \in [m-1] \cap I$, open ζ^i in an honest way; for $i \in [m+1, k] \cap I$, open ζ^i according to the step 4 of SIM; for $i = m \in I$, Sim opens ζ^i according to the step 4 of SIM except that, in the case of $q_m \nmid N_m$ and $b_m = 1$, it sets the opening of ζ^m to be the decommitment of $\tilde{c}^m$ (already computed in the previous step).

4. Run $Out_{\mathsf{Sim}} \leftarrow R^*(\{(b_i, dec_i))\}_{i\in I})$, and output $(\bar{b}, I, Out_{\mathsf{Sim}})$.

Observe that when $t = 0$, SIM_0^m computes the commitment c^m to 0 in case $q_m \nmid N_m$ and $b_m = 1$, and sets its opening to be the decommitment of an independent commitment $\tilde{c}^m$ to 1. That is, SIM_0^m acts exactly in the same way as SIM^{m-1}. We conclude the inequality (4) (and the Theorem 1) by the following two lemmas.

Lemma 5. $SIM_\ell^m \overset{c}{\approx} SIM^m$.

Lemma 6. *For all* $1 \le t \le \ell$, *and for all distingshuier* D_n *of size* T,

$$|\Pr[\mathsf{D}_n(SIM_{t-1}^m) = 1] - \Pr[\mathsf{D}_n(SIM_t^m) = 1]| < \frac{\epsilon}{k\ell}.$$

Due to space limitations, the proof of these two lemmas are provided in the full verison of this paper. □

6 Concurrent (T,ϵ)-Zero Knowledge and Witness Hiding in the BPK Model

In this section we present a very simple three-round concurrent (T, ϵ)-zero knowledge and witness hiding argument for NP in the BPK model. The construction relies on the *polynomial hardness* of factoring, and makes use of only two simple building blocks: the factoring-based encryption and the three round parallel version of Blum's protocol $(P_{\mathrm{B}}, V_{\mathrm{B}})$. Let a transcript of $(P_{\mathrm{B}}, V_{\mathrm{B}})$ be of the form (a, e, z), and P_{B}^1 and P_{B}^2 be the first and the second prover steps respectively.

In the key registration phase, an honest verifier generates two Blum integers N_0 and N_1 of length n, and stores *two* prime factors q_0 and q_1, $q_i|N_i$ for each $i \in \{0, 1\}$. It registers (N_0, N_1) as his public-key. In the proof phase, on input the verifier's public key (N_0, N_1) and the statement $x \in L$, the prover and the verifier execute $(P_{\mathrm{B}}, V_{\mathrm{B}})$ in which P_{B} proves the statement "$x \in L$ OR $\exists q$ *s.t.* $q|N_0$ or $q|N_1$". Denote such a prover by $P_{\mathrm{B}}(x \vee N_0 \vee N_1))$.

The formal description of our protocol follows.

$\mathsf{Protocol}_{czk}$:

Common input: $x \in R_L$, (N_0, N_1).
Private input to P: w s.t. $(x, w) \in R_L$.

$P \longrightarrow V$: Send $a \leftarrow P_{\mathrm{B}}^1(x \vee N_0 \vee N_1))$.

$V \longrightarrow P$: Send $e \leftarrow V_{\mathrm{B}}$.

$P \longrightarrow V$: $z = z_1||z_2||\cdots||z_\ell \leftarrow P_{\mathrm{B}}^2(x \vee N_0 \vee N_1)$, $\{\zeta_{i,j} \leftarrow \mathsf{Enc}_{N_i}(z_j)\}_{i\in\{0,1\} j\in[\ell]}$. Send $\{\zeta_{0,j}\}_{j\in[\ell]}$ and $\{\zeta_{1,j}\}_{j\in[\ell]}$.

V: $\hat{z} \leftarrow \{\mathsf{Dec}_N(\zeta_{0,j}, q_0)\}_{j\in[\ell]}$, $\tilde{z} \leftarrow \{\mathsf{Dec}_N(\zeta_{1,j}, q_1)\}_{j\in[\ell]}$. Accept iff $\hat{z} = \tilde{z}$ and $(a, e, \hat{z})$ is accepting.

Theorem 2. *Under the standard hardness assumption of factoring,* $\mathsf{Protocol}_{czk}$ *is an argument that satisfies the following properties:*

1. Concurrent (T, ϵ)-zero knowledge with concurrent soundness.
2. Concurrent witness hiding.
3. Concurrent zero knowledge with quasi-polynomial time simulator.

Proof. **Completeness** is obvious.

Concurrent Soundness. Suppose, towards a contradiction, that a cheating concurrent prover P^* initiates k sessions and makes the verifier accept a false statement $x \notin L$ with noticeable probability δ in one session. We can then construct an efficient algorithm Factor using P^* as a subroutine to factor a randomly chosen Blum integer with noticeable probability. Factor takes a Blum integer N as input, chooses two primes p, q ($\equiv 3 \bmod 4$) and a random $i \in \{0, 1\}$, sets N_i to be pq, N_{1-i} to be N. In the key registration phase, Factor registers (N_0, N_1) as his public key and keeps q as its secret key. In the proof phase, Factor chooses a random session, and try to obtain two accepting accpeting transcripts (a, e, z) and (a, e', z') and compute a witness q'(i.e., a prime factor of N_0 or N_1) from them.

It is not hard to show that q' is a prime factor of N_{1-i} with high probabiity, and this contradicts the hardness of factoring. The actual proof can be done by combining the standard analysis with a crucial observation, as mentioned in the introduction, that a successful cheating on session s means it will pass an *honest* verifier's check, which in turn implies that at least the both collections of ciphertexts in the last message can be decrypted to the same accepting z.

Concurrent (T, ϵ)-Zero Knowledge. Consider an arbitrary concurrent adversary V^* of polynomial size. We show there *exists* a simulator of polynomial size to establish the weak zero knowledge property.

Suppose that V^* registers k public keys $\{(N_0^i, N_1^i)\}_{i \in [k]}$ and initiates at most s sessions. As before, the simulator applies the nearly optimal extractor to factor all integers registered by V^* in the key registration phase. Once the simulator extracts a prime factor of one of (N_0^i, N_1^i), it can complete any session under the public key (N_0^i, N_1^i) successfully; if it fails for a public key (N_0^i, N_1^i), the simulator computes encryptions of zeros as its last message in the sessions under the public key (N_0^i, N_1^i).

Let Y_n be the distribution of V^*'s randomness, and the sampling algorithm Samp to be the V^*'s registration step. Set (T', δ) to be $((s(2\ell T_{enc} + T_p) + T), \frac{\epsilon}{4s\ell})$, where T_{enc}, T_p and T are the size of Enc, the honest prover of the Blum protocol (P_B, V_B) and the distinguisher respectively, and ϵ is the advantage of the distinguisher that we tolerate. By Lemma 4 we have a polynomial-size $(T', \delta = \frac{\epsilon}{4\ell})$-extractor $\mathsf{Ext} := \{\mathsf{Ext}_n\}_{n \in \mathbb{N}}$ against any circuit family of size T'.

On input s Yes instances $\bar{x} = \{x_i\}_{i \in [s]}$, the simulator proceeds as follows.

$\mathsf{Sim}(\bar{x})$:

1. $y \leftarrow Y_n$, $\{(N_0^i, N_1^i)\}_{i \in [k]} \leftarrow V^*(y)$.
2. $\{(q_0^i, q_1^i)\}_{i \in [k]} \leftarrow \mathsf{Ext}_n(\{(N_0^i, N_1^i)\}_{i \in [k]}, y)$.

3. For a session under the public key (N_0^i, N_1^i), do the following:
   (a) If $q_0^i|N_0^i$ or $q_1^i|N_1^i$, complete this session using the extracted prime factor as witness.
   (b) Otherwise, produce an honest message a in its first step. Upon receiving a challenge e, set $z = 0^\ell$, and compute $\{\mathsf{Enc}_{N_0^i}(z_j)\}_{i\in[\ell]}$ and $\{\mathsf{Enc}_{N_1^i}(z_j)\}_{i\in[\ell]}$ as the last message of this session.
4. Output the entire history when V^* terminates.

We are ready to prove the first part of Theorem 2. Suppose, towards a contradiction, that there exists a distinguisher D_n of size T such that

$$|\Pr[\mathsf{D}_n(\mathsf{View}_{V^*}^P)(\bar{x})) = 1] - \Pr[\mathsf{D}_n(\mathsf{Sim}(\bar{x})) = 1]| > \epsilon. \tag{5}$$

We order all s sessions according to its appearance, and construct the following hybrid simulators with all witnesses hardwired: Define $\mathsf{Sim}^0(\bar{x}, \bar{w})$ be the $\mathsf{Sim}(\bar{x}, \bar{w})$, and $\mathsf{Sim}^k(\bar{x}, \bar{w})$ as in the same way except that in each of the first k sessions it uses the real witness to complete a proof. Clearly, $\mathsf{Sim}^s(\bar{x}, \bar{w})$ is identical to the real interaction. From (5), there must exist a $m \in [s]$ such that

$$|\Pr[\mathsf{D}_n(\mathsf{Sim}^{m-1}(\bar{x}, \bar{w})) = 1] - \Pr[\mathsf{D}_n(\mathsf{Sim}^m(\bar{x}, \bar{w})) = 1]| > \frac{\epsilon}{s}\,. \tag{6}$$

Fix such a m, and for $t \in [2\ell]$, consider the sub-hybrid simulator $\mathsf{Sim}_t^m(\bar{x}, \bar{w})$:

$\mathsf{Sim}_t^m(\bar{x}, \bar{w})$:
1. Run step 1,2 of $\mathsf{Sim}^m(\bar{x}, \bar{w})$ and obtain $\{(N_0^i, N_1^i)\}_{i\in[k]}$ and $\{(q_0^i, q_1^i)\}_{i\in[k]}$.
2. For the session m under the public key (N_0^m, N_1^m), do the following:
   (a) If $q_0^i|N_0^i$ or $q_1^i|N_1^i$, act in the same way as $\mathsf{Sim}^m(\bar{x})$.
   (b) Otherwise, produce an honest message a in its first step. Upon receiving a challenge e, produce an accepting z using the real witness, set $z' = 0^t||z^{2\ell-t}$, where $z^{2\ell-t}$ is the suffix of $z||z$, and encrypt the first half bits of z' under N_0^i, their second half bits under N_1^i.

   For any other session, act in the same way as $\mathsf{Sim}^{m-1}(\bar{x}, \bar{w})$.
3. Output the entire history when V^* terminates.

Observe that $\mathsf{Sim}_{2\ell}^m(\bar{x}, \bar{w}) = \mathsf{Sim}^m(\bar{x}, \bar{w})$. It follows from the witness indistinguishability of the Blum protocol that $\mathsf{Sim}_0^m(\bar{x}, \bar{w}) \overset{c}{\approx} \mathsf{Sim}^{m-1}(\bar{x}, \bar{w})$ (with a negligible distinguishing gap). By (6), there must exist a $t \in [2\ell]$ such that

$$|\Pr[\mathsf{D}_n(\mathsf{Sim}_{t-1}^m(\bar{x})) = 1] - \Pr[\mathsf{D}_n(\mathsf{Sim}_t^m(\bar{x})) = 1]| > \frac{\epsilon}{4s\ell}. \tag{7}$$

Note that the only difference between $\mathsf{Sim}_{t-1}^m(\bar{x})$ and $\mathsf{Sim}_t^m(\bar{x})$ lies in the t-th ciphertext in case that the extractor fails to find any prime factors of the public key. Hence, if the inequality (7) holds, we can construct a size-T' circuit A_n with $(barx, \bar{w})$ hardwired, and show that it constradicts the (nearly) optimality of the extractor Ext_n. (The detailed proof can be found in the full version of this work.) This concludes the first part of Theorem 2.

The second part of Theorem 2 follows from the fact that (concurrent) (T, ϵ)-zero knowledge implies (concurrent) witness hiding (see [JKKR17] for the detailed proof). Here we just describe the underlying idea. For a given malicious verifier V^* of size T that can output a witness of a statement drawn from X_n at the end of a session with probability greater than some inverse polynomial ϵ, as we showed above, there exists a simulator of polynomial size such that V^* cannot distinguish the real interaction from simulation with probability greater than $\frac{\epsilon}{2}$. Combining the simulator and V^*, we will have a circuit family of polynomial size that breaks the hardness of X_n. Quasi-polynomial simulatability follows again from the second part of Lemma 4 directly. □

7 Simpler (T,ϵ)-Zero Knowledge and Analysis in the Plain Model

In this section we present a very simple delayed-input 2-round (T, ϵ)-zero knowledge argument for NP, and then sketch how to use our individual simulation technique to give a significantly simpler proof that the distinguisher-dependent simulatable zero knowledge protocols of [JKKR17,BKP19] also satisfy the stronger notion of (T, ϵ)-zero knowledge.

We build such an argument on a quasi-polynomial extractable perfectly binding commitment scheme Com [Pas03] (which can be based on sub-exponential hardness of factoring) and a NIWI proof system $(P_{\text{WI}}, V_{\text{WI}})$[10].

As usual, we denote by $P_{\text{WI}}(x \vee (N, c))$ the prover of the NIWI proof that proves to the verifier the statement "$x \in L$ OR $\exists\, q$ such that c is a commitment to q and $q|N$"

$\mathsf{Protocol}_{zk}$:

Private input to P: w s.t. $(x, w) \in R_L$.

$V \longrightarrow P$: $(N, q) \leftarrow \mathsf{Blum}(1^n)$. Send N to P.

$P \longrightarrow V$: $c \leftarrow \mathsf{Com}(0^n)$, $z = z_1\|z_2\|\cdots\|z_\ell \leftarrow P_{\text{WI}}(x \vee (N,c))$, $\{\zeta_j \leftarrow \mathsf{Enc}_N(z_j)\}_{j\in[\ell]}$. Send x, c and $\{\zeta_j\}_{j\in[\ell]}$ to V.

V: $z \leftarrow \{\mathsf{Dec}_N(\zeta_j, q)\}_{j\in[\ell]}$. Accept iff (x, z) is accepting.

Theorem 3. *Under the sub-exponential hardness assumption of factoring, $\mathsf{Protocol}_{zk}$ is a delayed-input interactive argument that satisfies all the following properties:*

1. *Delayed-input (T, ϵ)-zero knowledge.*
2. *Delayed-input witness hiding.*
3. *Delayed-input zero knowledge with quasi-polynomial time simulator.*

[10] One can also use two-round WI (such as [DN00]) here. We use NIWI (such as [GOS06]) to simplify our construction.

The soundness of this protocol is also straightforward. Note that a cheating prover P^* on a false statement $x \notin L$ with noticeable success probability δ implies that the message c sent by P^* is a commitment to a prime factor of N. This leads to a simple quasi-polynomial factoring algorithm Factor with success probability at least δ that contradicts the sub-exponential hardness of factoring: On input an integer N, it plays the role of the verifier and sends it to P^*; upon receiving the message c, it extracts a prime factor of N from c in quasi-polynomial time.

The proof of (T, ϵ)-zero knowledge, witness hiding and quasi-polynomial simulatability are essentially the same as in the previous section, we omit it here.

Upgrade the Distinguisher-Dependent Simulations. The work of [CLP15b] implies that existing distinguisher-dependent simulatable weak zero knowledge protocols of [JKKR17,BKP19] are also (T, ϵ)-zero knowledge. We note that both constructions of [JKKR17,BKP19] enjoy the two properties of (A, B) listed in Sect. 1.4, hence our individual simulation technique can also be applied to prove that they satisfy the stronger notion of (T, ϵ)-zero knowledge. For their 3-round protocols, one can view the verifier step as an NP instance (to which a solution will enable a successful simulation) sampler that takes as input its randomness and the first prover message a and outputs an instance (verifier message). To show the (T, ϵ)-zero knowledge property, we can construct an individual simulator in a similar way. The simulator applies a nearly optimal extractor (which is also given certain secret information $f(a)$ about the message a as an additional input[11]) to the sampler/verifier and tries to extract the corresponding witness, and then follows the residual strategy of the distinguisher-dependent simulator in [JKKR17,BKP19] after their extraction from the distinguisher oracle.

Acknowledgments. We would like to thank Takahiro Matsuda, Xinxuan Zhang and anonymous reviewers from Asiacrypt'20 and Crypto'19 for pointing out two errors in earlier versions of this paper, and for their valuable suggestions. We are supported by PlatON, the National Natural Science Foundation of China (Grant No. 61932019, No. 61772521 and No. 61772522), Key Research Program of Frontier Sciences, CAS (Grant No. QYZDB-SSW-SYS035).

References

[ACGS88] Alexi, W., Chor, B., Goldreich, O., Schnorr, C.-P.: RSA and rabin functions: certain parts are as hard as the whole. SIAM J. Comput. **17**(2), 194–209 (1988)

[11] This is in contrast to our settings, where the hard instances generated by the adversary depend only on its randomness. When these instances depend also on the first prover message a, the nearly optimal extractor usually needs to take as input some secret information about a, since in a proof by contradiction like ours, those algorithms D_n and A_n need these information to go through.

[AIR01] Aiello, B., Ishai, Y., Reingold, O.: Priced oblivious transfer: how to sell digital goods. In: Pfitzmann, B. (ed.) EUROCRYPT 2001. LNCS, vol. 2045, pp. 119–135. Springer, Heidelberg (2001). https://doi.org/10.1007/3-540-44987-6_8

[APV05] Alwen, J., Persiano, G., Visconti, I.: Impossibility and feasibility results for zero knowledge with public keys. In: Shoup, V. (ed.) CRYPTO 2005. LNCS, vol. 3621, pp. 135–151. Springer, Heidelberg (2005). https://doi.org/10.1007/11535218_9

[Bar01] Barak, B.: How to go beyond the black-box simulation barrier. In: Proceedings of the 42th Annual IEEE Symposium on Foundations of Computer Science - FOCS 2001, pp. 106–115. IEEE Computer Society (2001)

[BCC88] Brassard, G., Chaum, D., Crépeau, C.: Minimum disclosure proofs of knowledge. J. Comput. Syst. Sci. **37**(2), 156–189 (1988)

[BGI+17] Badrinarayanan, S., Garg, S., Ishai, Y., Sahai, A., Wadia, A.: Two-message witness indistinguishability and secure computation in the plain model from new assumptions. In: Takagi, T., Peyrin, T. (eds.) ASIACRYPT 2017. LNCS, vol. 10626, pp. 275–303. Springer, Cham (2017). https://doi.org/10.1007/978-3-319-70700-6_10

[BHY09] Bellare, M., Hofheinz, D., Yilek, S.: Possibility and impossibility results for encryption and commitment secure under selective opening. In: Joux, A. (ed.) EUROCRYPT 2009. LNCS, vol. 5479, pp. 1–35. Springer, Heidelberg (2009). https://doi.org/10.1007/978-3-642-01001-9_1

[BKP19] Bitansky, N., Khurana, D., Paneth, O.: Weak zero-knowledge beyond the black-box barrier. In: Annual ACM Symposium on the Theory of Computing - STOC 2019, pp. 1091–1102. ACM Press (2019)

[BP15] Bitansky, N., Paneth, O.: On non-black-box simulation and the impossibility of approximate obfuscation. SIAM J. Comput. **44**(5), 1325–1383 (2015)

[BP12] Bitansky, N., Paneth, O.: Point obfuscation and 3-round zero-knowledge. In: Cramer, R. (ed.) TCC 2012. LNCS, vol. 7194, pp. 190–208. Springer, Heidelberg (2012). https://doi.org/10.1007/978-3-642-28914-9_11

[CCH+19] Canetti, R., et al.: Fiat-Shamir: from practice to theory. In: Annual ACM Symposium on the Theory of Computing - STOC 2019, pp. 1082–1090. ACM Press (2019)

[CGGM00] Canetti, R., Goldreich, O., Goldwasser, S., Micali, S.: Resettable zero knowledge. In: Proceedings of the 32rd Annual ACM Symposium Theory of Computing- STOC 2000, pp. 235–244. ACM press (2000)

[CKPR01] Canetti, R., Kilian, J., Petrank, E., Rosen, A.: Black-box concurrent zero-knowledge requires omega(log n) rounds. In: Proceedings of the 33rd Annual ACM Symposium Theory of Computing- STOC 2001, pp. 570–579. ACM press (2001)

[CLP13] Chung, K.-M., Lin, H., Pass, R.: Constant-round concurrent zero knowledge from p-certificates. In: Proceedings of the 54th Annual Symposium on Foundations of Computer Science - FOCS 2013, pp. 50–59. IEEE Computer Society (2013)

[CLP15a] Chung, K.-M., Lin, H., Pass, R.: Constant-round concurrent zero-knowledge from indistinguishability obfuscation. In: Gennaro, R., Robshaw, M. (eds.) CRYPTO 2015. LNCS, vol. 9215, pp. 287–307. Springer, Heidelberg (2015). https://doi.org/10.1007/978-3-662-47989-6_14

[CLP15b] Chung, K.-M., Lui, E., Pass, R.: From weak to strong zero-knowledge and applications. In: Dodis, Y., Nielsen, J.B. (eds.) TCC 2015. LNCS, vol. 9014, pp. 66–92. Springer, Heidelberg (2015). https://doi.org/10.1007/978-3-662-46494-6_4

[Den17] Deng, Y.: Magic adversaries versus individual reduction: science wins either way. In: Coron, J.-S., Nielsen, J.B. (eds.) EUROCRYPT 2017. LNCS, vol. 10211, pp. 351–377. Springer, Cham (2017). https://doi.org/10.1007/978-3-319-56614-6_12

[DFG+11] Deng, Y., Feng, D., Goyal, V., Lin, D., Sahai, A., Yung, M.: Resettable cryptography in constant rounds – the case of zero knowledge. In: Lee, D.H., Wang, X. (eds.) ASIACRYPT 2011. LNCS, vol. 7073, pp. 390–406. Springer, Heidelberg (2011). https://doi.org/10.1007/978-3-642-25385-0_21

[DGL+16] Deng, Y., Garay, J., Ling, S., Wang, H., Yung, M.: On the implausibility of constant-round public-coin zero-knowledge proofs. In: Zikas, V., De Prisco, R. (eds.) SCN 2016. LNCS, vol. 9841, pp. 237–253. Springer, Cham (2016). https://doi.org/10.1007/978-3-319-44618-9_13

[DGS09] Deng, Y., Goyal, V., Sahai, A.: Resolving the simultaneous resettability conjecture and a new non-black-box simulation strategy. In: Proceedings of the 50th Annual Symposium on Foundations of Computer Science - FOCS 2009, pp. 251–260. IEEE Computer Society (2009)

[DK18] Deshpande, A., Kalai, Y.: Proofs of ignorance and applications to 2-message witness hiding. Cryptology ePrint Archive, Report 2018/896 (2018)

[DN00] Dwork, C., Naor, M.: Zaps and their applications. In: Proceedings of the 41th Annual IEEE Symposium on Foundations of Computer Science - FOCS 2000, pp. 283–293. IEEE Computer Society (2000)

[DNRS03] Dwork, C., Naor, M., Reingold, O., Stockmeyer, L.J.: Magic functions. J. ACM **50**(6), 852–921 (2003)

[DNS98] Dwork, C., Naor, M., Sahai, A.: Concurrent zero-knowledge. In: Proceedings of the 30rd Annual ACM Symposium Theory of Computing - STOC 1998, pp. 409–418. ACM press (1998)

[FGJ18] Fleischhacker, N., Goyal, V., Jain, A.: On the existence of three round zero-knowledge proofs. In: Nielsen, J.B., Rijmen, V. (eds.) EUROCRYPT 2018. LNCS, vol. 10822, pp. 3–33. Springer, Cham (2018). https://doi.org/10.1007/978-3-319-78372-7_1

[FKP19] Freitag, C., Komargodski, I., Pass, R.: Non-uniformly sound certificates with applications to concurrent zero-knowledge. In: Boldyreva, A., Micciancio, D. (eds.) CRYPTO 2019. LNCS, vol. 11694, pp. 98–127. Springer, Cham (2019). https://doi.org/10.1007/978-3-030-26954-8_4

[FLS99] Feige, U., Lapidot, D., Shamir, A.: Multiple noninteractive zero knowledge proofs under general assumptions. SIAM. J. Comput. **29**(1), 1–28 (1999)

[FS89] Feige, U., Shamir, A.: Zero knowledge proofs of knowledge in two rounds. In: Brassard, G. (ed.) CRYPTO 1989. LNCS, vol. 435, pp. 526–544. Springer, New York (1990). https://doi.org/10.1007/0-387-34805-0_46

[FS90] Feige, U., Shamir, A.: Witness indistinguishability and witness hiding protocols. In: Proceedings of the 22rd Annual ACM Symposium Theory of Computing- STOC 1990, pp. 416–426. ACM press (1990)

[GK96] Goldreich, O., Krawczyk, H.: On the composition of zero-knowledge proof systems. SIAM J. Comput. **25**(1), 169–192 (1996)

[GL89] Goldreich, O., Levin, L.: A hard-core predicate for all one-way functions. In: Proceedings of the 21th Annual ACM Symposium on the Theory of Computing - STOC 1989, pp. 25–32. ACM Press (1989)

[GMR89] Goldwasser, S., Micali, S., Rackoff, C.: The knowledge complexity of interactive proof systems. SIAM J. Comput. **18**(1), 186–208 (1989)

[Gol01] Goldreich, O.: Foundations of Cryptography, Volume Basic Tools. Cambridge University Press, Cambridge (2001)

[GOS06] Groth, J., Ostrovsky, R., Sahai, A.: Non-interactive zaps and new techniques for NIZK. In: Dwork, C. (ed.) CRYPTO 2006. LNCS, vol. 4117, pp. 97–111. Springer, Heidelberg (2006). https://doi.org/10.1007/11818175_6

[IR89] Impagliazzo, R., Rudich, S.: Limits on the provable consequences of one-way permutations. In: Proceedings of the 21th Annual ACM Symposium on the Theory of Computing - STOC 1989, pp. 44–61. ACM Press (1989)

[JKKR17] Jain, A., Kalai, Y.T., Khurana, D., Rothblum, R.: Distinguisher-dependent simulation in two rounds and its applications. In: Katz, J., Shacham, H. (eds.) CRYPTO 2017. LNCS, vol. 10402, pp. 158–189. Springer, Cham (2017). https://doi.org/10.1007/978-3-319-63715-0_6

[KP01] Kilian, J., Petrank, E.: Concurrent and resettable zero-knowledge in polyloalgorithm rounds. In: Proceedings of the 33rd Annual ACM Symposium Theory of Computing- STOC 2001, pp. 560–569. ACM press (2001)

[MR01] Micali, S., Reyzin, L.: Soundness in the public-key model. In: Kilian, J. (ed.) CRYPTO 2001. LNCS, vol. 2139, pp. 542–565. Springer, Heidelberg (2001). https://doi.org/10.1007/3-540-44647-8_32

[ORSV13] Ostrovsky, R., Rao, V., Scafuro, A., Visconti, I.: Revisiting lower and upper bounds for selective decommitments. In: Sahai, A. (ed.) TCC 2013. LNCS, vol. 7785, pp. 559–578. Springer, Heidelberg (2013). https://doi.org/10.1007/978-3-642-36594-2_31

[PA17] Ananth, P., Jain, A.: On secure two-party computation in three rounds. In: Kalai, Y., Reyzin, L. (eds.) TCC 2017. LNCS, vol. 10677, pp. 612–644. Springer, Cham (2017). https://doi.org/10.1007/978-3-319-70500-2_21

[Pas03] Pass, R.: Simulation in quasi-polynomial time, and its application to protocol composition. In: Biham, E. (ed.) EUROCRYPT 2003. LNCS, vol. 2656, pp. 160–176. Springer, Heidelberg (2003). https://doi.org/10.1007/3-540-39200-9_10

[Pas11] Pass, R.: Limits of provable security from standard assumptions. In: Proceedings of the 45rd Annual ACM Symposium Theory of Computing-STOC 2011, pp. 109–118. ACM press (2011)

[PRS02] Prabhakaran, M., Rosen, A., Sahai, A.: Concurrent zero knowledge with logarithmic round-complexity. In: Proceedings of the 43th Annual IEEE Symposium on Foundations of Computer Science - FOCS 2002, pp. 366–375. IEEE Computer Society (2002)

[RK99] Richardson, R., Kilian, J.: On the concurrent composition of zero-knowledge proofs. In: Stern, J. (ed.) EUROCRYPT 1999. LNCS, vol. 1592, pp. 415–431. Springer, Heidelberg (1999). https://doi.org/10.1007/3-540-48910-X_29

[SV12] Scafuro, A., Visconti, I.: On round-optimal zero knowledge in the bare public-key model. In: Pointcheval, D., Johansson, T. (eds.) EUROCRYPT 2012. LNCS, vol. 7237, pp. 153–171. Springer, Heidelberg (2012). https://doi.org/10.1007/978-3-642-29011-4_11

[TW87] Tompa, M., Woll, H.: Random self-reducibility and zero knowledge interactive proofs of possession of information. In: Proceedings of the 28th Annual Symposium on Foundations of Computer Science - FOCS 1987, pp. 472–482. IEEE Computer Society (1987)

[Xia11] Xiao, D.: (Nearly) round-optimal black-box constructions of commitments secure against selective opening attacks. In: Ishai, Y. (ed.) TCC 2011. LNCS, vol. 6597, pp. 541–558. Springer, Heidelberg (2011). https://doi.org/10.1007/978-3-642-19571-6_33

[Xia13] Xiao, D.: Errata to (nearly) round-optimal black-box constructions of commitments secure against selective opening attacks. In: Sahai, A. (ed.) TCC 2013. LNCS, vol. 7785, pp. 721–722. Springer, Heidelberg (2013). https://doi.org/10.1007/978-3-642-36594-2_40

[YZ07] Yung, M., Zhao, Y.: Generic and practical resettable zero-knowledge in the bare public-key model. In: Naor, M. (ed.) EUROCRYPT 2007. LNCS, vol. 4515, pp. 129–147. Springer, Heidelberg (2007). https://doi.org/10.1007/978-3-540-72540-4_8

Blockchains and Contact Tracing

KVaC: Key-Value Commitments for Blockchains and Beyond

Shashank Agrawal[1] and Srinivasan Raghuraman[2(✉)]

[1] Western Digital Research, Milpitas, USA
shashank.agrawal@wdc.com
[2] Visa Research, Palo Alto, USA
srraghur@visa.com

Abstract. As blockchains grow in size, validating new transactions becomes more and more resource intensive. To deal with this, there is a need to discover compact encodings of the (effective) state of a blockchain—an encoding that allows for efficient proofs of membership and updates. In the case of account-based cryptocurrencies, the state can be represented by a key-value map, where keys are the account addresses and values consist of account balance, nonce, etc.

We propose a new commitment scheme for key-value maps whose size does not grow with the number of keys, yet proofs of membership are of constant-size. In fact, both the encoding and the proofs consist of just two and three group elements respectively (in groups of unknown order like class groups). Verifying and updating proofs involves just a few group exponentiations. Additive updates to key values enjoy the same level of efficiency too.

Key-value commitments can be used to build dynamic accumulators and vector commitments, which find applications in group signatures, anonymous credentials, verifiable databases, interactive oracle proofs, etc. Using our new key-value commitment, we provide the most efficient constructions of (sub)vector commitments to date.

1 Introduction

Cryptocurrency space has grown quite rapidly since the introduction of Bitcoin [3] about a decade ago. The state of several leading cryptocurrencies like Ethereum [15], Ripple [26], EOS [13] and Stellar [24] can be represented by a key-value map $\mathcal{M}$ where *keys* are the public addresses of users and *values* are the attributes associated with them (balance amount, nonce, etc.). When Alice generates a transaction tx to transfer an amount x from her public key pk to Bob, the map $\mathcal{M}$ is used to check if pk has a balance of at least x. On confirmation of tx, balance of Alice and Bob (along with other bookkeeping information) is updated in $\mathcal{M}$.

In a cryptocurrency network, every node is expected to verify and store the state of the system. As the number of users increase and new accounts are created, the size of the key-value map grows, and the resource cost of running a

S. Moriai and H. Wang (Eds.): ASIACRYPT 2020, LNCS 12493, pp. 839–869, 2020.
https://doi.org/10.1007/978-3-030-64840-4_28

node increases. This drives a large proportion of users to rely on third parties to inform them of the state of the system, severely limiting the amount of decentralization in the network [11,12,27]. To provide some context, Ethereum has over 70 million accounts now [14] even though its not very widely used (5–10 transactions per second [16]). Upcoming currencies like Libra [23] can have a much higher throughput and are expected to have billions of accounts.

Key-Value Commitments. In this paper, we initiate a formal study of key-value commitments (KVC). These commitments allow one to produce succinct encodings of key-value maps that are amenable to both efficient membership proofs and additive updates.[1] We propose a new KVC KVaC (pronounced 'quack') in groups of unknown order, such as an RSA group or a class group [5], with the following properties:

- *Succinct encoding.* Commitment value consists of just two group elements *irrespective* of the number of items (key-value pairs) committed. If class groups of quadratic imaginary order targeting 100-bit security are used, then the commitment size would be 4096 bits or about half a kilobyte [18].
- *Succinct proofs & fast verification.* A proof to show that a certain item is in the commitment consists of just three group elements and only five exponentiations are required to verify a proof.
- *Fast updates.* Inserting new items to the map, updating values of existing items (additive updates), and updating membership proofs when items are added/changed can all be done quite efficiently—at most four exponentiations are required in any case. Furthermore, to update the value of an item, its existing value is not needed.
- *Trustless set-up.* If class groups are used as the underlying group here, then the encoding scheme could be bootstrapped in a trustless manner.
- *Aggregation & batching.* Multiple proofs can be aggregated to the size of a single proof and verified in the same amount of time as a single proof.

We prove the security of our construction under the RSA assumption in the random oracle model or the strong RSA assumption in the standard model.

Vector Commitments & Accumulators. KVCs can be used to construct and improve upon well-studied cryptographic primitives like accumulators [1,2,7,8, 25] and more recent ones like (sub)vector commitments (VC) [4,10,11,19,20,22]. Accumulators are used in group signatures, anonymous credentials, computation on authenticated data, decentralized bulletin boards, etc., and VCs have applications to verifiable databases with updates, interactive oracle proofs, etc.

VCs have been used to build accumulators [10] and vice versa [4]. We show how to build both of them from KVCs. In particular, we provide the first VC scheme where both public parameters and proofs consist of a constant number of group elements, the public parameters do not restrict the number of elements

[1] We do not intend key-value commitments to provide any sort of hiding for the keys or values committed, similar to how vector commitments do not intend to hide the vector elements [10].

that could be committed to, and all the VC algorithms require a constant number of group operations. Furthermore, the proofs can be batched to produce constant-size subvector openings. We also show how to build a dynamic accumulator from an (insert-only) KVC whose efficiency matches with the state-of-the-art. Thus, KVCs can be seen as a more general and flexible primitive.

We discuss our work in connection to VCs and accumulators in more depth in the following section.

1.1 Applications

Stateless Validation of Cryptocurrencies. Todd [27] first proposed the idea of a "stateless" blockchain where nodes participate in transaction validation without storing the entire state of the ledger, but rather only a short commitment to the state. Using our new key-value commitment scheme KVaC, one can build an account-based cryptocurrency where a node needs to store only two group elements (the commitment) to validate transactions. In the new currency, an account is represented by a key-value pair where key is a public key for a signature scheme (or a hash of it) and value consists of the account balance and a counter. (The counter helps to prevent replay attacks.) Suppose Alice has an account represented by $(pk, (v||ct))$ and she wants to transfer an amount b to a public key $pk^\star$. She will generate a transaction $tx = (pk, \sigma, v, ct, b, pk^\star, \pi)$ where σ is a signature on $(v, ct, b, pk^\star, \pi)$ under pk and π is a proof of the membership of $(pk, (v||ct))$ in the commitment.

A validator node, holding a commitment C, checks if σ is a valid signature, π is a valid proof w.r.t. C, and b is at most v. If all the checks pass, it updates the commitment using the efficient update algorithm Update of KVaC. The validator first executes Update with $(pk, -b||1)$ and C to produce a new commitment C' that reflects the change to Alice's account, and then executes Update with $(pk^\star, b||0)$ and C' to produce the final commitment C'' that reflects the changes to both the accounts. Here, KVaC's ability to update the value associated with $pk^\star$ without the knowledge of the original is very useful, otherwise senders would have to keep track of receivers' balances too.

Every time the commitment value changes, users need to update their proofs so that they remain valid. This puts some additional burden on users as they have to sync up with the blockchain frequently, which brings up a natural question: can the information required to update proofs be sublinear in the number of updates made? Unfortunately, this does not seem to be the case because the new and old values of commitment can be used to find out what updates have been made. Specifically, the lower bound of Camacho and Hevia can be extended to our setting as well [6].

Use of KVCs in blockchain also adds some extra overhead of generating and transmitting proofs, but they can be batched together and only one proof needs to be stored with every block.

Vector Commitments. Vector commitments (VC) were introduced by Catalano and Fiore [10]. VCs allow one to commit to an ordered sequence of values in such a way that one can later open the commitment at specific positions. They also allow updates to individual values and corresponding updates to proofs. The constructions of Catalano and Fiore, and those of Chepurnoy et al. [11] proposed later, have public parameters that scale *linearly* with the size of the vector. Though they suggest a way to cut down the parameters to a constant, it makes the cost of VC algorithms linear in the size of the vector.

Boneh et al. [4] take a different approach to build VCs. They provide a transformation from their accumulator construction which supports both membership and non-membership proofs. Though their construction does not put any restriction on the length of the vector, the vector elements are accumulated bit by bit. So the number of group operations required to insert new elements, generate membership proofs, etc. is linear in the bit-size of vector elements. Updates to values are not explicitly discussed but one could infer that it would have a similar cost. Lastly, their proofs contain seven group elements.

KVCs can be used to build a VC in a straightforward way, with keys playing the role of indices. Our KVC leads to a VC where the public parameters are of constant size, there is no restriction on the number of elements that could be committed, and proofs consist of just three group elements. Further, all the VC algorithms require a constant number of group operations. This improves upon all the known constructions.

Subvector Commitments. Lai and Malavolta [20] recently proposed the notion of subvector commitments (SVC). An SVC allows one to open a committed vector at a set of positions, where the opening size is independent of length of the committed vector and the number of positions to be opened. They show that the proofs (or openings) of Catalano and Fiore [10] can be extended for multiple elements without losing the succinctness. However, this also means that they inherit the limitations of Catalano and Fiore's constructions.

Membership proofs of our KVC can be batched, resulting in an SVC with succinct subvector openings—but without linear growth in public parameters.

Accumulators. Accumulators are a very well-studied cryptographic primitive with numerous applications. They can be based on RSA groups [2,8], Merkle hash trees [7], or bilinear maps [25]. See Baldimtsi et al. [1] for a thorough discussion of different types of accumulators and modular conversions between them. We show how to build a *dynamic positive* accumulator from an (insert-only) KVC whose efficiency matches with the state-of-the-art. (All accumulator algorithms need a constant number of group operations.) A dynamic accumulator supports both additions and deletions, and a positive one supports membership proofs.

1.2 More on Related Work

Comparison with Boneh et al. While Boneh et al.'s VC construction [4] is novel and efficient, their technique inherently works bit-by-bit. (They also discuss how to build KVCs from VCs.) The exponent is always a subset product of elements corresponding to the bits set to 1. It is not clear how to get rid of this restriction. This limitation also translates to updates as one would have to know which bits would have to be flipped from 0 to 1 and 1 to 0. This cannot be done simply using the knowledge of update value. Our construction takes a completely different approach by encoding the values directly as a linear function, which allows us to get past the bit-by-bit issues as well as handle updates while being oblivious to prior value (very important for blockchain applications). Our KVC algorithms involve constant number of group operations as opposed to linear in bit-length; the constants are small (between three and five); and, our proof size is three as opposed to seven.

Recent Work. Lately, vector commitments has been a very active area of research. Several new constructions have been proposed. We discuss a few of them here.

Campanelli et al. [9] study aggregation for subvector commitments. They introduce new incremental aggregation and disaggregation properties for SVCs. Incremental aggregation allows one to merge different subvector openings into a single concise opening, and to further aggregate merged openings (without knowing the entire committed vector). Disaggregation allows one to 'break down' openings into openings of subvectors. Campanelli et al. point out that though a form of aggregation is already present in the VC of Boneh et al. [4], it can be performed only once. They construct new VC schemes where openings can be aggregated an unbounded number of times.

Campanelli et al. provide two constructions with constant-size public parameters, a CRS in their case. However, the CRS needs to be 'specialized' for a length n before it can be used for commitment. The first construction, based on Boneh et al. [4], has a dependence on the bit-length of elements. Verification in the second construction, based on Catalano and Fiore [10], requires generation of n primes (unless they are already stored). Furthermore, Campanelli et al. do not consider updates to vector elements. Our KVC construction, on the other hand, can be used to build a VC that does not restrict the number of elements in a commitment and allows them to be updated. However, like Boneh et al., we can only support one-hop aggregation (we do not know how to further aggregate aggregated proofs).

Pointproofs [17] study aggregatable VCs in the cross-commitment setting. Proofs for subvectors of multiple commitments can be aggregated by any third party into a single proof for the multiple subvectors. When applied to smart contracts storage, Pointproofs reduces validators' storage requirements considerably. While Pointproofs have very short proofs, the public parameters are linear in the length of the vector. The scheme relies on a q-type assumption in a bilinear group. Further, in order to prove security of aggregation, they need to work in the algebraic group model.

Tomescu et al. [28] also study aggregatable subvector commitment and give an efficient construction in prime-order groups from constant-sized polynomial commitments. (They also provide a detailed and extensive overview of the literature.) Their public parameters also depend on the length of the vector though.

They discuss how to build a stateless cryptocurrency from their VC but the number of users n that need to be supported must be known in advance.

1.3 Organization

We first provide a technical overview of our construction (Sect. 2). We discuss two intermediate steps to building a KVC: an insert-only KVC that allows insertion of new items but no updates to existing ones, and an increment-only KVC that allows incrementing the values corresponding to keys but no inserts (it is assumed that all keys are initialized with value 0).

In Sect. 3, we describe the notation used in the paper, define key-value commitments formally, and state the assumptions we need to prove security. In Sects. 4 and 5, we build an insert-only KVC and a full KVC, respectively. We show how the former can be used to build accumulators and the latter naturally lends itself to vector commitments. Finally, in Sect. 6, we show how to batch membership proofs together.

We provide a formal description of the increment-only KVC in the full version of the paper.

2 Overview

In this section, we provide a technical overview of our construction of key-value commitments. Informally, a key-value commitment allows one to commit to a key-value map in such a way that it is later possible to open the commitment with respect to any specific key. To motivate our construction, we build up to it in three steps.

2.1 Insert-Only

We begin by describing an insert-only key-value commitment construction. By insert-only, we mean that we only insert key-value pairs into the commitment and do not the update the value corresponding to a key. Our key-value commitment C to the key-value map $\mathcal{M} = \{(k_i, v_i)\}_{i\in[q]} \subseteq \mathcal{K} \times \mathcal{V}$ takes the form

$$C_{\mathcal{M}} = \left(g^{\sum_{i\in[q]} v_i \prod_{j\in[q]\setminus\{i\}} z_j}, g^{\prod_{i\in[q]} z_i}\right),$$

where z_i are random strings[2] corresponding to the keys k_i. The crucial observation here is that the exponent in the first element of the commitment, namely $g^{\sum_{i\in[q]} v_i \prod_{j\in[q]\setminus\{i\}} z_j}$, is a linear function of the values v_i. The proof corresponding to a key $k_m \in \mathcal{K}_{\mathcal{M}}$ would be

$$\Lambda_{k_m} = \left(g^{\sum_{i\in[q]\setminus\{m\}} v_i \prod_{j\in[q]\setminus\{i,m\}} z_j}, g^{\prod_{i\in[q]\setminus\{m\}} z_i}\right)$$

[2] The precise requirement on $\{z_i\}$ will be described later.

which is essentially the key-value commitment of all the other key-value pairs in $\mathcal{M}$. Let us assume that the strings z_i can be publicly generated from the keys k_i, say by some hash function[3]. Then, the verification of the proof Λ_{k_m} for a key-value pair (k_m, v_m) would simply be the following checks:

$$\begin{aligned}\Lambda_{k_m,1}^{z_m} \cdot \Lambda_{k_m,2}^{v_m} &= \left(g^{\sum_{i\in[q]\setminus\{m\}} v_i \prod_{j\in[q]\setminus\{i,m\}} z_j}\right)^{z_m} \cdot \left(g^{\prod_{i\in[q]\setminus\{m\}} z_i}\right)^{v_m} \\ &= g^{\sum_{i\in[q]\setminus\{m\}} v_i \prod_{j\in[q]\setminus\{i\}} z_j} \cdot g^{v_m \prod_{i\in[q]\setminus\{m\}} z_i} \\ &= g^{\sum_{i\in[q]} v_i \prod_{j\in[q]\setminus\{i\}} z_j} \\ &= C_{\mathcal{M},1}\end{aligned}$$

and

$$\begin{aligned}\Lambda_{k_m,2}^{z_m} &= \left(g^{\prod_{i\in[q]\setminus\{m\}} z_i}\right)^{z_m} \\ &= g^{\prod_{i\in[q]} z_i} \\ &= C_{\mathcal{M},2}\end{aligned}$$

Note that the above design also describes a procedure to insert a key-value pair into the commitment. To insert a new pair (k_{q+1}, v_{q+1}) into $\mathcal{M}$, we set

$$C_{\mathcal{M}'} = \left(C_{\mathcal{M},1}^{z_{q+1}} \cdot C_{\mathcal{M},2}^{v_{q+1}}, C_{\mathcal{M},2}^{z_{q+1}}\right)$$

where $\mathcal{M}' = \mathcal{M} \cup \{(k_{m+1}, v_{m+1})\}$. Furthermore, the proof $\Lambda_{k_{q+1}}$ corresponding to the key k_{q+1} would be $C_{\mathcal{M}}$.

We also have a straightforward way to update proofs for the existing keys when a new key-value pair is inserted. For instance, on inserting (k_{q+1}, v_{q+1}), we can update the proof Λ_{k_m} corresponding to the key k_m with the help of the update information (k_{q+1}, v_{q+1}) as follows:

$$\Lambda'_{k_m} = \left(\Lambda_{k_m,1}^{z_{q+1}} \cdot \Lambda_{k_m,2}^{v_{q+1}}, \Lambda_{k_m,2}^{z_{q+1}}\right).$$

One can easily check that the modified proof would be successfully verified.

The final piece of the puzzle is key binding, i.e., it must be computationally infeasible for an adversary to produce a proof corresponding to a key k that verifies for a key-value pair (k, v) which is not in the key-value commitment. We analyze this as follows. Suppose an adversary comes up with a key-value pair (k, v) and a proof $\Lambda_k = (\Lambda_{k,1}, \Lambda_{k,2})$ corresponding to the key k. Let us assume that $k \in \mathcal{K}_{\mathcal{M}}$ (the other case is easier to handle). Let m denote the index of the key k in the map $\mathcal{M}$, i.e., let $k = k_m$. Let z_m be the string corresponding to k_m. We will, for reasons that will be clear shortly, require that z_m be an *odd* string.

[3] We will actually not require any private randomness in $\{z_i\}$, just that there is some concise representation of them. This will be clear from the fact that we publish the key for the hash function to enable its public evaluation.

Let v_m be the value corresponding to the key k_m in the commitment and let $\Lambda_{k_m} = (\Lambda_{k_m,1}, \Lambda_{k_m,2})$ be the corresponding proof. We first check that

$$\Lambda_{k,2}^{z_m} = C_{\mathcal{M},2}.$$

Suppose that the check passes. Then, with overwhelming probability,

$$\Lambda_{k,2} = g^{\prod_{i \in [q] \setminus \{m\}} z_i} = \Lambda_{k_m,2}.$$

This is because, otherwise,

$$\alpha = \frac{\Lambda_{k,2}}{\Lambda_{k_m,2}} \neq \pm 1$$

is a non-trivial z_mth root of unity. We know that such elements are hard to find without knowing the order of the group. In particular, this means that we have computed the order of the non-trivial element α.

We now proceed to the second and final check. We check that

$$\Lambda_{k,1}^{z_m} \cdot \Lambda_{k,2}^{v} = C_{\mathcal{M},1}.$$

Note that

$$\Lambda_{k_m,1}^{z_m} \cdot \Lambda_{k_m,2}^{v_m} = C_{\mathcal{M},1}.$$

and, with overwhelming probability, $\Lambda_{k,2} = \Lambda_{k_m,2}$. Hence

$$\left(\frac{\Lambda_{k,1}}{\Lambda_{k_m,1}}\right)^{z_m} = \Lambda_{k_m,2}^{v_m - v}.$$

We only care about the case $v_m \neq v$. Note that setting

$$\beta = \frac{\Lambda_{k,1}}{\Lambda_{k_m,1}}$$

and

$$\gamma = \Lambda_{k_m,2}^{v_m - v}$$

we have found β, a z_mth root of a non-trivial element γ, which should be hard to find in groups of unknown order.

Formally, we can show that if the RSA assumption holds, then computing β is indeed hard. This can be seen as follows. The exponent of g in $\Lambda_{k_m,2}$ contains numbers that are coprime to z_m. Furthermore, we will choose $\{z_i\}$ to be larger than the permitted value space, which ensures that $v_m - v$ is also coprime to z_m. Thus, if one can compute β, which is a z_mth root of γ, we can actually compute a z_mth root of g through an application of Shamir's trick, which would break the RSA assumption.

2.2 Increment-Only

We next describe an increment-only key-value commitment construction. By increment-only, we mean that values corresponding to *all* keys are initialized to 0 and we can just update them by some amount δ every time. We propose that our commitment C to a key-value map $\mathcal{M} = \{(k_i, v_i)\}_{i\in[q]} \subseteq \mathcal{K} \times \mathcal{V}$ takes the form

$$C_{\mathcal{M}} = g^{\prod_{i\in[q]} z_i^{v_i}},$$

where z_i are random primes corresponding to the keys k_i. Let us assume that the strings z_i can be publicly generated from the keys k_i, say by some hash function.

This construction is reminiscent of the RSA-based accumulator construction of Li et al. [21] and Boneh et al. [4]. The proof corresponding to a key $k_m \in \mathcal{K}_{\mathcal{M}}$ would need to consist of two parts, one to show that the exponent of z_m is at least v_m and one to show that it is at most v_m. The first part of the proof would be

$$\Lambda_{k_m,1} = g^{\prod_{i\in[q]\setminus\{m\}} z_i^{v_i}},$$

which is essentially the key-value commitment of all the other key-value pairs in $\mathcal{M}$. It can be used to show that the exponent of z_m is at least v_m by verifying that

$$\Lambda_{k_m,1}^{z_m^{v_m}} = C_{\mathcal{M}}.$$

The second part of the proof uses the idea from Li et al. [21] and Boneh et al. [4] that was used to build non-membership proofs. Basically, we would like to show that z_m is coprime to $\prod_{i\in[q]\setminus\{m\}} z_i^{v_i}$. This can be done by leveraging Bezout coefficients $a, b \in \mathbb{Z}$ such that

$$a \cdot z_m + b \cdot \prod_{i\in[q]\setminus\{m\}} z_i^{v_i} = 1.$$

2.3 Putting It All Together

We re-examine the insert-only key-value commitment, namely,

$$C_{\mathcal{M}} = \left(g^{\sum_{i\in[q]} v_i \prod_{j\in[q]\setminus\{i\}} z_j}, g^{\prod_{i\in[q]} z_i}\right)$$

and

$$\Lambda_{k_m} = \left(g^{\sum_{i\in[q]\setminus\{m\}} v_i \prod_{j\in[q]\setminus\{i,m\}} z_j}, g^{\prod_{i\in[q]\setminus\{m\}} z_i}\right)$$

The exponent of the first component of $C_{\mathcal{M}}$ is linear in the values that are being committed. Thus, in order to change the value corresponding to key k_m by δ, it is enough to perform the following operation:

$$C_{\mathcal{M}',1} = C_{\mathcal{M},1} \cdot g^{\delta \cdot \prod_{i\in[q]\setminus\{m\}} z_i}.$$

This means that one only needs to know the index m[4] and δ in order to perform an update on the value corresponding to the key k_m in the commitment. Let

$$\beta = g^{\prod_{i\in[q]\setminus\{m\}} z_i}.$$

Firstly, note that β can be generated publicly. However, one would have to generate all the z_i for $i \in [q] \setminus \{m\}$ (or retrieve it from some persistent storage) and then perform $q - 1$ exponentiations, making it a computationally intensive task. However, notice that

$$\Lambda_{k_m,2} = \beta.$$

Thus, if we assume that the party involved in the update of the mth element has access to Λ_{k_m}, we can assume that we have access to β and we do not have to recompute it every time an update is issued. However, we would like to overcome this limitation. For instance, in the case of a blockchain, a sender who wants to send another user some funds will not be able to update the key-value commitment to reflect the changes in the recipient's account efficiently unless they have access to the proof of the recipient.

Let us turn to the proofs. Note that if we perform an update at index m, the proof corresponding to the key k_m does not change. For $n \neq m$, we can update the proof corresponding to the key k_n by performing the following operation:

$$\Lambda_{k_n,1} = \Lambda_{k_n,1} \cdot g^{\delta \cdot \prod_{j\in[q]\setminus\{m,n\}} z_j}.$$

Let

$$\gamma = g^{\prod_{j\in[q]\setminus\{m,n\}} z_j}.$$

Again, note that γ can be generated publicly but it would be a computationally intensive task. The situation is even worse here because γ cannot be computed efficiently from any other information that is available as that would amount to taking z_mth roots of elements.

The construction we propose now circumvents all of these issues. It gets rid of indices and allows for efficient updates of the key-value commitment and proofs. Moreover, we can do so without involving the party (their proof) whose value is being modified. Our commitment C to the key-value map $\mathcal{M} = \{(k_i, v_i)\}_{i\in[q]} \subseteq \mathcal{K} \times \mathcal{V}$ takes the form

$$C_{\mathcal{M}} = \left(g^{\left(\sum_{i\in[q]} v_i \prod_{j\in[q]\setminus\{i\}} z_j\right) \cdot \prod_{i\in[q]} z_i^{u_i}}, g^{\prod_{i\in[q]} z_i^{u_i+1}} \right),$$

where u_i denotes the number of updates made to the value corresponding to the key k_i. With this form, insertion can be carried out in exactly the same way as in the case of the insert-only construction.

[4] While this is already pretty good, we ideally would like to get rid of the notion of an index and carry out an update just knowing the key k_m. We do achieve this in our construction.

More interestingly, if $C_{\mathcal{M}'}$ denotes the new commitment value after changing the value corresponding to key k_m by δ, then

$$\begin{aligned} C_{\mathcal{M}',1} &= C_{\mathcal{M},1}^{z_m} \cdot g^{\delta \cdot z_m^{u'_m} \prod_{i \in [q] \setminus \{m\}} z_i^{u_i+1}} \\ &= C_{\mathcal{M},1}^{z_m} \cdot g^{\delta \cdot z_m^{u_m+1} \prod_{i \in [q] \setminus \{m\}} z_i^{u_i+1}} \\ &= C_{\mathcal{M},1}^{z_m} \cdot g^{\delta \cdot \prod_{i \in [q]} z_i^{u_i+1}} \\ &= C_{\mathcal{M},1}^{z_m} \cdot C_{\mathcal{M},2}^{\delta}, \end{aligned}$$

where $u'_m = u_m + 1$ denotes the (new) total number of updates for key k_m. Note how using the number of updates $\{u_i\}$ in the exponents of the $\{z_i\}$ lets us perform an update without having to compute values akin to β (and γ while updating proofs) which have to miss some $\{z_i\}$ in the exponent, rendering their computation inefficient.

In fact, it is now easy to see that

$$C_{\mathcal{M}'} = \left(C_{\mathcal{M},1}^{z_m} \cdot C_{\mathcal{M},2}^{\delta}, C_{\mathcal{M},2}^{z_m} \right).$$

Thus, an update works exactly how an insert would and this is an important property our constructions enjoys that we will come back to later in seeing how this primitive fits into the blockchain setting. It can also be easily deduced now that this design has a very similar consequence on enabling update to proofs efficiently. In particular, recall that updating the values corresponding to keys and inserting a new key have similar effect. Since we know how to update proofs following an insert, we can update them in exactly the same way on an update to some value.

To prove key-binding, it will be crucial for a verifier to know precisely the number of updates that have been performed on the value corresponding to the key for which a proof is provided. If verifier is not aware of this, it is possible for an attacker to generate a "fake" proof and break key-binding. Indeed, the number of updates made to the values corresponding to each key is public in the blockchain setting, but we would not want parties to store this information as it grows linearly with the number of key-value pairs that are inserted into the commitment.

For this purpose, we can include in the commitment $C_{\mathcal{M}}$ an increment-only key-value commitment that stores the number of updates performed on each key. During verification, proofs would now have to contain a proof for the right number of updates that have been performed in addition to the proof for the value itself. In this way, the verifying party need not store the number of updates that have been made to the values corresponding to each of the keys. The final step is to observe that the second component of the key-value commitment, $C_{\mathcal{M},2}$, essentially acts as an increment-only key-value commitment for the number of updates. Thus, we do not need to add anything else to $C_{\mathcal{M}}$.

3 Preliminaries

3.1 Notation

For $n \in \mathbb{N}$, let $[n] = \{1, 2, \ldots, n\}$. Let $\lambda \in \mathbb{N}$ denote the security parameter. Let $|b|$ denote the bit-length of $b \in \mathbb{N}$. Let Primes denote the set of integer primes and $\mathsf{Primes}(\lambda)$ denote the set of integer primes less than 2^λ. Symbols in boldface such as $\mathbf{a}$ denote vectors. By a_i we denote the i-th element of the vector $\mathbf{a}$. For a vector $\mathbf{a}$ of length $n \in \mathbb{N}$ and an index set $I \subseteq [n]$, we denote by $\mathbf{a}|_I$ the sub-vector of elements a_i for $i \in I$ induced by I. By $\text{poly}(\cdot)$, we denote any function which is bounded by a polynomial in its argument. An algorithm $\mathcal{T}$ is said to be PPT if it is modeled as a probabilistic Turing machine that runs in time polynomial in λ. Informally, we say that a function is negligible, denoted by negl, if it vanishes faster than the inverse of any polynomial. If S is a set, then $x \leftarrow_\$ S$ indicates the process of selecting x uniformly at random from S (which in particular assumes that S can be sampled efficiently). Similarly, $x \leftarrow_\$ \mathcal{A}(\cdot)$ denotes the random variable that is the output of a randomized algorithm $\mathcal{A}$.

3.2 Key-Value Commitments

Informally, a key-value commitment allows one to commit to a key-value map in such a way that it is later possible to open the commitment with respect to any specific key. We require a key-value commitment to be *concise* in the sense that the size of the commitment string C is independent of the size of the map. Furthermore, it must be possible to update the map, by either adding new key-value pairs or updating the value corresponding to an existing key.

We set up the following notation for a key-value map: A key-value map $\mathcal{M} \subseteq \mathcal{K} \times \mathcal{V}$ is a collection of key-value pairs $(k, v) \in \mathcal{K} \times \mathcal{V}$. Let $\mathcal{K}_\mathcal{M} \subseteq \mathcal{K}$ denote the set of keys for which values have been stored in the map $\mathcal{M}$. We define a key-value commitment KVC as a non-interactive primitive that can be formally described via the following algorithms:

- $(\mathsf{pp}, C) \leftarrow_\$ \mathsf{KeyGen}(1^\lambda)$: On input the security parameter λ, the key generation algorithm outputs some public parameters pp (which implicitly define the key space $\mathcal{K}$ and value space $\mathcal{V}$) and the initial commitment C to the empty key-value map. All other algorithms have access to the public parameters.
- $(C, \Lambda_k, \mathsf{upd}) \leftarrow \mathsf{Insert}(C, (k, v))$: On input a commitment string C and a key-value pair $(k, v) \in \mathcal{K} \times \mathcal{V}$, the insertion algorithm outputs a new commitment string C, a proof Λ_k (that v is the value corresponding to k), and update information upd.
- $(C, \mathsf{upd}) \leftarrow \mathsf{Update}(C, (k, \delta))$: On input a commitment string C, a key $k \in \mathcal{K}$ and an update value δ[5], the update algorithm outputs an updated string C and update information upd. Note that this algorithm does not need the value corresponding to the key k.

[5] We assume updates are additive, i.e., updating a value v by δ amounts to changing v to $v + \delta$.

- $\Lambda_k \leftarrow \mathsf{ProofUpdate}(k, \Lambda_k, \mathsf{upd})$: On input a key $k \in \mathcal{K}$, a proof Λ_k for some value corresponding to the key k and update information upd, the proof update algorithm outputs an updated proof Λ_k.
- $1/0 \leftarrow \mathsf{Ver}(C, (k, v), \Lambda_k)$: On input a commitment string C, a key-value pair $(k, v) \in \mathcal{K} \times \mathcal{V}$ and a proof Λ_k, the verification algorithm either outputs 1 (denoting accept) or 0 (denoting reject).

For correctness, we require that for all $\lambda \in \mathbb{N}$, for all honestly generated public parameters $\mathsf{pp} \leftarrow_{\$} \mathsf{KeyGen}(1^\lambda)$, if C is a commitment to a key-value map $\mathcal{M}$, obtained by running a sequence of calls to Insert and Update, Λ_k is a proof corresponding to key k for any $k \in \mathcal{K}_{\mathcal{M}}$, generated during the call to Insert and updated by appropriate calls to ProofUpdate, then $\mathsf{Ver}(C, (k, v), \Lambda_k)$ outputs 1 with probability 1 if $(k, v) \in \mathcal{M}$.

To present the requirement formally, we define a correctness game. We have an adversary in this game to capture the arbitrary order in which inserts and updates can be applied to a commitment. We do not provide it any capability to do something beyond that.

Definition 1. *For a key-value commitment* KVC *and an adversary $\mathcal{A}$, we define a random variable $\mathcal{G}^{\mathsf{correct}}_{\mathsf{KVC},\lambda,\mathcal{A}}$ through a game between a challenger* CH *and $\mathcal{A}$ as follows:*

$\mathcal{G}^{\mathsf{correct}}_{\mathsf{KVC},\lambda,\mathcal{A}}$:

1. CH *samples* $(\mathsf{pp}, C) \leftarrow_{\$} \mathsf{KeyGen}(1^\lambda)$ *and sends them to $\mathcal{A}$.* CH *also maintains its own state comprising a key-value map $\mathcal{M} \subseteq \mathcal{K} \times \mathcal{V}$ initialized to the empty map, a key-proof map $\mathcal{P}$ initialized to the empty map, and the initial commitment value C.*
2. *$\mathcal{A}$ issues queries of one of the following forms:*
   - $(\mathsf{Insert}, (k, v))$: CH *checks if $\mathcal{M}$ contains a tuple of the form $(k, \cdot)$. If so,* CH *responds with $\perp$. If not,* CH *updates $\mathcal{M}$ to $\mathcal{M} \cup \{(k, v)\}$ and executes* $\mathsf{Insert}(C, (k, v))$ *to obtain a new commitment C, along with Λ_k and* upd. CH *then updates $\mathcal{P}$ to $\mathcal{P} \cup \{(k, \Lambda_k)\}$.*
   - $(\mathsf{Update}, (k, \delta))$: CH *checks if $\mathcal{M}$ contains a tuple of the form (k, v). If not,* CH *responds with $\perp$. If so,* CH *updates $\mathcal{M}$ to $(\mathcal{M} \cup \{(k, v + \delta)\}) \setminus \{(k, v)\}$ and executes* $\mathsf{Update}(C, (k, \delta))$ *to obtain a new commitment C, along with update value* upd.

   Any time $\mathcal{A}$ issues a query, CH *deals with the query as above and then performs the following updates and checks:*
   - *Let* upd *be the update information obtained by* CH *while processing $\mathcal{A}$'s most recent query. For each tuple $(k, \Lambda_k) \in \mathcal{P}$,* CH *updates Λ_k by executing* $\mathsf{ProofUpdate}(k, \Lambda_k, \mathsf{upd})$.
   - *For each tuple $(k, v) \in \mathcal{M}$ with the corresponding tuple $(k, \Lambda_k) \in \mathcal{P}$,* CH *obtains $b_k \leftarrow \mathsf{Ver}(C, (k, v), \Lambda_k)$. If for any k, $b_k = 0$, then* CH *outputs* failure *and terminates.*
3. CH *outputs* success.

The value of the random variable $\mathcal{G}^{\text{correct}}_{\mathsf{KVC},\lambda,\mathcal{A}}$ *is defined to be the output of* CH*, namely,* failure *or* success.

Definition 2 (Correctness). *A key-value commitment* KVC *is* correct *if for every adversary* $\mathcal{A}$*, the following probability is identically zero:*

$$\mathsf{Adv}^{\text{correct}}_{\mathsf{KVC},\mathcal{A}}(\lambda) = \Pr\left[\mathsf{failure} \leftarrow_\$ \mathcal{G}^{\text{correct}}_{\mathsf{KVC},\lambda,\mathcal{A}}\right]$$

The security requirement for key-value commitments is that of key binding. Informally, this says that it should be infeasible for any polynomially bounded adversary (with knowledge of pp) to come up with an *honestly generated* commitment and two proofs that certify to different values for the same key, or a single proof that certifies to a value for a key that has not been inserted. The adversary is, however, disallowed from executing Insert more than once with respect to any k. We present the requirement formally below. We first define a key-binding game.

Definition 3. *For a key-value commitment* KVC *and an adversary* $\mathcal{A}$*, we define a random variable* $\mathcal{G}^{\text{bind}}_{\mathsf{KVC},\lambda,\mathcal{A}}$ *through a game between a challenger* CH *and* $\mathcal{A}$ *as follows:*

$\underline{\mathcal{G}^{\text{bind}}_{\mathsf{KVC},\lambda,\mathcal{A}}:}$

1. CH *samples* $(\mathsf{pp}, C) \leftarrow_\$ \mathsf{KeyGen}(1^\lambda)$ *and sends them to* $\mathcal{A}$. CH *also maintains its own state comprising a key-value map* $\mathcal{M} \subseteq \mathcal{K} \times \mathcal{V}$ *initialized to the empty map and the initial commitment value* C.
2. $\mathcal{A}$ *issues queries of one of the following forms:*
   - $(\mathsf{Insert}, (k, v))$*:* CH *checks if* $\mathcal{M}$ *contains a tuple of the form* $(k, \cdot)$*. If so,* CH *responds with* $\perp$*. If not,* CH *updates* $\mathcal{M}$ *to* $\mathcal{M} \cup \{(k, v)\}$ *and executes* $\mathsf{Insert}(C, (k, v))$ *to obtain a new commitment* C.
   - $(\mathsf{Update}, (k, \delta))$*:* CH *checks if* $\mathcal{M}$ *contains a tuple of the form* (k, v)*. If not,* CH *responds with* $\perp$*. If so,* CH *updates* $\mathcal{M}$ *to* $(\mathcal{M} \cup \{(k, v+\delta)\}) \setminus \{(k, v)\}$ *and executes* $\mathsf{Update}(C, (k, \delta))$ *to obtain a new commitment* C.
3. $\mathcal{A}$ *sends a final output to* CH *of one of the following forms:*
   - *Type 1: a key* k *such that* $\mathcal{M}$ *does not contain a tuple of the form* $(k, \cdot)$*, a value* v*, and a proof* Λ_k.
   - *Type 2: a key* k *such that* $\mathcal{M}$ *contains a tuple of the form* $(k, \cdot)$*, a pair of values* (v, v') *where* $v \neq v'$*, and a pair of proofs* (Λ_k, Λ'_k).
4. CH *performs the following checks corresponding to* $\mathcal{A}$*'s output:*
   - *Type 1: if* $\mathsf{Ver}(C, (k, v), \Lambda_k) = 1$*, then* CH *outputs* failure*. Otherwise,* CH *outputs* success.
   - *Type 2: if* $\mathsf{Ver}(C, (k, v), \Lambda_k) = \mathsf{Ver}(C, (k, v'), \Lambda'_k) = 1$*, then* CH *outputs* failure*. Otherwise,* CH *outputs* success.

The value of the random variable $\mathcal{G}^{\text{bind}}_{\mathsf{KVC},\lambda,\mathcal{A}}$ *is defined to be the output of* CH*, namely,* failure *or* success.

Definition 4 (Key-binding). *A key-value commitment* KVC *is* key-binding *if for every PPT adversary $\mathcal{A}$, the following probability is negligible in λ:*

$$\mathsf{Adv}^{\text{bind}}_{\mathsf{KVC},\mathcal{A}}(\lambda) = \Pr\left[\mathsf{failure} \leftarrow_{\$} \mathcal{G}^{\text{bind}}_{\mathsf{KVC},\lambda,\mathcal{A}}\right].$$

Notice that in the definition of $\mathcal{G}^{\text{bind}}_{\mathsf{KVC},\lambda,\mathcal{A}}$, the commitment C is honestly generated by the challenger CH based on the queries issued by the adversary $\mathcal{A}$. Also note that the definition only uses the Insert and Update routines of the key-value commitment, as these are the only two that impact the value of the commitment. Indeed, the adversary can perform all operations by itself given the public parameters. However, the purpose of the game is to define the honestly generated commitment with respect to which the adversary will attempt to produce "fake" proofs. Definition 4 states that no PPT adversary will be able to do so.

We note that key-value commitments are not required to satisfy any sort of hiding property, although one can also define key-value commitments that are hiding. Informally, a key-value commitment is hiding if an adversary cannot distinguish whether a commitment was created to a key-value map $\mathcal{M}$ or to another key-value map $\mathcal{M}'$ even after learning the values corresponding to keys that have the same value in both maps.

KVC for Account-Based Cryptocurrency. In Sect. 1.1, we briefly discussed how a key-value commitment can be used to build an account-based cryptocurrency with stateless validation. When a validator receives a transaction $tx = (pk, \sigma, v, ct, b, pk^\star, \pi)$ to transfer an amount b from Alice's public key pk to Bob's public key $pk^\star$, it checks if σ is a valid signature on $(v, ct, b, pk^\star, \pi)$, π is a valid proof of the membership of $(pk, (v||ct))$ w.r.t. to the commitment state C, and b is at most v.

The validator can then execute Update with C and $(pk, -b||1)$ to produce a new commitment C' that reflects the change to Alice's account, but what should it do for Bob? Perhaps it should insert $pk^\star$ into C' if this is the first time that $pk^\star$ is being used in a transaction, or update it otherwise. However, there is no way for the validator to know this unless it keeps a copy of the blockchain. Fortunately, in our construction KVaC, insert and update work in the exact same way (see Fig. 2), so the validator could always just do an update. (The only difference between these operations is that the former outputs a proof whereas the latter doesn't.)

Let us look at the situation from Alice and Bob's perspective. While Alice has a proof π for her key pk that she can update, Bob may not have any proof for $pk^\star$ if this is the first time someone is sending money to him. We could help Bob generate a proof by including the latest state of the commitment value in every block. If the transaction tx is accepted into a block ℓ, Bob could use the commitment C' from block $\ell - 1$ to quickly generate a proof for $pk^\star$ by applying all the updates in block ℓ to C' except his own.

3.3 Assumptions

We describe in this section the various hardness assumptions that we will use in this work.

Groups of Unknown Order. We assume the existence of a randomized polynomial time algorithm $\mathsf{GGen}(\lambda)$ that takes as input the security parameter λ and outputs two integers a, b along with the description of a group $\mathbb{G}$ of unknown order in the range $[a, b]$ such that a, b and $a - b$ are all integers exponential in λ (similar to Boneh et al. [4]). We will suppress a, b when they are understood or not required.

RSA Assumption. Informally, the RSA assumption states that an adversary cannot compute a random root of a random group element. In the game, the challenger runs the generation algorithm $\mathsf{GGen}(\lambda)$ to obtain integers a, b such that a, b and $a - b$ are exponential in λ and the description of a group $\mathbb{G}$ of unknown order in the interval $[a, b]$. It also samples a random group element w and a random λ-bit prime ℓ, and outputs w and ℓ to the adversary. The adversary is then supposed to return an ℓth root u of w.

Definition 5 (RSA). *The RSA assumption holds for the algorithm* GGen *if for any PPT adversary $\mathcal{A}$, the following probability is negligible in λ:*

$$\mathsf{Adv}_{\mathcal{A}}^{\mathrm{RSA}}(\lambda) = \Pr\left[u^{\ell} = w : \begin{array}{c} (a, b, \mathbb{G}) \leftarrow_{\$} \mathsf{GGen}(\lambda) \\ w \leftarrow_{\$} \mathbb{G} \\ \ell \leftarrow_{\$} \mathsf{Primes}(\lambda) \\ u \leftarrow_{\$} \mathcal{A}(a, b, \mathbb{G}, w, \ell) \end{array}\right].$$

We would like to generalize the RSA assumption. For the assumption to make sense, we must maintain that ℓ is invertible modulo Q with overwhelming probability, where Q is the order of the group. If ℓ is a prime larger than Q, ℓ is certainly coprime to Q and hence invertible modulo Q. This also means that every element has an ℓth root. In particular, for any w, $u = w^{\ell^{-1}}$ is well-defined. Intuitively, the problem of finding an ℓth root should still be hard. This leads us to a generalized form of RSA.

Definition 6 (Generalized RSA). *The Generalized RSA assumption holds for the algorithm* GGen *if for any PPT adversary $\mathcal{A}$, the following probability is negligible in λ:*

$$\mathsf{Adv}_{\mathcal{A}}^{\mathrm{GRSA}}(\lambda) = \Pr\left[u^{\ell} = w : \begin{array}{c} (a, b, \mathbb{G}) \leftarrow_{\$} \mathsf{GGen}(\lambda), |b| = \zeta \\ w \leftarrow_{\$} \mathbb{G} \\ \ell \leftarrow_{\$} \mathsf{Primes}(\zeta + 1) \setminus [b] \\ u \leftarrow_{\$} \mathcal{A}(a, b, \mathbb{G}, w, \ell) \end{array}\right].$$

Strong RSA Assumption. Informally, the strong RSA assumption states that an adversary cannot compute any non-trivial root of a random group element. In the game, the challenger runs the generation algorithm $\mathsf{GGen}(\lambda)$ to obtain the description of a group $\mathbb{G}$ of unknown order. It also samples a random group element w and gives it to the adversary. The adversary is then supposed to return an ℓth root u of w for any odd prime ℓ of its choice. In particular, in the strong RSA assumption, the adversary gets to pick ℓ, while in the (regular) RSA assumption, the adversary is given a randomly chosen ℓ.

Definition 7 (Strong RSA). *The Strong RSA assumption holds for the algorithm* GGen *if for any PPT adversary $\mathcal{A}$, the following probability is negligible in λ:*

$$\mathsf{Adv}_{\mathcal{A}}^{\mathrm{SRSA}}(\lambda) = \Pr\left[\begin{array}{c} u^{\ell} = w \\ \ell \in \mathsf{Primes} \setminus \{2\} \end{array} : \begin{array}{c} (a, b, \mathbb{G}) \leftarrow_{\$} \mathsf{GGen}(\lambda) \\ w \leftarrow_{\$} \mathbb{G} \\ (u, \ell) \leftarrow_{\$} \mathcal{A}(a, b, \mathbb{G}, w) \end{array}\right].$$

4 An Insert-Only Key-Value Commitment

We begin by describing an insert-only key-value commitment KVC-Ins. By insert-only, we mean that we only insert key-value pairs into the commitment but do

- $\mathsf{KeyGen}(1^{\lambda})$: Sample the description of a group $(a, b, \mathbb{G}) \leftarrow_{\$} \mathsf{GGen}(\lambda)$ of unknown order in the range $[a, b]$ where a, b and $a - b$ are exponential in λ, and a random element $g \leftarrow_{\$} \mathbb{G}^{a}$. Set $\mathcal{V} = [0, a)$ and $\mathcal{K} = \{0,1\}^*$. Let ζ denote the bit-length of b, i.e., $\zeta = |b|$. Sample the description of a hash function H that maps arbitrary strings to unique primes from the set $\mathsf{Primes}(\zeta + 1) \setminus [b]^{b}$. Output $(\mathsf{pp}, C) = ((a, b, \mathbb{G}, g, H), (1, g))$.
- $\mathsf{Insert}(C, (k, v))$: Parse the input C as (C_1, C_2). Let $z = H(k)$. Set
$$\Lambda_k = C, \quad C = (C_1^z \cdot C_2^v, C_2^z), \quad \mathsf{upd} = (k, v).$$
Output $(C, \Lambda_k, \mathsf{upd})$.
- $\mathsf{ProofUpdate}(k, \Lambda_k, \mathsf{upd})$: Parse Λ_k as $(\Lambda_{k,1}, \Lambda_{k,2})$ and upd as $(\mathsf{upd}_1, \mathsf{upd}_2)$. Let $z = H(\mathsf{upd}_1)$. Set
$$\Lambda_k = \left((\Lambda_{k,1})^z \cdot (\Lambda_{k,2})^{\mathsf{upd}_2}, (\Lambda_{k,2})^z\right).$$
Output Λ_k.
- $\mathsf{Ver}(C, (k, v), \Lambda_k)$: Parse the input C as (C_1, C_2) and Λ_k as $(\Lambda_{k,1}, \Lambda_{k,2})$. Let $z = H(k)$. Check whether:
  - $v \in \mathcal{V}$ and $k \in \mathcal{K}$,
  - $(\Lambda_{k,2})^z = C_2$,
  - $(\Lambda_{k,1})^z \cdot (\Lambda_{k,2})^v = C_1$.

  If all the checks pass, output 1; else, output 0.

[a] A random element of $\mathbb{G}$ would be a generator of $\mathbb{G}$ with overwhelming probability and, at the very least, would not be of low order.

[b] Using existing techniques, we can sample hash functions that satisfy this property with high probability. For details, please refer to the full version.

Fig. 1. KVC-Ins: Insert-only KVC construction

not the update the value corresponding to a key. We also note that we are only concerned with the case of inserting values corresponding to distinct keys, i.e., we assume that the insert algorithm is not invoked with the same key more than once. The construction KVC-Ins is formally described in Fig. 1.

Completeness and Efficiency. The correctness of the scheme follows directly from inspection. Also note that all operations involve (at most) one hash computation, three exponentiations and one multiplication. The size of the key-value commitment is constant, namely, two group elements. This is also true of the proofs corresponding to keys.

4.1 Key Binding

If we model the hash function H in the construction as a random oracle, we can prove the key binding of KVC-Ins based on the generalized RSA assumption. We note that while applying the Definitions 3 and 4 for key binding to KVC-Ins, the adversary will not be allowed to issue any update queries (KVC-Ins is an insert-only commitment scheme).

Lemma 1. *Suppose there exists a PPT adversary $\mathcal{A}$ in the random oracle model that satisfies*

$$\mathsf{Adv}^{\mathsf{bind}}_{\mathsf{KVC\text{-}Ins},\mathcal{A}}(\lambda) = \epsilon,$$

where KVC-Ins *is the key-value commitment scheme defined in Fig. 1. Then, there exists a PPT adversary $\mathcal{B}$ such that*

$$\mathsf{Adv}^{\mathrm{GRSA}}_{\mathcal{B}}(\lambda) \geq \frac{\epsilon}{T_\lambda^2} - \mathsf{negl}(\lambda),$$

where T_λ denotes the running time of $\mathcal{A}$ parameterized by λ.

Proof. Assume the existence of an adversary $\mathcal{A}$ as stated in the lemma above. We now design the adversary $\mathcal{B}$. On obtaining $(a, b, \mathbb{G}) \leftarrow_\$ \mathsf{GGen}(\lambda)$ with $|b| = \zeta$, $w \leftarrow_\$ \mathbb{G}$ and $\ell \leftarrow_\$ \mathsf{Primes}(\zeta + 1) \setminus [b]$ from the challenger CH, $\mathcal{B}$ first guesses the number, q, of keys that $\mathcal{A}$ would issue hash queries for or insert into the commitment, and the index, m, of the key k_m which $\mathcal{A}$ would provide the "fake" proof for at the end of its execution. Note that each of these choices are limited in number by T_λ and hence $\mathcal{B}$ makes the correct guesses with probability greater than or equal to T_λ^{-2}.

$\mathcal{B}$ chooses $q-1$ unique primes $\{z_i\}_{i\in[q]\setminus\{m\}}$ at random from the set $\mathsf{Primes}(\zeta + 1) \setminus [b]$ that it will assign, under the map H, to the set of keys other than the one that $\mathcal{A}$ would provide the "fake" proof for. It computes

$$\pi = w^{\prod_{i\in[q]\setminus\{m\}} z_i}.$$

With all but negligible probability in λ, $\ell \neq z_i$ for any $i \in [q] \setminus \{m\}$. $\mathcal{B}$ sets $g = w$ and $z_m = \ell$. $\mathcal{B}$ sends $((a, b, \mathbb{G}, g), (1, g))$ to $\mathcal{A}$.

$\mathcal{B}$ maintains a key-value map $\mathcal{M} \subseteq \mathcal{K} \times \mathcal{V}$ initialized to the empty map and the initial commitment value $C = (1, g)$. Any time $\mathcal{A}$ issues the ith query, k_i, for the computation of H, $\mathcal{B}$ returns z_i and assigns $H(k_i) = z_i$. Any time $\mathcal{A}$ issues queries as in Definition 3, note that $\mathcal{B}$ has all the values it needs to make updates to C and $\mathcal{M}$ as defined in Definition 3 and Fig. 1. If $\mathcal{A}$ aborts at any point in time, $\mathcal{B}$ aborts as well. Assuming no aborts, finally, $\mathcal{A}$ responds with a tuple of the form

1. (k_m, v, Λ) where k_m wasn't inserted by $\mathcal{A}$, or
2. $(k_m, v, v', \Lambda, \Lambda')$ where k_m was inserted by $\mathcal{A}$ and $v \neq v'$.

Case 1: Let $C = (C_1, C_2)$ and $\Lambda = (\Lambda_1, \Lambda_2)$. Since $\mathsf{Ver}(C, (k_m, v), \Lambda) = 1$,

$$\Lambda_2^\ell = C_2.$$

Without loss of generality, we can assume that $\mathcal{A}$ inserted all keys that it queried the hash function for into the commitment (other than k_m).[6] Let $\mathcal{M} = \{(k_i, v_i)\}_{i \in [q] \setminus \{m\}}$ be the key-value map committed to in C. We have

$$C_2 = g^{\prod_{i \in [q] \setminus \{m\}} H(k_i)}.$$

Therefore,

$$\Lambda_2^\ell = w^{\prod_{i \in [q] \setminus \{m\}} z_i}.$$

Since $\ell \neq z_i$ for any $i \in [q] \setminus \{m\}$, ℓ is coprime to $\prod_{i \in [q] \setminus \{m\}} z_i$. $\mathcal{B}$ then computes integers θ_1, θ_2 such that

$$\theta_1 \cdot \ell + \theta_2 \cdot \prod_{i \in [q] \setminus \{m\}} z_i = 1.$$

Finally, $\mathcal{B}$ computes

$$u = w^{\theta_1} \Lambda_2^{\theta_2}.$$

Note that

$$\begin{aligned} u^\ell &= w^{\theta_1 \ell} \Lambda_2^{\theta_2 \ell} \\ &= w^{\theta_1 \ell} (\Lambda_2^\ell)^{\theta_2} \\ &= w^{\theta_1 \ell} (w^{\prod_{i \in [q] \setminus \{m\}} z_i})^{\theta_2} \\ &= w^{\theta_1 \cdot \ell + \theta_2 \cdot \prod_{i \in [q] \setminus \{m\}} z_i} \\ &= w. \end{aligned}$$

$\mathcal{B}$ forwards u to CH.

[6] If this is not the case, $\mathcal{B}$ can insert (arbitrary) values for the remaining keys after the fact to complete the reduction.

Case 2: Let $\Lambda' = (\Lambda'_1, \Lambda'_2)$. We claim that

$$\Lambda_2 = \Lambda'_2.$$

Since $\mathsf{Ver}(C, (k_m, v), \Lambda) = \mathsf{Ver}(C, (k_m, v'), \Lambda') = 1$,

$$\Lambda_2^\ell = C_2 = \Lambda_2'^\ell.$$

Let

$$\alpha = \frac{\Lambda_2}{\Lambda'_2}.$$

We have that $\alpha^\ell = 1$. Since ℓ is prime, if $\alpha \neq 1$, ℓ must be the order of α in $\mathbb{G}$. But ℓ is larger than the order of $\mathbb{G}$, which is not possible. Hence $\alpha = 1$.

Without loss of generality, we can assume that $\mathcal{A}$ inserted all keys that it queried the hash function for into the commitment. Let $\mathcal{M} = \{(k_i, v_i)\}_{i \in [q]}$ be the key-value map committed to in C. Consider the proof Λ_{k_m} corresponding to the key k_m defined by

$$\Lambda_{k_m} = (\Lambda_{k_m,1}, \Lambda_{k_m,2}),$$

where

$$\Lambda_{k_m,1} = g^{\sum_{i \in [q] \setminus \{m\}} v_i \prod_{j \in [q] \setminus \{i,m\}} H(k_j)}$$

and

$$\Lambda_{k_m,2} = g^{\prod_{i \in [q] \setminus \{m\}} H(k_i)}.$$

Clearly, $\mathsf{Ver}(C, (k_m, v_m), \Lambda_{k_m}) = 1$. In particular,

$$\Lambda_{k_m,2}^\ell = C_2.$$

Extending our previous argument, we have that

$$\Lambda_2 = \Lambda'_2 = \Lambda_{k_m,2} = g^{\prod_{i \in [q] \setminus \{m\}} H(k_i)}.$$

Since $\mathsf{Ver}(C, (k_m, v), \Lambda) = \mathsf{Ver}(C, (k_m, v'), \Lambda') = 1$, we have

$$(\Lambda_1)^\ell \cdot (\Lambda_2)^v = C_1 = (\Lambda'_1)^\ell \cdot (\Lambda'_2)^{v'}.$$

This implies that

$$\left(\frac{\Lambda_1}{\Lambda'_1}\right)^\ell = \left(g^{\prod_{i \in [q] \setminus \{m\}} H(k_i)}\right)^{v'-v}.$$

Let

$$\beta = \frac{\Lambda_1}{\Lambda'_1}$$

and

$$v' - v = \delta.$$

Note that $\beta^\ell = \pi^\delta$. This implies that

$$\beta^\ell = w^{\delta \prod_{i \in [q] \setminus \{m\}} z_i}.$$

Since $\mathcal{V} = [0, a)$, $|\delta| < a < b < \ell$, and since ℓ is prime, ℓ is coprime to δ. Also, since $\ell \neq z_i$ for any $i \in [q] \setminus \{m\}$, ℓ is coprime to $\prod_{i \in [q]\setminus\{m\}} z_i$. Hence, ℓ is coprime to $\delta \prod_{i \in [q]\setminus\{m\}} z_i$. $\mathcal{B}$ then computes integers θ_1, θ_2 such that

$$\theta_1 \cdot \ell + \theta_2 \cdot \delta \prod_{i \in [q]\setminus\{m\}} z_i = 1.$$

Finally, $\mathcal{B}$ computes

$$u = w^{\theta_1} \beta^{\theta_2}.$$

Note that

$$\begin{aligned} u^{\ell} &= w^{\theta_1 \ell} \beta^{\theta_2 \ell} \\ &= w^{\theta_1 \ell} (\beta^{\ell})^{\theta_2} \\ &= w^{\theta_1 \ell} (w^{\delta \prod_{i \in [q]\setminus\{m\}} z_i})^{\theta_2} \\ &= w^{\theta_1 \cdot \ell + \theta_2 \cdot \delta \prod_{i \in [q]\setminus\{m\}} z_i} \\ &= w. \end{aligned}$$

$\mathcal{B}$ forwards u to CH. This completes the proof.

Removing the Random Oracle Assumption. Intuitively, we need H to be a random oracle only because we are programming the challenge prime ℓ from the RSA assumption as one of the z's output by H. We can however get over this difficulty by letting H output arbitrary primes and letting the adversary choose ℓ as in the game for the strong RSA assumption.

Lemma 2. *Suppose there exists a PPT adversary $\mathcal{A}$ in the standard model that satisfies*

$$\mathsf{Adv}^{\mathsf{bind}}_{\mathsf{KVC\text{-}Ins},\mathcal{A}}(\lambda) = \epsilon,$$

where KVC-Ins *is the key-value commitment scheme defined in Fig. 1. Then, there exists a PPT adversary $\mathcal{B}$ such that*

$$\mathsf{Adv}^{\mathsf{SRSA}}_{\mathcal{B}}(\lambda) \geq \epsilon - \mathsf{negl}(\lambda).$$

A proof of this lemma can be found in the full version of the paper.

4.2 Accumulators

Observe that an insert-only key-value commitment directly gives us an accumulator that supports insertions and membership proofs (just use arbitrary keys). Our construction of an insert-only key-value commitment also provides for deletions because the proof corresponding to a key is the commitment of the remainder of the key-value map, which would be the new commitment. Existing proofs can be updated using the techniques of aggregation in Sect. 6. The idea is that given key-value commitments to the maps $\mathcal{M} \setminus \{(k, v)\}$ and $\mathcal{M} \setminus \{(k', v')\}$, it is possible to create a commitment to the map $\mathcal{M} \setminus \{(k, v), (k', v')\}$. Thus, KVC-Ins can be used to build optimal dynamic positive accumulators [1].

5 A Complete Key-Value Commitment

In this section, we provide our main construction of a key-value commitment. The construction KVaC is formally described in Fig. 2.

Completeness and Efficiency. The correctness of the scheme follows directly from inspection. Also note that all operations involve (at most) two hash computations, five exponentiations and two multiplications. The size of the key-value commitment is constant, namely, two group elements. This is also true of the proofs corresponding to keys.

5.1 Key Binding

If we model the hash function H in the construction as a random oracle, we can prove the key binding of KVaC based on the generalized RSA assumption.

Lemma 3. *Suppose there exists a PPT adversary $\mathcal{A}$ in the random oracle model that satisfies*

$$\mathsf{Adv}^{\mathrm{bind}}_{\mathsf{KVaC},\mathcal{A}}(\lambda) = \epsilon,$$

where KVaC *is the key-value commitment scheme defined in Fig. 2. Then, there exists a PPT adversary $\mathcal{B}$ such that*

$$\mathsf{Adv}^{\mathrm{GRSA}}_{\mathcal{B}}(\lambda) \geq \frac{\epsilon}{T_\lambda^3} - \mathsf{negl}(\lambda),$$

where T_λ denotes the running time of $\mathcal{A}$ parameterized by λ.

Proof. Assume the existence of an adversary $\mathcal{A}$ as stated in the lemma above. We now design the adversary $\mathcal{B}$. On obtaining $(a, b, \mathbb{G}) \leftarrow_{\$} \mathsf{GGen}(\lambda)$ with $|b| = \zeta$, $w \leftarrow_{\$} \mathbb{G}$ and $\ell \leftarrow_{\$} \mathsf{Primes}(\zeta + 1) \setminus [b]$ from the challenger CH, $\mathcal{B}$ first guesses the number, q, of keys that $\mathcal{A}$ would issue hash queries for or insert into the commitment, the index, m, of the key k_m which $\mathcal{A}$ would provide the "fake" proof for at the end of its execution, and u, the maximum number of updates performed on the value corresponding to any of the keys inserted by $\mathcal{A}$. Note that each of these choices are limited in number by T_λ and hence $\mathcal{B}$ makes the correct guesses with probability greater than or equal to T_λ^{-3}. We assume without loss of generality that $\mathcal{A}$ makes the same number of updates, u, to the values corresponding to each of the keys inserted into the commitment.

$\mathcal{B}$ chooses $q-1$ unique primes $\{z_i\}_{i \in [q] \setminus \{m\}}$ at random from the set $\mathsf{Primes}(\zeta + 1) \setminus [b]$ that it will assign, under the map H, to the set of keys other than the one that $\mathcal{A}$ would provide the "fake" proof for. It computes

$$\pi = w^{\prod_{i \in [q] \setminus \{m\}} z_i^{u+1}}.$$

With all but negligible probability in λ, $\ell \neq z_i$ for any $i \in [q] \setminus \{m\}$. $\mathcal{B}$ sets $g = w$ and $z_m = \ell$. $\mathcal{B}$ sends $((a, b, \mathbb{G}, g), (1, g))$ to $\mathcal{A}$.

- $\mathsf{KeyGen}(1^\lambda)$: Sample the description of a group $(a, b, \mathbb{G}) \leftarrow_\$ \mathsf{GGen}(\lambda)$ of unknown order in the range $[a, b]$ where a, b and $a - b$ are exponential in λ and a random element $g \leftarrow_\$ \mathbb{G}$. Set $\mathcal{V} = [0, a)$. Let the bit-length of b, $|b| = \zeta$. Set $\mathcal{K} = \{0,1\}^*$. Sample the description of a hash function H that maps arbitrary strings to unique primes from the set $\mathsf{Primes}(\zeta + 1) \setminus [b]$. Output $(\mathsf{pp}, C) = ((a, b, \mathbb{G}, g, H), (1, g))$.
- $\mathsf{Insert}(C, (k, v))$: Parse the input C as (C_1, C_2). Let $z = H(k)$. Set

$$\Lambda_k = ((C_1, C_2), (g, 1, 1), 0)^{a}, \quad C = (C_1^z \cdot C_2^v, C_2^z), \quad \mathsf{upd} = (\mathsf{insert}, (k, v)).$$

Output $(C, \Lambda_k, \mathsf{upd})$.

- $\mathsf{Update}(C, (k, \delta))$: Parse the input C as (C_1, C_2). Let $z = H(k)$. Set

$$C = \left(C_1^z \cdot C_2^\delta, C_2^z\right), \quad \mathsf{upd} = (\mathsf{update}, (k, \delta)).$$

Output (C, upd).

- $\mathsf{ProofUpdate}(k, \Lambda_k, \mathsf{upd})$: Parse the inputs Λ_k as $((\Lambda_{k,1}, \Lambda_{k,2}), (\Lambda_{k,3}, \Lambda_{k,4}, \Lambda_{k,5}), u_k)$ and upd as $(\mathsf{upd}_1, (\mathsf{upd}_2, \mathsf{upd}_3))$. Let $z = H(k)$. If $\mathsf{upd}_2 = k$, set

$$\Lambda_k = ((\Lambda_{k,1}, (\Lambda_{k,2})^z), (\Lambda_{k,3}, \Lambda_{k,4}, \Lambda_{k,5}), u_k + 1)\,.$$

Otherwise, let $\hat{z} = H(\mathsf{upd}_2)$. We assume that $z \neq \hat{z}$. Compute $\alpha, \beta \in \mathbb{Z}$ such that

$$\alpha \cdot z + \beta \cdot \hat{z} = 1.$$

Compute

$$\gamma = \beta \cdot \Lambda_{k,5} \bmod z.$$

Compute $\eta \in \mathbb{Z}$ such that

$$\gamma \cdot \hat{z} + \eta \cdot z = \Lambda_{k,5}.$$

Set

$$\Lambda_k = \left(\left((\Lambda_{k,1})^{\hat{z}} \cdot (\Lambda_{k,2})^{\mathsf{upd}_3}, (\Lambda_{k,2})^{\hat{z}}\right), \left((\Lambda_{k,3})^{\hat{z}}, \Lambda_{k,4} \cdot \Lambda_{k,3}^{\eta}, \gamma\right), u_k\right).$$

Output Λ_k.

- $\mathsf{Ver}(C, (k, v), \Lambda_k)$: Parse the inputs C as (C_1, C_2) and Λ_k as $((\Lambda_{k,1}, \Lambda_{k,2}), (\Lambda_{k,3}, \Lambda_{k,4}, \Lambda_{k,5}), u_k)$. Let $z = H(k)$. Check whether:
  - $v \in \mathcal{V}$ and $k \in \mathcal{K}$,
  - $u_k \in \mathbb{Z}_{\geq 0}$,
  - $(\Lambda_{k,2})^z = C_2$,
  - $(\Lambda_{k,1})^{z^{u_k+1}} \cdot (\Lambda_{k,2})^v = C_1$,
  - $(\Lambda_{k,3})^{z^{u_k+1}} = C_2$,
  - $(\Lambda_{k,4})^z \cdot (\Lambda_{k,3})^{\Lambda_{k,5}} = g$.

  If all the checks pass, output 1; else, output 0.

[a] It is possible to do away with one of these elements, but we keep them all here for ease of presentation.

Fig. 2. KVaC: Full KVC construction

$\mathcal{B}$ maintains a key-value map $\mathcal{M} \subseteq \mathcal{K} \times \mathcal{V}$ initialized to the empty map and the initial commitment value $C = (1, g)$. Any time $\mathcal{A}$ issues the ith query, k_i, for the computation of H, $\mathcal{B}$ returns z_i and assigns $H(k_i) = z_i$. Any time $\mathcal{A}$ issues queries as in Definition 3, note that $\mathcal{B}$ has all the values it needs to make updates to C and $\mathcal{M}$ as defined in Definition 3 and Fig. 2. If $\mathcal{A}$ made more than u updates to any key, $\mathcal{B}$ aborts. If $\mathcal{A}$ aborts at any point in time, $\mathcal{B}$ aborts as well. Assuming no aborts, finally, $\mathcal{A}$ responds with a tuple of the form

1. (k_m, v, Λ) where k_m wasn't inserted by $\mathcal{A}$, or
2. $(k_m, v, v', \Lambda, \Lambda')$ where k_m was inserted by $\mathcal{A}$ and $v \neq v'$.

Case 1: Let $C = (C_1, C_2)$ and $\Lambda = ((\Lambda_1, \Lambda_2), (\cdot, \cdot, \cdot), u_k)$. Since it is the case that $\mathsf{Ver}(C, (k_m, v), \Lambda) = 1$,

$$\Lambda_2^\ell = C_2.$$

Without loss of generality, we can assume that $\mathcal{A}$ inserted all keys that it queried the hash function for into the commitment (other than k_m). Let $\mathcal{M} = \{(k_i, v_i)\}_{i \in [q] \setminus \{m\}}$ be the map committed to in C. We have

$$C_2 = g^{\prod_{i \in [q] \setminus \{m\}} H(k_i)^{u+1}}.$$

Therefore

$$\Lambda_2^\ell = w^{\prod_{i \in [q] \setminus \{m\}} z_i^{u+1}}.$$

Since $\ell \neq z_i$ for any $i \in [q] \setminus \{m\}$, ℓ is coprime to $\prod_{i \in [q] \setminus \{m\}} z_i^{u+1}$. $\mathcal{B}$ then computes integers θ_1, θ_2 such that

$$\theta_1 \cdot \ell + \theta_2 \cdot \prod_{i \in [q] \setminus \{m\}} z_i^{u+1} = 1.$$

Finally, $\mathcal{B}$ computes

$$u = w^{\theta_1} \Lambda_2^{\theta_2}.$$

Note that

$$\begin{aligned} u^\ell &= w^{\theta_1 \ell} \Lambda_2^{\theta_2 \ell} \\ &= w^{\theta_1 \ell} (\Lambda_2^\ell)^{\theta_2} \\ &= w^{\theta_1 \ell} (w^{\prod_{i \in [q] \setminus \{m\}} z_i^{u+1}})^{\theta_2} \\ &= w^{\theta_1 \cdot \ell + \theta_2 \cdot \prod_{i \in [q] \setminus \{m\}} z_i^{u+1}} \\ &= w. \end{aligned}$$

$\mathcal{B}$ forwards u to CH.

Case 2: Let $\Lambda' = (\Lambda'_1, \Lambda'_2, (\cdot,\cdot,\cdot), u'_k)$. Following the key-binding proof of the increment-only construction (see the full version), we have that with overwhelming probability,

$$u = u_k = u'_k.$$

As in the proof of Lemma 1,

$$\Lambda_2 = \Lambda'_2.$$

Without loss of generality, we can assume that $\mathcal{A}$ inserted all keys that it queried the hash function for into the commitment. Let $\mathcal{M} = \{(k_i, v_i)\}_{i\in[q]}$ be the key-value map committed to in C. Consider the proof Λ_{k_m} corresponding to the key k_m defined by

$$\Lambda_{k_m} = (\Lambda_{k_m,1}, \Lambda_{k_m,2}),$$

where

$$\Lambda_{k_m,1} = g^{\left(\sum_{i\in[q]\setminus\{m\}} v_i \prod_{j\in[q]\setminus\{i,m\}} H(k_j)\right)\cdot \prod_{i\in[q]\setminus\{m\}} H(k_j)^u}$$

and

$$\Lambda_{k_m,2} = g^{\ell^u \cdot \prod_{i\in[q]\setminus\{m\}} H(k_i)^{u+1}}.$$

Clearly, $\mathsf{Ver}(C, (k_m, v_m), \Lambda_{k_m}) = 1$. In particular,

$$\Lambda_{k_m,2}^{\ell} = C_2.$$

Extending our previous argument, we have that

$$\Lambda_2 = \Lambda'_2 = \Lambda_{k_m,2} = g^{\ell^u \cdot \prod_{i\in[q]\setminus\{m\}} H(k_i)^{u+1}}.$$

Since $\mathsf{Ver}(C, (k_m, v), \Lambda) = \mathsf{Ver}(C, (k_m, v'), \Lambda') = 1$, we have

$$(\Lambda_1)^{\ell^{u+1}} \cdot (\Lambda_2)^v = C_1 = (\Lambda'_1)^{\ell^{u+1}} \cdot (\Lambda'_2)^{v'}.$$

This implies that

$$\left(\frac{\Lambda_1}{\Lambda'_1}\right)^{\ell^{u+1}} = \left(g^{\ell^u \cdot \prod_{i\in[q]\setminus\{m\}} H(k_i)^{u+1}}\right)^{v'-v}.$$

Let

$$\xi = \frac{\left(\frac{\Lambda_1}{\Lambda'_1}\right)^{\ell}}{g^{(v'-v)\cdot \prod_{i\in[q]\setminus\{m\}} H(k_i)^{u+1}}} = \frac{\left(\frac{\Lambda_1}{\Lambda'_1}\right)^{\ell}}{\pi^{v'-v}}.$$

We have that $\xi^{\ell^u} = 1$. Since ℓ is prime, the order of ξ in $\mathbb{G}$ must be a power of ℓ. But ℓ is larger than the order of $\mathbb{G}$, which is not possible. Hence $\xi = 1$, that is,

$$\left(\frac{\Lambda_1}{\Lambda'_1}\right)^{\ell} = \pi^{v'-v}.$$

Let

$$\beta = \frac{\Lambda_1}{\Lambda_1'}$$

and

$$v' - v = \delta.$$

Note that $\beta^\ell = \pi^\delta$. This implies that

$$\beta^\ell = w^{\delta \prod_{i\in[q]\setminus\{m\}} z_i^{u+1}}.$$

Since $\mathcal{V} = [0, a)$, $|\delta| < a < b < \ell$, and since ℓ is prime, ℓ is coprime to δ. Also, since $\ell \neq z_i$ for any $i \in [q] \setminus \{m\}$, ℓ is coprime to $\prod_{i\in[q]\setminus\{m\}} z_i^{u+1}$. Hence, ℓ is coprime to $\delta \prod_{i\in[q]\setminus\{m\}} z_i^{u+1}$. $\mathcal{B}$ then computes integers θ_1, θ_2 such that

$$\theta_1 \cdot \ell + \theta_2 \cdot \delta \prod_{i\in[q]\setminus\{m\}} z_i^{u+1} = 1.$$

Finally, $\mathcal{B}$ computes

$$u = w^{\theta_1} \beta^{\theta_2}.$$

Note that

$$\begin{aligned} u^\ell &= w^{\theta_1 \ell} \beta^{\theta_2 \ell} \\ &= w^{\theta_1 \ell} (\beta^\ell)^{\theta_2} \\ &= w^{\theta_1 \ell} (w^{\delta \prod_{i\in[q]\setminus\{m\}} z_i^{u+1}})^{\theta_2} \\ &= w^{\theta_1 \cdot \ell + \theta_2 \cdot \delta \prod_{i\in[q]\setminus\{m\}} z_i^{u+1}} \\ &= w. \end{aligned}$$

$\mathcal{B}$ forwards u to CH. This completes the proof.

Removing the random oracle assumption. As before, we can get rid of the need for a random oracle by leveraging the stronger form of RSA.

Lemma 4. *Suppose there exists a PPT adversary $\mathcal{A}$ in the standard model that satisfies*

$$\mathsf{Adv}^{\mathsf{bind}}_{\mathsf{KVaC},\mathcal{A}}(\lambda) = \epsilon,$$

where KVaC *is the key-value commitment scheme defined in Fig. 2. Then, there exists a PPT adversary $\mathcal{B}$ such that*

$$\mathsf{Adv}^{\mathrm{SRSA}}_{\mathcal{B}}(\lambda) \geq \epsilon - \mathsf{negl}(\lambda).$$

A proof of this lemma can be found in the full version of the paper.

Theorem 1. *The construction* KVaC *in Fig. 2 is a key-value commitment scheme for arbitrary keys and an exponentially large value space where the commitment is of constant size, the proof corresponding to any key is of constant size, and each operation requires only a constant number of hash computations, exponentiations or multiplications. The construction is key-binding (Definition 4) based on (i) the generalized RSA assumption in the random oracle model (Lemma 3), or (ii) the strong RSA assumption in the standard model (Lemma 4).*

5.2 Performing "Double" Exponentiations

In the verification procedure, one must compute z^{u_k+1}. While this is only a polynomial time computation (as u_k can only be polynomially large), we might want to avoid "double" exponentiations such as computing $(\Lambda_{k,1})^{z^{u_k+1}}$. This can be done by accumulating these values as they are computed per each update using standard accumulators such as those in the work of Boneh et al. [4] or the insert-only key-value commitment scheme construction in Fig. 1. This would only add one more group element to the commitment and a constant number (at most three) of hash computations, group exponentiations or multiplications to the operations.

5.3 Vector Commitments

A key-value commitment directly gives us a vector commitment. We can use the keys as indices. Using our construction for key-value commitments, the newly constructed vector commitment enjoys several benefits in comparison to prior constructions. For instance, additive updates on values can be performed by any party and corresponding updates to proofs can be made extremely efficiently. The commitment and the proofs are constant-sized and verification only involves a constant number of operations. An added benefit of constructing a vector commitment in this way is that the length of the vector being committed need not be known ahead of time, or, in fact, at any point in time. If one, however, did wish for a vector commitment with restrictions on the length of the vector that can be committed, or one which only allowed for appending elements, it can be trivially achieved through minor (black-box) modifications to our construction.

6 Aggregating Proofs

In this section, we describe how proofs corresponding to multiple keys can be combined, or "aggregated", into a single proof and "batch" verified in one shot. The first observation is that the proofs corresponding to keys in the increment-only construction described in the full version can be combined in a straightforward manner using the Shamir Trick described in the work of Boneh et al. [4], although this would only yield one-hop aggregation. We will discuss here how to combine proofs corresponding to multiple keys in the insert-only construction described in Fig. 1. In fact, the insert-only construction supports unbounded aggregation and disaggregation in the sense of Campanelli et al. [9]. Putting these techniques together, one can combine proofs corresponding to multiple keys for the full construction described in Fig. 2, but combined proofs cannot be combined further.

Suppose we had two proofs $\Lambda = (\Lambda_1, \Lambda_2)$ and $\Lambda' = (\Lambda'_1, \Lambda'_2)$ corresponding to two keys k and k' with values v and v' (with respect to the insert-only construction described in Fig. 1), and let the current state of the key-value commitment be $C = (C_1, C_2)$. Suppose $z = H(k)$ and $z' = H(k')$. Recall that if Λ and Λ' are valid proofs, it must be the case that

$$\Lambda_2^z = \Lambda_2'^{z'} = C_2$$

and

$$\Lambda_1^z \cdot \Lambda_2^v = \Lambda_1'^{z'} \cdot \Lambda_2'^{v'} = C_1.$$

In order to combine these two proofs, we would have to come up an "aggregated" proof $\Lambda'' = (\Lambda''_1, \Lambda''_2)$ whose "batch" verification would look like

$$\Lambda_2''^{zz'} = C_2$$

and

$$\Lambda_1''^{zz'} \cdot \Lambda_2''^{vz'+v'z} = C_1.$$

In other words, Λ'' represents a key-value commitment to the key-value pairs in C other than (k, v) and (k', v') which is realized by the fact that inserting (k, v) and (k', v') into Λ'' generates C.

We combine Λ and Λ' as follows. Since z and z' are distinct primes, compute $\alpha, \beta \in \mathbb{Z}$ such that

$$\alpha \cdot z + \beta \cdot z' = 1.$$

Set

$$\Lambda''_2 = \Lambda_2^\beta \cdot \Lambda_2'^\alpha$$

and

$$\Lambda''_1 = \frac{\Lambda_1^\beta \cdot \Lambda_1'^\alpha}{\Lambda_2''^{v\alpha + v'\beta}}.$$

Observe that

$$\Lambda_2''^{zz'} = \Lambda_2^{\beta zz'} \cdot \Lambda_2'^{\alpha zz'} = C_2^{\alpha z + \beta z'} = C_2$$

and

$$
\begin{aligned}
\Lambda_1^{\prime\prime zz'} \cdot \Lambda_2^{\prime\prime vz'+v'z} &= \frac{\Lambda_1^{\beta zz'} \cdot \Lambda_1^{\prime \alpha zz'}}{\Lambda_2^{\prime\prime v\alpha zz'+v'\beta zz'}} \cdot \Lambda_2^{\beta(vz'+v'z)} \cdot \Lambda_2^{\prime\alpha(vz'+v'z)} \\
&= \frac{(\Lambda_1^z \cdot \Lambda_2^v)^{\beta z'} \cdot \left(\Lambda_1^{\prime z'} \cdot \Lambda_2^{\prime v'}\right)^{\alpha z} \cdot (\Lambda_2^z)^{\beta v'} \cdot \left(\Lambda_2^{\prime z'}\right)^{\alpha v}}{C_2^{v\alpha+v'\beta}} \\
&= C_1^{\alpha z+\beta z'} \\
&= C_1.
\end{aligned}
$$

Notice that the aggregation procedure involves only two hash computations, five exponentiations and three multiplications. The size of the combined proof is the same as the sizes of each of the separate proofs and, by construction, the combined proof can be verified in one shot. Key-binding for the combined proof can be shown in exactly the same as was done for each of the separate proofs.

We can easily extend this procedure to combine more than two proofs. In particular, an aggregated proof can be combined with a regular proof or two aggregated proofs can be combined with each other.

Acknowledgement. We thank Asiacrypt 2020 reviewers for providing valuable feedback on the paper. We thank Benedikt Bünz for suggesting several improvements to the paper.

References

1. Baldimtsi, F., et al.: Accumulators with applications to anonymity-preserving revocation. In: 2017 IEEE European Symposium on Security and Privacy, EuroS&P 2017, Paris, France, 26–28 April 2017, pp. 301–315. IEEE (2017)
2. Benaloh, J., de Mare, M.: One-way accumulators: a decentralized alternative to digital signatures (extended abstract). In: Helleseth, T. (ed.) EUROCRYPT 1993. LNCS, vol. 765, pp. 274–285. Springer, Heidelberg (1994). https://doi.org/10.1007/3-540-48285-7_24
3. Bitcoin. https://bitcoin.org/
4. Boneh, D., Bünz, B., Fisch, B.: Batching techniques for accumulators with applications to IOPs and stateless blockchains. In: Boldyreva, A., Micciancio, D. (eds.) CRYPTO 2019, Part I. LNCS, vol. 11692, pp. 561–586. Springer, Cham (2019). https://doi.org/10.1007/978-3-030-26948-7_20
5. Buchmann, J., Hamdy, S.: A survey on IQ cryptography. In: Proceedings of Public Key Cryptography and Computational Number Theory, pp. 1–15 (2001)
6. Camacho, P., Hevia, A.: On the impossibility of batch update for cryptographic accumulators. In: Abdalla, M., Barreto, P.S.L.M. (eds.) LATINCRYPT 2010. LNCS, vol. 6212, pp. 178–188. Springer, Heidelberg (2010). https://doi.org/10.1007/978-3-642-14712-8_11
7. Camacho, P., Hevia, A., Kiwi, M., Opazo, R.: Strong accumulators from collision-resistant hashing. In: Wu, T.-C., Lei, C.-L., Rijmen, V., Lee, D.-T. (eds.) ISC 2008. LNCS, vol. 5222, pp. 471–486. Springer, Heidelberg (2008). https://doi.org/10.1007/978-3-540-85886-7_32

8. Camenisch, J., Lysyanskaya, A.: Dynamic accumulators and application to efficient revocation of anonymous credentials. In: Yung, M. (ed.) CRYPTO 2002. LNCS, vol. 2442, pp. 61–76. Springer, Heidelberg (2002). https://doi.org/10.1007/3-540-45708-9_5
9. Campanelli, M., Fiore, D., Greco, N., Kolonelos, D., Nizzardo, L.: Vector commitment techniques and applications to verifiable decentralized storage. Cryptology ePrint Archive, Report 2020/149 (2020). https://eprint.iacr.org/2020/149
10. Catalano, D., Fiore, D.: Vector commitments and their applications. In: Kurosawa, K., Hanaoka, G. (eds.) PKC 2013. LNCS, vol. 7778, pp. 55–72. Springer, Heidelberg (2013). https://doi.org/10.1007/978-3-642-36362-7_5
11. Chepurnoy, A., Papamanthou, C., Zhang, Y.: EDRAX: a cryptocurrency with stateless transaction validation. Cryptology ePrint Archive, Report 2018/968 (2018). https://eprint.iacr.org/2018/968
12. Dryja, T.: Utreexo: a dynamic hash-based accumulator optimized for the bitcoin UTXO set. Cryptology ePrint Archive, Report 2019/611 (2019). https://eprint.iacr.org/2019/611
13. EOS.io—Blockchain software architecture. https://www.eos.io
14. Etherchain – Evolution of the total number of Ethereum accounts. https://www.etherchain.org/charts/totalAccounts
15. Ethereum. https://www.ethereum.org/
16. Etherscan. https://etherscan.io/
17. Gorbunov, S., Reyzin, L., Wee, H., Zhang, Z.: Pointproofs: aggregating proofs for multiple vector commitments. Cryptology ePrint Archive, Report 2020/419 (2020). https://eprint.iacr.org/2020/419
18. Hamdy, S., Möller, B.: Security of cryptosystems based on class groups of imaginary quadratic orders. In: Okamoto, T. (ed.) ASIACRYPT 2000. LNCS, vol. 1976, pp. 234–247. Springer, Heidelberg (2000). https://doi.org/10.1007/3-540-44448-3_18
19. Krupp, J., Schröder, D., Simkin, M., Fiore, D., Ateniese, G., Nuernberger, S.: Nearly optimal verifiable data streaming. In: Cheng, C.M., Chung, K.M., Persiano, G., Yang, B.Y. (eds.) PKC 2016, Part I. LNCS, vol. 9614, pp. 417–445. Springer, Heidelberg (2016). https://doi.org/10.1007/978-3-662-49384-7_16
20. Lai, R.W.F., Malavolta, G.: Subvector commitments with application to succinct arguments. In: Boldyreva, A., Micciancio, D. (eds.) CRYPTO 2019, Part I. LNCS, vol. 11692, pp. 530–560. Springer, Cham (2019). https://doi.org/10.1007/978-3-030-26948-7_19
21. Li, J., Li, N., Xue, R.: Universal accumulators with efficient nonmembership proofs. In: Katz, J., Yung, M. (eds.) ACNS 2007. LNCS, vol. 4521, pp. 253–269. Springer, Heidelberg (2007). https://doi.org/10.1007/978-3-540-72738-5_17
22. Libert, B., Ramanna, S.C., Yung, M.: Functional commitment schemes: from polynomial commitments to pairing-based accumulators from simple assumptions. In: Chatzigiannakis, I., Mitzenmacher, M., Rabani, Y., Sangiorgi, D. (eds.) ICALP 2016. LIPIcs, vol. 55, pp. 30:1–30:14. Schloss Dagstuhl (2016). https://doi.org/10.4230/LIPIcs.ICALP.2016.30
23. Libra. https://libra.org/
24. Mazieres, D.: The stellar consensus protocol: a federated model for internet-level consensus. Stellar Development Foundation (2015)
25. Nguyen, L.: Accumulators from bilinear pairings and applications. In: Menezes, A. (ed.) CT-RSA 2005. LNCS, vol. 3376, pp. 275–292. Springer, Heidelberg (2005). https://doi.org/10.1007/978-3-540-30574-3_19
26. Ripple - One frictionless experience to send money globally. https://www.ripple.com

27. Todd, P.: Making UTXO set growth irrelevant with low-latency delayed TXO commitments. https://petertodd.org/2016/delayed-txo-commitments
28. Tomescu, A., Abraham, I., Buterin, V., Drake, J., Feist, D., Khovratovich, D.: Aggregatable subvector commitments for stateless cryptocurrencies. Cryptology ePrint Archive, Report 2020/527 (2020). https://eprint.iacr.org/2020/527

Catalic: Delegated PSI Cardinality with Applications to Contact Tracing

Thai Duong[1], Duong Hieu Phan[2], and Ni Trieu[3](✉)

[1] Google LLC, Menlo Park, USA
thaidn@google.com
[2] LTCI, Telecom Paris, Institut Polytechnique de Paris, Palaiseau, France
hieu.phan@telecom-paris.fr
[3] Arizona State University, Tempe, USA
nitrieu@asu.edu

Abstract. Private Set Intersection Cardinality (PSI-CA) allows two parties, each holding a set of items, to learn the size of the intersection of those sets without revealing any additional information. To the best of our knowledge, this work presents the first protocol that allows one of the parties to delegate PSI-CA computation to untrusted servers. At the heart of our delegated PSI-CA protocol is a new oblivious distributed key PRF (Odk-PRF) abstraction, which may be of independent interest.

We explore in detail how to use our delegated PSI-CA protocol to perform privacy-preserving contact tracing. It has been estimated that a significant percentage of a given population would need to use a contact tracing app to stop a disease's spread. Prior privacy-preserving contact tracing systems, however, impose heavy bandwidth or computational demands on client devices. These demands present an economic disincentive to participate for end users who may be billed per MB by their mobile data plan or for users who want to save battery life. We propose Catalic (ContAct TrAcing for LIghtweight Clients), a new contact tracing system that minimizes bandwidth cost and computation workload on client devices. By applying our new delegated PSI-CA protocol, Catalic shifts most of the client-side computation of contact tracing to untrusted servers, and potentially saves each user hundreds of megabytes of mobile data per day while preserving privacy.

Keywords: Private Set Intersection Cardinality · Contact tracing · Linkage attack

1 Introduction

Private Set Intersection (PSI) is a secure multiparty computation (MPC) technique that allows several parties, each holding a set of items, to learn the intersection of their sets without revealing anything else about the items. Over the past few years, practice has motivated the development of fast implementations

S. Moriai and H. Wang (Eds.): ASIACRYPT 2020, LNCS 12493, pp. 870–899, 2020.
https://doi.org/10.1007/978-3-030-64840-4_29

that make PSI practical. As of today, Google runs PSI together with third-party data providers to find target audiences for advertising and marketing campaigns [IKN+19]. Private Set Intersection Cardinality (PSI-CA) is a variant of PSI in which the parties learn the intersection size and nothing else. Recently, PSI-CA is used in the context of contact tracing to protect against linkage attacks [TSS+20]. In this work, we consider delegated PSI-CA in the semi-honest model. By "delegated," we refer to cases where the parties outsource their datasets to an untrusted cloud and let the cloud perform the PSI-CA computation on their behalf. At the end of the computation, the parties only learn the intersection size, while the cloud learns nothing. This setting is useful when some of the parties have limited computing power. For example, when a phone has to intersect its dataset with a large server-side database, it makes sense to delegate the phone's computation to the cloud for efficiency. To the best of our knowledge, this work is the first to consider delegated PSI-CA in the context of contact tracing to overcome the computational limitations of mobile devices.

We also explore the use of PSI-CA in privacy-preserving contact tracing (CT), an emerging technology that can help prevent the further spread of COVID-19 without violating individuals' privacy. Recently, there has been a significant amount of work on privacy-preserving CT [TPH+20, CGH+20, vABB+20, RPB20, Goo20a, MMRV20, LAY+20, AIS20, LTKS20, CDF+20, ABB+20, CKL+20, CBB+20, TZBS20]. Most contact tracing systems are decentralized and rely on Bluetooth Low Energy (BLE) wireless radio signals on mobile phones. These systems warn people about others they have been in contact with who have been diagnosed with the disease.

Most of the current decentralized CT systems impose a significant mobile data cost on end-users because they require them to download a large, new dataset every day. At the current peak, the US has nearly 40,000 new cases daily. With the current Apple-Google design, users have to download approximately 40,000 (cases) * 14 (keys per case) * 16 (bytes per key) = 8.96 MB each day. The number of cases could be significantly higher after social restrictions are lifted. Even with this cost, the current Apple-Google design remains susceptible to various attacks. For example, if Bob is diagnosed with the disease, he would upload daily diagnosis keys to the server. In this case, Bob's anonymous identifier beacons/tokens, as they are broadcast each day, can be linked to each other. This is called a linkage attack. The beacons can also be linked across days if Bob frequently appears at the same place and the same time (i.e., because it is on his commute route). At the time of writing, Apple and Google have not described how they are going to address this problem. DP3T has proposed a solution based on Cuckoo filters, but it requires even more data downloaded (Design 2, [TPH+20]). For 40,000 new daily infections, users would need to download 110 MB each day. Mobile service providers such as Google Fi charge $10/GB. This means, at 40,000 new cases per day, DP3T's Design 2 would cost each user $1/day, and the Apple-Google solution would cost $0.10/day (although we note that the Apple-Google design is more vulnerable to linkage attacks). Since contact tracing must be run continuously until a vaccine is available, it may last for months if not years. Therefore, the total cost to a single user could approach hundreds of dollars. In contrast, the network cost of our Catalic is on the order of a few hundred kilobytes and is independent of the server dataset size. We present details on comparisons between the systems' performance in Sect. 6.3.

The efficacy of contact tracing is proportional to the number of users. It is therefore crucial to the success of contact tracing to minimize the cost to these users. By applying our new lightweight delegated PSI-CA protocol, our Catalic system allows end users to delegate their computation to untrusted servers. As a result, the computation workload is almost free and the bandwidth cost is of a few hundred kilobytes, which is independent of the size of the server's database.

1.1 Our Contributions and Techniques

We design a modular approach for delegated PSI-CA that is secure against semi-honest parties. The main building block of our PSI-CA protocol, which we believe to be of independent interest, is oblivious distributed key PRF (Odk-PRF). Recall that, in oblivious PRF (OPRF), the sender learns (or chooses) a PRF key k, and the receiver learns $F(k, r)$, where F is a PRF and r is the receiver's input. The sender learns nothing about r, and the receiver learns nothing else. In Odk-PRF, the PRF key, input, and output are secret-shared among m parties. More precisely, an oblivious distributed key pseudorandom function (Odk-PRF) is a protocol that consists of a sender and m receivers. Each receiver has one XOR secret-shared of input r and learns the local PRF value $F(k_j, r_j)$, which is the result of the PRF on a secret-shared r_i with a secret-shared key k_j. The sender learns a combined PRF key $k = \bigoplus_{j=1}^{m} k_j$. If anyone collects all m local PRF evaluations, they can reconstruct the global PRF as $F(k, r)$. Such an actor is known as a combiner.

Our delegated PSI-CA protocol consists of two major phases. First, in the distributed PRF phase, the PSI-CA's receiver (who we will call Alice) distributes secret shares of her input $X = \{x_1, \ldots, x_n\}$ to m cloud servers, which run Odk-PRF with the PSI-CA's sender (called Bob) to obtain secret shares of the PRF output. Bob learns the combined PRF key k_i from this execution while each cloud server learns the local PRF value $F(k_{i,j}, r_{i,j})$ for each share $r_{i,j}$ of x_i, where $i \in [n], j \in [m]$. Among the cloud servers, Alice can choose a leader to reconstruct the PRF output $F(k_i, x_i)$ for each $x_i \in X$. In the second phase, Bob generates a set of key-value pairs $\{(F(k_i, y_i), v_i), \forall y_i \in Y\}$ where the key is the PRF output over his input $Y = \{y_1, \ldots, y_N\}$ and the value v_i is known to Alice. If any $x_i \in Y$, the cloud leader and Bob hold the same $F(k_i, x_i)$, so the cloud leader can obliviously obtain the correct value v_i by obliviously searching on Bob's key-value pairs. Otherwise, if $x_i \notin Y$, the corresponding value obtained is random. This concept can be viewed as Oblivious Programmable PRF, proposed in [KMP+17]. Now with a set of 'real" or 'fake" values v_i, the cloud leader permutes and sends them to Alice, who can compute how many items are in the intersection (PSI-CA) by counting how many "real" v_i there are, but can't learn anything about which specific items were in common (e.g., which v_i corresponds to the item x_j). Thus, the intersection set is not revealed. This brief overview ignores many important concerns—in particular, how Bob can coordinate PRF keys and items without revealing the identities of the items. A more detailed overview of the approach is presented in Sect. 4.

We motivate the design of our delegated PSI-CA protocol to build Catalic, a lightweight contact tracing system. As discussed in the introduction, most current decentralized systems impose a workload on end-users that has heavy bandwidth and computational costs. Catalic aims to minimize these costs. We will compare Catalic with other systems in Sect. 2.2 and Sect. 6.3. In Catalic, every client plays the role of a dealer by dividing each anonymous identifier beacon they collect into shares and giving each share to a cloud server of their choice. Finally, using the results of the cloud servers' computation, clients perform a simple calculation to check whether there is a match (e.g., one that indicates they are at risk). The distinguishing property of our system is that it allows the development of a collaborative and decentralized system of cloud servers all around the world. These servers are available to help users who have resource-constrained devices. Users can select among all available servers in the delegation. This choice is totally hidden from the view of any adversary and thus, unless a majority of all the servers around the world are corrupted, the whole system preserves privacy.

In summary, we make the following contributions:

- We propose a novel Delegated Private Set Intersection Cardinality (DPSI-CA) protocol. To the best of our knowledge, it is the first protocol that allows clients to delegate their PSI-CA computation to cloud servers. The computation and communication complexity of our DPSI-CA protocol is linear in the size of the smaller set $O(n)$, and is independent of the larger set's size.
- We design Catalic, a lightweight contact tracing system, that delegates client-side computation to untrusted servers. To the best of our knowledge, Catalic is the first system that outsources computation for contact tracing. Moreover, Catalic provides strong privacy guarantees that can prevent critical attacks (e.g., linkage attacks and false-positive claims).
- Finally, we implement building blocks of our PSI-CA protocol and estimate the protocol's performance. We show that the computational and network costs for the client are negligible. With the server database size $N = 2^{26}$, the client set size $n = 2^{12}$, and 2 cloud servers, without including the time spent waiting on the server's response, the client requires a running time of 2.17 milliseconds and only 190.48 KBs of communication. Our experiments show that Catalic is highly scalable.

2 Related Work and Comparison

2.1 Private Set Intersection

Private set intersection (PSI) has been motivated by many real-world applications such as contact discovery [CLR17], botnet detection [NMH+10], human genomes testing [KRT18]. The earliest PSI protocols are based on Diffie-Hellman assumptions [Sha80, Mea86, HFH99]. Over the last few years, there has been active work on efficient secure PSI [DCW13, PSSZ15, FHNP16, RR17, KMP+17, CLR17, PRTY19] with fast implementations that can process millions of items in seconds. However, these implementations only allow to output the intersection itself. In many scenarios (e.g., online marketing campaigns) it is preferable to compute some function of the intersection rather than to reveal the elements in the intersection. Limited work has focused on this so-called f-PSI problem. In this section, we focus on f-PSI constructions that support PSI-CA.

All current PSI-CA constructions are built in a setting where the sender and the receiver directly interact with each other in several interactive rounds to do the computation. Huang, Katz, and Evans [HEK12] propose an efficient sort-compare-shuffle circuit construction to implement f-PSI. Pinkas et al. [PSWW18, PSTY19] improve circuit-PSI using several hashing techniques. The main bottlenecks in the existing circuit-based protocols are the number of string comparisons and that computing the statistics (e.g., counts) of the associated values is done inside a generic MPC protocol, which is communication-expensive. Therefore, the current Diffie-Hellman Homomorphic encryption approach of [IKN+19] is still preferable in practice [Pos19], due to its more reasonable communication complexity. However, the protocol of [IKN+19] requires a certain amount of computation, which is still expensive in the mobile setting. Very recently, [TSS+20] combines DH-based PSI protocols [HFH99] and Private Information Retrieval [KO97] to reduce the communication cost of [IKN+19]. Their PSI-CA protocol requires 35 35 s to securely compute the intersection size for a server database size 5.6×10^6 and client set size 1120.

With the growth of cloud computing, delegating computation to cloud servers is more practical. There are a few works [Ker12, LNZ+14, ZX15, ATD17, QLS+18, ATMD19, ATD20] that consider the outsourcing (delegating) setting. Importantly, their protocols only compute the intersection itself. Most of the constructions are based on polynomials. Their core idea is that if the set X (respectively, Y) is represented as a polynomial f (respectively, g) whose roots are the set's elements, then the polynomial representation of the intersection $X \cap Y$ is $P = f \times r + g \times s$ where r and s are random polynomials, each of them secretly chosen by each party. An important property is that an item $x \in X \cap Y$ if and only if $f(x) = g(x) = 0$. Consequently, for each item x that appears in both sets X and Y, it holds that $P(x) = f(x) \times r(x) + g(x) \times s(x) = 0$ no matter which values $r(x)$ and $s(x)$ have. In the outsourcing setting, the parties encrypt and outsource the encrypted polynomials f and g to cloud servers that help to compute the polynomial P under homomorphic encryption. The servers then return the encrypted polynomial P to a receiver who figures out the intersection items by finding all roots of P. Because the valid roots of the polynomial are the items in the set intersection, it is not clear how to extend this idea to output only the intersection size without revealing the common elements. To the best of our knowledge, our DPSI-CA is the first protocol that allows the client (i.e., the receiver) to delegate their computation to cloud servers. The computation and communication complexity of our protocol is independent of the larger set size, and linear in the size of the smaller set $O(n)$.

2.2 Secure Contact Tracing

Global lockdown measures have been imposed all around the world and will cause severe social and economic problems. To relax the lockdown measures while keeping the ability to control the spread of the disease, technical tools for contact tracing have been introduced. The resulting applications try to log every instance a person is close to another smartphone-owner for a significant period of time.

The first method includes keeping logs of users' Global Positioning System (GPS) location data and asking them to scan Quick Response (QR) codes. However, GPS-based methods carry privacy risks because the GPS data may be sent to a centralized authority. Almost all nations are now focused on using another technology - wireless Bluetooth signals - to detect contact matches.

The main principle of Bluetooth-based approaches is to determine who has been in close physical proximity, determined by Bluetooth signals, to an individual who is diagnosed with the disease (a 'diagnosed user'). All methods require users to continually run a phone application that broadcasts pseudo-random Rolling Proximity Identifiers (RPI) representing the user and to record RPIs observed from phones in close proximity. Whenever a user is diagnosed positively with COVID-19, the application alerts all the devices from which it had received diagnosis RPIs during the infection window (e.g., 14 days for COVID-19).

There are two main categories of proposals: centralized and decentralized. In a centralized approach [Tra, Rob, NTK], the server generates RPIs and thus knows all the RPIs honestly used in the system. The model relies on a trusted third-party (e.g., a government health authority). It is therefore vulnerable to many privacy issues. In a decentralized approach like DP3T [TPH+20], PACT[CGH+20] and Apple/Google [Goo20a], each phone generates its own RPIs that are exchanged to another phone when a close contact event is detected. The RPI list never leaves a user's phone as long as the user is not diagnosed with the disease. This model removes the need of the trusted server, but is still vulnerable to several attacks like linkage attacks. For example, an attacker can install BLE-sniffing devices to different known physical locations and collect RPIs. By keeping track of when and where they received which tokens, the attacker can identify who has been diagnosed with the disease as well as the travel route of the individuals [Sei].

Recent analysis has shown that current centralized and decentralized digital contact tracing proposals come with their own benefits and risks [Vau20]. Against a malicious authority, the risk of mass surveillance is very high in centralized systems. This risk is lower in decentralized systems because the users generate their tokens themselves. However, the decentralized systems also endanger the anonymity of diagnosed people over other users, as the tokens of diagnosed people are broadcasted to everyone. [Vau20]: "centralized systems put the anonymity of all users in high danger, specially against a malicious authority, while decentralized systems put the anonymity of diagnosed people in high danger against anyone."

Several solutions have been proposed to prevent against linkage attack as well as to leverage the best of centralized and decentralized systems. As far as we know, there are three protocols in this direction.

- The Epione system [TSS+20], in which private set intersection protocols are used on top of decentralized systems: the diagnosis RPIs are not broadcasted. Instead, the user's query is done with the back-end server via an interactive secure computation protocol (PSI-CA). This system achieves both high privacy and a low volume of data to be downloaded. However, it requires each user to realize the high computation (w.r.t resource-constrained devices) of a two-round interactive protocol with the servers.
- The Pronto-C2, proposed by Avitabile *et al.* [ABIV20], in which instead of asking diagnosed people to send RPIs to the back-end server, they construct a system where smartphones anonymously and confidentially talk to each other in the presence of the back-end server. Informally, the back-end server helps users to establish shared Diffie-Hellman keys to check whether they are in contact with each other. The main shortcoming of this system is that the client still has to download a large database (as in the DP3T system) and this is not appropriate for resource-constrained devices.
- Finally, the DESIRE [DES] is presented as an evolution of the ROBERT protocol used in France [Rob]. In this system, for each contact between two phones, a Diffie-Hellman key exchange between is established and stored on each phone, which makes a high barrier for resource-constrained devices.

We observe that none of the above three schemes supports resource-constrained devices that have limited capacities for computation and storage. Our work solves this problem by introducing an efficient delegated PSI-CA. Our solution allows resource-constrained devices to fully perform the functionality of the contact tracing system while maintaining the user's privacy.

Catalic can also be considered as a generalization of the Epione system. Indeed, if the user plays the role of the cloud servers themselves, then Catalic is equivalent to Epione. This gives us the ability to design a flexible system that allows users with sufficiently powerful devices who do not trust cloud services to participate in contact tracing without cloud help.

3 Security Model and Cryptographic Preliminaries

This section introduces the notation, security guarantees, and cryptographic primitives used in the later sections. In this work, the computational and statistical security parameters are denoted by κ, λ, respectively. For $n \in \mathbb{N}$, we write $[n]$ to denote the set of integers $\{1, \ldots, n\}$.

3.1 Security Model

We consider a set of parties who have agreed upon a single functionality to compute and have also consented to give the final result to some particular

PARAMETERS: A PRF F, and two parties: receiver and sender.

BEHAVIOR:

- **Wait for input q from the receiver.**
- **Sample a random PRF seed k and give it to the sender.**
- **Give $F(k, q)$ to the receiver.**

Fig. 1. The OPRF ideal functionality

party. At the end of the computation, nothing is revealed by the computational process except the final output. In the real-world execution, the parties often execute the protocol in the presence of an adversary who corrupts a subset of the parties. In the ideal execution, the parties interact with a trusted party that evaluates the function in the presence of a simulator that corrupts the same subset of parties. There are two adversarial models and two models of collusion.

- *Adversarial model*: A *semi-honest* adversary follows the protocol but is curious and attempts to obtain extra information from the execution transcript. A *malicious* adversary can apply any arbitrary polynomial-time strategy to deviate from the protocol.
- *Collusion security*: A *colluding* model is considered as a single monolithic adversary that observes the possibility of collusion between the dishonest parties. Consequently, the model is secure if the joint distribution of those views can be simulated. In contrast, a *non-colluding* model is considered as independent adversaries, each observing the view of each independent dishonest party. The model is secure if the individual distribution of each view can be simulated.

In this work, we consider the semi-honest setting. The adversary can corrupt parties but as long as there are at least two non-corrupted *specific* servers involved in the protocol, the privacy of the users will be guaranteed. We describe more detail on the security of our DPSI-CA protocol and Catalic system in Sect. 4 and Sect. 6.3.

3.2 Cryptographic Primitives

Oblivious PRF An oblivious pseudorandom function (OPRF) [FIPR05] is a protocol in which a sender learns (or chooses) a random PRF seed s while the receiver learns $F(s, r)$, the result of the PRF on a single input r chosen by the receiver. The OPRF functionality is described in Fig. 1.

Distributed PRF. A distributed pseudorandom function (DPRF) is a protocol in which a PRF secret key sk is shared among n parties. Each party can locally compute a partial evaluation of the PRF on the same input x. A combiner who collects t partial evaluations can then reconstruct the evaluation $F(sk, x)$ of the PRF under the initial secret key.

Private Set Intersection Cardinality. Private set intersection cardinality (PSI-CA) is a two-party protocol that allows one party to learn the intersection size of their private sets without revealing any additional information. In this work, we consider PSI-CA in an untrusted third-party setting where the computation can be delegated to the third-party (e.g., cloud servers).

4 Cryptographic Protocols

In this section, we present more detail on our DPSI-CA construction which replies on our new cryptographic tool Odk-PRF. The DPSI-CA is later used as the main building block of our Catalic system described in Sect. 5.2.

4.1 Oblivious Distributed Key PRF

4.1.1 Definition

We introduce a new cryptographic notion of an oblivious distributed key pseudorandom function (Odk-PRF). Intuitively, the functionality is a hybrid of the distributed PRF and OPRF, with an additional feature that the PRF input is secret shared among m parties. Concretely, an oblivious distributed key PRF (Odk-PRF) is a protocol in which a server learns (or chooses) a random PRF key k. There are m clients, each has XOR secret share x_i of input point x. In Odk-PRF, each client learns $F(k_i, x_i)$, the result of the PRF on the *secret share input* x_i with a *secret share key* k_i of k. A combiner who collects all m PRF evaluations can then reconstruct the evaluation $F(k, x)$ as the PRF output on the input $x = \bigoplus_{i=1}^{m} x_i$ with the key $k = \bigoplus_{i=1}^{m} k_i$.

We present a formal definition of Odk-PRF functionality by considering the following algorithms:

- KeyGen takes a security parameter κ, and generates a PRF key as $\mathsf{KeyGen}(1^\lambda) \rightarrow k$.
- KeyShare takes a PRF key k as a master key and a number m, and generates m shared PRF keys as $\mathsf{KeyShare}(k, m) \rightarrow \{k_1, \dots, k_m\}$ such that $k = \bigoplus_{i=1}^{m} k_i$.
- KeyEval takes a shared PRF key k_i and a (shared) input x_i, and gives output $F(k_i, x_i) \rightarrow y_i$, where F is a PRF.

The correctness of our Odk-PRF is that if $k \leftarrow \mathsf{KeyGen}(1^\lambda)$ and $\{k_1, \dots, k_m\} \leftarrow \mathsf{KeyShare}(k, m)$, then $F(k, \bigoplus_{i=1}^{m} x_i) = \bigoplus_{i=1}^{m} F(k_i, x_i)$.

The security of the *oblivious distributed key* PRF (Odk-PRF) guarantees two following properties:

(1) Similar to the security guarantees of *distributed* PRF, any strict subset of the $F(k_i, x_i)$ hides $F(k, x)$, where $x = \bigoplus_{i=1}^{m} x_i$. Note that the distributed PRF

requires all the x_i values and x are the same (i.e, $x = x_1 = \ldots = x_m$) while in our Odk-PRF, the x_i values are XOR secret shares of x (i.e, $x = \bigoplus_{i=1}^{m} x_i$).

(2) Similar to the security guarantees of *oblivious* PRF, $F(k, x)$ reveals nothing about both x and k with very high probability (e.g., $2^{-\lambda}$).

4.1.2 OPRF's Instantiation

In an OPRF functionality for a PRF F, the receiver provides an input x; the functionality chooses a random key k, gives k to the sender and $F(k, x)$ to the receiver. In this work, we focus on the OPRF protocol [OOS17,KKRT16] which is based on inexpensive symmetric-key cryptographic operations (apart from a constant number of initial public-key operations). The protocol efficiently generates a large number of OPRF instances, which makes it a particularly good fit for our eventual contact tracing application. Note that the protocol of [KKRT16] achieves a slightly weaker variant of OPRF than what we have defined in Fig. 1, but the construction remains secure for our Odk-PRF protocol.

The work of [KKRT16] introduces BaRK-OPRF where the PRF key is a related pair (s, k). The first key s is a random secret value chosen by the sender, and when doing many "OPRF" instances, all instances have the same s (e.g. related key). The second key has a formula $k = t \oplus [C(x) \wedge s]$, where x is an input to OPRF, C is a pseudo-random function that has minimum distance κ, and $\wedge$ is bit-wise AND operator. In the construction of [OOS17], C is BCH code. The value t is chosen by the functionality (or the receiver), and has been considered as a PRF's output. e.g. the receiver gets $F(k, x) = t$.

Intuitively, for a BaRK-OPRF instance, the receiver can evaluate it on only one input (e.g., x) while the sender can evaluate this PRF at any point y by computing $F(k, y) = k \oplus [C(y) \wedge s]$. It is easy to see that $F(k, y) = t \oplus [(C(y) \oplus C(x)) \wedge s]$. If $x = y$ then $F(k, y) = t$, and thus, $(k, y) = F(k, x)$ as desired.

Briefly, the BaRK-OPRF construction has an additional key (i.e, the related key s) rather than the OPRF functionality defined in Fig. 1. To adapt the above OPRF variant for our Odk-PRF definition, we relax our KeyShare and KeyEval functions as follows. KeyShare only takes the second BaRK-OPRF key k as a master key, and generates secret shares of k as before KeyShare$(k, m) \rightarrow \{k_1, \ldots, k_m\}$. However, the KeyEval takes the shared PRF key k_i and the additional related PRF key s and gives output y_i as $F\big((k_i, s), x_i\big) \rightarrow y_i$.

4.1.3 Odk-PRF Construction from OPRF

We assume that there are m clients, each holds a value $x_{i \in [m]}$. When the clients act as PRF's receiver to provide m inputs $\{x_1, \ldots, x_m\}$ to the BaRK-OPRF functionality, the related key s and keys $\{k_1, \ldots, k_m\}$ are generated accordingly, where $k_i = t_i \oplus [C(x_i) \wedge s], \forall i \in [m]$. Each client, in turn, obtains $F(k_i, x_i) = t_i$, the result of the PRF on each single input x_i.

For Odk-PRF, we would like to produce a combined key by XORing all individual keys as $k = \bigoplus_{i=1}^{m} k_i$, a combined input value by XORing all corresponding

PRF inputs as $x = \bigoplus_{i=1}^{m} x_i$, and a combined output value by XORing all corresponding PRF outputs as $t = \bigoplus_{i=1}^{m} t_i$. To achieve the correctness of our Odk-PRF, the combined key k should be the same as the second BaRK-OPRF key generated by evaluating OPRF on the combined input value x. In other words, k must be written in a formula as $k = t \oplus [C(x) \wedge s]$.

We observe that $k = \bigoplus_{i=1}^{m} k_i = \bigoplus_{i=1}^{m} t_i \oplus [(\bigoplus_{i=1}^{m} C(x_i)) \wedge s]$, and if we define $F(k,x) := t$ then it is necessary to have XOR-homomorphic property for the function C so that k can be represented as $k = \bigoplus_{i=1}^{m} t_i \oplus [C(\bigoplus_{i=1}^{m} x_i) \wedge s] = t \oplus [C(x) \wedge s]$ as desired. By using a linear code [OOS17, PRTY20] for the function C , surprisingly Odk-PRF is implemented by evaluating OPRF. The Odk-PRF protocol is presented in Fig. 2. All functions KeyGen, KeyShare, and KeyEval are directly implemented from the protocol. Note that our Odk-PRF can support any type T (e.g., XOR, AND) of the combination of the individual keys k_i as long as the function C has T-homomorphic property. In this work, we use T as XOR.

Parameters: A server S, and m client $\mathcal{C}_1, \ldots, \mathcal{C}_m$; an OPRF primitive defined in Figure 1

Inputs: Each client $\mathcal{C}_m$ has input x_i, the server has no input.

Protocol:

- Each client $R_{i \in [n]}$ and the server S invoke an OPRF instance:
  - Client $\mathcal{C}_i$ acts as OPRF's client with input x_i
  - Server S acts as OPRF's sender. The server obtains a key k_i and a related key s which is the same for all OPRF instances.
  - Client $\mathcal{C}_i$ obtains a PRF value t_i
- Server outputs a master key $k = \bigoplus_{i=1}^{n} k_i$ and the related key s

Fig. 2. Our Odk-PRF Construction.

The security of Odk-PRF follows in a straightforward way from the security of its building blocks (e.g. OPRF). In particular, each PRF value t_i is independent of each other. In addition, $F(k,x)$ is indeed equal to $\bigoplus_{i=1}^{m} F(k_i, x_i)$. Therefore, any strict subset of the $F(k_i, x_i)$ reveals nothing about $F(k,x)$. Moreover, since OPRF is guaranteed to produce output indistinguishable from real, $F(k,x)$ reveals nothing about both x and k. Thus, we omit the proof of the following theorem.

Theorem 1. *The construction of Fig. 2 securely implements the oblivious distributed key PRF (Odk-PRF) defined in Sect. 4.1.1 in semi-honest setting, given the OPRF functionality described in Fig. 1.*

4.2 Delegated PSI-CA

In this section, we propose an efficient delegated PSI-CA in which the computation is delegated to the cloud servers.

4.2.1 Problem Definition

Definition 1. *In a delegated PSI-CA protocol, three kinds of parties are involved: a client $\mathcal{C}$, a backend server $\mathcal{S}$, and a set of m cloud servers $\mathcal{H}$. We assume that at most $m-1$ cloud servers are colluded, and the backend server does not collude with any cloud server. The delegated PSI-CA protocol Π computes a PSI-CA as follows: $\Pi : \perp \times (\{0,1\}^\star)^N \times (\{0,1\}^\star)^n \rightarrow \perp \times \perp \times f_{|\cap|}$ where, $\perp$ denotes the empty output, $\{0,1\}^\star$ denotes the domain of input item, N and n denote the set size, and f denotes the PSI-CA function. For every tuple of inputs $\perp$, a set X of size n, and a set Y of size N belonging to $\mathcal{H}, \mathcal{C}, \mathcal{S}$ respectively, the function outputs nothing $\perp$ to $\mathcal{H}$ and $\mathcal{S}$, and outputs $f_{|\cap|} = |X \cap Y|$ to $\mathcal{C}$.*

4.2.2 Technical Overview

The basic idea for our PSI-CA is to have the backend server $\mathcal{S}$ represent a dataset Y as a polynomial $P(y)$ by interpolating the unique polynomial of degree $(N-1)$ over the points $\{(y_1, r_1), \ldots, (y_N, r_N)\}$, where $R = \{r_1, \ldots, r_N\}$ is random and known by both $\mathcal{C}$ and $\mathcal{S}$. The backend server $\mathcal{S}$ sends the (plaintext) coefficients of the polynomial to a cloud server $\mathcal{H}$, who evaluates the received polynomial on each $x_i \in X$ (assuming X is known by $\mathcal{H}$) and obtains $P(x_i) = r'_i$. It is easy to see that if $x_i \in Y$, $r'_i \in R$. However, the cloud server cannot infer any information from r'_i since (s)he does not know R. To allow the client learn only the intersection size, the cloud server $\mathcal{H}$ sends a set $\{r'_1, \ldots, r'_n\}$ to the client in a randomly permuted order. Shuffling means the client can count how many items are in the intersection (PSI-CA) by checking whether $r'_i \in R$ but learns nothing about which specific item was in common (e.g. which r'_i corresponds to the item x_j). Thus, the intersection set is not revealed.

Note that the above brief overview assumes that the cloud server $\mathcal{H}$ knows X in the clear. To allow $\mathcal{H}$ to evaluate the polynomial without knowing the information of X, we propose to use our Odk-PRF primitive. In particular, the client secret shares its item $x_{i \in [n]}$ to a set of m non-colluding cloud servers, each $\mathcal{H}_{j \in [m]}$ receives a share $x_{i,j}$. All cloud servers $\mathcal{H}_{j \in [m]}$ invoke n Odk-PRF instances with the back-end server $\mathcal{S}$. For each Odk-PRF instance $i \in [n]$, the cloud server $\mathcal{H}_{j \in [m]}$ acts as one of Odk-PRF's clients with input $x_{i,j}$ and obtains PRF value $t_{i,j}$, while the back-end server $\mathcal{S}$ acts as a Odk-PRF's server and obtains Odk-PRF master key k_i and related key s. Let's $\mathcal{H}_m$ be a combiner, who can collect all $t_{i,j}$ from $\mathcal{H}_{j \in [m-1]}$ and reconstruct PRF value of item x_i as $F((k_i, s), x_i) \leftarrow \bigoplus_{j=1}^{m} t_{i,j}$.

The security of Odk-PRF guarantees that the $F((k_i, s), x_i)$ reveals nothing about x_i, k_i, and s to the combiner. For the rest of the paper, we omit the related key s, and use PRF key k_i to refer to the pair (k_i, s).

Recall that our goal is to have a cloud server (e.g. the combiner) to obtain the correct r_i from the polynomial's evaluation in a case that $x_i \in Y$, and random otherwise. To do so, the polynomial must be generated based on PRF values. The back-end server $\mathcal{S}$ has PRF key k_i from the Odk-PRF execution, thus $\mathcal{S}$ can evaluate PRF value on any input. There are n PRF keys $k_{i\in[n]}$ and N elements $y_{j\in[N]}$. The total PRFs needed to be evaluated is nN, and thus, the polynomial has a degree of $(nN-1)$, which is very expensive for interpolation and evaluation operations.

In order to address the above issue, similar to [PSSZ15], we use a hashing scheme to place items into several bins and then perform the polynomial's operations per bin. However, the cloud servers do not allow to know X, and thus cannot place the share $x_{i,j}$ into a corresponding bin. Therefore, in our protocol, the client $\mathcal{C}$ is required to map a set of X into the bins. Each $\mathcal{C}$'s bin contains at most one item. The backend server also hashes its items into bins, each contains a small number of inputs. The $\mathcal{C}$ secretly shares the item in its bin to the cloud servers, which later allows the cloud leader and the backend server to interpolate and evaluate the polynomial bin-by-bin efficiently. A more detailed overview of the approach and the hashing scheme is presented in the following section, prior to the presentation of the full protocol.

4.2.3 Cryptographic Gadgets

We review the basics of Cuckoo & Simple hashing scheme [PSSZ15], and Pack & Unpack Message [DCW13, KMP+17] to improve our DPSI-CA construction.

Cuckoo Hashing. In basic Cuckoo hashing, there are β bins denoted $B[1\ldots\beta]$, a stash, and k random hash functions $h_1, \ldots, h_k : \{0,1\}^\star \rightarrow [\beta]$. The client uses a variant of Cuckoo hashing such that each item $x \in X$ is placed in exactly one of β bins. Using the Cuckoo analysis [DRRT18] based on the set size $|X|$, the parameters β, k are chosen so that with high probability $(1-2^{-\lambda})$ every bin contains at most one item, and no item has to place in the stash during the Cuckoo eviction (.i.e. no stash is required).

Simple Hashing. The backend server maps its input set Y into β bins using the same set of k Cuckoo hash functions (i.e, each item $y \in Y$ appears k times in the hash table). Using a standard ball-and-bin analysis based on k, β, and the input size of client $|X|$, one can deduce an upper bound η such that no bin contains more than η items with high probability $(1-2^{-\lambda})$.

Pack&Unpack Message. A pack&unpack message consists of two algorithms:

- $\mathsf{pack}(S) \rightarrow \Pi$: takes a set S of key-value tuples $(a_i, b_i), \forall i \in [\eta]$, from a random distribution, then outputs a representation Π.
- $\mathsf{unpack}(\Pi, a) \rightarrow v$: takes a Π and a key a, then outputs value v.

Such a pack&unpack scheme should satisfy the following properties:

- Correctness: if $(a, b) \in S$ and $\Pi \leftarrow \mathsf{pack}(S)$ then $(a, \mathsf{unpack}(\Pi, a)) \in S$.
- Obliviousness: for $\mathsf{pack}(\{(a_1, b_1), \ldots, (a_\eta, b_\eta)\}) \rightarrow \Pi$, the distributions of $\mathsf{unpack}(\Pi, a)$ and $\mathsf{unpack}(\Pi, a')$ are indistinguishable when the b_i values are uniformly distributed.

There are several pack&unpack constructions presented in [KMP+17], with different tradeoffs in communication and computation cost. In this work, we use the following data structures:

1. Polynomial-based construction: $\mathsf{pack}(S)$ is implemented by interpolating a degree $(\eta - 1)$ polynomial Π over the points $\{(a_1, b_1), \ldots, (a_\eta, b_\eta)\}$. $\mathsf{unpack}(\Pi, a)$ is implemented by evaluating the polynomial Π on the key a. It is easy to see that Π satisfies correctness and obliviousness.
   The interpolation of the polynomial takes time $O(\eta \log(\eta)^2)$ field operations [MB72], which can be expensive for large η. The size of Π is $O(\eta)$.
2. Garbled Bloom filter (GBF) [DCW13]: given a collection of hash functions $H = \{h_1, \ldots, h_k \mid h_i : \{0,1\}^\star \rightarrow [\tau]\}$, a GBF is the array $\mathsf{GBF}[1\ldots, \tau]$ of strings. The GBF implements a key-value pair (a, b) in which the value associated with the key a is $b = \sum_{i=1}^{k} \mathsf{GBF}[h_i(a)]$. The GBF works as follows. The GBF is initialized with all entries equal to an empty string $\perp$. For each key-value pair (a, b), let $T = \{h_i(a) \mid i \in [k], \mathsf{GBF}[h_i(a)] = \perp\}$ be the relevant positions of GBF that have not yet been set. Abort if $T = \emptyset$. Otherwise, we choose random values for entries $\mathsf{GBF}[j], j \in [T]$, subject to $\sum_{i=1}^{k} \mathsf{GBF}[h_i(a)] = b$. For any remaining $\mathsf{GBF}[j] = \perp$, we replace $\mathsf{GBF}[j]$ with a randomly chosen value. The computation complexity is $O(\eta)$. The size of Π is also $O(\eta)$, however, its constant coefficient is high. The parameters k and τ are chosen so that the "Abort" event happens with negligible probability (e.g. $2^{-\lambda}$). We discuss parameter choice for GBF in Sect. 3.

4.2.4 Delegated PSI-CA Construction

Our semi-honest delegated PSI-CA protocol is presented in Fig. 3, following closely the description in the previous Sect. 4.2.2. The construction consists of four phases.

Recall that our construction requires that the client and backend server have the same set of random items R for computing PSI-CA final output. This can be done at the setup phase, where the backend server chooses a random seed s, and sends it to the client. Both parties can generate β random values as $R = \{r_1, \ldots, r_\beta\} \leftarrow PRG(s)$, where β is the number of bins in the Cuckoo's table.

In the tokens' distribution phase, the client hashes items X into β bins using the Cuckoo hashing scheme. For each bin $b \in [\beta]$, the client secret shares the item x_b in that bin to m cloud servers. To reduce the network costs, the client can sample $m - 1$ random seeds s_i, and sends each of them to one among $m - 1$

PARAMETERS:
- Set size n and N.
- A client $\mathcal{C}$, a backend server $\mathcal{S}$, and m cloud servers $\mathcal{H}_1, \dots, \mathcal{H}_m$
- A one-way hash function $H : \{0,1\}^* \rightarrow \{0,1\}^*$, and Cuckoo and Simple hashing scheme described in Section 4.2.3.
- A Odk-PRF primitive described in Section 4.1
- pack() and unpack() functions described in Section 4.2.3

INPUTS:
- Client $\mathcal{C}$ has input $X = \{x_1, \dots, x_n\}$
- Backend server $\mathcal{S}$ has input $Y = \{y_1, \dots, y_N\}$
- Cloud server $\mathcal{H}_{j\in[m]}$ has no input.

PROTOCOL:

I. **Setup phase**
- The backend server $\mathcal{S}$ chooses a random seed s, and sends it to the client.
- The client generates β random values $R = \{r_1, \dots, r_\beta\} \leftarrow PRG(s)$
- The back-end server $\mathcal{S}$ generates β random values from $PRG(s)$, permutes them, and gets $\{p_1, \dots, p_\beta\}$
- The client chooses $m-1$ random seeds $s_{i\in[m-1]}$, and sends s_i to $\mathcal{H}_{i\in[m-1]}$.

II. **Tokens distributed**
- The client hashes items X into β bins using the Cuckoo hashing scheme. Let $B_C[b]$ denote the item in the client's b^{th} bin (or a dummy item for empty bin).
- For each $b \in [\beta]$, and $x \in B_C[b]$, the client computes $x_b^m \leftarrow x \bigoplus_{j=1}^{m-1} PRG(s_i||b)$, and gives x_b^m to the cloud servers $\mathcal{H}_m$.
- For each $b \in [\beta]$, the cloud server $\mathcal{H}_{i\in[m-1]}$ computes $x_b^j \leftarrow PRG(s_i||b)$ as a share of item $x \in B_C[b]$.

III. **Server computation**
1. For each $b \in [\beta]$, cloud servers $\mathcal{H}_{j\in[m]}$ and back-end server $\mathcal{S}$ invoke an instance of Odk-PRF where:
   - $\mathcal{S}$ acts as Odk-PRF's server and obtains PRF key k_b
   - Each $\mathcal{H}_j$ acts as Odk-PRF's client with input x_b^j, and obtains PRF values t_b^j.
2. For all $j \in [m-1]$, each $\mathcal{H}_j$ sends $T_j = \{t_1^j, \dots, t_\beta^j\}$ to the combiner $\mathcal{H}_m$.
3. For each $b \in [\beta]$, the combiner $\mathcal{H}_m$ computes $t_b = \bigoplus_{j=1}^{n} t_\beta^j$
4. Let $\alpha = \lceil \frac{\beta}{m} \rceil$, the combiner $\mathcal{H}_m$ divides a set $\{t_1, \dots, t_\beta\}$ into m subsets $T_j = \{t_{(j-1)\alpha}, \dots, t_{j\alpha-1}\}$, and sends each T_j to $\mathcal{H}_j, \forall j \in [m-1]$.
5. The back-end server $\mathcal{S}$ hashes items Y into β bins using the Simple hashing. Let $B_S[b]$ denote the set of items in the bth bin
6. For each $b \in [\beta]$, $\mathcal{S}$ computes $u_{b,i} = F(k_b, y_i)$ for all $y_i \in B_L[b]$.
7. For each $b \in [\beta]$,
   - $\mathcal{S}$ generates a set of points $P = \{(H(u_{b,i}), p_b)) | y_i \in B_L[b])\}$ for all $b \in [(j-1)\alpha, j\alpha - 1]$, and sends $\Pi_b \leftarrow$ pack(P) to the cloud server $\mathcal{H}_j$ if $b \in [(j-1)\alpha, j\alpha - 1]$
   - $\mathcal{H}_j$ unpacks the received message using each element $t_j \in T_j$ as $v_j \leftarrow$ unpack$(\Pi_b, H(t_j))$, and then sends it to the combiner $\mathcal{H}_m$
8. After collecting all $v_{j\in[b]}$ from $\mathcal{H}_{j\in[m-1]}$, the combiner $\mathcal{H}_m$ permutes the set $V = \{v_1, \dots, v_b\}$ and sends it to $\mathcal{C}$.

IV. **Client's output**: $\sigma = |R \cap V|$.

Fig. 3. Our delegated PSI-CA construction.

cloud servers $\mathcal{H}_{j\in[m-1]}$ in the setup phase. For the item x_b in the bin b^{th}, the client computes a share $x_b^m \leftarrow x_b \oplus PRG(s_1||b) \oplus \ldots \oplus \mathsf{PRG}(s_{m-1}||b)$, and gives x_b^m to the cloud server $\mathcal{H}_m$. Having PRG seed s_i, other cloud server $\mathcal{H}_{j\in[m-1]}$ can generate the share x_b^j of x_b by computing $x_b^j \leftarrow PRG(s_j||b)$. It is easy to check that all the $x_b^j, \forall j \in [m]$, values are shares of x_b as $x_b = \bigoplus_{j=1}^{m} x_b^j$.

For each bin $b \in [\beta]$, the cloud servers $\mathcal{H}_{j\in[m]}$ and the back-end server $\mathcal{S}$ invoke a Odk-PRF instance such that $\mathcal{S}$ acts as a Odk-PRF's server and obtains PRF key k_b in Step (1,I) while the cloud leader $\mathcal{H}_m$ acts as a Odk-PRF's combiner and learns $t_b \leftarrow F(k_b, x_b)$ as described in Step (3,III). Unlike the brief overview described in section refsect:psicaspsoverview, the combiner $\mathcal{H}_m$ divides PRF values $\{t_1, \ldots, t_\beta\}$ into m groups, each group has $\alpha = \lceil \frac{\beta}{m} \rceil$ items as $T_j = \{t_{(j-1)\alpha}, \cdots, t_{j\alpha-1}\}$ except possibly the last group which may have less than α items (without loss of generality, we assume that β is divisible by m). The combiner $\mathcal{H}_m$ sends each set T_j to the cloud server $\mathcal{H}_j$. The main purpose of this step is to distribute the last computation phase (e.g. polynomial evaluation) to all cloud servers.

The backend server $\mathcal{S}$ hashes its input set Y into β bins using the Simple hashing. For each $b \in [\beta]$, $\mathcal{S}$ computes PRF value $u_{b,i} \leftarrow F(k_b, y_i)$ on every item y_i in that bin with the PRF key k_b obtained from the Odk-PRF execution. The backend server $\mathcal{S}$ then generates a set of points $P_b = \{(H(u_{b,i}), r_b)) | y_i \in B_S[b]\}$ for the bin $B_S[b]$ where H is a one-way hash function known by every participant, and r_b is in the random set R computed in the setup phase. $\mathcal{S}$ packs P_b as $\Pi_b \leftarrow \mathsf{pack}(P_b)$. If $b \in [(j-1)\alpha, j\alpha - 1]$, the backend server $\mathcal{S}$ sends Π_b to the corresponding cloud server $\mathcal{H}_j$. Each cloud server $\mathcal{H}_j$ unpacks the received message using every element $t_j \in T_j$ as $v_j \leftarrow \mathsf{unpack}(\Pi_b, H(t_j))$, and forwards the resulting value to the combiner $\mathcal{H}_m$.

After collecting all v_j values as $V = \{v_1, \ldots, v_\beta\}$, $\mathcal{H}_m$ permutes the set V and sends it back to the client, who computes $\sigma = |R \cap V|$ as an output of PSI-CA.

4.2.5 PSI-CA Security and Discussion

Theorem 2. *The PSI-CA construction of Fig. 3 securely implements the delegated PSI-CA functionality described in Definition 1 in semi-honest setting, given the Odk-PRF functionality described in Sect. 4.1.*

Proof. We exhibit simulators for simulating corrupt client, a set of corrupt cloud servers, and corrupt backend server respectively. We argue the indistinguishability of the produced transcript from the real execution.

Simulating Client. The simulator only sees a set of $v_{\pi(i)} = \mathsf{unpack}(t_i)$ messages in a randomly permuted order $\pi() : [\beta] \rightarrow [\beta]$ chosen by the cloud server combiner $\mathcal{H}_m$. We consider modifying this view as a set of $v_i = \mathsf{unpack}(t_{\pi^{-1}(i)})$. Using the abstraction of the unpack obliviousness we can replace term v_i with an independently random element for each $x_i \notin X \cap Y$. As long as the client and $\mathcal{H}_m$ do not collude, we can replace $\mathsf{unpack}(t_{\pi^{-1}(i)})$ with $\mathsf{unpack}(t)$ where t is a PRF value of a common item $x \in X \cap Y$ (i.e, the permutation hides the common items), and then replace $\mathsf{unpack}(t)$ with random element in R. In other words, the simulator only learns $|X \cap Y|$ and Y. The simulation is perfect.

Simulating Cloud Servers. Let Adv be a coalition of corrupt cloud servers. In our protocol, we assume that Adv has at most $m-1$ among m cloud servers. The simulator simulates the view of Adv, which consists of received shares from the client, Odk-PRF's randomness, pack messages from the backend server, and transcripts from the Odk-PRF ideal functionality. We consider two following cases:

- Security for the client $\mathcal{C}$: In Step (II) of our protocol, the client $\mathcal{C}$ secretly shares its input to m cloud servers. Since Adv contains at most $m-1$ corrupt cloud servers, Adv learns nothing from this step, and we can replace the share with random. Thanks to the cryptographic guarantees of the underlying Odk-PRF protocol, no information is revealed except the PRF output in Steps (III,3) and (III,4). We also assume that Adv does not collude with the backend server, the PRF outputs can be replaced with randoms. In Step (III,7), Adv evaluates unpack which also produces output indistinguishable from the real world.
- Security for the back-end server $\mathcal{S}$: In Step (III,7) of our protocol, $\mathcal{S}$ packs a set of key-value pairs $P = \{(H(u), p)\}$ via pack functionality, where $u = F(k, y)$ is a PRF value on the item $y \in Y$ with the key k obtained from Odk-PRF, and p is generated from the secret PRG seed. Because of Odk-PRF pseudorandomness property, we replace u with random. In our protocol, the cloud servers do not know the PRG seed, we can also replace p with random. The pack functionality takes a set of random pairs thus its distribution is uniform.

In summary, the output of Adv is indistinguishable from the real execution.

Simulating Back-End Server. When using the abstraction of our Odk-PRF functionality, the simulation is elementary.

Security Discussion. In our DPSI-CA, we require that the backend server does not collude with any cloud server. This requirement is for the security guarantee in Step (III,4) where each cloud server j^{th} can see a subset $T_j = \{t_{(j-1)\alpha}, \cdots, t_{j\alpha-1}\}$ of PRF outputs of the client's items in the buckets $[(j-1)\alpha, \ldots, j\alpha]$. If the cloud server j^{th} colludes with the back-end server, they can learn which specific items of these buckets are common by comparing T_j and the set of PRF outputs on $\forall y \in Y$.

Our protocol can be modified to make the above non-colluding requirement weaker. In particular, we can assume that there is a specific (instead of any) cloud server (e.g., the combiner $\mathcal{H}_m$) that does not collude with the backend server. With the new colluding assumption, $\mathcal{H}_m$ needs to play role of other cloud servers to perform unpack in Step (III,7). In other words, we modify our DPSI-CA construction in Fig. 3 by removing Step (III,4). The combiner $\mathcal{H}_m$ keeps the whole set $T = \{t_1, \ldots, t_\beta\}$ locally. The backend server $\mathcal{S}$ sends all $\mathsf{pack}(P_b)$ to the combiner $\mathcal{H}_m$ (instead of other cloud servers $\mathcal{H}_{j\in[m-1]}$). The $\mathcal{H}_m$ uses T to evaluate the corresponding pack(P_b) and obtains a set V which is forwarded to the client as before.

The modified protocol improves the security assumption of our DPSI-CA, but requires more computation on the cloud server combiner's side. Depending on the system specifications, the protocol can be adjusted to the appropriate design.

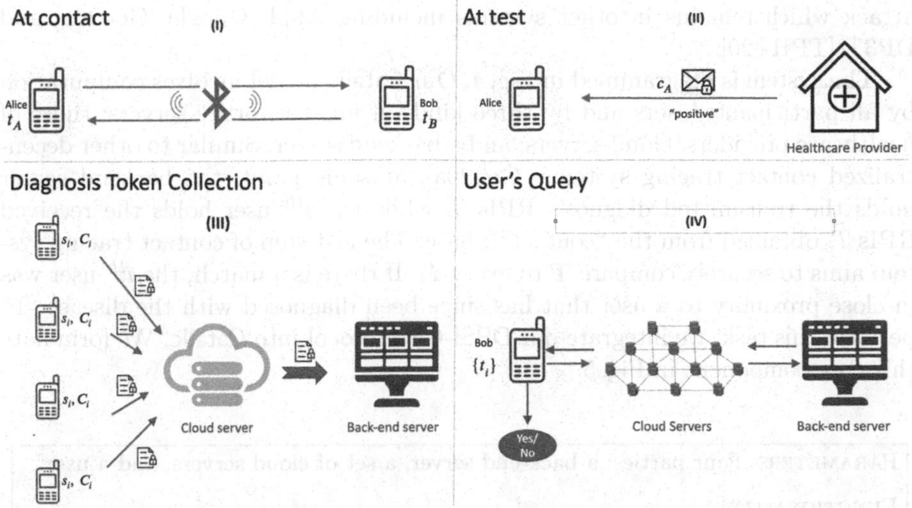

Fig. 4. The Overview of our Catalic System. (I) Tokens (RPIs) are exchanged when two users are in close proximity. (II) When a user is diagnosed by a healthcare provider, the user receives a certificate which indicates that (s)he tested positive with the disease. (III) the diagnosed user encrypts a pair of their PRG seed and the certificate using the public key of the backend server, and sends the encrypted values to the cloud server, who then permutates and transmits them to the backend server. Using its private key, the backend server decrypts the received ciphertexts and obtains a set of pairs including the PRG seed and associated certificate. The backend server checks whether the certificate is valid using the hospital key. If yes, the backend server generates the diagnosis tokens using the corresponding PRG. (IV) Each user invokes a DPSI-CA algorithm with the backend server via cloud servers, where the user's input is its received tokens and the server's input is the list of diagnosis tokens. The user learns only whether (or how many) tokens there are in common between the two sets.

5 Catalic System

5.1 System Overview

The Catalic system consists of five main phases. The first three steps are mostly the same as the BLE-based approaches such as Apple-Google [Goo20a]. In the third step, we can enhance the privacy w.r.t the prior methods by adding a Mix-Net system to shuffle the diagnosis tokens/keys. This prevents attackers from linking which tokens belong to which user, and thus protect the privacy of users who tested positive (so-called diagnosed users). The fourth step is the heart of our system where we allow a contract tracing app to delegate the secure matching computation to a decentralized system of untrusted cloud servers. Then based on the returned values, the user determines whether (s)he has been exposed to the disease. The secure matching allows Catalic to prevent against the linkage attack which remains in other systems including Apple-Google [Goo20a] and DP3T [TPH+20].

The system is diagrammed in Fig. 4. Our Catalic model involves computation by all participants/users and by three kinds of untrustworthy servers: those of healthcare providers, cloud servers, and a backend server. Similar to other decentralized contact tracing systems [Goo20a], at some point, the backend server holds the transmitted diagnosis RPIs $\mathbf{T}$ while the ith user holds the received RPIs $\widetilde{T}_i$ obtained from the "contact" phase. The last step of contact tracing system aims to securely compare $\mathbf{T}$ to every $\widetilde{T}_i$. If there is a match, the ith user was in close proximity to a user that has since been diagnosed with the disease. To perform this task, we integrate our DPSI-CA protocol into Catalic. We formulate this core component in Fig. 5.

PARAMETERS: Four parties: a back-end server, a set of cloud servers, and a user.

FUNCTIONALITY:
- Wait for the server with input set $\mathbf{T}$
- Wait for the user with input set $\widetilde{T}_i$
- Wait for the cloud servers with no input
- Give the user the intersection size $|\widetilde{T}_i \cap \mathbf{T}|$

Fig. 5. Our DPSI-CA gadget.

Each user delegates the PSI-CA computation to two (or more) non-colluding cloud servers (e.g., those run by Amazon, Google, or Apple). The backend server and the cloud servers jointly perform PSI-CA, and return the PSI-CA output to the user, who determines whether there is a match.

5.2 Catalic Extension

As mentioned in the previous section, each user delegates the PSI-CA computation to two or many cloud servers. The privacy of the user will be guaranteed if at least one of these servers is not corrupted. In practice, we can have a large network of cloud servers that helps the user to do this delegation. In this section, we briefly describe such a network and leave the concrete design for future work which goes beyond the scope of automated contact tracing.

DSUSH: Decentralized System of Untrusted Server-Helpers. We describe a decentralized system of untrusted servers as in Fig. 6, in which:

- Any server can ask to join DSUSH as a cloud server (so-called server-helper). Each one can be certified by the Authority, say the backend server. Whenever there is a proof that a cloud server is dishonest, this server will be removed from the system and blacklisted.
- Assume that the DSUSH has M server-helpers. Any client $\mathcal{C}$ can secretly choose any m among M server-helpers in DSUSH and run the delegated PSI-CA protocol described in Fig. 3 with these m server-helpers.

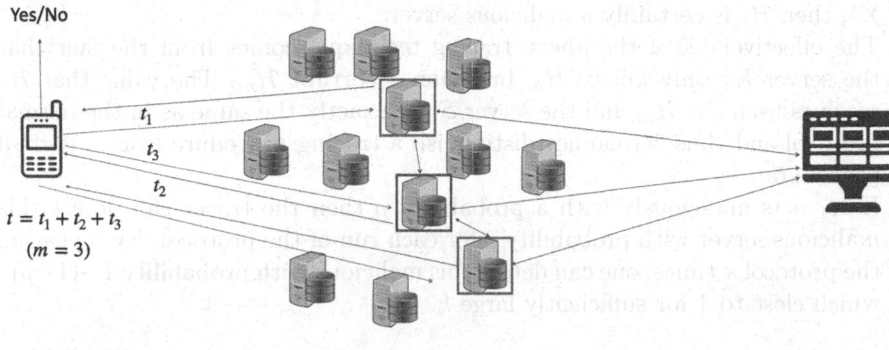

Fig. 6. DSUSH: Decentralised System of Untrusted Server-Helpers.

Client's Privacy. To break the privacy of the client $\mathcal{C}$, an outsider adversary has to corrupt all the m cloud servers chosen by $\mathcal{C}$.

5.2.1 Tracing Traitors for the Reliability of DSUSH.

Interestingly, we can employ techniques from traitor tracing to detect malicious cloud servers in DSUSH. Any cloud server can be traced if it acts as a malicious server. The tracing procedure can be realized without any notice: no server can tell if it is run in a normal process or in a tracing process. Traceability is the main feature that discourages cloud servers to behave maliciously.

Recall that in our delegated PSI-CA protocol described in Fig. 3, the client can choose $m \geq 2$ cloud servers with the following requirements:

- For all $j \in [m-1]$, the server-helper $\mathcal{H}_j$ interacts with cloud server-helper combiner $\mathcal{H}_m$.
- For all $j \in [m]$, the server-helper $\mathcal{H}_j$ interacts with the backend server $\mathcal{S}$.
- For all $j \in [m]$, the server-helper $\mathcal{H}_j$ interacts with the client $\mathcal{C}$.

From the above properties, we briefly show that anyone who possesses a diagnosis RPIs x that belongs to the set of diagnosis RPIs $Y = \{y_1, \ldots, y_N\}$ at the back-end server can do the tracing and becomes thus a tracer. Eventually, the back-end server can generate this special RPI x and add it to the list of the diagnosis RPIs Y.

Testing whether a suspected server-helper is malicious. The trace can test if a server, say $\mathcal{H}_1$, is a malicious as follow:

- Step 1: Tracer plays the role of the client $\mathcal{C}$ in the delegated PSI-CA protocol described in Fig. 3. The tracer can choose $n-1$ random dummy RPIs which are thus probably not in the backend server set Y of diagnosis RPIs. The tracer then defines X that contains x and these $n-1$ dummy RPIs.
- Step 2: The tracer sets $m = 2$, and chooses a trusted server $\mathcal{H}_m$ (the tracer can play himself/herself as the role of $\mathcal{H}_m$) and runs the protocol.
- Step 3: If the result returns at the end of the protocol is different than the correct value 1 (because x is the only element in the intersection of X and Y), then $\mathcal{H}_1$ is certainly a malicious server.
- The effectiveness of the above tracing technique comes from the fact that the server $\mathcal{H}_1$ only knows $\mathcal{H}_m$ but cannot corrupt $\mathcal{H}_m$. The value that $\mathcal{H}_1$ receives from the $\mathcal{H}_m$ and the server $\mathcal{S}$ are exactly the same as in the normal protocol and thus $\mathcal{H}_1$ cannot distinguish a tracing procedure from a normal procedure.
- If $\mathcal{H}_1$ acts maliciously with a probability p then the tracer can detect this malicious server with probability p for each run of the protocol. By repeating the protocol k times, one can detect this malicious with probability $1-(1-p)^k$ which close to 1 for sufficiently large k.

Testing whether a chosen set T of server-helpers contains a malicious server.

- Step 1: Identical as the above test of a suspected server-helper.
- Step 2: The tracer sets $m = |T| + 1$, and chooses a trusted server $\mathcal{H}_m$ (the tracer can play himself/herself as the role of $\mathcal{H}_m$) and runs the protocol.
- Step 3: If the result returned at the end of the protocol is different than the correct value 1, then the T contains at least a malicious server.
- The effectiveness of the above tracing technique comes from the fact that the server-helpers do not know each other and cannot collude to deter the computation. The servers in T only know $\mathcal{H}_m$ which is trusted and therefore cannot corrupt $\mathcal{H}_m$. The values that the servers in T receive from the $\mathcal{H}_m$ and the server $\mathcal{S}$ are exactly the same as in the normal protocol and thus T cannot distinguish a tracing procedure from a normal procedure.
- By repeating the protocol many times, the tracer can correctly determine with overwhelming probability whether T contains a malicious server.

Black-box Tracing. We can eventually generalize the above technique to get the black-box tracing. The tracer first set T to be the whole set in DSUSH. Then if T contains a malicious server then the tracer performs a binary search from T to be able to get the malicious servers.

5.2.2 Practical Implementation of DSUSH

DSUSH in Google-Apple setting. Google and Apple would allow their cloud servers all around the world to participate in a DSUSH. If these servers are trusted then the privacy of the users is preserved. If one of the two firms is malicious (or half of the servers are corrupted) then the privacy of a user who runs the delegated PSI-CA protocol described in Fig. 3 with m server-helpers will be broken with probability $\frac{1}{2^m}$ (m should be set around 40) assuming that the numbers of servers of Google and of Apple are the same and the choice of m server-helpers of the user is random. If both Google and Apple are malicious (all the servers are corrupted) then the privacy of the users will be broken, their tokens will also be revealed.

DSUSH in a general setting of proximity tracing.

- As far as the user knows an honest server in DSUSH (for example the server from his friend, his university, etc.) then the privacy is preserved.
- If the user randomly chooses a set of m server-helpers then the privacy will be broken only when all of these m server-helpers are malicious. Given the traceability, this case is quite improbable.

DSUSH itself could be an interesting platform and we leave a concrete design with formal proven properties of such a network to the future works.

6 Implementation and Performance

To demonstrate the practicality of our Catalic system, we evaluate each building block of our DPSI-CA protocol in C++. We run cloud server and backend server on a single server which has 2× 36-core Intel Xeon 2.30 GHz CPU and 256 GB of RAM. For evaluating the performance of the client, we do a number of experiments on a virtual Linux machine which has Intel Xeon 1.99 GHz CPU and 16 GB of RAM.

As detailed in Sect. 4, our Odk-PRF protocol builds on a specific OPRF variant [KKRT16, OOS17] from the open-source code [Rin]. Our polynomial pack and unpack implementation uses the NTL library [Sho] with GMP library and GF2X [GBZT] library installed for speeding up the running time. The implementation of the building blocks (pack/unpack, end-user's side) is available on Github: https://github.com/nitrieu/delegated-psi-ca.

6.1 Parameter Choices

All evaluations were performed with input item of 128 bits, a statistical security parameter $\lambda = 40$ and computational security parameter $\kappa = 128$. We perform DPSI-CA on the range of set sizes $N = \{2^{22}, 2^{24}, 2^{26}\}$ and $n = \{2^{10}, 2^{11}, 2^{12}\}$.

Cuckoo Hashing: Based on the experiment analysis [DRRT18], we choose cuckoo hashing parameters such that no stash is required with sufficiently low probability. Concretely, in our setting the client places its set into a Cuckoo table of size $\beta = 1.5n$ using 3 hash functions while the backend server using the same set of hash functions and maps its item y into three bins $\{h_1(y), h_2(y), h_3(y)\}$ (i.e., item y appears three times in the hash table with the high probability).

Polynomial Interpolation and Evaluation: Given m cloud servers, our DPSI-CA protocol requires the backend server to generate m polynomials, each of degree $N' \leftarrow \frac{3N}{m}$. Each cloud server must evaluate such a polynomial on $n' \leftarrow \frac{1.5n}{m}$ points. The best algorithms for interpolation incur $O(N' \log^2(N'))$ field operations which is expensive for a high-degree polynomial since N' is typically large (e.g. $N' = 2^{24}$). To speed up the computation complexity of our protocol, we map N' items into θ buckets, each has maximum d items. Instead of interpolating a polynomial of degree $N' - 1$, we interpolate multiple smaller polynomials of degree $d - 1$. Based on the analysis of the parameters [PSTY19], we choose $d = 2^{10}$, and because of $d << N'$ ($N' = 2^{24}$) there is a high probability that each bucket contains the same number of items. [PSTY19] shows that only 3% dummy items need to pad to the bucket to hide the actual bucket's size. Accordingly, the cloud server also maps its items into θ buckets and evaluates θ polynomials of small-degree $d - 1$. For communication and computation efficiency, the polynomial field size can be truncated to length $\lambda + \log(N'n')$ bits and the protocol will still be correct as long as there are no spurious collisions with probability $1 - 2^{-\lambda}$. In our experiment, we set the polynomial field size to be 80 bits to achieve a high probability of correctness of approximately $1 - 2^{-40}$.

Garbled Bloom Filter: The false-positive probability for a Garbled Bloom filter is the same as that of plain Bloom filter which has been well analyzed. Therefore, we choose 31 hash functions and the Garbled Bloom Filter of size $58N'$ to achieve the false-positive rate $(1 - e^{\frac{-31}{58}})^{31}$ which is close to $2^{-\lambda}$.

6.2 PSI-CA Performance

We demonstrate the scalability our protocol on the client side by evaluating it on the range of set sizes $n = \{2^{10}, 2^{11}, 2^{12}\}$ with the backend server set size $N = 2^{26}$ and the number of cloud servers $m = \{2, 8, 32, 64\}$. As mentioned above, the client maps n items into $1.5n$ bins using Cuckoo hashing. The client must send a seed of κ bits to $(m - 1)$ cloud servers and $1.5n\kappa$ bits to the cloud server combiner $\mathcal{H}_m$. For communication efficiency, the returned values from the cloud servers can be truncated to $\lambda + \log(3nN)$ bits for the correctness probability of $1 - 2^{-\lambda}$.

Table 1 presents the performance of our protocol on the client side. Note that the running time does not include the waiting time for the server's response. For $n = 2^{12}$ and $m = 2$, our protocol costs only 2.17 ms and 190 Kilobytes. Since the client's running time depends on the number of cloud servers involved in DPSI-CA, we are also interested in the protocol performance when increasing m. While the network cost is mostly stable, the computational cost increases $1.5\times$ if increasing $m = 2$ to $m = 32$. However, the client's running time is still under a few milliseconds which achieves our ultimate goal.

Table 2 presents the performance of our DPSI-CA protocol the cloud server's side on the range of the client set size $n = \{2^{10}, 2^{12}\}$ with the back-end server set size $N = \{2^{22}, 2^{24}, 2^{26}\}$ and $m = 2$ cloud servers. We assume that the backend servers uses m threads, each communicates with a single cloud server. In our

Table 1. Running time in millisecond and communication cost in kilobyte on the *client's slide* in our semi-honest delegated PSI-CA protocol with the back-end server set size $N = 2^{22}$; n and m are the client set size and the number of cloud servers, respectively. The running time does not include the waiting time from server's response.

	Running Time (milisecond)				Communication Cost (kilobyte)				
n	$m = 2$	$m = 8$	$m = 32$	$m = 64$	$m = 2$	$m = 8$	$m = 32$	$m = 64$	Asymptotic [bit]
2^{10}	0.48	0.48	3.01	5.1	47.63	47.73	48.11	48.62	$(m-1)\kappa + 1.5n\kappa$ $+ 1.5n(\lambda + \log(3nN))$
2^{11}	0.86	1.21	2.5	7.87	95.25	95.34	95.73	96.24	
2^{12}	2.17	2.77	3.01	8.76	190.48	190.58	190.96	191.47	

Table 2. Running time in minute and communication cost in megabyte on the *cloud server's side* in our semi-honest delegated PSI-CA protocol with 2 cloud servers; the client and back-end server set size is n and N, respectively. The running time does not include the waiting time for server's response.

Parameters		Running time (minute)						Communication cost (megabyte)					
Set size	N	2^{22}		2^{24}		2^{26}		2^{22}		2^{24}		2^{26}	
	n	2^{10}	2^{12}	2^{10}	2^{12}	2^{10}	2^{12}	2^{10}	2^{12}	2^{10}	2^{12}	2^{10}	2^{12}
OPRF		0.003	0.003	0.008	0.008	0.034	0.035	0.04	0.09	0.04	0.09	0.04	0.09
Pack &	Poly.	3.15	3.24	11.97	12.72	50.3	51.23	64.8	64.8	259.21	259.21	1036.83	1036.83
Unpack	GBF	0.44	0.44	1.87	1.89	7.91	7.98	3649	3649	14596	14596	60136	60136
Total	Poly.	3.2	3.28	12.1	12.86	50.84	51.78	**64.8**	**64.8**	**259.21**	**259.21**	**1036.83**	**1036.83**
	GBF	**0.49**	**0.49**	**2.00**	**2.03**	**8.45**	**8.53**	3649	3649	14596	14596	60136	60136

PSI-CA protocol, a cloud server requires to evaluate $1.5n$ Odk-PRF instances, and unpack $\frac{1.5n}{m}$ messages. The main cost of the computation is the waiting time of packing $\frac{3N}{m}$ messages by the backend server. We implement different pack and unpack constructions described in Sect. 4 with the parameter choices described in Sect. 6.1. We report the total cost of our protocol by aggregating the cost of building blocks. Table 2 shows the running time and communication cost of both polynomial-based and GBF-based DPSI-CA protocols. While the polynomial-based solution achieves the best communication cost, the GBF-based approach is fastest in the running time.

6.3 Catalic Discussion and Comparison

As discussed in Sect. 1, it is very important to design a contact tracing system that minimizes the client's effort. In this section we only focus on the performance comparison on the client's side. We note that our Catalic provides a reasonable computation and communication cost on the server's side, which presents in Table 2. The performance on the server side can be speed up since our protocol is very amenable to parallelization. Specifically, our algorithm can be parallelized at the level of buckets.

Table 3. Comparison of contact tracing systems with respect to privacy guarantees, required computational infrastructure, and computation and communication cost on the client's side. Infection status refers to identify who has been diagnosed with the disease. Travel route refers to recover travel route of the diagnosed individual. The system requires "# rounds" of interaction between client and server. Each user has $n = 2^{11}$ tokens/RPIs over 14 days of infection window. There are 2^{15} new diagnosed case per days. "neg" indicates the negligible cost of plaintext comparison operations in PACT.

Protocols	Linkage attack		System Req.		Client	
	Travel Route	Infection Status	# interactive Rounds	# Servers	Runtime (ms)	Comm. Cost (MB)
G& A [Goo20b]	Yes	Yes	1/2	1	331.96	7.34
DP3T [TPH+20]	No	Yes	1/2	1	0.02	469.76
PACT [CGH+20]	No	Yes	1/2	1	neg	1073.74
Epione [TSS+20]	No	No	2	2	394.01	1.27
Our Catalic	No	No	1	3	0.86	0.095

We estimate the Catalic performance in which the main computation cost is dominated by the DPSI-CA algorithm. We compare our Catalic with other systems include PACT [CGH+20], DP3T [TPH+20], Apple-Google [Goo20b], and Epione [TSS+20]. Note that PACT and DP3T publicly release tokens/RPIs of diagnosed users. Therefore, they are vulnerable to linkage attack which allows attackers to identify who has been diagnosed with the disease by keeping track of when and where they received which tokens. In the Apple-Google (A&G) approach, the daily diagnosis keys are publicly available which also allows attackers to learn the travel routes of the individual. Only Epione [TSS+20] keeps diagnosis keys/RPIs privately. However, it requires a certain amount of works on the client's side which we discuss later.

According to A&G approach, each user has about $k = 144$ new tokens per day. For the infection window, each client receives a total of approximately $n = 2^{11}$ over 14 days. If there are about $K = 2^{15} = 32,768$ new diagnosed cases per day, the total of new diagnosis RPIs is approximately $N = 2^{26}$ per day. We report detailed comparisons in Table 3, and here we describe how to get the numbers.

In A&G approach, the phone (user) has to download $14K$ new daily-diagnosis keys per day. Each key contains 128 bits thus the total communication cost is $14 \times 2^{15} \times 128$ (bits)= 7.34 MB. The phone also requires to compute $14Kk = 66,060,288$ AES operations. Since each AES requires 10 cycles, a phone with 1.99 99 GHz processor needs $66,060,288 \times \frac{10}{1.99 \times 10^9} = 0.33$ s to complete the contact tracing query.

In DP3T approach, the phone (user) has to download a Cuckoo filter of new diagnosis RPIs per day. To achieve the failure events with error probability $2^{-\lambda}$ per contact tracing instance (in line with our protocol), the false-positive rate of the Cuckoo filter would be $2^{40+\log(n)}$. Therefore, the Cuckoo filter stores for each item a 56-bit fingerprint. For $N = 2^{26}$ new diagnosis RPIs, the communication cost is $2^{26} \times 56$ (bits) = 469.76 MB. In terms of computation cost, the client requires to compute $2n$ AES hash functions for table lookup. The total running time is 0.02 ms.

In a simpler version of PACT approach, the phone (user) has to download all new diagnosis RPIs per day, each token has 128 bits. Therefore, the network cost is $2^{26} \times 128$ (bits) = 1073.74 MB for $N = 2^{26}$ new diagnosis RPIs. The PACT's client does not do any cryptographic operation, thus, we consider its running time to be negligible.

In Epione approach, the diagnosis keys/RPIs have never publicly available. The system also replies on PSI-CA for private matching which allows users to figure out whether they may have been exposed to the disease and nothing else. Epione proposes two PSI-CA protocols with different trade-offs in the communication and time complexity of the protocol and the security guarantees. Their fast variant is based on two-server PIR. It requires the servers do not collude each other, which has the same security guarantees in our Catalic. Therefore, we use the numbers reported in Epione to estimate the cost of their fast variant with the cache. The Epione's client needs to send and receive: $2k$ group elements, each of 256 bits; $2n$ PIR keys, each of $\kappa \log(N') = 128 \times \log(2^{18}) = 2304$ bits where $N' = 2^{18}$ is the bucket size after splitting $N = 2^{26}$ into 2^8 buckets; $2n$ PIR answers from servers, each of 159 (bits). The total communication cost is 1.79 MB. In terms of computation cost, the client requires to compute $2k$ group elements and $2n$ PIR queries. Using parameters for database shape, and implementation optimization of Epione, the running time is 394 milliseconds. Note that Epione requires two rounds of interaction between client and servers. Moreover, the running time of Epione's client is linear in the backend server's database.

In Catalic, Table 1 shows that our protocol requires only 0.86 milliseconds and 96 Kilobytes on the client's side. Note that the experiment uses 1 back-end server and 2 cloud servers, each with a single thread. As discussed in Sect. 5.2, if more cloud servers involve in the computation, it improves the security level as well as the scalability of our Catalic system.

Acknowledgments. We thank all anonymous reviewers and Ling Ren for insightful feedback. Ni Trieu was partially supported by NSF award #2031799 and Duong Hieu Phan was partially supported by the ANR ALAMBIC (ANR16-CE39-0006). Research conducted in part while Ni Trieu at University of California, Berkeley and Duong Hieu Phan at University of Limoges.

References

[ABB+20] Alsdurf, H., et al.: Covi white paper (2020)

[ABIV20] Avitabile, G., Botta, V., Iovino, V., Visconti, I.: Towards defeating mass surveillance and sars-cov-2: the pronto-c2 fully decentralized automatic contact tracing system. Cryptology ePrint Archive, Report 2020/493 (2020). https://eprint.iacr.org/2020/493

[AIS20] Fraunhofer AISEC: Pandemic contact tracing apps: Dp-3t, pepp-pt ntk, and Robert from a privacy perspective. Cryptology ePrint Archive, Report 2020/489 (2020). https://eprint.iacr.org/2020/489
[ATD17] Abadi, A., Terzis, S., Dong, C.: VD-PSI: verifiable delegated private set intersection on outsourced private datasets. In: Grossklags, J., Preneel, B. (eds.) FC 2016. LNCS, vol. 9603, pp. 149–168. Springer, Heidelberg (2017). https://doi.org/10.1007/978-3-662-54970-4_9
[ATD20] Abadi, A., Terzis, S., Dong, C.: Feather: lightweight multi-party updatable delegated private set intersection. Cryptology ePrint Archive, Report 2020/407 (2020). https://eprint.iacr.org/2020/407
[ATMD19] Abadi, A., Terzis, S., Metere, R., Dong, C.: Efficient delegated private set intersection on outsourced private datasets. IEEE Trans. Dependable Secure Comput. **16**(4), 608–624 (2019)
[CBB+20] Castelluccia, C., et al.: DESIRE: a third way for a European exposure notification system leveraging the best of centralized and decentralized systems. Working paper or preprint, May 2020
[CDF+20] Culler, D., et al.: CoVista: a unified view on privacy sensitive mobile contact tracing effort (2020)
[CGH+20] Chan, J., et al.: Pact: privacy sensitive protocols and mechanisms for mobile contact tracing (2020)
[CKL+20] Canetti, R., et al.: Privacy-preserving automated exposure notification. Cryptology ePrint Archive, Report 2020/863 (2020). https://eprint.iacr.org/2020/863
[CLR17] Chen, H., Laine, K., Rindal, P.: Fast private set intersection from homomorphic encryption. In: Thuraisingham, B.M., Evans, D., Malkin, T., Xu, D. (eds.) ACM CCS 2017, pp. 1243–1255. ACM Press, October/November 2017
[DCW13] Dong, C., Chen, L., Wen, Z.: When private set intersection meets big data: an efficient and scalable protocol. In: Sadeghi, A.-R., Gligor, V.D., Yung, M. (eds.) ACM CCS 2013, pp. 789–800. ACM Press, November 2013
[DES] Inria 3rd-way proposal for a European exposure notification system. https://github.com/3rd-ways-for-EU-exposure-notification/project-DESIRE
[DRRT18] Demmler, D., Rindal, P., Rosulek, M., Trieu, N.: PIR-PSI: scaling private contact discovery. Proc. Priv.c Enhanc. Technol. **4**, 2018 (2018)
[FHNP16] Freedman, M.J., Hazay, C., Nissim, K., Pinkas, B.: Efficient set intersection with simulation-based security. J. Cryptol. **29**(1), 115–155 (2016). https://doi.org/10.1007/s00145-014-9190-0
[FIPR05] Freedman, M.J., Ishai, Y., Pinkas, B., Reingold, O.: Keyword search and oblivious pseudorandom functions. In: Kilian, J. (ed.) TCC 2005. LNCS, vol. 3378, pp. 303–324. Springer, Heidelberg (2005). https://doi.org/10.1007/978-3-540-30576-7_17
[GBZT] Gaudry, P., Brent, R., Zimmermann, P., Thomé, E.: https://gforge.inria.fr/projects/gf2x/
[Goo20a] Apple and google privacy-preserving contact tracing. https://www.apple.com/covid19/contacttracing (2020)
[Goo20b] Privacy-safe contact tracing using bluetooth low energy. https://blog.google/documents/57/Overview_of_COVID-19_Contact_Tracing_Using_BLE.pdf (2020)
[HEK12] Huang, Y., Evans, D., Katz, J.: Private set intersection: are garbled circuits better than custom protocols? (2012)

[HFH99] Huberman, B.A., Franklin, M., Hogg, T.: Enhancing privacy and trust in electronic communities. In: Proceedings of the 1st ACM Conference on Electronic Commerce. EC 1999, pp. 78–86. ACM (1999)

[IKN+19] Ion, M., et al.: On deploying secure computing commercially: private intersection-sum protocols and their business applications. Cryptology ePrint Archive, Report 2019/723 (2019). https://eprint.iacr.org/2019/723

[Ker12] Kerschbaum, F.: Outsourced private set intersection using homomorphic encryption. In: Proceedings of the 7th ACM Symposium on Information, Computer and Communications Security. ASIACCS 2012, New York, NY, USA, pp. 85–86. Association for Computing Machinery (2012)

[KKRT16] Kolesnikov, V., Kumaresan, R., Rosulek, M., Trieu, N.: Efficient batched oblivious PRF with applications to private set intersection. In: Weippl, E.R., Katzenbeisser, S., Kruegel, C., Myers, A.C., Halevi, S. (eds.) ACM CCS 2016, pp. 818–829. ACM Press, October 2016

[KMP+17] Kolesnikov, V., Matania, N., Pinkas, B., Rosulek, M., Trieu, N.: Practical multi-party private set intersection from symmetric-key techniques. In: Thuraisingham, B.M., Evans, D., Malkin, T., Xu, D. (eds.) ACM CCS 2017, pp. 1257–1272. ACM Press, October/November 2017

[KO97] Kushilevitz, E., Ostrovsky, R.: Replication is not needed: single database, computationally-private information retrieval. In: Proceedings 38th Annual Symposium on Foundations of Computer Science, pp. 364–373 (1997)

[KRT18] Kolesnikov, V., Rosulek, M., Trieu, N.: SWiM: secure wildcard pattern matching from OT extension. In: Meiklejohn, S., Sako, K. (eds.) FC 2018. LNCS, vol. 10957, pp. 222–240. Springer, Heidelberg (2018). https://doi.org/10.1007/978-3-662-58387-6_12

[LAY+20] Liu, J.K., et al.: Privacy-preserving COVID-19 contact tracing app: a zero-knowledge proof approach. Cryptology ePrint Archive, Report 2020/528 (2020). https://eprint.iacr.org/2020/528

[LNZ+14] Liu, F., Ng, W.K., Zhang, W., Giang, D.H., Han, S.: Encrypted set intersection protocol for outsourced datasets. In: 2014 IEEE International Conference on Cloud Engineering, pp. 135–140 (2014)

[LTKS20] Liu, X., Trieu, N., Kornaropoulos, E.M., Song, D.: BeeTrace: a unified platform for secure contact tracing that breaks data silos. IEEE Data Eng. Bull. **43**(2), 108–120 (2020)

[MB72] Moenck, R., Borodin, A.: Fast modular transforms via division. In: 13th Annual Symposium on Switching and Automata Theory, College Park, Maryland, USA, 25–27 October 1972, pp. 90–96. IEEE Computer Society (1972)

[Mea86] Meadows, C.A.: A more efficient cryptographic matchmaking protocol for use in the absence of a continuously available third party. In: IEEE Symposium on Security and Privacy, pp. 134–137 (1986)

[MMRV20] Madhusudan, P., Miao, P., Ren, L., Venkatakrishnan, V.N.: Contrail: privacy-preserving secure contact tracing (2020). https://github.com/ConTraILProtocols/documents/blob/master/ContrailWhitePaper.pdf

[NMH+10] Nagaraja, S., Mittal, P., Hong, C.-Y., Caesar, M., Borisov, N.: BotGrep: finding P2P bots with structured graph analysis. In: Proceedings of the 19th USENIX Conference on Security, USENIX Security 2010, USA, p. 7. USENIX Association (2010)

[NTK] Pan-European privacy-preserving proximity tracing. https://github.com/pepp-pt/

[OOS17] Orrù, M., Orsini, E., Scholl, P.: Actively secure 1-out-of-N OT extension with application to private set intersection. In: Handschuh, H. (ed.) CT-RSA 2017. LNCS, vol. 10159, pp. 381–396. Springer, Cham (2017). https://doi.org/10.1007/978-3-319-52153-4_22

[Pos19] Google Blog Post. Helping organizations do more without collecting more data. Cryptology ePrint Archive, Report 2020/531 (2019). https://security.googleblog.com/2019/06/helping-organizations-do-more-without-collecting-more-data.html

[PRTY19] Pinkas, B., Rosulek, M., Trieu, N., Yanai, A.: SpOT-light: lightweight private set intersection from sparse OT extension. In: Boldyreva, A., Micciancio, D. (eds.) CRYPTO 2019. LNCS, vol. 11694, pp. 401–431. Springer, Cham (2019). https://doi.org/10.1007/978-3-030-26954-8_13

[PRTY20] Pinkas, B., Rosulek, M., Trieu, N., Yanai, A.: Psi from paxos: fast, malicious private set intersection. Cryptology ePrint Archive, Report 2020/193 (2020). https://eprint.iacr.org/2020/193

[PSSZ15] Pinkas, B., Schneider, T., Segev, G., Zohner, M.: Phasing: private set intersection using permutation-based hashing. In: Jung, J., Holz, T. (eds.) USENIX Security 2015, pp. 515–530. USENIX Association, August 2015

[PSTY19] Pinkas, B., Schneider, T., Tkachenko, O., Yanai, A.: Efficient circuit-based PSI with linear communication. In: Ishai, Y., Rijmen, V. (eds.) EUROCRYPT 2019. LNCS, vol. 11478, pp. 122–153. Springer, Cham (2019). https://doi.org/10.1007/978-3-030-17659-4_5

[PSWW18] Pinkas, B., Schneider, T., Weinert, C., Wieder, U.: Efficient circuit-based PSI via cuckoo hashing. In: Nielsen, J.B., Rijmen, V. (eds.) EUROCRYPT 2018. LNCS, vol. 10822, pp. 125–157. Springer, Cham (2018). https://doi.org/10.1007/978-3-319-78372-7_5

[QLS+18] Qiu, S., Liu, J., Shi, Y., Li, M., Wang, W.: Identity-based private matching over outsourced encrypted datasets. IEEE Trans. Cloud Comput. **6**(3), 747–759 (2018)

[Rin] Rindal, P.: libOTe: an efficient, portable, and easy to use Oblivious Transfer Library. https://github.com/osu-crypto/libOTe

[Rob] Robert - robust and privacy-preserving proximity tracing protocol. https://github.com/ROBERT-proximity-tracing/

[RPB20] Raskar, R., Pahwa, D., Beaudry, R.: Contact tracing: Holistic solution beyond bluetooth. IEEE Data Eng. Bull. **43**(2), 67–70 (2020)

[RR17] Rindal, P., Rosulek, M.: Malicious-secure private set intersection via dual execution. In: Thuraisingham, B.M., Evans, D., Malkin, T., Xu, D. (eds.) ACM CCS 2017, pp. 1229–1242. ACM Press, October/November 2017

[Sei] Seiskari, O.: BLE contact tracing sniffer PoC. https://github.com/oseiskar/corona-sniffer

[Sha80] Shamir, A.: On the power of commutativity in cryptography. In: de Bakker, J., van Leeuwen, J. (eds.) ICALP 1980. LNCS, vol. 85, pp. 582–595. Springer, Heidelberg (1980). https://doi.org/10.1007/3-540-10003-2_100

[Sho] Shoup, V.: NTL: a library for doing number theory. http://www.shoup.net/ntl/

[TPH+20] Troncoso, C., et al.: Decentralized privacy-preserving proximity tracing (2020)

[Tra] Tracetogether, safer together, a Singapore government agency website. https://www.tracetogether.gov.sg/

[TSS+20] Trieu, N., Shehata, K., Saxena, P., Shokri, R., Song, D.: Epione: lightweight contact tracing with strong privacy. IEEE Data Eng. Bull. **43**(2), 95–107 (2020)

[TZBS20] Trivedi, A., Zakaria, C., Balan, R., Shenoy, P.: WiFiTrace: network-based contact tracing for infectious diseases using passive WiFi sensing (2020)

[vABB+20] von Arx, S., et al.: Slowing the spread of infectious diseases using crowd-sourced data. IEEE Data Eng. Bull. **43**(2), 71–82 (2020)

[Vau20] Vaudenay, S.: Centralized or decentralized? The contact tracing dilemma. Cryptology ePrint Archive, Report 2020/531 (2020). https://eprint.iacr.org/2020/531

[ZX15] Zheng, Q., Xu, S.: Verifiable delegated set intersection operations on outsourced encrypted data. In: 2015 IEEE International Conference on Cloud Engineering, pp. 175–184 (2015)

Author Index

Printed in the United States
By Bookmasters